Scott Foresman/Silver Burdett supports the
National Standards for Music Education Grades 5-8

Developed by the Music Educators National Conference

Content Standard ☑ **Achievement Standard**

1
Singing, alone and with others, a varied repertoire of music

☐ **1a** Students sing accurately and with good breath control throughout their singing ranges, alone and in small and large ensembles

☐ **1b** Students sing with expression and technical accuracy a repertoire of vocal literature with a level of difficulty of 2, on a scale of 1 to 6, including some songs performed from memory

☐ **1c** Students sing music representing diverse genres and cultures, with expression appropriate for the work being performed

☐ **1d** Students sing music written in two and three parts

☐ **1e** Students who participate in a choral ensemble sing with expression and technical accuracy a varied repertoire of vocal literature with a level of difficulty of 3, on a scale of 1 to 6, including some songs performed from memory

Notes

2
Performing on instruments, alone and with others, a varied repertoire of music

☐ **2a** Students perform on at least one instrument[1] accurately and independently, alone and in small and large ensembles, with good posture, good playing position, and good breath, bow, or stick control

☐ **2b** Students perform with expression and technical accuracy on at least one string, wind, percussion, or classroom instrument a repertoire of instrumental literature with a level of difficulty of 2, on a scale of 1 to 6

☐ **2c** Students perform music representing diverse genres and cultures, with expression appropriate for the work being performed

☐ **2d** Students play by ear simple melodies on a melodic instrument and simple accompaniments on a harmonic instrument

☐ **2e** Students who participate in an instrumental ensemble or class perform with expression and technical accuracy a varied repertoire of instrumental literature with a level of difficulty of 3, on a scale of 1 to 6, including some solos performed from memory

Notes

SILVER·BURDETT

Making Music

1. E.g., band or orchestra instrument, keyboard instrument, fretted instrument, electronic instrument

National Standards for Music Education

Content Standard	✔	Achievement Standard

7

Evaluating music and music performances

☐ **7a** Students develop criteria for evaluating the quality and effectiveness of music performances and compositions and apply the criteria in their person listening and performing

☐ **7b** Students evaluate the quality and effectiveness of their own and others' performances, compositions, arrangements, and improvisations by applying specific criteria appropriate for the style of the music and offer constructive suggestions for improvement

Notes _____

_____

8

Understanding relationships between music, the other arts, and disciplines outside the arts

☐ **8a** Students compare in two or more arts how the characteristic materials of each art[4] can be used to transform similar events, scenes, emotions, or ideas into works of art

☐ **8b** Students describe ways in which the principles and subject matter of other disciplines taught in the school are interrelated with those of music[5]

Notes _____

_____

9

Understanding music in relation to history and culture

☐ **9a** Students describe distinguishing characteristics of representative music genres and styles from a variety of cultures[6]

☐ **9b** Students classify by genre and style (and, if applicable, by historical period, composer, and title) a varied body of exemplary (that is, high-quality and characteristic) musical works and explain the characteristics that cause each work to be considered exemplary

☐ **9c** Students compare, in several cultures of the world, functions music serves, roles of musicians,[7] and conditions under which music is typically performed

Notes _____

_____

4. E.g., sound in music, visual stimuli in visual arts, movement in dance, human interrelationships in theatre
5. E.g., language arts: issues to be considered in setting texts to music; mathematics: frequency ratios of intervals; sciences: the human hearing process and hazards to hearing; social studies: historical and social events and movements chronicled in or influenced by musical works
6. E.g., jazz, mariachi, gamelan
7. E.g., lead guitarist in a rock band, composer of jingles for commercials, singer in Peking opera

Used by permission of the Music Educators National Conference.

National Standards for Music Education

Content Standard ☑	Achievement Standard

3

Improvising melodies, variations, and accompaniments

☐ **3a** Students improvise simple harmonic accompaniments

☐ **3b** Students improvise melodic embellishments and simple rhythmic and melodic variations on given pentatonic melodies and melodies in major keys

☐ **3c** Students improvise short melodies, unaccompanied and over given rhythmic accompaniments, each in a consistent style, meter, and tonality

Notes _____

_____

_____

_____

_____

_____

4

Composing and arranging music within specified guidelines

☐ **4a** Students compose short pieces within specified guidelines,[2] demonstrating how the elements of music are used to achieve unity and variety, tension and release, and balance

☐ **4b** Students arrange simple pieces for voices or instruments other than those for which the pieces were written

☐ **4c** Students use a variety of traditional and nontraditional sound sources and electronic media when composing and arranging

Notes _____

_____

_____

_____

_____

_____

2. E.g., a particular style, form, instrumentation, compositional technique

National Standards for Music Education

Content Standard	✔		Achievement Standard

5 **Reading and notating music**

□ **5a** Students read whole, half, quarter, eighth, sixteenth, and dotted notes and rests in $\frac{2}{4}$, $\frac{3}{4}$, $\frac{4}{4}$, $\frac{6}{8}$, $\frac{3}{8}$, and *alla breve* meter signatures

□ **5b** Students read at sight simple melodies in both the treble and bass clefs

□ **5c** Students identify and define standard notation symbols for pitch, rhythm, dynamics, tempo, articulation, and expression

□ **5d** Students use standard notation to record their musical ideas and the musical ideas of others

□ **5e** Students who participate in a choral or instrumental ensemble or class sightread, accurately and expressively, music with a level of difficulty of 2, on a scale of 1 to 6

Notes _____

_____

_____

_____

_____

6 **Listening to, analyzing, and describing music**

□ **6a** Students describe specific music events[3] in a given aural example, using appropriate terminology

□ **6b** Students analyze the uses of elements of music in aural examples representing diverse genres and cultures

□ **6c** Students demonstrate knowledge of the basic principles of meter, rhythm, tonality, intervals, chords, and harmonic progressions in their analyses of music

Notes _____

_____

_____

_____

_____

SILVER·BURDETT

Making Music

3. E.g., entry of oboe, change of meter, return of refrain

SILVER·BURDETT
Making Music

Teacher's Edition
Part One
Grade 5

Editorial Offices: Glenview, Illinois • Parsippany, New Jersey • New York, New York
Sales Offices: Needham, Massachusetts • Duluth, Georgia • Glenview, Illinois
Coppell, Texas • Sacramento, California • Mesa, Arizona

ISBN: 0-382-36595-X

6 7 8 9 10 V064 13 12 11 10 09 08 07 06

Authors

PROGRAM AUTHORS

Jane Beethoven
Music Author/Consultant
Westport, Connecticut

Susan Brumfield
Texas Tech University
Lubbock, Texas

Patricia Shehan Campbell
University of Washington
Seattle, Washington

David N. Connors
California State University
at Los Angeles
Los Angeles, California

Robert A. Duke
University of Texas at Austin
Austin, Texas

Judith A. Jellison
University of Texas at Austin
Austin, Texas

Rita Klinger
Cleveland State University
Cleveland, Ohio

Rochelle Mann
Fort Lewis College
Durango, Colorado

Hunter C. March
University of Texas at Austin
Austin, Texas

Nan L. McDonald
San Diego State University
San Diego, California

Marvelene C. Moore
University of Tennessee
Knoxville, Tennessee

Mary Palmer
University of Central Florida
Orlando, Florida

Konnie Saliba
University of Memphis
Memphis, Tennessee

Will Schmid
Professor Emeritus
University of Wisconsin—
Milwaukee
Milwaukee, Wisconsin

Carol Scott-Kassner
Music Author/Consultant
Seattle, Washington

Mary E. Shamrock
Professor Emeritus, California
State University at Northridge
Minneapolis, Minnesota

Sandra L. Stauffer
Arizona State University
Tempe, Arizona

Judith Thomas
Music Education Consultant
West Nyack, New York

Jill Trinka
University of St. Thomas
St. Paul, Minnesota

CONTRIBUTING AUTHORS

Audrey A. Berger
University of Rhode Island
Kingston, Rhode Island

Roslyn Burrough
Clinician/Consultant
Brooklyn, New York

J. Bryan Burton
West Chester University
West Chester, Pennsylvania

Jeffrey E. Bush
Arizona State University
Tempe, Arizona

John M. Cooksey
University of Utah
Salt Lake City, Utah

Shelly C. Cooper
University of Arizona
Tucson, Arizona

Alice-Ann Darrow
Florida State University
Tallahassee, Florida

Scott Emmons
University of Wisconsin—
Milwaukee
Milwaukee, Wisconsin

Debra Erck
Austin Independent
School District
Austin, Texas

Anne M. Fennell
Vista Unified School District
Vista, California

Doug Fisher
San Diego State University
San Diego, California

Carroll Gonzo
University of St. Thomas
St. Paul, Minnesota

Larry Harms
University of Southern California
Los Angeles, California

Martha F. Hilley
University of Texas at Austin
Austin, Texas

Debbie Burgoon Hines
Consultant
DeSoto, Texas

Mary Ellen Junda
University of Connecticut
Storrs, Connecticut

Donald Kalbach
Consultant
Bound Brook, New Jersey

Shirley E. Lacroix
Rhode Island College
Providence, Rhode Island

Henry Leck
Butler University
Indianapolis, Indiana

Sanna Longden
Clinician/Consultant
Evanston, Illinois

Glenn A. Richter
University of Texas at Austin
Austin, Texas

Carlos Xavier Rodriguez
University of Iowa
Iowa City, Iowa

Kathleen D. Sanz
District School Board of
Pasco County
Tampa, Florida

Julie K. Scott
Southern Methodist University
Dallas, Texas

Gwyn Spell
Clinician/Consultant
Marietta, Georgia

Barb Stevanson
Austin Independent
School District
Austin, Texas

Kimberly C. Walls
Auburn University
Auburn, Alabama

Jackie Wiggins
Oakland University
Rochester, Michigan

Maribeth Yoder-White
Appalachian State University
Boone, North Carolina

Program Contributors

LISTENING MAP CONTRIBUTING AUTHORS

Patricia Shehan Campbell
Seattle, Washington

Jackie Chooi-Theng Lew
Salisbury, Maryland

Ann Clements
Federal Way, Washington

Kay Edwards
Oxford, Ohio

Scott Emmons
Milwaukee, Wisconsin

Sheila Feay-Shaw
Shoreline, Washington

Kay Greenhaw
Austin, Texas

David Hebert
Seattle, Washington

Hunter C. March
Austin, Texas

Will Schmid
Milwaukee, Wisconsin

Carol Scott-Kassner
Seattle, Washington

Mary E. Shamrock
Minneapolis, Minnesota

Sandra L. Stauffer
Tempe, Arizona

MOVEMENT CONTRIBUTING AUTHORS

Judy Lasko
New York, New York

Marvelene C. Moore
Knoxville, Tennessee

Dixie Piver
New York, New York

Wendy Taucher
New York, New York

Susan Thomasson
Demarest, New Jersey

Judith Thompson-Barthwell
Detroit, Michigan

TEACHER ADVISORY PANEL

Kathryn Amshoff
Humble, Texas

Bevra L. Carruth
Midland, Texas

Rebekah Dykhuis
Austin, Texas

Gwendolyn J. Farris
DeSoto, Texas

Richard Gabrillo
Georgetown, Texas

Maria Yolanda Garza
San Antonio, Texas

Mary Lee Gilliland
Memphis, Tennessee

Jacque Hall
Arlington, Texas

Shari Hazell
Canton, Michigan

Lynette Hubler
Bondurant, Iowa

Tracy Walsh Juarez
El Paso, Texas

Barbara Keaton
Arlington, Texas

Jim Lovell
Plano, Texas

Scott Mahaffey
San Antonio, Texas

Laura L. McGregor
Sugar Land, Texas

Carol Moeller
Carmel, Indiana

Sue Niemi
*Downingtown,
Pennsylvania*

Kathy Lee Peinado
El Paso, Texas

Domingo Porras
Edinburg, Texas

Joseph Puzzo
Washington, D.C.

Pam Ramirez
Brownsville, Texas

Emily Roden
Denton, Texas

Beth Russell
Noblesville, Indiana

Chrissie Horany Seligson
Arlington, Texas

Tanya Seslar
Denver, Colorado

Donna Shortal
Winter Park, Florida

Barb Stevanson
Austin, Texas

Roseanne Stuetz
Maywood, New Jersey

Cathy Warnock
Mesquite, Texas

Wendy Weeks
Abilene, Texas

Barbara White
Williamsville, New York

Recordings

RECORDING PERSONNEL

Executive Producer

Buryl Red, BR Productions

Associate Producers for Vocals

Bill and Charlene James, Tom Moore, J. Douglas Pummill, Michael Rafter, Robert Spivak, Jeanine Tesori, Linda Twine

Associate Producers for Instrumentals

Rick Baitz, Rick Bassett, Joseph Joubert, Bryan Louiselle, Michael Rafter, Buddy Skipper, Jeanine Tesori

Arrangers/Orchestrators

Rick Baitz, Rick Bassett, Jack Cortner, Bruce Coughlin, Cathy Elliott, Ned Ginsberg, Joseph Joubert, Dick Lieb, Bryan Louiselle, Chris McDonald, Gustavo Moretta, Valerie Naranjo, Janet Pummill, William Pursell, Buryl Red, Mick Rossi, Steve Shapiro, Buddy Skipper, Jeff Steinberg, Jeff Talman, Jeanine Tesori, David Thomas, Linda Twine, Dale Wilson, Ovid Young

Technical Engineering Staff

Jonathan Duckett, *supervisor*, Dave Darlington, Chris Miller, Tim Polashek, Amy Pummill, Patrick Pummill, Mick Rossi, Dan Rudin, William Santamaria, Bob Schaper, Ted Spencer, Jeff Talman, Tony Zimmerman

Instrumental Conductors

Bryan Louiselle, Michael Rafter, Buryl Red, Jeanine Tesori, Linda Twine

CHOIRS

Children's Choir Conductors and Choirs

Debbie Beinhorn
Beinhorn Singers

D. Shawn Berry
Bak Middle School of the Arts Boys Choir, Bak Middle School of the Arts Mixed Choir

Darrell Bledsoe
Darrell Bledsoe Children's Voices, Darrell Bledsoe Men's Chorus, Darrell Bledsoe Singers, Houston Vocal Edition, Richland Singers, Singing Boys of Houston, Spring Singers, Varsity Girls, Varsity Singers

Linda Bradberry
The Augusta Children's Choir

Madeline Bridges
The Nashville Children's Choir

Gregg Bunn
Lone Star Kids

Lori Casteel
Kidstyle Singers

Wayne Causey
The Cumberland Singers

Victor Cook
Victor Cook Singers

Debra Crowe
Debra Crowe Singers

David Czervinske
David Czervinske Children's Choir, David Czervinske Singers

Jerri Davidson
The Daggett Choir

Connie Drosakis
Bak Middle School of the Arts 6th Grade Treble Choir

Lynne Gackle
Miami Girls Choir

Ned Ginsburg
The Broadway Kids

Charlotte Greeson
Richland Singers

Joan Gregoryk
Chevy Chase Elementary Singers

Cathy Guajardo
Cathy Guajardo Singers

Jacque Hall
The Mary Moore Singers

Moses Hogan
The Moses Hogan Singers Youth Ensemble

Sandy Holland
The Charlotte Children's Choir

Eugenia Huanca
Eugenia Huanca Group

Laurie Jenschke
Eastman Children's Choir, Voices of Fredericksburg, Texas Children's Chorale

Brenda Jewell
The Nashville Children's Choir

Doug Jewett
The Smokey Mountain Children's Choir

Rebecca Johnson
The Sunshine Singers

Joseph Joubert
Joseph Joubert Singers

Mary Ellen Junda
The Treblemakers Children's Choir of the University of Connecticut

Jan Juneau
Woodland Singers

Henry Leck
The Indianapolis Children's Choir

Jeanine Tesori
Jeanine Tesori Singers

Carol Lockhart
The Carol Lockhart Singers

Chester Mahooty
American Indian Dance Theater

Albert McNeil
Albert McNeil Jubilee Singers

Jo Morris
Jo Morris Singers

Cynthia Nott
The Children's Chorus of Greater Dallas

Celia Ong
Asian American Youth Chorale

Rosalyn Payne
Step Chillin'

Ted Polk
Carrollton Singers

Douglas Pummill
Booker T. Washington Singers, Cantamos!, Children of the Heartland, The Dulcet Singers, Fiesta Americana, Heartland Youth, Heritage Children's Choir, Heritage Youth Choir, The New Horizons Show Choir, The North Texas Hispanic Choir, The Pan American Children's Choir, The Pan American Youth Choir, The Pan Asian Children's Choir, The Rainbow Children's Choir, The Rainbow Youth Choir, United in Youth

Eddie Quaid
Cypress Singers

Lynn Redmond
The Gwinnette Young Singers

Steve Roddy
The Houston Children's Choir, Steve Roddy Boys' Choir

Kenny Rodgers
Kenny Rodgers Singers

Betty Roe
McCullough Singers, Betty Roe Children's Choir

Reggie Royal
Calypso Royals

Sally Schott
South Houston Singers

Marilyn Shadinger
The Nashville Children's Choir

Martha Shaw
The Spivey Hall Children's Choir Chamber Ensemble

Kay Sherrill
Judson High School Chorale

Mark Slaughter
The Owensboro Children's Choir

Steve Stevens
The Seattle Boys Choir, The Seattle Children's Choir

Cameron Sullenburger
Wilson Middle School Varsity Boys Choir, Wilson Middle School Varsity Girls Choir, Wilson Middle School Varsity Mixed Choir

Sheryl Tallant
Kidstyle Singers

Barry Talley
Barry Talley Singers, Deer Park Singers

Julia Thorn
DeKalb County Children's Choir

Judy Tisch
Bammell Singers

Marie Tomlinson
Clitheroe Young Singers

Darryl Tookes
The Darryl Tookes Singers

Walter Turnbill
The Boys Choir of Harlem

Linda Twine
55th Street Jazz Singers, Linda Twine Singers

Tim Vaughn
La Porte Singers

Walt Whitman
The Soul Children of Chicago, The Walt Whitman Atlanta Singers, Walt Whitman's Soul Children

Linda Williams
Sundance Academy Singers, Westwind Singers

Judith Willoughby
The Temple University Children's Choir

Cheryl Wilson
Garland High School A cappella Choir, Garland High School A cappella Men, Garland High School A cappella Women

Janet Wilson
Janet Wilson Singers, Kid Connection

Karen Wolff
Cincinnati Children's Choir

Patrinell Wright
Total Experience Gospel Choir

Welcome music educators!

Silver Burdett MAKING MUSIC is an active, balanced, and comprehensive music program. It provides both sequential teaching of music elements and skills as well as theme-based instruction for music educators and students.

Kindergarten Big Book

Student Editions, Grades 1–6

- **Active music making** develops musical knowledge and skills.
- **Exceptional song literature and recordings** provide a strong foundation for instruction.
- **Balanced organization** presents a comprehensive music curriculum.
- **Proven content** reflects the National Standards for Music Education.

Active music making that supports your teaching

Student Editions

- Dynamic repertoire of song literature
- Opportunities to sing, listen to music, play instruments, read music, move to music, and connect to other disciplines

Big Books

- Big, bold, colorfully illustrated lessons
- Great for small-group and classroom instruction
- Many different musical experiences
- Sturdy easel for easy display
- One volume, Grades K–1; two volumes, Grade 2

Grades 1 and 2

Teacher's Editions

- Sequential instruction in Units 1–6
- Theme-based instruction in Units 7–12
- National Standards integrated throughout
- Consistent, three-step lesson plan

Recordings you'll want to carry everywhere

Ultraportable CD Cases

- Innovative design keeps you organized
- Lightweight and small so you can carry anywhere
- Removable pages for greater flexibility

Audio CD Booklets

- Quick, easy guide for each grade-level Audio CD package
- Comprehensive list of recorded tracks; includes information on performing groups, instrumentation, track length, page references, and special recorded features

Professional Recordings

- Superb sound quality—a higher standard in educational recordings
- Artists that people know and recognize
- Variety of children, youth, and adult vocal performers
- Varied and rich repertoire of listening selections
- Widest range of music genres, styles, and cultures—recorded with authenticity
- Tracks for stereo vocals, stereo performance, teach-a-part, sung pronunciation practice, dance practice and performance, interviews, and assessments

Resources that enhance your music teaching

Keyboard Accompaniments

- Keyboard accompaniments for classroom use and performances
- Easy-to-use, spiral-bound book—hard-back cover stays upright on any keyboard stand

Grade 5   Grade 1

Grade 3

Listening Map Transparency Package

- Visual guides for listening selections
- Easy-to-follow graphics that build skills in listening and understanding music
- Reproducible masters to support instruction

Resource Books

Reproducible masters are available to support the following:

- Pronunciation Practice Guides
- Graphic Organizers
- Assessments and Rubrics
- Music Reading Worksheets
- Music Reading Practice (1–6)
- Orff Arrangements
- Signing Activities
- Keyboard (2–6)
- Recorder (3–6)
- Activity Masters

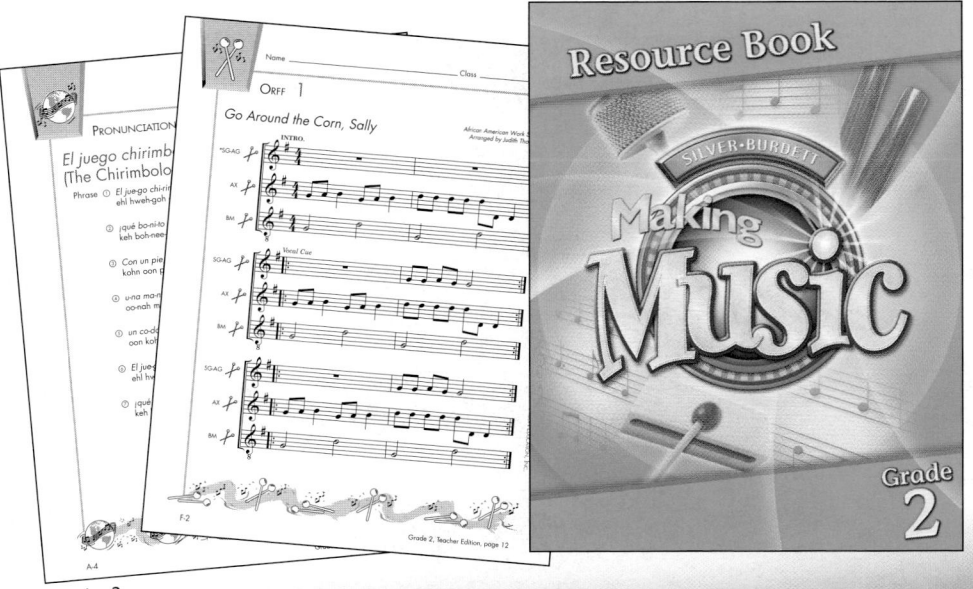

Grade 2

More resources for music instruction

Step into Music, Pre-Kindergarten

- Complete fine arts program that builds early music literacy and language skills
- Effective support for children's physical, emotional, social, and cognitive development

Silver Burdett MAKING MUSIC, Grades 7–8

- Modular organization for maximum teaching flexibility
- Active music-making experiences
- Comprehensive music instruction
- National Standards integrated throughout

MAKING MUSIC with Movement and Dance

- Easy-to-follow guide for movement and dance activities
- Folk dances, ethnic dances, and creative movement
- One volume—all grade levels

¡A cantar!

- Traditional and contemporary songs in Spanish
- Theme and element connections
- Recorded pronunciation practice
- Two CDs with all songs and literature
- Primary and Intermediate Levels

Bridges to Asia

- Additional lessons to explore the rich musical heritage of Asia
- Pronunciation practice for each song
- Four CDs with all songs and literature
- Primary and Intermediate Levels

New Activities for the Substitute Teacher

- Songs and activities for substitute teachers
- Song lyrics, teaching strategies, reproducible activity masters, and audio CD
- Integrated activities for all grade levels

Master Index and Correlations

- Comprehensive reference to simplify planning
- Grades K–8 index of all songs, speech pieces, listening selections, and more
- Pitch and Rhythm Index
- Thematic Index
- Reading and Phonics Correlations

Steps to MAKING MUSIC for sequential instruction

Silver Burdett MAKING MUSIC has a balanced, two-part organization. Part 1 is Steps to MAKING MUSIC, which comprises Units 1–6. Steps to MAKING MUSIC provides sequential instruction using elements, skills, and connections. These systematically progress from unit to unit and grade to grade.

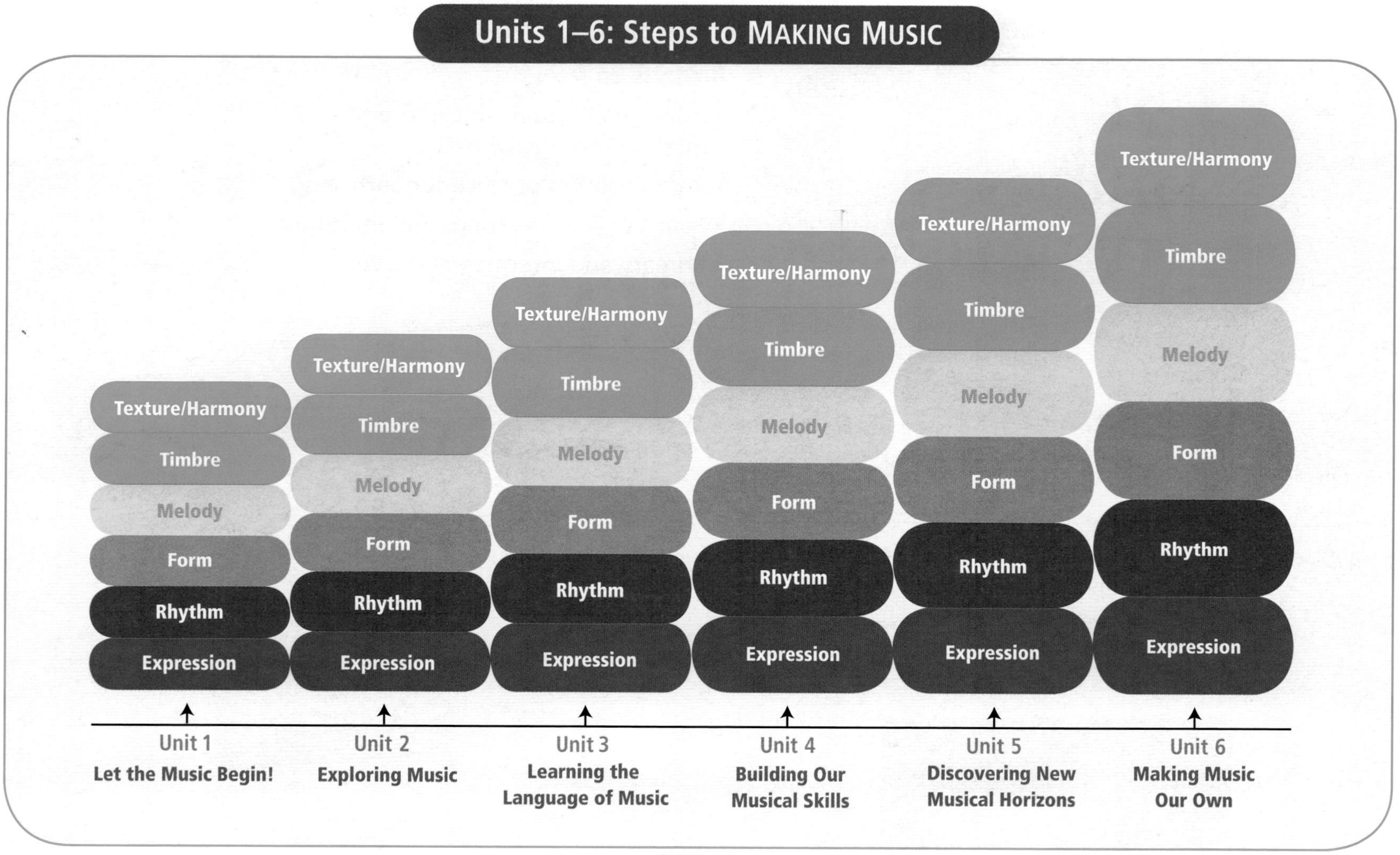

Units 1–6: Steps to MAKING MUSIC

Unit 1	Unit 2	Unit 3	Unit 4	Unit 5	Unit 6
Texture/Harmony	Texture/Harmony	Texture/Harmony	Texture/Harmony	Texture/Harmony	Texture/Harmony
Timbre	Timbre	Timbre	Timbre	Timbre	Timbre
Melody	Melody	Melody	Melody	Melody	Melody
Form	Form	Form	Form	Form	Form
Rhythm	Rhythm	Rhythm	Rhythm	Rhythm	Rhythm
Expression	Expression	Expression	Expression	Expression	Expression
Let the Music Begin!	**Exploring Music**	**Learning the Language of Music**	**Building Our Musical Skills**	**Discovering New Musical Horizons**	**Making Music Our Own**

Units 1–6: Steps to MAKING MUSIC

- Sequenced instruction to help students learn music elements and skills
- Gradual increase in skill levels that allows students to assimilate and apply learning
- 72 total music lessons—36 weekly core lessons plus 36 lessons to expand instruction

Paths to MAKING MUSIC for theme explorations

Paths to MAKING MUSIC is Part 2 of the program and includes Units 7–12. This section increases your students' music knowledge and skills through theme-based activities and lessons. The themes are coordinated from grade to grade so that all students can share related instruction.

Units 7–12: Paths to MAKING MUSIC

6	Exploring America's Music	Say It with Drums	Be a Star!	Sound Waves	Strike Up the Chorus	Celebrate the Day
5	Building America in Song	Music Around the World	In the Pop Style	Keepers of the Earth	We Sing!	Holidays in Song
4	Going Places U.S.A.	Bring Your Passport	Chasing a Dream	Earth, Sea, and Sky	Sing Out!	Sing and Celebrate
3	Singing America	Our World of Music	Fun and Games	This Beautiful Planet	Tuneful Tales	Holidays to Share
2	Music–U.S.A.	Home and Away	Creature Feature	Our Planet Earth	Perform a Story	Celebrate the Season
1	Making Music at School	My Family and Me	Adventures with Friends	The Great Outdoors	Imagination Station!	Days to Celebrate
K	All About Me	My Neighbors and Me	Imagine That!	Nature Walk	Look What I Can Do!	Celebrate with Me!
	↑	↑	↑	↑	↑	↑
	Unit 7 America Makes Music	Unit 8 From Home to the World	Unit 9 Expanding the Boundaries	Unit 10 Garden of the Earth	Unit 11 The Power of Performance	Unit 12 The Joy of Celebration

Units 7–12: Paths to MAKING MUSIC

- Thematic units aligned with themes commonly found in social studies, reading, science, and other curricular areas
- Terrific opportunities to make connections and present performances

Lesson Organization

Easy-to-teach, flexible, and inspiring lessons

Objective Bar focuses your students' learning. The yellow burst highlights the assessed item.

Lesson at a Glance lists critical information to streamline planning.

CD References make it easy to access your audio collection.

More Music Choices provide options for further practice.

Footnotes support your instruction and help you make connections.

Building Skills Through Music connects music learning to other curricular areas.

LESSON
Core **4**

Element: RHYTHM　　**Skill: PLAYING**　　**Connection: SOCIAL STUD**

LESSON AT A GLANCE

Element Focus　**RHYTHM** ♫ and ♫
Skill Objective　**PLAYING** Play sixteenth-note patterns
Connection　**SOCIAL STUDIES** Investigate the historical
Activity　　context of a railroad song

MATERIALS
• "Drill, Ye Tarriers"　　　　　　　　　**CD 3-16**
　Recording Routine: Intro (4 m.); v. 1; refrain; interlude (4 m.); v. 2; refrain; interlude (4 m.); v. 3, refrain; coda
• **Music Reading Practice, Sequence 6**　　**CD 3-18**
• **Dance Directions** for "Drill, Ye Tarriers" p. 554
• *Symphony No. 9*, Movement 1 (excerpt)　**CD 3-22**
• **Resource Book** p. E-7, F-6, I-6
• selected classroom percussion instruments

VOCABULARY
symphony　　　　　　movement

◆ ◆ ◆ ◆ National Standards ◆ ◆ ◆ ◆
1b Sing easy pieces with technical accuracy
2b Perform easy instrumental pieces with technical accuracy
5a Read quarter, eighth, sixteenth notes in duple meter
5d Use standard notation to record musical ideas
6a Listen and describe events in music using appropriate terms
8b Identify ways music relates to social studies

MORE MUSIC CHOICES
For more experience with sixteenth-note patterns:
"Camptown Races," p. 270

1 INTRODUCE

Have students listen to "Drill Ye Tarriers" **CD 3-16** and discuss the lyrics. Use the suggestions in Across the Curriculum below to engage students in a discussion of railroads.

Work to the Rhythm

In the 1880s, many different groups of immigrants helped to build American railroads. One of these groups was the Irish. **Sing** "Drill, Ye Tarriers," a song that tells of the hardships and injustices the railroad workers faced.

Listen for some clues in the text about what tarriers do.

CD 3-16

Drill, Ye Tarriers

Words and Music by Thomas C

VERSE
Cm

1. Ev - 'ry morn - ing at sev - en o' - clock There's twen - ty tar - ri - ers a
2. Our new fore - man is Dan ___ Mc - Cann, I'll tell you sure ___ he's a
3. Next time pay - day comes ___ a - round, Jim Goff was short ___ one

work - ing at the rock, And the boss comes a - long and he
blame ___ mean ___ man; Last ___ week a ____ prema - ture ___
buck, ___ he ___ found; "What ___ for?" says ___ he; then ___

says, "Keep still, And come down heav - y on the cast iron drill.
blast went off, And a mile in the air ___ went ___ Big Jim Goff.
this re - ply, "You're docked for the time ___ you were up in the sky.

54　Reading Sequence 6

Footnotes

MOVEMENT

▶ **Patterned Dance** Dancing is a natural part of Irish culture. It is said that when two Irishmen meet at a crossroad, they do a little jig. When the Irishmen who worked on the railroad had time to relax, they sang and danced. There were not many women at the railroad camps, so the men danced with each other, just as American cowboys and Argentine sailors did. See p. 554 for a movement pattern to accompany "Drill, Ye Tarriers."

BUILDING SKILLS THROUGH MUSIC

▶ **Math** Divide the class into two groups, with one group clapping the rhythm of the verse, the second group clapping a steady beat. Ask students to identify beats with one or more notes. Each beat will equal one [whole]. Review the fractions for 1/2 and 1/4. Have students identify fractions for each note. For example, an eighth note would equal 1/2; a sixteenth note would equal 1/4. Add the fractions for each beat, then for each measure.

54　Reading Sequence 6, p. 492

ACROSS THE CURRICULUM

8b ▶ **Social Studies** Students may enjoy reading and then creating a short historical-fact introduction to "Drill, Ye Tarriers" for performances. For interesting facts about the building of railroads across the United States, suggest they read *Ten Mile Day: And the Building of the Transcontinental Railroad* by Mary Ann Fraser (Henry Holt, 1996). This fascinating account of the building of the Transcontinental Railroad in 1869 explores the historical highlights and engineering feats, lives of the many ethnic groups who served as railroad workers, and the effects of the railroads on Native Americans.

Grade 5

REFRAIN

So drill, ye tar - ri - ers, drill, And drill, ye tar - ri - ers,

drill! Oh, it's work all day for sug - ar in your tay,

Down be-yond the rail - way, And drill, ye tar - ri - ers, drill!

Railroad Rhythms

Find the  and ♫♫ patterns in the song.

Sing the song again, and when one of these patterns comes along, sing the rhythm syllables instead of the words. Good luck!

Play the rhythm parts below with the refrain of "Drill, Ye Tarriers."

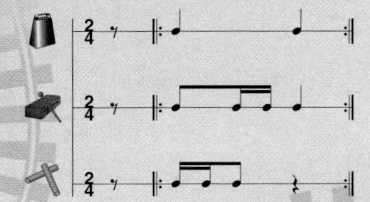

Listen to the ♫♫ pattern in this excerpt.

CD 3–22

 Symphony No. 9 ("From the New World")

Movement 1
by Antonín Dvořák

The name of this symphony, "From the New World," refers to the United States. Czech composer Antonín Dvořák [an-toh-NEEN d'VOHR-zhahk] wrote it at about the same time railroad workers were singing "Drill, Ye Tarriers."

Unit 2 **55**

2 DEVELOP

Reading

Ask volunteers to write three rhythms on the board:

♩♩♩♩ , ♫♩ , ♩♫

Set a steady beat and then have students

5a
- Read each rhythm with rhythm syllables.
- Look at the notation for "Drill, Ye Tarriers" and count how many times each sixteenth-note rhythm appears in the song. Then read the verse of the song with rhythm syllables.

For more practice performing sixteenth-note rhythms, see Music Reading Practice, Sequence 6 on p. 492 and Resource Book p. E-6.

Creating

5d
Add two beamed eighth notes, a quarter note, and a quarter rest to the rhythms on the board. Draw four blanks (two measures) on the board. Have students

- Decide how to fill in the blanks, using the patterns on the board. (The quarter note and quarter rest can be used only once.)
- Use standard symbols to notate rhythm in simple patterns and perform them using rhythm syllables. Then say their patterns one after another without silent beats in between.

Playing

Invite students to perform the instrumental parts on p. 55 with the refrain "Drill, Ye Tarriers."

Listening

6a
Play the excerpt from *Symphony No. 9* **CD 3-22** and ask students to listen for the *tiri-ti* rhythm.

3 CLOSE

Element: RHYTHM **ASSESSMENT**

1b **Performance/Observation** Have students play
2b their rhythm patterns, or those on p. 55, on selected percussion instruments as ostinatos, while singing "Drill, Ye Tarriers." Observe for rhythmic accuracy.

Systematic Instruction follows a consistent, three-step plan.

Song Notation on a white background improves readability.

National Standards at point of use identify your instructional goals.

Assessment allows you to monitor students' understanding.

SKILLS REINFORCEMENT

▶ **Recorder** To give students additional experience with rhythm patterns that use eighth and sixteenth notes, have them
2b compose a rhythmic piece to play on their recorders. Invite students to create and notate four, two-beat measures using quarter, eighth, and sixteenth notes. Using their recorders, have them play their compositions on the note G. Some students may want to accompany the verse of "Drill, Ye Tarriers" by playing their composition on G. They will need to repeat their four-measure pieces or have a friend play the second set of four measures.

Another time, have students play the rhythm of the words on the note G during the verse of the song. Make sure they say *daah* on each note so the rhythm is articulated clearly.

A countermelody for "Drill, Ye Tarriers" can be found on Resource Book p. I-6.

CHARACTER EDUCATION

▶ **Collaboration** To promote students' understanding of the skills necessary to collaborate with others, discuss singing and professional partnerships. Singing in a group requires vocal control and careful listening to achieve appropriate balance and blend. Individuals often must adjust their performance to benefit the group. Ask students what other situations require that individuals sacrifice control to help the group. (Accept various answers including team sports and medical teams.)

TECHNOLOGY/MEDIA LINK

5d **Notation Software** Have students notate their rhythm patterns from this lesson and print them before playing them.

Unit 2 *Exploring Music* **55**

The best music, the widest selection

Favorite songs, award-winning songs, exciting originals! Silver Burdett MAKING MUSIC provides quality song literature of lasting value. An exciting mix of songs and recordings supports every type of music-making experience—singing, playing instruments, moving, listening, creating, reading, and notating.

Music that models and instructs

Children's voices provide vocal modeling and adult voices demonstrate style, expression, and cultural authenticity.

- Student soloists
- Student vocal ensembles
- Student choirs
- Adult soloists
- Adult choirs
- Adult vocal ensembles

Music that represents diverse genres and styles

Your students experience, perform, and evaluate the most diverse range of music.

- Folk
- Traditional
- Multicultural
- Popular
- Contemporary
- Patriotic
- Seasonal
- Holiday

Recordings that support music learning

- Listening selections
- Dances
- Instrumental sound banks
- Montages
- Recorded poems and stories
- Recorded interviews
- Recorded assessments

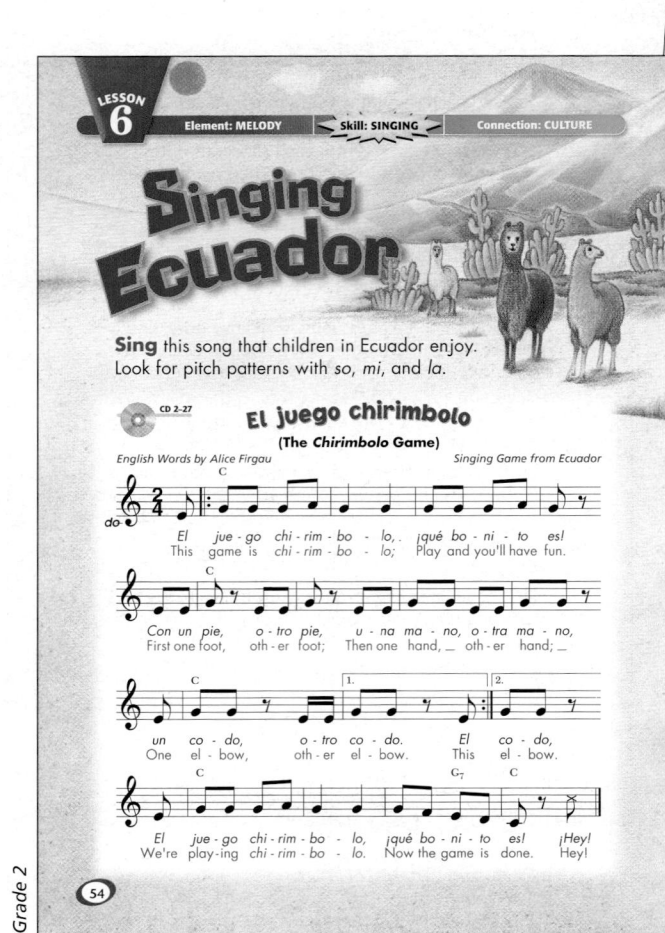

Recordings that express musical artistry

World-class performers, composers, and conductors inspire creative expression and performance.

- Ella Fitzgerald
- Ziggy Marley
- Gloria Estefan
- Yo-Yo Ma
- Itzhak Perlman
- Ludwig van Beethoven
- Leontyne Price
- Carlos Santana
- George Gershwin
- Wynton Marsalis
- The Boys Choir of Harlem
- Seiji Ozawa
- Tito Puente
- John Philip Sousa
- Johann Sebastian Bach
- Whitney Houston
- Duke Ellington, and hundreds more!

Music Literacy

Reading and writing music notation

A goal of Silver Burdett MAKING MUSIC is to help you develop your students' music literacy. Systematic instruction and practice opportunities permit all your students to become accomplished at reading and writing music notation.

Music Reading Lessons are clearly identified in both the Student Editions and Teacher's Editions.

Built-in Reading Sequences are referenced for access to more practice.

Instructional Strategies for Reading Music align with National Standards to meet your specific curricular goals.

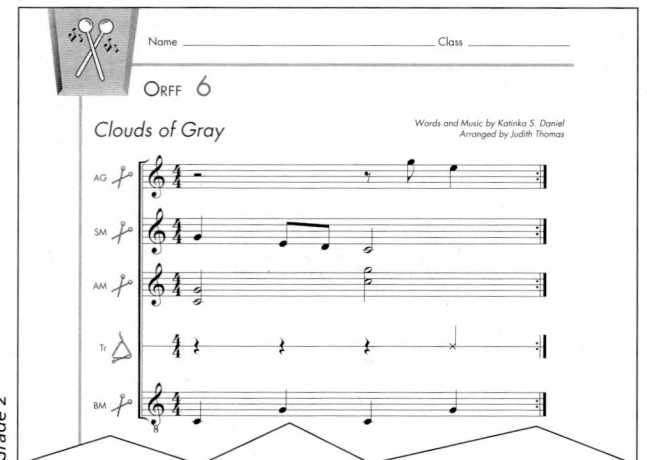

Orff Accompaniments add enrichment to many reading lessons.

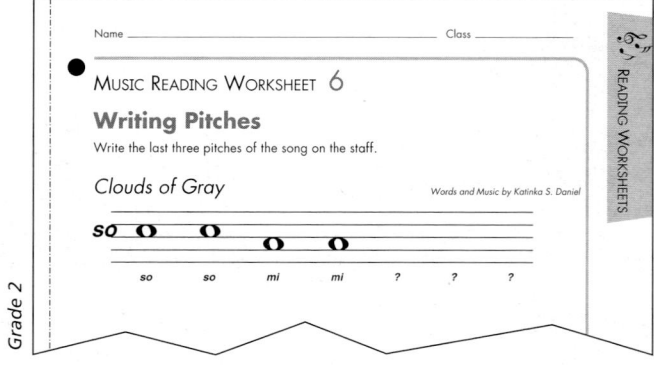

Music Reading Worksheets accompany every lesson to reinforce and extend music literacy.

Music Reading Practice Section reinforces melodic and rhythmic literacy. The section contains 24 Reading Sequences at each grade level for ample practice.

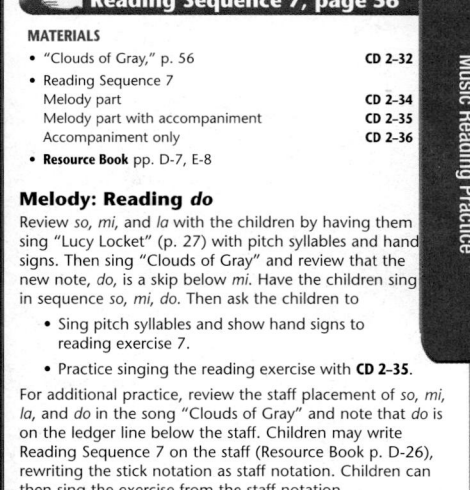

On-Page Pitch Ladder illustrates the hand signs used in reading sequences.

MIDI Tracks are provided for every Reading Sequence, allowing your students to practice individual parts at various tempos and keys.

Music Reading Practice Teacher's Edition Pages provide instructional strategies that make it easy to teach the reading lessons.

Audio CDs include both individual vocal and instrumental parts, as well as accompaniment tracks for each Reading Sequence.

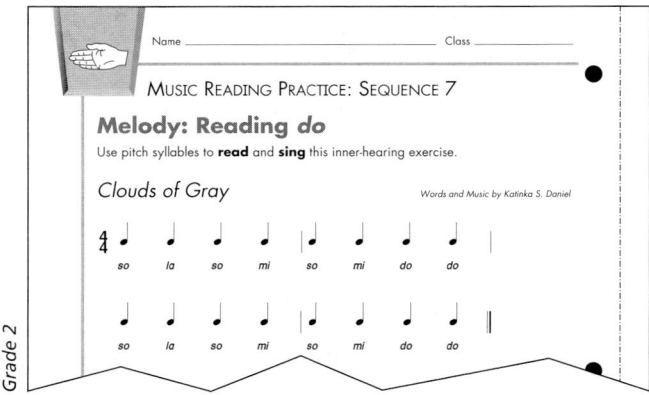

Music Reading Practice Worksheets support each Reading Sequence. Use the worksheets to create overhead transparencies for group instruction.

Performance Skills

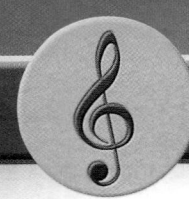

Activities for creative student performances

Developmentally appropriate vocal, instrumental, and movement experiences are core throughout Silver Burdett MAKING MUSIC. These varied musical experiences help you teach students critical aspects of expression, rhythm, form, melody, timbre, and texture/harmony.

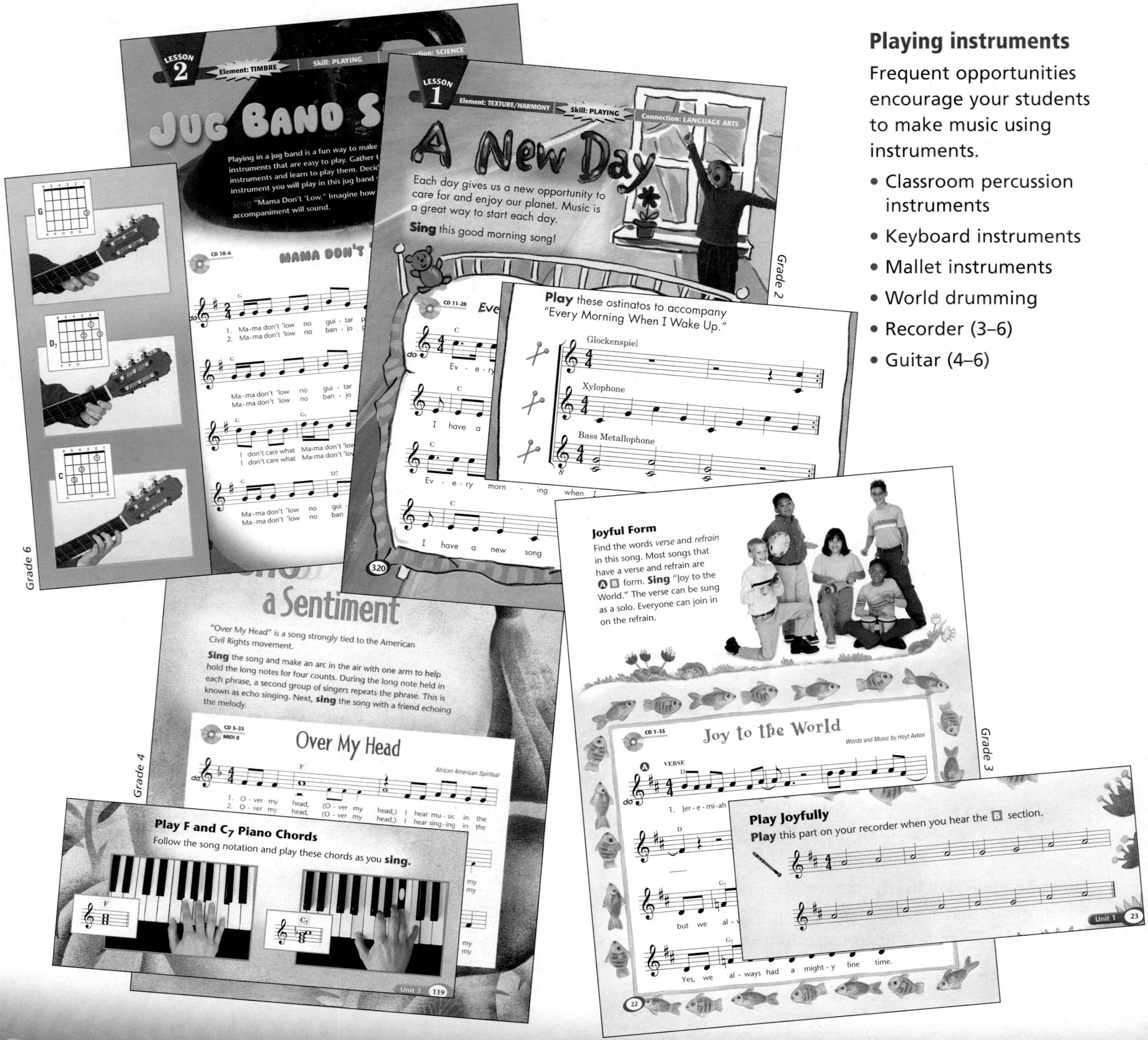

Playing instruments

Frequent opportunities encourage your students to make music using instruments.

- Classroom percussion instruments
- Keyboard instruments
- Mallet instruments
- World drumming
- Recorder (3–6)
- Guitar (4–6)

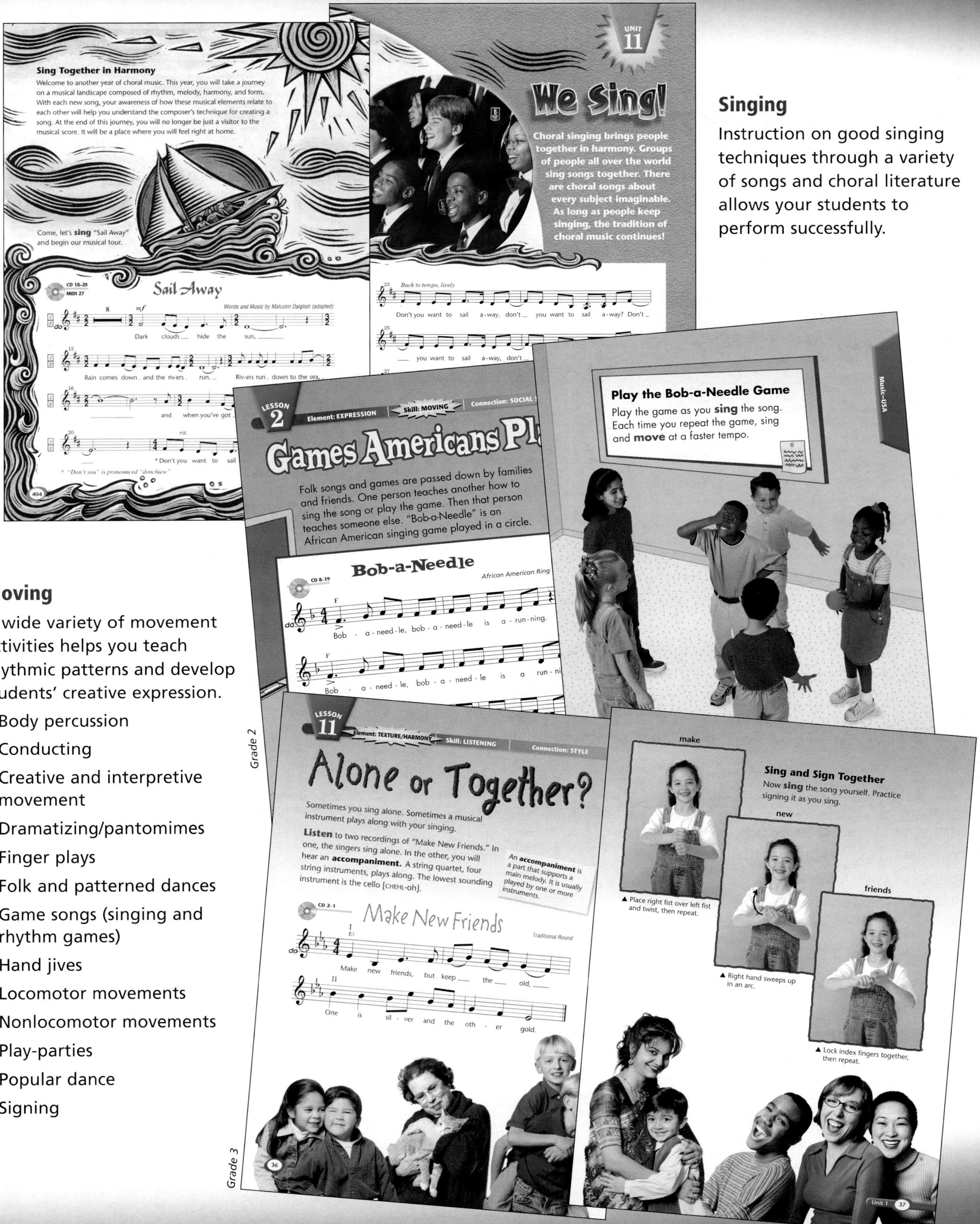

Singing

Instruction on good singing techniques through a variety of songs and choral literature allows your students to perform successfully.

Moving

A wide variety of movement activities helps you teach rhythmic patterns and develop students' creative expression.

- Body percussion
- Conducting
- Creative and interpretive movement
- Dramatizing/pantomimes
- Finger plays
- Folk and patterned dances
- Game songs (singing and rhythm games)
- Hand jives
- Locomotor movements
- Nonlocomotor movements
- Play-parties
- Popular dance
- Signing

Assessment to monitor learning and growth

Silver Burdett MAKING MUSIC provides a variety of tools to help you assess your students' music knowledge and skills. Choose from performance, written, and oral assessments according to your specific teaching style and instructional needs.

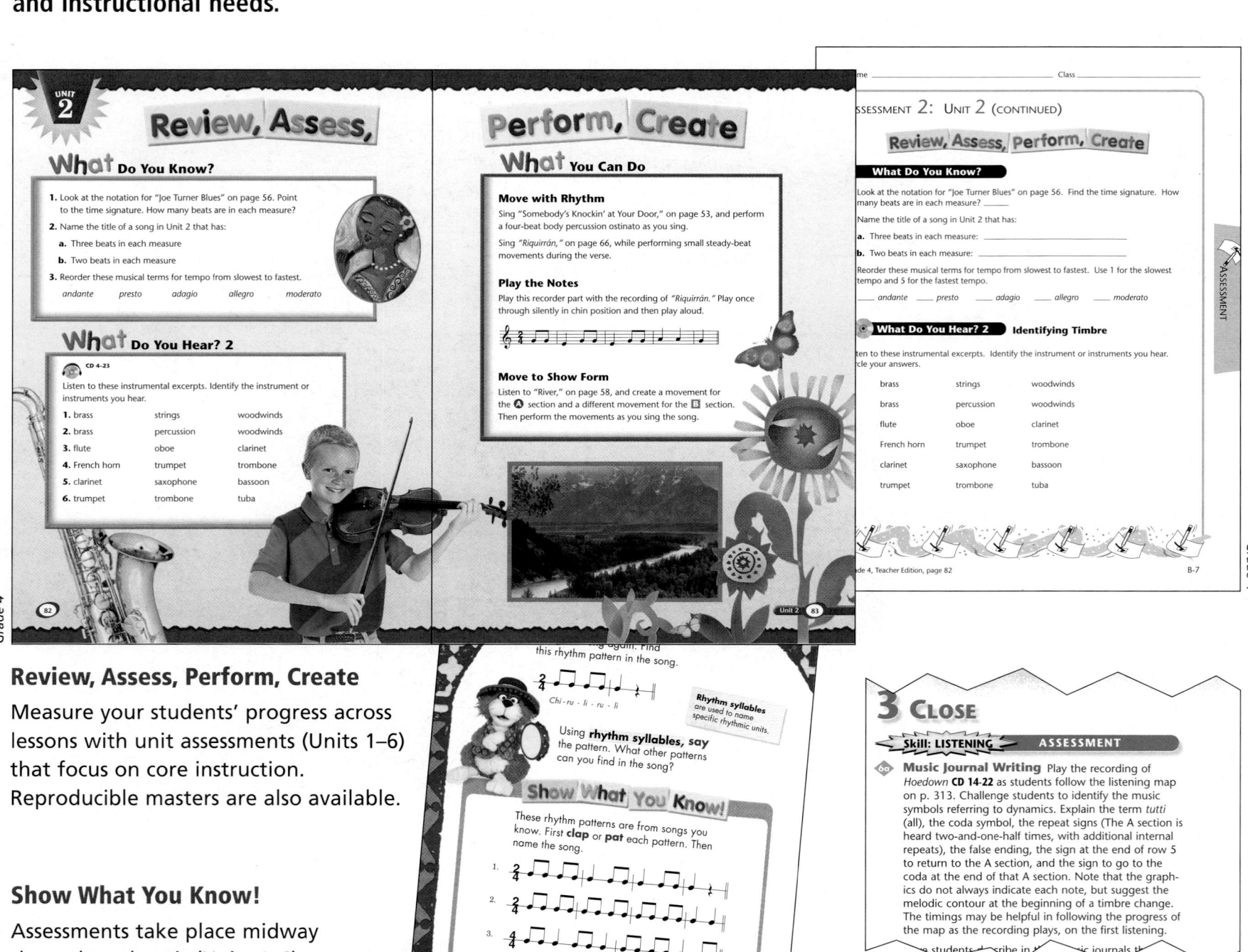

Review, Assess, Perform, Create

Measure your students' progress across lessons with unit assessments (Units 1–6) that focus on core instruction. Reproducible masters are also available.

Show What You Know!

Assessments take place midway through each unit (Units 1–6) to gauge your students' melodic and rhythmic skills. Reproducible masters are also available.

End-of-Lesson Assessment

Every lesson is designed to assess your students' understanding of a critical music element, skill, or connection.

National Standards Correlation for easy planning

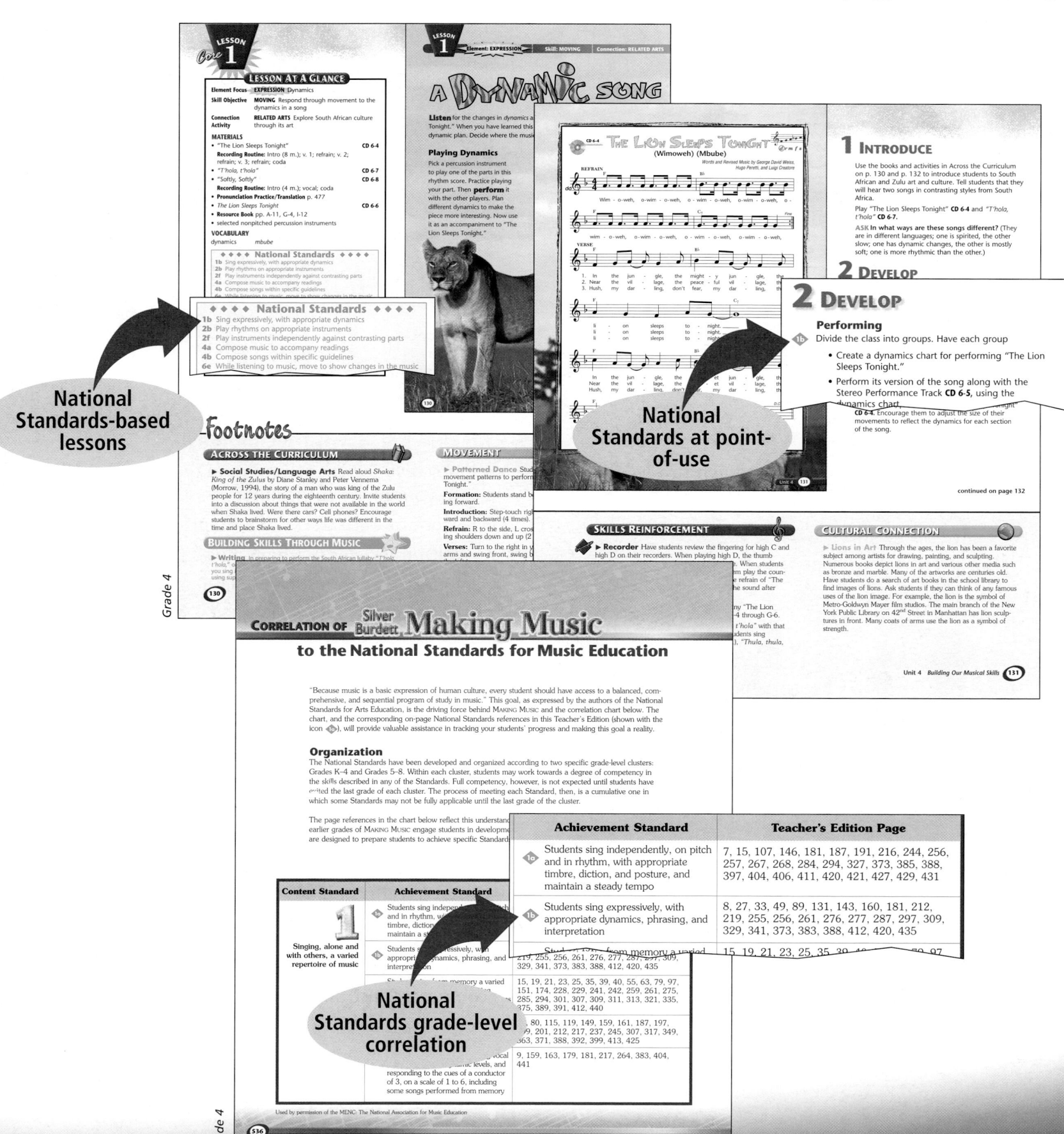

National Standards-based lessons

National Standards at point-of-use

National Standards grade-level correlation

Dynamic tools to motivate and engage students

MAKING MUSIC DVD

- Instructional video segments
- Signing activities
- Dances

MAKING MUSIC with Technology

- Innovative lessons to integrate technology into your music curriculum
- Dozens of MIDI tracks at each grade level
    MIDI tracks for teaching music elements
    MIDI tracks for music reading practice
    MIDI tracks for choral units (4–6)

Music Magic Video Library

- Versatile collection of 25 videos on topics ranging from melody and rhythm to keyboards, dancing, and music for special occasions
- Interviews with world-leading musicians, composers, instrument makers, and dancers

An online work center that revolutionizes teaching

SF SuccessNet

Online Lesson Planner and Teacher's Edition

Scott Foresman SuccessNet is a next-generation work center for Silver Burdett MAKING MUSIC teachers. It's a place where teachers can go to plan their lessons, streamline their work, and access standards-based instruction.

- Access instructional notes
- Create custom lesson plans
- Schedule lessons
- Organize resources
- Block out holidays
- Assign dates and times
- Save/edit lessons from year to year
- Print day, week, or monthly views

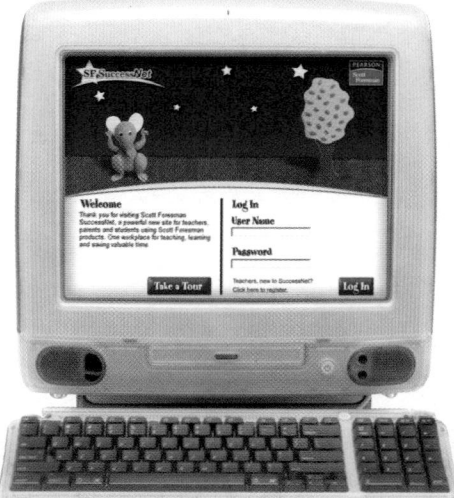

Online Resources for Teachers and Students

Take It to the NET at *www.sfsuccessnet.com* provides access to an entire collection of music resources.

- Theme musicals
- Grades K–8 index of all songs, listening selections, and more
- Standards-based practice
- Music reference articles
- Adaptations for meeting individual needs
- Rubrics—plus more!

Register Today!

To access Take It to the NET, follow three simple steps.

1 Go to *www.sfsuccessnet.com*

2 Click on the link to register

3 Enter the code **MakingMusic** (no spaces)

Note: You must register your students for **Take It to the NET** to access music reference articles.

Contents
Steps to Making Music

Unit 1 Let the Music Begin!

Unit 2 Exploring Music

= Core Lesson

= Music Reading Lesson

Unit 3 Learning the Language of Music

Unit 4 Building Our Musical Skills

⭐ = Core Lesson

= Music Reading Lesson

Unit 5 Discovering New Musical Horizons

Unit 6 Making Music Our Own

✦ = Core Lesson

= Music Reading Lesson

Paths to Making Music

Unit 7 Building America in Song

Unit 8 Music Around the World

= Core Lesson

= Music Reading Lesson

Unit 12 — Holidays in Song

Music Resources and Indexes

STEPS TO Making Music

Lesson	Elements	Skills	

LESSON 1 — CORE

Get Ready to Move

pp. 6–9

Element: Expression
Concept: p, mp, f, mf, subito
Focus: Dynamics

Secondary Element
Rhythm: patterns

National Standards
1b 2a 4a 5c 6b

Skill: Moving
Objective: Perform larger and smaller movements that correspond to dynamics in recorded music

Secondary Skills
- **Singing** Sing using dynamic
- **Moving** Move to the beat
- **Listening** Listen and describe the dynamic levels in the song
- **Listening** Listen for the dynamic changes in a Latin pop song
- **Listening** Listen and describe the contrasts between loud and soft
- **Creating** Create a composition that uses dynamics

SKILLS REINFORCEMENT
- **Playing** Play pop-rock percussion rhythms
- **Creating** Create compositions with loud and soft dynamics

LESSON 2

Ready for Rhythm

pp. 10–11

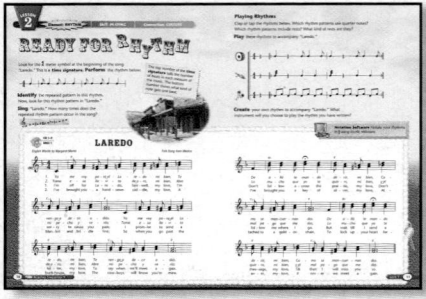

🖐 Reading Sequence 1, p. 490

Element: Rhythm
Concept: Meter
Focus: $\frac{4}{4}$ meter

Secondary Element
Harmony: 2-part singing

National Standards
1c 2a 4c 6c 8b

Skill: Playing
Objective: Create, notate, and play ostinato rhythms in $\frac{4}{4}$ meter.

Secondary Skills
- **Singing** Sing a cowboy song and discuss the lyrics
- **Reading** Read and identify time signatures
- **Playing** Play instrumental ostinatos to accompany the song

SKILLS REINFORCEMENT
- **Moving** Use body percussion with four-beat patterns
- **Recorder** Play a recorder part to accompany "Laredo"

LESSON 3

Reading Rhythms

pp. 12–13

🖐 Reading Sequence 2, p. 490

Element: Rhythm
Concept: Pattern
Focus: Syncopation

Secondary Element
Melody: pitch letter names

National Standards
1c 2a 5a 5c 6c 8b

Skill: Reading
Objective: Perform rhythm patterns, using syncopation.

Secondary Skills
- **Analyzing** Analyze to identify notes, rhythms, and their relationship to the beat
- **Singing** Sing the song while clapping the rhythm patterns

SKILLS REINFORCEMENT
- **Recorder** Play a countermelody
- **Mallets** Play an Orff arrangement to accompany the song

Connections

Music and Other Literature

Connection: Culture

Activity: Discuss the origins of a Latin dance (samba)

ACROSS THE CURRICULUM **Language Arts** Research favorite performers and recording artists, and organize materials for a presentation

MOVEMENT
Nonlocomotor Movement Move to show loud and soft dynamics
Popular Dances Learn salsa dance movements

SPOTLIGHT ON
The Grammy Awards Gloria Estefan and Leonard Bernstein
West Side Story Facts about *West Side Story*

TEACHER TO TEACHER **Staying Focused** Tips to help students during group work on compositions

BUILDING SKILLS THROUGH MUSIC **Language** Discuss the meaning of lyrics and a song title

Song "Get on Your Feet"

Listening Selections
Get on Your Feet
"Dance at the Gym" from *West Side Story* (excerpt)
"Samba" from *Divertimento for Orchestra* (excerpt)
M·U·S·I·C M·A·K·E·R·S
Gloria Estefan
Leonard Bernstein

More Music Choices
"Stand By Me," p. 46

ASSESSMENT

Performance/Observation Move to show the changes in dynamics

TECHNOLOGY/MEDIA LINK
Web Site Find information about Gloria Estefan and Leonard Bernstein

---

Connection: Culture

Activity: Discuss the meaning conveyed by the lyrics of a Mexican song

TEACHER TO TEACHER **Teaching Non-English Songs** How to use Pronunciation Practice recordings

CULTURAL CONNECTION
A Song from Mexico Information about Mexican folk ballads
Crossing the Prairie How people crossed the prairies as they moved west

BUILDING SKILLS THROUGH MUSIC **Language** Use the Story Map to discuss the lyrics

Songs
"Laredo" (Spanish)
"Laredo" (English)

More Music Choices
"Oh, Watch the Stars," p. 216
"¡Qué bonita bandera!" ("What a Beautiful Banner!") p. 294

ASSESSMENT

Portfolios Create an eight-beat rhythm ostinato pattern in $\frac{4}{4}$ meter to accompany the song; perform ostinato patterns on percussion instruments

TECHNOLOGY/MEDIA LINK
MIDI/Sequencing Software Notate a song and play the sequence to accompany a song

---

Connection: Culture

Activity: Discuss folk dance traditions from eastern Europe and perform a dance

ACROSS THE CURRICULUM **Social Studies** Read historical and geographical facts about Slovakia

CULTURAL CONNECTION **Work Songs** Purpose and history of work songs

BUILDING SKILLS THROUGH MUSIC **Writing** Create new lyrics for the song

Song "Morning Comes Early"

More Music Choices
"Fifty Nifty United States," p. 250
"Under the Sea," p. 372
"Rockin' Around the Christmas Tree," p. 466

ASSESSMENT

Performance/Observation Clap syncopated rhythm patterns while singing

TECHNOLOGY/MEDIA LINK
Notation Software Create and notate compositions with syncopation

Lesson	Elements	Skills	
LESSON 4 **CORE** **Syncopation Secrets** pp. 14–17 	**Element: Rhythm** **Concept:** Pattern **Focus:** Syncopated rhythms **Secondary Element** Melody: syncopated melodies **National Standards** 1c 2a 4a 5c 5d 6b 8a 8b 9a	**Skill: Playing** **Objective:** Play various rhythms that include syncopation **Secondary Skills** • **Singing** Sing and identify syncopated phrases • **Reading** Read and identify the syncopated rhythms • **Moving** Create movements to the words "Eliza Kongo" • **Listening** Listen to identify syncopation • **Creating** Create melodies with various rhythms, including syncopation	**SKILLS REINFORCEMENT** • **Playing** Play ostinato patterns to accompany the song • **Keyboard** Learn a syncopated keyboard accompaniment
LESSON 5 **CORE** **Bananas Form Bunches** pp. 18–21 	**Element: Form** **Concept:** Call and response **Focus:** Call-and-responses phrases **Secondary Element** Harmony: 2-part singing **National Standards** 1c 2c 3b 4a 5a 5c 6b 8a 8b	**Skill: Playing** **Objective:** Accompany a call-and-response song using rhythm instruments **Secondary Skills** • **Singing** Sing the responses in the song • **Moving** Create movement for the response part of the song • **Listening** Listen to two musicians perform the same song in different ways • **Improvising** Improvise call-and-response compositions • **Listening** Listen to call-and-response form in another musical style • **Playing** Play a rhythm score as an accompaniment	**SKILLS REINFORCEMENT** • **Creating** Create call-and-response compositions • **Listening** Use a Venn diagram to analyze two versions of "Day-O!"
LESSON 6 **Over the Ocean** pp. 22–23  Reading Sequence 3, p. 491	**Element: Melody** **Concept:** Pitch and direction **Focus:** Note names **Secondary Element** Form: call and response **National Standards** 1c 2a 3b 5c 8b	**Skill: Reading** **Objective:** Sing a melody and read from notation using note names **Secondary Skills** • **Singing** Sing the song and dramatize the motion of pulling ropes to raise the sails • **Reading** Find and name pitch syllables in the response • **Playing** Play the responses in the melody on keyboards, xylophone, or bells	**SKILLS REINFORCEMENT** • **Playing** Play chords to accompany the song • **Recorder** Learn a recorder accompaniment

Connections

Connection: Related Arts
Activity: Explore and discuss folk and visual art from the Caribbean

SPOTLIGHT ON **The Song** The story and history of the song

ACROSS THE CURRICULUM **Social Studies** Locate the Caribbean islands on a map and describe location using direction words

TEACHER TO TEACHER
Managing Composition Activities List criteria for a composition activity
Teaching Non-English Songs Using the recorded Pronunciation Practice

CULTURAL CONNECTION **Caribbean Crafts** Create Caribbean folk crafts

MOVEMENT **Creative Movement** Improvise movements for "Eliza Kongo

MEETING INDIVIDUAL NEEDS **Including Everyone** Earning instrument privileges to receive attention and praise

BUILDING SKILLS THROUGH MUSIC **Physical Education** Improvise locomotor movements

Connection: Social Studies
Activity: Discuss the the people, food, customs, and work life of the Caribbean

CULTURAL CONNECTION **Jamaica** Facts about Jamaica's economy and the origin of reggae music

CHARACTER EDUCATION **Respect** Discuss the need to respect differences in today's world.

ACROSS THE CURRICULUM **Social Studies** Read books to learn more about the Caribbean

SPOTLIGHT ON **The Performer** Facts about the popular singer Harry Belafonte

TEACHER TO TEACHER **Taking Turns During Improvisation** Creating calls in a call-and-response activity

BUILDING SKILLS THROUGH MUSIC **Theatre** Create and perform a dramatization of the song

Connection: Social Studies
Activity: Discuss the history of sailing ships

CULTURAL CONNECTION
Australia Read about the European settlement of Australia
History and Sailing Ships Research the steam engine and sailing ships

TEACHER TO TEACHER **Playing an Instrument—Silent Practice** Help students build confidence

BUILDING SKILLS THROUGH MUSIC **Reading** Discuss words that have multiple meanings

Music and Other Literature

Songs
"*Eliza Kongo*" (French)
"*Eliza Kongo*" (English)

Listening Selection *Saludo de Matanzas* (excerpt)
Arts Connection *Night at the Silver Slipper*

More Music Choices
"Happy Days Are Here Again," p. 284
"Rise Up, Shepherd, and Follow," p. 471

Song "Day-O!"

Listening Selections
Ain't That Love
Day-O! (excerpt)
M•U•S•I•C M•A•K•E•R•S
Harry Belafonte

More Music Choices
"Erie Canal," p. 262
"Go Down, Moses," p. 190

Song "Bound for South Australia"

More Music Choices
"Pollerita," p. 151
"Erie Canal," p. 262

ASSESSMENT

Performance/ Peer Critique Evaluate performances of syncopated rhythms
Show What You Know! Mid-unit assessment

TECHNOLOGY/MEDIA LINK
Notation Software Create and notate compositions with syncopation

ASSESSMENT

Performance/Observation Accompany a call-and-response song using rhythm instruments

TECHNOLOGY/MEDIA LINK
Web Site More information on Caribbean music and musicians

ASSESSMENT

Performance/Observation Sing the call using the letter names of the pitches

TECHNOLOGY/MEDIA LINK
Electronic Keyboard Improvise a folk accompaniment

Lesson	Elements	Skills

LESSON 7

Pentatonic Puzzle

pp. 24–25

Element: Melody
Concept: Tonality
Focus: Pentatonic patterns

Secondary Element
Rhythm 3/4 meter

National Standards
1c 3b 5b 8b

Skill: Singing
Objective: Read a pentatonic melody from notation

Secondary Skills
• **Reading** Read and review the pentatonic scale
• **Singing** Sing using pitch syllables and hand signs

SKILLS REINFORCEMENT
• **Creating/Playing** Compose and play variations of "Arirang" using pentatonic patterns
• **Mallets** Play an Orff arrangement to accompany the song

LESSON 8

CORE

Follow the Melody

pp. 26–27

🖐 Reading Sequence 4, p. 491

Element: Melody
Concept: Tonality
Focus: Pentatonic melody

Secondary Element
Rhythm: syncopation

National Standards
1b 1c 5b 8b

Skill: Reading
Objective: Sing and read from notation a pentatonic melody

Secondary Skills
• **Singing** Sing the notes of the pentatonic scale
• **Listening** Listen to identify pentatonic patterns

SKILLS REINFORCEMENT
• **Singing/Creating** Play a singing game using melody patterns
• **Signing** Perform a signing interpretation of "This Train"

LESSON 9

CORE

You Make the Timbre

pp. 28–31

Element: Timbre
Concept: Vocal Production
Focus: Vocal timbre

Secondary Element
Melody: melodic contour

National Standards
1a 1e 2a 4c 6a 6b 7b
8a 8b

Skill: Singing
Objective: Sing with good vocal technique and use good tone quality

Secondary Skills
• **Listening** Listen to recording and describe vocal quality
• **Moving** Move to show two-, three-, and four-beat patterns
• **Listening** Listen and describe the timbre of the voices in the recording

SKILLS REINFORCEMENT
• **Conducting** Use conducting motions to show time, space, energy, tempo, and dynamics
• **Recorder** Learn a countermelody for the song
• **Singing Voices** Learn to care for the singing voice
• **Keyboard** Learn a two-handed accompaniment

Connections

Music and Other Literature

Connection: Culture
Activity: Discuss the lyrics of a folk song from Korea

ACROSS THE CURRICULUM **Social Studies** Read about a student in Korea and compare the lifestyle to that of American students

CULTURAL CONNECTION *"Arirang"* Learn the origin of the lyrics to the song

BUILDING SKILLS THROUGH MUSIC **Language** Choose words that describe the emotions expressed by the singer.

Songs
"Arirang" (Korean)
"Arirang" (English)

More Music Choices
"Lahk gei mohlee," p. 317
"Meng Jian Nu," p. 194

ASSESSMENT

Performance/Observation
Use hand signs and pitch syllables while reading and singing pentatonic patterns

TECHNOLOGY/MEDIA LINK
Sequencing Software
Improvise and record two ostinato tracks

Connection: Social Studies
Activity: Read about the Underground Railroad

CULTURAL CONNECTION **Underground Railroad Code Words** How code words provided direction for escaping slaves

ACROSS THE CURRICULUM **Language Arts** Read about the lives of young people during the days of the Underground Railroad

BUILDING SKILLS THROUGH MUSIC **Science** Learn about constellations

Song "This Train"

More Music Choices
"All Through the Night," p. 105
"Da pacem, Domine" ("Grant us Peace"), p. 62

ASSESSMENT

Performance/Observation
Sing a pentatonic melody from notation using hand signs and pitch syllables

Show What You Know!
Mid-unit assessment

TECHNOLOGY/MEDIA LINK
Multimedia Use slides to show art from a production about the Underground Railroad

---

Connection: Science
Activity: Discuss the human respiratory system as it relates to vocal technique

MOVEMENT **Creative Movement** Create motions to show phrases in a song

ACROSS THE CURRICULUM **Science** Use illustrations and models to show parts of the body that support the singing voice

CULTURAL CONNECTION **Sunrise** Discuss the various cultural traditions of greeting the morning sun

AUDIENCE ETIQUETTE **Audience Behavior** Discuss appropriate theatre or concert etiquette

TEACHER TO TEACHER **The Art of Conducting** Use conducting sign language to convey ideas from the performers to the audience

BUILDING SKILLS THROUGH MUSIC **Science** Learn about the respiratory system

Song "Morning Has Broken"

Listening Selections
The Kerry Dance
Who Can Sail?
M•U•S•I•C M•A•K•E•R•S
Indianapolis Children's Choir

More Music Choices
"Uno, dos, y tres," p. 427
"Sail Away," p. 404

ASSESSMENT

Performance/Observation
Perform song in small groups for each other and have groups self-assess their vocal production

TECHNOLOGY/MEDIA LINK
Sequencing Software
Create new "timbre" arrangements

Lesson	Elements	Skills

LESSON 10 — Play an Ostinato!
pp. 32–33

Element: Texture/Harmony
Concept: Texture
Focus: Ostinato

Secondary Element
Melody: phrases

National Standards
1c　6b　7a　8b

Skill: Moving
Objective: Create ostinato movement patterns

Secondary Skills
- **Listening** Listen for repeated ostinato patterns
- **Listening** Listen to ostinatos played by different instruments

SKILLS REINFORCEMENT
- **Performing** Help students move, sing, and play simultaneously

---

LESSON 11 — Let Nature Sing
pp. 34–35

Element: Texture/Harmony
Concept: Texture
Focus: Melodic osinatos

Secondary Element
Melody: melodic sequence

National Standards
1a　2a　4c　6a　8b

Skill: Singing
Objective: Add ostinatos to create harmony

Secondary Skills
- **Singing** Sing an ostinato
- **Playing** Play an ostinato
- **Singing** Sing song with ostinato to change texture
- **Listening** Listen to layers of voices and follow a listening map

SKILLS REINFORCEMENT
- **Creating** Create additional verses for the song
- **Playing** Sing or play an additional ostinato with the song

---

LESSON 12 — CORE
Broadway Harmony
pp. 36–39

Element: Texture/Harmony
Concept: Two-part singing
Focus: Vocal harmony

Secondary Element
Melody: pitch and direction

National Standards
1d　2b　6a　6b　7b　8b

Skill: Listening
Objective: Discover how harmony is created by combining two different melodies

Secondary Skills
- **Listening** Listen and analyze a song recording
- **Singing** Sing the song and add harmony parts
- **Listening** Listen to the song and identify the pattern
- **Singing** Sing the song in parts

SKILLS REINFORCEMENT
- **Playing** Play a pattern on a melody instrument

Connections

Music and Other Literature

Connection: Culture

Activity: Participate in art projects relating to West African cultures

CULTURAL CONNECTION African Singing Discuss the importance of singing in African music and dance

ACROSS THE CURRICULUM **Art/Social Studies** Make simple art projects based on West African folk art design

BUILDING SKILLS THROUGH MUSIC Social Studies Identify locations of song origins on a world map

Songs
"*Funwa alafia*"
"Welcome, My Friends"
"*Kokoleoko*"

Listening Selection *Yo Lé Lé* (excerpt)

More Music Choices
"*Bantama kra kro,*" p. 308

ASSESSMENT

Performance/Observation
Create and perform an ostinato to accompany a song.

TECHNOLOGY/MEDIA LINK

Web Site Learn about West African drumming and vocal styles

Sequencing Software Record ostinatos and play back for self assessment

---

Connection: Science

Activity: Discuss plants and animals that might be encountered while hiking in the mountains

MEETING INDIVIDUAL NEEDS **Including Everyone** Find words about nature in a song

ACROSS THE CURRICULUM **Science** Research wilderness ecology and mountain environments

BUILDING SKILLS THROUGH MUSIC Language Discuss thirteenth century language

Song "I Love the Mountains"

Listening Selection *Sumer Is Icumen In* (excerpt)
Listening Map *Sumer Is Icumen In*

More Music Choices
"Oklahoma," p. 36
"*Zum gali gali,*" p. 401

ASSESSMENT

Performance/Observation
Perform the song, adding a melodic instrument to create layers of ostinatos

TECHNOLOGY/MEDIA LINK

Notation Software Create a melody using the rhythm pattern of a song

Transparency Use a listening map to analyze a canon

Connection: Social Studies

Activity: Discuss the location and economy of Oklahoma

ACROSS THE CURRICULUM **Social Studies** History and facts about Oklahoma

SPOTLIGHT ON The Musical Information on *Oklahoma!*

MEETING INDIVIDUAL NEEDS **Singing/Phrasing** Sing using proper posture and phrasing
Mnemonic Devices Discuss mnemonic devices and how they are used

CULTURAL CONNECTION A History of Pitch Syllables Discuss how pitch syllables were developed

CHARACTER EDUCATION **Collaboration** Discuss singing and professional partnerships

BUILDING SKILLS THROUGH MUSIC Social Studies Identify the words in the song that describe characteristics of Oklahoma

Song "Oklahoma"

Listening Selection
"Do-Re-Mi" from *The Sound of Music*
Interview with Rebecca Luker
Interview with Richard Rodgers

M·U·S·I·C M·A·K·E·R·S
Richard Rodgers and Oscar Hammerstein

More Music Choices
"*Canción Mixteca,*" p. 326
"*Hine mah tov,*" p. 431

ASSESSMENT

Performance/Observation
Use a rating system to observe how well students can sing using harmony parts with a song

TECHNOLOGY/MEDIA LINK

Web Site Learn more about musicals of Rodgers and Hammerstein

Electronic Keyboard Play chord roots to create an accompaniment

---

INTRODUCING THE UNIT

Unit 1 presents the first step in a sequenced approach to understanding music elements. Music skills—reading, performing, creating, listening, moving—are the means by which students gain an understanding of these concepts. Presented on p. 3 is a brief overview of the skills that are assessed in this unit. (See below and pp. 4–5 for unit highlights of related curricular experiences.)

For a more detailed unit overview, see Unit at a Glance, pp. 1a–1h.

UNIT PROJECT

Invite students to read the opening text on p. 2 of their books. Then have them

- Find and list ways of making music shown on pp. 2–3.
- Look through Unit 1 (pp. 2–39) to find other ways of making music, listening to music, or moving to music as shown in the photos and illustrations.

Have students begin a personal Music Journal. To start their journals, have them:

- List the ways they already make music, or musical skills they have.
- List the kinds of music they listen to or move to.
- List favorite songs.
- List favorite musicians or names of musicians or groups they know.
- Describe something they would like to learn about music.

During the unit, have students return to their Music Journal and add information to it. Encourage them to write about what they are learning, the skills they are developing, and the music they are performing or listening to both in school and at home.

You are the Musicians

Music is everywhere and musicians are everywhere, too. Musicians perform, compose, and listen to each other. You are already a musician! What musical things can you do? Get ready to embark upon new musical journeys.

A Patriotic March

Listen to this march composed by well-known American band leader Edwin Franko Goldman.

CD 1–1
On the Mall

**by Edwin Franko Goldman
as performed by the United States Army Field Band**
On the Mall was composed in March, 1923.

ACROSS THE CURRICULUM

Unit Highlights The following interdisciplinary activities in this unit are related to the music elements presented in the lessons. See Unit at a Glance pp. 1a–1h, for topical descriptions presented according to lesson sequence.

▶ **ART/RELATED ARTS**

- Create artwork based on West African cultures to display at musical performances (p. 32)
- Create crafts based on Caribbean folk traditions (p. 16)

▶ **LANGUAGE ARTS**

- Create and print bulletin board displays featuring favorite musical artists (p. 6)
- Read about the Underground Railroad (p. 26)

▶ **SCIENCE**

- Explore the physical mechanism of the singing voice (p. 28)
- Research wilderness ecology and mountain environments (p. 34)

▶ **SOCIAL STUDIES**

- Read about Slovakia (p. 12)
- Locate on a map the Caribbean sea and other islands (p. 15)
- Read about the people and customs of the Caribbean (p. 19)
- Read about a student in Korea (p. 24)
- Discuss the location and economy of Oklahoma (p. 36)

UNIT 1

LET THE MUSIC BEGIN!

Unit 1 **3**

MUSIC SKILLS
ASSESSED IN THIS UNIT

Reading Music: Rhythm

- Read ostinato rhythms in meter in 4 (p. 11)
- Read syncopated rhythm patterns (pp. 13, 17)

Reading Music: Pitch

- Read pitch syllables (*do, re, mi, so, la*) and note names (C, D, E, G, A) (p. 23)
- Read pentatonic patterns (pp. 25, 27)

Performing Music: Singing

- Sing the call in "Bound for South Australia" using letter names (p. 23)
- Sing "*Arirang*" using pitch syllables (p. 25)
- Sing "This Train" using hand signs and pitch syllables (p. 27)
- Sing "Morning Has Broken" using good vocal technique and tone quality (p. 31)
- Sing "Oklahoma" in 2-part harmony (p. 39)

Moving to Music

- Move to show changes in dynamics (p. 9)
- Perform an ostinato movement pattern (p. 33)

Performing Music: Playing

- Use nonpitched and pitched percussion to accompany a song (pp. 11, 21, 33)
- Perform layers of ostinatos using melodic instruments (p. 35)

Creating Music

- Compose a short composition that incorporates changes in dynamics (p. 9)
- Create a rhythm ostinato (pp. 11, 33)

Listening to Music

- Listen for changes in dynamics (p. 9)
- Listen for call-and-response form (p. 21)

CULTURAL CONNECTION

Unit Highlights The musical literature in this unit provides many opportunities for students to explore a variety of world cultures. See Unit at a Glance, pp. 1a–1h, for topical descriptions presented according to lesson sequence.

▶ **AFRICAN/AFRICAN AMERICAN**

- Learn about Underground Railroad code words (p. 26)
- Discuss the importance of singing in African music (p. 32)

▶ **ASIAN; AUSTRALIAN**

- Learn the origin of the lyrics to a folk song from Korea (p. 25)
- Read about the European settlement of Australia; Explore the history of sailing ships (p. 22)

▶ **CARIBBEAN**

- Explore the folk crafts of the Caribbean (p. 16)
- Read about Jamaica (p. 18)

▶ **EUROPEAN**

- Explore the history of work songs (p. 13)
- Read about various cultural traditions of greeting the day (p. 29)

▶ **LATIN AMERICAN**

- "Get on Your Feet" (p. 6)
- Explore the cultural significance of Mexican folk ballads; Research the historical significance of prairies (p. 11)

OPENING ACTIVITIES

MATERIALS

- "God Bless America" **CD 1-2**
  Recording Routine:
  Intro (11 m.); verse; refrain; interlude (2 m.); refrain; coda
- *On The Mall* **CD 1-1**
- finger cymbals or triangle; bass drum, snare drum, or hand drum

Listening

Invite students to listen to *On the Mall* **CD 1-1**. Ask students to identify the instruments they hear on the recording. Explain to them that the title *On the Mall* refers to the location where Edwin Franko Goldman's band performed in New York City's Central Park.

Singing

Play the recording of "God Bless America" **CD 1-2**. Invite students to listen to the verse and sing along with the refrain. Then play the recording again and invite them to sing the whole song.

Moving

Have students find the $\frac{4}{4}$ time signature at the beginning of "God Bless America." Help them recall that the top number indicates four beats in a measure and the bottom number indicates that the quarter note gets one beat. Invite students to create a four-beat movement pattern. Then play the recording and have them move to the music. You may also wish to have students conduct a four-beat pattern as they listen to "God Bless America."

Begin with Inspiration
Musicians create and perform music for themselves and for others. **Sing** "God Bless America." What ideas and feelings does this song inspire?

ASSESSMENT

Unit Highlights This unit includes a variety of strategies and methods, described below, to track students' progress and assess their understanding of lesson objectives. Reproducible masters for Show What You Know! and Review, Assess, Perform, Create can be found in the Resource Book.

▶ **FORMAL ASSESSMENTS**

The following assessments, using written language, cognitive, and performance skills, help teachers and students conceptualize the learning that is taking place.

- **Show What You Know!** Element-specific assessments, on the student page for Rhythm (p. 17) and Melody (p. 27)
- **Review, Assess, Perform, Create** This end-of-unit activity (pp. 40–41) can be used for review and to assess students' learning of the core lessons in this unit.

▶ **INFORMAL ASSESSMENTS**

At the close of each Teacher's Edition lesson in this unit, one of the following types of assessments is used to evaluate the learning of the key element focus or skill objective.

- Peer Critique (pp. 17, 33)
- Performance/Observation (pp. 9, 13, 21, 23, 25, 27, 35, 39)
- Performance/Self-Assessment (p. 31)
- Portfolios (p. 11)

▶ **RUBRICS**

Visit *www.sfsuccessnet.com* for rubrics to assess students' achievement in music skills.

Reading

Invite students to read the rhythm of the first phrase of the verse of "God Bless America." Have them tap or clap the rhythm and read using rhythm syllables. Then have students compare the rhythm of the first phrase to the remaining three phrases in the verse. Note that the last phrase is extended by one measure.

Playing

Have students find the rests in the notation for the verse of "God Bless America." Then have them play a triangle or finger cymbal during each rest as they sing the verse.

REFRAIN

God bless A-mer-i-ca, land that I love. Stand be-side her and guide her through the night with a light from a-bove. From the moun-tains, to the prai-ries, to the o-ceans, white with foam. God bless A-mer-i-ca, my home sweet home. God bless A-mer-i-ca, my home sweet home. ___

Unit 1   5

INNOVATIVE TEACHER SUPPORT FOR THIS UNIT

- **MAKING MUSIC DVD, Grade 5** contains video segments that support lessons, including signing and movement.
- **MAKING MUSIC with Movement and Dance** provides more opportunities for large group activities in music or physical education classes.
- **MAKING MUSIC with Technology** provides lesson plans for many technology applications; includes MIDI files.
- **¡A cantar!** features recorded songs and lessons from around the Spanish-speaking world; includes strategies for bilingual classes and for English-speaking teachers working with Spanish-speaking students.
- **Bridges to Asia** features recorded songs and lessons from Asian and Pacific region cultures.
- **www.sfsuccessnet.com** provides an online lesson planner to conveniently create lesson plans at school or at home. Includes rubrics for assessment, lesson modifications to meet the needs of all students, performance musicals based on program content, and more.

TECHNOLOGY/MEDIA LINK

Unit Highlights The following components are used in this unit to reinforce and expand students' understanding of music elements and related themes. See Unit at a Glance, pp. 1a–1h, for a descriptive listing according to lesson sequence.

▶ **ELECTRONIC KEYBOARD**

- Improvise accompaniments (p. 23)
- Play chord roots to create an accompaniment (p. 39)

▶ **MIDI/SEQUENCING SOFTWARE**

- Notate a song and play the sequence to accompany a song (p. 11)
- Improvise and record two ostinatos (p. 25)
- Create new "timbre" arrangements (p. 31)
- Record students' self-assessment ostinatos (p. 33)

▶ **NOTATION SOFTWARE**

- Create four-measure rhythm phrases (p. 13)
- Create and notate compositions with syncopation (p. 17)
- Create and notate a melody using the rhythm pattern of a song (p. 35)

▶ **TRANSPARENCY**

- Display a listening map to analyze a canon (p. 35)

▶ **WEB SITE**

- Go to *www.sfsuccessnet.com* to find more information about Gloria Estefan and Leonard Bernstein (p. 9); Caribbean music and musicians (p. 21); West African drumming and vocal styles (p. 33); and the musicals of Rodgers and Hammerstein (p. 39)

LESSON AT A GLANCE

Element Focus	**EXPRESSION** Dynamics
Skill Objective	**MOVING** Perform larger and smaller movements that correspond to dynamics in recorded music
Connection Activity	**CULTURE** Discuss the origins of a Latin dance (samba)

MATERIALS

• "Get on Your Feet" **CD 1-4**
  Recording Routine: Intro (8 m.); refrain; v. 1; refrain; v. 2; refrain; coda
• *Get on Your Feet* **CD 1-6**
• "Dance at the Gym" from *West Side Story* (excerpt) **CD 1-7**
• "*Samba*" from *Divertimento for Orchestra* (excerpt) **CD 1-8**
• world map

VOCABULARY

dynamics	*pianissimo*	*piano*	*mezzo piano*
subito piano	*forte*	*fortissimo*	*mezzo forte*
subito forte			

◆ ◆ ◆ ◆ National Standards ◆ ◆ ◆ ◆

1b Sing easy pieces with expression
2a Play instruments accurately in small ensembles
4a Compose short pieces, demonstrating unity and variety through music
5c Identify and define standard notation symbols for dynamics
6b Listen and analyze uses of dynamics in music from diverse cultures

MORE MUSIC CHOICES

For more practice with dynamics:
"Stand By Me," p. 46

Get Ready to MOVE

Music has energy—energy that inspires people to move, sing, or play. **Dynamics** are part of the energy of each song or composition. Experiment with different dynamics as you **sing** "Get on Your Feet."

Dynamics are the degrees of loudness and softness of sound.

CD 1-4

Get on Your Feet

Words and Music by John DeFaria, Clay Ostwald, and Jorge Casas

6

Footnotes

ACROSS THE CURRICULUM

▶ **Language Arts** Students can make their own books, portfolios, or classroom bulletin boards about the lives and musical accomplishments of their favorite performers. Newspapers, magazine articles, CD covers, and so on can be cut and pasted into their created books along with stories and facts about the performers. Have students write introductions, explanations, and critiques, organizing their material for presentation.

BUILDING SKILLS THROUGH MUSIC

▶ **Language** Write the title "Get on Your Feet" on the board. Ask students to brainstorm ideas of what message the composer might be trying to convey in a song with that title. Invite students to read the lyrics of the refrain and discuss the meaning. Then ask students to read verses 1 and 2. Lead a discussion on the meaning of the verses and how it relates to the song title.

SKILLS REINFORCEMENT

 ▶ **Playing** Invite students to play percussion instruments with "Get on Your Feet." Patterns that stress beats 2 and 4 are particularly appropriate for pop-rock style songs. Try these patterns, or encourage students to create their own.

1 INTRODUCE

Write the word *energy* on the board. Invite students to say the word loudly and softly. Then have students read the text on p. 6 in their books.

2 DEVELOP

Singing

1b Play the recording of "Get on Your Feet" **CD 1-4.** Have students sing along.

Moving

Play the recording again. Have students find the beat as they listen. Encourage them to move to the beat, using movements of their choice.

Listening

Have students read the information about dynamics on pp. 6 and 8 of their texts.

5c **ASK** What are dynamics? (Dynamics are the degrees of loudness and softness in music.)

SAY Point to the dynamic mark on p. 8 that shows the softest dynamic level (*pp*). Point to the dynamic mark that shows the loudest dynamic level (*ff*).

Then have students describe the dynamic levels in "Get on Your Feet."

Moving

Encourage students to explore movements that reflect changes in dynamics. (See Movement below.)

SAY Think about how your movements can show changes in dynamics. How can you move so that someone watching you would know if the music is loud or soft?

continued on page 8

MOVEMENT

▶ **Nonlocomotor Movement** Have students identify the loud and soft sections in the song. They can show the loud and soft sections by doing "pat-snap" to match the dynamics.

▶ **Popular Dance** Students can dance the salsa by doing these movements.

Step Left foot forward	"1"
Step Right foot backward	"and"
Step Left foot beside Right	"2"
Step Right foot backward	"1"
Step Left foot forward	"and"
Step Right foot beside Left	"2"

SPOTLIGHT ON

▶ **The Grammy Awards** Grammys are given in many categories of music, such as rock, pop, and classical. Gloria Estefan and Leonard Bernstein, music makers featured in this lesson, have both been Grammy winners.

Ask students to read more about the courageous life of a Grammy Award-winning artist in *Gloria Estefan* by Sue Boulais (Mitchell Lane, 1999).

Have students

- Experiment with movements that show soft dynamics.

- Experiment with movements that show loud dynamics.

- Move to "Get on Your Feet," showing the changes in dynamics with their movements.

Listening

Have students read about Gloria Estefan on p. 8 in their books. Play the Estefan recording *Get on Your Feet* **CD 1-6.**

Have students

- Read the information about *Dance at the Gym* on p. 9 in their books.

- Practice and then perform the salsa step with the recording. (See Movement, p. 7.)

Play the recording of *Dance at the Gym* **CD 1-7** and have students aurally identify this excerpt of music representing diverse genres.

6b **ASK How did the composer create the contrasts between loud and soft?** (Brass instruments and shouting voices are used in the loud sections; string instruments are used in the soft sections.)

Have students read the information about Leonard Bernstein. Share additional information about *West Side Story* from Spotlight On, p. 9.

SAY Leonard Bernstein also wrote orchestral music. Let's listen to another composition he wrote.

Have students

- Read the information about the samba dance at the bottom of p. 9.

- Use a map to trace the origin of the samba—from Africa, to Brazil, to the Caribbean.

- Identify terms and symbols related to dynamics. Find *subito* **p** and *subito* **f** marks on p. 9.

- Point to the *subito* **p** and *subito* **f** marks as they listen to the recording of *Samba* **CD 1-8.**

Latin Pop

Musicians use symbols to show dynamics in the music. Here are some examples.

pp = *pianissimo* = very soft
p = *piano* = soft
mp = *mezzo piano* = medium soft
mf = *mezzo forte* = medium loud
f = *forte* = loud
ff = *fortissimo* = very loud

Listen to Gloria Estefan's performance of *Get on Your Feet*. What dynamics do you hear? Think about ways you can **move** to *Get on Your Feet*. How can your motions match the dynamics of the song?

CD 1–6
Get on Your Feet

by John DeFaria, Clay Ostwald, and Jorge Casas performed by Gloria Estefan and Miami Sound Machine

Released on the 1989 album *Cuts Both Ways*, *Get on Your Feet* was one of Gloria Estefan and Miami Sound Machine's biggest successes.

M·U·S·I·C M·A·K·E·R·S
Gloria Estefan

Gloria Estefan (born 1957) has won two Grammy awards and is one of the most successful Latin performers. In 1975, she and her husband formed Miami Sound Machine. Inspired by the rhythms and dances of Cuba and other Latin American countries, Estefan's music has sold more than sixty million records.

8

TEACHER TO TEACHER

▶ **Staying Focused** Help students stay focused during group work on composition in the Creating section of the lesson. Use any of the following strategies.

- Make a chart of the directions or steps for composing and post it where students can refer to it as they work.

- Use whole-group instruction during the first few steps of the composing process to help students get started.

- Give students a limited time to work. Post a "Finish Time." Appoint a timekeeper in each group to remind the group about the time limit.

SKILLS REINFORCEMENT

4a
5c ▶ **Creating** Encourage students to notate the compositions from the Creating section on p. 9. Have them place dynamic symbols in their compositions. Then check the symbols as they perform their compositions.

Latin Dynamics

The islands in the Caribbean Sea have rich and varied musical traditions. The *mambo* is a dance that originated in Cuba and other Caribbean islands. Leonard Bernstein's *Dance at the Gym* was influenced by the music from Puerto Rico and other islands. **Listen** to the dynamics in *Dance at the Gym*. How are the first and second sections of the music different? How did the composer create contrasts between loud and soft in this piece?

1-7 Dance at the Gym

**from *West Side Story*
by Leonard Bernstein and Stephen Sondheim**
The Broadway musical *West Side Story* is based on William Shakespeare's play *Romeo and Juliet*.

M·U·S·I·C M·A·K·E·R·S
Leonard Bernstein

Leonard Bernstein (1918–1990) was one of the most famous American composers and conductors of the twentieth century. He played the piano and performed frequently when he was young. His life changed when Bruno Walter, a conductor of the New York Philharmonic, became ill and Bernstein conducted a concert in his place. Bernstein was soon conducting orchestras all over the world. He also composed music for symphony orchestras, choirs, and Broadway shows.

Listen to the rhythms of *Samba*. Point to the symbols below when you hear sudden changes in dynamics.

subito **p** = suddenly soft

subito **f** = suddenly loud

CD 1–8 Samba

**from *Divertimento for Orchestra*
by Leonard Bernstein**
The *samba* is a dance that originated in Africa. Later the *samba* moved to Brazil and to the Caribbean islands.

Unit 1   **9**

Creating

Divide the class into groups of three or four.

4a SAY Your assignment is to compose a piece that uses dynamics.

Have students

- Plan a 30-second composition that includes changes in dynamics. (Encourage students to use a variety of sounds in their compositions.)
- Invent a way to notate their compositions and include symbols for dynamics.

3 CLOSE

Element: EXPRESSION   ASSESSMENT

6b Performance/Observation Have students choose one of the recordings from the lesson.

SAY Listen for changes in dynamics. Move to show the changes you hear.

Play the recording and observe students' movements.

SPOTLIGHT ON

▶ **West Side Story** *West Side Story* opened on Broadway in September 1957. The musical became one of the most popular and best-known musical theater works of all time. The story, based on the book by Arthur Laurents, focuses on two gangs in New York City—the Jets and the Sharks. Conflict arises when Tony, a member of the self-named "American" gang (Jets), falls in love with Maria, whose brother is a member of the Puerto Rican gang (Sharks).

Among the original creative team for *West Side Story* was Leonard Bernstein (composer), Stephen Sondheim (lyricist), and Jerome Robbins (choreographer). All three went on to create many more musical and theatrical works.

TECHNOLOGY/MEDIA LINK

Web Site Have students go to *www.sfsuccessnet.com* to find information about Gloria Estefan and Leonard Bernstein.

LESSON 2

LESSON AT A GLANCE

Element Focus — **RHYTHM** $\frac{4}{4}$ meter

Skill Objective — **PLAYING** Create, notate, and play ostinato rhythms in $\frac{4}{4}$ meter

Connection Activity — **CULTURE** Discuss the meaning conveyed by the lyrics of a Mexican song

MATERIALS

- "Laredo" (Spanish) — **CD 1-9**
- "Laredo" (English) — **CD 1-10**
  Recording Routine: Intro (4 m.); v. 1; instrumental; v. 2; coda
- **Music Reading Practice, Sequence 1** — **CD 1-14**
- **Pronunciation Practice/Translation** p. 521
- **Resource Book** pp. A-2, C-7, E-2, I-2
- *guiro,* maracas, claves, drum

VOCABULARY

time signature

◆ ◆ ◆ ◆ National Standards ◆ ◆ ◆ ◆

1c Sing music from diverse cultures
2a Play instruments accurately in small ensembles
4c Arrange, using electronic media
6c Understand and use basic principles of rhythm in music analysis
8b Identify ways music relates to social studies

MORE MUSIC CHOICES

For more practice with $\frac{4}{4}$ meter:
"Oh, Watch the Stars," p. 216
"¡Que bonita bandera!" ("What a Beautiful Banner!") p. 294

1 INTRODUCE

Invite students to think about a friend or family member who lives in another town or city.

ASK How do you feel when you can't see this person for a while?

LESSON 2 — Element: RHYTHM | Skill: PLAYING | Connection: CULTURE

READY FOR RHYTHM

Look for the $\frac{4}{4}$ meter symbol at the beginning of the song "Laredo." This is a **time signature**. **Perform** the rhythm below:

> The top number of the **time signature** tells the number of beats in each measure of the music. The bottom number shows what kind of note gets one beat.

Identify the repeated pattern in this rhythm.
Now, look for this rhythm pattern in "Laredo."

Sing "Laredo." How many times does the repeated rhythm pattern occur in the song?

CD 1-9 MIDI 1

LAREDO

English Words by Margaret Marks   *Folk Song from Mexico*

```
1. Ya    me   voy    pa - ra el  La - re - do   mi  bien,   Te
2. Toma  e - sa      lla - vi - ta  de o - ro,  mi  bien,   Abre
1. I'm   off   for   La - re - do,  fare - well, my  love,  I'm
2. I've  brought you a  hand - sewn  sad - dle,  my  love,  A
```

```
ven - go a  de - cir   a - diós.  Ya   me   voy  pa - ra el  La -
mi  pe - cho  y  ve - rás;  Toma  e - sa  lla - vi - ta
sor - ry  to  cause  you  pain;  I  prom - ise  to  send  a
blan - ket  and  bri - dle  fine;  So  when  you  go  past  the
```

```
re - do,   mi  bien,   Te   ven - go a  de - cir   a - diós.
de o - ro,  mi  bien,  Abre  mi  pe - cho  y  ve - rás;
let - ter,  my  love,  To   say  when  we'll  meet  a - gain.
bunk - house, my  love, The  cow - boys  will  know  you're  mine.
```

10 — Reading Sequence 1

Footnotes

TEACHER TO TEACHER

▶ **Teaching Non-English-Language Songs** To give students an opportunity to hear a native speaker sing "Laredo" in Spanish, play Pronunciation Practice Track **CD 1-12.** Then distribute copies of Resource Book p. A-2, the Pronunciation Practice Guide, and use the Pronunciation Practice/Translation section, which begins on p. 521, to teach the Spanish version.

BUILDING SKILLS THROUGH MUSIC

▶ **Language** Display a transparency of the Story Map from Resource Book p. C-7. Discuss the headings to be completed. Invite students to listen to "Laredo" **CD 1-10** while following the words of verses 1 and 2. Ask students about possible causes of the situation and how the singer is facing the problem. Have students complete the diagram with their observations from listening to the song.

SKILLS REINFORCEMENT

▶ **Moving** Capture students' attention and challenge their moving skills by using a variety of body percussion rather than simple echo clapping. Pat one pattern, then snap the next, then stamp the next, and so on. To challenge students further, use more than one body percussion movement/sound within a four-beat pattern, such as

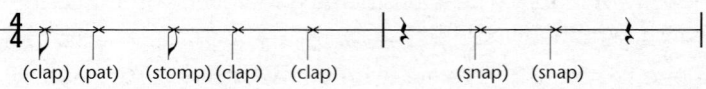

```
(clap) (pat) (stomp) (clap) (clap)  (snap) (snap)
```

▶ **Recorder** See Resource Book p. I-2, for a playing activity for "Laredo."

2a

Playing Rhythms

Clap or tap the rhythms below. Which rhythm patterns use quarter notes? Which rhythm patterns include rests? What kind of rests are they?

Play these rhythms to accompany "Laredo."

Create your own rhythm to accompany "Laredo." What instrument will you choose to play the rhythm you have written?

 Notation Software Notate your rhythms in $\frac{4}{4}$ using music software.

De   a - llá   te man - do   de - cir,   mi bien,   Co -
Lo   mu - cho   que yo   te   quie - ro,   mi bien,   y el
Don't   fol - low   a - cross   the   prai - rie,   my love,   Don't
I've   brought you   a   key   of   sil - ver,   my love,   At -

mo se   man - cuer - nan   dos.   De   a - llá   te man - do
mal pa - go que   me   das,   Lo   mu - cho   que yo   te
fol - low   me where   I   go.   But   wait till   I send   a
tached to   a   gold - en   chain,   To   lock up   your heart   for -

de - cir,   mi bien,   Co - mo se   man - cuer - nan   dos.
quie - ro,   mi bien,   y el   mal pa - go que   me   das.
mes - sage,   my love,   Till   then I   will miss   you   so.
ev - er,   my love,   If   nev - er   we meet   a - gain.

Unit 1   **11**

2 DEVELOP

Singing

Invite students to listen to "Laredo" **CD 1-10** and follow the lyrics. Discuss who is traveling (cowboy), where he is going and how (to Laredo on horseback), who he is leaving behind (his girlfriend), and what he has given her (a saddle, bridle, blanket, silver key, golden chain). Share information about songs from Mexico. See Cultural Connection below.

1c Have students sing the song.

Reading

6c Have students read about time signature, on p. 10, and identify the time signature of "Laredo."

Then have students read standard notation to

- Clap and say the rhythm pattern shown on p. 10.
- Find the pattern in the song.
- Clap and say the rhythm of the song.

For additional practice reading $\frac{4}{4}$ meter, see Music Reading Practice, Sequence 1 on p. 490 and Resource Book p. E-2.

Playing

2a Have students accompany "Laredo" with the instrumental ostinatos on p. 11.

3 CLOSE

Element: RHYTHM   ASSESSMENT

2a **Portfolios** Have students create an eight-beat rhythm ostinato pattern to accompany "Laredo." Have them notate their rhythm on paper. As they listen to the recording, they should softly tap the rhythm of their ostinato in the palm of their hand. Have them listen to the recording again while several students, selected by the teacher, perform their ostinato patterns on percussion instruments.

CULTURAL CONNECTION

8b ► **A Song from Mexico** One way of learning about people is to listen to their songs. Much can be learned about the nature and character of the people in rural Mexico from the content of the *corridos*—a type of narrative folk ballad. These folk ballads, such as "Laredo," tell of heroes, bandits, revolutions, and local politics, as well as of personal emotions and feelings. These are still composed regularly today about current figures and events.

► **Crossing the Prairie** The lyrics of the song "Laredo" include a reference to crossing the prairie. Have students research the meaning of *prairie*. Then have them find prairies on maps of the United States and Mexico. Finally, ask students to find out important events in the history of the United States in which people crossed prairies.

TECHNOLOGY/MEDIA LINK

4c **MIDI/Sequencing Software** Open the MIDI song file for "Laredo." Have students select the bass track and either a string bass or guitar pattern. Have them use quarter-note and half-note rhythms on the roots and fifths of the chords. Have them select a guitar or accordion pattern for the harmony track and record chord triads in quarter-note and half-note rhythms. Play the sequence to accompany "Laredo."

If time allows, students may add another track to the sequence, such as a violin or trumpet descant.

LESSON AT A GLANCE

Element Focus **RHYTHM** Syncopation

Skill Objective **READING** Perform rhythm patterns, including syncopation

Connection Activity **CULTURE** Discuss folk dance traditions from Eastern Europe and perform a dance

MATERIALS

- "Morning Comes Early" **CD 1-17**
  Recording Routine: Intro (4 m.); v. 1; interlude (4 m.); v. 2; coda
- **Music Reading Practice, Sequence 2** **CD 1-19**
- **Dance Directions** for "Morning Comes Early" p. 554
- **Resource Book** pp. D-2, E-3, F-3

VOCABULARY

syncopation

◆ ◆ ◆ National Standards ◆ ◆ ◆ ◆

1c Sing music from diverse cultures
2a Play instruments accurately alone and in small ensembles
5a Read quarter, eighth notes, and rests in duple meter
5c Identify standard notation symbols for rhythm
6c Understand and use basic principles of rhythm in music analysis
8b Identify ways music relates to social studies

MORE MUSIC CHOICES

For more practice with syncopated patterns:
"Fifty Nifty United States," p. 250
"Under the Sea," p. 372
"Rockin' Around the Christmas Tree," p. 466

1 INTRODUCE

Perform for students four-beat rhythm patterns consisting of quarter and eighth notes, that include syncopated patterns. Then review with them the known rhythms and their symbols (see Resource Book p. D-2).

READING RHYTHMS

Rhythm patterns are long and short sounds and silences that occur in relation to the beat. In some music the short sounds come in pairs.

In other music, the short sounds can stand alone. The short-long-short pattern below, written with eighth and quarter notes, is called **syncopation.**

Syncopation is rhythm in which important sounds begin on weak beats or weak parts of beats, giving a catchy, off-balance movement to the music.

12   Reading Sequence 2

Footnotes

ACROSS THE CURRICULUM

8b ▶ **Social Studies** After centuries of foreign rule (mostly by Hungary), the Slovaks joined with their neighbors, the Czechs, to form the new nation of Czechoslovakia in 1918. After the chaos of World War II, Czechoslovakia became a Communist nation within Soviet-ruled Eastern Europe. Soviet influence collapsed in 1989, and in 1993 the Slovaks and the Czechs agreed to separate peacefully. Ask students to find Slovakia on a map of Europe.

BUILDING SKILLS THROUGH MUSIC

▶ **Writing** Have students select phrases from "Morning Comes Early" that identify the occupation of the singer. Ask students to suggest other careers or occupations that cause people to rise early in the morning. Divide the class into groups. Have each group choose one suggested occupation and write new lyrics for the second phrase of the refrain (*To the green meadows, the herd I lead*). Invite the class to sing the song substituting the student created phrases.

SKILLS REINFORCEMENT

▶ **Recorder** Have students play this countermelody during the refrain of "Morning Comes Early." Before playing, students **2a** should clap and say the rhythm.

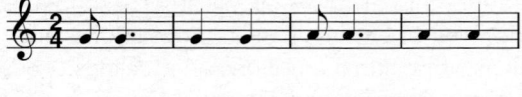

▶ **Mallets** See the Orff arrangement for "Morning Comes Early" in the Resource Book, p. F-3.

Catchy Rhythm

Syncopated rhythms can be found in many types of music, including this folk song from eastern Europe. **Listen** to "Morning Comes Early" while you **conduct** meter in 2. How many examples of the syncopated rhythm on page 12 can you **identify** in the song?

Compose and **perform** your own rhythms by combining different syncopated patterns in new ways.

CD 1-17

MORNING COMES EARLY

Slovak Folk Song

VERSE

1. Morn - ing comes ear - ly, the dew so bright.
2. Lis - ten, my com - rade, when work seems long,

Come with me, Lad - die, in day's first light.
Light - en each mo - ment with mer - ry song,

REFRAIN

Dawn o - ver - takes me, morn - ing a - wakes me,
Wel - come to - mor - row, wait not for sor - row,

To the green mead - ows, the herd I lead.
Mu - sic and laugh - ter are all we need!

Unit 1 13

Analyzing

Have students read standard notation to

5c • Identify quarter and eighth notes and quarter rests. Then recite the rhythm syllable for each.

6c • Describe its relationship to the beat as one sound on a beat (♩), two even sounds on a beat (♫), one silent beat (𝄽).

Ask students to keep a steady beat and listen as you clap the syncopated pattern on p. 12.

ASK How many beats did you pat during my clapped pattern? (two beats)

How many sounds did I clap? (three sounds)

What was the pattern of short and long sounds? (short-long-short)

5a Point out the syncopated figure on p. 12 and in the song notation.

SAY This rhythm pattern of short-long-short sounds is an example of syncopation.

Singing

1c Have students listen to the recording of "Morning Comes Early" **CD 1-17** while keeping a steady beat, then perform the song with accurate rhythm, demonstrating basic performance techniques. Discuss folk dance traditions from Eastern Europe. Share with students the information in Cultural Connection below.

3 CLOSE

Element: RHYTHM **ASSESSMENT**

1c **Performance/Observation** Have students sing "Morning Comes Early" **CD 1-17**, with half the class singing and conducting, and the other half clapping the rhythms from notation. They should then switch parts. Observe students' ability to accurately perform syncopated rhythm patterns

---

CULTURAL CONNECTION

8b ▶ **Work Songs** All over the world, people sing as they work. This helps to make the time go faster and the work more fun. If you had to get up early every day to take your cows up to the meadow, you might need a cheery song like "Morning Comes Early" to get you started. And in the evenings, when people gathered together, they often would dance to those same work songs. Women and men throughout eastern Europe sometimes dance separately as well as together. In this dance, the women dance in their own circle and the men dance around them.

See p. 554 for dance directions.

TECHNOLOGY/MEDIA LINK

5c **Notation Software** Divide the class into groups of three or four students. Give each student a blank sheet of staff paper. Have students

• Write a four-measure rhythm phrase using eighth, quarter, and half notes.

• Notate the completed phrase using notation software.

• Print.

• Perform works in groups, first as written, then as rounds.

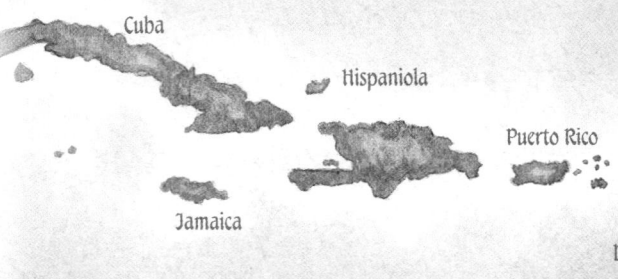
LESSON AT A GLANCE

Element Focus **RHYTHM** Syncopated rhythms

Skill Objective **PLAYING** Play various rhythms that include syncopation

Connection Activity **RELATED ARTS** Explore and discuss folk and visual art from the Caribbean

MATERIALS
- "*Éliza Kongo*" (French) **CD 1-23**
- "*Éliza Kongo*" (English) **CD 1-24**
  Recording Routine: Intro (8 m.); vocal; interlude (8 m.); vocal; coda
- **Pronunciation Practice/Translation** p. 522
- *Saludo de Matanzas* (excerpt) **CD 1-27**
- **Resource Book** pp. A-4, B-2, H-5
- mallet instruments, keyboards, or other melody instruments

VOCABULARY
syncopation

> ◆ ◆ ◆ ◆ **National Standards** ◆ ◆ ◆ ◆
> 1c Sing music from diverse cultures
> 2a Play instruments accurately in small ensembles
> 4a Compose short pieces, demonstrating unity and variety
> 5c Identify and define standard notation symbols for rhythm
> 5d Use standard notation symbols to record musical ideas
> 6b Listen and analyze uses of rhythm in music from diverse cultures
> 8a Show how different arts portray the same idea in unique ways
> 8b Identify ways music relates to the visual arts and social studies
> 9a Describe characteristics of music styles from a variety of cultures

MORE MUSIC CHOICES
For more practice with syncopation:
"Happy Days Are Here Again," p. 284
"Rise Up, Shepherd, and Follow," p. 471

Syncopation Secrets

"*Éliza Kongo*" is a rhythmic song from the Caribbean country of Dominica.

Listen for the syncopation in this song, then **sing** along with the recording.

CD 1-23

Éliza Kongo

Traditional Song from Dominica

Nou ka mou-té an-ro-a c'est la-peé
We're climb-ing up-ward, we're look-ing for peace.

É-li-za ___ Kon-
E-li-za ___ Con-

Nou ka mou-té an-ro-a c'est la-peé
We're climb-ing up-ward, we're look-ing for peace.

Nou ka mou-
We're climb-ing

go
go

É-li-za ___ Kon-go
E-li-za ___ Con-go

(14)

Footnotes

SPOTLIGHT ON

▶ **The Song** "*Éliza Kongo*" has many variants and multiple meanings. The roots of the song can be traced to descendants of people from central Africa to the Americas. One variant suggests that the singers are seeking their homeland or birthright. In a children's form of the song, the singers are trying to resolve a quarrel between Éliza Kongo and her friends.

BUILDING SKILLS THROUGH MUSIC

▶ **Physical Education** Invite students to improvise locomotor movements to perform with "*Éliza Kongo*." For more detailed instruction, see Movement, p. 16.

SKILLS REINFORCEMENT

▶ **Playing** Have students practice this ostinato in preparation for playing drums and adding them to the song.

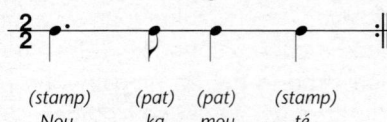

(stamp) (pat) (pat) (stamp)
Nou ka mou-té

To prepare for playing the xylophone pattern below, have students tap the pattern on their legs using the hands shown.

2a

É-li-za ___ Kon-go
(left) (right) (left) (right) (left)

▶ **Keyboard** See Resource Book, p. H-5, for a syncopated accompaniment for "*Éliza Kongo*."

Ay jou-joup, jou - joup, _ jou-joup nou ka _man-dé   Ay pawé-ou,
pawé-ou, _pawé-ou mwen ka _ vi - ni   Ay pawé-ou,
Oh jou-joup, jou - joup, _ jou-joup, We're ask - ing you,   Oh get set,
get set, _ get set, I'm com-ing now,   Oh get set,

go   É - li-za __ Kon-go
go   E - li-za __ Con-go

Where Is the Syncopation?

You have already identified syncopation by listening. You can already **read** this syncopated rhythm.

Look at "*Éliza Kongo*." Find measures that use this rhythm.

Where is the syncopation in this rhythm? **Perform** this rhythm, then **identify** it in "*Éliza Kongo*." Find other measures in the song that have syncopation.

Music of the Islands

In Dominica, both adults and children sing "*Éliza Kongo*." The singers stand in a circle, with one singer in the center. The person in the center sings the phrases on the upper staffs and improvises dance movements. Those in the circle sing the phrase "*Éliza Kongo*," clapping the following rhythms.

With your classmates, **perform** "*Éliza Kongo*," using the suggestions above.

Unit 1 **15**

continued on page 16

1 INTRODUCE

Invite students to echo four-beat and eight-beat rhythm patterns with you. Use different sounds such as clapping, snapping, and stamping. Include syncopation in some rhythms, such as

Write the pattern above on the board. Have students perform the pattern with accurate rhythm, demonstrating fundamental skills, and review the word *syncopation*. Then help students identify syncopation aurally.

ASK Does this rhythm include syncopation? (yes)

Then perform a different pattern, have students echo, and get their answer.

2 DEVELOP

Singing

6b Invite students to listen to *"Éliza Kongo"* **CD 1-23.** Have them signal each time they hear syncopation in the song.

After listening, have students look at "*Éliza Kongo*" in their books. Have them find the *Éliza Kongo* phrases (voice part 2) and sing them as you play the recording again.

1c Divide the class in half. Have one group sing the part 1 phrases and the other sing the part 2 phrases separately. Then have the groups sing their phrases together.

Reading

6b **ASK** Which of these is the best description of syncopation: short-short-long, short-long-short, long-short-short? [Say the patterns in rhythm.] (short-long-short)

ACROSS THE CURRICULUM

8b ▶ **Social Studies** Using a globe or world map, help students locate the Caribbean Sea and the islands mentioned in the lesson. Orient students to north, south, east, and west. Then help them to describe the location of the Caribbean Sea and islands, using direction words in sentences such as, "The Caribbean Sea is south of the United States" or "The Caribbean Sea is east of Mexico." Help them look for other islands and island nations and describe their locations using direction words.

TEACHER TO TEACHER

5c ▶ **Managing Composition Activities** Before beginning the composition activity in this lesson, establish criteria for the composition and write a list on the board. The list might include **5d** the following: The composition must be four measures long in $\frac{4}{4}$ meter; include one example of syncopation; the melody must use these notes—G, A, B, D, E; notate your composition.

▶ **Teaching Non-English Language Songs** Students become more sensitive to other cultures by singing songs in languages other than their own. To give students an opportunity to hear the special flavor of the original language, play the Pronunciation Practice Track **CD 1-26.** Then use the Pronunciation Practice/Translation section, which begins on p. 522, to teach the non-English version.

Unit 1 *Let the Music Begin!* **15**

Direct students to the text on p. 15 of their books. Have students read music that incorporates rhythmic patterns in various meters and

- Use standard terminology to describe the rhythm in the middle of p. 15 as short-long-short.
- Tap and say the rhythm, then find it in the song.
- Tap and say the next rhythm (short-long-short-long-long), noting the tie; find it in the song.

Ask students to look at "Éliza Kongo," p. 14. Divide the class. Have half the class tap and speak the rhythm of voice part 1 and the other half tap and speak the rhythm of part 2 (first two lines of the song only). Then have the groups switch parts.

Moving

8a Invite students to create movements for "Éliza Kongo" **CD 1-23.** Encourage them to use same or similar movements each time they hear the words Éliza Kongo in the song. Play the recording and invite students to move. Additional teaching suggestions can be found in Movement below.

Playing

Ask students to look at the instrumental parts at the top of p. 16 and identify the syncopated rhythms. Have them tap the rhythm of each part, then transfer to instruments. Invite them to perform the arrangement with accurate rhythm, demonstrating basic performance techniques, to accompany "Éliza Kongo."

Listening

6b Have students

- Identify the Caribbean islands on a map.
- Listen to *Saludo de Matanzas* **CD 1-27.**

Ask students to listen for syncopated patterns in the vocal and instrumental parts of the selection.

9a **SAY** Think about the music you have heard. Work with a partner to make a list of the characteristics of music from the Caribbean islands.

Island Syncopations

Play this arrangement to accompany "Éliza Kongo."

Arts **Connection**

Night at the Silver Slipper by Jackson Burnside, John Beadle, and Stan Burnside. This colorful Caribbean acrylic painting is a collective effort of visual artists and musicians. The painting was created as musicians improvised. ▶

Footnotes

CULTURAL CONNECTION

▶ **Caribbean Crafts** Learn more about the folk crafts of the Caribbean in *Art from Many Hands: Multicultural Art Projects* by Jo M. Schuman (Davis Publications, 1981). Students will enjoy crafting seed necklaces (Puerto Rico), island maracas (St. Thomas, Cuba), and silhouette stencils based on Haitian designs. Create a gallery of multicultural folk crafts to display student work at musical performances.

MOVEMENT

8a ▶ **Creative Movement** Encourage students to create their own movements for "Éliza Kongo." Allow them to experiment as they listen to the recording. Then gather students in a circle. Use students' ideas to create simple movements for the first two lines of the song, or use the following pattern.

Stamp, clap, stamp, clap,
shake fists right twice, left twice (repeat)

While the class sings and performs the movements above, have two or three students improvise their own movements or dances in the middle of the circle. During the second half of the song (*Jou-joup…*), have all students improvise their own dances in place. Ask each student in the middle to choose someone to take his or her place.

Listen for the syncopated rhythms in *Saludo de Matanzas*.

CD 1—27
Saludo de Matanzas

as performed by Afro Cuba de Matanzas

The city of Matanzas, located on the northwest coast of Cuba, is one of the historical centers of Afro-Cuban cultural traditions.

 Tune In

Saludo de Matanzas is a rumba from Cuba. Like many other Caribbean and Latin American dances, the rumba has elements of African, Spanish, and Native American dances.

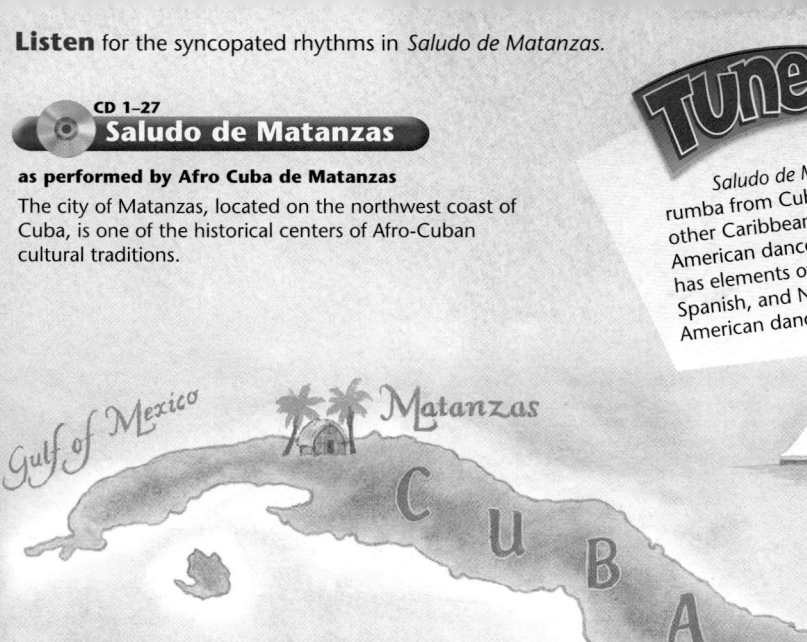

Show What You Know!

Using a rhythm instrument of your choice, **play** the following patterns.

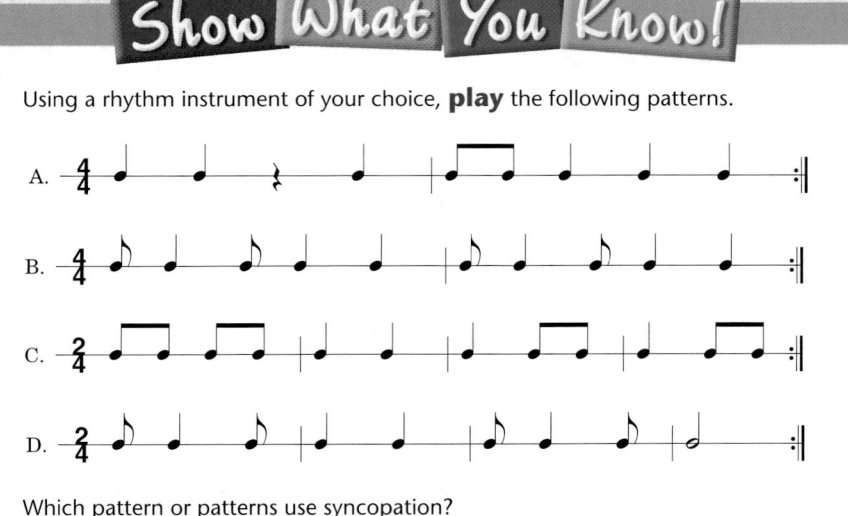

Which pattern or patterns use syncopation?

ASK If you had to describe the music to someone else, what would you say? (List students' answers on the board. *Syncopation* should be included among the answers.)

Creating

 Invite students to create melodic phrases with syncopation. Working individually, in pairs, or in small groups, have students

- Experiment with various rhythms by moving to, speaking, or playing the rhythms.

- Write music that incorporates rhythmic patterns in various meters. Write four measures of rhythm in $\frac{4}{4}$ meter and include at least one syncopated rhythm.

- Transfer the rhythms to a pitched instrument, such as a xylophone, keyboard, or bells.

- Use the pitch set G, A, B, C, D as a starting point for melodic exploration.

- Notate the melody using standard symbols to notate pitch in simple patterns.

3 CLOSE

Describing

 Focus students' attention on the Caribbean painting on p. 16. Ask students to identify concepts taught in the other fine arts and their relationship to music concepts. Lead a discussion of how the shapes and colors reflect the energy and rhythmic syncopation of a jazz "jam session." For ideas on creating Caribbean folk art, see Cultural Connection, p. 16.

 **Element: RHYTHM**   **ASSESSMENT**

Performance/Peer Critique Have students look at the Show What You Know activity on p. 17. (See Resource Book p. B-2.) Working individually or in pairs, have students read standard notation and

- Tap or clap and say each rhythm.

- Take turns playing rhythms on an instrument of their choice.

- Identify rhythms that include syncopation.

MEETING INDIVIDUAL NEEDS

▶ **Including Everyone** Drums are highly preferred instruments among students with and without special needs. Because instrument activities in this and the next lesson will be particularly motivating, assign instruments carefully. Rules for earning instrument privileges should be explicit, especially for students who are particularly active. When drum playing for *"Éliza Kongo"* is earned, students learn an adaptive and socially acceptable way to receive attention and praise from their peers and their teacher. Have students earn frequent but short playing periods in this and other lessons, and select rhythms for them that will allow all to have immediate success.

TECHNOLOGY/MEDIA LINK

Notation Software Have students use music software programs to create and notate compositions with syncopation. Encourage them to explore the various timbres available to capture the sounds and style of music from the Caribbean islands, as heard in this lesson.

LESSON AT A GLANCE

Element Focus **FORM** Call and response

Skill Objective **PLAYING** Accompany a call-and-response song using rhythm instruments

Connection Activity **SOCIAL STUDIES** Discuss the people, food, customs, and work life of the Caribbean

MATERIALS

- "Day-O!"   CD 1-28

  Recording Routine: Intro (2 m.); vocal; coda
- *Ain't That Love*   CD 1-30
- *Day-O!* (excerpt)   CD 1-31
- **Resource Book** pp. C-2, C-8
- xylophones, glockenspiels or bell sets, cowbell, drums, claves, maracas

VOCABULARY

call and response   calypso

◆ ◆ ◆ ◆ National Standards ◆ ◆ ◆ ◆

1c Sing music from diverse cultures

2c Perform instrumental music from diverse cultures

3b Improvise rhythmic variations on given melodies

4a Compose short pieces, demonstrating unity and variety through music

5a Read quarter notes and eighth notes in duple meter

5c Identify standard notation symbols for pitch

6b Listen and analyze uses of form, rhythm, pitch, and timbre in music from diverse cultures

8a Show how different arts portray the same idea in unique ways

8b Identify ways music relates to social studies

MORE MUSIC CHOICES

For more practice singing call-and-response songs:

"Erie Canal," p. 262

"Go Down, Moses," p. 190

BANANAS FORM BUNCHES

In Jamaica and other Caribbean islands, workers spend all night loading bananas on the boats to be shipped around the world. "Day-O!" is a song of boat loaders who are eager to go home.

Sing with the banana boat loaders in "Day-O!"

DAY-O!
(Banana Boat Loader's Song)

Folk Song from Jamaica

Day-o! Day-o! __ Day-light come _ and me wan' go home. wan' go home.

Work all night _ 'til de morn-in' come _ Day-light come _ and me wan' go home.

Stack ba-na - na 'til de morn-in' come. _ Day-light come _ and me wan' go home.

Come, Mis - ter Tal - ly - man, come tal - ly me ba - na - nas.
Came here for work, I did - n't come here for to i - dle.

Day-light come _ and me wan' go home. wan' go home.
Day-light come _ and me

18

Footnotes

CULTURAL CONNECTION

8b ► **Jamaica** Bananas, along with cocoa beans, fruit juices, coffee, citrus fruits, and coconuts, are important export crops from Jamaica. (Its main export is sugar cane.) Tourism and mineral production have also become very important.

Reggae, a syncopated Jamaican musical style, has achieved international popularity. It had a great influence on rock music in the 1960s, especially in Great Britain.

BUILDING SKILLS THROUGH MUSIC

► **Theatre** Invite students to sing "Day-O" **CD 1-28**. Lead students in a discussion of the song lyrics. Divide the class into groups of four to six students. Have each group create a dramatization of the song and perform it for the class.

CHARACTER EDUCATION

► **Respect** To encourage respect for differences among people, music, and cultures, question students about why such respect is needed in today's world. Ask the following questions: Why might such respect be more important today than thirty years ago? Do you think respecting differences today is easier, harder, or about the same as it was for your parents? Have students defend their responses. Guide them to understand that listening to and responding to a different style of music requires courage, self-discipline, and open-mindedness. Encourage students to recognize the musical differences in the two performances of "Day-O!" without labeling one performance as "better" than another.

1 INTRODUCE

5a Invite students to join you in echoing rhythms. Include syncopation in the patterns you perform. Challenge students by extending the echoes from four beats to eight beats. Then write this rhythm on the board and have students clap it.

SAY This rhythm is going to be your response to whatever I clap. Instead of echoing, clap this response every time.

Clap various patterns (calls), and have students clap the responses. Invite individual students to clap the "call" patterns.

2 DEVELOP

Singing

SAY The part you clapped that was the same each time is called a response. Listen to this song and identify the response.

Play the recording of "Day-O!" **CD 1-28.**

6b **ASK What is the response?** *(Daylight come and me wan' go home)*

Have students

- Read the text about the song on p. 18 in their books.
- **5c** Find the responses in the song.
- **1c** Sing the responses with the recording.
- Compare the upward and downward endings of the responses.

Moving

ASK We've been singing the response. What is the other part of the song called? (call)

continued on page 20

ACROSS THE CURRICULUM

8b ▶ **Social Studies** Help students explore more about the people, food, customs, work, family life, and songs of the Caribbean in the following books.

- *The Caribbean and its People* by T. W. Mayer (Thomson Learning, 1995)
- *Cooking the Caribbean Way* by Cheryl Davidson Kaufman (Lerner Publications, 1989)

Ask students to research the Caribbean area's banana crop, harvest, and transport. Invite students to discuss the following.

- How does "Day-O!" describe the work and feelings of the banana boat loaders?
- What were the banana boat workers doing when they would sing this song? (loading bananas)

SKILLS REINFORCEMENT

4a ▶ **Creating** Help students at varying skill levels create call-and-response compositions.

Reinforcement Some students may have difficulty creating their own call-and-response compositions. Allow these students to be successful by creating four-beat body percussion calls.

On Target Many students will be able to create call-and-response compositions. Invite these students to

- Improvise eight-beat body percussion calls.
- Answer each call with the response in "Day-O!"

Challenge Those students who master this lesson easily may be invited to improvise both a call and a response pattern and transfer them to glockenspiel or bells in G pentatonic.

8a Invite students to move to the call and response of "Day-O!" Have them

- Create one movement that they will all perform for every response.
- Practice their response movements with the music.
- Improvise individual movements during the call and perform the class movement during the response.
- Stand in a circle. Have individuals move (in the center) during the calls and everyone else move during the responses.

Playing

Have students clap this rhythm and speak the words printed below.

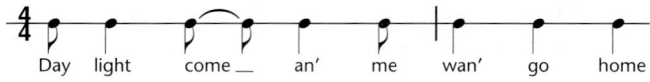

Day light come ___ an' me wan' go home

2c Have students pat the rhythm on their legs, then transfer the rhythm to xylophones, using the note B♭. Play during the response.

Listening

SAY Different musicians can perform the same song in different ways. Listen to this version of *Day-O!* and be ready to compare it to the one you already know.

To help students aurally identify excerpts of music from diverse cultures, play the recording of *Day-O!* **CD 1-31** performed by Harry Belafonte.

6b **ASK** **What did you hear that was the same as or similar to the version we sang?** (The words, rhythm, and melody are similar; there is still a call and response.)

What did you hear that was different? (The voices, instruments, and tempo are different.)

Which version do you prefer and why? (Accept various answers using music terms.)

How Will You Respond?

"Day-O!" is a song in call-and-response form. One person sings the call and the others answer with the response. **Create** a movement to go with the response as you **sing** the song.

People from the West Indies often improvise percussion accompaniments for their songs. **Play** one of the following rhythm patterns or improvise your own to accompany "Day-O!"

Listen to the calls and responses in this performance of *Ain't That Love.* **Sing** along on the response parts.

CD 1–30

Ain't That Love

by Ray Charles
as performed by Diane Schuur

Jazz singer Diane Schuur has won two Grammy awards.

Play the following rhythm patterns to accompany *Ain't That Love.*

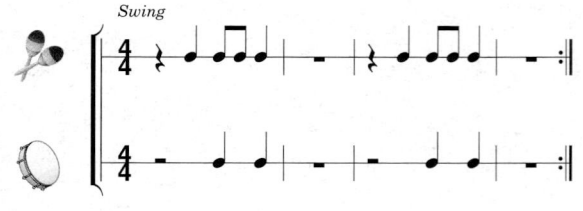

20

Footnotes

SPOTLIGHT ON

▶ **The Performer** Harry Belafonte (born 1927) began his singing career with popular music styles. He is best known, however, for his interpretations of the folk music of the United States and the Caribbean islands. In addition to his singing career, Belafonte has appeared as an actor in films, on television, and on Broadway, where he won a Tony Award for best supporting actor. Belafonte, a leader in breaking social and racial barriers, has a strong commitment to helping others. He received the 1986 Award of Appreciation from the American Music Center for his role in raising funds for African countries in need. On June 21, 2000, he was given the ASCAP Harry Chapin Humanitarian Award.

SKILLS REINFORCEMENT

6b ▶ **Listening** Use a comparison chart or Venn diagram to help students compare the two versions of "Day-O!" in this lesson. (See pp. C-2 and C-8 in the Resource Book.) If using the Venn diagram, have students write characteristics of the music in the left circle as they listen to one version of the song and in the right circle as they listen to the other version. Use the center overlap section to record characteristics that are the same or similar. Circle the differences that remain in the two circles.

MUSIC MAKERS
Harry Belafonte

American singer **Harry Belafonte** (born 1927) was born in Harlem, an area of New York City. He spent five years of his childhood in Jamaica. The music of Jamaica and other Caribbean islands influenced his recordings. His album *Calypso* was the first pop album to sell more than one milllion copies. Other Belafonte hits include "Jamaica Farewell" and "Matilda." Belafonte is considered the "King of Calypso."

Listen to Harry Belafonte perform *Day-O!* in traditional call-and-response calypso style. **Sing** the response part with the recording.

CD 1-31
Day-O!

Traditional Calypso from Jamaica as performed by Harry Belafonte
Many calypso songs, such as *Day-O!* have verses that tell a story about an event or experience.

 8b Refer students to the feature on Harry Belafonte on p. 21 and then lead a discussion of Caribbean life. (See Cultural Connection, p. 18, and Across the Curriculum, p. 19.)

Improvising

 3b Invite students to create rhythmic phrases for their own call-and-response compositions. For the responses, have students play the instrument parts for "Day-O!" (see p. 20). Set up a response group with instruments on one side of the room. Have students

- Improvise eight-beat body percussion calls to the response.
- Transfer the call rhythms to glockenspiels or bell sets in G pentatonic (G, A, B, D, E).

Allow students to improvise calls to the set responses.

3 CLOSE

Listening

6b Point out to students that call-and-response form is also used in other musical styles. Then play the recording of the jazz piece *Ain't That Love* **CD 1-30.**

Playing

Invite students to use the rhythm score at the bottom of p. 20 to accompany *Ain't That Love.*

Element: FORM   ASSESSMENT

1c
2c **Performance/Observation** Invite students to choose one of the rhythm parts at the top of p. 20 to accompany "Day-O!"

To reinforce the call-and-response form of the song, have one player act as the leader (call) as the others play the response. Observe students' ability to accurately perform the rhythm parts while singing the song.

TEACHER TO TEACHER

3b ▶ **Taking Turns During Improvisation** Engage students in a process for taking turns as they create their own calls in the Improvising section of the lesson above. Place the group of students playing the responses at one side of the room. Place three instruments opposite or facing the response group. Have improvisers line up behind the instruments, as though lining up for a relay race. Have the first person in line step forward and improvise, then go to the back of the line or take the place of one of the students playing in the response group.

TECHNOLOGY/MEDIA LINK

4c **Web Site** Invite students to visit *www.sfsuccessnet.com* for more information on Caribbean music and musicians.

LESSON AT A GLANCE

Element Focus   **MELODY** Note names

Skill Objective   **READING** Sing a melody and read from notation using note names

Connection Activity   **SOCIAL STUDIES** Discuss the history of sailing ships and their routes

MATERIALS

- "Bound for South Australia"   **CD 2-1**
  Recording Routine: Intro (2 m.); v. 1–5; coda
- **Music Reading Practice, Sequence 3**   **CD 2-3**
- **Resource Book** p. E-4, I-3
- keyboards, recorders, mallet instruments

VOCABULARY

call and response

> ◆ ◆ ◆ **National Standards** ◆ ◆ ◆ ◆
>
> **1c** Sing music from diverse cultures
> **2a** Play instruments accurately alone and in small ensembles
> **3b** Improvise melodic variations on given melodies
> **5c** Identify standard notation symbols for pitch
> **8b** Identify ways music relates to social studies

MORE MUSIC CHOICES

For more practice reading notes with letter names:
"Pollerita," p. 151

For another historical song about travel by water:
"Erie Canal," p. 262

1 INTRODUCE

8b   **SAY** Before the steam engine was invented, sailors relied on wind power in the sails to move the ships.

Discuss the map, sailing ships, and text on p. 23. See also Cultural Connection below.

Over the Ocean

"Bound for South Australia" is a sea shanty sung by sailors to help them work together. As they sang, they pulled the ropes that moved the sails. Can you imagine what the motions might look like? **Move** as you **sing** "Bound for South Australia."

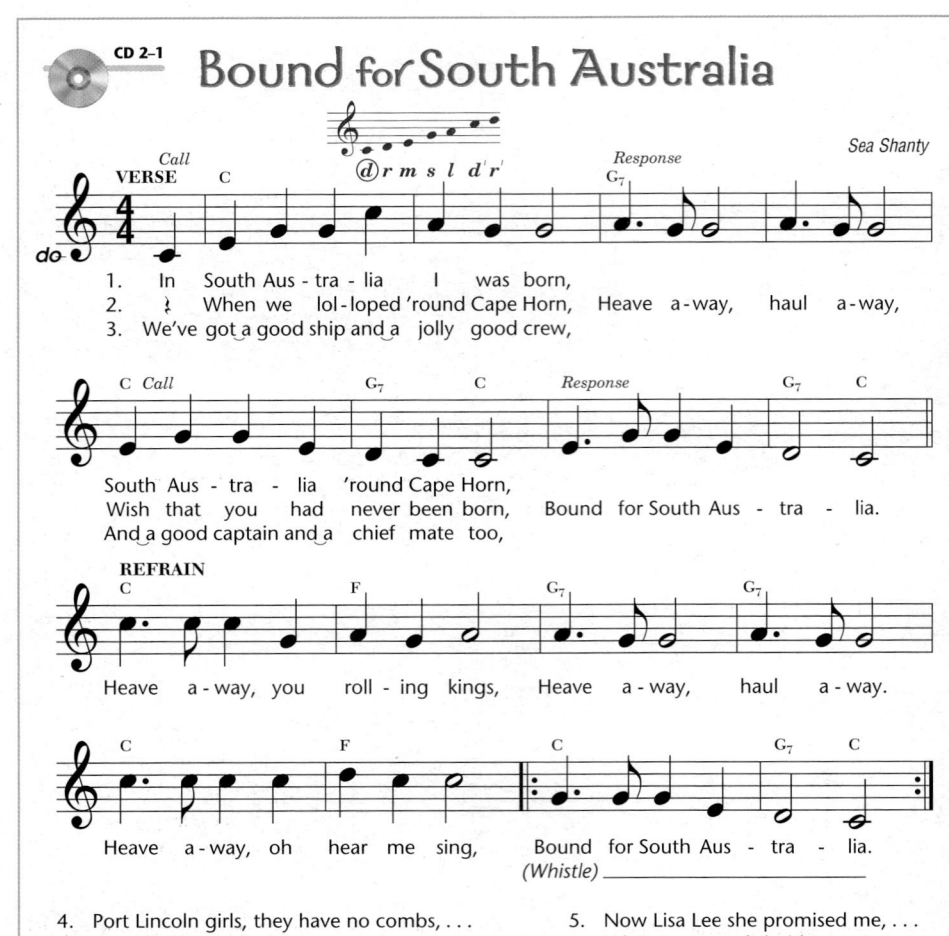

CD 2-1

Bound for South Australia

Sea Shanty

1. In South Aus-tra-lia I was born,
2. When we lol-loped 'round Cape Horn, Heave a-way, haul a-way,
3. We've got a good ship and a jolly good crew,

South Aus-tra-lia 'round Cape Horn,
Wish that you had never been born, Bound for South Aus-tra-lia.
And a good captain and a chief mate too,

REFRAIN

Heave a-way, you roll-ing kings, Heave a-way, haul a-way.

Heave a-way, oh hear me sing, Bound for South Aus-tra-lia.
(Whistle) _____

4. Port Lincoln girls, they have no combs, . . .
They do their hair with snapper bones, . . .
Refrain

5. Now Lisa Lee she promised me, . . .
When I returned she'd marry me, . . .
Refrain

Footnotes

SKILLS REINFORCEMENT

2a ▶ **Playing** "Bound for South Australia" can be accompanied using three chords—C, G7, and F. Help students find the chords on electric or acoustic keyboards. Bass notes for each chord can be played on bass xylophones or metallophones. Encourage students to accompany the song, using any of these instruments.

▶ **Recorder** See the Resource Book, p. I-3, for a playing activity for "Bound for South Australia."

BUILDING SKILLS THROUGH MUSIC

▶ **Reading** Invite students to listen to "Bound for South Australia" **CD 2-1** and determine the type of travel described in the song. Discuss other meanings or uses of the words "heave" and "haul." Have students locate other words and phrases that have more than one meaning. List words on the board that have multiple meanings and the ones appropriate for the song.

CULTURAL CONNECTION

▶ **Australia** Invite students to learn more about the European settlement of Australia in *My Place* by Nadia Wheatley (Kane Miller Books, 1994). The book contains interesting information about one particular place in Australia and the generations of children who have lived there.

▶ **History and Sailing Ships** Have students discover when the steam engine was invented. Previously, wind, sails, and (sometimes) oars were the "power" that moved ships. Have students search for additional information about sailing ships and how they were built.

If a world map is available, trace the route described in "Bound for South Australia." Port Lincoln is on the south coast of Australia.

Sailing, Sailing

Sing the response parts, first using pitch syllables, then the letter names of the notes.

Play the response parts of "Bound for South Australia" on recorder or keyboard.

RESPONSE

do — la so so la so so
A G G A G G

RESPONSE

do — mi so so mi re do
E G G E D C

Sailing from the East Coast of the United States to Australia was a very long trip that took many weeks. Ships had to travel all the way around South America by way of Cape Horn, then across the Pacific to Australia. ▼

Unit 1 **23**

2 DEVELOP

Singing

1c Play the recording of "Bound for South Australia" **CD 2-1.** Invite students to

- Move as though they were pulling the ropes to raise the sails on a ship as they listen to the song.
- Sing the song with the recording.

Reading

Have students find the words *Call* and *Response* in the song. Play the recording of "Bound for South Australia" and have students

- Listen to the calls and sing and move to the responses.
- 5c Find and name the pitch syllables in the response lines printed on p. 23.

Playing

2a Allow students to choose instruments to play the responses in the melody. Pairs of students can work together on keyboards, xylophones, or bells. Have them

- Review the note names for the responses.
- Find the notes on their instruments.
- Play the responses with the recording or while the class sings the song.

3 CLOSE

Element: MELODY   **ASSESSMENT**

1c
5c **Performance/Observation** Divide the class into two groups to demonstrate appropriate small-ensemble performance techniques, that can be used when performing in formal concerts. Have half the class sing the "calls" of "Bound for South Australia," using letter names of the pitches. The other half sings the responses.

TEACHER TO TEACHER

2a
5c ▶ **Playing an Instrument—Silent Practice** Add a "silent practice" step to students' playing experiences to help them build confidence. When learning to play the responses of "Bound for South Australia," have students

- Name the notes.
- Point to or finger the notes on the instruments they have chosen. (silent practice)
- Sing the pitch names and point to or finger the notes. (additional reinforcement prior to playing)
- Play the melody.

TECHNOLOGY/MEDIA LINK

Electronic Keyboard Help students improvise a folk accompaniment for "Bound for South Australia." Have students

- 5c Name the notes in the melody (C, D, E, G, A).
- Review where those pitches are located on a keyboard.
- Play the C-pentatonic scale with their right hands (thumb positioned on C, index on D, middle on E, stretch ring finger to G, pinky on A).
- 3b Choose a timbre that they think is appropriate for the song and improvise an ostinato using the C-pentatonic scale.
- 1c Play their ostinatos as the class sings the song.

LESSON AT A GLANCE

Element Focus **MELODY** Pentatonic patterns

Skill Objective **SINGING** Read a pentatonic melody from notation

Connection Activity **CULTURE** Discuss the meaning of the lyrics of a folk song from Korea

MATERIALS

- *"Arirang"* (Korean)   **CD 2-6**
- *"Arirang"* (English)   **CD 2-7**
  Recording Routine: Intro (4 m.); vocal; interlude (4 m.); vocal; coda
- **Pronunciation Practice/Translation** p. 522
- **Resource Book** pp. A-5, D-3, F-4
- melodic percussion instruments

VOCABULARY

scale   pentatonic

◆ ◆ ◆ National Standards ◆ ◆ ◆

1c Sing music from diverse cultures
3b Improvise melodic variations on given melodies
5b Sight-read melodies in treble clef
8b Identify ways music relates to language arts

MORE MUSIC CHOICES

For more practice with extended pentatonic patterns:
"Lahk gei mohlee," p. 317
"Meng Jian Nu," p. 194

1 INTRODUCE

Sing short pentatonic patterns for students, using a neutral syllable, such as *loo*. Have students

- Echo-sing each pattern as a group and individually.
- Show the melodic contour of each pattern with their hands, with chalk drawings at the board, or using a piece of yarn on the floor.

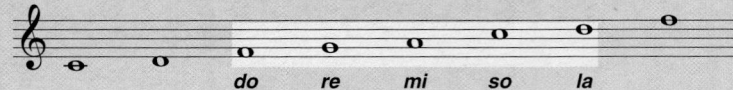

Pentatonic Puzzle

The melody of *"Arirang"* is based on a five-tone pattern called a **pentatonic** scale. (The prefix *penta* in Greek means "five.")

Sing the pentatonic scale in the color box, using hand signs.

Can you solve this pentatonic puzzle?

Look carefully at the notes outside the color box. Are they part of the pentatonic scale? In what way can a pentatonic scale have more than five notes?

> **Pentatonic** refers to music based on a five-tone scale.

do   re   mi   so   la

24

Footnotes

ACROSS THE CURRICULUM

▶ **Social Studies** Invite students to read more about the life of an elementary student in Korea in *Chi-Hoon: A Korean Girl* by Patricia McMahon (Boyd Mills, 1998). Ask students to compare Chi-Hoon's descriptions of family life, schoolwork, and dreams to their own lives in America.

BUILDING SKILLS THROUGH MUSIC

▶ **Language** Invite students to listen to *"Arirang"* **CD 2-7** and think of words to describe the feelings expressed by the singer. Discuss reasons for their choices and list them on the board. Have students listen to the song again and decide if any additional words should be added to the list. Ask students what characteristics from the music suggest the feelings represented on the list.

SKILLS REINFORCEMENT

3b ▶ **Creating/Playing** Encourage students to compose variations of *"Arirang"* using notes from the extended pentatone.

Have them play the pentatonic patterns from the song on Orff instruments, or use the black keys on a piano. Point out that on the piano, the black keys are found in groups of two's and three's. Play the black keys, starting with any group of two. The notes are *so, la, do, re, mi*.

▶ **Mallets** Students may enjoy learning the Orff accompaniment for *"Arirang"* in the Resource Book on p. F-4.

Music from Korea

Korea is a country with many different kinds of traditional music. This version of *"Arirang,"* one of the most popular songs in Korea, originated in Seoul. **Sing** *"Arirang"* and **listen** for its unique pentatonic sound.

CD 2-6

Arirang

English Words by Alice Firgau

Folk Song from Korea

A - ri - rang, __ A - ri - rang, __ a - ra - ri - yo, _____
A - ri - rang, __ A - ri - rang, __ a - ra - ri - yo, _____

A - ri - rang __ ko - ge - ro - nuh - muh - kan - da.
O - ver the __ hills _____ of __ A - ri - rang.

Chung - chun __ ha - nul - en __ pyul - do __ man - ko, _____
Voic - es __ call __ me from __ far __ a - way, _____

I - __ neh __ ka - sem - en __ su - sim - do man - ta
I _____ must __ fol - low, __ I __ can - not stay.

2 DEVELOP

Reading

Review the notes of the pentatonic scale, using Resource Book, p. D-3.

ASK Where are the steps and skips in the pentatonic scale? (All are steps except *mi* to *so*.)

Have students read standard notation and

- Use pitch syllables and demonstrate hand signs for the pitches.

5b
- Sing pitches as you point to them (in *F-do*).

Point out the missing notes on the staff by singing the interval from *do* to *low la*.

ASK Was the second sound higher or lower than *do*? (lower)

Is it a step or a skip away from *do*? (skip)

Name the note below *do* as *low la*. Show its hand sign as the same as *la* above *do*, but lower in space. Repeat the process with *low so* and then *high do*.

Singing

Have students

- Listen to *"Arirang"* **CD 2-6** while following the staff notation.

5b
- Sing with the recording, using pitch syllables and hand signs.

Discuss the literal meaning of the Korean lyrics. (See Cultural Connection below.)

3 CLOSE

Element: MELODY   ASSESSMENT

1c
5b
Performance/Observation Have students sing *"Arirang"* while following the notation, first using hand signs and pitch syllables and again using the song text. Observe students' ability to accurately read and perform the songs.

CULTURAL CONNECTION

8b ▶ *"Arirang"* Arirang refers to an imaginary hill, a place to which people aspire. *Arariyo* is a nonsense word. Line two speaks about going over the hills; line three about a clear, bright sky with many stars; and line four says that there are "many worries in my heart." Cultures throughout the world have similar ideas and hopes—the Promised Land, Shangri-La, nirvana.

Have students discuss, then write the meaning of the English lyrics in lines three and four. Where might the singer be going? What is calling him or her away? What might the singer find at the end of the journey? Might "going over the hills" refer to overcoming troubles and sorrows?

TECHNOLOGY/MEDIA LINK

3b **Sequencing Software** Have students improvise and record two ostinato tracks, using only the black keys on a keyboard. Students should assign the tracks the following roles.

- Track 1: A repeated pattern (one or two measures) using low notes
- Track 2: A short chordal, half-note pattern (two notes per chord) in the middle register

LESSON AT A GLANCE

Element Focus **MELODY** Pentatonic melody

Skill Objective **READING** Sing and read from notation a pentatonic melody

Connection Activity **SOCIAL STUDIES** Read about the Underground Railroad

MATERIALS

- "This Train" **CD 2-10**
  Recording Routine: Intro (4 m.); v. 1; interlude (2 m.); v. 2; interlude (2 m.); v. 3; interlude (2 m.); v. 1 reprise; coda
- **Music Reading Practice, Sequence 4** **CD 2-12**
- **Resource Book** pp. B-2, D-4, E-5, G-2
- selected melodic percussion instruments

VOCABULARY

pentatonic

◆ ◆ ◆ **National Standards** ◆ ◆ ◆

1b Sing easy pieces with technical accuracy
1c Sing music from diverse genres
5b Sight-read melodies in treble clef
8b Identify ways music relates to social studies

MORE MUSIC CHOICES

For more practice using hand signs and pitch syllables:
"All Through the Night," p. 105
"Da pacem, Domine" ("Grant Us Peace"), p. 62

1 INTRODUCE

8b Ask students to read and discuss the first two paragraphs of text on p. 26. (See Cultural Connection below and Across the Curriculm, p. 27, for more information on the Underground Railroad.) Then play the recording of "This Train" **CD 2-10**.

Follow the Melody

▲ Harriet Tubman was one of the "conductors" who led slaves on a journey to freedom on the Underground Railroad.

Railroads spread westward across the country during the Industrial Revolution in the mid-1800s. For African slaves, the "railroad" might represent a spiritual journey or, if it were the Underground Railroad, a special physical journey. This railroad used no trains or tracks. It was a secret network of people who helped runaway slaves find freedom in the North.

Spirituals were sometimes used to communicate code words and phrases about possible escape plans. A train "bound for glory," might be a group bound for freedom.

Sing the notes of the extended pentatonic scale going up and then down.
Read these pentatonic patterns. Then **sing** the melody using pitch syllables.

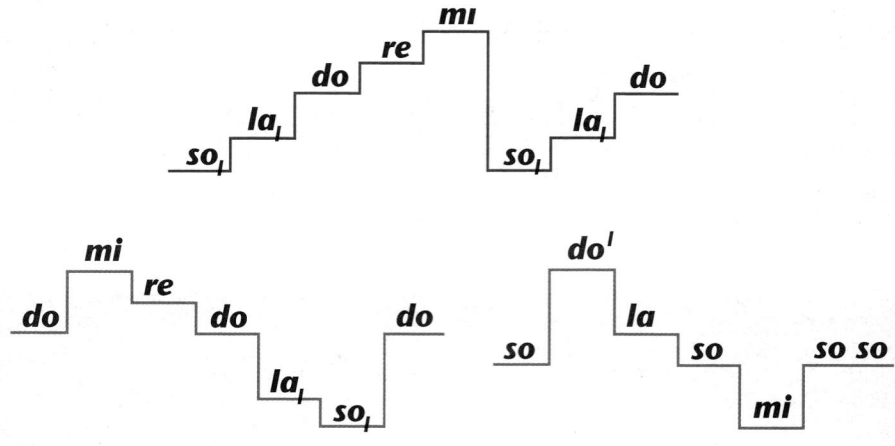

Sing "This Train," using pitch syllables. Can you find the pentatonic patterns?

26   Reading Sequence 4

Footnotes

CULTURAL CONNECTION

8b ▶ **Underground Railroad Code Words** The Underground Railroad was a system that helped slaves escape. Directions for the escape were often transmitted by coded words. For example, the *drinking gourd* indicated the Big Dipper; *River Jordan* was the Mississippi River; *baggage* referred to escaping slaves; *Canaan* was Canada; *gospel train* was the Underground Railroad itself; and *Moses* was Harriet Tubman.

BUILDING SKILLS THROUGH MUSIC

▶ **Science** Explain to students that before the Civil War, thousands of enslaved African Americans fled north to freedom. Traveling in secret at night, they looked to the stars for direction. They told each other to "follow the drinking gourd," the star pattern that points to the North Star. Today, this pattern is called the Big Dipper. Discuss the patterns of stars in the sky called constellations. Have students learn about other constellations.

SKILLS REINFORCEMENT

5b ▶ **Singing/Creating** Have students play a game: "Singing Secrets." Prepare for the game by having several melody flashcards in a box. One student draws a card from the box, reads the melody pattern, and sings it quietly to the next student. The second student sings it to a third, and so on, until the melody pattern has traveled around the room. The last person sings and then reads the original card. The object of the game is to pass the pattern from singer to singer without changing it! (See Resource Book p. D-4 for a selection of 16 melody patterns.)

 ▶ **Signing** For a sign interpretation of "This Train," see Resource Book p. G-2.

This Train

CD 2-10

s, l, ⓓ r m s l d'

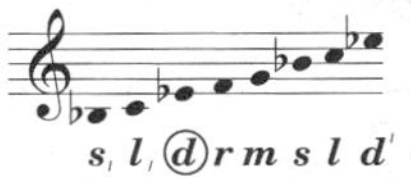

African American Spiritual

do

1. This train is bound for glo - ry, this train. __
2. This train don't pull no sleep - ers, this train. __
3. This train don't take your mon - ey, this train. __

This train is bound for glo - ry, this train. __
This train don't pull no sleep - ers, this train. __
This train don't take your mon - ey, this train. __

This train is bound for glo - ry, don't car - ry none but the good and ho - ly.
This train don't pull no sleep-ers, Don't pull __ nothin' but the right-eous peo-ple.
This train don't take your mon-ey, Pay your __ way with __ milk and hon-ey.

This train is bound for glo - ry, this train. __
This train is bound for glo - ry, this train. __
This train is bound for glo - ry, this train. __

Show What You Know!

do

Call   Response

Call   Response

Create and **perform** new response melodies for "Bound for South Australia," page 22. Choose your notes from the C-pentatonic scale (C-D-E-G-A).

Unit 1   27

2 DEVELOP

Singing

1b Sing short extended pentatonic patterns for students, using a neutral syllable, such as *loo*. Have students sing each pattern using pitch syllables and then hand signs.

Review the notes of the pentatonic scale (p. 24). Have students sing the notes of the extended pentatonic scale, ascending and descending.

Listening

Play the recording of "This Train" **CD 2-10** and have students

- Listen for the pentatonic patterns shown on p. 26.
- Identify the words that occur on each of the melody patterns *(is bound for glory)*.

ASK How are the melody patterns different? (Some notes are repeated in the song; the patterns on p. 26 only outline the contour of the melody.)

Reading

Have students

- Listen again to the recording of "This Train" while following the staff notation.
- **5b** Read "This Train" from staff notation using pitch syllables and hand signs.
- Clap and say the rhythm syllables.
- **1c** Sing again, this time singing the text.

For more experience reading pentatonic patterns, see Music Reading Practice, Sequence 4 on p. 491 and Resource Book p. E-5.

3 CLOSE

Element: MELODY   **ASSESSMENT**

1c **Performance/Observation** Have students sing "This Train." Then have them choose the first, second, or fourth phrase and sing it with hand signs and pitch syllables, then with the text. Observe students' success at each stage.

ACROSS THE CURRICULUM

8b ▶ **Language Arts** Can you imagine what it must have been like to have been a young boy or girl during the days of the Underground Railroad? Two fictional books based on actual events give accounts of just such young people. In *Which Way Freedom?* by Joyce Hansen (Camelot, 1992), a young slave named Obi makes a daring run from slavery and joins the army to help free his people. In *A Picture of Freedom: The Diary of Clotee, a Slave Girl* by Patricia McKissack (Scholastic, 1997), students can read about the struggles of a young girl's life on a Virginia plantation and her escape to freedom.

TECHNOLOGY/MEDIA LINK

Multimedia Have students add a multimedia dimension to the script of a production dealing with the Underground Railroad. Alternate freedom songs and spirituals with short readings. Use slides featuring student art depicting scenes and stories from the production. Encourage students to research ideas, focusing on the people involved, the history of the Underground Railroad, and the songs associated with it.

LESSON AT A GLANCE

Element Focus	**TIMBRE** Vocal timbre
Skill Objective	**SINGING** Sing with good vocal technique and use good tone quality
Connection Activity	**SCIENCE** Discuss the human respiratory system as it relates to vocal technique

MATERIALS

- "Morning Has Broken" **CD 2-16**
  Recording Routine: Intro (4 m.); v. 1; interlude (8 m.); v. 2
- *The Kerry Dance* **CD 2-15**
- *Who Can Sail?* **CD 2-18**
- **Resource Book** pp. H-6, I-4

VOCABULARY

vocal cords   diaphragm   timbre   contour

> ♦ ♦ ♦ ♦ **National Standards** ♦ ♦ ♦ ♦
>
> **1a** Sing accurately with good breath control
> **1e** In groups, sing moderately easy pieces from memory
> **2a** Play instruments accurately alone
> **4c** Arrange, using electronic media
> **6a** Listen and describe events in music using appropriate terms
> **6b** Listen and analyze uses of timbre and form in music from diverse cultures
> **7b** Students use specific criteria for evaluating their own performances
> **8a** Show how different arts portray the same idea in unique ways
> **8b** Identify ways music relates to science and social studies

MORE MUSIC CHOICES

For more practice using proper vocal technique:
"Uno, dos, y tres," p. 427
"Sail Away," p. 404

You Make the Timbre

Your voice is your own instrument! You take it with you wherever you go. Do you know how your voice works?

When you sing, air moves through your throat and your vocal cords vibrate. Your vocal cords are very small muscles used for speaking and singing. Your lungs are the air pump for your body. The air you need to speak and sing with comes from your lungs. Your diaphragm is a muscle that helps you breathe. When you sing, you use your diaphragm to help control the air flowing past your vocal cords.

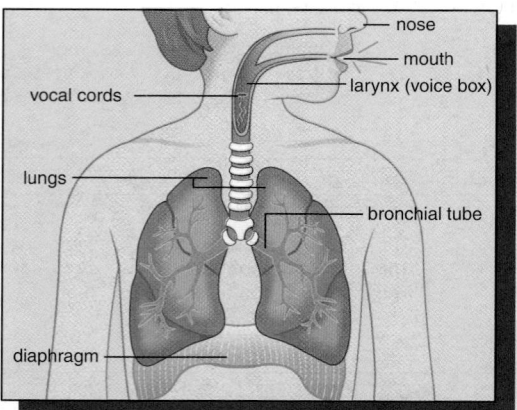

nose
mouth
larynx (voice box)
vocal cords
lungs
bronchial tube
diaphragm

▲ Good posture helps your vocal cords, lungs, and diaphragm work correctly.

Listen to this vocal performance of *The Kerry Dance.*

 CD 2–15
The Kerry Dance

by J.L. Molloy
as performed by Anthony Kearns, Ronan Tynan, and Finbar Wright
This performance was recorded live at Waterfront Hall in Belfast, Ireland.

The "Three Irish Tenors" (from left to right): Anthony Kearns, Ronan Tynan, Finbar Wright ▶

28

Footnotes

MOVEMENT

8a ▶ **Creative Movement** Have students listen to the recording of "Morning Has Broken" and show the phrases by pretending they are painting large arcs in the air with imaginary paintbrushes. Have students sing the song while showing the phrases. Encourage them to invent other movements that will also show the phrases. Their breathing should match their body movements.

BUILDING SKILLS THROUGH MUSIC

▶ **Science** Invite students to sing "Morning Has Broken" **CD 2-16** with good vocal technique. Focus students' attention on the picture of the respiratory system on p. 28. Have students draw and label an illustration of the respiratory system.

ACROSS THE CURRICULUM

8b ▶ **Science** Check out an anatomy illustration from the school library, or borrow an anatomy model from the science lab or from a science teacher. Show students parts of the body that support the singing voice.

- The spine is the foundation of good posture.
- The rib cage surrounds and protects the lungs.
- Air passes through the trachea and bronchial tubes on its way to the lungs.
- The sinuses provide extra resonating space for the voice. (Help students find their sinuses by tapping a tuning fork and placing it on the forehead above the eyebrow.)

Support Your Sound

"Morning Has Broken" is a traditional Gaelic melody from Ireland or Scotland. **Identify** the phrase markings in "Morning Has Broken" and trace the **contour** of the music.

Sing each phrase in one breath. Support your air flow by using your diaphragm.

Contour is the "shape" of a melody. The melody moves upward and downward in steps, leaps, and repeated tones.

CD 2-16
MIDI 2

Morning Has Broken

Words by Eleanor Farjeon
Traditional Gaelic Melody

@ r m s l t d r'

1. Morn - ing has bro - ken Like the first morn - ing,
2. Sweet the rain's new fall Sun - lit from heav - en,

Black - bird has spo - ken Like the first bird. _____
Like the first dew - fall On the first grass. _____

Praise for the sing - ing! Praise for the morn - ing!
Praise for the sweet - ness Of the wet gar - den,

Praise for them, spring - ing Fresh from the Word! _____
Sprung in com - plete - ness Where His feet pass. _____

Unit 1 29

1 INTRODUCE

Have students find a partner. Ask the members of each pair to think about how their voices work and to explain their thinking to their partner using standard teminology. Then play the recording of *The Kerry Dance* **CD 2-15** to illustrate proper vocal technique "in action."

2 DEVELOP

Singing

Invite students to read about their voices on p. 28 of their books.

8b Have students continue to work with a partner and quiz each other about the vocal cords, lungs, and diaphragm.

ASK What part of your body works like an air pump? (lungs)

Which muscle helps to control your air as you breathe, speak, and sing? (diaphragm)

What is the name of the small membranes that vibrate together when you talk or sing? (vocal cords)

1a Have students sing the first phrase of "Morning Has Broken" with collapsed posture and then with correct singing posture.

ASK What happened to your voices when you changed your posture? (Accept a variety of answers.)

Have students work in pairs and sing the phrase again, checking each other's posture.

Listening

Play the recording of "Morning Has Broken" **CD 2-16**. Have students

6b
- Trace the phrases in the music as they listen.
- Describe the timbre, or quality, of the singing voices.

continued on page 30

SKILLS REINFORCEMENT

▶ **Conducting** Have students explore the relationship between time, space, and energy. Write the words *time*, *space*, and *energy* on the board. Have students conduct a two-beat pattern to a familiar song, drumbeat, or other musical excerpt. Increase the tempo. Ask the students to describe what happens to their gestures (they get smaller, quicker, and may feel like they take more energy). Then slow the tempo of the musical example and ask students to describe what happens. Repeat the experiment with changes in dynamics.

▶ **Recorder** See Resource Book p. I-4 for a countermelody to be performed with "Morning Has Broken."

2a

CULTURAL CONNECTION

8b ▶ **Sunrise** Explore more about the ancient meanings, sights, and sounds of sunrise. Read and discuss the various cultural traditions surrounding people's greetings of the morning sun. Create a dramatic reading or readers' theatre from the text of the Caldecott Honor Book, *The Way to Start a Day* by Byrd Baylor (Simon & Schuster, 1986). Students could illustrate sections of the book and create scenery for a choral reading performance.

For more myths and legends of ancient peoples, read and dramatize *Sun, Moon and Stars* by Mary Hoffman (Dutton, 1998). This beautifully illustrated collection of folklore includes stories and poetry from China, Japan, Egypt, Korea, the Caribbean islands, and the Aztec and Navajo cultures.

Singing

To get them ready for singing, have students place their hands just below their rib cages to find their diaphragms. Have them breathe in and then hiss as they exhale to feel the muscle work.

SAY As we sing "Morning Has Broken," use your diaphragm to help control your air so you can sing each phrase in one breath.

 Have students sing with the recording **CD 2-16.** Then divide the class into groups of four or five.

SAY Practice "Morning Has Broken" in your group. Listen to each other, and think about what adjustments you can make so your voices blend, or work together.

Give students time to practice and then invite groups to sing for the class.

Moving

Invite students to describe what a conductor does.

ASK What is the conductor's job? How does a conductor move? (Accept a variety of answers.)

Have students move to show two-, three-, and four-beat patterns.

ASK What would your conducting movements look like if the meter is in 2 and the tempo is fast? (Allow students time to experiment.)

What would your conducting movements look like if the music is in triple meter and the tempo is slow? (Allow students time to experiment.)

SAY Conductors use other gestures to show loud and soft.

Model and have students

- Copy a crescendo motion—palms toward ceiling and arms rising.
- Copy a decrescendo motion—palms toward the floor and arms falling.

Following the Conductor

Singers perform together in a chorus by following a conductor. The conductor teaches the singers the music and uses conducting patterns to lead the group. These patterns tell the singers when to begin and end, and what tempo and dynamics to use.

Listen to the Indianapolis Children's Choir perform *Who Can Sail?* **Describe** the expression, phrasing, and vocal blend you hear in the performance.

CD 2-18
Who Can Sail?

**Folk Song from Scandinavia
as performed by the Indianapolis Children's Choir;
Henry Leck, conductor**

This "farewell" song is from a Swedish-speaking island that is part of Finland. It is located in the Baltic Sea.

Upgrade Your Singing!

Review "Morning Has Broken," on page 29, or choose another song that you like to sing. **Sing** the song with a small group. Check the list of suggestions below to improve your singing. Get ready to perform!

- Check your posture.
- Blend your voice with other singers in your group.
- Sing long phrases, using proper breath control.
- Sing with expression.
- Follow the conductor's gestures.

MIDI Create your own timbre arrangement by assigning sounds to each MIDI track for "Morning Has Broken."

30

Footnotes

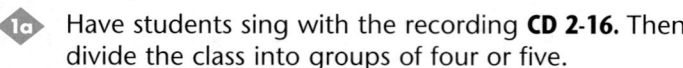
SKILLS REINFORCEMENT

▶ **Singing Voices** Help students learn to care for their singing voices. Post a list of "Good Singing Health" habits:

- Drink plenty of water.
- Sit or stand tall.
- Do not yell; it hurts your voice!

Help students who are singing off-pitch with this exercise. Draw a swooping upward line in the air. Have students copy your movement and swoop their voices upward. Continue with other movements and sounds.

▶ **Keyboard** See Resource Book p. H-6 for a two-handed broken chord accompaniment for "Morning Has Broken."

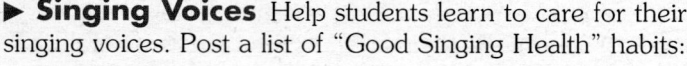
AUDIENCE ETIQUETTE

▶ **Audience Behavior** Encourage students to be actively involved listeners and to exhibit concert etiquette during varied live performances. Before they attend a performance, review appropriate concert or theater etiquette.

- Arrive on time for the performance and stay with your group at all times.
- Use soft voices while waiting for the performance to begin.
- Stay seated during the performance.
- Concentrate on listening and watching during the performance. Give the performers your full attention.
- No eating or drinking in the theater.
- Applaud with energy at the end of the performance.
- Tell your friends and family what you liked about the performance.

Indianapolis Children's Choir

Founded in 1986, the Indianapolis Children's Choir has performed all over the world. More than 1,000 children between the ages of 9 and 17 belong to the many choruses in the Indianapolis Children's Choir.

▲ Henry Leck is the conductor of the Indianapolis Children's Choir.

Unit 1   31

• Sing "Morning Has Broken" with a student conductor leading changes in dynamics.

Listening

Invite students to read the information on p. 31 about the Indianapolis Children's Choir and describe various music avocations.

Play the recording of the Indianapolis Children's Choir performing *Who Can Sail?* **CD 2-18.** Have students

• Move as though they are conducting the group.

6a
• Describe the timbre of the voices they hear in the recording. (Accept a variety of descriptions.)

3 CLOSE

Element: TIMBRE — **ASSESSMENT**

1e **Performance/Self-Assessment** Review "Morning Has Broken" **CD 2-16** by having the class sing the song. Divide students into three or four groups. Have each group

• Read "Upgrade Your Singing!" on p. 30.

• Practice "Morning Has Broken." (Encourage students to take turns conducting their groups. Hint: Due to the meter of the song, conductors may be limited to dynamics, phrase gestures, or showing the beat with a one-beat as though bouncing a ball.)

• Demonstrate appropriate small-ensemble performance techniques in their informal classroom concerts.

• Memorize the first verse, then watch the conductor.

7b Have groups perform with accurate intonation, demonstrating basic performance techniques. After they have performed, have groups self assess, verbally or in writing by applying criteria.

TEACHER TO TEACHER

▶ **The Art of Conducting** The conductor of a group is playing an instrument—the whole group. It is up to the conductor to interpret the wishes of the composer and to transmit those ideas to the group (and, ultimately, to the audience). This is done vocally in rehearsal, but the conductor must use a type of sign language in performance. It is the job of each of the performers to immediately respond to these signals.

The musical value of a selection to the listener is most often due to the decisions and effectiveness of the conductor.

SCHOOL TO HOME CONNECTION

▶ **Singing at Home** The urge to sing is universal. People all over the world use song for various purposes—to tell a story, to make a comment about an event or about life in general, or to capture a feeling. Have students list other reasons for singing. Then have them list activities they perform at home that they might accompany with singing.

TECHNOLOGY/MEDIA LINK

4c

MIDI/Sequencing Software Using the MIDI song file of "Morning Has Broken," have students create their own "timbre" arrangements by assigning their favorite sounds to each MIDI track.

LESSON AT A GLANCE

Element Focus   **TEXTURE/HARMONY** Ostinato

Skill Objective   **MOVING** Create ostinato movement patterns

Connection Activity   **CULTURE** Participate in art projects relating to West African cultures

MATERIALS

- "*Funwa alafia*"   **CD 2-19**
- "Welcome, My Friends"   **CD 2-20**

  Recording Routine: Intro (8 m.); vocal; interlude (4 m.); vocal; interlude (4 m.); vocal; coda
- **Pronunciation Practice/Translation** p. 522
- "*Kokoleoko*"   **CD 2-23**

  Recording Routine: Intro (2 m.); v. 1; instrumental; v. 2; instrumental; v. 3; instrumental; v. 4; coda
- *Yo Lé Lé (Fulani Groove)* (excerpt)   **CD 2-25**
- **Resource Book** p. A-5
- classroom rhythm instruments

VOCABULARY

ostinato

♦ ♦ ♦ ♦ **National Standards** ♦ ♦ ♦ ♦

1c Sing music from diverse cultures
6b Listen and analyze uses of pitch, rhythm, texture in music from diverse cultures
7a Create standards for evaluating performances
8b Identify ways music relates to social studies

MORE MUSIC CHOICES

For more practice singing African songs:
"*Bantama kra kro,*" p. 308

1 INTRODUCE

Invite students to look for and describe repeated patterns in the border art on pp. 32–33 and in objects in the room or in the clothing they are wearing.

PLAY AN OSTINATO!

Listen to "*Funwa alafia*" and "*Kokoleoko*," two songs from West Africa. Do you hear any repeated patterns in the songs?

Now it's your turn to **move** with the music. Choose a song and **create** a motion to go with the music. This pattern should last four or eight beats. Repeat it several times. Now move as you **sing**!

Your movement pattern is an illustration of **ostinato.**

> An **ostinato** is a repeated rhythm or melody pattern played throughout a piece or a section of a piece.

CD 2-19

FUNWA ALAFIA
(Welcome, My Friends)

English Words by Donald Scafuri   Folk Song from West Africa

Fun - wa   a - la - fia,   Ah - shay,   Ah - shay.
Wel - come,   my friends,   I   greet you   in peace.

Fun - wa   a - la - fia,   Ah - shay,   Ah - shay.
Wel - come,   my friends,   I   greet you   in peace.

Gankogui ▲

Gome ▶

32

Footnotes

CULTURAL CONNECTION

▶ **African Singing** Everywhere in Africa, music and dance are a part of all phases of daily life—economic, political, recreational, ceremonial, and so on. Virtually all African styles emphasize singing, primarily because song is used as an avenue of communication. Many of the languages in Africa are "tone" languages, in which pitch level carries meaning.

BUILDING SKILLS THROUGH MUSIC

▶ **Social Studies** To help students learn how to draw conclusions, have them sing "*Funwa Alafia*" and "*Kokoleoko*" while clapping the rhythm of each. Ask students to identify the repeated rhythm pattern in "*Funwa Alafia*" and the syncopated pattern in "*Kokoleoko.*" Review "*Éliza Kongo*" (p. 14), and "*Day-O!*" (p. 16). Have students identify the repeated rhythm patterns in these songs. Invite students to identify the places of origin of all the songs on a world map. Discuss possible reasons why the songs emphasize the same rhythm patterns.

ACROSS THE CURRICULUM

8b ▶ **Art/Social Studies** Supplement students' West African cultural experiences with art projects and displays in *The Kids' Multicultural Art Book: Art and Craft Experiences from Around the World* by Alexandra M. Terzian (Williamson Publishing, 1993). Learn how to make these simple art projects based on West African folk art designs: paper-weaving based on kente cloth from Ghana; akua'ba dolls based on Asante wooden dolls from Ghana; Wodaabe mirror pouches based on leather pouches from the Wodaabe people of Niger; and Korhogo mud cloths from the Ivory Coast. Display students' artwork at musical performances.

Kokoleoko

t d r m f

Folk Song from Liberia

do

G   C   G

1. Ko - ko - le - o - ko,   Ma - ma,   Ko - ko - le - o - ko,
2. A -   by,*   Sa - rah,   a -   by,
3. One __ more __ round, Te - te,   one __ more __ round,
4. Take __ your __ time, chick - en,   take __ your __ time,

G   D   G

Ko - ko - le - o - ko,   chick - en,   crow - ing   for   day.
A -   by,   chick - en,   crow - ing   for   day.
One __ more __ round, chick - en,   crow - ing   for   day.
Take __ your __ time, chick - en,   crow - ing   for   day.

*Aby means "goodbye."

Listen to this modern arrangement of a traditional West African song. How many ostinatos can you **identify**?

Improvise a movement ostinato with this music.

Yo Lé Lé (Fulani Groove)

Traditional Song from West Africa as performed by Youssou N'Dour and the Super Étoile

The opening words of this song—*Fluta Toro*—refer to a region in the West African country of Senegal.

Donno ▶

Dundun ▶

2 DEVELOP

Listening

6b Play the recordings of *"Funwa alafia"* **CD 2-19** and *"Kokoleoko"* **CD 2-23** and ask students to find repeated patterns in each song.

Moving

Play the recordings again and invite students to create an ostinato movement pattern for one of the songs that is four or eight beats long. Have students

1c
- Demonstrate patterns for each other.
- Move to the music again, this time while singing.

8b Share with students the resource listed in Across the Curriculum, p. 32, and encourage the class to choose an art project to accompany the performances of *"Funwa alafia"* and *"Kokoleoko."*

Listening

Play the recording of *Yo Lé Lé* **CD 2-25.**

6b **ASK Who is performing the ostinato in the music?** (Drummers; the rhythm of the string players is always similar, but the melody changes.)

3 CLOSE

Element: TEXTURE/HARMONY — **ASSESSMENT**

7a **Performance/Peer Critique** Have students work in small groups to create and perform a rhythm ostinato accompaniment to one of the songs in this lesson. Have students

- List three goals relating to the ostinato accompaniment.
- Perform the accompaniment while the class sings and moves to the song.
- Determine whether the goals were met.

SKILLS REINFORCEMENT

2c ▶ **Performing** Use the following teaching suggestions to help students move, sing, and play simultaneously.

Reinforcement Some students may have difficulty moving, playing, and singing at the same time. Ask these students to focus on moving to the beat as they listen to the song.

On Target Many students will be able to sing and move together. If this is difficult, have them alternate singing and moving. For example, students would sing line 1 of *"Funwa alafia"* and move to line 2.

Challenge Students who can move and play simultaneously may be invited to play ostinatos for the song while singing. Also, if students are playing smaller instruments, encourage them to move to the beat as they play.

TECHNOLOGY/MEDIA LINK

Web Site To learn more about West African drumming and vocal styles, visit *www.sfsuccessnet.com.*

7a **Sequencing Software** Use a digital audio program to record students' self-assessment ostinatos.

- Have students record their instrumental performance on one track and their singing performance on another track.
- When they are finished, students can play back their performance, then save the file as a WAV file.
- Have each group type their assessment of their recording.
- Post the WAVs and the self-assessments to the school Web site.

LESSON AT A GLANCE

Element Focus — **TEXTURE/HARMONY** Melodic ostinatos

Skill Objective — **SINGING** Add ostinatos to create harmony

Connection Activity — **SCIENCE** Discuss plants and animals that might be encountered while hiking in the mountains

MATERIALS

- "I Love the Mountains"   **CD 2-26**
  Recording Routine: Intro (4 m.); vocal; interlude (2 m.); ostinato 1 (2 times); ostinatos 1 and 2 (2 times); vocal with ostinatos; coda
- *Sumer Is Icumen In* (excerpt)   **CD 2-28**
- **Resource Book** p. F-5
- classroom melody instruments

VOCABULARY

ostinato   texture

◆ ◆ ◆ ◆ **National Standards** ◆ ◆ ◆ ◆

1a Sing accurately in small ensembles
2a Play instruments accurately in small ensembles
4c Compose, using electronic media
6a Listen and describe events in music using appropriate terms
8b Identify ways music relates to language arts and science

MORE MUSIC CHOICES

For more practice performing ostinatos:
"Oklahoma," p. 36
"Zum gali, gali," p. 401

1 INTRODUCE

8b Ask students to discuss their favorite objects in nature, such as trees and animals that they might encounter while hiking in the mountains. (See Across the Curriculum, p. 35) Then read the lyrics of "I Love the Mountains" to look for additional things about nature.

Let Nature Sing

People love to sing about the beauty of their surroundings.
Sing "I Love the Mountains."

CD 2–26

I Love the Mountains

Traditional

I love the moun-tains, I love the roll-ing hills,
I love the flow-ers, I love the daf-fo-dils,
I love the fire-side, When all the lights are low,
Boom-dee-ah - da, boom-dee-ah - da, Boom-de-ah - da, boom-dee-ah - da,
Boom!

Ostinato

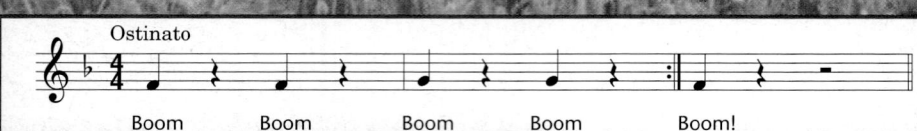

Boom   Boom   Boom   Boom   Boom!

Layers of sound can be used to create **harmony**. **Perform** the ostinato above to accompany "I Love the Mountains." You are singing in harmony when you sing the melody and the ostinato together.

Harmony is created when two or more different pitches sound at the same time.

34

Footnotes

MEETING INDIVIDUAL NEEDS

8b ▶ **Including Everyone** The song "I Love the Mountains" provides opportunities to focus on vocabulary. Have students find the words in the song that describe elements of nature *(mountains, rolling hills, daffodils)*. Encourage students to find and use more English words that describe elements of nature.

BUILDING SKILLS THROUGH MUSIC

▶ **Language** Ask students to look on p. 35 and read when *Sumer Is Icumen In* was written. (the thirteenth century) Have students read the words shown on the listening map on p. 35 and identify the words that were used in the thirteenth century that are similar to standard usage. Ask students to listen to and discuss the meaning of phrases in *Sumer Is Icumen In*.

SKILLS REINFORCEMENT

8b ▶ **Creating** Students can create additional verses for "I Love the Mountains." Ideas for first lines might include *I love the sunshine, I love the falling rain,* and so on.

2a ▶ **Playing** Invite students to sing or play the following additional ostinato with "I Love the Mountains."

doot   do-do   doot   do-do   doot

Lasting Beauty

Just as we do, people of earlier times sang about nature and their surroundings. **Listen** for ostinatos in this performance.

CD 2–28

Sumer Is Icumen In

**Thirteenth-Century Canon from England
as performed by the Purcell Consort of Voices**

Sumer Is Icumen In, a popular song from England during medieval times, is about the arrival of summer.

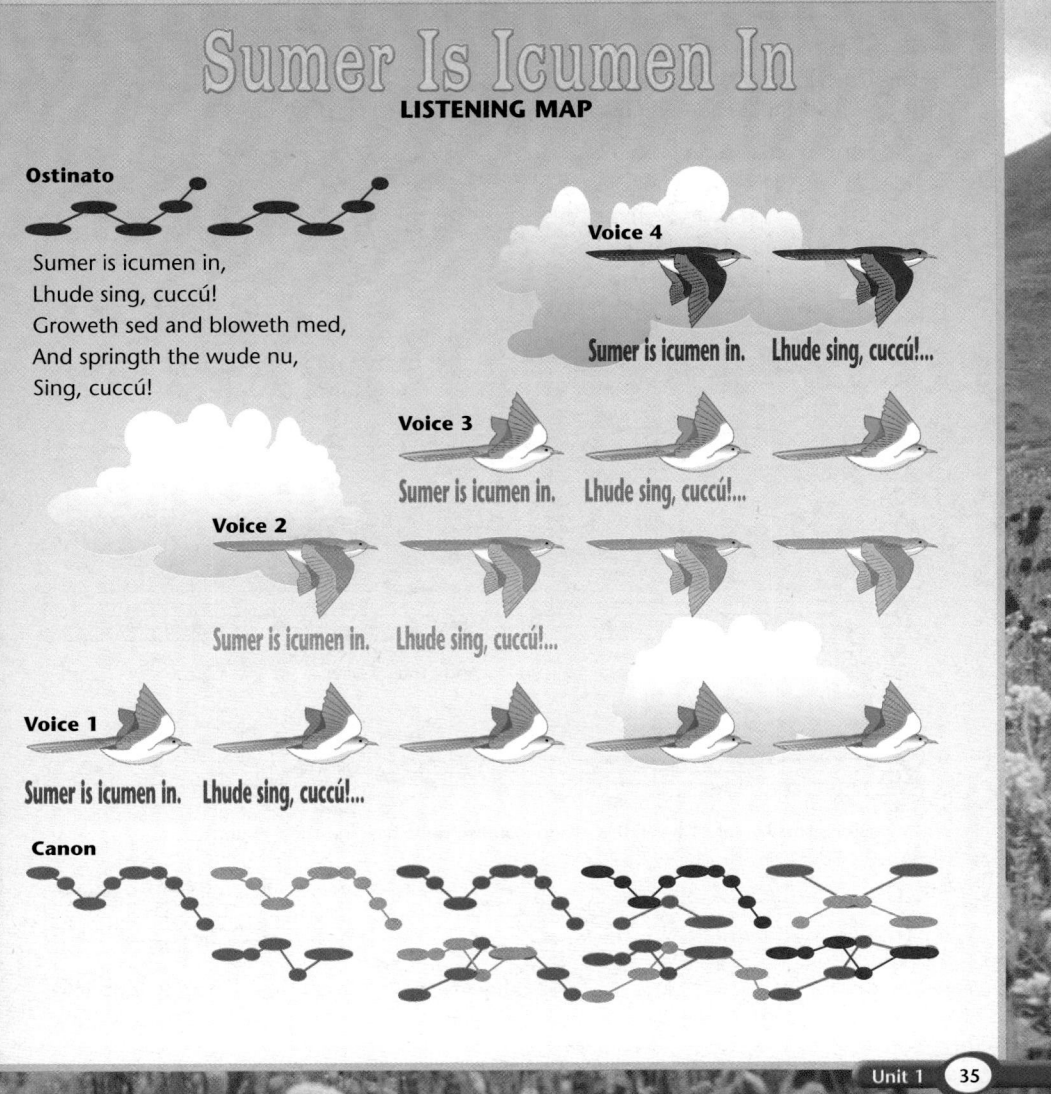

Sumer Is Icumen In
LISTENING MAP

Ostinato

Sumer is icumen in,
Lhude sing, cuccú!
Groweth sed and bloweth med,
And springth the wude nu,
Sing, cuccú!

Voice 4
Sumer is icumen in.   Lhude sing, cuccú!...

Voice 3
Sumer is icumen in.   Lhude sing, cuccú!...

Voice 2
Sumer is icumen in.   Lhude sing, cuccú!...

Voice 1
Sumer is icumen in.   Lhude sing, cuccú!...

Canon

Unit 1   35

Singing

1a Have students sing "I Love the Mountains" **CD 2-26** with the recording. Invite a small group to sing the ostinato at the bottom of p. 34 while the rest of the class sings the song.

6a **ASK What happened to the song when the ostinato was added?** (The texture became thicker.)

Playing

2a Invite a small group of students to play the ostinato on melody instruments while the rest of the class sings the song.

Students may also enjoy playing an Orff accompaniment with "I Love the Mountains." See Resource Book p. F-5.

Singing

1a Divide the class into groups; have one group sing the song and the other group sing the ostinato. Help students discover that the texture becomes thicker when the ostinato is added.

Listening

6a Play *Sumer Is Icumen In* **CD 2-28** as students follow the listening map on p. 35. Help students discover that the layering of voices and the use of ostinato create thicker texture.

3 CLOSE

Element: TEXTURE/HARMONY   ASSESSMENT

1a **Performance/Observation** Divide the class into small groups. Ask each group to select instruments to add to a performance of "I Love the Mountains." Have students perform the song several times, layering the instruments with the vocal performance.

2a

6a

ASK What happened to the texture as instruments were added? (The texture became thicker, thus adding more harmony.)

ACROSS THE CURRICULUM

8b ▶ **Science** Share the book *I Love the Mountains: A Traditional Song* by John Archambault (Silver Burdett Press, 1998), which sets the song text of "I Love the Mountains" within beautifully rendered block-cut construction-paper art. Invite students to discuss what they love or see—or wish they could see—while hiking in the mountains. Locate the nearest wilderness or park areas in your area, and challenge students to make a list of the most common plants, animals, and climatic features. Find books, pamphlets, and agencies that provide information about wilderness ecology in your area.

For more information about mountain environments, read *America's Mountains: A Guide to Plants and Animals* by Marianne D. Wallace (Fulcrum, 1999).

TECHNOLOGY/MEDIA LINK

4c

Notation Software Have students create, notate, and print their own melody using the same rhythm pattern found in "I Love the Mountains." Students should

- Be given "G" as a starting and ending pitch.
- Be given a range of pitches (D, E, F♯, G, A, B, C, D) to use.
- Make their melodies move by step as much as possible.

Transparency Display the listening map transparency for *Sumer Is Icumen In* as you play the recording. You may wish to point to each vocal entrance to help students follow along.

LESSON AT A GLANCE

Element Focus	**TEXTURE/HARMONY** Vocal harmony
Skill Objective	**LISTENING** Discover how harmony is created by combining two different melodies
Connection Activity	**SOCIAL STUDIES** Discuss the location and economy of Oklahoma

MATERIALS

- "Oklahoma" **CD 2-29**
  Recording Routine: Intro (16 m.); vocal; interlude (7 m.); repeat 2nd half vocal; coda
- "Do-Re-Mi" from *The Sound of Music* **CD 2-31**
- *Interview with Rebecca Luker* **CD 2-32**
- *Interview with Richard Rodgers* **CD 2-33**
- bells, keyboard, or other melodic instruments
- map of the United States

VOCABULARY

harmony

◆ ◆ ◆ ◆ National Standards ◆ ◆ ◆ ◆

1d Sing music written in two parts
2b Perform easy instrumental pieces with technical accuracy
6a Listen and describe events in music using appropriate terms
6b Listen and analyze uses of harmony and texture in music from diverse genres
7b Students use specific criteria for evaluating their own performances
8b Identify ways music relates to social studies

MORE MUSIC CHOICES

For more practice with vocal harmony:
"*Canción Mixteca,*" p. 326
"*Hine mah tov,*" p. 431

Broadway Harmony

Even before becoming a state in 1907, Oklahoma was a center of oil production, farming, and ranching. This adventurous period in the state's early history provided the setting for *Oklahoma!*, the 1943 Rodgers and Hammerstein production that set new standards for the Broadway musical.

Listen to the title song from the show. As you follow the music, **identify** at what point harmony is added by a group of backup singers.

 CD 2–29

Oklahoma

Words by Oscar Hammerstein II
Music by Richard Rodgers

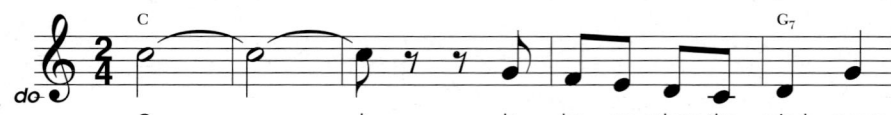

O - k - la - ho - ma, where the wind comes

sweep-in' down the plain, And the wav - in' wheat can

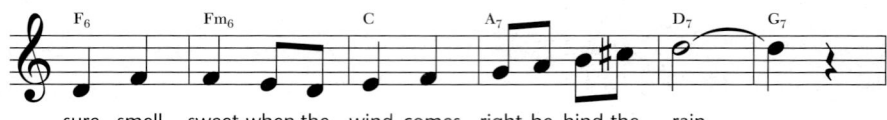

sure smell sweet when the wind comes right be-hind the rain. _____

O - k - la - ho - ma, ev - 'ry night my hon - ey lamb and

Footnotes

ACROSS THE CURRICULUM

8b ▶ **Social Studies** In the early 1800s, much of present day Oklahoma had been set aside for Native Americans. In 1889, the government opened up two million acres of land to settlers, an event in history known as the Oklahoma Land Rush. Oklahoma produces oil, coal, quarry stone, and cattle. Every year Native Americans from more than 100 tribal nations gather in Oklahoma City for a celebration of their heritage.

BUILDING SKILLS THROUGH MUSIC

▶ **Social Studies** Invite students to sing "Oklahoma." Have them identify words and phrases in the song that describe characteristics of the weather, topography, and agricultural products produced by the state. You may wish to invite students to develop an accompaniment for the song that creates sound effects for words from the song (for example, "wind" and "rain").

SKILLS REINFORCEMENT

2b ▶ **Playing** Have students play this pattern on a melody instrument. They can play along with the highlighted notes on p. 37.

1 INTRODUCE

8b Have students find Oklahoma on a map of the United States. (Oklahoma is in the west central region of the country.)

Inform students that oil production, cattle ranching, and farming have always been important to the state's economy. These activities play an important role in the play.

ASK What is the abbreviation for Oklahoma? (OK)

2 DEVELOP

Listening

Invite students to listen to "Oklahoma" **CD 2-29** to discover how the composer and lyricist introduce the name of the state and its abbreviation. (the long sustained "O" at the beginning and the "O.K.")

6b **ASK** What term best describes all voices singing the melody? (unison)

When did the voices sing in harmony? (the section of the song, on p. 37, in the color box)

Singing

Encourage students to sing along with the recording.

Focus students' attention on the harmony part on p. 38.

Invite students to sing the harmony part or play it on a melody instrument.

1d Divide the class into two groups and have them sing the song with the harmony part.

6b **ASK** What happened to the vocal texture when you sang in harmony? (It became thicker because another part was added.)

continued on page 38

▶ **The Musical** *Oklahoma!* is one of the longest running musicals in the history of the theater. The cast toured for three years in London and seven years in the United States. *Oklahoma!* changed the musical theater. Why? All musicals before *Oklahoma!* had songwriters, composers, and lyricists. After *Oklahoma!* the composers and lyricists had to become dramatists as well. Every song had to help develop the character and move the plot along. This was very difficult for most writers because not many people have all three abilities. *Oklahoma!* was the first collaboration of Rodgers and Hammerstein.

▶ **Singing/Phrasing** Breath support and control are needed to sing long phrases. Have students

• Check for appropriate singing posture.

• Exhale before inhaling so that the breath can be deep.

• Exhale on an *sss* sound for eight beats to sustain breath. (Repeat exercise until students can exhale for 16 to 20 beats.)

• Sing "Oklahoma" on *loo* with one breath per four-measure phrase.

• Sing the words with appropriate phrasing.

Lesson 12 Continued

Some students might enjoy the challenge of learning another harmony part. Invite them to sing or play the following part.

We be - long, We be - long to the land,

And the land we be - long — to is grand!

Listening

Inform students that the composer and the lyricist of "Oklahoma" collaborated to create several hit musicals, including *The Sound of Music*.

Invite students to listen to "Do-Re-Mi" from *The Sound of Music* **CD 2-31**. After several listenings, ask students to raise their hands when they hear both melodies in the song performed together.

Have students identify an ostinato-like pattern that is sung by the children while Maria sings the melody.

Singing

Have students

- Sing the melody part along with the recording of "Do-Re-Mi."
- Sing the harmony part along with the recording of "Do-Re-Mi."

Divide the class into two groups and have students sing the melody and harmony parts of "Do-Re-Mi" with the recording.

Invite students to

- Listen to the recorded interview **CD 2-32** with Rebecca Luker.
- Read the Music Makers feature on Richard Rodgers and Oscar Hammerstein, and listen to the recorded interview **CD 2-33** with Rodgers to learn how they created *Oklahoma!*
- Describe various music vocations.

Your Turn to Harmonize

The harmony part below was written to go with the section of "Oklahoma" shown in the color box. Learn to **sing** or **play** the part. Then perform it with the recording.

Ok - la - hom - a, Ok - la - hom - a,

Ok - la - hom - a, Ok - la - hom - a's grand!

Do-Re-Mi Equals Har-mo-ny

Listen to this performance of a song from another Rodgers and Hammerstein musical. Here, harmony is created by combining two different melodies.

 **CD 2-31**
Do-Re-Mi

from *The Sound of Music*
by Oscar Hammerstein II and Richard Rodgers
as performed by Rebecca Luker

The Sound of Music was the final musical written by this legendary team. It opened on Broadway in 1959.

 CD 2-32
Interview with Rebecca Luker

Rebecca Luker played the part of Maria von Trapp in the 1998 Broadway revival of *The Sound of Music*.

Rebecca Luker as Maria von Trapp ▶

 Visit **Take It to the Net** at *www.sfsuccessnet.com* to learn more about Rodgers and Hammerstein.

Footnotes

CULTURAL CONNECTION

▶ **A History of Pitch Syllables** Syllables assigned to each note of the scale have been used to help people read music since Guido d'Arezzo originated them in Europe during the eleventh century. D'Arezzo, a choir director, used the text of a well-known hymn to develop the syllables. Like "Do-Re-Mi," each phrase of the hymn began on the next higher pitch. The first note of the hymn was "C," and the first word was *Ut*. The second phrase of the hymn began on "D" and was sung on the syllable *re*. At first there were only six syllables: *ut, re, mi, fa, sol, la*. Later, *ti* was added, and *do* replaced *ut*. In a letter to a friend, d'Arezzo reported that the new syllables helped his choir boys learn in a few days what it previously required them many weeks to learn. Musicians still use d'Arezzo's syllables to help them learn music they've never heard before.

MEETING INDIVIDUAL NEEDS

▶ **Mnemonic Devices** In the song "Do-Re-Mi," Maria made use of a mnemonic device to help the von Trapp children learn the syllables of the scale. Mnemonic devices are a useful way to remember facts. Some people use a mnemonic device to remember the spaces of the treble staff: FACE. They use a different mnemonic device to remember the lines of the staff: Every Good Boy Does Fine. Tying a string on your finger to remember to take something home with you is a very old mnemonic device. Students might find it interesting to share mnemonic devices they use to remember something.

Richard Rodgers and Oscar Hammerstein II

The musicals by **Richard Rodgers** (1902–1979) and **Oscar Hammerstein II** (1895–1960) won 26 Tony awards, four Academy awards, two Pulitzer Prizes, and two Grammy awards. Rodgers composed the music and Hammerstein wrote the lyrics. Following the success of *Oklahoma!*, the team produced a string of Broadway hits, including *Carousel*, *South Pacific*, *The King and I,* and *The Sound of Music.*

CD 2–33

Interview with Richard Rodgers

In this historic interview, Rodgers discusses how he and Hammerstein created their first Broadway musical together—the groundbreaking production, *Oklahoma!*

▼ Oscar Hammerstein II

Richard Rodgers ▶

Unit 1 39

3 CLOSE

Element: TEXTURE/HARMONY — ASSESSMENT

7b **Performance/Observation** Have students sing "Oklahoma" with the harmony part on p. 38. Then use the following rating system to assess how well students can sing using harmony.

5 = Can sing any part of the melody or harmony accurately and independently

4 = Can sing any of the parts, but sometimes gets mixed up

3 = Can sing the melody and harmony with fair accuracy

2 = Can sing only the melody with fair accuracy

1 = Has difficulty singing the melody accurately

CHARACTER EDUCATION

▶ **Collaboration** To promote students' understanding of the skills necessary to collaborate with others, discuss singing and professional partnerships. Singing in a group requires vocal control and careful listening to achieve appropriate balance and blend. Individuals often must adjust their performance to benefit the group. Ask students what other situations require that individuals sacrifice control to help the group. (Accept various answers, including team sports and medical teams.)

Discuss the partnership between Richard Rodgers and Oscar Hammerstein. Ask students what personal traits are necessary if they are going to work effectively with other people. Invite students to write about whom they might like to collaborate with and the reasons why. Encourage them to consider the sacrifices they would have to make or the behaviors they would have to exhibit to work effectively with this person.

TECHNOLOGY/MEDIA LINK

Web Site To learn more about the musicals of Rodgers and Hammerstein, visit *www.sfsuccessnet.com.*

2b **Electronic Keyboard** Encourage students to play chord roots to generate and arrange auto-accompaniments for "Oklahoma."

• Have a student select an appropriate eight-beat pattern for "Oklahoma" from the auto-accompaniment bank of a MIDI keyboard.

• Let each student perform the accompaniment by playing the chord roots listed in the student text while the class sings.

• After several performers have played, have students choose the best arrangement/performance for a "concert."

UNIT 1 — Review and Assessment

WHAT DO YOU KNOW?

MATERIALS
- "This Train" — **CD 2-10**
- **Resource Book** p. B-3

Ask students to match the dynamic symbol with its definition.

Have students review "This Train," p. 27, and then identify the indicated notes in the music.

For a more formal assessment, you may wish to duplicate the Unit 1 assessment worksheet and have students work independently or in small groups to complete it. The worksheet is found on Resource Book p. B-3.

WHAT DO YOU HEAR?

MATERIALS
- *What Do You Hear? 1A* — **CD 2-34**
- **Resource Book** p. B-3

Review *timbre*. Play the pieces in *What Do You Hear? 1A* one or more times before students choose their answers. The worksheet is found on Resource Book p. B-3.

MATERIALS
- *What Do You Hear? 1B* — **CD 2-37**
- **Resource Book** p. B-3

Review the different forms discussed in this unit. Play "*Ise oluwa*" and ask students to identify the form of the song.

What Do You Know?

1. Name each dynamic symbol and point to the correct definition.
   - **a.** *p* — forte (loud)
   - **b.** *mf* — piano (soft)
   - **c.** *ff* — pianissimo (very soft)
   - **d.** *mp* — fortissimo (very loud)
   - **e.** *pp* — mezzo forte (medium loud)
   - **f.** *f* — mezzo piano (medium soft)

2. Look at the melody for "This Train," page 27. Where is *do*? Identify, by pointing in the music,
   - **a.** All the notes that are called *so*.
   - **b.** All the notes that are called *re*.
   - **c.** All the notes that are called *la*.
   - **d.** All the notes that are called *do*.

What Do You Hear? 1A

 CD 2–34

Listen to the following vocal timbres. Identify the voice(s) you hear.

1. male solo | female solo
2. children's chorus | mixed adult chorus
3. solo and chorus | chorus | solo

What Do You Hear? 1B

 CD 2–37

Listen to "*Ise Oluwa*." What is the musical form?

a. call and response **b.** verse/refrain

40

Footnotes

ANSWER KEY

▶ **What Do You Know?**

1. **a.** *piano* (soft)
   b. *mezzo forte* (medium loud)
   c. *fortissimo* (very loud)
   d. *mezzo piano* (medium soft)
   e. *pianissimo* (very soft)
   f. *forte* (loud)

2. **a.** *(so)* B♭—treble clef—first ledger space below middle C and on the third line (twelve)
   b. *(re)* (F)—treble clef—first space (six)
   c. *(la)* (C)—treble clef—first ledger line below staff and on the third space (five)
   d. *(do)*—E♭—treble clef—first line and fourth space (sixteen)

▶ **What Do You Hear? 1A**

1. male solo
2. children's chorus
3. solo and chorus

▶ **What Do You Hear? 1B**

b. call and response

Perform, Create

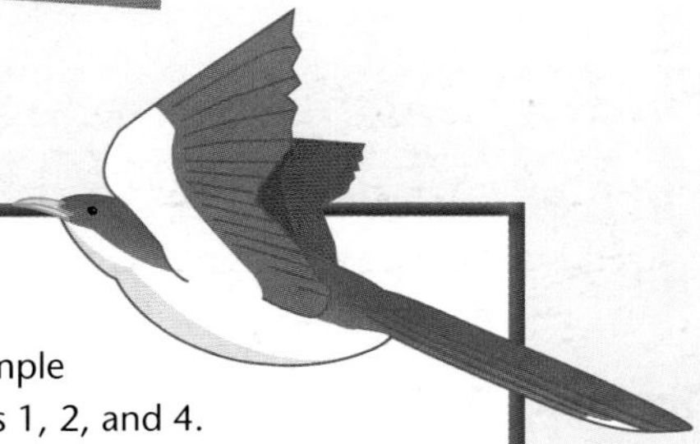

What You Can Do

Create a Response

Sing "This Train," on page 27. Then create a simple response part to sing or play at the ends of lines 1, 2, and 4.

Play a Rhythm

Look at the rhythm patterns below.

A 
B

- As the teacher plays a steady beat on a hand drum, play rhythm A on percussion instruments with the recording of "Funwa alafia."
- As the teacher plays a steady beat on a hand drum, play rhythm B on percussion instruments with the recording of "Kokoleoko."

Unit 1 41

MATERIALS
- "This Train"   CD 2-10
- "Funwa alafia"   CD 2-19
- "Kokoleoko"   CD 2-23
- **Resource Book** p. B-4
- classroom percussion instruments

Create a Melody

Review call-and-response form. Then play "This Train."

Ask students to identify the call. Invite each student to compose a response. (Classroom percussion instruments may be used.)

Notate a few of the responses on the board and ask students to play them.

Play a Rhythm

Play the recording of "Funwa alafia." Then play a steady beat on a hand drum while students—one by one—play rhythm A.

Do the same with "Kokoleoko." Ask students to play rhythm B.

Play a Game

Divide the class into two teams. Each time a team gives a response, if accepted, the team gets a point. The team with the most accepted answers wins. Students may give answers individually or confer with a team captain, who will answer for the team.

In the "Play a Rhythm" section, each correct rendition of the rhythm gets a point.

TECHNOLOGY/MEDIA LINK

Rubrics Visit *www.sfsuccessnet.com* for rubrics to assess students' achievement in music skills.

Lesson	Elements	Skills
 **LESSON 1** **CORE** **Expressing Friendship** pp. 46–49 	**Element: Expression** **Concept:** *Crescendo, Decrescendo* **Focus:** Dynamics **Secondary Element** Rhythm: ostinatos **National Standards** 1c 1d 2b 6b 7b 8b	**Skill: Singing** **Objective:** Sing a song, using expressive qualities **Secondary Skills** • **Moving** Move to vocal backup and dance steps • **Singing** Sing and add speech ostinatos to a song • **Listening** Listen to compare original artist and classroom versions of the song **SKILLS REINFORCEMENT** • **Listening** Listen and note contrast in dynamics • **Keyboard** Play a backup rhythm pattern
LESSON 2 **Move to the Beats** pp. 50–51 	**Element: Rhythm** **Concept:** Meter **Focus:** Meter in 2 **Secondary Element** Harmony: 2-part singing **National Standards** 1c 1d 2c 6c	**Skill: Moving** **Objective:** Create movements that demonstrate strong and weak beats **Secondary Skills** • **Singing** Sing the melody following the song notation • **Singing** Sing *do* on D, then *mi* on F♯ **SKILLS REINFORCEMENT** • **Guitar** Use guitar chords to accompany the song • **Keyboard** Play a left-handed accompaniment
LESSON 3 **Gold Rush Rhythms!** pp. 52–53  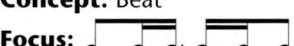 Reading Sequence 5, p. 492	**Element: Rhythm** **Concept:** Beat **Focus:** ♩ ♫ ♫, ♫ ♫ ♫ **Secondary Element** Form: verse/refrain **National Standards** 1c 2a 3b 5a 6c 8b	**Skill: Reading** **Objective:** Play rhythms, read from notation that includes ♫ ♫ ♫ and ♫ ♫ ♫ **Secondary Skills** • **Creating** Create simple accompaniments to the song **SKILLS REINFORCEMENT** • **Moving** Use body percussion to show note patterns • **Recorder** Play an accompaniment to the song

Connections

Music and Other Literature

Connection: Style

Activity: Discover that songs from the 1950s and 1960s still have appeal today

ACROSS THE CURRICULUM **Language Arts** Discuss how people can offer support to each other

CULTURAL CONNECTION **Signs of Friendship** Learn words for friend and friendship in different languages

CHARACTER EDUCATION **Friendship** List the characteristics of true friends

MOVEMENT **Patterned Dance** Add movement patterns to the song

SPOTLIGHT ON **The Performer** Facts about Ben E. King

BUILDING SKILLS THROUGH MUSIC **Physical Education** Perform a movement routine with the song

Song "Stand By Me"

Listening Selection *Stand By Me*
M·U·S·I·C M·A·K·E·R·S
Jerry Leiber and Mike Stoller

More Music Choices
"I Believe I Can Fly," p. 170
"Somewhere Out There," p. 368
"Lift Ev'ry Voice and Sing," p. 482

ASSESSMENT

Performance/Observation
Use a rubric to assess how well students can sing with the appropriate dynamics

TECHNOLOGY/MEDIA LINK
CD-ROM Explore accompaniment styles

Connection: Culture

Activity: Read about the lives of young people in nineteenth-century Mexico

ACROSS THE CURRICULUM **Language Arts** Read about young people growing up in nineteenth-century Mexican territories

MOVEMENT **Patterned Dance** Select two rhythm patterns and create foot patterns

BUILDING SKILLS THROUGH MUSIC **Writing** Write about the contributions of the featured instruments

Songs
"Adelita" (Spanish)
"Adelita" (English)

More Music Choices
"San Antonio Rose," p. 134
"*El carite*" ("The Kingfish"), p. 305

ASSESSMENT

Performance/Observation
Students will create and perform movements to show strong and weak beats

TECHNOLOGY/MEDIA LINK
MIDI/Sequencing Software Experiment with base and harmonic rhythm of a MIDI file

---

Connection: Social Studies

Activity: Explore the history of the California Gold Rush

ACROSS THE CURRICULUM **Social Studies** Read books about the California Gold Rush

MEETING INDIVIDUAL NEEDS **Including Everyone** Tips to help all students perform sixteenth-note rhythms

BUILDING SKILLS THROUGH MUSIC **Reading** Find phrases that express important ideas from the song

Song "California"

More Music Choices
"*Zum gali gali*," p. 401

ASSESSMENT

Performance/Observation
Observe students' abilities to read, play, and create rhythm patterns

Show What You Know!
Mid-unit assessment

TECHNOLOGY/MEDIA LINK
Web Site More information on the California Gold Rush

Lesson	Elements	Skills

LESSON 4

CORE

Work to the Rhythm

pp. 54–55

⟶ Reading Sequence 6, p. 492

Element: Rhythm
Concept: Pattern

Focus: ♩♫ and
♫♩

Secondary Element
Texture: ostinatos

National Standards
1b 2b 5a 5d 6a 8b

Skill: Playing
Objective: Play sixteenth-note patterns

Secondary Skills
• **Reading** Read rhythm patterns and identify them in notation
• **Creating** Create other rhythm patterns to the song
• **Playing** Perform instrumental parts with the song
• **Listening** Listen and identify the ♫♩ pattern

SKILLS REINFORCEMENT
• **Recorder** Perform a composition using eighth and sixteenth notes; play a countermelody

---

LESSON 5

CORE

New Land, New Verse

pp. 56–57

Element: Form
Concept: Same and different phrases
Focus: Verse/Refrain (AB Form)

Secondary Element
Rhythm: 6/8 meter

National Standards
1c 4c 6b 7a 8b

Skill: Singing
Objective: Sing a song in verse and refrain form

Secondary Skills
• **Listening** Listen to the recording and follow the lyrics
• **Singing** Sing the song with the recording and identify the form
• **Moving** Move using contrasting movements for the different sections

---

LESSON 6

A Song of Sequences

pp. 58–59

Element: Melody
Concept: Pattern
Focus: Melodic sequence

Secondary Element
Rhythm: 6/8 meter

National Standards
1c 2c 4c 6a 6b 8b

Skill: Singing
Objective: Sing a song that uses melodic sequence

Secondary Skills
• **Listening** Listen to identify similar phrases in the song
• **Playing** Play melody for phrases 1 and 2 on a keyboard or bells
• **Singing** Sing the song in Spanish
• **Listening** Listen to an excerpt using a short musical idea to build sequences

SKILLS REINFORCEMENT
• **Recorder** Play a countermelody on a recorder

Connection: Social Studies

Activity: Investigate the historical context of a railroad song

MOVEMENT **Patterned Dance** Add a patterned dance to "Drill, Ye Tarriers"

ACROSS THE CURRICULUM **Social Studies** Read about the building of the Transcontinental Railroad

CHARACTER EDUCATION **Collaborating** Discuss collaboration skills

BUILDING SKILLS THROUGH MUSIC **Math** Identify fractions for notation

Song "Drill, Ye Tarriers"

Listening Selection *Symphony No. 9, Movement 1* (excerpt)

More Music Choices
"Camptown Races," p. 270

ASSESSMENT

Performance/Observation
Have students play rhythm patterns on percussion instruments while singing the song

TECHNOLOGY/MEDIA LINK

Notation Software
Notate and print rhythm patterns from the lesson

Connection: Social Studies

Activity: Discuss immigration to the United States

ACROSS THE CURRICULUM **Social Studies/Language Arts** Read a book about the Ellis Island Oral History Project

SPOTLIGHT ON **Ellis Island** Facts on the famous immigration center

CHARACTER EDUCATION **Courage** Discuss situations that demand courage

SCHOOL TO HOME CONNECTION **Immigrants** Interview family and friends who have immigrated

BUILDING SKILLS THROUGH MUSIC **Language** Discuss characters in the song

Song "Away to America"

More Music Choices
"Twelve Gates to the City," p. 280
"Cattle Call," p. 344

ASSESSMENT

Performance/Observation
Perform a verse and refrain song highlighting the different sections

TECHNOLOGY/MEDIA LINK

MIDI/Sequencing Software Create "timbre" arrangements to illustrate different sections of the song

Connection: Culture

Activity: Connect Spanish explorations with Mexico and the southwest United States

TEACHER TO TEACHER **Invention** Explanation of this musical term

ACROSS THE CURRICULUM **Social Studies** Historical information about New Mexico

BUILDING SKILLS THROUGH MUSIC **Language** Discuss exaggeration in song text

Songs
"La ciudad de Juaja"
"The City of Juaja"

Listening Selection *Invention No. 5 in E-flat*

More Music Choices
"Autumn Canon," p. 148

ASSESSMENT

Performance/Observation
Observe students' ability to indicate when a sequence occurs in a song

TECHNOLOGY/MEDIA LINK

Notation Software
Notate song; then cut, paste, and transpose to create new melodies

Lesson	Elements	Skills
LESSON 7 **Step Up to *fa*** pp. 60–61  Reading Sequence 7, p. 493	**Element: Melody** **Concept:** Pitch and Direction **Focus:** *do, re, mi, fa, so, la* **Secondary Element** Form: verse/refrain **National Standards** 1a 1c 2c 4c 5a 6c	**Skill: Reading** **Objective:** Sing and read from notation that includes *do, re, mi, fa, so,* and *la* **Secondary Skills** • **Singing** Sing the pentatonic scale using hand signs and pitch syllables	**SKILLS REINFORCEMENT** • **Recorder** Play a countermelody along with the song • **Notating** Write motives using rhythm notation and pitch notation
LESSON 8 **CORE** **A Pitch for Peace** pp. 62–63  Reading Sequence 8, p. 493	**Element: Melody** **Concept:** Pitch and Direction **Focus:** *do, re, mi, fa, so, la* **Secondary Element** Texture: canons **National Standards** 1c 5a 5b 5c 6a 8b	**Skill: Reading** **Objective:** Sing and read notation, includes *do, re, mi, fa, so,* and *la* **Secondary Skills** • **Singing** Sing along with the recording • **Reading** Read and identify *do* by analyzing the key signature • **Listening** Listen to a canon and follow each entrance of the melody	
LESSON 9 **Percussion Near and Far** pp. 64–67 	**Element: Timbre** **Concept:** Instrumental sounds **Focus:** Percussion instruments **Secondary Element** Form: theme/variation **National Standards** 1c 2a 4c 5d 6a 6b 8b	**Skill: Listening** **Objective:** Listen to a composition for percussion ensemble **Secondary Skills** • **Listening** Listen and follow the listening map to identify the theme and variations • **Composing** Create, notate and perform a rhythm composition • **Singing** Sing an African song and focus on the pronunciation of the words • **Listening** Listen to a Montage of African Instruments • **Singing** Sing the different phrases of the song • **Listening** Listen and identify instruments heard in a section	**SKILLS REINFORCEMENT** • **Creating** Create an improvisation for percussion instruments • **Composing** Use percussion instruments to create rhythm variations

Connections

Music and Other Literature

Connection: Culture

Activity: Discuss characteristics of a Spanish lullaby

- **ACROSS THE CURRICULUM** **Social Studies** Research and locate the Basque region of Spain
- **TEACHER TO TEACHER** **Notation** Suggest steps to help students work individually to write notation
- **BUILDING SKILLS THROUGH MUSIC** **Language** Compare definitions and characteristics of lullabies

Songs
"A la puerta del cielo"
"At the Gate of Heaven"

More Music Choices
"Erie Canal," p.262
"Viva Jujuy," p. 228

ASSESSMENT

Performance/Observation
Perform the song using hand signs, pitch syllables and text

TECHNOLOGY/MEDIA LINK

Notation Software
Create an arrangement of the song

Connection: Related Arts

Activity: Explore how musicians and instruments can be depicted in art from a historical time period

- **SPOTLIGHT ON** **Capella Cantabile** Facts about this famous youth choral group
- **CULTURAL CONNECTION** **Vocal Forms** Information about the motet and madrigal
- **ACROSS THE CURRICULUM** **Language Arts** Discuss the meaning of Da pacem, Domine and what world peace would mean
- **BUILDING SKILLS THROUGH MUSIC** **Art** Discuss details of a painting

Songs
"Da pacem, Domine"
"Grant Us Peace"

Listening Selection Da pacem, Domine
Arts Connection Painting of Musicians

More Music Choices
"Colorado Trail," p. 276
"It Don't Mean a Thing," p. 336

ASSESSMENT

Performance/Observation
Read and perform the song reading the melody using pitch syllables and letter names

Show What You Know!
Mid-unit assessment

TECHNOLOGY/MEDIA LINK

Sequencing Software
Notate and transpose the melody; experiment with new timbres

Connection: Culture

Activity: Discuss the role of music in African culture

- **ACROSS THE CURRICULUM**
  Social Studies Background information on countries in West Africa
  Language Arts Read about legends of the world, and an African folktale
- **AUDIENCE ETIQUETTE** **Applause** Discuss when applause is appropriate during various kinds of performances
- **SPOTLIGHT ON** **The Composer** Facts about the composer/percussionist
- **CULTURAL CONNECTION** **Music in African Culture** The role of drumming in African culture
- **BUILDING SKILLS THROUGH MUSIC** **Language** Classify percussion instruments heard on a recording

Song "Ye jaliya da"

Listening Selections
Theme and Variations for Percussion
Montage of African Instruments
Oya (Primitive Fire)
Listening Map Theme and Variations for Percussion

M·U·S·I·C M·A·K·E·R·S
Babatunde Olatunji

More Music Choices
Yaudachi, p. 156
Conga Kings Grand Finale, p. 156
O'Sullivan's March, p. 157

ASSESSMENT

Observation/Music Journal Writing Have students follow a theme and variations using a listening map and write descriptions of each timbre in their journal

TECHNOLOGY/MEDIA LINK

Sequencing Software
Create an African-style sequence
Transparency Follow a listening map to analyze theme and variations

Lesson	Elements	Skills

LESSON 10 **CORE**
Singing Partners
pp. 68–71

Element: Texture/Harmony
Concept: Texture
Focus: Partner songs

Secondary Element
Rhythm: $\frac{3}{4}$ meter

National Standards
1b 1d 2d 4b 6c 7b 8b

Skill: Singing
Objective: Sing in harmony by performing two partner songs together

Secondary Skills
- **Playing** Play an accompaniment on keyboard or mallet instrument
- **Creating** Create an arrangement of the two songs

SKILLS REINFORCEMENT
- **Keyboard/Mallets** Accompany songs on keyboards or mallet instruments
- **Analyzing** Compare melodic phrases

LESSON 11 **CORE**
Partner Songs
pp. 72–75

Element: Texture/Harmony
Concept: Texture
Focus: Partner songs

Secondary Element
Texture: polyphony

National Standards
1c 2b 4a 4c 5a 6b 8b 9b

Skill: Singing
Objective: Sing in harmony by performing two partner songs together

Secondary Skills
- **Listening** Listen to the recording and follow the notation
- **Playing** Play the melodies notated on p. 75
- **Creating** Create and notate two melodies that can be played together

SKILLS REINFORCEMENT
- **Creating** Compose partner songs

LESSON 12 **CORE**
Harmony in Beauty and Song
pp. 76–79

Element: Texture/Harmony
Concept: Texture
Focus: Partner songs

Secondary Element
Timbre: instrumental sounds

National Standards
1b 1d 6b 6c 8b 9b

Skill: Singing
Objective: Sing in harmony by performing two partner songs together

Secondary Skills
- **Analyzing** Analyze by singing the songs separately, then comparing chord structure
- **Listening** Listen for a countermelody in a Sousa march

SKILLS REINFORCEMENT
- **Listening** Listen to another example of combining two different melodies

Connections

Music and Other Literature

Connection: Social Studies

Activity: Compare and contrast country and city life-styles

CULTURAL CONNECTION **Trick Roping** Facts about lassos and rope tricks

SPOTLIGHT ON **American Cowboys** Facts about cowboys, their origins, and their work.

TEACHER TO TEACHER **Slow vs. Fast Meter** Invite students to move to the music at different speeds.

ACROSS THE CURRICULUM **Language Arts** Read and dramatize poetry about cowboys

MEETING INDIVIDUAL NEEDS **English Language Learners** Use visuals to illustrate song lyrics

BUILDING SKILLS THROUGH MUSIC **Language** Discuss the thoughts and feelings expressed in the lyrics

Songs
"Home on the Range"
"Live in the City"
"Home on the Range/Live in the City"

Arts Connection
Singing Round Campfire

More Music Choices
"America, the Beautiful/Let Freedom Ring," pp. 76-77
"Play a Simple Melody," p. 72

ASSESSMENT

Performance/Self-Assessment Observe students' ability to perform the partner songs and have students assess and improve their own performance

TECHNOLOGY/MEDIA LINK
Sequencing Software
Sequence bass and harmonic rhythm parts in $\frac{3}{4}$ meter

---

Connection: Style

Activity: Explore the lives and music of popular composers of the American musical theatre

CULTURAL CONNECTION
"Humoresque" and *"Old Folks at Home"* Facts about the songs
Tin Pan Alley How the name became associated with popular music

ACROSS THE CURRICULUM **Language Arts** Create a bulletin board of famous popular composers

SPOTLIGHT ON
The Piano Facts about the piano and how it works
The Composer Biographical information about Irving Berlin

TEACHER TO TEACHER **Presenting Partner Songs** Suggestions for performing partner songs in a concert setting.

BUILDING SKILLS THROUGH MUSIC **Language** Discuss synonyms for the word "simple"

Song "Play a Simple Melody"

M·U·S·I·C M·A·K·E·R·S
Irving Berlin

More Music Choices
"Home on the Range," p. 69
"Live in the City," p. 71

ASSESSMENT

Performance/Observation Observe students' ability to perform the songs as partner songs

TECHNOLOGY/MEDIA LINK
CD-ROM Use *Band-in-a-Box* to create an accompaniment in ragtime style
Notation Software Notate and playback arrangements

Connection: Social Studies

Activity: Learn the origin of "America, the Beautiful"

ACROSS THE CURRICULUM
Language Arts Read about "America, the Beautiful" and Katharine Lee Bates
Language Arts Have students write about the beauty of America and illustrate their work

SPOTLIGHT ON
Katharine Lee Bates Information about the lyricist for "America, the Beautiful"
The United States Marine Corps Band Information about America's oldest professional musical organization

MEETING INDIVIDUAL NEEDS
Singing in Harmony Help students of different singing abilities to perform partner songs
Including Everyone Discuss freedom and equal access in America

BUILDING SKILLS THROUGH MUSIC **Social Studies** Discuss patriotic symbols used in America

Songs
"America, the Beautiful"
"Let Freedom Ring"
"America, the Beautiful/Let Freedom Ring"

Listening Selection *The Thunderer*
M·U·S·I·C M·A·K·E·R·S
John Philip Sousa

More Music Choices
"Home on the Range/Live in the City," pp. 69, 71
"Play a Simple Melody," p. 72

ASSESSMENT

Performance/Observation Observe students' ability to perform partner songs and describe how texture changes as parts are added

TECHNOLOGY/MEDIA LINK
Web Site More information about John Philip Sousa

INTRODUCING THE UNIT

Unit 2 presents the second step in a sequenced approach to understanding music elements. Music skills—reading, performing, creating, listening, moving—are the means by which students gain an understanding of these concepts. Presented on p. 43 is a brief overview of the skills that are assessed in this unit. (See below and pp. 44–45 for unit highlights of related curricular experiences.)

For a more detailed unit overview, see Unit at a Glance, pp. 41a–41h.

UNIT PROJECT

Ask students to imagine that they are explorers from another planet planning a trip to the United States. They have the the capability of traveling back and forth in time as well as space. They want to use this capability to explore music.

Have students look through Unit 2 and chart the times, places, and styles of music represented. (Suggestion: Lessons 2, 8, and 9 can be omitted since they are outside the primary thematic idea here.)

Divide the class into as many groups as there are lessons. Assign each group one of the song lessons. Have the group prepare a few sentences of invitation for the explorers to come and visit their song, time, and place. Allow time for groups to share these.

This activity can be expanded into a presentation for other students. For example, the refrain of "Away to America" can be used as the explorer's theme (replace the word "sail" with "fly"). The songs can be arranged and performed in any order.

Groove to the Bebop Style

In the early 1940s a new jazz style was created, called "bebop." Thelonious Monk, a pianist, and Charlie Parker, a saxophonist, became the center of the bebop style. Bebop is played by small groups, has fast tempos, intense melodies, and lots of improvisation.

Be Bop
by Toyomi Igus

I see the rhythm of **be** bop, the music of those jazz hipsters

who refuse to play the dance rhythms of swing and experiment with sound at Mintons' Playhouse in Harlem and the clubs of 52nd Street.

There, we dig the **flights of fancy** from Charlie Parker's sax, the **inventive harmonies** of Thelonious Monk's piano, and the **Latin rhythms** of Chano Pozo's congas.

There, in our zoot suits, porkpie hats and shades we are the living end.

I see the rhythm in the new sound, the new style, the new attitude— be bop.

ACROSS THE CURRICULUM

Unit Highlights The following interdisciplinary activities in this unit are related to the music elements presented in the lessons. See Unit at a Glance pp. 41a–41h, for topical descriptions presented according to lesson sequence.

▶ **LANGUAGE ARTS**

- Discuss the expressive nature of the lyrics of a song (p. 46)
- Read about young people growing up in nineteenth-century Mexican territories (p. 50)
- Read accounts of immigrants who came to the United States (p. 56)
- Read and write about the concept of world peace (p. 63)
- Read African folktales (p. 67)
- Read poetry of the Old West (p. 70)

- Create a bulletin board of popular composers of the American theatre (p. 72)
- Explore the origin of a well-known patriotic song (p. 76)
- Write paragraphs that express the beauty of the United States (p. 77)

▶ **SOCIAL STUDIES**

- Read about the lives of people seeking fortune during the California Gold Rush (p. 52)
- Research the construction of railroads in the United States (p. 54)
- Read about Spanish exploration and the history of New Mexico (p. 58)
- Research and locate the Basque region of Spain (p. 60)
- Learn about countries of West Africa (p. 64)

Unit 2 **43**

MUSIC SKILLS
ASSESSED IN THIS UNIT

Reading Music: Rhythm

- Read rhythm patterns using ♩ ♫ and ♫ ♩ (p. 53)
- Read rhythm patterns in meter in 2 (p. 55)

Reading Music: Pitch

- Read pitch syllables and note names (p. 61)
- Read a melody using pitch syllables and hand signs (p. 63)

Performing Music: Singing

- Sing "Stand By Me" using appropriate dynamics (p. 49)
- Perform a song in verse/refrain form (p. 57)
- Sing "*La ciudad de Juaja*" while indicating melodic sequence (p. 59)
- Sing a song with Spanish words (p. 61)
- Sing partner songs in groups (pp. 75, 79)

Moving to Music

- Create and perform movements for "*Adelita*" that show strong and weak beats (p. 51)
- Perform a movement routine to accompany a song (p. 48)

Performing Music: Playing

- Accompany "California" using original rhythm patterns (p. 53)
- Perform rhythm ostinatos (p. 55)

Creating Music

- Create rhythm patterns using ♩ ♫ and ♫ ♩ (p. 53)
- Create a group arrangement of two partner songs (p. 70)

Listening to Music

- Listen for different types of percussion timbres (p. 67)
- Listen for melodic sequences (p. 59)

CULTURAL CONNECTION

Unit Highlights The musical literature in this unit provides many opportunities for students to explore a variety of world cultures. See Unit at a Glance, pp. 41a–41h, for topical descriptions presented according to lesson sequence.

▶ AFRICAN

- Create student art projects based on African folk art (p. 66)

▶ AMERICAN REGIONAL

- Explore the art of trick roping (p. 68)
- Learn about Tin Pan Alley (p. 75)

OPENING ACTIVITIES

MATERIALS
• "Choo Choo Ch'Boogie"   **CD 2-38** **Recording Routine:** Intro (8 m.); v. 1; refrain; interlude (1 m.); v. 2; refrain; instrumental; v. 3; refrain; coda • "Be Bop" (poem) • keyboard, bass xylophone

Listening

Play the recording of "Choo Choo Ch'Boogie" **CD 2-38**. Ask students to snap their fingers on beats 2 and 4 to get the feel of the rhythm.

Singing

Invite students to sing along on the refrain of the song. Have them clap on beat 3 in measures 1, 3, 5 of the refrain.

Moving

In small groups or individually, have students develop arm movements for the refrain representing the wheels of a steam locomotive. Have them change direction for each phrase.

Playing

Students can accompany the refrain of "Choo Choo Ch'Boogie" by playing quarter notes on the chord roots (C and G) on either keyboard or bass xylophone.

Bebop Boogie
"Choo Choo Ch' Boogie" was written during the 1940s. Sing this song in the bebop jazz style, and move to the beat.

ASSESSMENT

Unit Highlights This unit includes a variety of strategies and methods, described below, to track students' progress and assess their understanding of lesson objectives. Reproducible masters for Show What You Know! and Review, Assess, Perform, Create can be found in the Resource Book.

▶ **FORMAL ASSESSMENTS**

The following assessments, using written language, cognitive, and performance skills, help teachers and students conceptualize the learning that is taking place.

- **Show What You Know!** Element-specific assessments, on the student page for Rhythm (p. 53) and Melody (p. 63)
- **Review, Assess, Perform, Create** This end-of-unit activity (pp. 80–81) can be used for review and to assess students' learning of the core lessons in this unit.

▶ **INFORMAL ASSESSMENTS**

At the close of each Teacher's Edition lesson in this unit, one of the following types of assessments is used to evaluate the learning of the key element focus or skill objective.

- Performance/Observation (pp. 49, 51, 53, 55, 57, 59, 61, 63, 75, 79)
- Observation/Music Journal Writing (p. 67)
- Performance/Self-Assessment (p. 71)

▶ **RUBRICS**

Visit *www.sfsuccessnet.com* for rubrics to assess students' achievement in music skills.

Creating

Use the poem "Be Bop" on p. 42 to develop a speech introduction for the song. Have individual students read lines. Have groups read the words printed in purple and red. If possible, have selected students add instrumental effects to underscore "flights of fancy" (saxophone), "inventive harmonies" (keyboard), and "Latin rhythms" (conga).

Song lyrics (under musical notation):

fel - lows named Mac, __ / Take me right back __ to the track, __
man with a knack, _ / So put it right back __ in the rack,
click - e - ty clack, __ / So take me back __ to the track,

REFRAIN
__ Jack. __ Choo __ choo _____ choo __
__ choo __ ch' boo - gie, __ Woo __ woo _____ woo __
__ woo __ ch' boo - gie, __ Choo __ choo _____ choo __
__ choo __ ch' boo-gie, Take me right back to the track, Jack. __

INNOVATIVE TEACHER SUPPORT FOR THIS UNIT

- **MAKING MUSIC DVD, Grade 5** contains video segments that support lessons, including signing and movement.
- **MAKING MUSIC with Movement and Dance** provides more opportunities for large group activities in music or physical education classes.
- **MAKING MUSIC with Technology** provides lesson plans for many technology applications; includes MIDI files.
- *¡A cantar!* features recorded songs and lessons from around the Spanish-speaking world; includes strategies for bilingual classes and for English-speaking teachers working with Spanish-speaking students.
- **Bridges to Asia** features recorded songs and lessons from Asian and Pacific region cultures.
- *www.sfsuccessnet.com* provides an online lesson planner to conveniently create lesson plans at school or at home. Includes rubrics for assessment, lesson modifications to meet the needs of all students, performance musicals based on program content, and more.

TECHNOLOGY/MEDIA LINK

Unit Highlights The following components are used in this unit to reinforce and expand students' understanding of music elements and related themes. See Unit at a Glance, pp. 41a–41h, for a descriptive listing according to lesson sequence.

▶ **CD-ROM**

- Explore accompaniment styles using *Band-in-a-Box* (p. 49)
- Create a new accompaniment using *Band-in-a-Box* (p. 75)

▶ **MIDI/SEQUENCING SOFTWARE**

- Sequence part for "*Adelita*" and choose appropriate sounds (p. 51)
- Create a "timbre" arrangement for "Away to America" (p. 57)
- Notate a song melody and experiment with timbre (p. 63)
- Record rhythm patterns (p. 67)
- Sequence bass and harmonic rhythm parts for partner songs (p. 71)

▶ **NOTATION SOFTWARE**

- Notate and print rhythm patterns (p. 55)
- Notate the first phrase of "*La ciudad de Juaja*" (p. 59)
- Create an arrangement of "*A la puerta del cielo*" (p. 61)
- Notate song arrangements (p. 75)

▶ **TRANSPARENCY**

- Display a listening map that illustrates a percussive orchestral piece (p. 67)

▶ **WEB SITE**

- Go to *www.sfsuccessnet.com* to find more information about popular music of the California Gold Rush (p. 53) and John Philip Sousa (p. 79).

LESSON AT A GLANCE

Element Focus   **EXPRESSION** Dynamics

Skill Objective   **SINGING** Sing a song, using expressive qualities

Connection Activity   **STYLE** Discover that songs from the 1950s and 1960s still have appeal today

MATERIALS

- "Stand By Me"   **CD 3-1**

  Recording Routine: Intro (10 m.); v. 1; refrain; v. 2; refrain; interlude (8 m.); refrain (2 times); coda
- *Stand By Me*   **CD 3-3**
- **Resource Book** p. G-3
- cymbal and brush

VOCABULARY

crescendo   decrescendo

◆ ◆ ◆ ◆ National Standards ◆ ◆ ◆ ◆

1c Sing music with appropriate expression
1d Sing music written in two parts
2b Perform easy instrumental pieces expressively
6b Listen and analyze uses of dynamics in music from diverse genres
7b Students use specific criteria for evaluating their own performances
8b Identify ways music relates to language arts

MORE MUSIC CHOICES

For more songs using expression and dynamics:

"I Believe I Can Fly," p. 170
"Somewhere Out There," p. 368
"Lift Ev'ry Voice and Sing," p. 482

Expressing Friendship

Music sends messages by expressing feelings and emotions. Some of these expressions are shown through dynamics. **Crescendo** and **decrescendo** are instructions for dynamic change.

Listen to "Stand By Me" and **identify** where you would place dynamic markings.

Crescendo means to gradually get louder.

Decrescendo means to gradually get softer.

CD 3-1

Stand By Me

Words and Music by Ben E. King, Jerry Leiber, and Mike Stoller

VERSE

1. When the night __ has come, _____
2. If the sky _____ that we __ look up - on

And the land __ is dark, And the moon __ is the on - ly
__ should crum-ble and fall, And the moun - tain should crum-ble __

light we'll see. No, I won't __ be a - fraid, No, I _____ won't
to the sea. I won't cry, __ I won't cry, __ No, I _____ won't

be a - fraid, Just as long __ as you stand, __ stand by __ me.
shed a tear,

46

Footnotes

ACROSS THE CURRICULUM

8b ▶ **Language Arts** Discuss the expressive nature of the lyrics of "Stand By Me." The singer expresses the need to feel supported by a friend or other important person. Ask students, "Who 'stands' by you in times of trouble?" Invite students to write about an experience where they reached out to someone for support during a challenging situation. Ask them to describe what this person did to make them feel better.

BUILDING SKILLS THROUGH MUSIC

▶ **Physical Education** Students may enjoy performing a movement routine with "Stand By Me." For more detailed instructions, see Movement p. 48.

SKILLS REINFORCEMENT

6b ▶ **Listening** Have students listen to "Somewhere Out There," p. 368. As they listen, ask students to write down the contrast in dynamics, making note of what makes each change of dynamics occur. (instrumentation)

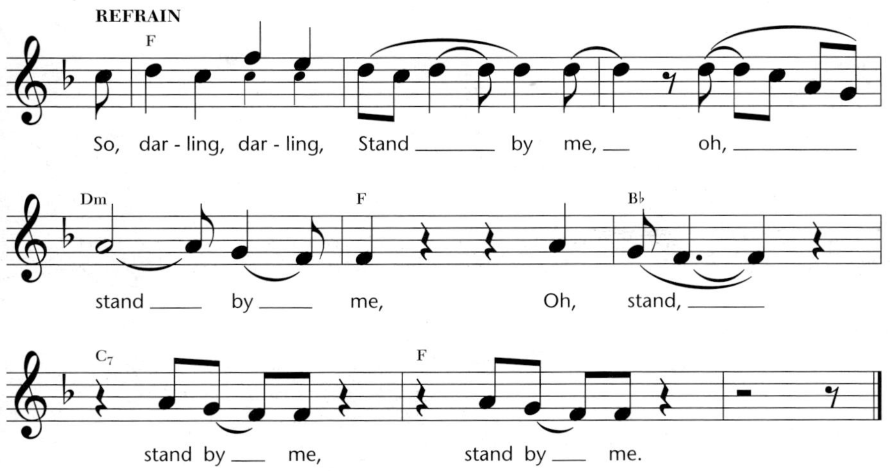

REFRAIN

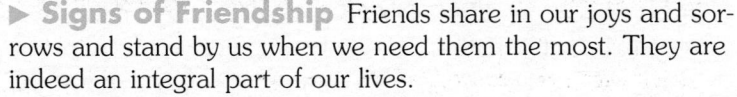

So, dar-ling, dar-ling, Stand _____ by me, _____ oh, _____

stand _____ by _____ me, Oh, stand, _____

stand by _____ me, stand by _____ me.

Many vocal groups in the 1960s were supported by backup singers, who often did dance steps behind the soloist.

Sing "Stand By Me" and add this "backup" vocal part.

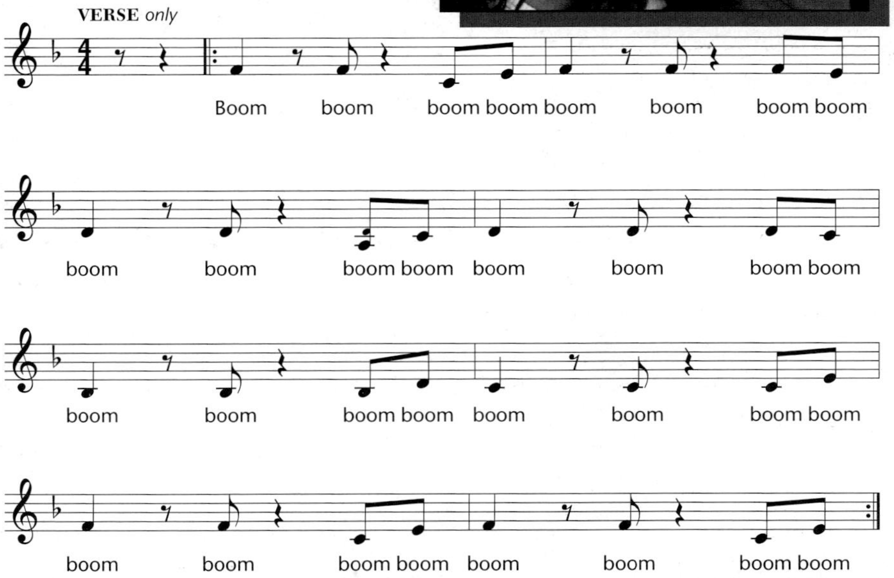

VERSE *only*

Boom boom boom boom boom boom boom boom

boom boom boom boom boom boom boom boom

boom boom boom boom boom boom boom boom

boom boom boom boom boom boom boom boom

1 INTRODUCE

SAY Styles and trends repeat. In fashion, in furniture, and even in music, things from previous generations are being recycled in today's society. A music style that is widely listened to is old-time rock 'n' roll. This music not only appeals to those of other generations, but has also caught on with the youth of today.

2 DEVELOP

Singing

Discuss with students the definition of *dynamics*.

SAY Degrees of loudness and softness in music are called dynamics. *Crescendo* means to gradually get louder. *Decrescendo* means to gradually get softer.

Have students

- Listen to "Stand By Me" **CD 3-1** and identify uses of *crescendo* and *decrescendo*.
- Identify other dynamics used in the recording.
- Sing the song with the recording, using dynamics they have identified.

SAY Many of the groups in the 1960s had a lead singer with vocal backup singers.

Have students practice the vocal backup part on p. 47.

Next ask for a few volunteers to pick out specific dynamics they would use on this part and sing this backup vocal while the rest of the class sings the melody.

Continue to pick different groups as backup singers and have them experiment with different dynamics.

continued on page 48

▶ **Signs of Friendship** Friends share in our joys and sorrows and stand by us when we need them the most. They are indeed an integral part of our lives.

Have students make a chart of the words *friend* and *friendship* in different languages. Here are a few to get started:

Language	Friend	Friendship
English	friend	friendship
German	die Freundin, der Freund	Freundschaft
Italian	amico, amica	amicìzia
Dutch	vriend	vriendschap
Esperanto	amikino	amikeco

▶ **Friendship** The song "Stand By Me" is about true friendship and loyalty. To help students understand the nature of true friendships and the potentially destructive power of false friendships, ask them to list the characteristics of real friends. Encourage students to identify which characteristics they possess and consider which characteristics they would like to develop further. Have students make a list of individuals they consider to be their true friends and indicate why each person's friendship is valued.

Unit 2 *Exploring Music* **47**

Lesson 1 Continued

Moving

SAY A common performance practice of vocal backup singers is to add dance steps behind the soloist.

When students have learned "Stand By Me," encourage them to add the movement routine shown on p. 48. See Movement below for more detailed information.

Singing

After a few groups have tried the movement, choose some voices to add the speech ostinato on p. 49 while others sing the melody. Then add the suspended cymbal part, also on p. 49.

Encourage students to demonstrate appropriate large-ensemble performance techniques when performing in formal or informal concerts. Have students

- Sing the melody with the backup vocal part.
- Add the movement routine to the melody and backup vocal.

- Add the suspended cymbal part and speech ostinato.

Listening

Invite students to

- Read the information on p. 49 about Jerry Leiber and Mike Stoller.
- Listen to the recording of *Stand By Me* **CD 3-3** performed by Ben E. King.
- Compare the original artist version with the recording used for classroom singing **CD 3-1**.

SAY Many different styles of popular music have evolved and developed since the 1950s and 1960s.

ASK Why are songs like "Stand By Me" considered to be "classics"? (accept a variety of answers)

Encourage students to think of other "classic" songs that they know, and share these with the class. Suggest that students make a list of titles and accompanying comments, and add this to their music journals.

Moving as a Backup Group

Now add these movement steps to your performance of "Stand By Me." Begin stepping on the word *night* and step on each beat.

You can repeat this pattern throughout the song.

Create other steps to accompany "Stand By Me.

48

Footnotes

MOVEMENT

▶ **Patterned Dance** Have students add these movement patterns to "Stand By Me." Begin stepping on the word *night* and step on each beat.

1 Step to the right (step-touch-step-touch).

2 Step to the left (step-touch-step-touch).

3 Repeat movements 1 and 2.

4 Walk forward beginning with the right foot (step-step-step-touch).

5 Walk backward beginning with the left foot (step-step-step-touch).

6 Repeat movements 4 and 5.

Repeat this pattern throughout the song.

SKILLS REINFORCEMENT

▶ **Keyboard** Using the F, Dm, B♭, and C₇ chords, have students play the rhythm pattern for the backup vocal part on p. 47.

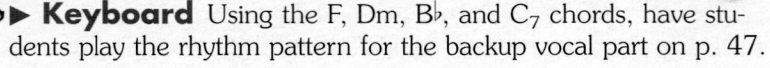

Add an Ostinato

Add a speech ostinato to "Stand By Me" while others sing.

Ostinato 1

Now add a cymbal struck with a cymbal brush. Use this pattern. Be sure to observe the *crescendos*.

Ostinato 2

M·U·S·I·C M·A·K·E·R·S
Jerry Leiber and Mike Stoller

Jerry Leiber (born 1933) and **Mike Stoller** (born 1933) are one of the most famous songwriting duos of all time. They have composed for many performers. They wrote "Yakety Yak" for the Coasters, "On Broadway" for the Drifters, and "Jailhouse Rock" for Elvis Presley. In 1964 they set up their own record label and had remarkable success. Eleven of their first 30 recordings made the Top 40, including such hits as "Chapel of Love" by the Dixie Cups and "Leader of the Pack" by the Shangri-Las. Leiber and Stoller were inducted into the Rock and Roll Hall of Fame in 1987.

Listen to the original version of *Stand By Me*, from 1961.

CD 3–3
Stand By Me

by Ben E. King, Jerry Leiber, and Mike Stoller as performed by Ben E. King

This was one of Ben E. King's hit songs. King's career fell on hard times in the late 1970s but was revived with the release of the motion picture *Stand By Me*, which featured this song.

---

3 CLOSE

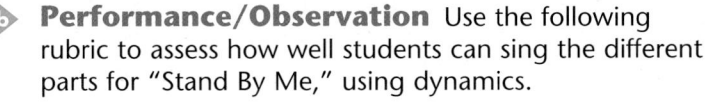

Element: EXPRESSION   ASSESSMENT

7b Performance/Observation Use the following rubric to assess how well students can sing the different parts for "Stand By Me," using dynamics.

4 = Can sing the melody accurately and independently with appropriate dynamics while another group sings vocal backup

3 = Can sing the vocal backup part accurately and independently with appropriate dynamics

2 = Can sing only the melody with fair accuracy and with limited dynamics

1 = Has difficulty singing the melody accurately and does not use dynamics

---

SPOTLIGHT ON

▶ **The Performer** Ben E. King (born 1938) sang doo wop with the Four Bs in high school. Later, he joined the Five Crowns and became its lead singer. Meanwhile, the Drifters were recording on their own with Clyde McPhatter as the lead. When McPhatter left, King became the lead singer of the Drifters. Their first recording together, "Save the Last Dance for Me," became an instant hit in 1959. Next followed "There Goes My Baby." King left the group in 1960 and recorded "Spanish Harlem" and "Stand By Me" as a solo artist. "Stand By Me" was originally an old gospel standard. King convinced Jerry Leiber and Mike Stoller to help him arrange it in pop style. "Stand By Me" became a huge success and is still well known today.

TECHNOLOGY/MEDIA LINK

CD-ROM Invite students to explore accompaniment styles using *Band-in-a-Box*.

- Prepare a *Band-in-a-Box* file with the melody and chord progressions to "Stand By Me."

- Have students take turns selecting different accompaniment styles to apply to the files as the class sings a verse of the song. Then discuss the appropriateness of the selected style.

- Ask students to determine why they were able to sing the song, no matter what accompaniment style was played. (The song's melody and harmony never change; only the accompaniment pattern applied to the harmony changes.)

LESSON AT A GLANCE

Element Focus	**RHYTHM** Meter in 2
Skill Objective	**MOVING** Create movements that demonstrate strong and weak beats
Connection Activity	**CULTURE** Read about the lives of young people in nineteenth-century Mexico

MATERIALS

- "Adelita" (Spanish)   **CD 3-4**
- "Adelita" (English)   **CD 3-5**

  Recording Routine: Intro (8 m.); vocal; interlude (8 m.); vocal; coda
- **Pronunciation Practice/Translation** p. 523
- **Resource Book** pp. A-6, H-7

VOCABULARY

duple meter

◆ ◆ ◆ ◆ **National Standards** ◆ ◆ ◆ ◆

1c Sing music from diverse cultures
1d Sing music written in two parts
2c Perform instrumental music from diverse cultures
6c Understand and use basic principles of meter in music analysis

MORE MUSIC CHOICES

For more practice with meter in 2:
"San Antonio Rose," p. 134
"El carite" ("The Kingfish"), p. 305

1 INTRODUCE

Have students pay close attention to the words as they listen to the recording of "Adelita" **CD 3-4.**

ASK Who is the singer? (a lovesick soldier)

What is he singing about? (his feelings for the beautiful Adelita)

Move to the Beats

Songwriters everywhere write love songs, and songs that talk about the person of their dreams. **Sing** this traditional Mexican song expressing the thoughts of a young man. **Move** to the **meter** in 2.

> **Meter** is the way beats of music are grouped, often in sets of two or three.

CD 3–4
MIDI 3

Adelita

English Words by Aura Kontra   Folk Song from Mexico

A-de-li-ta se lla-ma la jo-ven,
She is known as the young A-de-li-ta,

A quien yo quie-ro y no pue-do ol-vi-dar.
And she's the one that I love and can't for-get.

Y en el cam-po yo ten-go u-na ro-sa,
Like the ro-ses that bloom in the mea-dow,

Y con el tiem-po la voy a cor-tar,
Oh, she's the lov-li-est girl that I've met.

Si A-de-li-ta qui-sie-ra ser mi es-po-sa____
How I wish that she'd mar-ry this young sol-dier. ___

50

Footnotes

SKILLS REINFORCEMENT

2c ▶ **Guitar** Encourage students to use the guitar chords D, A₇, and G to accompany "Adelita," accenting the downbeat of each measure.

▶ **Keyboard** See Resource Book p. H-7 for a keyboard accompaniment to "Adelita."

BUILDING SKILLS THROUGH MUSIC

▶ **Writing** Ask students to look at the pictures on p. 51. Ask them to describe the differences between the guitar, *guitarrón*, and mandolin. Invite students to listen to "Adelita" **CD 3-4** and indicate when they hear the *guitarrón* and mandolin. Have students write two to three sentences describing the stylistic contribution of the featured instruments.

ACROSS THE CURRICULUM

▶ **Language Arts** Encourage students to read the following books about the lives of young people growing up in nineteenth-century Mexican territories.

- *Asi es Josefina, Meet Josefina, an American Girl* (The American Girls Collection) by Valerie Tripp (Pleasant Company Publications, 1997). A New Mexican girl in 1824 struggles to run her household after her mother dies. The book is a fascinating collection of historical photos, real-life narrative, maps, and artist's renditions of aspects of life in the Mexican territories—all from Josefina's point of view.

- *And Now Miguel* by Joseph Krumgold (HarperCollins Childrens, 1984). This is a Newbery Award-winning story about a boy's desire to be accepted as a grown man capable of traveling with other sheepherders to the mountain pastures.

D A7 D

Si A - de - li - ta fue - ra mi mu - jer. ___
How I wish A - de - li - ta were mine. ___

D D G

Le com - pra - rí a un ves - ti - do de se - da,
Then I would buy her a gown of silk and sat - in,

G D A7 D

Pa - ra lle - var - la a bai - lar al cuar - tel.
And she would dance through the night at my side.

Showing the Beat
Now let's give your feet a challenge. Make two groups.

Group 1: Move your feet to show the strong beats.

Group 2: Move on the weak beats.

▲ A Mexican musician plays a *guitarrón*, a very large bass guitar.

▲ A player strums a mandolin. Both the *guitarrón* and the mandolin can be heard on the recording of "Adelita."

Unit 2 51

2 DEVELOP

Singing

1c Encourage students to learn more about young people in Mexico during the nineteenth century. See Across the Curriculum, p. 50. Play the recording again and encourage students to sing the melody as they follow the music.

ASK How many beats are in each measure? (two)

Which beat is the strongest? (first)

SAY The grouping of strong and weak beats in a measure determine the meter of a song. The grouping of beats in "Adelita," with one strong and one weak beat per measure, is called duple meter.

Moving

6c Play "Adelita" **CD 3-4** again. Have students create body percussion patterns to show the strong and weak beats.

Singing

1d Ask students to sing *do* on D, then *mi* on F♯. Divide the class into groups, and sing *do* and *mi* together.

ASK What is the distance between these two pitches called? (an interval of a third)

Have students find where the harmony part begins on line 5. Form two groups, with one group singing the melody and the other singing the lower harmony part. Then have students exchange parts.

3 CLOSE

Skill: MOVING **ASSESSMENT**

Performance/Observation Have students work in small groups and create movements for "Adelita" showing the strong and weak beats of duple meter. Play the recording **CD 3-4**, and have groups take turns performing their movements for the class. Observe if students' movements are effective.

MOVEMENT

▶ **Patterned Dance** Work with two of the rhythm patterns from the song "Adelita:" *ta ti-ti* and *ti-ti-ti-ti*. Have students experiment with foot patterns using steps and heel touches. For example: step R touch L touch L *(ta ti-ti)* or step R touch L step L touch R *(ti-ti-ti-ti)*. After they have tried several options, ask them to share their patterns. Select two patterns for dancing to the song "Adelita," one pattern for the first 16 measures (the unison part of the recording) and the other for the second 16 measures (the section sung in harmony). This is one of many ways you could vary the patterns. Invite students to make suggestions.

TECHNOLOGY/MEDIA LINK

MIDI/Sequencing Software Mute all tracks in the "Adelita" MIDI song file, except the bass and harmonic rhythm. Display the tracks in notation view, and play for the class.

Then, have students unmute all the tracks and mute the bass and harmonic rhythm tracks. Next, have students sequence bass and harmony parts for "Adelita" (two separate tracks), based on the chord symbols printed above the music in the pupil text. Encourage students to use appropriate sound choices, such as acoustic guitar and bass.

LESSON 3

LESSON AT A GLANCE

Element Focus RHYTHM ♩ ♪♪ , ♪♪♪

Skill Objective READING Play rhythms, read from notation, that include ♩ ♪♪♪ , and ♪♪♪ ♩

Connection Activity SOCIAL STUDIES Explore the history of the California Gold Rush

MATERIALS
- "California" **CD 3-9**
  Recording Routine: Intro (4 m.); v. 1; refrain; interlude (2 m.); v. 2; refrain; interlude (2 m.); v. 3; refrain; interlude (2 m.); v. 4; refrain; interlude (2 m.); v. 5; coda
- **Music Reading Practice, Sequence 5** **CD 3-11**
- **Resource Book** pp. B-5, D-5, E-6, I-5
- selected rhythm instruments

VOCABULARY
rhythm   meter

> ◆ ◆ ◆ **National Standards** ◆ ◆ ◆ ◆
>
> **1c** Sing music from diverse genres
> **2a** Play instruments accurately in small ensembles
> **3b** Improvise rhythmic variations on given melodies
> **5a** Read rhythms in duple meter
> **6c** Understand and use basic principles of rhythm in music analysis
> **8b** Identify ways music relates to social studies

MORE MUSIC CHOICES
For more practice with eighth- and sixteenth-note patterns: "This Train," p. 27

1 INTRODUCE

1c Have students tap the steady beat as they listen to "California" **CD 3-9**, then tap the beat and sing the song. Use the resources in Across the Curriculum below to engage students in a discussion of the California Gold Rush.

GOLD RUSH RHYTHMS!

Gold in California was first discovered by James Marshall in early 1848 near a place called Sutter's Mill. In 1849, a traveling concert troupe known as the Hutchinson Family performed "California." They sang for a group of Massachusetts prospectors heading West to search for gold.

Sing "California" and **perform** a steady beat.

CD 3-9

CALIFORNIA

d r m s l d'

Folk Song from the United States

VERSE

1. We've formed our band, we are all well-manned to
2. O! don't you cry, nor ___ heave a sigh, For we'll
3. As the gold is *thar*, most ___ an-y *whar*, And they

jour — ney a — far to the prom — ised land,
all come ___ back a — gain ___ bye and bye,
dig it _____ out with an i — ron bar,

The gold — en ore is rich in store on the
Don't breathe a fear, nor shed a tear, But ___
And where 'tis thick with a spade or pick, They can

banks of the Sac — ra — men — to shore.
pa — tient — ly ___ wait for a — bout two year.
take out ___ lumps as heavy as brick.

52   Reading Sequence 5

Footnotes

SKILLS REINFORCEMENT

▶ **Moving** Have students show eighth-sixteenth and sixteenth-eighth patterns using body percussion (such as snap, clap, stamp, and slide). Have students create and perform the patterns while singing "California" and then form a circle and step while singing and performing the body percussion.

▶ **Recorder** See Resource Book p. I-5 for a recorder part to accompany "California."

BUILDING SKILLS THROUGH MUSIC

▶ **Reading** Choose 5–7 phrases from "California" that express important ideas from the song. Organize the phrases into a random order list and distribute to the class. Discuss the meaning of each phrase. Invite students to listen to "California" **CD 3-9** and identify the sequence of the phrases from the list.

ACROSS THE CURRICULUM

8b ▶ **Social Studies** For more about the California Gold Rush, invite students to read:

- *The Gold Rush* by Liza Ketchum (Little, Brown & Company, 1996) describes how dreams of "striking it rich" caused America's largest Western migration. The California Gold Rush had an immense effect on the migrants themselves, as well as on the Spanish settlers and the native Indian tribes.

- *The California Gold Rush: A Guide to the California Gold Rush* by Eugene R. Hart (Freewheel Pub., 1993) is an informative book that includes detailed descriptions of historical mining techniques. It also tells about places to visit in California where gold rush history and heritage have been carefully preserved.

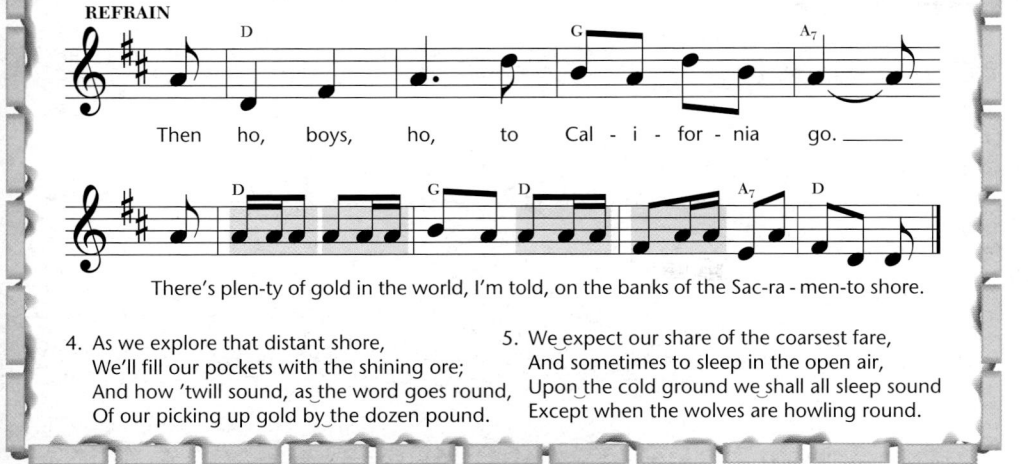

REFRAIN

Then ho, boys, ho, to Cal - i - for - nia go. _____

There's plen-ty of gold in the world, I'm told, on the banks of the Sac-ra - men-to shore.

4. As we explore that distant shore,
We'll fill our pockets with the shining ore;
And how 'twill sound, as the word goes round,
Of our picking up gold by the dozen pound.

5. We expect our share of the coarsest fare,
And sometimes to sleep in the open air,
Upon the cold ground we shall all sleep sound
Except when the wolves are howling round.

A rhythm pattern in music is a group of long and short sounds and silences used in different combinations.

Look at the color boxes in the last line of the song. Which color box contains a *short-short-long* rhythm pattern? Which color box contains a *long-short-short* rhythm pattern?

Show What You Know!

Read these patterns. Then **play** them on rhythm instruments.

1. $\frac{2}{4}$

2. $\frac{2}{4}$

Compose your own "Gold Rush Rhythm" and **perform** it with the song "California."

Tune In

In 1849, more than 80,000 "gold rushers" flocked to California to find their fortunes. They became known as the "forty-niners."

Unit 2 53

---

2 DEVELOP

Reading

Review known rhythms and their notation, using Resource Book p. D-5. Have students

- Echo clap two-beat patterns that include quarter notes, eighths, quarter rests, four-beamed sixteenths, beamed eighths and sixteenths.
- Identify each note and rest.
- Give the rhythm syllable name for each note.

Have students say the last line of "California" in rhythm as they pat the steady beat. Draw attention to the words *banks of the Sacramento*.

ASK What is the rhythm of the word *Sacramento*? *(ti-ti ti-ti)*

Have students pat the steady beat again, and listen as you clap the words *banks of the*.

ASK How many beats did you pat during my clapped pattern? (one)

How many sounds did you hear? (three)

What was the pattern of the sounds? (long-short-short)

Use Resource Book p. D-5 to point out the beamed eighth-two-sixteenth pattern. Have students compare this pattern to four-beamed sixteenth notes.

For extra reinforcement, see Music Reading Practice, Sequence 5 on p. 492 and Resource Book p. E-6.

3 CLOSE

Element: RHYTHM   ASSESSMENT

Performance/Observation Have students play the patterns in Show What You Know on p. 53. Then encourage students to create simple accompaniments to "California" using original patterns. Observe students' ability to accurately and independently perform sixteenth-note rhythms.

MEETING INDIVIDUAL NEEDS

 ▶ **Performing Rhythms** Help students at varying skill levels to perform sixteenth-note rhythms.

Reinforcement Some students may have difficulty singing and playing and . Invite these students to conduct a steady two-beat pattern as you point to the rhythm patterns highlighted on p. 53.

On Target Most students will be able to successfully sing or play sixteenth-note rhythms. For extra practice, perform an audible steady beat as they tap the rhythms, say the rhythm syllable names, and sing the rhythm patterns on a neutral syllable.

Challenge Invite students who easily master this lesson to create a rhythmic ostinato using and and perform it as everyone sings the refrain of "California."

TECHNOLOGY/MEDIA LINK

Web Site Encourage students to visit *www.sfsuccessnet.com* to learn about the popular music of the California Gold Rush.

LESSON AT A GLANCE

Element Focus   RHYTHM   ♪♪♩ and ♩♪♪

Skill Objective   PLAYING   Play sixteenth-note patterns

Connection Activity   SOCIAL STUDIES   Investigate the historical context of a railroad song

MATERIALS

- "Drill, Ye Tarriers"   **CD 3-16**
  Recording Routine: Intro (4 m.); v. 1; refrain; interlude (4 m.); v. 2; refrain; interlude (4 m.); v. 3, refrain; coda
- Music Reading Practice, Sequence 6   **CD 3-18**
- Dance Directions for "Drill, Ye Tarriers" p. 555
- *Symphony No. 9*, Movement 1 (excerpt)   **CD 3-22**
- **Resource Book** p. E-7, F-6, I-6
- selected classroom percussion instruments

VOCABULARY

symphony   movement

◆ ◆ ◆ National Standards ◆ ◆ ◆

1b   Sing easy pieces with technical accuracy
2b   Perform easy instrumental pieces with technical accuracy
5a   Read quarter, eighth, sixteenth notes in duple meter
5d   Use standard notation to record musical ideas
6a   Listen and describe events in music using appropriate terms
8b   Identify ways music relates to social studies

MORE MUSIC CHOICES

For more experience with sixteenth-note patterns:
"Camptown Races," p. 270

1 INTRODUCE

Have students listen to "Drill Ye Tarriers" **CD 3-16** and discuss the lyrics. Use the suggestions in Across the Curriculum below to engage students in a discussion of railroads.

Work to the Rhythm

In the 1880s, many different groups of immigrants helped to build American railroads. One of these groups was the Irish. **Sing** "Drill, Ye Tarriers," a song that tells of the hardships and injustices the railroad workers faced.

Listen for some clues in the text about what tarriers do.

CD 3–16

Drill, Ye Tarriers

Words and Music by Thomas Casey

l t ⓓ r m s l t d'

VERSE
Cm

do

1. Ev - 'ry morn-ing at sev - en o'-clock There's twen-ty tar-ri-ers a-
2. Our new fore-man is Dan ___ Mc-Cann, I'll tell you sure ___ he's a
3. Next time pay - day comes ___ a-round, Jim Goff was short ___ one ___

work - ing at the rock, And the boss comes a - long and he
blame ___ mean ___ man; Last ___ week a ___ prema - ture ___
buck, ___ he ___ found; "What ___ for?" says ___ he; then ___

says, "Keep still, And come down heav-y on the cast iron drill."
blast went off, And a mile in the air ___ went ___ Big Jim Goff.
this re - ply, "You're docked for the time ___ you were up in the sky."

Footnotes

MOVEMENT

▶ **Patterned Dance** Dancing is a natural part of Irish culture. It is said that when two Irishmen meet at a crossroad, they do a little jig. When the Irishmen who worked on the railroad had time to relax, they sang and danced. There were not many women at the railroad camps, so the men danced with each other, just as American cowboys and Argentine sailors did. See p. 554 for a movement pattern to accompany "Drill, Ye Tarriers."

BUILDING SKILLS THROUGH MUSIC

▶ **Math** Divide the class into two groups, with one group clapping the rhythm of the verse, the second group clapping a steady beat. Ask students to identify beats with one or more notes. Each beat will equal one [whole]. Review the fractions for 1/2 and 1/4. Have students identify fractions for each note. For example, an eighth note would equal 1/2; a sixteenth note would equal 1/4. Add the fractions for each beat, then for each measure.

ACROSS THE CURRICULUM

8b ▶ **Social Studies** Students may enjoy reading and then creating a short historical-fact introduction to "Drill, Ye Tarriers" for performances. For interesting facts about the building of railroads across the United States, suggest they read *Ten Mile Day: And the Building of the Transcontinental Railroad* by Mary Ann Fraser (Henry Holt, 1996). This fascinating account of the building of the Transcontinental Railroad in 1869 explores the historical highlights and engineering feats, lives of the many ethnic groups who served as railroad workers, and the effects of the railroads on Native Americans.

Railroad Rhythms

Find the  and  patterns in the song.

Sing the song again, and when one of these patterns comes along, sing the rhythm syllables instead of the words. Good luck!

Play the rhythm parts below with the refrain of "Drill, Ye Tarriers."

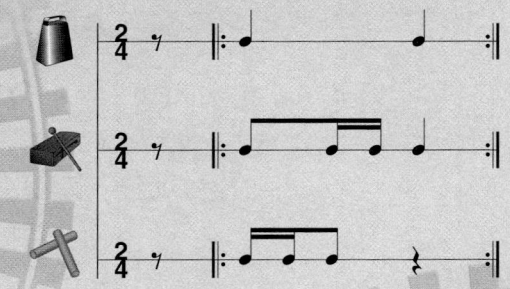

Listen to the pattern in this excerpt.

CD 3–22

Symphony No. 9 ("From the New World")

Movement 1
by Antonín Dvořák

The name of this symphony, "From the New World," refers to the United States. Czech composer Antonín Dvořák [an-toh-NEEN d'VOHR-zhahk] wrote it at about the same time railroad workers were singing "Drill, Ye Tarriers."

Unit 2 **55**

2 DEVELOP

Reading

Ask volunteers to write three rhythms on the board:

Set a steady beat and then have students

5a
- Read each rhythm with rhythm syllables.
- Look at the notation for "Drill, Ye Tarriers" and count how many times each sixteenth-note rhythm appears in the song. Then read the verse of the song with rhythm syllables.

For more practice performing sixteenth-note rhythms, see Music Reading Practice, Sequence 6 on p. 492 and Resource Book p. E-6.

Creating

5d Add two beamed eighth notes, a quarter note, and a quarter rest to the rhythms on the board. Draw four blanks (two measures) on the board. Have students

- Decide how to fill in the blanks, using the patterns on the board. (The quarter note and quarter rest can be used only once.)
- Use standard symbols to notate rhythm in simple patterns and perform them using rhythm syllables. Then say their patterns one after another without silent beats in between.

Playing

Invite students to perform the instrumental parts on p. 55 with the refrain "Drill, Ye Tarriers."

Listening

6a Play the excerpt from *Symphony No. 9* **CD 3-22** and ask students to listen for the *tiri-ti* rhythm.

3 CLOSE

Element: RHYTHM   **ASSESSMENT**

1b **Performance/Observation** Have students play their rhythm patterns, or those on p. 55, on selected percussion instruments as ostinatos, while singing "Drill, Ye Tarriers." Observe for rhythmic accuracy.

2b

SKILLS REINFORCEMENT

2b ▶ **Recorder** To give students additional experience with rhythm patterns that use eighth and sixteenth notes, have them compose a rhythmic piece to play on their recorders. Invite students to create and notate four, two-beat measures using quarter, eighth, and sixteenth notes. Using their recorders, have them play their compositions on the note G. Some students may want to accompany the verse of "Drill, Ye Tarriers" by playing their composition on G. They will need to repeat their four-measure pieces or have a friend play the second set of four measures.

Another time, have students play the rhythm of the words on the note G during the verse of the song. Make sure they say *daah* on each note so the rhythm is articulated clearly.

A countermelody for "Drill, Ye Tarriers" can be found on Resource Book p. I-6.

CHARACTER EDUCATION

▶ **Collaboration** To promote students' understanding of the skills necessary to collaborate with others, discuss singing and professional partnerships. Singing in a group requires vocal control and careful listening to achieve appropriate balance and blend. Individuals often must adjust their performance to benefit the group. Ask students what other situations require that individuals sacrifice control to help the group. (Accept various answers including team sports and medical teams.)

TECHNOLOGY/MEDIA LINK

5d **Notation Software** Have students notate their rhythm patterns from this lesson and print them before playing them.

LESSON AT A GLANCE

Element Focus   **FORM** Verse/Refrain (AB form)

Skill Objective   **SINGING** Sing a song in verse and refrain form

Connection Activity   **SOCIAL STUDIES** Discuss immigration to the United States

MATERIALS

• "Away to America"   **CD 3-23**

   Recording Routine: Intro (6 m.); first half v. 1; interlude (1 m.); second half v. 1; refrain; interlude (1 m.); v. 2; refrain; interlude (1 m.); v. 3; refrain; coda

VOCABULARY

form   verse   refrain

◆ ◆ ◆ ◆ National Standards ◆ ◆ ◆ ◆

1c Sing music from diverse genres
4c Compose using electronic media
6b Listen and analyze uses of form and timbre in music from diverse cultures
7a Create standards for evaluating performances
8b Identify ways music relates to social studies

MORE MUSIC CHOICES

For more practice with verse and refrain:
"Twelve Gates to the City," p. 280
"Cattle Call," p. 344

1 INTRODUCE

ASK Did you come to live in the United States from another place? Did your parents or grandparents emigrate from another country?

How did it (or how do you think it would) feel to be an immigrant? (Possible answers might include *exciting* because of the hope for a better life and *scary* because one is going to a new place with a different culture, customs, and perhaps a different language.)

Share information about Ellis Island in Spotlight On below.

New Land, New Verse

The first immigrants to arrive in America were from Western Europe. Since then, people have come to the United States from every part of the world. The trip to America was difficult and dangerous for many people. Many did not survive. Those who arrived showed amazing courage and strength.

The song "Away to America" has two parts—**verse** and **refrain. Sing** this song about one man's journey to a new world. Why did he want to come to America? From what country did he come?

> **Verse** refers to the section of a song that is sung before the refrain.
> **Refrain** is the part of a song that repeats, using the same melody and words.

56

Footnotes

ACROSS THE CURRICULUM

8b ▶ **Social Studies/Language Arts** Invite students to read *I Was Dreaming to Come to America: Memories from the Ellis Island Oral History Project* by Veronica Lawlor (Penguin Putnam, 1997). Real accounts of immigration to America are presented with photos of artifacts of the time. Folk art paintings express the immigrants' experience of dislocation, nostalgia for their homeland, and hopes for a bright future in a new land.

BUILDING SKILLS THROUGH MUSIC

▶ **Language** Invite the class to listen to "Away to America" **CD 3-23**. Lead the class in a discussion to determine the characters in the song. Choose one or more students to summarize the story in the song. Then discuss with students the singer's life and feelings. Ask students what part of the song made them come to their conclusions.

SPOTLIGHT ON

▶ **Ellis Island** On the coast of Ireland stands a statue dedicated to Annie Moore, the first immigrant to arrive in the U.S. in 1892 and pass through the gates of Ellis Island. Between 1892 and 1938 (the peak years were 1892–1924), great steamboats brought thousands of immigrants a day to America's "front door of freedom." Over 100 million Americans can trace their ancestry in the United States to a man, woman, or child whose courage brought them to New York's harbor, sometimes alone.

Many immigrants left whole families in the "old world" as well as traditions and customs. Ahead was a promising new life. With restrictions on immigration, Ellis Island closed its doors in 1954. Today, the Main Hall is a museum dedicated to the immigrants' stories—a lasting image of the "American dream."

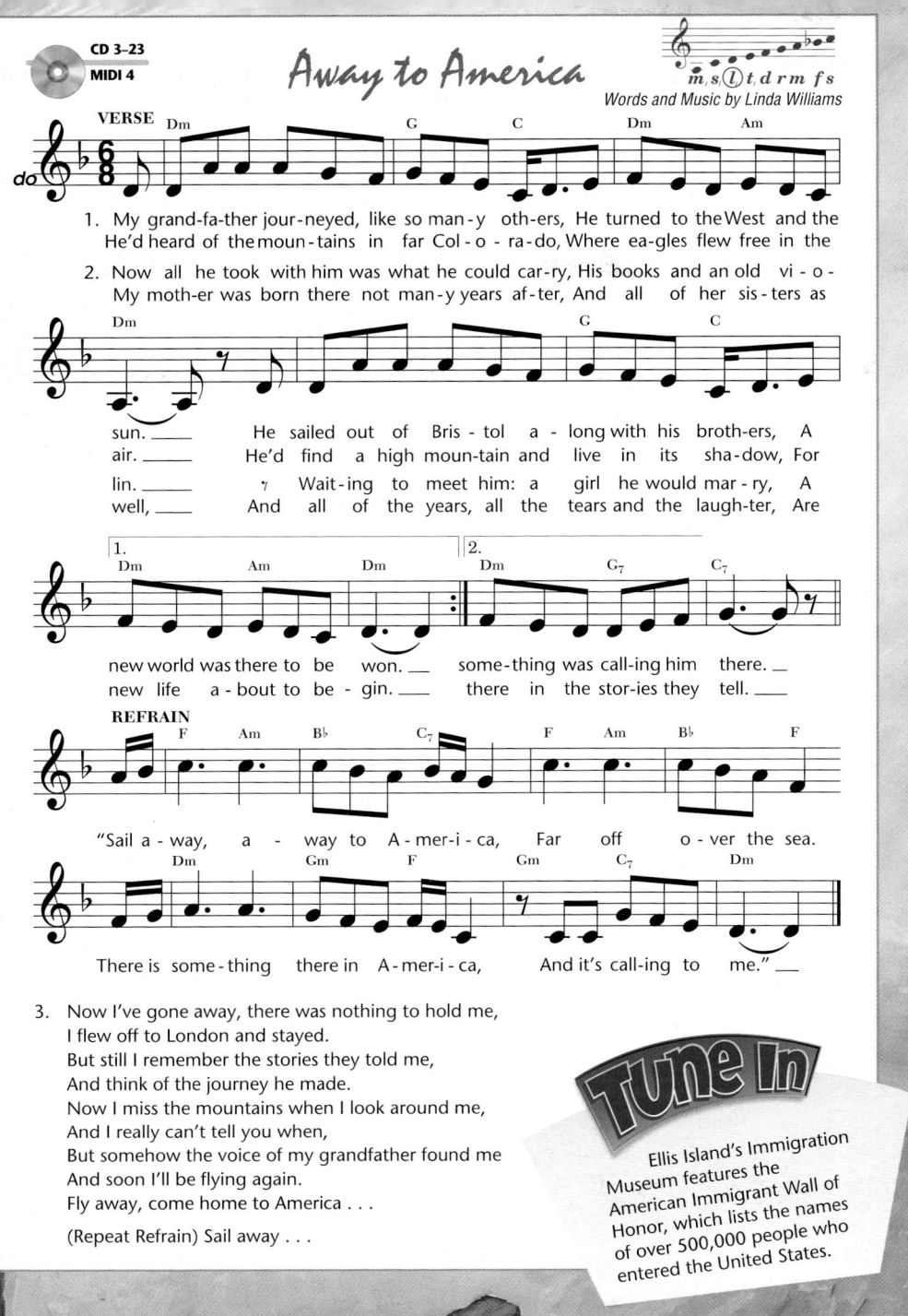

Away to America

Words and Music by Linda Williams

CD 3–23
MIDI 4

do

VERSE

1. My grand-fa-ther jour-neyed, like so man-y oth-ers, He turned to the West and the
He'd heard of the moun-tains in far Col-o-ra-do, Where ea-gles flew free in the

2. Now all he took with him was what he could car-ry, His books and an old vi-o-
My moth-er was born there not man-y years af-ter, And all of her sis-ters as

sun. _____ He sailed out of Bris-tol a-long with his broth-ers, A
air. _____ He'd find a high moun-tain and live in its sha-dow, For
lin. _____ Wait-ing to meet him: a girl he would mar-ry, A
well, _____ And all of the years, all the tears and the laugh-ter, Are

1.
new world was there to be won. ___ some-thing was call-ing him there. ___
new life a-bout to be-gin. ___ there in the stor-ies they tell. ___

2.

REFRAIN
"Sail a-way, a-way to A-mer-i-ca, Far off o-ver the sea.
There is some-thing there in A-mer-i-ca, And it's call-ing to me." ___

3. Now I've gone away, there was nothing to hold me,
I flew off to London and stayed.
But still I remember the stories they told me,
And think of the journey he made.
Now I miss the mountains when I look around me,
And I really can't tell you when,
But somehow the voice of my grandfather found me
And soon I'll be flying again.
Fly away, come home to America . . .

(Repeat Refrain) Sail away . . .

Tune In

Ellis Island's Immigration Museum features the American Immigrant Wall of Honor, which lists the names of over 500,000 people who entered the United States.

Unit 2 57

2 DEVELOP

Listening

8b Have students follow the words of "Away to America" **CD 3-23** as they listen to the recording.

ASK **What story does the song tell?** (about people leaving their country to find a new way of life)

Singing

1c Play the recording and have students sing along.

Have students look at the song.

ASK **Where are the words repeated?** (the last two lines of the song)

6b **What is this section called?** (refrain)

Have students look at the first three lines of the song.

ASK **Are the words repeated?** (no)

What is this part of the song called? (verse)

Have students read the text about verse and refrain on p. 56. Point out that the refrain of a song usually has a different melody than the verse.

Moving

Play the recording again. Have students

• Feel two beats to a measure.

• Use contrasting movements in the two sections.

3 CLOSE

Element: FORM — **ASSESSMENT**

7a **Performance/Observation** Have students work in groups. Ask each group to choose another song in verse/refrain form and decide on a way to perform the song that will highlight the two sections. When they are ready, have students present their ideas to the class and lead a class performance. Observe for effectiveness in students' performance choices.

CHARACTER EDUCATION

▶ **Courage** Help students to understand the courage needed to face certain life situations by discussing the bravery of people who immigrate to a new country or move to a different place. Ask them to describe appropriate and inappropriate individual and group responses to immigrants or newcomers today. Then ask students to list ways students might make such a transition easier for those who must make changes.

Have students describe other situations that demand courage. Invite interested students to describe a time when they felt afraid and/or courageous. Discuss ways they can feel more courageous even in the midst of adversity.

SCHOOL TO HOME CONNECTION

▶ **Immigrants** Ask students to talk with family members or friends who came to the United States as immigrants. Some questions they might ask are why the person wanted to come to the United States, how he or she felt on the immigration journey, and what adjustments he or she had to make in the new country.

TECHNOLOGY/MEDIA LINK

4c **MIDI/Sequencing Software** Using the MIDI song file of "Away to America," have students create their own "timbre" arrangements to illustrate the different sections of the form of the song. Have students explore various MIDI sounds for the melody and assign different MIDI sounds for the verse and the refrain.

LESSON AT A GLANCE

Element Focus   **MELODY** Melodic sequence

Skill Objective   **SINGING** Sing a song that uses melodic sequence

Connection Activity   **CULTURE** Connect Spanish explorations with Mexico and the southwest United States

MATERIALS

- "La ciudad de Juaja"   **CD 3-24**
- "The City of Juaja"   **CD 3-25**

  Recording Routine: Intro (4 m.); v. 1; refrain; interlude (4 m.); v. 2; refrain; coda
- **Pronunciation Practice/Translation** p. 523
- *Invention No. 5 in E-flat*   **CD 3-28**
- **Resource Book** p. A-7
- keyboard, recorder, bells

VOCABULARY

motive   sequence

◆ ◆ ◆ ◆ National Standards ◆ ◆ ◆ ◆

1c Sing music from diverse cultures
2c Perform instrumental music from diverse cultures
4c Compose, using electronic media
6a Listen and describe events in music using appropriate terms
6b Listen and analyze uses of pitch in music from diverse cultures
8b Identify ways music relates to social studies

MORE MUSIC CHOICES

For more experience with melodic sequence:
"Autumn Canon," p. 148

1 INTRODUCE

8b Introduce the song *"La cuidad de Juaja"* to students by sharing the information on Spanish explorations. (See Across the Curriculum below)

| Element: MELODY | Skill: SINGING | Connection: CULTURE |

A Song of Sequences

When Spanish explorers returned from the New World, they told unbelievable stories about what they had seen. *"La ciudad de Juaja"* makes fun of these "far out" stories.

Listen to *"La ciudad de Juaja"* and its lively melody. Then **sing** the song with the same lively feeling.

CD 3-24

La ciudad de Juaja
(The City of Juaja)

English Words by Ruth DeCesare

Folk Song from New Mexico

t @ r m f

VERSE

1. Des - de   la   ciu - dad   de   Jua - ja, _____
2. Los   ce - rros   son   de   tor - ti - llas, _____
1. From   the   far   cit - y   of   Jua - ja, _____
2. Hills   are   com - posed   of   tor - ti - llas, _____

me   man - dan   so - li - ci - tar, _____   que   me
las   que - bra - das   de   bu - ñue - los,   y   las
they   sent   a   card   to   in - vite   me,   so   I'd
val - leys   of   frit - ters   are   made, ___   and   the

va - ya,   que   me   va - ya   de un   te -
pie - dras,   fru - tas   cu - bier - tas,   pi - nos
come   and   see   a   place   so   strange   it
stones   and   fruit   and   pine   trees   are   with

so - ro   a   dis - fru - tar.
son   los   ca - ra - me - los.
cer - tain - ly   would   de - light   me.
car - a - mel   o - ver - laid. _____

58

Footnotes

TEACHER TO TEACHER

▶ **Invention** As a term for a short vocal or instrumental piece, the word *invention* was first used in France and England in the 1500s and then spread to other parts of western Europe. J. S. Bach wrote 15 two-part inventions for keyboard; the purpose was to give the player some technical practice, and to demonstrate some interesting aspect of composition. The obvious characteristics of this particular invention are sequence and imitation.

BUILDING SKILLS THROUGH MUSIC

▶ **Language** Invite students to sing "The City of Juaja" **CD 3-25** and identify phrases in the text that are not true. Discuss common places and things that are described with exaggeration. Invite students to develop new text to fit the rhythm of each verse. Verse 1 should include the students location; verse 2 can describe an imaginary place.

ACROSS THE CURRICULUM

8b ▶ **Social Studies** New Mexico is very closely tied to Mexico by its history, including all aspects of Spanish conquest and settlement. There is record of Spanish exploration there as early as 1540, and by 1700 the area that is now Mexico and the southwest U.S. was governed by the Spanish. In 1848 the southwest U.S. territory was ceded to the U.S. at the end of the Mexican-American War. New Mexico became a territory in 1858 and a state in 1912.

In order to get funding for their trips, the early Spanish explorers had to make great promises to their sponsors as to what they would find and what they would bring back. The people who occupied these territories found the "tall tales" rather fantastic and even humorous. From these stories, songs such as *"La ciudad de Juaja"* were created.

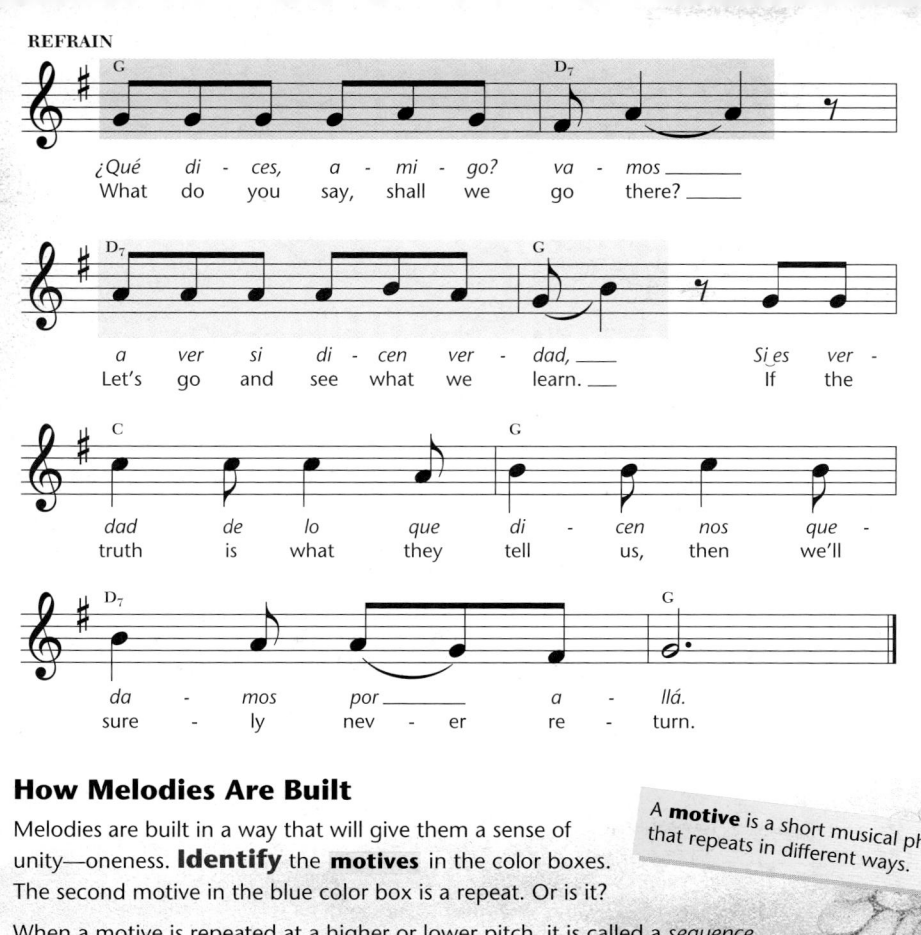

¿Qué di - ces, a - mi - go? va - mos _____
What do you say, shall we go there? _____

a ver si di - cen ver - dad, _____ Si es ver -
Let's go and see what we learn. _____ If the

dad de lo que di - cen nos que -
truth is what they tell us, then we'll

da - mos por _____ a - llá.
sure - ly nev - er re - turn.

How Melodies Are Built

Melodies are built in a way that will give them a sense of unity—oneness. **Identify** the **motives** in the color boxes. The second motive in the blue color box is a repeat. Or is it?

When a motive is repeated at a higher or lower pitch, it is called a *sequence*.

Listen for the following sequence in this piece by Johann Sebastian Bach.

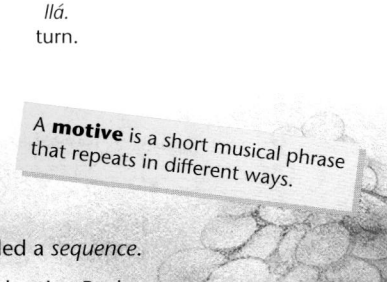
A **motive** is a short musical phrase that repeats in different ways.

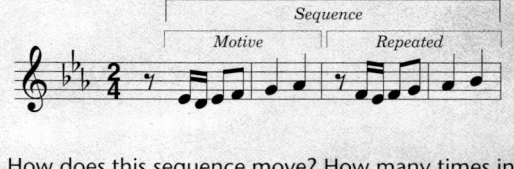

Sequence
Motive | Repeated

How does this sequence move? How many times in this piece is a sequence built from this motive?

CD 3–28
Invention No. 5 in E♭

by Johann Sebastian Bach
as performed by Glenn Gould

An "invention" is a short piece, usually for keyboard.

Unit 2 **59**

2 DEVELOP

Listening

6b Play the recording of "La ciudad de Juaja" **CD 3-24** and ask students to follow along in their books. Write the letter names F#-G-A-B-C-D on the board. Have students

* Sing the first line of "La ciudad de Juaja."
* Start on G and reorder the letter names on the board to match the melody.

ASK **What phrase in the song is similar to the first?** (phrase 2; the melody is the same, but it starts on a higher note)

SAY This structure is called a *sequence*.

Playing

2c Have students write the letter names of phrase 2 on the board, below those of phrase 1, and then play phrases 1 and 2 on keyboard or bells.

Singing

1c Use the Pronunciation Practice Track **CD 3-27** and Resource Book p. A-7 to help students sing "La ciudad de Juaja" in Spanish.

Listening

6b *Invention No. 5* **CD 3-28** uses a short musical idea to build sequences. Play the first few seconds and ask students to listen for the sequence shown on p. 59. Then play the entire piece.

ASK **How many times is the sequence played?** (9)

3 CLOSE

Element: MELODY — ASSESSMENT

1c **Performance/Observation** Ask students to sing
6a "La ciudad de Juaja" with their eyes closed, indicating when the sequence occurs by placing their hands in front of them at the two pitch levels. Observe students' ability to aurally recognize melodic sequences.

SKILLS REINFORCEMENT

▶ **Recorder** Have students play this countermelody on their recorders during the verse or the refrain of "La ciudad de Juaja." It uses mostly low D and E. Before playing, remind students they need very little air when playing notes in the low register. Make sure holes are covered securely with fingers flat, not arched.

TECHNOLOGY/MEDIA LINK

4c **Notation Software** Have students use notation software to notate the first phrase of "La ciudad de Juaja." (Be sure to set the key signature first.)

* Show them how to select the melody to cut, paste, and transpose notes.
* Have them cut, paste, and transpose the melody twice at successively higher or lower pitches.
* Then ask them to compose and notate an ending to the sequence.

Play the melodies back for students to follow the melodic contour with their hands and evaluate the melody ending.

LESSON AT A GLANCE

Element Focus **MELODY** *Do, re, mi, fa, so, la*

Skill Objective **READING** Sing a song, read from notation, that includes *do, re, mi, fa, so,* and *la*

Connection Activity **CULTURE** Discuss characteristics of a Spanish lullaby

MATERIALS

• "A la puerta del cielo" **CD 3-29**
• "At the Gate of Heaven" **CD 3-30**
  Recording Routine: Intro (8 m.); v. 1; refrain; interlude (4 m.); v. 2; refrain; coda
• **Music Reading Practice, Sequence 7** **CD 3-33**
• **Pronunciation Practice/Translation** p. 524
• **Resource Book** pp. A-8, D-6, E-8, I-7
• recorder

VOCABULARY

scale   pentatonic   half step   whole step

◆ ◆ ◆ ◆ National Standards ◆ ◆ ◆ ◆

1a Sing accurately in small ensembles
1c Sing music from diverse cultures
2c Perform instrumental music from diverse cultures
4c Arrange, using electronic media
5a Read eighth notes, quarter notes, half notes in duple meter
6c Understand and use basic principles of intervals in music analysis

MORE MUSIC CHOICES

For more practice with intervals:
"Erie Canal," p. 272
"Viva Jujuy," p. 228

1 INTRODUCE

1c Have students listen to "A la puerta del cielo" **CD 3-29** to learn the melody by rote, then sing along when they are ready. Discuss the features of this Spanish lullaby, such as slow tempo, even rhythms, Spanish lyrics, and gently rising and falling melody.

Step Up to fa

"A la puerta del cielo" is a lullaby that traveled with Spanish colonists to the New World.

Sing the first line of this song with pitch syllables. *Fa* is the note between *so* and *mi*.

s, t@rm f s l

CD 3-29

A la puerta del cielo
(At the Gate of Heaven)

English Words by Alice Firgau   Folk Song from Spain

VERSE

1. A la puer-ta del cie-lo ven-den za-pa-tos,
1. At the gate of Heav-en, new shoes they are sell-ing

Pa-ra an-ge-li-tos que an-dan des-cal-zos,
For the lit-tle an-gels who bare-foot are play-ing.

REFRAIN

Duér-me-te, ni-ño, duér-me-te, ni-ño,
Sleep now, my lit-tle child, sleep now, my lit-tle child,

Duér-me-te, ni-ño, a-rrú, a-rrú.
Sleep __ now, my dear child, a-rrú, a-rrú.

2. A los niños que duermen
   Dios los bendice,
   A las madres que velan
   Dios les asiste.
   Refrain

2. All the little children
   are blest while they're sleeping,
   And the mothers, too,
   will be blest, their watch keeping.
   Refrain

Footnotes

ACROSS THE CURRICULUM

8b ▶ **Social Studies** Invite students to research and locate the Basque region of Spain. What are the characteristic occupations of the native people of this region? How is their history and culture different from that of Spain? What are the region's most important landmarks and cultural centers?

BUILDING SKILLS THROUGH MUSIC

▶ **Language** Ask students to suggest definitions for "lullaby" and list them on the board. Next, ask them to recall subjects of lullabies that they know. Lead the class in a discussion on the common characteristics of lullabies and how they should be performed. Invite students to listen to "A la puerta del cielo" **CD 3-29** and identify similarities to the list of definitions on the board.

SKILLS REINFORCEMENT

5a ▶ **Recorder** Have students read the countermelody for "A la puerta del cielo" on Resource Book p. I-7, using hand signs. Then have them play the countermelody with the song.

2c **5a** ▶ **Notating** Have students write the following motives, first in rhythm notation in $\frac{4}{4}$. Then have them write the pitch notation using standard symbols on the staff in C-*do*.

so-fa-mi   do-re-mi-fa-so

so-fa-mi-re-do   mi-fa-mi-fa-mi

do-so-so-fa-mi-fa-so   mi-fa-so-do

Climb the Clouds

The step between *mi* and *fa* is called a half step because it is half the distance of a whole step. Can you hear the difference?

Sing the notes from *do* to *la* going up and down the "cloud ladder." Now try skipping around.

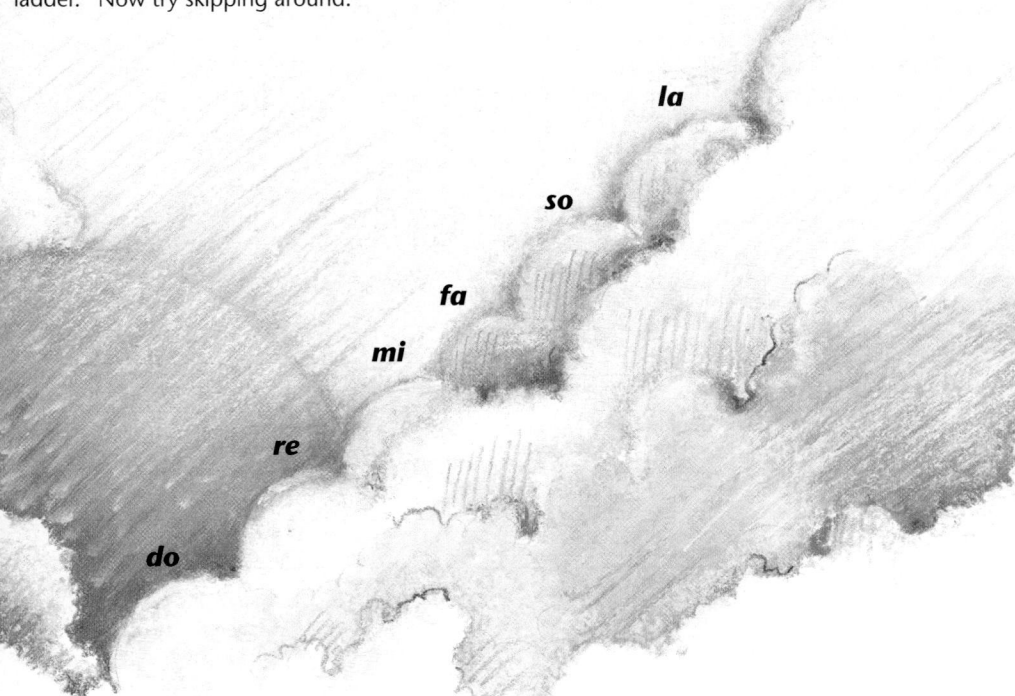

Fa on the Staff

When C is *do*, *fa* is F. The step from E to F is a half step.

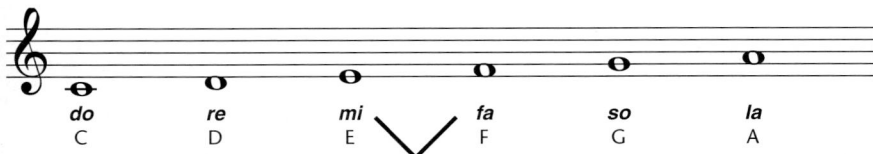

do	re	mi	fa	so	la
C	D	E	F	G	A

When F is *do*, *fa* is not B, but B♭. The pattern of whole and half steps must remain the same. This way, *mi* and *fa* are still a half step apart.

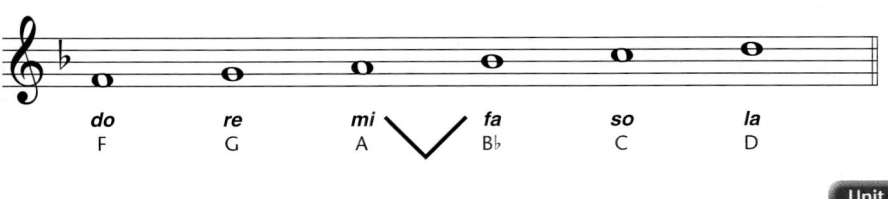

do	re	mi	fa	so	la
F	G	A	B♭	C	D

2 DEVELOP

Reading

 Review the notes of the F-*do* extended pentatonic scale (see Resource Book p. D-6). Have students sing the scale, ascending and descending.

Use pitch syllables to sing a descending *do*-pentachordal pattern for students (*so-fa-mi-re-do*). Hum *fa*.

ASK On which note did the pattern end? (*do*)

On which note did it begin? (*so*)

Where does the missing syllable (the note I'm humming) fall in the scale? (between *mi* and *so*)

SAY The note between *mi* and *so* is called *fa*.

Singing

Demonstrate the hand sign for *fa* and point to it on the pitch ladder on p. 61. Have students

- Sing the descending pattern with pitch syllables and hand signs.
- Sing all the known notes, from top to bottom.
- Sing the pattern *so-fa-so*, using hand signs. Then sing the pattern *mi-fa-mi*.

Explain that the distance between *fa* and *so* is called a whole step, while the distance between *fa* and *mi* is called a half step.

Have students read and discuss the information on p. 61 on whole and half steps.

For more practice reading *fa*, have students perform Music Reading Practice, Sequence 7 on p. 493 and Resource Book p. E-8.

3 CLOSE

Element: MELODY   **ASSESSMENT**

 Performance/Observation Have students sing "*A la puerta del cielo*" **CD 3-29** first using hand signs and pitch syllables, and again using the song text. (Refer to Pronunciation Practice Track **CD 3-32** and Resource Book p. A-8 to help students learn the Spanish lyrics.)

TEACHER TO TEACHER

▶ **Notation** Prepare students to work individually writing notation by providing ample opportunities to work as a group (at the board, on the overhead, with manipulatives). A writing exercise can be broken down into several steps, as follows:

1. Teacher sings pattern on neutral syllable; students echo back using hand signs and pitch syllables.
2. Teacher sings pattern on neutral syllable; students use inner hearing and show hand signs.
3. Teacher sings pattern on neutral syllable; students show hand signs and write pattern using pitch syllables.
4. Teacher sings pattern on neutral syllable, students determine the rhythm; then complete notation with pitch syllables.

TECHNOLOGY/MEDIA LINK

Notation Software Encourage students to use notation software to create their own arrangement of "*A la puerta del cielo*." Have students

- Set up the program for two staffs (one treble clef staff for the melody and one bass clef staff for the bass line).
- Choose the key of F (one flat).
- Notate the melody of "*A la puerta del cielo*" by selecting rhythmic values and then clicking on the staff to choose the pitch.
- Create a bass part on the bass staff by entering chord roots (see chord changes) with student-selected rhythms.
- Choose the best playback voices for their arrangement of the song.

LESSON AT A GLANCE

Element Focus   MELODY *Do, re, mi, fa, so, la*

Skill Objective   READING Sing a song, read from notation, that is based on a *do*-pentatonic scale

Connection Activity   RELATED ARTS Explore how musicians and instruments can be depicted in art from a historical time period

MATERIALS

- "*Da pacem, Domine*"   CD 3-38
- "Grant Us Peace"   CD 3-39
  Recording Routine: Intro (10 m.); vocal; interlude (10 m.); vocal; coda
- **Music Reading Practice, Sequence 8**   CD 4-1
- **Pronunciation Practice/Translation** p. 525
- *Da pacem, Domine*   CD 4-4
- **Resource Book** pp. A-9, B-5, E-9

VOCABULARY

transpose   canon

◆ ◆ ◆ ◆ National Standards ◆ ◆ ◆ ◆

1c Sing music from diverse genres
5a Read half notes, quarter notes in duple meter
5b Sightread melodies in treble clef
5c Identify standard notation symbols for pitch
6a Listen and describe events in music using appropriate terms
8b Identify ways music relates to art and language arts

MORE MUSIC CHOICES

For more experience with music and fine arts:
"Colorado Trail," p. 276
"It Don't Mean a Thing," p. 336

1 INTRODUCE

8b Point out the artwork on p. 63 and discuss how the musicians and the instruments (viol, flutes) are depicted. Lead students in a discussion to identify concepts taught in the other fine arts.

A Pitch for Peace

Melchior Franck [MEL-keeohr frahnk] (1573–1639) was a chapel conductor in Germany during the early 1600s. "*Da pacem, Domine*" is an example of his vocal music. **Sing** "*Da pacem, Domine*" using hand signs and pitch syllables.

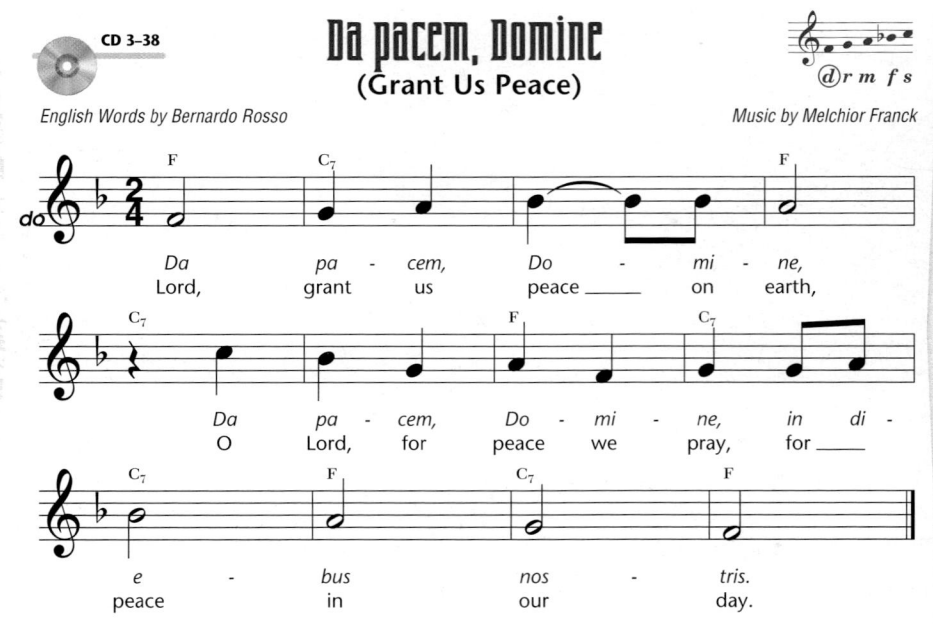

CD 3–38

Da pacem, Domine
(Grant Us Peace)

English Words by Bernardo Rosso   *Music by Melchior Franck*

Da   pa — cem,   Do — mi — ne,
Lord,   grant   us   peace ____ on   earth,

Da   pa — cem,   Do — mi — ne,   in di —
O   Lord,   for   peace   we   pray,   for ____

e   bus   nos   tris.
peace   in   our   day.

Layers of Melody

Listen to this performance of "*Da pacem, Domine.*" Follow each entrance of the melody as the parts overlap.

CD 4–4   Da pacem, Domine

by Melchior Franck
as performed by Capella Cantabile

Melchior Franck wrote over 600 pieces of music, including motets, madrigals, and instrumental dances.

Footnotes

SPOTLIGHT ON

▶ **Capella Cantabile** The Capella Cantabile choral group was founded in 1984 by conductor Alfred Tuzar. Capella Cantabile is one of the world's most famous youth choral groups. They have recorded for countless radio and television programs and have toured many European countries. The group sings only religious works, but their list of songs includes everything from seventeenth-century rounds to modern spirituals.

BUILDING SKILLS THROUGH MUSIC

▶ **Art** Ask students to look at *Painting of Musicians*, on p. 63. Have students suggest descriptions of the appearance of the musicians and instruments in the painting. Discuss details of the painting that are simple and complex, such as design, color, decoration, and ornamentation.

CULTURAL CONNECTION

8b ▶ **Vocal Forms** The **motet** was the most important form of polyphonic vocal music in Europe in the Middle Ages and the Renaissance. Written usually for three voices, the upper two voices complemented each other. The third voice, known as the *cantus firmus*, was written in a slower rhythm and could be sung by a tenor or played on an instrument. The *cantus firmus* was often based on a popular song of the day.

Another vocal form that flourished in the Renaissance was known as the **madrigal**. Each line of the madrigal has its own tune written for four to six voices and was generally performed unaccompanied (*a cappella*). Each line has its own melody, rather than the whole composition having a single melody with a harmonic accompaniment.

Show What You Know!

You performed *"Da pacem, Domine"* in F-*do*.

Any song can be transposed, or sung at a higher or lower pitch. **Sing** the version of *"Da pacem, Domine"* below, using hand signs and pitch syllables. Is this version higher or lower than the first version? Where is *do* in this version?

2 DEVELOP

Singing

1c Have students listen to *"Da pacem, Domine"* **CD 3-38** and then sing along with the recording.

Reading

5c Direct students' attention to the notation of *"Da pacem, Domine"* and have them find *do* by looking at the key signature (F-*do*). Explain that the last flat in a key signature is *fa*. In this song, there is only one flat, so it is *fa*. When B-flat is *fa*, F is *do*.

Have students determine the pitch-set, or scale, used in the song, from the lowest pitch to the highest. (*do-re-mi-fa-so*)

SAY This scale is a *do*-pentachord because *do* is the lowest note, there are five notes, and they are all next to each other, with no skips.

5b Have students read and sing *"Da pacem, Domine,"* first with pitch syllables and hand signs, then with letter names and hand signs, and finally with the lyrics.

You may also wish to have students perform Music Reading Practice, Sequence 8 on p. 493 and Resource Book p. E-9.

Listening

6a Have students listen to *"Da pacem, Domine"* **CD 4-4** to follow each entrance of the melody.

3 CLOSE

Element: MELODY   **ASSESSMENT**

5a **Performance/Observation** Have students

- Look at *"Da pacem, Domine,"* as notated in Show What You Know!, and determine *do*. (C)

- Read the melody, first using pitch syllables, and then using letter names.

Observe for melodic accuracy.

ACROSS THE CURRICULUM

8b ▶ **Language Arts** Encourage students to think about the meaning of the words in *"Da pacem, Domine."* Ask students to describe, either in discussion or in writing, what it would mean to truly have peace in the world. Invite students to read more about this theme in *The Day the Earth Was Silent* by Michael McGuffee (Inquiring Voices Press, 1996), an evocative story about children who work together to change the world for the better.

TECHNOLOGY/MEDIA LINK

5c **Sequencing Software** Have students

- Notate the melody patterns of *"Da pacem, Domine"* using standard symbols.

- Use the transpose function to hear and see it in other keys.

- Experiment with different instrumental sounds.

- Discuss which timbres fit the mood best, and why.

LESSON AT A GLANCE

Element Focus **TIMBRE** Percussion instruments

Skill Objective **LISTENING** Listen to a composition for percussion ensemble

Connection Activity **CULTURE** Discuss the role of music in African culture

MATERIALS
- "Ye jaliya da" **CD 4-7**
  Recording Routine: Intro (2 m.); vocal; interlude (8 m.); vocal; coda
- **Pronunciation Practice/Translation** p. 525
- *Theme and Variations for Percussion* **CD 4-5**
- *Montage of African Instruments* **CD 4-6**
- *Oya (Primitive Fire)* **CD 4-10**
- **Resource Book** p. A-9, C-6, J-4
- selected percussion instruments

VOCABULARY
percussion   idiophones
membranophones   theme and variations

◆ ◆ ◆ ◆ National Standards ◆ ◆ ◆ ◆
1c Sing music from diverse cultures
2a Play instruments accurately in small ensembles
4c Compose, using traditional sound sources and electronic media
5d Use standard notation to record musical ideas
6a Listen and describe events in music, using appropriate terms
6b Listen and analyze uses of timbre, dynamics, and form in music from diverse genres
8b Identify ways music relates to social studies and language arts

MORE MUSIC CHOICES
For more listening examples featuring percussion:
Yaudachi, p. 156
Conga Kings Grand Finale, p. 156
O'Sullivan's March, p. 157

Percussion Near and Far

Lightly stamp your foot on the floor…Pat your desk with your hand…

When you make sounds by striking something, you are playing **percussion.**

Make a list of instruments that fit this description. Which ones are pitched and which are nonpitched?

> **Percussion** instruments are pitched or nonpitched instruments that are played by striking, scraping, or shaking.

64

Footnotes

SKILLS REINFORCEMENT

▶ Creating Have students work in small groups to create an improvisation for percussion instruments. Students should include a variety of percussion instruments in their improvisations. Each instrument should have a distinct solo entrance. Invite each group to perform its improvisation for the class.

BUILDING SKILLS THROUGH MUSIC

▶ Language Display a transparency of the Semantic Map from Resource Book p. C-6. Write "Percussion Instruments" in the central box. Add "Shaking," "Scraping," and "Striking" as subcategory titles. Invite students to listen to *Theme and Variations for Percussion* **CD 4-5** and follow the listening map. Have them classify the percussion instruments they hear by the subcategories shown on the Semantic Map.

ACROSS THE CURRICULUM

▶ Social Studies Nigeria, Liberia, Chad, and the Ivory Coast are among the 15 countries that comprise the region known as West Africa. There are many large cities in this part of Africa, with large government and business buildings next to markets selling fish, animals, and fruits and vegetables. West Africa has become a world leader in the production of coffee, cacao, rubber, and palm oil.

Many people still live in small villages, in homes with traditional straw cone-shaped roofs. They do not have such everyday conveniences as electricity, running water, and indoor plumbing. Villagers make their living by farming or herding animals.

Percussion Variations

Listen to the various instruments used in *Theme and Variations for Percussion*. Point to the picture of each instrument as you hear it.

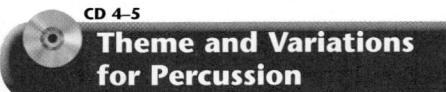
CD 4–5

Theme and Variations for Percussion

by William Kraft

The American composer William Kraft was born in Chicago in 1923. For many years, he was percussionist with the Los Angeles Philharmonic Orchestra.

Theme and Variations   LISTENING MAP

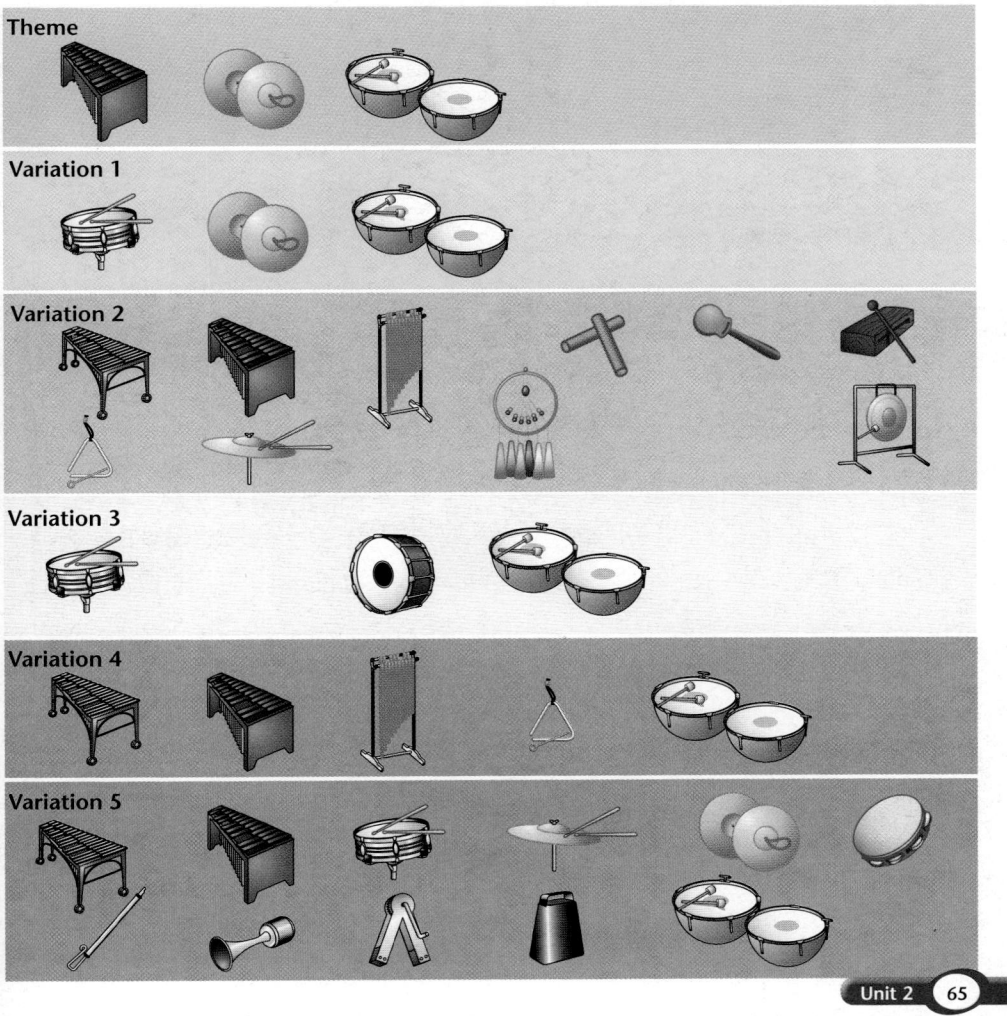

Theme

Variation 1

Variation 2

Variation 3

Variation 4

Variation 5

1 INTRODUCE

Conduct a review of percussion instruments by asking students to distinguish among a variety of musical timbres. Ask students to identify and name the instruments available in the classroom.

ASK If you were going to arrange the percussion instruments into categories or groups, what categories would you use and which instruments would belong to them? (pitched and nonpitched instruments)

Allow small groups of students to develop categories for classroom percussion instruments, then share their categories with the class.

2 DEVELOP

Listening

Invite students to turn to p. 64 and read the information about percussion instruments. Then have students preview the listening map on p. 65. Have them

- Identify the percussion instruments on the map.
- Review the term "theme and variations."

SAY The theme states a musical idea. Variations take the theme and change it in different ways. In *Theme and Variations for Percussion,* each variation is designed to showcase different percussion instruments.

To help students aurally identify excerpts of music from diverse genres, play the recording of *Theme and Variations for Percussion* **CD 4-5** and have students follow the map on p. 65 as they listen. Ask students to identify theme and variations form in the selection.

continued on page 66

AUDIENCE ETIQUETTE

▶ **Applause** Encourage students to be actively involved listeners and exhibit concert etiquette during varied live performances. Help them to know when to clap during various kinds of performances.

- **Orchestra/Band/Instrumental Ensemble/Choir—** Do not clap between movements in a symphony or other multi-section pieces of music. Wait until the conductor lowers his or her hands and steps off the podium before clapping.

- **Jazz—** During most jazz selections, different instrumentalists take turns improvising. It is appropriate to clap after each soloist is finished, even though musicians are still playing.

SPOTLIGHT ON

▶ **The Composer** William Kraft, a composer and a percussionist, was born in Chicago in 1923. During the 1950s, Kraft earned both bachelor and masters degrees from Columbia University in New York City. At that time, Columbia was the center of much cutting-edge experimental work in composition. From 1955 to 1981, he was timpanist with the Los Angeles Philharmonic Orchestra. He then became composer-in-residence for the Philharmonic, a position he held until 1985. Today, Kraft is still an active composer and teacher.

Use the following questions to help students focus their listening skills. Use all responses to engage students in a discussion of the composer's use of tempo, dynamics, timbre, and so on. Point out that there may be more than one "correct" answer. Encourage students to use standard terminology when explaining the performance on the recording.

 ASK Which variation was played in the slowest tempo? The quickest tempo?

 Which variation used only nonpitched percussion instruments?

Which variation was the softest? The loudest?

To learn more about the snare drum and xylophone, both featured in *Theme and Variations for Percussion*, refer students to Sound Bank pp. 518-519. Students can read descriptions of the instruments and listen to sound samples **CD 21-45**, **CD 21-55**.

Composing

 Have students

- Collaborate to create an eight-measure rhythm composition in a meter of their choice and notate it on the board.
- Clap or tap the rhythm.

SAY This rhythm is now our class theme, and we're going to create a set of percussion variations.

See Skills Reinforcement below to continue this activity.

Singing

 Next, have students

- Follow the music in their books as they listen to the recording of *"Ye jaliya da"* **CD 4-7** and focus their attention on the pronunciation of the words.
- Practice the words with Pronunciation Practice Track **CD 4-9** and Resource Book p. A-9.
- Sing the melody on a neutral syllable, such as *loo.*

 - Sing with the recording.

African Timbre

A wide variety of instruments are used by African musical groups. The different types of rattles and drums alone are quite numerous. In addition to percussion instruments, many different string instruments, flutes, and wooden or ivory horns can be found throughout the continent.

▲ *Axatse*
[ahks-AHT-see]

▲ *Mbira*
[m-BEE-rah]

▲ *Dundun*
[DOON - doon]

Listen to this montage of just a few African instruments.

CD 4–6
Montage of African Instruments

In this recording, the instruments are heard in the following order: *dundun, mbira,* and *axatse.*

66

Footnotes

SKILLS REINFORCEMENT

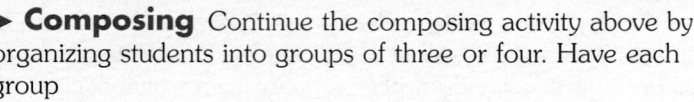

 ▶ **Composing** Continue the composing activity above by organizing students into groups of three or four. Have each group

- Practice the "theme" rhythm. Then create a variation on the rhythm using percussion instruments.
- Consider dynamics and tempo changes in its variation.
- Practice its variation and then perform it for the class.

After all groups have performed their variations, have students order them into a set to create a class "Theme and Variations" composition. Have the entire class perform the theme, then groups perform the variations in the order determined by students. Record the completed composition for student review and evaluation.

CULTURAL CONNECTION

▶ **Music in African Culture** Drums lie at the heart of African music. African musicians strive to communicate the many phases of life through music. Drums are played at many social and religious functions, including weddings and funerals. They have also been played to send messages over long distances.

Unlike in Western cultures, African drummers play more than just rhythms—they also play melodies. Drummers are highly respected members of society without whom no life cycle event would be complete.

Distant Drums

"*Ye jaliya da*" comes from West Africa. **Listen** for the *dundun, mbira,* and *axatse* as you sing.

 CD 4–7

Ye jaliya da

Folk Song from West Africa

Ye ja - li - ya   da ____   Al - lah le - ga ja - li - ya   da.

Ye ja - li - ya   da ____   Al - lah le - ga ja - li - ya   da.

M·U·S·I·C M·A·K·E·R·S

Babatunde Olatunji

Babatunde Olatunji [bah-bah-TOON-deh oh-lah-TOON-gee] (1927–2003) is the first West African drummer to become famous in the Western Hemisphere. Born in Nigeria, he spent his childhood listening to the drums that surrounded him. Many of his drum pieces have been inspired by his native country.

Listen to *Oya (Primitive Fire)*, a rhythmic depiction of the discovery of fire.

 CD 4–10
Oya (Primitive Fire)

written and performed by Babatunde Olatunji

Primitive Fire describes the lighting of the first fire, its mounting flames, and its slowly dying embers.

Listening

Invite students to turn to p. 66 and read about the African percussion instruments pictured on the page.

6a Play the recording of *Montage of African Instruments* **CD 4-6** and have students identify the instruments as they hear them.

Students may also read descriptions of the *axatse, mbira,* and *dundun* in the Sound Bank on pp. 514, 515, and 517.

Discuss with students the role of music in African culture. For more information, see Cultural Connection p. 66.

Singing

Play the recording of "*Ye jaliya da*" again. Have students

6b • Listen to each phrase, then sing along when it is repeated.

1c • Sing again, this time performing the entire song.

3 CLOSE

Listening

Have students read the information about the composition *Oya* and the artist Babatunde Olatunji on p. 67.

6b Then play the recording of *Oya* **CD 4-10.** Have students identify the instruments they hear, either verbally or in writing. Invite students to move to or play along with the music.

Element: TIMBRE ASSESSMENT

6b **Observation/Music Journal Writing** Play the recording of *Theme and Variations for Percussion* **CD 4-5** again and display the listening map transparency for the class. Invite individual students to point to each variation as it occurs in the music. Observe students' ability to aurally recognize the variations. Then ask students to write a brief description of each percussion timbre used in this piece.

 Unit 2 **67**

ACROSS THE CURRICULUM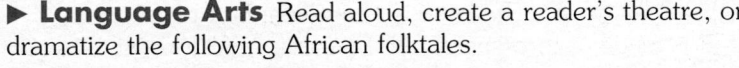

8b ▶ **Language Arts** Read aloud, create a reader's theatre, or dramatize the following African folktales.

• *Talk, Talk: An Ashanti Legend (Legends of the World Series)* by Deborah M. Chocolate (Troll, 1997). A delightful folktale about a farmer's surprise as stones, yams, a tree, and a dog begin to talk to him.

• *Mufaro's Beautiful Daughters: An African Tale* by John Steptoe (Lothrop Lee & Shepard, 1987). A beautifully illustrated African version of the Cinderella story.

• *Why the Sun and the Moon Live in the Sky: An African Folktale* by Elphinstone Dayrell (Houghton Mifflin, 1990). A story about the creation of the earth and sky.

TECHNOLOGY/MEDIA LINK

4c **Sequencing Software** Have students set three tracks to channel 10 (GM drum kit) and select a sound similar to an African percussion instrument. Then record a four-beat rhythm pattern on one track.

Select another sound for the next track and record a three-beat rhythm pattern. Record a two-beat pattern in the third track. Cut and paste each of the tracks carefully so that there are no rests between the repetitions and the tracks all end at 12 measures of four beats. Play all tracks at once while the class sings. Have students evaluate how well the sequence fits an African style.

Transparency Display the listening map transparency for *Theme and Variations for Percussion* as you play the recording.

LESSON AT A GLANCE

Element Focus	**TEXTURE/HARMONY** Partner songs
Skill Objective	**SINGING** Sing in harmony by performing two partner songs together
Connection Activity	**SOCIAL STUDIES** Compare and contrast country and city life-styles

MATERIALS

- "Home on the Range"   **CD 4-11**
  Recording Routine: Intro (8 m.); vocal; coda
- "Live in the City"   **CD 4-13**
  Recording Routine: Intro (4 m.); vocal; coda
- "Home on the Range/Live in the City"   **CD 4-15**
  Recording Routine: Intro (4 m.); vocal 1; interlude (8 m.); vocal 2; interlude (4 m.); vocals 1 & 2; coda
- **Resource Book** p. H-9
- keyboard, mallet instruments, bells

VOCABULARY

partner song   harmony

◆ ◆ ◆ National Standards ◆ ◆ ◆

1b Sing easy pieces with technical accuracy
1d Sing music written in two parts
2d Perform simple accompaniments by ear
4b Arrange pieces for voices and instruments
6c Understand and use basic principles of meter and chords in music analysis
7b Students use specific criteria for evaluating performances and offer constructive suggestions for improvement
8b Identify ways music relates to social studies and language arts

MORE MUSIC CHOICES

For more practice with partner songs:
"America, the Beautiful/Let Freedom Ring," pp. 76–77
"Play a Simple Melody," p. 72

Singing Partners

The cowboy's life on the range was lonely. Singing songs while driving cattle across the plains, and at night around the campfire, helped pass the time.

The words of "Home on the Range," a favorite song of the American West, were adapted from a poem written by Dr. Brewster Higley. First published in 1873, the song became popular again in the 1930s and was a favorite of President Franklin Roosevelt. **Sing** "Home on the Range."

Arts Connection

▲ *Singing Round Campfire,* P.V.E. Ivory, 1906.

Footnotes

SKILLS REINFORCEMENT

▶ **Keyboard/Mallets** Divide the class into three groups. Distribute keyboards, mallet percussion, or bells equally among groups. Have group 1 play the F chord (F-A-C); group 2, the C7 chord (C-E-G-B♭); and group 3, the B♭ chord (B♭-D-F). Have each group play its assigned chord at the appropriate time as the class sings "Home on the Range/Live in the City."

BUILDING SKILLS THROUGH MUSIC

▶ **Language** Lead students in a discussion of the lyrics of "Home on the Range" that describe the location of the singer. Discuss the thoughts and feelings the cowboy reveals about his work and the locale. Review "Laredo" on p. 10. Ask students how the two song's lyrics are similar and different.

CULTURAL CONNECTION

▶ **Trick Roping** The lasso is an integral part of a cowboy's life. It is made of three parts: the honda (a small loop at the end of the rope), the spoke (the unlooped end of the rope), and the loop (the large circle created by passing the spoke through the honda). A working cowboy uses it to catch a calf that has strayed from the herd. Some cowboys entertain their buddies with rope tricks. The tricks are named for the shape the lasso takes. They include the flat loop, the vertical loop, the Texas skip, and the butterfly. Trick roping was a popular competitive event in professional rodeos. The most famous "fancy roper" was Will Rogers, a vaudeville and radio performer from the early 1900s. Rogers spun a rope on stage while telling cowboy tales and jokes. A famous picture shows him performing the flat loop with thirty people standing in the middle of the loop!

Home on the Range

CD 4-11

s, l, t, @ r m f s

Traditional Song from the United States

Oh, give me a home where the buf - fa - lo roam, Where the

deer and the an - te - lope play; _____ Where sel - dom is

heard a dis - cour - a - ging word, And the skies are not cloud - y all

day. _____ Home, home on the range, _____ Where the

deer and the an - te - lope play; _____ Where sel - dom is heard a dis -

cour - a - ging word, And the skies are not cloud - y all day. _____

Unit 2 69

1 INTRODUCE

Have students

- Share their thoughts about the advantages and disadvantages of living in a rural area and living in a city.
- Listen to "Home on the Range" **CD 4-11** and "Live in the City" **CD 4-13.**
- Discuss what these songs say about living in the country and the city.

2 DEVELOP

Singing

Have students

- Sing "Home on the Range" **CD 4-11,** a song representative of American heritage, with the recording.
- Identify the $\frac{3}{4}$ time signature at the beginning of the song.

- Create a movement pattern that shows three beats to a measure, or conduct three-beat patterns.
- Sing "Home on the Range" while moving or conducting.

Then, have students turn to "Live in the City," on p. 71.

ASK What is the meter of this song? ($\frac{3}{4}$)

Have students

- Sing "Live in the City" **CD 4-13** with the recording.
- Create a different three-beat movement to perform with the song.
- Sing while moving in meter in 3.

continued on page 70

SPOTLIGHT ON

▶ **American Cowboys** In the 1860s, the U.S. saw the Great Plains as an area of expansion for raising cattle. The Great Plains became known as a "cattle kingdom" and out of it came a new kind of American—the cowboy. Cowboys—Native American, African American, Spanish, Mexican, and European—worked on ranches and rounded up the cattle to be herded to railroad centers. A chuck wagon carried the many needed items on the cattle drive. The team, which included six to eight cowboys, plus a cook, a trail boss, and one to care for the horses, was often on the trail for weeks at a time. The western cowboy adopted many Spanish words and skills of the *vaquero*, the Mexican cowboy. They wore *sombreros* (hats) and *chaps* (leg protectors), and they roped cattle with *lassos* or *lariats*.

TEACHER TO TEACHER

▶ **Slow vs. Fast Meter** $\frac{3}{4}$ meter has a different feel depending on the tempo. A slow $\frac{3}{4}$ feels lilting and tranquil. Though beat 1 is stressed, you feel all three beats in the measure at this tempo. A fast $\frac{3}{4}$ feels more raucous. You feel only beat 1.

Invite students to try "Home on the Range" at different speeds. Encourage them to show what the music feels like using their bodies. They may move around the room with a swagger or a lilt in their steps. They may conduct an imaginary orchestra. Your students will move if you provide a clear model and an inviting environment. As you watch your students, remember that their movements tell you what they are focusing on.

Unit 2 *Exploring Music* 69

6c **ASK In addition to the meter, what elements of music are the same in both songs?** (the key, the harmony, and chord structure)

What element of music is not the same? (the melody)

Explain that because the songs share meter, key, and chord structure, they can be sung at the same time as partner songs.

1d Divide the class into two groups—those who would like to live in a rural area and those who would like to live in a city. Invite the rural group to sing "Home on the Range," while the urban group sings "Live in the City" **CD 4-15.**

Exchange songs.

ASK What happens when the two songs are sung at the same time? (harmony is created)

Playing

Have students accompany each song using the bass xylophone/bass metallophone pattern on p. 70.

6c **ASK Do the songs use the same chords in the same pattern?** (yes)

SAY This chord structure allows the songs to be sung simultaneously.

Students may also enjoy playing a chordal accompaniment on keyboards or bells. (See Skills Reinforcement on p. 68.)

Creating

4b Divide the class into several groups and have each group create an arrangement of "Home on the Range" and "Live in the City." Ask each group to

- Create an appropriate musical introduction.
- Decide which song to sing first and which song to sing second before putting the songs together.
- Create a coda for the arrangement.
- Accompany the songs, using selected instruments.

Different Places

People choose to live in different places. Some people like a quiet country place, while others prefer living in cities, surrounded by sounds.

"Home on the Range" and "Live in the City" can be sung at the same time. When sung together, they are called **partner songs.** Partner songs share the same meter, chords, and key. What element of music do the two partners *not* share?

> **Partner songs** are two or more songs sung at the same time to create harmony.

Find "Live in the City." Then **perform** the two songs together.

Accompany Partner Songs

Play this part on bass xylophone or bass metallophone to accompany the partner songs.

Footnotes

SKILLS REINFORCEMENT

6c ▶ **Analyzing** Ask students to compare the melodic phrases in "Home on the Range" and "Live in the City," and then identify those phrases that are similar. Have students sing each pair of phrases, using hand signs and pitch syllables.

ACROSS THE CURRICULUM

8b ▶ **Language Arts** Encourage students to read about the poetry of the Old West in *Home on the Range: Cowboy Poetry* by Paul B. Janeczko (Dial, 1997). Invite them to dramatize their favorite cowboy poems and songs. They may also enjoy creating background scenery.

Live in the City

Words by Bryan Louiselle
Music by Buryl Red

CD 4–13

s, l, li, t, @ r m f s l

Some day __ I'll live in the city, __ I hear
mil - lions of peo - ple are run - ning __ a - round To the
mu - sic __ of tax - i horns blar - ing. __ Oh, what
I would - n't give for that beau - ti - ful sound. Yes, I'm
long - ing to be in __ the hus - tle __ and bus - tle: __
All night the lights are as bright as __ the __ day: They are
light - ing my way to the cit - y, __ And it's
there in the cit - y I know I will stay.

Sequencing Software Sequence parts that fit the chord symbols for "Home on the Range" and "Live in the City."

---

3 CLOSE

Element: TEXTURE/HARMONY — ASSESSMENT

7b **Performance/Self-Assessment** Have students sing "Home on the Range" and "Live in the City" together as partner songs **CD 4-15**. Have half the class sing "Home on the Range" and the other half sing "Live in the City."

Make a recording of the students' performance. Then play the recording and ask students to list ways to improve their harmony singing. List all possible improvements on the board.

Next, have students choose two or three "improvements." Allow time for them to practice, and then sing the songs again. Record their performance. Have students listen to their second recording and describe verbally or in writing how their singing improved.

MEETING INDIVIDUAL NEEDS

▶ **English Language Learners** Use visuals to illustrate "Live in the City." You may want to show pictures of New York or another large city. If possible, actual photographs are best. Have students name specific things in each photograph to help them extend and develop their vocabulary.

TECHNOLOGY/MEDIA LINK

Sequencing Software Invite students to arrange a simple accompaniment for "Home on the Range" and "Live in the City." Have students sequence bass parts and harmonic rhythm parts in meter in 3 that fit the chord symbols for the two songs.

If time permits, add melody tracks for "Home on the Range" and "Live in the City" to the sequence.

LESSON AT A GLANCE

Element Focus **TEXTURE/HARMONY** Partner songs

Skill Objective **SINGING** Sing in harmony by performing two partner songs together

Connection Activity **STYLE** Explore the lives and music of popular composers of the American musical theatre

MATERIALS

- "Play a Simple Melody" **CD 4-17**
  Recording Routine: Intro (4 m.); melody 1; interlude (4 m.); melody 2; interlude (4 m.); melodies 1 & 2
- keyboards, recorders, or other melody instruments

VOCABULARY

partner song   polyphonic texture

◆ ◆ ◆ ◆ **National Standards** ◆ ◆ ◆ ◆

1c Sing music from diverse genres
2b Perform two easy instrumental pieces with technical accuracy
4a Compose short pieces, demonstrating balance through music
4c Arrange, using electronic media
5a Read quarter, eighth, dotted, and whole notes in duple meter
6b Listen and analyze uses of texture in music from diverse genres
8b Identify ways music relates to language arts
9b Classify high-quality musical works by style and composer

MORE MUSIC CHOICES

For more practice with partner songs:
"Home on the Range," p. 68
"Live in the City," p. 71

Partner Songs

Partner songs are fun to sing. Irving Berlin, one of America's most loved songwriters, wrote a song in which the two sections can be sung as partner songs. Sing the first part of "Play a Simple Melody."

CD 4–17
Play a Simple Melody

Words and Music by Irving Berlin

PARTNER SONG 1:

Won't you play a sim-ple mel-o-dy
like my moth-er sang to me.
One with good old fash-ioned har-mo-ny.
Play a sim-ple mel-o-dy.

Footnotes

CULTURAL CONNECTION

▶ **"Humoresque" and "Old Folks at Home"** Czech composer Antonin Dvorák wrote the well-known "Humoresque" in 1894. Stephen Foster, one of America's most famous composers, wrote "Old Folks at Home" in 1851.

BUILDING SKILLS THROUGH MUSIC

▶ **Language** Invite students to suggest synonyms for the word "simple." List each synonym on the board and use each in a sentence to illustrate the meaning. Ask students how the composer described his idea of simple melodies.

ACROSS THE CURRICULUM

8b ▶ **Language Arts** Create a bulletin board of famous popular composers of the American musical theater (Jerome Kern, **9b** Richard Rodgers, Cole Porter, George Gershwin, Stephen Sondheim, and so on). Include the names of their most famous shows and song titles, and invite students to listen to selected examples in class.

For more about the life of Irving Berlin, encourage students to read *Say It With Music: A Story About Irving Berlin* by Tom Streissguth (Carolrhoda Books, 1993). This vividly written biography tells the story of the famous composer and describes the experiences and contributions of immigrants to America.

Play Me Some Rag

Now sing the second part of "Play a Simple Melody."

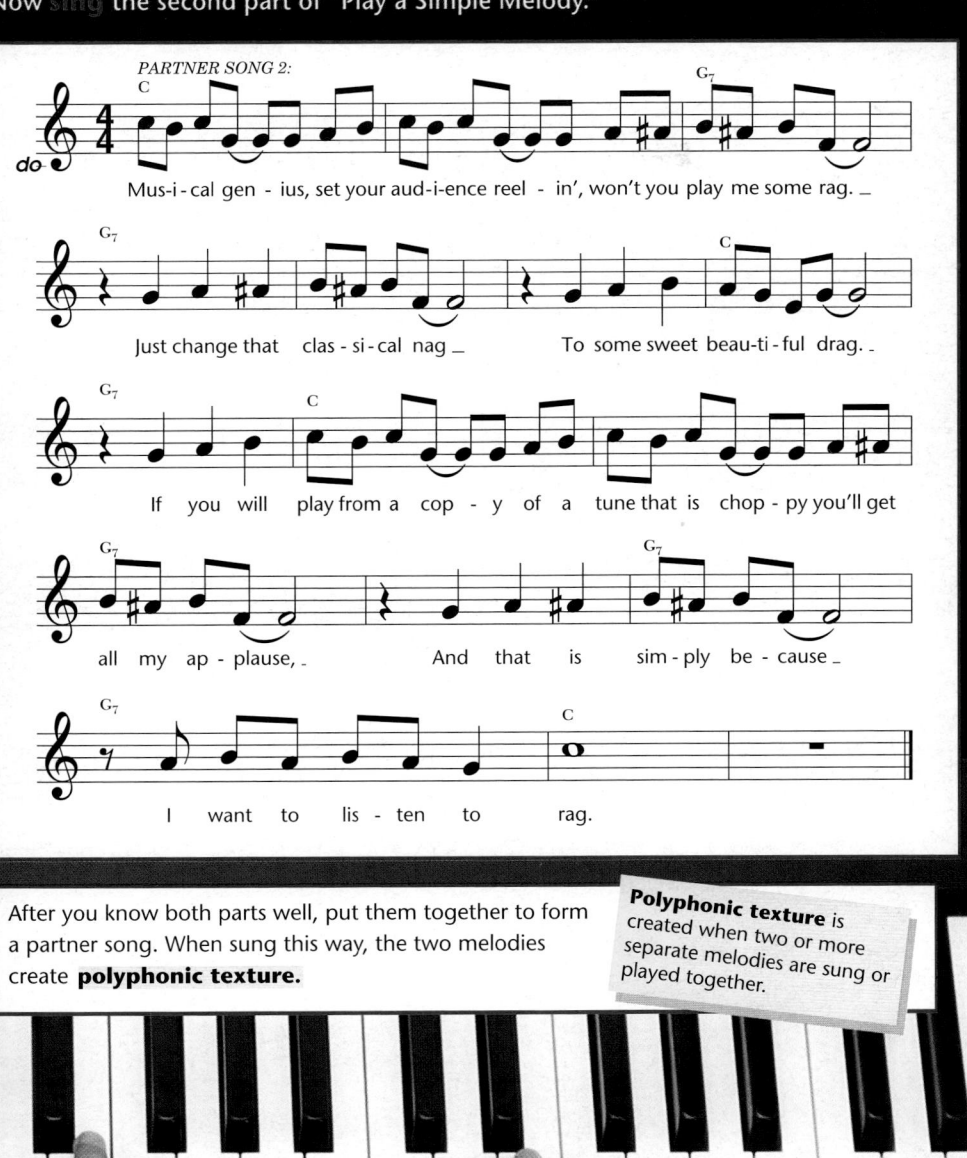

PARTNER SONG 2:

Mus-i-cal gen-ius, set your aud-i-ence reel-in', won't you play me some rag. _

Just change that clas-si-cal nag _ To some sweet beau-ti-ful drag. _

If you will play from a cop-y of a tune that is chop-py you'll get

all my ap-plause, _ And that is sim-ply be-cause _

I want to lis-ten to rag.

After you know both parts well, put them together to form a partner song. When sung this way, the two melodies create **polyphonic texture.**

Polyphonic texture is created when two or more separate melodies are sung or played together.

Unit 2 73

---

1 INTRODUCE

Remind students that partner songs are different songs that can be sung together because they have the same harmonic structure.

ASK Can you think of familiar songs that can be sung as partner songs? (The most familiar examples are "Row, Row, Row Your Boat," *"Frére Jacques,"* and "Three Blind Mice." Any two—or all three—of the songs can be sung as partner songs.)

Help students experiment briefly with their ideas for partner songs or with the songs suggested above.

2 DEVELOP

Listening

5a Play the recording of the first part of "Play a Simple Melody" (partner song 1) **CD 4-17** for students. Encourage them to follow the notation and words on p. 72 in their books.

Then play the second part of "Play a Simple Melody" (partner song 2), again asking students to follow along on p. 73 in their books.

ASK What was the same in both partner songs? (the meter, the key, the chord or harmonic structure, and the number of measures)

What was different? (the melody)

Singing

Have students

1c
- Sing the first part of "Play a Simple Melody" with the recording.

- Sing its partner song, the second part of "Play a Simple Melody," with the recording.

Divide the class into two groups. Have one group sing partner song 1 and the other group sing partner song 2. When this is successful, encourage groups to exchange parts.

continued on page 74

SKILLS REINFORCEMENT

4a ► **Creating** Help students compose their own partner songs using this set of simple steps.

1. Choose a short, familiar two-chord song and write the same number of bar lines on a blank piece of staff paper.

2. Determine where chord changes occur in the chosen song and write the same chord symbols above corresponding measures for the new song.

3. Find the number of beats per phrase in the song. Then create words that fit the length of each phrase.

4. Notate the rhythm of the new words. Then create a new melody using the new rhythm.

5. Notate the new melody in the blank measures.

SPOTLIGHT ON

► **The Piano** The piano is perhaps the most popular of all instruments. It is a member of the string family and the percussion family. When a pianist plays one of the keys on the keyboard, a hammer strikes a string causing the string to vibrate. The strings are attached to an iron frame that rests against a wooden soundboard. The soundboard magnifies the sound of the vibrating strings.

Although pianos have been around for centuries, they became the instrument we now know during the mid-1800s. Pianos were popular items found in many American homes in the late nineteenth and early twentieth centuries. Before the invention of the radio, phonograph, or television, it was the piano that many Americans turned to for relaxation and enjoyment during evening hours.

Unit 2 Exploring Music 73

Lesson 11 Continued

ASK What makes it possible to sing these two melodies at the same time? (they have the same chord structure)

SAY When we sing partner songs, the musical texture has a special name—polyphonic texture.

Direct students to p. 73 and read about polyphonic texture.

Direct students' attention to the information about Irving Berlin on p. 74 in their books. Discuss other Berlin songs that students might know or have heard.

(See Across the Curriculum p. 72, for a related classroom project.)

Playing

2b Direct students' attention to the melodies notated on p. 75. Invite volunteers to perform the melodies on two contrasting instruments (recorder and keyboard, for example) or as a duet on a keyboard or xylophone and metallophone.

Have students

- Perform each melody separately.
- Perform the melodies together.

6b **ASK** What do we call the musical texture when two different melodies are performed simultaneously? (polyphonic texture)

Creating

4a Have students work in small groups and create two short melodies that can be played together, or have them work as partners. Limit the pitches to C pentatonic (C, D, E, G, A). Suggest that their melodies start and end on C. Give students time to explore, then ask them to notate their melodies.

6b Have students play their partner melodies, one at a time, and then as partners. Ask the class to listen closely and apply criteria to determine whether the melodies are partners.

MUSIC MAKERS
IRVING BERLIN

Irving Berlin (1888–1989) was a Russian immigrant who came to the United States with his family in 1893, when he was five years old. Although Berlin could not read music, he composed about 1,500 songs. His songs are celebrated for their appealing melodies and easy-to-remember lyrics.

Three of Berlin's most popular songs are "White Christmas," "There's No Business Like Show Business," and "God Bless America." Berlin received a Grammy Lifetime Achievement Award in 1968.

▲ Irving Berlin performing (and recording) at his piano, a specially designed instrument that allowed Berlin to pl easily in different keys

74

Footnotes

Dvořák Meets Foster

This short piano piece combines two completely different melodies — *Humoresque,* by Antonín Dvořák, and *Old Folks at Home,* by Stephen Foster— to create another example of polyphonic texture. Play this piece on one piano. One person plays the top line while another person plays the bottom line. It will be easier if the bottom line is played an octave lower.

Using a keyboard or other melody instrument, create two short melodies that can be played together. Notate your melodies. Then ask a friend to be your musical partner.

3 CLOSE

Skill: SINGING   **ASSESSMENT**

1c **Performance/Observation** Have students sing both parts of "Play a Simple Melody" as partner songs, with the recording **CD 4-17.** Have half the class sing the first partner song and the other half sing the second partner song. Observe students' ability to maintain their assigned parts.

CULTURAL CONNECTION

▶ **Tin Pan Alley** Tin Pan Alley was originally the name of a district in New York occupied by music publishers. Many songwriters, arrangers, and music publishers located there. Tin Pan Alley and American popular music industry were one and the same. During this time, between the late 1880s until the middle of the twentieth century, many popular composers like Irving Berlin, Jerome Kern, George Gershwin, Cole Porter, and Richard Rodgers developed a type of popular song. This music had a melodic appeal, good form, new lyrics, and was very accessible. During the 1920s, America danced the Charleston. Tin Pan Alley provided the rhythm, and the fascination of new music knew no age limits.

TECHNOLOGY/MEDIA LINK

4c **CD-ROM** Have students use *Band-in-a-Box* to create and arrange a simple accompaniment for "Play a Simple Melody" by typing in the chord symbols and choosing a ragtime style. Complete the arrangement with an introduction and a coda.

Notation Software Have students use notation software to notate (Creating) and playback (Close) their arrangements. Post files to the school Web site.

LESSON AT A GLANCE

Element Focus	**TEXTURE/HARMONY** Partner songs
Skill Objective	**SINGING** Sing in harmony by performing two partner songs together
Connection Activity	**SOCIAL STUDIES** Learn the origin of "America, the Beautiful"

MATERIALS

- "America, the Beautiful"   **CD 4-19**
- "Let Freedom Ring"   **CD 4-21**
- "America, the Beautiful/Let Freedom Ring"   **CD 4-22**
  Recording Routine: Intro (6 m.); vocal
- *The Thunderer*   **CD 4-24**

VOCABULARY

harmony   texture   countermelody

◆ ◆ ◆ ◆ **National Standards** ◆ ◆ ◆ ◆

1b Sing easy pieces with technical accuracy
1d Sing music written in two parts
6b Listen and analyze uses of texture in music from diverse genres
6c Understand and use basic principles of chords in music analysis
8b Identify ways music relates to language arts and social studies
9b Classify high-quality musical works by composer

MORE MUSIC CHOICES

For more practice with partner songs:
"Home on the Range/Live in the City," pp. 68, 71
"Play a Simple Melody," p. 72

Harmony in Beauty and Song

Katharine Lee Bates was so impressed by the beauty of America that she created a poem, "America, the Beautiful." She later set the poem to the tune of an old hymn by Samuel A. Ward.

Sing "America, the Beautiful," one of our most beloved patriotic songs.

CD 4–19

America, the Beautiful

Words by Katharine Lee Bates

Music by Samuel A. Ward

O beau-ti-ful for spa-cious skies, For am-ber waves of grain,

For pur-ple moun-tain maj-es-ties A-bove the fruit-ed plain!

A-mer-i-ca! A-mer-i-ca! God shed His grace on thee,

And crown thy good with broth-er-hood, From sea to shin-ing sea!

Footnotes

ACROSS THE CURRICULUM

▶ **Language Arts** Read *America the Beautiful* by Katharine Lee Bates (Atheneum, 1993), a beautifully illustrated book to the text of the song. For information on the creation of this famous poem, read *Purple Mountain Majesties: The Story of Katharine Lee Bates and America the Beautiful* by Barbara Younger (Dutton, 1998). The students could read aloud or dramatize portions of this book.

BUILDING SKILLS THROUGH MUSIC

▶ **Social Studies** Invite the class to sing "America, the Beautiful." Using the United States flag, discuss the symbols on the flag, such as the stars and stripes and what they represent. Then have students discuss other patriotic symbols that are used in America.

SPOTLIGHT ON

8b ▶ **Katharine Lee Bates** Katharine Lee Bates (1859–1929) was a teacher, poet, and author. She was born in Falmouth, Massachusetts, in 1859. In the summer of 1893, Bates traveled by prairie wagon and mule up Pike's Peak in Colorado. She was very tired when she got to the top of the mountain, but she said, "When I saw the view, I felt great joy. All the wonder of America seemed displayed there, with sea-like expanse." Her joy inspired her to write the words for "America, the Beautiful." The poem first appeared on July 4, 1895, in a weekly journal called *The Congregationalist*. Bates received a small check from the journal, the only money she ever received for the poem. The poem was set to several different tunes. The tune that has become famous as "America, the Beautiful" was one originally written for another song by Samuel A. Ward (1847–1903).

Freedom Sings in Harmony

Sing "Let Freedom Ring." How is it similar to "America, the Beautiful"?

When sung together, "America, the Beautiful" and "Let Freedom Ring" create harmony.

1 INTRODUCE

8b Introduce "America, the Beautiful" by having students read the text on p. 76 in their books. Then share with students the information about Katharine Lee Bates and the origin of the song's words in Spotlight On, p. 76.

Have students

- Read the words of the song.
- Discuss the language used, such as *amber waves of grain,* and so on.

ASK What do the words mean? (accept various answers)

2 DEVELOP

Analyzing

1b Have students sing "America, the Beautiful" **CD 4-19** with the recording.

Ask students to look at "Let Freedom Ring" on p. 77 in their books.

SAY This is also a patriotic song. However, unlike "America, the Beautiful," it is a recently composed song.

Have the class sing "Let Freedom Ring" **CD 4-21** with the recording.

6c Have students compare the chord structure in both songs.

ASK Are the chords the same or different? (same)

SAY Because the chords are the same, the two melodies can be sung at the same time.

ASK What happens to the sound when two melodies are combined? (texture becomes thicker; harmony is expanded)

continued on page 78

MEETING INDIVIDUAL NEEDS

▶ **Singing in Harmony** Use the following suggestions to help all students perform partner songs.

Reinforcement Some students may have difficulty singing partner songs. Have these students form small groups to practice one of the partner songs in isolation.

On Target Many students will be able to successfully sing partner songs. For additional practice, invite all those wearing blue to sing one song and those not wearing blue to sing the other. These groupings force students to sometimes sing one of the partner songs while their neighbors sing the other.

Challenge Those students who master this lesson easily may be invited to perform one of the partner songs on keyboard or recorder to accompany the class.

ACROSS THE CURRICULUM

8b ▶ **Language Arts** Ask students to write paragraphs that begin "I think America is beautiful because . . ." Encourage students to illustrate their writings and display their work. Select students to read their compositions and to display their artwork at a performance that includes "America, the Beautiful."

Singing

Divide the class into two groups. Have one group sing "America, the Beautiful," and the other group sing "Let Freedom Ring" **CD 4-22.**

1d When students can sing each well, invite them to sing the songs together. Then have groups exchange songs and sing the two melodies together again.

Listening

Have students turn to p. 79 in their books and read about John Philip Sousa.

ASK **What famous band did Sousa lead?** (the United States Marine Corps Band)

Sousa is most famous for what kind of music? (marches)

Can you name a well-known Sousa march? (answers may vary, but students might know *Stars and Stripes Forever*)

Share information about the United States Marine Corps Band in Spotlight On below.

Listening

6b To help students aurally identify excerpts of music from diverse styles, play the recording of *The Thunderer* **CD 4-24.** Ask students to raise their hands if they hear a countermelody.

9b **ASK** **Did you hear a countermelody?** (yes)

What instruments play the countermelody? (brass)

Texture

Look at the two photos above. The one on the left shows a few mountain ridges. The one on the right shows several ridges that make up a mountain range. The number of lines or details in a piece of music, a photo, a painting, and so forth, is called **texture.**

Texture is the layering of sounds to create a thick or thin quality in music.

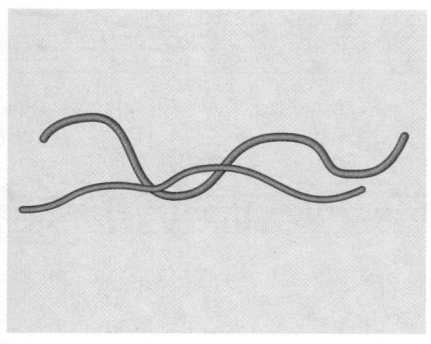 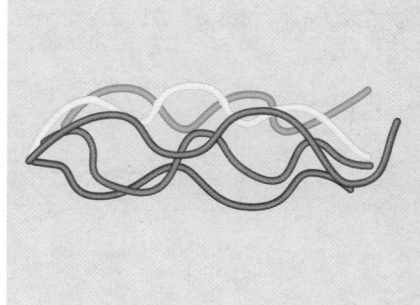

▲ If there are few lines, as in the photo at the top left of the page, we say the texture is thin.

▲ If there are several lines, as in the photo at the top right of the page, we say the texture is thick.

78

Footnotes

MEETING INDIVIDUAL NEEDS

▶ **Including Everyone** The majesty of the music and texts of "America, the Beautiful" and "Let Freedom Ring" provide an opportunity to sensitize students to issues concerning access in America. Students should know that federal and state laws now make it possible for people with disabilities to have more independence to travel and participate more fully in their communities. Give several examples (for example: lowered curbs; paths for wheelchairs in parks; accessible seating in concert halls; signing at public events; descriptions of events and sights in Braille). Have students watch for and relate situations that have either resulted in creating barriers or increasing access for people with disabilities.

SPOTLIGHT ON

▶ **The United States Marine Corps Band** America's oldest professional musical organization is the United States Marine Corps Band. Its primary mission is to provide music for the President of the United States and the commandant of the Marine Corps. It was established by an act of Congress in 1798 and was given the name "The President's Own" by President Thomas Jefferson, an accomplished musician himself.

In addition to year-round performances at the White House for ceremonies, receptions, and dinners, the band tours each fall through a region of the United States. This tour is a century-old tradition started by the band's legendary seventeenth director, John Philip Sousa.

Texture on the March

Listen to *The Thunderer*, composed by John Philip Sousa, America's "March King." You will hear two melodies played together on the repeat. What effect does this have on the texture?

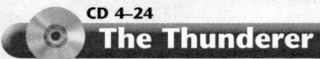

CD 4–24
The Thunderer
by John Philip Sousa

The Thunderer, one of more than 100 marches written by Sousa, was said to have been the composer's favorite.

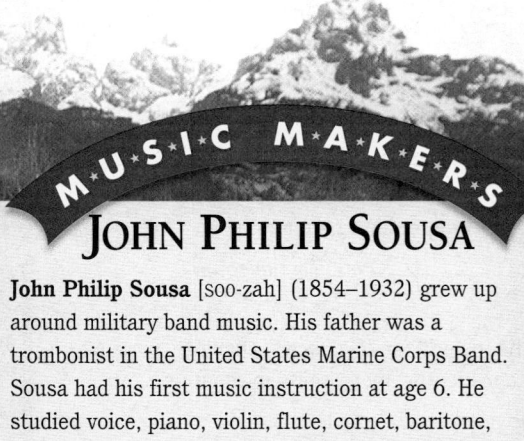

M·U·S·I·C M·A·K·E·R·S

JOHN PHILIP SOUSA

John Philip Sousa [soo-zah] (1854–1932) grew up around military band music. His father was a trombonist in the United States Marine Corps Band. Sousa had his first music instruction at age 6. He studied voice, piano, violin, flute, cornet, baritone, trombone, and alto horn. His father enlisted him in the Marines when he was 13 years old. After his discharge from the Marines, Sousa began performing on the violin and conducting orchestras for touring theater groups. In 1880 Sousa returned to his hometown, Washington, D. C., to lead the U.S. Marine Band. He became known as a brilliant bandmaster. After leaving the Marine Band, Sousa formed his own band and toured with his group until his death.

Tune In

Each branch of the military has its own band, but only the Marine Band is the official band of the President of the United States.

3 CLOSE

Element: TEXTURE/HARMONY **ASSESSMENT**

1d **Performance/Observation** Have students

- Write definitions of thin and thick texture.
- Form small groups.
- Sing "America, the Beautiful" and "Let Freedom Ring" simultaneously **CD 4-22**.

Pair weaker singers with stronger singers to give the weaker singers maximum encouragement and support.

Observe students' ability to accurately and independently perform the partner songs.

6b Have students describe how the texture changes as parts are added. (It becomes thicker.)

SKILLS REINFORCEMENT

6b ▶ **Listening** For an additional example of combining two different melodies, play the recording of "Do-Re-Mi" **CD 2-31**. Have students

- Determine the total number of different melodies used in the song. (3)
- Indicate which two melodies are sung at the same time. (Melodies 2 and 3)
- Map out the sequence of melodies. (1–1–2–3–2+3–1)
- Follow the sequence as the recording is played again and raise their hands when Melodies 2 and 3 are sung together.

SCHOOL TO HOME CONNECTION

▶ **Memorabilia** Have students take or find photographs of open spaces, cities and towns, and other places in the United States. Use the photographs to create a presentation to accompany the singing of "America, the Beautiful."

TECHNOLOGY/MEDIA LINK

Web Site To learn more about John Philip Sousa, invite students to visit *www.sfsuccessnet.com*.

WHAT DO YOU KNOW?

MATERIALS
- "*Da pacem, Domine,*" p. 62   **CD 3-38**
- **Resource Book** p. B-6

1. Write the five musical terms on the board. Ask students to match the musical terms on the left with the correct definitions by raising their hands.

2. Have students review the melody for "*Da pacem, Domine,*" p. 62. Ask them to find *do* and point to the notes in the music. (all *mi's, fa's* and *re's*)

For a more formal assessment, duplicate the Unit 2 assessment worksheet and have students work independently or in small groups to complete it. The worksheet is found on Resource Book p. B-6.

WHAT DO YOU HEAR?

MATERIALS
- *What Do You Hear?* 2   **CD 4-25**
- **Resource Book** p. B-6

Review the fact that meter refers to the way beats of music are grouped. Discuss duple meter (strong beat every two beats) and triple meter (strong beat every three beats).

Play the three examples, asking students to conduct as they listen and then choose their answers. The worksheet is found on Resource Book p. B-6.

What Do You Know?

1. Match the musical terms on the left with their correct definitions.

   a. *crescendo*   _____The part of a song that repeats, using the same melody and words

   b. *decrescendo*   _____Gradually get louder

   c. verse   _____The section of a song that is sung before the refrain

   d. refrain   _____Gradually get softer

2. Look at the melody for "*Da pacem, Domine,*" page 62. Where is *do*? Identify, by pointing in the music,

   a. All the notes that are called *mi.*

   b. All the notes that are called *fa.*

   c. All the notes that are called *re.*

What Do You Hear? 2

 CD 4–25

You will hear three songs. Listen and decide whether the music moves in meter in 2, or meter in 3.

1. Meter in 2   Meter in 3

2. Meter in 2   Meter in 3

3. Meter in 2   Meter in 3

Footnotes

ANSWER KEY

▶ What Do You Know?

1. a. *crescendo*—Gradually get louder

  b. *decrescendo*—Gradually get softer

  c. verse—The section of a song that is sung before the refrain

  d. refrain—The part of a song that repeats, using the same melody and words

2. a. *(fa)* B♭—treble clef third line (four)

  b. *(mi)* A—treble clef second space (five)

  c. *(re)* G—treble clef second line (five)

▶ What Do You Hear? 2

1. meter in 3

2. meter in 3

3. meter in 2

Perform, Create

What You Can Do

Choose Your Dynamics

Add *crescendo, decrescendo,* and other dynamics to the melody composition you created on page 75. Choose someone to help you perform your piece for the class.

Sing a Melody

Read the notation for *"A la puerta del cielo,"* page 60, using hand signs and pitch syllables. Then sing the song.

Keep a Journal

Keep a music journal. Divide it into three sections:
a. Vocabulary words
b. Musical forms
c. Lists of favorite songs and listening selections

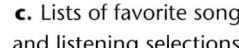

WHAT YOU CAN DO

MATERIALS
- *"A la puerta del cielo,"* p. 60   **CD 3-29**
- **Resource Book** p. B-7
- classroom percussion instruments

Play a Keyboard

Review dynamics that were learned in Unit 2. Invite students to volunteer to play the piano piece on p. 75 using *crescendo* and *decrescendo* in both parts. Ask another student to use different dynamics or the same piece in different places. Ask how dynamic differences can "change" a piece.

Sing a Melody

Have students review the notation for *"A la puerta del cielo,"* p. 60. Then have students individually or in small groups sing the song using hand signs and pitch syllables.

Keep a Journal

Have students start a music journal. The main sections could consist of vocabulary words, musical forms, and a list of favorite songs and listening selections. Another section could be favorite composers/performers. Invite students to include information from Unit 1, and continue updating information throughout the coming units. Encourage students not only to list words, forms, and songs, but also to describe any feelings about them.

TECHNOLOGY/MEDIA LINK

Rubrics Visit *www.sfsuccessnet.com* for rubrics to assess students' achievement in music skills.

Lesson	Elements	Skills

LESSON 1

CORE

Express Your Pride

pp. 86–89

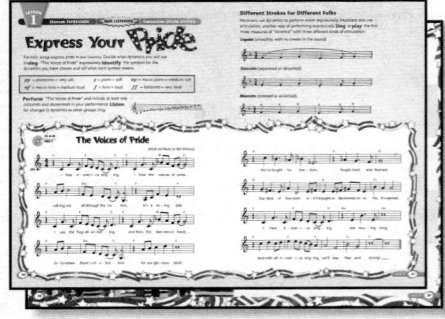

Element: Expression
Concept: Dynamics
Focus: Dynamics and articulation

Secondary Element
Rhythm: duration

National Standards
1a 1c 5c 6a 6c 8b 9c

Skill: Listening
Objective: Identify and describe dynamics and articulation

Secondary Skills
- **Singing** Choose dynamics for a song and perform
- **Reading** Read and describe the articulation markings
- **Moving** Demonstrate motions to conduct dynamic changes
- **Listening** Listen to the song and follow the listening map
- **Performing** Perform song with suggested articulation

SKILLS REINFORCEMENT
- **Conducting** Practice conducting a four-beat pattern
- **Vocal Development** Sing an exercise with a *crescendo* and *decrescendo*

LESSON 2

The Colors of Nature

pp. 90–93

Element: Rhythm
Concept: Pattern
Focus: $\frac{3}{4}$ meter

Secondary Element
Harmony: harmony in thirds

National Standards
1c 2a 4a 5a 5c 6c

Skill: Moving
Objective: Perform movement patterns in $\frac{3}{4}$ meter

Secondary Skills
- **Singing** Sing the song in Spanish and in English
- **Listening** Listen and move to show the meter of listening selection
- **Analyzing** Use a map to determine the origin of the song
- **Reading** Read the song and identify ties
- **Listening** Listen to the song and identify the hand claps
- **Singing** Sing the song in Spanish
- **Playing** Play small percussion instruments with the song

SKILLS REINFORCEMENT
- **Mallets** Create and play a xylophone accompaniment
- **Recorder** Play an accompaniment
- **Keyboard** Play a two-handed accompaniment
- **Moving** Help all students create body percussion patterns

---

LESSON 3

Music Lives On

pp. 94–95

Element: Rhythm
Concept: Pattern
Focus: Dotted-quarter and eighth notes

Secondary Element
Texture: imitation

National Standards
4c 5a 5d 6b 6c 8a

Skill: Reading
Objective: Read rhythm patterns in $\frac{3}{4}$

Secondary Skills
- **Listening** Listen to the song and determine a pattern of strong and weak beats
- **Analyzing** Analyze and use a tie to make the rhythm pattern of strong and weak beats
- **Listening** Listen to the recording and identify the dotted rhythm pattern

SKILLS REINFORCEMENT
- **Vocal Development** Exercise to improve student's intonation
- **Reading** Use music worksheet to reinforce patterns

Reading Sequence 9, p. 494

Connections

Music and Other Literature

Connection: Social Studies

Activity: Describe patriotic symbols and ways of expressing patriotism

ACROSS THE CURRICULUM **Language Arts** Read a book that celebrates America through poetry and art

CHARACTER EDUCATION **Pride** Discuss the meaning of and appropriate demonstration of pride

MOVEMENT **Creative Movement** Create choreography for the song

TEACHER TO TEACHER **Working in Groups** Assign students to groups with various levels of ability

MEETING INDIVIDUAL NEEDS **Cooperative Learning** Assign students in pairs to review dynamics and articulation

SCHOOL TO HOME CONNECTION **Pride** Interview friends and family about American pride

BUILDING SKILLS THROUGH MUSIC **Social Studies** Discuss the influence of patriotic songs

---

Song "The Voices of Pride"

Listening Selections
When Johnny Comes Marching Home
Listening Map *When Johnny Comes Marching Home*
M•U•S•I•C M•A•K•E•R•S
Roy Harris

More Music Choices
"*Hine mah tov*," p. 431
"Now's the Time," p. 445

ASSESSMENT

Observation Listen to selection and choose appropriate articulation terms

TECHNOLOGY/MEDIA LINK

Transparency Point to sections to help students follow a listening map

---

Connection: Culture

Activity: Participate in projects involving traditional Hispanic folk art and folktales

ACROSS THE CURRICULUM
Art Make art projects based on traditional Hispanic folk art
Language Arts Read Hispanic folktales

CULTURAL CONNECTION
The Art of Mexico Information about Hispanic folk art
Chiapas Information about the southernmost state in Mexico

MOVEMENT **Patterned Dance** Perform a patterned dance to the song

BUILDING SKILLS THROUGH MUSIC **Reading** Use song lyrics to describe sights in Mexico

---

Songs
"*De colores*" (Spanish)
"*De colores*" (English)
"*Chiapanecas*"
"The Girl from Chiapas"

Listening Selection *Janitzio* (excerpt)

More Music Choices
"Cattle Call," p. 344
"The Star-Spangled Banner," p. 488

ASSESSMENT

Performance/Observation Sing the song and move to show a three-beat pattern

TECHNOLOGY/MEDIA LINK

Notation Software Compose music in $\frac{3}{4}$ meter

Connection: Related Arts

Activity: Experience a poem about the lasting qualities of music

SPOTLIGHT ON **Music All Around Us** A time capsule representing music in America today

ACROSS THE CURRICULUM **Language Arts** Read a poem about the "infinite reach" of music

BUILDING SKILLS THROUGH MUSIC **Social Studies** Discuss things that change through time

---

Songs
"*Himmel und Erde*"
"Music Alone Shall Live"

Listening Selection *Viva la musica*
Poem "Music"

More Music Choices
"America, the Beautiful," p. 76

ASSESSMENT

Performance/Observation Sing the song and conduct a three-beat pattern

TECHNOLOGY/MEDIA LINK

Notation Software Notate the melody of a song and add chords

Lesson	Elements	Skills

LESSON 4 — CORE
Do You Feel the Rhythm?
pp. 96–99

Reading Sequence 10, p. 494

Element: Rhythm
Concept: Pattern
Focus: Dotted-rhythm patterns

Secondary Element
Harmony: chord changes

National Standards
1a 2a 5a 5d 6a 6b 6c 8b

Skill: Reading
Objective: Read from notation and perform dotted-rhythm patterns in $\frac{4}{4}$ time

Secondary Skills
• **Listening** Listen and discover the meter of the song
• **Performing** Conduct a four-beat pattern while listening to and singing the song
• **Analyzing** Analyze to determine which rhythm pattern is most like another
• **Playing** Play chords to accompany the song
• **Listening** Listen to the recording and compare the two versions of the song

SKILLS REINFORCEMENT
• **Listening** Clap rhythms to find dotted rhythms
• **Creating** Create a rhythm composition from notated rhythms on cards
• **Recorder** Play a countermelody

LESSON 5 — CORE
Form in Music
pp. 100–103

Element: Form
Concept: ABA
Focus: ABA form

Secondary Element
Rhythm: syncopation

National Standards
1c 2d 3a 4c 5d 6a 6b 8a 8b

Skill: Playing
Objective: Play an accompaniment to reinforce the concept of ABA form

Secondary Skills
• **Analyzing** Listen to the song to analyze story elements and form
• **Singing** Sing the song in the selection
• **Playing** Play the xylophone part to accompany the refrain of the song
• **Listening** Listen to the selection and discuss form and timbre
• **Analyzing** Compare and contrast painting to music selections
• **Moving** Create movements to show ABA form

SKILLS REINFORCEMENT
• **Creating** Create contrasting ostinatos for A and B sections
• **Creating** Improvise an instrumental accompaniment in ABA form
• **Mallets** Play an Orff arrangement

LESSON 6
A New Note
pp. 104–105

Reading Sequence 11, p. 495

Element: Melody
Concept: Pattern
Focus: Melodic Patterns using *ti*

Secondary Element
Rhythm: patterns

National Standards
1c 2a 4c 5a 5d 8b

Skill: Reading
Objective: Read and sing from notation melodic patterns using low *ti*

Secondary Skills
• **Singing** Echo-sing patterns
• **Analyzing** Discover low *ti*
• **Singing** Sing the *la-ti-do* pattern and then the song
• **Listening** Listen to a related listening selection

SKILLS REINFORCEMENT
• **Keyboard** Play descant with song
• **Signing** Learn a sign interpretation of the song
• **Notating** Complete a music reading worksheet
• **Reading** Practice *low ti* through composition and improvisation

Connections

Music and Other Literature

Connection: Related Arts
Activity: Discover how a pastoral scene is presented in a song and in a painting

- **ACROSS THE CURRICULUM**
  - **Language Arts** Read a book about a family of sheepherders from New Mexico
  - **Language Arts** Read a poem about the life of a shepherd
- **SPOTLIGHT ON** **The Artist** Information about Frank Reed Whiteside
- **TEACHER TO TEACHER**
  - **Program Music** Use visualization while listening to program music
  - **Reading New Rhythm Patterns** Use ties to create new rhythms
- **BUILDING SKILLS THROUGH MUSIC** **Language** Use sound effects to accompany the poem

Song "Don't You Hear the Lambs?"

Listening Selection *Don't You Hear the Lambs?*

Arts Connection *The Shepherd*

M·U·S·I·C M·A·K·E·R·S
Mike Seeger

Poem "The Shepherd"

More Music Choices
"Ama-Lama," p. 142

ASSESSMENT

Performance/Observation
Match rhythm patterns to song rhythms and perform patterns

Show What You Know!
Mid-unit assessment

TECHNOLOGY/MEDIA LINK

Sequencing Software
Use digital audio to record and evaluate a performance

Connection: Related Arts
Activity: Discover structure in music and art

- **TEACHER TO TEACHER** **Hearing Chord Changes** Move to show chord changes
- **CULTURAL CONNECTION** **Spirituals** Historic and cultural context of spirituals
- **ACROSS THE CURRICULUM**
  - **Social Studies** Read about the founding of the Fisk School and the Jubilee Singers
  - **Language Arts** Read poems and determine their similar structure
- **AUDIENCE ETIQUETTE** **A Museum Visit** Create a set of behavior guidelines for visiting museums
- **BUILDING SKILLS THROUGH MUSIC** **Theatre** Create a dramatization of an African American spiritual

Song "Joshua Fought the Battle of Jericho"

Listening Selections *Standin' in the Need of Prayer*

Arts Connection *Going to Church*

More Music Choices
"Happy Days Are Here Again," p. 284
"Sing, Sing, Sing!" p. 340

ASSESSMENT

Performance/Observation
Perform the song in groups and demonstrate form

TECHNOLOGY/MEDIA LINK

Sequencing Software
Compose music in ABA form using sequencing software

Connection: Culture
Activity: Discuss the culture of Wales

- **CULTURAL CONNECTION** **Wales** Background information about Wales
- **BUILDING SKILLS THROUGH MUSIC** **Math** Compute the average number of Haydn's compositions written each year

Song "All Through the Night"

Listening Selection *All Through the Night*

M·U·S·I·C M·A·K·E·R·S
Franz Joseph Haydn

More Music Choices
"I Love the Mountains," p. 34
"Blowin' in the Wind," p. 382

ASSESSMENT

Performance/Observation
Sing the song with pitch syllables and hand signs including low *ti*

TECHNOLOGY/MEDIA LINK

MIDI/Sequencing Software Use MIDI song file to explore tempo, dynamics, and orchestration

Lesson	Elements	Skills

LESSON 7   CORE
Same Note...Different Place
pp. 106–107

> Reading Sequence 12, p. 495

Element: Melody
Concept: Pattern
Focus: Melodic patterns using low *ti*

Secondary Element
Texture: countermelody

National Standards
1c   2a   5a   5d   6c

Skill: Reading
Objective: Read and sing from notation melodic patterns using *low ti*

Secondary Skills
- **Singing** Sing the song in Hebrew with the recording
- **Analyzing** Review that the distance between low *ti* and *do* is half a step
- **Reading** Identify *ti* in the patterns

SKILLS REINFORCEMENT
- **Notating** Write a countermelody
- **Recorder** Practice leaps on recorders and accompaniment
- **Mallets** Play an Orff arrangement

LESSON 8
Learn by Ear and Eye
pp. 108–109

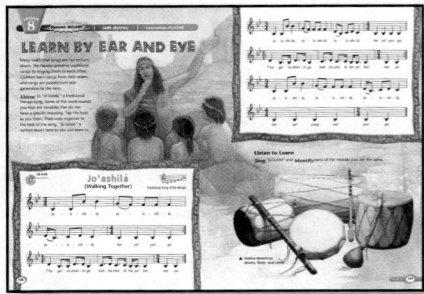

Element: Melody
Concept: Pattern
Focus: Melodic Patterns

Secondary Element
Rhythm: meter

National Standards
1c   2c   6a   6c   8b

Skill: Moving
Objective: Move to the beat of a Navajo song

Secondary Skills
- **Singing** Sing and follow song notation; identify like phrases in the melody
- **Moving** Walk to the beat while reflecting on an important Navajo concept

SKILLS REINFORCEMENT
- **Listening** Discover the traditional timbres found in Native American music

---

LESSON 9   CORE
Winds of the World
pp. 110–113

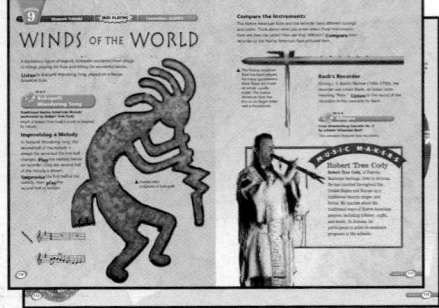

Element: Timbre
Concept: Instrumental
Focus: Flute and recorder timbres

Secondary Element Form: question and answer

National Standards
2a   2d   3b   4c   6a   6b   7b   8b

Skill: Playing
Objective: Play improvised and composed melodies on recorder

Secondary Skills
- **Listening** Describe sounds of Native American instruments in selection
- **Improvising** Improvise an eight-beat melody using given notes
- **Listening** Compare recorders to Native American flutes; recognize recorder timbre in an orchestral work
- **Composing** Compose melodies on given notes
- **Listening** Describe sounds of Japanese flutes

SKILLS REINFORCEMENT
- **Recorder** Post a list of recorder tips
- **Listening** Listen to flute selections

Connections

Music and Other Literature

Connection: Culture

Activity: Discuss the significance of the Torah in Jewish heritage

ACROSS THE CURRICULUM **Social Studies** Discover more about Jewish heritage

CULTURAL CONNECTION **The Torah** Information about the Torah

BUILDING SKILLS THROUGH MUSIC **Language** Discuss the theme of the song

Songs
"*Dundai*" (Hebrew)
"*Dundai*" (English)

More Music Choices
"*Ego sum pauper*" ("Nothing Do I Own"), p. 158

ASSESSMENT

Performance/Observation
Sing the song with pitch syllables to demonstrate low *ti*

Show What You Know!
Mid-review assessment

TECHNOLOGY/MEDIA LINK
Web Site More information about Middle Eastern music.

Connection: Culture

Activity: Discuss Navajo art and history

CULTURAL CONNECTION **Navajo Art** Characteristics and cultural significance of Navajo artwork

SPOTLIGHT ON **The Navajo Nation** History of the relocation

SCHOOL TO HOME CONNECTION **Cultures** Share symbols of culture and heritage

BUILDING SKILLS THROUGH MUSIC **Language** Write about about a nursery rhyme, story, or song learned from elders

Song "*Jo'ashila*"

More Music Choices
"Haliwa-Saponi Canoe Song," p. 302
"Zuni Sunrise Call," p. 396
"Green Corn Song," p. 462

ASSESSMENT

Performance/Observation
Sing the song with movement to demonstrate melodic pattern

TECHNOLOGY/MEDIA LINK
Electronic Keyboard Play drum and rattle sounds to accompany the song

---

Connection: Science

Activity: Discuss acoustical principles related to the construction of flutes

SPOTLIGHT ON **The Legend of Kokopelli** Legend of an ancestral spirit of the Hopi group

CULTURAL CONNECTION
Native American Flutes Information on the spiritual and social importance of flutes
Flutes Around the World Stories about flutes from different cultures

ACROSS THE CURRICULUM **Math** Measure and graph the lengths of flutes, recorders, or whistles; discover that the length of the air column is related to the pitch of the note being played

CHARACTER EDUCATION **Respect** Discuss the meaning of respect

SCHOOL TO HOME CONNECTION **Create Instruments** Design and construct wind instruments

BUILDING SKILLS THROUGH MUSIC **Language** Describe timbre and performance styles of different flutes

Listening Selections
Kokopelli Wandering Song
"Allegro" from *Brandenburg Concerto No. 4* (excerpt)
Shika no tone (The sound of Deer Calling to One Another) (excerpt)
Syrinx
Prelude to the Afternoon of a Faun (excerpt)
M·U·S·I·C M·A·K·E·R·S
  Robert Tree Cody
  Claude Debussy
Arts Connection *Woman Playing Shakuhachi*

More Music Choices
"Haliwa-Saponi Canoe Song," p. 302
"Green Corn Song," p. 462

ASSESSMENT

Performance/Observation
Improvise question and answer phrases on recorder or flute

TECHNOLOGY/MEDIA LINK
Web Site More information about flutes around the world

Lesson	Elements	Skills

LESSON 10
Songs About Nature

pp. 114–115

Element: Texture/Harmony
Concept: Harmony
Focus: Descant

Secondary Element
Form: AABA

National Standards
1d 2a 6a 7b 8b

Skill: Singing
Objective: Sing a song with a descant

Secondary Skill
• **Listening** Listen and follow the notation of the melody

SKILLS REINFORCEMENT
• **Playing** Play descant on recorder or band instruments
• **Recorder** Play a countermelody

LESSON 11
Singing Together

pp. 116–117

Element: Texture/Harmony
Concept: Harmony
Focus: Countermelody

Secondary Element
Rhythm: duration

National Standards
1d 2a 2d 5c 7b 8b

Skill: Singing
Objective: Sing a song with a counter-melody

Secondary Skills
• **Listening** Listen to hear the meter of a song
• **Playing** Accompany the song on keyboard and perform the countermelody on pitched instruments

SKILLS REINFORCEMENT
• **Guitar** Accompany the song using chords
• **Mallets** Play an Orff arrangement

LESSON 12   CORE
Sing of America's Beauty

pp. 118–121

Element: Texture/Harmony
Concept: Harmony
Focus: Countermelody

Secondary Element
Timbre: instrumental

National Standards
1d 2a 2d 3a 5c 6b 7b
8a 8b

Skill: Playing
Objective: Accompany a song on key-board

Secondary Skills
• **Listening** Listen for harmony in the song
• **Singing** Sing the melody with the harmony added
• **Performing** Play chord accompaniment on keyboard; improvise using different rhythm patterns
• **Listening** Listen and discuss instrumentation in selection
• **Creating** Create a new verse for the song
• **Listening** Discuss recording melodies

SKILLS REINFORCEMENT
• **Performing** Perform an arrangement with added accompaniments
• **Mallets** Play an Orff arrangement
• **Guitar** Play a guitar accompaniment

Connections

Music and Other Literature

Connection: Language Arts
Activity: Relate a poem about a tree to a folk song from Wales

- **ACROSS THE CURRICULUM** **Language Arts** Read a poem about the beauty of trees
- **CULTURAL CONNECTION** **Arbor Day** Information about Arbor Day
- **BUILDING SKILLS THROUGH MUSIC** **Science** Discuss the importance of trees in the environment

Song "The Ash Grove"

Poem "Trees"

More Music Choices
"Roll On, Columbia," p. 116
"This Land Is Your Land," p. 118

ASSESSMENT

Music Journal Writing Self evaluation in singing harmony and song learned in harmony

TECHNOLOGY/MEDIA LINK
MIDI/Sequencing Software Use MIDI song file as an aid to learning melody and descant parts

---

Connection: Social Studies
Activity: Locate on a map places mentioned in the text of a song

- **ACROSS THE CURRICULUM** **Social Studies** Locate places mentioned in the song lyrics
- **TEACHER TO TEACHER** **Countermelodies** Tips for teaching countermelodies
- **SCHOOL TO HOME CONNECTION** **Class Project** Research the most important river or waterway in the region and create a class song or poem
- **BUILDING SKILLS THROUGH MUSIC** **Social Studies** Discuss the natural geography features and man-made changes listed in the text of the song

Song "Roll On, Columbia"

More Music Choices
"Battle Hymn of the Republic," p. 274

ASSESSMENT

Performance/Observation Perform a song with a countermelody

TECHNOLOGY/MEDIA LINK
Sequencing Software Use digital audio to record melody and countermelody

---

Connection: Related Arts
Activity: Discuss ways in which a similar topic is presented in different art forms

- **ACROSS THE CURRICULUM**
  Social Studies Locate on a map places mentioned in song lyrics
  Language Arts Read a book about the life and music of Woody Guthrie
- **SPOTLIGHT ON**
  Woody Guthrie Information about the singer/songwriter
  The Composer Information about Virgil Thomson
- **TEACHER TO TEACHER** **Ribbon of Highway** Use a road atlas to trace highway routes across the United States from coast to coast
- **BUILDING SKILLS THROUGH MUSIC** **Reading** Discuss how dynamic changes emphasize different ideas expressed in the song

Song "This Land is Your Land"

Listening Selections
This Land Is Your Land
"Finale" from *The River Suite* (excerpt)
Poem "The River" (excerpt)

More Music Choices
"Deck the Hall," p. 474

ASSESSMENT

Performance/Observation Perform the song with countermelody and assess competence

TECHNOLOGY/MEDIA LINK
MIDI/Sequencing Software Use MIDI song file as an aid for learning melody and descant parts of song

INTRODUCING THE UNIT

Unit 3 presents the next step in a sequenced approach to understanding music elements. Music skills—reading, performing, creating, listening, moving—are the means by which students gain an understanding of these concepts. Presented on p. 83 is a brief overview of the skills that are assessed in this unit. (See below and pp. 84–85 for unit highlights of related curricular experiences.)

For a more detailed unit overview, see Unit at a Glance, pp. 81a–81h.

UNIT PROJECT

Invite students to make a "Music in Style" class list of musical styles they know. Organize the list in three columns: Style, Characteristics, and Example. Working as a class, have students add three or four styles to the list. For example, they might add "rock" in the Style column; "uses guitars, drums, keyboards, and vocals" in the Characteristics column; a rock musician or "group" in the Example column.

Explain to students they will be adding to the "Music in Style" list as they work on Unit 3. Invite them to

• Preview the songs by looking through the unit.

• Identify any styles of music they recognize.

You may wish to add style words to the list as students identify them. Add characteristics and examples from each lesson.

What Makes a Swing Song Swing?

During the 1940s, jazz bands and singers made swing music popular in the United States. Swing was a dance, too! In a swing song, the eighth notes are performed in swing rhythm, unevenly instead of evenly.

Tap the rhythm below using even eighth notes. Then tap the rhythm with "swing" eighth notes. Find this rhythm in "Teach Me to Swing," on page 84.

ACROSS THE CURRICULUM

Unit Highlights The following interdisciplinary activities in this unit are related to the music elements presented in the lessons. See Unit at a Glance pp. 81a–81h, for topical descriptions presented according to lesson sequence.

▶ **ART/RELATED ARTS**

• Create art projects based on traditional Hispanic folk art (p. 90)

▶ **LANGUAGE ARTS**

• Read a book that celebrates America through poetry and art (p. 86)

• Read a hispanic folk tale (p. 90)

• Read and discuss a poem about music (p. 95)

• Read a book about a family of sheepherders in New Mexico (p. 96)

• Read a poem about a shepherd's life (p. 98)

• Read poems and determine their structure (p. 102)

• Read a well-known poem about trees (p. 114)

• Read books about the qualities of America and the life and music of Woody Guthrie (p. 120)

▶ **MATHEMATICS**

• Discover the relationship between length of instruments and pitch of notes (p. 111)

▶ **SOCIAL STUDIES**

• Learn about the Fisk School and the Fisk University Jubilee Singers (p. 101)

• Learn about Jewish heritage (p. 106)

• Locate places on a map; research facts and information about the region (p. 116)

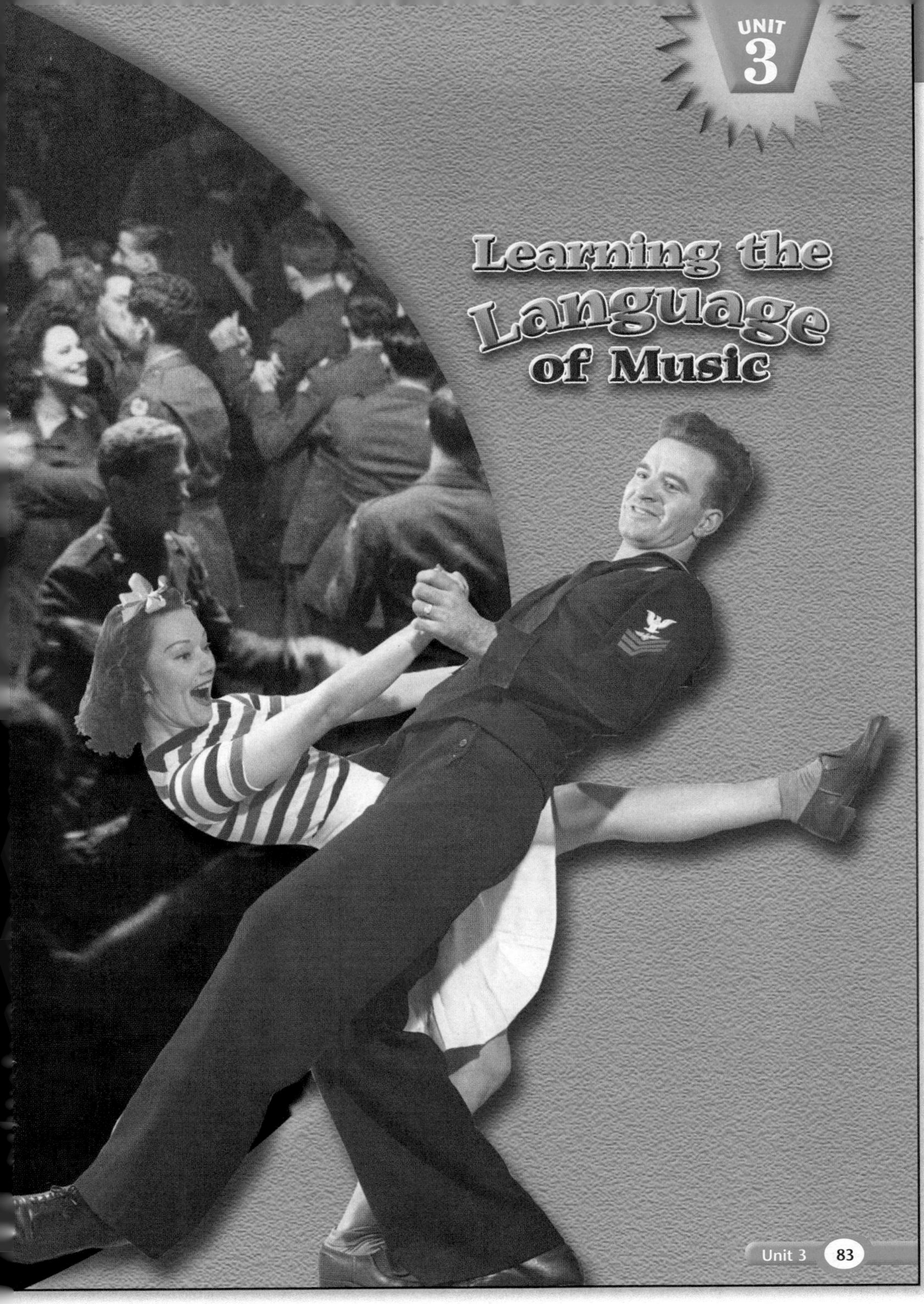

Learning the Language of Music

MUSIC SKILLS ASSESSED IN THIS UNIT

Reading Music: Rhythm

- Read and count the rhythm of a song in $\frac{3}{4}$ meter (p. 95)
- Read and count dotted rhythms in meter in 4 (p. 99)

Reading Music: Pitch

- Identify *la-ti-do* patterns in a song; read a song melody using pitch syllables and hand signs (p. 105)
- Read a song from staff notation using pitch syllables and hand signs (p. 107)

Performing Music: Singing

- Sing songs from Mexico in $\frac{3}{4}$ meter (p. 92)
- Sing a folk hymn from the Southern United States (p. 99)

Moving to Music

- Move to show three-beat patterns in a song (p. 92)
- Create movements to show ABA form (p. 103)

Performing Music: Playing

- Perform an accompaniment using percussion and melody instruments (p. 103)
- Play melody patterns on recorder (p. 113)

Creating Music

- Improvise three-beat ostinatos (p. 92)
- Compose melody patterns for recorder using D,F, G, A, and C (p. 113)

Listening to Music

- Listen and identify articulation (p. 89)
- Listen and compare two versions of an American folk hymn (p. 99)

CULTURAL CONNECTION

Unit Highlights The musical literature in this unit provides many opportunities for students to explore a variety of world cultures. See Unit at a Glance, pp. 81a–81h, for topical descriptions presented according to lesson sequence.

▶ AFRICAN/AFRICAN AMERICAN

- Discuss historical and cultural context of spirituals (p. 101)
- Read about an African girl who learns to play the songs of native birds on her flute (p. 112)

▶ AMERICAN REGIONAL

- Discover the history and traditions of Arbor Day (p. 115)

▶ EUROPEAN

- Explore the history and culture of Wales (p. 104)
- Learn about the Torah and its relation to the Christian Bible (p. 107)

- Read a story of a flute player who plays the songs of nature (p. 112)

▶ LATIN AMERICAN

- Learn about visual arts and crafts of Mexico (p. 91)
- Read about the Mexican state of Chiapas (p. 92)

▶ NATIVE AMERICAN

- Discuss symbols in Navajo artwork (p. 108)
- Explore the spiritual and social importance of flutes in the Native American culture (p. 110)

OPENING ACTIVITIES

> **MATERIALS**
> - "Teach Me to Swing" **CD 4-28**
>   **Recording Routine:** Intro (4 m.); vocal

Moving

Divide the class into two groups. Invite one group to create movements for the first section of "Teach Me to Swing." Explain to students that in swing style, eighth notes have an uneven feel. Encourage them to mirror this uneven feel in the movements they create. Suggest that they try to bring out the meaning of the words.

Invite the second group to create movements for the scat singing section of the song. Have students make their movements considerably different from those of the first group.

Analyzing

Review and practice with the class any parts of the song that might be difficult for them.

Call attention to

- The indication at the top left of the score showing the two eighth notes are played as a quarter-eighth triplet.
- The $\frac{4}{4}$ time signature, the repeat signs, and the first and second endings.
- The *D.C. al Coda* and review its meaning.

Sing that Swing!

Sing "Teach Me to Swing." Swing songs sometimes include "scat" singing. **Listen** for the scat parts and swing!

Teach Me to Swing
Words and Music by Kirby Shaw

ASSESSMENT

Unit Highlights This unit includes a variety of strategies and methods, described below, to track students' progress and assess their understanding of lesson objectives. Reproducible masters for Show What You Know! and Review, Assess, Perform, Create can be found in the Resource Book.

▶ **FORMAL ASSESSMENTS**

The following assessments, using written language, cognitive, and performance skills, help teachers and students conceptualize the learning that is taking place.

- **Show What You Know!** Element-specific assessments, on the student page for Rhythm (p. 98) and Melody (p. 107)
- **Review, Assess, Perform, Create** This end-of-unit activity (pp. 122–123) can be used for review and to assess students' learning of the core lessons in this unit.

▶ **INFORMAL ASSESSMENTS**

At the close of each Teacher's Edition lesson in this unit, one of the following types of assessments is used to evaluate the learning of the key element focus or skill objective.

- Performance/Observation (pp. 93, 95, 99, 103, 105, 107, 109, 113, 117, 121)
- Observation (p. 89)
- Music Journal Writing (p. 115)

▶ **RUBRICS**

Visit *www.sfsuccessnet.com* for rubrics to assess students' achievement in music skills.

Improvising

Practice any difficult parts such as the quarter-note triplets, the slides, and the syncopated rhythms. Have students say the scat words slowly at first. After students can speak the piece in rhythm, encourage them to sing the song.

INNOVATIVE TEACHER SUPPORT FOR THIS UNIT

- **MAKING MUSIC DVD, Grade 5** contains video segments that support lessons, including signing and movement.
- **MAKING MUSIC with Movement and Dance** provides more opportunities for large group activities in music or physical education classes.
- **MAKING MUSIC with Technology** provides lesson plans for many technology applications; includes MIDI files.
- *¡A cantar!* features recorded songs and lessons from around the Spanish-speaking world; includes strategies for bilingual classes and for English-speaking teachers working with Spanish-speaking students.
- **Bridges to Asia** features recorded songs and lessons from Asian and Pacific region cultures.
- *www.sfsuccessnet.com* provides an online lesson planner to conveniently create lesson plans at school or at home. Includes rubrics for assessment, lesson modifications to meet the needs of all students, performance musicals based on program content, and more.

Unit 3 **85**

TECHNOLOGY/MEDIA LINK

Unit Highlights The following components are used in this unit to reinforce and expand students' understanding of music elements and related themes. See Unit at a Glance, pp. 81a–81h, for a descriptive listing according to lesson sequence.

▶ **ELECTRONIC KEYBOARD**

- Play drum and rattle sounds with a Native American song (p. 109)

▶ **MIDI/SEQUENCING SOFTWARE**

- Record a class accompaniment and assess the performance (p. 99)
- Sequence eight-measure melodies (p. 103)
- Incorporate tempo, dynamic, and orchestration changes for a MIDI song file (p. 105)
- Use a MIDI song file to help students learn the melody and descant of a song (p. 115)

- Record a two-part song and assess tone pitch and accuracy (p. 117)
- Use a MIDI song file to help students learn the melody and countermelody of a song (p. 121)

▶ **NOTATION SOFTWARE**

- Notate a piece in $\frac{3}{4}$ meter (p. 93)
- Notate a song melody (p. 95)

▶ **TRANSPARENCY**

- Display a listening map illustrating an orchestral piece (p. 89)

▶ **WEB SITE**

- Go to *www.sfsuccessnet.com* for more information about Middle Eastern music (p. 107) and flutes from around the world (p. 113)

LESSON AT A GLANCE

Element Focus   **EXPRESSION** Dynamics and articulation

Skill Objective   **LISTENING** Identify and describe dynamics and articulation

Connection Activity   **SOCIAL STUDIES** Describe patriotic symbols and ways of expressing patriotism

MATERIALS

- "The Voices of Pride"   CD 4-30
   Recording Routine: Intro (4 m.); vocal; interlude (6 m.); vocal
- "When Johnny Comes Marching Home"   CD 9-13
- *When Johnny Comes Marching Home*   CD 4-32
- writing paper
- **Resource Book** p. J-5

VOCABULARY

dynamics	*crescendo*	*decrescendo*
legato	*staccato*	*marcato*

◆ ◆ ◆ ◆ National Standards ◆ ◆ ◆ ◆

1a Sing accurately in small ensembles
1c Sing music with appropriate expression
5c Identify and define standard symbols for articulation and dynamics
6a Listen and describe events in music using appropriate terms
6c Understand and use basic principles of meter in music analysis
8b Identify ways music relates to language arts
9c Compare, in several cultures, functions music serves

MORE MUSIC CHOICES

For more practice with dynamics and articulation:
"*Hine mah tov,*" p. 431
"*Now's the Time,*" p. 445

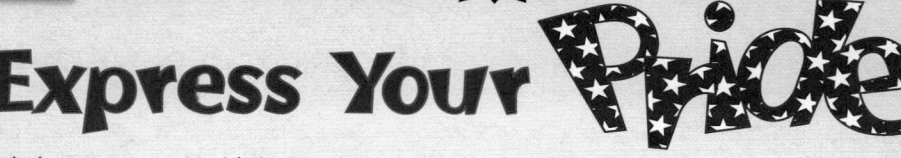

Express Your Pride

Patriotic songs express pride in our country. Decide what dynamics you will use to **sing** "The Voices of Pride" expressively. **Identify** the symbols for the dynamics you have chosen and tell what each symbol means.

pp = *pianissimo* = very soft	*p* = *piano* = soft	*mp* = *mezzo piano* = medium soft
mf = *mezzo forte* = medium loud	*f* = *forte* = loud	*ff* = *fortissimo* = very loud

Perform "The Voices of Pride" and include at least one *crescendo* and *decrescendo* in your performance. **Listen** for changes in dynamics as other groups sing.

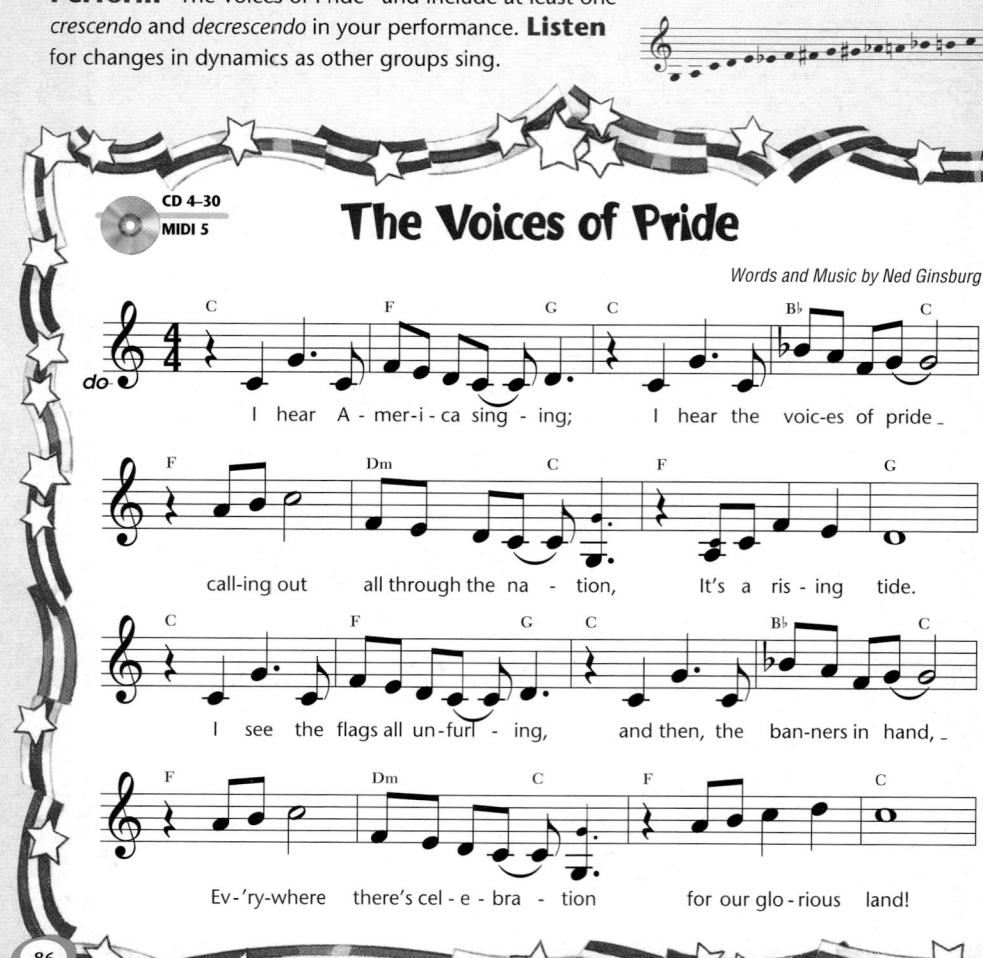

CD 4–30
MIDI 5

The Voices of Pride

Words and Music by Ned Ginsburg

I hear A-mer-i-ca sing-ing; I hear the voic-es of pride
call-ing out all through the na-tion, It's a ris-ing tide.
I see the flags all un-furl-ing, and then, the ban-ners in hand,
Ev-'ry-where there's cel-e-bra-tion for our glo-rious land!

Footnotes

ACROSS THE CURRICULUM

8b ▶ **Language Arts** *Celebrate America: In Poetry and Art* by Nora Panzer (Editor) (Hyperion, 1994) is a collection of poetry organized into five sections: the country's landscape, its melting pot makeup, city and rural life, American history, and American pastimes. The poetry is beautifully paired with paintings, sculpture, drawings, and photographs from the National Museum of American Art at the Smithsonian.

BUILDING SKILLS THROUGH MUSIC

▶ **Social Studies** Lead students in a discussion of the lyrics of "The Voices of Pride." Have students list other patriotic songs that they know. Discuss the influence of patriotic songs in our culture and the reasons why we sing them.

SKILLS REINFORCEMENT

6c ▶ **Conducting** Help students locate the time signature for "The Voices of Pride." (4/4) Then have them practice conducting a beat pattern in 4, in both slow and fast tempos. (See p. 211 for the conducting pattern in 4.) When students become proficient with the beat pattern, remind them that conductors also indicate expression by changing the size and style of their conducting movements. Invite students to conduct as they sing or listen to "The Voices of Pride."

Different Strokes for Different Folks

Musicians use dynamics to perform music expressively. Musicians also use articulation, another way of performing expressively. **Sing** or **play** the first three measures of "America" with three different kinds of articulation:

Legato (smoothly, with no breaks in the sound)

Staccato (separated or detached)

Marcato (stressed or accented)

We've fought for free - dom, fought hard and learned;

Our kind of free-dom is - n't bought or be-stowed on us. No, it's earned.

I hear A - mer - i - ca sing - ing one rous - ing song.

And with all A - mer - i - ca sing-ing, we'll stay free and strong! ____

Invite students to share their ideas about patriotism.

ASK What does the word *patriotic* mean to you? (Answers will vary.)

How do people show patriotism? (Possible answers include flying the flag, celebrating patriotic holidays, being active in their communities, and voting.)

2 DEVELOP

Listening

Invite students to find objects or symbols that represent the United States in the room and in the art on pp. 86–89. (flag, use of red, white, and blue) Then have students read lyrics from "The Voices of Pride."

 ASK What words or phrases in "The Voices of Pride" express patriotism? (*flags all unfurling, our glorious land,* and so on)

How would you sing to show pride? (Answers will vary; encourage students to consider dynamics.)

Discuss with students the dynamic markings and terms on p. 86, and then play "The Voices of Pride" **CD 4-30.** Encourage students to follow the notation on pp. 86–87 and listen for dynamics in the song.

ASK Where did you hear a *crescendo*? (on the last line of the song)

Singing

Invite students to

- Sing "The Voices of Pride" with the recording.
- Choose and describe the dynamics they will use.
- Perform the song again, with attention to the chosen dynamics.

continued on page 88

CHARACTER EDUCATION

▶ **Pride** To encourage an understanding of pride, discuss with students what it means to have pride and how we demonstrate pride appropriately. Ask students about aspects of their life for which they feel pride. You may wish to use the following question. Why do you feel prideful about these areas? Discuss the difference between pride and arrogance. Invite students to share situations in which they observed prideful or arrogant behavior. Ask them the following questions. How might the arrogant behavior be modified to more appropriately demonstrate pride? What behaviors could have made the prideful behavior appear more arrogant? Brainstorm ways in which the school environment and activities promote school pride, for example school colors, school song, school mascot and so on.

MOVEMENT

▶ **Creative Movement** Invite students to create choreography for "The Voices of Pride." Divide the class into four groups. Assign each group two phrases of the song, and have students invent movements to perform with their assigned phrases. To get students started, ask them to think of how someone looks when feeling proud (standing tall, smiling). Movements may be simple (waving or marching) or more elaborate. Use the students' ideas to create a class choreography for the entire song.

Reading

 5c Invite students to sing the opening phrases of "America" by memory. Have students examine the three versions of the opening phrase of the song, on p. 87, and identify symbols referring to articulation. Ask students to describe the markings found above the notes.

SAY The marks you see are called articulation marks. They show you how to perform the same melody three different ways.

 1a Have students identify terms referring to articulation. Ask them to read the definition of *legato* and then sing the first phrase of "America" in legato style. Do the same for *staccato* and *marcato*.

Moving

Ask students if they have ever seen a conductor lead a music group. Allow volunteers to describe what a conductor does. Point out that conductors use specific movements and gestures to show the elements of music, including meter, tempo, dynamics, and articulation.

Invite students to demonstrate motions they might use to conduct *crescendo, decrescendo,* and each of the three articulations shown on p. 87.

Listening

Ask students to sing the first verse of "When Johnny Comes Marching Home" **CD 9-13**, on p. 180. Then focus their attention on the listening map for *When Johnny Comes Marching Home,* on p. 89. (You may wish to use the timings in parentheses to check the progress through the map on the first listening.)

6a Help students

- Identify the dynamic symbols and terms on the map.
- Identify the instruments pictured on the map.
- Locate and understand the coda symbol and *coda.* Identify the terms and symbols, *rit.* and *a tempo,* relating to tempo.
- Understand that they must return to the A section after the B section.

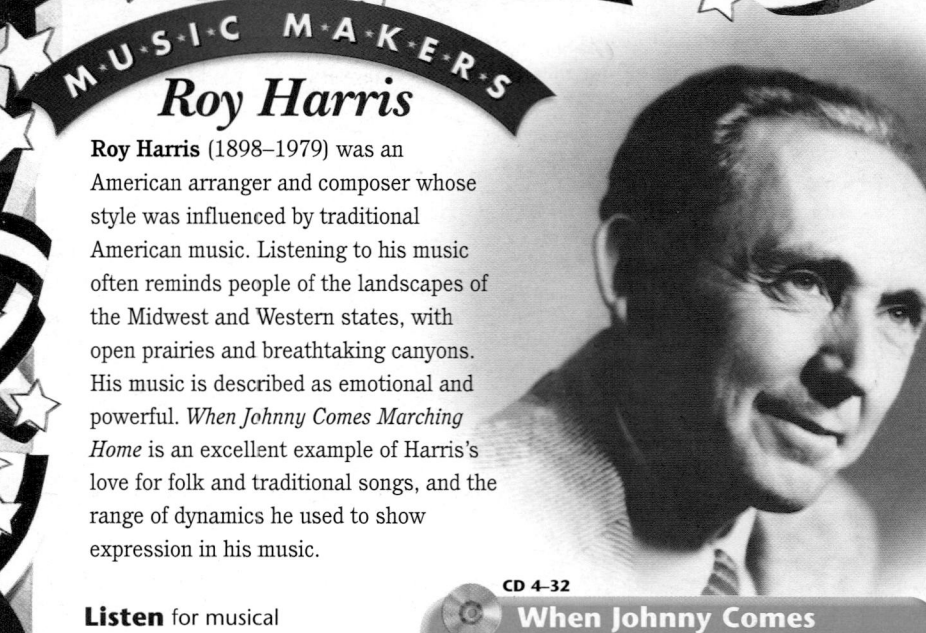

M·U·S·I·C M·A·K·E·R·S

Roy Harris

Roy Harris (1898–1979) was an American arranger and composer whose style was influenced by traditional American music. Listening to his music often reminds people of the landscapes of the Midwest and Western states, with open prairies and breathtaking canyons. His music is described as emotional and powerful. *When Johnny Comes Marching Home* is an excellent example of Harris's love for folk and traditional songs, and the range of dynamics he used to show expression in his music.

Listen for musical expression in *When Johnny Comes Marching Home.* What expressive qualities can you **describe**?

CD 4–32

When Johnny Comes Marching Home

by Patrick S. Gilmore
arranged by Roy Harris

When Johnny Comes Marching Home was first published in 1863—the third year of the Civil War. Gilmore was a bandmaster in the Union army.

88

Footnotes

TEACHER TO TEACHER

▶ **Working in Groups** When students are working in smaller groups, they will have many different types of activities to complete (read, quiz each other, determine dynamics, and so on). Review the tasks and the strengths of different students and anticipate in what ways they will be most successful. You may want to assign one or two students as co-leaders to lead each specific task (for example, skilled readers read aloud to the entire group; a student leads a review of dynamics and symbols). Establish group rules (for example: everyone should have an opportunity to talk; one person talks at a time; everyone listens to the person talking).

SKILLS REINFORCEMENT

 ▶ **Vocal Development** To help students perform independently, with accurate intonation, demonstrating fundamental skills, give them a starting pitch in the middle register, and have them sing the following exercise.

Conduct and have students sing *One and two and three and four and four and three and two and one* as they *crescendo* and *decrescendo.*

Students should follow the dynamic changes in your conducting pattern. Make sure they do not *decrescendo* too quickly or lose breath support.

Once students can do this vocalise, have them use a neutral syllable such as *doo* or *noo*, quarter notes instead of eighth notes, and 12 beats instead of 8 beats.

As you **listen** to *When Johnny Comes Marching Home*, follow the melody and listen for the dynamics and form as shown in the listening map.

When Johnny Comes Marching Home
LISTENING MAP

Introduction

ppp —————— mf ———— ff $< sfp >$

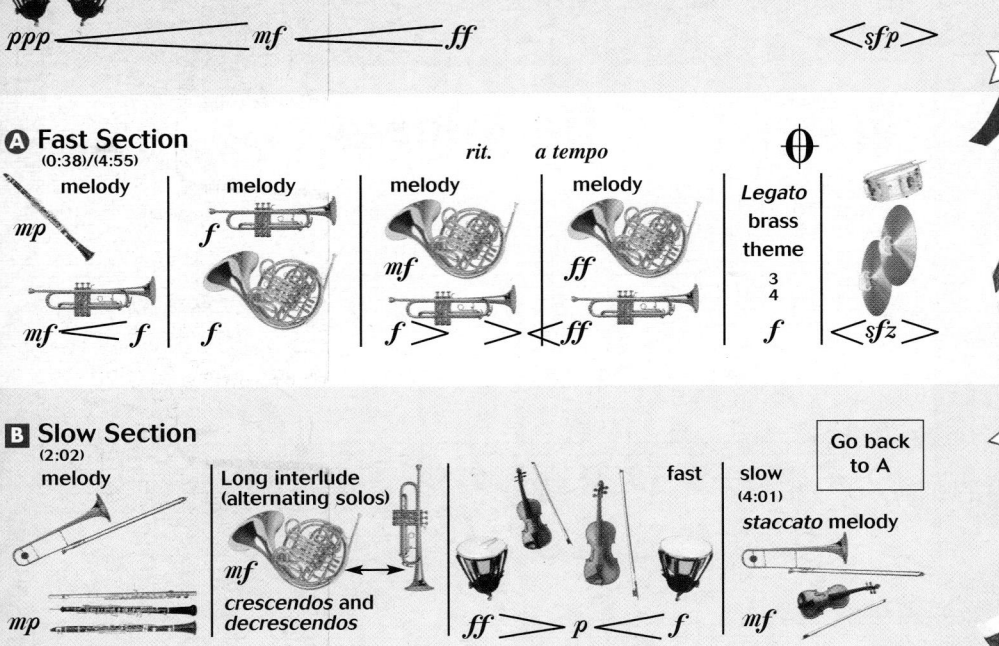

A Fast Section
(0:38)/(4:55)

rit.   *a tempo*

melody   melody   melody   melody

Legato brass theme

mp f mf ff

3
4

$mf < f$ | f | $f > < ff$ | f | f | $< sfz >$

B Slow Section
(2:02)

melody

Long interlude (alternating solos)

Go back to A

fast   slow (4:01)

staccato melody

mf
crescendos and *decrescendos*

mp

$ff > p < f$ mf

Coda (6:15) slower

tutti

fff fff

• Listen to *When Johnny Comes Marching Home* **CD 4-32** as they follow the listening map.

ASK What dynamics did you hear in the introduction? (mostly *forte* and *fortissimo*)

For a sound sample of the timpani, featured in *When Johnny Comes Marching Home*, have students listen to **CD 21-49**. For a photo and description of the instrument, have them refer to the Sound Bank on p. 518.

3 CLOSE

Performing

Review "The Voices of Pride." Have students suggest phrases in the song in which the use of *legato*, *staccato*, or *marcato* might be appropriate.

1c Have students perform the song with the suggested articulation, using a student conductor. You may wish to record the performance and replay it later for students.

Skill: LISTENING   **ASSESSMENT**

6a **Observation** Have students write the terms *legato*, *staccato*, and *marcato* on three separate sheets of paper. As the recording of *When Johnny Comes Marching Home* **CD 4-32** is played, have students choose and display the term that best describes the articulation that is used in the music. Observe that students can correctly identify the articulation in the selection using standard terminology in explaining music.

MEETING INDIVIDUAL NEEDS

6a ▶ **Cooperative Learning** Group students into pairs for practice and review of dynamics and articulation marks in this lesson. Ask partners to take turns performing and then quizzing each other on dynamic and articulation terms and symbols, as found on pp. 86–87. Allow students time to work together. Then quiz the entire class on dynamics. After each question, ask students to

• Think about the answer.
• Discuss it with their partners.
• Share their answers with the class.

SCHOOL TO HOME CONNECTION

▶ **Pride** Have students interview friends, older adults, and family members by asking them to complete this statement: "I am proud to be an American because _____." Invite students to read their interview information aloud. Use selected responses to introduce a performance of "The Voices of Pride."

TECHNOLOGY/MEDIA LINK

Transparency Display the listening map transparency for *When Johnny Comes Marching Home*. Point to each section of the piece to help students follow along. Then invite students to point to the sections as they listen again.

LESSON AT A GLANCE

Element Focus RHYTHM $\frac{3}{4}$ meter

Skill Objective **MOVING** Perform movement patterns in $\frac{3}{4}$ meter

Connection Activity **CULTURE** Participate in projects involving traditional Hispanic folk art and folktales

MATERIALS

- "De colores" (Spanish) **CD 5-1**
- "De colores" (English) **CD 5-2**
  Recording Routine: Intro (9 m.); vocal; interlude (5 m.); vocal
- **Pronunciation Practice/Translation** p. 525
- "Chiapanecas" **CD 5-7**
- "The Girl from Chiapas" **CD 5-8**
  Recording Routine: Intro (8 m.); vocal; interlude (8 m.); vocal
- **Pronunciation Practice/Translation** p. 526
- *Janitzio* (excerpt) **CD 5-6**
- **Resource Book** pp. A-10, A-11, F-9, H-11, I-8
- xylophones, recorder, keyboard

VOCABULARY

meter   time signature

◆ ◆ ◆ ◆ National Standards ◆ ◆ ◆ ◆

1c Sing music from diverse cultures
2a Play instruments accurately in small ensembles
4c Compose using electronic media
5a Read dotted half notes, half notes and quarter notes
5c Identify standard notation symbols for rhythm
6c Understand and use basic principles of meter in music analysis

MORE MUSIC CHOICES

For more practice with meter in 3:
"Cattle Call," p. 344
"The Star-Spangled Banner," p. 488

The Colors of Nature

In Mexico City, brilliant flowers spill from window boxes and form bright patterns in the parks. In rural villages, orange, salmon red, or aqua stucco walls shimmer in the sun. **Sing** "De colores," a song that describes the beauty of the simple things of life. As you sing, feel the meter in 3.

CD 5–1
MIDI 6

De colores

English Words by Alice Firgau

Folk Song from Mexico

De ___ co - lo - res, ___ De co - lo - res se vis - ten los
Wher ___ the mead - ows, ___ when the mead - ows burst forth in the

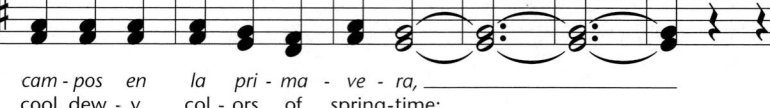

cam - pos en la pri - ma - ve - ra, _____
cool, dew - y col - ors of spring-time; _____

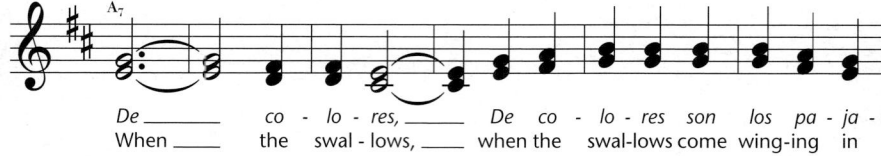

De ___ co - lo - res, ___ De co - lo - res son los pa - ja -
When ___ the swal - lows, ___ when the swal-lows come wing-ing in

ri - tos que vie - nen de a - fue - ra, _____
clouds of bright col - ors from far - off; _____

90

Footnotes

ACROSS THE CURRICULUM

▶ **Art** Encourage students to make art projects based on traditional Hispanic folk art found in *The Kids' Multicultural Art Book: Art & Craft Experiences from Around the World* by Alexandra M. Terzian (Williamson, 1993).

▶ **Language Arts** Share with students *The Story of Colors/La Historia de los Colores: A Bilingual Folktale from the Jungles of Chiapas* by Subcomandante Marcos (Cinco Puntos Press, 1999).

BUILDING SKILLS THROUGH MUSIC

▶ **Reading** Invite students to use the text on p. 90 and the English words of "De colores" to list descriptions of spring that are frequent sights in Mexico. Play "De colores" **CD 5-1** and have students match the instrument timbres heard on the recording to items on the list.

SKILLS REINFORCEMENT

▶ **Mallets** Encourage students to use xylophones to create a simple accompaniment for "De colores." Have students play the lowest pitch of each chord on the bass xylophone, and the upper two pitches on soprano or alto xylophones.

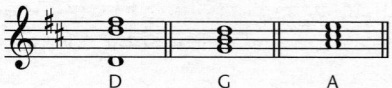

D   G   A

Make a chord chart for students to follow, or use body percussion to help them follow the chord changes—for example,

C = pat-clap-clap

F = snap-clap-clap

G = tap shoulders

De _____ co - lo - res, _____ De co - lo - res es el ar - co
When _____ the rain - bow, _____ when the rain - bow spreads rib - bons of

i - ris que ve - mos lu - cir, _____ y por e - so los
col - or all o - ver the sky; _____ Then I know why the

gran - des a - mo - res de mu - chos co - lo - res me
splen - dors of true love are great and their col - ors, the

1.
gus - tan a mí. _____
best ones of all. _____

2.
gus - tan a mí. _____
best ones of all. _____

Listen to the Rhythm

Move to the beat of *"De colores."* Look at the time signature to find the number of beats in each measure. **Create** motions that show the strong beats.

Listen for meter in 3 in *Janitzio*. Where does the meter change?

CD 5–6
Janitzio

by Silvestre Revueltas

This piece is a musical description of a lake island in the Mexican state of Michoacán. Janitzio is famous for its festivals, beautiful flowers, and calm lake waters.

1 INTRODUCE

Play the recording of *"De colores"* **CD 5-1.** Use the resources in Across the Curriculum on p. 90 to engage students in related projects.

2 DEVELOP

Singing

Have students

1c
- Read the text on p. 90.
- Find the words *De colores* in the song lyrics.

Play *"De colores"* **CD 5-1.** Invite students to

- Listen to the song and sing the words *De colores* each time they occur.
- Use the Pronunciation Practice Tracks **CD 5-4, CD 5-5** and Resource Book p. A-10 to learn the Spanish lyrics.
- Sing the song in Spanish with the recording.

Moving

5a
Have students create a three-beat movement pattern. Ask them to perform the pattern as they listen to or
6c
sing *"De colores."*

ASK What symbol in the written music for *"De colores"* shows that there are three beats in each measure? (time signature)

Point out the time signature in the notation on p. 90. Have students find two measures in the song with three quarter notes.

Listening

Play the recording of *Janitzio* **CD 5-6** and invite students to move to show the meter.

CULTURAL CONNECTION

▶ **The Art of Mexico** The visual arts and crafts of Mexico feature bright, clear colors, and bold designs. The native populations were creating ceramics, sculpture, and weavings by the time the Spaniards arrived in the 1500s. As a result, characteristics of Mexican art were integrated into European techniques and themes. In the 1920s and 1930s, the Mexican government promoted the painting of large wall murals on public buildings that depicted Mexican history. These murals are noted for their use of strong color.

SKILLS REINFORCEMENT

▶ **Recorder** For a recorder part to accompany *"De colores,"* see Resource Book p. I-8.

▶ **Keyboard** Students can play a two-handed accompaniment with *"De colores"* that reinforces meter in 3. Use these three positions:

Analyzing

Have students look at a map of Mexico to locate a state with a name similar to the song title "*Chiapanecas*." (Chiapas) After they locate and identify Chiapas, ask them to find the word *chiapaneca* in the refrain. Help them to determine that the word means "girl from Chiapas."

Reading

 Ask students to look at Section A and identify and count all the ties that have a bar line between them.

ASK **What note value might be used if the bar line was not there?** (half note)

Point out that in this situation, the only way to indicate a two-beat sound is with a tie. Play the recording of "*Chiapanecas*" **CD 5-7** and ask students to follow the notation. Each time a tie occurs, have them say "tie," holding it for two beats and clapping on beat two (the downbeat).

Listening

 Play the recording again. Ask students to follow the song notation, listen for the section with the hand claps, and count how many times these claps occur. Students may be invited to sing and clap during that section. Have students

- Invent body percussion patterns that demonstrate the feeling of 3 beats in a group.
- Fit them to the tempo of the song.

Select three patterns for the class to perform during the three sections of the song. Divide the class into three groups; each group can perform its three-beat pattern during the appropriate section while the other two groups sing.

Singing

 Have students

- Use the Pronunciation Practice Track **CD 5-10** and Resource Book p. A-11 to learn the Spanish lyrics.
- Sing the song in Spanish with the recording.

Celebrate with Dance

"*Chiapanecas*" is a traditional Mexican dance song that celebrates life and love. **Compare** the meter of this song to "*De colores*."

Listen for the section that includes two hand claps. How many times do you hear the hand claps in that section? Now, **sing** "*Chiapanecas*."

CD 5–7

Chiapanecas
(The Girl from Chiapas)

English Words by Don Kalbach

Folk Song from Mexico

Un cla - vel co - rté, ____ por la sie - rra fui ____ ca - mi -
I was go - ing home, ___ I was all a - lone, ___ when I

ni - to de ____ mi ran - cho. Co - mo el vien - to fue ___
spied a red ____ car - na - tion, Rid - ing like the wind _

____ mi ca - ba - llo fiel ____ á lle - var - me has-ta ____ su la - do,
____ on my trust - y horse _ I came to your side, ___ my dar - ling.

Lin - da flor de a - bril ____ to - ma es - te cla - vel ____ que te
Love - ly girl of spring, _ take this flow'r I bring, ___ which I

brin - do con ____ pa - sión. No me di - gas no, ____ que en tu
glad - ly of - fer you. Please don't tell me no, ____ I a -

bo - ca es - tá ____ el se - cre - to de ____ mi a - mor.
dore you so, ____ And I give you all ____ my love.

92

Footnotes

CULTURAL CONNECTION

▶ **Chiapas** Chiapas is the southernmost state in Mexico, with the Pacific Ocean as its southern border and the country of Guatemala to the east. Its capital city is Tuxtla Guitérrez. About a quarter of the population is Native American, particularly of Mayan origin and speak their own languages. Economically, the state is primarily agricultural– corn and beans are produced for in-state consumption. Coffee, chocolate, cotton, fish, and bananas are the main export products. Several sites are of significant interest to tourists. San Cristobal de las Casas is an important colonial city with interesting architecture; Palenque and Bonampak are significant ancient Mayan cities.

SKILLS REINFORCEMENT

▶ **Moving** Use the following teaching suggestions to help all students create body percussion patterns.

Reinforcement For students who have difficulty inventing a body percussion pattern, assign something simple. For example, "clap pat pat" often works well. Remind them to keep their movements small. Let this be one of the patterns selected for the group activity, so these students can participate.

On Target Students capable of maintaining a body percussion pattern should also

- sing the song
- change patterns for each of the 3 sections

Challenge Those students who can easily do the above activities can be asked to develop body percussion patterns that include rests and eighth notes. These students can also be asked to invent patterns for nonpitched percussion instruments.

Sheet music: "Chiapanecas"

Cuan-do la no-che lle-gó (clap) (clap) y con su man-to de a-
Night falls when day-time is through, *And with its man-tle of*

zul (clap) (clap) el blan-co ran-cho cu-brió (clap)
blue, *Cov-ers the ranch with its hue*

(clap) y al-le-gre el bai-le em-pe-zó. (clap) (clap)
Now we dance all the night through.

Bai - la, mi Chia-pa-ne-ca, bai -
Bai - la, mi Chia-pa-ne-ca, bai -
Danc - ing, my Chia-pa-ne-ca, Danc -
Danc - ing, my Chia-pa-ne-ca, Danc -

la, bai - la con gar - bo, Bai - la
la, bai - la con gar - bo, que en el
ing, grace - ful - ly danc - ing, Danc - ing
ing, grace - ful - ly danc - ing, You - are

1.
sua - ve ra - yo de luz. ____
like a smooth ray of light. ____

2.
bai - le la rei-na e - res tú, Chia-pa - ne - ca gen - til. (clap) (clap)
like a queen when you dance, Chia-pa - ne - ca, so dance!

Playing

Invite students to play small percussion instruments with "*Chiapanecas.*" Help them to choose appropriate instruments and play during

- The initial rest in each phrase of Section A.
- The hand claps in Section B.
- The measures of rest at the end of Section A and the two measures of rest in the first ending of Section C.

All instruments should play on the last six quarter notes of the song and the final two handclaps.

Moving

Students may enjoy performing a patterned dance with "*Chiapanecas.*" (See Movement below) Have students practice the movements in place first, then have them form a line and perform it with the recording **CD 5-7.** Play Section C of the song one or more times to give partners an opportunity to develop their improvisation.

3 CLOSE

Skill: MOVING   **ASSESSMENT**

Performance/Observation Have students move to show three-beat patterns as they sing "*Chiapanecas*" and "*De colores.*" Then invite students to improvise three-beat rhythm ostinatos to accompany the song. Observe that students' movements accurately reflect meter in 3.

MOVEMENT

▶ **Patterned Dance** Invite students to perform the following movements to "*Chiapanecas.*"

Formation: Students stand in pairs, facing each other in a line.

A section   mm. 2-3 Step left, right together (on the downbeats)

mm. 4-5 Step right, left together

mm. 6-7 Step left, right together

mm. 8-9 Step right, step left behind, step right

mm. 10-17 Repeat sequence, starting to the right

B section   Move three steps forward and clap twice. Repeat throughout.

C section   Students can improvise movements for the C section. Partners may choose to sway in the same direction and add an elbow swing for the last five measures.

TECHNOLOGY/MEDIA LINK

Notation Software Using notation software, provide students with an opportunity to compose in $\frac{3}{4}$ meter. Help students find and select $\frac{3}{4}$ meter and open a new file for composing. Allow time for students to compose and then have them share their pieces. Print out compositions and post them in a "Composer's Corner" in your room, the students' classroom, or a special place in your school.

LESSON AT A GLANCE

Element Focus RHYTHM Dotted-quarter and eighth notes

Skill Objective READING Read rhythm patterns in $\frac{3}{4}$

Connection Activity RELATED ARTS Experience a poem about the lasting qualities of music

MATERIALS

- "Himmel und Erde" **CD 5-11**
- "Music Alone Shall Live" **CD 5-12**
  - **Recording Routine:** Intro (4 m.); vocal; interlude (4 m.); vocal; coda
- **Pronunciation Practice/Translation** p. 527
- **Music Reading Practice, Sequence 9** **CD 5-15**
- *Viva la musica!* **CD 5-18**
- "Music" (poem)
- **Resource Book** pp. A-13, D-9, E-10

VOCABULARY

tie   time signature   round

◆ ◆ ◆ **National Standards** ◆ ◆ ◆

4c Arrange, using electronic media
5a Read dotted-quarter and eighth notes
5d Use standard notation to record musical ideas
6b Listen and analyze uses of rhythm in diverse cultures
6c Understand basic principles of meter and rhythm
8a Show how different arts portray the same emotion

MORE MUSIC CHOICES

For more practice with dotted-quarter/eighth-note patterns: "America, the Beautiful," p. 76

1 INTRODUCE

8a Have students read the English text for *"Himmel und Erde."* Then engage students in the activity described in Across the Curriculum, p. 95.

Music Lives On

This song from Germany can be sung as a round. After you learn to **sing** it in unison, sing it in three parts. Try the German words, too.

Perform the groups of beats by patting the first beat of each measure on your knees, and snapping your fingers on beats 2 and 3.

Take turns conducting meter in 3 as the class sings "Music Alone Shall Live" in unison or as a round.

▲ Title page of a 16th-century music score

 **CD 5-11**

Himmel und Erde
(Music Alone Shall Live)

s, l, t@ r m f s l

Round from Germany

I
Him - mel und Er - de müss - en ver - gehn;
All things shall per - ish from un - der the sky;

II
a - ber die Mu - si - ca, a - ber die Mu - si - ca,
Mu - sic a - lone shall live, Mu - sic a - lone shall live,

III
a - ber die Mu - si - ca blei - bet be - stehn.
Mu - sic a - lone shall live, nev - er to die.

94 ☞ Reading Sequence 9

Footnotes

SPOTLIGHT ON

▶ **Music All Around Us** Suggest to students that they create an imaginary time capsule representing all the different kinds of music heard and played in America today. What different kinds of music would be placed in that capsule? Which artists would be included?

BUILDING SKILLS THROUGH MUSIC

▶ **Social Studies** Invite students to sing "Music Alone Shall Live." Ask them to list things that have changed and today are found in different forms (answers may include methods of transportation, clothing and hair styles, and entertainment media). Direct students to look at the two examples of music notation on p. 94. Ask them to find similarities and differences in the 16th century score and the notation for "Music Alone Shall Live."

SKILLS REINFORCEMENT

▶ **Vocal Development** To help students perform with accurate intonation, demonstrating fundamental skills, remind them to listen carefully to themselves and to each other. On the board write a C-major scale, from middle C to third-space C and back down. Use a contrasting color for the pitches *do, mi,* and *so.* Have students sing the scale with pitch syllables and hand signs. Then have students divide into three groups and sing the scale in a three-part canon at the third (group 2 starts when group 1 reaches *mi,* group 3 starts when group 2 reaches *mi*), ending on the notes *do* (group 1), *mi* (group 2), and *so* (group 3).

▶ **Reading** See Resource Book p. D-9 for a lesson-related Music Reading worksheet.

Round and Round

As you say *Mu-sic a-lone shall live* in rhythm, tap the beat with your foot.

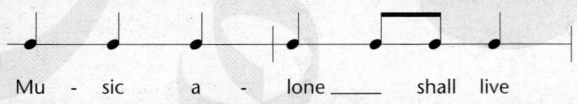

Try it again, and this time **perform** the rhythm pattern below while you say the words. Does the pattern always match each syllable of the words?

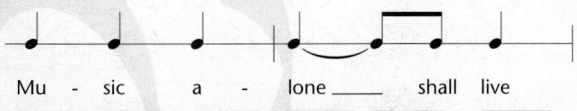

Mu - sic   a -   lone _____   shall   live

Did you notice that the rhythm pattern doesn't match up with the second syllable of *alone*? We can use the tie to show that the sound lasts for one and a half beats.

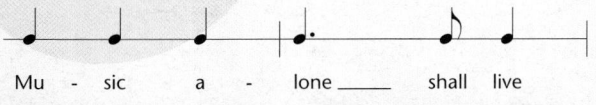

Mu - sic   a -   lone _____   shall   live

But there is an easier way to write the same rhythm, using a dotted quarter note and an eighth note.

Mu - sic   a -   lone _____   shall   live

How many times can you find this pattern in the song?

Listen to another round from Germany. Can you **identify** the same dotted rhythm pattern from "Music Alone Shall Live"?

CD 5–18
Viva la musica!

by Michael Praetorius

Michael Praetorius (1571–1621) was an organist, composer, and musicologist. Much of his music was based on Lutheran hymns and on the Latin mass still in use by the Lutheran church of his time.

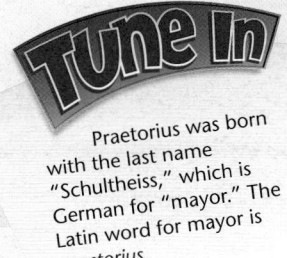

Praetorius was born with the last name "Schultheiss," which is German for "mayor." The Latin word for mayor is *praetorius*.

Unit 3   95

2 DEVELOP

Listening

Clap three-beat rhythm patterns that include dotted rhythms and rests. As students echo-clap, help them determine that each pattern has three beats.

Then have students

6b
- Pat the steady beat while listening to *"Himmel und Erde"* **CD 5-11.**
- Determine the pattern of strong and weak beats. (sets of 3—strong, weak, weak) (Remind students that $\frac{3}{4}$ time has three beats in each measure.)

Analyzing

6c Have students keep a steady beat as they say in rhythm *music alone shall live.* Then clap the first rhythm pattern on p. 95.

ASK Does the pattern have the same rhythm as the words? (No; on the syllable *lone,* the pattern has two sounds while the syllable has only one.)

5d Use a tie to make the rhythm pattern the same as that of the words. Then have students clap the rhythm.

5a Have students find other places in the song where a dotted-quarter/eighth-note pattern occurs.

For more practice, have students refer to Music Reading Practice, Sequence 9 on p. 494 in their books. (See also Resource Book p. E-10.)

Listening

Play the recording of *Viva la musica!* **CD 5-18** and ask students to listen for the same dotted rhythm pattern from *"Himmel und Erde."*

3 CLOSE

Element: RHYTHM   **ASSESSMENT**

5a **Performance/Observation** Have students read, clap, and count the rhythm of *"Himmel und Erde."* Then have them sing the song while conducting in 3 (see p. 217). Observe for rhythmic accuracy.

ACROSS THE CURRICULUM

8a ▶ **Language Arts** Discuss with students the meaning of the text for *"Himmel und Erde."* Why do people all over the world need music in their lives? Share with students the following poem about the "infinite reach" of music.

Music
by Mary L. O'Neill

Music is a tale told in sounds
Of such infinite reach
All time, all life, all tongues
Are in its speech.
Music is the sound of events
So moving, in its classic or its blue,
The heart nods recognition: "I was there.
And I have felt that, too . . ."

TECHNOLOGY/MEDIA LINK

4c **Notation Software** Have students notate the melody of *"Himmel und Erde."* After students notate the melody, give them the opportunity to add more staves and to notate a second part using the chord roots found above the staff. If time permits, have students explore different playback timbres for the song.

Unit 3   *Learning the Language of Music*   **95**

LESSON AT A GLANCE

Element Focus **RHYTHM** Dotted-rhythm patterns

Skill Objective **READING** Read from notation and perform dotted-rhythm patterns in $\frac{4}{4}$ time

Connection Activity **RELATED ARTS** Discover how a pastoral scene is presented in a song and in a painting

MATERIALS

- "Don't You Hear the Lambs?" **CD 5-19**

  Recording Routine: Intro (4 m.); v. 1; refrain; interlude (4 m.); v. 2; refrain
- **Music Reading Practice, Sequence 10** **CD 5-21**
- *Don't You Hear the Lambs?* **CD 5-24**
- "The Shepherd" (poem)
- **Resource Book** pp. B-8, D-11, E-11, I-9

VOCABULARY

tie

◆ ◆ ◆ ◆ National Standards ◆ ◆ ◆ ◆

1a Sing accurately in small ensembles
2a Play instruments accurately alone and in small ensembles
5a Read quarter notes, dotted notes, eighth notes in duple meter
5d Use standard notation to record musical ideas
6a Listen and describe events in music using appropriate terms
6b Listen and analyze uses of rhythm in music from diverse cultures
6c Understand and use basic principles of rhythm and meter in music analysis
8b Identify ways music relates to science, the visual arts, and language arts

MORE MUSIC CHOICES

For more practice with eighth-note/dotted-quarter patterns: "Ama-Lama," p. 142

Do You Feel the Rhythm?

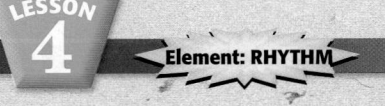

Conduct "Don't You Hear the Lambs?" in $\frac{4}{4}$ meter as you **listen** to the recording. Notice that the song begins on beat three.

Arts Connection

▲ *The Shepherd* was painted by Frank Reed Whiteside (1866–1929), who was an art teacher as well as a professional painter.

Footnotes

ACROSS THE CURRICULUM

▶ **Language Arts** Encourage students to read *And Now Miguel* by Joseph Krumgold (HarperTrophy, 1984), a deeply moving Newbery Award–winning book about a New Mexican family of sheepherders. Young Miguel longs to be accepted as a man so he can accompany the other sheepherders to the mountain summer pastures.

BUILDING SKILLS THROUGH MUSIC

▶ **Language** Write the poem "The Shepherd" (p. 98) on the board. Divide the class into eight groups and assign each group one phrase of the poem. Ask each group to arrange sound effects to accompany their phrase. Ask a student from each group to read their phrase as the rest of the group accompanies. Ask other students to evaluate the accompaniment choices and discuss how the text influenced the choice.

SKILLS REINFORCEMENT

6c ▶ **Listening** Clap four-beat patterns for students, using known rhythms. Include dotted-quarter/eighth and eighth/dotted-quarter rhythms in some patterns. Have individual students indicate whether or not each pattern contains a dotted rhythm, and which dotted pattern was included.

5d ▶ **Creating** Invite students to write music that incorporates rhythmic patterns in various meters. Divide students into groups of four and assign each group either $\frac{2}{4}$, $\frac{3}{4}$, or $\frac{4}{4}$ time. Each student in the group will compose one measure using known rhythms and notate it on a blank card. The group members can then put their cards together to form a rhythm composition. Invite each group to perform its composition for the class by clapping or by playing classroom percussion instruments.

Do You Hear the Singing?

"Don't You Hear the Lambs?" is an "old-time" folk song. These were songs that came from an old-time theme.

Sing "Don't You Hear the Lambs?"

CD 5-19

Don't You Hear the Lambs?

Folk Hymn from the Southern United States

VERSE

1. Don't you hear the lambs a - cry - in' on the
2. Don't you see the stars a - shin - in' on the

oth - er green shore? Don't you hear the lambs a -
oth - er green shore? Don't you see the stars a -

cry - in'? O, good _ shep-herd, go feed my sheep.
shin - in'? O, good _ shep-herd, go feed my sheep.

REFRAIN

Some for Paul and some for Si - las, some for to

make _ my heart re - joice. Don't you hear the lambs a -

cry - in'? O, good _ shep-herd, go feed my sheep.

Unit 3   97

continued on page 98

1 INTRODUCE

5a Clap four-beat rhythm patterns using quarter notes, quarter rests, eighth notes, dotted-quarter/eighth patterns, and eighth-note/dotted-quarter patterns.

Have students

- Echo-clap each pattern both as a group and individually.
- Determine the number of beats in each pattern. (four)

2 DEVELOP

Listening

Have students

6c
- Pat the steady beat while listening to "Don't You Hear the Lambs?" **CD 5-19.**
- Discover the meter of the song by determining the pattern of strong and weak beats. (strong, weak, weak, weak) (Focus students' attention on the time signature, and remind them that $\frac{4}{4}$ time has four beats in each measure.)

Performing

6b Have students conduct a four-beat pattern while listening to "Don't You Hear the Lambs?" and while singing the song as a group. Ask volunteers to take turns conducting the class. Be sure to start singing on beat 3.

SPOTLIGHT ON

8b ▶ **The Artist** Frank Reed Whiteside (1866–1929) was born in Philadelphia and studied at the Pennsylvania Academy of Fine Arts. He continued his education at the Academie Julian in Paris. From 1902–1921, he taught art in various schools, including the Pennsylvania Academy. When he had time to paint, however, he particularly liked to paint the ceremonies of the Zuni Indians, with whom he had lived for an extensive period. He also liked to paint the Apaches and Hopis of Arizona.

Whiteside's work was all but forgotten until the 1970s when the Phoenix Art Museum rediscovered him. Two of his paintings are now on display in the White House.

TEACHER TO TEACHER

▶ **Program Music** Program music is music that is inspired by an idea or "program" outside the music itself. This idea is often in the title of the work or in the program notes. For example, if the title were "Blue Mountain," you might be picturing a blue mountain when you heard the piece. The idea might also be in a painting, such as *The Shepherd* by Whiteside.

Help students visualize the music by calling their attention to the painting. Ask them what the lambs are doing. (bleating, walking, eating grass) Ask what the shepherd is going to do (feed sheep). Encourage students to visualize the scene in the painting as they listen to the music.

Analyzing

Have students

- Clap the four rhythm patterns on p. 98.

- Compare each rhythm with the rhythm of the words *other green* from measure 3 of the song.

- Determine which rhythm pattern is most like *other green.* (pattern 4)

- Use a tie to make rhythm pattern 4 match the rhythm of the words *other green.*

ASK How can we use a tie to make this rhythm fit the words *other green?* (add a tie between the second and third notes)

Have students clap the rhythm they created.

Ask students to tap the steady beat as you clap the rhythm of the word *other.*

ASK How many beats did you tap as I clapped the pattern? (2) **How many sounds did I clap?** (2) **Were they both the same length?** (No, the first sound is shorter and the second is longer.)

Have students clap the eighth/dotted-quarter rhythm.

SAY This two-beat rhythm pattern of short and long sounds can be written an easier way, using an eighth note and a dotted quarter note, as shown on p. 98.

See Resource Book p. D-11 for a Music Reading worksheet to use with this activity.

Music Reading Practice, Sequence 10 on p. 494 and Resource Book p. E-11 can also be used for extra reinforcement.

Reading

Have students read standard notation and

- Find the dotted-quarter/eighth patterns in the notation of "Don't You Hear the Lambs?" on p. 97.

- Read, clap, and say the rhythm of the song using rhythm syllables.

Do You See the Patterns?

These four-beat patterns contain rhythms that you already know. Tap the beat with your foot while you **read**, clap, and count them, using rhythm syllables.

Which pattern is closest to the rhythm of the words in the third full measure of "Don't You Hear the Lambs?" Try saying the words *other green* in tempo while clapping each pattern.

You can use the tie to make pattern 4 above fit the rhythm of the words.

oth - er _____ green

You can use an eighth note and a dotted quarter note to show the same rhythm a different way:

oth - er _____ green

Now you are ready to **read** and **perform** the rhythm of "Don't You Hear the Lambs?" using rhythm syllables.

Using a grand staff, **notate** the refrain of "Don't You Hear the Lambs?" on the top staff. On the bottom staff, notate an accompaniment using D-major and C-major chords. Use a rhythm pattern in your accompaniment that includes the dotted quarter note and eighth note.

Footnotes

SKILLS REINFORCEMENT

▶ **Recorder** Students can play this recorder countermelody during the verse of "Don't You Hear the Lambs?" See Resource Book p. I-9 for an expanded part, with accompanying directions.

ACROSS THE CURRICULUM

▶ **Language Arts** Read the following poem by William Blake, English poet and artist (1757–1827), that describes the life of a shepherd.

The Shepherd
by William Blake

How sweet is the shepherd's sweet lot!
From the morn to the evening he strays;
He shall follow his sheep all the day,
And his tongue shall be filled with praise.
For he hears the lambs' innocent call,
And he hears the ewes' tender reply;
He is watchful while they are in peace,
For they know when their shepherd is nigh.

Sing and Play

Follow the music on page 97 and accompany "Don't You Hear the Lambs?" using either of the chords below. Choose a guitar, an Autoharp, a keyboard, or a mallet instrument and **play** your chord when it occurs in the song.

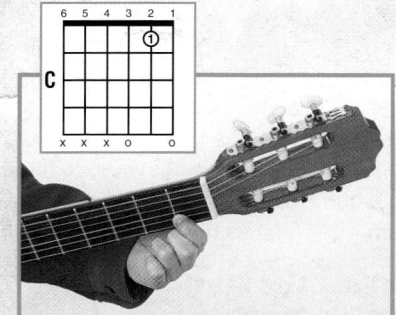

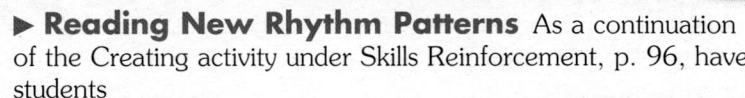

MUSIC MAKERS

Mike Seeger — The Seeger Family

The Seeger family has been a vital part of American music for over 50 years. The patriarch, Charles Louis Seeger, was a musician and inventor. His wife, Ruth Crawford Seeger, was a distinguished composer and music educator. There are seven Seeger children, including Peggy, Mike, and Pete. Mike plays several dozen instruments and has recorded many traditional and new folk songs. All members of the Seeger family have a passion for traditional music.

Listen to Mike, Peggy, and Penny Seeger perform their version of *Don't You Hear the Lambs?*

CD 5–24
Don't You Hear the Lambs?

Folk Hymn from the Southern United States as performed by Mike, Peggy, and Penny Seeger

Many favorite Christmas songs are folk songs. Folk songs are usually simple so many people can sing and play them.

Unit 3 99

1a • Sing the song **CD 5-19**, performing with accurate rhythm, demonstrating basic performance techniques.

Playing

2a Encourage a group of students to learn to play the D and C chords on guitar or Autoharp. Have the instrumentalists follow the chord symbols in the music and accompany a classroom performance of "Don't You Hear the Lambs?"

Listening

6a Once students have read about the Seeger family, on p. 99, play the recording of *Don't You Hear the Lambs?* **CD 5-24.** Then ask students to compare the two versions of the song.

ASK Which version do you prefer and why? (Accept various answers and encourage students to use music terms to explain their preference.)

8b Engage students in a discussion of the painting on p. 96 (see Teacher to Teacher, p. 97).

3 CLOSE

Notating

5d Distribute copies of Resource Book p. B-8. Review the directions in the Show What You Know activity on p. 98 and have students notate, using standard symbols, and perform their arrangements.

Element: RHYTHM   **ASSESSMENT**

5a **Performance/Observation** Focus students' attention once again on the rhythm patterns on p. 98. Ask
6c students to decide which of the rhythm patterns match rhythms in "Don't You Hear the Lambs?" Have them identify the words that match the rhythms and the measure numbers in which the rhythms occur. Have students read, clap, and count the rhythms from the song notation on p. 97. Then have students end the lesson by singing the song. Observe for rhythmic accuracy.

TEACHER TO TEACHER

5a ▶ **Reading New Rhythm Patterns** As a continuation of the Creating activity under Skills Reinforcement, p. 96, have students

- Share their rhythm compositions with the other groups.
- Invite each group to change the rhythm by drawing ties on the music.
- Clap the new rhythm patterns.

TECHNOLOGY/MEDIA LINK

Sequencing Software Using digital audio, record the class playing chordal accompaniment on guitars or other chordal instruments, singing the melody, and adding a bass part, on all separate tracks. Ask students to assess the recorded performance, including whether the dotted-rhythm patterns were performed accurately.

LESSON AT A GLANCE

Element Focus	**FORM** ABA form
Skill Objective	**PLAYING** Play an accompaniment to reinforce the concept of ABA form
Connection Activity	**RELATED ARTS** Discover similar structure in music and art

MATERIALS

* "Joshua Fought the Battle of Jericho"   **CD 5-25**
  Recording Routine: Intro (4 m.); vocal
* *Standin' in the Need of Prayer*   **CD 5-26**
* alto and bass xylophones
* guitars or keyboard
* **Resource Book** p. F-12

VOCABULARY

ABA form

◆ ◆ ◆ ◆ National Standards ◆ ◆ ◆ ◆

1c Sing music from diverse cultures
2d Perform simple accompaniments
3a Improvise simple harmonic accompaniments
4c Compose, using traditional sound sources and electronic media
5d Use standard notation to record musical ideas
6a Listen and describe events in music using appropriate terms
6b Listen and analyze uses of form in music from diverse cultures
8a Show how different arts portray the same idea in unique ways
8b Identify ways music relates to the visual arts, social studies, and language arts

MORE MUSIC CHOICES

For more practices with ABA form:
"Happy Days Are Here Again," p. 284
"Sing, Sing, Sing!" p. 340

Form in Music

Spirituals tell ancient stories in song form. **Sing** "Joshua Fought the Battle of Jericho," a spiritual about a biblical hero. Look for a section of the song that repeats.

Follow the Music

"Joshua Fought the Battle of Jericho" is a song in **ABA form.** Which part of the song is the **A** section? Which part is the **B** section? Now that you have identified the form, learn to **play** the following parts during the **A** section.

> In **ABA form**, the first and last sections are the same. The middle section is different.

100

Footnotes

TEACHER TO TEACHER

6a ▶ Hearing Chord Changes Use movement to help students recognize chord changes in "Joshua Fought the Battle of Jericho." As students listen to or sing the song, have them pat the half-note beat on their knees. Change to patting shoulders in A section measures 3 and 7, where the chord changes. In the B section, change to shoulders in measures 4 and 7. Moving in this way will help students remember to shift patterns when playing the accompaniment on instruments.

BUILDING SKILLS THROUGH MUSIC

▶ Theatre Divide the class into groups. Have each group create a dramatization through movement of "Joshua Fought the Battle of Jericho." Ask them to create different movements for the A and B sections. Have each group perform their movements for the class.

SKILLS REINFORCEMENT

2d ▶ Creating Help all students to create rhythm ostinatos by using the teaching suggestions below.

5d **Reinforcement** For some students, creating rhythm ostinatos to accompany "Joshua Fought the Battle of Jericho" may be difficult. Ask them to hand clap on beats 2 and 4 of the song.

On Target Many students will be able to create rhythm ostinatos. If they are having difficulty, invite them to work in pairs or small groups.

Challenge Students who can easily create rhythm ostinatos may be invited to create A-section and B-section ostinatos that highlight the form of the song.

Joshua Fought the Battle of Jericho

CD 5-25

African American Spiritual

REFRAIN **A**

si₁ (l₁) t₁ d r m l

Josh - ua fought the bat - tle of _____ Jer - i - cho, _____

Jer - i - cho, _____ Jer - i - cho, _____

Josh - ua fought the bat - tle of _____ Jer - i - cho, _____

And the walls came tum - blin' down. *Fine*

VERSE **B**

You can talk a - bout your king of Gid - e - on, _____

You can talk a - bout your man of Saul, _____

But there's none like good old Josh - u - a

At the bat - tle of Jer - i - cho. *D.C. al Fine*

Unit 3 **101**

continued on page 102

1 INTRODUCE

Invite students to engage in a simple storytelling game. Have them work in groups of three to invent a story they can tell the class in one minute or less, and then have them share their stories with the class.

2 DEVELOP

Analyzing

Write words that describe story elements such as *characters, plot, time,* and *place* on the board.

SAY Some songs tell stories. Listen to this song and find out what the story is about.

Play "Joshua Fought the Battle of Jericho" **CD 5-25** and have students listen for story elements and list them.

ASK Who is the main character in this story-song? (Joshua)

Where did the story take place? (Jericho)

What is the plot of the story? (Joshua marched around the walls of Jericho until the walls came tumbling down.)

SAY This song has an A section and a B section. The A section is the first part of the song.

ASK Where does the A section begin? (measure 1)

Where does it end? (Answers may include double bar line, measure 8, the word *down,* or the *Fine* sign.)

Where does the B section begin? (measure 9, the words *you can talk*)

Which section do you hear twice? (the A section)

Have students identify ABA form in the song by creating a diagram.

 CULTURAL CONNECTION

▶ **Spirituals** Spirituals are a part of the rich African American musical tradition. They have been sung for hundreds of years and for many purposes. Some, like "Joshua Fought the Battle of Jericho," refer to ancient biblical stories. Some spirituals are songs of longing for a better place and a better life. Others protested the conditions and circumstances of slavery, while others celebrated freedom. Invite students to investigate the meaning of the spirituals found in their books. Help them work together to list spirituals they know and can sing together.

 **ACROSS THE CURRICULUM**

▶ **Social Studies** Read aloud or encourage students to read the story of the founding of the Fisk School (now Fisk University) and its world-renowned Jubilee Singers in *A Band of Angels* by Deborah Hopkinson (Atheneum, 1999). The story is told through the voice of a descendant of an original member of the Jubilee Singers, Ella Sheppard. To raise money for the African American college, music teacher George White took his group on tour in the late 1860s. The audiences were not interested in the popular music the group offered. When they sang the spirituals of their own heritage, the Jubilee Singers quickly became world famous. Combine this book with a listening activity to one of the many recordings by the Fisk University Jubilee Singers.

Singing

1c Play "Joshua Fought the Battle of Jericho" again and invite students to sing along. For variety, have the whole class sing the A section and soloists or small groups sing the B section.

Playing

To prepare students for the playing activity on p. 100, have them move to the rhythm of each instrumental part as they sing the refrain of "Joshua Fought the Battle of Jericho."

2d Divide players into three groups—one to play the alto xylophone part, one to play the bass xylophone part, and one to play the tambourine part. Have students

- Identify the pitches in the xylophone parts by letter name.
- Review the movement for each xylophone part.
- Transfer the movements to instruments.
- Accompany the A section of the song as the class sings.

Listening

6b Play *Standin' in the Need of Prayer* **CD 5-26.** Invite students to follow the form of the piece by using the illustration on p. 103.

Discuss the recording, encouraging students to use standard terminology in explaining voices.

ASK Who sings the melody in the A section? (full choir)

Who sings the melody during the B section? (call—small group; response—full choir)

What words are repeated in both sections? (*Standin' in the need of prayer*)

One More Time–with Guitar

"Joshua Fought the Battle of Jericho" uses just the Dm and A₇ chords in the **B** section. Learn to **play** these chords on guitar. Then follow the chord symbols in the music and **improvise** your own rhythm to accompany the song.

 Arts Connection ▲ *Going to Church* was painted by the American artist William H. Johnson (1901–1970). As in music, form is an important element in the visual arts. What hints of ABA form, such as balance and repetition, can you identify in this painting?

102

Footnotes

ACROSS THE CURRICULUM

▶ **Language Arts** Invite students to read poems and determine their structure. One fine poetry source for students is *The 20th Century Children's Poetry Treasury*, edited by Jack Prelutsky (Alfred A. Knopf, 1999).

8b Students may also enjoy writing a poem in ABA form. One idea to get them started is to write a three-stanza poem using the same first and third stanzas.

SKILLS REINFORCEMENT

3a ▶ **Creating** Encourage students to improvise an instrumental accompaniment to emphasize the ABA form for the poems written in the poetry activity in Across the Curriculum.

▶ **Mallets** For an expanded Orff arrangement of "Joshua Fought the Battle of Jericho," see Resource Book p. F-12.

What's the Form?

Listen to *Standin' in the Need of Prayer*. Does it follow the same form as "Joshua Fought the Battle of Jericho"?

CD 5–26

Standin' in the Need of Prayer

African American Spiritual as performed by the Moses Hogan Chorale

The Moses Hogan Chorale is based in New Orleans, Louisiana. In 1996, the group was invited to perform at the World Choral Symposium in Sydney, Australia.

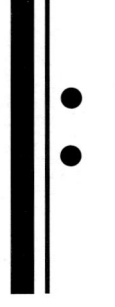
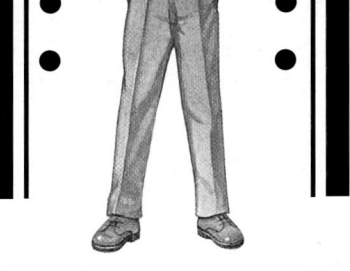

Brother

Sister

Mother

Father

Deacon

Preacher

Analyzing

8a Have students examine the painting on p. 102 and identify concepts taught in the other fine arts. Ask them **8b** to suggest specific elements of unity and variety that help to give the painting structure and form. For example, the structures at the upper right and left corners provide balance, while the figures in the center provide contrast and a focus for the setting.

Relate this use of structure and form to the ABA form of "Joshua Fought the Battle of Jericho" and *Standin' in the Need of Prayer*.

Moving

8a Working in small groups, have students

- Listen to *Standin' in the Need of Prayer*.
- Create movements to show the ABA form.
- Practice their movements with the recording.
- Perform their movements for the class.

3 CLOSE

Element: FORM **ASSESSMENT**

1c **Performance/Observation** Divide the class into three groups and help students plan a formal classroom **2d** performance of "Joshua Fought the Battle of Jericho" that includes the following.

- Group 1: Singers.
- Group 2: Tambourine and xylophone players to perform the parts on p. 100 with the A section.
- Group 3: Guitar or keyboard players to accompany the B section of the song (see p. 102).

Encourage students to demonstrate appropriate small-ensemble performance techniques, when performing in formal concerts.

Observe that students assigned to instrumental parts perform during the appropriate section of the song.

AUDIENCE ETIQUETTE

▶ **A Museum Visit** Visiting a museum or visual-arts display can be a great way to correlate music studies with other art forms. Before attending an exhibit, provide background information about what the students will see. Have them look for specific works or symbols in works during their visit. For example, paintings that include images of instruments or ballet dancers. Invite students to create a set of behavior guidelines, such as

- Stay with your group and listen to the teacher.
- Wear comfortable clothes and shoes; leave backpacks and purses at home.
- Art can be fragile and sensitive. Oils from hands damage art, so don't touch.
- Discussing and analyzing art in the museum is encouraged, but be courteous to other viewers by keeping voices low.

TECHNOLOGY/MEDIA LINK

4c **Sequencing Software** Divide the class into small groups. Ask students to use classroom instruments or classroom keyboards to compose two eight-measure melodies using notes from the C-pentatonic scale. Ask them to limit rhythmic values to quarter notes, half notes, eighth notes, and dotted halves. Have students choose one melody to be the A section and one to be the B section. As the groups finish, have them take turns sequencing their melodies in ABA form. Remind students how to use the sequencing software's copy and paste functions. After they have completed the activity, encourage students to trade B sections with other groups and sequence these as well.

LESSON AT A GLANCE

Element Focus   **MELODY** Melodic patterns using *ti*

Skill Objective   **READING** Read and sing from notation melodic patterns using low *ti*

Connection Activity   **CULTURE** Discuss the culture of Wales

MATERIALS

- "All Through the Night"   **CD 5-28**
  Recording Routine: Intro (2 m.); v. 1; v. 2
- **Music Reading Practice, Sequence 11**   **CD 5-29**
- *All Through the Night*   **CD 5-27**
- **Resource Book** pp. D-12, D-13, E-12, G-5
- barred instruments

VOCABULARY

scale   key signature   whole step   half step

◆ ◆ ◆ ◆ **National Standards** ◆ ◆ ◆ ◆

1c Sing music from diverse cultures
2a Play instruments accurately alone
4c Arrange, using electronic media
5a Read whole, half, quarter, eighth, and dotted notes in duple meter
5d Use standard notation to record musical ideas
8b Identify ways music relates to social studies

MORE MUSIC CHOICES

For more songs with low *ti* patterns:
"I Love the Mountains," p. 34
"Blowin' in the Wind," p. 382

1 INTRODUCE

Sing short melodic patterns containing *ti* for students, using neutral syllables (such as *loo*).

Element: MELODY   **Skill: READING**   **Connection: CULTURE**

A New Note

"All Through the Night" is a beautiful Welsh lullaby. **Listen** to determine how many times you hear the phrase *all through the night*. Do the notes in this phrase move upward or downward?

This time as you listen, **sing** the phrase each time it occurs. Use hand signs and pitch syllables for the notes you know. (Hum the new note.) **Describe** the new note. How does it sound compared to *la*? How does it sound compared to *do*?

The note between *la₁* and *do* is called *ti₁*. Since it is below *do*, it is called *low ti*.

la₁   *ti₁*   *do*

Use the key signature in "All Through the Night" to find *do*. Can you also find each *ti₁* in the song? **Sing** the song using pitch syllables and hand signs. Then **read** the song using letter names.

A Classical Arrangement

Listen to this performance of *All Through the Night*, sung in Welsh.

CD 5–27
All Through the Night

Traditional Melody from Wales
arranged by Franz Joseph Haydn
performed by Angelika Kirschlager

Haydn's arrangement of this famous Welsh song uses a piano and string instrument accompaniment.

Footnotes

CULTURAL CONNECTION

8b ▶ **Wales** Wales is a part of the island of Great Britain. Its landscape of mountains, hills, and coast is filled with castles and ancient monuments, churches, and museums. A famous Welsh choir is the Royal National Eisteddfod that performs at the summer festival for music, poetry, and dance. Historically, Wales has ancient standing stone ruins of Norman castles and harbors which once sent tall ships halfway around the world.

BUILDING SKILLS THROUGH MUSIC

▶ **Math** Discuss with students the information about the life of Franz Joseph Haydn found on p. 105. Select individual students to determine the age of Haydn at the time of his death. Then ask students to compute the average number of compositions per year if he began composing at different ages, for example, 12, 18, 21, and so on.

SKILLS REINFORCEMENT

▶ **Keyboard** Students can play the following descant for "All Through the Night" one octave higher than written.

2a

CD 5-28
MIDI 7

All Through the Night

Verse 1 by Harold Boulton
Verse 2 Attributed to Thomas Oliphant

Melody from Wales

1. Sleep, my child, and peace at-tend thee All through the night;
2. While the moon her watch is keep - ing All through the night;

Guard - ian an - gels God will send thee All through the night.
While the wea - ry world is sleep - ing All through the night.

Soft the drow - sy hours are creep - ing, Hill and vale in slum - ber steep-ing,
O'er thy spir - it gent - ly steal-ing, Vi - sions of de - light re - veal-ing,

I my lov - ing vig - il keep - ing All through the night.
Breathes a pure and ho - ly feel - ing All through the night.

MUSIC MAKERS

Franz Joseph Haydn

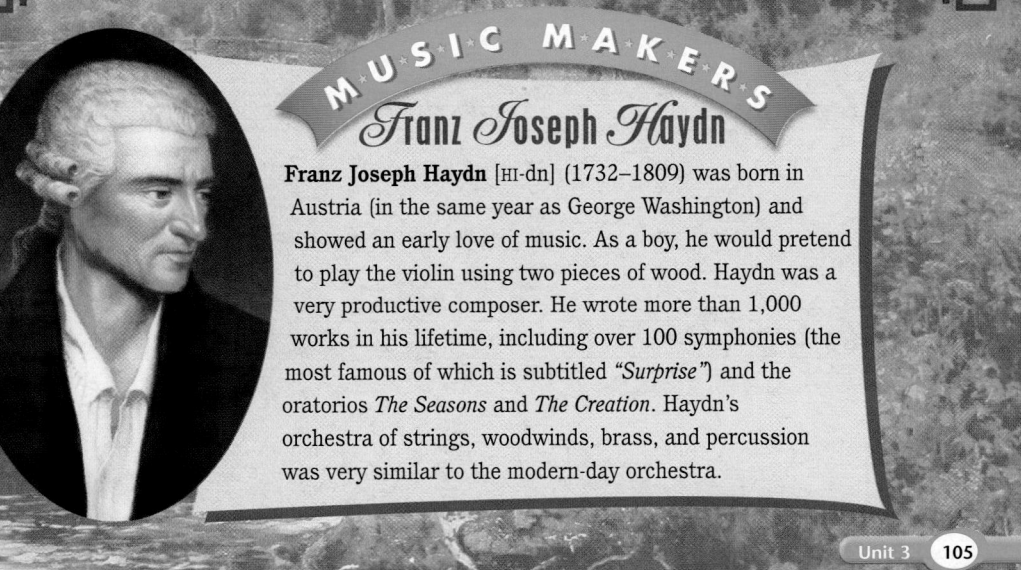

Franz Joseph Haydn [HI-dn] (1732–1809) was born in Austria (in the same year as George Washington) and showed an early love of music. As a boy, he would pretend to play the violin using two pieces of wood. Haydn was a very productive composer. He wrote more than 1,000 works in his lifetime, including over 100 symphonies (the most famous of which is subtitled *"Surprise"*) and the oratorios *The Seasons* and *The Creation*. Haydn's orchestra of strings, woodwinds, brass, and percussion was very similar to the modern-day orchestra.

Unit 3 **105**

---

2 DEVELOP

Singing

Have students echo-sing the patterns you modeled and then play the patterns on barred instruments, using F as *do.*

Analyzing

 Play "All Through the Night" **CD 5-28** and have students learn the melody by rote.

Write the known notes of the F-*do* scale on the board, using a question mark for *low ti.* Have students sing the known notes, using pitch syllables. Hum the note shown with a question mark *(ti₁).*

ASK Where does the "hummed" note fall in the scale? (between *la₁* and *do*)

SAY The note between *la₁* and *do* is called *ti₁.* It is below *do,* so it is called low *ti.* The space between *ti₁* and *do* is a half step. The space between *la₁* and *ti₁* is a whole step.

See Resource Book p. D-12 for more activities using *ti₁.*

Singing

 Following the sequence on p. 104, have students sing and read with hand signs the *la₁-ti₁-do* pattern from "All Through the Night." Then have them sing the entire song from notation.

Listening

Play the Haydn arrangement of *All Through the Night* **CD 5-27,** which is sung in Welsh. Share information about Wales in Cultural Connection on p. 104.

3 CLOSE

Skill: READING **ASSESSMENT**

Performance/Observation Ask students to look at "All Through the Night" and find the low *la₁-ti₁-ti₁-do* patterns (mm. 3–4, 7–8, 15–16) and other patterns with *low ti.* Have students use pitch syllables and hand signs to sing the song while reading from the notation. Observe for melodic accuracy.

SKILLS REINFORCEMENT

▶ **Signing** For a sign interpretation of "All Through the Night," refer to Resource Book p. G-5.

▶ **Notating** Using Resource Book p. D-13, have students create six one-measure melodic patterns containing *low ti.* Have students

- Notate the rhythm of the patterns as you play them.
- Write the pitch syllables for each pattern as you sing them.
- Notate each pattern on the staff in F-*do.*

TECHNOLOGY/MEDIA LINK

MIDI/Sequencing Software Play the MIDI song file for "All Through the Night." Ask students what the words of the song mean. Encourage students to suggest tempo, dynamic, and orchestration changes for the music. Play the file again, using various suggestions. After each hearing, ask students if the mood of the song changed.

LESSON AT A GLANCE

Element Focus   **MELODY** Melodic patterns using *low ti*

Skill Objective   **READING** Read and sing from notation melodic patterns using *low ti*

Connection Activity   **CULTURE** Discuss the significance of the Torah in Jewish heritage

MATERIALS
- *"Dundai"* (Hebrew)   **CD 5-34**
- *"Dundai"* (English)   **CD 5-35**
  Recording Routine: Intro (4 m.); vocal; interlude (4 m.); vocal 2; coda
- **Music Reading Practice, Sequence 12**   **CD 5-38**
- **Pronunciation Practice/Translation** p. 527
- **Resource Book** pp. A-14, B-8, D-14, E-13, F-14
- selected melodic percussion instruments

VOCABULARY
diatonic scale

◆ ◆ ◆ ◆ National Standards ◆ ◆ ◆ ◆
1c Sing music from diverse cultures
2a Play instruments accurately in small ensembles
5a Read half, quarter, eighth, and dotted notes in duple meter
5d Use standard notation to record musical ideas
6c Understand and use basic principles of intervals in music analysis

MORE MUSIC CHOICES
For more practice with *ti* patterns:
"Ego sum pauper" ("Nothing Do I Own"), p. 158

1 INTRODUCE

Share with students the information about the Torah in Cultural Connection, p. 107, and invite discussion.

Same Note...
Different Place

"Dundai" is a Hebrew folk song about the Torah, the holy book of the Jewish faith.

You have learned that the new note between *low la* and *do* is *low ti*. Can you find *low ti* in the scale?

do   la,   ti,   do   re   mi   fa   so   la

Now look at the last note of the song. What is the tonic? Can you find *low ti* in the melody?

Read and **sing** *"Dundai."*

CD 5-34

Dundai

English Version by David Eddleman   *Folk Song from Israel*

l t d r m f s l

E - rets   Yis - ra - el,   b' - li   To - rah.
Yal - de   Yis - ra - el,   lim - du   To - rah.
Land   of   Is - ra - el,   a   na - tion   whole,
Learn   its   ho - ly   ways   that   make   us   wise,

Hi   k' - guf____   b' - li   n'sha - ma.
Hiz - ku,   im - tsu   nish - mat   ha - u - ma.
We   the   bod - y,   our   To - rah   the   soul.
Strength   is   giv - en   us   from   Is - rael's   prize.

106   Reading Sequence 12

Footnotes

ACROSS THE CURRICULUM

▶ **Social Studies** To help students discover more about Jewish heritage, see the many activities in *Learning About Other Cultures: Literature, Celebrations, Games, and Art Activities* by John Gust and J. Meghan McChesney (Teaching and Learning Company, 1995).

BUILDING SKILLS THROUGH MUSIC

▶ **Language** Invite students to sing *"Dundai"* in Hebrew and English **CD 5-34, CD 5-35**. Lead the class in a discussion on the main idea or theme of the song. Select individual students to share suggestions and to explain the reasons for their choice. List suggestions on the board and discuss the significance of items on the list.

SKILLS REINFORCEMENT

5d ▶ **Notating** Have students use Resource Book p. D-14 to write a countermelody for *"Dundai"* in staff notation.

▶ **Recorder** When they are ready, have students play the part below as others sing *"Dundai."*

2a

▶ **Mallets** An Orff arrangement of *"Dundai"* can be found on p. F-14 of the Resource Book.

Dun - dai, dun - dai, _____ dun - dai dai,

Dun - dai, dun - dai, _____ dun - dai dai.

Show What You Know!

Identify *ti* in each of these patterns. Then **sing** the pattern using hand signs and pitch syllables.

1. do
2. do
3. do

This phrase is from a song in Unit 3. **Sing** the phrase using hand signs and pitch syllables. Where is *ti*? What is the name of the *song*?

do

2 DEVELOP

Singing

Sing short melodic patterns containing *low ti* for students. Use a neutral syllable, such as *loo,* for *low ti.* Have some patterns start and end on *la,* to introduce the minor sound of *"Dundai."*

 Play *"Dundai"* **CD 5-34** and have students sing along. Use the Pronunciation Practice Track **CD 5-37** and Resource Book A-14 to help students learn the Hebrew words.

Analyzing

Review all known notes in the scale on p. 106. Then have students

- Sing the known notes of the scale, ascending and descending, starting on *la⌐*(D) and hum *ti⌐.*
- Sing measures 3–4 of *"Dundai,"* using pitch syllables. (Hum *ti⌐.*)

ASK What note is between low *la* and *do?* (*low ti*)

Have students sing the phrase, adding *ti.* Explain that the distance between *low ti* and *do* is a half step, while the distance between *low ti* and *la* is a whole step.

For additional practice with *low ti,* have students perform Music Reading Practice, Sequence 12 on p. 495 and Resource Book p. E-13.

3 CLOSE

Reading

Read the directions for the Show What You Know activity on p. 107 with students. (The phrase shown at the bottom of the page is from *"Himmel und Erde,"* p. 94.) See Resource Book p. B-8 for the corresponding worksheet.

Skill: READING **ASSESSMENT**

 Performance/Observation Have students sing *"Dundai,"* reading from staff notation and using pitch syllables and hand signs. Observe for melodic accuracy.

CULTURAL CONNECTION

▶ **The Torah** The word *Torah* has two meanings. In a limited sense, it refers to the entire Jewish Bible. In its broader sense, it refers to the whole body of Jewish law and teachings.

The Christian Bible is divided into the Old Testament and New Testament. In Jewish tradition, there is no "Old Testament." The so-called Old Testament is known as the Written Torah or the Tanakh. The Hebrew names of its first five books are derived from the first few words of the book: Genesis, Exodus, Leviticus, Numbers, and Deuteronomy.

The scriptures used in synagogue services are written in Hebrew calligraphy on parchment scrolls. The Torah scrolls are kept covered with fabric, and they are often ornamented with silver crowns on the handles and a silver breastplate on the front.

TECHNOLOGY/MEDIA LINK

Web Site To learn more information about Middle Eastern music, visit *www.sfsuccessnet.com.*

LESSON AT A GLANCE

Element Focus   **MELODY** Melodic patterns

Skill Objective   **MOVING** Move to the beat of a Navajo song

Connection Activity   **CULTURE** Discuss Navajo art and history

MATERIALS
- *"Jo'ashilá"*   **CD 5-43**
  Recording Routine: Intro (4 m.); vocal
- **Pronunciation Practice/Translation** p. 527
- **Resource Book** p. A-15
- drum

VOCABULARY
vocables

◆ ◆ ◆ **National Standards** ◆ ◆ ◆

1c Sing music from diverse cultures
2c Perform instrumental music from diverse cultures
6a Listen and describe events in music using appropriate terms
6c Understand and use basic principles of rhythm and intervals in music analysis
8b Identify ways music relates to social studies

MORE MUSIC CHOICES

For more experience with Native American songs:
"Haliwa-Saponi Canoe Song," p. 302
"Zuni Sunrise Call," p. 396
"Green Corn Song," p. 462

1 INTRODUCE

Play a drum beat and invite students to walk to the beat. Challenge them by varying the tempo. Then invite students to link arms with a partner and try walking together to the beat.

ASK What must you do to be able to walk together? (listen to the beat, match steps with partner)

Element: MELODY | **Skill: MOVING** | **Connection: CULTURE**

LEARN BY EAR AND EYE

Many traditional songs are not written down. The Navajo preserve traditional songs by singing them to each other. Children learn songs from their elders, and songs are passed from one generation to the next.

Listen to *"Jo'ashilá,"* a traditional Navajo song. Some of the word sounds you hear are vocables that do not have a specific meaning. Tap the beat as you listen. Then walk together to the beat of the song. *"Jo'ashilá"* is written down here so you can learn it.

CD 5–43

Jo'ashilá
(Walking Together)
Traditional Song of the Navajo

Jo - 'a - shi - lá, Jo - 'a - shi - lá,

Jo - 'a - shi - lá, hei yei' yun ga.

T'oo ga' ni-zhón - ní-go bah ho-zhó lá hei ya' hei', nee ya.

108

Footnotes

CULTURAL CONNECTION

▶ **Navajo Art** Symbols in artworks express the beliefs or ideas of a culture. Designs and colors can have certain meanings. For example, in Navajo artworks, stalks of corn symbolize the Navajo ceremonial system as well as a staple food of life. Four mountains symbolize the mountains that form the boundaries of the Navajo homeland. The Navajo people create beautiful rugs, silver jewelry, pottery, and paintings (including sand paintings). Traditional symbols are often included in these artworks.

BUILDING SKILLS THROUGH MUSIC

▶ **Language** Direct students to read the information on p. 108. Discuss the oral tradition of children learning songs and rhymes from their elders. Ask students to write a brief paragraph about a nursery rhyme, song, or story they learned from one of their elders.

SKILLS REINFORCEMENT

2c
6a
▶ **Listening** Have students list the timbres they heard in *"Jo'ashilá."* (voice, drum, flute) These are traditional timbres in many Native American cultures. Help students recognize that the drum is played with a steady beat and without accents. This is unlike most classical and popular music, which often have an accent on the first beat of each measure. Accents heard in some traditional songs are used to show honor or to signal the end of the song. Invite students to play a traditional Native American drumbeat with *"Jo'ashilá."*

Jo - 'a-shi-lá,   Jo - 'a-shi-lá,   Jo - 'a-shi-lá,   hei yei' yun ga.

T'oo ga' ni-zhón - ní-go   bah ho-zhó lá hei ya' hei',   nee ya.

Jo - 'a - shi - lá,   Jo - 'a - shi - lá,   Jo - 'a - shi - lá,

hei   yei'   yung   wei'   yun - ga.

Listen to Learn

Sing "Jo'ashilá" and **identify** parts of the melody that are the same.

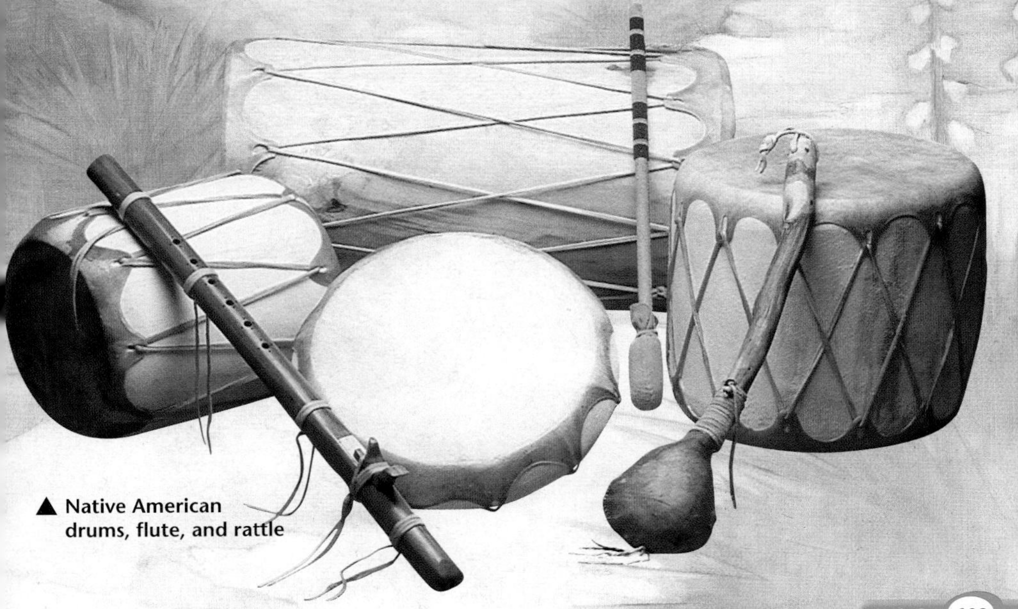

▲ Native American drums, flute, and rattle

2 DEVELOP

Moving

 Play "Jo'ashilá" **CD 5-43.** Invite students to tap the beat and then step lightly to the beat.

SAY "Jo'ashilá" is a song from the Navajo culture. In English, it means "Walking Together."

Have students choose a partner and form a circle facing counterclockwise. Play the recording again as partners link arms and walk to the beat.

Singing

SAY Native American people learned songs by listening and repeating what they heard.

Play the Pronunciation Practice Track **CD 5-45** and have students echo-sing each phrase of "Jo'ashilá." (Refer also to Resource Book p. A-15.)

Invite students to follow the notation on p. 108 as they sing the song. Then have them identify phrases of the melody that are the same, using pitch letter names. (measures 1–4, 8–11, 15–18; measures 5–7, 12–14)

3 CLOSE

Moving

Point out the word *hozhó,* which means "walk in beauty"—an important Navajo concept. Invite students to walk to the music again, as they think about "walking in beauty."

For additional information on the art and history of the Navajo Nation, discuss Cultural Connection, p. 108, and Spotlight On, below, with students.

Element: MELODY   ASSESSMENT

Performance/Observation Have students walk to the beat of "Jo'ashilá" and sing the phrase that starts with *Jo'ashilá* each time it occurs. Observe that students accurately perform the phrase.

SPOTLIGHT ON

▶ **The Navajo Nation** In 1864, the Navajo people were forced to walk three hundred miles from their homeland to southern New Mexico by the U.S. military. More than 2,500 people died of disease, depression, and starvation. In 1868, the survivors returned to their homeland, called *"Dinetah."* Today, the Navajo Nation is located in the Four Corners area of the United States where Utah, Arizona, New Mexico, and Colorado meet.

SCHOOL TO HOME CONNECTION

▶ **Cultures** Music, arts, and crafts are expressions of a culture's identity. Invite students to think about objects in their homes that tell something about their families or cultures. Have them describe the music, art, or artifact and its meaning. Invite students to bring the art, craft items, or music to class, or invite family members to class to share symbols of their culture and heritage.

TECHNOLOGY/MEDIA LINK

Electronic Keyboard After students have learned to sing "Jo'ashilá," select two students per keyboard to play Native American drum and rattle sounds along with the recording.

LESSON AT A GLANCE

Element Focus   **TIMBRE**   Flute and recorder timbres

Skill Objective   **PLAYING**   Play improvised and composed melodies on recorder

Connection Activity   **SCIENCE**   Discuss acoustical principles related to the construction of flutes

MATERIALS

- *Kokopelli Wandering Song*   **CD 6-1**
- *Allegro* from *Brandenburg Concerto No. 4* (excerpt)   **CD 6-2**
- *Shika no tone* (*The Sound of Deer Calling to One Another*) (excerpt)   **CD 6-3**
- *Syrinx*   **CD 6-4**
- *Prelude to the Afternoon of a Faun* (excerpt)   **CD 6-5**
- slide whistle
- recorders
- flute (if available)

VOCABULARY

recorder

◆ ◆ ◆ ◆ National Standards ◆ ◆ ◆ ◆

2a   Play instruments accurately alone and in small ensembles
2d   Perform simple melodies by ear
3b   Improvise melodic variations on given melodies
4c   Compose, using traditional sound sources
6a   Listen and describe events in music using appropriate terms
6b   Listen and analyze uses of timbre in music from diverse cultures
7b   Students evaluate the music they hear
8b   Identify ways music relates to math, science, and social studies

MORE MUSIC CHOICES

For more practice with Native American flute:
"Haliwa-Saponi Canoe Song," p. 302
"Green Corn Song," p. 462

WINDS OF THE WORLD

A mysterious figure of legend, Kokopelli wandered from village to village, playing his flute and telling his wonderful stories.

Listen to *Kokopelli Wandering Song,* played on a Native American flute.

CD 6–1
Kokopelli Wandering Song

Traditional Native American Melody performed by Robert Tree Cody
Much of Robert Tree Cody's music is inspired by nature.

Improvising a Melody

In *Kokopelli Wandering Song*, the second half of the melody is always the same but the first half changes. **Play** the melody below on recorder. Only the second half of the melody is shown. **Improvise** the first half of the melody, then **play** the second half as written.

▲ Pueblo relief sculpture of Kokopelli

(110)

Footnotes

SPOTLIGHT ON

8b ▶ **The Legend of *Kokopelli*** The word *Kokopelli* refers to a kachina ancestral spirit of the Hopi tribe. It is said that *Kokopelli* looks like wood (*koko*) and has a hump (*pilau*). *Kokopelli* is depicted as a stick figure form playing the flute in carved art that appears on rock formations throughout the southwest United States and northwest Mexico.

BUILDING SKILLS THROUGH MUSIC

▶ **Language** Distribute copies of the Semantic Map on p. C-6 of the Resource Book. Have students label the center box "Flutes" and the surrounding boxes with names of the flutes presented on pp. 110-113. Invite students to listen to aural examples of each. Then ask them to add words to the Semantic Map that describe timbres of each type of flute.

CULTURAL CONNECTION

8b ▶ **Native American Flutes** Many, but not all, Native American tribes use flutes to make music. Most of the Native American flute music heard today comes from Plains tribes. The flute was most often used by young men for courting. It was believed that a beautifully played song could win a young woman's heart. Each Native American flute is unique. There is not a standard length or width, so each flute has its own sound. Flutes are usually made of cedar. The flute maker must hollow out the cedar branch to create the flute. Legend says that the maker replaces the inner part of the branch with his or her heart.

Compare the Instruments

The Native American flute and the recorder have different tunings and scales. Think about what you know about these instruments. How are they the same? How are they different? **Compare** your recorder to the Native American flute pictured here.

▲ The Native American flute has been played for many generations. Most flutes are made of wood, usually cedar. The Native American flute has five or six finger holes and a thumbhole.

Bach's Recorder

During J. S. Bach's lifetime (1685–1750), the recorder was called *flauto,* an Italian term meaning "flute." **Listen** to the sound of the recorders in this concerto by Bach.

CD 6–2
Allegro

**from *Brandenburg Concerto No. 4*
by Johann Sebastian Bach**
This concerto features two recorders.

MUSIC MAKERS

Robert Tree Cody

Robert Tree Cody, of Dakota-Maricopa heritage, lives in Arizona. He has traveled throughout the United States and Europe as a traditional dancer, singer, and flutist. He teaches about the traditional ways of Native American peoples, including folklore, crafts, and music. In Arizona, he participates in artist-in-residence programs in the schools.

Unit 3 111

---

1 INTRODUCE

8b Have students experiment with whistle sounds. Show them a slide whistle. Help students discover that

- The sound becomes lower as the tube gets longer.
- The air travels over an edge in the opening of the whistle, which makes the air column vibrate.

Tell students that flutes produce sound in the same way as whistles. Different cultures produce many types of flutes.

2 DEVELOP

Listening

6a Play *Kokopelli Wandering Song* **CD 6-1.** Invite students to tap the beat lightly as they listen and then use standard terminology to describe the sound of the instrument they hear.

8b Have students look at and read about the *Kokopelli* artwork on p. 110. Share with students the legend of *Kokopelli* in Spotlight On on p. 110. Then have them read about the Native American flute and about Robert Tree Cody on p. 111. For more information about Native American flutes, see Cultural Connection on p. 110.

Playing

Have students

2d
- Echo as you play four-beat patterns on the recorder, using these notes:

- Look at the melody on p. 110 and show the fingering for each note.
- Play the melody together.

continued on page 112

▶ **Recorder** Some students may need extra help with recorder playing. Post a list of "Recorder Tips" to help students problem-solve their own playing. Tips may include:

- Place the left hand on top.
- Cover the holes completely.
- Rest the mouthpiece lightly on the lower lip.
- Press the upper lip against the mouthpiece with the bottom lip over the teeth.
- Start each note with *daah* and blow gently.

Circulate among students to check hand and finger position. Encourage students to choose a "recorder buddy" with whom to practice and share information.

ACROSS THE CURRICULUM

8b ▶ **Math** Have students measure and graph the lengths of flutes, recorders, or whistles. For example, have students finger the note "B" on a soprano recorder, then measure the distance from the whistle hole on the top of the recorder to the first open hole. The distance is the length of the air column that is vibrating when the recorder is played. Compare the measurement of different notes that are lower than "B." Repeat similar measurements for other flutes and whistles. Help students discover that the length of the air column is related to the pitch of the note played: the lower the pitch, the longer the vibrating air column.

Improvising

3b Write the pitches shown on p. 111 in the side column on the board. Invite students to improvise an eight-beat melody using those notes. Allow time to practice.

SAY We will be playing in question/answer style. Your improvisations will be the questions. The answer is the melody in your book.

3b Demonstrate by playing an eight-beat improvisation. Have students answer by playing the melody on p. 110 in their books. Invite pairs or trios of students to take turns improvising the "questions" as the class plays the "answer" phrase.

Listening

Have students compare their recorders to the Native American flute shown on p. 111.

ASK How are your recorders similar to the Native American flute? (Both have holes in the front; both are flutes; both have a whistle hole; sounds get lower as fingers are added.)

How are your recorders different from the Native American flute? (Native American flute is made of cedar; some students' recorders may be plastic; only the recorder has a hole for the thumb in the back; Native American flute has an animal carving at the whistle hole, which is used to adjust the sound)

SAY Native American flutes and recorders have both been used for many years. In Europe in the early 1700s, J.S. Bach used the recorder as part of the orchestra.

6b To help students aurally identify excerpts of music from diverse periods, invite them to listen to *Allegro* from
7b Bach's *Brandenburg Concerto No. 4* **CD 6-2.** Have them hold up their recorders each time they hear recorders in the music.

6b Play *Shika no tone* **CD 6-3.**

ASK How would you describe the sound of this flute? (Answers will vary.)

A Special Flute

The *shakuhachi* [shah-koo-HAH-chee] is a Japanese flute made of bamboo. The basic notes are D, F, G, A, and C. **Play** these notes on your recorder. Then **compose** a melody using these notes.

Shakuhachi players can create special effects by sliding their fingers and trilling or fluttering their tongues as they play.

What special effects can you **create** on the recorder? Add them to your melody.

Arts Connection

◀ Painting by Diana Ong of woman playing *shakuhachi*. The *shakuhachi* has been played for more than a thousand years. The instrument has four holes in the front and one in the back.

Listen to this excerpt featuring a *shakuhachi*. **Describe** the special effects that you hear.

CD 6–3
Shika no tone

Traditional Song from Japan as performed by Yamato Ensemble

Shika no tone (The Sound of Deer Calling to One Anoth[er]) is a *shakuhachi* composition that dates from the eighteenth century.

Tune In

At one time, the *shakuhachi* was played by Japanese priests who wore wicker baskets over their heads to hide their identities. They walked through the streets listening to conversations while playing soft tunes on their *shakuhachis*.

112

Footnotes

CULTURAL CONNECTION

▶ **Flutes Around the World** Many different kinds of flutes are found in cultures all over the world. Students may enjoy reading these stories about flutes from different cultures.

- *The Flute Player/La Flautista* by Robyn Eversole (Orchard Books, 1995). Originally in Spanish, this book is the story of a flute player who plays the songs of nature for neighbors living in an apartment building.

- *The Song of Six Birds* by Rene Deetlefs (Dutton Books, 2000). A young African girl learns to play the songs of native birds on her flute.

CHARACTER EDUCATION

▶ **Respect** To encourage students to demonstrate respectful behavior, discuss with them the meaning of respect (to have high regard or esteem for, to treat with courteous and considerate behavior.) Describe how individuals show respect for themselves (for example, behavior, attire, walking, talking, and so on) and authority figures such as teachers and parents. Question students about why it is important to show respect for others. Lead students to understand that it is important to be respectful of those who are different from, as well as similar to, them.

Song of the Flute

The flute is the oldest known wind instrument. Almost every culture has some kind of flute, but the flute we are most familiar with was designed by Theobald Boehm. The flute is played by blowing across a hole near one end of the instrument. The number of holes and keys on the flute has changed over the centuries.

◀ The modern flute is a long metal tube with 13 main holes, several smaller ones, and many keys of different shapes and sizes.

MUSIC MAKERS
Claude Debussy

Claude Debussy (1862–1918) was an important composer of the late nineteenth and early twentieth centuries. He began a movement in French music called Impressionism. Early in his life, Debussy wrote unusual music for the piano. He created dream-like moods using unusual harmonies, rhythms, and whole-tone scales.

Listen to *Syrinx*, a composition by Debussy for solo flute.

CD 6–4
Syrinx

by Claude Debussy
performed by James Galway
Debussy named this piece after a water nymph in the legend of Pan.

Now **listen** to the opening of *Prelude to the Afternoon of a Faun*, which features the flute with orchestra.

CD 6–5
Prelude to the Afternoon of a Faun

by Claude Debussy
This piece is about a faun, a mythical creature that is half man and half beast. This music was featured in the Disney film *Fantasia*.

Tune In

In music, Impressionism uses mood or atmosphere instead of emotion or story to convey the composer's intention.

Invite students to read about the Japanese *shakuhachi* on p. 112. Help students measure a line 1'9" long—the length of a traditional *shakuhachi*. Then ask students to compare the size of the *shakuhachi* to that of their recorders.

Have students turn to Sound Bank p. 517 for a detailed description of the *shakuhachi*. Play **CD 21-43** for an additional sound sample of the instrument.

Composing

4c Help students find the basic notes of the *shakuhachi* on p. 112. (D, F, G, A, C) Ask students to name each note and show the fingering for it on a recorder. Invite students to echo as you play four-beat patterns using these notes. Then have them create their own melodic phrases using these pitches.

Listening

Invite students to read about the modern orchestral flute on p. 113. If possible, show one to students.

6b Play *Syrinx* **CD 6-4** so students can hear the sound of a solo orchestral flute. Have them close their eyes and move one hand with the melody as they listen.

6a Play *Prelude to the Afternoon of a Faun* **CD 6-5**. Have students signal when they hear the flute.

Play **CD 21-31** from the Sound Bank for an additional sound clip of the flute.

3 CLOSE

Skill: PLAYING — **ASSESSMENT**

2a
3b **Performance/Observation** Invite students to play an improvised "question" phrase and the written "answer" phrase from p. 110 on recorder. Or, have students play the melodies they composed from p. 112. Students may play individually or in pairs. As you listen to the players, have other students practice by moving their fingers only (not blowing). Observe students' ability to accurately perform the phrases.

SKILLS REINFORCEMENT

6b ▶ **Listening** For additional experience with flute timbre, have students listen to and evaluate for personal preferences the following selections.

- *Camino de piedra* **CD 7-34** (panpipes)
- *Daybreak Vision* **CD 18-11** (Native American flute)
- *The Honiesuckle* **CD 21-20** (recorder)
- *Variations on Simple Gifts* **CD 9-19** (flute)

SCHOOL TO HOME CONNECTION

8b ▶ **Create Instruments** Have students design their own wind instruments. Make a list of possible materials (bamboo, cardboard tubes, PVC pipe, rubber hoses, and so on). Create a class composition for students' aerophone inventions.

TECHNOLOGY/MEDIA LINK

Web Site To learn more information about other flutes around the world, visit *www.sfsuccessnet.com*. Some flutes you might read about include fife, ocarina, and panpipes.

LESSON AT A GLANCE

Element Focus — **TEXTURE/HARMONY** Descant

Skill Objective **SINGING** Sing a song with a descant

Connection Activity **LANGUAGE ARTS** Relate a poem about trees to a folk song from Wales

MATERIALS

- "The Ash Grove"   **CD 6-6**

  Recording Routine: Intro (4 m.); vocal; interlude (4 m.); vocal; coda
- **Resource Book** p. I-10
- "Trees" (poem)

VOCABULARY

descant

♦ ♦ ♦ National Standards ♦ ♦ ♦

1d Sing music written in two parts
2a Play instruments accurately alone and in small ensembles
6a Listen and describe events in music using appropriate terms
7b Students use specific criteria for evaluating their own performances
8b Identify ways music relates to science

MORE MUSIC CHOICES

For more practice with descants/countermelodies:
"Roll On, Columbia," p. 116
"This Land Is Your Land," p. 118

1 INTRODUCE

8b Read the poem "Trees" (see Across the Curriculum below). Ask students to list all the different trees they know. Help students discover that

- An ash is a type of tree.
- A grove is a group of trees standing together, usually without undergrowth.

SONGS ABOUT NATURE

There are many different ways to create harmony. You've already done this by singing ostinatos and partner songs. A **descant** provides another way to sing in harmony.

Sing "The Ash Grove," a folk song from Wales.

Read the lyrics before you sing, to understand what the song is all about.

> A **descant** is another melody that decorates the main tune, usually placed above the main melody.

CD 6-6 MIDI 8

THE ASH GROVE

Folk Song from Wales

Descant

2. The ash   grove   is   speak -
   The light   through   its   branch -

Melody

1. Down yon - der green _ val - ley where stream - lets ___ me -
   Or   at   the   bright _ noon - tide In   sol - i - ___ tude
2. The   ash grove, how _ grace - ful, how plain - ly ___ 'tis
   When - ev - er the ___ light through its branch - es ___ is

ing,   The harp   plays   lan - guage for   me.
es   Brings fac -   es   gaz - ing on   me.

an - der, When twi - light ___ is ___ fad - ing   I   pen - sive - ly   rove,
wan - der, A - mid the ___ dark _ shades of the lone - ly ash   grove.
speak - ing, The harp through _ it ___ play - ing has lan - guage for me;
break - ing, A host of ___ kind _ fac - es is   gaz - ing on   me.

114

Footnotes

SKILLS REINFORCEMENT

2a ▶ **Playing** Give one or more students the opportunity to play the descant for "The Ash Grove" on instruments as the class sings the song. (Don't forget that some instruments, such as trumpets and clarinets, will have to transpose the music.)

▶ **Recorder** A countermelody for the "The Ash Grove" can be found on Resource Book p. I-10.

BUILDING SKILLS THROUGH MUSIC

▶ **Science** After students have learned the song "The Ash Grove" and heard the poem "Trees," share the information found in the Cultural Connection. Lead students in a discussion of the importance of trees in the environment.

ACROSS THE CURRICULUM

▶ **Language Arts** Introduce students to the well-known poem "Trees" by Joyce Kilmer.

I think that I shall never see
A poem lovely as a tree.
A tree whose hungry mouth is prest
Against the earth's sweet flowing breast;
A tree that looks at God all day,
And lifts her leafy arms to pray;
A tree that may in summer wear
A nest of robins in her hair;
Upon whose bosom snow has lain;
Who intimately lives with rain.
Poems are made by fools like me,
But only God can make a tree.

The notation for "The Ash Grove" with lyrics:

(2.) My friends come before me And
(1.) 'Tis there where the black-bird is cheer-ful-ly sing-ing, Each
(2.) The friends of my child-hood a-gain are be-fore me, Each

wak-en mem-'ries as I roam. Its leaves
war-bler en-chants with his note from the tree. Ah, then lit-tle
step wakes a mem-'ry as free-ly I roam; With soft whis-pers

rus-tle o'er me, The ash grove,
think I of sor-row or sad-ness; The ash grove en-
la-den, its leaves rus-tle o'er me, The ash grove, the

ash grove is my home.
chant-ing spells beau-ty for me.
ash grove a-lone is my home.

2 DEVELOP

Listening

Have students

- Look at the notation for "The Ash Grove" on p. 114 and follow the "roadmap" of the song.
- Read the text of "The Ash Grove" and discuss its meaning.

6a Play "The Ash Grove" **CD 6-6**, inviting students to follow the notation for the melody as they listen.

ASK Was the song sung in unison or harmony? (verse 1: unison; verse 2: harmony)

Explain to students that

- A descant was added to the second verse to create harmony.
- A descant is a second melody, usually higher than the main melody.
- The descant and melody create harmony when performed together.

Singing

1d Invite students to sing "The Ash Grove" melody with the recording. Then have students sing the descant with the recording. Finally, have students sing in two parts with the recording.

3 CLOSE

Element: TEXTURE/HARMONY   ASSESSMENT

7b **Music Journal Writing** Have students apply criteria to evaluate their own progress in harmony singing, by asking them to enter their assessments in their music journals. Also, ask them to list all the songs they can sing in harmony.

CULTURAL CONNECTION

8b ▶ **Arbor Day** Each year, citizens of the United States set aside a special day to plant trees. The holiday is called Arbor Day, and it began in Nebraska in 1872. Discouraged that his state had very few trees, Sterling J. Morton, a newspaper publisher, encouraged his fellow Nebraskans to beautify their state by planting trees. He offered prizes for the persons who planted the most trees. More than one million trees were planted by April 10 of that year, and Nebraskans celebrated the first Arbor Day. Today, Arbor Day is observed individually by state.

Invite students to develop two lists. One list should include information about the role of trees in the environment. (For example, trees purify the air, serve as a habitat for animals, and filter water.) The second list should include ideas about the role of trees for humans. (For example, trees provide food and shelter.)

TECHNOLOGY/MEDIA LINK

MIDI/Sequencing Software Use the MIDI song file for "The Ash Grove" to help students learn the vocal parts.

- Display the melody and descant tracks in graphic notation view. Mute the other tracks to help students focus; then play the file.
- Help students learn the melody. Play the melody alone and ask students to sing along. Follow the same procedure to help students learn the descant.
- Next, play both tracks as students rehearse first the melody and then the descant.
- Finally, play both tracks as half the students sing the melody and half sing the descant.

LESSON AT A GLANCE

Element Focus **TEXTURE/HARMONY** Countermelody

Skill Objective **SINGING** Sing a song with a countermelody

Connection Activity **SOCIAL STUDIES** Locate on a map places mentioned in the text of a song

MATERIALS

- "Roll On, Columbia" **CD 6-8**

  Recording Routine: Intro (4 m.); v. 1; refrain; v. 2; refrain; v. 3; refrain; v. 4; refrain
- map of the United States and Canada
- keyboard; selected melody instruments
- **Resource Book** p. F-15

VOCABULARY

countermelody   polyphonic texture

◆ ◆ ◆ ◆ National Standards ◆ ◆ ◆ ◆

1d Sing music written in two parts
2a Play instruments accurately in small ensembles
2d Perform simple accompaniments by ear
5c Identify standard notation symbols for pitch
7b Students use specific criteria for evaluating their own performances
8b Identify ways music relates to social studies

MORE MUSIC CHOICES

For more practice with descants/countermelodies:
"The Battle Hymn of Republic," p. 274

1 INTRODUCE

8b **ASK** **What are some of the main rivers that flow through the United States?** (Mississippi, Missouri, Colorado, Columbia, Ohio, and others)

Discuss the importance of rivers. (They provide recreation, food, water, and hydroelectric power.)

Singing Together

The Columbia River is one of our country's most spectacular rivers. **Listen** to "Roll On, Columbia." **Sing** the melody of the refrain. Then sing the **countermelody**. **Sing** the two parts together to experience polyphonic texture.

> A **countermelody** is played or sung at the same time as the main melody.

CD 6-8

Roll On, Columbia

Words by Woody Guthrie   Music Based on "Goodnight, Irene" by Huddie Ledbetter and John A. Lomax

s, l, t @ rm fs l ta

VERSE

1. Green Doug - las fir where the wa - ters cut through,
2. Oth - er big riv - ers add ___ pow - er to you,
3. At Bonne - ville now there are ships in the locks, The
4. And on up the ri - ver is the Grand Cou - lee Dam, The

Down her wild moun - tains and can - yons she flew,
Yak - i - ma, Snake, and the Klick - i - tat, too.
wa - ter has ris - en and cov - ered the rocks.
big - gest thing built by the hand of a man,

Ca - na - di - an North-west to the o - cean so blue,
7 Sand - y, Wil - lam - ette, and the Hood Riv - er, too,
7 Ship - loads a - plen - ty are ___ soon past the docks,
To run the great fact' - ries and ___ wa - ter the land,

Roll on, Co - lum - bia, roll on. _____

TRO – © Copyright 1936 (renewed), 1957 (renewed) and 1963 (renewed) Ludlow Music, Inc., New York, NY. Used by Permission.

116

Footnotes

ACROSS THE CURRICULUM

8b ▶ **Social Studies** Ask students to locate each of the places mentioned in the text of "Roll On, Columbia" on a map of the Pacific Northwest region. Have them label the references on the map. Challenge students to research information about the Columbia River region, such as the names of Native American groups in the region.

BUILDING SKILLS THROUGH MUSIC

▶ **Social Studies** Have students review the words of "Roll On, Columbia" by singing the song. Ask selected students to locate phrases in the song that identify natural geography features and list them on the board. Then ask them to locate words or phrases that describe or name man-made changes and add them to the list on the board.

TEACHER TO TEACHER

1d ▶ **Countermelodies** A countermelody is an independent melody that is sung in conjunction with the melody. Typically, countermelodies are well suited for students who have a fully developed head voice. Teach the countermelody for "Roll On, Columbia" using these steps:

- Students sing the refrain melody.
- Students sing the melody; the teacher sings the countermelody.
- Teach the countermelody by rote, echoing each phrase.
- Students sing the countermelody; the teacher sings the melody.
- One group of students sings the countermelody and another group sings the melody.

REFRAIN

Rolling a - long, Rolling a - long,
Roll on, _____ Co - lum - bia, roll on.

Rolling a - long, _____ Co - lum - bia, roll on. Your
Roll on, _____ Co - lum - bia, roll on. Your

pow - er turns dark - ness to dawn,
pow - er is turn - ing our dark - ness to dawn,

Roll on, Co - lum - bia, roll on, roll on.
Roll on, Co - lum - bia, roll on. _____

2 DEVELOP

Listening

 Play "Roll On, Columbia" **CD 6-8.** Invite students to discover where the Columbia River is located and how the river helps the people who live nearby. Then have students trace the Columbia River on a map of the United States and locate the places named in the song.

Singing

Direct students' attention to the notation for "Roll On, Columbia." Help them recognize that the song has a countermelody that is sung only on the refrain.

Help students learn to sing the countermelody. Then divide the class into two groups to sing the song in two parts with the recording.

Playing

Invite students to accompany the song using a keyboard. Point out the time signature ($\frac{3}{4}$) and the chords needed to accompany the song (F, B♭, C₇).

Have students follow the chord symbols in the music and play each chord on the downbeat (beat 1).

Encourage students to perform the countermelody on xylophone, bells, or other melody instruments.

3 CLOSE

Element: TEXTURE/HARMONY   ASSESSMENT

Performance/Observation In small groups, have students perform "Roll On, Columbia," with all students singing the verse, and some singing the countermelody while others sing the melody during the refrain. Observe that students can independently and accurately sing the countermelody.

SKILLS REINFORCEMENT

▶ **Guitar** To accompany "Roll On, Columbia" on guitar, have students use a capo on fret 3 and play the following chords:

- F = D
- B♭ = G
- C₇ = A₇

▶ **Mallets** An Orff arrangement of "Roll On, Columbia" can be found on p. F-15 of the Resource Book.

SCHOOL TO HOME CONNECTION

▶ **Class Project** Invite students to research ten or more facts about the most important river or waterway in their region including: the source of the river, its mouth and tributaries, key sites along its banks, dams and other structures, and historical activities on the river. Use the descriptions to create a class song or poem about it.

TECHNOLOGY/MEDIA LINK

Sequencing Software Have groups of four students record the two parts of "Roll On, Columbia" on separate tracks of a digital recording program and then self-assess their tone and pitch accuracy.

LESSON AT A GLANCE

Element Focus   **TEXTURE/HARMONY** Countermelody

Skill Objective   **PLAYING** Accompany a song on keyboard

Connection Activity   **RELATED ARTS** Discuss ways in which a similar topic is presented in different art forms

MATERIALS

- "This Land Is Your Land"   **CD 6-10**

  Recording Routine: Intro (10 m.); refrain; v. 1; refrain; v. 2; refrain; v. 3; refrain
- *This Land Is Your Land*   **CD 6-12**
- *Finale* from *"The River" Suite*   **CD 6-13**
- "The River" (narrative)
- **Resource Book** p. F-17
- keyboard
- map of the United States

VOCABULARY

countermelody

◆ ◆ ◆ ◆ National Standards ◆ ◆ ◆ ◆

1d Sing music written in two parts
2a Play instruments accurately alone and in small ensembles
2d Perform simple accompaniments by ear
3a Improvise simple harmonic accompaniments
5c Identify standard notation symbols for pitch
6b Listen and analyze uses of harmony and timbre in music from diverse genres
7b Students use specific criteria for evaluating their own performances
8a Show how different arts portray the same idea in unique ways
8b Identify ways music relates to social studies

MORE MUSIC CHOICES

For more practice with songs with descants or countermelodies:

"Deck the Hall," p. 474

Sing of America's Beauty

"This Land Is Your Land" is probably the most popular song composed by Woody Guthrie. **Sing** the melody of the refrain. Then **sing** the countermelody. How is the countermelody different from the main melody?

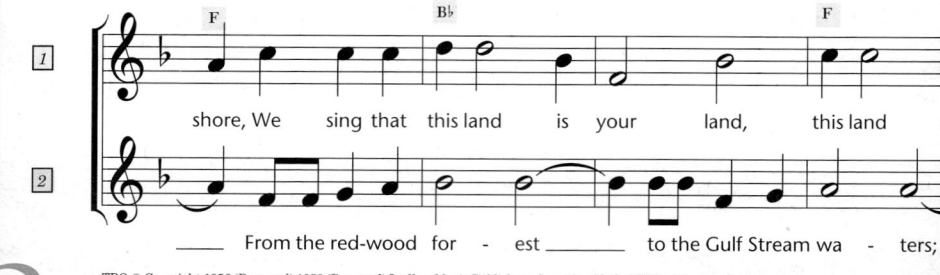

This Land Is Your Land

Words and Music by Woody Guthrie
Countermelody by Ruth Tutell

TRO © Copyright 1956 (Renewed) 1958 (Renewed) Ludlow Music Publishers, Inc., New York, NY Used by Permission.

118

Footnotes

ACROSS THE CURRICULUM

8b ▶ **Social Studies** Use a map of the United States to help students locate the various places mentioned in "This Land Is Your Land." You may wish to take the states mentioned in the song—California, Maine, Montana, and New York—and divide the class into four groups, one for each state. Have each group research and report to the class on "its" state. Information might include location, history, resources, and population.

BUILDING SKILLS THROUGH MUSIC

▶ **Reading** Invite students to sing "This Land Is Your Land" and decide how dynamic changes can be used to emphasize different ideas expressed in the song. Select individual students to show dynamic changes either by conducting with the right hand and varying the size of the beat or by raising or lowering the left hand to show *crescendo* and *decrescendo*.

SPOTLIGHT ON

▶ **Woody Guthrie** Woodrow Wilson ("Woody") Guthrie (1912–1967) was one of America's most famous folk singers and composers. He was born in Okemah, Oklahoma, but spent much of his life traveling around the United States. He wrote songs about ordinary people and about the natural beauty of America. A year before Guthrie died, he received the Department of the Interior's Conservation Service Award in recognition of the work he did to make the American people aware of their heritage and the land.

Unfortunately, Guthrie suffered from Huntington's disease, a progressive deterioration of the brain, and he died at a relatively young age.

F **C₇** **F** *Fine*

1

mine, Yes, it's made for you and me. _____

2

_____ This land was made for you and me. _____

VERSE

F **B♭** **F**

1. As I was walk - ing _____ that rib - bon of high - way, __
2. I've roamed and ram - bled _____ and I fol-lowed my foot - steps __
3. When the sun comes shin - ing _____ and I _____ was stroll - ing __

F **C₇** **F**

_____ I saw a - bove me _____ that end - less sky - way, __
_____ to the spar - kling sands of _____ her dia-mond des - erts, __
_____ And the wheat-fields wav - ing _____ and the dust clouds roll - ing, __

F **B♭** **F**

_____ I saw be - low me _____ that gold - en val - ley, __
_____ And all a - round me _____ a voice was sound - ing, __
_____ As the fog was lift - ing _____ a voice was chant - ing, __

F **C₇** **F** *D.C. al Fine*

_____ This land was made for you and me. _____
_____ "This land was made for you and me." _____
_____ "This land was made for you and me." _____

Unit 3 119

1 INTRODUCE

8b Read the words to "This Land Is Your Land" and invite students to locate the place names on a map (see Across the Curriculum on p. 120).

2 DEVELOP

Listening

6b Play "This Land Is Your Land" **CD 6-10.** Ask students to raise their hands when they hear a part that is sung in harmony. Then ask them to look at the song notation on pp. 118–119 and identify which lines are written in harmony.

Singing

1d Invite students to sing the melody of "This Land Is Your Land" with the recording. Then direct students' attention to the harmony part. Help them notice that

- Different states are mentioned in the harmony part.
- The harmony part goes both higher and lower than the melody.
- The harmony part is called a countermelody.

Explain that descants and countermelodies are similar, but descants are usually played or sung above the melody, while countermelodies go below the melody at least part of the time. Encourage students to notice where the countermelody for "This Land Is Your Land" goes above and below the melody.

Have students

- Learn the countermelody, using the recording.
- Perform this song representative of American heritage in two parts with the Stereo Performance Track **CD 6-11.**

continued on page 120

SKILLS REINFORCEMENT

2d ▶ **Performing** Divide students into small groups and invite them to create instrumental accompaniments for "This Land Is Your Land." Have groups perform their arrangements for the class. Some groups may wish to create rhythmic accompaniments, while others may wish to include chords.

 ▶ **Mallets** An Orff arrangement of "This Land Is Your Land" can be found on p. F-17 of the Resource Book.

TEACHER TO TEACHER

▶ **Ribbon of Highway** Using a road atlas, have students make an outline of the map of the United States and trace a route across the states, from coast to coast. One such highway is Route 30, which is also called Lancaster Pike, the Mormon Pioneer National Historical Trail, and the Lincoln Highway. Another coast-to-coast route is Interstate 80. Have students match up the names of the different routes for each state.

Unit 3 *Learning the Language of Music* **119**

Performing

2a Refer students to p. 120 and invite them to perform a keyboard accompaniment to "This Land Is Your Land."

Help them discover that

5c
- Chord symbols for the accompaniment are printed above the staff in the notation on pp. 118–119.
- The time signature ($\frac{2}{2}$) lets them know to play twice per measure.

3a When students are comfortable playing the chords, encourage them to improvise an accompaniment using different rhythm patterns.

Listening

6b Play the recording of *This Land Is Your Land* **CD 6-12**, as performed by Woody Guthrie.

ASK On what instrument is Guthrie accompanying himself? (guitar)

Creating

Encourage students to create a new verse for "This Land Is Your Land." Students may enjoy substituting locations in their area for those in the song.

Listening

8a Read the excerpt from the narrative to the documentary film *The River* directed by Pare Lorentz. Have students pick out the names of all the different rivers mentioned in the narrative. Point out that each of these rivers eventually flows into the Mississippi—the main "character" in the film.

6b Play *Finale* from *"The River" Suite* **CD 6-13** and have students identify excerpts of music representing diverse genres.

ASK Are there any melodies that you recognize? ("The Bear Went Over the Mountain")

Play the recording again while a student volunteer gives a dramatic reading of the written narrative excerpt.

Keyboard Harmony

The harmony in "This Land Is Your Land" is based on the three chords shown below.

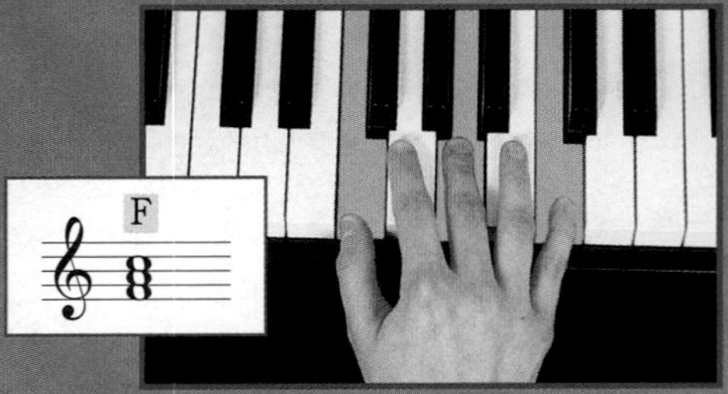

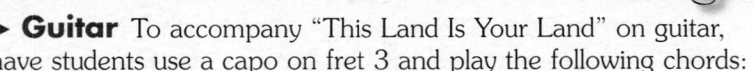

Play the chords on keyboard to accompany the song. Follow the chord symbols above the music as you play.

Roaming with Woody

Fortunately for music lovers everywhere, Woody Guthrie recorded many of his songs before a serious illness ended his career. **Listen** to one of his early recordings of *This Land Is Your Land.*

CD 6–12
This Land Is Your Land

written and performed by Woody Guthrie

When Guthrie wrote this song in 1940, the final line of each verse was sometimes sung *God blessed America for me.*

Footnotes

ACROSS THE CURRICULUM

▶ **Language Arts** Share a delightful book called *This Land Is Your Land* by Woody Guthrie and Kathy Jakobsen (Little, Brown & Company, 1998). The lyrics of the song and relevant quotations about America are set in a background of oil paintings reminiscent of the 1920s and 1930s. The book is a tribute to America's diverse population, geographical regions, and unifying belief in freedom.

Students can read more about the life and music of Woody Guthrie in *Lives of the Musicians: Good Times, Bad Times (and What the Neighbors Thought)* by Kathleen Krull (Harcourt, 1993).

SKILLS REINFORCEMENT

▶ **Guitar** To accompany "This Land Is Your Land" on guitar, have students use a capo on fret 3 and play the following chords:

2d
- F = D
- B♭ = G
- C₇ = A₇

River Inspirations

The music of American composer Virgil Thomson (1896–1989) was frequently inspired by the beauty and grandeur of our country. In 1937, he wrote music to accompany *The River,* a documentary film about the Mississippi River.

Listen to this excerpt from *"The River" Suite.* **Identify** sections in which different melodies are played at the same time.

CD 6–13
Finale

from *"The River" Suite*
by Virgil Thomson

Thomson incorporated many folk songs into his music. Do you recognize the melody of "The Bear Went Over the Mountain" in *Finale*?

This excerpt, from the narrative to the film *The River,* names the tributaries that flow to the Mississippi River. Pare Lorentz was the director of the documentary.

The River

by Pare Lorentz

Down the Yellowstone, the Milk, the White, and Cheyenne;
The Cannonball, the Musselshell, the James, and the Sioux;
Down the Judith, the Grand, the Osage, and the Platte,
The Skunk, the Salt, the Black, and Minnesota;
Down the Rock, the Illinois, and the Kankakee,
The Allegheny, the Monongahela, Kanawha, and Muskingum;
Down the Miami, the Wabash, the Licking and the Green,
The Cumberland, the Kentucky, and the Tennessee;
Down the Ouachita, the Wichita, the Red, and Yazoo—
Down the Missouri, three thousand miles from the Rockies;
   Down the Ohio, a thousand miles from the Alleghenies;
Down the Arkansas, fifteen hundred miles from the Great Divide;
   Down the Red, a thousand miles from Texas;
Down the great Valley, twenty-five hundred miles from Minnesota,
   Carrying every rivulet and brook, creek and rill,
Carrying all the rivers that run down two-thirds the continent—
   The Mississippi runs to the Gulf.

Unit 3 **121**

---

3 CLOSE

Element: TEXTURE/HARMONY ASSESSMENT

7b **Performance/Observation** Use the following rubric to assess how well students can perform "This Land Is Your Land."

5 = Can sing the melody and countermelody accurately and independently

4 = Can sing the refrain or verse accurately and independently

3 = Can sing the melody and countermelody with fair accuracy

2 = Can sing only the melody with fair accuracy

1 = Has difficulty singing the melody accurately

SPOTLIGHT ON

▶ **The Composer** Virgil Thomson (1896–1989) was inspired by cowboy songs, folk tunes, hymns, baroque fugues, patriotic songs, and dances. He was chief music critic of the *New York Herald Tribune* for 14 years.

Thomson's *"The River" Suite* has four movements. The first movement, *The Old South,* has subtle hints of "Dixie." The second movement, *Industrial Expansion in the Mississippi Valley,* depicts a Saturday night celebration, with a jazz trombone using lots of glissandos. The slow movement, *Soil Erosion and Floods,* starts with the "river motif," which is introduced by the horn. The *Finale* has a string of melodies leading to a hymn tune used in "Dixie."

TECHNOLOGY/MEDIA LINK

1d **MIDI/Sequencing Software** Use the MIDI song file for "This Land Is Your Land" to help students learn the vocal parts.

- Display the melody and descant tracks in graphic notation view. Mute the other tracks to help students focus; then play the file.

- Help students learn the melody. Play the melody alone and ask students to sing along. Follow the same procedure to help students learn the countermelody.

- Next, play both tracks as students rehearse first the melody and then the countermelody.

- Finally, play both tracks as half the students sing the melody and half sing the countermelody.

Unit 3 *Learning the Language of Music* **121**

UNIT 3 — Review and Assessment

WHAT DO YOU KNOW?

MATERIALS
- "This Land is Your Land," p. 118   **CD 6-10**
- **Resource Book** pp. B-8

Review pitch syllables with the class. Then, invite students to look at the last four measures of the refrain of "This Land is Your Land" and find *do*. Once they have decided that *do* is F, write the F-major scale on the board and encourage them tell you which pitch syllable goes with each note. Have students read and answer the questions independently.

Review the definitions of *legato*, *staccato*, and *marcato*. Invite students to make vocal sounds with each articulation. For example, suggest that they say a very smooth *dah-dah-dah* for the *legato*, a *tut-tut-tut* for *staccato*, and a *tahk-tahk-tahk* for *marcato*. Play each line for the class and ask students to answer the articulation questions.

WHAT DO YOU HEAR?

MATERIALS
- "The Stars and Stripes Forever"   **CD 6-14**
- *What Do You Hear? 3*
- **Resource Book** p. B-8

Review the terms for the dynamics with students. Tell them that they will hear four excerpts from *Stars and Stripes Forever* and need to listen for the dynamics and articulation. Play *What Do You Hear? 3*. For a formal assessment, duplicate the Unit 3 assessment worksheet found on Resource Book p. B-8.

What Do You Know?

1. Look at the last four measures of the refrain of "This Land Is Your Land," on page 118, in which *do* is in the first space.

   a. Point to all the notes called *so*.
   b. Point to all the notes called *re*.
   c. Point to all the notes called *ti*.

2. Look at the three phrases below.

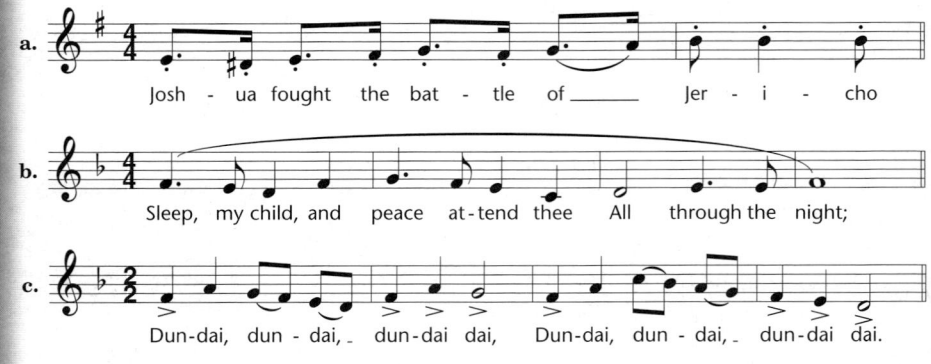

a. Josh - ua fought the bat - tle of _____ Jer - i - cho

b. Sleep, my child, and peace at-tend thee   All   through the night;

c. Dun-dai, dun - dai, _ dun-dai dai,   Dun-dai, dun - dai, _ dun-dai dai.

   - Point to the phrase that should be performed in a *legato* style.
   - Point to the phrase that should be performed in a *marcato* style.
   - Point to the phrase that should be performed in a *staccato* style.

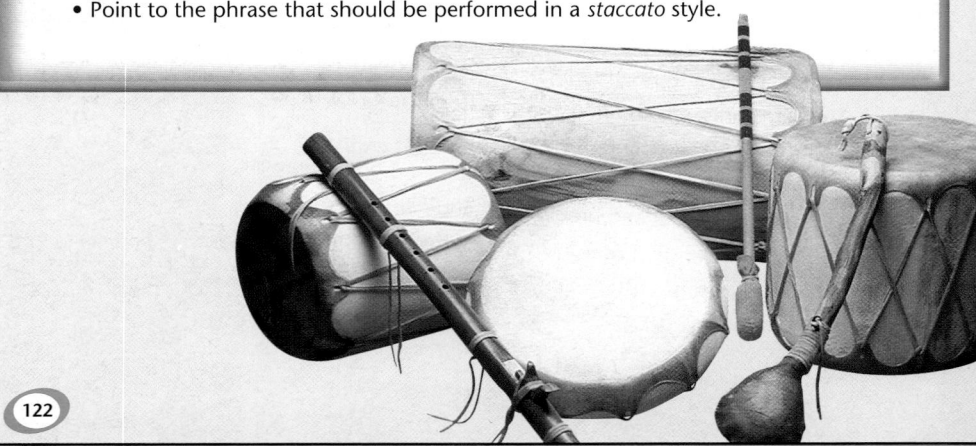

122

ANSWER KEY

▶ What Do You Know?

1. **a.** *(so)* C—treble clef, first ledger line below the staff (one)
   b. *(re)* G—treble clef, second line (four)
   c. *(ti)* E—treble clef, first line (two)

2. Line l should be performed in *staccato* style.
   Line 2 should be performed in *legato* style.
   Line 3 should be performed in *marcato* style.

▶ What Do You Hear?

1. **a.** *Crescendo*
2. **b.** *Legato*
3. **b.** *Marcato*
4. **b.** *Fortissimo*

Perform, Create

What Do You Hear? 3

 CD 6–14

Listen to four excerpts from *The Stars and Stripes Forever*. Following each excerpt, point to the words that best describe the dynamics or articulation you hear in the music.

1. a. *Crescendo*   **b.** *Forte*

2. a. *Staccato*   **b.** *Legato*

3. a. *Legato*   **b.** *Marcato*

4. a. *Pianissimo*   **b.** *Fortissimo*

What You Can Do

Sing and Show Hand Signs

Sing "*Himmel und Erde*," page 94, using hand signs and pitch syllables. Then sing the song with the lyrics.

Sing and Conduct

Sing "All Through the Night," page 105, and conduct the beat while following the notation. Sing the song, using rhythm syllables and then the lyrics.

Create a Rhythm Pattern

Create a four-measure rhythm pattern in $\frac{3}{4}$ meter using ♩ ♩ ♩. ♩. ♪. Be sure to include rests.

Now perform your rhythm pattern on an instrument of your choice.

WHAT YOU CAN DO

MATERIALS	
• "*Himmel und Erde*," p. 94	**CD 5-11**
• "All Through the Night," p. 104	**CD 5-28**
• **Resource Book** p. B-10	
• classroom percussion instruments	

Sing and Show Hand Signs

Tell the class that "*Himmel und Erde*" is great for practicing hand signs and pitch syllables. State that *do* is on the first space F and *so* is on C. After reviewing hand signs with the class, have students sing the song with both hand signs and pitch syllables. Finally, encourage students to sing the song with the words.

Sing and Conduct

Invite students to look at "All Through the Night." Tell them that they will now have a chance to be *maestros* and conduct this lovely song. Have them pick up a pencil "baton" in their right hands. Ask in what meter "All Through the Night" is written. ($\frac{4}{4}$)

Demonstrate the conducting pattern and ask students to follow along with you. They should keep their movements very flowing.

When the piece is ended, students should "cut off" the sound by using a circle. Encourage students to first conduct the song as they sing. Then, invite volunteers to come up and conduct while the class sings and follows.

Create a Rhythm Pattern

Invite students to use the examples below to create a four-measure rhythm pattern in $\frac{3}{4}$ meter. Have students include the dotted-quarter/eighth-note pattern (*tam-ti*) in their work. Encourage volunteers to play their patterns for the class.

TECHNOLOGY/MEDIA LINK

Rubrics Visit *www.sfsuccessnet.com* for rubrics to assess students' achievement in music skills.

Lesson	Elements	Skills	

LESSON 1 — CORE
Expressive Sounds

pp. 128–131

Element: Expression
Concept: Dynamics and tempo
Focus: Expressive use of rhythm and timbre

Secondary Element
Harmony: chord changes including I, IV, and V

National Standards
1a 1c 2d 6b 7a 9a

Skill: Listening
Objective: Listen to an example of *jaro-cho* style from Mexico

Secondary Skills
- **Listening** Listen to a recording and discuss style
- **Singing** Sing lyrics in Spanish and experiment with expression
- **Listening** Listen to a recording and discuss the instruments used
- **Playing** Play chord roots on selected instruments
- **Moving** Learn a simple dance step for the song

SKILLS REINFORCEMENT
- **Creating** Create a rhythm to perform with the song
- **Singing** Have one group sing and other groups accompany with vocal chord tones

---

LESSON 2
Upbeats

pp. 132–135

Element: Rhythm
Concept: Beat
Focus: Upbeat

Secondary Element
Melody: pitch and direction

National Standards
1c 2b 2c 5a 5b

Skill: Singing
Objective: Sing songs with phrases that begin with an upbeat

Secondary Skills
- **Reading** Read notation and identify the upbeats
- **Playing** Play keyboard or bell accompaniment
- **Reading** Identify phrases with one or two upbeats in the song
- **Playing** Play a xylophone or metallophone accompaniment
- **Listening** Listen to the recording

SKILLS REINFORCEMENT
- **Mallets** Play a xylophone accompaniment
- **Mallets** Play a xylophone or metallophone accompaniment

LESSON 3
Rhythm of the Rails

pp. 136–137

Element: Rhythm
Concept: Beat
Focus: ♩. ♪

Secondary Element
Melody: intervals

National Standards
1a 2a 4c 5a 6c 8a 8b

Skill: Reading
Objective: Read rhythm patterns using ♩. ♪

Secondary Skills
- **Singing** Sing the song while following the notation
- **Analyzing** Find another dotted rhythm pattern and compare

SKILLS REINFORCEMENT
- **Reading** Read and perform a counter rhythm
- **Recorder** Play a countermelody
- **Mallets** Perform an Orff arrangement

👉 Reading Sequence 13, p. 496

Connections

Music and Other Literature

Connection: Style

Activity: Identify features of *jarocho* style

ACROSS THE CURRICULUM
Language Arts Read a book about the life and career of Ritchie Valens
Social Studies Information on Veracruz

CULTURAL CONNECTION **Jarocho Ensemble** Information about the instruments in the ensemble

SPOTLIGHT ON **Folklórico Dance** Information on the cultural significance of Mexican dance

CHARACTER EDUCATION **Respect** Consider ways to be more accepting and understanding of other cultures

BUILDING SKILLS THROUGH MUSIC **Reading** Discuss possible meanings of the song title

Songs
"*La bamba*" (Spanish)
"*La bamba*" (English)

Listening Selections
La bamba (Ritchie Valens)
La bamba (*son jarocho*) (excerpt)
M•U•S•I•C   M•A•K•E•R•S
   Ritchie Valens

More Music Choices
"Imbabura," p. 203
"*Canción Mixteca*," (Mixteca Song), p. 326

ASSESSMENT

Music Journal List expressive musical qualities needed for exciting performance

TECHNOLOGY/MEDIA LINK
Web Site More information on *conjunto jarocho* Mexican music

---

Connection: Style

Activity: Explore origins of music with different styles

SPOTLIGHT ON
Jamaica Background information on the country
San Antonio Facts about the city

CULTURAL CONNECTION
Carribean Music History of the music
Western Swing Information about the style of music

ACROSS THE CURRICULUM **Science** Discuss the building materials of different areas and how geography or weather might have an impact on them

BUILDING SKILLS THROUGH MUSIC **Social Studies** Discuss the significance of the Alamo in American history

Songs
"Hosanna, Me Build a House"
"San Antonio Rose"

Listening Selection *New San Antonio Rose*
M•U•S•I•C   M•A•K•E•R•S
   Bob Wills

More Music Choices
"This World," p. 168
"Connemara Lullaby," p. 232

ASSESSMENT

Performance/Observation Sing and play ostinatos with an upbeat

TECHNOLOGY/MEDIA LINK
Web Site More information on Caribbean music as well as country music and musicians

---

Connection: Social Studies

Activity: Discuss the impact of railroads in the United States

MOVEMENT **Creative Movement** Create movements for the song

ACROSS THE CURRICULUM **Social Studies/Math** Learn about the impact of railroads on the development of the United States; calculate distances mentioned in the song

SCHOOL TO HOME CONNECTION **Railroads** Ask family and friends about train travel experiences

BUILDING SKILLS THROUGH MUSIC **Writing** Write a brief paragraph about life as a hobo

Song "Wabash Cannon Ball"

More Music Choices
"Battle Cry of Freedom," p. 272

ASSESSMENT

Performance/Observation Sing the song and conduct meter in 2 accurately

TECHNOLOGY/MEDIA LINK
Sequencing Software Create a rhythm accompaniment to a song

Lesson	**Elements**	**Skills**

LESSON 4 CORE

Sounds of Scotland

pp. 138–141

Reading Sequence 14, p. 496

Element: Rhythm
Concept: Pattern
Focus: Dotted rhythm patterns

Secondary Element
Form: verse/refrain

National Standards
1c 1d 2c 5a 5d 6c 8a
8b 9a

Skill: Reading
Objective: Sing and read from notation of a song containing dotted eighth/sixteenth note rhythm patterns

Secondary Skills
• **Reading** Read the rhythm of the song using rhythm syllables
• **Singing** Conduct a four-beat pattern while singing the song
• **Moving** Learn a Scottish country dance
• **Reading** Read a different rhythm pattern

SKILLS REINFORCEMENT
• **Keyboard** Play two handed accompaniment
• **Creating** Write a counterrhythm
• **Recorder** Play a countermelody
• **Singing** Practice singing in thirds

LESSON 5 CORE

A Nonsense Rondo

pp. 142-145

Element: Form
Concept: Rondo
Focus: Rondo form

Secondary Element
Expression: dynamics and articulation

National Standards
1a 2a 4c 5a 6b 7b 8a

Skill: Playing
Objective: Perform a rondo for voices and percussion instruments

Secondary Skills
• **Analyzing** Listen to a selection and identify rondo form
• **Singing** Listen to the song and follow notation, then sing the song
• **Moving** Perform a movement routine with the song
• **Playing** Perform an Orff arrangement in rondo form
• **Listening** Listen to a selection and identify the theme

SKILLS REINFORCEMENT
• **Creating** Create an art piece to visually represent rondo form
• **Recorder** Use practice exercises to learn to play a trill

---

LESSON 6

A Scale of Major Importance
pp. 146-147

Reading Sequence 15, p. 497

Element: Melody
Concept: Tonality
Focus: Diatonic major scale

Secondary Element
Rhythm: duration

National Standards
1c 5a 5c 6c 8b

Skill: Reading
Objective: Sing a song and read from notation that is based on the diatonic major scale

Secondary Skills
• **Singing** Sing the song in Spanish
• **Analyzing** Read intervals in the C scale and identify half steps
• **Notating** Notate the C-major scale on the staff

SKILLS REINFORCEMENT
• **Reading** Read and notate F, G, and D scales

Connections

Music and Other Literature

Connection: Culture

Activity: Explore Scottish culture

MOVEMENT   **Patterned Dance** Learn a Scottish country-dance

ACROSS THE CURRICULUM
Social Studies Learn information about Scotland
Language Arts/Drama Read and present a Scottish folktale

MEETING INDIVIDUAL NEEDS   **Including Everyone** Learn rhythm patterns with a partner

CULTURAL CONNECTION   **Scottish Language** The languages used in Scotland

SCHOOL TO HOME CONNECTION   **Local Bagpipers** Invite Scottish or Celtic bagpipers to visit and share information about heritage

BUILDING SKILLS THROUGH MUSIC   **Language** Discuss the musical characteristics and timbres important to the performance of the songs

Songs
"Scotland the Brave"
"Loch Lomond"

Listening Selection *Scottish Medley*

More Music Choices
"Colorado Trail," p. 276

ASSESSMENT

Performance/Observation
Sing the song with rhythm syllables to demonstrate understanding of pattern

Show What You Know!
Mid-unit assessment

TECHNOLOGY/MEDIA LINK
Web Site More information about the Gaelic music of Scotland and Ireland

---

Connection: Related Arts

Activity: Read a poem in rondo form

ACROSS THE CURRICULUM   **Language Arts** Read a poem and discuss the form

SPOTLIGHT ON   **The Concerto** Facts about the musical form

MEETING INDIVIDUAL NEEDS
Moving Suggestions to help students perform the movement activity
Including Everyone Tips to help students with special needs play instruments

TEACHER TO TEACHER   **Substituting Instruments** Suggestions for substituting instrument parts

BUILDING SKILLS THROUGH MUSIC   **Theatre** Create a dramatization for the poem

Song "Ama-Lama"

Listening Selection *Concerto No. 1 for Horn and Orchestra in D Major, ":Rondo"*
Poem "Beavers in November" (excerpt)
M·U·S·I·C M·A·K·E·R·S
Wolfgang Amadeus Mozart

More Music Choices
Cotton Boll Rag, p. 333

ASSESSMENT

Performance/Peer Critique Perform a rondo with rhythmic accuracy and ensemble balance

TECHNOLOGY/MEDIA LINK
Notation Software
Notate musical phrases to show rondo

Connection: Mathematics

Activity: Examine the numerical sequence and interval relationship in a musical scale

CULTURAL CONNECTION   **Christmas in Mexico** Information about Mexican festivities

TEACHER TO TEACHER   **Intervals** Help students to name diatonic intervals

BUILDING SKILLS THROUGH MUSIC   **Social Studies** Discuss family traditions for celebrations

Songs
"*Las velitas*"
"Candles Burning Bright"

More Music Choices
"*Viva Jujuy*," p. 228

ASSESSMENT

Performance/Observation
Sing song and accurately perform diatonic scale patterns

Show What You Know!
Mid-unit assessment

TECHNOLOGY/MEDIA LINK
Notation Software
Notate and print major scales

Lesson	Elements	Skills

LESSON 7

A Song of Seasons
pp. 148-149

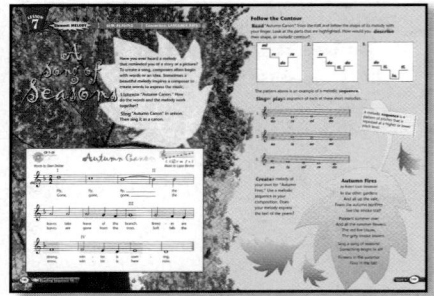

Reading Sequence 16, p. 497

Element: Melody
Concept: Pattern
Focus: Melodic sequence

Secondary Element
Texture: canons

National Standards
1b 1d 2e 5c 5d 6c 8b

Skill: Reading
Objective: Sing a song from notation that includes melodic sequences

Secondary Skills
- **Singing** Learn the song by rote
- **Analyzing** Analyze the melodic contour and melodic sequence of the song

SKILLS REINFORCEMENT
- **Notating** Notate a short melodic pattern
- **Mallets** Play an Orff arrangement

LESSON 8

CORE
Listen to the Patterns
pp. 150-153

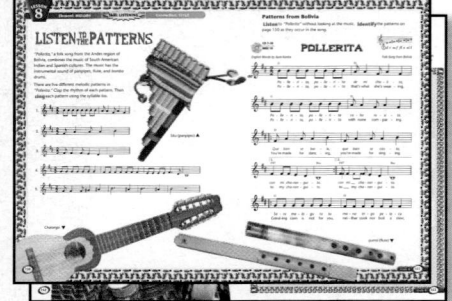

Element: Melody
Concept: Pattern
Focus: Melodic patterns

Secondary Element
Rhythm: pattern

National Standards
1a 1c 4a 5a 5b 6a 6b 8b

Skill: Listening
Objective: Listen to and identify various melodic patterns

Secondary Skills
- **Reading** Read notation with pitch and rhythm syllables
- **Singing** Learn a song in English and Spanish
- **Listening** Listen to the selections and discuss instrumentation
- **Creating** Create melodic visuals and use them to create new melody

SKILLS REINFORCEMENT
- **Listening** Discuss the timbre of the instruments discussed in the lesson

---

LESSON 9

CORE
A Drum Roll, Please
pp. 154-157

Element: Timbre
Concept: Instrumental
Focus: Percussion

Secondary Element
Rhythm: patterns

National Standards
2b 5a 6a 6b 7a 8b

Skill: Playing
Objective: Perform a piece for percussion ensemble

Secondary Skills
- **Listening** Listen to and describe drum timbres
- **Playing** Play a hand drum using different techniques
- **Reading** Read and clap the rhythm of percussion ensemble parts, then transfer to instruments

SKILLS REINFORCEMENT
- **Listening** Listen to and describe several drum selections

Connections

Music and Other Literature

Connection: Language Arts

Activity: Discuss a poem about autumn

SPOTLIGHT ON **The Composer and Lyricist** Information about Lajos Bárdos and Sean Deibler

ACROSS THE CURRICULUM **Language Arts** Discuss autumn and create a student-illustrated poem about the coming of autumn

BUILDING SKILLS THROUGH MUSIC **Art** Create a visual of the melodic movement in the song

Song "Autumn Canon"
Poem "Autumn Fires"

More Music Choices
"I Love the Mountains," p. 34

ASSESSMENT

Performance/Observation Sing a song in canon; create sequences from provided patterns

TECHNOLOGY/MEDIA LINK

Notation Software Create and notate melodic sequences and transpose the melody

---

Connection: Style

Activity: Discuss musical instruments used in the music of the Andes

CULTURAL CONNECTION
Native Americans of Bolivia Discuss the ethnic diversity of Bolivia
A Loyal Companion Learn about the llama

ACROSS THE CURRICULUM
Social Studies Facts about Bolivia
Language Arts Share a humorous poem and read a book about the children of Bolivia

MOVEMENT **Patterned Dance** Learn a dance for the song

SPOTLIGHT ON **The Performers** Information about Andes Manta and Inti-Illimani

BUILDING SKILLS THROUGH MUSIC **Reading** Identify similarities and differences between instrumental timbres

Songs
"Pollerita" (Spanish)
"Pollerita" (English)

Listening Selections
Camino de piedra
Amores hallarás
Listening Map *Amores hallarás*
Poem "The Llama"

More Music Choices
"Imbabura," p. 203
"El carite" ("The Kingfish"), p. 305
"Viva Jujuy," p. 228

ASSESSMENT

Observation Identify patterns as they appear in the song recording

TECHNOLOGY/MEDIA LINK

Transparency Display listening map
MIDI/Sequencing Software Locate melodic phrases and identify melodic contours

---

Connection: Culture

Activity: Discuss the role of drums in various cultures

ACROSS THE CURRICULUM
Social Studies/Language Arts Locate the geographical areas associated with the listening examples and describe each percussion group
Language Arts Read about a Japanese drum festival

AUDIENCE ETIQUETTE **Specific Venues and Genres** Discuss appropriate behavior for different venues

MEETING INDIVIDUAL NEEDS **Different Drummers** Alternatives for performing drum patterns

CULTURAL CONNECTION **Taiko** Information about *taiko* drums

CHARACTER EDUCATION **Diversity** Consider personal characteristics or attributes that cross cultural barriers

BUILDING SKILLS THROUGH MUSIC **Social Studies** Discuss the prominent musical characteristics of listening selections

Listening Selections
Malagueña (excerpt)
Birdland (excerpt)
Wipe Out
Yaudachi (excerpt)
Conga Kings Grand Finale (excerpt)
O'Sullivan's March

More Music Choices
Theme and Variations for Percussion, p. 65
"Jo'ashilá," p. 108

ASSESSMENT

Performance/Peer Critique Perform in percussion ensembles and describe changes in timbre with added instrumentss

TECHNOLOGY/MEDIA LINK

Web Site More information on percussion instruments from around the world

Lesson	Elements	Skills	
LESSON 10 **Where You Lead...I Will Follow** pp. 158-159 	**Element: Texture/Harmony** **Concept:** Texture **Focus:** Two-part canon **Secondary Element** Timbre: instrumental **National Standards** `1d` `2a` `6b` `7a` `8a`	**Skill: Singing** **Objective:** Perform a song as a two-part canon **Secondary Skills** • **Singing** Sing the song in two groups • **Listening** Listen to instruments and describe the texture	**SKILLS REINFORCEMENT** • **Recorder** Play a recorder ostinato
LESSON 11 **CORE** **Round and Round** pp. 160-161 	**Element: Texture/Harmony** **Concept:** Texture **Focus:** Three-part rounds **Secondary Element** Tonality: minor **National Standards** `1c` `1d` `2a` `6b` `7b`	**Skill: Moving** **Objective:** Perform a circle dance to accompany a three-part round **Secondary Skills** • **Listening** Listen to and identify the tonality of the song and its texture • **Singing** Sing phrases in groups • **Playing** Play phrases on mallet instruments • **Moving** Learn a movement routine	**SKILLS REINFORCEMENT** • **Recorder** Play a recorder ostinato • **Keyboard** Play the song on keyboard
LESSON 12 **Rounds** pp. 162–163 	**Element: Texture/Harmony** **Concept:** Texture **Focus:** Round **Secondary Element** Timbre: vocal **National Standards** `1a` `1d` `4c` `5d` `7a` `8a`	**Skill: Singing** **Objective:** Sing a three-part round **Secondary Skills** • **Singing** Sing the song in three groups • **Comparing** Discuss the relationship between poetry and music	**SKILLS REINFORCEMENT** • **Singing** Sing independently of other groups

Connections

Music and Other Literature

Connection: Related Arts

Activity: Recognize that imitation is also used in visual arts

ACROSS THE CURRICULUM **Visual Art** Study the art form and subjects of visual artist M. C. Escher

TEACHER TO TEACHER **Response Songs** Suggestions on singing canons

BUILDING SKILLS THROUGH MUSIC **Writing** Discuss different interpretations of the meaning of the song text

Songs
"Ego sum pauper"
"Nothing Do I Own"

Listening Selection "Allegretto poco mosso" from *Sonata in A Minor* (excerpt)
M∙U∙S∙I∙C M∙A∙K∙E∙R∙S
Isaac Stern

More Music Choices
"I Love the Mountains," p. 34
Sumer Is Icumen In, p. 35

ASSESSMENT

Performance/Peer Critique Sing song in canon in small groups and evaluate

TECHNOLOGY/MEDIA LINK
MIDI/Sequencing Software Use the song file to help sing the canon

Connection: Culture

Activity: Explore the cultural background of a Jewish dance

MOVEMENT **Patterned Dance** Learn a dance for the song

TEACHER TO TEACHER **Teaching Tip** Suggestions for teaching rounds

BUILDING SKILLS THROUGH MUSIC **Social Studies** Identify similar musical characteristics in two songs

Song "Tumba"

Arts Connection 15th Century Woodcut Mosaic of Jerusalem

More Music Choices
"Himmel und Erde" ("Music Alone Shall Live"), p. 94
Viva la musica, p. 95
"Ego sum pauper" (Nothing Do I Own"), p. 158

ASSESSMENT

Performance/Observation Sing, play and move to show three-part round

TECHNOLOGY/MEDIA LINK
Sequencing Software Play "Tumba" as a MIDI round

Connection: Language Arts

Activity: Read and discuss a poem about music

ACROSS THE CURRICULUM **Language Arts** Use a poem as a performance introduction

SPOTLIGHT ON **Music Education** History of public school music education

BUILDING SKILLS THROUGH MUSIC **Social Studies** Identify dates when states were added to the United States

Song "O Music"

Poem "In Music Meeting"
M∙U∙S∙I∙C M∙A∙K∙E∙R∙S
Lowell Mason

More Music Choices
"Da pacem, Domine" ("Grant Us Peace"), p. 62

ASSESSMENT

Performance/Peer Critique Sing song as a round and discuss

TECHNOLOGY/MEDIA LINK
Notation Software Notate bass line for "O Music"

INTRODUCING THE UNIT

Unit 4 presents the next step in a sequenced approach to understanding music elements. Music skills—reading, performing, creating, listening, moving—are the means by which students gain an understanding of these concepts. Presented on p. 125 is a brief overview of the skills that are assessed in this unit. (See below and pp. 126–127 for unit highlights of related curricular experiences.)

For a more detailed unit overview, see Unit at a Glance, pp. 123a–123h.

UNIT PROJECT

SAY All things are accomplished through a series of "small steps." Often, we are given a manual to help us accomplish our goal or task.

Have students work in pairs and choose a simple common task (for example, tying a shoe, making a peanut butter and jelly sandwich, or sharpening a pencil, and so on) for which they will write a step-by-step manual. One student should write the directions. The other student will try to complete the task by reading the instructions and following them. Allow time for each pair to edit and revise the directions as needed.

Invite each pair to present their manual to the class and discuss the accuracy of their instructions.

You may wish to designate an area in the classroom to display the student manuals.

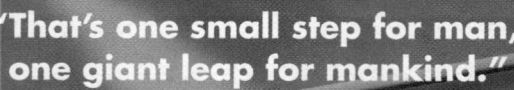

"That's one small step for man, one giant leap for mankind."

(American Astronaut Neil Armstrong, July 20, 1969, at10:56 PM EST)

Make a Difference!

"One Small Step," on page 126, is about making a difference. Doing one small thing can open another door or lead us down a different path. Like Neil Armstrong, we too can be leaders by taking one small step, one step at a time.

Learning music is like taking one step at a time. You learn musical skills a little at a time and build on them. Then you use these skills to experience music and to share what you have learned with others.

124

ACROSS THE CURRICULUM

Unit Highlights The following interdisciplinary activities in this unit are related to the music elements presented in the lessons. See Unit at a Glance, pp. 123a–123h, for topical descriptions presented according to lesson sequence.

▶ **ART/RELATED ARTS**

- Explore imitation and canon in visual arts (p. 158)

▶ **LANGUAGE ARTS**

- Read about the life and career of Richie Valens (p. 128)
- Read and dramatize a Scottish folktale (p. 141)
- Read an excerpt of a poem and discuss its AABACA form (p. 142)
- Create a class poem using descriptions of autumn (p. 149)
- Share a humorous poem; read a book about the children of Bolivia (p. 152)

- Read about a 1576 event in Japan (p. 156)
- Use poem as an introduction to a performance (p. 162)

▶ **MATHEMATICS**

- Caculate the distance between each location mentioned in a song (p. 136)

▶ **SCIENCE**

- Discuss factors to consider when building a dwelling in Jamaica (p. 133)

▶ **SOCIAL STUDIES**

- Discuss the history and culture of Veracruz, Mexico (p. 130)
- Discuss the impact of railroads in the United States (p. 136)
- Read about Scottish bagpipes (p. 139)
- Locate Bolivia on a map and discuss its history and culture (p. 152)
- Find geographical areas associated with listening examples (p. 154)

UNIT 4

Building Our Musical Skills

MUSIC SKILLS ASSESSED IN THIS UNIT

Reading Music: Rhythm

- Read and sing a song with sixteenth-note rhythms (p. 137)
- Read and perform a song using rhythm syllables (p. 141)

Reading Music: Pitch

- Read and sing a song using pitch syllables and hand signs (p. 147)
- Read and sing melodic pattens using pitch syllables (p. 149)

Performing Music: Singing

- Perform a song with upbeats (p. 135)
- Perform a song in rondo form (p. 145)
- Sing a canon (p. 159)

Moving to Music

- Perform movements to illustrate ABACA form (p. 143)
- Perform a movement routine with a two-part round (p. 161)

Performing Music: Playing

- Perform an instrumental accompaniment (p. 135)
- Perform an accompaniment in ABACA form (p. 145)

Creating Music

- Create melodic sequences from musical phrases (p. 149)
- Create eight-measure melodies from visuals (p. 153)

Listening to Music

- Listen and compare two versions of a Mexican folk song (p. 129)
- Listen for rhythm patterns in a song (p. 153)

CULTURAL CONNECTION

Unit Highlights The musical literature in this unit provides many opportunities for students to explore a variety of world cultures. See Unit at a Glance, pp. 123a–123h, for topical descriptions presented according to lesson sequence.

▶ AMERICAN REGIONAL

- Explore the origins and influences of western swing during the 1930s (p. 134)

▶ ASIAN

- Discuss the Japanese *taiko* (p. 156)

▶ CARIBBEAN

- Discuss the origins and different styles of Caribbean music (p. 132)

▶ EUROPEAN

- Discover the differences between English, Gaelic, and Lowland Scots (p. 140)

▶ LATIN AMERICAN

- Learn about the various instruments used in a *jarocho* ensemble (p. 129)
- Discuss the events of Mexico's nine-day Christmas celebration (p. 146)
- Discuss the culture and ethnic diversity of Bolivia (p. 150)
- Recognize the llama's importance to the lifestyle of the Andes (p. 152)

OPENING ACTIVITIES

MATERIALS

- "One Small Step" **CD 6-18**

  Recording Routine: Intro (4 m.); v.1; v. 2

Analyzing

Have students look at "One Small Step." Ask them if they can find any areas that might cause difficulty. Practice those areas with the class.

Point out that the meter changes from $\frac{4}{4}$ to $\frac{2}{4}$ several times. Ask students to locate the meter changes in the notation.

Review the routine of the song with students. Make note of the first and second endings, the repeat sign, the *del segno*, and the *coda*.

Singing

Invite students to sing "One Small Step" with the recording **CD 6-18**. Monitor students to make sure they are blending their voices properly.

Students may also enjoy performing a pat-clap-snap body percussion pattern on the words "one small step."

Step by Step

Sing "One Small Step." In what ways can you make a difference?

Words and Music by Jay Althouse and Sally K. Albrecht

ASSESSMENT

Unit Highlights This unit includes a variety of strategies and methods, described below, to track students' progress and assess their understanding of lesson objectives. Reproducible masters for Show What You Know! and Review, Assess, Perform, Create can be found in the Resource Book.

▶ **FORMAL ASSESSMENTS**

The following assessments, using written language, cognitive, and performance skills, help teachers and students conceptualize the learning that is taking place.

- **Show What You Know!** Element-specific assessments, on the student page, for Rhythm (p. 141) and Melody (p. 147).
- **Review, Assess, Perform, Create** This end-of-unit activity (pp. 164–165) can be used for review and to assess students' learning of the core lessons in this unit.

▶ **INFORMAL ASSESSMENTS**

At the close of each Teacher's Edition lesson in this unit, one of the following types of assessments is used to evaluate the learning of the key element focus or skill objective.

- Music Journal Writing (p. 131)
- Observation (p. 153)
- Performance/Observation (pp. 135, 137, 141, 147, 149, 161)
- Performance/Peer Critique (pp. 145, 157, 159, 163)

▶ **RUBRICS**

Visit *www.sfsuccessnet.com* for rubrics to assess students' achievement in music skills.

One small step bring-ing us all a lit-tle bit clos-er,

one small step, be-gin-ning to - day. If we all join hand in hand, ev-'ry

na - tion, ev - 'ry land, ___ we can take

one small step and lead the way. way.

So man-y col-ors, so man-y names. We are man-y; we are one.

We are all the same. ___

one small step. One small step. One small step leads the way.

I can see a world . . . Let me lead the way.

Moving

Divide the class into five groups. Ask each group to create movement for a part of the song—taking "one small step" toward completing it.

Invite group 1 to work with measures 1–10; group 2 measures 11–18; group 3 measures 25–32 (8 measures repeated); group 4, measures 33–38; and group 5 develop movement for the *coda*.

Groups should work together to integrate and perform the movement for the entire piece.

INNOVATIVE TEACHER SUPPORT FOR THIS UNIT

- **MAKING MUSIC DVD, Grade 5** contains video segments that support lessons, including signing and movement.
- **MAKING MUSIC with Movement and Dance** provides more opportunities for large group activities in music or physical education classes.
- **MAKING MUSIC with Technology** provides lesson plans for many technology applications; includes MIDI files.
- **¡A cantar!** features recorded songs and lessons from around the Spanish-speaking world; includes strategies for bilingual classes and for English-speaking teachers working with Spanish-speaking students.
- **Bridges to Asia** features recorded songs and lessons from Asian and Pacific region cultures.
- **www.sfsuccessnet.com** provides an online lesson planner to conveniently create lesson plans at school or at home. Includes rubrics for assessment, lesson modifications to meet the needs of all students, performance musicals based on program content, and more.

TECHNOLOGY/MEDIA LINK

Unit Highlights The following components are used in this unit to reinforce and expand students' understanding of music elements and related themes. See Unit at a Glance, pp. 123a–123h, for a descriptive listing according to lesson sequence.

▶ **MIDI/SEQUENCING SOFTWARE**

- Display the notation view of the MIDI song file to locate melodic phrases and identify melodic contour (p. 153)
- Use MIDI song file to help learn the parts of the canon (p. 159)

▶ **NOTATION SOFTWARE**

- Notate four-measure musical phrases to show an ABACA rondo (p. 145)
- Notate and print three major scales (p. 147)
- Create and notate melodic sequences (p. 149)
- Notate the bass line of a song and compose a harmonic and percussion accompaniment (p. 163)

▶ **SEQUENCING SOFTWARE**

- Create a rhythm accompaniment to a song (p. 137)
- Record the melody of "Tumba" and use the sequencing software to create a round (p. 136)

▶ **TRANSPARENCY**

- Display a listening map and point to the sections to help students follow along (p. 153)

▶ **WEB SITE**

- Go to *www.sfsuccessnet.com* for more information on *conjunto jarocho* (p. 131); Caribbean music styles, country music and musicians (p. 135); Gaelic music of Scotland and Ireland (p. 141); and percussion instruments around the world (p. 157)

LESSON AT A GLANCE

Element Focus	**EXPRESSION** Expressive use of rhythm and timbre	
Skill Objective	**LISTENING** Listen to an example of *jarocho* style from Mexico	
Connection Activity	**STYLE** Identify features of *jarocho* style	

MATERIALS
- "La bamba" (Spanish) — **CD 6-20**
- "La bamba" (English) — **CD 6-21**
  Recording Routine: Intro (8 m.); vocal; coda
- **Pronunciation Practice/Translation** p. 528
- *La bamba* (Ritchie Valens) — **CD 6-24**
- *La bamba (son jarocho)* (excerpt) — **CD 6-25**
- lower-pitched barred instruments, keyboard
- **Resource Book** p. A-16
- map of Mexico

VOCABULARY
conjunto jarocho   chord   ostinato

◆ ◆ ◆ ◆ National Standards ◆ ◆ ◆ ◆
1a Sing accurately in small ensembles
1c Sing music representing diverse genres and cultures
2d Perform simple accompaniments by ear
6b Listen and analyze uses of rhythm and timbre in music from diverse cultures
7a Students evaluate the music they hear
9a Describe characteristics of music styles from a variety of cultures

MORE MUSIC CHOICES
For more experience with Latin American rhythm and timbre:
"Imbabura," p. 202
"*Canción Mixteca*," (Mixteca Song), p. 326

EXPRESSIVE SOUNDS

"La bamba" is a folk dance with expressive rhythms. The instruments used and the percussive sounds of the dancers reflect the familiar sounds of the Veracruz region of Mexico.

Listen to "La bamba." How do the rhythm and timbre add to the expressive qualities of the melody? What is the style of this music?

CD 6–20

La bamba

Folk Song from Mexico
Adapted and Arranged by Ritchie Valens

Pa-ra bai-lar la bam-ba.
⁊ Hear the beat of the bam-ba.
Pa-ra bai-lar la bam-
⁊ Hear the beat of the bam-

-ba se ne-ce-si-ta un-a po-ca de gra-cia.
-ba. To dance the bam-ba, you need to be grace-ful.

Un-a po-ca de gra-cia pa-ra mi pa-ra ti
Oh, you need to be grace-ful ___ to dance __ the bam-

___ ya a-rri-ba a-rri-ba; y'a-rri-ba y'a-
-ba; You need to be play-ful. I will __ dance the

rri-ba por ti se-ré ___ por ti se-ré ___ por ti se-ré.
bam-ba, Oh I will dance, ___ I will dance the bam-ba, I will dance the bam-

128

Footnotes

ACROSS THE CURRICULUM

▶ **Language Arts** Encourage students to learn about the life and career of Ritchie Valens by reading *Ritchie Valens: The First Latino Rocker* by Beverly Mendheim (Bilingual Review, 1990). The book offers 23 pages of photographs of Valens' career, as well as a comprehensive discography and bibliography.

BUILDING SKILLS THROUGH MUSIC

▶ **Reading** Have students look at the song title "La bamba" and make a list of possible meanings. List suggestions on the board and discuss reasons for each. Ask students to locate places in the song lyrics that give the meaning of "La bamba." Invite students to describe the characteristics of the dance described in the song lyrics.

SKILLS REINFORCEMENT

2d ▶ **Creating** Many Latin American songs can benefit from added percussion parts, because these additions emphasize the energetic rhythms that characterize Latin American music. Have students add an improvised rhythm with the maracas on "La bamba." Hint—although there are seemingly endless possibilities, only certain maraca rhythms really "work" with this song. Make sure you allow ample time for students to determine what the best rhythms are, and they will find that the resulting sounds are surprisingly authentic.

Music notation for "La bamba" with lyrics:

C₇ / F / B♭ / C₇

_____ Yo no soy mar - i - ne - ro. / Yo no soy mar - i -
- ba, I'll go up and _ dance it. / But no sail - or am

F / B♭ / C₇

ne - ro, soy cap - i - tan; _____ soy cap - i - tan, _____
I, but for you I'll be; _____ For you I'll be, _____

F / B♭ / C₇ / Last time to Coda ⊕ F / B♭

_____ soy cap - i - tan. _____ Bam - ba _____ bam -
_____ For you I'll be. _____ Dance the _____ bam -

C₇ / F / B♭ / C₇ / F / B♭

- ba, bam - ba _____ bam - ba, bam - ba, _____ bam -
- ba, dance the _____ bam - ba, Dance the _____ bam -

D.S. al Coda

C₇ / F / B♭ / C₇

- ba, bam - ba _____ bam... Pa - ra bai - lar la bam -
- ba, bam - ba, _____ dance. _ Hear the beat of the bam -

⊕ Coda / F / B♭ / C₇ / Repeat ad lib.

Bam - ba, _____ bam - ba!
Dance the _____ bam - ba!

Unit 4 **129**

Lead a discussion on popular and folk music here in the United States. Help students understand that each country of the world may have a different kind of music that is the most popular there.

SAY Today we will listen to music in the *son jarocho* style that is popular in part of Mexico.

ASK What is folk music? (Accept a variety of answers.)

What is popular music? (Accept a variety of answers.)

2 DEVELOP

Listening

Have students

- Read the text on p. 130 about Ritchie Valens.
- Locate the Mexican state of Veracruz on a map. (Refer also to Across the Curriculum, p. 130.)
- Focus on the song "La bamba" on pp. 128–129.

SAY This is a traditional song from Veracruz that was made popular throughout the United States by Ritchie Valens in the early days of rock 'n' roll music.

6b Have students listen to the recording of "La bamba" **CD 6-20.**

ASK Which musical elements are used to help express the mood of the music? (rhythm and timbre)

What is the style of this music? (Latin pop)

Have students listen to the Ritchie Valens version of *La bamba* **CD 6-24.**

9a **ASK What is the style of this music?** (rock 'n' roll version of a folk song)

What qualities are used that establish style in the music? (rhythm and timbre)

continued on page 130

CULTURAL CONNECTION

9a ▶ **Jarocho Ensemble** The instruments used by *jarocho* musicians come from the string and percussion families. One is likely to see *arpas* (harps), the *bocona* (a four-string bass), the *quijada* (literally the jaw of the burro), and violins. Other essential instruments seen in the ensemble are the *jarana,* an eight-stringed guitar, and a *requinto,* a small four-stringed guitar plucked with a thin cowhorn pick. Occasionally, *panderos* (tambourines) are used.

Another essential feature of *jarocho* style is the *tarima,* the foot-high platform of cedar planks. This is where the dancers supply rhythms with their feet, interacting with the other musicians by following and sometimes dictating the direction of the music.

SPOTLIGHT ON

▶ **Folklórico Dance Traditions** In each state of Mexico, as well as in specific geographic and cultural regions, dances represent the unique cultural heritage. The folklórico dance traditions of Mexico are of three types: 1. Danza—dances, usually religious in nature, that are performed in ritual and community settings. 2. Mestizo—dances reflecting European influences in either steps, theme, instrumentation, or a combination of the above. Mestizo dances are also generally religious in nature. 3. Bailes Regionales—dances primarily social in origin and manifestation, presented in community and theatrical performances. Most of the dances presented by Ballet Folklórico groups in the United States and Mexico are Bailes Regionales.

Unit 4 *Building Our Musical Skills* **129**

ASK **What qualities can you identify about this song that makes it good for dancing?** (steady beat, good tempo for moving, syncopated rhythms, and enthusiasm of the singer)

Have students listen again and identify the elements in the music that indicate this is early rock 'n' roll. (the instruments, the drumbeat, guitar)

Singing

Have students

- Learn the Spanish lyrics of *"La bamba"* by echo-singing with the Pronunciation Practice Track **CD 6-23.** (You may also have them refer to Resource Book p. A-16.)

- Sing *"La bamba"* **CD 6-20** in Spanish with the recording.

- Learn the following vocal ostinato.

Bam - bam   bam - ba

- Sing the song again, with some students singing the ostinato.

ASK **How could this song be performed so that it would be good for quiet resting rather than dancing?** (slow tempo, soft dynamics, gentle singing, more straightforward rhythms, perhaps leave the drums out)

Invite students to experiment with singing *"La bamba"* in this manner.

Listening

Organize students into small groups. Tell them that they are going to listen to a more traditional version of the song, as played by a *"conjunto jarocho"* (jarocho ensemble). See Cultural Connection, p. 129, and discuss the instruments used. (*arpa, requinto, jarana,* and guitar) See Spotlight On, p. 131, for information on the performers.

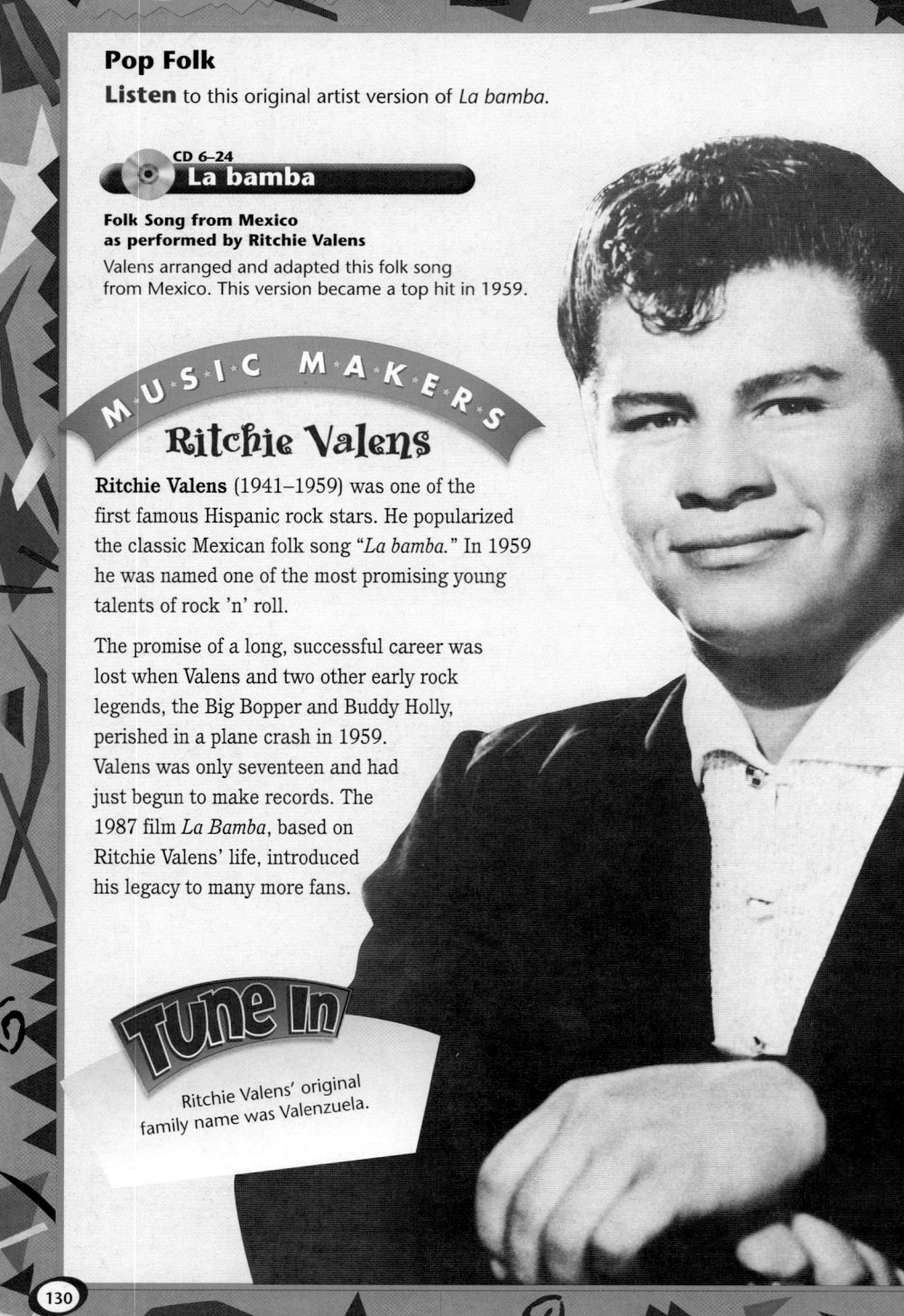

Pop Folk

Listen to this original artist version of *La bamba.*

CD 6-24
La bamba

Folk Song from Mexico
as performed by Ritchie Valens

Valens arranged and adapted this folk song from Mexico. This version became a top hit in 1959.

MUSIC MAKERS
Ritchie Valens

Ritchie Valens (1941–1959) was one of the first famous Hispanic rock stars. He popularized the classic Mexican folk song *"La bamba."* In 1959 he was named one of the most promising young talents of rock 'n' roll.

The promise of a long, successful career was lost when Valens and two other early rock legends, the Big Bopper and Buddy Holly, perished in a plane crash in 1959. Valens was only seventeen and had just begun to make records. The 1987 film *La Bamba,* based on Ritchie Valens' life, introduced his legacy to many more fans.

Tune In

Ritchie Valens' original family name was Valenzuela.

130

Footnotes

SKILLS REINFORCEMENT

▶ **Singing** Vocal chording identifies the singing of chord tones as accompaniment to a song. Organize the class into four groups. As group 4 sings the melody of *"La bamba,"* have the other groups accompany using the following vocal chording.

	I	IV	V
Group 1:	so	la	so
Group 2:	mi	fa	re
Group 3:	do	do	ti

ACROSS THE CURRICULUM

▶ **Social Studies** The state of Veracruz, in the eastern part of Mexico, has been called one of the most enjoyable places to vacation. Visitors to Veracruz enjoy watching its lively port, which is frequented by many foreign vessels. They also like its generally warm climate, beautiful beaches, and interesting museums. In the evening, visitors often like to sip a cold drink in a sidewalk cafe in the plaza. There, they also hear the sounds of the marimba played by strolling musicians. The tourist might also see the great fortress called the *Castillo de San Juan de Ulua,* which was featured in the climactic chase scene in the movie *Romancing the Stone.*

The fortress, unfortunately, did a poor job of protecting the state. Over the years, Veracruz suffered invasions by the Spanish, English, Dutch, French, and the United States.

Traditional Folk

You've heard Ritchie Valens' version of *La bamba*. Now **listen** to *La bamba* as performed in the *jarocho* [hah-ROH-choh] style from the Mexican state of Veracruz. This *jarocho* ensemble includes the instruments shown below.

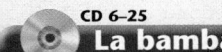
CD 6–25
La bamba

Folk Song from Mexico
as performed by Los Pregoneros del Puerto

The musicians are all native *Veracruzano*s who have performed together for 25 years.

Jarocho ensemble (left to right):
arpa, two requintos, jarana ▼

For more information about and sounds of the *arpa, jarana,* and *requinto* refer to Sound Bank pp. 514, 516, and 517 and **CD 21-21**, **CD 21-37**, and **CD 21-41**.

6b Play the recording of *La bamba* **CD 6-25.** Then have each group discuss what is different about this style from the early rock 'n' roll version they heard before (not just the names of instruments, but also how they are used).

Have groups share their findings. Ask each group which version they prefer and why using music terminology.

Playing

2d Help students identify the tones of the vocal ostinato as the roots of the chords used to support *"La bamba"*: I (F), IV (B♭), V_7 (C_7). Have some students play these roots on bass bars, xylophone bars, or keyboard.

Have students

1c • Sing *"La bamba"* **CD 6-20.**

• Add the vocal ostinato.

• Add the instrumental chord roots.

Encourage students to demonstrate appropriate small-ensemble performance techniques in their informal classroom concerts.

Moving

Have students learn a simple "dance" step to accompany *"La bamba"*: side right-close/side left-close in each measure, clapping on each "close."

3 CLOSE

Element: EXPRESSION   ASSESSMENT

7a **Music Journal** Ask students in pairs or threes to make a list in their music journals of the expressive musical qualities needed to make an exciting, danceable version of *"La bamba."* Encourage students to use standard terminology in explaining music.

CHARACTER EDUCATION

▶ **Respect** The world is made up of many different kinds of music, each of which is an expression of the people and culture that created it. Encourage students to consider ways they can be more accepting and understanding of other cultures. (For example, learn the language, become familiar with the traditions and customs, and so on.)

Ask students to brainstorm a list of positive and negative words used to describe people who are different. Ask students: Which words show respect and which do not? How does hearing and/or using these words make you and others feel? Why do people often respond with disrespect when they see someone who is different from them? Explain to students that being respectful and accepting of people who are different often demands courage. It may require them to go "against the crowd" and stand for what they know is right. Have students list some ways they can respond appropriately to negative comments they hear about people who are different.

TECHNOLOGY/MEDIA LINK

Web Site Go to *www.sfsuccessnet.com* to learn more about *conjunto jarocho* Mexican music.

LESSON AT A GLANCE

Element Focus **RHYTHM** Upbeat

Skill Objective **SINGING** Sing songs with phrases that begin with an upbeat

Connection Activity **STYLE** Explore origins of music with different styles

MATERIALS

- "Hosanna, Me Build a House" **CD 6-26**
  Recording Routine: Intro (4 m.); v. 1; interlude (4 m.); v. 2; coda
- "San Antonio Rose" **CD 6-28**
  Recording Routine: Intro (4 m.); vocal; coda
- *New San Antonio Rose* **CD 6-30**
- keyboard or resonator bells, bass xylophone
- map of Texas

VOCABULARY

upbeat   syncopation   calypso

◆ ◆ ◆ ◆ **National Standards** ◆ ◆ ◆ ◆

1c Sing music from diverse cultures
2b Perform easy instrumental pieces with technical accuracy
2c Perform instrumental music from diverse cultures
5a Read quarter notes and eighth notes in duple meter
5b Sightread melodies in treble clef

MORE MUSIC CHOICES

For more experiences with upbeats:
"This World," p. 168
"Connemara Lullaby," p. 232

Upbeats

A song that begins before the first beat of a measure begins on an **upbeat**.

Sing "Hosanna, Me Build a House."

Can you **identify** phrases in this song that begin on an upbeat?

Upbeats are sometimes called weak beats because they lead to the next note, a strong beat.

 CD 6–26

Hosanna, Me Build a House

t, (d) r m f s l t d'
Calypso Song from Jamaica

1., 2. Ho - san - na, me build a house, oh, __ Ho - san - na, me build a house, oh, __ Ho - san - na, me build a house, oh, __ I built it on the

san - dy ground. Me house built on a san - dy ground, __
sol - id ground. Me house built on a sol - id ground, __

132

Footnotes

SPOTLIGHT ON

▶ **Jamaica** Jamaica was governed by Great Britain for more than 300 years. Both its language and customs reflect British and African influences. English is the official language, though many Jamaicans speak a local English dialect that includes elements of African, Spanish, and French. One of the most internationally famous styles of Caribbean music is reggae. Reggae began in Jamaica in the late 1960s, and spread in popularity through such performers as Jamaican singer Bob Marley.

BUILDING SKILLS THROUGH MUSIC

▶ **Social Studies** Have students locate San Antonio on a map of Texas. Share the information found in Spotlight On. Then discuss the significance of the Alamo in American history.

CULTURAL CONNECTION

▶ **Caribbean Music** Music history in the Caribbean began with Native Americans who lived there before the Europeans and Africans arrived. Their instruments included rattles, slit-drums made from hollowed logs, and other percussion instruments. But by 1600, most Native Americans of the Caribbean had perished. By the twentieth century, with the advent of phonograph records and radio, popular dance music styles emerged. These include the calypso from Trinidad; the *merengue* from Dominican Republic and Haiti; and the *rumba* and *mambo* from Cuba. Although music from each of the islands is more different than alike, a few common traits can be identified. Tempos are lively, with great use of syncopation; vocals frequently use call and response; and ostinatos are used extensively.

It will fall, you see. Me house built with sand all 'round,
It'll stand up, you see. Me house built on sol-id ground,

It will fall, you see. The rain will __ wet it up (ha, ha), The
It'll stand up, you see. No, the rain can't __ wet it up (ha, ha), The

sun will burn it ____ up (ha, ha), The breeze will shake it ____
sun can't burn it ____ up (ha, ha), The breeze can't shake it ____

up (ha, ha), The storm come blow it ____ down (ha, ha). Me
up (ha, ha), The storm can't blow it ____ down (ha, ha). Me

house can nev-er ____ be (no, no), Me house too weak, you __
house will ev-er ____ be (yes, yes), Me house too strong, you __

see (no, no), Me house will not stand (no, no), ____
see (yes, yes), Me house will ever stand (yes, yes), ____

Storm blow it on - to the ground (ha, ha).
Storm can't __ bring it to ground (ha, ha).

1 INTRODUCE

Lead a discussion of the lyrics of "Hosanna, Me Build a House" and relate them to the sandy beaches and tropical storms of the Caribbean islands. Then share with students the origins of calypso music as described in Cultural Connection on p. 132.

5a Play the recording **CD 6-26** and invite students to follow the music in their books.

2 DEVELOP

Reading

Have students read the text on p. 132.

ASK How many times does the upbeat occur in "Hosanna, Me Build a House"? (13)

Have students identify the phrases that begin on an upbeat. Then play the recording **CD 6-26** and invite students to sing along.

Playing

Ask students to play a D-major scale on keyboard or resonator bells, then sing it using hand signs.

On the board or a visual, notate the four bass xylophone patterns under Skills Reinforcement below.

5b Ask students to sing the patterns (in a comfortable range) using letter names and pat each pattern on knees before transferring to keyboard or mallet instruments.

1c Have students sing the song with the instrumental
2b accompaniment.

► **Mallets** The following bass xylophone patterns can be used to accompany "Hosanna, Me Build a House."

2b

► **Science** Ask students to find Jamaica on a world map and describe its location. Explain to students that the words of the song "Hosanna, Me Build a House" describe concerns about building a sturdy shelter in Jamaica. Ask students what those concerns might be and what weather conditions affect them.

Discuss with students the materials used to build dwellings in their area and what geographical or weather considerations are factors.

Reading

5a Invite students to listen to "San Antonio Rose" **CD 6-28** while following the song notation on p. 134.

ASK How many times does a phrase begin with two upbeats? (4)

How many times does a phrase begin with one upbeat? (6)

1c Have students divide into groups of two. While following the notation and listening to the recording, have one student clap the two upbeats. Ask the other student to clap the single upbeat. Both should always clap to the downbeat. Play the recording again and invite students to sing along.

Playing

Select a group of students to practice the bass xylophone/bass metallophone part found in Skills Reinforcement on p. 135. Once they can play the part proficiently, invite them to perform it as an accompaniment to "San Antonio Rose."

Listening

Invite students to listen to Bob Wills' performance of *New San Antonio Rose* **CD 6-30**.

Encourage students to use standard terminology in explaining musical performances.

ASK How is this version different than the version you just sang? (Accept various answers.)

Have students read the information about Bob Wills on p. 135. Lead a discussion on western swing, the style of music he helped popularize. For more information, see Cultural Connection below.

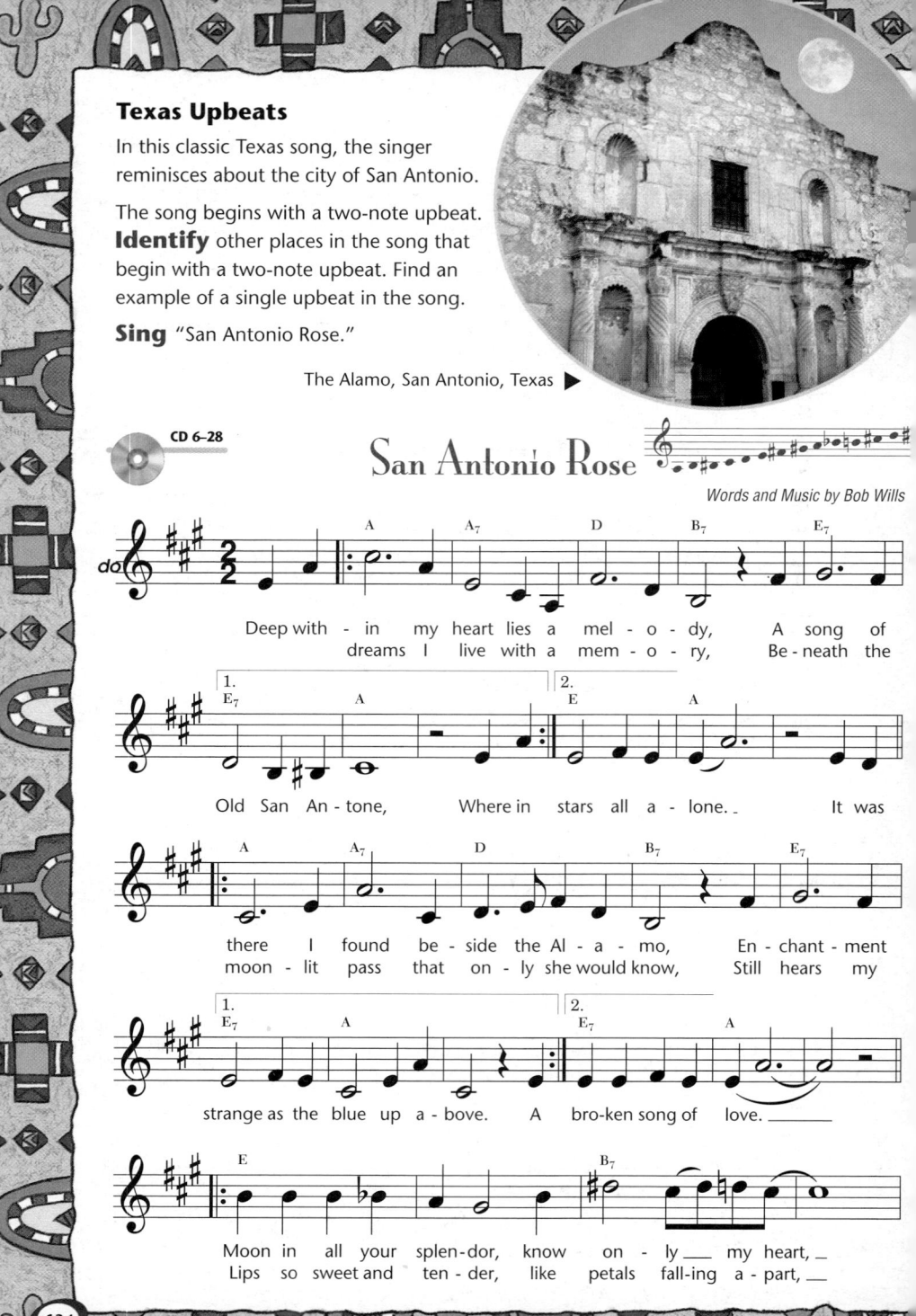

Texas Upbeats

In this classic Texas song, the singer reminisces about the city of San Antonio.

The song begins with a two-note upbeat. **Identify** other places in the song that begin with a two-note upbeat. Find an example of a single upbeat in the song.

Sing "San Antonio Rose."

The Alamo, San Antonio, Texas ▶

CD 6-28

San Antonio Rose

Words and Music by Bob Wills

Deep with-in my heart lies a mel-o-dy, A song of
dreams I live with a mem-o-ry, Be-neath the

Old San An-tone, Where in stars all a-lone. It was

there I found be-side the Al-a-mo, En-chant-ment
moon-lit pass that on-ly she would know, Still hears my

strange as the blue up a-bove. A bro-ken song of love. ___

Moon in all your splen-dor, know on-ly ___ my heart, __
Lips so sweet and ten-der, like petals fall-ing a-part, __

Footnotes

CULTURAL CONNECTION

▶ **Western Swing** Bob Wills developed a style of music called western swing, or as it is sometimes referred to, western jazz. When it came about in the 1930s, the swing music of big bands led by Benny Goodman and Glenn Miller was popular. Thus, the term "swing" carried over to Wills' music. Western music, like the music of the big bands, was popular for dancing. It was heavily influenced by jazz, combining syncopation and improvisation. Wills later added brass and reed instruments to his band, a revolutionary decision at the time.

SPOTLIGHT ON

▶ **San Antonio** The Coahuiltec Indians resided in the vicnity of modern-day San Antonio prior to the arrival of white settlers. After it was explored by the Spanish in the 1500s, present day Texas was claimed by France from 1685 until 1690. The Spanish then reclaimed the land. In 1691, they renamed the Indian village of Yanaguana, *San Antonio*, after Saint Anthony of Padua. San Antonio was officially established by Spain in 1718. That same year, Father Antonio Olivares founded the *San Antonio de Valero*, which was later called the Alamo.

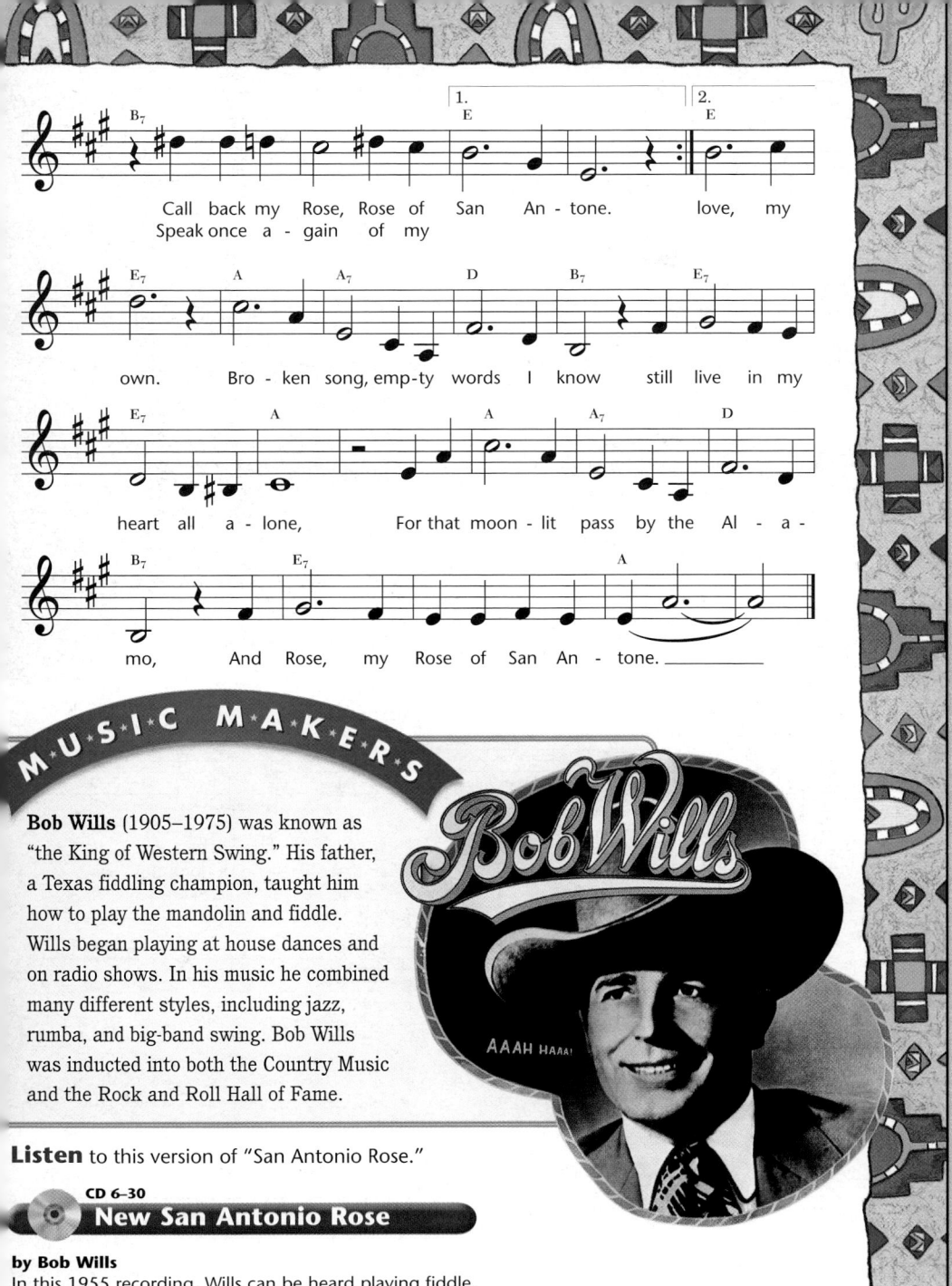

Call back my Rose, Rose of San An - tone.
Speak once a - gain of my

love, my
own. Bro - ken song, emp-ty words I know still live in my

heart all a - lone, For that moon - lit pass by the Al - a -

mo, And Rose, my Rose of San An - tone. _____

M·U·S·I·C M·A·K·E·R·S

Bob Wills (1905–1975) was known as "the King of Western Swing." His father, a Texas fiddling champion, taught him how to play the mandolin and fiddle. Wills began playing at house dances and on radio shows. In his music he combined many different styles, including jazz, rumba, and big-band swing. Bob Wills was inducted into both the Country Music and the Rock and Roll Hall of Fame.

Listen to this version of "San Antonio Rose."

CD 6–30
New San Antonio Rose

by Bob Wills
In this 1955 recording, Wills can be heard playing fiddle.

Unit 4   135

3 CLOSE

1c **Performance/Observation** Challenge students to sing "Hosanna, Me Build a House" or "San Antonio Rose" from memory. Have small groups practice together, then sing for the class.

2c As groups become more proficient, have students add the instrumental accompaniment to their performance. Observe and assess students' ability to accurately perform the upbeats.

SKILLS REINFORCEMENT

2b ▶ **Mallets** The following bass xylophone/bass metallophone part can be used to accompany "San Antonio Rose."

Bass Xylophone/Bass Metallophone
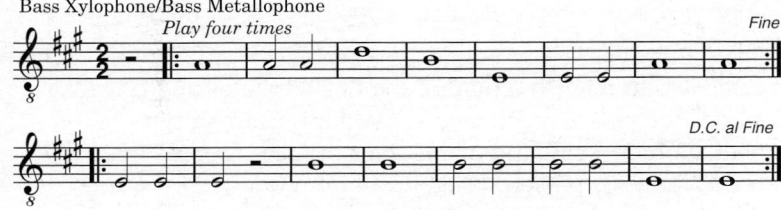
Play four times   *Fine*

D.C. al Fine

TECHNOLOGY/MEDIA LINK

Web Site To learn more about Caribbean music, as well as country music and musicians, visit *www.sfsuccessnet.com.*

Unit 4 *Building Our Musical Skills*   **135**

LESSON AT A GLANCE

Element Focus RHYTHM

Skill Objective READING Read rhythm patterns using

Connection Activity SOCIAL STUDIES Discuss the impact of railroads in the United States

MATERIALS

- "Wabash Cannon Ball" **CD 7-1**
  Recording Routine: Intro (10 m.); v. 1; refrain; interlude (10 m.); v. 2; refrain; coda
- Music Reading Practice, Sequence 13 **CD 7-3**
- Resource Book pp. D-16, E-14, F-18, I-11

VOCABULARY

tie

◆ ◆ ◆ ◆ National Standards ◆ ◆ ◆ ◆

1a Sing accurately in small ensembles
2a Play instruments accurately in small ensembles
4c Compose, using electronic media
5a Read dotted eighth/sixteenth patterns in duple meter
6c Understand and use basic principles of rhythm in music analysis
8a Show how different arts portray the same idea in unique ways
8b Identify ways music relates to social studies

MORE MUSIC CHOICES

For more experience with:
"Battle Cry of Freedom," p. 272

1 INTRODUCE

Ask students to read the text on p. 136. Then play the recording of "Wabash Cannon Ball" **CD 7-1** and invite students to sing along. Share with students and discuss the information on railroads in the United States in Across the Curriculum, below.

RHYTHM OF THE RAILS

During the late 1800s, as a result of the Industrial Revolution, many factory workers were laid off from their jobs and took to the rails. These "hobos" hopped freight trains from one town to the next to make a living.

Listen to "Wabash Cannon Ball." It tells about a mythical train that could take a hobo anywhere. Legend has it that the train was so fast it flew right off the track and headed for the stars!

CD 7-1

Wabash Cannon Ball

f, s, l, t,(d)r m s Traditional

VERSE

1. From the coast of the At-lan-tic to the wide Pa-cif-ic shore,
   name of great im-por-tance that is known by one and all,
2. There are cit-ies of im-por-tance that are reached a-long the way,
   Spring-field and De-ca-tur and Pe-or-ia, Mon-tre-al,

From the warm and sun-ny South-land to the
It's the West-ern com-bi-na-tion called the
Chi-ca-go and Saint Lou-is and Rock
On the West-ern com-bi-na-tion called the

1. isle of Lab-ra-dor, There's a Wa-bash Can-non Ball.
2. Is-land, San-ta Fe, And ___

Footnotes

MOVEMENT

8a ▶ Creative Movement Have students explore ways to show rhythm patterns using body percussion. Discuss different possibilities for creating sounds (snap, clap, pat, stamp, slide) and then decide on which sounds are best suited for each rhythm. Perform these patterns while singing "Wabash Cannon Ball." Then have them try stepping to the beat in a circle while singing and performing the body percussion.

BUILDING SKILLS THROUGH MUSIC

▶ Writing Direct students' attention to the text at the top of p. 136. Discuss the life and reasons why people became "hobos." Have students write a brief paragraph using the writing prompt, "If I were a hobo, I'd hop a train and go to..."

ACROSS THE CURRICULUM

8b ▶ Social Studies/Math Invite students to discuss the impact of railroads on the development of the United States. How did railroads change our country's history? How were travel and commerce accomplished before the building of transcontinental railways?

Ask students to refer to a map of the United States and Canada. Locate all the places mentioned in "Wabash Cannon Ball" in sequential order. Using the map's scale of miles, approximate the number of miles a person would travel from one place to the next in the song. Estimate how long each part of the trip would have taken in the 1800s and today. Compare the time required for those journeys with the same journeys made by airplane.

REFRAIN

Just lis-ten to the jin-gle, the rum-ble, and the roar

Of the might-y lo-co-mo-tive as she streams a-long the shore,

Hear the thun-der of the en-gine, hear the lone-some whis-tle call,

It's the West-ern com-bi-na-tion called the Wa-bash Can-non Ball.

Find the Rhythm

Read, clap, and count the rhythm below. Where does this rhythm match the rhythm of the first line of "Wabash Cannon Ball"? Where is it different?

We can use the *tie* to make the rhythm match the song.

But there is an easier way to write the tied rhythm, using a dotted eighth note. It looks like this.

You can use this symbol to show two uneven sounds on the beat. How many times can you find 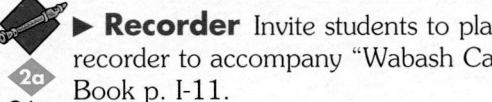 in the song? Can you find a pattern that is similar but not quite the same?

Unit 4 **137**

2 DEVELOP

Reading

5a Have students read the rhythm patterns on p. 137 using rhythm syllables. Invite them to sing "Wabash Cannon Ball" **CD 7-1** and clap the rhythms when they occur in the song.

Have students look at the highlighted rhythm in the song and identify the words, the measure, and the beat on which it occurs.

Singing

1a Discuss the time signature and demonstrate a $\frac{2}{4}$ con-ducting pattern (see p. 217). Have students conduct and sing the song while following the rhythm of the notation.

3 CLOSE

Analyzing

6c Have students work in pairs to find the other rhythm in the song that uses a dotted eighth note and a sixteenth note. (the rhythm for *Cannon* in both verse and refrain)

ASK How is this rhythm similar to the other rhythm that uses a dotted eighth note and a sixteenth note? (Both use the same notes; both have two unequal sounds in one beat.)

How is it different? (It is short/long; the other is long/short.)

You may also wish to use Music Reading Practice, Sequence 13 on p. 496 and Resource Book p. E-14 to further reinforce dotted-eighth/sixteenth-note rhythms.

Skill: READING   **ASSESSMENT**

1a
5a **Performance/Observation** Have students sing "Wabash Cannon Ball" while they follow the notation and conduct meter in 2. Circulate among them to observe their rhythm-reading comprehension.

SKILLS REINFORCEMENT

5a ▶ **Reading** Have students read, clap, and count the rhythm on Resource Book, p. D-16, and then perform it as a counter-rhythm while singing "Wabash Cannon Ball."

2a ▶ **Recorder** Invite students to play a countermelody on recorder to accompany "Wabash Cannon Ball." See Resource Book p. I-11.

2a ▶ **Mallets** See Resource Book, p. F-18, for an Orff arrange-ment of "Wabash Cannon Ball."

SCHOOL TO HOME CONNECTION

▶ **Railroads** Invite students to ask older relatives and friends about their train travel experiences over the years. Students may then report their findings to the class.

TECHNOLOGY/MEDIA LINK

4c **Sequencing Software** Encourage students to compose a rhythm accompaniment for "Wabash Cannon Ball" using a sequencing program. Each pattern should contain at least one dotted-eighth/sixteenth-note figure. Set the time signature to $\frac{2}{4}$ and the count-off to four measures.

LESSON AT A GLANCE

Element Focus **RHYTHM** Dotted rhythm patterns

Skill Objective **READING** Sing and read from notation a song containing dotted eighth/sixteenth note rhythm patterns

Connection Activity **CULTURE** Explore Scottish culture

MATERIALS

- "Scotland the Brave" **CD 7-6**
  Recording Routine: Intro (5 m.); vocal; instrumental; vocal; coda
- **Music Reading Practice, Sequence 14** **CD 7-8**
- "Loch Lomond" **CD 7-13**
  Recording Routine: Intro (4 m.); v. 1; refrain; interlude (2 m.); v. 2; refrain; interlude (2 m.); v. 3; refrain; coda
- *Scottish Medley* **CD 7-11**
- **Dance Directions** for *Ms. Maggie's Jig* p. 556
- **Resource Book** pp. B-11, D-18, E-15, H-12, I-12–13

VOCABULARY

verse   refrain

◆ ◆ ◆ ◆ National Standards ◆ ◆ ◆ ◆

1c Sing music from diverse cultures
1d Sing music written in two parts
2c Perform instrumental music from diverse cultures
5a Read dotted eighth and sixteenth notes in duple meter
5d Use standard notation to record musical ideas
6c Understand and use basic principles of rhythm and form in music analysis
8a Show how different arts portray the same idea in unique ways
8b Identify ways music relates to social studies
9a Describe characteristics of music styles from a variety of cultures

MORE MUSIC CHOICES

For more practice with ♩. ♪ and ♪ ♩.:
"Colorado Trail," p. 276

Sounds of Scotland

Bagpipes are a well-known part of Scottish music. "Scotland the Brave" was originally used as a bagpipe tune for marching.

Listen to "Scotland the Brave."
Identify a rhythm pattern that is used throughout the song.

Pictured, from left to right, are the Celtic harp (*clarsach*), fiddle, and lute. ▶

CD 7-6

Scotland the Brave

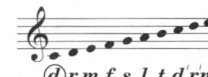

Words by Cliff Hanley

Traditional Melody from Scotland

Hark, when the night is fall - ing, Hear! Hear the pipes are call - ing,

Loud - ly and proud - ly call - ing, down through the glen.

There, where the hills are sleep - ing, Now feel the blood a - leap - ing,

High as the spir - its of the old High - land men.

Footnotes

MOVEMENT

8a ▶ **Patterned Dance** Scottish country dances are social and friendly. They are similar to the longways dances of the rest of the British Isles, but have more elegance because of the influence from seventeenth and eighteenth-century French court dances.

Invite students to learn *Ms. Maggie's Jig*, a Scottish country dance based on the traditional Scottish *Cumberland Reel*. See p. 556 in this book for dance directions.

BUILDING SKILLS THROUGH MUSIC

▶ **Language** Invite students to sing "Scotland the Brave." List musical characteristics and timbres that are important to the performance. Then ask students to listen to "Loch Lomond" and again list important musical characteristics and timbres. Have students compare the songs using the Venn Diagram on p. C-8 of the Resource Book.

SKILLS REINFORCEMENT

▶ **Keyboard** Have students play a two-handed accompaniment for "Scotland the Brave." See Resource Book p. H-12.

2c ▶ **Creating** Encourage students to use familiar rhythms to create rhythmic phrases for a counter-rhythm to the refrain of "Loch Lomond" or "Scotland the Brave." See Resource Book p. D-18.

2c ▶ **Recorder** Have students play countermelodies on recorder to accompany "Scotland the Brave" and "Loch Lomond." See Resource Book pp. I-12 and I-13.

A Scottish Rhythm

Dotted rhythms are often used in Scottish music. How many times do you find these dotted rhythm patterns in "Scotland the Brave"?

Read and clap "Scotland the Brave," using rhythm syllables. Now you are ready to **sing** the song.

Listen to *Bonnie Dundee, Off She Goes,* and *Donald's Awa'* in this medley of traditional Scottish songs.

CD 7–11
Scottish Medley

as performed by Steve Kendall and His Glencastle Sound

This medley can also accompany a Scottish country dance called *Ms. Maggie's Jig.* Your teacher can help you learn the steps.

Bagpipes ▶

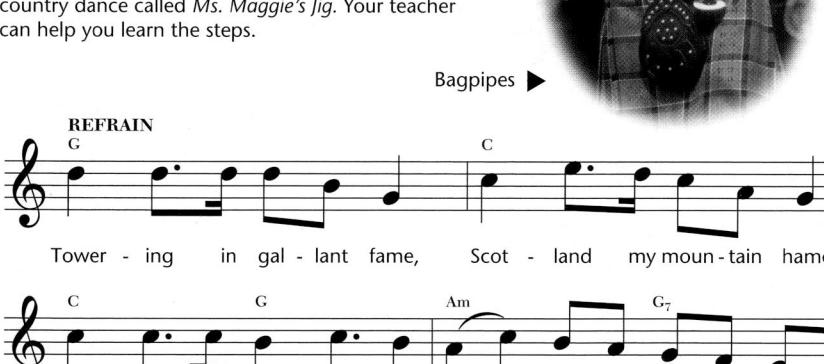

REFRAIN

Tower - ing in gal - lant fame, Scot - land my moun - tain hame,

High may your proud stan - dards glo - rious - ly wave for - ev - er.

Land of my high en - deav - or, Land of the shin - ing riv - er,

Land of my heart for - ev - er, Scot - land the brave.

---

1 INTRODUCE

8b Lead a discussion with students about the bagpipe and its place in Scottish culture (see Across the Curriculum, below).

2 DEVELOP

Reading

On the board, write rhythm patterns in $\frac{4}{4}$ using ♩, ♫, 𝄽, ♬.

Then add rhythm patterns that include ♪. ♪.

5a Using rhythm syllables, have students

- Perform each pattern with accurate rhythm, demonstrating fundamental skills.
- Determine the number of beats in each pattern. (four)

Review the dotted eighth/sixteenth-note pattern from the previous lesson. Remind students that this pattern

- Contains a dotted eighth note and a sixteenth note.
- Has two unequal sounds in one beat. (long/short)

Have students

- Locate the dotted eighth/sixteenth-note patterns in the notation for "Scotland the Brave."
- Read the rhythm for "Scotland the Brave" using rhythm syllables.

6c Clap the rhythm again as they listen to the recording **CD 7-6.**

For more practice reading dotted rhythm patterns, see Music Reading Practice, Sequence 14 on p. 496 and Resource Book p. E-15.

continued on page 140

ACROSS THE CURRICULUM

8b ▶ **Social Studies** The bagpipe has surfaced throughout history in almost every kind of culture. In Scotland there are four sizes of bagpipe, each from a different region. It has been used as a military instrument in Scotland since the 1500s; it has a place in any important occasion, from weddings to funerals. Scottish bagpipes tend to have a larger wind bag than most others, enabling the player to stand tall with head held high while playing. Ask students what they already know about Scotland. Make a list of their responses. (These may include kilts, bagpipes, Loch Ness Monster, clans, and so on.) Point out the tartan plaid art border in this lesson. Challenge students to gather more information on these subjects using the school or public library.

MEETING INDIVIDUAL NEEDS

▶ **Including Everyone** Playing an ostinato pattern can be difficult for students who have not thoroughly learned the basic rhythm pattern. Model and have them imitate the basic rhythm pattern several times before repeating it as an ostinato. They should pat the rhythm using the dominant hand that they will use to play. When most students are successful imitating the single rhythm pattern, lengthen the pattern to two, three, and four continuous repetitions. Add more repetitions only when most students are successful performing the shorter pattern. Have them work with a partner modeling and imitating the single and repeated patterns.

Singing

Focus students' attention on the time signature in "Scotland the Brave" and remind them that each measure in $\frac{4}{4}$ time has four beats. Demonstrate the conducting pattern for meter in 4 (see p. 217).

Have students

 6c
- Conduct a four-beat pattern while listening to "Scotland the Brave" **CD 7-6.**

1c
- Conduct a four-beat pattern while singing "Scotland the Brave" as a group.

Moving

Invite students to

- Listen to the traditional songs in *Scottish Medley* **CD 7-11.**
- Learn the steps to *Ms. Maggie's Jig,* a Scottish country dance. See Movement, p. 138.

8a
- Perform the dance with *Scottish Medley.*

Singing

Invite students to listen to "Loch Lomond" **CD 7-13.** Then discuss the meaning of the text, using Cultural Connection below.

6c Draw attention to the form (verse and refrain) and the meter ($\frac{4}{4}$) of "Loch Lomond." Help students discover that both "Scotland the Brave" and "Loch Lomond" have the same meter and form. Then have students

- Learn the refrain of "Loch Lomond" by rote and sing with the recording when ready.

1c
- Conduct a four-beat pattern as they sing.

Reading

5a Have students locate the dotted-eighth/sixteenth-note patterns in the notation for "Loch Lomond." (line 1, p. 141)

Have students say the words of the last line of "Loch Lomond" as they keep a steady beat. (The last line of both the first verse and the refrain are the same.)

Another Scottish Tune

Have you ever heard a Scottish person speak? Most Scots speak English, but two other languages are spoken there. One is Gaelic, and the other is Lowland Scots. Lowland Scots sounds a lot like English, but you may not recognize all the words.

Listen to "Loch Lomond." Find the unfamiliar Lowland Scots words, along with a new rhythm pattern.

CD 7-13

Loch Lomond

s, l, t,@ r m f s l

Folk Song from Scotland

VERSE
F Gm C₇

1. By ___ yon bon-nie banks and by yon bon-nie braes,
2. 'Twas ___ there that we part-ed in yon shad-y glen,
3. The ___ wee bird-ies sing and the wild flow-ers spring,

F Bb F

Where the sun shines bright on Loch Lo - mond,
On the steep, steep side of Ben Lo - mond,
While in sun - shine the wa - ters are sleep - in';

Bb F Gm C₇

Where me and my true love were ev - er wont to gae,
Where pur - ple in hue, ___ the High-land hills we view,
The bro - ken heart kens nae sec - ond spring a - gain,

F Bb F C₇ F

On the bon - nie, bon-nie banks of Loch Lo - mond.
An' the moon ___ com-in' out in the gloam - in'.
Tho' the wae ___ fo' may cease frae their greet - in'.

Footnotes

SKILLS REINFORCEMENT

1d ▶ **Singing** Singing in parallel thirds, as in the refrain of "Loch Lomond," is challenging because the melody and harmony parts are so similar. To help students, have them

- Sing scales in thirds.
- Sing easy folk songs or phrases in thirds before trying more advanced pieces.
- Begin the two parts in unison or contrary motion if possible.
- Sing the melody as you model the harmony part.

CULTURAL CONNECTION

▶ **Scottish Language** Although English is spoken by most people in Scotland, there are two other languages spoken there. One is Gaelic, and the other is Lowland Scots. Scots sounds a lot like English, but there are some words that may not be familiar. The following examples are from "Loch Lomond."

Loch—Lake
braes—river banks
gloamin'—twilight
gae—go
kens—knows
nae—no
waefo'—woeful, sorrowful
frae—from
greetin'—crying, weeping.

REFRAIN

Oh, ye'll take the high road, and I'll take the low road,

And I'll be in Scot-land a-fore ye,

But me and my true love we'll nev-er meet a-gain

On the bon-nie, bon-nie banks of Loch Lo-mond.

Show What You Know!

Read these rhythm patterns from "Scotland the Brave" and "Loch Lomond," using rhythm syllables. **Identify** the line in the song that matches each rhythm pattern. Then, clap each pattern as you **sing** the words.

1. $\frac{4}{4}$

2. $\frac{4}{4}$

5a Discuss with students the rhythm of the words *bonnie, bonnie*. Help students determine that there are two unequal sounds on each beat (short/long). Show them how the rhythm would look using four sixteenth notes, with the last three tied; then show them the easier way to write the rhythm: .

3 CLOSE

Reading

5a Have students read music that incorporates rhythmic patterns in various meters and

9a
- Find all the sixteenth/dotted eighth figures in "Loch Lomond" and identify the measure, the beat, and the words on which they occur. (Point out that, among musicians, this rhythmic figure is known as the "Scottish snap.")

- Sing "Loch Lomond" **CD 7-13** while following the notation.

- Describe and compare the dotted eighth/sixteenth and sixteenth/dotted eighth figures.

6c **ASK How are these two figures similar?** (Both use the same notes and have two unequal sounds in one beat.)

How are they different? (One is short/long, the other is long/short.)

Element: RHYTHM **ASSESSMENT**

Performance/Observation Have students

5a
- Follow the directions for the activities in Show What You Know on p. 141. (See Resource Book p. B-11 for the corresponding worksheet.) Circulate among students to observe their rhythm-reading comprehension.

1c
- Sing "Scotland the Brave" **CD 7-6** and "Loch Lomond" **CD 7-13** using rhythm syllables and then with the song text.

Observe and assess students' accuracy in performing the dotted rhythm patterns.

ACROSS THE CURRICULUM

▶ **Language Arts/Drama** Students may enjoy reading and dramatizing the Caldecott Award-winning Scottish folktale *Always Room for One More* by Sorche NicLeadhas (Henry Holt, 1982). In this charming story, old Lachie McLachlan stands on his porch and invites strangers in for shelter from Scotland's windy storms. "There's room galore. Och, come awa' in! There's room for one more, always room for one more!" Lachie McLachlan's hospitality eventually backfires when his house is overflowing with travelers. The story comes complete with instructions on how to speak in a Scottish brogue and would be excellent in performances for younger students.

SCHOOL TO HOME CONNECTION

▶ **Local Bagpipers** Find out if there are any Scottish or Celtic bagpipers in your area. (The local Musicians' Union or a Scottish cultural organization might be good sources to contact.) Invite them to visit the class and to play for students in ceremonial dress. Ask pipers to share stories about tartan plaids, clans, Highland Games, and bagpipe history.

TECHNOLOGY/MEDIA LINK

Web Site Go to *www.sfsuccessnet.com* to learn more about the Gaelic music of Scotland and Ireland.

LESSON AT A GLANCE

Element Focus	**FORM** Rondo form
Skill Objective	**PLAYING** Perform a rondo for voices and percussion instruments
Connection Activity	**RELATED ARTS** Read a poem in rondo form

MATERIALS

- "Ama-Lama" **CD 7-15**

  Recording Routine: Intro (4 m.); vocal A; vocal B; vocal A; vocal C; vocal A; interlude (4 m); vocal A; vocal B; vocal A; vocal C; vocal A; coda

- *Concerto No. 1 for Horn and Orchestra in D major,* **CD 7-17** "Rondo"
- **Resource Book** p. I-14
- alto xylophone; bass xylophone; tambourine, conga drum; temple blocks; cabasa
- various found objects from classroom

VOCABULARY

rondo   coda

◆ ◆ ◆ ◆ **National Standards** ◆ ◆ ◆ ◆

1a Sing accurately in small ensembles
2a Play instruments accurately in small ensembles
4c Compose, using electronic media
5a Read quarter, sixteenth, and dotted notes in duple meter
6b Listen and analyze uses of form in music from diverse genres
7b Students use specific criteria for evaluating their own performances
8a Show how different arts portray the same idea in unique ways

MORE MUSIC CHOICES

For more practice with rondo form:
"*Cotton Boll Rag,*" p. 333

Element: FORM | **Skill: PLAYING** | **Connection: RELATED ARTS**

A NONSENSE RONDO

The lyrics of most songs are about people, places, or activities. Sometimes, though, the words of a song don't have a meaning. These are called "nonsense songs."

"Ama-Lama" is a nonsense song in **rondo** form.

Sing the song in **A B A C A** form. Notice that this rondo adds a coda at the end.

> A **rondo** is a musical form in which the first section always returns. The most common rondo form is ABACA.

(142)

Footnotes

SKILLS REINFORCEMENT

▶ **Creating** Have students create "rondo art" by making an art piece to visually represent rondo form (ABACA). Divide the class into small groups of two or three students and distribute materials such as colored construction paper, cardboard, string, markers, crayons, scissors, glue, and tape. Invite them to create a five piece mobile using the form indicator shapes on pp. 142–143.

BUILDING SKILLS THROUGH MUSIC

▶ **Theatre** Have students read the poem "Beavers in November" found in Across the Curriculum. Divide the class into three groups for the A, B, and C sections and have them create a dramatization for their assigned section.

ACROSS THE CURRICULUM

8a ▶ **Language Arts** Students will enjoy a creative reader's theatre activity using an excerpt from the poem "Beavers in November" by Marilyn Singer. Invite students to discuss the AABACA form of the poem.

This stick here
That stick there
   Mud, more mud, add mud,
    good mud
That stick here
This stick here
   Mud more mud, add mud,
    good mud
   You pat
   I gnaw
   I pile
   You store

This stick here
That stick there
   Mud, more mud, add mud,
    good mud
   You guard
   I pack
   I dig
   You stack
That stick here
This stick there
   Mud, more mud, add mud,
    good mud

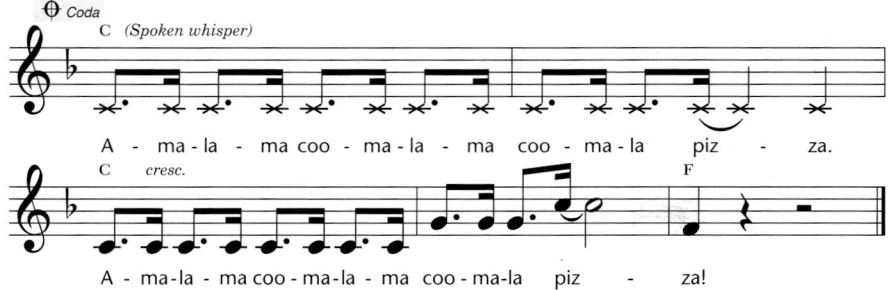

A - ma-la - ma coo - ma-la - ma coo - ma-la piz - za.

A - ma-la - ma coo - ma-la - ma coo - ma-la piz - za!

Move to the Rondo

As you **listen** to "Ama-Lama," **move** to show the rondo form of the song.

▲ Walk around the circle with a step-touch movement while snapping on the off-beat (beats 2 and 4).

▲ Stop and face the center of the circle. Lean in and out of the circle while doing a "fist spin." Raise hands in the air on *a-pizza!*

▲ Using small steps, walk into the circle for four beats, out for four beats, and repeat.

Unit 4 **143**

continued on page 144

1 INTRODUCE

Invite students to locate five different found objects in the classroom. Three should be the same (for example, three pencils). The other two objects should be different from one another (for example, an eraser and a marker).

Review ABA form by asking students to arrange three of their five found objects to represent ABA. Make sure students use two of the same items to represent the A section, along with a different item to represent the B section.

Write the letters ABACA on the board. Have students arrange their found objects to illustrate the form.

SAY When ABACA form occurs in music, it is called rondo form.

ASK How many times will you hear the A section? (three)

How many other sections will you hear? (two; a B section and a C section)

Share with students an excerpt from the poem "Beavers in November" (See Across the Curriculum, p. 142).

ASK What is the form of the poem? (rondo)

2 DEVELOP

Analyzing

Play "Ama-Lama" **CD 7-15** and have students identify rondo form in the song as they point to the corresponding found object.

ASK What is the form of "Ama-Lama"? (rondo)

Ask students to look at the song notation and determine the order in which the song will be sung.

MEETING INDIVIDUAL NEEDS

▶ **Moving** Use the following teaching suggestions to help all students perform the movement activity for "Ama-Lama."

Reinforcement Some students may have difficulty walking to the beat, snapping on the offbeat, and singing "Ama-Lama." Give these students the option of omitting the snaps until they are comfortable walking to the beat and singing the song.

On Target Many students will be able to successfully perform the snaps on the offbeat as they move and sing. Monitor these students to ensure they are singing the song as they perform the dance.

Challenge Students who can perform the dance movements with ease while singing the song may enjoy an extra challenge. Have them play the tambourine part or the cabasa part from p. 144 while they sing and move.

Unit 4 *Building Our Musical Skills* **143**

Singing

1a Invite students to listen to "Ama-Lama" again while following the song notation. Then have students sing the song.

Moving

8a To further reinforce rondo form, invite students to perform a movement activity with "Ama-Lama." Have students form a circle and perform the following movements.

- A section: Students walk around the circle with a step-touch movement while snapping on the off beats (beats 2 and 4).
- B section: Students stop and face the center of the circle. Lean in and out while doing a "fist spin." Raise hands in the air on *a-pizza*!
- C section: Using small steps, students walk into the circle for four beats, out for four beats, and repeat.

Playing

5a Prepare students to play the percussion rondo on p. 144–145. Have them

2a

- Clap the rhythm of each instrumental part in the A section.
- Clap the rhythm of each instrumental part in the B section.
- Clap the rhythm of each instrumental part in the C section.

When students have learned the percussion rondo, they may perform it as an accompaniment to "Ama-Lama."

Playing in Rondo Form

Clap the rhythm of each section of this rondo. **Perform** the rondo on percussion instruments to accompany "Ama-Lama." **Describe** the differences between the Ⓐ, Ⓑ, and Ⓒ sections.

Arranged by Julie Scott

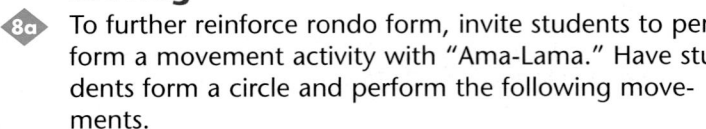

Footnotes

TEACHER TO TEACHER

▶ **Substituting Instruments** Here are a few suggestions for substituting instrument parts for this lesson.

- If you do not have all the instruments that are called for in the accompaniment for "Ama-Lama," substitute another instrument. For example, if you do not have a conga drum, use any type of drum that you have.
- You can substitute instruments of similar timbre for ones that you do not have. For example, if you do not have a cabasa, you may use maracas instead. If you do not have temple blocks, you can use any type of wood blocks.

SKILLS REINFORCEMENT

▶ **Recorder** The recorder countermelody on Resource Book p. I-14 contains a trill that some students may not be comfortable playing. To help them learn to play the trill, review the fingerings for C and D and have them play the following exercises.

Next, have students play rapidly from C to D, tonguing the first C and slurring all of the D's and C's in between. Select some students to play the trill during the B section of "Ama-Lama."

Listen to a Rondo

This is the A section theme of a rondo by Mozart.

Listen to the beginning of *Rondo (Allegro)*.

Now, **listen** to the entire rondo. Raise your hand each time you hear the theme of the A section.

CD 7–17
Rondo (Allegro)

from *Concerto No. 1 for Horn and Orchestra in D Major*
by Wolfgang Amadeus Mozart
as performed by Dennis Brain and the Philharmonia Orchestra

This concerto was written in 1791, the year Mozart died.

M·U·S·I·C M·A·K·E·R·S

Wolfgang Amadeus Mozart

Wolfgang Amadeus Mozart [moht-sahrt] (1756–1791) was born in Salzburg, Austria. He demonstrated an amazing musical talent from a very young age. He wrote one of his earliest compositions at age five. His father, Leopold, traveled with the young Wolfgang and his sister throughout Europe. The children performed for the public, as well as for nobility. Mozart's travels greatly influenced his composition style.

Unit 4 **145**

Listening

6b Refer students to the theme printed on p. 145. Explain that this is the A section theme in a listening selection composed by W. A. Mozart. Play it for students on a melody instrument.

Play "Rondo" from *Concerto No. 1 for Horn and Orchestra in D major* **CD 7-17**. Ask students to raise their hand each time they hear the theme.

Invite students to read the information about Wolfgang Amadeus Mozart on p. 145 in their texts.

3 CLOSE

Element: FORM   ASSESSMENT

2a **Performance/Peer Critique** Divide the class into two groups and have students perform "Ama-Lama"
7b with the percussion instrument parts on p. 144.

Encourage students to demonstrate appropriate large-ensemble performance techniques when performing in formal and informal concerts.

Allow groups to switch roles and then ask students to assess their own and each others' performances. Assess for rhythmic accuracy, ensemble balance, and the ability to accurately perform rondo form.

MEETING INDIVIDUAL NEEDS

▶ **Including Everyone** For students with special needs, consider the following options that may enable them to play instruments with greater success.

- Assign students with limited fine motor skills to larger instruments, such as bass xylophones, metallophones, or large drums.

- For students with limited mobility in one hand, allow him or her to play barred instruments with only one mallet. Talk with the student's parent or physical therapist to determine whether they would prefer for the student to try using both hands.

- Ask your music instrument supplier if they carry adaptive instruments, instrument mounts for wheelchairs, and adaptive mallets. Many companies make very useful products for students with special needs.

TECHNOLOGY/MEDIA LINK

4c **Notation Software** Before class, prepare a handout with three contrasting four-measure musical phrases. Invite students to use the phrases from the handout to notate an ABACA rondo on the computer using their notation software. Encourage students to play back and print their work. For a challenge, have students compose their own four-measure phrases and create another rondo.

LESSON AT A GLANCE

Element Focus | **MELODY** Diatonic major scale

Skill Objective | **READING** Sing a song and read from notation that is based on the diatonic major scale

Connection Activity | **MATHEMATICS** Examine the numerical sequence and interval relationship in a musical scale

MATERIALS

- "Las velitas" — **CD 7-18**
- "Candles Burning Bright" — **CD 7-19**
  Recording Routine: Intro (4 m.); vocal; instrumental; vocal; coda
- **Music Reading Practice, Sequence 15** — **CD 7-22**
- **Pronunciation Practice/Translation** p. 528
- **Resource Book** pp. A-17, B-11, D-20, E-16
- staff paper

VOCABULARY

diatonic scale whole step half step interval

◆ ◆ ◆ ◆ National Standards ◆ ◆ ◆ ◆

1c Sing music from diverse cultures
5a Read quarter, half, dotted, and whole notes in duple meter
5c Identify standard notation symbols for pitch
6c Understand and use basic principles of intervals in music analysis
8b Identify ways music relates to social studies

MORE MUSIC CHOICES

For more practice with diatonic patterns:
"Viva Jujuy," p. 228

1 INTRODUCE

Explain to students that they can use easy math to count the number of half steps in a major scale (12) and work with the numerical sequence in a scale to find intervals. See Skills Reinforcement, p. 147.

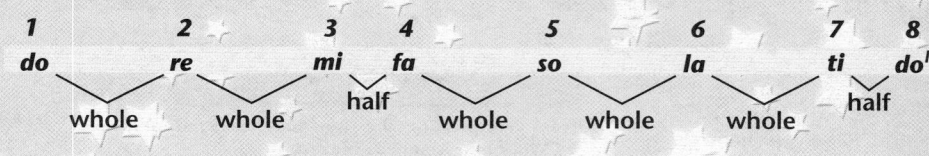

A Scale of Major Importance

Now that you know *ti*, you're ready for a new scale. This scale uses *do-re-mi-fa-so-la-ti-do*ˡ in an arrangement of whole and half steps. The half-steps occur between *mi* and *fa* and between *ti* and *do*ˡ. This pattern makes up a scale called the **diatonic major scale.**

> A **diatonic scale** uses sever different notes. It is called "major" when the *tonic*, or home note, is *do*.

1		2		3	4		5		6		7	8
do		re		mi	fa		so		la		ti	doˡ
	whole		whole		half	whole		whole		whole	half	

Look at the pattern of whole and half steps. **Sing** the diatonic major scale.

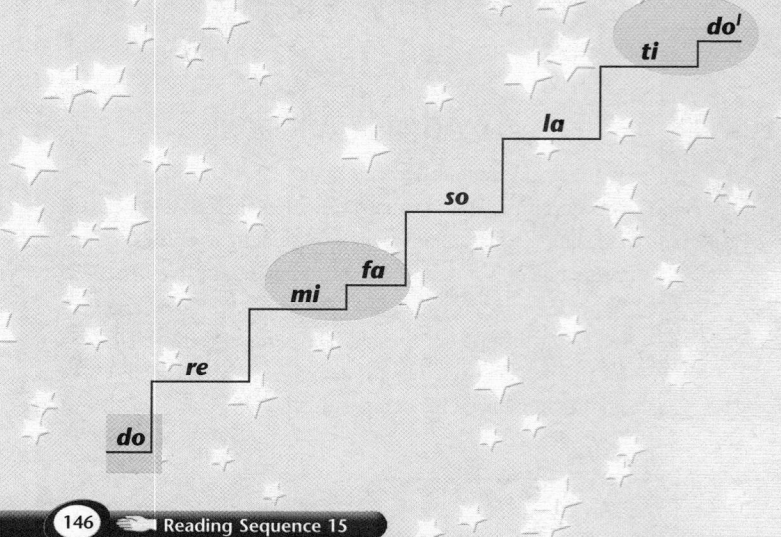

do
re
mi fa
so
la
ti doˡ

Footnotes

CULTURAL CONNECTION

8b ▶ **Christmas in Mexico** In Mexico, Christmas is celebrated for nine days. Christmas Eve, the ninth day, is marked with dancing and special treats. The highlight of the festivities is the breaking of the *piñata,* which is hung high above an open space.

For a delightful story of a Christmas star, to dramatize and illustrate, see *Pancho's Pinata* by Stefan Czerneki (Hyperion, 1992).

BUILDING SKILLS THROUGH MUSIC

▶ **Social Studies** Invite students to sing "*Las velitas.*" Share the information from Cultural Connection about the *piñata* used for festivities in Mexico. Lead students in a discussion about family traditions that they may have for celebrations.

TEACHER TO TEACHER

6c ▶ **Intervals** To help students name diatonic intervals,

- Sing the first interval from a familiar song, using pitch syllables, and have students name the song and the interval.
- Have students sing all of the intervals in order, from perfect unison *do–do* to perfect octave *do-do*ˡ.
- Have students sing an interval using pitch syllables and then say the interval name.

Read and Sing

"*Las velitas*" is based on the diatonic major scale. Does it use all the notes?

Las velitas
(Candles Burning Bright)

English Words by Donald Scafuri

Folk Song from Mexico

CD 7–18

Her-mo-sas ve-li-tas, en la ob-scu-ri-dad. Ha-blan de la es-
See the lit-tle can-dles shin-ing in the night, Tell-ing of a

tre-lla de la Na-vi-dad. Ved nues-tras ve-li-tas,
star with beams of ho-ly light. See our love-ly can-dles,

ved que a-lum-bran bien. Ha-blan de la es-tre-lla que bri-lló en Be-lén.
let them lead the way To a qui-et vil-lage where a ba-by lay.

Show What You Know!

Do and high do are shown on the staff below.

Complete the scale. Write in the missing pitch syllables and add their letter names.

do   mi   fa   do'
C   —   —   F   —   —   —   C

Sing the scale using pitch syllables.

---

2 DEVELOP

Singing

1c Invite students to listen to the recording of "*Las velitas*" **CD 7-18** and then learn the melody by rote using Pronunciation Practice Track **CD 7-21** and Resource Book p. A-17.

Analyzing

6c Have students sing the C-*do* scale, ascending and descending, from the pitch ladder on p. 146.

ASK Between which notes do half steps occur? (between *mi* and *fa,* and between *ti* and *do*)

SAY This scale uses all the notes from *do* to *do'* and contains both whole and half-step intervals. *Do* is the first degree of the diatonic major scale.

Have students sing the scale again, using pitch syllables, numbers (*do* = 1), and hand signs.

For further practice reading the diatonic major scale, refer to Music Reading Practice, Sequence 15 on p. 497 or Resource Book p. E-16.

3 CLOSE

Notating

Draw students' attention to the Show What You Know activity on p. 147. (See Resource Book p. B-11.)

SAY When C is *do*, the pattern of whole steps and half steps occurs according to keyboard structure, because the steps between E and F, and B and C are half-steps. So, the notes from C to C form the major scale without using any sharps or flats.

5c Have students notate the C-major scale on the staff and then sing it using pitch syllables and hand signs.

Skill: READING   ASSESSMENT

5a **Performance/Observation** Have students sing "*Las velitas*" using pitch syllables and hand signs, and **6c** then the lyrics. Observe students' ability to perform diatonic scale pitches.

SKILLS REINFORCEMENT

▶ **Reading** Tell students that when C is *do*, the pattern of whole and half steps falls into place naturally (according to keyboard structure) because the steps from E to F and B to C are half steps. But when other notes are *do*, the pattern must be created using flatted or sharped notes. Help students figure out the notes needed for other major scales and then write them on the staff. (Start with scales on F, G, and D.) Have them use the pattern of whole and half steps from *do* to *do'* to figure out the notes needed for each scale. See the Reading Music Worksheet on Resource Book pp. D-20 and D-21, for reading and writing the diatonic major scale.

TECHNOLOGY/MEDIA LINK

5c **Notation Software** Tell students that they are to notate, **6c** print, and hand in three major scales (C, G, and F). For each scale, have them

- Select the key signature corresponding to the scale's starting note.
- Set the time signature to $\frac{4}{4}$ (or common time) and use standard symbols to notate meter in simple patterns.
- Enter a quarter note for each note of the scale, both upward and downward. Do not repeat the top note. Make the last note value a half note.
- Play back the scale using the program's playback function.
- Print the scale.
- Describe the combination of whole steps and half steps.

LESSON AT A GLANCE

Element Focus   **MELODY** Melodic sequence

Skill Objective   **READING** Sing a song from notation that includes melodic sequences

Connection Activity   **LANGUAGE ARTS** Discuss a poem about autumn

MATERIALS

- "Autumn Canon"   **CD 7-25**
  Recording Routine: Intro (6 m.); v. 1 in unison; interlude (6 m.); v. 2 in 4-part canon; coda
- **Music Reading Practice, Sequence 16**   **CD 7-27**
- "Autumn Fires" (poem)
- **Resource Book** pp. D-22, E-17, F-19

VOCABULARY

sequence   melodic contour

◆ ◆ ◆ ◆ National Standards ◆ ◆ ◆ ◆

1b Sing easy pieces with technical accuracy
1d Sing music written in two, three parts
2e In instrumental ensembles, perform moderately easy pieces with technical accuracy
5c Identify standard notation for pitch
5d Use standard notation to record musical ideas
6c Understand and use basic principles of intervals in music analysis
8b Identify ways music relates to language arts

MORE MUSIC CHOICES

For more experience with melodic sequences:
"I Love the Mountains," p. 34

1 INTRODUCE

8b Have students read the poem "Autumn Fires" on p. 149. Then have them read the lyrics to "Autumn Canon," and relate the two texts. The text of "Autumn Fires" looks back ("pleasant summer over") and that of "Autumn Canon" looks ahead ("winter is coming"). See Across the Curriculum, for a related activity.

A Song of Seasons

Have you ever heard a melody that reminded you of a story or a picture? To create a song, composers often begin with words or an idea. Sometimes a beautiful melody inspires a composer to create words to express the music.

Listen to "Autumn Canon." How do the words and the melody work together?

Sing "Autumn Canon" in unison. Then sing it as a canon.

CD 7–25

Autumn Canon

l, t, d r m f s l

Words by Sean Deibler
Music by Lajos Bárdos

I
Fly,   fly,   fly, _____ the
Gone,   gone,   gone, _____ the

III
leaves   take   leave   of   the   branch.   Breez - es   are
leaves   are   gone   from   the   trees.   Soft   falls   the

IV
strong,   win - ter   is   com - ing.
snow,   win - ter   is   here   now.

148   Reading Sequence 16

Footnotes

SPOTLIGHT ON

▶ **The Composer and Lyricist** Lajos Bárdos (1899–1986), the composer of "Autumn Canon," was a conductor and musicologist. He lived in Budapest, Hungary.

Sean Deibler, who wrote the words for "Autumn Canon," is a conductor, singer, clarinetist, and the music director for the Music Group of Philadelphia. The Hungarian government has honored him for promoting Hungarian music.

BUILDING SKILLS THROUGH MUSIC

▶ **Art** Invite students to sing "Autumn Canon" **CD 7-25** and trace the melodic movement in the air. Distribute crayons or markers and ask students to create a visual of the melodic movement that includes a representation of note durations. Students should use contrasting colors to show sections that are similar and different.

SKILLS REINFORCEMENT

5d ▶ **Notating** Use the Music Reading Worksheet on Resource Book, p. D-22, to let students practice notating simple melodic patterns as sequences. Encourage students to

- Compose a short melodic pattern, then use it as a sequence to create a melody.
- Play their original melodies on melodic instruments.

▶ **Mallets** See Resource Book, p. F-19, for an Orff arrangement of "Autumn Canon."

2e

Follow the Contour

Read "Autumn Canon" from the staff and follow the shape of its melody with your finger. Look at the parts that are highlighted. How would you **describe** their shape, or melodic contour?

1. 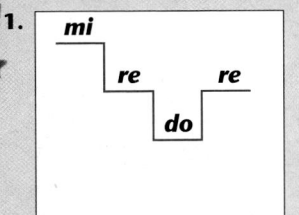 **2.** 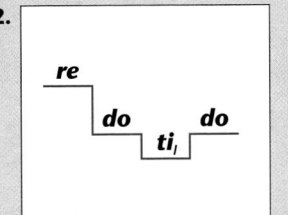 **3.**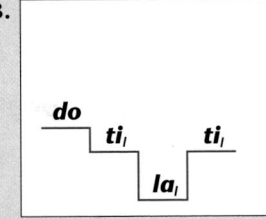

The pattern above is an example of a melodic **sequence**.

Sing or **play** a sequence of each of these short melodies.

> A melodic **sequence** is a pattern of pitches that is repeated at a higher or lower pitch level.

Create a melody of your own for "Autumn Fires." Use a melodic sequence in your composition. Does your melody express the text of the poem?

Autumn Fires
by Robert Louis Stevenson

In the other gardens
And all up the vale,
From the autumn bonfires
See the smoke trail!

Pleasant summer over
And all the summer flowers,
The red fire blazes,
The grey smoke towers.

Sing a song of seasons!
Something bright in all!

Flowers in the summer
Fires in the fall!

Unit 4 **149**

---

2 DEVELOP

Singing
Play "Autumn Canon" **CD 7-25** and have students learn the melody by rote.

Analyzing

1b
5c
Ask students to look at the notation for "Autumn Canon" on p. 148. Have students find *la* on the staff, using the key signature. (*do* is F, *la* is D) Invite students to read the song from staff notation, first with pitch syllables and hand signs and then with letter names. Have students sing the words.

6c **ASK** How would you describe the shape, or melodic contour, of measures 6–11? (Three notes go down by step, then one goes up by step.)

What happens in measures 8–9 and 10–11? (These are two sequences of measures 6–7.)

SAY When a pattern in a song is repeated and starts on a different note, a melodic sequence results.

1b Have students sing the melodic sequence (measures 6–11) with pitch syllables and hand signs. Then, have them sing the sequence again, this time continuing upward in the same pattern in six measures.

For more practice with melodic sequences, see Music Reading Practice, Sequence 16 on p. 497 and Resource Book p. E-17.

3 CLOSE

Element: MELODY — **ASSESSMENT**

1d **Performance/Observation** Invite students to sing the song in canon, up to four parts, if possible.

5c Create visuals of these phrases in C-*do*: *do, re, mi, do; so, la, so, mi; do, mi, so, do; so, fa, mi, re, do.* Have students sing the patterns, then create sequences from them. Observe and assess the students' ability to read the notated melodic sequence and to demonstrate appropriate large-ensemble performance techniques that can be used in formal or informal concerts.

ACROSS THE CURRICULUM

8b ▶ **Language Arts** Ask students to describe the things they would see, feel, taste, and hear as autumn arrives in those places where there are seasonal changes. Make a list of all the students' descriptions (frost crystals glistening on window panes; sweet apple cider steaming in mugs; crunchy, crinkly leaves on the sidewalk; fat squirrels hurrying up and down trees to store their winter food; brown flat grass; crisp wind; football and marching bands on TV).

Create a student-illustrated class poem about the coming of autumn. Have students recite, dramatize, and move creatively to their original work. Use it as an introduction during performances of "Autumn Canon."

TECHNOLOGY/MEDIA LINK

5d **Notation Software** Invite students to create and notate a melodic sequence using notation software. Ask them to create a two-measure melody. Show students how to highlight and select the melody so as to cut, paste, and transpose notes.

Have students cut, paste, and transpose the melody twice at successively higher or lower pitches. This will make a six-measure melody. Have students create a two-measure ending for the melody. Listen to the melodies before printing and posting them on a bulletin board.

Have the class select one melody and write lyrics for it.

Core 8

LESSON AT A GLANCE

Element Focus   **MELODY** Melodic patterns

Skill Objective   **LISTENING** Listen to and identify various
melodic patterns

Connection   **STYLE** Discuss musical instruments used in
Activity   the music of the Andes

MATERIALS
- *"Pollerita"* (Spanish)   **CD 7-30**
- *"Pollerita"* (English)   **CD 7-31**
  Recording Routine: Intro (10 m.); vocal;
  instrumental
- **Pronunciation Practice/Translation** p. 529
- *Camino de piedra*   **CD 7-34**
- *Amores hallarás*   **CD 7-35**
- "The Llama" (poem)
- **Resource Book** p. A-18
- map of South America

VOCABULARY
melodic patterns

◆ ◆ ◆ ◆ National Standards ◆ ◆ ◆ ◆
1a Sing accurately alone and in small ensembles
1c Sing music from diverse cultures
4a Compose short pieces, demonstrating unity and variety
through music
5a Read eighth, quarter, dotted, and whole notes in duple meter
5b Sightread melodies in treble clef
6a Listen and describe events in music using appropriate terms
6b Listen and analyze uses of pitch and timbre in music from
diverse cultures
8b Identify ways music relates to social studies

MORE MUSIC CHOICES
For more practice singing songs from South America:
"Imbabura," p. 203
"El carite," (The Kingfish) p. 305
"Viva Jujuy," p. 228

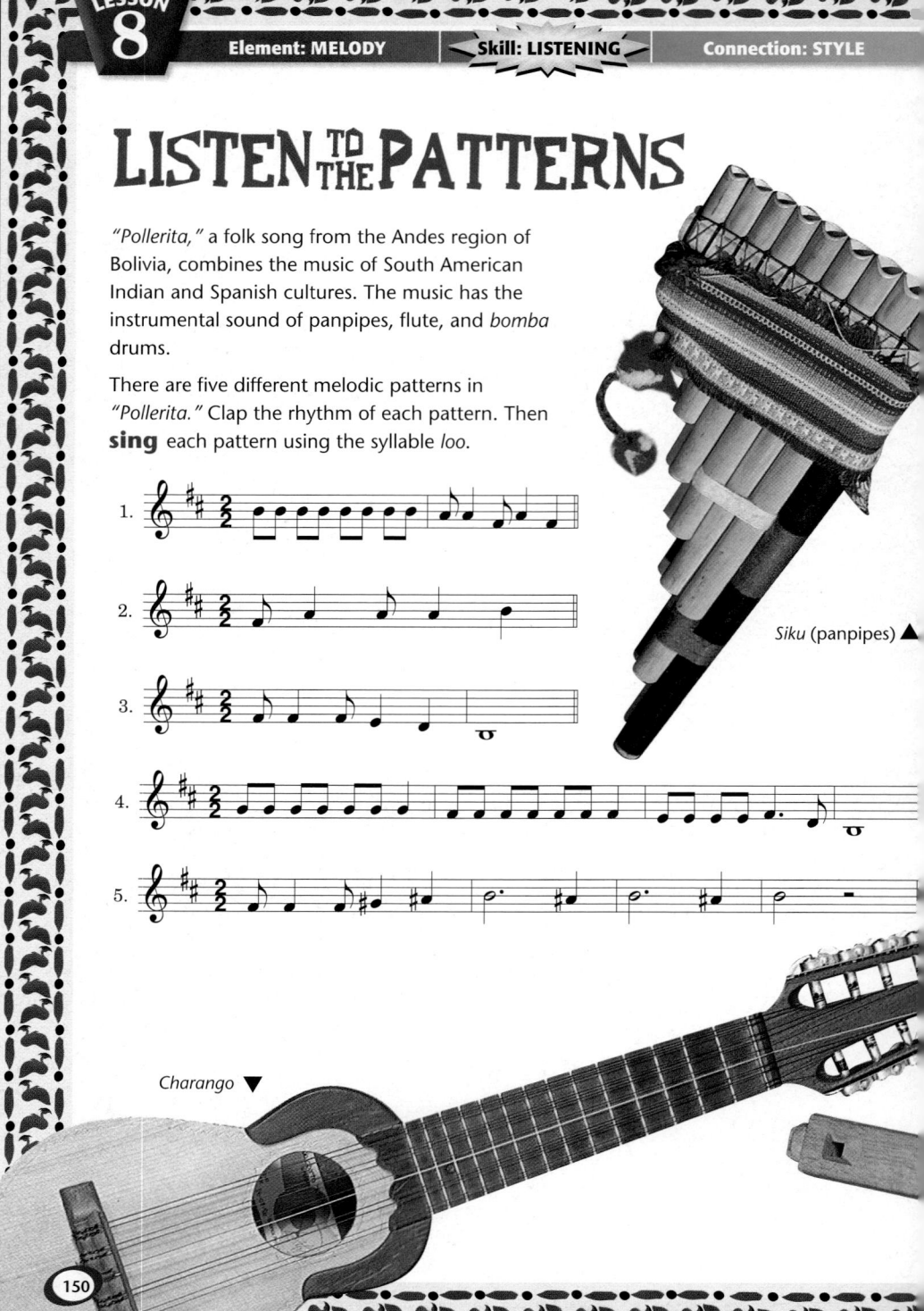

LISTEN TO THE PATTERNS

"Pollerita," a folk song from the Andes region of
Bolivia, combines the music of South American
Indian and Spanish cultures. The music has the
instrumental sound of panpipes, flute, and *bomba*
drums.

There are five different melodic patterns in
"Pollerita." Clap the rhythm of each pattern. Then
sing each pattern using the syllable *loo.*

Siku (panpipes) ▲

Charango ▼

150

Footnotes

CULTURAL CONNECTION

8b ▶ **Native Americans of Bolivia** Over half of Bolivia's
population is of Native American descent, represented mostly
by the Aymara and Quechua peoples. Many Bolivians are of
mestizo (mixed parentage) ancestry, chiefly Spanish and Native
American. Encourage students to research the music and culture
of the Andes region and share their findings with the class.

BUILDING SKILLS THROUGH MUSIC

▶ **Reading** Review information about flutes found on pp. 110-113. Have
students refer to the Semantic Map for flutes that they previously prepared
or develop a Semantic Map. Direct students to label additional boxes on the
map for the *quena* and *siku*. Listen to *"Pollerita"* **CD 7-30** and ask students
to describe the timbre of each instrument. Invite them to add descriptive
terms to their Semantic Maps. Ask students to identify similarities and differences between the flutes listed on their Semantic Maps.

ACROSS THE CURRICULUM

▶ **Social Studies** Bolivia is a country of sharp contrasts. The
Andes mountains, some of the highest in the world, are in the
western part of Bolivia. The eastern part is tropical rain forest.
Bolivia is rich in minerals, but most Bolivians are farmers. They
raise cotton and soybeans to sell, and potatoes, corn, wheat,
rice, and sugarcane to eat. The official language is Spanish,
but over half the people are Native Americans with their own
languages.

Have students locate Bolivia on a map of South America. Ask
students to consult their social studies textbook or an encyclopedia
to find out who were the first European explorers to "discover"
this area of the world. When did these explorers arrive in South
America? Who were the original inhabitants of South America?

Patterns from Bolivia

Listen to *"Pollerita"* without looking at the music. **Identify** the patterns on page 150 as they occur in the song.

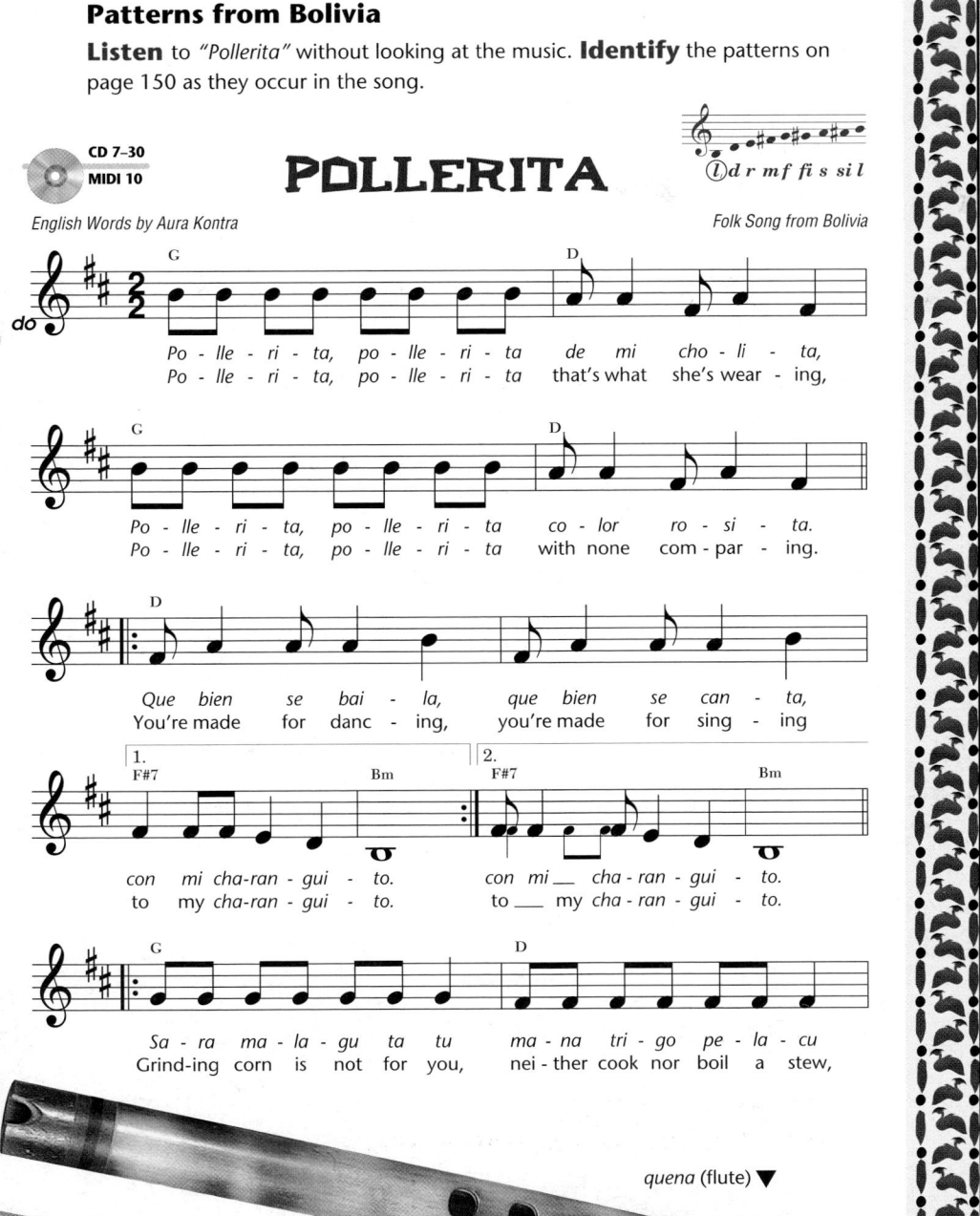

CD 7-30
MIDI 10

POLLERITA

(i) d r mf fi s si l

English Words by Aura Kontra

Folk Song from Bolivia

Po - lle - ri - ta, po - lle - ri - ta de mi cho - li - ta,
Po - lle - ri - ta, po - lle - ri - ta that's what she's wear - ing,

Po - lle - ri - ta, po - lle - ri - ta co - lor ro - si - ta.
Po - lle - ri - ta, po - lle - ri - ta with none com - par - ing.

Que bien se bai - la, que bien se can - ta,
You're made for danc - ing, you're made for sing - ing

con mi cha - ran - gui - to. | con mi __ cha - ran - gui - to.
to my cha - ran - gui - to. | to __ my cha - ran - gui - to.

Sa - ra ma - la - gu ta tu ma - na tri - go pe - la - cu
Grind - ing corn is not for you, nei - ther cook nor boil a stew,

quena (flute) ▼

Unit 4 **151**

---

1 INTRODUCE

Ask students to look at the song *"Pollerita"* on pp. 150–151.

SAY *"Pollerita"* is a folk song from Bolivia. The word *pollerita* means a full, pleated skirt. A *charango* is a small guitar-like string instrument. At one time, charangos were made from armadillo shells. A *charanguito* is a smaller version of the charango.

Have students read the words of *"Pollerita"* and then describe what the song is about.

2 DEVELOP

Reading

5a Have students listen to the recording of *"Pollerita"* **CD 7-30** as they follow the music in their books.

Have students

5a
- Look at the five patterns on p. 150.
- Use rhythm syllables to speak the rhythm of each pattern.
- Perform each pattern independently, with accurate rhythm, demonstrating fundamental skills.

5b
- Sing each pattern using pitch syllables.

Invite students to listen to *"Pollerita"* again and hold up one finger when they hear the music for pattern 1, two fingers for pattern 2, and so on.

Ask students to speak the words of *"Pollerita,"* first in English and then in Spanish. (Explain that the words in lines 5 and 6 are not Spanish but are of Native American origin.) Point out the repeat signs and be sure students understand the "road map" for the song.

continued on page 152

MOVEMENT

▶ **Patterned Dance** *"Pollerita"* Formation: Partners facing; girls pantomime shaking frilly skirts; boys' hands on waists.

M. 1–4:	Basic footwork pattern (step-hop, step-hop, step, step, step, rest), moving toward partner. Repeat.
M. 5–6:	Right elbow turn with partner, left hands held high; step-hop four times, moving in a circle.
M. 7–8:	Basic footwork pattern (see above).
M. 9–10:	Left elbow turn with partner.
M. 11–12:	Basic footwork pattern, moving back to place.
M. 13–15:	Step-hops in place.
M. 16:	Clap *ti-ta ti-ta* (rest).
M. 17–20:	Repeat M. 13–16.
M. 21–24:	Right elbow turn.
M. 25–26:	Left elbow turn.
M. 27–29:	Step-hop back to place.
M. 30:	Clap *ti-ta ti-ta* (rest).

SKILLS REINFORCEMENT

▶ **Listening** Prepare students for the listening activities in this lesson by sharing the following information.

- The *charango*, traditionally made from the shell of an armadillo, has five double sets of strings over a long fretted neck. The strings are strummed or plucked with the fingernails, producing a sharp, high-pitched sound.

- The *quena*, a notched flute, has a mouthpiece carved in a bamboo cane. It was originally carved from llama bones.

- The panpipes, or *siku*, has two rows of pipes joined as a pair. One row has pipes closed at the bottom and the other has open pipes.

Singing

Have students

- Use the Pronunciation Practice Track **CD 7-33** to echo-sing the Spanish words of *"Pollerita."* You may wish to refer to Resource Book p. A-18.

1c
- Sing *"Pollerita"* in English **CD 7-31** and in Spanish **CD 7-30.**

Listening

6b Have students listen to *Camino de piedra* **CD 7-34** and distinguish among a variety of musical timbres. Then using information in Skills Reinforcement, p. 151, discuss with students some of the traditional Andean instruments used in this recording.

ASK **What instruments do you hear?** (panpipes, *quena* [flute], *charango,* drum)

What similarities can you hear between *Camino de piedra* and *"Pollerita"*? (The instrumentation is similar; both pieces are rhythmic and energetic; both use a lot of melodic repetition.)

SAY This next listening selection, *Amores hallarás,* means "Love can be found," and is a festival song from Ecuador, Bolivia, and elsewhere in the Andes.

Invite students to find Ecuador and Bolivia on a map and then find the Andes.

While looking at the listening map on p. 153, ask students to find the following:

- Repeat sign
- *D.C.*
- 1st and 2nd endings
- *D. S. al Coda*
- *Coda*

Ma - na chu - ño pun - ti - co.
Sing and dance the whole day through.

Que bien se bai - la que bien se can - ta
You're made for danc - ing, you're made for sing - ing

1.
con mi cha - ran - gui - to.
to my cha - ran - gui - to.

2.
con mi cha - ran - gui - to. _____
to my cha - ran - gui - to. _____

Listen to *Camino de piedra,* a piece inspired by music of the Andes. What instruments do you hear? What similarities can you hear between *Camino de piedra* and *"Pollerita"*?

CD 7–34
Camino de piedra

by Wilson López
as performed by Andes Manta

Camino de piedra means "the rocky road." The instruments and rhythm patterns are typical of Andean music.

Bolivian musicians, Carnival Tarabuco ▼

(152)

Footnotes

CULTURAL CONNECTION

▶ **A Loyal Companion** The llama is an important animal in the Andes mountains of western South America. Fossil footprints found in California indicate that llamas originated in North America. The structure of their feet makes llamas great mountain animals. Each foot has two toes with toenails. (The toenails are used as an Andean rattle called the *chajchas.*) The bottoms of their feet have soft, but leathery cushions that provide excellent traction. People in the Andes breed llamas as pack animals, as well as for their wool, meat, and dung (used for fuel). Llamas make good pets. They are calm, loyal, intelligent, easy to train, and especially gentle with children.

ACROSS THE CURRICULUM

▶ **Language Arts** Share this classic humorous poem with students.

The Llama
by Ogden Nash

The one-l lama, he's a priest.
The two-l llama, he's a beast.
And I will bet a silk pajama,
There isn't any three-l lllama!

Encourage students to read *The Children of Bolivia* by Jules M. Hermes (Carolrhoda Books, 1995) for more pictures and information on the people, culture, and land of Bolivia. The book includes beautiful color photographs of traditional festivals, dances, music, and clothing.

Map Out a Form

The listening map below shows the form of *Amores hallarás*.

Trace each section of the music as you **listen**.

CD 7–35
Amores hallarás
by Victor M. Salgado
as performed by Inti-Illimani

Inti-Illimani is a Chilean ensemble whose members perform on more than 30 instruments. The group was formed in 1967 by engineering students at Santiago Technical University.

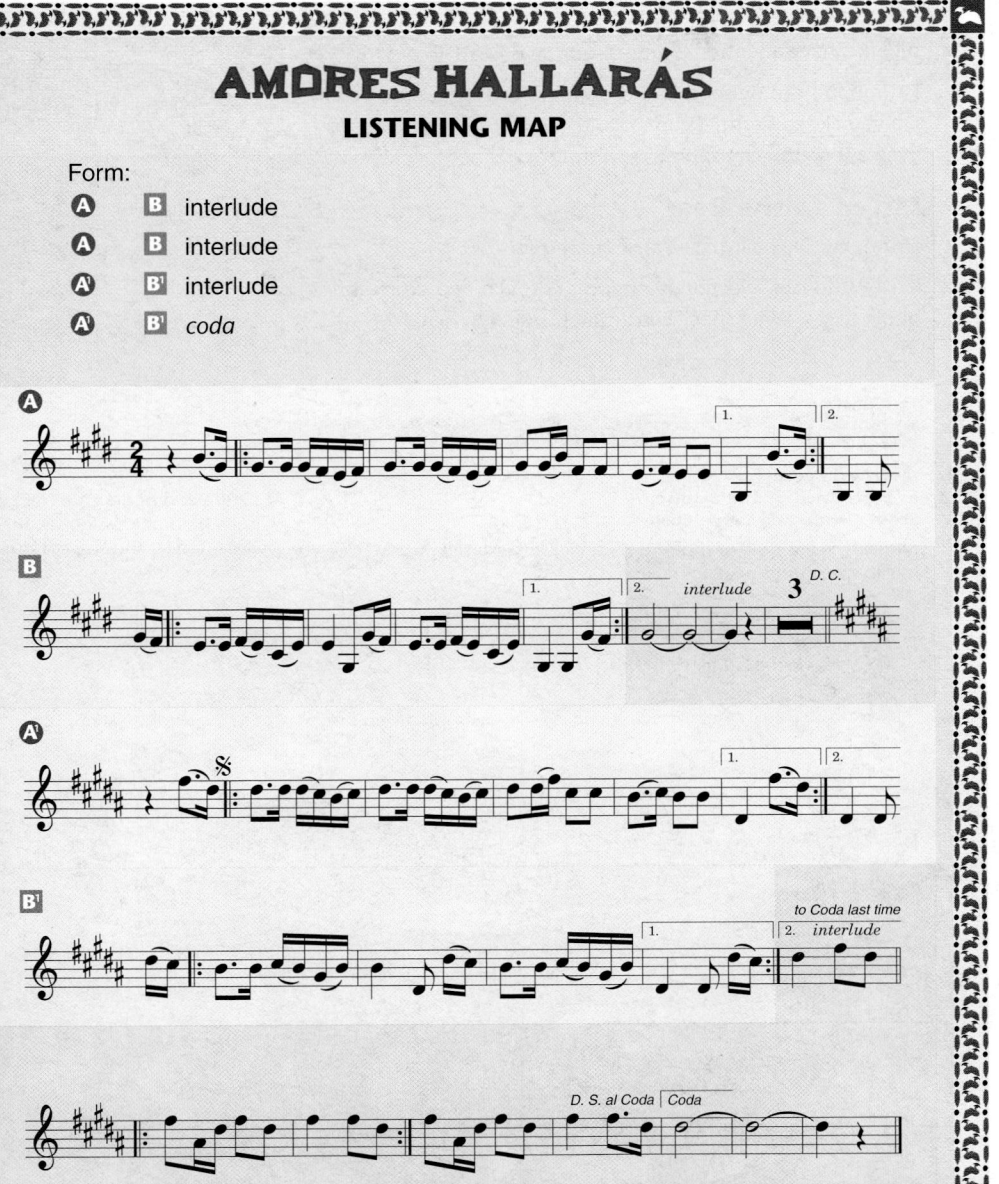

AMORES HALLARÁS
LISTENING MAP

Form:
- Ⓐ Ⓑ interlude
- Ⓐ Ⓑ interlude
- Ⓐ' Ⓑ' interlude
- Ⓐ' Ⓑ' *coda*

Point to the different signs as students follow the melody while listening to *Amores hallarás* **CD 7-35**. This may take multiple listenings.

6b **ASK** What type of solo instrument is used? (flute, or *quena*)

What instruments are used to accompany the flutes? (string instruments, including the *charango*)

Share with students the information about the performers, Andes Manta and Inti-Illimani. (See Spotlight On below.) Lead students in a discussion of various music avocations.

3 CLOSE

Creating

Create five different melodic visuals from phrases of *"Pollerita."* Notate the melody only, not the rhythm.

Play or sing the visuals in random order. Have students hold up 1–5 fingers to identify which visual you are performing.

1a Ask volunteers to take turns singing the visuals at random for the class to identify.

4a Divide the class into small groups. Invite students to use segments from the visuals to create a new melody. Suggest that groups create an eight-measure melody. Let them know that they may repeat or change a motive, if they wish. Suggest that students end their melodies on B.

Have students sing or play their new melodies.

Skill: LISTENING   **ASSESSMENT**

5a **Observation** Have students listen to the recording of **6a** *"Pollerita"* **CD 7-30** and identify excerpts of music representing diverse cultures. Ask students to point to each pattern on p. 150 as it appears in the song.

SPOTLIGHT ON

▶ **The Performers** In Ecuador in the late 1970s, five talented friends and relatives formed a group called Andes Manta. With its blend of music of the Inca Empire, the sounds of the rain forest, and Latin rhythms, the group has captivated audiences at home and in the United States. In their performances, they play more than 35 instruments, including six-foot long panpipes (*siku*), llama toenail rattles (*chajchas*), and four-foot long flutes (*moxenos*).

Members of Inti-Illimani, from Chile, were engineering students who met in the 1960s. In performance, Inti-Illimani plays more than 30 wind, string, and percussion instruments to create a mural of the sacred places, carnivals, and daily lives of the people of Chile, Peru, Bolivia, Ecuador, and Argentina.

TECHNOLOGY/MEDIA LINK

6b **Transparency** Display the listening map transparency for *Amores hallarás* as you play the recording. Point to each section of the piece on the first listening to help students follow along. On subsequent listenings, invite a student to point to the sections.

MIDI/Sequencing Software Display the notation view of the MIDI song file for *"Pollerita."* Have students

5a • Locate the melodic phrases that correspond to the visuals in the Creating activity above.

6b • Start the playback in different locations to identify the melodic contours.

LESSON AT A GLANCE

Element Focus **TIMBRE** Percussion

Skill Objective **PLAYING** Perform a piece for percussion ensemble

Connection Activity **CULTURE** Discuss the role of drums in various cultures

MATERIALS

- *Malagueña* (excerpt) **CD 8-1**
- *Birdland* (excerpt) **CD 8-2**
- *Wipe Out* **CD 8-3**
- *Yaudachi* (excerpt) **CD 8-4**
- *Conga Kings Grand Finale* (excerpt) **CD 8-5**
- *O'Sullivan's March* **CD 8-6**
- hand drums, conga drums, bongo drums, rattles, bells, selected percussion instruments

VOCABULARY

drum and bugle corps   *taiko*   *bodhran*

◆ ◆ ◆ ◆ National Standards ◆ ◆ ◆ ◆

2b Perform easy instrumental pieces with technical accuracy

5a Read quarter, eighth, sixteenth, and dotted notes in duple meter

6a Listen and describe events in music using appropriate terms

6b Listen and analyze uses of timbre in music from diverse genres and cultures

7a Students evaluate the music they perform

8b Identify ways music relates to social studies

MORE MUSIC CHOICES

For more choices on various drums:

Theme and Variations for Percussion, p. 65

"*Jo' ashilá*", p. 108

A Drum Roll, Please

All of us have an internal drum—our heartbeat!

Drumming can be soothing; drumming can stir us into action. Do you like to drum? Drums come in many different shapes. Even a tabletop can sound like a drum.

Listen to the Beat

Drums can be heard in all styles of music.

Listen to this selection featuring the sound of a drum and bugle corps. What specific instruments do you hear?

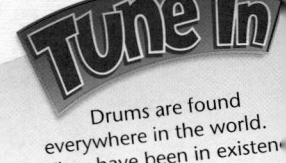

Drums are found everywhere in the world. They have been in existence for at least 6,000 years.

CD 8–1
Malagueña

by Ernesto Lecuona as performed by the Madison Scouts Drum and Bugle Corps

Malagueña is a style of music and dance from the region of Málaga in southern Spain.

▼ Drum and bugle corps include marching percussion section of bass, tenor, and snare drums, as well as cymbals.

154

Footnotes

ACROSS THE CURRICULUM

8b ▶ **Social Studies/Language Arts** Ask students to locate the geographical areas associated with the listening examples in the lesson on a world map. Invite them to write paragraphs in their journals describing each world percussion group, how the instruments are played, and the sound of the percussion from each listening example. Encourage students to use correct musical terminology in their descriptions.

BUILDING SKILLS THROUGH MUSIC

▶ **Social Studies** Invite students to listen to **CD 8-1, CD 8-2, CD 8-3, CD 8-4, CD 8-5,** and **CD 8-6** and decide what are the most prominent musical characteristics of each performance, including specific percussion timbres represented. List the titles on the board and discuss how each is similar and different.

SKILLS REINFORCEMENT

6a ▶ **Listening** The following selections feature additional types of drums. Have students aurally identify excerpts of music from diverse styles and then write a short description of each.

- "*Ah ya Zane*" **CD 13-26**
- *Oya (Primitive Fire)* **CD 4-10**
- *Saludo de Matanzas* **CD 1-27**
- *Theme and Variations for Percussion* **CD 4-5**

Listen to the sounds of a famous jazz band. How is the drum used in this song?

CD 8–2
Birdland
by Joe Zawinul
as performed by the Buddy Rich Big Band
Buddy Rich was a musician his entire life. At age four he was featured as a solo performer, nicknamed "Traps, the Drum Wonder."

The Buddy Rich Big Band was one of the best bands of the 1960s, and Rich himself is widely accepted as the greatest jazz drummer of all time. ▶

Listen to an exciting drum solo in this popular 1960s rock song, *Wipe Out*. Does the drum make you want to dance?

CD 8–3
Wipe Out
written and performed by the Surfaris
The Surfaris got their start as teenagers by playing dance music at local skating rinks and halls. *Wipe Out* is their best-known song.

The Surfaris got their name by combining the words "surfing safari," a common phrase used by surfers hunting good waves. Surf music was very popular in the early 1960s. ▶

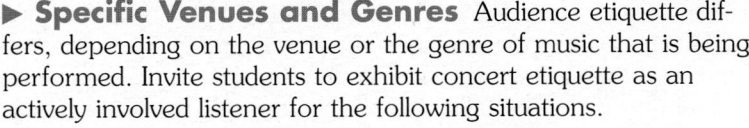

Unit 4 **155**

1 INTRODUCE

Ask students to name as many different kinds of drums and as many different kinds of music that use drums as they can. Discuss answers and then explain that drums are found in almost every culture throughout the world.

The drum shell holds the drum head or heads and acts as a resonator. Drums come in many shapes. Some, like bass drums, are cylindrical. Some drums of China, India, and Africa are barrel-shaped. Middle Eastern drums sometimes have a goblet shape. Drums like the Irish *bodhran* and the classroom hand drum, which have a very shallow shell, are called frame drums.

2 DEVELOP

Listening
ASK How are the drums pictured on pp. 154–157 alike and how are they different? (Answers may include: different sizes, different shapes, one or two heads.)

6b Invite students to listen to and identify examples of each kind of drum.

Have students listen to:

* *Malagueña* **CD 8-1**

ASK What instruments do you hear? (bass drums, snare drums, trumpet, trombone, and tuba)

* *Birdland* **CD 8-2**

ASK What kind of drum do you hear? (snare drum)

Is it the only instrument you hear? (no; double bass, keyboard, trumpet, trombone, brush cymbal)

What is the style of the music? (jazz)

continued on page 156

AUDIENCE ETIQUETTE

▶ **Specific Venues and Genres** Audience etiquette differs, depending on the venue or the genre of music that is being performed. Invite students to exhibit concert etiquette as an actively involved listener for the following situations.

* A rock concert held outdoors. (It is appropriate to move, dance, clap, and sing along with the music.)
* A half-time show. (Stand or sit to watch the band. It is appropriate to cheer for the performance.)
* A chorus, band, or orchestra concert in an auditorium. (Quiet and stillness are best. Applaud only at the end of pieces.)
* A jazz concert. (Audiences tend to nod or tap feet to the music. It's okay to applaud after a solo, even if the piece is not over.)
* A special event with "background music." (It is appropriate to talk quietly or even to eat while the music plays.)

MEETING INDIVIDUAL NEEDS

▶ **Different Drummers** Students need many opportunities to feel positive about their capabilities in front of their peers. Clapping rhythms while counting and reading may be difficult for students who learn more easily by imitating aural models or performing patterns from previous lessons. Help transfer by having all students practice patterns using the motor movements required for each drum. Observe patterns that are performed successfully and assign a pattern and a "cool" drum to a student who will benefit from praise and attention. After rehearsing and sharing one drum with a kind partner, partners can perform (each on a drum) in a small ensemble. Be sure to cue "applause" for group performances.

Lesson 9 Continued

- *Wipe Out* **CD 8-3**

ASK What kind of drum do you hear? (drum set, which includes cymbals, snare, and bass)

What is the style of music? (rock 'n' roll)

SAY You will hear different sounds of drums from different cultures, and the different sounds similar drums can make when used in different styles of music. Let's listen to some drums and drummers from other parts of the world.

- *Yaudachi* **CD 8-4**

ASK What are the drum sounds describing in this selection? (sounds of an evening storm)

How does the drummer produce the effect of the storm? (low slow drum roll that gradually becomes louder and faster)

- *Conga Kings Grand Finale* **CD 8-5**

ASK What happens in this selection that is different from all the other examples? (Each of the Conga Kings is introduced and plays a solo.)

What other instruments do you hear? (No other instrument is played.)

- *O'Sullivan's March* **CD 8-6**

ASK What is the drum in this selection? *(bodhran)*

How is the *bodhran* used? (to keep the steady beat)

Have students compare and contrast the different drums and the way the drums are used in each selection using standard terminology in explaining musical instruments. (Accept a variety of answers.)

ASK How is the use of the drums alike? (Accept a variety of answers.)

How is it different? (Accept a variety of answers.)

Have students read more about the *bodhran*, conga drum, bongo drums and *taiko* on pp. 514 and 518 of the Sound Bank.

Distant Drums

Drums are found everywhere in the world and are closely associated with ceremonies. Sometimes drums are housed in sacred places.

Listen to the Soh Daiko Taiko Drummers perform *Yaudachi*. They are playing traditional Japanese drums called *taiko*.

CD 8–4
Yaudachi

as performed by Soh Daiko Taiko Drummers

Soh means "peace, harmony, and working together." The Soh Daiko Taiko musicians needed all of these attributes when they started their careers using garbage cans, old tires, and barrels as practice instruments.

◀ *Taiko* means "big drum" in Japanese. These drums are traditionally used for ceremonies, but now are played also for entertainment.

Listen to these conga and bongo drums from Latin America.

CD 8–5
Conga Kings Grand Finale

Written and performed by the Conga Kings

The bongos are played with the fingers. Bongo players usually play a counter-rhythm to the main rhythm. Conga drums (shown below) are tall drums with high, medium, and low pitches.

Congas are played with the hands and palms. Since performances on congas and bongos are usually improvised, they are often included in jazz ensembles. ▼

 156

Footnotes

ACROSS THE CURRICULUM

▶ **Language Arts** Students may enjoy reading *Drums of Noto Hanto* by J. Alison James, and illustrated by Tsukushi (DK Publishing, 1999). This book retells the story of an event that happened in 1576 on the shores of Japan. Villagers of Nabune, Japan, on the coast of Noto Hanto, cleverly frighten away invading samurai warriors by wearing fearful masks and drumming furiously on thundering drums. The book layers the sounds of the drums, the culture, and the beauty of the masks. Each year a festival is held on the seacoast to commemorate this historical event.

CULTURAL CONNECTION

▶ *Taiko* The word *taiko* is used in different ways. It can mean the art of Japanese drumming in modern times, or it can mean the actual drum named *taiko*. In Japanese, *taiko* actually means "big fat drum," but not all *taiko* are big and fat. There are many different shapes and sizes of *taiko*, as well as different styles of *taiko* music. Some styles use other instruments, such as gongs, cymbals, flutes, and rattles. Usually, *taiko* are played with sticks called *bachi*. Only in classical *taiko* music is the hand used to play other types of drums. The two main types of *taiko* are ones with nailed heads and ones with heads connected with hoops and rope.

A *bodhran* is a large Irish drum that is held by a crossbar under the drum's head. **Listen** to the *bodhran* in *O'Sullivan's March* by the Chieftains.

O'Sullivan's March

Traditional Irish Tune as performed by the Chieftains

This song showcases the dark, low sound of the *bodhran* as it keeps the beat for the other musicians.

◄ The Chieftains are one of the best-known Irish music groups. They play many traditional Irish instruments, including the *bodhran*.

Rhythm and Improvisation

Play this percussion ensemble, adding one part at a time until all parts sound good together.

Then, **improvise** new solo parts to go with the ensemble. Use bells, talking drums *(dundun),* or other percussion instruments.

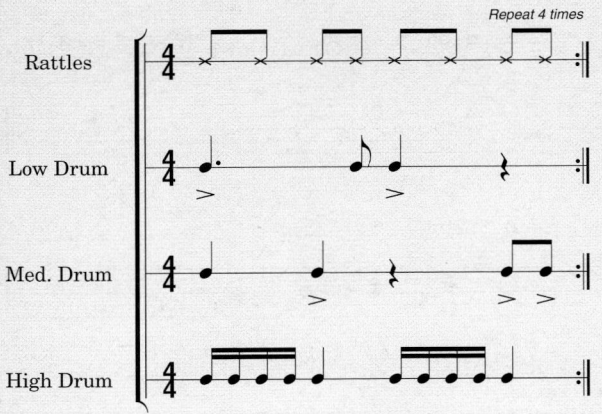

Playing

Demonstrate different ways to play a hand drum (with hand in the middle, with hand near the rim, using a mallet). Invite students to describe the different timbres that the various playing techniques produce.

Explain that conga drums are played with the palms of the hands, and the bongos are played with the fingers.

Distribute as many drums as possible to the class. Clap some rhythm patterns for students, and have them echo on the drums individually.

Reading

5a Ask the class to speak and clap the rhythm of the percussion ensemble parts on p. 157. Have students practice one of the parts using body percussion before transferring to drums.

2b Transfer to rattles and drums, layering the parts of the ensemble. Ask students to describe the changes in timbre as the parts are added. Encourage them to improvise solo parts on bells and other percussion instruments over the ensemble accompaniment.

3 CLOSE

Element: TIMBRE  **ASSESSMENT**

Performance/Peer Critique Divide the class into small groups for a performance of the percussion ensemble.

Have each group decide whether they will play the piece slowly, moderately, quickly, or use a combination of tempos.

2b Invite each group to perform the piece as notated for the rest of the class.

7a Ask listeners to describe the changes in timbre that result and evaluate the performance of each group.

CHARACTER EDUCATION

► **Diversity** Drums can be found in almost every culture throughout the world. Because of this, they are a uniting musical element between cultures. Encourage students to consider other personal characteristics or attributes that cross cultural barriers. Ask students the following questions. How are people of different cultures similar? Why is it important to consider common traits among people of various cultures? Divide the class into pairs and ask students to talk to their partner and make a list of ways they are similar to each other. Then have students write about what they learned from the experience, including their perceptions of their partner prior to and following the activity.

TECHNOLOGY/MEDIA LINK

Web Site For more information on percussion instruments from around the world, go to *www.sfsuccessnet.com.*

LESSON AT A GLANCE

Element Focus	TEXTURE/HARMONY	Two-part canon
Skill Objective	SINGING	Perform a song as a two-part canon
Connection Activity	RELATED ARTS	Recognize that imitation is also used in the visual arts

MATERIALS

- "Ego sum pauper" **CD 8-7**
- "Nothing Do I Own" **CD 8-8**
  - **Recording Routine:** Intro (6 m.); vocal (unison); interlude (6 m.); vocal (2-part canon); coda
- **Pronunciation Practice/Translation** p. 529
- *Sonata in A major* "Allegretto poco mosso" (excerpt) **CD 8-11**
- **Resource Book** p. A-19

VOCABULARY

canon   unison   polyphonic texture

◆ ◆ ◆ ◆ National Standards ◆ ◆ ◆ ◆

1d Sing music written in two parts
2a Play instruments accurately alone and in small ensembles
6b Listen and analyze uses of harmony in music from diverse genres
7a Students evaluate the music they perform
8a Show how different arts portray the same idea in unique ways

MORE MUSIC CHOICES

For more practice with imitative form:
"I Love the Mountains," p. 34
Sumer Is Icumen In, p. 35

1 INTRODUCE

Explain that a canon is a musical version of "Follow the Leader." The voice that "leads" a canon is called the initiating voice. The voice that follows is called the imitating voice.

8a Imitation can also be used in paintings, drawings, and other visual arts. See Across the Curriculum below.

Where You Lead... I Will Follow

In a two-part **canon,** one part leads and the other part follows.

Listen to "Ego sum pauper." You will hear the voices sing the canon. You will also hear an instrumental canon. **Identify** the instrument.

Sing "Ego sum pauper" in unison. Then **perform** the song as a two-part canon.

> A **canon** is a musical composition in which the parts imitate each other. One part begins, or leads, and the other part follows.

CD 8-7 MIDI 11

Ego sum pauper
(Nothing Do I Own)

Traditional

d s l t (d) r m'

E - go sum pau - per.
Noth-ing do I own.
Ni - hil ha - be - o
Poor of things I live,

E - go sum pau - per.
Noth-ing do I own.
Ni - hil ha - be -
Poor of things I

Cor me - um da - bo.
But my heart I give.

o
live,
Cor me - um da - bo.
But my heart I give.

(158)

Footnotes

▶ Recorder Review with students the fingering for high D and C on their recorders. Remind them to move their thumb slightly away from the thumb hole when playing high D. Students can play the ostinato below as others sing "Ego sum pauper."

BUILDING SKILLS THROUGH MUSIC

▶ Writing Invite students to sing the canon "Ego sum pauper" **CD 8-7, 8-8** in Latin and English. Select individual students to share their interpretation of the meaning of the text. Discuss different interpretations among students. Ask students to write a complete sentence that expresses their personal opinion about the meaning of the words of the song.

ACROSS THE CURRICULUM

8a ▶ Visual Arts Imitation and canon appear in visual arts as well as in music. The famous Dutch visual artist M.C. Escher (1898–1972) is known for his detailed black-and-white lithographs, many in strikingly clear imitative and canonic design. His subjects include reptiles, birds, butterflies, humans, city scenes, and water, in which students can easily see visual representations of different forms. See Escher's remarkable work in *M.C. Escher: 29 Master Prints* (Harry N. Abrams, 1983).

Students will enjoy coloring the imitative and canonic puzzle designs in *The M.C. Escher Coloring Book: 24 Images to Color* (Harry N. Abrams, 1995). Students may wish to complete the large poster included with the book as a class project. Display the artworks on bulletin boards and at performances.

A Canon for Instruments

Listen to this selection and **identify** the instruments that play the leader and the follower.

CD 8–11
Allegretto poco mosso

from *Sonata in A Major*
by César Franck
as performed by Isaac Stern

Belgian composer César Franck [frahnk] (1822–1890) wrote this sonata for violin and piano at age 63.

MUSIC MAKERS
Isaac Stern

Isaac Stern (1920–2001) was one of the leading violinists of our time. Stern was born in Russia and came to America when he was ten months old. He began playing the violin at the age of eight and made his recital debut at the age of thirteen. He has been recognized for his dedication to teaching young musicians all over the world. Stern was featured in the 1981 Academy Award-winning documentary *From Mao to Mozart*. He also appeared in the motion picture *Music of the Heart*, about a dedicated and determined violin teacher in Harlem. Stern served as president of Carnegie Hall. In 1960 he played a major role in saving Carnegie Hall from being demolished.

Isaac Stern is famous for his work with young musicians. *From Mao to Mozart* featured Stern using music to connect with people of all ages in China, "first as musicians, then as friends."
▼

Unit 4   159

2 DEVELOP

Singing

Invite students to sing "*Ego sum pauper*" **CD 8-7** in unison. Use the Pronunciation Practice Track **CD 8-10** and Resource Book p. A-19 to help students learn the Latin words.

1d Divide the class into two groups—initiating voices and imitating voices—and have students sing the song as a two-part canon.

ASK Did you sing in unison or harmony? (harmony)

Help students discover that the harmony was created when they sang the same melody at different times and that the two parts together resulted in polyphonic texture.

Listening

Have students listen to *Allegretto poco mosso* **CD 8-11.**

ASK How many instruments did you hear? (two)

6b **What instruments did you hear?** (violin and piano)

Ask a volunteer to read aloud the information on p. 159 about the violinist Isaac Stern.

6b Play the recording once again. Have students raise their hands when the violin and piano are in canon.

ASK Which instrument is the leader, and which is the follower? (The piano begins as the leader; later, the violin is the leader.)

Invite students to read more about the violin on p. 519 of the Sound Bank.

3 CLOSE

Element: TEXTURE/HARMONY —— ASSESSMENT

1d
7a **Performance/Peer Critique** Divide the class into small groups, with strong singers in each group. Have two groups at a time perform "*Ego sum pauper*" in canon. Allow students in the audience to make constructive comments on each performance.

TEACHER TO TEACHER

▶ **Response Songs** Two-voice canons are similar to echo songs—one voice leads and the other follows. Canons are more challenging for the young singer because the initiating voice does not wait for the imitating voice to echo the initial phrase. "*Ego sum pauper*" is a "beginner" canon, perfect for young singers. The initiating voice sustains a pitch, while the imitating voice sings the echo. When students are comfortable singing "*Ego sum pauper*" in two parts, you may wish to add the challenge of singing it as a three-part canon. Group 3 will begin when Group 2 reaches the second measure of the melody.

TECHNOLOGY/MEDIA LINK

1d **MIDI/Sequencing Software** Use the MIDI song file for "*Ego sum pauper*" to help students learn to sing the canon. Have students

- Sing the melody with voice 1 and voice 2 tracks.
- Sing voice 2 while the two tracks play.
- Add voice 3 to voice 2.
- Continue until they can sing in three parts.

After students can sing their parts, make a recording of their singing in a digital audio program for them to enjoy hearing.

LESSON AT A GLANCE

Element Focus	**TEXTURE/HARMONY** Three-part rounds
Skill Objective	**MOVING** Perform a circle dance to accompany a three-part round
Connection Activity	**CULTURE** Explore the cultural background of a Jewish dance

MATERIALS

- "Tumba"   **CD 8-12**

  Recording Routine: Intro (4 m.); vocal (3-part round); coda
- **Dance Directions** for "Tumba" p. 557
- selected barred instruments, including alto metallophone, bass metallophone, bass xylophone; tambourine
- **Resource Book** p. H-13

VOCABULARY

round   polyphonic texture

◆ ◆ ◆ ◆ National Standards ◆ ◆ ◆ ◆

1c Sing music from diverse cultures
1d Sing music written in three parts
2a Play instruments accurately in small ensembles
6b Listen and analyze uses of harmony and texture in music from diverse cultures
7b Students use specific criteria to evaluate their own performances

MORE MUSIC CHOICES

For more practice with rounds:
"*Himmel und Erde*" ("Music Alone Shall Live"), p. 94
Viva la musica, p. 95
"*Ego sum pauper*" (Nothing Do I Own"), p. 158

1 INTRODUCE

Review canon and polyphonic texture. Have students look at "Tumba" [TOOM-bah]. Tell them that it has three phrases and uses nonsense syllables.

and ROUND and ROUND and ROUND and

Jewish pioneers came to Palestine from all over the world to establish a new country, Israel. Pioneers from Eastern Europe brought "Tumba" with them.

"Tumba" is a **round. Sing** the song in unison.

Next **sing** "Tumba" as a two-part or three-part round.

> **Rounds** are compositions in which the parts enter in succession, singing the same melody.

Arts Connection   ▲ 15th Century Woodcut Mosaic of Jerusalem, by Gianni Dagli Orti

160

Footnotes

SKILLS REINFORCEMENT

▶ **Recorder** Students can play a recorder ostinato as others sing "Tumba," using Part III of the round as the ostinato. (Have students change the whole notes to quarter-quarter-half.)

2a

▶ **Keyboard** Students can play "Tumba" on keyboard, using the fingering shown on p. H-13 in the Resource Book.

2a

BUILDING SKILLS THROUGH MUSIC

▶ **Social Studies** Invite the class to sing "*Dundai*" **CD 5-34** and then "Tumba" **CD 8-12**. Ask students to identify musical characteristics that are the same (for example, key signature, meter, repetition of phrases, rhythm patterns). Distribute copies of the Comparison Chart from Resource Book p. C-2 and have students list similarities in the left column and differences in the right column.

MOVEMENT

▶ **Patterned Dance** "Tumba" was sung by the Central and Eastern European Jewish pioneers of the early twentieth century who worked to bring life to the desert land that became Israel. "Tumba" is often described in song collections as being "from Palestine," as the area was called until becoming Israel in 1948. The song is not, however, of the Palestinian people, or even of Israeli origin. It comes from the same tradition as klezmer music and dance, that of the Ashkenazi Jewish people (rather than the Sephardic or Yemenite or Oriental Jewish people whose backgrounds are from other parts of the world).

Dance Directions for "Tumba" can be found beginning on p. 557.

Tumba

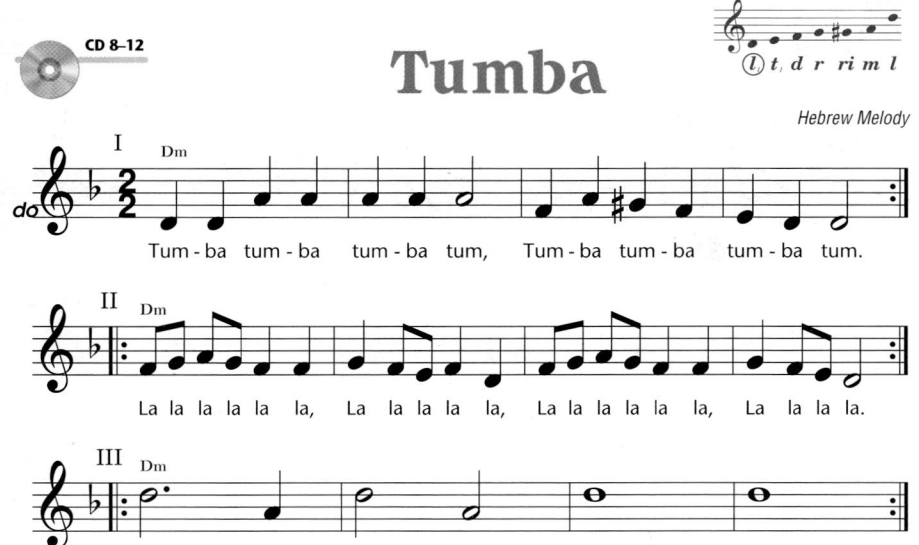

Hebrew Melody

I Dm
Tum - ba tum - ba tum - ba tum, Tum - ba tum - ba tum - ba tum.

II Dm
La la la la la la, La la la la la la, La la la la la la, La la la la.

III Dm
Tum - ba, Tum - ba, Tum - ba.

... and Round

Play the following accompaniment for "Tumba" to add more harmony to the song.

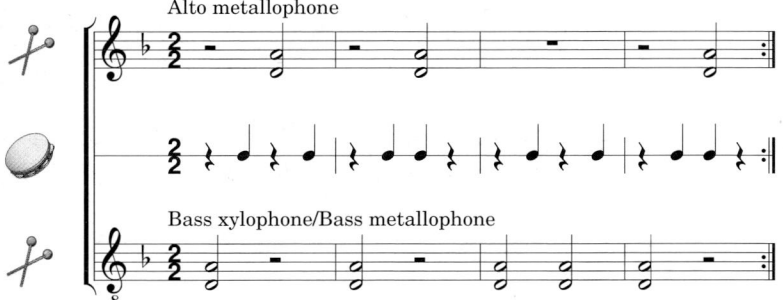

Alto metallophone

Bass xylophone/Bass metallophone

Dance A-Round

There is no traditional dance to "Tumba." You can form three circles; one circle within another circle, within another circle. Then **create** your own movements to dance a round.

---

2 DEVELOP

Listening

Play "Tumba" **CD 8-12.**

6b   **ASK Is the song in major or minor?** (minor)

Is the song in unison or harmony? (harmony)

What is the texture? (polyphonic)

Which phrase *sounds* the fastest? (the second phrase because it has many eighth notes)

Which phrase *sounds* the slowest? (the last phrase because it has the longest note values but the tempo is the same)

Singing

1c **1d** Divide the class into three groups; assign a phrase from "Tumba" to each group. Encourage students to sing the song in three parts by having each group continue repeating its assigned part as the other parts enter.

Playing

2a Have the members of each group learn to play their phrase on barred instruments. Have each group repeat its phrase as the other groups enter, layering the parts. Then have each group perform the phrases in succession so as to play the song as a round.

Students may also play the percussion parts on p. 161 as an accompaniment to "Tumba."

3 CLOSE

Moving

Help students learn a movement routine and its cultural background to reinforce the polyphonic texture of "Tumba." See Movement, p. 160.

Element: TEXTURE/HARMONY   ASSESSMENT

7b **Performance/Observation** Organize the class into three performing groups and have students sing, play, and move to "Tumba." Observe that each group can perform its part accurately and independently.

TEACHER TO TEACHER

▶ **Teaching Tip** Rounds are difficult for most young singers to perform. They hear other parts around them as they try to sing their own part. This may confuse inexperienced singers and cause them to lose concentration. To help students perform rounds more successfully, divide the round into phrases.

Assign a group of students to sing each phrase as an ostinato. Have Group 1 sing phrase 1. When Group 1 repeats the phrase, Group 2 begins. Group 3 begins when Group 2 repeats its phrase. Allow students to enjoy listening to the harmonies by having all singers continue until Group 3 has repeated its phrase several times. A slowing of tempo in the last two measures provides an effective ending.

TECHNOLOGY/MEDIA LINK

Sequencing Software As a class, transform "Tumba" into a MIDI round. First, help students use MIDI sequencing software to record the melody. You will need to either use projection equipment or connect the computer to a television. When the melody is successfully sequenced, have students create a round by

- Using "click and drag" to select the entire melody.
- Pasting the melody into a new track beginning in m. 5.
- Pasting the melody into a third track beginning in m. 9.

Students may wish to lengthen the round by pasting a repetition of the entire melody at the end of each track.

LESSON AT A GLANCE

Element Focus   **TEXTURE/HARMONY** Round

Skill Objective   **SINGING** Sing a three-part round

Connection Activity   **LANGUAGE ARTS** Read and discuss a poem about music

MATERIALS

• "O Music"   **CD 8-15**

   Recording Routine: Intro (4 m.); vocal (unison); interlude (4 m.); vocal (3-part round); coda

• "In Music Meeting" (poem)

VOCABULARY

round   phrase   harmony

◆ ◆ ◆ ◆ National Standards ◆ ◆ ◆ ◆

1a Sing accurately in small ensembles
1d Sing music written in three parts
4c Compose, using electronic media
5d Use standard notation to record musical ideas
7a Students evaluate the music they perform
8a Show how different arts portray the same idea in unique ways

MORE MUSIC CHOICES

For more practice with rounds:
"*Da pacem, Domine*" ("Grant Us Peace"), p. 62

1 INTRODUCE

Discuss the text on p. 162 with students. Have students read about Lowell Mason on p. 163 and then invite them to listen to "O Music" **CD 8-15.**

ROOUNDS

Lowell Mason, the composer of "O Music," was the first public school music teacher in the United States.

"O Music" is a three-part round. **Sing** it first in unison and then as three repeated phrases, sung by three groups.

After you know the song very well, sing it as a traditional round.

 **CD 8–15**

 m, f, s, l, t @ r m f s l

O MUSIC

Words and Music by Lowell Mason
Arranged by Doreen Rao

O __ mu - sic, sweet _ mu - sic, thy _ prais - es we will sing;

We _ will _ tell of the _ pleas - ures and _ hap - pi - ness you _ bring.

Mu - sic,   mu - sic,   let the cho - rus sing.

Footnotes

ACROSS THE CURRICULUM

8a ▶ **Language Arts** The poem in the student text on p. 163 is from *Song and Dance: Poems*, selected by Lee Bennett Hopkins (Simon and Schuster, 1997). Read "In Music Meeting" as an introduction in performances of Lowell Mason's "O Music." Combine performances of this song with advocacy speeches about the history of American music education and the importance of a music curriculum in every school.

BUILDING SKILLS THROUGH MUSIC

▶ **Social Studies** Display a map or chart showing the dates when states and territories were added to the United States. Ask students to identify states that were part of our country in 1792, the year Lowell Mason was born. Ask students how many states were included in 1872, the year he died.

SKILLS REINFORCEMENT

▶ **Singing** Use the following teaching suggestions to help all students perform rounds.

Reinforcement Some students may have difficulty singing in parts. Have these students form small groups and practice the song in unison.

On Target Many students will be able to successfully sing a round. For extra support, group students with strong, independent singers. Be sure to discourage students from covering their ears to block out other voices and singing loudly or shouting.

Challenge Those students who easily master this lesson may be invited to perform a round with individual singers performing each part.

In Music Meeting
by Victoria Forrester

Amid the sound,
The silent,
unsung greeting:
We sing together
And our voices
Touch,
In music meeting.

MUSIC MAKERS

Lowell Mason

Lowell Mason (1792–1872) was born near Boston, Massachusetts, less than twenty years after the American Revolution. Mason was a performer, composer, and teacher. As a young man, he traveled by horse throughout the northeastern part of the United States teaching people how to sing and how to read music. Mason believed that everyone should learn to sing and read music. He proposed that music be taught in public schools as part of the curriculum. The School Committee of Boston accepted his proposal, and in 1838 music became a part of the curriculum in the public schools of Boston.

2 DEVELOP

Singing

1a Have students sing along in unison with "O Music" **CD 8-15.** Divide the class into three groups and assign a part to each. Ask the groups to sing and repeat their assigned parts together in harmony. Have each student try a different vocal part than he or she learned earlier. Then encourage students to sing all three parts consecutively. You may want students to try the method of learning rounds described in Teacher to Teacher, p. 161, and in Skills Reinforcement, p. 162.

1d Finally, ask the class to sing the song as a round.

Comparing

8a Invite students to read and discuss the poem "In Music Meeting" on p. 163. Encourage students to talk about the relationship between poetry and music.

ASK How are we brought together as people when we sing? What skills and behaviors do we have to master in order to sing well with others? (Accept a variety of answers.)

3 CLOSE

Element: TEXTURE/HARMONY — ASSESSMENT

1d **Performance/Peer Critique** Have students form groups (approximately 10 per group) to perform "O Music" as a round.

7a Have each group perform for the class. Invite the remaining students to listen and to give constructive comments on each performance.

SPOTLIGHT ON

▶ **Music Education** Before Lowell Mason introduced music education to the public schools in Boston, people attended singing schools to learn how to sing and read music. Singing masters often taught music classes so people would buy music books from them. They traveled from place to place, staying in each town long enough to teach the public how to use their newly purchased music books. Because singing schools were only held for a few weeks at a time, both city dwellers and pioneers took advantage of every lesson offered. Attending a singing master's classes became a popular form of socializing. Historians now recognize that the singing school movement laid the foundation for music education today.

TECHNOLOGY/MEDIA LINK

4c
5d
Notation Software Use music notation software to help students understand harmony and $\frac{4}{4}$ time. Have students notate a repeating bass line for "O Music." Ask them to compose a harmonic accompaniment part on another staff, using quarter notes and quarter rests. Measures 2, 6, and 10 will have D-major triads. All other measures will use G triads. Use complete triads, or select only one note of the triad per beat.

Students may wish to notate a four-measure percussion part on a third staff if time allows.

Review and Assessment

Review, Assess,

WHAT DO YOU KNOW?

MATERIALS
• **Resource Book** p. B-12

Review the concept of texture with the class by discussing the meaning of unison, countermelody, and three-part round. Ask which of the three forms has the thickest texture (three-part round) and which has the thinnest (unison). Then ask students to complete the matching activity on p. 164.

Invite students to review Lesson 9, *A Drum Roll, Please* (p. 154) with a partner. Have the partners ask each other questions about the chapter until they both know the information contained in it.

For a more formal assessment, you may wish to duplicate the Unit 4 assessment worksheet and have students work independently or in small groups to complete it. The worksheet is found on Resource Book p. B-11.

WHAT DO YOU HEAR?

MATERIALS
• *What Do You Hear? 4*   **CD 8-17**
• **Resource Book** p. B-13

Review the melody patterns from *"Pollerita"* on p. 150. Have the class sing and clap each one with you. Invite students to listen to *What Do You Hear? 4*. Have them work with a partner to identify each melody pattern as it is heard.

What Do You Know?

Match the Texture
Look at each type of song that is described on the left. Then point to the picture on the right that best represents the texture.

1. A three-part round

a.

2. A song with a countermelody

b.

3. A song sung in unison

c.

Fill in the Blanks
1. The music of the Irish group the Chieftains includes the _____ drum.

   a. snare   **b.** conga   **c.** bodhran

2. *Taiko* means _____ in Japanese.

   a. bass drum   **b.** big drum   **c.** snare drum

3. There are many styles of drumming. Drummer Buddy Rich's playing style would be classified as _____.

   a. jazz style   **b.** folk style   **c.** rock style

What Do You Hear? 4

 **CD 8–17**

Look at the melody patterns on page 150. Point to the pattern that matches the one you hear.

Footnotes

ANSWER KEY

▶ **What Do You Know?**

1. c. (a three-part round)

2. a. (a song with a countermelody)

3. b. (a song sung in unison)

1. c. (bodhran)

2. b. (big drum)

3. a. (jazz style)

▶ **What Do You Hear?**

1. Pattern 3

2. Pattern 1

3. Pattern 4

4. Pattern 5

5. Pattern 2

Perform, Create

What You Can Do

Listen, Conduct and Sing

Listen to "Scotland the Brave," page 138, and conduct the beat while following the notation. Sing the song, using rhythm syllables and then the song text.

Create a Rondo

Use the two rhythm patterns below, plus a contrasting pattern of your own, to create a rhythm rondo.

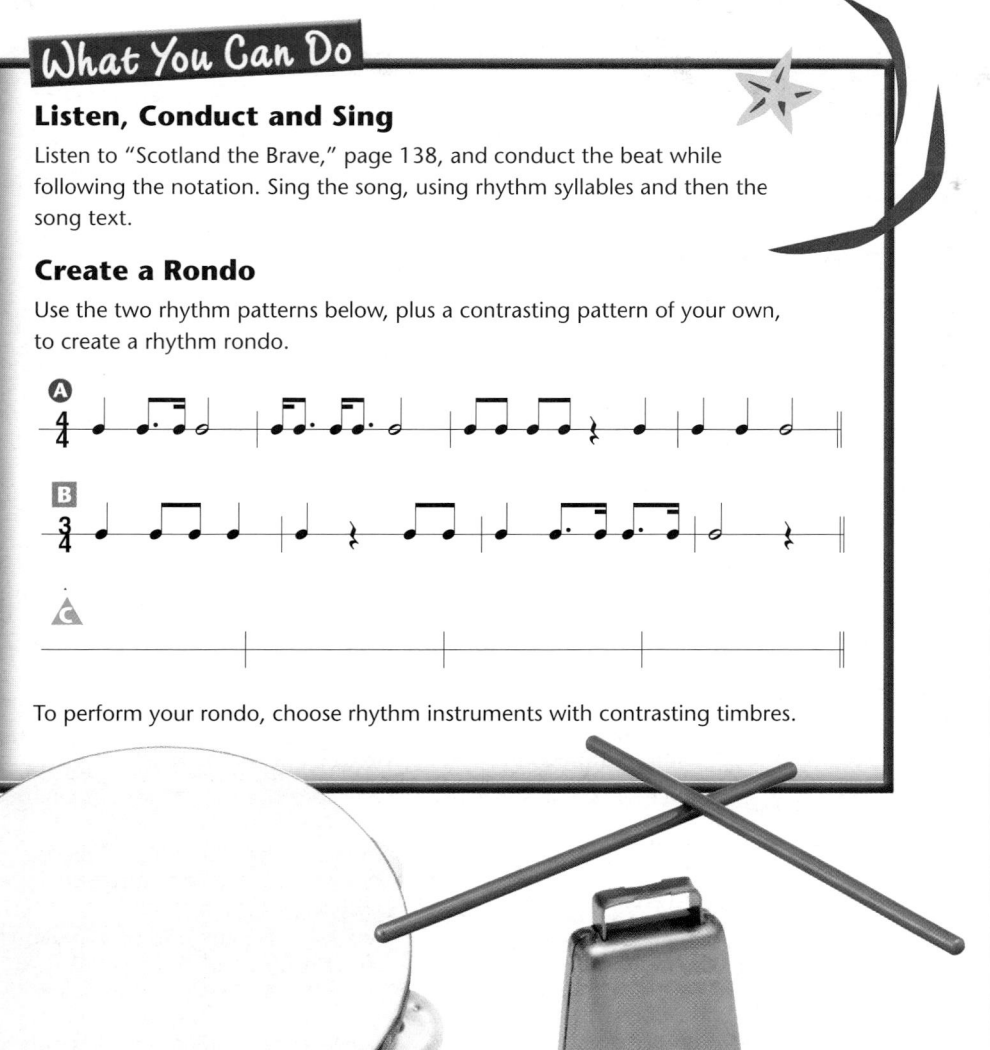

To perform your rondo, choose rhythm instruments with contrasting timbres.

WHAT YOU CAN DO

> **MATERIALS**
> * "Scotland the Brave," p. 138   **CD 7-6**
> * **Resource Book** p. B-14
> * nonpitched percussion instruments

Sing and Conduct

Invite the class to turn to "Scotland the Brave" **CD 7-6** on p. 138. Review the four-beat conducting pattern with the class, including the preparatory beat and the cutoff. Invite the class to conduct the four-beat pattern while they sing the piece on a neutral syllable, like *dah*. When they can do this comfortably, have them conduct the piece while singing with pitch syllables. Then, ask them to conduct while they sing the song with words.

Invite a student to volunteer to conduct while the class sings. Suggest that the conductor help the class by breathing visibly when the class is to breathe.

Create a Rondo

Review rondo form with the class (ABACA). Tell students that today they will be writing a part of a rondo. Give them permission to put it in the meter of their choice but to make each meter different.

Have the class clap the rhythm of the A and B sections, keeping the beat with a foot, if necessary. Then, choose a composer to clap the newly created C section. Select a few of the rondos for the class to play on nonpitched percussion instruments.

TECHNOLOGY/MEDIA LINK

Rubrics Visit *www.sfsuccessnet.com* for rubrics to assess students' achievement in music skills.

Lesson	Elements	Skills	
LESSON 1 **CORE** **Expression Takes Flight** pp. 170–173 	**Element: Expression** **Concept:** Articulation **Focus:** Slurs and accents **Secondary Element** Form: D.S. al Coda, D.C. al Coda **National Standards** 1b 2b 5c 6a 6b 7b 8b	**Skill: Singing** **Objective:** Sing expressively, observing slurs **Secondary Skills** • **Listening** Listen to the song and follow the notation • **Singing** Sing along with the repeated sections • **Reading** Identify markings that indicate the order of sections • **Singing** Sing the entire song and follow markings in the music • **Reading** Locate ties and slurs in the music • **Playing** Play an ostinato accompaniment on recorder • **Listening** Listen to a selection with accents	**SKILLS REINFORCEMENT** • **Arranging** Create performance arrangements of the song • **Reading** Practice identifying music notation symbols by playing a game
LESSON 2 **Simple or Compound** pp. 174-177  **Reading Sequence 17, p. 498**	**Element: Rhythm** **Concept:** Meter **Focus:** Compound meter **Secondary Element** Melody: pattern **National Standards** 1c 2c 4c 5a 6c 8a	**Skill: Reading** **Objective:** Sing and accompany from notation songs in compound meter **Secondary Skills** • **Singing** Sing and conduct a two-beat pattern to song • **Listening** Listen to and compare two songs • **Singing** Sing a song with a compound meter • **Listening** Listen to the recording and tap the steady beat • **Playing** Play a chordal guitar accompaniment with the song • **Moving** Learn a patterned dance	**SKILLS REINFORCEMENT** • **Reading** Complete a music reading worksheet • **Mallets** Play an Orff accompaniment for *"Las estrellitas del cielo"* • **Performing** Show the difference between simple and compound meters using movement • **Mallets** Play an Orff accompaniment for *"Don Alfonso"*
LESSON 3 **CORE** **Name a New Meter** pp. 178-179  **Reading Sequence 18, p. 498**	**Element: Rhythm** **Concept:** Meter **Focus:** $\frac{6}{8}$ meter **Secondary Element** Form: verse/refrain **National Standards** 1c 2a 3b 6c 8b	**Skill: Reading** **Objective:** Sing and accompany from notation a song in $\frac{6}{8}$ meter **Secondary Skills** • **Listening** Listen and answer questions about meter • **Singing** Sing the song and perform an ostinato	**SKILLS REINFORCEMENT** • **Reading** Read a music worksheet on compound meter • **Recorder** Play an accompaniment • **Keyboard** Play a chord accompaniment

Connections

Music and Other Literature

Connection: Language Arts
Activity: Read poetry with expression

ACROSS THE CURRICULUM
Language Arts Read poetry aloud with expression
Language Arts Write a story, poem or essay about aspirations
MOVEMENT **Moving with Expression** Create movements for each section of the song
TEACHER TO TEACHER **Recorder Tips** Develop and post a list of "Recorder Reminders"
AUDIENCE ETIQUETTE **Critical Listening** Practice critical listening skills
BUILDING SKILLS THROUGH MUSIC **Writing** Rewrite the song text in different forms

Song "I Believe I Can Fly"

Listening Selection The Firebird, "Infernal Dance"
Listening Map The Firebird, "Infernal Dance"

More Music Choices
"When Johnny Comes Marching Home," p. 180
"I Vow to You, My Country," p. 418

ASSESSMENT

Performance/Peer Critique Sing the song to evaluate performance of slurs

TECHNOLOGY/MEDIA LINK
Notation Software Experiment with adding slurs to notated music
Transparency Display the listening map transparency

Connection: Related Arts
Activity: Discuss the use of rhythm in a painting and a song

TEACHER TO TEACHER **Meter** Tips on how to explain simple and compound meter
CULTURAL CONNECTION **The Way of the Saint** The legend of Santiago de Compostela
SPOTLIGHT ON
The Artist Facts about Joan Miró
The Composer Facts about Joaquín Rodrigo
MOVEMENT **Patterned Dance** Learn a dance in the sevillana style
BUILDING SKILLS THROUGH MUSIC **Social Studies** Locate Spain on a world map or globe

Songs
"Las estrellitas del cielo"
"Stars of the Heavens"
"Don Alfonso" (Spanish)
"Don Alfonso" (English)

Listening Selections
Concierto Madrigal for Two Guitars and Orchestra, "Caccía a la española"
Arts Connection Creatures in the Night
M·U·S·I·C M·A·K·E·R·S
The Romero Family

More Music Choices
"La ciudad de Juaja" ("The City of Juaja"), p. 58

ASSESSMENT

Performance/Observation Sing the song with accompaniment, demonstrating compound meter

TECHNOLOGY/MEDIA LINK
Notation Software Create eight-measure melodies using stepwise movement

---

Connection: Social Studies
Activity: Discuss the ancient kingdom of Northumbria

ACROSS THE CURRICULUM **Social Studies** Facts about Northumbria, England
BUILDING SKILLS THROUGH MUSIC **Reading** Identify words in song text that have multiple meanings

Song "Blow the Wind Southerly"

More Music Choices
"Away to America," p. 57

ASSESSMENT

Performance/Observation Sing the song and perform body percussion to show the meter
Show What You Know! Mid-unit assessment

TECHNOLOGY/MEDIA LINK
Electronic Keyboard Play root position arpeggios

Lesson	Elements	Skills	

LESSON 4

March to the Beat

pp. 180–183

Element: Rhythm
Concept: Meter
Focus: $\frac{6}{8}$ meter

Secondary Element
Melody: tonality

National Standards
1a 1d 2b 3b 4c 5a 6b
7a 8b

Skill: Playing
Objective: Play rhythm pattern in $\frac{6}{8}$ meter

Secondary Skills
• **Singing** Sing song in rhythm
• **Reading** Speak and clap some common rhythms
• **Singing** Speak the song text in rhythm and sing the song
• **Creating** Create a body percussion ostinato
• **Listening** Listen to a work song
• **Reading** Read and identify common rhythms

SKILLS REINFORCEMENT
• **Recorder** Play a countermelody

LESSON 5

CORE

A Musical Idea

pp. 184–187

Element: Form
Concept: Theme and variation
Focus: Theme-and-variation form

Secondary Element
Expression: dynamics

National Standards
1c 2a 4a 4c 6b 8a 8b

Skill: Listening
Objective: Identify theme and variations using different instrumental timbres

Secondary Skills
• **Singing** Sing Shaker song
• **Creating** Create a variation of a familiar song
• **Analyzing** Research and analyze other compositions by the composer

SKILLS REINFORCEMENT
• **Creating** Create variations of other simple melodies
• **Recorder** Play an accompaniment

LESSON 6

A New Scale

pp. 188–189

Element: Melody
Concept: Pattern
Focus: Natural minor scale

Secondary Element
Harmony: chords

National Standards
1a 1c 2a 4c 5b 5c 8b

Skill: Reading
Objective: Read and sing a song in natural minor

Secondary Skills
• **Singing** Sing the song with the recording
• **Reading** Read the A-minor scale with hand signs and using pitch syllables, numbers, and letter names

SKILLS REINFORCEMENT
• **Keyboard** Play a chord accompaniment
• **Reading** Complete a music reading worksheet

Reading Sequence 19, p. 499

Connections

Connection: Social Studies
Activity: Explore the historical background of a song

- **TEACHER TO TEACHER** **Historical Research** Tips on how to do historical research
- **ACROSS THE CURRICULUM**
  Social Studies Read about the American Civil War
  Social Studies Information about the expansion of the railroads
- **CHARACTER EDUCATION** **Diversity** Discuss advances that increased awareness of diversity
- **CULTURAL CONNECTION** The Legacy of Songs How songs become a part of cultural history
- **MEETING INDIVIDUAL NEEDS** **Including Everyone** Tips to help all students coordinate movements on beats 1 and 4
- **BUILDING SKILLS THROUGH MUSIC** **Language** Identify the story elements in the songs

Connection: Culture
Activity: Discuss Shaker culture

- **SPOTLIGHT ON**
  The Folk Tune Information about "Simple Gifts"
  The Choreographer Facts about Martha Graham
- **CULTURAL CONNECTION** Shakers Facts on the community of the Shakers
- **ACROSS THE CURRICULUM** **Language Arts** Read a book about Shaker culture
- **MOVEMENT** Creative Movement Create a movement for each variation
- **CHARACTER EDUCATION** **Perseverance** Discuss plans to achieve goals
- **BUILDING SKILLS THROUGH MUSIC** Social Studies List important facts about two composer's lives

Connection: Social Studies
Activity: Explore the relationship between music and historical events

- **SPOTLIGHT ON** The Song Background information on the song
- **ACROSS THE CURRICULUM** **Social Studies** Research American Revolutionary soldiers
- **BUILDING SKILLS THROUGH MUSIC** **Writing** Write about the relationship between music and historical events

Music and Other Literature

Songs
"When Johnny Comes Marching Home"
"Pat Works on the Railway"

More Music Choices
"Erie Canal," p. 262
"Battle Hymn of the Republic," p. 274
"Colorado Trail," p. 276

Song "Simple Gifts"

Listening Selections
Variations on Simple Gifts
Interview with Aaron Copland
Listening Map *Variations on Simple Gifts*
M·U·S·I·C M·A·K·E·R·S
Aaron Copland

More Music Choices
American Salute, p. 275

Song "Johnny Has Gone for a Soldier"

More Music Choices
"Old Abram Brown," p. 222
"Pat Works on the Railway," p. 182
"Erie Canal," p. 262

ASSESSMENT

Performance/Self-Assessment Perform song with accompaniment and movement and evaluate rhythmic accuracy

TECHNOLOGY/MEDIA LINK

Sequencing Software
Compose a $\frac{6}{8}$ military-style drum accompaniment

ASSESSMENT

Musical Journal Writing List instruments and description of one variation from the listening selection

TECHNOLOGY/MEDIA LINK

Notation Software
Create an arrangement of the song

ASSESSMENT

Performance/Observation Read and sing the song with pitch syllables and hand signs to show natural minor

TECHNOLOGY/MEDIA LINK

Notation Software
Notate natural minor scales and compose a melody

Lesson	Elements	Skills

LESSON 7 — CORE
Melody in Minor

pp. 190–193

Reading Sequence 20, p. 499

Element: Melody
Concept: Pattern
Focus: Harmonic minor scale

Secondary Element Form: call and response

National Standards
1a 1c 2c 5c 6a 6b 6c 8b

Skill: Reading
Objective: Read and sing from notation a song in harmonic minor

Secondary Skills
- **Singing** Sing the song and discover a new note
- **Reading** Identify the new note called *si*
- **Notating** Notate the harmonic minor scale
- **Listening** Listen to another song in harmonic minor

SKILLS REINFORCEMENT
- **Recorder** Play the simplified melody of a song
- **Reading** Complete a music reading worksheet

LESSON 8
Searching for Scales

pp. 194–195

Element: Melody
Concept: Pattern
Focus: Pentatonic scale

Secondary Element
Expression: articulation

National Standards
1c 2a 6b 8b

Skill: Playing
Objective: Read and perform from notation pentatonic patterns to accompany a song

Secondary Skills
- **Listening** Listen to the song recording for a five-tone scale
- **Singing** Sing a song in Mandarin with the recording
- **Reading** Read and play the instrumental parts

SKILLS REINFORCEMENT
- **Playing** Perform an ensemble accompaniment

LESSON 9 — CORE
A String of Strings

pp. 196–199

Element: Timbre
Concept: Instrumental
Focus: String Instruments

Secondary Element
Rhythm: meter

National Standards
1c 2b 6b 8b

Skill: Listening
Objective: Listen to and identify various string instruments

Secondary Skills
- **Singing** Sing a provided melody line
- **Playing** Play the melody on instruments

Connections

Music and Other Literature

Connection: Social Studies

Activity: Explore the role of African American spirituals during the time of slavery

ACROSS THE CURRICULUM
Language Arts Information on the lyrics of the song
Social Studies Read a book about the secret codes of the Underground Railroad

TEACHER TO TEACHER **Intervals** Develop skills for hearing intervals

SPOTLIGHT ON
African American Spirituals Information about the history of spirituals
Heroes Historical legends, heroes, and mystical figures

BUILDING SKILLS THROUGH MUSIC **Social Studies** Discuss why the songs are spirituals

Song "Go Down, Moses"

Listening Selections
Sometimes I Feel Like a Motherless Child
M•U•S•I•C M•A•K•E•R•S
  Mahalia Jackson

More Music Choices
"*¡Qué bonita bandera!*" ("What a Beautiful Banner!"), p. 294

ASSESSMENT

Performance/Observation
Read and sing the song with accurate intervals
Show What You Know!
Mid-unit assessment

TECHNOLOGY/MEDIA LINK
Video Library Watch a video on call-and-response form

Connection: Culture

Activity: Discuss a historical figure taken from Chinese folklore, on which a folk song is based

CULTURAL CONNECTION **Language** Learn about the Mandarin language

SPOTLIGHT ON **The Song** Background information about the song

BUILDING SKILLS THROUGH MUSIC **Writing** Write new lyrics for the song

Song
"*Meng Jian Nu*" (Mandarin)
"*Meng Jian Nu*" (English)

More Music Choices
"*Yüe liang wan wan*", p. 314

ASSESSMENT

Performance/Observation
Set up instruments in G pentatonic and perform instrumental parts

TECHNOLOGY/MEDIA LINK
Web Site More information on Chinese folk music

Connection: Culture

Activity: Explore the cultural context of a variety of string instruments

TEACHER TO TEACHER **Instruments** Research on string instruments

ACROSS THE CURRICULUM
Science Learn about the structure and production of string instrument sound
Language Arts Read a book about musical instruments

SPOTLIGHT ON
Keyboard Instruments Information about various keyboard instruments
The Harp Background on the instrument

CULTURAL CONNECTION
African Musical Bows Discuss kinds of African bows
An African American Instrument Information about the banjo

BUILDING SKILLS THROUGH MUSIC **Writing** List facts about different plucked-string instruments

Listening Selections
Zither Montage
Keyboard Instrument Montage
Plucked String Montage
Eriskummainen kantele

More Music Choices
"*Cho'i hát bội*" ("The Theater Game"), p. 318
Julie-O, p. 311
Sindhi-Bhairavi, p. 320

ASSESSMENT

Music Journal Writing
Listen to and identify string instruments

TECHNOLOGY/MEDIA LINK
Web Site More information about string instruments of the world

---

Lesson	Elements	Skills	
LESSON 10 **CORE** **Calypso Walk** pp. 200–201 	**Element: Texture/Harmony** **Concept:** Harmony **Focus:** I and V₇ chords **Secondary Element** Rhythm: patterns **National Standards** 1c 2c 4c 6b 6c 9a	**Skill: Playing** **Objective:** Play a I-V₇ chord accompaniment **Secondary Skills** • **Listening** Listen and follow notation of song to discover chord changes • **Reading** Read notation to determine the key of the song • **Listening** Identify which instrument plays the melody in the selection	**SKILLS REINFORCEMENT** • **Mallets** Play an Orff accompaniment
LESSON 11 **Nothing More Than I and IV** pp. 202–203 	**Element: Texture/Harmony** **Concept:** Harmony **Focus:** I and IV chords **Secondary Element** Rhythm: meter in 3 **National Standards** 1a 1c 3a 6c 8b	**Skill: Singing** **Objective:** Sing a song with I and IV chords **Secondary Skills** • **Listening** Listen to the recording and identify the I and IV chords • **Singing** Sing the song in Spanish • **Playing** Play appropriate chords to accompany the song	**SKILLS REINFORCEMENT** • **Playing** Tips to help all students perform keyboard accompaniments
LESSON 12 **Too Much Talk** pp. 204–205 	**Element: Texture/Harmony** **Concept:** Harmony **Focus:** I, IV, and V₇ chords **Secondary Element** Melody: pattern **National Standards** 1a 1c 2c 3a 6b 6c 9a	**Skill: Playing** **Objective:** Play an accompaniment using the I, IV, and V₇ chords **Secondary Skills** • **Singing** Sing the song with the recording • **Listening** Listen to the source recording and compare • **Improvising** Improvise a backup vocal accompaniment on chord roots	**SKILLS REINFORCEMENT** • **Singing** Sing the chord roots and learn to harmonize by ear

Connections	Music and Other Literature	
Connection: Culture **Activity:** Associate calypso style with specific cultures of the Caribbean **ACROSS THE CURRICULUM** **Language Arts** Read a book of Jamaican poetry **CULTURAL CONNECTION** **Calypso Style** Information about the song style **BUILDING SKILLS THROUGH MUSIC** **Social Studies** Determine which songs originated in the islands of the Caribbean Sea	**Song** "Mango Walk" **Listening Selections** *Jamaican Rumba* **More Music Choices** "Day-O!" p. 18	**ASSESSMENT** **Performance/Self-Assessment** Sing and play chord accompaniment on resonator bells **TECHNOLOGY/MEDIA LINK** **CD-ROM** Create a Caribbean accompaniment for the song
Connection: Social Studies **Activity:** Discuss the Imbabura region of Ecuador **CULTURAL CONNECTION** **Imbabura** Information about the Imbabura region of Ecuador **MOVEMENT** **Nonlocomotor Movement** Perform a hand-jive routine to illustrate the I-IV chord progression **BUILDING SKILLS THROUGH MUSIC** **Language** Identify phrases in the song text that illustrate the singer's feelings	**Songs** "Imbabura" (Spanish) "Imbabura" (English) **More Music Choices** "*Pollerita*," p. 151 "*Amores hallarás*," p. 153 "*Viva Jujuy*," p. 228	**ASSESSMENT** **Performance/Observation** Sing the song and play the chordal accompaniment accurately **TECHNOLOGY/MEDIA LINK** **CD-ROM** Create an eight-measure chord progression using I and IV chords
Connection: Style **Activity:** Discover that I, IV, and V_7 chords were popular with early rock 'n' roll musicians **SPOTLIGHT ON** **The Composer and Lyricist** Information about Jerry Leiber and Mike Stoller **ACROSS THE CURRICULUM** **Language Arts** Perform a dramatization of "likes" and "dislikes" **SCHOOL TO HOME CONNECTION** **Interviews** Interview older family members about relationships with their parents **BUILDING SKILLS THROUGH MUSIC** **Social Studies** Discuss the term "rock 'n' roll"	**Song** "Yakety Yak" **Listening Selections** *Yakety Yak* M•U•S•I•C M•A•K•E•R•S The Coasters **More Music Choices** "Linstead Market," p. 241	**ASSESSMENT** **Performance/Peer Critique** Perform a three-chord accompaniment with the song **TECHNOLOGY/MEDIA LINK** **Electronic Keyboard** Use auto-accompaniment in a rock 'n' roll style

INTRODUCING THE UNIT

Unit 5 presents the next step in a sequenced approach to understanding music elements. Music skills—reading, performing, creating, listening, moving—are the means by which students gain an understanding of these concepts. Presented on p. 167 is a brief overview of the skills that are assessed in this unit. (See below and pp. 168–169 for unit highlights of related curricular experiences.)

For a more detailed unit overview, see Unit at a Glance, pp. 165a–165h.

UNIT PROJECT

Have students read "The New Colossus" by Emma Lazarus on p. 166. Discuss with students the following:

- To what does the phrase "Brazen giant of Greek fame" refer?
- Why is the statue called "Mother of Exiles"?
- Who were the "Exiles"?
- Why were they coming to America?
- What does the statue symbolize?

Encourage students to ask their parents or grandparents about the country their family immigrated from.

Invite students to create a large world map in the classroom. On the map, have them indicate the various countries of origin from which their families may have come from.

Encourage students to collect pictures and objects that are representative of their family homelands to be displayed with the map.

A New Horizon

Immigrants who travel to the United States take a big step towards a new life. For many who arrived in the last century by boat, the first image of this new life was the inspiring sight of the Statue of Liberty. The poem "The New Colossus" is set on a tablet within the statue's pedestal. Read the poem and then **listen** to a choral setting of the text.

CD 8–22
The New Colossus

The New Colossus

by Emma Lazarus

Not like the brazen giant of Greek fame,
With conquering limbs astride from land to land;
Here at our sea-washed, sunset gates shall stand
A mighty woman with a torch, whose flame
Is the imprisoned lightning, and her name
Mother of Exiles. From her beacon-hand
Glows world-wide welcome; her mild eyes command
The air-bridged harbor that twin cities frame.
"Keep, ancient lands, your storied pomp!" cries she
With silent lips. "Give me your tired, your poor,
Your huddled masses yearning to breathe free,
The wretched refuse of your teeming shore.
Send these, the homeless, tempest-tost to me,
I lift my lamp beside the golden door!"

Setting Poetry to Music

The Mormon Tabernacle Choir is one of the best-known and loved choral organizations in the United States. **Listen** as they perform Irving Berlin's setting of Emma Lazarus' poem.

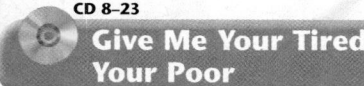

CD 8–23
Give Me Your Tired, Your Poor

by Emma Lazarus and Irving Berlin
as performed by the Mormon Tabernacle Choir

The Mormon Tabernacle Choir has toured all over the world and has released more than 130 recordings.

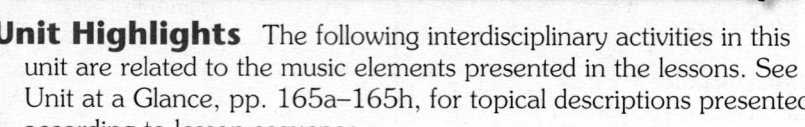

ACROSS THE CURRICULUM

Unit Highlights The following interdisciplinary activities in this unit are related to the music elements presented in the lessons. See Unit at a Glance, pp. 165a–165h, for topical descriptions presented according to lesson sequence.

▶ **LANGUAGE ARTS**

- Read poems aloud and experiment with different expressive qualities (p. 170)
- Write about personal hopes, dreams, or goals (p. 172)
- Read a book about a Shaker village (p. 185)
- Discuss information about the text of an African American spiritual (p. 190)
- Explore the history of a variety of musical instruments and their place among a certain culture or period of time (p. 198)

- Read a book of Jamaican poems (p. 200)
- Create and perform dramatized narrations (p. 205)

▶ **SCIENCE**

- Discover the structure and production of string instrument sound (p. 196)

▶ **SOCIAL STUDIES**

- Learn about Northumbria (p. 178)
- Explore events in the Civil war (p. 180)
- Discuss how the transcontinental railroad changed American lifestyle (p. 182)
- Research and discuss the soldiers of the Revolutionary War (p. 189)
- Read a book about the secret codes of the Underground Railroad (p. 192)

UNIT 5

Discovering New Musical Horizons

Unit 5 **167**

MUSIC SKILLS
ASSESSED IN THIS UNIT

Reading Music: Rhythm

- Read rhythms in compound meter (pp. 177, 179)

Reading Music: Pitch

- Read a song in natural minor using pitch syllables and hand signs (p. 189)
- Read a song in harmonic minor using pitch syllables and hand signs (p. 193)

Performing Music: Singing

- Accurately sing slurs in a song (p. 173)
- Sing a song in $\frac{6}{8}$ meter (p. 183)
- Sing a rock 'n' roll song (p. 205)

Moving to Music

- Move to show duple meter of a song (p. 183)
- Perform a hand jive in meter in 3 (p. 202)

Performing Music: Playing

- Accurately perform an accompaniment with slurs (p. 173)
- Perform a counter-rhythm as an ostinato (p. 179)
- Accompany a song in $\frac{6}{8}$ meter (p. 183)
- Set up a G-pentatonic scale on resonator bells and accompany a pentatonic song (p. 195)
- Perform an accompaniment using the I and V_7 chords (p. 201) and the I and IV chords (p. 203)
- Accompany a rock 'n' roll song (p. 205)

Creating Music

- Create body percussion ostinatos to accompany a song (p. 182)
- Create a backup vocal accompaniment for a rock 'n' roll song (p. 205)

Listening to Music

- Listen for variations on a theme (p. 187)
- Listen to and describe string instruments (p. 199)

CULTURAL CONNECTION

Unit Highlights The musical literature in this unit provides many opportunities for students to explore a variety of world cultures. See Unit at a Glance, pp. 165a–165h, for topical descriptions presented according to lesson sequence.

▶ **AFRICAN/AFRICAN AMERICAN**

- Discuss the various types of African musical bows (p. 197)
- Explore the origins and evolution of the banjo (p. 198)

▶ **AMERICAN REGIONAL**

- Discuss the origins and history of the Shakers (p. 184)

▶ **ASIAN**

- Learn about the Mandarin language (p. 194)

▶ **CARIBBEAN**

- Discuss the unique characteristics of Calypso music and its importance in the Jamaican community (p. 200)

▶ **EUROPEAN**

- Discuss the legend of Santiago de Compostela (p. 175)

▶ **LATIN AMERICAN**

- Learn about the people of Otavalo, Ecuador (p. 202)

OPENING ACTIVITIES

MATERIALS
- "This World"   **CD 8-24**
  Recording Routine:
  Intro (4 m.); vocal
- "The New Colossus" (poem)   **CD 8-22**
- Give Me Your Tired, Your Poor   **CD 8-23**
- various nonpitched percussion instruments

Listening

Have students listen to the poem "The New Colossus" **CD 8-22** by Emma Lazarus. Discuss with students the meaning and significance of this poem in our culture.

Then invite students to listen to *Give Me Your Tired, Your Poor* **CD 8-23**, a choral setting of the poem they just read and listened to.

Singing

Play the recording of "This World" **CD 8-24** and invite students to sing along. Ask them to tap on beats 1 and 3 while they sing.

Playing

Students also may be invited to perform ostinatos on nonpitched percussion instruments to accompany "This World."

From Sea to Shining Sea

Sing "This World." In what ways might the lyrics reflect the thoughts and feelings of a new immigrant to this country?

![ASSESSMENT]

Unit Highlights This unit includes a variety of strategies and methods, described below, to track students' progress and assess their understanding of lesson objectives. Reproducible masters for Show What You Know! and Review, Assess, Perform, Create can be found in the Resource Book.

▶ **FORMAL ASSESSMENTS**

The following assessments, using written language, cognitive, and performance skills, help teachers and students conceptualize the learning that is taking place.

- **Show What You Know!** Element-specific assessments, on the student page, for Rhythm (p. 179) and Melody (p. 193).
- **Review, Assess, Perform, Create** This end-of-unit activity (pp. 206–207) can be used for review and to assess students' learning of the core lessons in this unit.

▶ **INFORMAL ASSESSMENTS**

At the close of each Teacher's Edition lesson in this unit, one of the following types of assessments is used to evaluate the learning of the key element focus or skill objective.

- Musical Journal Writing (pp. 187, 199)
- Performance/Observation (pp. 177, 179, 189, 193, 195, 203)
- Performance/Peer Critique (pp. 173, 205)
- Performance/Self-Assessment (pp. 183, 201)

▶ **RUBRICS**

Visit *www.sfsuccessnet.com* for rubrics to assess students' achievement in music skills.

throw it all a-way. ___ This

bring back yes-ter-day. ___ This

world, this world, my mind holds this world, my

mind holds this world in its hands. ___ This

world in its hands. _____

Analyzing

Discuss the meaning of the words "This World." Bring out the following points.

- The singer has dominion over his or her thoughts.
- One's attitude can help to control one's reality.
- The singer can look to the future or can look back on yesterday.
- The singer can turn night (symbolizing a negative outlook) to day (symbolizing a positive outlook).

Use the following question for class discussion.

ASK Did the immigrants to the United States, referred to in the poem, have a positive or negative outlook? (positive)

INNOVATIVE TEACHER SUPPORT FOR THIS UNIT

- **MAKING MUSIC DVD, Grade 5** contains video segments that support lessons, including signing and movement.
- **MAKING MUSIC with Movement and Dance** provides more opportunities for large group activities in music or physical education classes.
- **MAKING MUSIC with Technology** provides lesson plans for many technology applications; includes MIDI files.
- **¡A cantar!** features recorded songs and lessons from around the Spanish-speaking world; includes strategies for bilingual classes and for English-speaking teachers working with Spanish-speaking students.
- **Bridges to Asia** features recorded songs and lessons from Asian and Pacific region cultures.
- **www.sfsuccessnet.com** provides an online lesson planner to conveniently create lesson plans at school or at home. Includes rubrics for assessment, lesson modifications to meet the needs of all students, performance musicals based on program content, and more.

TECHNOLOGY/MEDIA LINK

Unit Highlights The following components are used in this unit to reinforce and expand students' understanding of music elements and related themes. See Unit at a Glance, pp. 165a–165h, for a descriptive listing according to lesson sequence.

► **CD-ROM**

- Use *Band-in-a-Box* to create a Caribbean-style accompaniment (p. 201)
- Create an eight-measure chord progression using I and IV chords (p. 203)

► **ELECTRONIC KEYBOARD**

- Accompany a song by playing *arpeggios* (p. 179)
- Use the auto-accompaniment feature (p. 205)

► **NOTATION SOFTWARE**

- Add slurs to a composition (p. 173)

- Create eight-measure melodies (p. 177)
- Create an original arrangement of a Shaker song (p. 187)
- Notate natural minor scales and compose a melody (p. 189)

► **SEQUENCING SOFTWARE**

- Compose a drum accompaniment in $\frac{6}{8}$ meter (p. 183)

► **VIDEO LIBRARY/DVD**

- Watch a video to reinforce the concept of call-and-response form (p. 193)

► **WEB SITE**

- Visit *www.sfsuccessnet.com* to learn more about the music of China and Taiwan (p. 195) and string instruments from around the world (p. 199)

LESSON AT A GLANCE

Element Focus   **EXPRESSION** Slurs and accents

Skill Objective   **SINGING** Sing expressively, observing slurs

Connection Activity   **LANGUAGE ARTS** Read poetry with expression

MATERIALS

- "I Believe I Can Fly"   **CD 8-26**
  Recording Routine: Intro (4 m.); vocal; coda
- *The Firebird*, "Infernal Dance"   **CD 8-28**
- soprano recorders

VOCABULARY

slur   accent   *legato*   *staccato*

> ◆ ◆ ◆ ◆ **National Standards** ◆ ◆ ◆ ◆
>
> **1b** Sing easy pieces with expression
> **2b** Perform easy instrumental pieces expressively
> **5c** Identify standard notation symbols for expression
> **6a** Listen and analyze uses of form in music from diverse cultures
> **6b** Listen and analyze uses of dynamics in music from diverse cultures
> **7b** Students use specific criteria for evaluating their own performances
> **8b** Identify ways music relates to language arts

MORE MUSIC CHOICES

"When Johnny Comes Marching Home," p. 180
"I Vow to You, My Country," p. 418

Expression Takes Flight

You can do anything! You can accomplish things that may seem impossible at first. The key to success is believing in yourself. "I Believe I Can Fly" is a song that expresses this belief.

Musicians communicate by performing with expression. They use their own ideas, and they follow expression marks in the music. One type of expression mark is called a **slur.**

Identify all the slurs that occur in "I Believe I Can Fly." Then **sing** the song.

A **slur** indicates that a syllable is sung on more than one pitch.

CD 8–26

I Believe I Can Fly

Words and Music by R. Kelly

s, l, t, @ r m f s

1. I used to think that I could not go
     I was on the verge of break - ing

on,   And life was noth - ing but an aw - ful
down.   Some - times si - lence can seem so

song.   But now I know the mean - ing of true
loud.   There are mir - a - cles in life I must a -

love.   I'm lean - ing on the ev - er - last - ing
chieve,   But first I know it starts in - side of

170

Footnotes

ACROSS THE CURRICULUM

8b ▶ **Language Arts** Consult with a classroom teacher or school librarian to select short poems that are appropriate for fifth graders to read aloud with expression. Then determine how they will make their reading expressive by

- Varying the dynamics, pitch level, or timbres of their voices.
- Using solo as well as group reading.
- Varying the speed or pace of their reading, or using pauses.
- Repeating lines of the poem.

BUILDING SKILLS THROUGH MUSIC

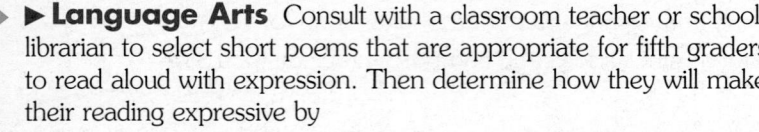

▶ **Writing** Invite students to listen to "I Believe I Can Fly" **CD 8-26** and observe where the singers take breaths. Divide the class into two groups. Assign one group to rewrite the song lyrics in poetic form and the other group to write the lyrics in complete sentences. Have each group read their version while taking breaths at appropriate places to emphasize the assigned form.

MOVEMENT

▶ **Moving with Expression** To prepare for creative movement, have students mirror you as you move to show phrases of "I Believe I Can Fly." Use a single large arching movement for each two-measure phrase. Play the recording and have students move with you as they listen. Then arrange the students into groups of four or more. Have each group choose a section of the song and create movements that they can perform with that section. For example, one group might choose the first verse (beginning section) of the song and another might choose the "I Believe I Can Fly" section. Providing props such as scarves, streamers, or colorful paper plates may help groups or individuals feel more comfortable.

1 INTRODUCE

Invite students to read aloud short poems. Encourage them to use expressive qualities in their readings. Help them to identify concepts taught in the other fine arts and their relationships to music. For more information, see Across the Curriculum on p. 170.

Invite students to think about their own abilities, acomplishments, and achievements.

ASK What do you do well? How hard did you have to work to be good at what you do? Who encouraged you? (Accept a variety of answers.)

2 DEVELOP

Listening

Have students read the information in their books on p. 170.

Play "I Believe I Can Fly" **CD 8-26** and have students follow the notation in their books as they listen.

6a ASK Which section of the song was repeated? (the section that begins with the words "I Believe I Can Fly")

Singing

Play the recording of "I Believe I Can Fly" **CD 8-26** and invite students to sing along with the repeated sections.

Reading

5c Have students find and identify markings in the music that indicate the order of sections (for example, repeat signs, first and second endings, *D.C. al Coda,* and the sign and *Coda* markings)

Have students find the first ending.

ASK Where do we go at the end of the first ending? (back to the repeat sign at the beginning)

Have students find the second ending, then follow the music to the *D.S. al Coda* marking.

ASK Where do we go when we see *D.S. al Coda*?

continued on page 172

TEACHER TO TEACHER

▶ **Recorder Tips** To help students with the recorder part for this lesson, you may wish to provide various tips and visual supports for their playing. Prior to playing, have students create a list of "Recorder Reminders" such as

- Position left hand on top
- Cover holes completely
- Use gentle air
- Start the sound with a *daah*

Alternatively, you can post the list of "Recorder Reminders" somewhere in the classroom.

SKILLS REINFORCEMENT

▶ **Arranging** Have students create their own performance arrangements of "I Believe I Can Fly." Review with students the performance options they have learned during the lesson, including singing the song, singing while observing slurs, and playing a recorder ostinato. Then have students brainstorm other options for their arrangements. For example, they may wish to add

- Changes in dynamics
- Sections for solo singing and whole group singing
- Movement
- Nonpitched percussion ostinatos or accompaniment highlights

Lesson 1 Continued

(Go back to the sign and sing to the *Coda* sign.)

Have students find the sign in the fifth line of the music. Then have them follow the music until they reach the *Coda* sign.

ASK What happens when we get to the *Coda* sign? (skip to the *Coda*)

Singing

Play the recording again and invite students to sing the song. Encourage them to follow the signs in the music and to sing the entire song.

Reading

 Direct students to the first line of "I Believe I Can Fly" to identify symbols referring to articulation.

ASK How many short curved lines do you see in the first line of music? (three)

What are these curved lines called? (ties)

What does a tie do? (connects two pitches that are the same)

Direct students to the sixth line of the song.

SAY Look at the curved line for the notes over the word "do" in measure 10.

ASK How is this curved line different than a tie? (The line connects pitches that are not the same.)

Tell the students that this is a slur and have them read the definition of slur on p. 170 in their books. Then challenge them to find other ties and slurs in "I Believe I Can Fly."

Singing

Tell students that a slur is an expression mark in music that tells musicians to perform in a certain way.

ASK If you see a slur in the music, how should those notes be sung? (*legato*, or smoothly)

Play the recording again. Invite students to sing and observe the slurs.

Playing with Expression

Slurs can be sung or played on instruments. **Play** the recorder part below. Experiment by playing *staccato* (detached) and then *legato* (smoothly), with slurs. **Play** during the verses of "I Believe I Can Fly."

Play eight times

Another Mark of Expression

Another way to communicate expression is through the use of **accents.**

Listen for accents in this piece by Igor Stravinsky.

An **accent** (>) indicates that a note should be sung or played with more emphasis than the other notes.

172

Footnotes

ACROSS THE CURRICULUM

▶ **Language Arts** "I Believe I Can Fly" is a song about inspiration, hope, and belief in one's own abilities. Have students listen to the song and think about their own aspirations. Then invite them to write a story, poem, or short essay about hopes, dreams, or goals they wish to accomplish. Encourage them to include a description of why the goal is important to them and why they believe they can achieve it.

Alternatively, you may wish to have them write about something they have already accomplished and how they did so. Encourage students to think about what or who gives them confidence and about how they overcome obstacles. You may wish to assemble student writing samples into an "I Can…" display on a bulletin board or in a class notebook.

SKILLS REINFORCEMENT

5c ▶ **Reading** To reinforce students' abilities to identify and define music notation symbols, play a "Symbol Search" game using "I Believe I Can Fly." When you call out the name of a musical symbol, students must find the symbol in the music, point to it, and then be able to define it (tell what it means to a musician). Symbols included in this lesson are

- repeat sign
- second ending
- the *dal segno* sign
- tie
- first ending
- *D.S. al Coda*
- *Coda*
- slur

You may also wish to include other symbols in the game, such as treble clef, flat sign, a note on a ledger line, half rest, a group of four sixteenth notes, and so on.

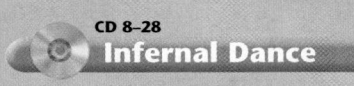

from *The Firebird*
by Igor Stravinsky
as performed by the New York Philharmonic; Pierre Boulez, conductor

The Firebird was written as ballet music. It was first performed on June 25, 1910, in Paris, France.

Infernal Dance LISTENING MAP

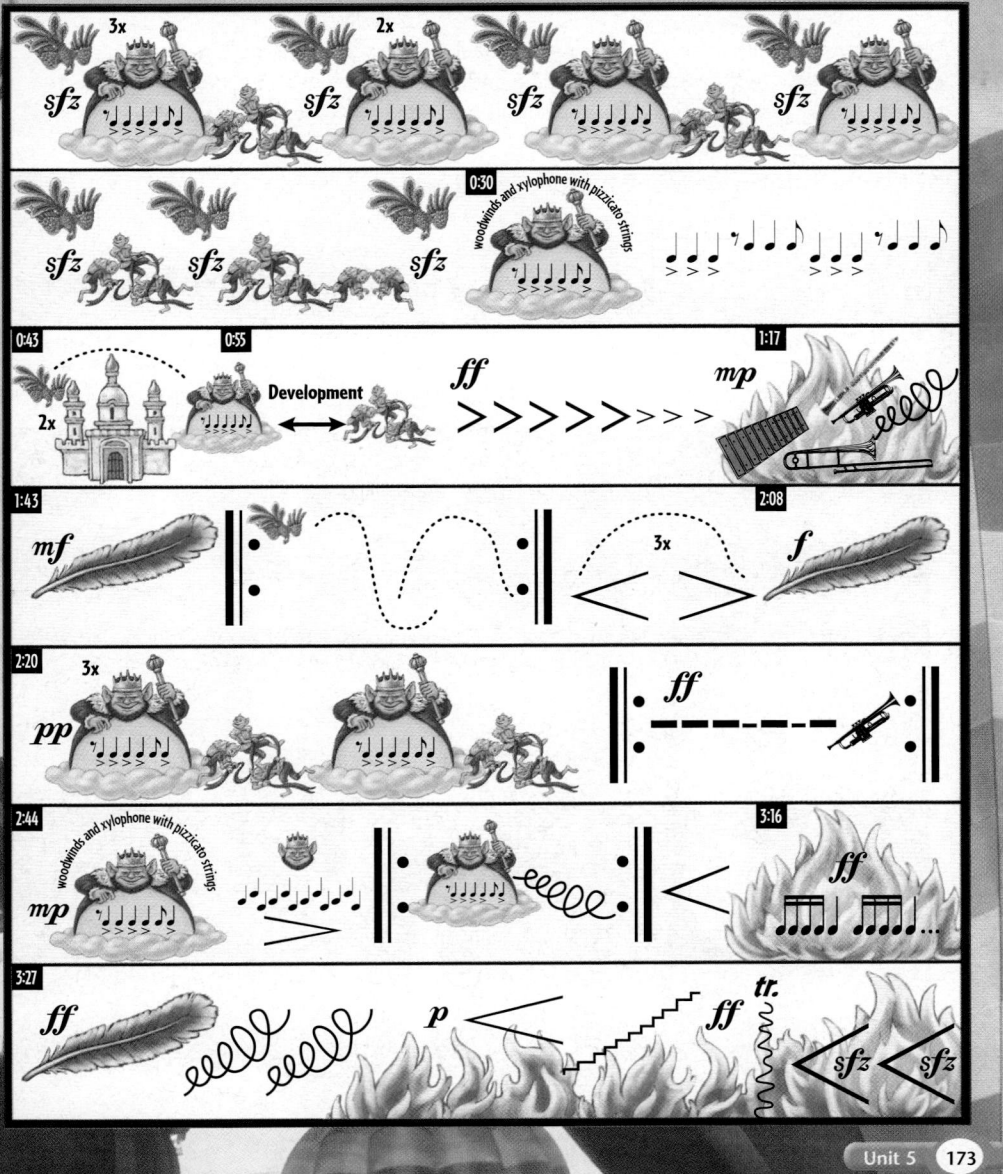

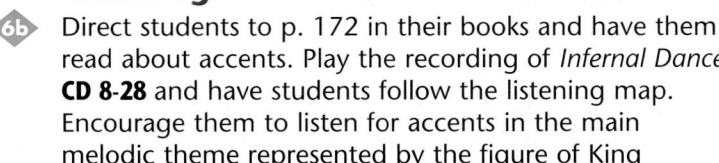

Unit 5 **173**

Playing

2b Have students read "Playing with Expression" on p. 172 in their books. Distribute soprano recorders to the class.

Model how to play *staccato* and *legato* for students, then allow them to experiment with *staccato* and *legato* playing.

Have students identify terms referring to articulation.

ASK Should you play this ostinato *staccato* or *legato*? (*legato*)

> **How do you know?** (Slur marks indicate *legato* playing.)

Have students play the recorder ostinato during the verses of "I Believe I Can Fly."

Listening

6b Direct students to p. 172 in their books and have them read about accents. Play the recording of *Infernal Dance* **CD 8-28** and have students follow the listening map. Encourage them to listen for accents in the main melodic theme represented by the figure of King Katschei throughout the listening map.

Use the indicated timings to help students follow the listening map.

3 CLOSE

SKILL: SINGING   **ASSESSMENT**

7b **Performance/Peer Critique** Divide the class into groups of four to six students. Tell students that groups will be assessed for accurate performance of slurs. Play the recording of "I Believe I Can Fly" **CD 8-26** and have groups practice singing the song. Some groups may wish to add the recorder ostinato to their performance. Play the recording again. Have students take turns listening to and evaluating other groups.

AUDIENCE ETIQUETTE

▶ **Critical Listening** Students who practice active listening skills, including analysis and critique of music they hear in the classroom, will be more attentive at live performances. To promote critical listening skills, have students

- Follow visual maps of the music as they listen. Look for listening maps that illustrate or highlight form, dynamics, instrumentation, or other musical elements.

- Respond to music through movement to show the style, tempo, instrumentation, or other musical elements found in the selection.

- Respond to music in class by writing about what they hear in a listening log.

TECHNOLOGY/MEDIA LINK

Notation Software Using notation software, have students experiment with adding slurs to notated music. You may wish to provide students with a melody, or you may have them compose their own melodies within parameters you suggest (for example, a four measure melody in the key of C). After students have added slurs to the melody, have them sing or play the melody and observe the slurs they have written.

Transparency Display the listening map transparency for *Infernal Dance* as you play the recording. Encourage students to listen for dynamic contrasts and instrumental timbre.

LESSON AT A GLANCE

Element Focus   **RHYTHM** Compound meter

Skill Objective   **READING** Sing and accompany from notation songs in compound meter

Connection Activity   **RELATED ARTS** Discuss the use of rhythm in a painting and a song

MATERIALS

- *"Las estrellitas del cielo"*   **CD 8-29**
- "Stars of the Heavens"   **CD 8-30**

   Recording Routine: Intro (4 m.); vocal; instrumental; vocal

- **Music Reading Practice, Sequence 17**   **CD 8-33**
- **Pronunciation Practice/Translation** p. 529
- *"Don Alfonso"* (Spanish)   **CD 9-2**
- *"Don Alfonso"* (English)   **CD 9-3**

   Recording Routine: Intro (free/2 m.); v.1; interlude (6 m.); v.2; Interlude (6 m.); v.3; coda

- *Concierto Madrigal for Two Guitars and Orchestra,*   **CD 9-1**
   "Caccía a la española"
- **Pronunciation Practice/Translation** p. 530
- **Dance Directions** for *"Don Alfonso"* p. 558
- **Resource Book** pp. A-19, A-20, D-23, E-18, F-20, F-21
- finger cymbals, triangle

VOCABULARY

simple meter   compound meter   ostinato

◆ ◆ ◆ National Standards ◆ ◆ ◆

1c Sing music from diverse cultures
2c Perform instrumental music from diverse cultures
4c Compose, using electronic media
5a Read quarter, eighth, dotted notes in duple meter
6c Understand and use basic principles of rhythm in music analysis
8a Show how different arts portray the same idea in unique ways

MORE MUSIC CHOICES

For more practice with compound meter:
"La ciudad de Juaja" ("The City of Juaja"), p. 58

Simple or Compound

Music from Spain often has a gentle, swaying feel. Before you sing *"Las estrellitas del cielo,"* **listen** to the recording and keep a steady beat. Can you feel the strong and weak beats? Pat the strong beats on your knees and softly clap the weak beats.

Look at these rhythm patterns. Which one fits the song?

Now clap each of these rhythm patterns as you **sing** the song. Which pattern feels more comfortable?

Arts Connection

Creatures in the Night by Joan Miro, 1950 ▼

174 Reading Sequence 17

Footnotes

SKILLS REINFORCEMENT

6c ▶ **Reading** See Resource Book, p. D-23, for a Music Reading Worksheet to accompany this lesson.

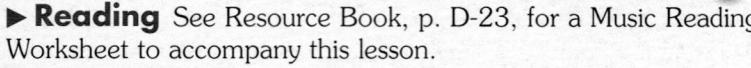
▶ **Mallets** An Orff accompaniment for *"Las estrellitas del cielo"* can be found on Resource Book p. F-20.

2c
BUILDING SKILLS THROUGH MUSIC

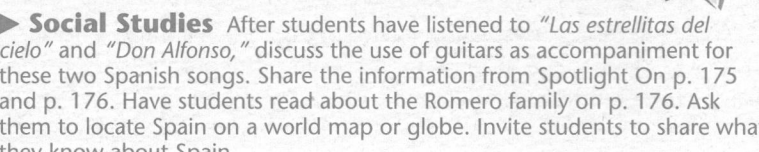
▶ **Social Studies** After students have listened to *"Las estrellitas del cielo"* and *"Don Alfonso,"* discuss the use of guitars as accompaniment for these two Spanish songs. Share the information from Spotlight On p. 175 and p. 176. Have students read about the Romero family on p. 176. Ask them to locate Spain on a world map or globe. Invite students to share what they know about Spain.

TEACHER TO TEACHER

▶ **Meter** Students should feel and describe the difference between simple and compound meter before learning to read rhythmic figures that occur in $\frac{6}{8}$. Once they understand that *simple* and *compound* are terms used to describe the underlying pulse or subdivision of each beat, while *duple, triple,* and *quadruple* refer to the number of beats per measure, they will be able to read and notate rhythmic figures in compound meter as easily as those in simple meter.

CD 8-29
MIDI 12

Las estrellitas del cielo
(Stars of the Heavens)

English Words by Aura Kontra

Folk Song from Spain

Las es-tre-lli-tas del cie-lo
Stars of the heav-ens are wink-ing,

Bri-llan con su luz de
With sil-v'ry light they are

pla-ta. San-tia-go las fué sem-bran-do
twin-kling. A heav-en-ly rid-er came jing-ling

Con sus es-pue-las de pla-ta.
With sil-v'ry spurs, star-light sprin-kling.

That Stubborn Ostinato

Ostinato is an Italian word that means "stubborn." And that's what an ostinato is! It repeats and repeats throughout the music. As you sing "*Las estrellitas del cielo*" again, add an ostinato by clapping or playing this rhythm.

Create another ostinato to **perform** with "*Las estrellitas del cielo.*"

Simple or Compound?

When the beat is subdivided into groups of two, the meter is called **simple meter.** When it is subdivided into groups of three, it is called **compound meter.**

Is the meter of "*Las estrellitas del cielo*" simple or compound?

> **Simple and compound meter** describes the way beats in music can be subdivided into groups of two and three.

Unit 5 **175**

---

1 INTRODUCE

6c Discuss the feeling of "rhythm" in the painting by Miró. Then have students listen to *"Las estrellitas del cielo"*

8a **CD 8-29** while keeping a steady beat. Discuss the rhythm in the music and how it relates to the painting. (Answers will vary.)

2 DEVELOP

Singing

Have students

* Conduct a two-beat pattern while listening to *"Las estrellitas del cielo"* **CD 8-29.**

1c
* Sing the song while conducting.

Reading

SAY This song has two beats in each measure. But not all songs with two beats to a measure are the same. This has to do with the way each beat is subdivided.

Have students

5a
* Read, clap, and count the rhythm patterns on p. 174.

* Sing the song as they clap each pattern.

6c **ASK** Which rhythm pattern feels more comfortable? (the two groups of three eighth notes)

Discuss the text at the bottom of p. 175.

SAY Because the beats in this song are subdivided into groups of three, the meter is compound.

5a Invite students to clap the ostinato on p. 175 to accompany the song.

For additional practice reading in compound meter, see Music Reading Practice, Sequence 17 on p. 498 and Resource Book p. E-18.

CULTURAL CONNECTION

▶ **The Way of the Saint** The literal translation of the lyrics of "*Las estrellitas del cielo*" is "The little stars of heaven shine with their silvery light." Santiago (Saint James) de Compostela is a city in northwestern Spain. It has been a destination for pilgrims since the ninth century, when the bones of the apostle James the Great were allegedly discovered there. According to legend, the hermit Pelagius had a vision and the burial place of James was revealed to him. The place of the grave was surrounded in a miraculous light. A church was built, and James was named patron saint of Spain. A later legend says that the name *Compostela* comes from the words *Campus Stellae* or *star field,* after the miraculous starlight that showed the place of the grave. Pilgrims may sing "*Las estrellitas del cielo*" as they approach the site.

SPOTLIGHT ON

▶ **The Artist** Joan Miró (1893-1983) was born in Barcelona, Spain. At age fourteen, he attended business school in Barcelona, as well as the School of Fine Arts there. After three years of studying art, Miró dropped out of school to become a clerk. He began his art study again in 1912 after suffering a mental breakdown. Miró's first solo show opened in 1918 in a Barcelona gallery. His work was greatly inspired by his love for his native country, Spain. Miró remains one of Spain's most well-known abstract and Surrealist artists.

Listening

Have students listen to the recording of "Don Alfonso" **CD 9-2** and compare the song to "Las estrellitas del cielo."

ASK How are these songs similar? (Both are in Spanish and both have the same swaying feel; both songs have guitar in the accompaniment.)

Singing

Have students practice the Spanish text of "Don Alfonso" with the Pronunciation Practice Tracks **CD 9-5, 9-6** and Resource Book p. A-20.

1c Then have students sing "Don Alfonso" while conducting a two-beat pattern.

6c **ASK** When the beat subdivides into groups of three, what is the meter called? (compound meter)

SAY The meter is determined by the way the beat subdivides (either simple or compound) and the number of beats in each measure. When a song in compound meter has two beats per measure, it is described as compound duple meter.

Listening

Invite students to listen to *Caccía a la española* **CD 9-1** performed by Pepe and Angel Romero. Ask them to tap the steady beat when they hear it. Point out to students that in most measures of this piece, the beat is subdivided into groups of three, as in "Don Alfonso."

Have students read the information on p. 176 about the Romero family.

Playing

Some students may enjoy performing a chordal guitar accompaniment with "Don Alfonso." Have students practice the Dm, Gm, and A7 chords shown on p. 177. When they are comfortable, invite them to accompany the song while others sing.

More About Meter

"Don Alfonso" is another song from Spain. Like "Las estrellitas del cielo," it also has a swaying feel.

Listen to the recording and tap the steady beat. Is the beat subdivided into groups of two, or subdivided into groups of three?

Spanish Guitars

Listen to this selection by the Spanish composer Joaquín Rodrigo. When you hear a steady beat, tap along with the recording. In most measures, the beat is subdivided into groups of three, as in "Don Alfonso."

CD 9-1
Caccía a la española
from *Concierto Madrigal for Two Guitars and Orchestra*
by Joaquín Rodrigo
as performed by Pepe and Angel Romero

Joaquín Rodrigo became blind at the age of three, due to illness.

M·U·S·I·C M·A·K·E·R·S

The Romero Family

The Romero Family of Spain is known as the "Royal Family of the Guitar." Celin, Pepe, and Angel Romero carry on the teachings passed down to them by their father, Celedonio.

Celedonio Romero (1913–1996) was mostly self-taught on the guitar. He went on to study at the Conservatory of Málaga in Spain. He was not allowed to perform outside of Spain due to government regulations. In 1957, Celedonio and his family settled in the United States.

Celin Romero (born 1936) is the oldest of Celedonio's sons. His first professional concert was at age seven at the Radio National de España. Today, he continues to perform worldwide.

Pepe Romero (born 1944) has also performed worldwide. He was the recipient of the "Premio Andalucía de Müsica," one of the most prestigious awards in Spain.

Angel Romero (born 1946), in addition to performing on the concert stage, has been involved in performing and composing music for film. In 1995, he received an Ariel, Mexico's equivalent of the American Academy Award, for his work in this genre.

◀ The Romero Family (clockwise from left): Angel, Pepe, Celin, and Celedonio (seated)

176

Footnotes

SKILLS REINFORCEMENT

6c ▶ **Performing** Have students explore ways to show the difference between simple and compound meters using their bodies, scarves, or ribbons. Discuss different possibilities for using sounds (snap, clap, pat, stamp, slide) and space, and decide which are best suited for each meter. Have students perform these patterns while singing familiar songs in each meter. Then try stepping the beat in a circle while singing and performing the body percussion.

▶ **Mallets** An Orff accompaniment for "Don Alfonso" can be found on Resource Book p. F-21.

SPOTLIGHT ON

▶ **The Composer** Joaquín Rodrigo (1901-1999) was born in Sagunto (Valencia), Spain on November 22, 1901. After suffering with diphtheria, he lost his sight when he was only three years old. At the age of eight he began studying piano and violin and by age sixteen he was a student at the Conservatory in Valencia. By the time he was 22, he had composed his first pieces: *Suite for Piano*, *Dos Esbozos* (Two Sketches) *for Violin*, and *Siciliana for Cello*. Rodrigo wrote all his works in Braille, later dictating them to a copyist. He composed eleven concertos for various instruments, more than sixty songs, choral and instrumental works, and music for theater and films.

Sing *"Don Alfonso."* Is the song in simple meter or in compound meter?

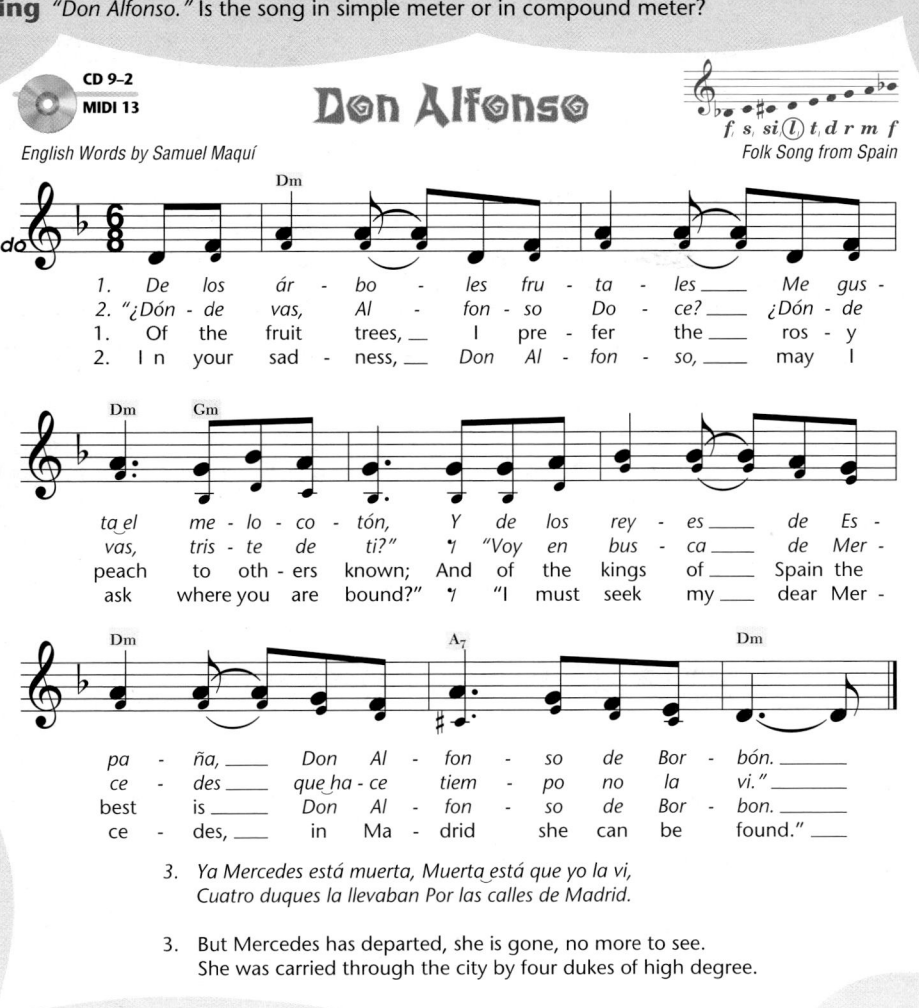

CD 9–2
MIDI 13

Don Alfonso

English Words by Samuel Maquí

Folk Song from Spain

f, s, si l, t, d r m f

1. De los ár - bo - les fru - ta - les _____ Me gus -
2. "¿Dón - de vas, Al - fon - so Do - ce?_____ ¿Dón - de
1. Of the fruit trees, _____ I pre - fer the _____ ros - y
2. In your sad - ness, _____ Don Al - fon - so, _____ may I

ta el me - lo - co - tón, Y de los rey - es _____ de Es -
vas, tris - te de ti?" ¬ "Voy en bus - ca _____ de Mer -
peach to oth - ers known; And of the kings of _____ Spain the
ask where you are bound?" ¬ "I must seek my _____ dear Mer -

pa - ña, _____ Don Al - fon - so de Bor - bón. _____
ce - des _____ que ha - ce tiem - po no la vi." _____
best is _____ Don Al - fon - so de Bor - bon. _____
ce - des, _____ in Ma - drid she can be found." _____

3. Ya Mercedes está muerta, Muerta está que yo la vi,
Cuatro duques la llevaban Por las calles de Madrid.

3. But Mercedes has departed, she is gone, no more to see.
She was carried through the city by four dukes of high degree.

Play these chords on guitar to accompany *"Don Alfonso."*

Unit 5 177

Moving

Invite students to learn a patterned dance to perform with *"Don Alfonso."* For more detailed instruction, see Movement below.

3 Close

Skill: READING   **ASSESSMENT**

1c 2c **Performance/Observation** Have students demonstrate appropriate large-ensemble performance techniques when performing in formal or informal concerts. Ask students to

- Sing *"Las estrellitas del cielo"* and *"Don Alfonso"* from notation.

- Describe the subdivision of the beat (three eighth notes).

- Accompany the songs by playing the ostinato on p. 175 on light percussion instruments, such as finger cymbals and triangle.

Observe and assess students' ability to sing and accompany from notation a song in compound meter.

MOVEMENT

▶ **Patterned Dance** *"Don Alfonso"* is in the flamenco song and dance style called *sevillana* [she-vee-AH-nah], named for the Spanish city of Seville where it originated. The *sevillana* is sung and danced to the accompaniment of guitar and castanets. The pain and sad emotions expressed by the words and music are interpreted by dancers with strong movements and stern facial expressions. Dancers may stamp, clap, and snap their fingers. Watchers show appreciation and encouragement by shouts of *"Ole!"* For Dance Directions, see p. 558 in this book.

TECHNOLOGY/MEDIA LINK

4c **Notation Software** Challenge students to create eight-measure melodies, using stepwise movement like that found in *"Las estrellitas del cielo."* Have students

- Use a notation program in the computer lab, at home, or in the classroom computer center.

- Choose a meter $\frac{6}{8}$ or $\frac{4}{4}$.

- Begin and end their pieces on the note E.

- Notate their pieces by selecting the desired rhythmic value and then clicking on the musical staff to choose the pitch.

- Play back and edit their pieces.

LESSON AT A GLANCE

Element Focus	**RHYTHM** $\frac{6}{8}$ meter	
Skill Objective	**READING** Sing and accompany from notation a song in $\frac{6}{8}$ meter	
Connection Activity	**SOCIAL STUDIES** Discuss the ancient kingdom of Northumbria	

MATERIALS

- "Blow the Wind Southerly" **CD 9-8**
  Recording Routine: Intro (4 m.); refrain; v. 1; refrain; interlude (4 m.); refrain; v. 2; refrain; coda
- **Music Reading Practice, Sequence 18** **CD 9-10**
- **Resource Book** pp. B-15, E-19, F-22, H-14, I-15

VOCABULARY

rhythm	duple meter	time signature
simple meter	compound meter	

◆ ◆ ◆ ◆ National Standards ◆ ◆ ◆ ◆

1c Sing music from diverse cultures
2a Play instruments accurately alone
3b Improvise rhythmic variations on given melodies
6c Understand and use basic principles of rhythm in music analysis
8b Identify ways music relates to social studies

MORE MUSIC CHOICES

For more practice with $\frac{6}{8}$ meter:
"Away to America," p. 57

1 INTRODUCE

Clap two-beat rhythm patterns from "Blow the Wind Southerly." Have students echo-clap each pattern and identify the number of beats in each pattern. (two)

Tell students that the rhythm patterns occur in a song from an area of England called Northumbria. Then share the information in Across the Curriculum.

NAME A NEW METER

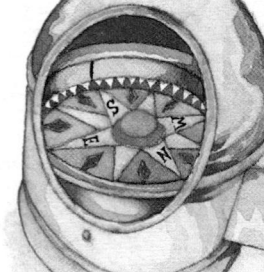

Every country that borders an ocean has songs and stories about the sea. "Blow the Wind Southerly" is one of many such songs. Can you think of others?

Identify the pattern of strong and weak beats as you **listen** to "Blow the Wind Southerly." Which rhythm pattern below fits best with the song?

simple   compound

Create an ostinato in $\frac{6}{8}$ compound meter and **perform** it as you **sing** the song.

m, f, s, l, t,@ r m f fis l

 CD 9-8 BLOW THE WIND SOUTHERLY

Folk Song from Northumbria

REFRAIN

Blow the wind south - er - ly, south - er - ly, south - er - ly,

Blow the wind south o'er the bon - ny blue sea;

Blow the wind south - er - ly, south - er - ly, south - er - ly,

Fine

Blow bon - ny breeze __ my true love to me.

Footnotes

SKILLS REINFORCEMENT

▶ **Reading** Have students use E-19 for more practice with compound meter.

▶ **Recorder** Have students learn and play the recorder part for "Blow the Wind Southerly" on p. I-15 in the Resource Book.

2a

BUILDING SKILLS THROUGH MUSIC

▶ **Reading** Have students review the text of "Blow the Wind Southerly" by singing all the verses. Ask students to identify words in the song that have multiple meanings or that are not common usage. Discuss alternate meanings for the words. Select individual students to give their interpretation of the main idea of the song.

ACROSS THE CURRICULUM

8b ▶ **Social Studies** Northumbria is made up of Northumberland, Cleveland, and Durham counties in the northeastern part of England. Carved out by the Saxons centuries ago, this ancient kingdom once stretched from the Firth of Forth (a narrow inlet of the sea) in Scotland to the banks of the Humber River in Yorkshire. During the thirteenth and fourteenth centuries, the land was ravaged by terrible battles between the warring English and Scots. Many "border ballads" were written about their struggles for power. Invite volunteers to research and report on the battles between the English and Scots.

VERSE

1. He told me last night there were ships in the off-ing, And
2. I stood by the light-house that last time we part-ed, 'Til

I hur-ried down to the deep roll-ing sea; But my
dark-ness came down o'er the deep roll-ing sea; And no

eye could not see it, wher-ev-er might be it, The
long-er I saw the bright bark of my true love, Oh,

D. C. al Fine

bark that is bear-ing my true love to me.
blow bon-ny breeze ___ and bring him to me.

Simple and Compound Meter

In simple meter, the bottom number of the time signature represents the beat. In $\frac{2}{4}$ the beat note is ♩. In compound meter the beat note is ♩.

Show What You Know!

Clap these patterns in compound meter. Use the patterns to **create** a counter-rhythm. Then **perform** your counter-rhythm as you **sing** "Blow the Wind Southerly."

1. $\frac{6}{8}$ ♪♪♪ ♩. | ♪♪♪ ♩. ‖
2. $\frac{6}{8}$ ♩. ♪ | ♪♪♪ ♪ ♩. ‖

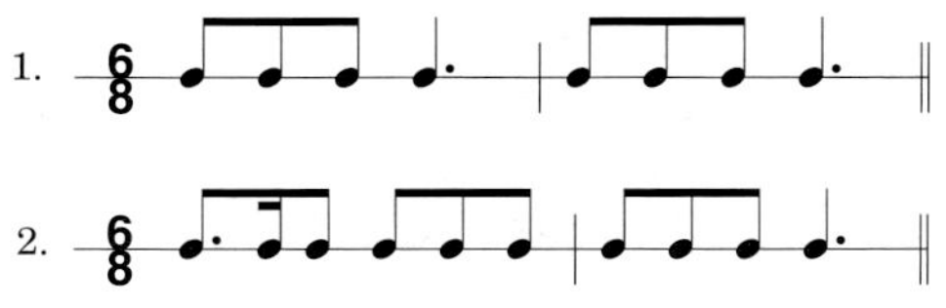

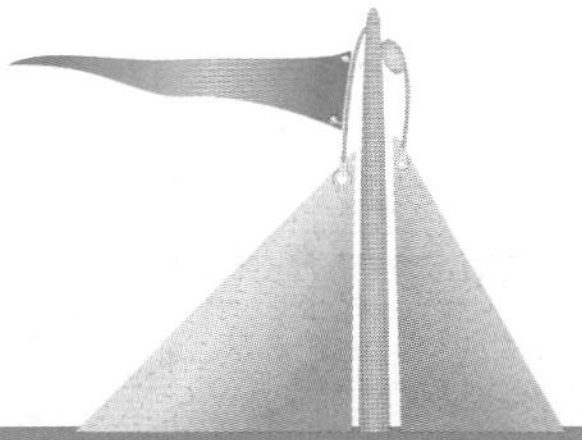

2 DEVELOP

Listening

Have students keep a steady beat as they listen to "Blow the Wind Southerly" **CD 9-8.**

6c **ASK Is this song in duple or triple meter?** (It is in duple meter, two beats to each measure.)

Is this song in simple duple or compound duple meter? (It is in compound meter, because the beat subdivides into threes.)

Creating and Singing

1c Have students create an ostinato in $\frac{6}{8}$ meter and perform it as they sing the song.

Reading

Discuss time signature and encourage students to use standard terminology in explaining music notation.

6c **ASK In a time signature, what represents the beat in simple meter?** (the bottom number)

In $\frac{2}{4}$ time, what is the beat note? (quarter)

What is the beat note in $\frac{6}{8}$ time? (dotted quarter)

What does the bottom number represent? (the subdivision or the pulse note [eighth note])

Draw attention to the time signature of the song.

SAY The time signature for compound duple is $\frac{6}{8}$. There are two beats in each measure, each with three pulses, for a total of six eighth notes in each measure.

For a related reading activity, see p. 498 and Resource Book p. E-19.

3 CLOSE

Element: RHYTHM | **ASSESSMENT**

1c **Performance/Observation** Following the directions in Show What You Know, have students sing
3b "Blow the Wind Southerly" while performing a body percussion counter-rhythm as an ostinato. (See Resource Book p. B-15.) Observe students' ability to perform the body percussion accurately.

SKILLS REINFORCEMENT

▶ **Keyboard** Students can play a two-handed broken-chord accompaniment for the refrain of "Blow the Wind Southerly,"
2a using the following positions. An accompaniment for the verse can be found in the Resource Book, p. H-14.

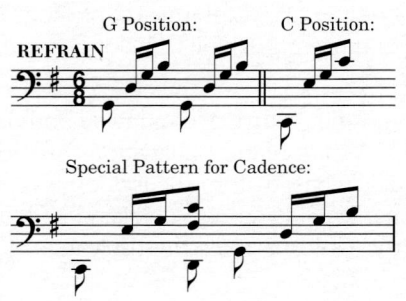

G Position: C Position:
REFRAIN

Special Pattern for Cadence:

TECHNOLOGY/MEDIA LINK

2a **Electronic Keyboard** Have pairs of students alternate playing *arpeggios* in root position on beats 1 and 2 to accompany "Blow the Wind Southerly."

LESSON AT A GLANCE

Element Focus	**RHYTHM** $\frac{6}{8}$ meter
Skill Objective	**PLAYING** Play rhythm patterns in $\frac{6}{8}$ meter
Connection Activity	**SOCIAL STUDIES** Explore the historical background of a song

MATERIALS

- "When Johnny Comes Marching Home" **CD 9-13**

  Recording Routine: Intro (8 m.); v. 1; interlude (8 m.); v. 2; interlude (8 m.); v. 3; coda

- "Pat Works on the Railway" **CD 9-15**

  Recording Routine: Intro (6 m.); v. 1; refrain; interlude (4 m.); v. 2; refrain; interlude (4 m.); v. 3; refrain; coda

- **Resource Book** p. F-24
- bass xylophone/bass metallophone, alto xylophone/alto metallophone, alto glockenspiel/soprano glockenspiel, tambourine, hand drum, triangle, claves

VOCABULARY

duple meter   verse   refrain   countermelody

◆ ◆ ◆ ◆ National Standards ◆ ◆ ◆ ◆

1a Sing accurately in small ensembles
1d Sing music written in two parts
2b Perform easy instrumental pieces with technical accuracy
3b Improvise rhythmic variations on given melodies
4c Compose, using electronic media
5a Read eighth, quarter, dotted notes in duple meter
6b Listen and analyze uses of rhythm in music from diverse genres
7a Students evaluate the music they perform
8b Identify ways music relates to social studies

MORE MUSIC CHOICES

For other songs that relate to historical events:

"Erie Canal," p. 262

"Battle Hymn of the Republic," p. 274

"Colorado Trail," p. 276

March To The Beat

The Civil War was a momentous event in American history. The war produced songs, such as "When Johnny Comes Marching Home," that have become part of our musical tradition.

Sing "When Johnny Comes Marching Home." **Move** to show its duple meter.

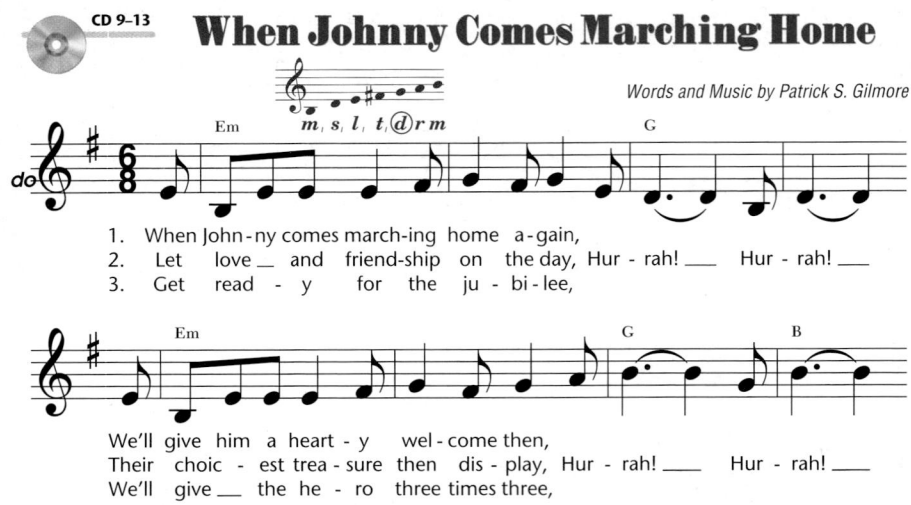

CD 9-13 When Johnny Comes Marching Home

Words and Music by Patrick S. Gilmore

1. When John-ny comes march-ing home a-gain,
2. Let love __ and friend-ship on the day, Hur - rah! ___ Hur - rah! ___
3. Get read - y for the ju - bi-lee,

We'll give him a heart - y wel - come then,
Their choic - est trea - sure then dis - play, Hur - rah! ___ Hur - rah! ___
We'll give __ the he - ro three times three,

The _ men will cheer, _ the boys will shout, The la - dies they _ will all turn out,
And _ let each one _ per-form some part, To fill with joy _ the war-rior's heart,
The _ laur - el wreath _ is read - y now To place up - on _ his roy - al brow,

And we'll shout "Hur - rah" when john-ny comes march-ing home! __

180

Footnotes

TEACHER TO TEACHER

▶ **Historical Research** If students would like to learn more about a part of history, tell them that one of the best ways is to talk to a person who actually lived through the experiences they are interested in. If such a person is not available, students might look for articles and letters that were written at the time.

BUILDING SKILLS THROUGH MUSIC

▶ **Language** Review the elements of stories such as location, time, characters, and plot. Have students listen to "When Johnny Comes Marching Home" **CD 9-13** and determine the story elements. Then have them listen to "Pat Works on the Railway" **CD 9-15** while reading the song text. Ask students to compare their ideas about the song with the information on p. 182 in their book. Have students identify phrases from the song that reveal how the singer felt about his work.

ACROSS THE CURRICULUM

8b ▶ **Social Studies** Invite students to learn more about the people and events of the American Civil War by reading:

- *Civil War: Garments, History, Legends and Lore* by Gina Capaldi (Frank Schaffer Publications, 1999). This history/activity book is full of interesting photographs and diaries, as well as museum exhibits of clothing and other artifacts of this period.

- *Broken Drum* by Edith Morris Hemingway and Jacqueline Cosgrove Shields (White Mane Publications, 1996). This poignant, historically-based story focuses on a real-life 12-year-old boy, Charles E. King, who enlisted as a drummer for Company F of the Union army's Pennsylvania 49th Volunteers, 1861–1862.

▲ Civil War Drum Corps. Photo by Timothy H. O'Sullivan, 1863

Tune In

"When Johnny Comes Marching Home" was written by a Union army bandmaster, Patrick S. Gilmore, in 1863.

Percussion Patterns

Play these rhythm patterns on percussion instruments throughout the song.

Create a body percussion ostinato with a partner. **Perform** the ostinato as you **sing** the song.

1 INTRODUCE

Have students read the words of "When Johnny Comes Marching Home."

ASK What is the message of the text? (Everyone wants the war to end and the soldiers to return home to a joyous welcome.)

So they can better understand the period in which this song was written, share with students the resources listed in Across the Curriculum, p. 180.

2 DEVELOP

Singing

1a Encourage students to sing this song representative of American heritage along with the recording **CD 9-13.** Have them move to show the duple meter—two beats to a measure.

Reading

Write on the board some common rhythms in $\frac{6}{8}$ meter that are found in the song.

Have students

5a
- Speak and then clap each rhythm.
- Echo-clap each rhythm on the board and identify which rhythm it is.

Singing

Have students

- Speak the words of "When Johnny Comes Marching Home" in rhythm.
1a
- Sing the song again with the recording.

Playing

Ask students to

- Read music that incorporates rhythmic patterns in various meters. Look at the percussion patterns on p. 181 in their books.
5a
- Clap each pattern.

continued on page 182

CHARACTER EDUCATION

▶ **Diversity** Help students to understand the diverse nature of our contemporary world and the subsequent increased need for acceptance of those who are different from us. Discuss the impact of railroad expansion on American society (for example, increased trade and travel, increased awareness of diversity as people experienced other parts of the country). What twentieth-century advances have made it easier for our society to experience diversity? (Answers may include air travel, Internet, and telecommunications.) How should we respond to people who are different from us? Why should we respond in these ways? Lead students to understand that the global nature of our world makes diversity a part of everyday life; thus, acceptance of people, customs, music, and cultures that are different from us is crucial.

CULTURAL CONNECTION

▶ **The Legacy of Songs** Songs are part of every culture and some become a part of cultural history. Some songs tell stories, such as ballads. Others recount events in history. Peoples who did not have written languages used songs and stories to preserve their history. Some songs were used to convey messages, such as those of the Underground Railroad. Some are patriotic and were used to bolster morale or recount events. Other songs, such as work songs, were used to encourage laborers. Songs are used for ceremonies, for celebrations, for rituals, to celebrate life, and mourn death. What kinds of songs of today do students envision might become part of history?

2b
- Transfer the patterns to percussion instruments and play them as an accompaniment to "When Johnny Comes Marching Home."

Creating

 **3b** Have students find partners. Ask them to create body percussion ostinatos to accompany "When Johnny Comes Marching Home," and perform their ostinatos while singing the song.

Listening

 8b **SAY** In the mid-1800s, railroads were being built throughout the United States at a rapid rate. This is one of the songs that helped the workers survive long and strenuous work hours. Many of these workers were Irish American immigrants.

See Across the Curriculum, below, for more information on the building of the railroads.

6b Play the recording of "Pat Works on the Railway" **CD 9-15** so that the class can hear the strong pulse in duple meter. Ask students to imagine sledge hammers hammering down twice in each measure.

Reading

Ask students to echo-clap the first two measures of "Pat Works on the Railway."

 5a **ASK** **Are there other measures with exactly the same rhythm?** (measures 3–4 and 5–6)

Have students

- Turn to "When Johnny Comes Marching Home" on p. 180 and identify two-measure groups with the same rhythm or nearly the same rhythm as in measures 1 and 2 in "Pat Works on the Railway." (measures 9–10 and 11–12)
- Clap and speak the words of both the verse and refrain of "Pat Works on the Railway."
- Sing "Pat Works on the Railway" with **CD 9-15.**
- **1d** Add the countermelody on the refrain after verses 2 and 3.

Rhythm of the Rails

During the mid-1800s, railroads spread throughout the country. The coast-to-coast expansion was completed in 1869. A golden spike joined the Union Pacific and Central Pacific Railways at Promontory Summit, north of Salt Lake City.

"Pat Works on the Railway" is a humorous song that helped workers survive their strenuous labor. **Listen** to the song to hear how the music imitates the sound of building the railroad.

As you **sing** the song, **create** movements to show the meter.

 CD 9–15 MIDI 14 **Pat Works on the Railway**

Irish American Railroad Song

VERSE *Solo* Em

1. In eight - een hun - dred and for - ty - one, I
2. In eight - een hun - dred and for - ty - two, I
3. It's "Pat, do this," ___ and "Pat, do that," With -

G / Em

put my cor - du - roy breech - es on, I put my cor - du - roy
left the old ___ world for the new, Oh, spare me the luck ___ that
out a stock - ing or cra - vat, And no - thing but ___ an

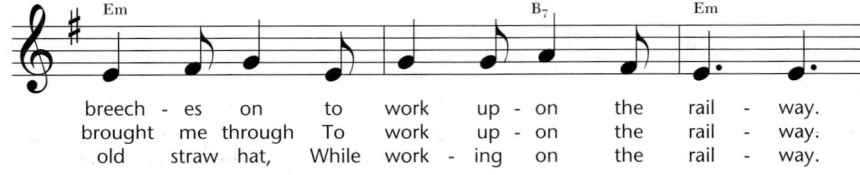

Em / B7 / Em

breech - es on to work up - on the rail - way.
brought me through To work up - on the rail - way.
old straw hat, While work - ing on the rail - way.

182

Footnotes

 ## SKILLS REINFORCEMENT

 ▶ **Recorder** To help develop right hand dexterity, students can play this recorder countermelody to "Pat Works on the Railway." Begin by playing each measure from the counter-melody and have students echo on their recorders. Then play two-measure phrases and have students echo. Repeat as necessary.

VERSE

ACROSS THE CURRICULUM

 8b ▶ **Social Studies** What happened after that gold spike joined the two railroads at Promontory Point in 1869? The railroads kept expanding! Four more transcontinental lines were finished by 1893, giving many towns their own railroad stations. So many people migrated West that nine new states joined the nation between 1867 and 1897. Trade between the coasts was opened because of the new railroads. Western states shipped lumber and minerals to the East. The eastern states shipped fin-ished goods, such as stoves, clothing, and furniture to the West. Railroads also enabled people to travel from coast to coast.

Play the score below to accompany "Pat Works on the Railway."

3 CLOSE

Playing

Have students

5a
- Pat the rhythm of each part in the score on p. 183.
- Transfer the rhythm to mallet instruments and tambourine.

2b
- Play the score to accompany the refrain of "Pat Works on the Railway."

Element: RHYTHM   **ASSESSMENT**

Performance/Self-Assessment Divide the class into three groups for a combined performance of "When Johnny Comes Marching Home," organized as follows:

- Group 1—Move to show the duple meter of the song.

2b
- Group 2—Accompany the song using the percussion parts on p. 181.

1a

7a
- Group 3—Sing the song. Encourage students to demonstrate appropriate large-ensemble performance techniques when performing in formal or informal concerts. Allow groups to switch roles.

After each performance, allow time for students to evaluate the rhythmic accuracy of the singing and playing.

MEETING INDIVIDUAL NEEDS

▶ **Including Everyone** Use the following teaching strategies to help all students coordinate movements on beats 1 and 4.

Reinforcement Have students close their eyes, relax, and listen to the music while seated and use any silent movements (pat, tap their foot, upper body) to "feel" the beat.

On Target Most students will "naturally" feel two beats. Tell them that the "natural" feel of the beat is the most important and that trying to "feel" six may seem awkward.

Challenge Those students who easily master this activity may be invited to create alternate movements to perform on beats 1 and 4.

TECHNOLOGY/MEDIA LINK

4c
Sequencing Software Encourage students to compose a $\frac{6}{8}$ military-style drum accompaniment for "When Johnny Comes Marching Home" using a sequencing program. Set the time signature to $\frac{6}{8}$ and the count-off to two measures.

Send students one at a time to record one drum track with repeating $\frac{6}{8}$ patterns.

Play combinations of the tracks at once to accompany the class when it sings the song.

LESSON AT A GLANCE

Element Focus **FORM** Theme-and-variation form

Skill Objective **LISTENING** Identify theme and variations using different instrumental timbres

Connection Activity **CULTURE** Discuss Shaker culture

MATERIALS

- "Simple Gifts" **CD 9-17**

  Recording Routine: Intro (4 m.); vocal; interlude (4 m.); vocal; coda
- *Variations on Simple Gifts* **CD 9-19**
- *Interview with Aaron Copland* **CD 9-20**
- barred instruments
- **Resource Book** p. I-16

VOCABULARY

theme and variations

◆ ◆ ◆ ◆ National Standards ◆ ◆ ◆ ◆

1c Sing music from diverse cultures
2a Play instruments accurately
4a Compose short pieces, demonstrating unity and variety through music
4c Arrange, using electronic media
6b Listen and analyze uses of form in music from diverse genres
8a Show how different arts portray the same idea in unique ways
8b Identify ways music relates to social studies

MORE MUSIC CHOICES

For more practice with theme-and-variation form:
American Salute, p. 275

A Musical Idea

People express ideas in many ways. You can ask, "How are you doing?" or "How are you feeling?" These are variations of "How are you?"

A musical statement or theme can do the same. How can music be varied, while keeping some elements the same? The idea is called **theme and variations.**

Let's use the song "Simple Gifts" as our musical "theme." **Sing** "Simple Gifts" to become familiar with the melody.

> **Theme and variations** is a musical form in which each section is a modification of the initial theme.

CD 9–17

Simple Gifts

s, t, d r m f s
Shaker Song

'Tis the gift to be sim - ple, 'Tis the gift to be free, 'Tis the gift to come down where we ought to be, And when we find our-selves _ in the place just _ right, 'Twill _ be in the val - ley of love and de-light.

184

Footnotes

SPOTLIGHT ON

▶ **The Folk Tune** "Simple Gifts" is a Shaker folk tune that has acquired the status of an American classic. One of its most famous settings is found in Aaron Copland's variations on the tune, which conclude his ballet *Appalachian Spring*.

BUILDING SKILLS THROUGH MUSIC

▶ **Social Studies** Invite students to read the information about Aaron Copland on p. 187 in their books and list important facts about his life. Have students listen to the *Interview with Aaron Copland* **CD 9-20** and add additional facts to their list. Review the information on p. 9 about Leonard Bernstein and ask students to list information about his life. Distribute copies of the Venn Diagram from Resource Book p. C-6. Have students label each circle with the name of one of the composers. Ask them to complete the diagram by adding information specific to each composer and information that the composers share.

CULTURAL CONNECTION

8b ▶ **Shakers** The Shakers are a community of people founded in 1747 in England. This group of dissenting Quakers separated from its church and emigrated, like the Pilgrims, to America in search of religious freedom.

"Simple Gifts" is the most famous Shaker tune, well-suited to their rhythmic swaying and "dancing" when the spirit moved them. The Shakers consciously insulated themselves from the world and practically became extinct as their numbers dwindled. Today, the only remaining Shaker community is in Sabbathday Lake, Maine.

The Shakers are known for their simple, distinctive furniture and folk craft designs, which are both beautiful and highly functional. The Shakers believe that "Anything may be called perfect which perfectly answers the purpose for which it was designed."

Variations on a Theme

In his ballet *Appalachian Spring*, Aaron Copland used the theme of "Simple Gifts" to create a set of variations. **Listen** to the variations on this theme.

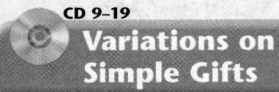

CD 9–19

Variations on Simple Gifts

from *Appalachian Spring*
by Aaron Copland

The ballet *Appalachian Spring* was choreographed by Martha Graham and premiered in 1944.

When true sim-pli-ci-ty is gained, To bow and to bend we —

shan't be a-shamed, To turn, turn will be our de-light, Till by

turn - ing, turn - ing we come 'round right.

Unit 5 **185**

1 INTRODUCE

Invite students to read aloud the information about theme and variations on p. 184. Ask students to look around the classroom to find examples of theme and variations. (Possible answers might include: teacher's desk, students' desks; classroom door, closet door; bookshelves, bookracks, bookcases, and so on.)

2 DEVELOP

Singing

1c Have students sing "Simple Gifts" **CD 9-17** with the recording. Discuss the information about Shaker culture
8b in Cultural Connection, p. 184.

Creating

Discuss how music can be varied and yet maintain common elements.

2a Sing and then play the first phrase of the familiar song "Twinkle Twinkle Little Star" on barred instruments.

4a Help students create melodic phrases for four different variations of this phrase. Some suggestions include high/low, slow/fast, straight rhythm/jazzy, major/modal.

ASK Can you think of other variations? (Engage students in the Skills Reinforcement activity below to help them come up with answers.)

Listening

SAY The composer Aaron Copland is best known for composing music that listeners can relate to. He used the tune "Simple Gifts" for the closing section of his ballet *Appalachian Spring*, and later wrote an arrangement of the song for his first set of *Old American Songs*, published in 1950.

continued on page 186

ACROSS THE CURRICULUM

8b ▶ **Language Arts** For more history and photos of this interesting group of Americans, see *Shaker Home* by Raymond Bial (Houghton Mifflin, 1994). Focused on the Shaker village of Pleasant Hill, Kentucky, the book features the architecture, farm life, seeds, tools, and everyday furniture and home items of the people who lived there. Customs, beliefs, clothing, and community traditions as well as the Shakers' ideal of simplicity are explained.

SKILLS REINFORCEMENT

4a ▶ **Creating** After exploring "theme and variations" by having students create variations to "Twinkle Twinkle Little Star," ask students to create their own variations of other simple melodies (for example, "Ode to Joy"). This time, instead of providing them with suggestions for variations such as "high-low, slow-fast," ask them to play their variations and answer the question: "How have you changed the original melody?" Encourage them to use technical vocabularies that extend from the basic concepts of melody, rhythm, dynamics, tone color, harmony, texture, and form.

Make a chart on the board and check each concept that was
 manipulated.

▶ **Recorder** For a countermelody to "Simple Gifts," see Resource Book, p. I-16.

Unit 5 *Discovering New Musical Horizons* **185**

Play the recording of *Variations on Simple Gifts* **CD 9-19** and ask students to raise their hands when they hear parts of the folk song in the variation. Have them listen again and follow the listening map on p. 186.

6b **SAY** Aaron Copland created these variations using instruments of different timbre.

Play the recording again and have students point to the groups of instruments as they hear them. Ask students to identify the terms and symbols related to dynamics found in the listening map.

Encourage students to use standard terminology in explaining musical instruments.

ASK What instruments did you hear in *Variations on Simple Gifts*? (instruments on map)

Introduction: flute and strings (*pp*)

Theme: clarinet, flute, oboe, and harp accompany (*mp*)

Variation 1: oboe and bassoon; French horn accompanies (still quiet)

Variation 2: low strings; high strings and French horn follow (fuller sound)

Interlude: woodwinds

Variation 3: brass; strings occasionally run quickly around melody in accompaniment

Variation 4: bassoon, oboes, and clarinet; low strings accompany (softer dynamics)

Variation 5: full orchestra (a rich *ff* sound)

Invite students to read more about the clarinet on p. 514 in the Sound Bank. For an additional sound sample of the clarinet, play **CD 21-25.**

Invite students to read the information on Aaron Copland on p. 187 in their books.

Share the information on Martha Graham, who choreographed the ballet *Appalachian Spring,* in Spotlight On, p. 187.

Same—but Different

Listen to *Variations on Simple Gifts* and follow the listening map below.

Variations on Simple Gifts LISTENING MAP

| Introduction *pp* | Theme *mp* | Variation 1 *mf* | Variation 2 *mf–f* |

| Variation 3 *mf* | Variation 4 *mp* | Variation 5 *ff* |

186

Footnotes

MOVEMENT

8a ▶ **Creative Movement** There are five variations for "Simple Gifts." Make a cassette for each variation and then divide the class into four groups. Pass out cassettes for variations 1–4.

Give students enough time to listen to their variation. Then have students create an appropriate movement for their variation. Suggest to students that each movement variation should end with appropriate "ending" movement or pose. As a group, create movement for the fifth variation that incorporates ideas from the first four.

CHARACTER EDUCATION

▶ **Perseverance** To help students recognize the importance of perseverance in setting and working toward goals, discuss how the Shakers planned and sacrificed in their search for religious freedom. Then lead a discussion about the students' goals, their plans for achieving them, and the challenges they foresee as they work to accomplish their goals. Have each student write their specific goal at the top of a paper, then make two columns underneath. Label one column "Benefits of Attaining My Goal" and the other "Choices or Sacrifices I Will Make to Reach My Goal." At the bottom of the paper, have each student describe his or her step-by-step plan for attaining this goal, including a time line. Encourage students to check their plan throughout the year and evaluate their progress toward this goal.

Sound Variations

What instruments did you hear in *Variations on Simple Gifts*? **Describe** at least one way the composer varied the theme.

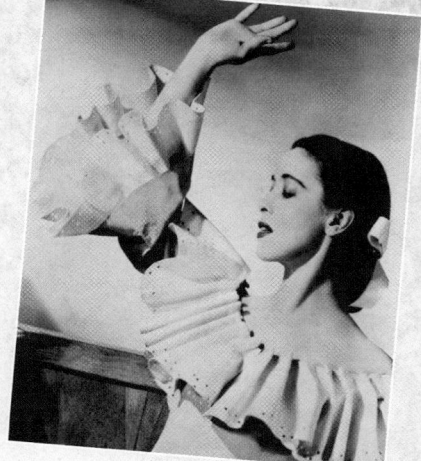

◀ Choreographer and dancer Martha Graham

AARON COPLAND

Aaron Copland [KOHP-land] (1900–1990) was a composer, an author, and a conductor. Although he never went to college, he became a respected instructor at Harvard University. Copland searched the musical and folk literature of America to find themes and story ideas for his compositions. His ballets *Rodeo* and *Billy the Kid* feature American folk tunes and jazz. "Simple Gifts," a Shaker hymn from Pennsylvania, was another source of inspiration. Copland used this melody in his ballet *Appalachian Spring*. This ballet became his most popular work and won him a Pulitzer Prize. Copland believed that classical music could express the spirit of America's beauty and historical traditions, and could be enjoyed by everyone.

CD 9–20
Interview with Aaron Copland

This historic interview with Copland was conducted in the mid-1960s.

Unit 5 **187**

Have students listen to the recorded interview **CD 9-20** with Aaron Copland and describe his vocation as a composer. Discuss with students how composing can also be an avocation.

3 CLOSE

Analyzing

Have students

- Research the titles of additional compositions by Aaron Copland.
- Share their research with the class.
- Keep their reports in their music journals.

Skill: LISTENING   **ASSESSMENT**

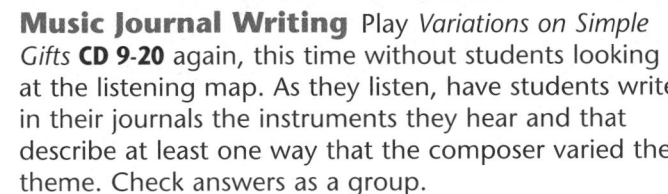

6b **Music Journal Writing** Play *Variations on Simple Gifts* **CD 9-20** again, this time without students looking at the listening map. As they listen, have students write in their journals the instruments they hear and that describe at least one way that the composer varied the theme. Check answers as a group.

SPOTLIGHT ON

▶ **The Choreographer** Martha Graham (1894–1991) was a dance legend who had immense impact on the world of choreography and dance performance. Her methods are routinely taught in studios all over the world and are part of the air every contemporary dancer breathes. At the age of 22, she found her destiny—dance; her mission "to chart the graph of the heart." She launched her own company when she was 35 and established the school of modern dance at Bennington College. She taught many movie actors and actresses as she turned out in rapid succession a decade-long series of dance dramas in the 1940s. Did she invent modern dance? No, but she came to represent it. Her reputation rests primarily on commissions to choreograph scores by such noted composers as Aaron Copland and Samuel Barber.

TECHNOLOGY/MEDIA LINK

4c **Notation Software** Have students use notation software to create their own arrangement of "Simple Gifts." Have students

- Set up the program for two staffs (one treble clef staff for the melody and one bass clef staff for a bass line) and choose the key of F (one flat).
- Use standard symbols to notate pitch in simple patterns.
- Notate the melody of "Simple Gifts" by selecting rhythmic values and then clicking on the staff to choose the pitch.
- Create a bass part on the bass staff by entering chord roots (see chord changes) with student-selected rhythms.

Tranparency Display the listening map transparency for *Variations on Simple Gifts* and have students listen and follow.

LESSON AT A GLANCE

Element Focus	**MELODY** Natural minor scale	
Skill Objective	**READING** Read and sing a song in natural minor	
Connection Activity	**SOCIAL STUDIES** Explore the relationship between music and historical events	

MATERIALS

- "Johnny Has Gone for a Soldier"　　　　　**CD 9-21**
  Recording Routine: Intro (8 m.); v. 1; interlude (2 m.); v. 2; interlude (2 m.); v. 3; coda
- Music Reading Practice, Sequence 19　　　**CD 9-23**
- Resource Book pp. D-25, E-20, H-16

VOCABULARY

scale	natural major	whole step
half step	interval	major scale

◆ ◆ ◆ ◆ National Standards ◆ ◆ ◆ ◆

1a Sing accurately in small ensembles
1c Sing music from diverse genres and from diverse cultures
2a Play instruments accurately alone
4c Compose, using electronic media
5b Sight read melodies in treble clef
5c Identify standard notation symbols for pitch
8b Identify ways music relates to social studies

MORE MUSIC CHOICES

For more practice with natural minor patterns:
"Old Abram Brown," p. 222
"Pat Works on the Railway, " p. 182
"Erie Canal," p. 262

1 INTRODUCE

Invite students to read the text on p. 188 about the song "Johnny Has Gone for a Soldier." See also Spotlight On below, for a discussion on the relationship between music and historical events.

A New Scale

Irish immigrants brought the melody of "Johnny Has Gone for a Soldier" to America. This version of the song comes from John Allison, whose family lived near Buttermilk Hill, on the west bank of the Hudson River, in New York. One of Allison's ancestors heard it sung as he marched with George Washington's army during the Revolutionary War.

Listen to "Johnny Has Gone for a Soldier" and notice the haunting quality of its melody.

 CD 9-21

Johnny Has Gone for a Soldier

Song of the American Revolution
Collected by John Allison

1. There I sat on But-ter-milk Hill, Who could blame me
2. Me oh my, I loved __ him so, Broke my heart to
3. I'll sell my flax, I'll sell __ my wheel, Buy my love a

cry my fill; And ev-'ry tear would __
see him go, And on-ly time will __
sword of steel, So it in bat-tle __

turn a mill; John-ny has gone for a sol-dier.
heal my woe; John-ny has gone for a sol-dier.
he may wield; John-ny has gone for a sol-dier.

 188 Reading Sequence 19

Footnotes

SPOTLIGHT ON

8b ▶ **The Song** "Johnny Has Gone for a Soldier" is a lovely melody that was brought to America by Irish immigrants. It is an old Irish folk tune associated with the years between 1691 and 1745, when the Irish were fighting with the French. This folk song was sung by sailors, lumberjacks, and colonists, all using their own versions. The melody was also sung during the Revolutionary War when Washington marched his soldiers near Buttermilk Hill on the west bank of the Hudson River.

BUILDING SKILLS THROUGH MUSIC

▶ **Writing** Have students read the information on p. 188 and sing the song "Johnny Has Gone for a Soldier." Share the information from Spotlight On with students. Ask them to write a brief paragraph about the relationship between music and historical events.

SKILLS REINFORCEMENT

2a ▶ **Keyboard** Students can play a left-handed broken-chord accompaniment for "Johnny Has Gone for a Soldier" based on the following chord positions:

Am:　Em:　C:　G:　F:

See Resource Book, p. H-16, for the complete left-hand accompaniment.

5b ▶ **Reading** See Resource Book, p. D-25, for a Music Reading Worksheet to accompany this lesson.

Relative Scales

You know that the notes from *do* to *do'* produce a scale called the diatonic major scale. The special sound of this scale comes from its pattern of whole steps and half steps. Let's learn a new scale, called the **natural minor scale.** It uses the same notes as the major scale, but they're arranged in a different pattern of whole steps and half steps.

> The **natural minor scale** is an arrangement of eight tones with a pattern of steps as follows: whole, half, whole, whole, half, whole, whole.

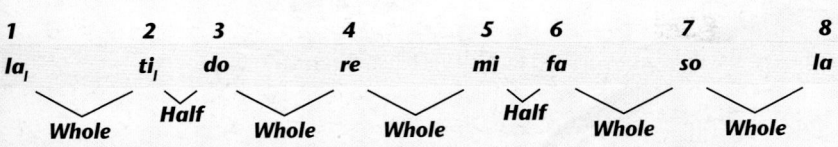

1	2	3	4	5	6	7	8
la,	ti,	do	re	mi	fa	so	la

Whole — Half — Whole — Whole — Half — Whole — Whole

Identify where the half steps occur. **Sing** the natural minor scale, using pitch syllables. Because its tonic is *la,* it sounds different.

la, ti, do re mi fa so la

Read and **sing** "Johnny Has Gone for a Soldier." How many pitches of the natural minor scale can you find in this melody?

2 DEVELOP

Singing

1c Have students sing "Johnny Has Gone for a Soldier" **CD 9-21** with the recording.

Reading

Have students read the text at the top of p. 189 and examine the natural-minor scale step pattern.

ASK Between which notes do half steps occur? (between *ti,* and *do* and *mi* and *fa*)

SAY This scale uses all the notes from *low la* to *la*. This pattern of whole and half steps is called the *natural minor* scale. *La* is its tonic, or home tone.

1a Have students sing the scale using numbers (*la,* = 1).

5c Have students read the remaining text on p. 189 and look at the staff notation of the scale.

SAY When A is *la,* the pattern of whole steps and half steps occurs naturally, because the steps between E and F, and B and C are half steps.

5c Have students read the A-minor scale with hand signs and using pitch syllables, numbers, and letter names.

For more practice reading the natural minor scale, refer to Music Reading Practice, Sequence 19 on p. 499 and Resource Book p. E-20.

3 CLOSE

Skill: READING   ASSESSMENT

1c **Performance/Observation** Have students read and sing "Johnny Has Gone for a Soldier," first with **5b** pitch syllables and hand signs and again using the lyrics.

Observe students' ability to accurately perform the notes of the natural minor scale found in the song.

ASK Does the melody use all the notes of the natural minor scale? (No, there is no *fa,* or F.)

ACROSS THE CURRICULUM

8b ▶ **Social Studies** Ask students to research information about American Revolutionary War soldiers. What was their average age? What were conditions like for these soldiers? How long did they serve during this war? What were some of the major battles during this war? What was the role of African Americans and Native Americans during the American Revolution?

For the little-known, important story of the contribution of over 5,000 African Americans who fought during this war, see *Come All You Brave Soldiers: Blacks in the Revolutionary War* by Clinton Cox (Scholastic, 1999).

TECHNOLOGY/MEDIA LINK

4c **Notation Software** Have students notate two natural minor **5c** scales, using quarter notes and beginning on the notes D (D-E-F-G-A-B♭-C-D) and E (E-F♯-G-A-B-C-D-E). Ask students to

- Describe the combination of whole steps and half steps used in each scale.
- Choose one of the scales and select the key signature corresponding to the scale's starting note.
- Set up four measures in a time signature of $\frac{4}{4}$.
- Compose a natural minor melody, using only the notes of the scale. (Begin and end on the first note of the scale.)
- Print the melody for classroom performance and discussion.

LESSON AT A GLANCE

Element Focus	**MELODY** Harmonic minor scale
Skill Objective	**READING** Read and sing from notation a song in harmonic minor
Connection Activity	**SOCIAL STUDIES** Explore the role of African American spirituals during the time of slavery

MATERIALS

- "Go Down, Moses" **CD 9-26**
  Recording Routine: Intro (4 m.); v. 1; refrain; interlude (2 m.); v. 2; refrain; interlude (2 m.); v. 1; refrain; coda
- Music Reading Practice, Sequence 20 **CD 9-28**
- *Sometimes I Feel Like a Motherless Child* **CD 9-33**
- **Resource Book** pp. B-15, D-27, E-21
- selected melodic percussion instruments

VOCABULARY

harmonic minor scale   accidental

◆ ◆ ◆ ◆ National Standards ◆ ◆ ◆ ◆

1a Sing accurately in small ensembles
1c Sing music from diverse cultures
2c Perform instrumental music from diverse cultures
5c Identify standard notations, symbols for pitch
6a Listen and describe events in music using appropriate terms
6b Listen and analyze uses of pitch and form in music from diverse cultures
6c Understand and use basic principles of intervals in music analysis
8b Identify ways music relates to social studies

MORE MUSIC CHOICES

For more practice with harmonic minor patterns:
"¡Que bonita bandera!" ("What a Beautiful Banner!") p. 294

MELODY IN MINOR

In the years before slavery was abolished in the United States, many slaves related the trials and tribulations of biblical heroes to their own suffering. The African American spiritual "Go Down, Moses" tells about the ancient Hebrews held captive in Pharaoh's Egypt. But the song also had its own meaning for those under the bondage of slavery in America.

Listen to "Go Down, Moses." How many times do you hear the phrase *Let my people go*?

Footnotes

ACROSS THE CURRICULUM

▶ **Language Arts** For more background information about the text of the African American spiritual "Go Down, Moses," encourage students to read *Moses in Egypt* by Lynne Reid Banks (Dreamworks, 1998). The book uses photos from the motion picture *The Prince of Egypt* to re-tell the story of Moses and the exodus of the Jews from Egypt.

BUILDING SKILLS THROUGH MUSIC

▶ **Social Studies** Invite students to sing "Go Down, Moses" **CD 9-26** and then discuss how parts of the text are emphasized. Have them identify instruments and voices heard on the recording. Lead students in a discussion of the techniques used by singers. Invite students to listen to *Sometimes I Feel Like a Motherless Child* **CD 9-33** and repeat the discussion. Have them compare the two songs and discuss why they think the songs are called spirituals.

SKILLS REINFORCEMENT

▶ **Recorder** Review with students the recorder fingering for G♯. Then have students play the simplified melody shown below during the response of each verse of "Go Down, Moses."

2c

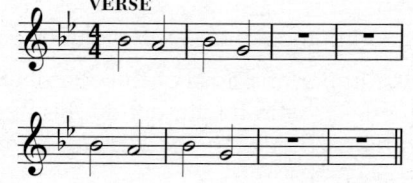

Steps and Skips

Sing the phrase *Let my people go* each time it occurs in the recording. Use hand signs and pitch syllables for the notes you know. (Hum the new note).

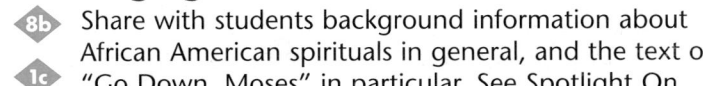

Now **analyze** the phrase by answering these questions.

• In what direction do the notes in this phrase move?

• How many *different* pitches did you sing?

• Where are the steps?

• Where are the skips?

The new note between *so* and *la* is called *si*. It is a half step higher than *so* and a half step lower than *la*. It shares a place on the staff with *so*, but you can tell them apart because *si* is always marked with an **accidental.**

Accidental signs are used to show altered pitches. The most common signs (which raise or lower a pitch by a half step) are sharps (♯), flats (♭), and naturals (♮).

Background photo: Replica of the nineteenth-century slave ship *Amistad*

▲ A family standing in front of the Civil Rights Memorial at the Southern Poverty Law Center, 1990

Unit 5 **191**

1 INTRODUCE

Sing short harmonic minor patterns, using a neutral syllable such as *loo*. Have students echo-sing each pattern on *loo* as a group and individually.

2 DEVELOP

Singing

8b Share with students background information about African American spirituals in general, and the text of

1c "Go Down, Moses" in particular. See Spotlight On, below, and on p. 192.

Then play the recording of "Go Down, Moses" **CD 9-26.** Have students listen and learn the melody by rote, then sing along when they are ready.

Draw students' attention to the phrase *Let my people go.*

6b **ASK How many times did you hear this phrase in each verse?** (two times)

How many times did you hear the phrase in the refrain? (one time)

Reading

1a Have students turn to p. 191 and

• Read the Steps and Skips text. Sing the pitch syllables for the phrase *Let my people go,* using the step diagram.

• Sing the phrase with hand signs, humming the missing note.

6c • Compare the missing note *(si)* to the other known notes.

ASK How does the missing note sound in relation to *so* and *la*? (It sounds higher than *so* and lower than *la*.)

continued on page 192

TEACHER TO TEACHER

▶ **Intervals** Once students have a firm knowledge of scale steps as whole and half steps (along with clear aural perception of the difference), intervals may be introduced. At this point, whole and half steps should be named as either major seconds or minor seconds; students should use the terms interchangeably. Introduction of the other intervals will follow later.

Students can then see that the interval from *fa* to *si* is still a second, because *si* is the next note in the scale; however, since it is even larger than a major second (three half steps away), it is called an augmented second.

SPOTLIGHT ON

8b ▶ **African American Spirituals** African American spirituals were learned by oral tradition because slaves were not allowed to learn to read or write. Spirituals often contained secret messages about the Underground Railroad. (See Cultural Connection, p. 26.) This "railroad" was a series of shelters for escaping slaves. Other spirituals expressed the longing of the slaves for freedom. After the Civil War, African American colleges and universities sent choirs on tours in the United States and Europe to sing spirituals, thus spreading their popularity. The most famous of these groups was the Fisk Jubilee Singers, from Fisk University in Nashville, Tennessee.

Unit 5 *Discovering New Musical Horizons* **191**

SAY The note between *so* and *la* is a half step away from each. This new note is called *si*. *Si* will always be marked with an accidental, or a sign used to show an altered pitch.

Demonstrate the hand sign for the new note *si*. Have students sing the phrase again, this time using *si*.

Reading

Have students read standard notation and

- Examine the step pattern shown on p. 192.
- Sing the known notes of the harmonic minor scale in G-*la,* using pitch syllables and hand signs. (You hum the note *si*.)
- Review that the hummed missing note is the new note *si*.

ASK Between what notes do half steps occur when *si* is in the scale? (between *ti_|* and *do*, *mi* and *fa,* and *si* and *la*)

SAY This scale uses all the notes from *low la* to *la*, but *si* is used instead of *so*. This pattern of whole and half steps makes up the harmonic minor scale. *La* is its tonic, or home tone; *la* is the first degree of the harmonic minor scale. Let's figure out what the other scale degrees are.

Have students

- Sing the complete scale, using pitch syllables and hand signs.
- Sing the scale in numbers (*la_|* = 1).

Divide the class in half; have one group sing pitch syllables while the other half sings numbers. Exchange parts. Remind students to demonstrate appropriate small-ensemble performance techniques.

For additional experience reading the harmonic minor scale, have students perform Music Reading Practice, Sequence 20 on p. 499 and Resource Book p. E-21.

A New Minor Scale

You have already learned that the notes from *low la* to *la* produce a scale called the *natural minor scale*. But when *si* replaces *so* in a minor scale, it makes a new scale — the **harmonic minor scale.**

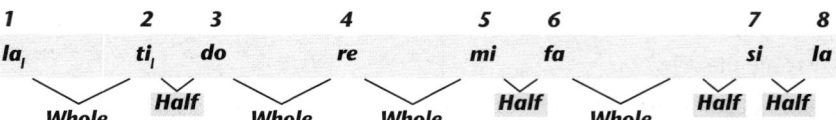

The **harmonic minor scale** is an arrangement of eight tones with a pattern of steps as follows: whole, half, whole, whole, half, whole + half, half.

Look at the pattern of whole and half steps in the harmonic minor scale. **Sing** the scale, using pitch syllables.

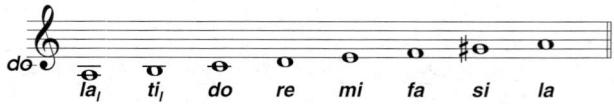

Step Up to the Staff

Look at the staff below. This is the harmonic minor scale, in A -*la*. We can also call it the A-minor scale. (Remember that *si* will always be marked with an accidental.)

Read and **sing** the scale, using pitch syllables and hand signs. Can you **identify** the note name of *si*?

Sing "Go Down, Moses." Then **identify** *si* each time it occurs in the music. (Its first appearance is shown in the color box.)

Group of freed slaves, 1862, who worked with the 13th Massachusetts Infantry Regiment during the American Civil War ▼

Footnotes

ACROSS THE CURRICULUM

▶ **Social Studies** For more information on the secret codes of the Underground Railroad and stories of men and women who risked their lives to help thousands of slaves find freedom, invite students to read *The Underground Railroad* by Raymond Bial (Houghton Mifflin Co., 1995).

SPOTLIGHT ON

 ▶ **Heroes** Throughout history humankind has had legends, heroes, and mystical figures that inspire folk songs. David, the shepherd boy, is celebrated for his courage in the face of the giant whom he slew with a single stone. He became King David. Daniel, an Israelite slave in Egypt, became a symbol of courage against the king when he disobeyed orders to eat certain foods that were forbidden by his religion. He was thrown into a den of lions, but was saved. Joshua, one of Israel's first generals, came to the city of Jericho, the home of a fierce nomad tribe known as the Amalekites. Jericho was surrounded by two walls. Joshua had his people march around the walls and "shout" at the walls. The walls came tumbling down. Moses led his people from the bonds of slavery, which was the inspiration for the African American spiritual "Go Down, Moses."

The Queen of Spiritual Singers

Listen to a performance of another African American spiritual that is based on the harmonic minor scale.

Sometimes I Feel Like a Motherless Child

African American Spiritual as performed by Mahalia Jackson

The African American civil rights leader and educator W. E. B. Du Bois (1868–1963) used the phrase "sorrow song" to describe emotionally poignant spirituals such as this.

MUSIC MAKERS
Mahalia Jackson

Mahalia Jackson (1912–1972) has been called "the true queen of spiritual singers." She was born in New Orleans, Louisiana, where, as a child, she sang in her father's church choir. A pioneer interpreter of gospel music, she insisted that gospel preceded jazz, affected jazz, and gave it inspiration and new forms. She sang only songs she believed in—positive anthems that reflected the spirit. The first gospel song she wrote and recorded was her personal statement: *I'm Going to Move on Up a Little Higher.* Her rich, deep contralto voice was one of the great voices of the century.

Jackson sang at the inauguration of President John F. Kennedy and for Dr. Martin Luther King Jr., when he delivered his "I Have a Dream" speech. She was inducted into the Rock and Roll Hall of Fame in 1997.

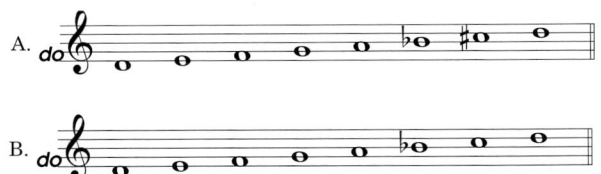
Show What You Know!

Using pitch syllables, **read** and **sing** each of these minor scales. Which scale is natural minor? Which one is harmonic minor?

A.

B.

Notating

5c Draw students' attention to the staff notation of the scale on p. 192 in their books.

Have students read the A-harmonic minor scale. Then write the G-harmonic minor scale on a staff. Have students sing the scale in pitch syllables and hand signs, with numbers, and with letter names.

Listening

Ask students to read about Mahalia Jackson in their books, p. 193. Then play the recording of *Sometimes I Feel Like a Motherless Child* **CD 9-33.**

ASK On what scale is this spiritual based? (harmonic minor)

6a Ask students to raise their hands when they hear the *si* in the melody.

3 CLOSE

Have students complete the Show What You Know activity on p. 193. See Resource Book, p. B-15, for the corresponding worksheet. (Scale A is harmonic minor; scale B is natural minor.)

 Skill: READING　　ASSESSMENT

1c **Performance/Observation** Have students

6c
- Look at "Go Down, Moses," on p. 190, once again.
- Find *do* on the staff, using the key signature (*do* = A).
- Find *low la* to discover the tonic (*la* = G).
- Read the song from staff notation, using pitch syllables and hand signs, letter names, and then the text.

Observe students' ability to sing the intervals accurately.

SKILLS REINFORCEMENT

5c ▶ **Reading** See Resource Book p. D-27 for Music Reading Worksheets to accompany this lesson. Worksheet activities **6c** include

- Singing the notes of the harmonic-minor scale, using a pitch ladder.
- Reading and notating harmonic-minor scales, starting on D and E.

TECHNOLOGY/MEDIA LINK

Video Library To reinforce the concept of call and response in "Go Down, Moses," show "Great Gettin' Up Morning" by the Albert McNeil Singers. Have students identify who is performing the call and who is performing the response, and notice whether the response stays the same or changes.

LESSON 8

LESSON AT A GLANCE

Element Focus	**MELODY** Pentatonic scale	
Skill Objective	**PLAYING** Read and perform from notation pentatonic patterns to accompany a song	
Connection Activity	**CULTURE** Discuss a historical figure taken from Chinese folklore, on which a folk song is based	

MATERIALS

- "Meng Jian Nu" (Mandarin) **CD 10-1**
- "Meng Jian Nu" (English) **CD 10-2**
  Recording Routine: Intro (4 m.); vocal; interlude (4 m.); vocal; coda
- **Pronunciation Practice/Translation** p. 530
- **Resource Book** p. A-21
- resonator bells, soprano/alto metallophones

VOCABULARY

pentatonic

◆ ◆ ◆ ◆ **National Standards** ◆ ◆ ◆ ◆

1c Sing music from diverse cultures
2a Play instruments accurately in small ensembles
6b Listen and analyze uses of pitch in music from diverse cultures
8b Identify ways music relates to social studies

MORE MUSIC CHOICES

For more experience with pentatonic scales:
"Yüe liang wan wan," p. 314

1 INTRODUCE

8b **SAY** Many folk songs tell a story about a person or event. These stories sometimes become folk legends. For example, many Chinese men participated in building the great Pacific railroad in the United States. To help endure the hardships, they would recall legends of their home country.

Searching For Scales

The song "Meng Jian Nu" is based on an old Chinese legend that tells the story of a devoted wife. Her husband, Wan Chi Liang, had gone away to help build the Great Wall. After many months with no word from him, Meng Jian Nu went to look for him. The song does not say if she ever found him.

Sing "Meng Jian Nu" and **listen** for the sound of a special five-tone scale.

CD 10-1

Meng Jian Nu

English Words by Alice Firgau

Folk Song from China

Zheng yu_____ mei_____ hua, shi xing_____
Blos - soms from cher - ries fall, Fra - grance fills ___ the

chung, _____ Jia jia _____ hu ___ hu
air; _____ Spring - time brings _ hap - pi - ness,

tian hon_____ deng, _____ Ran_____ jia
New Year __ with - out care. _____ But for me

zhang _____ fu _____ tuan _ yuan_____ ju, _____
there's _ no ___ spring, _ Sad - ness _ fills my heart. _____

Meng _ Jian Nu de___ zhang _ fu zou chan_____ cheng. _____
Wan _ Chi Liang has _ gone a - way And now we _ are _ a - part. _____

(194)

Footnotes

CULTURAL CONNECTION

▶ **Language** The official language of the People's Republic of China is Mandarin. Other languages are also spoken, but Mandarin is used in business, the media, education, and all printed and visual material. The sound of each syllable is the same in length and stress, because the language is based on tones rather than on accents. Each vowel sound has four different inflections (tones) that contribute to the meaning of a word.

BUILDING SKILLS THROUGH MUSIC

▶ **Writing** Have students locate words or phrases in the text of "Meng Jian Nu" that identify the season of the year. Have them discuss reasons for their choices. Ask students to identify important traditions, holidays, or seasonal changes associated with specific months. Assign students to work with a partner to write new lyrics that can be substituted for the text of the song.

SPOTLIGHT ON

8b ▶ **The Song** Meng Jian Nu was the eldest daughter of the Jian family and one of the most famous figures of Chinese folklore. The story is as old as the Great Wall itself, built in the third century B.C. Her legend inspired poets for centuries. It is sung in musical dramas as well as in folk songs in many dialects. One version consists of four verses, stating the sorrows for the four seasons; another has 12 verses, one for each month of the year.

Play a Pentatonic Scale

The melody of "Meng Jian Nu" is built on a pentatonic scale — a scale that consists of only five notes. For a review, line up bells to form a G-major scale. **Play** the scale. It is the diatonic major scale.

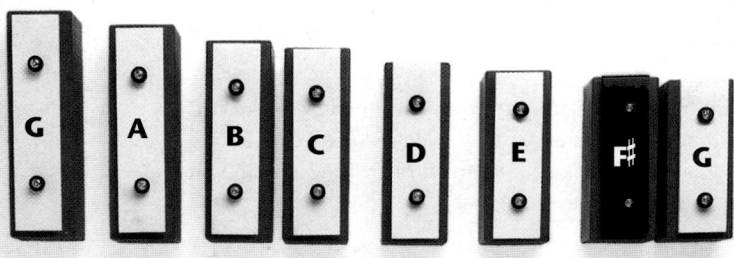

Now remove the bells for C, F♯, and the high G.

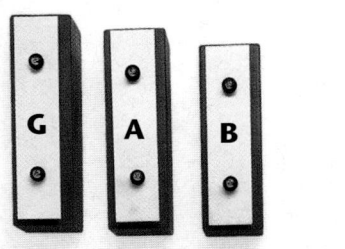 

Play the scale. It has a very different sound. The pentatonic scale is used in the folk music of many countries, not only in Asia, but in Europe and America as well. **Play** these pentatonic parts as others **sing** the song.

2 DEVELOP

Listening

Share the information in Spotlight On, p. 194. Then have students listen to the recording of "Meng Jian Nu" **CD 10-1.**

6b **SAY** Listen for the sound of a five-tone scale.

ASK Where have you heard this sound before? (Accept various answers.)

Singing

1c Have students listen to the Pronunciation Practice Track **CD 10-4.** (You may also wish to use Resource Book p. A-21.) Then have them sing the song along with the recording, first in Mandarin and then in English.

Playing

2a Have students read the text on p. 195. Review the diatonic scale and then play it on resonator bells. Then remove the bells for C, F♯, and low G and play this scale.

ASK What is the name of the scale that has only five notes? (pentatonic scale)

3 CLOSE

Reading

Have students practice playing the pentatonic parts on p. 195. (The metallophone will use D below *do.*)

Skill: PLAYING   ASSESSMENT

Performance/Observation Ask students to

2a • Set up a G-major scale and then play the scale.

• Remove the bells to make this a G-pentatonic scale, then play the scale.

1c • Play the parts on p. 195 while the class sings "Meng Jian Nu."

Observe students' ability to construct the G-pentatonic scale and perform the instrumental accompaniment.

SKILLS REINFORCEMENT

▶ **Playing** Have students play

2a • The melody of "Meng Jian Nu" on the recorder.

• The melodic rhythm on the woodblock.

• Finger cymbals on the fourth beat of each measure.

Invite students to use this ensemble to accompany the singing of "Meng Jian Nu."

TECHNOLOGY/MEDIA LINK

Web Site Go to *www.sfsuccessnet.com* for more information on the music of China and Taiwan.

LESSON AT A GLANCE

Element Focus **TIMBRE** String instruments

Skill Objective **LISTENING** Listen to and identify various string instruments

Connection Activity **CULTURE** Explore the cultural context of a variety of string instruments

MATERIALS

- Zither Montage — **CD 10-5**
- Keyboard Instrument Montage — **CD 10-6**
- Plucked String Montage — **CD 10-7**
- Eriskummainen kantele — **CD 10-8**
- selected melody instruments

VOCABULARY

zither	hammered dulcimer	koto
dan tranh	piano	clavichord
harpsichord	sitar	banjo
harp	guitar	lute
ud	kantele	

◆ ◆ ◆ ◆ National Standards ◆ ◆ ◆ ◆

1c Sing music from diverse cultures
2b Perform easy instrumental pieces
6b Listen and analyze uses of timbre in music from diverse cultures
8b Identify ways music relates to science and social studies

MORE MUSIC CHOICES

For more experience with string timbre:
"Cho'i hát bội" ("Crescent Moon"), p. 318
Julie-O, p. 311
Sindhi-Bhairavi, p. 320

A String of Strings

All cultures have string instruments. Most string instruments are plucked. Some are struck with mallets, and a few are bowed like the violin. String instruments differ greatly from one country to another. They are thought to have evolved from an early instrument that resembled a hunting bow.

One group of string instruments is the zither family. In zithers, the strings are stretched over one or more bridges. Instruments in this group include the Japanese *koto*, the Vietnamese *dan tranh*, and the hammered dulcimer.

The *koto* and the *dan tranh* are similar in structure, with both instruments having up to 17 strings.

Koto ▶

▲ Hammered Dulcimer

Listen to these zithers and **describe** the sound of each.

CD 10–5
Zither Montage

This montage features the hammered dulcimer, the *koto*, and the *dan tranh*.

(196)

Footnotes

TEACHER TO TEACHER

▶ **Instruments** Ask students to research more information on one of the instruments presented in this lesson. Provide questions such as the following for students to answer.

- How many strings does the instrument have?
- What is it made of?
- How is it similar to or different from other string instruments?

BUILDING SKILLS THROUGH MUSIC

▶ **Writing** Review the names and characteristics of instruments from the *Plucked String Montage* found on pp. 196-199. Distribute copies of the Semantic Map from Resource Book p. C-6. Have students label the center box "Plucked Strings" and the surrounding boxes with instrument names. Have them add facts about each instrument in the appropriate box. Lead students in a discussion of how the plucked-string instruments are similar and different.

ACROSS THE CURRICULUM

8b ▶ **Science** Instruments with vibrating strings are classified as chordophones. Instruments in this family have strings as the tone-producing element. These strings are always stretched between fixed points. Sounds are produced when the strings are plucked, struck, or scraped. String instruments are more recent than percussion and wind instruments. In pre-Columbian America before the sixteenth century, string instruments were virtually unknown. The number of strings on instruments of different cultures can range from one, like the *berimbau* of Brazil, to the 16-string Japanese *koto*, to the modern Western concert harp with 46 or 47 strings.

Keyboards

In the mid-1900s, musicians became interested in performing music from earlier eras on historic, or "period" instruments. This caused a revival of interest in the harpsichord.

Keyboard string instruments include the piano, clavichord, and harpsichord. The harpsichord was developed in the late 1400s and was the most widely used keyboard instrument until the piano was invented in the early 1700s.

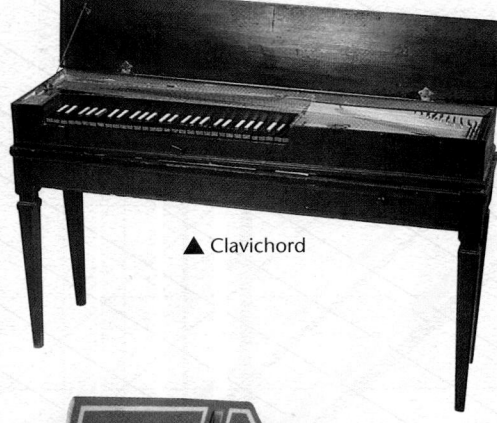
▲ Clavichord

▲ Harpsichord

Listen to these keyboard instruments and **compare** the sounds of each. What adjectives will you use?

 CD 10–6
Keyboard Instrument Montage

This montage highlights the piano, clavichord, and harpsichord.

▲ Piano

1 INTRODUCE

SAY Just as an artist uses different colors in a painting, a composer uses different instruments to express his or her musical ideas. Some instruments produce a bright sound while others are muted and soft. In this lesson you will explore the colors of various string instruments from different cultures.

For more information on string instruments, share with students Across the Curriculum, p. 196, and Cultural Connection below.

2 DEVELOP

Listening

Have students

- Look at the instruments on pp. 196–199.
- Notice the groupings: zither family, keyboard instruments, plucked strings, and the Finnish *kantele.*

ASK What string instruments are not pictured? (among others, traditional strings of the European or Western orchestra)

Which instruments on these pages are familiar to you and why? (Answers will vary.)

Ask students to

- Read about and listen to the sounds of the instruments in *Zither Montage* **CD 10-5**, p. 196 (hammered dulcimer, *koto*, and *dan tranh*).
- Describe the sound of each instrument.

Play *Keyboard Montage* **CD 10-6** (piano, clavichord, harpsichord) after the class reads the text on p. 197. Share with students the additional information on keyboard instruments in Spotlight On below.

ASK How would you describe the sounds of these instruments? (Answers will vary.)

continued on page 198

SPOTLIGHT ON

▶ **Keyboard Instruments** Keyboard instruments fall into two categories: those whose strings are struck, such as the clavichord and the piano, and those that are plucked, such as the harpsichord. The clavichord and piano are closely related to the hammered dulcimer and the harpsichord is related to the psaltery, an ancient instrument of the zither family, whose strings are plucked by the fingers or by plectra. The harpsichord has *jacks*, with *plectra* that pluck the strings. The piano has hammers that strike the strings when the piano keys are depressed.

When playing a piano, varying pressure on the keys and the use of the damper pedal produces louder and softer sounds. When playing the harpsichord, hand pressure does not affect the volume. Before the development of the modern piano in the nineteenth century, harpsichords were very popular.

CULTURAL CONNECTION

▶ **African Musical Bows** The most common string instruments in Africa are musical bows, including the following.

Earth Bow A flexible pole is stuck into the ground and is bent at an angle. At one end a string is attached and the loose end of the string is fastened to a piece of bark, wood, or stone. This is planted in a hole in the ground. The hole becomes a resonator, amplifying the sound when the string is plucked.

Mouth Bow A string is tightly tied to both ends of a flexible pole. Pulled into an arch shape, a bow is formed. The string is held in the mouth while being struck. The mouth cavity acts as a resonator.

Resonator-bow This is a kind of mouth bow, but in the middle a calabash resonator is attached.

Lesson 9 Continued

How might you compare and contrast the sounds? (Encourage students to describe similarities and differences.)

Next, have students read about and listen to *Plucked String Montage* **CD 10-7**, p. 198 *(sitar, banjo, harp, guitar, lute, ud)*. Point out that these instruments are played by plucking the strings.

ASK With which instruments are you familiar? (Most students are familiar with harp and guitar.)

At this point, share the information about the banjo and harp. See Cultural Connection below and Spotlight On, p. 199.

 ASK How did you become familiar with these instruments? (Answers will vary.)

Have students listen to *Plucked String Montage* again and

- Describe the sound of each instrument using standard terminology.
- Analyze why the instruments sound different. (Remind students that plucking or striking a string will produce different sounds.)

For additional listening experiences with the harp, harpsichord, and *koto* play **CD 21-36**, **CD 21-35**, and **CD 21-38**. Students may also read detailed descriptions of the instruments on p. 516 in the Sound Bank.

Singing

 Have students sing the traditional Finnish Kalevala melody, p. 199, first on a neutral syllable and then with letter names or numbers. (Note the $\frac{5}{4}$ meter.)

Strings Are for Picking

Harps and lyres are played by plucking the strings.

Other plucked instruments include the *sitar* of India, banjos, guitars, lutes, and the Arabic instrument called the *ud*.

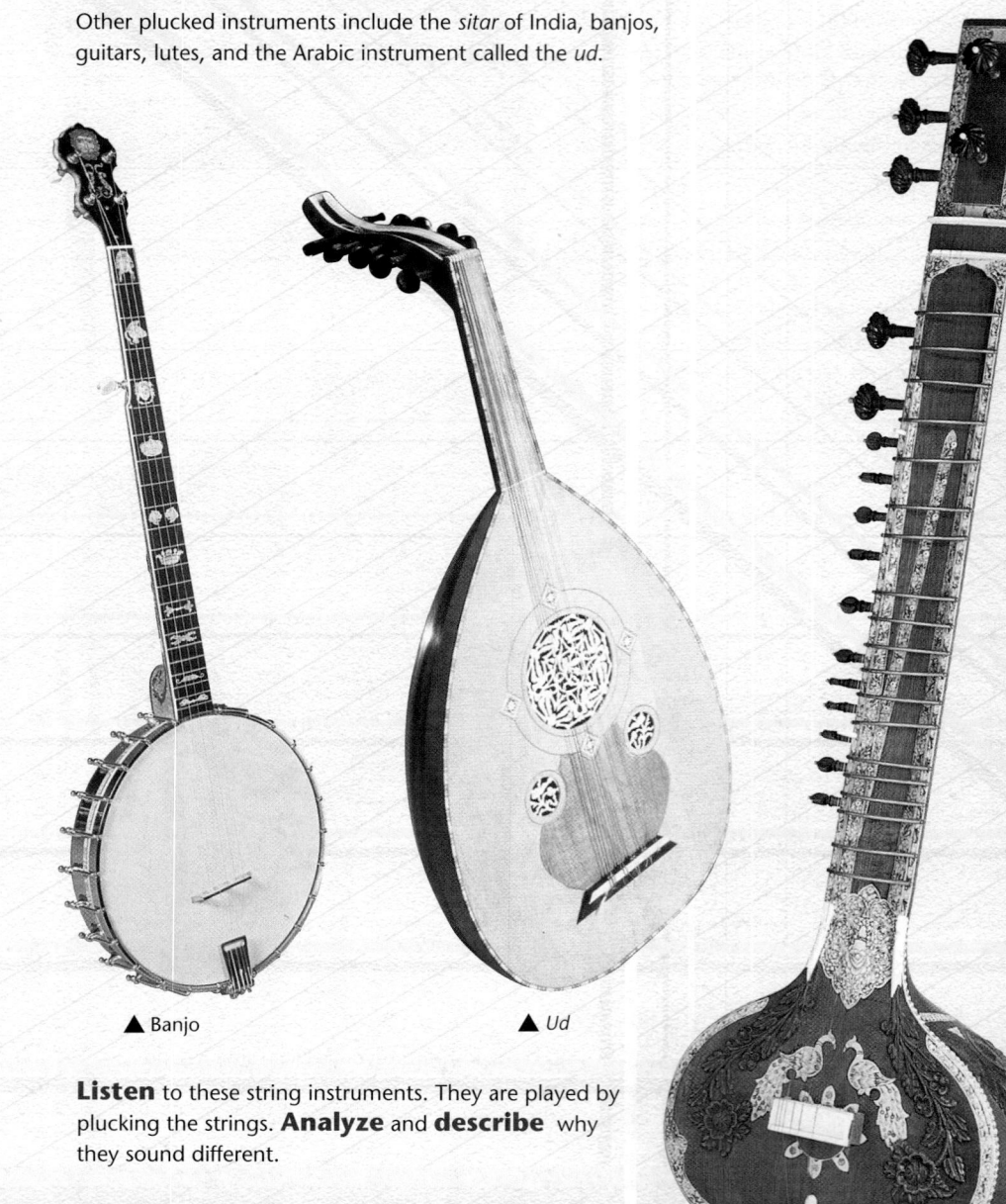

▲ Banjo   ▲ Ud

Listen to these string instruments. They are played by plucking the strings. **Analyze** and **describe** why they sound different.

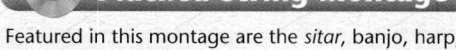 **CD 10–7**
Plucked String Montage

Featured in this montage are the *sitar*, banjo, harp, guitar, lute, and *ud*.

▲ Sitar

 198

Footnotes

CULTURAL CONNECTION

 ▶ **An African American Instrument** A type of banjo was brought to the United States by enslaved Africans in the seventeenth century. (A possible ancestor is the *bania* [BAHN-yah], a similar instrument found in West Africa.) The modern banjo has a long, fretted neck, five steel strings, and a calfskin or plastic soundbox stretched over a hoop, or rim. The strings are picked with the fingers or brushed with the nails. Once popularized by minstrel shows in the nineteenth century and jazz bands in the twentieth century, the banjo is now mainly associated with bluegrass and other folk music.

ACROSS THE CURRICULUM

▶ **Language Arts** Students will enjoy an unusually interesting and highly interactive book, *Musical Instruments: From Flutes Carved of Bone, to Lutes, to Modern Electric Guitars* (Scholastic Voyages of Discovery: Music and Performing Arts) (Scholastic Trade, 1994). The book is designed somewhat like an interactive CD-ROM that allows readers to explore and discover the history of a wide variety of musical instruments related to the art of the period or culture. Interesting strobe photographs are included to show musicians in actions demonstrating many instruments.

Finnish Strings

The *kantele* is a small string instrument used for hundreds of years in Finland and still used today. The traditional *kantele* has five strings that are plucked. The modern version has 12 to 46 metal strings. The *kantele* is a national symbol of Finland.

Other instruments with four to six strings that are plucked are the psaltery and the lap dulcimer. If you have one of these instruments in your classroom, you can play this beautiful folk melody.

◀ Finnish girl playing the *kantele*

Traditional Kalevala Melody from Finland

Listen to the lyrical sound of Finnish *kanteles* as they accompany a solo singer in this selection.

CD 10–8
 **Eriskummainen kantele**

by Kurki-Suonio
as performed by Loituma
The English title of this selection is *The Peculiar Kantele*. Both five-string and ten-string *kanteles* are heard in this performance.

Playing

2b Have students play the traditional Finnish Kalevala melody on xylophones, glockenspiels, resonator bells, or keyboard.

Listening

Ask students to

- Read the text on p. 199 in their books.
- Identify aurally-presented exerpts of music representing diverse cultures. Recognize the sound of the *kantele* as they listen to *Eriskummainen kantele* **CD 10-8**, a folk song from Finland.

3 CLOSE

Element: TIMBRE   **ASSESSMENT**

6b **Music Journal Writing** To assess students' understanding of timbre in string instruments, have them

- Review the photos and descriptions of string instruments in this lesson.
- Listen to excerpts of the string instruments, in random order.
- Distinguish among a variety of musical timbres. Write in their journals the names of the instruments and a short description of each as they listen.
- Choose partners and compare answers.

SPOTLIGHT ON

▶ **The Harp** The harp is an ancient instrument. According to some references, harps in some form existed in every age of human history. It was popular in ancient Greece and Rome.

The harp is one of the musical instruments adopted by a country as a national symbol. At one time it appeared in the British flag to represent Ireland. Welsh bards were famous harpists. Every noble household had a harp that was handed down through the generations. Many families boasted about their harpist or family of harpists. In England in the early Victorian days, a refined family would always have someone who could play flute, and another family member would usually accompany that person on the harp.

TECHNOLOGY/MEDIA LINK

Web Site To learn more about different string instruments from around the world, visit *www.sfsuccessnet.com*.

LESSON AT A GLANCE

Element Focus	**TEXTURE/HARMONY** I and V_7 chords
Skill Objective	**PLAYING** Play a I–V_7 chord accompaniment
Connection Activity	**CULTURE** Associate calypso style with specific cultures of the Caribbean

MATERIALS

- "Mango Walk"   **CD 10-9**
  Recording Routine: Intro (4 m.); vocal; instrumental; vocal; coda
- *Jamaican Rumba*   **CD 10-11**
- **Resource Book** p. F-26
- claves, maracas, cowbell
- classroom melody instruments

VOCABULARY

accompaniment   harmony

◆ ◆ ◆ **National Standards** ◆ ◆ ◆ ◆

1c Sing music from diverse cultures
2c Perform instrumental music from diverse cultures
4c Compose, using electronic media
6b Listen and analyze uses of harmony and timbre in music from diverse cultures
6c Understand and use basic principles of chords in music analysis
9a Describe characteristics of music styles from a variety of cultures

MORE MUSIC CHOICES

For more practice playing the I and V_7 chords:
"Day-O!" p. 18

1 INTRODUCE

Show students a map of the Caribbean to locate the island of Jamaica. Tell them calypso originated in Jamaica and "Mango Walk" is a typical calypso song. Share with students the information in Cultural Connection below.

Calypso Walk

Do you know where Jamaica is? You'll find this beautiful island in the Caribbean Sea. Jamaican musicians have given us a great deal of lively, danceable music. Some musicians, such as Bob Marley and his son, Ziggy, have achieved international fame.

This Jamaican calypso song can be accompanied by two chords: I and V_7. **Listen** to "Mango Walk" and **identify** the chord changes. Follow the chord symbols above the music as you listen.

CD 10–9

Mango Walk

s, t @ r m f s l

Calypso Song from Jamaica

$C_7(V_7)$ ... $F(I)$
My bro-ther did-a tell me that you go man-go walk,

$C_7(V_7)$ ... $F(I)$
You go man-go walk, you go man-go walk.

$C_7(V_7)$ ... $F(I)$
My bro-ther did-a tell me that you go man-go walk

$C_7(V_7)$ ... $F(I)$
And steal all the num-ber 'lev-en.

200

Footnotes

ACROSS THE CURRICULUM

▶ **Language Arts** Students will discover many things about the people, land, customs, and traditions of Jamaica in *Under the Breadfruit Tree: Island Poems* by Monica Gunning (Boyds Mills, 1998). These poems are written from the perspective of a Jamaican girl, the author, who grew up surrounded by many colorful family members and friends in this island culture.

BUILDING SKILLS THROUGH MUSIC

▶ **Social Studies** Echo-clap selected rhythm patterns from "Mango Walk," "Day-O!" (p. 18), and "Hosanna, Me Build a House" (p. 132). Ask students to identify songs that include some of the rhythm patterns clapped. List class suggestions on the board. Have students determine which songs from their list originated in the islands of the Caribbean Sea. Discuss other characteristics that are common to songs listed.

CULTURAL CONNECTION

9a ▶ **Calypso Style** Calypso is a song style usually associated with Carnival in Jamaica, Trinidad, and other islands in the Caribbean. One unique aspect of a calypso song is the lyrics. Calypso lyrics are usually invented words that may have no literal meaning, but serve an aesthetic function within the calypso. The text helps the song flow more smoothly, with only moderate regard for content or conventional sense. The singer may give special significance to these made-up words that are understood within the cultural community, but may not be understood elsewhere. New texts are set to familiar melodies every year and become an important part of the Carnival celebration.

Chords to Play

Play the F (I) and C₇ (V₇) chords on the marimba or other mallet instruments.

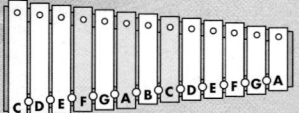 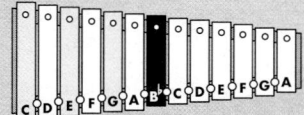

Use these chords to accompany "Mango Walk." **Play** a chord on the first beat of each measure. Which chord will you play first? When do you change chords? By accompanying the melody of "Mango Walk" with chords, you create a thicker texture. Next, **play** the following rhythm accompaniment with the chord accompaniment.

Sing "Mango Walk" with the chord and rhythm accompaniment.

Ready to Rumba

Arthur Benjamin borrowed the melody of "Mango Walk" for his composition *Jamaican Rumba*. **Listen** for the texture and chord changes.

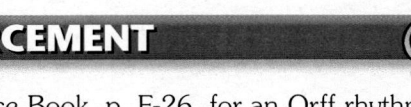
CD 10–11
Jamaican Rumba

by Arthur Benjamin
as performed by the Cleveland Pops Orchestra
Much of the music of this composer was influenced by the sounds and rhythms of Latin America and the West Indies.

Unit 5   **201**

---

2 DEVELOP

Listening

1c **6b** Invite students to follow the music in their books as they listen to "Mango Walk" **CD 10-9.** Ask them to raise their hands each time the chords change. Then have them sing the song.

Reading

6c **SAY** Look at the notation to determine the key of the song (F) and the chords used to harmonize the song. (F and C₇) In the key of F, the F chord is I and the C₇ chord is V₇.

Playing

2c Have students

- Read the information at the top of p. 201.
- Play the chordal accompaniment while the rest of the class sings the song.

SAY Accompanying a melody with chords creates homophonic texture. Now add the rhythmic accompaniment on p. 201.

Listening

6b Play *Jamaican Rumba* **CD 10-11.**

ASK **What instrument plays the melody?** (a viola)

What is the texture? (homophonic)

What melodies did you hear? ("Mango Walk" and a new melody)

3 CLOSE

Skill: PLAYING **ASSESSMENT**

1c **2c** **Performance/Self-Assessment** Have students sing "Mango Walk" while accompanying the song with the F (I) and C₇ (V₇) chords on resonator bells or hand chimes. Invite students to apply criteria to evaluate their performance and make suggestions for improvement.

SKILLS REINFORCEMENT

2c ▶ **Mallets** See Resource Book, p. F-26, for an Orff rhythm and mallet accompaniment for "Mango Walk."

TECHNOLOGY/MEDIA LINK

4c **CD-ROM** To build a Caribbean accompaniment for "Mango Walk" using *Band-in-a-Box,* have students

- Set the key to F major, chorus to end after 8, total choruses to 1, and uncheck "Overall Loop."
- Type C₇ at the beginning of mm. 1, 3, 5, and 7. Type F at the beginning of mm. 2, 4, 6, and 8.
- Under the song menu, generate a two-bar ending.
- Select a Caribbean style from the style menu.
- Under the edit menu, generate an introduction.
- Click play to hear the accompaniment and then perform chords to a steady beat using classroom instruments.

LESSON AT A GLANCE

Element Focus **TEXTURE/HARMONY** I and IV chords

Skill Objective **SINGING** Sing a song with I and IV chords

Connection Activity **SOCIAL STUDIES** Discuss the Imbabura region of Ecuador

MATERIALS

- "Imbabura" (Spanish) **CD 10-12**
- "Imbabura" (English) **CD 10-13**
  Recording Routine: Intro (8 m.); v. 1; v. 2; v. 3; interlude (8 m.); v. 4; coda
- **Pronunciation Practice/Translation** p. 531
- **Resource Book** p. A-22
- keyboard or Autoharp

VOCABULARY

chord interlude

◆ ◆ ◆ ◆ **National Standards** ◆ ◆ ◆ ◆

1a Sing accurately in small ensembles
1c Sing music from diverse cultures
2a Play instruments accurately in small ensembles
6c Understand and use basic principles of chores in music analysis
8b Identify ways music relates to social studies

MORE MUSIC CHOICES

For more experience with music from South America:
"*Pollerita*," p. 151
"*Amores hallarás*," p. 153
"*Viva Jujuy*," p. 228

1 INTRODUCE

Invite students to read the text on p. 202 about the Ecuadorian province of Imbabura. Lead students in a discussion about this region. Share Cultural Connection, below with them.

Nothing More Than I and IV

Imbabura

ECUADOR

PERU

Imbabura, a province in the South American country of Ecuador, is known for its beautiful lakes and mountains. The province is home to several volcanoes. The Pan-American Highway takes tourists through this beautiful area of the country. The song "Imbabura" praises the beauty of this area of South America.

Listen to "Imbabura." Notice the harmony uses only two chords: I and IV.

Sing "Imbabura." Then, **perform** an accompaniment to the song on keyboard, using the C (I) and F (IV) chords, as shown in the music.

C(I)   F(IV)

202

Footnotes

CULTURAL CONNECTION

8b ▶ **Imbabura** "Imbabura" is sung by the people from Otavalo, Ecuador, known for its huge handicraft market. Otavaleños play intricate rhythms on 10-stringed guitars called *charangos*. They play melodies on panpipes and flutes and sing songs in both Spanish and the indigenous language, Quichua. The flutes and panpipes were originally made of bamboo, but many Ecuadorians today use plastic tubes since they last longer and the sound quality is just as good.

BUILDING SKILLS THROUGH MUSIC

▶ **Language** Have students locate Ecuador on a world map and describe its geographic features. Invite students to listen to **CD 10-13** and follow the English text for "Imbabura" to locate phrases that tell how the singer feels about the area. Select individual students to identify phrases that explain the reason for each.

MOVEMENT

6c ▶ **Nonlocomotor Movement** As students sing or listen to "Imbabura" have them perform the following hand jive routine to illustrate the I-IV chord progression. The jive will also help reinforce the triple meter of the song.

C (I)

	Pat	Clap	Raise index finger
(beats)	1	2	3

F (IV)

	Pat	Clap	Raise index finger
(beats)	1	2	3

Imbabura

CD 10–12

English Words by Don Kalbach

Folk Song from Ecuador

do

1.,4. Im - ba - bu - ra de mi vi - da, tú se - rás la
1.,4. Im - ba - bu - ra, sing your prais - es, You're the best of

pre - fe - ri - da, por - que a to - dos das al - ber - gue
all the plac - es, For your shel - ter free - ly giv - en,

co - mo si fue - ran tus hi - jos.
As if we were all your chil - dren.

Fine

2. To - dos los e - cua - to - ria - nos te de - di - ca -
3. De mi co - ra - zón la due - ña has de ser, Im -
2. All the Ec - ua - do - rians love you, And they sing their
3. You have won my heart for - ev - er; It is yours, Im -

mos can - cio - nes pa - ra tus her - mo - sos
ba - bu - re - ña, por - que yo ad - mi - ro tus
prais - es of you, For the beau - ty of your
ba - bu - re - ña, For I love your lakes and

1.   2. *D.C. al Fine*

la - gos, que nos brin - dan sus ha - la - gos.
pren - das, tus mu - jé - res y tus
wa - ters, And de - lights that they have brought us.
wa - ters, And your peo - ple and your flo - res.
                                                    flow - ers.

Unit 5   **203**

2 DEVELOP

Listening

Invite students to listen to "Imbabura" **CD 10-12**.

SAY As you listen to "Imbabura," determine how many different chords are used to accompany the song.

Have students listen to the song again and raise their right hand when they hear the I chord and raise their left hand when they hear the IV chord.

Singing

Invite students to sing "Imbabura" **CD 10-13** in English with the recording. Then have students listen to the Pronunciation Practice Track **CD 10-15** and use Resource Book, p. A-22, to learn the Spanish words. Encourage them to sing the song in Spanish with the recording.

Playing

Help students

- Discover that the two chords used to accompany the song are the C chord (C-E-G) and the F chord (F-A-C).
- Play C and F chords on keyboard or Autoharp.

Organize the class into two different groups: a C chord group and F chord group.

Encourage students to accompany the song by playing the appropriate chords on the first beat of each measure.

3 CLOSE

Element: TEXTURE/HARMONY   ASSESSMENT

Performance/Observation Divide the class into groups of six. Have each group prepare a formal performance of "Imbabura," singing and playing a C and F chordal accompaniment. Assess students' ability to play and change chords at the same time and to demonstrate appropriate small-ensemble performance techniques. These same techniques should be used in formal concerts.

SKILLS REINFORCEMENT

▶ **Playing** Use the following teaching strategies to help students of varying skill levels perform keyboard accompaniments.

Reinforcement Some students may have difficulty accompanying the song using the keyboard chords. Allow these students to play only the root of the chord with the hand of their choice.

On Target Most students will be able to accompany the song using the I and IV chords. If this is still difficult, have these students keep their thumb on C and move their fifth finger from G to A as the chord progression changes.

Challenge Those students who easily master this lesson may be asked to play the melody of the song while others play the accompaniment or play the melody with the progression changes.

TECHNOLOGY/MEDIA LINK

CD-ROM After discussing I and IV chords with students, reinforce the sound of the chord functions by having students enter their own eight-measure chord progressions into *Band-in-a-Box.* Instruct them to begin and end with a I chord. Encourage students to sing chord roots as the program plays back the chord progression.

LESSON AT A GLANCE

Element Focus   TEXTURE/HARMONY   I, IV, and V_7 chords

Skill Objective   PLAYING   Play an accompaniment using the I, IV, and V_7 chords

Connection Activity   STYLE   Discover that I, IV, and V_7 chords were popular with early rock 'n' roll musicians

MATERIALS

• "Yakety Yak"   **CD 10-17**

     Recording Routine: Intro (2 m.); v. 1; v. 2; v. 3; instrumental; v. 4; coda

• *Yakety Yak*   **CD 10-16**

• keyboards, xylophones

VOCABULARY

chord   harmony   accompaniment

◆ ◆ ◆ ◆ National Standards ◆ ◆ ◆ ◆

1a   Sing accurately in small ensembles

1c   Sing music from diverse genres

2c   Perform instrumental music from diverse genres

3a   Improvise simple harmonic accompaniments

6b   Listen and analyze uses of timbre and texture in music from diverse genres

6c   Understand and use basic principles of chords in music analysis

9a   Describe characteristics of music genres from a variety of cultures

MORE MUSIC CHOICES

For more practice with I, IV, and V_7 chords: "Linstead Market," p. 241

1 INTRODUCE

9a   Play "Yakety Yak" **CD 10-17**, and tell students that it is harmonized with I, IV, and V_7 chords. Stress the fact that these chords were popular with many early rock 'n' roll musicians. Invite students to read the information on p. 204 and share Spotlight On with them.

Too Much Talk

Rock 'n' roll, one of the most enduring styles in popular music, began in the 1950s. This music was usually accompanied by electric guitars and keyboards and had a driving percussion beat. Rock harmony was—and remains—simple, usually including only three basic chords: I, IV, and V_7.

Sing "Yakety Yak," an early rock 'n' roll hit. **Play** the C (I), F (IV), and G_7 (V_7) chords on keyboard or guitar to accompany the melody. The chord symbols in the music will tell you when to change chords.

M·U·S·I·C   M·A·K·E·R·S

The Coasters

The Coasters was a band that became very popular in the late 1950s. Using humor and upbeat rhythms, the group sang its way into the hearts of American teenagers. In 1957 the Coasters reached number one on the rhythm and blues charts with their hit songs *Searchin'* and *Young Blood*. Their other classics include *Charlie Brown*, *Poison Ivy*, and *Yakety Yak*. In 1987 they were inducted into the Rock and Roll Hall of Fame.

Listen to the "original artist" recording of *Yakety Yak*.

   **CD 10–16**
       Yakety Yak

by Jerry Leiber and Mike Stoller as performed by the Coasters

204

Footnotes

SPOTLIGHT ON

▶ **The Composer and Lyricist** Jerry Leiber (b. 1933) and Mike Stoller (b. 1933) composed some of the most spirited and enduring rock 'n' roll hit songs. The pair teamed as songwriters shortly after they met in Los Angeles in 1950. Leiber wrote the lyrics and Stoller composed the music. Elvis Presley and other rock stars recorded their songs. The talented team was inducted into the Rock and Roll Hall of Fame in 1987. "Stand By Me," another big hit composed by the duo, is on p. 46.

BUILDING SKILLS THROUGH MUSIC

▶ **Social Studies** Ask students to read the term "rock 'n' roll" and tell what they know about it. List their responses on the board. Invite students to listen to *Yakety Yak* **CD 10-16** and describe how the music reflects the suggestion list and information found in their books.

SKILLS REINFORCEMENT

1a   ▶ **Singing** Encourage students to sing the chord roots by letter name while playing the chords with the recording of "Yakety Yak." Later, invite students to substitute *doo* or another neutral syllable for the chord roots. When students are secure singing the roots on a neutral syllable, challenge them to sing the lyrics of the song on the roots of the chords. This technique will help them learn to harmonize by ear. Some students may carry this ability into their adult life whenever they sing certain style songs in harmony.

Yakety Yak

s l t d

Words and Music by Jerry Leiber and Mike Stoller

CD 10–17

1. Take out the pa - pers and the trash,
2. Just fin - ish clean - ing up your room.

Or you don't get no spend - ing cash.
Let's see that dust fly with that broom.

If you don't scrub that kitch - en floor,
Get all that gar - bage out of sight,

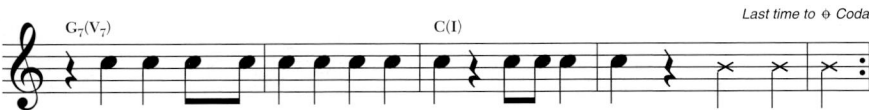

Last time to ⊕ Coda

You ain't gon - na rock 'n' roll no more. Yak-et-y Yak! *(Spoken) Don't talk back.*
Or you don't _ go out Fri-day night.

⊕ *Coda* 3

Yak - et - y Yak! *(Spoken) Don't talk back.*

3. You just put on your coat and hat.
   And walk yourself to the Laundromat.
   And when you finish doing that,
   Bring in the dog and put out the cat . . .

4. Don't you give me no dirty looks.
   Your father's hip; he knows what cooks.
   Just tell your hoodlum friends outside,
   You ain't got time to take a ride . . .

Backup

Many rock groups have backup singers that provide harmony.

Perform a backup vocal accompaniment for "Yakety Yak."

Unit 5 **205**

---

2 DEVELOP

Singing

 Help students follow the routine of the song. Then have them sing the song with the recording **CD 10-17**.

Playing

Divide the class into three groups. Ask students to find the I (C), IV (F), and V₇ (G₇) chords in the song and identify the notes used in each chord. Have each group play one note in each chord on xylophones or keyboards.

Have students

- Determine which notes of the C, F, and G₇ chords they will play.

- Practice playing the chords, then play the chords on the first beat of each measure while they sing the song with the recording.

Listening

Have students listen to the original artist recording of *Yakety Yak* **CD 10-16** and compare this performance to the version they played. Ask students which version they preferred and to use musical terms to explain why.

Improvising

Have students improvise a backup vocal accompaniment for "Yakety Yak" using the I, IV, and V₇ chords. Have them sing on a neutral syllable the chord tones they played earlier.

3 CLOSE

Skill: PLAYING   **ASSESSMENT**

Performance/Peer Critique Have small groups of students perform an instrumental accompaniment for "Yakety Yak" as the rest of the class sings.

Invite students to assess each group's accuracy in playing three-chord harmonic accompaniment. Guide students in providing meaningful and respectful evaluation of performances.

ACROSS THE CURRICULUM

▶ **Language Arts** Encourage students to create a dramatized narration to pair in performance with the song "Yakety Yak." Make class lists of "Things We Hate to Hear from Our Parents" and "Things We Most Like to Hear from Our Parents." Select students to read or dramatize scenes from both lists to provide drama and comedy as needed.

SCHOOL TO HOME CONNECTION

▶ **Interviews** Encourage students to ask older family members what their parents used to nag them about! Use these ideas as part of an amusing dramatic narration entitled "Some Things Never Change!"

TECHNOLOGY/MEDIA LINK

 Electronic Keyboard Have students use the auto-accompaniment feature of a MIDI keyboard to accompany "Yakety Yak" in a rock 'n' roll style. As one student presses the key for each chord root, the keyboard will generate rhythmic and harmonic patterns. Others may play block chords on the beat or improvised harmonic patterns.

WHAT DO YOU KNOW?

MATERIALS
• **Resource Book** p. B-16

Have students read and answer the questions independently and then check their answers with a partner before sharing answers with the rest of the class.

For a more formal assessment, duplicate the Unit 5 assessment worksheet and have students work independently or in small groups to complete it. The worksheet is found on Resource Book p. B-16.

WHAT DO YOU HEAR?

MATERIALS
• *What Do You Hear? 5A*   **CD 10-19**
• **Resource Book** p. B-16

Review the differences between $\frac{4}{4}$, $\frac{2}{4}$, and $\frac{6}{8}$. If possible, give examples of each meter. Then have students work with a partner to identify the meter of each selection on the recording.

MATERIALS
• *What Do You Hear? 5B*   **CD 10-22**
• **Resource Book** p. B-16

Ask students to name three techniques that are used when playing string instruments. (bowing, plucking, striking) Give an example of each and tell when each would be used. Then invite students to work with a partner to identify the musical examples.

What Do You Know?

Fill in the Blanks

1. A mark that indicates to sing or play a note with more emphasis than the other notes is called _____.

    a. a tie   **b.** a slur   **c.** an accent

2. A musical form in which each section is a modification of the initial theme is called _____.

    a. verse and refrain   **b.** solo and chorus   **c.** theme and variations

3. The arrangement of eight tones with a step pattern of whole, half, whole, whole, half, whole, whole is a _____ scale.

    a. diatonic   **b.** major   **c.** natural minor

What Do You Hear? 5A

 CD 10–19

Listen to the following musical excerpts as you conduct the meter. Identify the meter of each selection and point to your answer.

1. $\frac{4}{4}$ meter $\frac{6}{8}$ meter
2. $\frac{6}{8}$ meter $\frac{2}{4}$ meter
3. $\frac{6}{8}$ meter $\frac{4}{4}$ meter

What Do You Hear? 5B

 CD 10–22

Listen to the following musical excerpts of string instruments and identify whether the instrument you hear is plucked, bowed, or struck.

1. plucked   bowed   struck
2. plucked   bowed   struck
3. plucked   bowed   struck

206

Footnotes

ANSWER KEY

▶ **What Do You Know?**

1. c. (an accent)
2. c. (theme and variations)
3. c. (natural minor)

▶ **What Do You Hear? 5A**

1. $\frac{4}{4}$ meter—*When the Saints Go Marching In*

2. $\frac{2}{4}$ meter—*Give My Regards to Broadway*

3. $\frac{6}{8}$ meter—*When Johnny Comes Marching Home*

▶ **What Do You Hear? 5B**

1. plucked (violin)
2. bowed (cello)
3. struck (double bass)

Perform, Create

What You Can Do

Play Chords

As the group sings "Mango Walk," page 200, accompany the singers on Autoharp or keyboard. Be sure to play the I and V₇ chords at the appropriate time.

Create a Melodic Poem

- Read the poem *Who Has Seen the Wind?* by Christina Rossetti.

Who Has Seen the Wind?

by Christina Rossetti

Who has seen the wind?

Neither I nor you:

But when the leaves hang trembling,

The wind is passing through.

Who has seen the wind?

Neither you nor I;

But when the leaves bow down their heads,

The wind is passing by.

- Work together in two groups to create a melody. Group 1 should create a melody in C major, ending on C, to accompany lines 1–4 of the poem. Group 2 should create a melody in A minor, ending on A, to accompany lines 5–8.
- Play and sing your melodies for the other groups. Review each performance. Which melody did you like best and why? How could you improve it?

WHAT YOU CAN DO

MATERIALS
- "Mango Walk," p. 200   CD 10-9
- "Who Has Seen the Wind?," p. 207 (poem)
- **Resource Book** p. B-17
- Autoharp or keyboard

Play Chords

Invite the class to sing "Mango Walk" on p. 200. Tell them that it is easy to accompany this piece because there are only two chords to learn: I and V₇. Explain how the two chords are developed from the F-major scale. Give each student an Autoharp or a keyboard, and invite the players to practice the two chords until they can switch between them easily. Then, while students sing, ask them to play the correct chord on the first beat of each measure.

Create a Melodic Poem

Tell students that many professional composers set poetry to music. Ask them to read aloud "Who Has Seen the Wind?" by Christina Rossetti, on p. 207. Ask them what words they think are important. Encourage them to bring out the meaning of these words in their music. Invite students also to notice what syllables are stressed. Tell them that a stressed syllable must fall on the accented beat of the measure.

Arrange the class in two groups. Have one group write the composition in a major key and the second group in a minor key. Allow students to participate in the group of their choice. If time allows, have students do an individual composition. Encourage volunteers to perform their work for the class.

TECHNOLOGY/MEDIA LINK

Rubrics Visit *www.sfsuccessnet.com* for rubrics to assess students' achievement in music skills.

Lesson	Elements	Skills

LESSON 1 — CORE: Let's Rock!

pp. 212–215

Element: Expression
Concept: Tempo
Focus: Tempo

Secondary Element
Harmony: chord changes I, IV and V

National Standards
1c 2a 4c 6c 8b 9a 9b

Skill: Playing
Objective: Play a percussion accompaniment for a blues progression in a rock style

Secondary Skills
- **Listening** Listen to and discuss the tempo of the song
- **Singing** Sing along with the recording and focus on lyrics
- **Creating** Create other verses to the song
- **Analyzing** Analyze blues influence in the song

SKILLS REINFORCEMENT
- **Singing** Sing the song at different tempos
- **Analyzing** Create a blues melody, and identify the "bent" notes
- **Recorder** Play two countermelodies

LESSON 2 — Musical Patterns

pp. 216–217

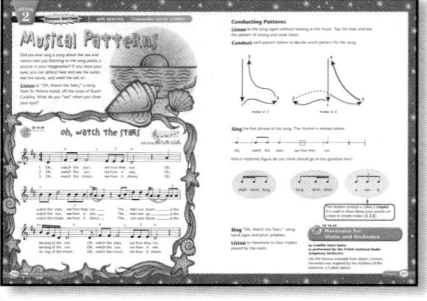

Reading Sequence 21, p. 500

Element: Rhythm
Concept: Pattern
Focus: Triplets

Secondary Element
Rhythm: meter in 2, 3, and 4; conducting patterns

National Standards
1c 2a 4c 5a 6c 8b

Skill: Reading
Objective: Read and sing from notation a song containing triplets

Secondary Skills
- **Listening** Listen to the song while keeping a steady beat
- **Conducting** Conduct different patterns in 2, in 3 and in 4
- **Listening** Listen for triplets in a listening selection

SKILLS REINFORCEMENT
- **Keyboard** Play an accompaniment using triplets
- **Recorder** Play a countermelody
- **Reading** Complete a Music Reading worksheet

LESSON 3 — CORE: A Different Meter

pp. 218–221

Element: Rhythm
Concept: Meter
Focus: Meter in 5

Secondary Element
Form: A B A

National Standards
4c 6b 6c 7a 8a 8b 9a

Skill: Moving
Objective: Move to meter in 5

Secondary Skills
- **Listening** Listen to song in meter in 5
- **Listening** Listen to a jazz selection in meter in 5
- **Moving** Move to a jazz selection

SKILLS REINFORCEMENT
- **Creating** Create body percussion patterns for meter in 5
- **Analyzing** Compare meter in 5 to meter in 4

Connections

Music and Other Literature

Connection: Style

Activity: Identify examples of blues style in a rock 'n' roll song of the 1950s

TEACHER TO TEACHER **Pitch Patterns** Suggestions for learning pitch patterns

SPOTLIGHT ON **Elvis Aron Presley** Information on the performer

ACROSS THE CURRICULUM **Language Arts** Write new song lyrics

MEETING INDIVIDUAL NEEDS **Including Everyone** Developing social skills and appropriate behavior

CHARACTER EDUCATION **Respect** Discuss ways to be accepting of differences

BUILDING SKILLS THROUGH MUSIC **Language** Identify words in song text which are not standard usage

Song "Hound Dog"

More Music Choices
"Basin Street Blues," p. 354
"Good Mornin', Blues," p. 224
"St. Louis Blues," p. 352

ASSESSMENT

Performance/Observation
Sing and play an accompaniment for the song at an appropriate tempo

TECHNOLOGY/MEDIA LINK

CD-ROM Create an accompaniment for the song

Connection: Social Studies

Activity: Discuss the history and culture of St. Helena Island, SC

ACROSS THE CURRICULUM **Language Arts** Develop minidramas to perform with the song

CULTURAL CONNECTION **St. Helena Island** History and culture

SCHOOL TO HOME CONNECTION **Science** Research which constellations and planets are visible in the area

BUILDING SKILLS THROUGH MUSIC **Science** Discuss how the sun and moon light the earth

Song "Oh, Watch the Stars"

Listening Selections
Havanaise for Violin and Orchestra (excerpt)

More Music Choices
"Turn, Turn, Turn," p. 378
"*Se va el caimán*" (The Alligator), p. 306

ASSESSMENT

Performance/Observation
Follow notation and perform a triplet pattern

TECHNOLOGY/MEDIA LINK

Notation Software
Compose and notate a layered rap containing triplets

Connection: Related Arts

Activity: Learn a Turkish folk dance

SPOTLIGHT ON **Ali Pasha** Information on the political leader

ACROSS THE CURRICULUM
Social Studies Learn about the geography and history of Turkey
Language Arts Read about the history, people and culture of Turkey

MOVEMENT
Patterned Dance Learn a patterned dance to *Ali Pasha*
Patterned Dance Learn a patterned dance to *Take Five*

TEACHER TO TEACHER **Meter in 5** Help students develop a feel for uneven meter

BUILDING SKILLS THROUGH MUSIC **Social Studies** Discuss the architecture and clothing of Turkey

Listening Selections
Ali Pasha
Take Five
M·U·S·I·C M·A·K·E·R·S
Dave Brubeck

More Music Choices
Eriskummainen kantele, p. 199

ASSESSMENT

Performance/Observation
Perform movement using meter in 5 at the appropriate time

TECHNOLOGY/MEDIA LINK

Sequencing Software
Compose and sequence rhythmic rondos in meter in 5

Lesson	Elements	Skills	

LESSON 4

The Long and Short of It

pp. 222–223

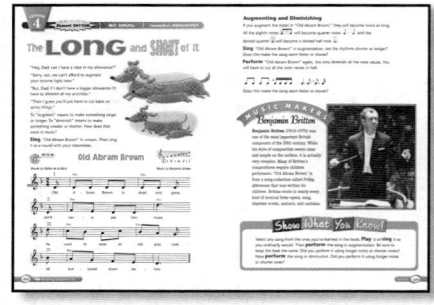

👉 Reading Sequence 22, p. 500

Element: Rhythm
Concept: Duration
Focus: Augmentation and diminution

Secondary Element
Texture: round

National Standards
1a 4c 5a 6c 8b

Skill: Singing
Objective: Perform a song in augmentation and in diminution

Secondary Skills
- **Singing** Sing the song and conduct a two-beat pattern
- **Reading** Read the rhythm and sing the song in augmentation and diminution

SKILLS REINFORCEMENT
- **Singing** Sing variations of the D minor scale

LESSON 5

CORE
A Form of Blues

pp. 224–227

Element: Form
Concept: 12-bar form
Focus: 12-bar blues form

Secondary Element
Harmony: chord changes I, IV, and V7

National Standards
1c 2c 3a 3c 6a 6b 6c
8b 9a 9b

Skill: Listening
Objective: Listen to a blues song

Secondary Skills
- **Singing** Sing a blues song and discuss the lyrics
- **Playing** Play the chords to accompany a song
- **Creating** Create other verses for the song
- **Improvising** Improvise melodies to the new verses
- **Analyzing** Analyze the form of the song
- **Listening** Listen to the selection and follow the listening map

SKILLS REINFORCEMENT
- **Improvising** Improvise in F pentatonic
- **Keyboard** Improvise an accompaniment

LESSON 6

Love of Country

pp. 228–229

Element: Melody
Concept: Tonality
Focus: Major and minor triads

Secondary Element
Rhythm: meter in 5/4

National Standards
1c 2a 6a 6c 9a

Skill: Singing
Objective: Sing a song that is in minor tonality

Secondary Skills
- **Listening** Listen to and move to show sections
- **Analyzing** Analyze the use of major and minor in a song
- **Listening** Listen to the selection and identify the form

SKILLS REINFORCEMENT
- **Analyzing** Analyze the tonal center of a song

Connections

Connection: Mathematics

Activity: Relate the concept of augmentation and diminution to specific numerical values

ACROSS THE CURRICULUM **Math** Compute proportional numerical values for notes

SPOTLIGHT ON **The Song** Background information on the song

BUILDING SKILLS THROUGH MUSIC **Social Studies** Create a time line of musicians

Connection: Style

Activity: Explore the traditional performance characteristics of blues

TEACHER TO TEACHER
How to Improvise Tips on improvising in blues style
Guitar Capo Suggestion on simplifying an accompaniment
Guitar Strum Suggestion for a guitar strum for the song

SPOTLIGHT ON **Different Kinds of Blues** Information on country, classic, and urban blues

CULTURAL CONNECTION **Blues Style** Information on the development of blues style

ACROSS THE CURRICULUM **Language Arts** Read the effect of blues style on African American art and poetry

BUILDING SKILLS THROUGH MUSIC **Social Studies** Identify the musical characteristics of each performance

Connection: Culture

Activity: Discuss the customs and culture of Argentina

TEACHER TO TEACHER **Other Languages** Suggestions on teaching foreign language lyrics

SPOTLIGHT ON **The Composer** Information about Alberto Ginastera

ACROSS THE CURRICULUM **Language Arts** Research the culture and customs of Argentina

BUILDING SKILLS THROUGH MUSIC **Reading** Discuss the imagery in songs

Music and Other Literature

Song "Old Abram Brown"
M•U•S•I•C M•A•K•E•R•S
Benjamin Britten

More Music Choices
"Autumn Canon," p. 148
"*Las velitas*" ("Candles Burning Bright"), p. 147
"*Still, Still, Still*" ("Sleep, Dearest Child"), p. 468

Song "Good Mornin', Blues"

Listening Selections
Country Blues
Walkin' Blues
Listening Map *Walkin' Blues*
M•U•S•I•C M•A•K•E•R•S
Muddy Waters

More Music Choices
"St. Louis Blues," p. 352
"Basin Street Blues," p. 354

Songs
"*Viva Jujuy*" (Spanish)
"*Viva Jujuy*" (English)

Listening Selection *Danza del trigo* (excerpt)
M•U•S•I•C M•A•K•E•R•S
Alberto Ginastera

More Music Choices
"Pat Works on the Railway," p. 182

ASSESSMENT

Performance/Observation
Sing the song in augmentation and diminution
Show What You Know!
Mid-unit assessment

TECHNOLOGY/MEDIA LINK
Notation Software Create an arrangement of the song

ASSESSMENT

Observation Identify 12-bar blues form by indicating chord changes while listening to the song

TECHNOLOGY/MEDIA LINK
CD-ROM Improvise in jazz swing
Transparency Display the transparency to follow form

ASSESSMENT

Performance/Observation
Develop a performance of the song

TECHNOLOGY/MEDIA LINK
Web Site More information on the music and composers of Argentina

Lesson	Elements	Skills

LESSON 7

CORE

A Song of the Sea

pp. 230-231

Reading Sequence 23, p. 501

Element: Melody
Concept: Tonality
Focus: Mixolydian mode

Secondary Element
Rhythm: upbeat

National Standards
1a 1c 5c 6c 8b

Skill: Reading
Objective: Read and sing from notation a song in mixolydian mode

Secondary Skills
- **Singing** Sing the notes of the G-so scale
- **Playing** Play the major, natural minor and mixolydian scales

SKILLS REINFORCEMENT
- **Reading** Read mixolydian scales
- **Playing** Play mixolydian scales

LESSON 8

A Song from Ireland

pp. 232–235

Reading Sequence 24, p. 501

Element: Melody
Concept: Tonality
Focus: Dorian mode

Secondary Element
Rhythm: $\frac{6}{8}$ meter

National Standards
1c 2a 4c 5c 6c 8b

Skill: Reading
Objective: Read and sing from notation a song in dorian mode

Secondary Skills
- **Moving** Create movements for the song
- **Performing** Accompany the song
- **Listening** Listen to a selection and identify the dorian melody

SKILLS REINFORCEMENT
- **Recorder** Play a countermelody
- **Playing** Tips to help all students perform the accompaniment

---

LESSON 9

CORE

Keyboard Technology

pp. 236–239

Element: Timbre
Concept: Keyboard
Focus: Keyboard timbre

Secondary Element
Expression: dynamics

National Standards
4c 6b 8b

Skill: Listening
Objective: Listen to and compare the timbre of a variety of keyboard instruments

Secondary Skills
- **Analyzing** Analyze the physical structure of a harpsichord
- **Listening** Listen to the harpsichord selection
- **Analyzing** Analyze the physical structure of a piano
- **Listening** Listen to the piano selection
- **Analyzing** Analyze the physical structure of a synthesizer
- **Listening** Listen to the synthesizer selections

SKILLS REINFORCEMENT
- **Analyzing** Analyze the structure of a piano, harpsichord, and a synthesizer

Connections

Music and Other Literature

Connection: Social Studies

Activity: Investigate the history of the whaling industry and the use of whaling songs

TEACHER TO TEACHER **Aural Perception** Use aural examples of whole and half steps

ACROSS THE CURRICULUM
Social Studies Research information about whaling
Language Arts Read a story of sea travel

BUILDING SKILLS THROUGH MUSIC **Social Studies** Determine the setting, place, and time of the song

Song "The Greenland Whale Fishery"

More Music Choices
"Don't You Hear the Lambs?" p. 97

ASSESSMENT

Performance/Observation
Sing the song with pitch syllables and hand signs

Show What You Know!
Mid-unit assessment

TECHNOLOGY/MEDIA LINK
Web Site More information on sea shanties and seafaring songs

---

Connection: Social Studies

Activity: Discuss a geographic region in Ireland

MEETING INDIVIDUAL NEEDS **Gifted and Talented Students** Research Irish music

CULTURAL CONNECTION **Connemara** Information about the Connemara region of Ireland

TEACHER TO TEACHER **Different Modes** Tips for teaching modes

ACROSS THE CURRICULUM **Language Arts** Write a short poem about Ireland

SPOTLIGHT ON The Composer Information about Ralph Vaughan Williams

AUDIENCE ETIQUETTE **Rehearsal Etiquette for Performers** Learn appropriate behaviors for rehearsal

BUILDING SKILLS THROUGH MUSIC **Social Studies** List the mountain ranges in the United States and locate them on a map

Song "Connemara Lullaby"

Listening Selection *Fantasia on Greensleeves*
M•U•S•I•C M•A•K•E•R•S
Ralph Vaughan Williams

More Music Choices
"The Greenland Whale Fishery," p. 230

ASSESSMENT

Performance/Observation
Read the song with pitch syllables, hand signs, and letter names

TECHNOLOGY/MEDIA LINK
Notation Software Compose a melody with accompaniment in dorian mode

---

Connection: Science

Activity: Relate the sound of an instrument to the technology available at the time the instrument was developed

ACROSS THE CURRICULUM
Science The evolution of the recording of language
Science Research the newest sound technologies

SPOTLIGHT ON
The Harpsichord Information about the instrument
The Piano Information about the instrument

MEETING INDIVIDUAL NEEDS **Challenge** Research the technology of other keyboard instruments

TEACHER TO TEACHER **More Technology** Research development of electronics used in music

BUILDING SKILLS THROUGH MUSIC **Writing** Describe in writing the timbre of an instrument

Listening Selections
Two-Part Invention in A Major (harpsichord)
Two-Part Invention in A Major (piano)
Two-Part Invention in A Major (synthesizer)
Come Out and Play (excerpt)
Snowflakes are Dancing
M•U•S•I•C M•A•K•E•R•S
Robert Moog
Isao Tomita

More Music Choices
Invention No. 5 in E-flat, p. 59
Scott Joplin's New Rag, p. 335

ASSESSMENT

Observation Identify instrument timbre from selections

TECHNOLOGY/MEDIA LINK
Electronic Keyboard Create a "voice map" for an electronic keyboard

---

Lesson	Elements	Skills

LESSON 10

Harmonizing Folk Music

pp. 240–241

**Element:
Texture/Harmony**
Concept: Harmony
Focus: Primary chords

Secondary Element
Form: verse/refrain

National Standards
1c 2c 3a 6c 8b

Skill: Playing
Objective: Play chords on keyboard to accompany a song

Secondary Skill
• **Singing** Sing the song to discover form and harmony

SKILLS REINFORCEMENT
• **Guitar** Play a chord accompaniment
• **Recorder** Play a countermelody

LESSON 11

**CORE
Two-Part Singing**

pp. 242–243

**Element:
Texture/Harmony**
Concept: Harmony
Focus: Two-part harmony

Secondary Element
Timbre: vocal

National Standards
1c 1d 2a 4c 6c 7b 8b
9a

Skill: Singing
Objective: Sing a song in two-part harmony

Secondary Skills
• **Analyzing** Analyze notation to discover chord structure
• **Listening** Listen to a recording and determine harmony
• **Playing** Play accompaniment for a song

SKILLS REINFORCEMENT
• **Vocal Development** Review vocal techniques
• **Guitar** Play an accompaniment

LESSON 12

Music in Three Parts

pp. 244–245

**Element:
Texture/Harmony**
Concept: Harmony
Focus: Three-part harmony

Secondary Element
Form: solo/chorus

National Standards
1c 1d 2a 4c 6c 8b

Skill: Singing
Objective: Sing a song in three-part harmony

Secondary Skill
• **Playing** Play an accompaniment to a song

SKILLS REINFORCEMENT
• **Recorder** Play a countermelody
• **Signing** Perform a sign interpretation of the song

Connections

Music and Other Literature

Connection: Culture

Activity: Discuss Jamaican culinary customs referred to in a calypso song

ACROSS THE CURRICULUM **Language Arts/Social Studies** Read a book of Jamaican poems

CULTURAL CONNECTION **Culinary Customs** Information on the foods of Jamaica

BUILDING SKILLS THROUGH MUSIC **Social Studies** Substitute English words for Jamaican words

Song "Linstead Market"

More Music Choices
"*Imbabura*," p. 203
"Oh, Freedom," p. 392

ASSESSMENT

Performance/Observation Play chords on keyboard to accompany the song

TECHNOLOGY/MEDIA LINK
MIDI/Sequencing Software Improvise a bass part using the I, IV, and V_7 chords

---

Connection: Genre

Activity: Explore the historical tradition of African American spirituals

ACROSS THE CURRICULUM **Social Studies** Read a book about African American musicians

CHARACTER EDUCATION **Responsibility** Discuss responsibility to help someone in distress

BUILDING SKILLS THROUGH MUSIC **Writing** Compare dynamic changes in two different performances

Song "Ev'ry Time I feel the Spirit"

More Music Choices
"Camptown Races," p. 270
"*Canción Mixteca*," p. 326

ASSESSMENT

Performance/Self-Assessment Sing a song in two parts with accompaniment and record for assessment of the harmony parts

TECHNOLOGY/MEDIA LINK
MIDI/Sequencing Software Compose "fills" based on I, IV, and V_7 chord tones

---

Connection: Culture

Activity: Explore the association of a song with the civil rights movements of different countries

CULTURAL CONNECTION "Kum ba yah" Information about a Liberian civil rights song

TEACHER TO TEACHER **Singing in Harmony** Tips on singing in three-part harmony

BUILDING SKILLS THROUGH MUSIC **Social Studies** Write a paragraph about the use of the song in the American civil rights movement

Song "*Kum ba yah*"

More Music Choices
"Freedom is Coming," p. 415
"*'Ūlili E*," p. 441

ASSESSMENT

Performance/Peer Critique Perform a song in three parts and assess intonation, diction, phrasing, and tone quality

TECHNOLOGY/MEDIA LINK
Sequencing Software Notate an instrumental version of the song

INTRODUCING THE UNIT

Unit 6 presents the next step in a sequenced approach to understanding music elements. Music skills—reading, performing, creating, listening, moving—are the means by which students gain an understanding of these concepts. Presented on p. 209 is a brief overview of the skills that are assessed in this unit. (See below and pp. 210–211 for unit highlights of related curricular experiences.)

For a more detailed unit overview, see Unit at a Glance, pp. 207a–207h.

UNIT PROJECT

Discuss with students the meaning of the unit title. Ask students how they can make music their own. (through selection and repeated contact so that it feels comfortable that it could "belong" to you)

Divide the class into twelve groups. Assign each group one lesson in the unit. Ask each group to plan a short introduction of its song to the rest of the class, preparing them for what they will hear. No pre-judgment should be included (For example, "This will be great" or "You won't like this much, but.")

After the unit has been completed, this activity can be expanded into a presentation.

- A central character can be developed who is looking for musical friends.
- Each of the unit songs (or a selection from the lesson) can be introduced by a group posing as the originator of the song.
- Groups can present their selections by singing with recorded accompaniment or with keyboards or performing movement.

The British Are Coming

The musical blending of country, rhythm and blues, and folk styles produced many different types of rock. In the 1960s, bands from England launched a "British Invasion" of the American rock scene. Two legendary figures, John Lennon and Paul McCartney, were the main songwriting members of the most famous English rock group of all—the Beatles.

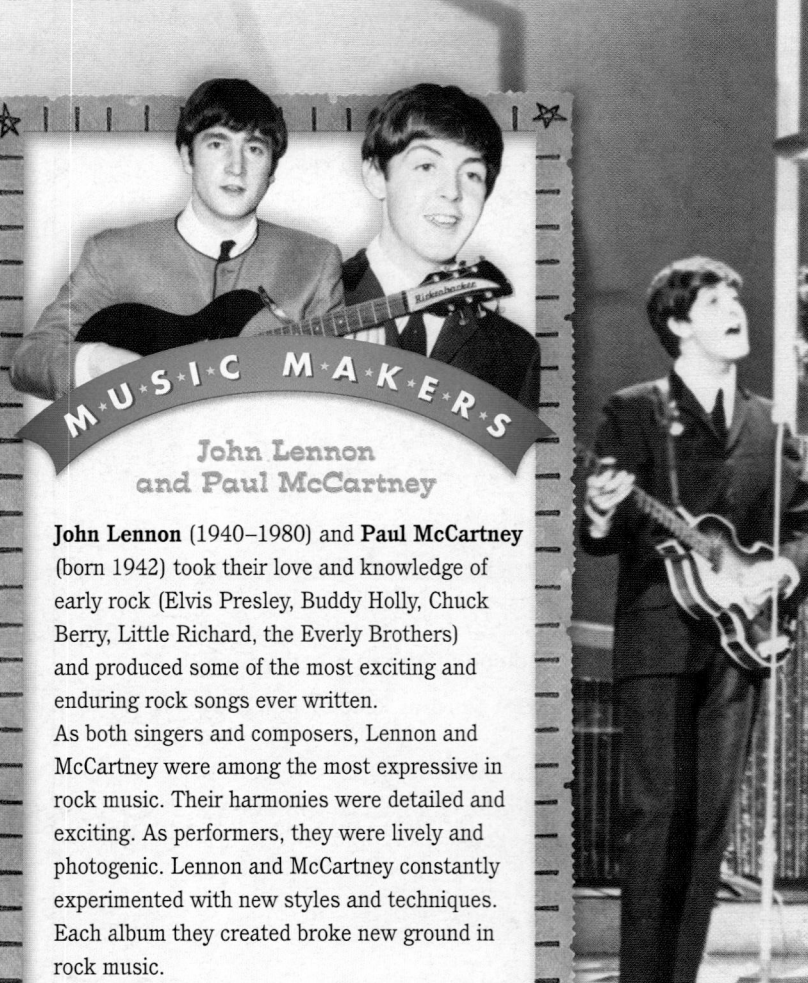

MUSIC MAKERS

John Lennon and Paul McCartney

John Lennon (1940–1980) and **Paul McCartney** (born 1942) took their love and knowledge of early rock (Elvis Presley, Buddy Holly, Chuck Berry, Little Richard, the Everly Brothers) and produced some of the most exciting and enduring rock songs ever written.

As both singers and composers, Lennon and McCartney were among the most expressive in rock music. Their harmonies were detailed and exciting. As performers, they were lively and photogenic. Lennon and McCartney constantly experimented with new styles and techniques. Each album they created broke new ground in rock music.

208

ACROSS THE CURRICULUM

Unit Highlights The following interdisciplinary activities in this unit are related to the music elements presented in the lessons. See Unit at a Glance, pp. 207a–207h, for topical descriptions presented according to lesson sequence.

▶ **LANGUAGE ARTS**

- Write new lyrics for a rock 'n' roll song (p. 213)
- Develop minidramas, legends, and narrations song (p. 216)
- Read books about the history, culture, people, and land of Turkey (p. 218)
- Read a poem by Langston Hughes and compare it to the form the lyrics of a blues song (p. 226)
- Research the customs and culture of Argentina (p. 229)
- Read a story about sea travel (p. 231)
- Write a short poem about Ireland and a melody to go with it (p. 234)

- Read poems written through the eyes of a young girl growing up in Jamaica (p. 240)

▶ **MATHEMATICS**

- Compute proportional numeric values for notes (p. 222)

▶ **SCIENCE**

- Discuss the technological evolution in the recording of language (p. 236)
- Research the newest sound technologies (p. 238)

▶ **SOCIAL STUDIES**

- Locate Turkey on a map and learn about its history (p. 218)
- Research and discuss whales and the history of whaling (p. 231)
- Read a book about the Fisk Jubilee Singers (p. 242)

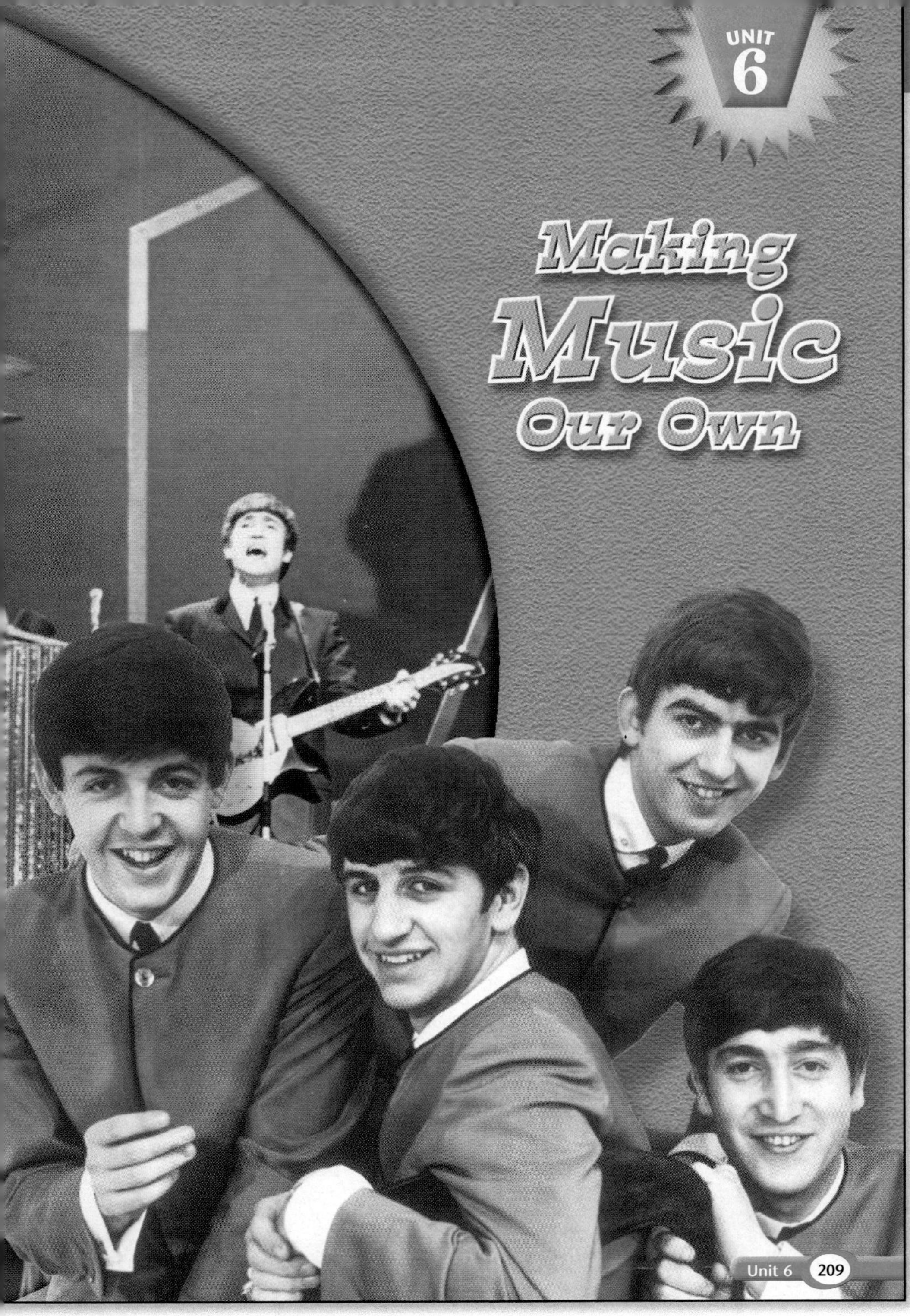

Making Music Our Own

MUSIC SKILLS ASSESSED IN THIS UNIT

Reading Music: Rhythm

- Read and perform triplets in meter in 4 (p. 217)
- Read and perform augmented and diminished rhythms (p. 223)

Reading Music: Pitch

- Read and perform a song in mixolydian mode using pitch syllables and hand signs, letter names, and lyrics (p. 231)
- Read and perform a song in dorian mode using pitch syllables and hand signs (p. 235)

Performing Music: Singing

- Sing a popular song at a convincing rock 'n' roll tempo (p. 215)
- Sing a song that shifts from major and minor (p. 229)

Moving to Music

- Perform a meter-in-5 movement (p. 221)
- Perform movements for each phrase in an Irish folk song (p. 233)

Peforming Music: Playing

- Perform an accompaniment on rhythm and mallet instruments to a rock 'n' roll song (p. 215)
- Perform a chordal accompaniment using the I, IV, V$_7$ chords (p. 241)

Creating Music

- Improvise body percussion patterns (p. 219)
- Create a new verse for a blues song (p. 226)

Listening to Music

- Listen to a blues song and identify the I, IV, and V$_7$ chords (p. 227)
- Listen to excerpts of different keyboard instruments and identify them (p. 239)

CULTURAL CONNECTION

Unit Highlights The musical literature in this unit provides many opportunities for students to explore a variety of world cultures. See Unit at a Glance, pp. 207a–207h, for topical descriptions presented according to lesson sequence.

▶ AFRICAN/AFRICAN AMERICAN

- Learn about the history of the song *"Kum ba yah"* (p. 244)
- Explore the origins of the blues style (p. 225)

▶ AMERICAN REGIONAL

- Discover information about St. Helena Island, South Carolina (p. 217)

▶ CARIBBEAN

- Read about the culinary customs of Jamaica (p. 240)

▶ EUROPEAN

- Learn about the Connemara region of Ireland (p. 232)

Unit 6 *Making Music Our Own* **209**

OPENING ACTIVITIES

MATERIALS
- "There's a Place" **CD 10-25**
  Recording Routine:
  Intro (5 m.); vocal; coda
- xylophones, keyboard or mallet instruments

Listening

Invite students to listen to "There's a Place" **CD 10-25** and think about a place they go when they feel happy or sad. Invite volunteers to share their responses.

Singing

Have students listen to the song again. Establish the sound of *do* (C). Ask students to listen to the melodic pattern on the first word *there* and determine the pitch syllables *(mi-re-do-re-mi)*. Have students sing these pitches.

Have students sing *so-ti-do*, then *so-fa-mi*. Divide the group; have half sing each pattern, then combine them. Write these patterns on the board, with help from the class (G-B-C, G-F-E). Then play "There's a Place" again. Ask students to look for the places in the song where this pattern is used, and sing along on the words in those places.

Playing

Have several students figure out how to play the *mi-re-do-re-mi* pattern on xylophones. Have others learn *so-ti-do* and *so-fa-mi* on glockenspiels, metallophones, bells, or keyboard.

Performing

Have students play the patterns at the appropriate times while everyone sings the song.

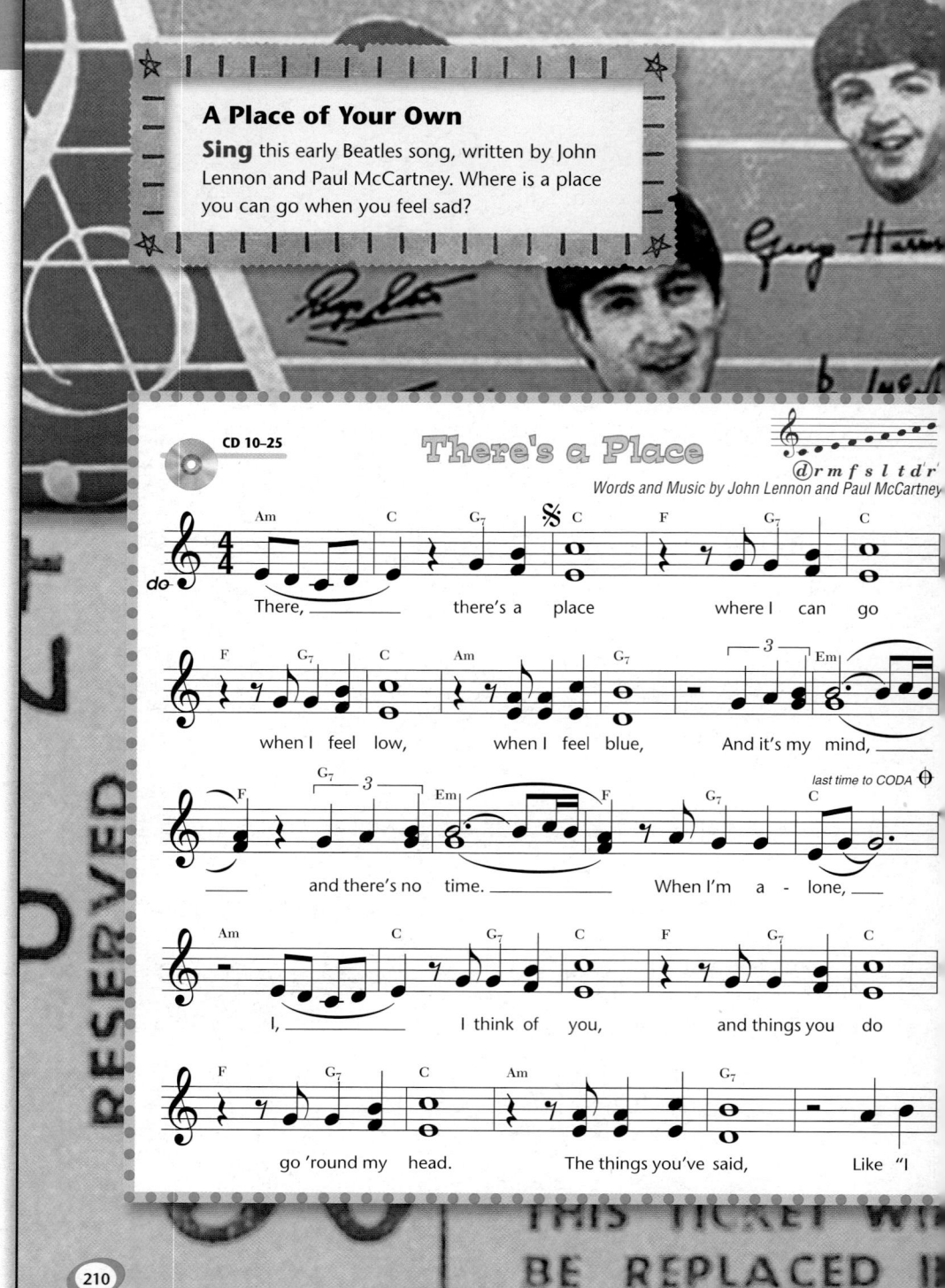

A Place of Your Own

Sing this early Beatles song, written by John Lennon and Paul McCartney. Where is a place you can go when you feel sad?

There's a Place

Words and Music by John Lennon and Paul McCartney

There, ____ there's a place where I can go when I feel low, when I feel blue, And it's my mind, ____ and there's no time. ____ When I'm a-lone, ____ I, ____ I think of you, and things you do go 'round my head. The things you've said, Like "I

210

ASSESSMENT

Unit Highlights This unit includes a variety of strategies and methods, described below, to track students' progress and assess their understanding of lesson objectives. Reproducible masters for Show What You Know! and Review, Assess, Perform, Create can be found in the Resource Book.

▶ **FORMAL ASSESSMENTS**

The following assessments, using written language, cognitive, and performance skills, help teachers and students conceptualize the learning that is taking place.

- **Show What You Know!** Element-specific assessments, on the student page, for Rhythm (p. 223) and Melody (p. 231).
- **Review, Assess, Perform, Create** This end-of-unit activity (pp. 246–247) can be used for review and to assess students' learning of the core lessons in this unit.

▶ **INFORMAL ASSESSMENTS**

At the close of each Teacher's Edition lesson in this unit, one of the following types of assessments is used to evaluate the learning of the key element focus or skill objective.

- Observation (pp. 227, 239)
- Performance/Observation (pp. 215, 217, 221, 223, 229, 231, 235, 241)
- Performance/Peer Critique (p. 245)
- Performance/Self-Assessment (p. 243)

▶ **RUBRICS**

Visit *www.sfsuccessnet.com* for rubrics to assess students' achievement in music skills.

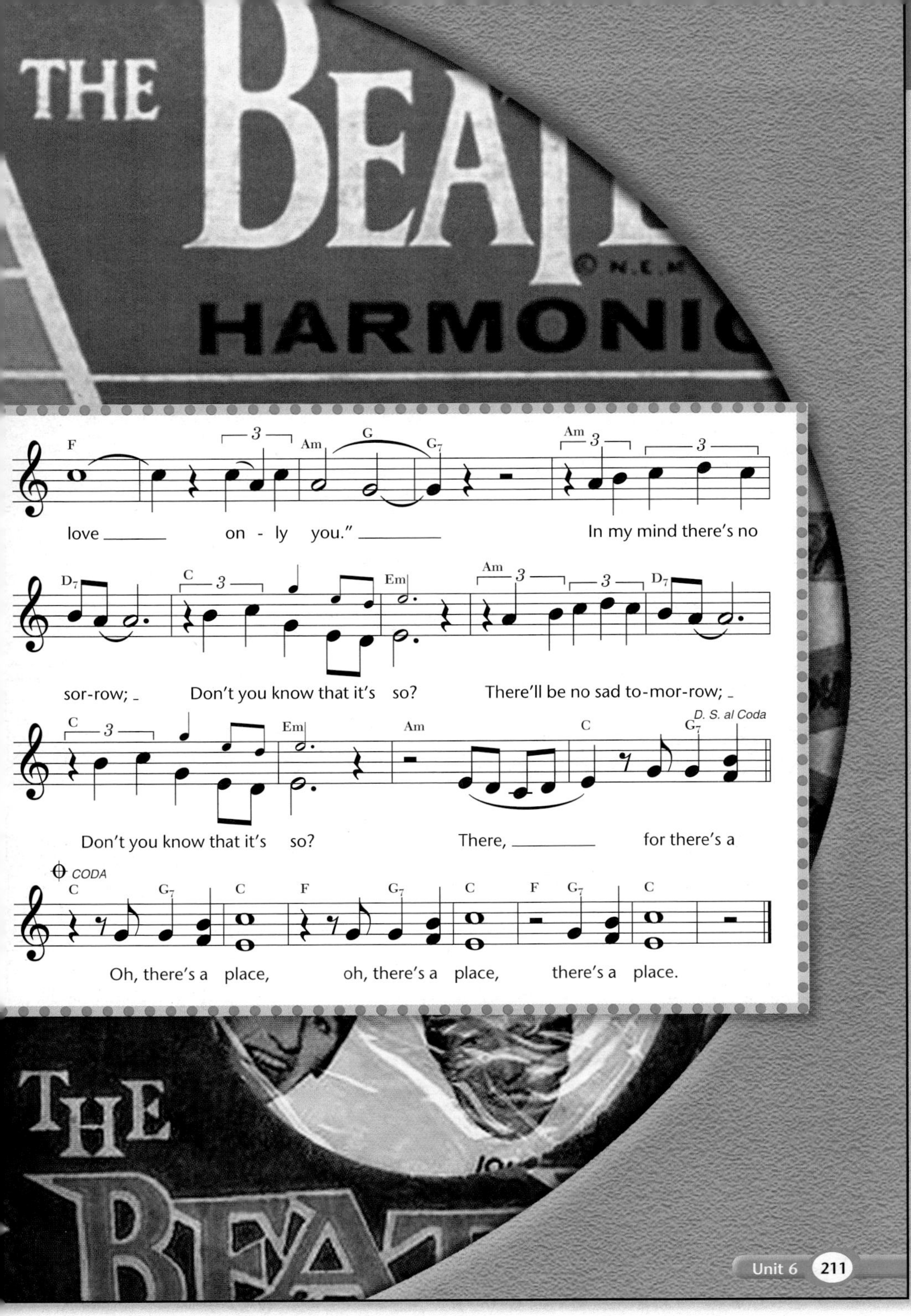

The sheet music with lyrics:

love _____ on - ly you." _____ In my mind there's no

sor-row; _ Don't you know that it's so? There'll be no sad to-mor-row; _

Don't you know that it's so? There, _____ for there's a
D. S. al Coda

CODA
Oh, there's a place, oh, there's a place, there's a place.

Moving

Ask students to find a gentle movement that can be used to keep the beat of the song—it should be one that can be seen but not heard (visible but not audible). Have students use their movement through the song, but change it in some small way every time they hear a long note value (for example, on *place, go,* and *low*). The change can be direction, height, or the body part doing the movement. Have students listen and move to the entire song. (Many variations in how they move are acceptable.)

INNOVATIVE TEACHER SUPPORT FOR THIS UNIT

- **MAKING MUSIC DVD, Grade 5** contains video segments that support lessons, including signing and movement.
- **MAKING MUSIC with Movement and Dance** provides more opportunities for large group activities in music or physical education classes.
- **MAKING MUSIC with Technology** provides lesson plans for many technology applications; includes MIDI files.
- *¡A cantar!* features recorded songs and lessons from around the Spanish-speaking world; includes strategies for bilingual classes and for English-speaking teachers working with Spanish-speaking students.
- **Bridges to Asia** features recorded songs and lessons from Asian and Pacific region cultures.
- *www.sfsuccessnet.com* provides an online lesson planner to conveniently create lesson plans at school or at home. Includes rubrics for assessment, lesson modifications to meet the needs of all students, performance musicals based on program content, and more.

Unit 6   **211**

TECHNOLOGY/MEDIA LINK

Unit Highlights The following components are used in this unit to reinforce and expand students' understanding of music elements and related themes. See *Unit at a Glance,* pp. 207a–207h, for a descriptive listing according to lesson sequence.

▶ **CD-ROM**
- Create an accompaniment for a rock 'n' roll song (p. 215)
- Use *Band-in-a-Box* to learn how to improvise (p. 227)

▶ **ELECTRONIC KEYBOARD**
- Create a voice map and explore the different sounds available (p. 239)

▶ **MIDI/SEQUENCING SOFTWARE**
- Compose and sequence rhythmic rondos in meter in 5 (p. 221)
- Improvise a bass part using the I, IV, and V_7 chords (p. 241)

- Compose "fills" based upon I, IV, and V_7 chord tones (p. 243)
- Notate an instrumental version of the song (p. 245)

▶ **NOTATION SOFTWARE**
- Compose and notate a layered rap that contains triplets (p. 217)
- Create an arrangement of a song (p. 223)
- Compose a melody with accompaniment in dorian mode (p. 235)

▶ **TRANSPARENCY**
- Display a listening map to follow the form of a selection (p. 227)

▶ **WEB SITE**
- Visit *www.sfsuccessnet.com* for more information on the music and composers of Argentina (p. 229) and shanties and seafaring songs (p. 231)

Unit 6 *Making Music Our Own*   **211**

LESSON AT A GLANCE

Element Focus   **EXPRESSION** Tempo

Skill Objective   **PLAYING** Play a percussion accompaniment for a blues progression in a rock style

Connection Activity   **STYLE** Identify examples of blues style in a rock 'n' roll song of the 1950s

MATERIALS

- "Hound Dog"   **CD 10-27**
  Recording Routine: Intro (4 m.); vocal; coda
- **Resource Book** p. I-17
- alto xylophones, bass xylophone, drums

VOCABULARY

tempo   blues

◆ ◆ ◆ National Standards ◆ ◆ ◆

1c Sing music from diverse genres
2a Play instruments accurately in small ensembles
4c Arrange, using electronic media
6c Understand and use basic principles of rhythm in music analysis
8b Identify ways music relates to language arts and social studies
9a Describe characteristics of music styles from a variety of cultures
9b Classify high-quality works by genre

MORE MUSIC CHOICES

For more experience with tempo and blues style:
"Basin Street Blues," p. 354
"Good Mornin', Blues," p. 224
"St. Louis Blues," p. 352

Let's Rock!

The song most often associated with Elvis Presley, the "king" of rock 'n' roll, is "Hound Dog." It was popular in the 1950s.

Listen to "Hound Dog." What gives this song its energy?

CD 10–27
MIDI 15

Hound Dog

Words and Music by Jerry Leiber and Mike Stoller

You ain't noth-in' but a hound dog, — cry - in' all the time.

You ain't noth-in' but a hound dog, — cry - in' all the time.

Well, — you ain't nev-er caught a rab-bit, and you ain't no friend of mine.

When they said you was high-classed, — well, that — was just a lie.

212

Footnotes

TEACHER TO TEACHER

▶ **Pitch Patterns** In helping students learn pitch patterns such as the instrumental parts for "Hound Dog," make sure that from the very beginning, the correct pitches are heard as the letter patterns are learned. Sing letters, speak letters and play the pitches, or speak letters while students play pitches. The goal is for students to learn a sequence of tones, not letters.

BUILDING SKILLS THROUGH MUSIC

▶ **Language** Review the lyrics of "Hound Dog" by having students sing the song. Select individual students to identify words or phrases that are not standard usage and list on the board. Have students work individually or with a partner to make one phrase of the song's lyrics reflect standard usage. Ask them to chant the new phrases while keeping a steady beat.

SPOTLIGHT ON

▶ **Elvis Aron Presley** The first musical "event" for Elvis Presley (1935–1977) was winning the prize of $5 at a local song contest at age ten. In his late teens, he cultivated a "rebel" look—long hair and flamboyant clothes. He was "discovered" by Sun Records when he cut a single for his mother's birthday. Within a short time he began performing on radio programs and touring in neighboring states. His style combined country with rhythm 'n' blues, and evolved into early rock 'n' roll. Among many successful recordings was the best selling double-sided single ever: "Hound Dog" backed by "Don't Be Cruel." Before long, Elvis began acting in films. The fourth, *King Creole* (1958), is considered his best. Graceland, his home in Memphis, Tennessee, is now a museum that attracts a constant stream of visitors.

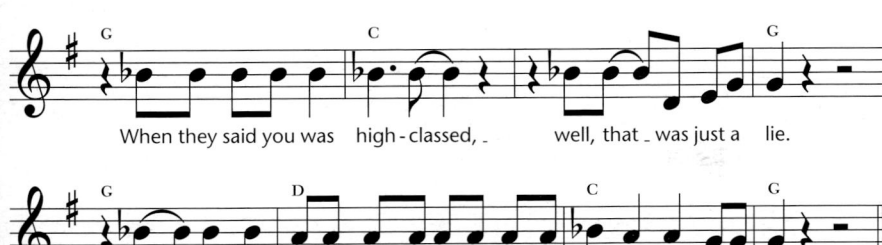

When they said you was high-classed, _ well, that _ was just a lie.

Well, _ you ain't nev-er caught a rab-bit and you ain't no friend of mine. _

Even a Hound Dog Can Be Expressive

How do you think "Hound Dog" would sound if you sang it very slowly? Try it and see how it works.

How does your musical expression change when you sing "Hound Dog" in different tempos?

When played and sung at a slow tempo, it sounds a little "bluesy," doesn't it?

These illustrations express different styles. What kind of music might go with each illustration?

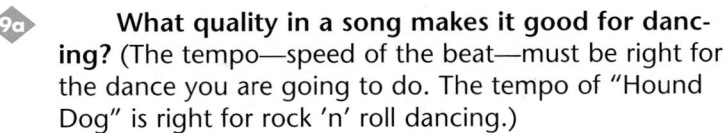

1 INTRODUCE

Listening

Ask students to share what they know about Elvis Presley. See Spotlight On, p. 212. Tell students that "Hound Dog" **CD 10-27** was Elvis's top single. Play the recording for the class.

ASK Since the words are really directed at a person, not a dog, what does it mean? (This is an insulting song, telling somebody he or she isn't worth much.)

What would the listeners of the song be doing? (The listeners would be dancing.)

9a What quality in a song makes it good for dancing? (The tempo—speed of the beat—must be right for the dance you are going to do. The tempo of "Hound Dog" is right for rock 'n' roll dancing.)

6c How would "Hound Dog" sound at a much slower tempo? (Answers will vary.)

Have students sing the song at a slower tempo to see how the slow speed affects the song. Ask them to identify a term that can be used as a tempo indicator or symbol at the beginning of each version "Hound Dog." See Skills Reinforcement below for related suggestions.

2 DEVELOP

Singing

1c
9a Ask students to sing the song with the recording **CD 10-27**, paying attention to the construction of the lyrics. (The first two lines are the same, the third line is different, the ending words rhyme.) Tell them this form, AAB, is the scheme for the lyrics of a blues song.

Creating

Students may enjoy creating positive verses for "Hound Dog." Try replacing *hound dog* with *good guy,* and *ain't no* with *are a* (line 3). See Across the Curriculum below.

continued on page 214

SKILLS REINFORCEMENT

1c ► **Singing** Terms indicating tempo have flexible meanings according to style, type of ensemble, preference of the performers and so on. *Andante* in one situation will be slower than in another. Bring a metronome to class (a student who takes music lessons may enjoy bringing one from home). Tell students that the tick of the metronome indicates the number of beats per minute. Write on the board these five tempo terms: *adagio* (slow), *andante* (moderate), *allegretto* (moderately quick), *allegro* (fast), and *presto* (very fast). Have the class sing "Hound Dog" at different metronome speeds. Develop a class consensus on what metronome markings would match each of the five tempo terms when applied to this song. For example, *allegretto* = M.M. 112.

ACROSS THE CURRICULUM

8b ► **Language Arts** To help students write new song lyrics to "Hound Dog," you may have to provide an example, such as "You're my ever lovin' angel, Helpin' all the time. You're my ever lovin' angel, Helpin' all the time. Well, you can't never ever walk away 'cause you're a friend of mine."

Lesson 1 Continued

Have students

- Form small groups.
- Sing the tune of "Hound Dog" before starting on the new lyrics.
- **8b** Create new words, making sure that the words fit the rhythm of the melody and that the last syllables of lines 2 and 3 rhyme. (See Across the Curriculum, p. 213.)
- Write the new words in their music journals.
- Share their new songs with the class.

Analyzing

9a Point out to students that, in addition to the AAB form of the lyrics in "Hound Dog," the blues influence can be seen in the lowered third in the melody. See Skills Reinforcement, p. 215.

9b **ASK** **What makes rock music "rock"?** (a set of characteristics that give it a unique style)

SAY One of the most important characteristics of rock style is the backbeat.

Have students examine the backbeat charts on p. 215.

SAY Most music in duple meter ($\frac{2}{4}$ or $\frac{4}{4}$) accents beats 1 and 3, with beat 3 less stressed than beat 1.

6c **ASK** **Where are the stresses in chart number 1?** (beats 1 and 3)

Where are the stresses in chart number 2? (beats 2 and 4)

SAY Let's clap the beats in the first chart.

Let's clap the beats in the second chart.

Playing Rock 'n' Roll

Play this part on a bass xylophone as you sing "Hound Dog."

Next add these parts, using xylophones, as others sing.

Now add these percussion parts for a classroom rock-style sound.

High drum

Low drum

Cymbals

Footnotes

MEETING INDIVIDUAL NEEDS

▶ **Including Everyone** Students with poor social skills who have not learned to self-monitor their performance nor to respond to cues from others may seek peer approval in inappropriate ways. Work out two discrete signals to use when the student is doing well and when he or she begins inappropriate behavior. Anticipate inappropriate responses to "Hound Dog" (or other activities) and discretely remind the student at the beginning of class of the signals and your high expectations for his or her "having a good day." Use behavior signals *early and frequently*, especially at the start of any inappropriate behavior. Have the student use the signals for self-monitoring.

CHARACTER EDUCATION

▶ **Respect** Discuss the diverse genres of music available today and how this diversity perpetuates the need for increased appreciation and acceptance of differences. Explain to students that familiarity with, and understanding of, that which is different leads to appreciation. Ask students how they should respond to different kinds of music and to different people. Discuss how people often respond when they hear music or see someone that is different from what they know or understand. You may wish to question students further about responding positively to diversity. Which responses are appropriate? How could inappropriate responses be modified? How should you react when you hear someone respond negatively to music or people with which you aren't familiar? Discuss with students things they can say and ways to help others be more accepting of differences.

What Makes It Rock?

What makes rock music sound different from other kinds of music—jazz, folk, or a symphony? Rock is a *style* of music. It has a set of characteristics that makes it sound unique.

One of the most important characteristics of rock style is the *backbeat*.

Most music that is in $\frac{4}{4}$ meter has a stress on the first and third beats of the measure, with the third beat less accented than the first beat.

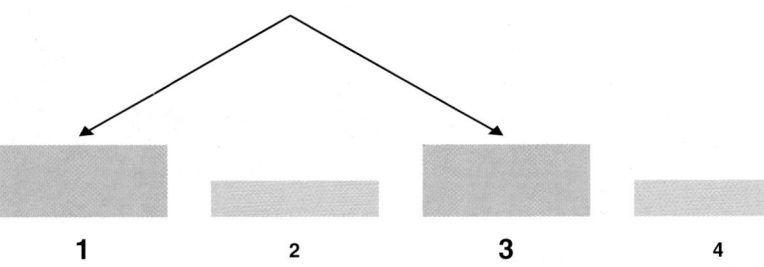

1   2   3   4

The backbeat in rock is on the second and fourth beats.

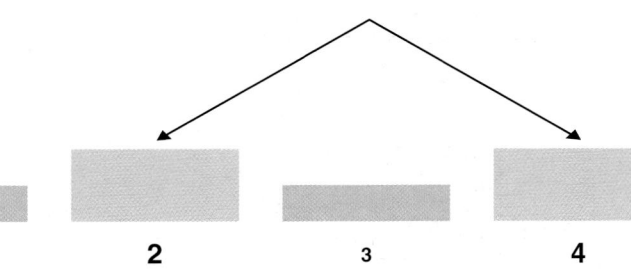

1   2   3   4

The percussion part you learned has a strong backbeat in the low drum.

 **MIDI** Use the "Hound Dog" song file with sequencing software to experiment with a variety of tempos.

6c Have students

- Repeatedly count aloud to four, with a strong beat feeling, in the tempo of "Hound Dog."
- Divide into two groups; one group says *one* and *three*, the other group says *two* and *four*.
- Say *one* and *three* and clap on beats 2 and 4.
- Think *one* and *three* and clap on beats 2 and 4. (It will be easier if some movement is added to beats 1 and 3—bouncing arms or head, for example.)

Playing

2a Have students look at the instrumental parts on p. 214. Assign or have students choose instruments. Then have students

- Practice the bass xylophone part.
- Add the other xylophone parts.
- Play the low drum backbeat pattern, stressing beats 2 and 4.
- Add the high drum part and then the cymbals.

As each new part is learned, add it to the parts already known and accompany the song as the class sings. Since the percussion parts begin on the word *hound*, add two bars of introduction identical to the first bar played. Have students start singing right after beat 1 of the second introductory bar.

3 CLOSE

Element: EXPRESSION   **ASSESSMENT**

1c
2a **Performance/Observation** Have students sing "Hound Dog" while performing the accompaniment on rhythm and mallet instruments. Observe that students perform at a convincing rock 'n' roll tempo and demonstrate appropriate large-ensemble performance techniques in an informal concert.

SKILLS REINFORCEMENT

9a ▶ **Analyzing** The song "Hound Dog" is built on a "blues scale" (lowered third, lowered seventh), an alteration of a standard major scale. These notes are "bent." (In the notation on pp. 212-213, the lowered third in the melody is B♭.) Help students find the "blue notes" of other major scales (for example, C, D, F, A) to strengthen the concept. Suggest that they improvise or compose short melodies on keyboard or synthesizer (or even using their voice) that incorporate these notes. Do the resulting melodies sound like the blues? Listen to or perform other blues songs to see if the students can identify the "bent" notes.

▶ **Recorder** See Resource Book p. I-17 for two countermelodies to accompany "Hound Dog."

2a

TECHNOLOGY/MEDIA LINK

4c **CD-ROM** Encourage students to create a simple accompaniment for "Hound Dog" and explore various rock styles. Have students

- Start *Band-in-a-Box*. Under song settings, set the key to G major, the chorus to end after 24, total choruses to 1, and uncheck "Overall Loop" and "Embellish Chords."
- Type the chord symbols in each bar.
- Select a rock style from the Style (sty) menu.
- Under the Edit menu, select intro bars to generate an introduction for the song.
- Click Play to hear the accompaniment and sing along.

LESSON AT A GLANCE

Element Focus RHYTHM Triplets

Skill Objective READING Read and sing from notation a song containing triplets

Connection Activity SOCIAL STUDIES Discuss the history and culture of St. Helena Island, SC

MATERIALS

- "Oh, Watch the Stars" CD 10-29
  Recording Routine: Intro (4 m.); v. 1; interlude (2 m.); v. 2; interlude (2 m.); v. 3; coda
- **Music Reading Practice, Sequence 21** CD 10-31
- *Havanaise for Violin and Orchestra* (excerpt) CD 10-34
- **Resource Book** pp. D-28, E-22, H-17, I-18

VOCABULARY

rhythm meter time signature triplet

◆ ◆ ◆ ◆ National Standards ◆ ◆ ◆ ◆

1c Sing music from diverse cultures
2a Play instruments accurately, alone and in small ensembles
4c Compose, using electronic media
5a Read half, quarter, eighth notes in duple meter
6c Understand and use basic principles of rhythm in music analysis
8b Identify ways music relates to language arts, social studies, and science

MORE MUSIC CHOICES

For more practice with triplets:
"Turn, Turn, Turn," p. 378
"*Se va el caimán*" ("The Alligator"), p. 306

1 INTRODUCE

Clap different four-beat rhythmic patterns.

6c Have students echo-clap each pattern, as a group and individually. Then have them determine the number of beats in each pattern. (four beats)

Musical Patterns

Did you ever sing a song about the sea and notice how just listening to the song paints a picture in your imagination? If you close your eyes, you can almost hear and see the water, feel the waves, and smell the salt air.

Listen to "Oh, Watch the Stars," a song from St. Helena Island, off the coast of South Carolina. What do you "see" when you close your eyes?

CD 10–29

oh, watch the stars

Folk Song from South Carolina

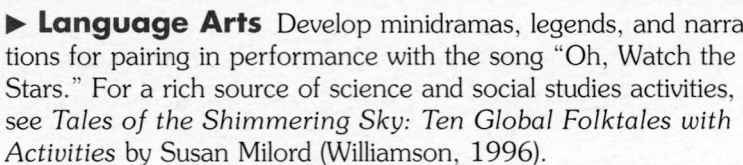

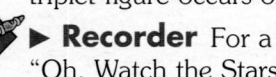

1. Oh, watch the stars, see how they run, Oh,
2. Oh, watch the sun, see how it sets, Oh,
3. Oh, watch the moon, see how it shines, Oh,

watch the stars, see how they run. ____ The _ stars run down _____ at the
watch the sun, see how it sets. ____ The _ stars rise up _____ at the
watch the moon, see how it shines. _ The _ sun runs down _____ at the

set-ting of the sun. Oh, watch the stars, see how they run.
set-ting of the sun. Oh, watch the sun, see how it sets.
ris-ing of the moon. Oh, watch the moon, see how it shines.

Footnotes

ACROSS THE CURRICULUM

8b ▶ **Language Arts** Develop minidramas, legends, and narrations for pairing in performance with the song "Oh, Watch the Stars." For a rich source of science and social studies activities, see *Tales of the Shimmering Sky: Ten Global Folktales with Activities* by Susan Milord (Williamson, 1996).

BUILDING SKILLS THROUGH MUSIC

▶ **Science** Discuss the lyrics of the song "Oh, Watch the Stars." Then discuss with students the fact that the sun is the reason for day and night. Ask students how sun lights up Earth. Have a student hold a globe tilted at a 23 degree angle and slowly turn it clockwise. Using a flashlight from several feet away, shine the light on the globe. Then ask students how the moon lights up Earth. (The moonlight is actually sunlight.) Discuss that their part of the earth is not facing the sun at night, however, the sun's light reaches the moon and the moon bounces it to Earth.

SKILLS REINFORCEMENT

▶ **Keyboard** Students can play an accompaniment for "Oh, Watch the Stars" using triplets. See Resource Book p. H-17.
2a They can play it using closest position I, IV, and V chords. The triplet figure occurs on beat 4.

▶ **Recorder** For a recorder countermelody to accompany "Oh, Watch the Stars," see Resource Book p. I-18.

▶ **Reading** Use the Music Reading worksheet on Resource Book, p. D-28, to reinforce students' understanding of triplets.

Conducting Patterns

Listen to the song again without looking at the music. Tap the beat and feel the pattern of strong and weak beats.

Conduct each pattern below to decide which pattern fits the song.

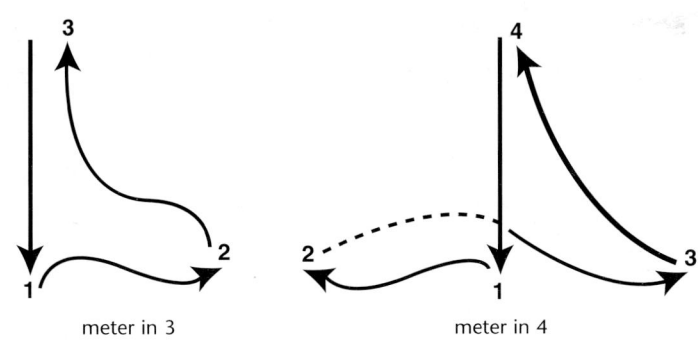

meter in 3   meter in 4

Sing the first phrase of the song. The rhythm is written below.

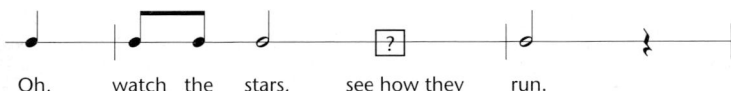

Oh,   watch the   stars,   see how they   run.

Which rhythmic figure do you think should go in the question box?

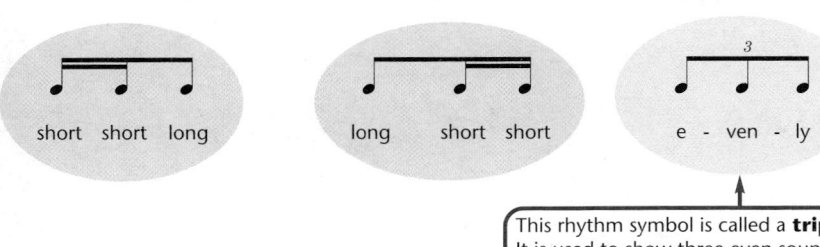

short short long   long   short short   e - ven - ly

This rhythm symbol is called a **triplet**. It is used to show three even sounds on a beat in simple meter ($\frac{2}{4}, \frac{3}{4}, \frac{4}{4}$).

Sing "Oh, Watch the Stars," using hand signs and pitch syllables.

Listen to *Havanaise* to hear triplets played by the violin.

CD 10-34
Havanaise for Violin and Orchestra

by Camille Saint-Saëns
as performed by the Polish National Radio Symphony Orchestra

Like the famous example from Bizet's *Carmen*, *Havanaise* was inspired by the rhythms of the *habanera*, a Cuban dance.

Unit 6   **217**

2 DEVELOP

Listening
 Lead students in a discussion about St. Helena Island, South Carolina. See Cultural Connection footnote below. Then play the recording of "Oh, Watch the Stars" **CD 10-29** while students keep a steady beat.

Conducting
Have students conduct patterns in 2, in 3, and in 4 to determine which one best fits the song.

ASK Which meter felt most comfortable when you conducted the song? (meter in 4)

Have students clap the rhythm pattern on p. 217 as they say the words of the first phrase of the song. (You clap the missing rhythm.)

ASK What words are on the beat that I clapped? *(see how they)*

Were the sounds all the same length? (yes)

Have students look at the triplet figure on p. 217.

SAY Because there are three eighth notes on the beat instead of two, the number 3 is written above the notes. We call this figure a triplet. Now fill in the missing rhythm.

Reading
For additional practice reading triplets, see Music Reading Practice, Sequence 21 on p. 500 and Resource Book p. E-22.

Listening
Have students listen for the triplets played by the violin in *Havanaise for Violin and Orchestra* **CD 10-34**

3 CLOSE

Element: RHYTHM ► **ASSESSMENT**

Performance/Observation Have students sing "Oh, Watch the Stars" while following the notation and conducting a four-beat pattern. Observe students' ability to perform the triplet rhythm accurately.

CULTURAL CONNECTION

▶ **St. Helena Island** The folk song "Oh, Watch the Stars" is from St. Helena Island, South Carolina. This island is part of a chain of about a hundred islands in the Atlantic Ocean off the coast of South Carolina, Georgia, and northern Florida. In the early nineteenth century, St. Helena had a number of large cotton plantations. After the Civil War, the federal government distributed land on the Sea Islands to former slaves who had developed their own culture and language. The language, called Gullah, is a synthesis of some West African languages, including Hausa, Igbo, and Yoruba, and colonial English. Some Gullah words the students may recognize are *goober*, which means peanut, and *gumbo*, which means okra.

SCHOOL TO HOME CONNECTION

▶ **Science** Ask students what constellations and planets are clearly visible this time of year in the night sky in their area. Encourage them to find out from newspapers, almanacs, star charts, family members, and other sources.

TECHNOLOGY/MEDIA LINK

Notation Software Invite students to create and notate rhythmic phrases for a layered rap that contains triplets.

LESSON AT A GLANCE

Element Focus **RHYTHM** Meter in 5

Skill Objective **MOVING** Move to meter in 5

Connection Activity **RELATED ARTS** Learn a Turkish folk dance

MATERIALS
- *Ali Pasha* **CD 10-35**
- *Take Five* **CD 10-37**
- **Dance Directions** for *Ali Pasha* p. 559

VOCABULARY
meter

◆ ◆ ◆ ◆ National Standards ◆ ◆ ◆ ◆

4c Compose, using electronic media
6b Listen and analyze the uses of rhythm in music from diverse cultures and genres
6c Understand and use basic principles of meter in music analysis
7a Create standards for evaluating performances
8a Show how different arts portray the same idea in unique ways
8b Identify ways music relates to social studies
9a Describe characteristics of music genres and styles from a variety of cultures

MORE MUSIC CHOICES

For more experience with meter in 5:

Eriskummainen kantele, p. 199

A Different Meter

Most of the music we listen to is in some form of duple or triple meter. In some countries, especially in eastern and southeastern Europe, meter in 5 is common.

Listen to this example from the Republic of Turkey. Each measure contains five beats.

CD 10–35
Ali Pasha

Folk Song from Turkey
The historical figure Ali Pasha [PAH-shah] was an 18th-century governor of a Greek province of the Ottoman Empire.

Listen again and this time count out the meter by tapping each finger on your book. Begin with your thumb on 1. Your little finger should fall on beat 5. On which fingers will the accent fall?

$1 \; 2 \; 3 \; 4 \; 5$

Create a body percussion pattern that shows the combination of accented and unaccented beats in meter in 5.

218

Footnotes

SPOTLIGHT ON

8b ▶ **Ali Pasha** Ali Pasha (1741–1822) became provincial governor of a Greek area of the Ottoman Empire in 1788. Through ongoing illegal and nasty tactics, he extended his area of governance significantly. Overcome by his own hunger for power, he refused to take orders from the head of the empire (the Sultan) in the capital city of Constantinople. In the interest of centralizing the government, his removal was necessary. His allies deserted him and he was assassinated in 1822.

BUILDING SKILLS THROUGH MUSIC

▶ **Social Studies** Share the information about Turkey found in Across the Curriculum p. 218. Have students look at the photo. Ask them to describe in detail the architecture of the buildings. Then have students look at the dancers on p. 219 and describe the detail of the clothes they are wearing. Divide the class into small groups. Have each group select either architecture or clothing to compare and contrast what they see on the pages to that of their community.

ACROSS THE CURRICULUM

8b ▶ **Social Studies** Locate Turkey on a world map. Challenge volunteers to research about the history of Turkey and its main city, Istanbul (formerly the city of Constantinople), and report their findings to the class.

▶ **Language Arts** For more information on this country's history, people, culture, and land, invite interested students to read *Turkey (Cultures of the World)* by Sean Sheehan (Benchmark Books, 1996) and *Turkey in Pictures (Visual Geography Series)* by Steve Feinstein (Lerner Publications, 1998).

Ali Pasha Folk Dance

People in Turkey have used these dance movements for hundreds of years. They still dance this way today.

▼ The leader on the end carries a handkerchief in her right hand. She uses it to signal changes in the steps.

▼ The *Ali Pasha* dance is performed in lines. Sometimes dancers hold each other's hands by hooking their little fingers together.

1 INTRODUCE

Give students, working in pairs or in small groups, this task: Make a short phrase or sentence starting with a three-syllable word accented on the first syllable, followed by a two-syllable word. Examples: *Mys-te-ry nov-el; Beau-ti-ful rain-bow.*

Ask groups to share their phrases quickly and write them on the board. Review the requirement that the first and the fourth syllables are to be the accented ones.

2 DEVELOP

Listening

 To help students aurally identify excerpts of music representing diverse periods, ask them to listen to *Ali Pasha* **CD 10-35** and notice that the syllables fall in this same pattern. Students can hear the pattern even though they don't know the Turkish language.

Point out that most of the music we listen to is in duple or triple meter, but this music has a meter of 5.

Ask students to

- Count the five beats by tapping their fingers, starting with their thumb as 1.
- Listen again to *Ali Pasha* to determine which beats are the strongest.
- Relate these to the five-beat meter diagram on p. 218.

Moving

Ask students to suggest body percussion patterns that show patterns of five beats, with the same strong sound used on beat 1 and beat 4 (for example: PAT-snap-snap PAT-snap).

continued on page 220

MOVEMENT

 ▶ **Patterned Dance** All over the world and all through history, people who are oppressed, or feel put down, try to deal with their misery by making up satirical songs about those who mistreat them. Can you think of some present-day examples? The folk song *Ali Pasha* makes fun of a very cruel official and military general of the Ottoman Turkish Empire. The dance has movements that are typical of the way people danced in Turkey in those days and also today.

Formation: One or more lines or open circles with hands joined at shoulder height (W position). Sometimes people hook little fingers (the pinkie hold). The leader is at the right end holding a kerchief in his/her free hand to signal changes in the step. For complete dance instructions for *Ali Pasha,* see p. 559.

SKILLS REINFORCEMENT

 ▶ **Creating** To reinforce the concept of meter in 5, have students develop body percussion patterns. First have them practice with different ways to group five-beat patterns. For example, start with a familiar grouping where the first and third beats are emphasized: **1**–2–**3**–4–5. Then have them work with a grouping where the first and fourth beats are emphasized: **1**–2–3–**4**–5. Invite them to experiment with other groupings, emphasizing different beats or alternating groupings in a sequence.

To extend the activity, invite students to transfer their pattern sequences to percussion instruments.

Lesson 3 Continued

Once a usable pattern is suggested, ask students to

- Perform it, making sure the beats are evenly spaced.
- Read their word phrases from the board, one right after the other in a steady rhythm, as they repeat the body percussion pattern.

Divide the class into four groups; have each group

- Perform the body percussion pattern once, in sequence, without missing a beat between groups.
- Perform the pattern softly as they listen again to the recording of *Ali Pasha* **CD 10-35.**

8b Provide the historical information about *Ali Pasha* from Spotlight On, p. 218. Have a student locate and show Turkey on a map or a globe. Mention events in American history that took place at a roughly parallel time: 1776—Declaration of Independence; 1789—first Constitutional Congress.

ASK **What do you think accounts for the song being rather lively, even though the events it talks about are rather serious?** (The lively mood may express happiness that Ali Pasha is no longer around to make lives miserable. Also, the song is for dancing.)

See Movement, p. 219, and invite students to learn the routine and perform it with the recording of *Ali Pasha* **CD 10-35.**

Listening

Have students

- Listen to the recording of *Take Five* **CD 10-37.**
- **6c** Count the five beats by tapping their fingers, starting with their thumb as 1.
- Read the information about Dave Brubeck on p. 220.

Another Take on Meter

Listen to the jazz piece *Take Five,* another "take" on meter in $\frac{5}{4}$. The percussion and piano introduction sets up the following five-beat pattern.

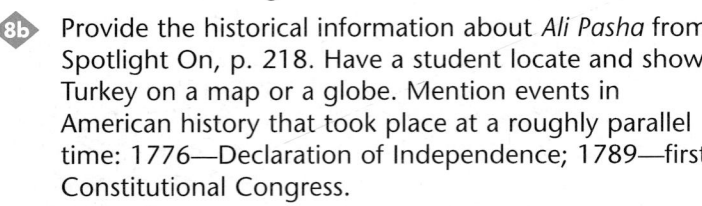

CD 10-37
Take Five

by Paul Desmond
as performed by the Dave Brubeck Quartet
This piece was made famous by the jazz quartet founded by pianist Dave Brubeck in the late 1950s. When first released, *Take Five* was at the top of the pop charts for months.

Tune In

Although *Take Five* became Brubeck's signature tune, it was actually composed by saxophonist Paul Desmond. It uses drummer Joe Morello's idea of $\frac{5}{4}$ meter.

M·U·S·I·C M·A·K·E·R·S
Dave Brubeck

Dave Brubeck (born 1920 in Concord, California) is one of the 20th century's most important jazz composers and performers. In 1959 the Dave Brubeck Quartet cut its first album using experimental meters and rhythms. That album, *Time Out,* was the first jazz album to sell over one million copies. Brubeck has performed for four presidents (Kennedy, Johnson, Reagan, and Clinton) and was elected to the *Downbeat Hall of Fame.* Brubeck was one of the first musicians to have a star on the Hollywood Walk of Fame. He holds six honorary degrees and has appeared on the cover of *Time* magazine.

Footnotes

MOVEMENT

8a ▶ **Patterned Dance** Have students form a circle, arms at sides, one foot in front of the other. Have them

- Listen to *Take Five* and count the meter in 5 aloud.
- Add accents by stepping on counts 1 and 4 to divide the meter into groupings of 3 and 2.
- Counts 1–2–3: Step forward on right foot, swing arms forward and upward.
- Counts 4–5: Step back on left foot, swing arms back, feet together.
- Counts 1–2–3: Step forward on left foot, swing arms forward and upward.
- Counts 4–5: Step back on right foot and then left, swing arms back, feet together.

TEACHER TO TEACHER

▶ **Meter in 5** Developing the feeling for an uneven meter such as 5 is a process requiring practice; it will be easy for very few students. As in acquiring other skills, short exposures and exercises over the course of several (or many) lessons will bring about the security needed. (For students having difficulty, revert to numbers; have them count "1 2 3" and "1 2" and then listen to how the "1s" come in different places when these are combined.)

Moving in Five

Take Five follows this form:

1. Introduction: Percussion and piano set up the pattern of five beats.
2. Theme: a short melody played by the saxophone.
3. The saxophone "takes a ride," or improvises a solo.
4. The drummer "takes a ride," improvising a solo.
5. The theme returns in the saxophone.

Feeling an irregular meter is easy if you do it with motions. Try this movement with the saxophone theme. Each section lasts eight measures.

◀ **Count 1–2–3:**
Step forward on the right foot as you swing your arms upward.

Count 4–5: ▶
Step back on the left foot. Then swing your arms back as you bring your feet together.

...eat the entire five-beat pattern, beginning with the left foot.)

Moving

8a Have students practice the movements suggested on p. 221. (See also Movement, p. 220.) Have them

- Coordinate the movements with counting aloud.
- Listen again to *Take Five* **CD 10-37.**
- Add the movements they have practiced to the ABA sections of the recording.

3 CLOSE

> **Element: RHYTHM** | **ASSESSMENT**

6c **Performance/Observation** Ask students to

- Perform the meter-in-5 movement during the ABA sections of *Take Five* and to improvise body percussion patterns during the two solo sections (saxophone and drums).
- Perform two different patterns, one for each solo.
- Move to the entire piece, as planned.

Students can also decide on what to do during the introduction (snap fingers, count aloud, and so on).

7a Set up a format for small ensemble performances of the *Take Five* movement. Observe students' ability to perform the movement patterns at the appropriate time in the form of the piece.

SKILLS REINFORCEMENT

6b ▶ **Analyzing** The feeling of meter in 5 can be stabilized by performing it together with a pattern of 4. Ask students to count "1 2 3 4," as described in Teacher to Teacher, p. 220. With it, put a five-syllable word such as *Con-stan-ti-no-ple* (there can be a secondary accent on either the third or fourth syllables).

Then ask them to perform a four-beat clap-snap-snap-snap pattern along with a four-syllable word such as *Min-ne-so-ta* (with accents on first and third syllables).

Divide the class in half, one group for each of the patterns above. The four-syllable group performs its pattern five times while the five-syllable group performs its pattern four times. The syllable speed must remain steady and synchronized. Trade patterns so everyone can experience both patterns.

TECHNOLOGY/MEDIA LINK

4c **Sequencing Software** Invite students to use standard symbols and write music that incorporates rhythmic patterns in various meters. Have students compose and sequence rhythmic rondos in meter in 5. Have them begin by drawing, on lined notebook paper, five percussion staves of four bars each. Remind them to include a $\frac{5}{4}$ time signature at the beginning. Using quarter notes, eighth notes, half notes, dotted quarters, and dotted half notes and their corresponding rests, have students

- Compose the first four measures, the A section, making sure that each measure contains five beats.
- Transfer it to the third and fifth line (the returns of A).
- Compose the B and C sections.

LESSON AT A GLANCE

Element Focus   **RHYTHM** Augmentation and diminution

Skill Objective   **SINGING** Perform a song in augmentation and in diminution

Connection Activity   **MATHEMATICS** Relate the concept of augmentation and diminution to specific numerical values

MATERIALS

- "Old Abram Brown"   **CD 10-38**

  Recording Routine: Intro (4 m.); vocal; instrumental; interlude (4 m.); 4-part round twice; coda

- **Music Reading Practice, Sequence 22**   **CD 11-1**

- **Resource Book** pp. B-18, D-30, E-23, F-27

VOCABULARY

rhythm	meter	time signature
augmentation	diminution	

◆ ◆ ◆ ◆ National Standards ◆ ◆ ◆ ◆

1a Sing accurately, with good breath control
4c Arrange, using electronic media
5a Read and notate known rhythms in simple meter
6c Understand and use basic principles of rhythm in music analysis
8b Identify ways music relates to math

MORE MUSIC CHOICES

For more experience with augmentation and diminution:
"Autumn Canon," p. 148
"Las velitas" ("Candles Burning Bright"), p. 147
"Still, Still, Still" ("Sleep, Dearest Child"), p. 468

1 INTRODUCE

6c Clap four-beat rhythm patterns, consisting of quarter notes, eighth notes, and half notes. Have students echo-clap each pattern using rhythm syllables. Then have them determine the number of beats in each pattern. (four beats)

The LONG and SHORT of It

"Hey, Dad, can I have a raise in my allowance?"

"Sorry, son, we can't afford to *augment* your income right now."

"But, Dad, if I don't have a bigger allowance I'll have to *diminish* all my activities."

"Then I guess you'll just have to cut back on some things."

To "augment" means to make something larger or longer. To "diminish" means to make something smaller or shorter. How does that work in music?

Sing "Old Abram Brown" in unison. Then sing it as a round with your classmates.

 CD 10–38   **Old Abram Brown**

Words by Walter de la Mare   Music by Benjamin Britten

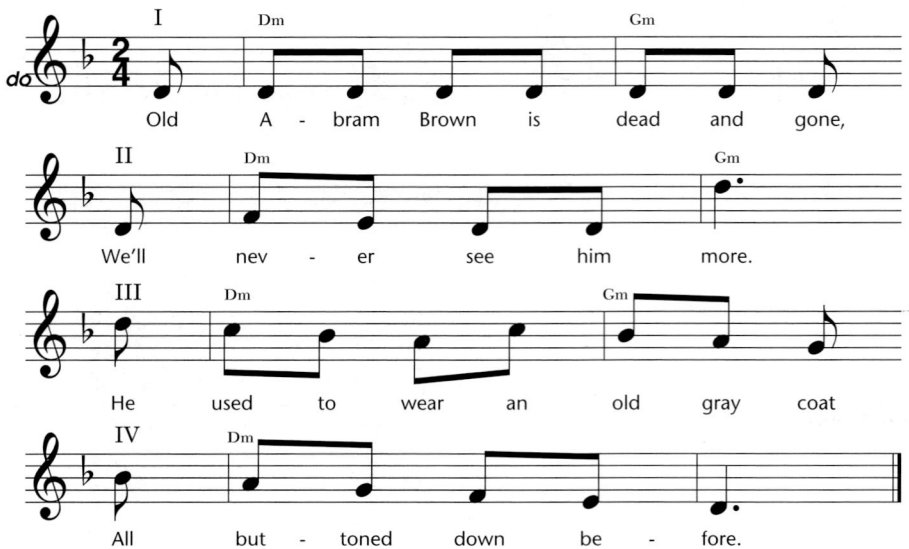

I — Old A-bram Brown is dead and gone,
II — We'll nev-er see him more.
III — He used to wear an old gray coat
IV — All but-toned down be-fore.

Footnotes

ACROSS THE CURRICULUM

8b ▶ **Math** Have students choose a phrase from one of the songs listed under More Music Choices above and compute the proportional numerical value of each note. The following example is from "Autumn Canon" (using $\frac{4}{4}$ meter).

Augmentation	8	8	8	4–4	4–4	4–2–2	8
Original	4	4	4	2–2	2–2	2–1–1	4
Diminution	2	2	2	1–1	1–1	1–.5–.5	2

BUILDING SKILLS THROUGH MUSIC

▶ **Social Studies** Have students create a time line using the following musicians and their dates: Benjamin Britten (1913–1976); Dave Brubeck (b. 1920); Muddy Waters (1915–1983); Alberto Ginastera (1916–1983); Ralph Vaughan Williams (1872-1958); Robert Moog (b. 1934); Isao Tomita (b. 1932).

SKILLS REINFORCEMENT

1a ▶ **Singing** Write the D-minor scale on the staff. Have descending *mi–do* and *la* in a different color. Write pitch syllables underneath. Have students

- Sing from la_l to *la* with pitch syllables and hand signs. (A scale from la_l to *la* is a minor scale.)

- Sing *la-do-mi* and identify it as a minor chord. In the key of D minor it is the tonic chord or I chord. Show on staff.

- Sing la_l-do-mi-la-mi-do-la_l and identify this as a minor arpeggio. An *arpeggio* is a broken chord. Show on staff.

- Sing the minor scale and arpeggio individually.

Augmenting and Diminishing

If you augment the notes in "Old Abram Brown," they will become twice as long. All the eighth notes ♫ will become quarter notes ♩ ♩ and the dotted quarter ♩. will become a dotted half note ♩..

Sing "Old Abram Brown" in augmentation. Are the rhythms shorter or longer? Does this make the song seem faster or slower?

Perform "Old Abram Brown" again, this time diminish all the note values. You will have to cut all the note values in half.

Does this make the song seem faster or slower?

Benjamin Britten

Benjamin Britten (1913–1976) was one of the most important British composers of the 20th century. While his style of composition seems clear and simple on the surface, it is actually very complex. Many of Britten's compositions require children performers. "Old Abram Brown" is from a song collection called *Friday Afternoons* that was written for children. Britten wrote in nearly every kind of musical form–opera, song, chamber works, oratorio, and cantatas.

Show What You Know!

Select any song from the ones you've learned in the book. **Play** it or **sing** it as you ordinarily would. Then **perform** the song in augmentation. Be sure to keep the beat the same. Did you perform it using longer notes or shorter notes? Now **perform** the song in diminution. Did you perform it using longer notes or shorter ones?

Unit 6   223

---

2 DEVELOP

Singing

1a Have students conduct a two-beat pattern while listening to and then singing "Old Abram Brown" **CD 10-38.**

Reading

5a Have students read and clap the rhythm of the song.

6c **ASK How can the rhythm change to make the words sound twice as slow, without slowing down the steady beat?** (Make each note value twice as long.)

8b Provide copies of the Reading Music Worksheet on Resource Book p. D-30. Have students identify the note values and clap the rhythm as they say the words of the first line of the song notated in quarter notes.

SAY When note values are made twice as long, the rhythm is augmented.

Help students sing the song in augmentation.

SAY The opposite of augmentation is *diminution*. To diminish a rhythm, note values are cut in half.

Have students identify the note values, clap the rhythm of the song notated in eighth notes, and sing it in diminution. For more experience with the mathematical concept of augmentation/dimunition, see Across the Curriculum, p. 222.

Have students perform Music Reading Practice, Sequence 22 on p. 500 (also found on Resource Book p. E-23) for more practice reading augmented and diminished rhythms.

3 CLOSE

Element: RHYTHM   ASSESSMENT

1a **Performance/Observation** Divide the class into two groups. Have one group sing "Old Abram Brown" **6c** the way it is written and the other group sing it in augmentation. Then switch groups and have one group sing it as written and the other in diminution. Observe students' ability to maintain a steady beat while performing each version.

SPOTLIGHT ON

▶ **The Song** No one is sure if "Old Abram Brown" was a real person, but we do know that this rhyme was already well-known and sung by children in England by 1849. In play, the name of the "deceased" was often substituted for "Old Abram Brown," and despite its rather grim lyrics, children were reported to have sung it at a brisk and cheerful pace.

The rhyme was often sung in America to the tune of "Old Lang Syne," but Benjamin Britten composed a haunting original tune which he set for boys' voices in his 1935 collection, *Friday Afternoons*. Britten notes the text as "anonymous," from *Tom Tiddler's Ground* by Walter de la Mare.

Britten dedicated the collection to his brother and the boys of Clive House, Prestatyn. He wrote the pieces for their school music classes, which met on Friday afternoons.

TECHNOLOGY/MEDIA LINK

4c **Notation Software** Have students create their own arrangement of the round "Old Abram Brown." Have them

- Set up the program for four staff lines.
- Choose the key of D minor (one flat).
- Notate, two times through, the top staff of "Old Abram Brown" by selecting the desired rhythmic value and then clicking on the musical staff to choose the pitch.
- Notate the other voices in a similar manner, remembering to stagger the round's entrances.
- Choose the best playback voices for their arrangement of the song.

LESSON AT A GLANCE

Element Focus   **FORM** 12-bar blues form

Skill Objective   **LISTENING** Listen to a blues song

Connection Activity   **STYLE** Explore the traditional performance characteristics of blues

MATERIALS

- "Good Mornin', Blues"   **CD 11-7**

    Recording Routine: Intro (4 m.); v. 1; instrumental; v. 2; coda

- *Country Blues*   **CD 11-9**
- *Walkin' Blues*   **CD 11-10**
- **Resource Book** p. H-19
- Autoharp, keyboard, guitar

VOCABULARY

blues

◆ ◆ ◆ ◆ National Standards ◆ ◆ ◆ ◆

1c Sing music from diverse genres

2c Perform instrumental music from diverse genres

3a Improvise simple harmonic accompaniments

3c Improvise melodies with consistent tonality

6a Listen and describe events in music using appropriate terms

6b Listen and analyze uses of pitch, harmony, timbre, and form in music from diverse genres

6c Understand and use basic principles of tonality, chords, and harmonic progressions in music analysis

8b Identify ways music relates to social studies and language arts

9a Describe characteristics of music genres and styles from a variety of cultures

9b Classify high-quality musical works by genre

MORE MUSIC CHOICES

For more experience with blues style:

"St. Louis Blues," p. 352

"Basin Street Blues," p. 354

A Form of BLUES

What does it mean to have the blues? Did you know that this expression comes from an African American musical style that has been around for more than one hundred years?

How can we identify a blues song? One way is through the lyrics. Look at "Good Mornin', Blues" and **analyze** the form, or pattern, of the lyrics. Which lines are the same? How would you **describe** the form? Blues singers often improvise their lyrics on the spot. What do you think they do as they sing the second line? Of course! They think up the last line!

Sing "Good Mornin', Blues" with a "blues" feeling.

Good Mornin', Blues

CD 11-7

Edited with New Additional Material by Alan Lomax

New Words and New Musical Arrangement by Huddie Ledbetter

1. Good morn - in', blues,   Blues, how do you   do?

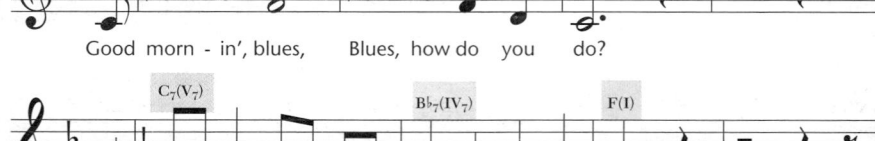

Good morn - in', blues,   Blues, how do you   do?

I'm   do-in' all right, ____Good morn-in', how are   you?

2. I sent for you yesterday, Here you come a-walkin' today.   *(2 times)* Got your mouth wide open, You don't know what to say.

TRO—© Copyright 1959 (Renewed) Folkways Music Publishers, Inc., New York, NY. Used by permission.

Footnotes

SKILLS REINFORCEMENT

3a ▶ **Improvising** At the end of each phrase in "Good Mornin', Blues," have one student improvise on a barred instrument set up in F pentatonic. This will last for six beats (from bar 3, beat 2 through bar 4, beat 3; and the same for bars 7–8 and 11–12).

BUILDING SKILLS THROUGH MUSIC

▶ **Social Studies** Display a transparency of the Semantic Map from Resource Book p. C-6 with "Blues" written in the center box. Label the surrounding boxes with the titles "Good Mornin', Blues," *Country Blues*, and *Walkin' Blues*. Have students listen to **CD 11-7**, **CD 11-9**, and **CD 11-10** and identify characteristics of each performance including vocal and instrumental timbre.

TEACHER TO TEACHER

▶ **How to Improvise** The "feel" for improvising during the allotted spaces in a blues form develops through aural familiarity. Have students listen to "Good Mornin', Blues" and other blues pieces and play during the improvisation breaks with "air mallets" to develop a sense of how many beats a short improvisation will fill. Once a few students catch on, the ability will spread.

2c ▶ **Guitar Capo** To accompany "Good Mornin', Blues" on guitar (see Teacher to Teacher, p. 226), it will be easier for students to place a capo on fret 3 and substitute the following chords:

F = D; B♭7 = G7; C7 = A7

Country Blues

The blues can be about anything that gets you down. Listen to *Country Blues* to discover why the singer is feeling blue.

CD 11–9
Country Blues

written and performed by Muddy Waters

Muddy Waters was famous for his bottleneck guitar playing. He would play guitar using a steak bone, pocket knife, brass tube, or bottleneck. Can you hear any of these sounds in this recording?

M·U·S·I·C M·A·K·E·R·S

Muddy Waters

Muddy Waters (1915–1983) was one of the most influential guitarists of the 20th century. The city of Chicago is known for its special kind of blues music, and Waters was the musician who defined the Chicago blues. His first hit song, *I Can't Be Satisfied*, was so popular in Chicago that he had a hard time buying a copy for himself! He taught himself to play the guitar using a slide and became one of the best musicians in the city. When Waters and his band members challenged other bands to contests, they almost always won the contest!

Unit 6 **225**

1 INTRODUCE

9a Ask students to share what they already know about music that is called "blues." List their responses on the board using two categories—lyrics and music. Continue the discussion by sharing the information in Spotlight On and Cultural Connection below.

Listening

Have students

- Look at the lyrics of "Good Mornin', Blues" on p. 224.

- Listen to the recording of "Good Mornin', Blues" **CD 11-7.** (Point out to students that the soloist does not perform the notation exactly as it is written. She performs in a "blues" style—"bending" the melody and rhythm.)

6b
- Discuss the things they heard and compare this to their list.

- Discuss any additional characteristics of blues that were not on the original list, using standard terminology in explaining musical performances.

2 DEVELOP

Singing

1c Ask students to sing along with the recording of "Good Mornin', Blues" **CD 11-7.** Lead students in a discussion about the lyrics of the song.

ASK What are the lyrics of the "blues" about? (generally, something that makes you feel sad)

6b **What is the form or pattern of the lyrics?** (A blues text consists of short verses. Each verse has three lines. The first two lines are the same, and the ending of the third line rhymes with the ending of the other two.)

continued on page 226

SPOTLIGHT ON

9a ▶ **Different Kinds of Blues** As a twentieth-century African American vocal style, blues can be categorized as follows:

- **Country blues**—A male singer with an acoustic, steel-string guitar (as in the songs in this lesson). Great freedom in improvising both the words and the accompaniment.

- **Classic blues**—A female singer accompanied by a New Orleans style jazz band or pianist. Words and melodies are composed, allowing for interpretation, but not free invention. Formal stage presentation. Flowered from 1920–1930.

- **Urban blues**—A male singer leading an instrumental group. Flowered after World War II (1945–1960). Composed lyrics; much vocal improvisation.

CULTURAL CONNECTION

9b ▶ **Blues Style** Blues was without question a product of African American culture in the late nineteenth and early twentieth century. The spiritual provided hope during slavery times for a better life in the hereafter. The blues developed after slavery officially ended. It was a personal lament for situations causing sadness, but often the song ended by suggesting the difficult situation wouldn't last forever. A great upsurge of interest in the blues among white musicians and listeners came in the 1960s as part of the folk music revival.

Unit 6 *Making Music Our Own* **225**

Lesson 5 Continued

Listening

6a Have students

- Read the text about Muddy Waters on p. 225.
- Listen to the recording of *Country Blues* **CD 11-9**.

ASK What blues effects can you identify in Muddy Waters' performance? (bottleneck guitar playing, vocal and instrumental improvisation, "bent" notes)

Playing

Have students

2c
- Learn to play chords shown on p. 226 on Autoharp, guitar, or keyboard.
- Accompany a class performance of "Good Mornin', Blues."

See Teacher to Teacher below for tips on playing a rhythm-and-blues strum.

Creating

Play the recording of "Good Mornin', Blues" **CD 11-7** again. Ask students to sing along and think about another verse they could add that would fit the AAB form of the lyrics.

8b Assist students in working out another verse for "Good Mornin', Blues." Point out that each line must fit into nine beats (not counting the two additional beats in the dotted half note). In this song the first word *good* is an unstressed "pickup" to the nine beats. A visual framework may be provided by drawing nine vertical lines on the board to use as a guide for fitting in student suggestions. Remind students to think of the melody and see if the words fit. Stressed syllables must fall on strong beats (1 and 3). Quarter notes may replace half notes. Examples:

I need to write a new verse for this song,

Oh, I need to write a new verse for this song,

Just a few short words 'cause it can't be very long.

Improvising

3c Encourage students to improvise melodies for their new verses. Help students write the rhythmic notation above

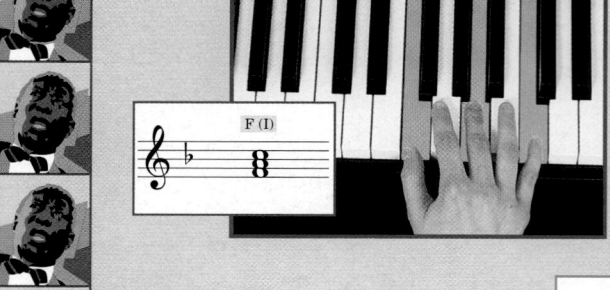

Blues in F
Learn to **play** these chords on keyboard to accompany "Good Mornin', Blues."

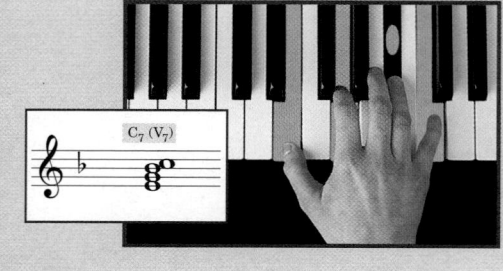

Create your own blues lyrics based on the rhyme scheme of "Good Mornin', Blues." Then **improvise** a melody to accompany your song.

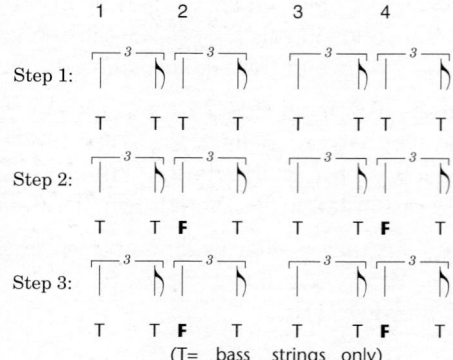

226

Footnotes

ACROSS THE CURRICULUM

8b ▶ Language Arts The blues style affected the art and poetry of many African American artists. *The Dream Keeper and Other Poems* by Langston Hughes (Random, 1996) uses dialect to portray the sound of the blues. Compare the poem's form and lyrics to that of the song "Good Mornin', Blues."

TEACHER TO TEACHER

2c ▶ Guitar Strum Have students play a rhythm-and-blues strum with "Good Mornin', Blues." (T = thumb; F = full strum)

	1	2	3	4
Step 1:	T	T T T	T	T T T
Step 2:	T	T F T	T	T F T
Step 3:	T	T F T	T	T F T

(T= bass strings only)

Walkin' Blues

Listen to the blues sound of *Walkin' Blues*. How would you **describe** the feeling expressed in the music?

Walkin' Blues

written and performed by Robert Johnson

Robert Johnson (1912–1938) was one of the greatest of the Delta bluesmen. His guitar playing was legendary. Listen for the guitar solos at the beginning and end of *Walkin' Blues*.

Walkin' Blues LISTENING MAP

Verses 1-2

Verses 3-5

 CD 11-10

---

the new verses for the song using standard symbols to notate meter and rhythm in simple patterns.

Analyzing

To help students aurally identify excerpts of music representing diverse periods, have them

6c
- Listen to "Good Mornin', Blues" **CD 11-7** again and count the total number of bars in the song (12).
- Build a chart showing the chords that belong in each bar:

F	F	F	F
B♭₇	B♭₇	F	F
C₇	B♭₇	F	F

- Identify F as the key of this song.

3a Using a keyboard chart, assist students in identifying F as tone 1 of the F scale, B♭ as tone 4, and C as tone 5. Remind them that Roman numerals are used to indicate chords. Help students convert the chart to Roman numerals (F = I; B♭₇ = IV₇; C₇ = V₇). See Skills Reinforcement below and encourage students to play a keyboard improvisation with "Good Mornin', Blues."

Listening

Have students

- Examine the blues chord progression outlined in the listening map on p. 227.

6b
- Listen to the recording of *Walkin' Blues* **CD 11-10** as they follow the listening map.

3 CLOSE

Element: FORM — **ASSESSMENT**

6a **Observation** Observe students as they

6c
- Make three cards, one each for the I, IV, and V₇ chords.
- Listen to the recording again and hold up the appropriate cards to show 12-bar blues form as they hear the chord changes in "Good Mornin', Blues."

SKILLS REINFORCEMENT

▶ Keyboard Students can play an improvisation with "Good Mornin', Blues" using LH tritones and RH F-blues pentascale
3a (F, A♭, B♭, C♭, C♮).

For a more detailed treatment of this activity, see Resource Book p. H-19.

TECHNOLOGY/MEDIA LINK

3a **CD-ROM** Use *Band-in-a-Box* as a tool for learning improvisation. As students sing "Good Mornin', Blues," have them enter the jazz swing style accompaniment for this song. Have students

- Sing the song with the *Band-in-a-Box* accompaniment.
- Mark the keyboard's middle octave F, A♭, and E♭ with tape.
- Improvise at the end of measures 3 and 4, 7 and 8, and 11 and 12.

Transparency Display the listening map transparency for *Walkin' Blues* as you play the recording. Invite a student to point to each section of the piece at the appropriate time in the music.

LESSON AT A GLANCE

Element Focus **MELODY** Major and minor triads

Skill Objective **SINGING** Sing a song that is in minor tonality

Connection Activity **CULTURE** Discuss the customs and culture of Argentina

MATERIALS

- "Viva Jujuy" (Spanish) **CD 11-11**
- "Viva Jujuy" (English) **CD 11-12**

  Recording Routine: Intro (20 m.); vocal; instrumental

- **Pronunciation Practice/Translation** p. 531
- *Danza del trigo* (excerpt) **CD 11-15**
- **Resource Book** p. A-23
- barred instruments, guitar, keyboard

VOCABULARY

scale   major scale   minor scale

◆◆◆◆ National Standards ◆◆◆◆

1c Sing music from diverse cultures

2a Play instruments accurately in small ensembles

6a Listen and describe events in music using appropriate terminology

6c Understand and use basic principles of tonality, intervals, and chords in music analysis

9a Describe characteristics of music styles from a variety of cultures

MORE MUSIC CHOICES

For more practice with minor tonality:
"Pat Works on the Railway," p. 182

1 INTRODUCE

Point out Argentina on a map. Then point out the northwest area of the country bordering Peru and Bolivia. Invite students to research and share information on Argentina. (See Across the Curriculum on p. 229.) Tell them that "Viva Jujuy" is a folk song from this region.

Love of Country

Every nation has songs that express love of one's country. "Viva Jujuy," from Argentina, South America, is such a song. Jujuy is a province in the far northwest corner of the country, bordering Bolivia and Peru. A deep gorge, called Humahuaqueña [oo-mah-wah-KEH-nyah], is located there.

Listen to and then **sing** "Viva Jujuy."

CD 11-11
MIDI 16

Viva Jujuy

English Words by Aura Kontra   *Folk Song from Argentina*

t, d r m s (l) d'

Am   C   F   G₇   C

do

Vi - va Ju - juy, ____ vi - va la pu - na,   Vi - va mi a - ma - da.
Long live Ju - juy, ____ long live the high land, Long live my true love.

F   C   E₇   Am

Vi - van los ce - rros   pin - ta - rra - jea - dos   De mi que - bra - da.
Long live the can - yon   and loft - y moun - tains   Soar - ing high a - bove.

F   G₇   C   F   G₇   C

De mi   que - bra - da   Hu - ma - hua - que - ña.
Soar - ing high   a - bove Hu - ma - hua - que - ña.

F   C   E₇   Am

No te se - pa - res   De mis a - mo - res   Tu e - res mi due - ña.
I'll nev - er leave you. I'll not for - sake you. I be - long to you.

228

Footnotes

TEACHER TO TEACHER

▶ **Other Languages** It is important for students to try to learn song lyrics in another language. Students who speak only English need to extend themselves. However, care needs to be taken not to destroy interest in a song experience by devoting too much time in any given lesson to correct language skill. Making an effort at the language and then finishing the melody by singing *la la la* may sometimes better serve the overall objectives of a lesson.

BUILDING SKILLS THROUGH MUSIC

▶ **Reading** Review the songs "America, the Beautiful" (p. 76) and "This Land is Your Land" (p. 118). Ask students why they think the phrases "for amber waves of grain" and "and the wheat fields waving" were included in the two songs. Discuss reasons why the Argentinean composer Alberto Ginastera would include a wheat dance as part of a ballet.

SPOTLIGHT ON

▶ **The Composer** A highly respected Argentinean composer, Alberto Ginastera (1916–1983) is considered an interpreter of Argentinean culture in the larger format of Western art music. He was born in Buenos Aires; as an adult, he both taught music and held administrative positions in institutions of higher learning. The ballet *Estancia* was commissioned in 1941 by the American Ballet Caravan Company. It was first performed in 1952 at the Teatro Colón in Buenos Aires. Ginastera's first venture abroad was from 1945 to 1947 in the United States. He later spent much time in the United States and Europe, though he continued to hold various teaching posts in Argentina. In the late 1960s he moved to Geneva, Switzerland, and lived there until his death. (The pronunciation of the composer's surname is a reflection of his Italian heritage.)

Travel to a Different Tune

The two most common scales are major and minor. Every major scale has a relative minor scale with the same exact pitches. But the two scales start and end on different pitches. They share the same key signature. The major scale begins on *do;* the minor scale begins on *la.*

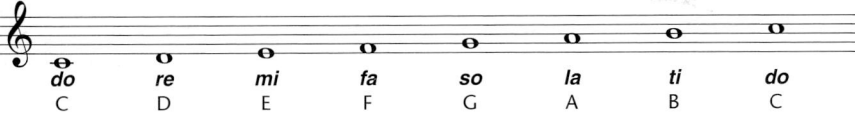

do	re	mi	fa	so	la	ti	do
C	D	E	F	G	A	B	C

la	ti	do	re	mi	fa	so	la
A	B	C	D	E	F	G	A

Sing the first two lines of *"Viva Jujuy."* Is the melody based on the major scale or the minor scale?

MUSIC MAKERS
Alberto Ginastera

Alberto Ginastera [jee-nah-STEH-rah] (1916–1983) was a 20th century composer from Argentina. At age 7, he began studying the piano, and at age 12, he entered a music conservatory. Early in his career, Ginastera's music expressed strong feelings of Argentinian nationalism. In mid-career, his style changed and he began writing large, dissonant works that reflected the trends of the time.

Listen to *Danza del trigo*, one of Ginastera's earliest compositions. Can you **identify** which scale is used?

CD 11–15
Danza del trigo

from *Estancia*
by Alberto Ginastera
as performed by the Simón Bolívar Symphony Orchestra; Eduardo Mata, conductor

Estancia was a ballet written in 1941. The ballet includes dances showing Argentinian life. *Danza del trigo* is a wheat dance.

Unit 6 **229**

---

2 DEVELOP

Listening
6a Ask students to listen to *"Viva Jujuy"* **CD 11-11**, patting the steady beat for the A section, and tapping the shoulders (crossing arms over chest) for the B section.

Singing
1c Help students learn the Spanish words of *"Viva Jujuy,"* using the Pronunciation Practice Track **CD 11-14** and Resource Book p. A-23, before singing the song.

Analyzing
Have students play the two scales on p. 229.

9a **SAY** *"Viva Jujuy"* demonstrates a very common characteristic of Andean songs—the shift from minor to major and back again.

2a Set up an A-minor triad and a C-major triad on one or more barred instruments (guitar or keyboard can also be used). Have students sing once again while small groups of students play these chords as they occur in the score.

Listening
6a Play *Danza del trigo* **CD 11-15**. Have students listen for major and minor tonalities and identify the form (ABA).

The A section is quiet, with two solo themes; the B section is played by full orchestra. The A section has major/minor contrasts: first theme—flute, major; second theme—horns, minor. The last chord is major. When the A section returns at the end, both themes are major; this time a violin replaces the flute.

3 CLOSE

Element: MELODY   **ASSESSMENT**

1c **Performance/Observation** Have students develop a performance of *"Viva Jujuy."* Observe their ability to perform in major and minor tonalities.

SKILLS REINFORCEMENT

6c ▶ **Analyzing** Sound the A-minor chord and have students sing the A-minor scale as it appears on p. 229. Help students notice that the A-minor chord acts as the center for the entire scale. Repeat the procedure, using the C-major chord and the C-major scale. Next, ask those playing the chords to play them to the steady beat whenever those chords are used in *"Viva Jujuy."* Section A: measures 1, 2, 4, 6, 8; Section B: measures 10, 12, 14, 16. These chords are acting as the tonal center at these points. Point out that Section A starts in minor, switches to major, but ends in minor. Section B starts in major and switches to minor at the end.

ACROSS THE CURRICULUM

▶ **Language Arts** Invite students to research the customs and culture of Argentina and share the information with the class. One print resource is the book *Argentina in Pictures (Visual Geography Series)* by E. W. Egan (Lerner Publications, 1994).

TECHNOLOGY/MEDIA LINK

Web Site For more information on the music and composers of Argentina, visit *www.sfsuccessnet.com.*

LESSON AT A GLANCE

Element Focus **MELODY** Mixolydian mode

Skill Objective **READING** Read and sing from notation a song in mixolydian mode

Connection Activity **SOCIAL STUDIES** Investigate the history of the whaling industry and the use of whaling songs

MATERIALS
- "The Greenland Whale Fishery" **CD 11-16**
  Recording Routine: Intro (8 m.); v. 1; v. 2; v. 3; v. 4; v. 5; coda
- **Music Reading Practice, Sequence 23** **CD 11-18**
- **Resource Book** pp. B-18, D-32, E-24
- resonator bells

VOCABULARY

whole step	half step	major scale
minor scale	mode	mixolydian

◆ ◆ ◆ ◆ National Standards ◆ ◆ ◆ ◆
1a Sing accurately in small ensembles
1c Sing music from diverse cultures
5c Identify standard notation symbols for pitch and rhythm
6c Understand and use basic principles of intervals in music analysis
8b Identify ways music relates to science and social studies

MORE MUSIC CHOICES
For more practice with mixolydian mode:
"Don't You Hear the Lambs?" p. 97

1 INTRODUCE

1a Sing short mixolydian (*so* to *so′*) melodic patterns in G-*so* using a neutral syllable. Have students echo-sing each pattern on *loo* and then using pitch syllables (give *so* as a starting pitch).

A SONG OF THE SEA

By the mid-1800s, whaling had become a vital industry in the New England states. Whale oil was used in lamps, lighthouse beacons and street lights, and in soap, varnish, and paint. Whalebone was strong and flexible. It was used to make canes, umbrellas, carriage springs, and shoehorns.

Whaling was a dangerous occupation. Many songs were written about the adventures of the whalers at sea.

Sing "The Greenland Whale Fishery," a whaling song that was first sung in Britain and then passed to Newfoundland sailors.

◀ Many sailors spent their spare time at sea doing scrimshaw. Scrimshaw involves engraving a design on polished ivory or whalebone with a sharp tool, and filling in the lines with ink. Today, a manufactured material called alabastrite is used as a substitute for whalebone.

CD 11-16

The Greenland Whale Fishery

Newfoundland Version of a British Sea Song

1. It was in the ___ year of ___ fif - ty - five, On ___
2. Bark - er ___ was our ___ cap - tain's name, Our ___
3. Our ___ mate a - loft on the fore - top stood With a

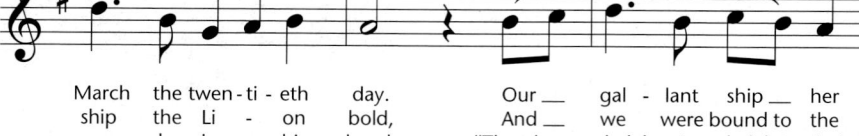

March the twen - ti - eth day. Our ___ gal - lant ship ___ her
ship the Li - on bold, And ___ we were bound to the
spy - glass in ___ his hand. "There's a whale! A whale! A whale -

an - chors weighed, And to sea we sailed a - way, brave boys, And to
north - ern seas ___ To face the storms and cold, brave boys, To ___
fish!" he cries, "And he's arch - ing toward the land, brave boys, And he's

Footnotes

SKILLS REINFORCEMENT

6c ▶ **Reading** See Resource Book pp. D-32 and E-24 for more practice with mixolydian mode.

▶ **Playing** Have students determine which bars are needed to play various mixolydian scales on resonator bells. Ask them to use their knowledge of whole and half steps to play various mixolydian scales on a keyboard.

BUILDING SKILLS THROUGH MUSIC

▶ **Social Studies** Review the elements of stories by discussing the sections of the Story Map from Resource Book p. C-7. Have students listen to verse 1 of "The Greenland Whale Fishery" **CD 11-16** to determine the setting, time, and place of the song. Distribute copies of the Story Map to students. Ask students to record the sequence of events in verses 2 and 3 on their Story Maps.

TEACHER TO TEACHER

▶ **Aural Perception** It is very important that students have a clear *aural* perception of whole and half steps, as well as an intellectual understanding of those concepts. Each time a new scale or mode is introduced, the need for sharped or flatted notes should be preceded by an aural example. For example, when deriving the G-mixolydian scale, students should be allowed to *hear* the notes from G to G and to *identify* the note that does not fit the correct pattern of whole and half steps.

While it may seem redundant to repeat this process in every key, it is necessary for students' later work with key signatures. Otherwise, their understanding of sharps and flats will be theoretical at best. They must understand, for instance, that B♭ is not just another name for B; it is a completely different pitch. The two notes happen to share the same place on the staff.

sea	we _____	sailed _____	a	-	way.
face	the _____	storms	and		cold.
arch	- ing _____	toward _____	the		land."

4. We struck that whale and away he went
With a flourish of his tail.
He upset our boat, we lost one man,
But did not gain that whale, brave boys,
But did not gain that whale.

5. "My gallant crew, don't be dismayed
By the losing of a man,
For Providence will have its way
That a man do all he can, brave boys,
That a man do all he can."

A Whale of a Scale

You know about scales built on *do*, the major scale, and *la*, the minor scale.
Did you know that each of the other notes has its own scale?
These scales are called *modes*. The *so* scale is known as the mixolydian scale.

Sing *so* to *so'* using hand signs. Start on G.

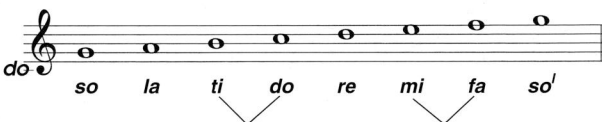

The mixolydian scale can also be sung from *do* to *do'*. To keep the pattern of
whole and half steps, we need a new note, *ta*, in the place of *ti*. *Ta* is the note
between *la* and *ti*. It is a half step lower than *ti*, and a half step higher than *la*.

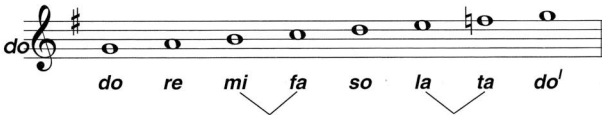

Sing this mixolydian scale both ways, first with G = *so*, then G = *do*. Which set
of pitch syllables will you use to sing "The Greenland Whale Fishery"?

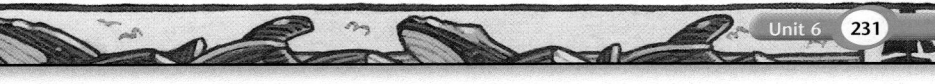

Line up a set of resonator bells in a C-major scale pattern: C-D-E-F-G-A-B-C.

Next, rearrange the bells from A to A to show a natural minor scale. What
bells will you use to show a mixolydian scale? **Play** each scale.

2 DEVELOP

Singing

8b Ask students to read the opening text on p. 230.
1c Encourage volunteers to do research on whaling songs.
See Across the Curriculum below.

Play "The Greenland Whale Fishery" **CD 11-16** and have
students learn the melody by rote.

1a Have students sing the notes of the G-*so* scale, ascending
and descending, using pitch syllables and hand signs.

ASK Between which notes do half steps occur?
(between *mi* and *fa* and between *ti* and *do*)

SAY This scale uses all the notes from *so* to *so'* and
contains both whole- and half-step intervals. This
arrangement of whole and half steps makes up the
mixolydian scale. We can create the mixolydian scale
starting on *do* by using a new note, *ta*, to form
the pattern.

Have students sing the scale again, using pitch syllables
and hand signs, and then numbers (*so*=1).

Playing

6c Draw attention to the Show What You Know activity
and have students play and compare the arrangement
of whole and half steps for the major, natural minor,
and mixolydian scales. See Resource Book p. B-18 for
the corresponding worksheet.

3 CLOSE

Skill: READING   **ASSESSMENT**

Performance/Observation Have students

5c • Look at "The Greenland Whale Fishery" and figure
out the pitch syllables in G-*so*, then in G-*do*.

1c • Read the song from staff notation, using pitch
syllables and hand signs, letter names, and then
singing the lyrics.

Observe students' ability to read and sing mixolydian
mode.

ACROSS THE CURRICULUM

8b ▶ **Social Studies** Today, whale hunting has been declared
illegal in many countries, and many whale species are classified
as endangered. Invite students to conduct the following research.

• Prepare a brief oral report on the history of whaling.

• Identify other songs about whaling.

• Locate pictures and descriptions of different kinds of whales.

▶ **Language Arts** Read aloud a lyrical story of sea travel in
Seabird by Hollings C. Holling (Houghton Mifflin, 1978). The
story is told through the adventures of Seabird, a carved ivory
gull, that is present through four generations of sailors and their
seafaring adventures.

TECHNOLOGY/MEDIA LINK

Web Site Visit *www.sfsuccessnet.com* for more information
on sea shanties and seafaring songs.

LESSON AT A GLANCE

Element Focus **MELODY** Dorian mode

Skill Objective **READING** Read and sing from notation a song in dorian mode

Connection Activity **SOCIAL STUDIES** Discuss a geographic region in Ireland

MATERIALS

- "Connemara Lullaby" **CD 11-21**

  Recording Routine: Intro (6 m.); vocal; interlude (4 m.); vocal; coda
- **Music Reading Practice, Sequence 24** **CD 11-23**
- *Fantasia On Greensleeves* **CD 11-26**
- **Resource Book** p. E-25
- bass xylophone, bass metallophones, triangle, soprano recorder

VOCABULARY

whole step	half step	interval
minor scale	mode	dorian

◆ ◆ ◆ ◆ National Standards ◆ ◆ ◆ ◆

1c Sing music from diverse cultures
2a Play instruments accurately in small ensembles
4c Compose, using electronic media
5c Identify standard notation symbols for pitch and rhythm
6c Understand and use basic principles of intervals in music analysis
8b Identify ways music relates to social studies

MORE MUSIC CHOICES

For more experience with modes:
"The Greenland Whale Fishery," p. 230

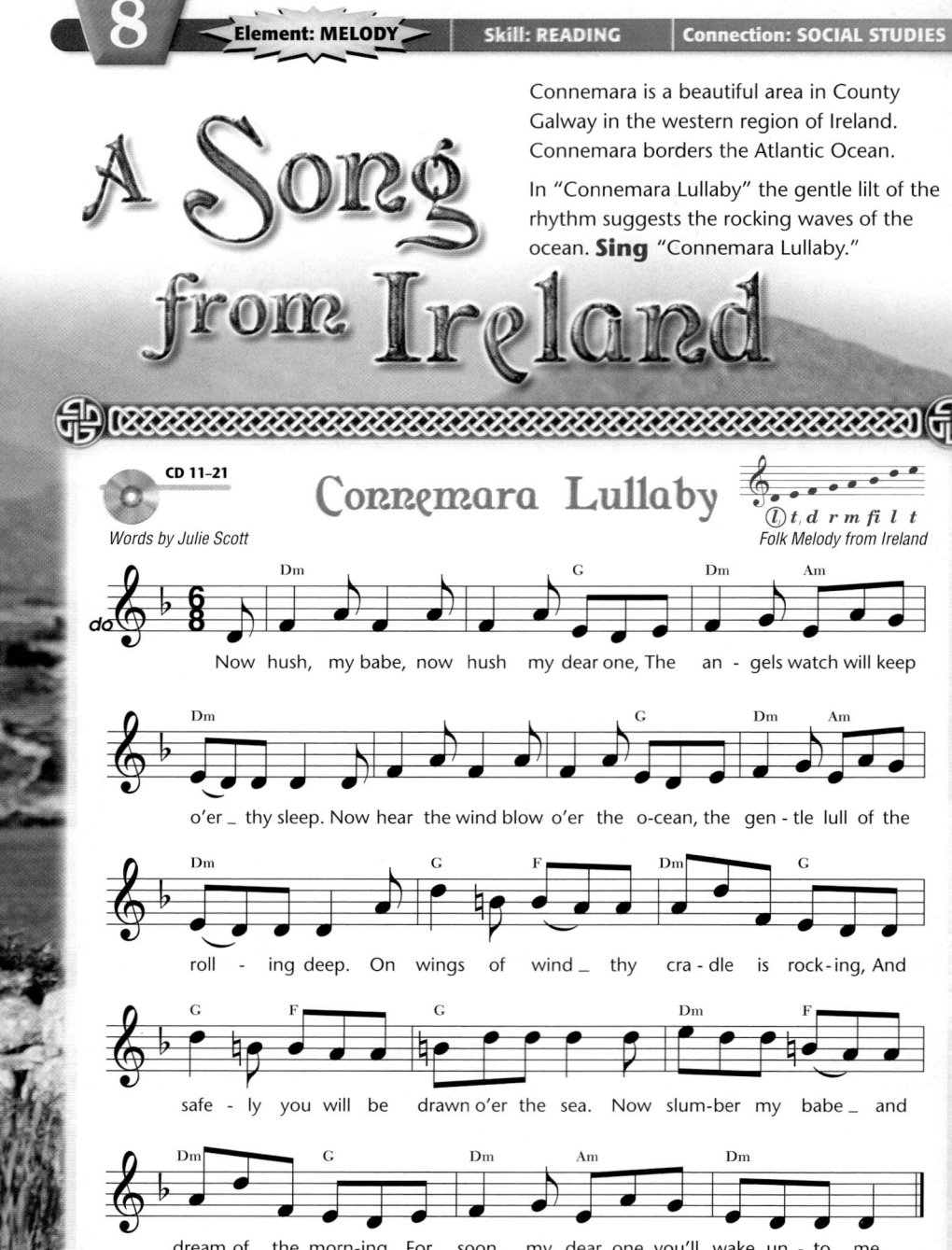

A Song from Ireland

Connemara is a beautiful area in County Galway in the western region of Ireland. Connemara borders the Atlantic Ocean.

In "Connemara Lullaby" the gentle lilt of the rhythm suggests the rocking waves of the ocean. **Sing** "Connemara Lullaby."

CD 11-21

Connemara Lullaby

Words by Julie Scott

l, d r m f l t
Folk Melody from Ireland

Now hush, my babe, now hush my dear one, The an - gels watch will keep o'er _ thy sleep. Now hear the wind blow o'er the o-cean, the gen - tle lull of the roll - ing deep. On wings of wind _ thy cra - dle is rock-ing, And safe - ly you will be drawn o'er the sea. Now slum-ber my babe _ and dream of the morn-ing, For soon, my dear one, you'll wake un - to me.

232

Footnotes

MEETING INDIVIDUAL NEEDS

▶ **Gifted and Talented Students** Invite any students who have a special interest in the music of Ireland to do additional research on Irish music in the library or on the Internet. Ask them to report to their music class on topics such as famous folk songs of Ireland, folk instruments of Ireland, or irish folk dancing.

BUILDING SKILLS THROUGH MUSIC

▶ **Social Studies** Direct students to look at the map of Ireland on p. 233. Share the information on Connemara from the Cultural Connection footnote. Discuss the information on the Twelve Bens mountain range. Have students list mountain ranges in the United States and locate them on a map.

CULTURAL CONNECTION

8b ▶ **Connemara** The Connemara region of Ireland is located in the western region of the country. Many different landscapes are found within this area, including bogs, mountains, and rugged coastlines. The Twelve Bens mountain range rises out of the east. The highest point of the Twelve Bens, Benbaun, is located in the Connemara National Park. Encompassing more than 5,000 acres, Connemara National Park draws many visitors, many of whom come to see the pure bred Connemara ponies that live throughout the park.

A New Mode

"Connemara Lullaby" is in the dorian mode. The dorian scale begins on *re*.

Sing from *re* to *re'* using hand signs. Start on D.

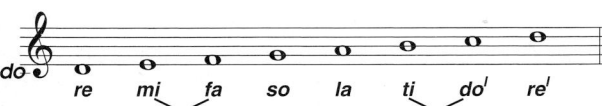

The dorian scale can also be sung from *la₁* to *la*. To keep the pattern of whole and half steps, we need a new pitch syllable, *fi*, in place of *fa*.

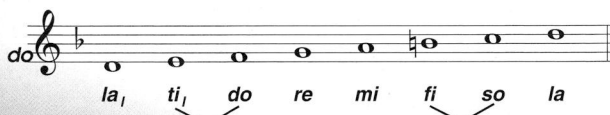

Sing this dorian scale both ways, first with D=*re*, then D=*la₁*. Which set of pitch syllables will you use to sing "Connemara Lullaby"?

ATLANTIC OCEAN

IRELAND

Connemara

1 INTRODUCE

8b Invite students to read the information on p. 232. Have them locate Ireland on a world map or globe and then lead them in a discussion about the Connemara region of Ireland. For more information, see Cultural Connection below.

Ask students if any of them have ever been on a boat ride in the ocean. If so, allow a few of them to share their experience.

2 DEVELOP

Reading

Sing short dorian melodic patterns in D-*re* using a neutral syllable. Have students echo-sing each pattern on *loo* and then use pitch syllables (give *re* as a starting pitch).

Invite students to listen to "Connemara Lullaby" **CD 11-21**. Then have them sing the D-*re* scale (shown on p. 233), ascending and descending, using pitch syllables and hand signs.

ASK Between which notes do half steps occur? (between *mi* and *fa* and between *ti* and *do'*)

SAY This scale uses all notes from *re* to *re'*. This arrangement of whole and half steps makes up the dorian scale.

Have students sing the scale again, this time beginning on D-*la*.

ASK What is the interval between *fa* and *so*? (a whole step)

ASK What is the interval between *fi* and *so*? (a half step)

1c Have students find *fi* in "Connemara Lullaby" and then sing the song using pitch syllables.

6c For additional practice reading in dorian mode, see Music Reading Practice, Sequence 24 on p. 501 and Resource Book p. E-25

TEACHER TO TEACHER

▶ **Different Modes** Most folk music of North America tends to be ionian (major), aeolian (natural minor), mixolydian, or dorian. These (along with the harmonic and melodic form of minor) are the modes with which most students need to be familiar. It is often helpful to explain the construction of modal scales by showing that any pitch can be the starting note of any of the modes. Students can sing all the modes from the same starting pitch simply by singing up eight half steps, and applying the proper placement of the two half steps.

do – do' Ionian *so – so'* Mixolydian

re – re' Dorian *a – la'* Aeolian

mi – mi' Phrygian *ti – ti'* Locrian

fa – fa' Lydian

SKILLS REINFORCEMENT

▶ **Recorder** Have students play the countermelody below to accompany "Connemara Lullaby."

2a

Moving

Have students create movements for "Connemara Lullaby." Divide the class into four groups and assign each one of the four phrases of the song. Have each group stand along one of the walls in the room. Play the recording **CD 11-21**. As their phrase is sung, each group should move into the middle of the room with swaying motions on the steady beat. Encourage students to match their movements to the contour of the melody.

Performing

2a Ask students to look at the accompaniment on p. 234. Prepare them to play the accompaniment by tapping the rhythm of each part to the steady beat. Have students practice the bass xylophone/bass metallophone part. When they can play the part comfortably, invite them to accompany "Connemara Lullaby." Then invite selected students to add the triangle part to the accompaniment. Have students perform the song again, this time with the mallet accompaniments.

Some students may enjoy learning the recorder part in the Skills Reinforcement footnote on p. 233. Invite these students to perform the recorder part along with the accompaniment part on p. 234.

Listening

Invite students to read the information on p. 235. Play the following dorian melody on keyboard or recorder for students.

Playing the Waves of the Sea

Perform this accompaniment with "Connemara Lullaby." Feel the steady beat as you **play**.

Bass Xylophone/Bass Metallophone

Footnotes

ACROSS THE CURRICULUM

▶ **Language Arts** Divide the class into small groups of two or three. Have students write a short, four-line poem about Ireland. The poem may be serious or humorous. Then invite each group to write a melody in dorian mode for their poem.

SPOTLIGHT ON

▶ **The Composer** Ralph Vaughan Williams (1872-1958) was considered to be a nationalistic composer of his day. Like Sibelius in Finland and Bartók in Hungary, Vaughan Williams had a great affinity for the folk music of his native England. He published arrangements of English folk songs and also composed original melodies in the English folk song style. Vaughan Williams composed nine symphonies, numerous pieces for chorus, and music for eleven films.

SKILLS REINFORCEMENT

▶ **Playing** Use the following teaching strategies to help all students perform the accompaniment part on p. 234.

Reinforcement Some students may have difficulty performing the bass xylophone/bass metallophone part. Pair these students with a partner and allow them to practice together.

On Target Many students will be able to perform both parts comfortably. Invite these students to choose a part and accompany the song.

Challenge Invite interested students to create a new triangle part to perform with the other parts.

Listen for Dorian Mode

"Greensleeves" is an English folk tune that you might recognize.

Listen to *Fantasia on Greensleeves* by Ralph [RAFE] Vaughan Williams. This piece is in ABA form. Listen for dorian mode in the B section.

CD 11–26
Fantasia on Greensleeves

by Ralph Vaughan Williams
as performed by the London Symphony Orchestra;
John Georgiadis, conductor

In addition to "Greensleeves," Vaughan Williams used another English folk tune, "Lovely Joan," in this piece.

M·U·S·I·C M·A·K·E·R·S
Ralph Vaughan Williams

Ralph Vaughan Williams (1872–1958) was born in Gloucestershire, England. As a young boy, he studied piano with his aunt. He developed an interest in composition and later went on to attend the Royal College of Music in London. During his education there, he formed a friendship with fellow student and composer Gustav Holst. The two offered each other constructive comments on their compositions. In addition to composing, Vaughan Williams collected over 800 English folk songs. He used many of them in his own music.

Unit 6 **235**

Point out to students that this melody contains a B natural and is in dorian mode like "Connemara Lullaby." Explain to students that they will hear this dorian melody in the B section of *Fantasia on Greensleeves.*

Invite students to listen to *Fantasia on Greensleeves* **CD 11-26**, raising their hand when they hear the dorian melody.

Select individual students to read aloud the information on p. 235 about Ralph Vaughan Williams.

3 CLOSE

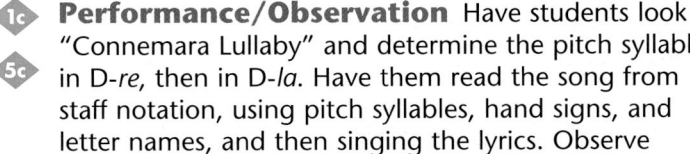

Element: MELODY | **ASSESSMENT**

1c **5c** **Performance/Observation** Have students look at "Connemara Lullaby" and determine the pitch syllables in D-*re*, then in D-*la*. Have them read the song from staff notation, using pitch syllables, hand signs, and letter names, and then singing the lyrics. Observe students' ability to read and perform in dorian mode.

AUDIENCE ETIQUETTE

▶ **Rehearsal Etiquette for Performers** Productive rehearsals prepare musicians for the best performance possible. Help students develop a set of "rehearsal etiquette" guidelines, such as

- Be on time.
- Converse with friends only after the rehearsal is finished.
- Come prepared for rehearsal with a pencil and your music.
- Listen to others in your section and to other sections.
- Listen to all instructions.
- Be attentive to your personal space, and respect the space of others.
- Say "thank you" to the leaders of the group at the end of rehearsal.

TECHNOLOGY/MEDIA LINK

4c **Notation Software** Encourage students to compose a melody with accompaniment in dorian mode. Have them

- Improvise melodies on an Orff instrument or recorder in dorian mode on D.
- Notate the melody on the top staff of a notation file.
- Add a staff beneath the melody line for a bass accompaniment part. They may use the same drone used to accompany "Connemara Lullaby."
- Listen to their compositions and write an assessment of the strengths and weaknesses of their work.

LESSON AT A GLANCE

Element Focus   **TIMBRE** Keyboard timbre

Skill Objective   **LISTENING** Listen to and compare the timbre of a variety of keyboard instruments

Connection Activity   **SCIENCE** Relate the sound of an instrument to the technology available at the time the instrument was developed

MATERIALS

- *Two-Part Invention in A Major* (harpsichord)   **CD 11-27**
- *Two-Part Invention in A Major* (piano)   **CD 11-28**
- *Two-Part Invention in A Major* (synthesizer)   **CD 11-29**
- *Come Out and Play* (excerpt)   **CD 11-30**
- *Snowflakes Are Dancing*   **CD 11-31**

VOCABULARY

timbre

◆◆◆◆ National Standards ◆◆◆◆

4c Arrange, using electronic media

6b Listen and analyze uses of timbre in music from diverse genres

8b Identify ways music relates to science

MORE MUSIC CHOICES

For more experiences with piano timbre:

Invention No. 5 in E-flat, p. 59

Scott Joplin's New Rag, p. 335

Keyboard Technology

When composers wrote music hundreds of years ago, they wrote for instruments of their day. The technology of each era helped those historic instruments evolve into instruments we know today.

Listen to this short keyboard composition. It is performed on a harpsichord, the instrument for which it was originally composed.

CD 11–27
Two-Part Invention in A Major

by Johann Sebastian Bach as performed on harpsichord by Kathleen McIntosh

The harpsichord used for this recording is similar to the one Bach used when he composed this piece in 1723.

The strings on a harpsichord are plucked to make their sound.

236

Footnotes

ACROSS THE CURRICULUM

8b ▶ **Science** Technological evolution can be readily seen in the recording of language (the written word). Work backwards. Now we have word processing programs, both keyboard and voice activated; 25–30 years ago the typewriter was still widely used. The invention of the printing press (Gutenberg, 1450) was the landmark development before computers. Handwritten language has many variations in the implements used, from chisel and stone to felt-tip pen.

BUILDING SKILLS THROUGH MUSIC

▶ **Writing** Have students look at the instrument photos on pp. 236-239. Invite them to listen to **CD 11-27, CD 11-28,** and **CD 11-29.** Have students select one performance and, using musical vocabulary, write a brief letter describing the timbre of the instrument to someone who has never heard the instrument.

SPOTLIGHT ON

▶ **The Harpsichord** A harpsichord is a string keyboard instrument widely used in Europe from the sixteenth to eighteenth centuries, with periodic revivals in the nineteenth and twentieth centuries. Harpsichords sometimes have several sets of strings that sound an octave above or below the basic set; octaves can be coupled together so that two or more sets sound at once. Instruments also can have more than one keyboard or manual.

Harpsichords range from small and simple in design to large and elaborate. Some instruments are colorful and decorated with intricate painted designs.

Bach Today

Although the harpsichord was the most popular keyboard instrument in Bach's time, the piano soon took its place.

Listen again to Bach's *Invention*, this time played on a modern piano.

 CD 11–28

Two-Part Invention in A Major

by Johann Sebastian Bach as performed on piano by Glenn Gould

Gould specialized in playing Bach on the piano.

In the 20th century, Robert Moog [mohg], inventor and physicist, was one of the people who applied new technology to the keyboard. In 1964 he invented one of the first synthesizers.

Musicians representing styles from classical to rock quickly became interested in this new development.

Now **listen** to Bach's *Invention* played on a Moog synthesizer.

CD 11–29

Two-Part Invention in A Major

by Johann Sebastian Bach as realized on synthesizer

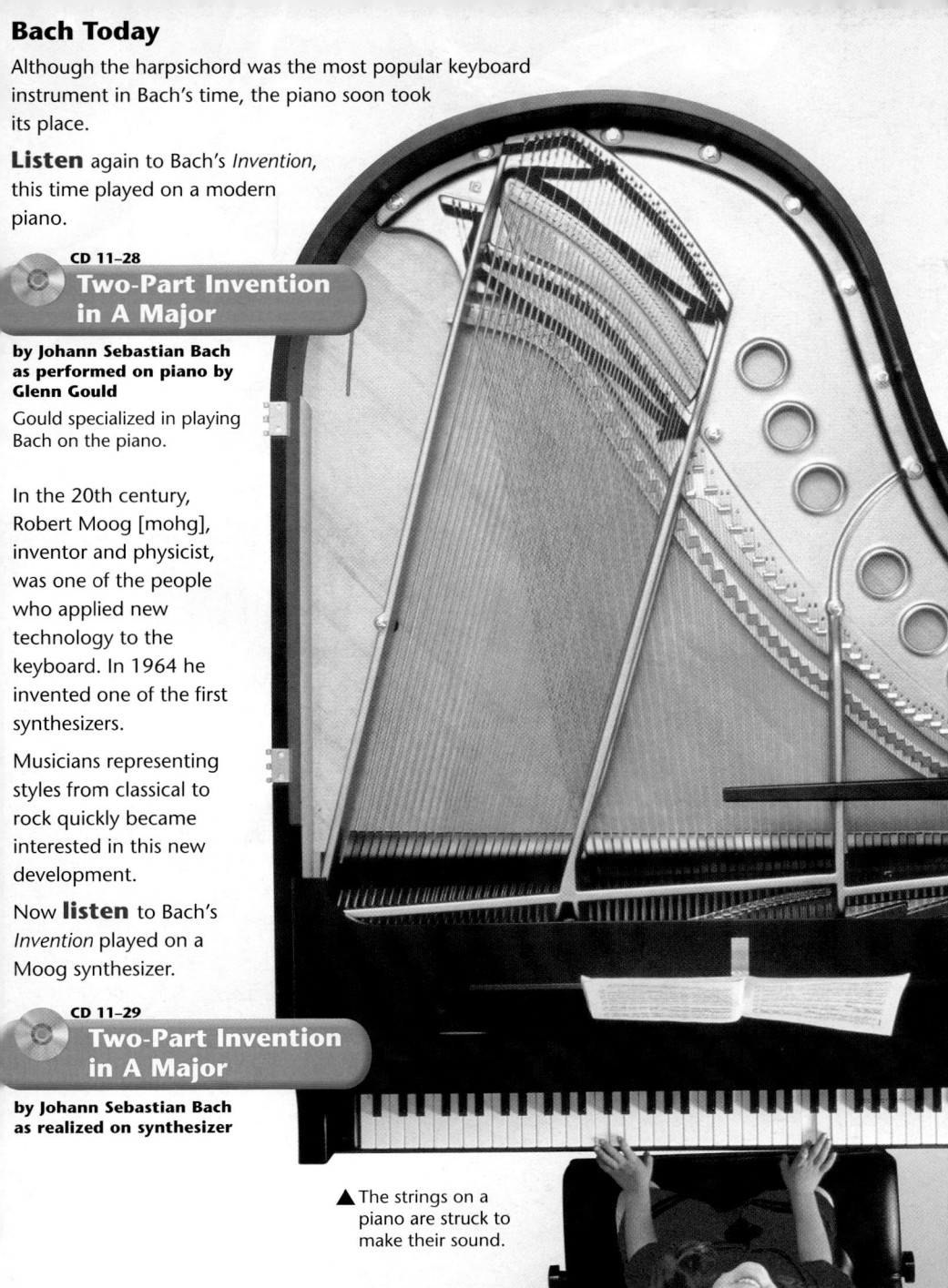

▲ The strings on a piano are struck to make their sound.

Unit 6 **237**

1 INTRODUCE

Write the word *technology* on the board. Ask students to quickly make lists of all the words this term brings to mind. (Some possible answers include computers, Internet, CD-ROM, and so on.) Then ask students to make lists relating to "music technology." (Answers might include synthesizer, MIDI, MP-3, and so on.)

While this is going on, ask one or more students to look up the word *technology* in the dictionary and be ready to report at this point. Very likely, none of the words above will be included in the definition. Instead, *technology* means "applied science"—applying whatever scientific principles and facts known at a particular time in history to making things work. Point out that there has always been technology; the difference now is that many advances have come in a very short time period.

Use information in Across the Curriculum, p. 236, to continue this discussion.

Tell students that this lesson will include several examples of musical keyboard technology.

2 DEVELOP

Analyzing

8b Ask a student to hold a length of wire or nylon cord taut between the hands. Have another student pluck this string with a toothpick, moving upward. Identify this as the technological basis for the harpsichord (see Spotlight On, p. 236).

Have students examine the photo of the harpsichord on p. 236.

ASK Why didn't we hear any sound from the plucked string? (Because in order to be heard, the vibrating string must be amplified by a resonator. That is what the body of the instrument does.)

continued on page 238

SKILLS REINFORCEMENT

8b ▶ **Analyzing** The best reinforcement for understanding the technology of instruments is first-hand demonstration and observation. Arrange for students to look at the interior of a piano, with someone knowledgeable to explain the layout of strings, hammers, keys, and so on. Ask students if they know someone who has a portable harpsichord that can be brought in for demonstration. Ask a local high school music teacher or university music educator to recommend a student or faculty member who can perform on a synthesizing instrument for students at your school. Invite that individual to talk about his or her instrument(s) and the technology involved in its creation and musical performance.

MEETING INDIVIDUAL NEEDS

▶ **Challenge** Have interested students look up and report on technology of other keyboard instruments, such as the pipe organ, accordion, clavichord, hurdy-gurdy, fortepiano, and harmonium. Assist students with finding recordings to demonstrate the sounds of these instruments.

Lesson 9 Continued

Listening

 Have students listen to the harpsichord version of the *Two-Part Invention in A Major* **CD 11-27**.

SAY This piece was written for the harpsichord. Present-day harpsichords, and those in Bach's time, have several courses of strings and several keyboards (manuals). The player can vary the texture and dynamics by coupling one or more courses of strings.

(Point out to students that a "course" is more than one string tuned to the same pitch.)

Analyzing

This time, have a student hold two pieces of cord close and parallel to each other. Have another student hold a spoon by the handle, with the bottom of the spoon bowl facing the stretched cords. Allow the spoon bowl to fall gently onto the two stretched cords. This is the "hammer" principle underlying the construction of the piano.

Refer students to the photo of the piano on p. 237.

SAY Sound is produced on a piano by hammers striking tuned strings, making the strings vibrate. The sound is amplified by the soundboard. The piano was first called the *pianoforte* because it can play both soft *(piano)* and loud *(forte)*; now it is usually called piano.

If a piano is available, allow students to view the interior mechanism. See Skills Reinforcement, p. 237, for additional ideas.

Listening

Have students

• Listen to the piano performance of the *Two-Part Invention in A Major* **CD 11-28**.

• Describe the differences they hear between the harpsichord and piano versions, both in the timbre and in the way the piece is played (interpretation).

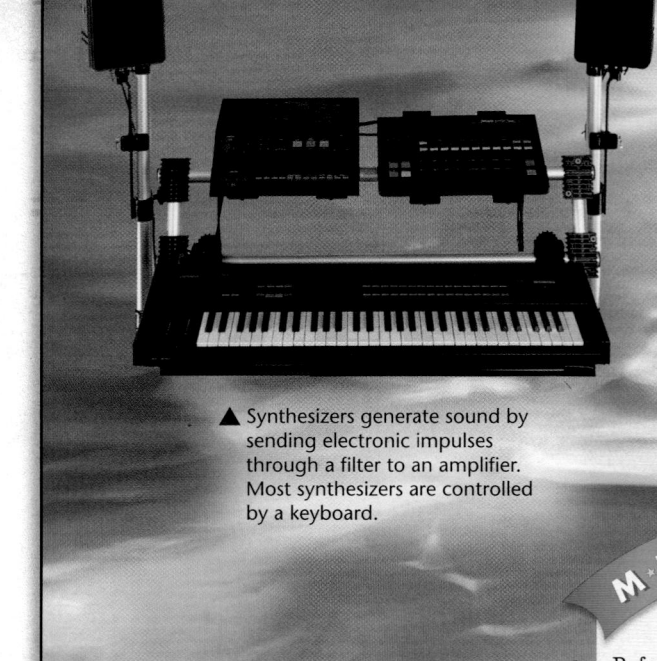

▲ Synthesizers generate sound by sending electronic impulses through a filter to an amplifier. Most synthesizers are controlled by a keyboard.

Listen to *Come Out and Play* played o a Moog synthesizer.

CD 11–30
Come Out and Play

by Brian Holland
as performed by Meco Eno and Uli Nomi

Come Out and Play is performed on a presen day synthesizer. The digital technology used is similar to that used in CD players and computers.

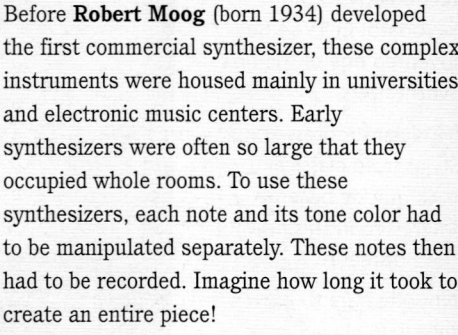

MUSIC MAKERS
Robert Moog

Before **Robert Moog** (born 1934) developed the first commercial synthesizer, these complex instruments were housed mainly in universities and electronic music centers. Early synthesizers were often so large that they occupied whole rooms. To use these synthesizers, each note and its tone color had to be manipulated separately. These notes then had to be recorded. Imagine how long it took to create an entire piece!

In 1964, Moog introduced his first synthesizer for the commercial market. Soon other companies began to compete with Moog. As a result, he developed the Minimoog, a small portable instrument that quickly became popular with rock groups. The Minimoog could play pre-set manufactured sounds. This encouraged more performers to use synthesizers.

In many ways, Robert Moog can be thought of as the father of the music synthesizer.

238

Footnotes

ACROSS THE CURRICULUM

▶ **Science** Challenge students to find out all they can about the newest sound technologies, including how digital recordings are produced, examples of modern synthesizing musical instruments, the use of synthesizers in today's popular music, and so on. Ask students for ideas on how they can search for this information (internet, music stores, catalogs, and so on). Create a "Synthesized Music" bulletin board, with information and up-to-date pictures about instruments, recordings, performers, playback devices, and computer-assisted musical instruments and compositions.

SPOTLIGHT ON

▶ **The Piano** The piano developed in Western Europe over the course of the late eighteenth and early nineteenth centuries to fill the need for a keyboard instrument that could play gradations of loud and soft. By 1860, it had reached the form in which it now continues, with seven octaves of keys. Many different designs for the hammer mechanism and various types of pedals were tried. A set of three strings (but just two strings for very low pitches) is strung side by side for each pitch; these must be tuned exactly alike.

Impression: Snowflakes

Listen to this version of the piano piece *Snowflakes Are Dancing*, played on a Moog synthesizer. **Describe** how the tone colors of the synthesizer capture the image of snowflakes swirling in the wind.

CD 11–31

Snowflakes Are Dancing

from *Children's Corner Suite*
by Claude Debussy
performed by Isao Tomita

Snowflakes Are Dancing portrays the hypnotic effect that comes from watching the falling snow.

M·U·S·I·C M·A·K·E·R·S

Isao Tomita

Isao Tomita [toh-mee-tah], born in 1932 in Tokyo, Japan, first studied art history. He eventually chose music as his profession. While much of Tomita's music is written for television and films, he also wrote the theme music for the Japanese gymnastics team at the 1956 Olympics. Since 1973 his music has been created mostly for electronic instruments but also, on occasion, for traditional Japanese instruments.

Unit 6 **239**

Analyzing

Refer students to the material on p. 237 that introduces the synthesizer.

 SAY Sound waves can be produced and controlled electronically by connecting various control devices that shape the sound that is desired. These sound waves are fed through an amplifier and exit through speakers so that we can hear them.

Have students read the Music Makers material on p. 238 about Robert Moog, a pioneer in developing this musical technology for commercial use.

Listening

Have students

- Listen to the synthesizer performance of *Two-Part Invention in A Major* **CD 11-29.**
- Describe what they hear, both in the timbre and the interpretation.

As an example of the variety of sounds and musical styles the Moog synthesizer is capable of producing, play the recording of *Come Out and Play* **CD 11-30,** performed by Meco Eno and Uli Nomi.

Ask students to read about Isao Tomita on p. 239 and then listen to his version of Debussy's *Snowflakes Are Dancing* **CD 11-31.**

For additional sound samples of the harpsichord, piano, and synthesizer, play **CD 21-35, CD 21-40,** and **CD 21-47** for students. They also can read detailed descriptions of the instruments on pp. 516-518 of the Sound Bank.

3 CLOSE

Element: TIMBRE — **ASSESSMENT**

 Observation After reviewing the three performances of Bach's *Invention,* give a timbre quiz by playing brief segments in random order. Write the terms "harpsichord," "piano," and "synthesizer" on the board so students only have to write 1, 2, or 3. Observe students' ability to accurately recognize instrument timbre.

TEACHER TO TEACHER

▶ **More Technology** Invite students who are science oriented to research particular developments of electronics used in music. These could include:

- Theremin.
- Tape technology used in the 1940s and early 1950s.
- *Musique concrete* (French—acoustic sounds recorded and used in composing).
- *Elektronische musik* (German—sounds created by oscillators).
- Electronic music in the United States, such as the Buchla, Arp, sampler, the latest MIDI (Musical Instrument Digital Interface), and the sequencer.

Have students make a time line with pictures and descriptions.

TECHNOLOGY/MEDIA LINK

 Electronic Keyboard Have students complete a "voice map" for the classroom electronic keyboard as they explore the different sounds available. Ask students

- "Which sounds would you use the most?"
- "Which sounds are most like acoustic instruments you know?"

LESSON AT A GLANCE

Element Focus   **TEXTURE/HARMONY** Primary chords

Skill Objective   **PLAYING** Play chords on keyboard to accompany a song

Connection Activity   **CULTURE** Discuss Jamaican culinary customs referred to in a calypso song

MATERIALS

- "Linstead Market"   **CD 11-32**
  Recording Routine: Intro (4 m.); v. 1; refrain; v. 2; refrain; v. 3; refrain; v. 1; refrain; coda
- **Resource Book** p. I-19
- keyboard

VOCABULARY

primary chords

◆ ◆ ◆ National Standards ◆ ◆ ◆ ◆

1c Sing music from diverse cultures
2c Perform instrumental music from diverse cultures
3a Improvise simple harmonic accompaniments
6c Understand and use basic principles of intervals, chords, and harmonic progressions in music analysis
8b Identify ways music relates to social studies and language arts

MORE MUSIC CHOICES

For more practice playing primary chords:
"*Imbabura*," p. 203
"Oh, Freedom," p. 392

1 INTRODUCE

6c Invite students to read the information on p. 240. Help students determine how the D, G, and A_7 chords are built on the first, fourth, and fifth notes of the D-major scale. Then help them to understand that in the key of D: I is D, IV is G, and V_7 is A_7.

SAY Musicians call the I, IV, and V_7 *primary chords.*

HARMONIZING Folk Music

Each style of folk music appeals to the people who create, perform, and listen to it. It is usually simple enough that almost everyone can understand it.

Most folk music, whether it comes from Latin America, the Caribbean, or the United States, can be accompanied by three chords; I, IV, and V_7.

Sing "Linstead Market" and **listen** for the three chords used in the harmony. The three chords used are D (I), G (IV), and A_7 (V_7).

240

Footnotes

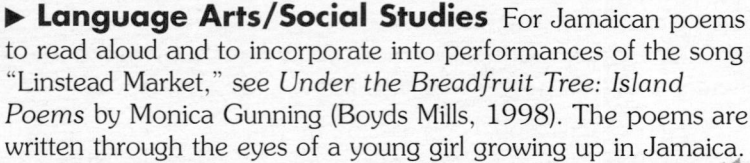

ACROSS THE CURRICULUM

8b ▶ **Language Arts/Social Studies** For Jamaican poems to read aloud and to incorporate into performances of the song "Linstead Market," see *Under the Breadfruit Tree: Island Poems* by Monica Gunning (Boyds Mills, 1998). The poems are written through the eyes of a young girl growing up in Jamaica.

BUILDING SKILLS THROUGH MUSIC

▶ **Social Studies** Have students sing "Linstead Market." Share the meaning of the words *ackee, gutty, dem tan,* and *nyam grab* listed in the side column on p. 241. Have students sing the song again, substituting English words. Then have them make a list of different foods that they eat for breakfast. Arrange the class in small groups. Invite each group to write new words to the verses by substituting the names of breakfast foods from the list.

CULTURAL CONNECTION

8b ▶ **Culinary Customs** The 7,000 islands of the Caribbean are known for their abundance of fruits, such as mangos, bananas, passion fruit, and coconuts. Staple foods of the region include callaloo (leafy greens), Scotch Bonnet chili peppers (very hot), and land crabs. The national dish of Jamaica is ackee and saltfish. It is made with dried salted cod and cooked ackee, a fruit that is poisonous if eaten raw.

Learn more about the fascinating people, customs, and land of this Caribbean Island in *Jamaica in Pictures (Visual Geography Series)* by Anne Egan (Lerner Publications, 1997).

CD 11–32
MIDI 17

Linstead Market

Calypso Song from Jamaica

t d r m f s l t d'

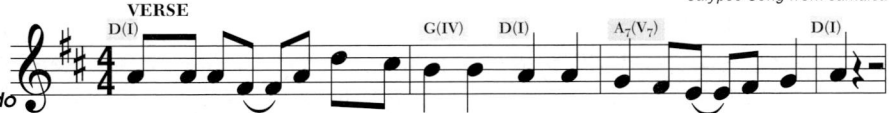

VERSE

do

1. Car - ry me ack - ee go   a   Lin-stead Mar - ket, Not a quat - ty would sell.
2. Ev - er - y - bod - y   come _   feel them, feel them, Not a quat - ty would sell.
3. Make _ me call _ it loud - er "Ack - ee, Ack - ee," Red and pret - ty dem tan.

Car-ry me ack - ee go   a   Lin-stead Mar - ket, Not a quat - ty would sell.
Ev-er - y - bod - y   come _   feel them, feel them, Not a quat - ty would sell.
La-dy come buy _ your Sun - day morn-ing break-fast, Rice and ack - ee nyam gran'.

REFRAIN

Oh,   no,   not a   mite, not a bite,   What a   Sat - ur-day night.

Oh,   no,   not a   mite, not a bite,   What a   Sat - ur-day night.

Playing I, IV, and V₇ chords

Play the D, G, and A₇ chords on the keyboard to accompany "Linstead Market."

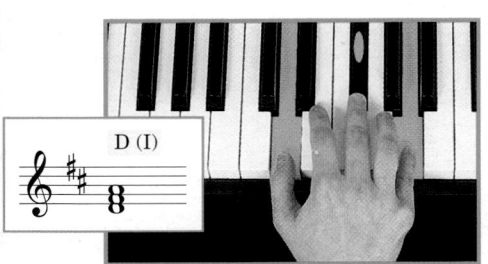

D (I)

G (IV)

A₇ (V₇)

Unit 6   241

2 DEVELOP

Singing

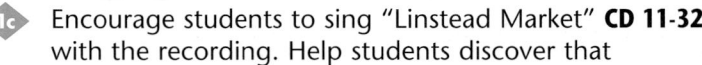

Encourage students to sing "Linstead Market" **CD 11-32** with the recording. Help students discover that

- The song has a verse and refrain.
- The harmony for the verse uses I, IV, and V₇ chords.
- The harmony for the refrain uses only the I and V₇ chords.

Challenge students to sing the lyrics of the song on chord roots. (*Ackee* means "red fruit"; *quatty* means "small sum of money"; *dem tan* means "they are"; *nyam grab* means "taste good.") Then select a small group of students to sing the lyrics on chord roots while the rest of the class sings the melody with the recording.

Share with students information on Jamaican culinary customs. See Cultural Connection, p. 240.

Playing

Have students look carefully at the notation of the chords on p. 241. Have students

- Say the notes used in each chord.
- Find and play the chords on keyboards.
- Play the chord accompaniment while singing the song.

3 CLOSE

Element: TEXTURE/HARMONY ─ **ASSESSMENT**

Performance/Observation As students perform the chords on keyboards to accompany "Linstead Market,"observe and assess their ability to change chords at the appropriate time.

SKILLS REINFORCEMENT

▶ **Guitar** Give students the opportunity to accompany "Linstead Market" on guitar. For a less complex accompaniment, have students play 1, 2, or 3 strums on measures that use the D chord throughout (allow time for stopping before the chord changes in the next measure).

For some students, the guitar might pose too great a challenge. Their hands might be too small to fit around the guitar's neck, or they might have difficulty holding the instrument properly. The baritone ukulele, which is tuned to the same four pitches as the upper strings of a guitar, might offer a good alternative for these students. Its nylon strings are easier for young fingers to press against the fret board.

▶ **Recorder** See Resource Book p. I-19 for a countermelody to accompany "Linstead Market."

TECHNOLOGY/MEDIA LINK

MIDI/Sequencing Software Have students open the MIDI song file for "Linstead Market" and invite them to improvise a bass part using the I, IV, and V₇ chords. Have students

- Select a bass voice on their MIDI keyboards.
- Play repeated chord roots on the steady beat as the MIDI track for "Linstead Market" plays.
- Play the roots and fifths of the chords.
- Play arpeggiated chords for the bass part.

Other students may play percussion instruments.

LESSON AT A GLANCE

Element Focus **TEXTURE/HARMONY** Two-part harmony

Skill Objective **SINGING** Sing a song in two-part harmony

Connection Activity **GENRE** Explore the historical tradition of African American spirituals

MATERIALS

- "Ev'ry Time I Feel the Spirit" **CD 11-34**
  Recording Routine: Intro (4 m.); refrain; v. 1; refrain; v. 2; refrain; coda
- resonator bells

VOCABULARY

verse   refrain   unison   harmony

◆ ◆ ◆ ◆ **National Standards** ◆ ◆ ◆ ◆

1c Sing music from diverse genres
1d Sing music written in two parts
2a Play instruments accurately in small ensembles
4c Compose, using electronic media
6c Understand and use basic principles of chords and harmonic progressions in music analysis
7b Students use specific criteria for evaluating performances and offer constructive suggestions for improvement
8b Identify ways music relates to social studies
9a Describe characteristics of music from a variety of genres

MORE MUSIC CHOICES

For more practice with songs in two-part harmony:
"Camptown Races," p. 270
"Canción Mixteca," p. 326

1 INTRODUCE

9a **SAY** From its early development among enslaved Africans in the nineteenth century, the African American spiritual has become one of the best-known American musical styles. The most important historical feature in spirituals, the message of the lyrics, is communicated through expressive singing.

For more information, see Across the Curriculum below.

Two-Part Singing

In most traditional music, the human voice is the primary melody instrument. In this arrangement of "Ev'ry Time I Feel the Spirit," the voices sing in two-part harmony on the refrain. The verses are in unison. Learn both the harmony and melody parts. Then **sing** them together.

 CD 11-34 MIDI 18

Ev'ry Time I Feel the Spirit

African American Spiritual

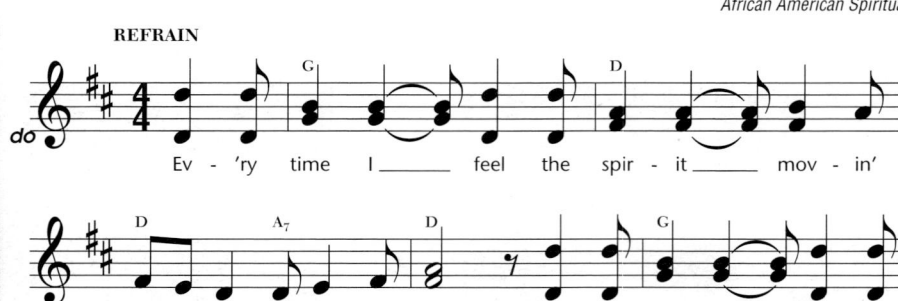

REFRAIN

Ev - 'ry time I _____ feel the spir - it _____ mov - in'

in my heart _____ I will pray; Ev - 'ry time I _____ feel the

spir - it _____ mov - in' in my heart _____ I _____ will pray.

(242)

Footnotes

ACROSS THE CURRICULUM

8b ▶ **Social Studies** Read about the African American musicians who founded the famous Fisk Jubilee Singers in 1871 in Nashville, Tennessee. Read aloud *A Band of Angels: A Story Inspired by the Jubilee Singers* by Deborah Hopkinson (Atheneum, 1999). The book presents the story through the eyes of one of the group's founding members, Ella Sheppard Moore. Pair a reading of this book with recordings of spirituals by the Jubilee Singers and other groups.

BUILDING SKILLS THROUGH MUSIC

▶ **Writing** Have students sing "Ev'ry Time I Feel the Spirit" using dynamic changes and stylistic interpretations they feel are appropriate. Then have them listen to the recording **CD 11-34**. Distribute copies of the Comparison Chart from Resource Book p. C-2. Have students compare dynamic changes in their performance with dynamic changes in the recording.

CHARACTER EDUCATION

▶ **Responsibility** Encourage students to consider their responsibility for helping people in distress. Ask students if they feel a responsibility to help those who are less fortunate. Discuss students' responses. Point out that those who provided shelter for enslaved African Americans on the Underground Railroad demonstrated great courage, integrity, compassion, and persistence. Discuss the character traits needed to take responsibility to assist someone in distress.

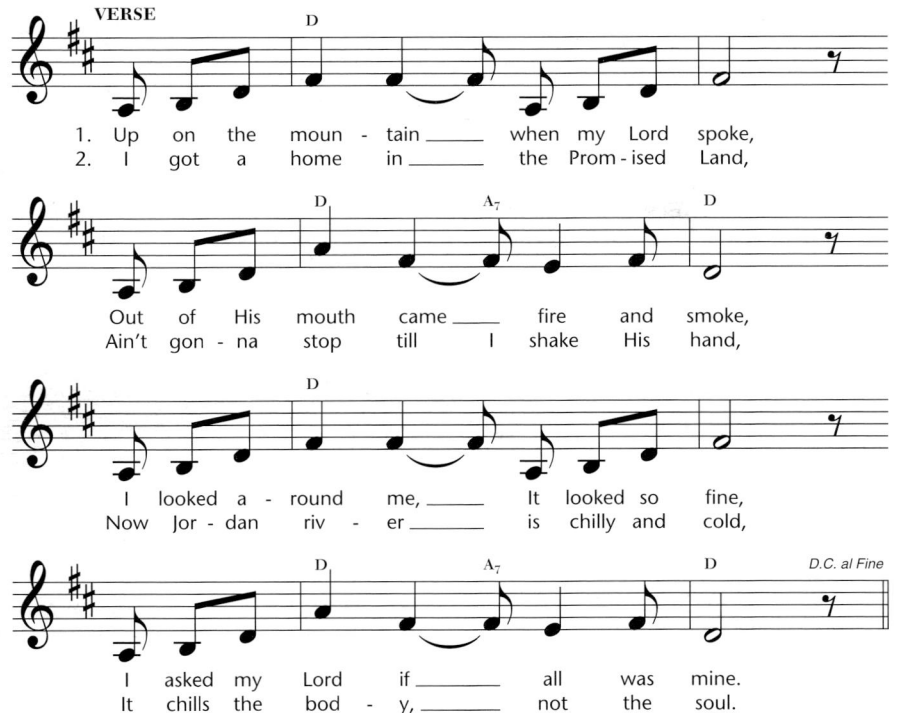

VERSE

1. Up on the moun-tain _____ when my Lord spoke,
2. I got a home in _____ the Prom-ised Land,

Out of His mouth came _____ fire and smoke,
Ain't gon-na stop till I shake His hand,

I looked a-round me, _____ It looked so fine,
Now Jor-dan riv-er _____ is chilly and cold,

I asked my Lord if _____ all was mine.
It chills the bod-y, _____ not the soul.

Three-Part Playing

During the refrain, **play** these parts on resonator bells to add more harmony.

PLAYER 1

PLAYER 2

PLAYER 3

2 DEVELOP

Analyzing

6c Ask students to look at the song "Ev'ry Time I Feel the Spirit" and

- Notice that the I (D), IV (G), and V₇ (A₇) chords are used to harmonize the song.
- Discover that the IV chord is used only in the refrain.

Listening

6c Play "Ev'ry time I Feel the Spirit" **CD 11-34.**

ASK Is the song in unison or in harmony? (The verse is in unison and the refrain has harmony.)

How many different voice parts are in the refrain? (two)

Singing

1d Invite students to sing the melody with the recording. Then divide the class into two groups. Have one group sing the harmony part with the recording. Students can then sing the song in two parts with the recording.

Playing

2a Have students look at the parts for resonator bells on p. 243. Assign parts and have students add the parts to a performance of the song.

3 CLOSE

Element: TEXTURE/HARMONY **ASSESSMENT**

1c **Performance/Self-Assessment** Have students sing "Ev'ry Time I Feel the Spirit" in two parts and with
2a the resonator bell accompaniment on p. 243.
7b Encourage students to demonstrate appropriate small-ensemble performance techniques in their informal classroom concerts. Record the performance and allow students to evaluate their performance of the harmony parts and offer suggestions for improvement.

SKILLS REINFORCEMENT

1c ▶ **Vocal Development** Review vocal techniques with students. Have students stand tall, relax their shoulders, and concentrate on good breath control. Students need to be aware of long phrases, and not taking a breath in the middle of a phrase. Invite students to perform "Ev'ry Time I Feel the Spirit" with accurate intonation, demonstrating basic performance techniques.

▶ **Guitar** Many African American spirituals have been adopted by folk singers who accompany their singing with guitars. Invite students to sing and play a guitar accompaniment for "Ev'ry Time I Feel the Spirit" using the I, IV, and V₇ chords in the key of D.

TECHNOLOGY/MEDIA LINK

4c **MIDI/Sequencing Software** Have students compose "fills" based upon I, IV, and V₇ chord tones. Have students

- Open the MIDI song file for "Ev'ry Time I Feel the Spirit" and add one blank track for fills.
- Display the melody track and the blank track.
- Locate good locations for fills (during long tones or breaks in the melody).
- Improvise fills based on the chord symbol at those locations.
- Sequence the fills into the blank track.
- Play all tracks.

LESSON AT A GLANCE

Element Focus   **TEXTURE/HARMONY** Three-part harmony

Skill Objective   **SINGING** Sing a song in three-part harmony

Connection Activity   **CULTURE** Explore the association of a song with the civil rights movements of different countries

MATERIALS
- *"Kum ba yah"*   **CD 11-36**
   Recording Routine: Intro (4 m.); refrain; v. 1; refrain; v. 2; refrain; v. 3; refrain; coda
- **Resource Book** p. G-7
- resonator bells, metallophones

VOCABULARY
chord   harmony   call and response

> ◆ ◆ ◆ ◆ **National Standards** ◆ ◆ ◆ ◆
> **1c** Sing music from diverse cultures
> **1d** Sing music written in three parts
> **2a** Play instruments accurately in small ensembles
> **4c** Arrange, using electronic media
> **6c** Understand and use basic principles of chords and harmonic progressions in music analysis
> **8b** Identify ways music relates to social studies

MORE MUSIC CHOICES
For more practice with songs in three-part harmony:
"Freedom Is Coming," p. 415
"'Ūlili E," p. 441

1 INTRODUCE

8b Encourage students to read the introductory text on p. 244. Follow this with a discussion about the role of the song "*Kum ba yah*" in worldwide civil rights movements. For more information, see Cultural Connection below.

Music in Three Parts

"*Kum ba yah*" is a long-time favorite song for singing around a campfire or in other social settings. The words have been translated as "come by you," "come by me," and "come by here." During the American Civil Rights movement of the 1960s, the song became a call for freedom and equal rights.

Sing the melody of *"Kum ba yah,"* then learn the harmony parts and **sing** it in three-part harmony.

Kum ba yah

Traditional Song from Liberia

(244)

 Footnotes

CULTURAL CONNECTION

8b ▶ **"Kum ba yah"** "*Kum ba yah*" has been attributed to Liberia, in West Africa, the site of the exportation of many slaves to the Americas. Liberia is also one of the principal countries to which English-speaking Africans repatriated following their emancipation, and so the song may have traveled with Liberians from shore to shore. In the 1960s, the song became a banner-cry of freedom for African Americans.

BUILDING SKILLS THROUGH MUSIC

▶ **Social Studies** Have students read the information about "*Kum ba yah*" on p. 244. Share the information in the Cultural Connection footnote. Have students write a brief paragraph about why they think the song "*Kum ba yah*" was used in the American civil rights movement of the 1960s. Ask volunteers to share their paragraphs.

SKILLS REINFORCEMENT

▶ **Recorder** Students can play Parts 1 and 2 of "*Kum ba yah*" as notated in their book. Part 3 is more difficult because it **2a** includes notes that are out of the range of the soprano recorder. The countermelody below can be substituted for Part 3.

▶ **Signing** For a sign interpretation of "*Kum ba yah,*" refer to Resource Book p. G-7.

Play in Three Parts

When you've learned the song, **play** the chords on metallophones or resonator bells to accompany it.

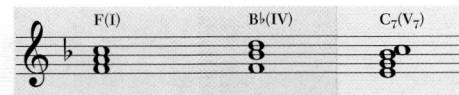

◀ Ladysmith Black Mambazo, a singing group from South Africa

1. Some - one's sing - in', Lord,
2. Some - one's pray - in', Lord, *Kum ba yah!*
3. Some - one's shout - in', Lord,

Some - one's
Some - one's
Some - one's

sing - in', Lord,
pray - in', Lord, *Kum ba yah!*
shout - in', Lord,

Some-one's sing - in', Lord,
Some-one's pray - in', Lord, *Kum ba*
Some-one's shout - in', Lord,

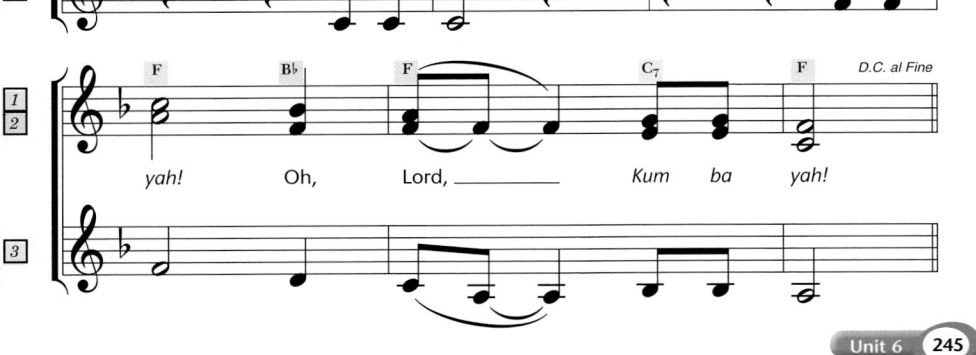

yah!   Oh,   Lord, _____   *Kum ba yah!*

Unit 6   **245**

2 DEVELOP

Singing

1c Encourage students to sing the melody of *"Kum ba yah"* **CD 11-36** with the recording.

6c **ASK** Is the song mostly in unison or in harmony? (It is mostly in harmony.)

    When is it not in harmony? (during the solo sections of the verse)

    What chords are used to harmonize the song? (I [F], IV [B♭], V₇ [C₇]).

Help students discover

- The call and response treatment of the verse.
- The relationship between the harmony parts and the notes of the I, IV, and V chords.

1d Divide the class into three groups and have students sing the entire song in three parts. See Teacher to Teacher below for related information.

Invite individuals or small groups of students to sing the solo sections of the verse while the rest of the class sings the response.

Playing

2a Draw attention to the chords on p. 245. Using resonator bells or metallophones, have students play the chords as an accompaniment to the song.

3 CLOSE

Element: TEXTURE/HARMONY **ASSESSMENT**

1c **Performance/Peer Critique** Have a group of students perform *"Kum ba yah"* in three parts. Have another group offer suggestions for improvement by commenting on performance of the harmony parts. Use the same process to assess intonation, diction, phrasing, and tone quality. Switch groups.

TEACHER TO TEACHER

1d ▶ **Singing in Harmony** Although some teachers have success teaching young singers to sing in harmony by teaching one part at a time, the procedure is time-consuming and frustrating for many inexperienced singers. Another approach allows students to sing the song in harmony by concentrating only on one short pattern that is repeated many times throughout the song. New patterns are introduced only when the singers are ready. Singing the opening pattern of *"Kum ba yah,"* built on the tonic chord, might be a major accomplishment for some students and should be viewed as such by the teacher. Students might need several revisits to the song to learn to sing all the patterns and eventually perform the entire piece in harmony. For them, the feeling of accomplishment when they finally sing the song in harmony will be well worth the many revisits.

TECHNOLOGY/MEDIA LINK

4c **Sequencing Software** Have students notate an instrumental version of *"Kum ba yah."* Have students

- Set up the program for three staff lines.
- Choose the key of F major.
- Choose the time signature of ¾ and use standard symbols to notate meter in simple patterns.
- Notate each part, both melody and harmony, of *"Kum ba yah"* by selecting the desired rhythmic value and then clicking on the musical staff to choose the pitch.
- Choose the best instrumental playback voices for their arrangements of the song.

Unit 6   *Making Music Our Own*   **245**

WHAT DO YOU KNOW?

MATERIALS
• **Resource Book** p. B-19

Have students read and answer the questions independently and then check their answers with a partner before sharing answers with the class.

For a more formal assessment, duplicate the Unit 6 assessment worksheet and have students work independently or in small groups to complete it. The worksheet is found on Resource Book p. B-19.

WHAT DO YOU HEAR?

MATERIALS	
• *What Do You Hear? 6A*	**CD 12-1**
• **Resource Book** p. B-19	

Review how a major chord is made and how a minor chord is made. Play some of each, asking the class to identify whether they are quality of major or minor. Have students listen to the recording and identify what they hear.

MATERIALS	
• *What Do You Hear? 6B*	**CD 12-5**
• **Resource Book** p. B-19	

Review and discuss the differences between the harpsichord, the piano, and the synthesizer. Invite students to describe the differences in sound quality. Then ask students to work with a partner to identify the instruments they hear in the recording.

What Do You Know?

1. Which of the following are expressive qualities?

  a. form   **b.** tempo   **c.** dynamics

2. Meter in 5 means _____.

  a. the music has only five measures   **b.** there is no such meter   **c.** there are five beats in a measure

3. In music, blues is an expression, a feeling, and a _____.

  a. meter   **b.** form   **c.** verse

4. The dorian scale begins on _____.

  a. *do*   **b.** *la*   **c.** *re*

What Do You Hear? 6A

 CD 12–1

Listen to the following excerpts. Each time a number is called, point to the word that describes the tonality. Is it major or minor?

1. major   minor

2. major   minor

3. major   minor

4. major   minor

What Do You Hear? 6B

 CD 12–5

Listen to the following excerpts. For each, point to the name of the instrument you hear.

1. harpsichord   piano   synthesizer

2. harpsichord   piano   synthesizer

3. harpsichord   piano   synthesizer

246

Footnotes

ANSWER KEY

▶ **What Do You Know?**

1. c. dynamics

2. c. There are five beats in a measure

3. b. form

4. c. *re*

▶ **What Do You Hear? 6A**

1. major—*"Vive l'amour"* (excerpt)

2. minor—*"Drill, Ye Tarriers"* (excerpt)

3. minor—*"Hava nagila"* (excerpt)

4. major—*"Orange Blossom Special"* (excerpt)

▶ **What Do You Hear? 6B**

1. piano

2. harpsichord

3. synthesizer

Perform, Create

Create a 12-bar Blues Song

- Compose your own 12-bar blues song (see the form of "Good Mornin', Blues," page 224, for an example).
- Notate your melody in the key of C.

Show the Meter

Listen to *Ali Pasha* and *Take Five*. Perform steady-beat movements that reflect the accent pattern of the meter in 5.

Sing in Harmony

Practice singing in two- and three-part harmony by reviewing these songs in Unit 6:

"Linstead Market," page 241

"Ev'ry Time I Feel the Spirit," page 242

"Kum ba yah," page 244

Working in small groups,

- Choose one song.
- Decide who will sing the melody and who will sing the harmony parts.
- Practice each part.
- Perform your song for the teacher and the other groups.
- Discuss how well each group was able to sing in two or three parts. Then offer suggestions that will help each group improve its performance.

Unit 6 **247**

WHAT YOU CAN DO

MATERIALS

• "Good Mornin', Blues," p. 224	**CD 11-7**
• *Ali Pasha*, p. 218	**CD 10-35**
• *Take Five*, p. 220	**CD 10-37**
• "Linstead Market," p. 241	**CD 11-32**
• "Ev'ry Time I Feel the Spirit," p. 242	**CD 11-34**
• "*Kum ba yah*," p. 244	**CD 11-36**

Create a 12-bar Blues Song

Invite students to sing "Good Mornin', Blues." Then divide the class into four groups and encourage them to write their own 12-bar blues song in the key of C. Ask for suggestions of topics suitable for blues material, and suggest that the words be in a three-line stanza. Then review the 12-bar blues form. Tell students that to be authentic, the first four measures should be based on the I chord. The next two measures must be based on the IV chord, the next two on the I chord again. The next one should be based on the V chord, then one measure on IV, and the last two on the I chord. Encourage students to sing and play their compositions.

Show the Meter

Have the class listen to *Ali Pasha* and *Take Five* while patting the steady beat. Caution them not to wait for that "sixth beat" before starting again.

Sing in Harmony

Invite students to sing songs in harmony. Divide the class into three groups. If students are very comfortable, they can sing one-on-a-line. If not, try to have several students on each part. Help students decide who is on what line, putting the higher voices on top. Ask students to clap the beat and say the rhythm of each line. Then ask the groups to sing each line individually. Give each group a keyboard instrument so that they may practice each line before putting them together. Then have the groups sing in harmony.

TECHNOLOGY/MEDIA LINK

Rubrics Visit *www.sfsuccessnet.com* for rubrics to assess students' achievement in music skills.

PATHS TO Making Music

Lesson	Elements	Skills

LESSON 1
Spiritual Style
pp. 256-259

Element: Rhythm
Concept: Beat
Focus: Syncopation

Secondary Element
Form: verse/refrain

National Standards
1c 2a 5a 6c 8b 9a

Skill: Creating
Objective: Create new verses containing syncopation to a spiritual

Secondary Skills
• **Singing** Sing and tap a steady beat
• **Listening** Listen to a selection and follow the notation
• **Moving** Sing and move to the song
• **Reading** Read the song notation and locate the dotted-quarter/eighth-note pattern
• **Performing** Perform the songs together

SKILLS REINFORCEMENT
• **Recorder** Play a countermelody
• **Keyboard** Perform a keyboard accompaniment
• **Mallets** Play an Orff arrangement
• **Keyboard** Tips to help all students perform a keyboard accompaniment

LESSON 2
Dance to the Music
pp. 260-261

Element: Texture/Harmony
Concept: Harmony
Focus: Two-chord harmony

Secondary Element
Form: verse/refrain

National Standards
1a 2b 6a 8b

Skill: Playing
Objective: Accompany a song with two-chord harmony

Secondary Skills
• **Singing** Sing the song and compare the melody of the verse and refrain
• **Listening** Listen to the selection and identify the instrument

SKILLS REINFORCEMENT
• **Recorder** Play a countermelody

LESSON 3
Miles and Miles
pp. 262-263

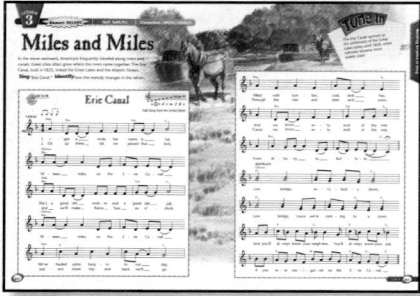

Element: Melody
Concept: Tonality
Focus: Minor and major tonalities

Secondary Element
Form: verse/refrain

National Standards
1a 6c 8b

Skill: Singing
Objective: Sing in minor and major tonalities

Secondary Skills
• **Analyzing** Analyze and identify pitches and tonality of verse and refrain
• **Singing** Sing the song and alternate the solo and chorus parts

SKILLS REINFORCEMENT
• **Reading** Discover the difference between tied and slurred notes

Connections

Music and Other Literature

Connection: Style

Activity: Discuss and compare a spiritual and an Early American hymn

MEETING INDIVIDUAL NEEDS **English Language Learners** Use a word bank and sentence starters to aid comprehension

SPOTLIGHT ON
African American Spirituals Facts about spirituals
Sacred Harp Spirituals Facts about a different spiritual style

ACROSS THE CURRICULUM
Language Arts Create a journal log of different versions of the same songs
Language Arts Read a book about the song author

BUILDING SKILLS THROUGH MUSIC **Language** Discuss the meaning of the song text

Songs
"Down by the Riverside"
"The Promised Land"

Listening Selection *Amazing Grace*

More Music Choices
"Joshua Fought the Battle of Jericho,"
p. 101
"Ev'ry Time I Feel the Spirit," p. 242
"Simple Gifts," p. 184

ASSESSMENT

Music Journal Writing/Performance Listen to and compare songs; perform original lyrics containing syncopation

TECHNOLOGY/MEDIA LINK
Web Site More information on African American gospel music and spirituals

---

Connection: Culture

Activity: Learn about the mountain dulcimer

ACROSS THE CURRICULUM **Language Arts** Read folk legends about pioneer America

SPOTLIGHT ON **Mountain Dulcimer** Facts about the instrument

BUILDING SKILLS THROUGH MUSIC **Art** Draw a scene that depicts an aspect of the westward expansion

Song "Shady Grove"

Listening Selection *Cedar Swamp*

More Music Choices
"California," p. 52

ASSESSMENT

Performance/Peer Critique Sing a song in small groups with accompaniment and assess

TECHNOLOGY/MEDIA LINK
Web Site More information about Appalachian music and instruments

---

Connection: Social Studies

Activity: Discover that Americans traveled westward to settle the Great Lake states using the Erie Canal

MEETING INDIVIDUAL NEEDS **English Language Learners** Create a semantic map to help with comprehension

ACROSS THE CURRICULUM **Social Studies** Develop map skills and trace the Erie Canal

BUILDING SKILLS THROUGH MUSIC **Math** Compute the miles traveled each day by the singer on the Erie Canal

Song "Erie Canal"

More Music Choices
"El carite" ("The Kingfish"), p. 305

ASSESSMENT

Performance/Interview Sing a song and discuss tonalities of verse and refrain

TECHNOLOGY/MEDIA LINK
Web Site More information about the songs of the western movement

Lesson	Elements	Skills

LESSON 4

Songs of the Sea
pp. 264-265

Element: Form
Concept: Call and response
Focus: Call-and-response form

Secondary Element
Rhythm: upbeat

National Standards
1c 3c 6a 6b 8b

Skill: Singing
Objective: Sing using call-and-response form

Secondary Skills
- **Singing** Sing the song
- **Listening** Listen to and discuss a related selection

SKILLS REINFORCEMENT
- **Vocal Development** Use call-and-response singing to match pitches
- **Recorder** Perform an exercise to accompany the song
- **Mallets** Play an Orff accompaniment

LESSON 5

A Special Ride
pp. 266-269

Element: Timbre
Concept: Instrumental
Focus: Instruments imitating train sounds

Secondary Element
Expression: tempo and articulation

National Standards
1a 2d 6a 6b 8b 9a

Skill: Listening
Objective: Listen to a selection in which instruments imitate train sounds

Secondary Skills
- **Singing** Examine the lyrics of the song to find the form; identify the blue notes
- **Creating** Experiment with other instruments to make train sounds
- **Moving** Perform a special dance with the song

SKILLS REINFORCEMENT
- **Keyboard** Create train sound effects
- **Creating** Make a list of train sounds and the instruments that can produce the sounds

---

LESSON 6

19th Century Pop
pp. 270-271

Element: Texture/Harmony
Concept: Harmony
Focus: Parallel Thirds

Secondary Element
Form: verse/refrain

National Standards
1d 2a 5d 6b 8b

Skill: Singing
Objective: Sing both melody and harmony parts in parallel thirds

Secondary Skill
- **Listening** Listen and distinguish harmony and melody in song notation

SKILLS REINFORCEMENT
- **Recorder** Play a countermelody
- **Mallets** Play an Orff arrangement
- **Keyboard** Play a two-hand accompaniment

Connections

Music and Other Literature

Connection: Social Studies

Activity: Become acquainted with the tradition of singing shanties on sailing ships

SPOTLIGHT ON **Shanties** Facts about types of shanties

ACROSS THE CURRICULUM **Language Arts** Discuss and write an essay about the lyrics of "Shenandoah"

BUILDING SKILLS THROUGH MUSIC **Language** List the similarities and differences in music characteristics between two versions of the song

Song "Shenandoah"

Listening Selection *Shenandoah*
Arts Connection *The Clipper Ship*

More Music Choices
"Go Down, Moses," p. 190
"Day-O!," p. 18

ASSESSMENT
Performance/Observation Research and perform other call-and-response songs correctly

TECHNOLOGY/MEDIA LINK
Sequencing Software Create a call-and-response melody

Connection: Social Studies

Activity: Discuss the history of trains in the United States

ACROSS THE CURRICULUM
Social Studies Discuss and research railroads in the United States
Language Arts Dramatize poetry about transportation

SPOTLIGHT ON **The Orange Blossom Special** Information about this famous train

MEETING INDIVIDUAL NEEDS **Inclusion** Alternatives for patterned dance movements

MOVEMENT **Patterned Dance** Perform a dance to a bluegrass song

BUILDING SKILLS THROUGH MUSIC **Language** Describe the locations where the singer of the song would like to travel

Song "Orange Blossom Special"

Listening Selection *Orange Blossom Special*
Listening Map *Orange Blossom Special*

More Music Choices
"Wabash Cannon Ball," p. 136
"Pat Works on the Railway," p. 182

ASSESSMENT
Observation/Music Journal Writing Write descriptions of instrument timbres heard in a listening selection

TECHNOLOGY/MEDIA LINK
MIDI/Sequencing Software Use MIDI file to create a bluegrass band song
Transparency Use the listening map to track the elements of the song

Connection: Culture

Activity: Discuss the background of a Stephen Foster song

SPOTLIGHT ON **The Composer** Facts about Stephen Foster

CULTURAL CONNECTION **A Day at the Races** Background on the song; discussion of horseracing

BUILDING SKILLS THROUGH MUSIC **Social Studies** Write new lyrics to the song to describe a different event

Song "Camptown Races"

M·U·S·I·C M·A·K·E·R·S
Stephen Collins Foster

More Music Choices
"Day-O!," p. 18
"Laredo," p. 10

ASSESSMENT
Performance/Observation Sing a song in thirds and assess accuracy

TECHNOLOGY/MEDIA LINK
Notation Software Compose a harmony part based on thirds

Lesson	Elements	Skills	
LESSON 7 **Comin' Home** pp. 272-275 	**Element: Texture/Harmony** **Concept:** Texture **Focus:** Descant **Secondary Element** Timbre: instrumental **National Standards** 1c 1d 5a 6a 6b 8b	**Skill: Creating** **Objective:** Explore a parody to a well-known song **Secondary Skills** • **Singing** Compare and contrast different sets of lyrics • **Listening** Listen and identify instruments heard in a recording • **Reading** Read melody and countermelody and discuss contrast • **Singing** Sing melody and countermelody in groups • **Listening** Listen and indicate statement of the melody	**SKILLS REINFORCEMENT** • **Singing** Sing alternate lyrics to the song melody • **Keyboard** Play a chord accompaniment
LESSON 8 **Singing on the Trail** pp. 276-277 	**Element: Form** **Concept:** abac **Focus:** abac form **Secondary Element** Timbre: Instrumental **National Standards** 1c 2d 4c 6b 8b	**Skill: Playing** **Objective:** Play guitar to accompany an abac song **Secondary Skills** • **Analyzing** Analyze the song form before singing • **Listening** Listen to the selection and compare it to the song	**SKILLS REINFORCEMENT** • **Reading** Discover and discuss the pitches in a song • **Recorder** Play an accompaniment
LESSON 9 **Send the Word** pp. 278-279 	**Element: Melody** **Concept:** Pattern **Focus:** Motive **Secondary Element** Expression: tempo and articulation **National Standards** 1b 3b 5d 8b 9b	**Skill: Singing** **Objective:** Sing short melodic patterns in a patriotic song **Secondary Skills** • **Singing** Sing the song paying attention to tempo, diction, and energy • **Playing** Play the motive on various instruments • **Listening** Compare two patriotic songs	**SKILLS REINFORCEMENT** • **Improvising** Improvise patterns of the song on instruments

Connections

Music and Other Literature

Connection: Social Studies

Activity: Learn how songs were used in context of the Civil War

TEACHER TO TEACHER **Listening Preparation** Use the Sound Bank to help identification

CHARACTER EDUCATION **Courage** Discuss character traits needed by soldiers during wartime

ACROSS THE CURRICULUM
Social Studies Read accounts of life during the Civil War
Social Studies Background of song melody

AUDIENCE ETIQUETTE **Preparing to Attend a Performance** How to prepare to attend a live performance

BUILDING SKILLS THROUGH MUSIC **Social Studies** Locate the Northern and Southern states that were involved in the Civil War

Songs
"Battle Cry of Freedom"
"Battle Hymn of the Republic"

Listening Selection *American Salute*
Arts Connection *Yankee Volunteers Marching to Dixie*

More Music Choices
"The Ash Grove," p. 114
"Roll On, Columbia," p. 116
"This Land Is Your Land," p. 118

ASSESSMENT

Performance/Peer Critique Sing songs with a descant and a rhythm interlude, and evaluate peers

TECHNOLOGY/MEDIA LINK

Web Site More information about music during the American Civil War period

Connection: Related Arts

Activity: Discuss an engraving by an American artist of the cowboy era

ACROSS THE CURRICULUM **Language Arts** Share poetry and songs about the Old West

SPOTLIGHT ON **The Artist** Facts about Frederic Remington

BUILDING SKILLS THROUGH MUSIC **Language** Discuss the memories mentioned in the song

Song "Colorado Trail"

Listening Selection *Colorado Trail*
Arts Connection *Engraving by Remington*

More Music Choices
"Cattle Call," p. 344
"Home on the Range," p. 69

ASSESSMENT

Performance/Observation Perform a song and demonstrate the form of a piece

TECHNOLOGY/MEDIA LINK

Sequencing Software Compose a bass part for the song

Connection: Social Studies

Activity: Discuss the role of patriotic songs during World War I

SPOTLIGHT ON **The Composer** Facts about George M. Cohan

ACROSS THE CURRICULUM **Social Studies** Discuss historical information about World War I

BUILDING SKILLS THROUGH MUSIC **Writing** Rewrite the song text as complete sentences

Song "Over There"

Listening Selection *I'm a Yankee Doodle Dandy*
M·U·S·I·C M·A·K·E·R·S
George M. Cohan

More Music Choices
"America, the Beautiful," p. 76

ASSESSMENT

Performance/Observation Sing a song and identify melodic sections containing a motive

TECHNOLOGY/MEDIA LINK

Notation Software Notate and play back bugle calls

Lesson	Elements	Skills	
LESSON 10 **Gospel Calling** pp. 280-281 	**Element: Timbre** **Concept:** Vocal timbre **Focus:** Vocal and instrumental timbre **Secondary Element** Form: verse/refrain **National Standards** 1c 2c 6b	**Skill: Listening** **Objective:** Listen and compare two African American gospel performances **Secondary Skills** • **Listening** Listen to the recording and identify instruments • **Analyzing** Identify the song form • **Listening** Compare the differences in vocal timbre	**SKILLS REINFORCEMENT** • **Keyboard** Play a keyboard accompaniment
LESSON 11 **Better Times Ahead...** pp. 282-283 	**Element: Texture/Harmony** **Concept:** Harmony **Focus:** Chords **Secondary Element** Rhythm: meter **National Standards** 1b 2d 8b	**Skill: Playing** **Objective:** Play an instrumental accompaniment using appropriate chords **Secondary Skills** • **Singing** Sing alternate verses to a song • **Listening** Compare two versions of the same song	**SKILLS REINFORCEMENT** • **Playing** Experiment with playing chord accompaniment by ear
LESSON 12 **Another Challenge** pp. 284-285 	**Element: Rhythm** **Concept:** Pattern **Focus:** Syncopation **Secondary Element** Melody: pitch and direction **National Standards** 1a 6b 7a 8b	**Skill: Singing** **Objective:** Sing syncopated rhythm patterns **Secondary Skill** • **Reading** Locate and practice clapping syncopated rhythms	
LESSON 13 **The Sign of the Times** pp. 286-289 	**Element: Rhythm** **Concept:** Pattern **Focus:** Syncopation **Secondary Element** Melody: pitch and direction **National Standards** 1c 2e 4c 5a 5c 6a 7b 8b 9a	**Skill: Creating** **Objective:** Create new verses and movements to show syncopation **Secondary Skills** • **Listening** Listen to a recording and discuss the lyrics • **Reading** Practice the syncopated rhythms exercise • **Singing** Sing the song with the recording • **Listening** Listen to a selection and discuss syncopation and blue notes	• **Reading** Practice the rhythm of the first measure of the song • **Singing** Sing the song and practice syncopations • **Moving** Create movements to the song **SKILLS REINFORCEMENT** • **Reading** Read and clap syncopated rhythms • **Mallets** Play an Orff arrangement • **Reading** Complete an exercise to practice syncopation

Connections

Music and Other Literature

Connection: Genre
Activity: Learn about Thomas A. Dorsey and the beginning of the gospel movement in the 1920s and 1930s

TEACHER TO TEACHER **The Singing/Listening Connection** Learn good singing traits by listening to quality artist recordings

SPOTLIGHT ON **The History of Gospel Music** Information about Thomas A. Dorsey and his music

BUILDING SKILLS THROUGH MUSIC **Art** Draw a visual representation of the song text

Song "Twelve Gates to the City"

Listening Selection *What Could I Do*
M·U·S·I·C M·A·K·E·R·S
  Thomas A. Dorsey

More Music Choices
"Joshua Fought the Battle of Jericho," p. 101
"Go Down, Moses," p. 190
"Ev'ry Time I Feel the Spirit," p. 242

ASSESSMENT

Music Journal Writing Describe the sound of the voices and instruments in the recording

TECHNOLOGY/MEDIA LINK

Web Site More information about African American blues and jazz music

---

Connection: Social Studies
Activity: Relate a song to a historical event

SPOTLIGHT ON **The Performer** Advice from Woody Guthrie

ACROSS THE CURRICULUM **Social Studies** Background of the Great Depression

SCHOOL TO HOME CONNECTION **The Homeless** Read a book about homeless children

BUILDING SKILLS THROUGH MUSIC **Social Studies** Decribe the characteristics of two versions of the song

Song "Goin' Down the Road Feelin' Bad"

Listening Selection *Goin' Down the Road Feelin' Bad*
M·U·S·I·C M·A·K·E·R·S
  Woody Guthrie

More Music Choices
"Roll On, Columbia," p. 116
"This Land Is Your Land," p. 118

ASSESSMENT

Performance/Observation Perform the song with accompaniment, using appropriate chords

TECHNOLOGY/MEDIA LINK

Sequencing Software Record and critique a classroom performance of a song

---

Connection: Social Studies
Activity: Explore how America pulled itself out of the Great Depression

SPOTLIGHT ON **Music to Make You Happy** Music to "cure the blues"

CULTURAL CONNECTION **1930s-1940s** Discuss the contribution of radio and movies during this time

ACROSS THE CURRICULUM **Social Studies** Overview of Roosevelt and the New Deal

SCHOOL TO HOME CONNECTION **Great Depression to World War II** Interview people who lived through the Great Depression

BUILDING SKILLS THROUGH MUSIC **Writing** Write a paragraph about the importance of the New Deal

Song "Happy Days Are Here Again"

More Music Choices
"Éliza Kongo," p. 14
"Morning Comes Early," p. 13

ASSESSMENT

Performance/Self-Assessment Clap the steady beat while singing syncopated rhythms in the song

TECHNOLOGY/MEDIA LINK

Web Site More information about 1930s music

Connection: Social Studies
Activity: Discuss social change in the 1960s and early 1970s, as expressed through songs

SPOTLIGHT ON **The 1960s** Overview of the civil rights movement

CULTURAL CONNECTION **Social Issues** Background on civil rights and war issues of the 1960's and 1970's

ACROSS THE CURRICULUM **Social Studies/Language Arts** Search newspapers for current issues

CHARACTER EDUCATION **Social Responsibility** Discuss how to respond to social concerns

BUILDING SKILLS THROUGH MUSIC **Language** Complete sentences based on song text

Songs
"If I Had a Hammer"
"Woke Up This Morning"

Listening Selection *Where Have All the Flowers Gone?*

More Music Choices
"Stand By Me," p. 46
"You've Got a Friend," p. 366
"Turn, Turn, Turn," p. 378

ASSESSMENT

Performance/Music Journal Writing Perform and record a song with movements to show syncopation

TECHNOLOGY/MEDIA LINK

Web Site More information about songs of the Civil Rights movement

INTRODUCING THE UNIT

Unit 7 presents a thematic approach to understanding music elements. This unit features work songs, spirituals, sea shanties, and cowboy songs. Presented on p. 251 is a brief overview of the skills that are assessed in this unit. (See below and pp. 252–253 for unit highlights of related curricular experiences.)

For a more detailed unit overview, see Unit at a Glance, pp. 249a–249h.

UNIT PROJECT

This unit presents the perfect opportunity to develop a class musical. This musical can be presented at a PTA meeting, at a school assembly, or at a special concert.

To organize the musical, have students

- Learn to sing the songs in the unit. Feature soloists or small groups on some verses.
- Add instruments such as guitars, Autoharps, or other folk instruments wherever possible. (The Stereo Performance Track for each song can also be used as accompaniment.)
- Develop a narration or story between songs. (The narration can include short sections of important documents such as the Gettysburg Address.)
- Include dances or other small theatrical skits with the songs.
- Create simple costumes that help portray the message of the musical.
- Organize a gallery of historical images that can be displayed around the performance venue or used as a slide background to the musical.
- Invite parents or prominent community members to observe the presentation.

Singing Across the Country

Pack your bags for a musical journey across America. We'll start "Down by the Riverside," travel along the "Erie Canal," hop on "The Orange Blossom Special" for a fun time at "Camptown Races," and then move on to the "Colorado Trail." These are just a few of the songs that people sang as they built America.

Sing "Fifty Nifty United States" and add movement for a special performance.

★★★★★★★★★★★★★★★

Arts Connection

▼ *Map* by Jasper Johns, 1963. Encaustic and collage on canvas

(250)

ACROSS THE CURRICULUM

Unit Highlights The following interdisciplinary activities in this unit are related to the music elements presented in the lessons. See Unit at a Glance, pp. 249a–249h, for topical descriptions presented according to lesson sequence.

▶ **LANGUAGE ARTS**

- Create journals to keep records of songs (p. 257)
- Share the story of John Newton (p. 258)
- Read folk legends and stories of pioneer America (p. 260)
- Discuss the lyrics of a song and write poems and essays (p. 265)
- Read aloud and dramatize poetry about trains and other forms of transportation; write new poetry about transportation (p. 268)
- Read poetry and perform songs about the Old West (p. 276)
- Search newspapers for current issues and write your feelings about them (p. 287)

▶ **SOCIAL STUDIES**

- Trace the route of the Erie Canal (p. 262)
- Explore facts about railroads (p. 266)
- Read accounts of life during the Civil War (p. 273)
- Discover the origin of a popular Civil War song (p. 274)
- Learn historical information about World War I (p. 279)
- Discuss information about the Great Depression (p. 283)
- Read facts about the New Deal (p. 285)

CD 12–8

Fifty Nifty United States

Words and Music by Ray Charles

s l t, d r m f s l

Fif - ty   nif - ty   U - nit - ed States from   thir-teen o - rig - i - nal   col - o - nies;

Fif - ty   nif - ty   stars in   the flag that   bil-lows so beau-ti-f'ly   in __ the breeze.

Each   in - di - vid - u - al   state con - trib-utes   a qual-i - ty   that is great.

Each   in - di - vid - u - al   state de - serves a   bow, we sa - lute them now.

Unit 7   251

Building America in Song

America has always been a singing country. In this unit, we will explore songs that tell the stories of America's history.

MUSIC SKILLS
ASSESSED IN THIS UNIT

Reading Music: Rhythm
- Say the lyrics of a song in rhythm while maintaining a steady beat (p. 285)
- Identify and read dotted-quarter/eighth note rhythm patterns in a song (p. 258)

Reading Music: Pitch
- Learn melody and harmony parts of a song (p. 271)
- Locate the melody and descant parts of a song (p. 274)

Performing Music: Singing
- Perform new verses for a song (p. 259)
- Sing a folk song from the United States (p. 261)
- Sing songs in call and response form (p. 265)

Moving to Music
- Create and perform body movements (p. 289)
- Perform a movement with a bluegrass song (p. 269)

Performing Music: Playing
- Accompany a folk song on Autoharp or guitar (p. 261)
- Accompany a cowboy song (p. 277)
- Accompany a song on keyboard, Autoharp, or guitar (p. 283)

Creating Music
- Create new verses for an African American spiritual (p. 259)
- Create new verses to a civil rights song (p. 289)

Listening to Music
- Listen to a selection and follow a listening map (p. 268)
- Listen and compare two African American spirituals (p. 281)

CULTURAL CONNECTION

Unit Highlights   The musical literature in this unit provides many opportunities for students to explore a variety of world cultures. See Unit at a Glance, pp. 249a–249h, for topical descriptions presented according to lesson sequence.

▶ **AMERICAN REGIONAL**

- Discuss the background of a song and the history of horse racing (p. 271)
- Explore the impact of radio and movies during the 1930's and 1940's (p. 284)
- Discuss the civil rights and war issues of the 1960's and 1970's (p. 286)

OPENING ACTIVITIES

MATERIALS
- "Fifty Nifty United States"   **CD 12-8**

    Recording Routine:
    Intro (2 m.); vocal

Listening

Invite students to listen to "Fifty Nifty United States"
CD 12-8 as they follow the notation in their books.

Reading

Ask students to identify the
- A and B sections of the song.
- Key signatures and tonic for each section
- Measures containing syncopated rhythm

Singing

After students have learned the first phrase through
Connecticut, ask them to look at the second phrase,
Delaware through *Indiana,* to discover that it is somewhat
like a sequence (a similar pattern repeated a step higher).
Then ask them to find where the *Alabama* melody returns
(Oklahoma). Use the recording to help students practice
and memorize the song.

252

ASSESSMENT

Unit Highlights This unit includes a variety of strategies and
methods, described below, to track students' progress and assess their
understanding of lesson objectives.

▶ **INFORMAL ASSESSMENTS**

At the close of each Teacher's Edition lesson in this unit, one of the
following types of assessments is used to evaluate the learning of the
key element focus or skill objective.

- Music Journal Writing (pp. 259, 269, 281, 289)
- Performance/Interview (p. 263)
- Performance/Observation (pp. 265, 271, 277, 279, 283)
- Performance/Peer Critique (p. 275)
- Performance/Self-Assessment (p. 285)

▶ **RUBRICS**

Visit *www.sfsuccessnet.com* for rubrics to assess students'
achievement in music skills.

ho, Il-li-nois, In-di-an-a;

I-o-wa, Kan-sas, Ken-tuck-y, Lou-i-si-an-a, Maine,

Mar-y-land, Mas-sa-chu-setts, Mich-i-gan; Min-ne-

so-ta, Mis-sis-sip-pi, Mis-sou-ri, Mon-tan-a, Ne-

bras-ka, Ne-vad-a;

New Hamp-shire, New Jer-sey, New Mex-i-co, New York,

Improvising

Use the ragtime rhythms found in the A section as a basis for a rhythmic improvisation. Have students

- Establish a basic "boom-chick" rhythm ostinato like the left hand of a ragtime piano player. Use body percussion, voice sounds, or instruments.
- Play solos using rhythm instruments, body percussion, or voice sounds) on the rhythms of any of the measures of the A section.

INNOVATIVE TEACHER SUPPORT FOR THIS UNIT

- **MAKING MUSIC DVD, Grade 5** contains video segments that support lessons, including signing and movement.
- **MAKING MUSIC with Movement and Dance** provides more opportunities for large group activities in music or physical education classes.
- **MAKING MUSIC with Technology** provides lesson plans for many technology applications; includes MIDI files.
- *¡A cantar!* features recorded songs and lessons from around the Spanish-speaking world; includes strategies for bilingual classes and for English-speaking teachers working with Spanish-speaking students.
- **Bridges to Asia** features recorded songs and lessons from Asian and Pacific region cultures.
- *www.sfsuccessnet.com* provides an online lesson planner to conveniently create lesson plans at school or at home. Includes rubrics for assessment, lesson modifications to meet the needs of all students, performance musicals based on program content, and more.

TECHNOLOGY/MEDIA LINK

Unit Highlights The following components are used in this unit to reinforce and expand students' understanding of music elements and related themes. See Unit at a Glance, pp. 249a–249h, for a descriptive listing according to lesson sequence.

▶ **MIDI/SEQUENCING SOFTWARE**

- Create a call-and-response melody (p. 265)
- Explore MIDI sounds and select timbres for each track (p. 269)
- Notate and compose the bass part for a cowboy song (p. 277)
- Record a chordal accompaniment (p. 283)

▶ **NOTATION SOFTWARE**

- Create a harmony part based on thirds (p. 271)
- Notate and play back bugle calls (p. 279)

▶ **TRANSPARENCY**

- Use a transparency to help students follow a listening map (p. 269)

▶ **WEB SITE**

- Go to *www.sfsuccessnet.com* for more information on gospel music and spirituals (p. 259); Appalachian music and instruments (p. 261); westward movement (p. 263); music and songs of the American Civil War (p. 275); African American blues and jazz music (p. 281); music of the 1930's (p. 285); songs of the Civil Rights movement (p. 289)

Moving

After students know how to sing "Fifty Nifty United States," teach them this show choir routine. (It will be helpful to number the measures of the song 1–108.)

Formation: Students stand across the room in three or four lines.

Measures 1–2: March in place.

Measures 3–4: Thirteen students from center of lines march forward while remainder of students march in place.

Measures 5–6: Thirteen students march back to place and join others who are marching.

Measures 7–8: March in place.

Measures 9–10: Stand in place, extending both arms forward from the chest, with palms facing upward.

Measure 11: Bring arms to sides.

Measure 12: March to melodic rhythm.

Measures 13–14: Stand in place.

Measure 15: Bow on *serve.*

Measure 16: Salute on syllable *lute.*

North, south, east, west, in our calm ob - jec - tive o - pin - ion, *(name of*

home state) is the best of the Fif - ty nif - ty U - nit - ed States from

thir - teen o - rig - i - nal col - o - nies, Shout 'em, scout 'em, Tell all a - bout 'em,

One by one till we've giv - en a day to ev - 'ry state in the good old

U. S. A.

Measures 17–25: Repeat measures 1–8.

Measure 26: Step on beat 1; stand in place on beats 2, 3, and 4.

Measure 27: Raise arms to ceiling.

Measures 28–84: Have students create movements that represent individual states. For example, the names of the fifty states begin with nineteen different letters of the alphabet. Students can be arranged in nineteen groups, each representing one of those letters, and each group can create a statue movement for the states that begin with its letter.

Measures 85–86: Point north, east, south, and west with both hands.

Measure 87–88: Stand in place.

Measures 89–90: All perform the movement that was created by the group for this state.

Measures 91–99: Repeat measures 1–8.

Measure 100: Repeat measure 26.

Measures 101–102: Raise left arm slowly toward ceiling and back to place on last beat.

Measures 103–104: Repeat measures 101–102 with right arm.

Measures 105–108: Raise both arms slowly.

LESSON AT A GLANCE

Element Focus **RHYTHM** Syncopation

Skill Objective **CREATING** Create new verses containing syncopation to a spiritual

Connection Activity **STYLE** Discuss and compare a spiritual and an early American hymn

MATERIALS

- "Down by the Riverside"   **CD 12-10**

  Recording Routine: Intro (4 m.); v. 1; refrain; interlude (4 m.); v. 2; refrain; interlude (4 m.); v. 3; refrain; coda

- "The Promised Land"   **CD 12-12**

  Recording Routine: Intro (4 m); vocal; interlude (4 m); vocal

- *Amazing Grace*   **CD 12-14**

- **Resource Book** pp. F-28, H-20

VOCABULARY

spiritual   syncopation

tempo   gospel

◆ ◆ ◆ ◆ **National Standards** ◆ ◆ ◆ ◆

1c Sing music from diverse genres
2a Play instruments accurately alone and in small ensembles
5a Read eighth notes in duple meter
6c Understand and use basic principles of rhythm and intervals in music analysis
8b Identify ways music relates to social studies and language arts
9a Describe characteristics of music styles from a variety of cultures

MORE MUSIC CHOICES

For more practice singing African American spirituals:
"Joshua Fought the Battle of Jericho," p. 101
"Ev'ry Time I Feel the Spirit," p. 242
For more practice singing early American hymn tunes:
"Simple Gifts," p. 184

| Element: RHYTHM | Skill: CREATING | Connection: STYLE |

Spiritual STYLE

American spirituals were popular from 1820–1860 among both African and European Americans. The spiritual gave voice to enslaved African Americans who longed for the promised land of freedom.

Sing this spiritual and **identify** the syncopated patterns.

CD 12–10
MIDI 18

Down by the Riverside

s, l, t, (d) di r ri m f

African American Spiritual

VERSE

1. Gon - na lay down my sword and shield, __
2. Gon - na join hands with ev - 'ry one, __
3. Gon - na ring out a song of joy, __

Down by the riv - er - side, ____

Down by the riv - er - side, ____

Down by the riv - er - side, ____

Gon - na lay down my sword and shield, __
Gon - na join hands with ev - 'ry one, __
Gon - na ring out a song of joy, __

256

Footnotes

MEETING INDIVIDUAL NEEDS

▶ **English Language Learners** Developing entirely new verses may be difficult for students who are less fluent with English. You may want to use sentence starters, or frames, such as "Gonna' lay down my _____ and _____." You may also want to use a word bank and encourage students to complete the sentence starters with words they know from the bank.

BUILDING SKILLS THROUGH MUSIC

▶ **Language** Have students read the lyrics of "Down by the Riverside" and discuss ideas about the meaning of the text. Ask students to write a sentence to explain their own interpretation. Then have students read the song lyrics again and find phrases that reflect the lives of people today.

SPOTLIGHT ON

8b ▶ **African American Spirituals** During the period of slavery before the Civil War, African American spirituals were learned by oral tradition. The spirituals often contained secret messages about the Underground Railroad—a series of way stations and shelters for escaping slaves. For example, the song "Oh, Won't You Sit Down?" says *See those children dressed in red/Must be the children that old Moses led.* Slave owners thought the verse was about the Old Testament prophet Moses, but the verse referred to Harriet Tubman, the black Moses who led her people to freedom. After the Civil War, African American colleges and universities sent choirs on tours in the United States and Europe to sing spirituals, helping to popularize them.

Down by the riv-er-side, _____

And stud-y _____ war no more. _____

REFRAIN

I ain't gon-na stud-y _____ war no more,

I ain't gon-na stud-y _____ war no more,

I ain't gon-na stud-y _____ war no

1.
more. _____ I ain't gon-na more.
2.

Create new verses to "Down by the Riverside" by making up only one line of text.

- Start with the word *Gonna.*
- Make sure your line contains a total of eight syllables.
- Place your new text on lines 1 and 5 of the song.
- Write at least three new verses; then try them out by yourself and with your classmates.

1 INTRODUCE

8b ASK What do you know about spirituals? (Students may describe the feelings expressed in spirituals or the singing styles they have heard.)

How do you think spirituals were learned? (They were learned by listening to others sing them. Slaves, for example, were forbidden to learn to read or write.)

2 DEVELOP

Singing

1c Have students sing "Down by the Riverside" **CD 12-10** with the recording, while tapping the steady beat and following the notation on pp. 256–257.

5a ASK Where are the syncopations in the verse?
6c (Measures 2, 4, 6, 8, 10, 12, and 13; measures 1 and 9 have a quarter-note/half-note syncopation.)

1c Have students sing "The Promised Land" **CD 12-12** with the recording while tapping the steady beat and following the notation on p. 258.

ASK Are there any syncopated measures in "The Promised Land"? (no)

9a Using standard terminology in explaining music notation, discuss one of the major differences between African American (syncopation) and Sacred Harp (lack of syncopation) spirituals.

Listening

9a Have students look at the Sacred Harp version of "Amazing Grace" on p. 259 in their books. Share the information in Spotlight On, p. 259. Then play *Amazing Grace* **CD 12-14** as students follow the shape notes in the arrangement shown on p. 259.

continued on page 258

ACROSS THE CURRICULUM

▶ **Language Arts** When songs are learned orally (aurally), they change quite a bit. Each person makes a song his or her own, and variations occur—both in the music and in the lyrics. Songs learned from written music tend to stay the same longer, because the written notation keeps reminding people to sing it the same way. As this unit progresses, ask students to find other versions of the songs they are learning.

Students can create journals to keep records of songs they may know in different versions. They can also record stories or songs that have been passed down in their families.

SKILLS REINFORCEMENT

▶ **Recorder** Have students play this countermelody during the refrain of "Down by the Riverside."

2a

▶ **Keyboard** For a keyboard activity for "Down by the Riverside," see Resource Book p. H-20.

▶ **Mallets** An Orff arrangement of "Down by the Riverside" can be found on p. F-28 of the Resource Book.

Lesson 1 Continued

Invite students to look at the mountain dulcimer on p. 259 and read the information in the photo caption. Have students read an additional description of the instrument on p. 515 in the Sound Bank and listen to a sound sample **CD 21-28**.

Creating

Encourage each student to write new verses to "Down by the Riverside" by simply making up one phrase. Share some samples of verses people have created over the years: *Gonna shake hands around the world; Gonna light up this world of mine.* See also Meeting Individual Needs on p. 256.

Moving

After students can sing "Down by the Riverside" with ease, have them stand and move to this foot pattern:

Left-together-right-together

Add a backbeat clap on the "together" (beat 2) of each measure. Encourage students to clap by hitting their fingers into the palm of the other hand. This creates a better sound than the "splat" of palm against palm.

Reading

Have students look at the notation for "The Promised Land."

ASK How many times does the dotted-quarter/ eighth-note pattern occur? (4)

Ask students to listen to the recording again **CD 12-12** and count the dotted-quarter/eighth-note pattern using rhythm syllables each time it occurs.

The Sacred Harp

European Americans also created their own style of religious song that was different from the African American spiritual. Many of these spirituals, hymns, and anthems were collected in a book called *The Sacred Harp*.

Sing "The Promised Land," a well-known hymn from the early nineteenth century. The melody below is taken directly from *The Sacred Harp* collection.

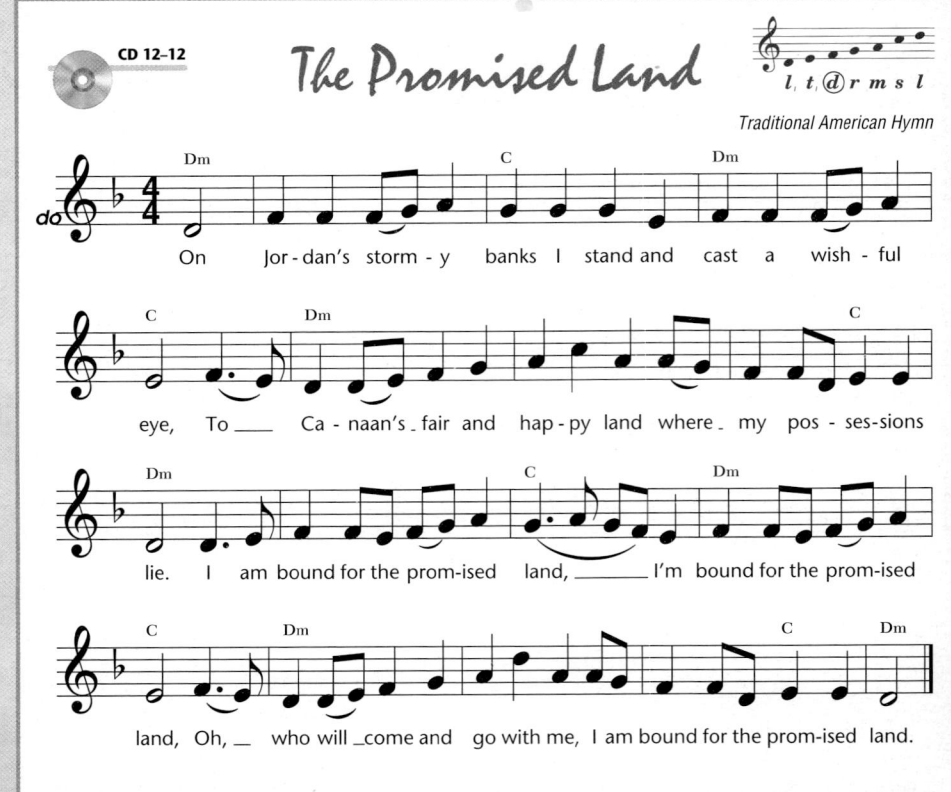

258

Footnotes

ACROSS THE CURRICULUM

▶ **Language Arts** Share with students the story of John Newton, the author of the text of "Amazing Grace," in *Amazing Grace: The Story of the Hymn* by Linda Granfield (Tundra Books, 1997).

Newton was a former British slave trader who saw the error of his ways and eventually became a minister and strong advocate against slavery. Newton wrote "Amazing Grace" during a terrible storm at sea. This frightening experience was the beginning of his change of heart.

SKILLS REINFORCEMENT

▶ **Keyboard** Use the following suggestions to help all students perform a keyboard accompaniment to "The Promised Land."

Reinforcement Some fifth-grade students may have minimal experience playing the keyboard. Have these students play only the first two notes of the C and Dm chords.

On Target Most students will be able to proficiently perform three-note piano chords. Ask these students to play the C and Dm chords to accompany the song.

Challenge Interested students may be invited to play the melody of "The Promised Land" with the right hand and the C and Dm chords with the left hand while the rest of the class sings the song.

A Shape-Note Hymn

Listen to this performance of *Amazing Grace*, which is based on the shape-note arrangement shown below.

CD 12–14

Amazing Grace

Early American Hymn
as performed by the Sacred Harp Singers

This version of *Amazing Grace* is similar to the way you might hear the song sung today.

◀ The mountain dulcimer, from the Appalachian region of the United States, is often used to accompany folk and hymn singing. The strings are usually strummed with picks, quills, or the thumb.

The Sacred Harp hymns were notated using shape notes. Each shape stood for a tone syllable—*fa, so, la,* or *mi*. This is how "Amazing Grace" looks in the Sacred Harp book. The melody is in the tenor part, the third line down. ▼

3 CLOSE

Performing

1c Have students perform "Down by the Riverside" and "The Promised Land"—two types of American spirituals—as part of a group of songs representing pre-Civil War America.

Element: RHYTHM   **ASSESSMENT**

6c **Music Journal Writing/Performance** Have students compare and contrast the styles of the two songs in this lesson by answering the following questions.

ASK Which song has little or no syncopation?
("The Promised Land")

Which song is performed at a faster tempo?
("Down by the Riverside")

In which song is it easier to create new verses?
("Down by the Riverside")

Which song uses only two chords?
("The Promised Land")

Students can write, then discuss, their answers.

Then invite students to perform the new verses they created for "Down by the Riverside."

ASK Which phrases in your lyrics contain syncopation?

SPOTLIGHT ON

▶ **Sacred Harp Spirituals** The music of *The Sacred Harp*, or white spiritual, tradition is named after *The Sacred Harp*, the principal book of hymns that originated in the early nineteenth century. The shape notes used to teach people how to sing these songs also gave these hymns the name "fasola" songs. Early American pioneers called the shaped notes "buckwheat" notes. The melody (tenor part) and the soprano part are often doubled by both men and women, giving the songs a thicker texture.

TECHNOLOGY/MEDIA LINK

Web Site For more information on African American gospel music and spirituals, visit *www.sfsuccessnet.com*.

LESSON AT A GLANCE

Element Focus **TEXTURE/HARMONY** Two-chord harmony

Skill Objective **PLAYING** Accompany a song with two-chord harmony

Connection Activity **SOCIAL STUDIES** Learn about the mountain dulcimer

MATERIALS

- "Shady Grove" **CD 12-15**

  Recording Routine: Intro (4 m.); refrain; v. 1; refrain; interlude (4 m.); refrain; v. 2; refrain; interlude (4 m.); refrain; v. 3; refrain; coda

- *Cedar Swamp* **CD 12-17**
- Autoharp, guitar
- **Resource Book** p. I-20

VOCABULARY

harmony   pentatonic

◆ ◆ ◆ ◆ National Standards ◆ ◆ ◆ ◆

1a Sing accurately with good breath control
2b Perform easy instrumental pieces expressively
6a Listen and analyze uses of timbre in music from diverse cultures
8b Identify ways music relates to social studies

MORE MUSIC CHOICES...

For more practice singing early American tunes:
"California," p. 52

1 INTRODUCE

8b **SAY** The westward expansion of the United States was carried out by rugged pioneer families who carved out their new lives in the wilderness. Groups of settlers valued those individuals who could sing and play for dances– a great diversion at the end of the day. "Shady Grove" was one of the tunes used for dances during this period.

Explain to students that many of these pioneer families settled in the Appalachian mountain region of the

Dance to the Music

As Americans moved westward from the original thirteen colonies, they took their music with them. One of their favorite pastimes was dancing to the music of fiddles, harmonicas, and banjos. Mountain dulcimers were also used to accompany songs.

Sing "Shady Grove," an Appalachian song that was sung during the westward movement.

CD 12-15

Shady Grove

d r m s l d'

Folk Song from the United States

REFRAIN
Em — D — Em — (D) — Em
do

Shad - y Grove,   my   lit - tle love,   Shad - y Grove I   know,

Em — D — Em — (D) — Em
Fine

Shad - y Grove,   my   lit - tle love,   Bound for the Shad - y   Grove.

VERSE
Em — D — Em — (D) — Em

1. Cheeks as   red   as a   bloom-in' rose,   Eyes of the deep-est   brown,   You
2. Went to   see   my __ Shad - y Grove,   Stand-in' __ in   the   door,   ⁊
3. Wish I   had   a ___ big fine horse,   Corn to __ feed him   on,   ⁊

Em — D — Em — (D) — Em
D. C. al Fine

   are   the dar - lin'   of   my __heart,   Stay till   the sun goes   down.
   Shoes and stock-ings   in   her __hand,   Little bare __ feet on the floor.
   Pretty little girl   to   stay   at __home,   Feed him __ when I'm   gone.

(260)

Footnotes

ACROSS THE CURRICULUM

► Language Arts For interesting folk legends and stories of pioneer America, ask students to read aloud selections within *From Sea to Shining Sea: A Treasury of American Folklore and Folk Songs* compiled by Amy L. Cohn (Scholastic, 1993).

BUILDING SKILLS THROUGH MUSIC

► Art Building on the content of the lesson and the text of "Shady Grove," invite students to draw a scene that depicts an aspect of the westward expansion.

SPOTLIGHT ON

► Mountain Dulcimer The mountain dulcimer, also known as the Appalachian or lap dulcimer, evolved in the southern Appalachian mountains from a zither found in German immigrant settlements in Pennsylvania. Although it dates back to the early 1800s, the present-day instrument developed in the early 1900s. By this time, the mountain dulcimer was recognized as an integral part of Appalachian culture even though not everyone in the region was familiar with the instrument. Through the music of performers such as Jean Ritchie, the mountain dulcimer gained a national and international following in the 1940s and 1950s that continues today.

Accompany the Song

Play the Em and D chords on Autoharp or guitar to accompany the song.

Listen to *Cedar Swamp*, performed on the dulcimer.

Jill Trinka playing the dulcimer. ▼

CD 12–17
Cedar Swamp

Folk Song from the United States as performed by Jill Trinka, dulcimer

Cedar Swamp is included in the Jean Ritchie collection *Folk Songs of the Southern Appalachians.*

Unit 7 **261**

---

southern United States. Lead students in a discussion about the mountain dulcimer, an instrument that developed in this region. For information, see Spotlight On, p. 260.

2 DEVELOP

Singing

1a Have students sing the refrain of "Shady Grove" with **CD 12-15**.

SAY Look at the melody of the refrain and then look at the melody of the verse.

ASK Are they the same or different? (They are almost the same, but the verse has different rhythms to accommodate the lyrics.)

Sing up and down the major pentatonic scale based on D (D E F♯ A B). Show students that these are the notes used in "Shady Grove."

Playing

2b Demonstrate how to play the Em and D chords on the Autoharp and guitar.

Have students practice strumming down strokes on quarter or half notes on the chord sequence to the song. The D chord in parenthesis is optional.

Listening

6a Have students listen to *Cedar Swamp* **CD 12-17** performed by Jill Trinka.

ASK What instrument is heard on this recording? (the mountain dulcimer)

3 CLOSE

Element: TEXTURE/HARMONY — ASSESSMENT

Performance/Peer Critique Divide the class into two groups. Have one group sing "Shady Grove" while the other group accompanies on Autoharp or guitar. After the performance, allow students to critique their performance and offer suggestions for improvement. Have groups switch parts and repeat.

SKILLS REINFORCEMENT

▶ **Recorder** Invite students to play the following countermelody to accompany "Shady Grove."

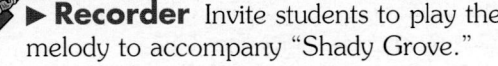

This activity can also serve as preparation for playing the fuller-sounding countermelody on Resource Book p. I-20. Advanced players may enjoy the challenge of playing the melody of "Shady Grove" as other students play one of the countermelodies.

TECHNOLOGY/MEDIA LINK

Web Site To learn more about Appalachian music and instruments, visit *www.sfsuccessnet.com.*

Element Focus **MELODY** Minor and major tonalities

Skill Objective **SINGING** Sing in minor and major tonalities

Connection Activity **SOCIAL STUDIES** Discover that Americans traveled westward to settle the Great Lake states using the Erie Canal

MATERIALS

• "Erie Canal"   CD 12-18

  Recording Routine: Intro (4 m.); v. 1; refrain; interlude (4 m.); v. 2; refrain; coda

• **Resource Book** p. C-6

• **Dance Directions** for "Erie Canal" p. 560

VOCABULARY

major scale   minor scale

syncopation   tonality

◆ ◆ ◆ ◆ **National Standards** ◆ ◆ ◆ ◆

1a Sing accurately alone and in large ensembles

6c Understand and use basic principles of tonality and rhythm in music analysis

8b Identify ways music relates to social studies

MORE MUSIC CHOICES

For more practice with major and minor tonalities:

"*El carite*" ("The Kingfish"), p. 305

1 INTRODUCE

8b Share the information in Across the Curriculum, below, and explain that the Erie Canal connected the Hudson River with the Great Lakes. The canal gave American settlers a much easier way of moving westward before the railroads were built.

Have the class listen to the recording of "Erie Canal" **CD 12-18.**

Miles and Miles

In the move westward, Americans frequently traveled along rivers and canals. Great cities often grew where the rivers came together. The Erie Canal, built in 1825, linked the Great Lakes and the Atlantic Ocean.

Sing "Erie Canal." **Identify** how the melody changes in the refrain.

CD 12-18

Erie Canal

Folk Song from the United States

s, l, t, d r m f fis

VERSE

Solo   Dm   Gm   A₇

1. I got a ___ mule, her name is ___ Sal,
2. Git up there, ___ Sal, we passed that ___ lock,

Chorus Dm

Fif - teen ___ miles on the E - rie Ca - nal! ___

Solo Dm   Gm   A₇

She's a good old ___ work - er and a good old ___ pal,
And ___ we'll make ___ Rome ___ 'fore ___ six o' - clock,

Chorus Dm

Fif - teen ___ miles on the E - rie Ca - nal! ___

Solo F   C

We've hauled some barg - es in our ___ day,
Just one more trip and back we'll ___ go

262

Footnotes

▶ **English Language Learners** A semantic map can help students who are less fluent in English understand the meaning of the lyrics of "Erie Canal." Start by writing the phrase *canal trip* on the board, with a circle around it. As students learn the song, add sections for each verse. For example, draw a line from the central circle to a new circle and write *barges;* then from that second circle, add the words *lumber, coal,* and *hay.* For a semantic map master, see Resource Book p. C-6.

▶ **Math** Have students compute the miles traveled each day by the singer on the Erie Canal. Have them divide 363 (the length of the Erie canal) by 5 (the number of days it usually took to travel the canal).

8b ▶ **Social Studies** Show students a map of New York state. Have them connect Buffalo, Rochester, Syracuse, Utica, Schenectady, and Albany. This is roughly the route of the 363 miles of the Erie Canal. Opened in 1825, it led to the development of the Great Lakes states as well as the economic dominance of New York City. After 1850, trade on the Erie Canal declined because railroads were becoming more prominent. Today it and other smaller canals together form the New York State Barge Canal System. The Erie Canal is still used for barge and pleasure-boat traffic, but its five-day trip is no longer economically feasible.

The Erie Canal opened up the settlement of the Great Lakes states until 1850, when railroads became more widely used.

Dm   **A₇**

Filled with lum - ber, coal, and _____ hay,
Through the rain and sleet and _____ snow,

Dm   **Gm**   **A₇**

And we know _____ ev - 'ry inch of the way
'Cause we know _____ ev - 'ry inch of the way

Dm   **C₇**

From Al - ba - ny _____ to _____ Buf - fa - lo. _____

REFRAIN
Chorus
F   **C₇**

Low bridge, ev - 'ry - bod - y down,

F   **C₇**   **F**

Low bridge, 'cause we're com - ing to a town;

F   **C₇**   **F**   **C₇**

And you'll al - ways know your neigh-bor, You'll al - ways know your pal,

F   **B♭**   **F**   **C₇**   **F**

If you ev - er nav - i - gat - ed on the E - rie Ca - nal. _____

2 DEVELOP

Analyzing

6c   Have students

- Identify the first three pitches of the verse as A, D, and F. Sing the triad with D as the root.
- Cover the fermata and middle C at the end of the verse and identify the D as the root of the same triad.

ASK Does this triad have a major or a minor sound? (minor)

Identify the first and last notes of the refrain by letter name (A and C at first, then F at the end). Sing the triad, with F as the root.

ASK Does this triad have a major or a minor sound? (major)

SAY The melody of the verse is minor and the melody of the refrain is major, but they share the same key signature.

Singing

1a   Have the class sing "Erie Canal" **CD 12-18**, alternating the solo and chorus parts.

3 CLOSE

Element: MELODY   ASSESSMENT

Performance/Interview Have students sing "Erie Canal" again. Then ask them to summarize the difference in tonality between the verse and the refrain.

1a
6c

SKILLS REINFORCEMENT

6c   ▶ **Reading** Have students clap and say the rhythm of the verse. Then have them look for tied notes and discover the rhythm of the tied notes. (Note: A good way to do this is to ignore the ties at first, then add them back in.)

Have students clap and say the rhythm. Lead them to discover the difference between tied notes (same pitch) and slurred notes (different pitches).

TECHNOLOGY/MEDIA LINK

Web Site To learn more about songs of the western movement, visit *www.sfsuccessnet.com.*

LESSON AT A GLANCE

Element Focus **FORM** Call-and-response form

Skill Objective **SINGING** Sing using call-and-response form

Connection Activity **SOCIAL STUDIES** Become acquainted with the tradition of singing shanties on sailing ships

MATERIALS

• "Shenandoah"   CD 12-21

   Recording Routine: Intro (4 m.); v. 1; interlude (2 m.); v. 2; interlude (2 m.); v. 3; interlude (2 m.); v. 4; coda

• *Shenandoah*   CD 12-23

• **Resource Book** pp. C-2, F-30, I-21

VOCABULARY

call and response   shanty

◆ ◆ ◆ ◆ National Standards ◆ ◆ ◆ ◆

1c Sing music from different genres
3c Improvise melodies with consistent tonality
6a Listen and describe events in music using appropriate terms
6b Listen and analyze uses of form in music from diverse cultures
8b Identify ways music relates to social studies and language arts

MORE MUSIC CHOICES

For more experience with call-and-response form:
"Go Down Moses," p. 190
"Day-O!," p. 18

1 INTRODUCE

8b **SAY** Between 1800 and 1900, America became a major world power partly because of its sailing ships. The ships were used for trading, whaling, and transportation to places like San Francisco for the gold rush. When a clipper ship was ready to leave port, the crew would sing a shanty like "Shenandoah" while raising the anchor. (See Spotlight On below, for more information on shanties.)

Songs of the Sea

The tradition of sea shanties began with sailors on the ocean. On board the tall ships, a shantyman was paid to lead the crew in singing to lighten the work. Sea shanties were sung to raise the anchor, hoist the sails, or pump out the ship. They were also sung in the crew's quarters for relaxation. As early Americans moved inland, many of the sea shanties became river songs.

Sing "Shenandoah," a well-known American sea shanty.

Identify the *call* (shantyman) and *response* (crew) form.

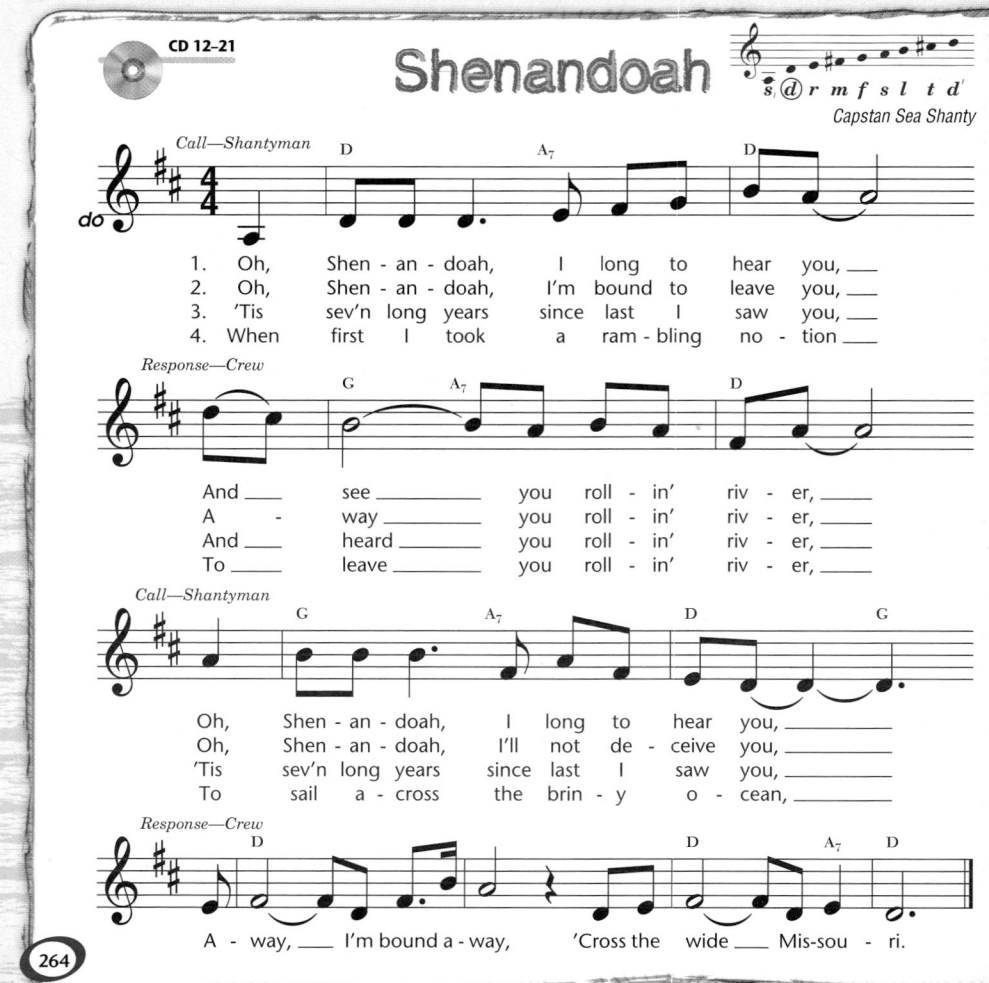

CD 12-21

Shenandoah

Capstan Sea Shanty

Call—Shantyman

1. Oh, Shen-an-doah, I long to hear you, ___
2. Oh, Shen-an-doah, I'm bound to leave you, ___
3. 'Tis sev'n long years since last I saw you, ___
4. When first I took a ram-bling no-tion ___

Response—Crew

And ___ see _____ you roll-in' riv-er, _____
A - way _____ you roll-in' riv-er, _____
And ___ heard _____ you roll-in' riv-er, _____
To ___ leave _____ you roll-in' riv-er, _____

Call—Shantyman

Oh, Shen-an-doah, I long to hear you, _____
Oh, Shen-an-doah, I'll not de-ceive you, _____
'Tis sev'n long years since last I saw you, _____
To sail a-cross the brin-y o-cean, _____

Response—Crew

A - way, ___ I'm bound a - way, 'Cross the wide ___ Mis-sou - ri.

264

Footnotes

SKILLS REINFORCEMENT

▶ **Vocal Development** Use call-and-response singing to monitor students' ability to match pitches. They can begin by imitating the "call," then create suitable responses.

▶ **Recorder** For a recorder exercise to accompany "Shenandoah," see Resource Book p. I-21.

▶ **Mallets** An Orff arrangement of Shenandoah" can be found on p. F-30 of the Resource Book.

BUILDING SKILLS THROUGH MUSIC

▶ **Language** Distribute copies of the Comparison Chart from Resource Book p. C-2. Have students listen to the two versions of "Shenandoah" **CD 12-21, CD 12-23** and describe the musical characteristics of each. Ask students to complete the chart by listing similarities and differences, including melody, rhythm, tempo, timbres, and texture.

SPOTLIGHT ON

8b ▶ **Shanties** Here are some of the different types of shanties that might have been heard in the nineteenth century.

• *Capstan* shanties for bringing up the anchor. Men marched around the spool-like capstan, pushing on bars coming out like spokes on a wheel.

• *Halyard* shanties for raising sails. Men pulled hard on the ropes, all at the same time.

• *Short haul* (drag) shanties for pumping out the ship or raising small sails.

The other main category, the *forecastle* (foke-s'l) shanty, was for leisure time in the crew's quarters, called the forecastle, near the front of the ship.

Ship Ahoy!

Listen to Paul Robeson, a great African American bass, sing *Shenandoah*.

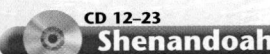

CD 12-23
Shenandoah

Capstan Sea Shanty
as performed by Paul Robeson

Capstan sea shanties were sung during the long tedious job of pulling the anchor in. Many of these shanties have long melodies and many verses.

Arts Connection

▲ *The Clipper Ship* by Alistair Ross. After the War of 1812, America became a major seafaring nation with large clipper ships trading in ports all over the world. All along the East Coast men shipped out of cities to go whaling, or to trade American textiles for goods in other seaports.

2 DEVELOP

Singing

1c Have students

- Sing the crew lines (lines 2 and 4) of "Shenandoah" **CD 12-21** in a full-bodied sound. (Point out that the crew sang together to make the work easier by moving together around the capstan, a large spool on the deck, to bring up the anchor rope or chain.)

- Sing the shantyman's calls, followed by the crew responses.

6b • Sing in groups, with some taking the part of the shantyman and everyone singing the crew parts.

Ask for volunteers to sing the calls as solos, with the class singing the responses.

Listening

6a Play the recording of Paul Robeson singing *Shenandoah* **CD 12-23.**

ASK Does this version sound like a work song? Why or why not? (Answers will vary.)

Are the verses and the melody the same or different as those on p. 264? (different)

Why do you think that is? (Because of oral tradition, many different versions exist.)

3 CLOSE

Element: FORM **ASSESSMENT**

Performance/Observation Ask students to find other songs in call-and-response form. (See More Music Choices on p. 264.) Divide the class into two groups ("call" and "response"). Have the groups sing their parts. Observe if the groups sing at the appropriate time.

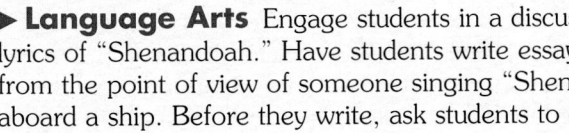
ACROSS THE CURRICULUM

8b ▶ **Language Arts** Engage students in a discussion of the lyrics of "Shenandoah." Have students write essays or poems from the point of view of someone singing "Shenandoah" aboard a ship. Before they write, ask students to consider these questions.

- Where is the Shenandoah River?
- Where is the person singing the song?
- How long has this person been at sea?
- Where is the person in the song going?

TECHNOLOGY/MEDIA LINK

3c **Sequencing Software** Have students

- In pairs, use the black keys on a MIDI keyboard to improvise, record, and play back a call-and-response melody.

- Start the sequencing program and select a track for recording. Set the record mode to wait for a note.

- Play for eight beats (two measures). (One student will play in a high octave, one should play in a low octave.)

- Save the sequences, and play them for the class.

- Evaluate which calls and responses fit well.

LESSON AT A GLANCE

Element Focus **TIMBRE** Instruments imitating train sounds

Skill Objective **LISTENING** Listen to a selection in which instruments imitate train sounds

Connection Activity **SOCIAL STUDIES** Discuss the history of trains in the United States

MATERIALS

- "Orange Blossom Special" **CD 12-24**
  Recording Routine: Intro (4 m.); v. 1; interlude (2 m.); v. 2; interlude (2 m.); v. 3; coda
- *Orange Blossom Special* **CD 12-26**
- **Dance Directions** for "Orange Blossom Special" p. 561
- recorders, woodblock, claves, Autoharp

VOCABULARY

timbre   bluegrass   blues

◆ ◆ ◆ ◆ National Standards ◆ ◆ ◆ ◆

1a Sing accurately with good breath control
2d Perform simple accompaniments by ear
6a Listen and describe events in music using appropriate terms
6b Listen and analyze uses of timbre and form in music from diverse genres
8b Identify ways music relates to social studies and language arts
9a Describe characteristics of music styles from a variety of cultures

MORE MUSIC CHOICES

For more experience with songs connected to the railroad-tradition:

"Wabash Cannon Ball," p. 136
"Pat Works on the Railway," p. 182

A SPECIAL RIDE

The Orange Blossom Special was Florida's "Distinguished Winter Train." It traveled the east coast to Florida from 1925 until 1953.

Listen as the harmonica and fiddle imitate the sound of a train. Then **sing** "Orange Blossom Special."

Orange Blossom Special, 1938 ▶

CD 12–24
MIDI 20

Orange Blossom Special

@ r m a m f s l t

Words and Music by Ervin T. Rouse

do

1. Look - a yon - der com - in', _____
2. I'm go - in' down _____ to Flori - da _____
3. Talk a - bout _____ a - trav - 'lin', _____

com - in' down that rail - road ___ track!
and get some sand in my _____ shoes.
she's the fast - est train on the _____ line.

Hey, look - a yon - der com - in', _____
Or may - be Cal - i - for - nia _____
Talk a - bout _____ a - trav - 'lin', _____

266

Footnotes

SKILLS REINFORCEMENT

▶ **Keyboard** Students will enjoy playing train sound effects on the lower end of the keyboard. Have them play a cluster of these notes—C, D, E♭, F, G, and A—whenever they wish to insert the sound of a train whistle as others sing "Orange Blossom Special." You might have several students each play two or three of the tones. Encourage students to experiment with other tone clusters and decide which clusters work best.

2d

BUILDING SKILLS THROUGH MUSIC

▶ **Language** Ask students to read the lyrics of "Orange Blossom Special" and explain the singer's interest in the train. Have students describe the location(s) where the singer would like to travel. Ask them to look at the map on p. 268 and identify the places mentioned in the song where the Orange Blossom Special did not travel.

ACROSS THE CURRICULUM

8b ▶ **Social Studies** Between the Civil War (1861–1865) and World War I (1914–1918), railroads became the most important form of transportation in the United States. Not until well into the twentieth century did the automobile and the airplane challenge the dominance of the railroad.

Today trains are an important form of transportation, but not a dominant one. People still ride on trains from the Northeast to Florida. Some trains have special cars that can carry the passengers' automobiles. When the train arrives at the destination, the cars are unloaded and the people can drive wherever they want to go.

If time permits, ask students to work in small groups to research a railroad line in their state. Have them present reports to the class and include maps of these railway routes.

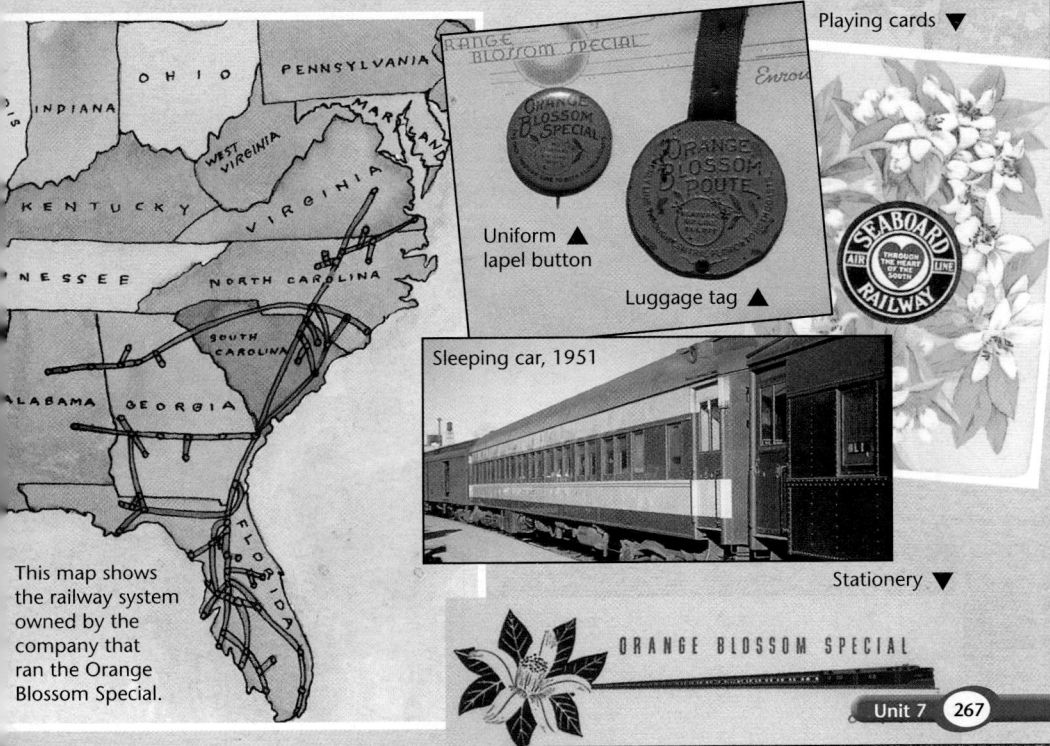

It's the | Or - ange | Blos - som | Spe - cial
I'll | ride that | Or - ange | Blos - som | Spe - cial
It's that | Or - ange | Blos - som | Spe - cial

bring - in' my | ba - by ___ back.
and | lose ___ these | New ___ York ___ blues.
roll - in' down the | Sea - board ___ line.

com - in' down | that | rail - road | track!
and | get some sand | in - my | shoes.
she's the | fast - est train | on the | line.

Souvenirs of the Orange Blossom Special

Playing cards ▼

Uniform lapel button ▲

Luggage tag ▲

Sleeping car, 1951

Stationery ▼

ORANGE BLOSSOM SPECIAL

This map shows the railway system owned by the company that ran the Orange Blossom Special.

1 INTRODUCE

8b **SAY** Railroads began to be built in America in the 1830s. Ever since, Americans have had a fascination with trains and have written many songs about them.

Share with students the information in Across the Curriculum on p. 266 about the history of trains in the United States.

2 DEVELOP

Listening

6a Have students listen to the recording of "Orange Blossom Special" **CD 12-24**, one of the most famous songs written about a train. Discuss examples of the harmonica and fiddle imitating the sound of a train. Share with the class the information about the Orange Blossom Special in Spotlight On, below.

Singing

Have students look at the lyrics of "Orange Blossom Special."

ASK **What pattern do you see in the lyrics of this song?** (aab)

9a Point out that this pattern is used in African American blues form.

Have students sing the melody from line 2 at the words *railroad track*. Point out that the E♭ is a flatted third of the scale—another feature borrowed from African American blues.

Share with students that the flatted note is called a "blue note" by musicians.

ASK **Where else do you find a blue note in this song?** (E♭ in the last line)

1a Lead the class in singing the entire melody with the recording.

continued on page 268

Unit 7 **267**

SPOTLIGHT ON

8b ▶ **The Orange Blossom Special** This train operated between the cities of New York, Philadelphia, Baltimore, and Washington and Florida from 1925 to 1953. Florida-bound passengers could choose either Miami or St. Petersburg as their destination. The Orange Blossom Special received great praise from its passengers for its food and attentive service. It was also one of the first trains to have air conditioning installed, in 1934.

The Blossom was a part of the Seaboard Air Line Railway, which had other routes in the southern states, as the map shows. Although the Orange Blossom Special was inaugurated over 75 years ago and has not run for half a century, there are people who worked on or around this train and who remember how special it was.

MEETING INDIVIDUAL NEEDS

▶ **Inclusion** Students who have motor impairments can still participate in the "Orange Blossom Special" movement described on p. 269. Depending on their special need, they might be able to play an instrument to accompany the dance. If this is not possible, they might do a vocal percussion activity or whistle to imitate the sound of the train. Perhaps they might join hands with another student to become part of the "tunnel" that others go through or become part of the train if assisted by another student. The visually impaired student can also participate in the movement activity by being taught the dance by an assistant and by being guided by the assistant during the activity.

Lesson 5 Continued

Listening

6b Invite students to listen to the recording of *Orange Blossom Special* **CD 12-26** performed by the Stanley Brothers and follow the listening map on p. 268. Have students listen and identify the timbre of specific instruments and articulations such as *pizzicato*, scratch fiddle, and picking banjo, as depicted in the map. On subsequent listenings, encourage students to follow the I, I, IV, V$_7$ chord progressions depicted in panels 2 and 4, and the blues form of the verse.

Creating

2d Challenge students to discover techniques for using classroom instruments to imitate train sounds to accompany "Orange Blossom Special." For instance, they may

- Play woodblocks or claves, keeping the tempo to imitate the engine, listening for guitar and banjo.
- Rub a string of an Autoharp to imitate the rumble of a train.
- Imitate a train's whistle on recorders.

Have students keep a record of the technique they have chosen.

See Skills Reinforcement below for a related activity.

All Aboard!

Listen to this bluegrass performance of *Orange Blossom Special* as you follow the listening map below.

CD 12–26
Orange Blossom Special

**by Ervin T. Rouse
as performed by the Stanley Brothers**

Carter and Ralph Stanley are well-known bluegrass musicians from the mountains of Virginia.

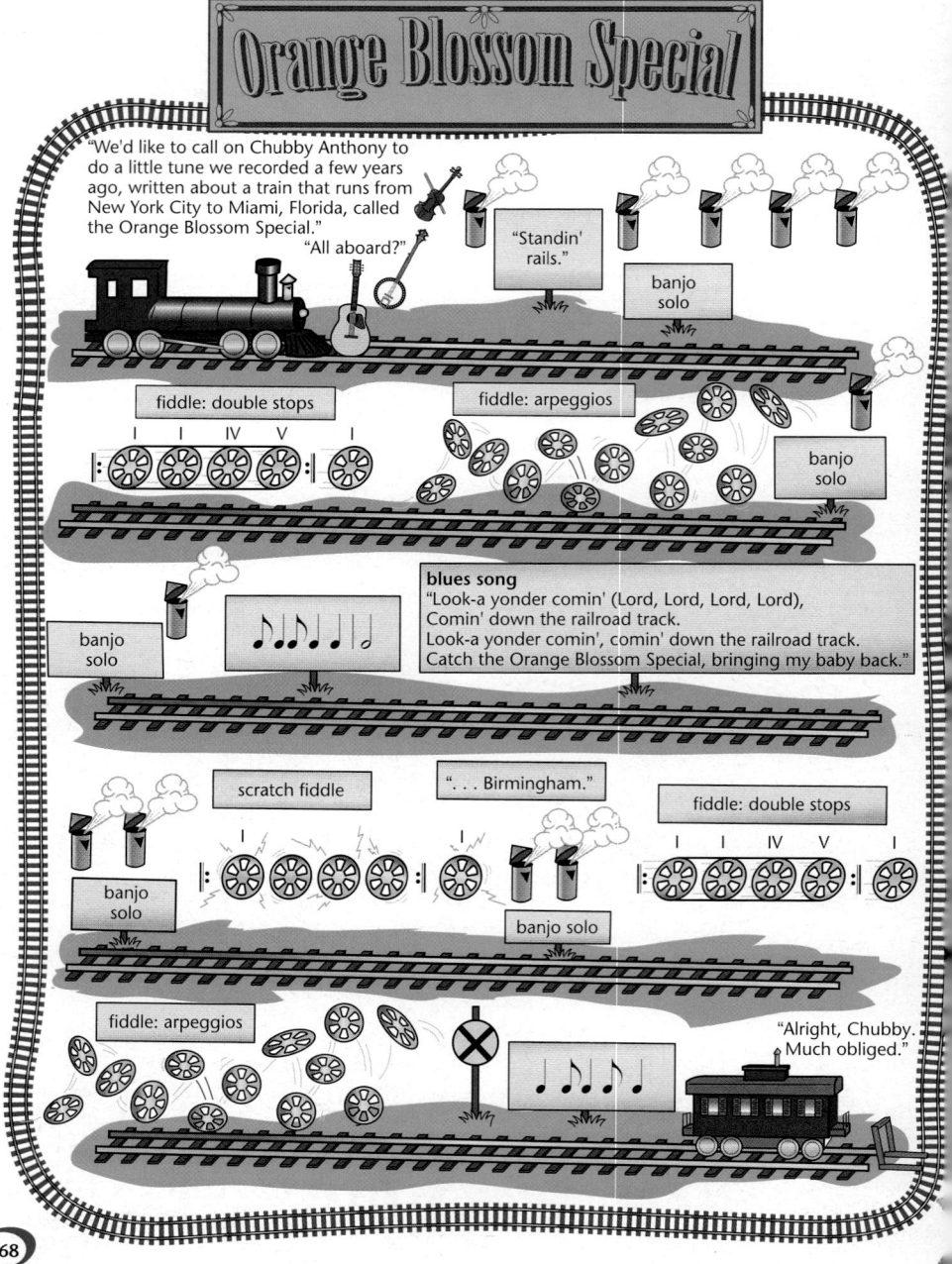

Orange Blossom Special

"We'd like to call on Chubby Anthony to do a little tune we recorded a few years ago, written about a train that runs from New York City to Miami, Florida, called the Orange Blossom Special."

"All aboard?"

"Standin' rails."

banjo solo

fiddle: double stops — I I IV V I

fiddle: arpeggios

banjo solo

banjo solo

blues song
"Look-a yonder comin' (Lord, Lord, Lord, Lord),
Comin' down the railroad track.
Look-a yonder comin', comin' down the railroad track.
Catch the Orange Blossom Special, bringing my baby back."

scratch fiddle

". . . Birmingham."

fiddle: double stops — I I IV V

banjo solo

banjo solo

fiddle: arpeggios

"Alright, Chubby. Much obliged."

(268)

Footnotes

SKILLS REINFORCEMENT

▶ **Creating** Ask students to make a list of train sounds (steam escaping, brakes screeching, wheels clattering) and the instruments they think would imitate that sound.

Have students find other songs in this book that are about trains. ("Choo Choo Ch' Boogie," p. 44; "Drill, Ye Tarriers," p. 54; "Wabash Cannon Ball," p. 136; "Pat Works on the Railway," p. 182). Invite students to choose one or more of these songs and create a performance that incorporates the train "sound effects."

ACROSS THE CURRICULUM

8b ▶ **Language Arts** Invite students to read aloud and dramatize unusual poetry about trains and other forms of transportation from *Roll Along: Poems on Wheels,* collected by Myra Cohn Livingston (Margaret McElderry, 1993). There are 50 highly evocative and interesting poems in this anthology about transportation. Many unique sounds, words, and rhythms, as well as created words are used in these unusual and engaging poems designed to capture the sights and sounds of trains and other forms of transportation.

Invite students to form groups and write new poems about transportation.

The *Orange Blossom Special* Dance

To **perform** this dance about a special train, **move** in a circle and then go through a "tunnel."

Moving

See Movement below and Meeting Individual Needs on p. 267 to help students perform a dance routine with "Orange Blossom Special."

3 CLOSE

 **Skill: LISTENING** ASSESSMENT

Observation/Music Journal Writing Have students

- Listen to *Orange Blossom Special* **CD 12-26.**
- Focus on the violin (fiddle) timbre, while following on the listening map.
- Focus on the banjo timbre, then on that of the guitar, tapping the steady beat throughout the selection.

The movement of students' fingers across the page should correspond to the events like whistle imitations from the fiddle, sections showing changes in mood, chord progression, and the printed lyrics.

Ask students to write brief descriptions of the timbres used in *Orange Blossom Special.*

 **MOVEMENT**

▶ **Patterned Dance** "Orange Blossom Special" has become a well-known Appalachian dance tune. The musicians may use their instruments to make train sounds. They sometimes start playing slowly, like a train pulling out of the station, and then increase the tempo as the train gathers speed. Some play very fast to show their virtuosity.

A dance to go with this music can be found on p. 561. It is a grand march based on traditional figures, including arches and tunnels. The arches and tunnels evoke the motion of a train going through a railroad tunnel.

 TECHNOLOGY/MEDIA LINK

MIDI/Sequencing Software Use the MIDI song file for "Orange Blossom Special" to have students explore instrument sounds and select timbres for each track. Ask students to make the song resemble a bluegrass band as much as possible. Discuss the pros and cons of using MIDI voices.

Transparency For students who have difficulty tracking the various elements of the *Orange Blossom Special* listening map, use the transparency for the map and an overhead projector. Encourage students to follow the map individually, but occasionally give them helpful hints on the overhead.

LESSON AT A GLANCE

Element Focus	**TEXTURE/HARMONY** Parallel thirds
Skill Objective	**SINGING** Sing both melody and harmony parts in parallel thirds
Connection Activity	**CULTURE** Discuss the background of a Stephen Foster song

MATERIALS

- "Camptown Races" **CD 12-29**

  Recording Routine: Intro (8 m.); v. 1; refrain; interlude (4 m.); v. 2; refrain; coda

- **Resource Book** pp. F-31, H-21

VOCABULARY

solo

◆ ◆ ◆ ◆ National Standards ◆ ◆ ◆ ◆

1d Sing music written in two parts
2a Play instruments accurately alone and in small ensembles
5d Use standard notation to record musical ideas
6b Listen and analyze uses of harmony and form in music from diverse genres
8b Identify ways music relates to social studies

MORE MUSIC CHOICES

For more experience with harmony in thirds:
"Day-O!" p. 18
"Laredo," p. 10

1 INTRODUCE

8b **SAY** Stephen Foster was the best-known American composer of the nineteeth century. "Camptown Races" is a lively song that was very popular at mid-century. Share with students the background information on the song in Cultural Connection, p. 271.

19ᵗʰ CENTURY POP

"Camptown Races" was written by Stephen Foster in 1850. It "topped the charts" in its day.

Listen to "Camptown Races" and **sing** along on the response part.

 **CD 12–29**

Camptown Races
t, ⓓ r m f s l d'

Words and Music by Stephen Foster

VERSE *Solo* ... *Chorus*

1. The camp-town la - dies sing this song, Doo - dah! doo - dah!
2. The long tail filly and the big black horse, Doo - dah! doo - dah!

The camp-town race - track five miles long, Oh! doo-dah day!
They fly the track and they both cut a-cross, Oh! doo-dah day!

I come down there with my hat caved in, Doo - dah! doo - dah!
The blind horse stickin' in a big mud hole, Doo - dah! doo - dah!

270

Footnotes

SPOTLIGHT ON

▶ **The Composer** Stephen Foster (1826–1864) was born on July 4, 1826, near Pittsburgh, Pennsylvania. Between 1846 and 1850, he lived in Cincinnati, Ohio, and after signing a contract with a New York publisher, he moved to New York, where he died in 1864. Foster's only trip to the South was in 1852 when he took a steamboat trip down the Ohio and Mississippi rivers to New Orleans.

BUILDING SKILLS THROUGH MUSIC

▶ **Social Studies** Have students read the lyrics of "Camptown Races" and discuss things the singers saw at the races. Ask students to list events people attend today for entertainment. Divide the class into groups to write new lyrics that tell about a different event. Invite students to perform the new verses with **CD 12-30**.

SKILLS REINFORCEMENT

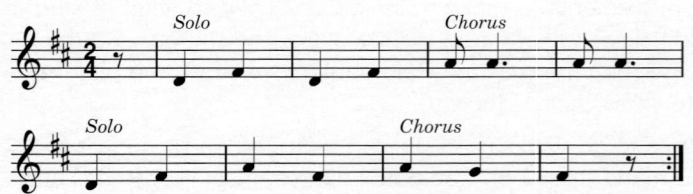

▶ **Recorder** Have students play this recorder countermelody with "Camptown Races."

2a

Solo ... *Chorus*

Solo ... *Chorus*

 ▶ **Mallets** An Orff arrangement of "Camptown Races" can be found on p. F-31 of the Resource Book.

▶ **Keyboard** For a keyboard accompaniment for "Camptown Races" using syncopation, see Resource Book p. H-21.

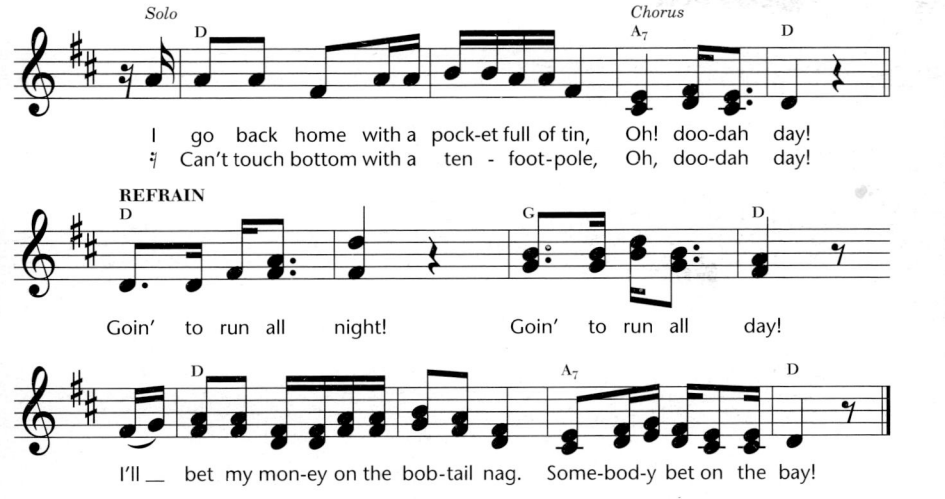

Solo | I go back home with a pock-et full of tin, Oh! doo-dah day!
2. Can't touch bottom with a ten - foot-pole, Oh, doo-dah day!

REFRAIN
Goin' to run all night! Goin' to run all day!

I'll __ bet my mon-ey on the bob-tail nag. Some-bod-y bet on the bay!

MUSIC MAKERS
Stephen Collins Foster

Stephen Collins Foster (1826–1864) added hit after hit to his long list of popular tunes. Steering away from the "conventional" songs of the day, Foster's new "minstrel" sound made him one of the most popular composers of the 19th century. In addition to his biggest hit, "Camptown Races," he wrote such favorites as "Oh! Susanna," "My Old Kentucky Home," "Jeanie with the Light Brown Hair," and "Old Folks at Home." Most of Stephen Foster's songs were about the South, even though he lived most of his life in Pennsylvania and New York.

Create an American song bag (a collection of your favorite songs) for your music class. Write the title, composer, origin, and a special fact about each song on a 3x5 card. Put the song in a bag decorated with symbols from America's history. Keep your song bag for review.

Unit 7 **271**

2 DEVELOP

Listening

Have students follow the notation in their books as they listen to the recording of "Camptown Races" **CD 12-29.**

Invite them to sing along, in unison, on the chorus parts.

Discuss the notation, encouraging students to use standard terminology in explaining music notation.

6b ASK Which section is in unison, and which section has a harmony part? (The solo is sung in unison; the chorus has a harmony part.)

How is the harmony part created? (It follows the contour of the melody, only the pitches are a third lower. This is called parallel thirds.)

3 CLOSE

Singing

Invite students to sing the melody with the recording. Then, have them

- Learn the harmony part for the chorus responses.
1d - Learn the harmony part on the refrain; then put the parts together and sing the entire song.

Skill: SINGING   **ASSESSMENT**

Performance/Observation Use the following rubric to assess students' ability to sing "Camptown Races" in parallel thirds.

5 = Can sing both the melody and harmony accurately and independently

4 = Can sing the melody and most of the harmony accurately and independently

3 = Can sing the melody accurately but cannot yet sing the harmony part throughout

2 = Can sing the melody with fair accuracy

1 = Has difficulty singing the melody accurately

CULTURAL CONNECTION

8b ▶ A Day at the Races "Camptown Races" was written in 1850. The song created such notoriety for the town in which the racetrack was located that the town was forced to change its name to Irvington, New Jersey. Its original name was Camptown.

Horse racing was a competitive event that started around 4500 B.C. when nomadic tribesmen domesticated the horse. Today, all thoroughbreds are descended from only three horses. Professional racing started in England between 1702–1714. In the United States, organized racing began only after the Civil War. While viewed as a social event by the wealthy, American racing was rife with crime until the American Jockey Club regulated it in 1894.

TECHNOLOGY/MEDIA LINK

5d Notation Software Have students create a harmony part based on thirds. Have them

- Create a notation file and notate the melody of a chosen song.

- Work in pairs to add an alto harmony part in thirds below or above the melody.

- Play back their compositions and find any notes that need to be changed.

- Change the identified notes, then print their compositions.

LESSON 7

LESSON AT A GLANCE

Element Focus   **TEXTURE/HARMONY** Descant

Skill Objective   **CREATING** Explore a parody to a well-known song

Connection Activity   **SOCIAL STUDIES** Learn how songs were used in the context of the Civil War

MATERIALS

- "Battle Cry of Freedom"   **CD 12-31**
  Recording Routine: Intro (4 m.); v. 1; refrain; interlude (2 m.); v. 2; refrain; coda
- "Battle Hymn of the Republic"   **CD 12-33**
  Recording Routine: Intro (5 m.); v. 1; v. 2; coda
- *American Salute*   **CD 12-35**

VOCABULARY

descant   countermelody

◆ ◆ ◆ National Standards ◆ ◆ ◆

1c Sing music from diverse genres
1d Sing music written in two parts
5a Read dotted notes in duple meter ($\frac{4}{4}$)
6a Listen and describe events in music using appropriate terms
6b Listen and analyze uses of rhythm timbre, and texture in music from diverse genres.
8b Identify ways music relates to social studies

MORE MUSIC CHOICES

For more practice with descants:
"The Ash Grove," p. 114
"Roll On, Columbia," p. 116
"This Land Is Your Land," p. 118

LESSON 7

Element: TEXTURE/HARMONY   **Skill: CREATING**   **Connection: SOCIAL STUDIES**

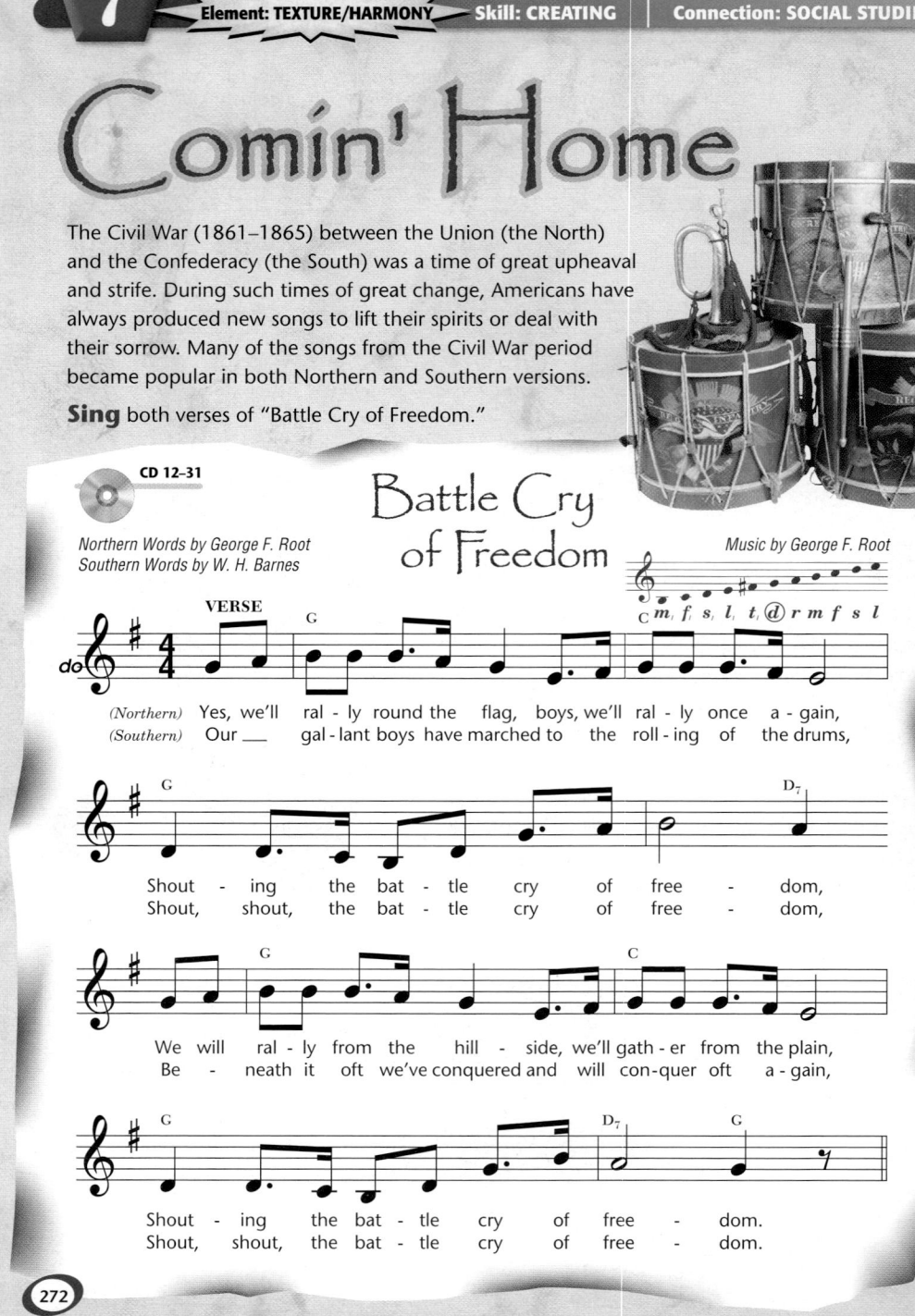

Comin' Home

The Civil War (1861–1865) between the Union (the North) and the Confederacy (the South) was a time of great upheaval and strife. During such times of great change, Americans have always produced new songs to lift their spirits or deal with their sorrow. Many of the songs from the Civil War period became popular in both Northern and Southern versions.

Sing both verses of "Battle Cry of Freedom."

 CD 12–31

Battle Cry of Freedom

Northern Words by George F. Root
Southern Words by W. H. Barnes

Music by George F. Root

(Northern) Yes, we'll ral - ly round the flag, boys, we'll ral - ly once a - gain,
(Southern) Our ___ gal - lant boys have marched to the roll - ing of the drums,

Shout - ing the bat - tle cry of free - dom,
Shout, shout, the bat - tle cry of free - dom,

We will ral - ly from the hill - side, we'll gath - er from the plain,
Be - neath it oft we've conquered and will con-quer oft a - gain,

Shout - ing the bat - tle cry of free - dom.
Shout, shout, the bat - tle cry of free - dom.

272

Footnotes

TEACHER TO TEACHER

▶ **Listening Preparation** Before asking students to identify the specific instruments heard on the recording of "Battle Cry of Freedom," consider using the Sound Bank (p. 514).

BUILDING SKILLS THROUGH MUSIC

▶ **Social Studies** After students have examined the Northern and Southern verses of the song, discuss the North and South. Distribute an outline of the United States. Have students outline the states involved in the Civil War. Ask them to outline the Northern states in one color and the Southern states in a different color.

CHARACTER EDUCATION

▶ **Courage** To help students understand the human aspect of war, list the character traits needed by soldiers during wartime (for example, commitment, integrity, courage, self-discipline, and so on). Ask students to give examples of specific situations in which each of these traits might be tested. For example, if a soldier is told to "go to the front line," he or she would face tremendous danger and would need great courage and self-discipline. Invite students to interview individuals who have participated in a war or military conflict about their feelings and the character traits they found important during this experience. Share the list of character traits created by students and question the former soldier about the accuracy of the list. Invite the veteran to add other traits that he or she found important during military service.

272

REFRAIN

The Un - ion for - ev - er, Hur - rah, boys, Hur - rah!
Our Dix - ie for - ev - er, she's never at a loss.

Down with the trai - tor, Up with the star;
Down with the eag - le and up with the cross;

While we ral - ly round the flag, boys, ral - ly once a - gain,
We'll __ ral - ly round the bonny flag, we'll ral - ly once a - gain,

Shout - ing the bat - tle cry of free - dom.
Shout, shout the bat - tle cry of free - dom.

◀ "Drummer Jackson"

Arts Connection

▲ Yankee Volunteers
Marching to Dixie, 1862

Unit 7 **273**

1 INTRODUCE

SAY The songs of the American Civil War are some of America's best known. They came out of a very difficult period in our history.

"Battle Cry of Freedom" was a popular song of the soldiers of the North. Southern soldiers also had their own words. Discuss some of the background of the Civil War.

Refer to Across the Curriculum below for resource suggestions.

2 DEVELOP

Singing

Have students examine both the Northern and Southern verses to "Battle Cry of Freedom."

ASK Do you think that these two verses would normally be sung together? (No; they are different sets of words that were sung to the same melody.)

What words refer to the Northern soldiers? (Union, star, eagle)

What words refer to the Southern soldiers? (gallant, Dixie, cross)

Have students listen to the recording of "Battle Cry of Freedom" **CD 12-31** as they follow the music in their books. When they can, encourage them to sing along.

ASK For what purpose do you think a song like this was sung? (to rally the troops into battle; to strengthen support back home)

Have students sing both verses of the song.

Listening

Have students listen to the recording of "Battle Cry of Freedom" **CD 12-31.** (See Teacher to Teacher on p. 272 for a suggested preparation activity.)

ASK What group of instruments is heard most? (brass)

continued on page 274

ACROSS THE CURRICULUM

▶ **Social Studies** Invite students to read the following accounts of life during the Civil War.

Behind the Blue and Grey: The Soldier's Life in the Civil War by Delia Ray (Demco, 1996). This interesting book is full of photographs, diaries, letters, and stories about soldiers' personal experiences during this era.

Black, Grey and Blue: African Americans in the Civil War by James Haskins (Simon & Schuster Children's, 1998) reveals a new perspective about African Americans during the Civil War.

Separate Battle: Women and the Civil War by Ina Chang (Demco, 1996) offers a unique view of this historical period based on the little-known contributions and involvement of many Northern and Southern women.

SKILLS REINFORCEMENT

▶ **Singing** Have students sing "John Brown's Body" to the tune of "Battle Hymn of the Republic." (See Across the Curriculum, p. 274, for historical information on John Brown.)

John Brown's body lies a-mold'ring in the grave, *(3 times)*
His soul goes marching on.

John Brown died that the slaves might be free, *(3 times)*
His soul goes marching on.

What specific instruments do you recognize?
(cornet, tuba, snare drum, and bells)

Reading

Have students look at "Battle Hymn of the Republic" **CD 12-33** on pp. 274–275 and locate the melody and descant parts of the refrain.

Review the meaning of descant. Then play the recording.

ASK How do the notes of the descant move—in the same direction as the melody or independently? (independently)

Point out that the descant is a countermelody that harmonizes with the melody of the refrain.

Singing

After the class has sung the melody of the entire song, help students learn the descant. Divide the class into two groups—one group to sing the melody, the other group to sing the descant. Switch groups so that everyone sings both parts.

See Across the Curriculum below and share the history of "Battle Hymn of the Republic" with the class.

Listening

Before listening to *American Salute,* **CD 12-35,** have students sing "When Johnny Comes Marching Home," p. 180. This is a well-known song of the American Civil War. Morton Gould uses it as the basis for his composition.

Have students listen to *American Salute.* On a repeat listening, have them indicate when each new statement of the melody occurs. Encourage them to describe how its treatment is distinctive in each variation.

Marching On

In the North, "Battle Hymn of the Republic" was the best-known song of the Civil War. Learn the descant part and **sing** it on the refrain.

"Battle Hymn of the Republic" has gone through many lyric changes and has been sung for various purposes. **Create** your own words to this melody.

Footnotes

SKILLS REINFORCEMENT

▶ **Keyboard** Have students play a steady four-quarter-note beat using A♭, D♭, and E♭₇ chords to accompany "Battle Hymn of the Republic." Alternatively, they can play just the root notes— A♭, D♭, and E♭—rather than the complete chords.

Note: If using a transposing electronic keyboard, have students play chords one-half step lower than those listed—G, C, and D₇. They are much easier to play on a keyboard.

ACROSS THE CURRICULUM

▶ **Social Studies** The origin of the tune used for "Battle Hymn of the Republic" was "Say, Brothers, Will You Meet Us?" a religious song. John Brown was an abolitionist who was hung in 1859 after his attack on the armory in Harpers Ferry, West Virginia.

Poet Julia Ward Howe heard Union troops singing "John Brown's Body" (see Skills Reinforcement, p. 273) and was stirred to write more appropriate words. Published in 1861 by *Atlantic Monthly* magazine, her "Battle Hymn of the Republic" became the theme song of the Union and perhaps one of the best-known American songs of all time. She went on to become an important early advocate for women's rights.

REFRAIN
Descant

Glo - ry, glo - ry, hal - le - lu - jah!

Glo - ry, glo - ry, hal - le - lu - jah!

Glo - ry, glo - ry, hal - le - lu - jah!

Glo - ry, glo - ry, hal - le - lu - jah!

Glo - ry, glo - ry, hal - le - lu! His

Glo - ry, glo - ry, hal - le - lu - jah! His

truth is march - ing, march - ing on.

truth is march - ing on.

Listen to Morton Gould's *American Salute*. What familiar Civil War melody do you hear?

 CD 12–35
American Salute

by **Morton Gould**
as performed by the **Philadelphia Orchestra; Eugene Ormandy, conductor**

Morton Gould was a Pulitzer Prize-winning composer who used American themes in much of his music.

Unit 7 **275**

ASK How does Morton Gould use the rhythm of the opening phrase of the song pattern as a motive throughout this piece? (It is used as trumpet calls and echoes from the battlefield.)

SAY People often put new words to old tunes. When the words are humorous or poke fun at something serious, the result is called a parody.

Creating

Have students create their own words to "Battle Hymn of the Republic." Some possible topics might include

- The environment.
- School. *(We're from ____ ____ ____school.)*
- Recent items in the news.
- Homework.

Plan a class performance of students' parodies.

3 CLOSE

Element: TEXTURE/HARMONY — **ASSESSMENT**

Performance/Peer Critique Have students plan a performance that includes both songs in this lesson. Keep a tape recording of the performance. Here are some ideas.

- The class divides into two sections: Section 1 sings the Northern version of "Battle Cry of Freedom," Section 2 sings the Southern version.
- Students create a rhythm interlude using patterns from one of the songs.
- All sing "Battle Hymn of the Republic," taking turns singing the descant.
- Add a spoken or played introduction and coda.

Have students listen to evaluate their performances.

AUDIENCE ETIQUETTE

▶ **Preparing to Attend a Performance** Students are more attentive during live performances when they are prepared for what they will see and hear. To help students prepare, have them

- Research and summarize information about the featured performers and composers.
- Listen to recordings of the music they will hear. Engage students in the music through movement, listening maps, written responses, or singing/playing themes or rhythms.
- Read information about the music, including plots or story lines.
- Prepare interview questions for musicians who visit the school or classroom, or write a letter to musicians they have heard in live performances.

SCHOOL TO HOME CONNECTION

▶ **Civil War Research** The American Civil War was a significant turning point in the history of the United States. Ask students to research that era. What were the major changes that occurred because of that conflict? What were some famous battles, speeches, and leaders associated with the Civil War? Invite students to discuss this period with a relative or friend.

TECHNOLOGY/MEDIA LINK

Web Site To learn more about the music and songs of the American Civil War period, visit *www.sfsuccessnet.com*.

LESSON AT A GLANCE

Element Focus   **FORM** abac form

Skill Objective   **PLAYING** Play guitar to accompany an abac song

Connection Activity   **RELATED ARTS** Discuss an engraving by an American artist of the cowboy era

MATERIALS

- "Colorado Trail"   **CD 12-36**
  Recording Routine: Intro (4 m.); vocal; interlude (4 m.); vocal; coda
- *Colorado Trail*   **CD 13-1**
- **Resource Book** p. I-22
- guitar, Autoharp

VOCABULARY

phrase   form

◆ ◆ ◆ National Standards ◆ ◆ ◆ ◆

1c Sing music from diverse genres
2d Perform simple accompaniments by ear
4c Compose, using electronic media
6b Listen and analyze uses of form in music from diverse genres
8b Identify ways music relates to art and language arts

MORE MUSIC CHOICES

For more experience with cowboy songs:
"Cattle Call," p. 344
"Home on the Range," p. 69

1 INTRODUCE

8b As students examine the artwork on p. 277, share and discuss information on cattle drives in the Old West (see Across the Curriculum, p. 344) and the artist Frederic Remington (see Spotlight On, p. 277).

Singing on the Trail

The heyday of the American cowboy was the period following the Civil War until 1885. Many war veterans went West in search of adventure or work opportunities. Many ended up as cowboys, often working for less than a dollar a day.

Sing "Colorado Trail." Which phrases use the same melody?

CD 12-36

Colorado Trail

Cowboy Song

Eyes like a morn-ing star, cheeks like a rose,

Lau - ra was a pret-ty girl, ev-'ry-bod - y knows.

Weep all ye lit - tle rains, wail winds, _ wail,

All a - long, a - long, a - long the Col - o - ra - do Trail.

276

Footnotes

SKILLS REINFORCEMENT

▶ **Reading** Lead students to discover that there are only five different notes used in "Colorado Trail" (D, E, F♯, A, B). Ask students to identify the type of scale on which this melody is based. (pentatonic)

▶ **Recorder** For a recorder part to accompany "Colorado Trail," see Resource Book p. I-22. Have students identify the form of the recorder part (abac) before playing.

BUILDING SKILLS THROUGH MUSIC

▶ **Language** Have students identify phrases from "Colorado Trail" that are memories and those that describe scenes from the trail. Discuss how and why both are important to the cowboy. Ask students to suggest other things the cowboy would remember or see on the cattle drive.

ACROSS THE CURRICULUM

8b ▶ **Language Arts** Invite students to read poetry and perform songs based on themes of the Old West in *Singing Our Way West: Songs and Stories of America's Westward Expansion* by Jerry Silverman (Milbrook, 1998) and *Home on the Range: Cowboy Poetry* by Paul Janeczko (Dial, 1997).

Invite students to read or dramatize selected poems or stories as introductions to performances of songs of the Old West.

Strumming Cowboys

Learn to **play** one of the chords below to accompany "Colorado Trail" on guitar.

Sounds of the Trail

Listen to this recording of *Colorado Trail* and **compare** it to the version of the song on page 276. How is it the same? How is it different?

CD 13–1
Colorado Trail

Cowboy Song
arranged by Matthias Gohl
This rendition was featured in the film *The West.*

Arts Connection

This hand-colored engraving by American artist and sculptor Frederic Remington (1861–1909) depicts cowboys trailing cattle.

Unit 7   277

---

2 DEVELOP

Analyzing

Play the recording of "Colorado Trail" **CD 12-36** as students follow the music on p. 276.

6b **ASK** What lines are almost the same? (lines 1 and 3)

If you label those lines letter "a", what letters would you give to lines 2 and 4? ("b" and "c")

Help students identify and outline the "abac" phrase form of the song.

1c Have students sing "Colorado Trail" **CD 12-36** with the recording.

Playing

2d Students can take turns adding a guitar (or Autoharp) accompaniment to "Colorado Trail." Have students

- Review the fingering for the D and A₇ chords.
- Use an appropriate strum.
- Accompany the song, substituting the D chord for the E₇ and G chords.
- Review the fingering for the E₇ and G chords. Add them where indicated.

Note: For students with limited ability, the song can be accompanied using only the D chord throughout.

Listening

Invite students to listen to *Colorado Trail* **CD 13-1** and compare it to the version they just sang.

3 CLOSE

Skill: PLAYING   **ASSESSMENT**

1c **Performance/Observation** Have students plan a
2d performance of "Colorado Trail," incorporating activities from this lesson. Observe and assess their ability to

- Play accurately on guitar or Autoharp.
- Sing accurately and clearly.
- Demonstrate the form of the piece by singing on some phrases and playing on others.

SPOTLIGHT ON

▶ **The Artist** Frederic Remington (1861–1909) was born in Canton, New York, on October 4, 1861. As a boy, he developed a lifelong love of horses and the outdoors. After studying art at Yale, Remington traveled to Montana in 1881 and fell in love with the West.

Frederic Remington's major artistic achievements include pen-and-ink drawings and illustrations, paintings, and his famous 22 bronze sculptures. A considerable number of Remington's works appeared in magazine articles and books about the West. The epitaph on his gravestone is "He knew horses." A museum of his work is located at his boyhood home in Ogdensburg, New York, on the St. Lawrence Seaway.

TECHNOLOGY/MEDIA LINK

4c **Sequencing Software** Have students compose a bass part for a cowboy song. They can

- Choose a guitar timbre and record the melody of "Colorado Trail" in step-time on one track.
- Choose a string bass timbre and record a bass part using quarter-note roots and fifths, according to the chord symbols.
- Select a guitar patch for a harmony track and record chords in any rhythm pattern they choose.
- Play back the sequence to accompany class singing.

LESSON AT A GLANCE

Element Focus **MELODY** Motive

Skill Objective **SINGING** Sing short melodic patterns in a patriotic song

Connection Activity **SOCIAL STUDIES** Discuss the role of patriotic songs during World War I

MATERIALS
- "Over There" **CD 13-3**
  Recording Routine: Intro (free tempo); vocal 1; instrumental; vocal 2
- *I'm a Yankee Doodle Dandy* **CD 13-2**
- selected melody instruments

VOCABULARY
motive

◆ ◆ ◆ ◆ **National Standards** ◆ ◆ ◆ ◆

1b Sing easy pieces with expression
3b Improvise melodic variations on given melodies
5d Use standard notation to record musical ideas
8b Identify ways music relates to language arts and social studies
9b Classify high-quality musical works by genre

MORE MUSIC CHOICES
For more practice with motives:
"America, the Beautiful," p. 76

1 INTRODUCE

8b **9b** During World War I, both patriotic songs in this lesson helped to keep up morale among fighting troops and the public back home. Play the recording of "Over There" **CD 13-3** and ask students to listen to the lyrics.

ASK What elements make this song patriotic? (upbeat tempo and optimism of the lyrics)

Send the Word

America entered World War I (1914–1918) in 1917. In order to stir American patriotism and support, vaudeville songwriters like George M. Cohan wrote songs such as "You're a Grand Old Flag" and "Over There."

Sing "Over There," and share in the enthusiasm of the lyrics and the upbeat rhythm. Then **identify** the part of the melody that repeats throughout the song.

M·U·S·I·C M·A·K·E·R·S
George M. Cohan

George M. Cohan (1878–1942)—American musical theater actor, composer, singer, dancer, playwright, director, and producer—added his support of the war with his hit "Over There." The song was as popular as his other show stoppers, "You're a Grand Old Flag, "I'm a Yankee Doodle Dandy," and "Give My Regards to Broadway."

Listen to another spirited patriotic favorite from George M. Cohan.

 CD 13–2
I'm a Yankee Doodle Dandy
by George M. Cohan
I'm a Yankee Doodle Dandy, from the musical *Little Johnny Jones,* premiered on November 17, 1904. This song was one of Cohan's early successes.

278

Footnotes

SKILLS REINFORCEMENT

3b ▶ **Improvising** "Over There" lies in an easy range for many instruments. Find out which students play band or orchestra instruments. Challenge them to improvise patterns using the first three notes of the song. This three-note motive imitates a bugle call, such as might be played in the military.

A trumpet player can play bugle calls on open tones, using only the embouchure and no valves.

BUILDING SKILLS THROUGH MUSIC

▶ **Writing** Invite students to sing "Over There." Discuss the meaning of the lyrics of each phrase. Have students work individually or in pairs to rewrite the text for each phrase as a complete sentence. Choose students to read their sentences in song order. Discuss with students how George M. Cohan made the lyrics and rhythm appealing to people.

SPOTLIGHT ON

▶ **The Composer** George M. Cohan (1878–1942) was born on the third of July (not on the fourth as he sings in *I'm a Yankee Doodle Dandy*). Cohan's other famous songs include "You're a Grand Old Flag" and "Give My Regards to Broadway." He started his performing career as a child in his family's vaudeville act. By age 23, he had produced his first full-length musical in New York City.

Over There

CD 13–3

Words and Music by George M. Cohan

s, l, t, @ r m f s

do

O - ver there, o - ver there,

Send the word, send the word o - ver there

That the Yanks are com-ing, the Yanks are com-ing, The

drums rum tum - ming ev - 'ry - where.

So pre - pare, say a pray'r,

Send the word, send the word to be - ware

We'll be o - ver, we're com - ing o - ver, And we

won't come back 'till it's o - ver o - ver there.

Visit **Take It to the Net** at www.sfsuccessnet.com to learn more about George M. Cohan.

Building America in Song

2 DEVELOP

Singing

8b Refer to Across the Curriculum below and discuss in more detail the historical context of "Over There" **CD 13-3**.

Have students

1b
- Read about George M. Cohan on p. 278. (See also Spotlight On, p. 278.)
- Sing "Over There" with the recording, paying attention to tempo, diction, and energy level.
- Look at the first three notes in the melody and identify them as a *motive*—a melodic pattern used many times during the song.

Playing

Ask students to play the first three notes of "Over There" on melody instruments. Encourage students to use keyboards, recorders, mallet instruments, or guitars. (On the guitar, use open strings 2, 3, and 4.)

Listening

9b Have students listen to *I'm a Yankee Doodle Dandy* **CD 13-2**, another of Cohan's patriotic songs that was sung during World War I.

ASK What do *I'm a Yankee Doodle Dandy* and "Over There" have in common? (use of the words *Yanks* and *Yankee;* fast rousing tempo; major key; Broadway songs)

3 CLOSE

Element: MELODY   **ASSESSMENT**

Performance/Observation Ask students to sing "Over There" and indicate, with raised hands, those sections of the melody that are based on the three-note motive. Observe that students correctly identify the motive each time it occurs.

ACROSS THE CURRICULUM

8b ▶ **Social Studies** Called the Great War, World War I (1914–1918) pitted the Central Powers of Germany, Austria-Hungary, Turkey, and Bulgaria against the Allies of Russia, France, Great Britain, Italy, Romania, the United States, and others. The expression *in the trenches* comes from the fact that both sides fought much of the war from deep trenches dug in the ground. Gas warfare (mustard gas) also became a grim feature of World War I. Although the United States was very reluctant to get into the war, in 1917 it finally sent an Expeditionary Force eventually amounting to 4,355,000 men. U.S. casualties numbered 126,000. Germany (1,773,700), Russia (1,700,000), France (1,375,800), and Austria-Hungary (1,200,000) suffered the highest casualties.

TECHNOLOGY/MEDIA LINK

5d **Notation Software** Give students blank sheets of staff paper. Have them write their own bugle calls, using the first three notes of "Over There." They can also add high D. Divide students into groups, and have them notate their bugle calls using notation software. When possible, have students play back their work using the computer. Have students print out their work and share it with classmates and parents.

LESSON AT A GLANCE

Element Focus — **TIMBRE** — Vocal and instrumental timbre

Skill Objective — **LISTENING** — Listen and compare two African American gospel performances

Connection Activity — **GENRE** — Learn about Thomas A. Dorsey and the beginning of the gospel movement in the 1920s and 1930s.

MATERIALS
- "Twelve Gates to the City"   **CD 13-5**
  Recording Routine: Intro (4 m.); refrain; v. 1; refrain; interlude (4 m.); refrain; v. 2; refrain; coda
- *What Could I Do*   **CD 13-7**
- keyboard

VOCABULARY

blues   jazz   gospel

◆ ◆ ◆ ◆ National Standards ◆ ◆ ◆ ◆

1c Sing music from diverse genres
2c Perform instrumental music from diverse genres
6b Listen and analyze the uses of timbre in music from diverse genres

MORE MUSIC CHOICES...

For more practice in singing African American spirituals:
"Joshua Fought the Battle of Jericho," p. 101
"Go Down, Moses," p. 190
"Ev'ry Time I Feel the Spirit," p. 242

1 INTRODUCE

SAY The African American gospel movement had its roots not only in spirituals, but also in blues and jazz. Musicians such as Thomas A. Dorsey added the blues and jazz style to traditional African American hymns and spirituals to help create the excitement of gospel music.

Element: TIMBRE | **Skill: LISTENING** | **Connection: GENRE**

Gospel Calling

In the late 1920s, a blues pianist named Thomas A. Dorsey added elements of blues and jazz to the African American spiritual and hymn tradition. He helped create a style that became known as gospel music.

Listen to "Twelve Gates to the City," a traditional spiritual that is arranged here in gospel style.
Describe the voices and the accompanying instruments on the recording.

CD 13–5

Twelve Gates to the City

African American Spiritual

Oh, ___ what a beau-ti-ful ci-ty; ___ Oh, ___ what a

beau-ti-ful ci-ty; ___ Oh, ___ what a beau-ti-ful ci-ty; ___

Twelve gates _ to the ci-ty, a-hal-le-lu. ___

1. My Lord built ___ the ci-ty, ___ Ci-ty was just ___ four

square, Said he want-ed his child-ren ___ to

meet him in ___ the air, And there's twelve gates _ to the

280

Footnotes

TEACHER TO TEACHER

▶ **The Singing/Listening Connection** Students who admire the style of popular singers will probably include vocal elaboration and embellishment in their singing. Students learn to sing in a stylistic manner through a combination of listening and singing. Repeated listening to quality artist recordings will lead students to incorporate good singing traits into their own style of singing.

BUILDING SKILLS THROUGH MUSIC

▶ **Art** Invite students to listen to "Twelve Gates to the City" **CD 13-5**. Have them draw a visual representation of the text in the song. Ask students to share their pictures and analyze whether the visual representation matches the lyrics.

SPOTLIGHT ON

▶ **The History of Gospel Music** Thomas A. Dorsey was the self-described "son of a preacher man." After a successful career as a jazz and blues pianist, he started writing gospel songs in 1929 at the beginning of the Great Depression. Although his early gospel songs had religious lyrics, the instrumental style contained many of the elements of his blues and jazz background. This was highly controversial in the early 1930s, and many African American churches banned the use of this "brash" new music in their services. In addition to Dorsey's "Precious Lord, Take My Hand" and "What Could I Do," his other well-known song is "There Will Be Peace in the Valley."

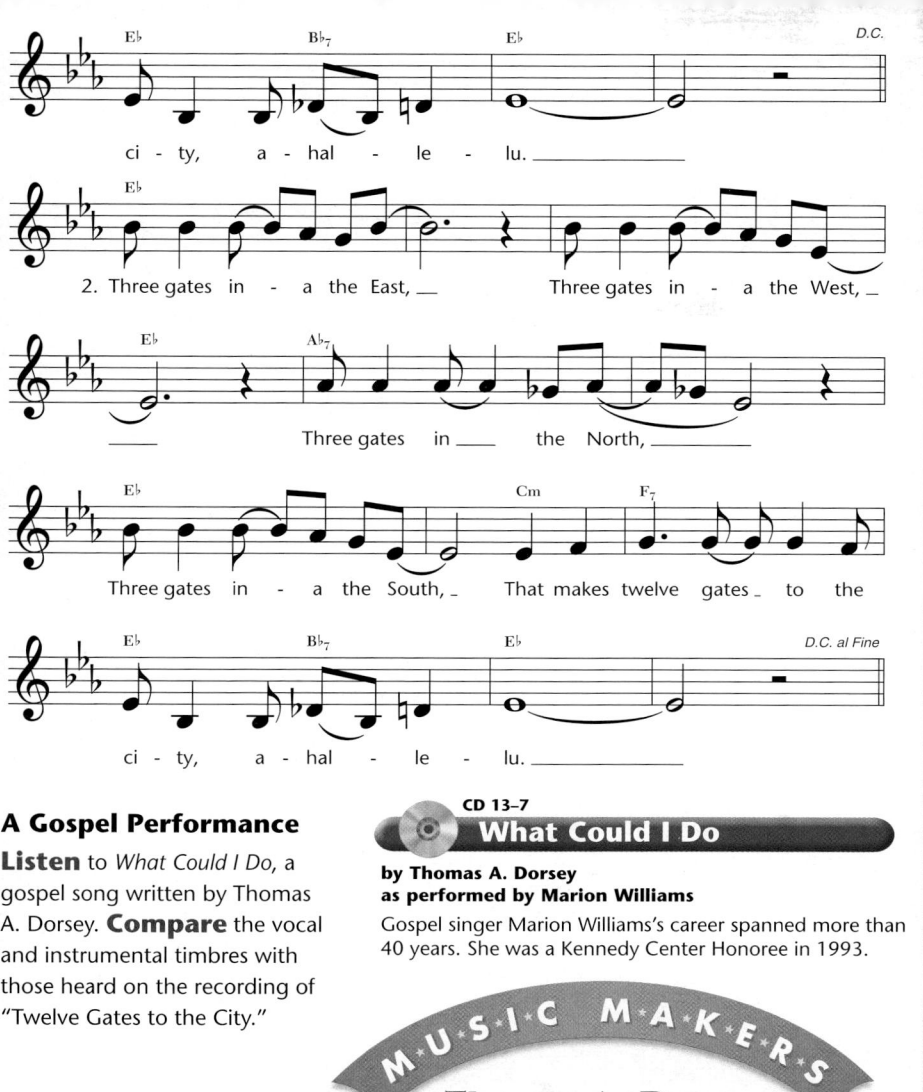

city, a - hal - le - lu.

2. Three gates in - a the East, ___ Three gates in - a the West, ___

___ Three gates in ___ the North, _____

Three gates in - a the South, ___ That makes twelve gates _ to the

city, a - hal - le - lu. _____

A Gospel Performance

Listen to *What Could I Do*, a gospel song written by Thomas A. Dorsey. **Compare** the vocal and instrumental timbres with those heard on the recording of "Twelve Gates to the City."

CD 13–7
What Could I Do

by Thomas A. Dorsey
as performed by Marion Williams

Gospel singer Marion Williams's career spanned more than 40 years. She was a Kennedy Center Honoree in 1993.

M·U·S·I·C M·A·K·E·R·S

Thomas A. Dorsey

Thomas Andrew Dorsey (1899–1993) is known as the "father of gospel music." He was born in Georgia and began his career playing in theaters and clubs. He later played with legendary blues vocalist Ma Rainey. After the deaths of his wife and son, Dorsey wrote "Precious Lord, Take My Hand," one of the best-loved gospel songs of the twentieth century. He founded the first independent publisher of African American gospel music.

Unit 7 281

Lead students in a discussion about Thomas A. Dorsey and how he helped create African American gospel music. See Spotlight On, p. 280 for more information.

2 DEVELOP

Listening

6b Have students listen to "Twelve Gates to the City" **CD 13-5**.

ASK What instruments do you hear on the recording? (piano, electric organ, drums, tambourine, bass)

Analyzing

Ask students to look at the notation for "Twelve Gates to the City" and identify the verse/refrain or AB form.

ASK What phrase occurs in the refrain, verse 1, and verse 2? (*"Twelve gates to the city, a-hallelu"*)

1c Have students sing "Twelve Gates to the City" with the recording **CD 13-5**.

Ask students to read the information on p. 281 about Thomas A. Dorsey.

Listening

6b Invite students to listen to *What Could I Do* **CD 13-7** performed by well-known gospel singer Marion Williams.

Encourage students to use standard terminology in explaining voices.

ASK What differences do you hear in vocal timbre on this recording compared to "Twelve Gates to the City"? (*What Could I Do* features a solo female voice; "Twelve Gates to the City" features a gospel choir.)

ELEMENT: TIMBRE   ASSESSMENT

6b **Music Journal Writing** Play the recordings of "Twelve Gates to the City" **CD 13-5** and *What Could I Do* **CD 13-7** again. Have students describe in their music journals the sound of the voices and instruments heard on the recordings. Ask them to list the similarities and differences in the two recordings.

SKILLS REINFORCEMENT

2c ▶ **Keyboard** Use the following suggestions to help all students perform a keyboard accompaniment for "Twelve Gates to the City."

Reinforcement Students who have difficulty playing the E♭ and B♭7 chords may play a steady quarter note beat using the root notes of these chords.

On Target Many students will be able to play the E♭ and B♭7 chords. Ask these students to accompany the refrain of "Twelve Gates to the City."

Challenge Invite interested students to accompany the entire song playing the Cm and F7 chords in addition to the E♭ and B♭7 chords.

TECHNOLOGY/MEDIA LINK

Web Site For more information about African American blues and jazz, visit *www.sfsuccessnet.com*.

LESSON AT A GLANCE

Element Focus TEXTURE/HARMONY Chords

Skill Objective PLAYING Play an instrumental accompaniment using appropriate chords

Connection Activity SOCIAL STUDIES Relate a song to a historical event

MATERIALS

• "Goin' Down the Road Feelin' Bad" **CD 13-8**

  Recording Routine: Intro (4 m.); v. 1; interlude (4 m.); v. 2; interlude (4 m.); v. 3; interlude (4 m.); coda

• *Goin' Down the Road Feelin' Bad* **CD 13-10**

• guitar, Autoharp, keyboard

VOCABULARY

harmony   chord

◆ ◆ ◆ ◆ **National Standards** ◆ ◆ ◆ ◆

1b Sing easy pieces with expression
2d Perform simple accompaniments by ear
8b Identify ways music relates to social studies

MORE MUSIC CHOICES

For more experience with songs by Woody Guthrie:
"Roll On, Columbia," p. 116
"This Land Is Your Land," p. 118

1 INTRODUCE

8b **SAY** During the Great Depression and Dust Bowl of the 1930s, many Americans lost their homes and jobs. They were forced to hit the road in search of ways to feed their families. Their feelings are reflected in the Dust Bowl ballad "Goin' Down the Road Feelin' Bad."

See Across the Curriculum, p. 283, for more information on this period in American history.

Better Times Ahead...

The stock market crash of 1929 brought a decade of hardship to many Americans. The severe drought of the 1930s added to this misery by creating the Dust Bowl. Thousands of people suffered as the land dried up. Many were forced to migrate to other parts of the country.

Sing this song about the feelings of many Americans at this very difficult time.

CD 13–8

Goin' Down the Road Feelin' Bad

Words and Melody Adapted and Arranged by John A. Lomax and Alan Lomax

1. I'm go-in' down the road feel-in' bad,
2. I ain't_ got but one old lous-y dime,
3. I'm go-in' where the cli-mate suits my clothes,

Lord, I'm go-in' down the road feel-in' bad,
Lord, I ain't_ got but one old lous-y dime,
Lord, I'm go-in' where the cli-mate suits my clothes,

Well, I'm go-in' down the road feel-in' bad, Lord,
Well, I ain't_ got but one old lous-y dime, Lord,
Well, I'm go-in' where the cli-mate suits my clothes, Lord,

Lord, And I ain't gon-na be treat-ed this-a-way.
Lord, But I'll find me _ a new dol-lar some old day.
Lord, 'Cause I ain't gon-na be treat-ed this-a-way.

TRO–Copyright 1947 (Renewed) Ludlow Music, Inc., New York, NY. Used by Permission.

282

Footnotes

SPOTLIGHT ON

▶ **The Performer** Woody Guthrie (1912–1967) was a prolific writer who wrote pages of new poetry and lyrics every day. Here is some advice he gave to those who want to write songs.

You know you are as good a songwriter as there is, but you might not believe it. If you don't believe it, that's why you're not. All you have to do is sit down and write up what's wrong and how to fix it. That's all there is to it.

BUILDING SKILLS THROUGH MUSIC

▶ **Social Studies** Invite students to listen to the two versions of "Goin' Down the Road Feelin' Bad" **CD 13-8, CD 13-10** and describe the characteristics of each performance. Distribute copies of the Venn Diagram from Resource Book p. C-8. Have students compare the two recordings using the Venn Diagram.

SKILLS REINFORCEMENT

2d ▶ **Playing** Remind students that the note D can belong to several chords: D, B minor, G, and several others. Ask students

• What is the last note of the song? (D) What is the key signature? (D major—so a D chord is clearly called for.)

• What chords include the note D? (in D major, the I [D] and IV [G] chords; and the VI [B minor] chord)

Have students memorize the first verse, then add harmonies "by ear." Challenge them to use alternative chords. For instance, the B in measure 2 fits with the B minor, G, or E chords. Students' ears will tell them which one is right.

Have students experiment with harmonies for the entire song.

Folk Guitar Chords

Play the following chords on guitar to accompany "Goin' Down the Road Feelin' Bad."

Listen to Woody Guthrie's performance of *Goin' Down the Road Feelin' Bad.*

CD 13-10
Goin' Down the Road Feelin' Bad

adapted, arranged, and performed by
Woody Guthrie and Lee Hays
This song was sung by many Dust Bowl farmers as they left their devastated homes and fields in hope of finding a better life.

M·U·S·I·C M·A·K·E·R·S

Woody Guthrie

Woody Guthrie (1912–1967) was one of the most important American folk music artists of the 20th century. He was born in Oklahoma, one of the hardest-hit states during the Dust Bowl years. Along with other folk music legends like Pete Seeger and Leadbelly, Guthrie had a major influence on the next generation of folk artists, such as Bob Dylan and Joan Baez.

Unit 7 **283**

Building America in Song

2 DEVELOP

Singing

1b Have students sing "Goin' Down the Road Feelin' Bad" **CD 13-8**, with the recording. Encourage students to sing some of Woody's other verses.

- *I'm going where them dust storms never blow* (3 times)
- *They say I'm a dust bowl refugee* (3 times)
- *I'm looking for a job with honest pay* (3 times)

Playing

2d Have students add harmony to the song by playing an accompaniment on guitar, Autoharp, or keyboard. They can play the D, G, and A₇ chords printed above the music in their books.

Students who have trouble with the full G chord on guitar can play a one-finger version of G (press string 1 at fret 3; strum strings 4 through 1).

Consider also adding any available classroom instruments.

Listening

Play for students Woody Guthrie's recording of *Goin' Down the Road Feelin' Bad* **CD 13-10**.

ASK How does this recording of the song differ from the version on p. 283? Which version do you prefer? (Accept a variety of answers.)

3 CLOSE

Skill: PLAYING   ASSESSMENT

Performance/Observation Have students take turns playing guitar, Autoharp, or keyboard to accompany "Goin' Down the Road Feelin' Bad." Observe whether they use the appropriate chords in their accompaniments.

ACROSS THE CURRICULUM

8b ▶ **Social Studies** The period from 1929 to the beginning of World War II (1941) was known as the Great Depression. Industrial stocks lost much of their value, 11,000 U.S. banks failed, and farm prices fell. During the 1930s, a severe drought in the Midwest states turned the land into a huge Dust Bowl. The dust storms were so large that roads and houses were buried, and clouds from the storms were observed hundreds of miles away. More than half the people abandoned their farms or houses and left the area.

To help bring the United States out of the Great Depression, President Roosevelt and his administration created many government projects that put people to work. Woody Guthrie wrote a song about one of the projects—government dams ("Roll On, Columbia").

SCHOOL TO HOME CONNECTION

▶ **The Homeless** Encourage students to read and discuss with the class *Lives Turned Upside Down: Homeless Children in Their Own Words and Photographs* by Jim Hubbard (Simon & Schuster Children's, 1996), a sensitive portrayal of several children who are homeless.

TECHNOLOGY/MEDIA LINK

Sequencing Software Using digital audio, record the class playing chordal accompaniment on guitars or other chordal instruments, singing the melody, and adding a bass part, all on separate tracks. Ask students to describe the strong points and weak points of the recorded performance.

LESSON AT A GLANCE

Element Focus **RHYTHM** Syncopation

Skill Objective **SINGING** Sing syncopated rhythm patterns

Connection Activity **SOCIAL STUDIES** Explore how America pulled itself out of the Great Depression

MATERIALS

- "Happy Days Are Here Again" **CD 13-11**

  Recording Routine: Intro (8 m.); vocal (AABA); instrumental B; vocal (A); coda

VOCABULARY

syncopation

◆ ◆ ◆ ◆ **National Standards** ◆ ◆ ◆ ◆

1a Sing accurately in small ensembles
6b Listen and analyze uses of rhythm in music from diverse genres
7a Students evaluate the music they perform
8b Identify ways music relates to social studies

MORE MUSIC CHOICES

For more practice in singing syncopated rhythms:

"*Éliza Kongo*," p. 14

"Morning Comes Early," p. 13

1 INTRODUCE

8b **SAY** In the Great Depression many people lost their jobs, their homes, their farms, and their livelihood. Share the information in Across the Curriculum, p. 285, to help students understand how Franklin D. Roosevelt's New Deal gave people hope that times were going to get better. Point out that "Happy Days Are Here Again" became FDR's political theme song.

ANOTHER CHALLENGE

The Great Depression of the early 1930s brought mass unemployment and long food lines. Many people looked to popular entertainment for a temporary escape from their hardships. One song, written in the same year as the stock market crash, gained unexpected popularity. With its catchy, syncopated rhythms, and optimistic lyrics, "Happy Days Are Here Again" expressed new hope for better days. It went on to become the theme song of President Franklin D. Roosevelt's efforts to lead the country out of the Depression.

Listen to and then **sing** "Happy Days Are Here Again." Can you **identify** the repeated syncopated rhythm pattern?

▲ Food line on East 25th St., New York City, 1931

CD 13–11

HAPPY DAYS ARE HERE AGAIN

Words by Jack Yellen

Music by Milton Ager

Hap - py days — are here a - gain! — The skies a - bove — are
All to - geth - er shout it now! — There's no one who — can

clear a - gain. — Let us sing a song — of cheer a - gain, — hap - py
doubt it now. — So let's tell the world — a - bout it now, — hap - py

284

Footnotes

SPOTLIGHT ON

▶ **Music to Make You Happy** When people are feeling "down and out," they often turn to music. This was certainly true during the Great Depression of the 1930s. Movie musicals and westerns starring dancers, singers, and cowboys like Fred Astaire, Ginger Rogers, Gene Kelly, Gene Autry, and Bing Crosby provided an escape from the harsh realities of life. Many large dance halls thrived on the crowds of people that came to "dance their troubles away."

BUILDING SKILLS THROUGH MUSIC

▶ **Writing** Share the information in Across the Curriculum, p. 285. Ask students to write a brief paragraph about the importance of the projects that enabled people to work after the Great Depression.

CULTURAL CONNECTION

8b ▶ **1930s–1940s** Despite the Great Depression and the Dust Bowl, FDR's New Deal and other events brought hope to many people. In 1936 an African American named Jesse Owens inspired our nation by winning four gold medals in the Olympic Games in Berlin, Germany.

Movies and radio broadcasts helped the American public look on the lighter side. The main attractions of this time were *King Kong* (1933) and *The Wizard of Oz* (1939). The radio entertained the public with variety shows, soap operas, and quiz shows. In addition to the news, some of the more popular shows were adventure series, such as *The Lone Ranger*, *Superman*, and *Dick Tracy*. The classic radio broadcast was *The War of the Worlds* (1938), which sent Americans into a panic for several hours, fearing invasion by Martians.

days are here a - gain!
days are here a - gain!

Your cares and

trou-bles are gone.   There'll be no more from now on.

▲ Ticker tape parade,
November 28, 1931,
Los Angeles, California

Franklin Delano Roosevelt ▶

2 DEVELOP

Reading

Have students

- Listen to the recording of "Happy Days Are Here Again" **CD 13-11**, while following the music.
- Locate the syncopations in the song. (tied notes; all half notes and dotted half notes in lines 1 and 2; and line 4, mm. 1 and 5)
- Practice clapping the tied notes *without* the ties; then add the ties to create the syncopation.
- Sing "Happy Days Are Here Again" with the recording.
- See Spotlight On and Cultural Connection, p. 284, and discuss how music and other forms of popular entertainment helped people get through the Great Depression.

3 CLOSE

Skill: SINGING   **ASSESSMENT**

Performance/Self-Assessment Have students show that they understand that syncopation is meaningful only in its relationship to the beat. Have them

- Clap or tap a steady beat
- Say the lyrics of "Happy Days Are Here Again" in rhythm while keeping the beat.
- Keep the beat and at the same time sing the lyrics.

Note: Aim for individual independence. It may be necessary to modify the exercise to accommodate individual abilities. Have students keep a record in their journals of the level they attain; they should try to advance as they are able.

ACROSS THE CURRICULUM

▶ **Social Studies** President Franklin D. Roosevelt and his administration created many government projects that put people to work, such as the National Reconstruction Administration (NRA), the Civilian Conservation Corps (CCC), the Tennessee Valley Authority (TVA), and the Works Progress Administration (WPA). The WPA built many of the beautiful national and state parks that are still part of the American landscape. The CCC put young people to work in rural areas planting trees and, in the process, gave them something to live for. The New Deal, greatly aided by First Lady Eleanor Roosevelt, also helped create more opportunities for African Americans, other minorities, and women.

SCHOOL TO HOME CONNECTION

▶ **Great Depression to World War II** Encourage students to interview older people in the community who lived through the Great Depression. Ask them some of these questions.

- What was life like during the Depression?
- Do you remember President Roosevelt? The New Deal? War bonds? Victory gardens? Rationing?
- What changes came about when World War II started?

TECHNOLOGY/MEDIA LINK

Web Site Go to *www.sfsuccessnet.com* to learn more about the music of the 1930s.

LESSON AT A GLANCE

Element Focus **RHYTHM** Syncopation

Skill Objective **CREATING** Create new verses and movements to show syncopation

Connection Activity **SOCIAL STUDIES** Discuss social change in the 1960s and early 1970s, as expressed through songs

MATERIALS

- "If I Had a Hammer"   **CD 13-13**
  Recording Routine: Intro (4 m.); verses 1–3; interlude (2 m.); v. 4; coda
- "Woke Up This Morning"   **CD 13-16**
  Recording Routine: Intro (8 m.); v. 1; v. 2; v. 3; coda
- *Where Have All the Flowers Gone?*   **CD 13-15**
- **Resource Book** p. F-33

VOCABULARY

syncopation

◆ ◆ ◆ ◆ National Standards ◆ ◆ ◆ ◆

1c Sing music with appropriate expression

2e In instrumental ensembles, perform moderately easy pieces with technical accuracy

5a Read half notes, quarter notes, eighth notes, dotted notes in duple meter

5c Identify standard notation symbols for pitch

6a Listen and describe events in music using appropriate terms

7b Students use specific criteria for evaluating performances, and offer constructive suggestions for improvement

8b Identify ways music relates to social studies and language arts

9a Describe characteristics of music genres from a variety of cultures

MORE MUSIC CHOICES

For more experience with songs of the 1960s and 1970s:

"Stand By Me," p. 46

"You've Got a Friend," p. 366

"Turn, Turn, Turn," p. 378

THE Sign OF THE Times

On November 22, 1963, President John F. Kennedy was assassinated. This tragic event launched a decade of social triumphs and tragedies that deeply affected our nation. As always, America's folk music voiced the feelings, hopes, and dreams of the American people. Songs about civil rights, equality for all, environmental concerns, and peace echoed throughout the country.

"Ask not what your country can do for you—ask what you can do for your country."
— JFK Inaugural address, January 20, 1961

"If I Had a Hammer" is a song that raised a few warnings. **Sing** it and then **create** other verses that might reflect the concerns of the present decade.

Footnotes

SPOTLIGHT ON

▶ *Clearwater* Pete Seeger launched a campaign in 1969 to help clean up the Hudson River in New York. He led a small group of river-lovers to try to change the conditions that were destroying the Hudson. The group wanted to reclaim a neglected and polluted historical natural treasure. So they built a boat, the sloop *Clearwater*, and used it as a movable classroom to teach people how to care for our threatened waterways.

BUILDING SKILLS THROUGH MUSIC

▶ **Language** Ask students to write a sentence to complete one of the following statements: "If I Had a Hammer, Bell, or Song, I'd..." Invite students to share their sentences with the class.

CULTURAL CONNECTION

8b ▶ **Social Issues** During the 1960s and early 1970s, there was a rising tide of protest against America's involvement in the Vietnam War. Unlike the popular support for participation in World War II, many Americans felt that the struggle in Vietnam was internal and best left to the Vietnamese to decide.

Encouraged by African American civil rights gains in the 1950s and 1960s, women expanded the issue of equality to include much more than voting rights. The main concerns of the women's movement from the 1960s to today are for economic, political, and social equality.

IF I HAD A HAMMER

Words and Music by Lee Hays and Pete Seeger

1. If I had a ham-mer, ____ I'd ham-mer in the morn-ing,
2. If I had a bell, ____ I'd ring it in the morn-ing,
3. If I had a song, ____ I'd sing it in the morn-ing,
4. Well, I got a ham-mer, ____ And I ____ got a bell, ____

I'd ham-mer in the eve - ning ____
I'd ring it in the eve - ning ____
I'd sing it in the eve - ning ____ All o - ver this land,
And I ____ got a song to sing.

I'd ham-mer out dan - ger, ____ I'd ham-mer out a warn-ing,
I'd ring ____ out dan - ger, ____ I'd ring ____ out a warn-ing,
I'd sing ____ out dan - ger, ____ I'd sing ____ out a warn-ing,
It's the ham-mer of jus - tice, ____ It's the bell ____ of ____ free - dom, ____

I'd ham-mer out
I'd ring ____ out
I'd sing ____ out love be-tween my broth-ers and my sis-ters,
It's the song a-bout

All ____ o - ver this land.

"If I Had a Hammer" (The Hammer Song) TRO—© Copyright 1958 (Renewed) 1962 (Renewed) Ludlow Music, Inc., New York, NY. Used by Permission.

The song *Where Have All the Flowers Gone?* expresses many of the social concerns of the 1960s. **Listen** to Pete Seeger's performance.

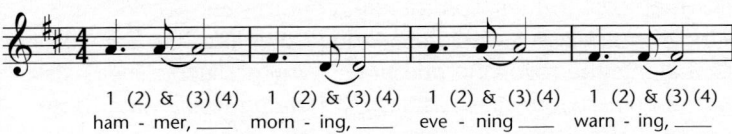

CD 13–15

Where Have All the Flowers Gone?

written and performed by Pete Seeger

Where Have All the Flowers Gone?, written in 1961, was inspired by the novel *And Quiet Flows the Don.*

Unit 7 **287**

Building America in Song

1 INTRODUCE

8b **SAY** The 1960s and early 1970s were times of great civil unrest and change. Americans took on the issues of civil rights, the Vietnam War, women's rights, and the environment. Like the Civil War and the Great Depression, the process of social change during this period produced a number of songs, many of which remain popular today.

Engage the class in a discussion of the major events and memorable music of this time period. See Cultural Connection, p. 286, Across the Curriculum, below, and Spotlight On, p. 289, for more information and related projects.

2 DEVELOP

Listening

1c Have students

- Read the text on p. 286.
- Listen to "If I Had a Hammer" **CD 13-13** while following the music on p. 287.

ASK What dangers do you think this song was warning about in the 1960s? (injustice, lack of free-dom for some, lack of love and trust between people)

Discuss with students whether they think these are dangers that still need warnings today.

Reading

5a To prepare students to sing the syncopated rhythms in "If I Had a Hammer," have them practice the syncopation exercise in Skills Reinforcement below.

Singing

Have students sing "If I Had a Hammer" with the recording.

continued on page 288

SKILLS REINFORCEMENT

5a ▶ **Reading** Have students clap the beats in four meter in "If I Had a Hammer"; add "and" to beat 2; clap but do not say beats 2, 3, and 4; then say the lyrics.

1 (2) & (3)(4) 1 (2) & (3)(4) 1 (2) & (3)(4) 1 (2) & (3)(4)
ham - mer, ____ morn - ing, ____ eve - ning ____ warn - ing, ____

2e ▶ **Mallets** An Orff arrangement of "Woke Up This Morning" can be found on p. F-33 of the Resource Book.

ACROSS THE CURRICULUM

8b ▶ **Social Studies/Language Arts** Ask students to search newspapers for articles about issues of concern to them person-ally; for example, hunger, diseases, poverty, crime, injustice. Invite students to share their articles. Then encourage them to write a poem or journal entry expressing their feelings about a situation or current event. How can they personally work toward peaceful change?

Lesson 13 Continued

Listening

6a Play the recording of Pete Seeger performing *Where Have All the Flowers Gone?* **CD 13-15.** Ask students to describe Seeger's use of syncopation in the melody.

ASK Does the singer perform the syncopation the same way for each verse? (No; the syncopation is varied, to reflect the rhythm of the lyrics.)

Have students

- Follow the music as they listen to the recording of "Woke Up This Morning" **CD 13-16.**
- Listen again, carefully following the sequence of verses.

5c • Find the flatted thirds (B-flats) in verse 2. (*mind on* and *freedom*)

9a Point out that the blues flatted third is one of the hallmarks of the African American musical tradition.

Reading

5a Have students practice the rhythm of the first measure of "Woke Up This Morning" **CD 13-16.** See Skills Reinforcement below for a preparation activity.

ASK Where else in the song do you find this same syncopated rhythm? (measures 5 and 9)

Singing

Have students

- Practice the syncopated rhythms at the beginning of verse 2.

1c • Sing the entire song.

Ask students to sing these other traditional verses to "Woke Up This Morning."

Walkin' and talkin' with my mind stayed on freedom
(three times)

Ain't-a no harm to keep your mind stayed on freedom
(three times)

A King's Dream

The latter part of the 1960s was a difficult time. The Vietnam War was still raging, and cries for freedom and peace continued to echo across the nation. A song of hope became a moment of silence when another leader was taken away. On April 4, 1968, Martin Luther King, Jr. was assassinated, and another dream remained unfulfilled.

"Woke Up This Morning" is an older African American song that was revived during the Civil Rights movement.

Sing this song and **create** additional verses that reflect King's dream.

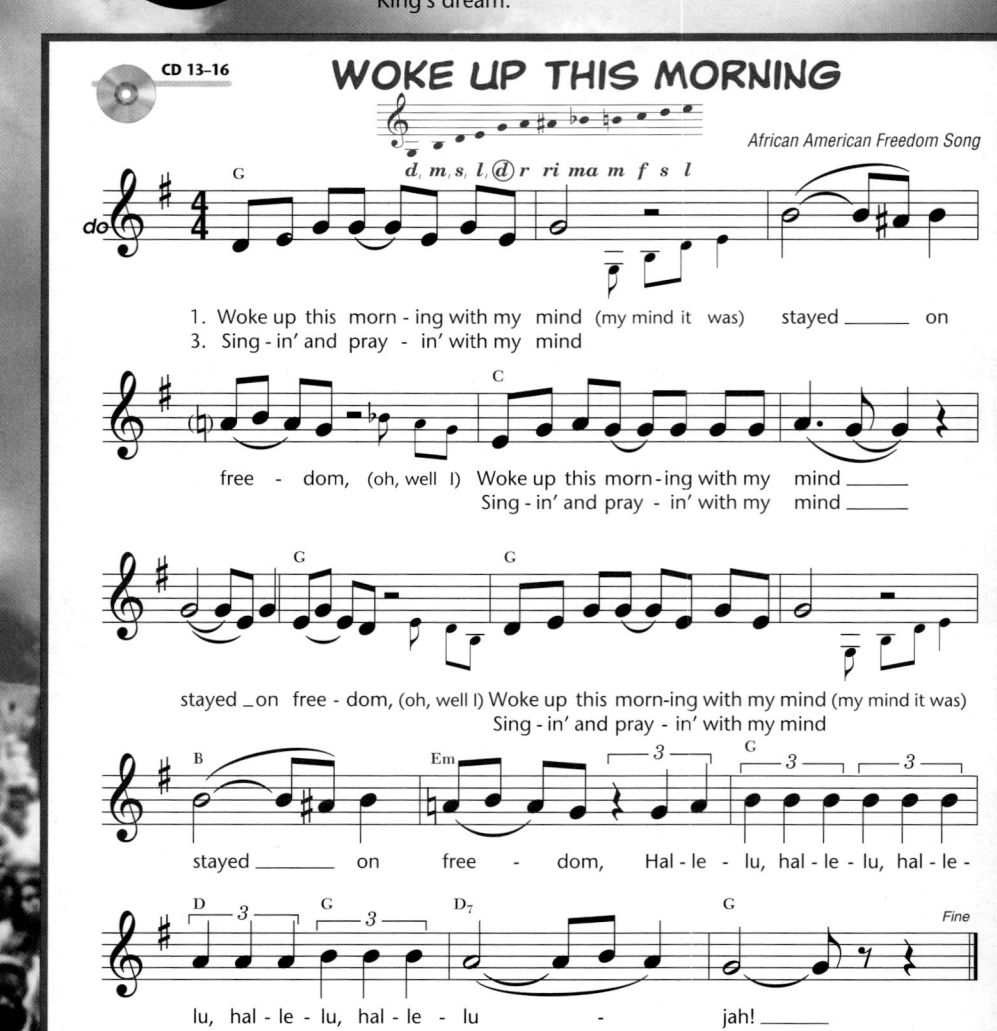

CD 13–16

WOKE UP THIS MORNING

African American Freedom Song

1. Woke up this morn - ing with my mind (my mind it was) stayed _____ on free - dom, (oh, well I) Woke up this morn-ing with my mind _____
3. Sing - in' and pray - in' with my mind Sing - in' and pray - in' with my mind _____

stayed _ on free - dom, (oh, well I) Woke up this morn-ing with my mind (my mind it was) Sing - in' and pray - in' with my mind

stayed _____ on free - dom, Hal - le - lu, hal - le - lu, hal - le -

lu, hal - le - lu, hal - le - lu - jah! _____

288

SKILLS REINFORCEMENT

▶ **Reading** Direct students' attention to the rhythm of the melody on the word *Hallelu*. The notes are quarter-note triplets—they take the space of two quarter notes (half the measure in $\frac{4}{4}$ meter).

Have students write four quarter notes in $\frac{4}{4}$ meter. Above the notes, have students write quarter-note triplets and then take turns clapping the parts. This will help students perform quarter-note triplets correctly.

CHARACTER EDUCATION

▶ **Social Responsibility** To encourage students to consider social responsibility, discuss the role they should or could play in alleviating current social woes. List various social issues and concerns that exist in their community, country, and world (for example, homelessness, poverty, inequality, littering, and so on). Ask students the following questions. Why do such issues exist? What, if any, is your responsibility in helping to alleviate these problems? How can you express your concerns about a social issue in a respectful manner? Help students understand that responding to social concerns in a respectful, responsible, manner requires courage, compassion, and self-discipline. Select one local issue on which to focus. Determine what students could do to make a difference in this local issue. For example, if homelessness is a concern, students could determine what needs the local homeless have, collect these items, and donate them to a shelter.

2. Walk   walk (doo doo doo) walk   walk   walk   walk with my mind on free-dom,

Walk   walk   walk   walk (a-well-a) walk   walk   with my mind on free-dom,

Ah _____   walk   walk   walk   walk

Unit 7 **289**

Creating

Encourage students to make up new verses for "Woke Up This Morning" by using the formula of singing the same new line of text three times.

Moving

Students can also add their own movements to "Woke Up This Morning" by swaying or stepping on the phrase *walk, walk.*

3 CLOSE

Skill: CREATING    **ASSESSMENT**

Performance/Music Journal Writing Have students

- Create and perform body movements to show syncopation in "Woke Up This Morning."
- Keep a written record of the movements.
- Create new verses to "Woke Up This Morning" using syncopation.
- Sing "Woke Up This Morning" with the new verses and the body movement.

7b Videotape a performance of "Woke Up This Morning" for class assessment, including constructive suggestions for improvement.

SPOTLIGHT ON

8b ▶ **The 1960s** The 1960s were an era of social protest and nonviolent demonstrations for civil rights. "If I Had a Hammer" was sung to symbolize social protests. Peter, Paul, and Mary, a popular folk group, sang this song on the steps of the Lincoln Memorial at the 1963 March on Washington, D.C., the same day and place where the Reverend Martin Luther King, Jr., gave his famous "I Have a Dream" speech to hundreds of thousands of people gathered on the Capitol Mall.

Invite students to read more about this important event in *The March on Washington, 1963: Gathering to Be Heard* by Tricia Andryszewski (Millbrook, 1996).

TECHNOLOGY/MEDIA LINK

Web Site To learn more about songs of the Civil Rights movement, visit *www.sfsuccessnet.com.*

Lesson	Elements	Skills	

LESSON 1
Move to the Music

pp. 294–297

Element: Rhythm
Concept: Pattern
Focus: Rhythm patterns from Latin America and the Middle East

Secondary Element
Harmony: thirds

National Standards
1c 1d 2c 6b 7a 8b 9a

Skill: Moving
Objective: Perform a Latin American song with rhythmic clapping

Secondary Skills
- **Singing** Sing with harmony and a clapping pattern
- **Playing** Accompany a song on guitar and unpitched percussion instruments
- **Listening** Listen and identify flamenco clapping and dancing rhythms
- **Singing** Clap a rhythm pattern while singing
- **Playing** Play a drumming pattern
- **Singing** Sing the songs with instrumental accompaniment

SKILLS REINFORCEMENT
- **Guitar** Use a capo to play chords
- **Mallets** Play an Orff arrangement
- **Keyboard** Play an accompaniment
- **Recorder** Play a countermelody

LESSON 2
Dancing in Friendship

pp. 298–301

Element: Melody
Concept: Tonality
Focus: Pitch syllables

Secondary Element
Harmony: layered melodies

National Standards
1c 2a 2d 5a 6b 6c 8b

Skill: Singing
Objective: Sightread a song using pitch syllables

Secondary Skills
- **Singing** Sing the song in three languages
- **Moving** Dance the *hora* and *debky* to related songs
- **Playing** Play a guitar accompaniment

SKILLS REINFORCEMENT
- **Analyzing** Play chords to reinforce chord function
- **Recorder** Play a countermelody

LESSON 3
Singing Stories

pp. 302–307

Element: Rhythm
Concept: Pattern
Focus: Rhythm patterns

Secondary Element Form: verse/refrain

National Standards
1c 2c 3b 5a 7a 8b

Skill: Reading
Objective: Sing songs that include repeated rhythm patterns

Secondary Skills
- **Singing** Sing the song with the recording
- **Moving** Perform a patterned dance
- **Reading** Identify major and minor tonalities and compare rhythm patterns
- **Singing** Sing the song and tap the rhythm
- **Playing** Play the provided rhythms with the song
- **Singing** Sing the song in Spanish
- **Playing** Play a two-chord guitar accompaniment
- **Singing** Sing the songs expressively

SKILLS REINFORCEMENT
- **Mallets** Play an Orff arrangement
- **Recorder** Play a countermelody
- **Reading** Identify and clap rhythm patterns

Connections

Music and Other Literature

Connection: Culture

Activity: Explore Puerto Rican and Arabic cultural traditions

CULTURAL CONNECTION
Puerto Rico Facts about Puerto Rico
Modern Day Egypt Facts about Egypt

TEACHER TO TEACHER Clapping Experiment with different clapping sounds

ACROSS THE CURRICULUM Social Studies Read a book about flags of many countries

MEETING INDIVIDUAL NEEDS Performing Tips to help all students perform hand claps in the song

SCHOOL TO HOME CONNECTION Culture Learn about different cultures

BUILDING SKILLS THROUGH MUSIC Social Studies Research and draw flags

Songs
"¡Qué bonita bandera!"
"What a Beautiful Banner!"
"Ah ya Zane"
"Zane from Abedeen"

Listening Selection *Río de la miel*
M·U·S·I·C M·A·K·E·R·S
Francisco Sánchez Gómez

More Music Choices
"Se va el caiman" ("The Alligator"), p. 306

ASSESSMENT
Performance/Self-Assessment Sing and clap selected rhythms accurately

TECHNOLOGY/MEDIA LINK
Web Site More information about the music and folk instruments of Latin America and the Middle East

---

Connection: Related Arts

Activity: Learn to dance an Arabic line dance and an Israeli circle dance

ACROSS THE CURRICULUM Social Studies Research the building of the nation of Israel in the late 1940s

CULTURAL CONNECTION Israel Facts about Israel

MOVEMENT
Patterned Dance Learn to dance the *hora*
Patterned Dance Learn to dance the *debky*

TEACHER TO TEACHER Guitar Chords Play a guitar accompaniment

SCHOOL TO HOME CONNECTION Community Involvement Share information about Israeli and Arabic cultures

BUILDING SKILLS THROUGH MUSIC Language Identify phrases from the song that describe the feelings of the singers

Song "Tzena, tzena"

Listening Selection *Ala Da'lona*

More Music Choices
"Dundai," p. 106
"Ah ya Zane" ("Zane from Abedeen"), p. 297

ASSESSMENT
Performance/Observation Perform a song in sections with pitch syllables and lyrics

TECHNOLOGY/MEDIA LINK
MIDI/Sequencing Software Use the MIDI file to dance to faster tempos

---

Connection: Social Studies

Activity: Become familiar with story songs as a form of literature

SPOTLIGHT ON Vocables Facts about vocables
Musical Instruments of South America Facts about South American instruments

CULTURAL CONNECTION Haliwa-Saponi Indians Facts about the Haliwa-Saponi tribe
Venezuela Facts about Venezuela
Colombia Facts about Colombia

MOVEMENT Patterned Dance Learn a single-file line movement routine

CHARACTER EDUCATION Values and Traditions Discuss the importance of values and traditions

ACROSS THE CURRICULUM Social Studies/Science Read books about the Amazon rain forest

TEACHER TO TEACHER Guitar Chords Play a guitar accompaniment

BUILDING SKILLS THROUGH MUSIC Language Research and write descriptions of the alligator

Songs
"Haliwa-Saponi Canoe Song"
"El carite"
"The Kingfish"
"Se va el caimán"
"The Alligator"

Listening Selection *Haliwa- Saponi Canoe Song*
M·U·S·I·C M·A·K·E·R·S
Haliwa-Saponi Singers

More Music Choices
"Los reyes de Oriente" ("The Kings from the East"), p. 480

ASSESSMENT
Performance/Self-Assessment Plan and create a performance of the song and evaluate

TECHNOLOGY/MEDIA LINK
MIDI/Sequencing Software Record percussion lines for song melody

Lesson	Elements	Skills

LESSON 4

Singing Games

pp. 308–309

Element: Melody
Concept: Pattern
Focus: Call-and-response patterns

Secondary Element
Harmony: thirds

National Standards
1c　1d　5a　7b　8b　9c

Skill: Singing
Objective: Sing a game song from West Africa

Secondary Skills
- **Singing** Sing the song in parts
- **Moving** Play a stone-passing game with song

LESSON 5

Fiddle Relatives

pp. 310–313

Element: Timbre
Concept: Instrumental
Focus: String Instruments

Secondary Element
Expression: dynamics

National Standards
6a　6b　8b

Skill: Listening
Objective: Distinguish the sound of string instruments in a guided listening experience

Secondary Skill
- **Creating** Create a one-stringed spike fiddle

SKILLS REINFORCEMENT
- **Listening** Listen to Sound Bank selections

LESSON 6

Celebrate Nature

pp. 314–317

Element: Melody
Concept: Tonality
Focus: Pentatonic melody

Secondary Element Form: phrase structure

National Standards
1c　2c　3a　5c　6c　7a　8a　8b

Skill: Singing
Objective: Perform songs that are based on a pentatonic scale

Secondary Skills
- **Singing** Sing the song in Mandarin
- **Playing** Identify and play an ostinato
- **Creating** Create an ostinato and improvise accompaniment
- **Singing** Compare two songs and sing the song in Taiwanese
- **Playing** Play provided ostinatos

SKILLS REINFORCEMENT
- **Moving** Interpret nature imagery through dramatized movement

---

Connections

Music and Other Literature

Connection: Culture
Activity: Learn a traditional Akan game to accompany a song

- **ACROSS THE CURRICULUM** **Social Studies** Read books to learn about the people, art, and customs of Ghana
- **CULTURAL CONNECTION** **Akan of Ghana** Facts about people that speak the Akan language
- **SCHOOL TO HOME CONNECTION** **Decorating Stones** Research patterns and designs of West African countries to decorate stones for the game
- **BUILDING SKILLS THROUGH MUSIC** **Math** Create a graph to represent the length of the call and response

Songs
"Bantama kra kro" (Akan)
"Bantama kra kro" (English)

More Music Choices
"Funwa alafia" ("Welcome, My Friends"), p. 32
"O, Desayo," p. 411

ASSESSMENT
Performance/Observation Sing a call-and-response song; use a rubric to assess ability

TECHNOLOGY/MEDIA LINK
Video Library Watch *Percussion Instruments* to learn about West African percussion

---

Connection: Science
Activity: Explore the acoustics and construction of string instruments

- **CULTURAL CONNECTION** **Spike Fiddle** Facts about the instrument
- **ACROSS THE CURRICULUM**
  Arts and Crafts Make a simple spike fiddle
  Science Facts about the construction and function of a violin
- **SPOTLIGHT ON**
  Turtle Island String Quartet Facts about the group
  The Composer Facts about Aaron Copland
  The Ballet Facts about *Rodeo*
- **TEACHER TO TEACHER** **String Instruments** Learn about electronic string instruments
- **BUILDING SKILLS THROUGH MUSIC** **Social Studies** Describe the appearance and sound of instruments

Listening Selections
Picking Red Chestnuts
Julie-O
Solo Flight (excerpt)
Hoedown

Listening Map *Hoedown*
M·U·S·I·C M·A·K·E·R·S
The Turtle Island String Quartet

More Music Choices
Zither Montage, p. 196
The Fourth of July, p. 489

ASSESSMENT
Music Journal Writing Listen to a recording and describe instrumental timbre

TECHNOLOGY/MEDIA LINK
Transparency Identify sections of a song using a listening map

---

Connection: Culture
Activity: Become acquainted with the importance of nature in Chinese culture

- **CULTURAL CONNECTION** **Mandarin** Facts about the dialect **Bamboo** Facts about the symbolism of bamboo
- **TEACHER TO TEACHER** **Guitar Drone** Discuss the use of guitar in Asian music
- **SPOTLIGHT ON** **The Moon in Chinese Art** Discuss the use of the moon to represent immortality
- **ACROSS THE CURRICULUM**
  Language Arts Share a sample of books on Chinese painting
  Visual Arts Collect artwork depicting moon shapes in art
- **SCHOOL TO HOME CONNECTION** **Moon Songs** Make a list of songs that mention the moon
- **BUILDING SKILLS THROUGH MUSIC** **Language** Identify words in the song text that have multiple meanings

Songs
"Yüe liang wan wan"
"Cresent Moon"
"Jasmine Flowers"
"Lahk gei mohlee"

Arts Connection *Chinese Ink Painting of Panda*

More Music Choices
"Hitotsu toya" ("Temple Bells"), p. 478

ASSESSMENT
Performance/Self-Assessment Sing and accompany one song and evaluate the performance

TECHNOLOGY/MEDIA LINK
Video Library Watch a video about Chinese music

Lesson	Elements	Skills

LESSON 7
Music and Theater

pp. 318–319

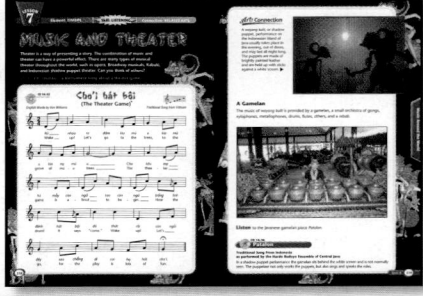

Element: Timbre
Concept: Instrumental
Focus: Time-keeping gongs of the Javanese gamelan

Secondary Element
Melody: intervals

National Standards
◆1c◆ ◆6b◆ ◆8b◆ ◆9a◆

Skill: Listening
Objective: Listen to a performance by a Javanese gamelan

Secondary Skill
• **Singing** Learn a song in English and Vietnamese and discuss

SKILLS REINFORCEMENT
• **Moving** Practice body percussion to perform with a song

LESSON 8
Musical Feelings

pp. 320–321

Element: Expression
Concept: Expressive tempo
Focus: Tempo

Secondary Element
Form: AB

National Standards
◆1c◆ ◆3c◆ ◆6b◆ ◆8b◆ ◆9a◆ ◆9c◆

Skill: Listening
Objective: Listen to a traditional song from India and identify expressive qualities

Secondary Skill
• **Reading** Discuss the melody of the song
• **Singing** Sing an open fifth drone to imitate the sound of an instrument

SKILLS REINFORCEMENT
• **Creating** Improvise a melody around a tonal center

LESSON 9
Dance of Joy

pp. 322–325

**Element:
Texture/Harmony**
Concept: Chord
Focus: I and V_7 chords

Secondary Element
Expression: tempo

National Standards
◆1c◆ ◆2c◆ ◆2d◆ ◆5c◆ ◆6c◆ ◆7b◆ ◆9a◆

Skill: Singing
Objective: Sing and accompany a folk song from Mexico using I and V_7 chords

Secondary Skills
• **Listening** Listen for chord changes in a song recording
• **Analyzing** Learn how the I and V_7 chord are built
• **Playing** Play parts with a song; create a duet between the melody and chords of a song

• **Singing** Sing and discuss the theme of the song

SKILLS REINFORCEMENT
• **Recorder** Tips to help all students perform a recorder countermelody
• **Keyboard** Play an accompaniment
• **Mallets** Play an Orff arrangement
• **Analyzing** Identify pentatonic scales

LESSON 10
Love for the Homeland

pp. 326–327

**Element:
Texture/Harmony**
Concept: Harmony
Focus: Two-part harmony

Secondary Element
Melody: pitch and direction

National Standards
◆1c◆ ◆5b◆ ◆6c◆

Skill: Singing
Objective: Sing a Spanish song in two-part harmony

Secondary Skill
• **Analyzing** Analyze the way the notes of the harmony part move

SKILLS REINFORCEMENT
• **Vocal Development** Sing a major scale in a two-part round

Connections

Music and Other Literature

Connection: Related Arts

Activity: Become acquainted with the art of Indonesian shadow puppet theater

ACROSS THE CURRICULUM **Art/Language Arts** Read books about multicultural art projects to gather ideas

CULTURAL CONNECTION **Wayang Kulit** Facts about the shadow plays

BUILDING SKILLS THROUGH MUSIC **Theatre** Develop short skits in groups

Songs
"Cho'i hát bội"
"The Theater Game"

Listening Selection *Patalon*
Arts Connection *Indonesian shadow puppets*

More Music Choices
"Meng Jian Nu," p. 194

ASSESSMENT

Music Journal Writing Listen to a selection and describe the Javanese gamelan family

TECHNOLOGY/MEDIA LINK

Web Site More information about Javanese and Balinese gamelans

---

Connection: Culture

Activity: Explore the cultural traditions that surround Indian music

ACROSS THE CURRICULUM **Social Studies** Read books about the Indian festival of lights

CULTURAL CONNECTION **"Ragupati Ragava Raja Ram"** Facts about the song

SCHOOL TO HOME CONNECTION **Cultural Exploration** Explore different kinds of ethnic foods

BUILDING SKILLS THROUGH MUSIC **Writing** Create a new title for the song

Song "Ragupati Ragava Raja Ram"

Listening Selection *Sindhi-Bhairavi*
M·U·S·I·C M·A·K·E·R·S
Ravi Shankar

More Music Choices
"Morning Has Broken," p. 29
"Simple Gifts," p. 184

ASSESSMENT

Music Journal Writing Describe the expressive qualities of the music and instruments

TECHNOLOGY/MEDIA LINK

Web Site More information about the music instruments of India

---

Connection: Culture

Activity: Discover common themes used in songs from Latin America

ACROSS THE CURRICULUM **Social Studies** Read a book about and discuss immigrants in America

CHARACTER EDUCATION **Compassion and Caring** Discuss different types of love expressed in songs

TEACHER TO TEACHER **Mallet Instruments** Use resonator bells to play a melody in a hocket ensemble

CULTURAL CONNECTION **Vihuela** Facts about the instrument

AUDIENCE ETIQUETTE **Educating the Audience** Develop a set of audience etiquette guidelines

BUILDING SKILLS THROUGH MUSIC **Social Studies** Share information about countries in Latin America

Songs
"La Jesusita" (Spanish)
"La Jesusita" (English)
"Love is on Our Side"

More Music Choices
"De colores," p. 90
"La ciudad de Juaja" ("The City of Juaja"), p. 58

ASSESSMENT

Performance/Peer Critique Sing and accompany in groups using the I and V₇ chords

TECHNOLOGY/MEDIA LINK

MIDI/Sequencing Software Use the MIDI file to identify the chord changes

---

Connection: Culture

Activity: Explore the history and culture of Mexico

TEACHER TO TEACHER **Assigning Voice Parts** Tips for grouping students for voice parts

CULTURAL CONNECTION **Mexican History and Culture** Read books about the history and culture of Mexico

BUILDING SKILLS THROUGH MUSIC **Language** Identify phrases in the song text where the singer describes feelings

Songs
"Canción Mixteca"
"Mixteca Song"

More Music Choices
"De colores," p. 90
"Qué bonita bandera" ("What a Beautiful Banner!"), p. 294
"Río, río" ("River, River"), p. 370

ASSESSMENT

Performance/Observation Sing the song in two-part harmony

TECHNOLOGY/MEDIA LINK

Web Site More information about the music of Mexico

UNIT 8 INTRODUCTION

INTRODUCING THE UNIT

Unit 8 presents a thematic approach to understanding music elements. This unit will expand students' knowledge of music through lively dance rhythms from the Caribbean, songs from the Middle East, and instruments from Asia. Presented on p. 291 is a brief overview of the skills that are assessed in this unit. (See below and pp. 292–293 for unit highlights of related curricular experiences.)

For a more detailed unit overview, see Unit at a Glance, pp. 289a–289f.

UNIT PROJECT

Unit 8 is about celebrating things that make us different and the things that bring us together through music. Because so much of multicultural education emphasizes the differences, this unit can be a good opportunity to stress the connections—those things that bind us together as human beings.

Invite students to organize a multimedia project that emphasizes the connections among cultures.

Have students

• Learn the songs in the unit focusing on the themes of each lesson. Bring examples from their own cultural background.

• Take the themes of each lesson (clapping, dancing, story songs, singing games, and so on) and build a multi-media presentation highlighting some or all of these connections.

The multimedia presentations can be in a number of forms such as a video presentation or a museum-type installation or display.

Distant Lands

Let's travel beyond our borders—around the world. We'll sing folk songs in Spanish, dance a few Middle Eastern dances, play an African game, visit an Indonesian shadow puppet play, and listen to a world-renowned sitarist from India.

▼ Bagpiper

Israeli Folk dancers dressed in traditional costume ▼

▲ Accordion (left) and maraca players

290

ACROSS THE CURRICULUM

Unit Highlights The following interdisciplinary activities in this unit are related to the music elements presented in the lessons. See Unit at a Glance, pp. 289a–289f, for topical descriptions presented according to lesson sequence.

▶ **ART**

• Make a simple spike fiddle (p. 310)
• Collect pictures of nature and moon shapes in art and use them in various creative projects (p. 316)

▶ **LANGUAGE ARTS**

• Share books on Chinese painting (p. 315)
• Read books about multicultural art projects to gather ideas (p. 318)

▶ **SCIENCE**

• Read a book about a group of young American students who travel the Amazon rain forest (p. 305)
• Discover facts about the construction of a violin (p. 312)

▶ **SOCIAL STUDIES**

• Learn about the flags of different countries and a famous Puerto Rican sports superstar (p. 295)
• Discuss and research the settlement of Israel in the 1940's (p. 298)
• Read about the people, art, and customs of Ghana (p. 308)
• Learn about the Indian festival of lights (p. 320)
• Discuss the struggles of immigrant groups (p. 322)

Music Around the World

Let us travel to new places and explore new musical traditions. We will celebrate the things that make us different, and focus on what brings us together through music.

Ravi Shankar performing on the *sitar* ▼

MUSIC SKILLS
ASSESSED IN THIS UNIT

Reading Music: Rhythm

- Read and clap rhythms to accompany a song (p. 297)
- Read, tap, and say the rhythms in a Spanish song (p. 304)

Reading Music: Pitch

- Practice a three-part song using pitch syllables (p. 301)
- Read and identify identical phrases in a song (p. 306)

Performing Music: Singing

- Sing a song from Puerto Rico (p. 297)
- Sing a multicultural song during a class performance (p. 307)

Moving to Music

- Perform the *hora* and *debky* (p. 300)
- Perform a movement routine with a Native American selection (p. 303)

Performing Music: Playing

- Perform a rhythm accompaniment with a class performance (p. 307)
- Accompany a song during a class performance (p. 317)
- Accompany a class performance of a Spanish song (p. 325)

Creating Music

- Improvise accompaniment patterns (p. 316)
- Create a pentatonic accompaniment (p. 317)

Listening to Music

- Listen to an orchestral selection and follow a listening map (p. 313)
- Listen to a gamelan selection and describe the instrument sound (p. 319)

CULTURAL CONNECTION

Unit Highlights The musical literature in this unit provides many opportunities for students to explore a variety of world cultures. See Unit at a Glance, pp. 289a–289f, for topical descriptions presented according to lesson sequence.

▶ AFRICAN/AFRICAN AMERICAN

- Discover facts about the Akan of Ghana (p. 308)

▶ ASIAN

- Discuss facts about the Mandarin dialect (p. 314)
- Learn about the bamboo plant (p. 317)
- Discuss history and facts about the *wayang kulit* (p. 318)
- Explore the meaning of a traditional Indian song (p. 320)

▶ EUROPEAN

- Discuss the origins and history of the *vihuela* (p. 324)

▶ LATIN AMERICAN

- Discover history and facts about Puerto Rico (p. 294)
- Learn about the geography and natural wonders of Venezuela (p. 304)
- Explore the geography of Columbia (p. 307)
- Explore books about the history and culture of Mexico (p. 326)

▶ MIDDLE EASTERN

- Explore facts about modern day Egypt (p. 297)
- Learn about the background and origins of Israel (p. 298)

▶ NATIVE AMERICAN

- Discover facts about the Haliwa-Saponi (p. 302)

OPENING ACTIVITIES

MATERIALS

- "Beyond Borders"   **CD 13-18**
  Recording Routine:
  Intro (5 m.); v. 1; v. 2; coda

Listening

Invite students to listen to "Beyond Borders" **CD 13-18** as they follow the notation in their books. Discuss with students what they believe the song is about.

Reading

Ask students to look at the notation and

- Locate the *D.C., Coda,* and double bars.
- Identify where the time signature changes from meter in 4 to meter in 6.
- Identify melodic phrases that are the same or similar. (mm. 5–8 and mm. 1–4 are similar: the phrases are similar in lines 4, 5, and 6 of the last three lines)

Many Voices Singing

Sing "Beyond Borders," a song that describes the power of music to unite people across time and distance.

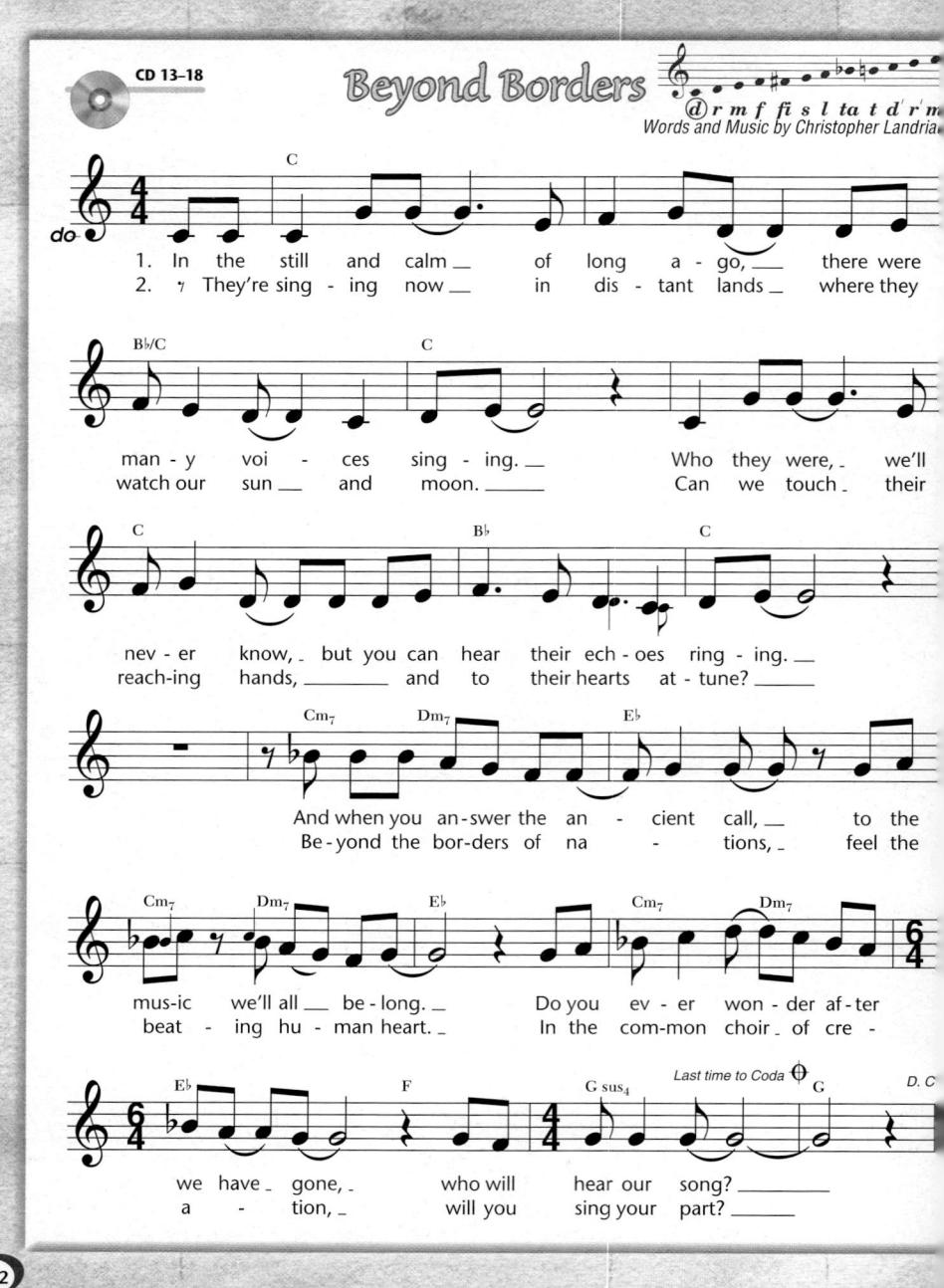

ASSESSMENT

Unit Highlights This unit includes a variety of strategies and methods, described below, to track students' progress and assess their understanding of lesson objectives.

▶ **INFORMAL ASSESSMENTS**

At the close of each Teacher's Edition lesson in this unit, one of the following types of assessments is used to evaluate the learning of the key element focus or skill objective.

- Music Journal Writing (pp. 313, 319, 321)
- Performance/Observation (pp. 301, 309, 327)
- Performance/Peer Critique (p. 325)
- Performance/Self-Assessment (pp. 297, 307, 317)

▶ **RUBRICS**

Visit *www.sfsuccessnet.com* for rubrics to assess students' achievement in music skills.

Singing

Point out to students that the first four measures of the melody are repeated. Help them to read and count the syncopated rhythms in the last line on p. 292.

After students have learned p. 292, ask them to look at p. 293 and sing the last three lines. Discuss with students how the lines are similar and different from the last three lines on p. 293. This similar-but-different theme can be a metaphor for the whole unit.

Have students learn the *Coda* and then sing the entire song with the recording **CD 13-18**.

Coda

For mu-sic is __ to hu-man-i-ty, like

twink-ling is __ to a star, __ and the sec-rets held __ in the songs __

__ we sing __ shine light on who we are. ___

Bey-ond the bor-ders of na - tions, _ feel the

beat-ing hu-man heart. _ In the com-mon choir _ of cre -

a - tion, _ will you sing your part? _____

Unit 8 293

INNOVATIVE TEACHER SUPPORT FOR THIS UNIT

- **MAKING MUSIC DVD, Grade 5** contains video segments that support lessons, including signing and movement.
- **MAKING MUSIC with Movement and Dance** provides more opportunities for large group activities in music or physical education classes.
- **MAKING MUSIC with Technology** provides lesson plans for many technology applications; includes MIDI files.
- *¡A cantar!* features recorded songs and lessons from around the Spanish-speaking world; includes strategies for bilingual classes and for English-speaking teachers working with Spanish-speaking students.
- **Bridges to Asia** features recorded songs and lessons from Asian and Pacific region cultures.
- *www.sfsuccessnet.com* provides an online lesson planner to conveniently create lesson plans at school or at home. Includes rubrics for assessment, lesson modifications to meet the needs of all students, performance musicals based on program content, and more.

TECHNOLOGY/MEDIA LINK

Unit Highlights The following components are used in this unit to reinforce and expand students' understanding of music elements and related themes. See Unit at a Glance, pp. 289a–289f, for a descriptive listing according to lesson sequence.

▶ MIDI/SEQUENCING SOFTWARE

- Experiment with tempo using a MIDI File (p. 301)
- Explore MIDI sounds and select timbres for each track (p. 307)
- Use a MIDI file to accompany a song (p. 325)

▶ TRANSPARENCY

- Use a transparency to help students follow a listening map (p. 313)

▶ VIDEO LIBRARY/DVD

- View a video showcasing West African percussion ensembles (p. 309)
- Show a video highlighting two traditional Chinese instruments (p. 317)

▶ WEB SITE

- Go to *www.sfsuccessnet.com* for more about music and folk instruments of Latin America and the Middle East (p. 297); Javanese and Balinese gamelans (p. 319); instruments of India (p. 321); music of Mexico (p. 327)

LESSON AT A GLANCE

Element Focus **RHYTHM** Rhythm patterns from Latin America and the Middle East

Skill Objective **MOVING** Perform a Latin American song with rhythmic clapping

Connection Activity **CULTURE** Explore Puerto Rican and Arabic cultural traditions

MATERIALS

- *"¡Qué bonita bandera!"*   **CD 13-20**
- *"What a Beautiful Banner!"*   **CD 13-21**

  Recording Routine: Intro (8 m.); verse; refrain; interlude (8 m.); refrain; coda

- *"Ah ya Zane"*   **CD 13-26**
- *"Zane from Abedeen"*   **CD 13-27**

  Recording Routine: Intro (4 m.); vocal; interlude (3 m.); vocal

- *Río de la miel*   **CD 13-25**
- **Pronunciation Practice/Translation** p. 532
- **Resource Book** pp. A-24, A-26, F-37, H-22
- claves, drums, guitar

VOCABULARY

flamenco

◆ ◆ ◆ ◆ National Standards ◆ ◆ ◆ ◆

1c Sing music from diverse cultures
1d Sing music written in two parts
2c Perform instrumental music from diverse cultures
6b Listen and analyze uses of rhythm in music from diverse cultures
7a Students evaluate the music they perform
8b Identify ways music relates to social studies
9a Describe characteristics of music genres from a variety of cultures

MORE MUSIC CHOICES

For more practice with Latin American rhythm:
"Se va el caiman" ("The Alligator"), p. 306

Move to the Music

All around the world, people clap interesting rhythms as they sing. Clapping or tapping your fingers is like dancing with your hands—something you can do even when you can't get up and move around.

Clap the strong beats as you **sing** "*¡Qué bonita bandera!*", a lively song about the flag of Puerto Rico.

CD 13–20

¡Qué bonita bandera!
(What a Beautiful Banner!)

English Words by Samuel Maqui   *Folk Song from Puerto Rico*

A - zul, blan - ca y___ co - lo - ra - da, y en el
Blue and white and red __ are the col - ors, with a

me - dio tie - ne un es - tre - lla. Bo - ni - ta, se -
pure white star in the cen - ter. A beau - ti - ful

ñor - es, es la ban - de - ra Puer - to - ri - que - ña.
ban - ner is the flag of our Puer - to Ri - co!

REFRAIN

¡Qué bo - ni - ta ban - de - ra! ¡Qué bo - ni - ta ban - de - ra!
What a beau - ti - ful ban - ner! What a beau - ti - ful ban - ner!

¡Qué bo - ni - ta ban - de - ra es la ban - de - ra Puer - to - ri - que - ña!
What a beau - ti - ful ban - ner is the flag of our Puer - to Ri - co!

294

Footnotes

CULTURAL CONNECTION

8b ▶ **Puerto Rico** Puerto Rico is a possession of the United States, and its capital is San Juan. Juan Ponce de Leon claimed Puerto Rico for Spain in 1508, and it remained Spanish until the United States took over in 1898. Puerto Rico's population is almost entirely Hispanic. Spanish is the major language, although English is a required second language. There are about 2.7 million Puerto Ricans living on the U.S. mainland.

BUILDING SKILLS THROUGH MUSIC

▶ **Social Studies** Have students sing *"¡Qué bonita bandera!"* **CD 13-20**. Discuss the flag of Puerto Rico. Ask students to draw the flag. Have them research and draw on the opposite side of their paper flag(s) from where they were born or where their ancestors were born.

TEACHER TO TEACHER

▶ **Clapping** Students love to clap loudly. Invite them to experiment with the sounds of different kinds of clapping, including

- One-finger claps
- Two fingers into the palm
- Cupped-hand claps
- Partial-hand claps

Have students describe the volume and sound of each kind of clap. Then allow them to choose different kinds of clapping for different purposes. Suggest that the volume of the clapping be lower than the volume of singing.

Fun with Rhythm

"*¡Qué bonita bandera!*" features a lively Puerto Rican rhythm typical of the islands of the Caribbean. The underlying eighth notes in this piece are grouped as 3 + 3 + 2, instead of the usual 4 + 4. Pay special attention to the accents as you **perform** these patterns.

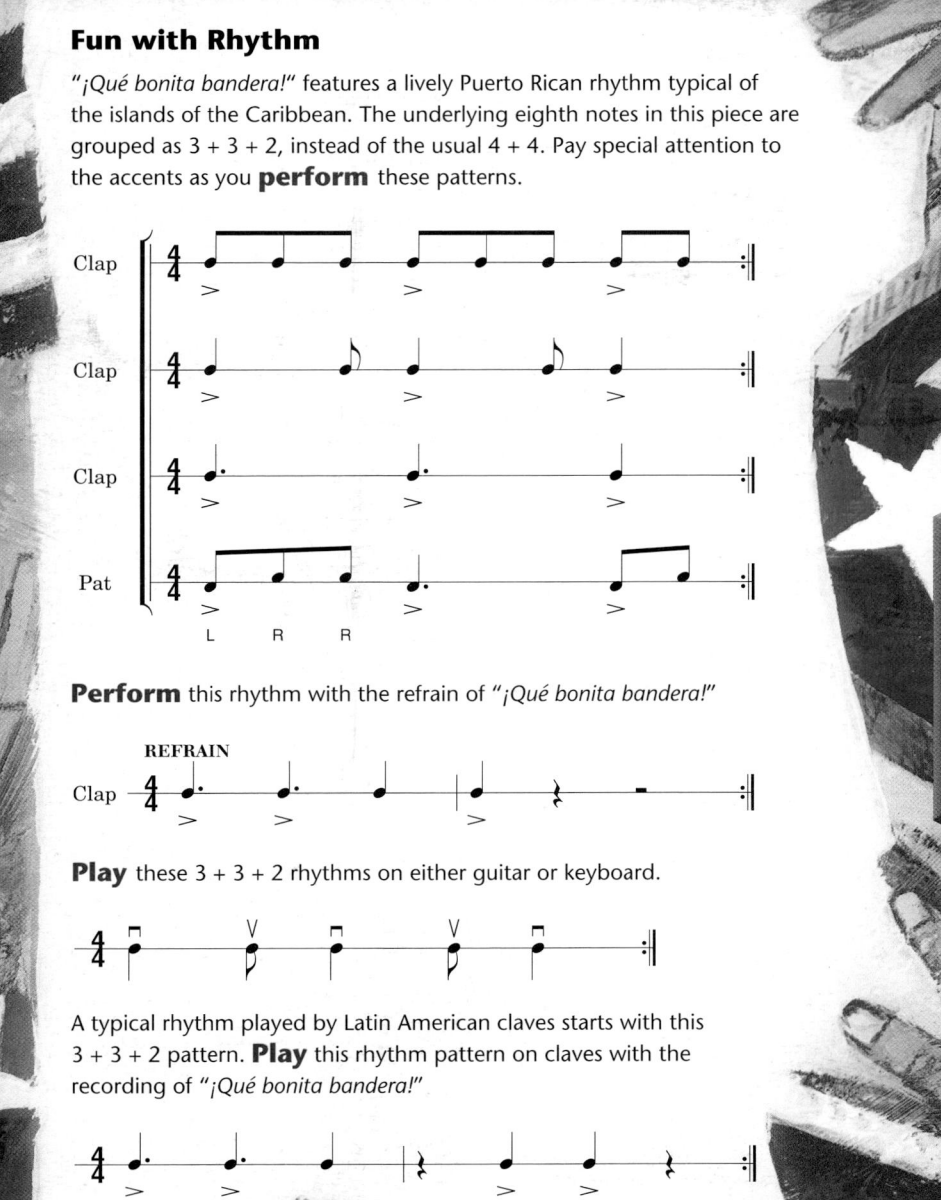

Perform this rhythm with the refrain of "*¡Qué bonita bandera!*"

Play these 3 + 3 + 2 rhythms on either guitar or keyboard.

A typical rhythm played by Latin American claves starts with this 3 + 3 + 2 pattern. **Play** this rhythm pattern on claves with the recording of "*¡Qué bonita bandera!*"

Unit 8 295

continued on page 296

1 INTRODUCE

Ask students to think about music that is so alive that they can hardly sit still—that invites them to tap their toes, clap their hands, get up, and dance or sway to the music. Introduce the idea that these are just some of the ways people all over the world respond to music.

2 DEVELOP

Moving

Have students

- Read about rhythms on p. 295.
- Clap a steady, even beat while listening to "*¡Qué bonita bandera!*" **CD 13-20.**
- Clap the accented eighth-note exercises on p. 295, saying "1-2-3, 1-2-3, 1-2" as they clap.
- Pat the left-right rhythm on their thighs.
- Divide into three equal groups and do the top three lines of rhythms as a round twice through.
- Contrast this with the usual grouping of eight eighth notes (4 + 4) by clapping those patterns.
- Divide into two groups: group 1 pats even quarter notes on thighs while group 2 claps the top three lines; then switch roles.
- Clap the rhythm labeled *Refrain* and perform it with the recording of "*¡Qué bonita bandera!*"

 ## SKILLS REINFORCEMENT

▶ **Guitar** To accompany "*¡Qué bonita bandera!*" beginning guitar students will find it easier to capo at fret 3 and play the following chord substitutes:

- Cm = Am
- G_7 = E_7
- Fm = Dm

▶ **Mallets** An Orff arrangement for "*Ah ya Zane*" can be found in the Resource Book, p. F-37.

ACROSS THE CURRICULUM

▶ **Social Studies** Students will enjoy learning about the flags of many countries in *The World of Flags* by William Crampton (Rand McNally & Co., 1994). Ask students to make a large painted or construction paper reproduction of the Puerto Rican flag to use in performances of "*¡Qué bonita bandera!*" and include student narration about the meaning of the flag's color and design.

Invite interested students to read about the life of a famous Puerto Rican sports superstar in *Pride of Puerto Rico: The Life of Roberto Clemente* by Paul Robert Walker (Harcourt Brace, 1991).

Lesson 1 Continued

Singing

Refer to Cultural Connection, p. 294, and share information about Puerto Rico with the class. See Across the Curriculum, p. 295, for a project idea involving the Puerto Rican flag.

Have students

• Learn the Spanish-language refrain to *"¡Qué bonita bandera!"* by using the Pronunciation Practice Track **CD 13-23**. Refer to Pronunciation Practice Guide on Resource Book p. A-24.

• Sing the refrain and add the clapping pattern.

• Sing the entire melody, with clapping on the refrain, along with **CD 13-20**.

• Learn the harmony part for the refrain using the Pronunciation Practice Track **CD 13-24**; then sing the refrain with both parts and clapping.

• Sing the entire song with the recording.

Playing

Encourage students to accompany *"¡Qué bonita bandera!"* with *claves* (or other nonpitched percussion instruments) and the guitar strum shown on p. 295. See also Skills Reinforcement below for additional playing activities.

Listening

Invite students to listen to the clapping and dancing rhythms in the flamenco selection, *Río de la miel* **CD 13-25** on p. 296.

Fiery Footwork

The flamenco dance is one of Spain's best-known cultural traditions. Clapping is an important element. **Listen** to this exciting flamenco performance of *Río de la miel*. Do you hear the overlapping rhythms of the clapping hands and stomping feet?

M·U·S·I·C M·A·K·E·R·S

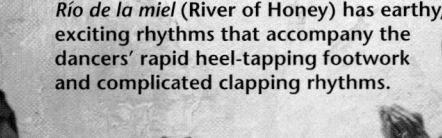

Francisco Sánchez Gómez

Francisco Sánchez Gómez (born 1947), better known as Paco de Lucía, is considered to be one of the greatest living flamenco guitarists. Introduced by his father to the flamenco guitar style, he showed an early understanding of the music. Gómez began to play professionally at the age of thirteen. By the beginning of the 1970s, he was known the world over. In 1975 he gave a famous concert at the Royal Theater in Madrid.

 **CD 13-25**
Río de la miel

written and performed by Francisco Sánchez Gómez

Río de la miel (River of Honey) has earthy, exciting rhythms that accompany the dancers' rapid heel-tapping footwork and complicated clapping rhythms.

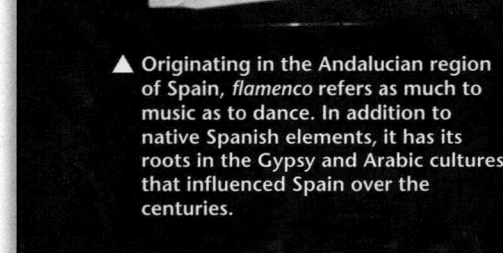

▲ Originating in the Andalucian region of Spain, *flamenco* refers as much to music as to dance. In addition to native Spanish elements, it has its roots in the Gypsy and Arabic cultures that influenced Spain over the centuries.

296

Footnotes

SKILLS REINFORCEMENT

▶ **Keyboard** See Resource Book, p. H-22, for a keyboard part to accompany *"¡Qué bonita bandera!"*

▶ **Recorder** Students can play this 3 + 3 + 2 countermelody during the refrain of *"¡Qué bonita bandera!"*

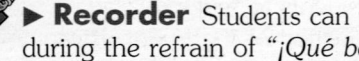
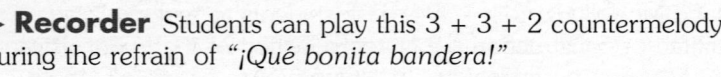

MEETING INDIVIDUAL NEEDS

▶ **Performing** Use the following suggestions to help all students perform the hand claps in *"Ah ya Zane."*

Reinforcement Some students may not be able to move their arms well enough to clap to the beat of the song. Have these students pat with one hand on his or her leg, rather than clap two hands.

On Target Most students will be able to clap with both hands. These students can perform the hand claps in the song as written.

Challenge Interested students may be invited to improvise a hand clap pattern to accompany the last line of the song.

A Different Rhythm

This lively dance song from Cairo, Egypt, includes a simple clapping pattern performed at face level.

Sing "Ah ya Zane."

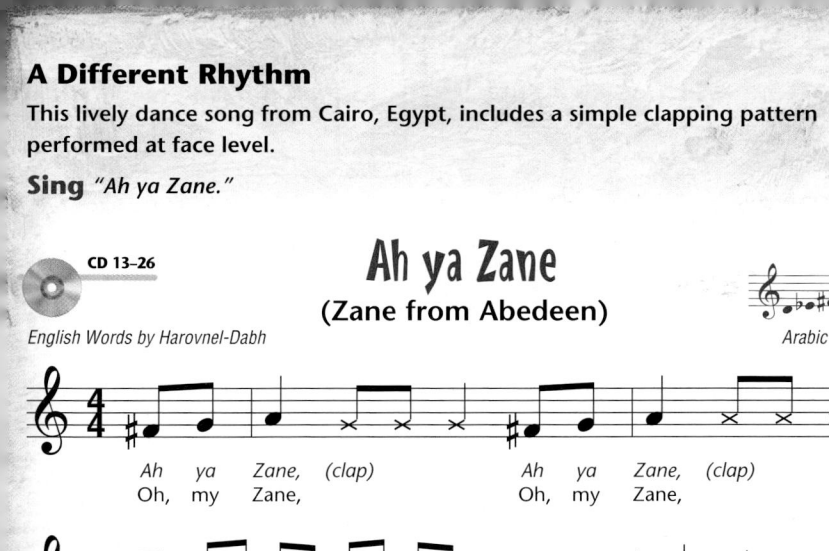

CD 13–26

Ah ya Zane
(Zane from Abedeen)

English Words by Harovnel-Dabh

Arabic Folk Song

Ah ya Zane, (clap)   Ah ya Zane, (clap)
Oh, my Zane,   Oh, my Zane,

Ah ya Zane _ el __ A - be - deen; (clap)   Ya ward, (clap)
Oh, my Zane _ el __ A - be - deen;   Come walk,

Ya __ ward - im - fet - tah, bay - nil - ba - sa - teen.
Come _ walk _ in the gar - den, walk _ in the gar - den with me.

The Arabic *doumbek* part in "Ah ya Zane" is named *baladi*. **Play** this drum part to accompany the song.

High
Low

The *doumbek* (also spelled *dumbek*) can be heard in the recording of "Ah ya Zane." The instrument gets its name from the low tone ("doum") in the center of the drum and the high sharp tone ("bek" or "tek") played on the edge of the drum. ▶

Music Around the World

Unit 8   **297**

Singing

Introduce "Ah ya Zane" by explaining that singing, clapping, and moving are also an important part of music-making in the Middle East. Point out that "Ah ya Zane" is an Arabic song from Egypt; then share with students the information about Egypt in Cultural Connection below.

Have students

- Listen to the recording of "Ah ya Zane" **CD 13-25** and follow the melody and lyrics in their books. (You may wish to have them clap where indicated in the music.)

- Use the Pronunciation Practice Track **CD 13-29** to learn the Arabic words. Refer to Pronunciation Practice Guide in Resource Book, p. A-26.

1c
- Sing and clap "Ah ya Zane" with the recording.

Playing

2c Teach students how to play the *baladi* rhythm on the *doumbek*. If a *doumbek* is not available, substitute other drums such as bongos or two hand drums that produce low and high pitches.

Have students play the *doumbek* part along with the singing and clapping of "Ah ya Zane."

Singing

Invite students to perform expressively, first from notation and then from memory, music from diverse cultures. Have them perform "¡Que bonita bandera!," then "Ah ya Zane" with appropriate instrumental parts.

3 CLOSE

Element: RHYTHM   **ASSESSMENT**

1c
1d **Performance/Self-Assessment** Divide the class into two groups. Have one group sing "¡Qué bonita bandera!" while the other group claps selected rhythms
7a from p. 295. Then allow groups to switch. After each performance, discuss with students the accuracy of their rhythmic clapping.

CULTURAL CONNECTION

8b ▶ **Modern Day Egypt** Egypt is the most populous nation in the Arab world. After Nigeria, it is the second most populous country in Africa. Cairo, Egypt's capital, is the largest city in both Africa and the Middle East. The fertile Nile River valley and delta is home to 99 percent of the Egyptian population. Arabic is the official language, spoken by almost all Egyptians. Most Egyptians are Sunni Muslims, but other religious groups include Coptic Christians, Greek Orthodox, Roman Catholics, and Jews.

SCHOOL TO HOME CONNECTION

▶ **Culture** Find out which families in your school and community have connections to Spanish and Arabic language and culture. Plan a special "Music Around the World" concert with families setting up cultural information tables as a bazaar before the concert and during intermission.

TECHNOLOGY/MEDIA LINK

9a
Web Site Go to *www.sfsuccessnet.com* to learn more about the music and folk instruments of Latin America and the Middle East.

LESSON AT A GLANCE

Element Focus **MELODY** Pitch syllables

Skill Objective **SINGING** Sightread a song using pitch syllables

Connection Activity **RELATED ARTS** Learn to dance an Arabic line dance and an Israeli circle dance

MATERIALS

- *"Tzena, tzena"*   CD 13-30

  Recording Routine: Intro (4 m.); Hebrew verse; interlude (8 m.); Arabic verse; interlude (8 m.); English verse

- **Resource Book** p. A-27
- **Pronunciation Practice/Translation** p. 533
- **Dance Directions** for *"Tzena, tzena"* p. 562
- *Ala Da'lona*   CD 14-1
- **Dance Directions** for *Ala Da'lona* p. 563

VOCABULARY

hora   debky

◆ ◆ ◆ ◆ **National Standards** ◆ ◆ ◆ ◆

1c Sing music from diverse cultures
2a Play instruments accurately alone and in small ensembles
2d Perform simple accompaniments by ear
5a Read whole notes, half notes, quarter notes in duple meter
6b Listen and analyze uses of form in music from diverse cultures
6c Understand and use basic principles of chords in music analysis
8b Identify ways music relates to social studies

MORE MUSIC CHOICES

For more practice singing songs in Hebrew:
"Dundai," p. 106

For more practice singing songs in Arabic:
"Ah ya Zane" ("Zane from Abedeen"), p. 297

DANCING in Friendship

In 1998, in anticipation of the fiftieth anniversary of the birth of Israel, the well-known song "Tzena, tzena" was remade to promote peace in the Middle East by changing the English verse and adding verses in both Hebrew and Arabic.

Sing "Tzena, tzena" in English. Then learn both the Hebrew and the Arabic verses.

CD 13–30
MIDI 21

TZENA, TZENA

Hebrew Words by Yehlel Haggiz   English Words by Gordon Jenkins
Arabic Words by Salman Natour   (with one line altered by Pete Seeger)
Music by Issachar Miron

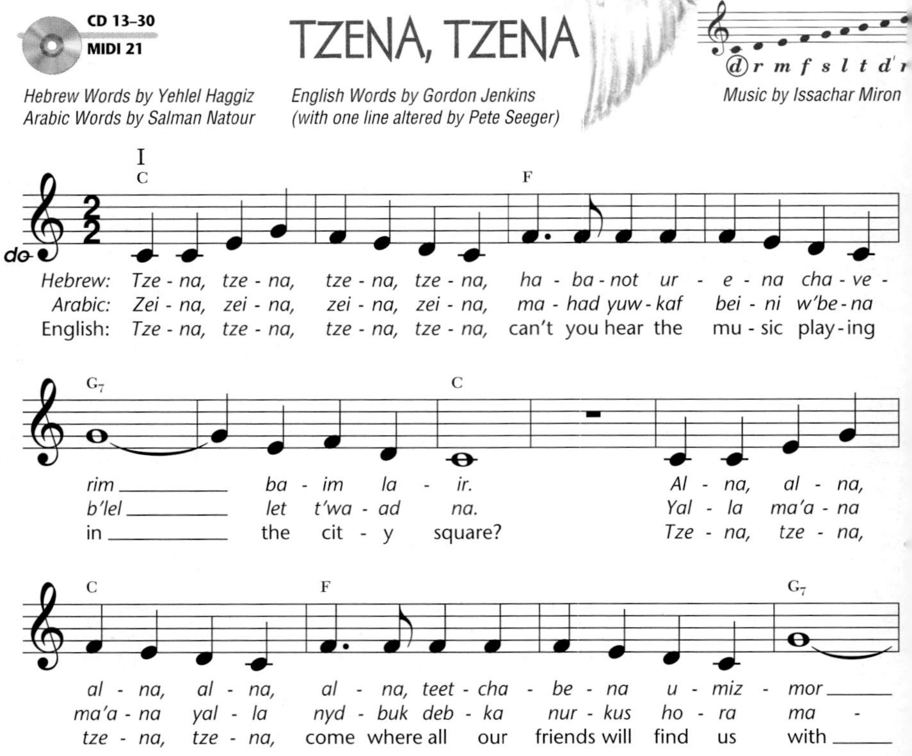

Hebrew: Tze - na, tze - na, tze - na, tze - na, ha - ba - not ur - e - na cha - ve -
Arabic: Zei - na, zei - na, zei - na, zei - na, ma - had yuw - kaf bei - ni w'be - na
English: Tze - na, tze - na, tze - na, tze - na, can't you hear the mu - sic play - ing

rim ___ ba - im la - ir. Al - na, al - na,
b'lel ___ let t'wa - ad na. Yal - la ma'a - na
in ___ the cit - y square? Tze - na, tze - na,

al - na, al - na, al - na, teet - cha - be - na u - miz - mor ___
ma'a - na yal - la nyd - buk deb - ka nur - kus ho - ra ma ___
tze - na, tze - na, come where all our friends will find us with ___

298

Footnotes

ACROSS THE CURRICULUM

8b ▶ **Social Studies** *"Tzena, tzena"* is a folk song and dance about the building of the nation of Israel in the late 1940s. Ask students to research the settlement of this new country in an ancient land. Who came to Israel? How did the immigrants travel to their new home? What were some of the challenges of establishing a new homeland? What other groups of people live in Israel and the surrounding countries?

BUILDING SKILLS THROUGH MUSIC

▶ **Language** Ask students to read the English lyrics of *"Tzena, tzena"* and describe the feelings of the singers. Have students identify phrases from the song that support their responses. Divide the class into groups to plan a performance that expresses the mood of the song by changes in dynamics and tempo.

CULTURAL CONNECTION

8b ▶ **Israel** In 1998, Israel celebrated the fiftieth anniversary of its founding as a modern state in 1948. *"Tzena, tzena"* was remade with both Hebrew and Arabic lyrics to promote peace in the Middle East. After Israel was established as a homeland for Jews, immigrants came from all parts of the world—one of the largest groups coming from the former Soviet Union. The non-Jewish population of Israel (approximately 15 percent) consists mainly of Arabs. Israel has recently been in negotiation with the Palestine Liberation Organization over a homeland for Palestinians. The official languages of Israel are Hebrew and Arabic, although languages such as English and Russian are commonly spoken in homes.

(Musical notation for "Tzena, tzena" with lyrics in three languages — Hebrew transliteration, Hebrew, and English)

Section II

yach - dav na - shir. Tze - na, tze - na,
- 'as ad na. Zei - na, zei - na,
the danc - ers there. Tze - na, tze - na,

ha - ba - not ur - e - na cha - ve - rim ba - im la - ir.
yal - la ghan - nu ma'a - na ah - lan bi - kom ya - as - ha -
join the cel - e - bra - tion, there'll be peo - ple there from ev - 'ry

Al - na, al - na, al - na, teet - cha - be - na
- ab. Zei - na, zei - na, yal - la rud - du ma'a - na
na - tion. Dawn will find us laugh - ing in the sun - light,

Section III

u - miz - mor yach - dav na shir. Tze - na,
yal - la ya kul lell - ah bab. Zei - na,
danc - ing in the cit - y square. Tze - na,

tze - na, (clap) tze - na, tze - na, tze - na, tze - na, tze - na,
zei - na, nur - kus ho - ra nyd - buk deb - ka yal - la
tze - na, come and dance the ho - ra, dance the deb - ka,

tze - na, tze - na, tze - na, tze - na, Tze - na, tze - na, (clap) tze - na,
hu - bi ad u' - ma ba - ad - na Zei - na, zei - na, ghan - nu
sing with me, we'll dance to - geth - er. Tze - na, tze - na, when the

tze - na, tze - na, tze - na, tze - na, tze - na, tze - na, tze - na!
ma'a - na ghan - nu ma'a - na, ghan - nu zei - na, zei - na, zei - na!
band is play - ing, my heart's say - ing: Tze - na, tze - na, tze - na!

Unit 8 **299**

1 INTRODUCE

8b **SAY** One of the great ways of bridging cultural gaps is to involve people in cultural exchanges or art festivals where they come to realize that they have more in common than they may have thought. This version of *"Tzena, tzena"* is just such an attempt.

Share with students the background information on *"Tzena, tzena"* and Israel in Across the Curriculum and Cultural Connection, p. 298.

2 DEVELOP

Singing

Play the recording of *"Tzena, tzena"* **CD 13-30** and have students follow along in their books.

6b **ASK** Which phrases of the melody of *"Tzena, tzena"* repeat? (Each section—ABA—has a second half that repeats.)

What key is *"Tzena, tzena"* **in?** (C major)

5a Have students

- Review the pitch syllables used in the song.
- Sightread the melody of *"Tzena, tzena,"* using pitch syllables.
- Sing the English words to *"Tzena, tzena"* with the recording.
- Learn the Hebrew lyrics by listening to and echoing the Pronunciation Practice Track **CD 13-34.**

1c - Practice the Hebrew lyrics at slower tempos, then sing the Hebrew lyrics with the recording.
- Learn the Arabic lyrics by listening to and echoing the Pronunciation Practice Track **CD 13-35.** (Refer to the Pronunciation Practice Guide or Resource Book p. A-27.)

continued on page 300

SKILLS REINFORCEMENT

6c ▶ **Analyzing** Use the structure of melody and chords in *"Tzena, tzena"* to teach or reinforce students' knowledge of chords and chord functions.

- Show students how the triad built on the first note of the scale (I) is outlined in measure 1. Then show them how to play it on a keyboard, using fingers 1, 3, and 5.
- Transfer this chord knowledge and playing position to the F chord (IV) built on the fourth note of the scale.
- Transfer this chord knowledge and playing position to the G chord (V) built on the fifth note of the scale.

MOVEMENT

▶ **Patterned Dance** The *hora* came to Israel in the early twentieth century, when the land was called Palestine (Israel became a nation in 1948). The *hora* was brought by settlers from Romania, where they enjoyed popular circle dances. In fact, the word *hora* means "circle dance." The Israeli *hora* was originally done in closed circles with hands joined with neighbors' hands and held down at the sides ("V" position) or on neighbors' shoulders ("T" position). In Israel, the traditional *hora* moves to the left (clockwise), although nowadays *horas* can move in either direction. The steps are high and joyous, with leaps and kicks.

For Dance Directions, see p. 562.

Unit 8 *Music Around the World* **299**

- Practice the Arabic lyrics at slower tempos, then sing the Arabic lyrics with the recording.

1c
- Sing *"Tzena, tzena"* **CD 13-30** in all three languages with the recording.

- Divide into three groups and sing *"Tzena, tzena"* **CD 13-32** in English as a round.

Moving

Invite students to perform movement from diverse cultures. Ask them to follow the Dance Directions pp. 300–301 and dance the *hora* with *"Tzena, tzena"* and the *debky* (also called *debke, dubka,* or *debka*) with the recording of *Ala Da'lona* **CD 14-1.** See Movement, below, and on p. 299 for more information on the dances.

Playing

2d
Encourage students to accompany *"Tzena, tzena"* on guitar. See Teacher to Teacher, below, for a helpful performance suggestion.

Two Cultures Shake Hands . . .

The *hora* and the *debky* are dances that come from people who live in the Middle East. The steps are quite similar, but there are some interesting differences in style.

Listen to *"Tzena, tzena"* and dance the *hora*.

How to Dance the Hora

The *hora* came to Israel in the early twentieth century when the land was called Palestine. The word *hora* means "circle dance"; the traditional *hora* moves to the left (clockwise). The steps are high and joyous, with leaps and kicks.

1. Step left.
2. Step right (in front or in back of left foot).
3. Step left.

4. Lift right foot and swing it slightly to the left.
5. Step right.
6. Repeat step 4. Then repeat steps 1–6.

300

Footnotes

MOVEMENT

8b ▶ **Patterned Dance** The *debky* is one of the most common dances of the Arabic people who live in Lebanon, Jordan and Syria, as well as the Palestinian people. The word means *line dance,* and traditional *debkas* are often done in short lines. Hands are generally joined down at the side, while dancers move shoulder to shoulder in a tight formation to the right (counterclockwise). Although the step pattern is almost the same as the Israeli *hora, debky* steps are more up-and-down, as well as sharp and powerful, with stamps and knee movements.

For Dance Directions, *see* p. 563.

TEACHER TO TEACHER

2d ▶ **Guitar Chords** To accompany *"Tzena, tzena,"* beginning guitar students will find it easier to capo at fret 3 and play the following chord substitutes:

- C = A
- G_7 = E_7
- F = D

. . . and Dance

The *debky*, which means "line dance," is one of the most common dances of the Arabic people.

Listen to *Ala Da'lona*, form a line, join hands, and dance!

CD 14–1
Ala Da'lona

Arabic Folk Song

This recording also features the *oud* [ood], a string instrument that has been used in the Middle East for more than 1,000 years.

How to Dance the Debky

The *debky* is often performed in short lines. Hands are generally joined down at the side, with dancers moving shoulder to shoulder in a tight formation to the right. The *debky* steps are up-and-down, with stamps and knee movements.

1. Step right.
2. Step left (in front or in back of right foot).
3. Step right.

4. Step right foot (in place) and stamp left foot (next to right).
5. Step left.
6. Repeat step 4. Then repeat steps 1–6.

Unit 8 **301**

3 CLOSE

Skill: SINGING — **ASSESSMENT**

1c **Performance/Observation** Divide the class into three groups: Part I, Part II, and Part III. Have each **5a** group perform its section of *"Tzena, tzena"* using pitch syllables. Then have students perform the song as a three-part partner song (in which each group repeats its part only) or as a three-part round. Encourage students to use the Hebrew, Arabic, and English text. Observe students for pitch accuracy.

SKILLS REINFORCEMENT

▶ **Recorder** Students can play a countermelody on their recorders to accompany *"Tzena, tzena"* as others sing and **2a** dance. Have them feel two beats in each measure as they play. Remind students to move their fingers together when playing leaps. More advanced recorder players should try playing Part II of the song melody.

SCHOOL TO HOME CONNECTION

▶ **Community Involvement** Invite community resource people to share information about Israeli and Arabic cultures. An additional project might include sampling traditional Middle Eastern foods made by parents or supplied by community resources.

TECHNOLOGY/MEDIA LINK

MIDI/Sequencing Software Add excitement to dancing the *hora* and the *debky* by gradually increasing the tempo. Open the MIDI song file of *"Tzena, tzena"* and set the file to repeat continuously. Start with a slow tempo, then increase it as students become more proficient.

Unit 8 *Music Around the World* **301**

LESSON AT A GLANCE

Element Focus **RHYTHM** Rhythm patterns

Skill Objective **SINGING** Sing songs that include repeated rhythm patterns

Connection Activity **LANGUAGE ARTS** Become familiar with story songs as a form of literature

MATERIALS
- "Haliwa-Saponi Canoe Song"   **CD 14-3**
  Recording Routine: Intro; vocal
- *"El carite"*   **CD 14-6**
- *"The Kingfish"*   **CD 14-7**
  Recording Routine: Intro (8 m.); v. 1; refrain; interlude (8 m.); v. 2; refrain; coda
- *"Se va el caimán"*   **CD 14-10**
- *"The Alligator"*   **CD 14-11**
  Recording Routine: Intro (16 m.); v. 1; refrain; interlude (8 m.); v. 2; refrain; interlude (16 m.); v. 3; refrain
- **Pronunciation Practice/Translation** p. 534
- **Resource Book** pp. A-30, A-31, F-39, I-23
- *Haliwa-Saponi Canoe Song*   **CD 14-5**
- *guiro, claves,* tambourine

VOCABULARY

ballad   vocables   major scale   minor scale

◆ ◆ ◆ ◆ **National Standards** ◆ ◆ ◆ ◆

1c Sing music from diverse cultures
2c Perform instrumental music from diverse cultures
2e In instrumental ensembles, perform moderately easy pieces with technical accuracy
3b Improvise rhythmic variations on given melodies
5a Read eighth and sixteenth notes in duple meter
7a Create standards for evaluating performances
8b Identify ways music relates to social studies and language arts

MORE MUSIC CHOICES

For more practice singing story songs:
"Los reyes de Oriente" ("The Kings from the East"), p. 480

Singing Stories

The legends of many cultures are often about heroes, ways of learning how to live, or a moment of history. When stories are set to song, they become more powerful and more memorable.

The "Haliwa-Saponi Canoe Song" is a dance song about traveling in a canoe. The song uses **vocables** instead of words. Vocables have no specific meaning, but among the Haliwa-Saponi, the meaning of this song is clear. It is about teaching the young the importance of canoeing and how this ties into the history of their people.

Vocables are sung or spoken syllables that do not have a specific meaning.

CD 14-3

Haliwa-Saponi Canoe Song

Native American Song of the Haliwa Saponi
Transcribed by J. Bryan Burton

Drums (continue throughout)

We ya we we ya we we ya we,

Ya we ___ ya o-we; Ya we ya we we ya we we ya we,

Fine

Ya we ___ ya o-we. Ya we ha ya we ha yo-we;

Ya we ___ ya o-we. Ya we ha ya we ha yo-we;

1. Ya we ___ ya o-we. Ya 2. we ___ ya o-we.

D.S. al Fine

302

Footnotes

▶ **Vocables** Most Native American songs use vocables—syllables that do not have a literal meaning. The vocable sounds usually match the vowel sound of the tribal language. Vocables may be sung throughout the whole song and may sometimes be combined with spoken text. "Haliwa-Saponi Canoe Song" features vocables.

BUILDING SKILLS THROUGH MUSIC

▶ **Language** Select students to summarize the story sequence in *"Se va el caimán."* Discuss parts of the story that could reflect actual events and those that are imaginary. Have students work individually or in pairs to research and write descriptions of the alligator, his habitat, and the type of food that is typically eaten by alligators.

CULTURAL CONNECTION

8b ▶ **Haliwa-Saponi Indians** The Haliwa-Saponi tribe, descendants of the Saponi, Tuscarora, and Nansemond, merged to make up the third largest Native American tribe in North Carolina. Originally habitants of Virginia and North Carolina, the Haliwa-Saponi migrated northward during the mid-eighteenth century and became associated with the Iroquois Confederation. The name *Haliwa* represents Halifax and Warren counties, where the Haliwa-Saponi tribe lives today.

Listen to this performance of *Haliwa-Saponi Canoe Song* as you follow the music. Find the lowest and highest notes. Is the range of the music narrow or wide?

CD 14-5
Haliwa-Saponi Canoe Song

Native American Song of the Haliwa-Saponi as performed by the Haliwa-Saponi Singers
This recording features Native American drums and bells.

MUSIC MAKERS
Haliwa-Saponi Singers

The Haliwa-Saponi Singers are a group of Native Americans from the Saponi people. The Haliwa portion of their name comes from the place in which they live—Halifax and Warren Counties of North Carolina. The Haliwa-Saponi hold a big pow-wow every year in April. A pow-wow is a celebration with music, dancing, and food—something like a family reunion.

Music Around the World

Unit 8 **303**

1 INTRODUCE

8b Invite students to share stories from their childhood. Ask them what the messages of the stories were. Share with students the idea that stories can be sung as well as told and that they are probably our oldest form of person-to-person entertainment and education.

2 DEVELOP

Singing

Have students look at "Haliwa-Saponi Canoe Song" on p. 302 and read the information about vocables.

Tell students that songs can communicate a story or theme from one generation to the next.

Have students

- Look for repeat signs, endings, and *D.S. al Fine* in "Haliwa-Saponi Canoe Song"; then move their fingers along the staves to indicate the routine of the song.

5a
- Follow the music and vocables of "Haliwa-Saponi Canoe Song" **CD 14-3** while they listen to the recording and tap the beat.

1c
- Sing the song with the recording.

Moving

Have students move to "Haliwa-Saponi Canoe Song." See Movement below for specific directions.

Invite students to perform movement from diverse cultures. They may enjoy performing the patterned dance with *"Uno, dos, y tres"* (see Movement, p. 428) that also uses a line formation.

continued on page 304

MOVEMENT

▶ **Patterned Dance** Invite students to perform the following movement routine with "Haliwa-Saponi Canoe Song."

- Form groups of three or four dancers (in a canoe) in a single-file line behind the front dancer. Place your hands on the waist of the dancer in front of you.
- Move as groups (canoes), first to the left in a small side-step motion: L R L R L R L R 1 & 2 & 3 & 4 &
- Then to the right: R L R L R L R L 1 & 2 & 3 & 4 &
- The person at the front of each line becomes the "navigator" and leads the group forward in a clockwise circle. The leader's arms should imitate a paddling motion.
- Move around the room as multiple canoes follow the leader.

CHARACTER EDUCATION

▶ **Values and Traditions** To help students understand the importance of values and traditions, discuss how songs communicate stories or themes that express values. You may wish to ask students the following questions. What values are expressed in the 3 songs in this lesson? What values and traditions do you have and how have they been communicated to you? How are the values expressed in the 3 songs in this lesson similar to your values and traditions? How are they different? Where do you learn values and establish traditions? (school, family, and so on)

Unit 8 *Music Around the World* **303**

Listening

Invite students to listen to Haliwa-Saponi Canoe Song **CD 14-5** and compare it to the version they just performed.

Ask students to read the information on p. 303 about the Haliwa-Saponi Singers.

Reading

Have students

- Read the story of *"El carite,"* a typical ballad (story song), and summarize the story for each other.

5a
- Find the final notes of the verse (F) and the refrain (D); then locate the final chords of each section (F and Dm). (Point out that this song has a verse in F major and a refrain in Dm, which share the same key signature.)

- Listen to *"El carite"* **CD 14-6** and raise their hands when they hear the shift from major to minor.

- Sing *"El carite"* **CD 14-7** in English along with the recording.

- Focus on the verse, then tap and say the rhythms of each phrase.

- Learn the Spanish lyrics, using the Pronunciation Practice Track **CD 14-9** and Resource Book p. A-30.

1c
- Sing the song in Spanish with the recording **CD 14-6**.

ASK Which phrases have similar rhythms? (phrases 1, 2, and 3)

What new or different rhythms are there in the refrain?

Ballads

Venezuela is a beautiful country with dramatic scenic contrasts: the snowcapped Andes in the west, the Amazonian jungles in the south, the Gran Sabana plateau with its flat-topped mountains in the east, and white-sand beaches along the Caribbean coast. This is a perfect setting for singing and telling stories.

Stories are a way of passing on our values—what we believe. When stories are set to song, they are called ballads.

Sing *"El carite,"* a ballad that describes a very successful fishing expedition.

Choose one of the parts below to **perform** a Latin rhythm with *"El carite."*

REFRAIN
(Play 4 times)

304

Footnotes

CULTURAL CONNECTION

▶ **Venezuela** Venezuela is a beautiful country with huge scenic contrasts: the snowcapped Andes in the west, the Amazonian jungles in the south, the Gran Sabana plateau with its flat-topped mountains in the east, and the white-sand beaches along the Caribbean coast. Venezuela's natural wonders include Lake Maracaibo (South America's largest lake), the Orinoco River (South America's third longest), Angel Falls (the world's highest waterfall), and a wide variety of exotic plants and animals (jaguar, ocelot, tapir, armadillo, anteater, and the anaconda snake).

SPOTLIGHT ON

▶ **Musical Instruments of South America** There is a wide variety of instruments played in South America. Some percussion instruments (mainly of African derivation, some native Indian) include conga drums, claves, guiros and rattles. The string instruments, from Spanish influence, include the *charango* (a small 10-string instrument with armadillo back), harp, *cuatro* (four strings), *tiple* (three strings), mandolin, violin, and guitar. The wind instruments are native South American and include panpipes and *quena* (Andean end-blown flute).

CD 14-6

El carite
(The Kingfish)

s, (l) t, d r m f s si l t

Folk Song from Venezuela
Arranged by Jerry Silverman

VERSE

A - yer sa - lió la lan - cha Nue - va Es - par - ta.
The Nue - va Es - par - ta set sail yes - ter - day, ___

Sa - lió con - fia - da a re - co - rrer los ma - res.
Set out so brave - ly to sail a - cross the o - cean.

En - con - tró un pez de fuer - zas muy li - je - ro.
It met a fish that was so ver - y trick - y.

Que a - ga - rra los an - zue - los y re - vien - ta los gua - ra - les.
It grap-pled with our fish-hooks and it smashed up our fish box - es.

REFRAIN

Co - mo la cos-ta es bo - ni - ta, Yo me ven - go di - vir - tien - do;
Oh, the coast-line is so pret - ty, As I sailed ___ a - long for pleas - ure;

Pe - ro ___ me vie - ne si - guien-do de fue - ra u - na pi - ra - gui - ta.
But I saw ap - proach-ing swift - ly a ca - noe off in the dis - tance.

"El carite" (the Kingfish) from *Songs of Latin America* by Jerry Silverman. Arr. by Jerry Silverman. Copyright © 1994 by Mel Bay® Publications, Inc. All Rights Reserved. Used by Permission.

Music Around the World

Unit 8 **305**

Singing

1c Have students sing both the verse and refrain of *"El carite,"* tapping the rhythm during the verse and the beat during the refrain.

Playing

2c Allow a group of students the opportunity to learn the rhythm parts on p. 304. Have the instrumentalists practice each rhythm at a moderate tempo before they accompany a classroom performance of *"El carite."*

2e Invite students to add a recorder countermelody to the performance. (See Skills Reinforcement below.)

continued on page 306

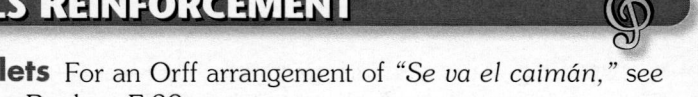 ACROSS THE CURRICULUM

▶ **Social Studies/Science** For a fascinating real-life story of a faraway place, encourage students to read *Adventures in the Amazon Rain Forest* (*Ultimate Field Trip, No. 1*) by Susan E. Goodman (Aladdin, 1999). It is a touching photo essay of a group of young American students who travel to the Amazon rain forest to learn about the people, as well as the animal and plant life of the area.

For more science activities, stories, and songs about the rain forest ecosystem, suggest students read *Exploring the Rain Forest: Science Activities for Kids* by Anthony D. Fredericks (Fulcrum, 1996).

SKILLS REINFORCEMENT

▶ **Mallets** For an Orff arrangement of *"Se va el caimán,"* see Resource Book p. F-39.

▶ **Recorder** See Resource Book p. I-23 for a descending-pattern countermelody for *"El carite."*

2c

Lesson 3 Continued

Singing

Have students

- Read the story of *"Se va el caimán,"* a ballad about a fanciful alligator.

5a - Listen to *"Se va el caimán"* **CD 14-10** and follow the music.

- Sing *"Se va el caimán"* **CD 14-11** in English along with the recording.

- Learn the Spanish lyrics, using the Pronunciation Practice Track **CD 14-9** and Resource Book p. A-31.

1c - Sing the song in Spanish **CD 14-10** with the recording.

- Look at the notation of the song.

ASK **Which phrases are the same?** (phrases 1 and 2, 3 and 4, and 5 and 6)

Playing

2c *"Se va el caimán"* has three chords—C, G, and G₇,—but students can play the song using C and G₇.

Write the following chart on the board.

C / G₇ / / / C /

This pattern can be used to accompany the entire song, strumming on the beat. Divide students into two groups. Have one group play the C chord and the other play the G₇ chord to accompany the song. Then have groups switch chords and accompany the song again. Finally, encourage all students to play both chords, switching between the two, to accompany the song. See Teacher to Teacher below for suggested chord substitutes.

Another Singing Tale

Colombia is located in northwestern South America. It is bordered by Ecuador and Peru on the south, Brazil and Venezuela on the east, and Panama on the northwest.

With its snowcapped peaks (in the Andes mountains) and tropical regions, Colombia is another perfect setting for story-telling. **Sing** the Colombian song *"Se va el caimán,"* which tells a wonderful, exaggerated story. As you sing, notice the many repeated patterns. How many different patterns can you **identify**?

CD 14–10
MIDI 22

Se va el caimán
(The Alligator)

English Words by Aura Kontra

Dance Song from Colombia

VERSE

1. Voy a em-pe-zar mi re-la-to___ con a-le-gría y con a-fán. ___
2. Lo que co-me es-te cai-mán___ yo le ten-go ad-mi-ra-ción, ___
1. Let me tell a sil-ly sto-ry___ on a light and hap-py note, ___
2. What this ga-tor has for din-ner___ is a won-der to be-hold, ___

Voy a em-pe-zar mi re-la-to___ con a-le-gría y con a-fán, ___
Lo que co-me es-te cai-mán___ yo le ten-go ad-mi-ra-ción, ___
Let me tell a sil-ly sto-ry___ on a light and hap-py note. ___
What this ga-tor has for din-ner___ is a won-der to be-hold. ___

Por el rí-o Mag-da-le-na___ se vol-vió un hom-bre cai-mán, ___
Co-me que so y co-me pan___ con re-fre-scos de li-món, ___
On the riv-er Mag-da-le-na,___ a ga-tor likes to float, ___
There is cheese and there is bread___ and lem-on-ade served cold. ___

Por el rí-o Mag-da-le-na___ se vol-vió un hom-bre cai-mán.
Co-me que so y co-me pan___ con re-fre-scos de li-món.
On the riv-er Mag-da-le-na,___ a ga-tor likes to float.
There is cheese and there is bread___ and lem-on-ade served cold.

Footnotes

SKILLS REINFORCEMENT

5a ▶ **Reading** After students have sung *"Se va el caimán,"* challenge them to identify and then clap the following rhythm patterns from the song.

TEACHER TO TEACHER

2c ▶ **Guitar Chords** To accompany *"Se va el caimán,"* beginning guitar students will find it easier to capo at fret 3 and play the following chord substitutes:

- C = A
- G₇ = E₇

REFRAIN

Se va_el cai - mán, se va_el cai - mán,
Oh, there he goes, oh, there he goes;

Se va pa - ra Ba-rran - qui - lla,
He's leav-ing for Ba-ran - qui - lla;

Se va_el cai - mán, se va_el cai - mán,
Oh, there he goes, oh, there he goes;

Se va pa - ra Ba-rran - qui - lla.
He's leav-ing for Ba-ran - qui - lla.

1.

2.
to verses 2 and 3 / last time

va pa - ra Ba-rran - qui - lla.
leav-ing for Ba-rran - qui - lla.

va pa - ra Ba-rran - qui - lla.
leav-ing for Ba-rran - qui - lla.

3. Al otro lado del río
    pescaron una mojarra, (2 times)
    Y del buche le sacaron
    él que toca la guitarra. (2 times)
Refrain

3. On the far side of the river,
    fishermen reeled in a perch, (2 times)
    It had swallowed the guitarist,
    now they've called off the search. (2 times)
Refrain

MIDI Create new rhythm patterns and add them to the "Se va el caimán" song file.

Music Around the World

Singing

Invite students to perform expressively, first from notation and then from memory, music from diverse cultures. Have them perform "Haliwa-Saponi Canoe Song," then "El carite" or "Se va el caiman."

3 CLOSE

Element: RHYTHM | **ASSESSMENT**

 Performance/Self-Assessment Have students choose one of the songs from this lesson and plan a performance that includes singing and a rhythm accompaniment of their choice. Allow students to establish their own criteria for an effective performance of the song they have selected. Then, give them time to practice. Tape record their performance and invite students to describe how well they met the criteria they established.

CULTURAL CONNECTION

▶ **Colombia** Colombia is located in northwestern South America. It is bordered by Ecuador and Peru on the south, Brazil and Venezuela on the east, and Panama on the northwest. It has coastlines on both the Pacific and the Caribbean. Colombia, whose capital city is Bogota, is the fourth-largest country in Latin America. Coffee is one of Colombia's most important exports. Colombia has both snowcapped peaks (Andes mountains) and tropical regions. Colombia claims the highest number of species of plants and animals of any country in the world. There are more than 1,500 recorded species of birds! (more than in the whole of Europe and North America combined)

TECHNOLOGY/MEDIA LINK

 MIDI/Sequencing Software Prepare the classroom computer/keyboard to play back the MIDI song file for "Se va el caimán." Assign students to groups of three or four. Have students

- Listen to the playback of the MIDI file.
- Turn off all percussion tracks.
- Create several new tracks for recording percussion parts (channel 10).
- Choose keyboard percussion instruments and improvise percussion parts.
- Record several percussion lines that complement the melody.

LESSON 4

LESSON AT A GLANCE

Element Focus   **MELODY** Call-and-response patterns

Skill Objective   **SINGING** Sing a game song from West Africa

Connection Activity   **CULTURE** Learn a traditional Akan game to accompany a song

MATERIALS

- *"Bantama kra kro"* (Akan)   **CD 14-14**
- *"Bantama kra kro"* (English)   **CD 14-15**
  Recording Routine: Intro (4 m.); vocal; interlude (4 m.); vocal; coda
- **Pronunciation Practice/Translation** p. 536
- **Resource Book** p. A-34
- stones (or substitutes)
- map of West Africa

VOCABULARY

call and response

◆ ◆ ◆ ◆ National Standards ◆ ◆ ◆ ◆

1c Sing music from diverse cultures
1d Sing music written in two parts
5a Read dotted notes in duple meter
7b Students use specific criteria for evaluating their own performances
8b Identify ways music relates to social studies, art, and literature
9c Compare, in several cultures, functions music serves

MORE MUSIC CHOICES

For more practice singing songs from West Africa:
"Funwa alafia" ("Welcome, My Friends"), p. 32
"O, Desayo," p. 411

1 INTRODUCE

Ask students to describe the games they have played that include some sort of movement, chant, rhythm, or song.

Singing GAMES

All over the world, both children and adults love to pass the time playing musical games. These singing games often include moving or dancing, passing something, complicated clapping patterns, or just singing the right thing at the right time. How many games can you remember that include music?

Sing *"Bantama kra kro,"* a game song from Ghana about delicious pastries made in the town of Bantama.

CD 14-14

Bantama kra kro

English Words by George Nkwame   Song from the Akan People of Ghana

Ban - ta - ma kra kro, meh yeh den na m'an - ya bi ma - dzi
Ban - ta - ma's the town where all the most de - li - cious pas - tries are,

Kra kro __ deh deh iyi, meh yeh den na m'an - ya bi ma - dzi
Sweet treats __ to try and buy, it real - ly is - n't ve - ry far;

Kra kro __ kra kro, meh yeh den na m'an - ya bi ma - dzi
If I've __ no mon - ey for the sweets a - top the pas - try cart,

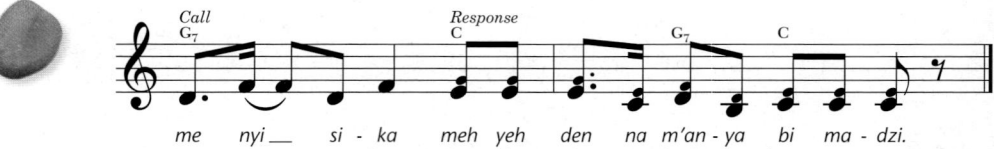

me nyi __ si - ka meh yeh den na m'an - ya bi ma - dzi.
How can __ I buy that de - li - cious look - ing hon - ey tart?

308

Footnotes

ACROSS THE CURRICULUM

8b ▶ **Social Studies** Students will enjoy learning a folktale from the Akan people of Ghana in *Spider and the Sky God: An Akan Legend* (Legend of the World Series), by Deborah M. Newton Chocolate (Troll, 1997).

For more about the people, art, and customs of Ghana, read *West Africa: Ghana (Ancient and Living Cultures Series)* by Mira Bartok and Christine Ronan (GoodYear, 1992).

BUILDING SKILLS THROUGH MUSIC

▶ **Math** While singing *"Bantama kra kro,"* have students pat a steady beat on the call and clap a steady beat on the response. Ask them to count the total number of beats for each (3 beats for the call, 5 beats for the response). Have students work with a partner to create a graph that represents the length of the call and response with either an icon or line.

CULTURAL CONNECTION

▶ **Akan of Ghana** Akan is the language spoken in dialects by groups of people living in the south-central forest zone and coastal areas of Ghana and in southeastern Ivory Coast. The Ashanti and Fante are probably the best-known Akan groups in Ghana. The Akan are well known for their commercial cacao farming and gold mining. Several types of Akan cloth have become well known throughout the world, including the block-printed *adinkra*, the hand-woven *kente*, the appliquéd *akunin-tam* and *asafo* flags, and the factory-made Java and wax prints. *Adinkra* symbols often embody some form of proverb. The wooden comb *dua afe* is a symbol of beauty, love, fondness, patience, prudence, and care.

Playing Games

In Ghana, West Africa, as in other parts of the world, stone-passing games are common. People sit in a circle and pass smooth stones in rhythm while they sing.

Play the stone-passing game for *"Bantama kra kro"* by forming a circle and following this simple plan.

Tap, tap—Hold stone in right hand and tap it on the ground in front of you.

Pass—Right hand passes stone to right in front of the next person, and drops the stone on word *pass.*

Grab—On the word *grab,* right hand grabs the stone the person to left has passed you.

Follow the rhythm pattern below and play this game while you **sing** *"Bantama kra kro."* As the game proceeds, gradually speed up the tempo.

Unit 8 309

2 DEVELOP

Singing

8b Help students locate Ghana, West Africa, on a map and then share information about the Akan people. See Cultural Connection, p. 308.

1c Have students follow the music and lyrics of *"Bantama kra kro"* **CD 14-14** as they listen to the recording.

5a

ASK **Which lines of the song are similar?** (lines 1 and 3; 2 and 4)

Have students

- Sing the melody (lower notes) of the responses.
1d - Sing the harmony (upper notes) of the responses.
- Sing the responses in harmony.
- Divide into two groups: group 1 sings both the call and the melody; group 2 joins in on the harmony on the responses.

Moving

9c Have students practice the stone-passing game. When they are ready, add the song.

3 CLOSE

Skill: SINGING **ASSESSMENT**

7b **Performance/Observation** Assess each student's abilities to sing the call or response according to the following rubric:

4 Sings the call or response part accurately while passing the stones

3 Sings the call or response part with fair accuracy while passing the stones

2 Sings the call part and struggles with passing the stones

1 Sings the call part with some inaccuracy and struggles with passing the stones

---

MOVEMENT

▶ **Game Song** Use the following activity to help students play the stone-passing game for *"Bantama kra kro."*

Sit in a circle and practice saying these words together: *Tap, tap, pass, grab* (keep repeating). Without the stones, practice the following motions, using only your right hand (left hand behind back) as you say the words.

- "Tap, Tap" an imaginary stone on the floor directly in front of you.
- "Pass" the imaginary stone to the next person to your right.
- "Grab" the new stone in front of you.

SCHOOL TO HOME CONNECTION

8b ▶ **Decorating Stones** Encourage students to find and decorate interesting stones and sticks for use in the game *"Bantama kra kro."* Invite students to research the colorful patterns and designs of West African countries, as seen in the *kente* cloth and other folk arts. Students should know the meanings of designs, colors, and patterns as they decorate their stones and sticks.

TECHNOLOGY/MEDIA LINK

Video Library Show the video *Percussion Instruments* to students to present a performance by a percussion ensemble from the West African country of Senegal.

LESSON AT A GLANCE

Element Focus   **TIMBRE**   String instruments

Skill Objective   **LISTENING**   Distinguish the sound of string instruments in a guided listening experience

Connection Activity   **SCIENCE**   Explore the acoustics and construction of string instruments

MATERIALS

- *Picking Red Chestnuts*   **CD 14-19**
- *Julie-O*   **CD 14-20**
- *Solo Flight* (excerpt)   **CD 14-21**
- *Hoedown*   **CD 14-22**
- **Resource Book** p. C-6
- violin, guitar, or other available string instruments

VOCABULARY

timbre   spike fiddle

◆ ◆ ◆ ◆ National Standards ◆ ◆ ◆ ◆

6a Listen and describe events in music using appropriate terms such as change in sections, instrumental entrances
6b Listen and analyze uses of timbre in music from diverse cultures/genres
8b Identify ways music relates to science and social studies

MORE MUSIC CHOICES

For more practice with string instrument timbre:
Zither Montage, p. 196
Plucked String Montage, p. 198

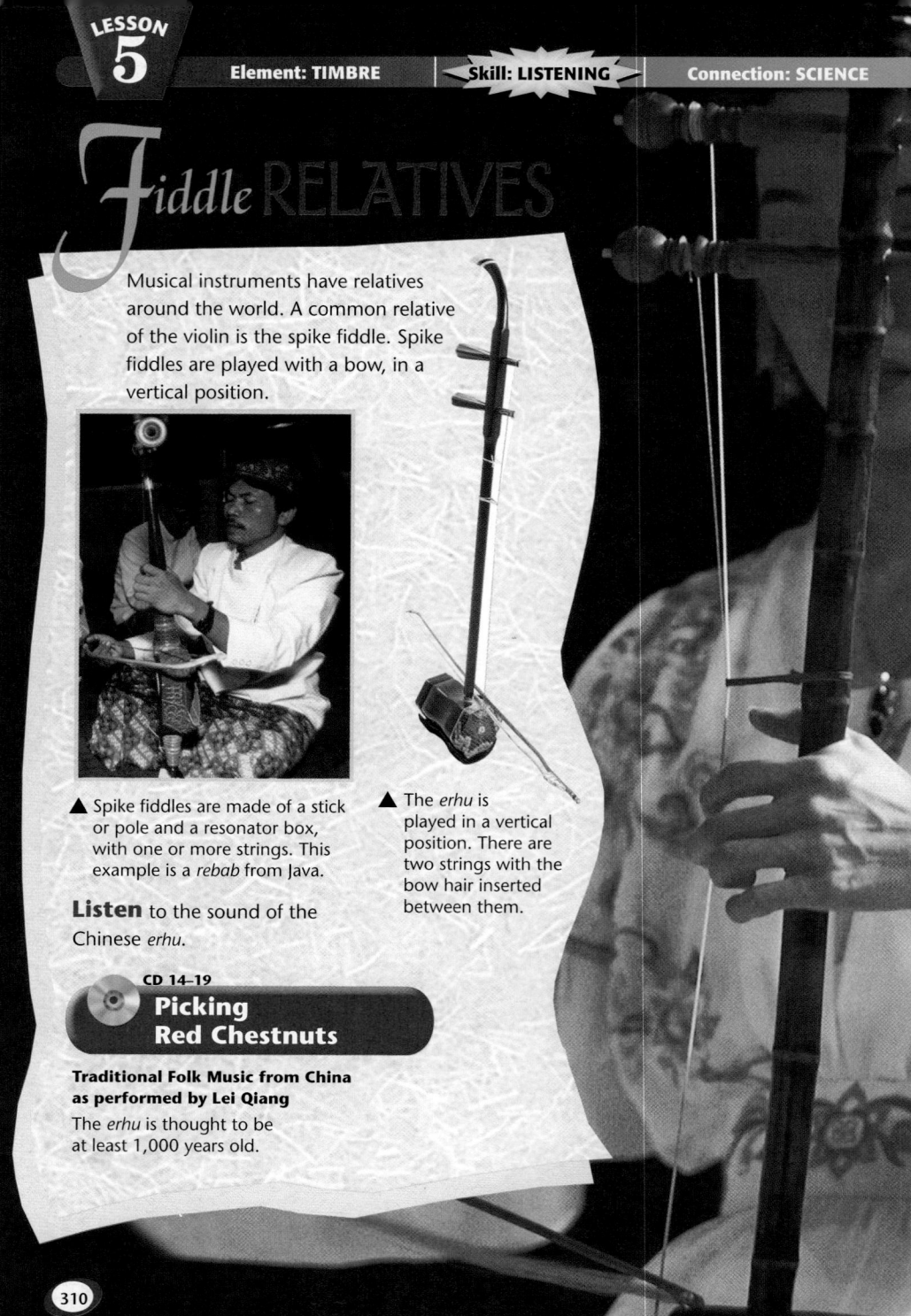

Fiddle RELATIVES

Musical instruments have relatives around the world. A common relative of the violin is the spike fiddle. Spike fiddles are played with a bow, in a vertical position.

▲ Spike fiddles are made of a stick or pole and a resonator box, with one or more strings. This example is a *rebab* from Java.

▲ The *erhu* is played in a vertical position. There are two strings with the bow hair inserted between them.

Listen to the sound of the Chinese *erhu*.

CD 14–19
Picking Red Chestnuts

Traditional Folk Music from China as performed by Lei Qiang
The *erhu* is thought to be at least 1,000 years old.

310

Footnotes

CULTURAL CONNECTION

 ▶ **Spike Fiddle** Spike fiddles are very simple string instruments composed of a stick or pole, a resonator (a gourd, box, turtle shell, or anything hollow), and a string. The pole is inserted through the resonator, and the string is tied from the end of the pole to the surface of the resonator. Most spike fiddles are played with a bow, but they can also be plucked. They are found in many cultures, especially in Asia, the Middle East, and Africa.

BUILDING SKILLS THROUGH MUSIC

▶ **Social Studies** Distribute copies of the Semantic Map from Resource Book p. C-6 to students. Have students label the center box "String Instruments" and write the names of string instruments found on pp. 310–312 in the surrounding boxes. Ask them to add descriptions such as appearance and sound of each of the instruments to the Semantic Map.

ACROSS THE CURRICULUM

 ▶ **Arts and Crafts** Follow these steps to make a simple spike fiddle. Materials needed: 18" long 1" dowel or stick, a fairly large tin can, two eye screws, about 2' of wire.

1. Make a hole in both sides of the can large enough for the dowel to pass snugly through. Then insert the dowel so that it sticks out about 2" on one side and about 12" on the other.

2. Screw the eye screws into each end of the dowel. Then attach the wire firmly to the screw on the short end of the dowel; then pass the wire over the middle of the closed end of the can and attach it to the screw at the long end of the dowel. Tighten the wire by turning the screws. The wire will produce a sound when plucked or bowed.

A New Sound

The entire European violin family (violin, viola, cello, string bass) is related to the spike fiddle. Their four strings are stretched over hollow, rounded bodies of different shapes. They are usually bowed, but can be plucked and struck in various ways to make interesting sounds.

Read about the Turtle Island String Quartet. Then **listen** to the group's cellist perform *Julie-O*. **Describe** the sounds of the cello. How do you think the performer produces them?

CD 14–20
Julie-O

written and performed by Mark Summer, cellist, the Turtle Island String Quartet

The Turtle Island String Quartet took its name from creation stories found in Native American folklore.

MUSIC MAKERS

The Turtle Island String Quartet

The Turtle Island String Quartet is a traditional type of chamber music group with a very different sound. The members play the traditional string quartet instruments (violin, viola, and cello), but arrange and perform music in a wide variety of styles. These include folk, bluegrass, jazz, Indian music, funk, New Age, hip-hop, and Latin music, in addition to the usual classical string repertoire. The musicians even improvise while playing classical music, bringing back a practice that is over 200 years old.

Music Around the World

Unit 8　311

---

1 INTRODUCE

Ask students to list as many different types of string instruments as they can. Ask them to arrange their lists into sub-categories of their own choice; for example: "orchestra strings," "folk music strings," "amplified strings," and so on.

2 DEVELOP

Listening

Have students

- Read the information on pp. 310–311 about the spike fiddle and its relatives.
- Discuss the photos on p. 310 and compare the look and playing positions of the spike fiddle and the *erhu* with those of the classical European violin. (See Skills Reinforcement below.)
- Listen to *Picking Red Chestnuts* **CD 14-19** and then discuss the timbre of the *erhu*.

Creating

Have students

- Construct a simple one-stringed spike fiddle following the instructions in Across the Curriculum, p. 310.
- Discuss and demonstrate the parts necessary to make a string instrument and how they function. (See Across the Curriculum, p. 312.)
- Identify and demonstrate the vibrating string, the starter (the means for initiating the sound), and the resonator on a violin, guitar, or other available string instruments. Then identify the same features on the *erhu*.

continued on page 312

SKILLS REINFORCEMENT

▶ Listening See Sound Bank, p. 514 and **CD 21-30, CD 21-54** for recordings of and information on the *erhu* and the violin.

SPOTLIGHT ON

▶ Turtle Island String Quartet David Balakrishnan had to write music for his master's thesis at Antioch University West in 1985. The music that he wrote, however, was so different that it required a unique group of musicians to handle it. It required classically trained musicians who could also feel comfortable with the jazz medium. After some searching, he found just the right people—and the Turtle Island String Quartet was formed. Joining Balakrishnan was Darol Anger (replaced by Evan Price), Mark Summer, and Danny Seidenberg. The quartet has included such elements as rhythm and blues and African rhythms.

Listening

ASK What instruments make up a typical string quartet? (2 violins, 1 viola, 1 cello)

Have students

- Discuss the kind of classical music string quartets traditionally play (four-movement compositions by Haydn, Mozart, and Beethoven, as well as contemporary composers).

- Read about the Turtle Island String Quartet, on p. 311, and how they have widened the boundaries for the string quartet.

 Play the recording of *Julie-O* **CD 14-20** and have students listen for the string timbre.

ASK How does this timbre compare with that of the *erhu?* (Accept all valid answers.)

Refer to Teacher to Teacher, p. 313, and explain to students how a MIDI controller (whether a violin, cello, guitar, wind, voice, or keyboard) simply gives signals to the synthesizer for what pitches and what timbres to play. So a violin can sound like an organ, a drum, a trumpet, or an electric rock guitar.

As an example of MIDI violin, play the recording of *Solo Flight* **CD 14-21** by Susie Hansen.

The Fiddle Goes Digital

The new digital Zeta MIDI violin is capable of sounding like any instrument—an organ, a brass instrument, a drum, or an electric guitar.

The MIDI violin does this by using digital sounds stored in a synthesizer. Because the resonator box is no longer important (as in the solid-body electric guitar), the shape of the body of the MIDI violin can be very different from that of a regular violin.

Listen to Susie Hansen play the Zeta MIDI violin. How can you tell that this is not a regular acoustic violin?

CD 14–21
Solo Flight

written and performed by Susie Hansen
Susie Hansen is a rising star in the field of Latin jazz. This selection also features Mark Gutierrez on piano.

Rodeo Strings

Listen to *Hoedown* from Aaron Copland's ballet *Rodeo*. The listening map on page 313 shows how the composer combined string instruments with other sections of the orchestra.

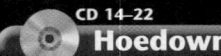

CD 14–22
Hoedown

from *Rodeo*
by Aaron Copland
as performed by the London Symphony Orches

Copland based the music for *Hoedown* on a square dance tune. At the time this music was written (1942), it was unusual for a composer to make violins in an orchestra sound like country fiddles.

Midi violins ▼

312

Footnotes

ACROSS THE CURRICULUM

▶ **Science** Violin strings, when played, vibrate. That vibration causes a vibration in the eardrum, and sound is heard. The thick strings vibrate more slowly than the thin ones, giving a lower pitch. The strings when shortened (with a finger) or tightened (with a peg) give a higher sound. The bridge transfers energy from the string vibration into the body, giving the violin its characteristic bright timbre. The body of the violin acts as a resonating chamber, since the belly and back plates can vibrate up and down. The air inside vibrates much like a bottle when air is blown across the top. The body also transmits vibrations in the air around it. Finally, the violin needs a vibration starter, such as a finger or a bow. The bow allows the player to energize the vibrating string and play sustained notes.

SPOTLIGHT ON

▶ **The Composer** See p. 187 for biographical information on Aaron Copland, and a recorded interview with the composer.

▶ **The Ballet** *Rodeo* was composed by Aaron Copland and the libretto, as well as the choreography, was done by Agnes de Mille. The 1942 work included tap dancing as well as movements reminiscent of the American West. Subtitled *The Courting at Burnt Ranch*, it is the story of a cowgirl who wants to get married. To meet her true love, she tries to become one of the cowhands. One of the most memorable scenes from this ballet is "Hoedown." It is joyous, boisterous, rhythmic, and spontaneous.

The first performance of *Rodeo* was at the Metropolitan Opera House in New York, and was danced by Ballet Russe of Monte Carlo.

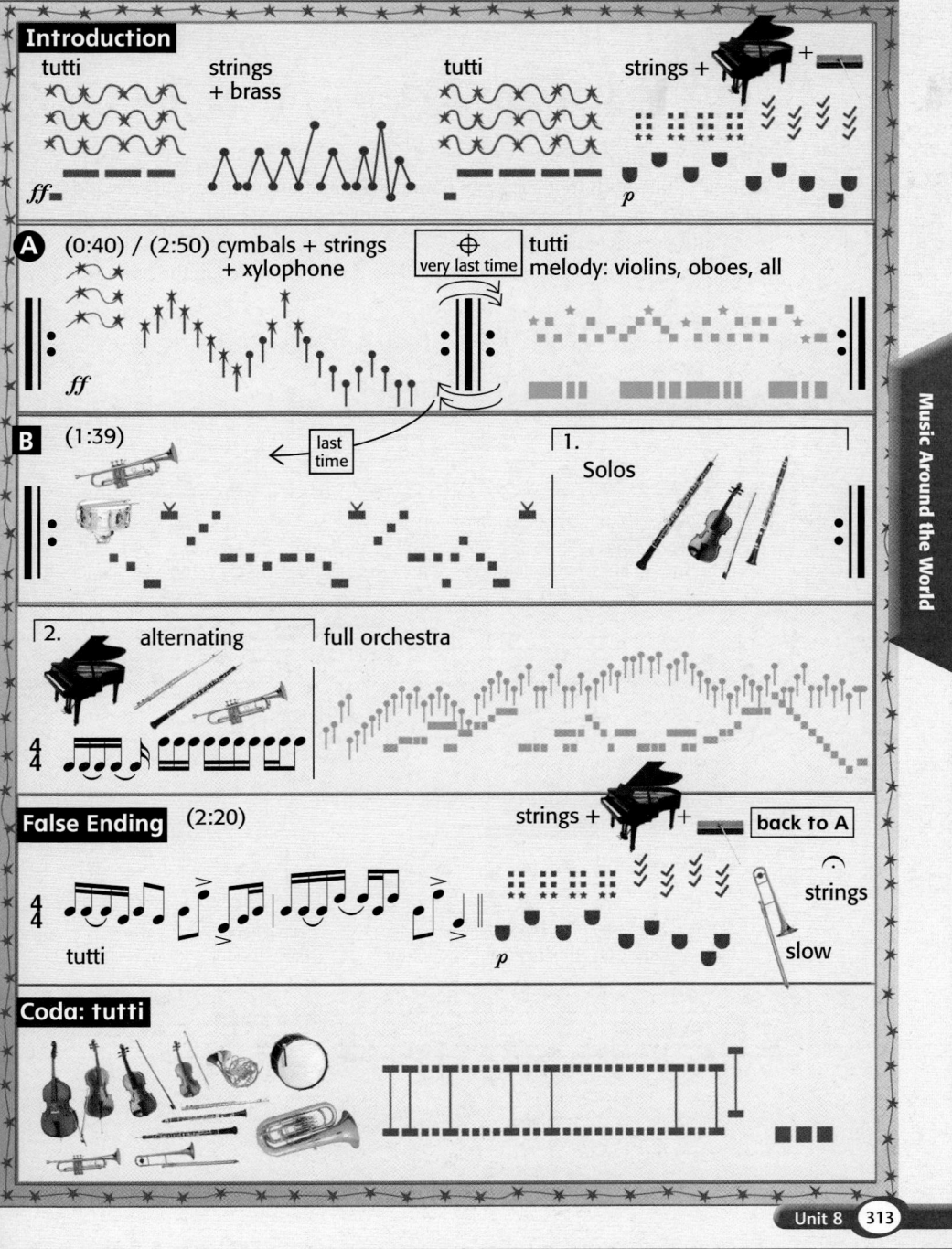

Hoedown
LISTENING MAP

Introduction

tutti

strings + brass

tutti

strings +

ff

A (0:40) / (2:50) cymbals + strings + xylophone

very last time

tutti melody: violins, oboes, all

ff

B (1:39)

last time

1.

Solos

2. alternating   full orchestra

4/4

False Ending (2:20)

strings +   + back to A

4/4

tutti   *p*   strings

slow

Coda: tutti

3 CLOSE

Skill: LISTENING   **ASSESSMENT**

6a **Music Journal Writing** Play the recording of *Hoedown* **CD 14-22** as students follow the listening map on p. 313. Challenge students to identify the music symbols referring to dynamics. Explain the term *tutti* (all), the coda symbol, the repeat signs (the A section is heard two-and-one-half times, with additional internal repeats), the false ending, the sign at the end of row 5 to return to the A section, and the sign to go to the coda at the end of that A section. Note that the graphics do not always indicate each note, but suggest the melodic contour at the beginning of a timbre change. The timings may be helpful in following the progress of the map as the recording plays, on the first listening.

Have students describe in their music journals the sound of the string instruments and how the composer combined these instruments with the other orchestral timbres. See Technology/Media Link below for tips on using the listening map transparency.

TEACHER TO TEACHER

▶ **String Instruments** The new MIDI violins, violas, cellos, and basses often have a futuristic look to them, with bodies made of specially molded plastic. The one thing they have in common with regular acoustic string instruments is the fingerboard and placement of the strings. When the strings are bowed or plucked, the vibration, articulation, dynamics, and other information is sent to a MIDI controller/synthesizer. The pitch-to-MIDI converter then recognizes the analog notes and converts the analog signal into digital MIDI information. This MIDI information allows the controller/synthesizer to create sounds and/or send digital information to other MIDI devices, thus allowing it to access computer software programs such as music notation and publishing programs.

TECHNOLOGY/MEDIA LINK

Transparency Display the listening map transparency for *Hoedown* as you play the recording. You may wish to point to each section of the piece on the first listening to help students follow along. On subsequent listenings, invite a student to point to the sections as you play the recording.

LESSON AT A GLANCE

Element Focus	**MELODY** Pentatonic melody
Skill Objective	**SINGING** Perform songs that are based on a pentatonic scale
Connection Activity	**CULTURE** Become acquainted with the importance of nature in Chinese culture

MATERIALS

- "Yüe liang wan wan"   **CD 14-23**
- "Crescent Moon"   **CD 14-24**
  Recording Routine: Intro (8 m.); vocal; interlude (8 m.); vocal; coda
- **Pronunciation Practice/Translation** p. 536
- "Jasmine Flowers"   **CD 14-27**
  Recording Routine: Intro (4 m.); v. 1; interlude (2 m.); v. 2; interlude (2 m.); v. 3; coda
- "Lahk gei mohlee"   **CD 14-29**
  Recording Routine: Intro (4 m.); vocal; coda
- **Resource Book** pp. A-35, A-36
- xylophones, woodblock, bells

VOCABULARY

pentatonic

◆ ◆ ◆ ◆ National Standards ◆ ◆ ◆ ◆

1c Sing music from diverse cultures
2c Perform instrumental music from diverse cultures
3a Improvise simple harmonic accompaniments
5c Identify standard notation symbols for pitch
6c Understand and use basic principles of tonality and intervals in music analysis
7a Create standards for evaluating performances
8a Show how different arts portray the same scene in unique ways
8b Identify ways music relates to social studies and art

MORE MUSIC CHOICES

For more practice singing pentatonic songs:
"Hitotsu toya" ("Temple Bells"), p. 478

Celebrate Nature

Songs and paintings that celebrate nature are common throughout the world. In China the image of the moon in its different phases has been the source of much musical inspiration. **Sing** "Yüe liang wan wan," a song that symbolizes new hope for a better life. How many different notes are used in the melody?

CD 14-23

Yüe liang wan wan
(Crescent Moon)

English Words by Elaine Nienow   Folk Song from China

跑 马 溜 溜 的 山___ 上 一 朵 溜 溜 的
Pao ma liu liu di shan___ shang yi duo liu liu di
Cres - cent moon float-ing on a cloud O'er the crest of the

云 哟 端 端 溜 溜 的 照___ 在
yün yo Duan duan liu liu dee zhao___ zai
moun - tain. Sil - ver gem in a sat - in crown,

康 定 溜___ 溜 的 城 哟 月 亮 弯___
Kang ding liu - liu di cheng yo. Yüe liang wan___
Rest - ing on the roy - al moun-tain. Pale moon, new moon,

弯___ 康 定 溜 溜 的 城 哟
wan___ Kang ding liu - liu di cheng yo.
cres - cent moon___ Shin - ing bright-ly o - ver K'an - ting.

314

Footnotes

CULTURAL CONNECTION

8b ▶ **Mandarin** The Chinese text of "Yüe liang wan wan" is Mandarin, the official language of the People's Republic of China. Mandarin is used in education, business, and the media. It is spoken in Taiwan (Republic of China) and by Chinese who have emigrated to other countries. Mandarin is written with characters that can represent objects or ideas. Mandarin syllables tend to sound the same in length and stress, because this language is based on tones rather than on accents.

BUILDING SKILLS THROUGH MUSIC

▶ **Language** Ask students to identify words in the lyrics of "Crescent Moon" that have multiple meanings and give the alternate meaning of each. Have them identify words or phrases that relate to performance styles or qualities.

TEACHER TO TEACHER

▶ **Guitar Drone** Although the guitar is not commonly used in Asian music, the song "Yüe liang wan wan" can be accompanied by guitar tuned to a drone. The notes can be determined with some experimentation, although D, A, and E are possibilities. Some experimentation can also be used when determining the most effective way to play the strings. Some suggestions include using metal finger picks or tapping the strings lightly with a drum stick. In these cases, the guitar is being used purely as a "sound source" as opposed to traditional guitar-playing style, but its demonstrated versatility should make the instrument even more exciting and attractive to your students.

"Crescent Moon" Ostinato

Play this pattern on a mallet instrument to accompany "Yüe liang wan wan."

(last measure)

Choose two or more of the following notes and **improvise** your own part to play with the song.

*Arts* **Connection**

▲ Chinese ink painting of a panda by Wu Zhoren.
Paintings made of or depicting bamboo are common throughout East and Southeast Asia, because bamboo is so abundant in this part of the world. Painters work for many hours to produce just the right brush strokes in a painting of a bamboo plant.

Unit 8　315

Music Around the World

1 INTRODUCE

8a Explain the concept of a "frozen moment" in which nature is captured in a photograph, a painting, or a song.

ASK Have you ever been to a place so beautiful that you wanted to take a photograph so you could remember it forever? (Accept a variety of answers.)

2 DEVELOP

Singing

8a Share with the class the information in Spotlight On below about the important symbolic meaning the image of the moon has in Chinese art forms.

Have students

- Read the English lyrics for "Yüe liang wan wan" ("Crescent Moon") and discuss the images.
- Echo sing the Mandarin words to "Yüe liang wan wan" as you play the Pronunciation Practice Track **CD 14-26.** (Refer also to Resource Book p. A-35.)
- **1c** Sing "Yüe liang wan wan" **CD 14-23** in Mandarin with the recording.

8a Have students identify concepts taught in the other fine arts and their relationship to music. Then have them look at the bamboo painting on p. 315 and read the accompanying information. Share with students the additional information in Cultural Connection, p. 317. Emphasize the attention given to brush strokes and calligraphy in China, Korea, and Japan.

Have students

- Look for nature images in the English lyrics of "Yüe liang wan wan."
- Sing the English words to "Yüe liang wan wan" **CD 14-24** with the recording.

ASK How many other songs can you name that are about the moon? (Accept all valid answers.)

continued on page 316

SPOTLIGHT ON

8a ▶ **The Moon in Chinese Art** The moon has greatly influenced the ideas for many of the Chinese poems, paintings, and pieces of music. The message is one of immortality. As students listen and sing "Yüe liang wan wan," invite them to listen for the rich sound of the *erhu,* a violinlike instrument. Mention that the sound of the *erhu* is often associated with moments of contemplation shared beneath the light of the moon.

ACROSS THE CURRICULUM

▶ **Language Arts** Share with students the following books on Chinese painting.

- *Chinese Brush Painting: Workstation/Brush and Tools* by I-Ching (Workstations, 1995)
- *Chinese Brushwork in Calligraphy and Painting: Its History, Aesthetics and Techniques* by Kwo Da-Wei (Dover, 1990)
- *Chinese Landscape Painting for Beginners: A Practical Course* by Audrey Quigley (Sterling, 1993)

Lesson 6 Continued

Encourage students to ask family members and friends to help them think of other "moon" songs.

Playing

Have students

- Prepare to play the mallet ostinato on p. 315 by patting the rhythm pattern on their legs or on the floor.

- Identify the pitches in the ostinato.

- Practice the ostinato on xylophones and then perform it with *"Yüe liang wan wan."*

Creating

Have students

- Create their own ostinatos, using the notes suggested on p. 315.
- Improvise accompaniment patterns to *"Yüe liang wan wan."*
- Play the new ostinatos with the recording.

Singing

Have students

- Follow the English lyrics and melody for "Jasmine Flowers" **CD 14-27** as they listen to the recording.

ASK What nature images are in this song? (moon, jasmine flowers)

- Sing "Jasmine Flowers" with the recording.

Ask students to listen to and compare "Jasmine Flowers" to *"Lahk gei mohlee."*

ASK What is the same? (the melody; the rhythm is similar)

What is different? (Chinese characters and lyrics; English lyrics)

SAY "Jasmine Flowers" and *"Lahk gei mohlee"* are the same song, except the lyrics are in different languages.

Flowers of the Moon

This folk song, originally from southern China, is about a girl who compares herself to jasmine flowers. **Listen** to the lyrics to discover what the young girl is asking for.

CD 14–27

Jasmine Flowers

Words by Rebecca Schwan

Folk Song from Taiwan

1. White jas-mine flow-ers of the Sixth Moon are fair,
2. White jas-mine flow-ers of the Sixth Moon are fair,
3. White jas-mine flow-ers of the Sixth Moon are fair,

And there's a young lad who's no-ble and fine.
Love - ly lass has nev - er been found.
Lass - es a - lone are sor - ry and sad.

Love - ly flow-ers rare - ly ev - er grow all a - lone;
Flowers and lass - es should nev - er be a - lone;
Love - ly flow-ers should be bloom-ing side by side.

Fair lone - ly lass can be sad, so sad.
Sad is the love - ly lass who's nev - er, nev - er found.
When will the lass be found and nev - er be a - lone?

Play the following parts on glockenspiel or resonator bells, finger cymbals, and woodblock to accompany "Jasmine Flowers."

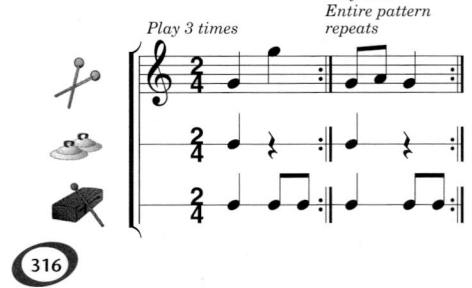

Play 3 times

Play once Entire pattern repeats

316

Footnotes

ACROSS THE CURRICULUM

▶ **Visual Arts** Ask students to collect their favorite photographs of nature. From available resources, make a class bulletin board or have students do their own nature photograph portfolios.

Invite students to photograph, illustrate, and find artwork depicting beautiful crescent moon shapes in art from China and other countries. Display the student's original work in an art show at musical performances. Themes for student artwork could be linked to the cultural origins and song text meanings of each of the musical selections the students perform.

SKILLS REINFORCEMENT

▶ **Moving** The song *"Yüe liang wan wan"* is full of vivid artistic imagery of the crescent moon, mountains, nightingales, and lotus blossoms. Ask students to design simple scenery or props, inspired by the song text words and images, and use them within a dramatized movement staging of this beautiful Chinese folk song.

Spring Flowers

This folk song from Taiwan celebrates the beauty of nature. **Listen** to the notes used in this song and compare the melody to that of "Jasmine Flowers."

CD 14-29

Lahk gei mohlee

Words by Hsy Ping-Ting
Transliterated by Han Kuo-Huang

Folk Song from Taiwan

六 月 茉 莉 真 正 美
Lahk gei ___ moh lee ___ jeen jeeahn ___ shwee,

郎 君 生 著 你 都 真 古 椎
long goon ___ sheen jway lee go jeen ___ go jwee.

好 花 難 得 成 雙 對
Hoh hway lahn ___ dee ___ sheen ___ shiong ___ dwee,

身 邊 哪 沒 娘 啊 你 都 上 刻 虧
sheen bean nah moh new ah lee - goh shiong ___ keh ___ kwee.

Unit 8 **317**

Then have students

- Echo sing the Taiwanese words to *"Lahk gei mohlee"* with the recording of the Pronunciation Practice Track **CD 14-31**. (Refer also to Resource Book p. A-36.)

1c

- Sing *"Lahk gei mohlee"* **CD 14-29** in Taiwanese with the recording.

SAY Both *"Lahk gei mohlee"* and *"Yüe liang wan wan"* are songs that use the pentatonic scale (do-re-mi-so-la).

6c **ASK Which of these pitch syllables is the tonic, or home tone, for each song?** (*"Yüe liang wan wan"* is based on *la* and therefore has a "minor" modal character; *"Lahk gei mohlee"* is based on *so* and has a somewhat "major" modal character.)

Playing

Have students

2c

- Practice the ostinatos on p. 316, then play them with the recording of "Jasmine Flowers" **CD 14-27**.
- Use the same ostinatos to accompany *"Lahk gei mohlee"* **CD 14-29**.

3 CLOSE

Element: MELODY **ASSESSMENT**

1c **Performance/Self-Assessment** Have students
2c choose one of the songs from this lesson and plan a
7a performance that includes singing and an improvised pentatonic accompaniment. Allow students to establish their own criteria for an effective performance of the song they have selected. Then give them time to practice. Tape record their performance, then invite students to describe how well they had met the criteria they established.

CULTURAL CONNECTION

▶ **Bamboo** Bamboo is commonly known as the "friend of China." Bamboo, pine, and plum trees are also known as the "three friends of winter." Since bamboo does not die in the winter but remains green even in very cold weather, it is considered a symbol for long friendship and as a bearer of happiness.

Bamboo also symbolizes moral character which is flexible (like the trunk of the bamboo) and bends to the times but returns to its upright form. It also symbolizes modesty because the leaves of the bamboo droop.

SCHOOL TO HOME CONNECTION

▶ **Moon Songs** Ask students to work with their parents, grandparents, or friends to think of songs that mention the moon in the title or lyrics. Make a bulletin board or special list somewhere in the room.

TECHNOLOGY/MEDIA LINK

Video Library Show the video *String Instruments: Bowed* to highlight two traditional Chinese instruments.

LESSON AT A GLANCE

Element Focus   **TIMBRE** Time-keeping gongs of the Javanese gamelan

Skill Objective   **LISTENING** Listen to a performance by a Javanese gamelan

Connection Activity   **RELATED ARTS** Become acquainted with the art of Indonesian shadow puppet theater

MATERIALS

- "Cho'i hát bội"   **CD 14-32**
- The Theater Game   **CD 14-33**
  Recording Routine: Intro (4 m.); vocal; interlude (4 m.); vocal
- **Pronunciation Practice/Translation** p. 537
- *Patalon*   **CD 14-36**
- **Resource Book** p. A-37

VOCABULARY

gamelan

◆ ◆ ◆ ◆ National Standards ◆ ◆ ◆ ◆

1c Sing music from diverse cultures

6b Listen and analyze uses of rhythm and timbre in music from diverse cultures

8b Identify ways music relates to language arts and drama

9a Describe characteristics of music genres from a variety of cultures

MORE MUSIC CHOICES

For more practice singing Asian songs:

"Meng Jian Nu," p. 194

1 INTRODUCE

Ask students to think of times they have seen or used puppets to tell a story. Point out that before television, live theater in homes and communities was even more important than it is today.

MUSIC AND THEATER

Theater is a way of presenting a story. The combination of music and theater can have a powerful effect. There are many types of musical theater throughout the world, such as opera, Broadway musicals, Kabuki, and Indonesian shadow puppet theater. Can you think of others?

Sing "Cho'i hát bội," a Vietnamese song about a theater game.

CD 14-32

Cho'i hát bội
(The Theater Game)

English Words by Kim Williams   Traditional Song from Vietnam

Rù _____ nhau ra đám kia mú u kia mú
Wake _____ up! Let's go to the trees, to the

u kia nọ mú u. _____ Cha kêu mẹ _____
grove of mú - u trees. _____ The thea - ter _____

hú mấy còn ngủ _____ tao còn ngủ _____ trống linh
game is a - bout _____ to be - gin. Hear the

đánh hát bội đó thức rồi còn ngồi
drum! It says "come." Wake up! Let's _____

đây sao chẳng đi coi họ hát cho'i.
go, for the play is lots of fun.

318

Footnotes

ACROSS THE CURRICULUM

8b ▶ **Art/Language Arts** For art projects to use with performances of music from Southeast Asia, see *The Kids' Multicultural Art Book* by Alexandra Terzian (Econo-Clad, 1999) and *Art from Many Hands: Multicultural Art Projects* by Jo Miles Schuman (Davis, 1981). Projects include Vietnamese Tet Festival dragon puppets, Thai hanging owl kites, Indonesian shadow puppets, and batik fabric designs.

BUILDING SKILLS THROUGH MUSIC

▶ **Theatre** Have students learn the song "Cho'i hát bội." Divide the class into groups. Distribute cards with the name of a place, person (people), and time to each group (house, family, morning; playground, children, after school). Have them develop a short skit based on the words that are on their card. Ask students to sing the song before each group performs their skit.

CULTURAL CONNECTION

8b ▶ **Wayang Kulit** In Java, the shadow plays are performed in villages and towns for holidays, religious festivals, weddings, births and other celebrations. As the darkness comes, people gather in front of the white screen ready to see the plays put on by the *dalang* or puppeteer. The *dalang* tells the story, manipulates the figures (which he makes), does the voices and sound effects, sings, and cues the gamelan players. Most shadow plays are based on two epic stories from India—the *Mahabarata* and the *Ramayana*—and a mixture of Buddhist, Muslim, Hindu, and local folklore. Gamelan players respond to the timing and direction of the *dalang*. The gamelan repertoire usually consists of an overture, traveling music, character pieces, and battle music.

Arts Connection

A *wayang kulit,* or shadow puppet, performance on the Indonesian island of Java usually takes place in the evening, out of doors, and may last all night long. The puppets are made of brightly painted leather and are held up with sticks against a white screen. ▶

A Gamelan

The music of *wayang kulit* is provided by a gamelan, a small orchestra of gongs, xylophones, metallophones, drums, flutes, zithers, and a *rebab.*

Listen to the Javanese gamelan piece *Patalon.*

CD 14–36
Patalon

Traditional Song From Indonesia
as performed by the Hardo Budoyo Ensemble of Central Java

In a shadow puppet performance the gamelan sits behind the white screen and is not normally seen. The puppeteer not only works the puppets, but also sings and speaks the roles.

Unit 8 **319**

2 DEVELOP

Singing

Have students read the English lyrics for *"Cho'i hát bôi."*

ASK Where does the theater take place? (in the grove of *mú u* trees)

How is the play announced? (with a drum)

Have students

- Echo sing the Vietnamese words to *"Cho'i hát bôi,"* using the Pronunciation Practice Track **CD 14-35.** (Refer also to Resource Book p. A-37)

1c
- Sing *"Cho'i hát bôi"* **CD 14-32** in Vietnamese with the recording.

- Perform the song with the snap-clap movement described in Skills Reinforcement below.

Listening

8b Have students read the information on p. 319 and then discuss Indonesian *wayang kulit* shadow puppet theater and the gamelan accompaniment. Include in the discussion the information in Cultural Connection, p. 318.

6b Play the recording of *Patalon* **CD 14-36,** which is music for the *wayang kulit* played by a gamelan from Java. Help students identify the timbre of specific instruments listed on p. 319.

3 CLOSE

Skill: LISTENING **ASSESSMENT**

6b
9a **Music Journal Writing** Play the recording of *Patalon* again and ask students to describe in their music journals the individual and combined sounds of the Javanese gamelan. Have students group the instruments by family (percussion, winds, strings).

SKILLS REINFORCEMENT

6b ▶ **Moving** Have students practice the following rhythm pattern, which is typically found in Vietnamese theater songs.

snap   snap   clap

Then have students perform this pattern with *"Cho'i hát bôi."*

TECHNOLOGY/MEDIA LINK

Web Site To learn more about Javanese and Balinese gamelans, visit *www.sfsuccessnet.com.*

LESSON AT A GLANCE

Element Focus   **EXPRESSION** Tempo

Skill Objective   **LISTENING** Listen to a traditional song from India and identify expressive qualities

Connection Activity   **CULTURE** Explore the cultural traditions that surround Indian music

MATERIALS

- *"Ragupati Ragava Raja Ram"*   **CD 15-2**
  Recording Routine: Intro (22 m.); refrain; v. 1; refrain; instrumental; v. 2; refrain; v. 1; refrain (no repeat)
- *Sindhi-Bhairavi*   **CD 15-1**
- **Pronunciation Practice/Translation** p. 538
- **Resource Book** p. A-38

VOCABULARY

drone

◆ ◆ ◆ ◆ National Standards ◆ ◆ ◆ ◆

1c Sing music from diverse cultures
3c Improvise melodies with consistent tonality
6b Listen and analyze uses of timbre in music from diverse cultures
8b Identify ways music relates to social studies
9a Describe characteristics of music genres from a variety of cultures
9c Compare, in several cultures, functions music serves

MORE MUSIC CHOICES

For more practice with expression:
"Morning Has Broken," p. 29
"Simple Gifts," p. 184

1 INTRODUCE

8b Locate India on a map and share information about India from the resource listed in Across the Curriculum below. Invite students to read about Ravi Shankar.

Musical Feelings

Music expresses what words cannot. People of all countries and cultures around the world use music in many different ways.

In India, music is sometimes used as an accompaniment to meditation or devotional activities.

Listen to *"Ragupati Ragava Raja Ram,"* a Hindu song that is well known in India.

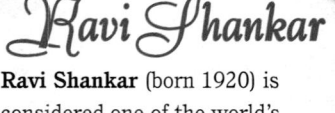

MUSIC MAKERS

Ravi Shankar

Ravi Shankar (born 1920) is considered one of the world's greatest sitar players. He rocketed to international stardom during the 1960s when George Harrison of the Beatles helped to popularize the sitar in the West. Shankar performs traditional Indian classical music and has experimented with using the sitar in other styles of music.

Listen to Ravi Shankar's performance of *Sindhi-Bhairavi*. How would you describe the sound of the sitar?

CD 15–1
Sindhi-Bhairavi

Traditional Raga from India as performed by Ravi Shankar

The sitar is associated with the sound of India, and used mainly for playing classical Indian music.

320

Footnotes

ACROSS THE CURRICULUM

8b ▶ **Social Studies** Invite students to read about the Indian festival of lights, Diwali, and other fascinating celebrations of people all over the world in *Children Just Like Me* and *Celebrations!* by Barnabas and Anabel Kindersley (DK Publishing, 1997). Pictures of children from a variety of cultures are set within pages full of interesting photos and facts about food, games, legends, customs, artifacts, and other information about celebrations in each season of the year.

BUILDING SKILLS THROUGH MUSIC

▶ **Writing** Invite students to listen to *"Ragupati Ragava Raja Ram"* **CD 15**-2 and think of an English title for the song. Discuss the suggestions and reasons for each. Have students read the information on p. 320 and decide which titles would be most appropriate. Ask students to select the titles that they would accept.

CULTURAL CONNECTION

8b ▶ ***"Ragupati Ragava Raja Ram"*** The words of this prayer song talk about God giving wisdom to everyone. Because India is a country with large Hindu and Muslim populations, *"Ragupati Ragava Raja Ram"* addresses each group by using both words for God (Ishware = Hindu; Allah = Muslim). India's greatest leader, Mahatma Gandhi, lived his life in a way that paid respect to all religions. Here are some of his quotes:

- "Intolerance is itself a form of violence and an obstacle to the growth of a true democratic spirit."

- "I do not want my house to be walled in on all sides, and my windows to be closed. Instead, I want the cultures of all lands to be blown about my house as freely as possible. But I refuse to be blown off my feet by any."

Ragupati Ragava Raja Ram

CD 15-2

Traditional Hindu Song · Traditional Melody

REFRAIN

Ra - gu - pa - ti ra - ga - va ra - ja ____ Ram

Pa - ti - ta pa - va - na Si - ta ____ Ram.

VERSE

1. Si - ta Ram jai Si - ta ____ Ram,
2. Ish - ware Al - lah te - re ____ nam,

Pa - ti - ta pa - va - na Si - ta ____ Ram.
Sub - be - ko sun - mut - ti de bha - ga - wan.

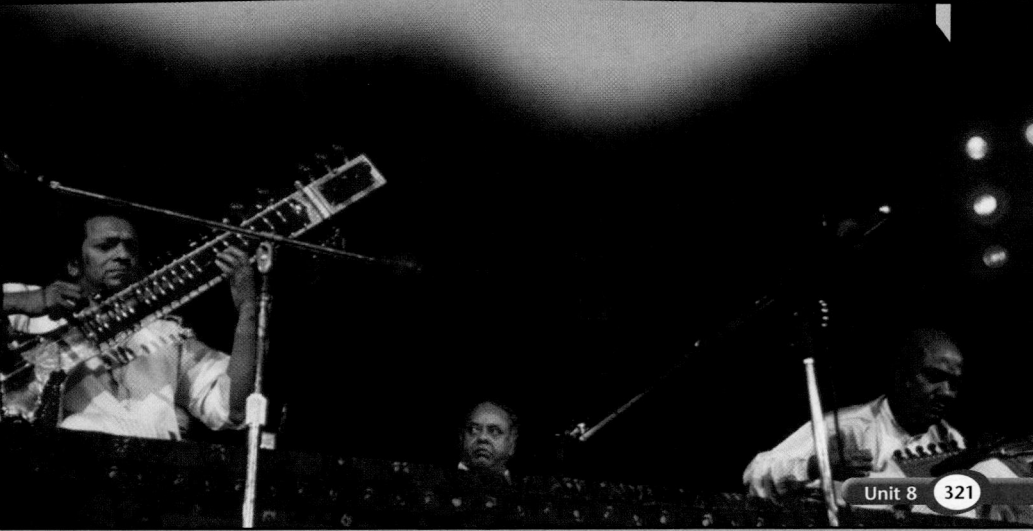

Unit 8 321

2 DEVELOP

Reading

Discuss with students how the melody of *"Ragapati Ragava Raja Ram"* moves around the note E that is reinforced by the *tamboura* (a four-string drone).

Listening

Have students

1c
9c
- Sing the *tamboura* drone notes E and B, using an open-lipped "n" sound to simulate the nasal sound of the drone. Stagger the breathing to make a continuous sound.

- Listen to *"Ragupati Ragava Raja Ram"* **CD 15-2** while following the music on p. 321.

9a
- Discuss how increasing the tempo affects the expression of the music. Share with them that this is a common practice in the music of India, particularly in instrumental pieces.

For a detailed description of the *sitar*, have students refer to Sound Bank p. 518. For an additional listening experience with the *sitar*, play **CD 21-44**.

3 CLOSE

Skill: LISTENING ASSESSMENT

6b **Music Journal Writing** Play the recording of Ravi Shankar performing *Sindhi-Bhairavi* **CD 15-1**, a traditional song from India. Ask students to describe in their music journals the expressive qualities of the music and the sound of the sitar.

SKILLS REINFORCEMENT

3c **6b** ▶ **Creating** One of the organizing principles of Indian music is the tendency for the melody to hint at, but avoid sounding overtly like, a tonal center. *"Ragupati Ragava Raja Ram"* and *Sindhi-Bhairavi* are both fine examples of this principle in action. This is because the tonal center is constantly present in the drone. After extensive listening and discussion of these examples, have students improvise melodically on available instruments around a tonal center provided by a drone (a guitar tuned to the tonic and fifth, the notes of the *tamboura,* is ideal). To make this task more comprehensible, you can ask students to identify and notate the tonal center and the surrounding notes, thereby limiting the possibilities of played notes on the melodic instrument.

SCHOOL TO HOME CONNECTION

▶ **Cultural Exploration** Invite students to learn more about India and other world cultures by exploring the many kinds of ethnic food restaurants in your city or town. Encourage students to learn about other cultures by inviting parents and grandparents to share favorite ethnic dishes at a school multicultural food fair.

TECHNOLOGY/MEDIA LINK

Web Site Go to *www.sfsuccessnet.com* to learn more about the music instruments of India.

LESSON AT A GLANCE

Element Focus **TEXTURE/HARMONY** I and V₇ chords

Skill Objective **SINGING** Sing and accompany a folk song from Mexico using I and V₇ chords

Connection Activity **CULTURE** Discover common themes used in songs from Latin America

- "La Jesusita" (Spanish) **CD 15-5**
- "La Jesusita" (English) **CD 15-6**

  Recording Routine: Intro (8 m.); vocal; interlude (8 m.); vocal
- **Pronunciation Practice/Translation** p. 538
- "Love Is on Our Side" **CD 15-9**

  Recording Routine: Intro (4 m.); vocal; coda
- **Resource Book** pp. A-39, F-41, H-23, I-24
- resonator bells, keyboards, guitars, Autoharps

VOCABULARY

chord

◆ ◆ ◆ ◆ National Standards ◆ ◆ ◆ ◆

1c Sing music from diverse genres

2c Perform instrumental music from diverse cultures

2d Perform simple accompaniments by ear

5c Identify standard notation symbols for pitch

6c Understand and use basic principles of intervals and chords in music analysis

7b Students use specific criteria for evaluating their own performances, and offer constructive suggestions for improvement

9a Describe characteristics of music genres from a variety of cultures

MORE MUSIC CHOICES

For more practice singing songs from Mexico:

"De colores," p. 90

"La ciudad de Juaja" ("The City of Juaja"), p. 58

Dance of Joy

"*La Jesusita*" is a Mexican song that describes a courtship. The first phrase in the lyrics is an invitation to dance. Enjoy the *mariachi* style of the recording as you sing.

CD 15-5
MIDI 23

La Jesusita

English Words by Aura Kontra

Folk Song from Mexico

s, l, t, (d) r m f s

VERSE

Va - mos al bai - le y ve - rás que bo - ni - to _____
Will you go danc - ing with me, how de - light - ful,

Don - de se a - lum - bran con vein - te lin - ter - nas.
Where twink - ling lights fill the air with their bright - ness.

Don - de se bai - lan las dan - zas mo - der - nas, _____
Where those who go know the steps to the mu - sic, _____

Don - de se bai - la de mu - cho va - ci - lón. _____
Let's join our friends as they dance the night a - way. _____

Fine

322

Footnotes

ACROSS THE CURRICULUM

▶ **Social Studies** Invite students to discuss the various languages and groups of people who make up the population of America's largest cities. What are some of the struggles recent immigrant groups face in adjusting to life in a new country? For a sensitive and unique look at the life of a young Mexican immigrant within a modern urban setting, read *Barrio: Jose's Neighborhood* by George Ancona (Harcourt Brace, 1998).

BUILDING SKILLS THROUGH MUSIC

▶ **Social Studies** On a map of the Western Hemisphere, have students identify countries that are in Latin America. Ask them to share information they know about the area, including information about percussion instruments that originated there. Ask students to describe the timbre of each instrument. Invite students to listen to "*La Jesusita*" **CD 15-5** and identify instrument timbres on the recording that match the instrument timbres they just discussed.

CHARACTER EDUCATION

▶ **Compassion and Caring** To help students understand the reasons for the theme of love in music, discuss the popularity of love songs. Ask students to compile a class list of love songs and determine what aspect of love (lost love, friendship, love for family, love for country) is expressed in each song. Have students work in small groups to research additional love songs, determining the kind of love expressed in each song. Ask them to consider the different types of love discussed and explain ways to demonstrate caring for each type. For example, how would a parent show love?

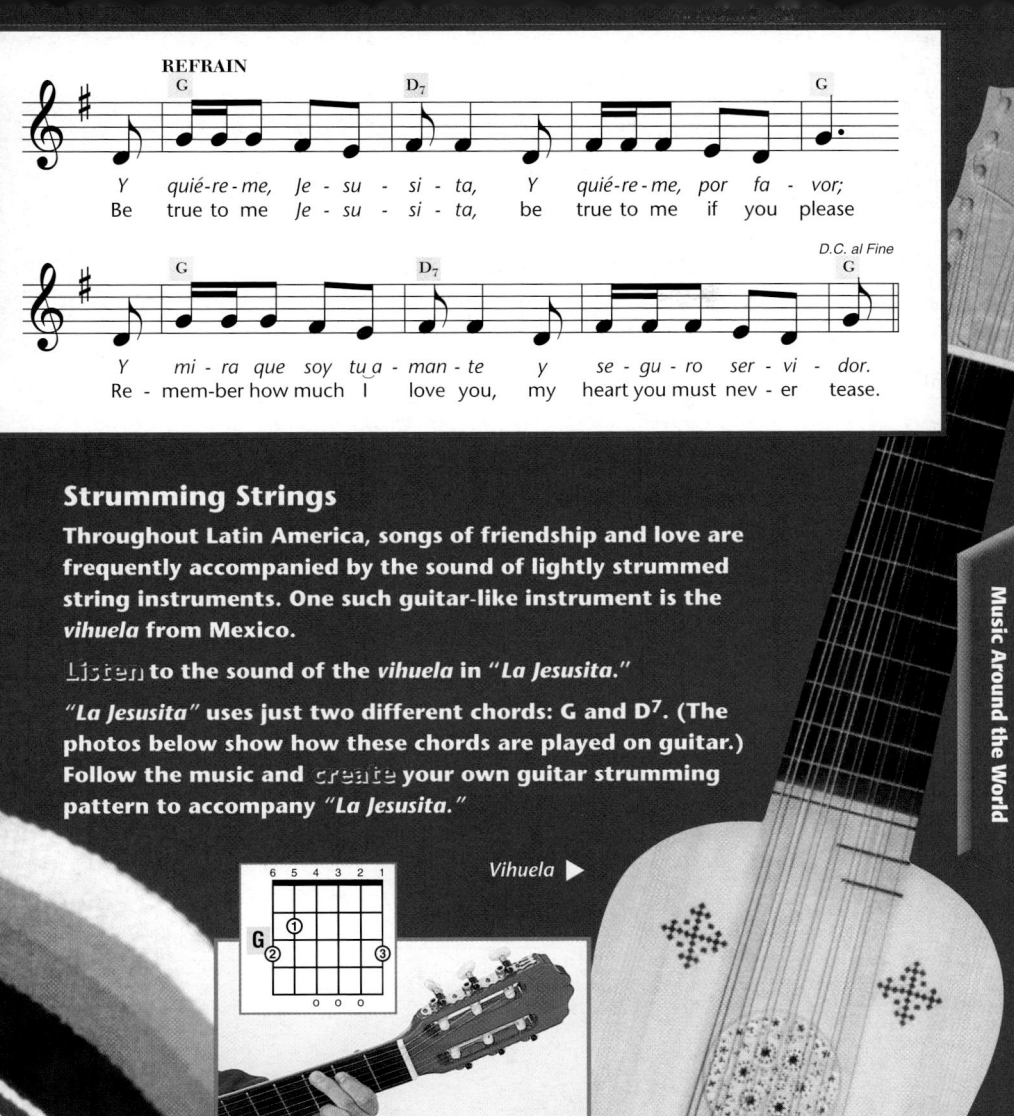

REFRAIN

G　　　　　　　　　　　　D₇　　　　　　　　　　　　G

Y　quié-re-me,　Je-su-si-ta,　Y　quié-re-me,　por　fa-vor;
Be　true to me　Je-su-si-ta,　be　true to me　if　you　please

G　　　　　　　　　　　　D₇　　　　　　　　　　　D.C. al Fine G

Y　mi-ra　que　soy　tu a-man-te　y　se-gu-ro　ser-vi-dor.
Re-mem-ber how much　I　love you,　my　heart you must nev-er　tease.

Strumming Strings

Throughout Latin America, songs of friendship and love are frequently accompanied by the sound of lightly strummed string instruments. One such guitar-like instrument is the *vihuela* from Mexico.

Listen to the sound of the *vihuela* in *"La Jesusita."*

"La Jesusita" uses just two different chords: G and D⁷. (The photos below show how these chords are played on guitar.) Follow the music and create your own guitar strumming pattern to accompany *"La Jesusita."*

Vihuela ▶

Music Around the World

Unit 8　**323**

---

1 INTRODUCE

ASK Can you imagine a culture anywhere on the planet that has no form of love songs?

Ask students to name some hit songs that are currently popular that are about love. Point out that love songs are probably the biggest category of songs that exists.

2 DEVELOP

Listening

9a Play the recording of *"La Jesusita"* **CD 15-5** and ask students to focus on the chord changes in the music, as played by the *vihuela.*

Invite students to read about the *vihuela,* on p. 323. Share the additional information in Cultural Connection, p. 324; then play the recording again.

For a detailed description of the *vihuela,* have students turn to p. 519 in the Sound Bank and listen to **CD 21-53.**

Singing

Have students

- Read the English lyrics for *"La Jesusita."*
- Echo sing the Spanish words to *"La Jesusita"* with the Pronunciation Practice Track **CD 15-8.** (Refer also to Resource Book p. A-39.)
- **1c** Sing *"La Jesusita"* **CD 15-5** in Spanish with the recording.

continued on page 324

TEACHER TO TEACHER

▶ **Mallet Instruments** A hocket ensemble works like a bell choir—each student has one pitch and must play that pitch when it comes up in a melody. As long as resonator bells are already available for *"La Jesusita,"* have students work out the melody by themselves (with one resonator bell per student), then play it for the class. It may help to elect a conductor for each group.

SKILLS REINFORCEMENT

▶ **Recorder** Use the following suggestions to help all students perform a recorder accompaniment to *"La Jesusita."*

2c **Reinforcement** Some fifth graders may have minimal experience playing the recorder. Have these students perform the following countermelody during the refrain of *"La Jesusita."*

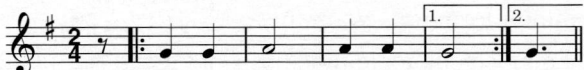

On Target Most students will be able to perform on the recorder proficiently. These students may be asked to perform the countermelody found on Resource Book p. I-24.

Challenge Interested students may be invited to improvise their own countermelody to perform on the verse or refrain of *"La Jesusita."*

Unit 8 *Music Around the World* **323**

Analyzing

Have students

- Build a G chord and D_7 chord on the board and then play each chord on bells.

- Find the G and D_7 chords outlined in the melody of "La Jesusita."

- Play the G and D_7 chords on guitar, keyboard, or mallet instruments with the recording. (See p. 283 for an illustration of the partial G chord for guitar.)

- Learn that the G chord is built on the first note of the G-major scale; therefore, the chord is called the I chord. The D_7 chord is built on the fifth note of the scale and is called the V_7 chord.

ASK Does anyone know why the Roman numeral V has a "7" after it? (because there is an added tone a 7th above the root—call the D chord root "1" and count up to C)

Playing

See Skills Reinforcement p. 323 for more instrumental parts to perform with "La Jesusita."

Have students

- Set up tone bells (keyboard or other mallet instruments) with the pentatonic scale pitches (C, D, F, G, A, C, D) for the melody of "Love Is on Our Side."

- Sing and play through D, F, G, A, C, D, C, A, G, F, D, C, D to establish the la-based minor pentatonic scale.

- Play the first four phrases of the song on keyboard or mallet instruments; then add the block triads for the Dm and F chords played by another player (this makes a good piano duet).

- Work out how to play the triads for the progression Dm, C, B♭, C, Dm; then build an instrumental duet consisting of the melody and the chords.

Family and Friends

Sing "Love Is on Our Side," a popular song about family and friends. What feeling do you get from the rhythm of the music? What meaning do you get from the lyrics?

Footnotes

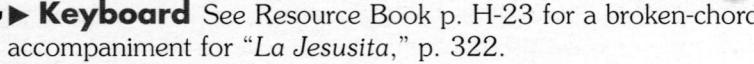

SKILLS REINFORCEMENT

 ▶ **Keyboard** See Resource Book p. H-23 for a broken-chord accompaniment for "La Jesusita," p. 322.

 ▶ **Mallets** See Resource Book p. F-41 for an Orff arrangement of "La Jesusita," p. 322.

▶ **Analyzing** A pentatonic scale can be any five notes, but the most common form uses do-re-mi-so-la.

The la-based minor pentatonic mode used in "Love Is on Our Side" is also the mode sometimes used to play blues. (Refer students to "Good Mornin', Blues," p. 224.)

CULTURAL CONNECTION

 ▶ **Vihuela** The vihuela is a stringed instrument that was developed during the Renaissance. Its name is Spanish for "one that is plucked." It was used for Spanish courtly music, much as the way a lute was used in Italy and other countries. One theory has it that the vihuela was developed from the lute, which was developed from the oud, an instrument that the Moors played. Not wanting to use a Moorish instrument, the Spanish flattened the back and called it a "Christian lute." Actually, the vihuela is a member of the viol family. It became the grandfather of the modern guitar, although the strings of the vihuela and the guitar are tuned differently. Of all the vihuelas in Renaissance Spain, only one, which is in a museum in Paris, survived. What did survive in quantity, though, are wonderful collections of Renaissance vihuela music, which are still played and enjoyed today.

We're ___ all ___ on that ___ train, ___

There's ___ where ___ hope be - gins. ___

D. C. (verse 2) al Coda

○ Coda

side, ___ That ___ love ___

___ is on ___ our side.

Mexican family making a *piñata* ▼

Singing

Have students

- Sing "Love Is on Our Side" **CD 15-9** with the recording.
- Discuss the theme of this song.

3 CLOSE

 Element TEXTURE/HARMONY — ASSESSMENT

7b **Performance/Peer Critique** Divide the class into two groups. While one group sings *"La Jesusita"* **CD 15-5**, have the other group accompany the song on selected instruments, using the I and V₇ chords. Allow groups to switch roles. After each performance, invite students to evaluate the singing and playing and offer suggestions for improvement.

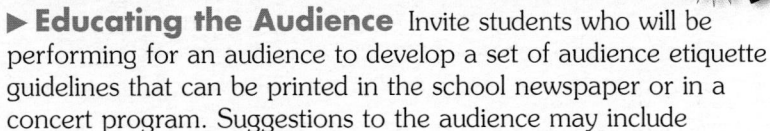

AUDIENCE ETIQUETTE

▶ **Educating the Audience** Invite students who will be performing for an audience to develop a set of audience etiquette guidelines that can be printed in the school newspaper or in a concert program. Suggestions to the audience may include

- Be punctual for the concert.
- Turn all pagers, cell phones, and other electronic equipment to the silent mode.
- No flash photography during the performance.
- If video cameras are allowed, do not place them in the aisles or between seats. Do not block the view of other audience members.
- Hold applause until the end of a selection.
- Do not bring food or drinks to the concert.

TECHNOLOGY/MEDIA LINK

2c **MIDI/Sequencing Software** Have students open the MIDI song file for *"La Jesusita."*

Point out that the nylon-string guitar part (track 5) follows the chord changes in the song. To play this part on keyboard, have students

- Play G and D alternately in an even rhythm when the G chord is indicated in the music.
- Play A and D in the same way when the D_7 chord is indicated.
- Isolate the melody and drum tracks, and selected guitar, trumpet, and fiddle tracks.
- Play the keyboard part with the song file.

Unit 8 *Music Around the World* **325**

LESSON AT A GLANCE

Element focus   **TEXTURE/HARMONY** Two-part harmony

Skill Objective   **SINGING** Sing a Spanish song in two-part harmony

Connection Activity   **SOCIAL STUDIES** Explore the history and culture of Mexico

MATERIALS

• "Cancón Mixteca"   **CD 15-11**
• "Mixteca Song"   **CD 15-12**
   Recording Routine: Intro (4 m.); vocal; coda
• **Pronunciation Practice/Translation** p. 539
• **Resource Book** p. A-40

VOCABULARY

melody   harmony

◆ ◆ ◆ ◆ **National Standards** ◆ ◆ ◆ ◆

1c Sing music from diverse cultures
5b Sightread melodies in treble clef
6c Understand and use basic principles of intervals in music analysis

MORE MUSIC CHOICES

For more practice singing two-part songs in Spanish:
"De colores," p. 90
"Qué bonita bandera," (What a Beautiful Banner!) p. 294
"Río, río," (River, River) p. 370

1 INTRODUCE

Ask students to think about the feelings of someone who has left his or her homeland to live in a different country.

SAY "Cancón Mixteca" is a song from Mexico that expresses feelings of being homesick and sadness.

Love for the Homeland

Have you ever thought about what it would be like if you left your home and moved away to a distant country?

What would you miss about the United States if you moved to a different country? What would you miss about your state?

Listen to "Cancón Mixteca," a song about leaving Mexico and feeling homesick.

As you **listen**, find where the voices sing in two-part harmony.

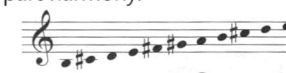

CD 15–11

Canción Mixteca
(Mixteca Song)

English Words by Don Kalbach   Words and Music by José López Alavés

¡Que le - jos es - toy del sue - lo don-de he na - ci - do!
I've come ver - y far, so far from my na - tive home - land! _

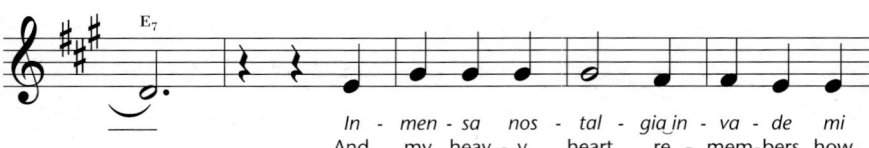

In - men - sa nos - tal - gia_in - va - de mi
And my heav - y heart re - mem-bers how

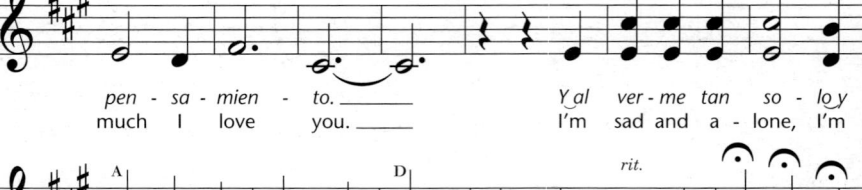

pen - sa - mien - to. _____   Y al ver-me tan so - lo y
much I love you. _____   I'm sad and a - lone, I'm

tris - te cual ho - ja_al vien - to,   qui - sie - ra llo -
just like a leaf that's blow - ing,   And I want to

326

Footnotes

TEACHER TO TEACHER

▶ **Assigning Voice Parts** Since fifth graders' voices are in the process of changing, it is difficult to assign students to a certain voice part and expect them to sing the part all year long. However, there is not time in class to spend checking and regrouping students for singing parts. When teaching two-part music, teach both parts to all students.

BUILDING SKILLS THROUGH MUSIC

▶ **Language** Discuss reasons why people are required to move or travel long distances from their homes. Ask students to identify phrases in the English lyrics of "Cancón Mixteca" where the singer describes his or her feelings. Have students suggest ways the lyrics could be revised to correspond to different situations today.

CULTURAL CONNECTION

▶ **Mexican History and Culture** For more information on the history and culture of Mexico, as well as interesting class projects about Mexico, guide students to read the following books:

• *Mexico: The People (Lands, Peoples, and Cultures)* by Bobbie Kalman (Crabtree, 2001)
• *Welcome to Josephina's World (1824): Growing Up on America's Southwest Frontier* by Yvette La Pierre, Peg Ross, and Jodi Everett (Pleasant Co., 1991)
• *Mexico: 40 Activities to Experience Mexico Past and Present* by Susan Milfords (Williamson, 2003)

rar, quisie-ra mo-rir de sen-ti-mien-to. ___
sigh, and I want to cry when I think of you. ___

¡Oh tie-rra del sol! (¡Oh tie-rra del sol!) Sus-
Oh, land of the sun! (Oh, land of the sun!) I

pi-ro por ver-te, a-ho-ra que le-jos (a-
live just to see you, I'm far from my home-land (I'm

ho-ra que le-jos) yo vi-vo sin luz sin a-mor. ___
far from my home-land) And I am with-out light or love. ___

Y al ver-me tan so-lo y tris-te cual
I'm sad and a-lone, I'm just like a

ho-ja al vien-to, qui-sie-ra llo-
leaf that's blow-ing, And I want to

rar, quisie-ra mo-rir de sen-ti-mien-to. ___
sigh, and I want to cry when I think of you. ___

Sing of Mexico

Sing "*Canción Mixteca*" in harmony. First, **sing** the melody. Then sing the harmony, which begins on line *3* of the song. Finally, divide into two groups and **sing** both parts together.

Unit 8 **327**

(side tab) Music Around the World

Lead students in a discussion about Mexican culture and history. For more information, see Cultural Connection on p. 326.

2 DEVELOP

Singing

Ask students to look at the notation for "*Canción Mixteca.*"

ASK Is "*Canción Mixteca*" sung in unison or two parts? (both)

1c Have students

- Practice singing the melody and harmony parts on a neutral syllable. **5b**
- Echo sing the Spanish words of the song using Pronunciation Practice Tracks **CD 15-14, CD 15-15** and Resource Book p. A-40.

Analyzing

Ask students to look at the harmony part for "*Canción Mixteca.*"

6c **ASK** Do the notes of the harmony part move by step or leap? (both)

When does the harmony part echo the melody? (mm. 33-34 and mm. 41-43)

Have all students sing the harmony part with the recording **CD 15-11.**

3 CLOSE

Element: **TEXTURE/HARMONY** — **ASSESSMENT**

1c **Performance/Observation** Have students sing "*Canción Mixteca*" in two-part harmony with the recording **CD 15-11.**

As they sing, listen to the two-part harmony and observe whether the two groups were successful at singing the parts accurately and independently.

SKILLS REINFORCEMENT

▶ **Vocal Development** To improve students' skill at singing parallel thirds, have them warm up by singing a major scale in a two-part round. Divide the class into two groups and have the students

- Sing a major scale on quarter notes using pitch syllables, starting on C or D. Do not repeat any notes.
- Sing the scale in a two-part round as you conduct. (Group I begins, and Group II begins two beats later)
- Sing the scale as a round again, but be prepared to stop and hold any pitches to tune the thirds.

When students feel confident with this exercise, have them sing it in four groups as a four-part round.

TECHNOLOGY/MEDIA LINK

Web Site To learn more about the music of Mexico, visit *www.sfsuccessnet.com.*

Lesson	Elements	Skills	
LESSON 1 **Ragtime and the New Century** pp. 332–335 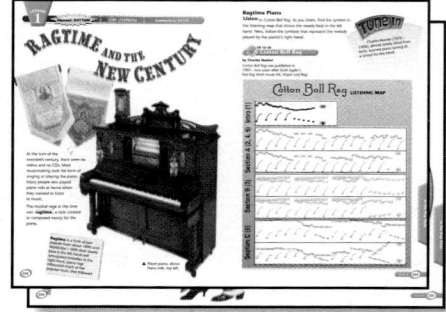	**Element: Rhythm** **Concept:** Pattern **Focus:** Syncopation **Secondary Element** Form: ABC **National Standards** 6b 8a 8b 9a	**Skill: Listening** **Objective:** Identify elements of ragtime syncopation in a listening selection **Secondary Skills** • **Listening** Listen to the recording and follow the listening map • **Moving** Perform a cakewalk to the song • **Moving** Learn the "Ragtime Dance"	
LESSON 2 **Swing With the Big Bands** pp. 336–339  	**Element: Melody** **Concept:** Pitch and direction **Focus:** Repeated notes **Secondary Element** Rhythm: syncopation **National Standards** 1c 2c 4c 5b 6b 7a 8a 8b 9a	**Skill: Singing** **Objective:** Perform a song from the swing era containing repeated notes **Secondary Skills** • **Analyzing** Discuss the visual elements of swing style • **Playing** Play song chords on keyboard • **Listening** Listen to and discuss another version of a song • **Playing** Play response section of a song on pitched instrument • **Moving** Read about and perform an appropriate movement to the song • **Listening** Listen to the song and list the elements of swing that it includes	**SKILLS REINFORCEMENT** • **Keyboard** Tips to help all students perform a keyboard accompaniment
LESSON 3 **Scat Singing** pp. 340–343  	**Element: Melody** **Concept:** Pitch and direction **Focus:** Melodic ornamentation **Secondary Element** Harmony: two-part **National Standards** 1d 2c 6a 6b 7a 8b 9a 9b	**Skill: Singing** **Objective:** Improvise using scat syllables and melodic ornamentation **Secondary Skills** • **Analyzing** Analyze the form of a song • **Singing** Sing the song in two parts • **Playing** Play a chord accompaniment on selected instruments • **Listening** Listen to and discuss selection containing scat singing • **Listening** Listen to a selection with a listening map to hear instruments and style • **Moving** Perform a basic swing dance pattern with selection	**SKILLS REINFORCEMENT** • **Recorder** Play an accompaniment

Connections

Music and Other Literature

Connection: Style

Activity: Perform a dance that reflects elements of ragtime style

CULTURAL CONNECTION
Ragtime Background on the musical style
Cakewalk History of the dance

ACROSS THE CURRICULUM
Science Structure of the player piano
Language arts Read books about the ragtime era

SPOTLIGHT ON
The Composer Information about Charles Hunter
Joplin's Rag Information on the listening selection

MOVEMENT **The Cakewalk Game** Learn to play the cakewalk game

BUILDING SKILLS THROUGH MUSIC **Social Studies** Create a Keyboard Instrument timeline

---

Listening Selections
Cotton Boll Rag
North Carolina Breakdown
Scott Joplin's New Rag

Listening Map *Cotton Boll Rag*

Poem "Ragtime"
M·U·S·I·C M·A·K·E·R·S
Scott Joplin

More Music Choices
"Morning Comes Early," p. 13
"Éliza Kongo," p. 14

ASSESSMENT

Music Journal Writing Compare the meter and syncopation of two recording selections

TECHNOLOGY/MEDIA LINK
Transparency Display listening map and give suggestions

Connection: Related Arts

Activity: Discover how swing era style can be expressed through the visual arts

SPOTLIGHT ON
The Artist Information about Michele Wood
Swing Dancing Background of the dance style

ACROSS THE CURRICULUM
Art Discuss Art Deco
Social Studies The social changes of the 1920s

CULTURAL CONNECTION **Swing** Information about 1930s-1940s musical style

CHARACTER EDUCATION **Respect** Discuss how actions demonstrate respect

BUILDING SKILLS THROUGH MUSIC **Language** Write a new version of the song lyrics

---

Song "It Don't Mean a Thing (If It Ain't Got That Swing)"

Listening Selection *It Don't Mean a Thing If It Ain't Got That Swing*

Arts Connection
I see the rhythm
M·U·S·I·C M·A·K·E·R·S
Duke Ellington

More Music Choices
"Sing, Sing, Sing!" p. 340

ASSESSMENT

Performance/Peer Critique Perform a song with appropriate pitch and style, and evaluate the performance

TECHNOLOGY/MEDIA LINK
Video Library View jazz video on song from lesson

Connection: Style

Activity: Discuss scat singing and the sound of the big bands during the swing era

CULTURAL CONNECTION **Technological Advances** The effect of the rapid development of technology

SPOTLIGHT ON
The Performer Information about Diane Schuur
The Performer Information about Glenn Miller

TEACHER TO TEACHER **Big Band Instrumentation** Discuss certain swing instruments

ACROSS THE CURRICULUM **Social Studies** Read a book on American popular music

MOVEMENT **Popular Dance** Learn the basic swing step

BUILDING SKILLS THROUGH MUSIC **Social Studies** Develop a time line

---

Song "Sing, Sing, Sing!"

Listening Selections
How High the Moon
Pennsylvania 6-5000
M·U·S·I·C M·A·K·E·R·S
Ella Fitzgerald

Listening Map *Pennsylvania 6-5000*

More Music Choices
"It Don't Mean a Thing (If It Ain't Got That Swing)," p. 336
"Now's the Time," p. 445

ASSESSMENT

Performance/Observation Ornament the melody of a well-known song and experiment with scat singing

TECHNOLOGY/MEDIA LINK
Transparency Use listening map to point out excerpts from Pennsylvania 6-5000
CD-ROM Enter and play back chord progressions and rhythms

Lesson	Elements	Skills	
LESSON 4 **On the Lone Prairie** pp. 344–347 	**Element: Rhythm** **Concept:** Meter **Focus:** Meter in 3 **Secondary Element** Melody: pattern **National Standards** 1c 2a 5c 6b 7b 8b 9a	**Skill: Singing** **Objective:** Sing a song in triple meter that includes yodeling **Secondary Skills** • **Playing** Play provided instrumental accompaniment • **Listening** Listen to a duet version of a song selection	**SKILLS REINFORCEMENT** • **Keyboard** Play an ostinato accompaniment • **Recorder** Play an accompaniment
LESSON 5 **Home Sweet Home** pp. 348–351 	**Element: Rhythm** **Concept:** Beat **Focus:** Steady beat **Secondary Element** Melody: phrases **National Standards** 1c 2b 3b 5a 6b 7b 8b 9a	**Skill: Moving** **Objective:** Perform steady-beat movements in a country line dance **Secondary Skills** • **Listening** Listen to a country song to determine instruments and mood • **Singing** Sing a song and tap the steady beat • **Performing** Perform the rhythm accompaniment with the song • **Listening** Listen to and discuss the selection by a country music group • **Listening** Listen to a selected recording and review it	**SKILLS REINFORCEMENT** • **Recorder** Play an accompaniment
LESSON 6 **Singing the Blues** pp. 352–353 	**Element: Form** **Concept:** Blues **Focus:** 12-bar blues **Secondary Element** Harmony: chords **National Standards** 2b 3b 4c 6c 7b 9a	**Skill: Playing** **Objective:** Perform a 12-bar blues chord progression **Secondary Skills** • **Singing** Discuss blues styles and sing the song • **Playing** Accompany the song with chords • **Listening** Listen to a selection and discuss the performer and style	**SKILLS REINFORCEMENT** • **Recorder** Tips to help all students perform a recorder accompaniment • **Keyboard** Play a tritone accompaniment • **Mallets** Play an Orff accompaniment

Connections

Connection: Social Studies

Activity: Become aware of the role of cowboys in the expansion of the American West

MEETING INDIVIDUAL NEEDS **Boys' Changing Voices** Tips on helping adolescent boys' voices

ACROSS THE CURRICULUM **Social Studies** Discuss the life of a cowboy

CULTURAL CONNECTION **Dance** Explore country line dance

TEACHER TO TEACHER
Young Singers Review the use of healthy vocal techniques
Resource Materials Teacher resources on American country music

SPOTLIGHT ON **The Singer** Information about Eddy Arnold

BUILDING SKILLS THROUGH MUSIC **Language** List the important musical characteristics of the song

Connection: Related Arts

Activity: Explore country style line dancing

TEACHER TO TEACHER **Classroom Project** Create a bulletin board display or portfolios of popular recording artists

CULTURAL CONNECTION
Country Music Roots Origin of country music
The Grande Ole Opry History of the Grand Ole Opry

SPOTLIGHT ON
Country Music Background and origin of country music
The Musician Information about Eddie Rabbitt

MOVEMENT **Line Dance** Learn a line dance routine

SCHOOL TO HOME CONNECTION **Country Performers** Create a bulletin board of country recording stars

BUILDING SKILLS THROUGH MUSIC **Language** Experiment with articulation styles

Connection: Style

Activity: Explore elements of blues style

SPOTLIGHT ON **The Singer** Information about Bessie Smith

BUILDING SKILLS THROUGH MUSIC **Language** Rewrite words and phrases with correct style, grammar, and spelling

Music and Other Literature

Song "Cattle Call"

Listening Selection *Cattle Call*
M•U•S•I•C M•A•K•E•R•S
   LeAnn Rimes

More Music Choices
"Orange Blossom Special," p. 266
"Rocky Top," p. 348

Song "Rocky Top"

Listening Selections
Tennessee River
I Love a Rainy Night
M•U•S•I•C M•A•K•E•R•S
   Alabama

More Music Choices
"Home on the Range," p. 69
"Cattle Call," p. 344

Song "St. Louis Blues"

Listening Selection *St. Louis Blues*
M•U•S•I•C M•A•K•E•R•S
   Bessie Smith

More Music Choices
"Good Mornin', Blues," p. 224

ASSESSMENT

Performance/Self Assessment Perform a song with an accompaniment and evaluate the performance

TECHNOLOGY/MEDIA LINK
Video Library View a country fiddle duet

ASSESSMENT

Performance/Peer Critique Perform a line dance with a song and evaluate the performance

TECHNOLOGY/MEDIA LINK
Web Site More information about country music and musicians
Video Library View lesson on country singer

ASSESSMENT

Performance/Peer Critique Create a 12-bar blues song and evaluate

TECHNOLOGY/MEDIA LINK
CD-ROM Create a jazz swing style accompaniment for the song

Lesson	Elements	Skills

LESSON 7

Upbeat Blues

pp. 354–355

Element: Rhythm
Concept: Pattern
Focus: Syncopated rhythmic motive

Secondary Element
Form: verse/refrain

National Standards
1c 2a 5c 6c 7a 8b 9a

Skill: Singing
Objective: Sing a blues song containing a syncopated rhythmic motive

Secondary Skills
- **Reading** Read rhythms in the song notation
- **Playing** Play a motive on unpitched instruments

LESSON 8

Rock 'n' Roll 'n' Sing

pp. 356–359

Element: Texture/Harmony
Concept: Harmony
Focus: Blues chord progression

Secondary Element
Rhythm: beat

National Standards
2d 6a 6b 8a 8b 9a

Skill: Playing
Objective: Accompany a rock 'n' roll song using a standard blues chord progression

Secondary Skills
- **Listening** Listen to several rock 'n' roll songs and study the chord progressions and rhythms
- **Moving** Learn a dance for a listening selection

SKILLS REINFORCEMENT
- **Keyboard/Guitar** Accompany a song with a blues chord progression
- **Analyzing/Notating** Transpose a chord progression and play it with another selection

---

LESSON 9

The Soul of the Music

pp. 360–363

Element: Rhythm
Concept: Beat
Focus: Backbeat

Secondary Element
Form: D.S al Coda/Coda

National Standards
1e 2a 2c 5a 6a 6b 9a

Skill: Singing
Objective: Sing a soul song containing backbeat rhythms

Secondary Skills
- **Listening** Listen for the backbeats in a song
- **Singing** Sing the song and clap the backbeat
- **Reading** Identify syncopated patterns in a song
- **Playing** Play the melody rhythm on a hand drum or tambourine with a song

SKILLS REINFORCEMENT
- **Guitar** Play a strumming rhythm pattern to accompany the song
- **Analyzing** Explore the primary chords used in a song

Connections

Music and Other Literature

Connection: Genre

Activity: Recognize that not all blues are sad

- **ACROSS THE CURRICULUM** **Social Studies** View a video about the history of jazz; use a map to trace its migration
- **SPOTLIGHT ON** **New Orleans Jazz** Background information about this unique style
- **CULTURAL CONNECTION** **The Blues Era** History of the style
- **BUILDING SKILLS THROUGH MUSIC** **Social Studies** Locate cities that are famous for blues on a map

Song "Basin Street Blues"

More Music Choices
"This Train," p. 27
"Mango Walk," p. 200

ASSESSMENT

Performance/Peer Critique Sing and play a rhythmic motive and evaluate success

TECHNOLOGY/MEDIA LINK

Video Library Watch video to see a performance of a jazz song

---

Connection: Related Arts

Activity: Perform the Twist, a dance that was popular during the early rock 'n' roll era

- **ACROSS THE CURRICULUM** **Social Studies** Research rock 'n' roll
- **CULTURAL CONNECTION** **The 1950s** Discuss the history and culture of the decade
- **AUDIENCE ETIQUETTE** **Get There Early!** Describe the advantages of arriving early
- **SPOTLIGHT ON**
  The Performer Information about Chubby Checker
  Rock 'n' Roll Background of the style
- **SCHOOL TO HOME CONNECTION** **Fifty Plus** Interview older family members and friends about rock 'n' roll artists
- **BUILDING SKILLS THROUGH MUSIC** **Language** Create a Venn diagram listing musical characteristics of two performing groups

Listening Selections
Rock Around the Clock
Bye Bye Love
The Great Pretender
The Twist

M·U·S·I·C M·A·K·E·R·S
The Platters

More Music Choices
"Hound Dog," p. 212
"Dancin' in the Street," p. 361

ASSESSMENT

Performance/Observation Play an accompaniment to a song with the correct chord progressions

TECHNOLOGY/MEDIA LINK

Web Site More information about the music and performing artists of the 1950s

---

Connection: Genre

Activity: Become familiar with the characteristics of classic soul music

- **ACROSS THE CURRICULUM**
  Language Arts Read a book about soul artists and their music
  Language Arts Read books about Motown soul artists and their music
- **MOVEMENT**
  Popular Dances/Then Research dances from the first half of the 20th century
  Popular Dances/Now Discuss current popular dance
- **SPOTLIGHT ON** **The Performers** Information about Martha Reeves and the Vandellas
- **CHARACTER EDUCATION** **Emotional Expression** Discuss inappropriate and appropriate means of expressing emotions
- **BUILDING SKILLS THROUGH MUSIC** **Language** Identify unique qualities of a performer

Song "Dancin' in the Street"

Listening Selections
Dancin' in the Street
Soulville
M·U·S·I·C M·A·K·E·R·S
Aretha Franklin

More Music Choices
"Get on Your Feet," p. 6

ASSESSMENT

Performance/Observation Sing a song and clap the backbeats

TECHNOLOGY/MEDIA LINK

Web Site More information on popular music of the 1960s

INTRODUCING THE UNIT

The different styles of music in this unit create a time line that illustrates some of the social and technological changes of the twentieth century. Topics include the player piano, "big band" sound, scat singing, country, blues, gospel, and the evolution of a unique style called "rock 'n' roll."

Presented on p. 329 is a brief overview of the skills that are assessed in this unit. (See below and pp. 329–330 for unit highlights of related curricular experiences.)

For a more detailed unit overview, see Unit at a Glance, pp. 327a–327f.

UNIT PROJECT

This unit celebrates American popular music from the end of the nineteenth century to the present. Throughout this unit students will encounter important musical styles and some of the key personalities who helped create them.

Invite students to organize a "Trip Down Memory Lane" that showcases some of the significant forms of American popular music.

Have students

- Go through each lesson, learn the songs, and listen to examples of each style.
- Learn other activities in the lesson that exemplify each style.
- Interview their grandparents or other older members of the community about some of the styles of music studied. Gather information about how they listened or danced to the music when they were young.
- Collect examples of clothing worn during some of the eras studied or other items such as record jackets.
- Take the stylistic themes of each lesson and build a presentation highlighting these lessons. Divide into teams to work on different lessons or styles.
- Share the presentation with other students, parents and relatives, school administrators, and community members.

Popular Music Sweeps the Nation

New styles of popular music began to sweep across the country in the twentieth century. Music played an important role in expressing society's happenings, hopes, dreams, and feelings. Almost every style of music had a dance to go with it— from the cakewalk to the jitterbug to rock 'n' roll.

328

ACROSS THE CURRICULUM

Unit Highlights The following interdisciplinary activities in this unit are related to the music elements presented in the lessons. See Unit at a Glance, pp. 327a–327f, for topical descriptions presented according to lesson sequence.

▶ **ART**

- Learn about the Art Deco period (p. 336)

▶ **LANGUAGE ARTS**

- Share books about the ragtime era (p. 334)
- Read about soul artists of Motown (p. 360)
- Share books about Motown artists (p. 362)

▶ **SCIENCE**

- Discover facts about the player piano (p. 332)

▶ **SOCIAL STUDIES**

- Discuss social changes in the 1930s and swing music (p. 338)
- Write about the popularity of swing music in the 1930s and 1940s (p. 342)
- Learn about the life of a cowboy (p. 344)
- Share a video about jazz history and artists (p. 354)
- Research rock 'n' roll artists of the 1950s (p. 356)

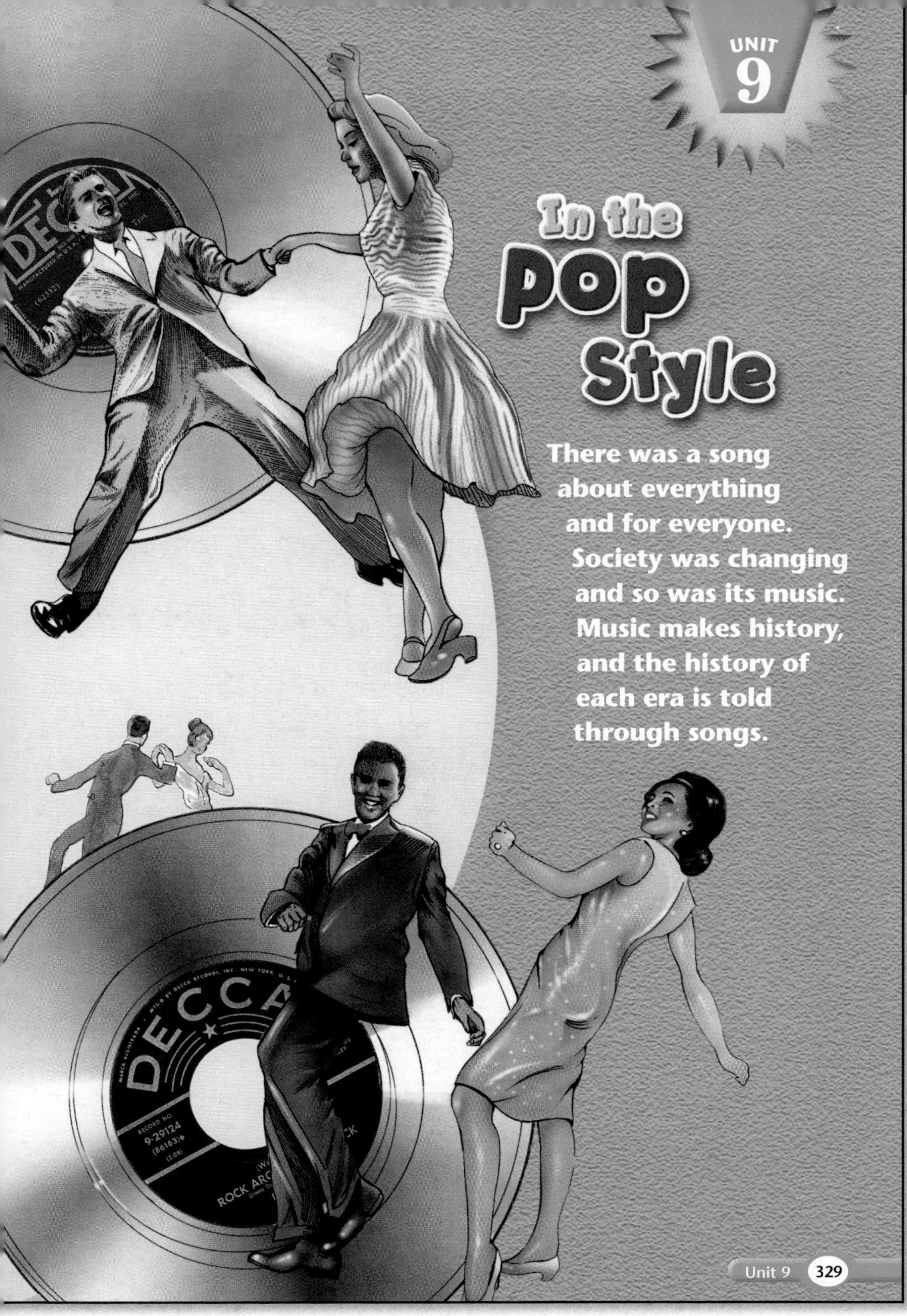

In the Pop Style

UNIT 9

There was a song about everything and for everyone. Society was changing and so was its music. Music makes history, and the history of each era is told through songs.

Unit 9 **329**

MUSIC SKILLS
ASSESSED IN THIS UNIT

Reading Music: Rhythm
- Read and tap a ragtime rhythm (p. 334)
- Read and clap a syncopated pattern (p. 362)

Reading Music: Pitch
- Read and identify pitches in a scat song (p. 341)
- Read notation for a keyboard ostinato accompaniment (p. 346)

Performing Music: Singing
- Perform a song in swing style (p. 339)
- Sing a song using scat syllables (p. 343)
- Perform a cowboy song (p. 347)
- Sing a blues song (p. 355)

Moving to Music
- Conduct meter in 2 (p. 335)
- Perform a country line dance (p. 351)

Performing Music: Playing
- Perform an accompaniment with a cowboy song (p. 347)
- Perform backbeats while singing a song (p. 363)

Creating Music
- Improvise new rhythms for a chordal accompaniment (p. 338)
- Create a blues-style text and melody (p. 353)

Listening to Music
- Listen for meter in two ragtime selections (pp. 333, 335)
- Listen for blues chords in a rock 'n' roll selection (p. 359)

CULTURAL CONNECTION

Unit Highlights The musical literature in this unit provides many opportunities for students to explore a variety of world cultures. See Unit at a Glance, pp. 327a–327f, for topical descriptions presented according to lesson sequence.

▶ **AMERICAN REGIONAL**
- Explore facts about ragtime (p. 332)
- Learn about the cakewalk dance (p. 334)
- Discover facts about swing music (p. 337)
- Discuss the effect of technological advances on music (p. 340)
- Learn about various styles of American popular dancing (p. 345)
- Explore the history of country music (p. 348)
- Learn about the Grand Ole Opry (p. 351)
- Discuss the blues era of music (p. 355)
- Discover facts about the 1950s (p. 356)

OPENING ACTIVITIES

<table>
<tr><td colspan="2">MATERIALS</td></tr>
<tr><td>• "Land of a Thousand Dances"</td><td>CD 15-16</td></tr>
<tr><td colspan="2">Recording Routine:
Intro (4 m.); v. 1; refrain; interlude (24 m.);
refrain; v. 2; refrain; coda</td></tr>
</table>

Listening

Ask students to read the information on p. 330 about dance crazes that swept the country during the 1960s. Then play "Land of a Thousand Dances" **CD 15-16.** Encourage students to sing along on the refrain in unison.

Singing

Have students look at the refrain.

ASK **Where does the harmony part begin in the refrain?** (measure 7)

Divide the class into two groups. Have one group learn the melody part and the other group learn the harmony part. When they are comfortable singing their parts, ask them to switch. This will ensure that all students are able to sing both the melody and harmony parts.

Invite the class to sing "Land of a Thousand Dances" with the Stereo Performance Track **CD 15-17.**

Music for Dancing

Roll up the rug and get ready to dance! After Chubby Checker created "The Twist" in the 1960s, lots of new dance crazes swept the country. "Land of a Thousand Dances" mentions many of those dances, such as "the mashed potato."

Sing this flashback favorite with its popular "na-na" chorus.

ASSESSMENT

Unit Highlights This unit includes a variety of strategies and methods, described below, to track students' progress and assess their understanding of lesson objectives.

▶ **INFORMAL ASSESSMENTS**

At the close of each Teacher's Edition lesson in this unit, one of the following types of assessments is used to evaluate the learning of the key element focus or skill objective.

- Music Journal Writing (p. 335)
- Performance/Observation (pp. 343, 359, 363)
- Performance/Peer Critique (pp. 339, 351, 353, 355)
- Performance/Self-Assessment (p. 347)

▶ **RUBRICS**

Visit *www.sfsuccessnet.com* for rubrics to assess students' achievement in music skills.

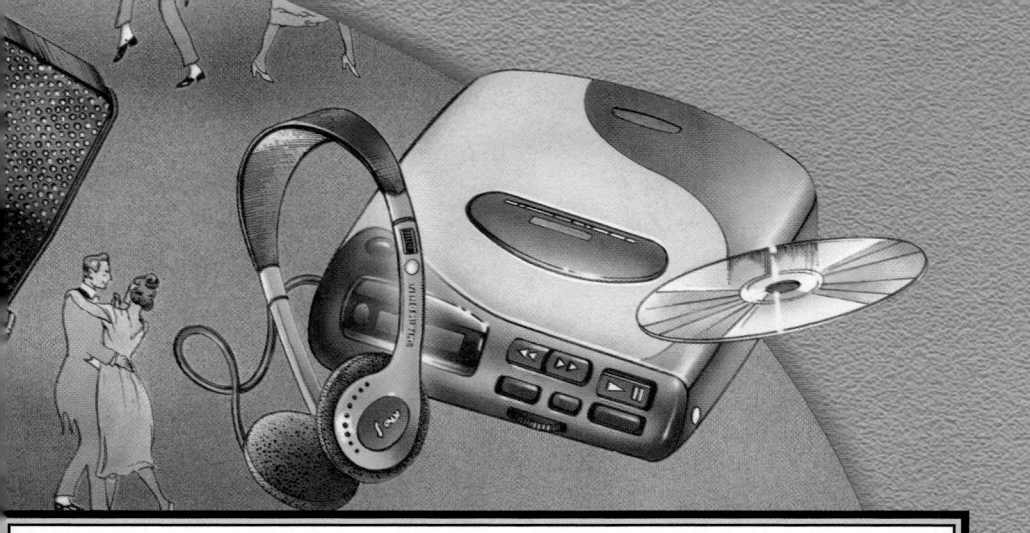

Moving

Encourage students to move to the beat while they sing "Land of a Thousand Dances." Some students may enjoy improvising movements or creating a movement routine to perform.

REFRAIN

Na na na na na ____ na na na na ____ na na na na

na na na na na. ____ Na na na na na. ____

na na na na ____ na na na na

Last time to Coda *Last time to Coda* 1. F **23**

na na na na na.

2. F *D.S. al Coda* Coda F

na na na na na.

INNOVATIVE TEACHER SUPPORT FOR THIS UNIT

- **MAKING MUSIC DVD, Grade 5** contains video segments that support lessons, including signing and movement.
- **MAKING MUSIC with Movement and Dance** provides more opportunities for large group activities in music or physical education classes.
- **MAKING MUSIC with Technology** provides lesson plans for many technology applications; includes MIDI files.
- **¡A cantar!** features recorded songs and lessons from around the Spanish-speaking world; includes strategies for bilingual classes and for English-speaking teachers working with Spanish-speaking students.
- **Bridges to Asia** features recorded songs and lessons from Asian and Pacific region cultures.
- **www.sfsuccessnet.com** provides an online lesson planner to conveniently create lesson plans at school or at home. Includes rubrics for assessment, lesson modifications to meet the needs of all students, performance musicals based on program content, and more.

Unit 9 331

TECHNOLOGY/MEDIA LINK

Unit Highlights The following components are used in this unit to reinforce and expand students' understanding of music elements and related themes. See Unit at a Glance, pp. 327a–327f, for a descriptive listing according to lesson sequence.

▶ **CD-ROM**

- Arrange a swing style accompaniment using *Band-in-a-Box* (p. 343)
- Learn improvisation using *Band-in-a-Box* (p. 353)

▶ **TRANSPARENCY**

- Display a listening map transparency to help students follow a selection (p. 335, 343)

▶ **VIDEO LIBRARY/DVD**

- Share a video showcasing a jazz performance (p. 339)
- Show a video featuring a country fiddle duet (p. 347)
- Share a video showcasing a blues performance (p. 355)

▶ **WEB SITE**

- Go to *www.sbgmusic.com* for more information on country music and musicians (p. 351); music and performing artists of the 1950's (p. 359); popular music of the 1960's (p. 363)

LESSON AT A GLANCE

Element Focus   **RHYTHM** Syncopation

Skill Objective   **LISTENING** Identify elements of ragtime syncopation in a listening selection

Connection Activity   **STYLE** Perform a dance that reflects elements of ragtime style

MATERIALS
- *Cotton Boll Rag*   **CD 15-18**
- "Ragtime" (poem)
- *North Carolina Breakdown*   **CD 15-19**
- *Scott Joplin's New Rag*   **CD 15-21**
- **Dance Directions** for *North Carolina Breakdown* p. 564
- **Dance Directions** for *Scott Joplin's New Rag* p. 565

VOCABULARY
ragtime   syncopation

◆ ◆ ◆ ◆ National Standards ◆ ◆ ◆ ◆
6b Listen and analyze uses of rhythm and form in music from diverse genres

8a Show how different arts portray the same idea in unique ways

8b Identify ways music relates to dance and science

9a Describe characteristics of music styles from a variety of cultures

MORE MUSIC CHOICES
For more practice with syncopation:

"Morning Comes Early," p. 13

"Éliza Kongo," p. 14

RAGTIME AND THE NEW CENTURY

'PIANOLA'

At the turn of the twentieth century, there were no radios and no CDs. Most musicmaking took the form of singing or playing the piano. Many people also played piano rolls at home when they wanted to listen to music.

The musical rage at the time was **ragtime**, a style created or composed mostly for the piano.

Ragtime is a form of jazz popular from about 1890 until World War I. With their steady beat in the left hand and syncopated melodies in the right hand, piano rags influenced much of the popular music that followed.

▲ Player piano, above. Piano rolls, top left.

332

Footnotes

CULTURAL CONNECTION

▶ **Ragtime** Ragtime began in the 1890s and peaked in 1915. Since recording technology was in its infancy, popular music of this era was spread mostly by way of sheet music. Tin Pan Alley, for example, referred to a street in New York City lined with publishers who hired composers to turn out as many tunes as possible. Ragtime music was written for many dance forms, including the march, the cakewalk (an elegant dance of the day), and the two-step.

BUILDING SKILLS THROUGH MUSIC

▶ **Social Studies** Have students prepare a Keyboard Instrument time line that begins in 1700, using a scale of 25 years=6 inches. Ask students to review information about keyboard instruments from pp. 236–239 and list the names of keyboard instruments with dates on the time line (Harpsichord 1723, Piano 1860, Player Piano 1897, Synthesizer 1964).

ACROSS THE CURRICULUM

8b ▶ **Science** The player piano, patented in 1897 by organ builder Edwin Scott Votey, is an automatic instrument consisting of a piano and a mechanical device that plays it. A roll of paper with perforations punched into it passes over a bar with holes corresponding to each of the keys of the piano. When a perforation on the piano roll aligns with a hole on the mechanism, the suction created by pumping pedals draws air through the hole and causes the piano to sound. Most rolls were produced mechanically, although some were punched during an actual performance. Rolls produced by a performer could reproduce the nuances of dynamics and rhythm of the actual performance. Families frequently spent evenings and weekends listening to music played on the player piano.

Ragtime Piano

Listen to *Cotton Boll Rag*. As you listen, find the symbol in the listening map that shows the steady beat in the left hand. Next, follow the symbols that represent the melody played by the pianist's right hand.

Charles Hunter (1876 - 1906), almost totally blind from birth, learned piano tuning at a school for the blind.

CD 15–18
Cotton Boll Rag

by Charles Hunter

Cotton Boll Rag was published in 1901—two years after Scott Joplin's first big sheet music hit, *Maple Leaf Rag*.

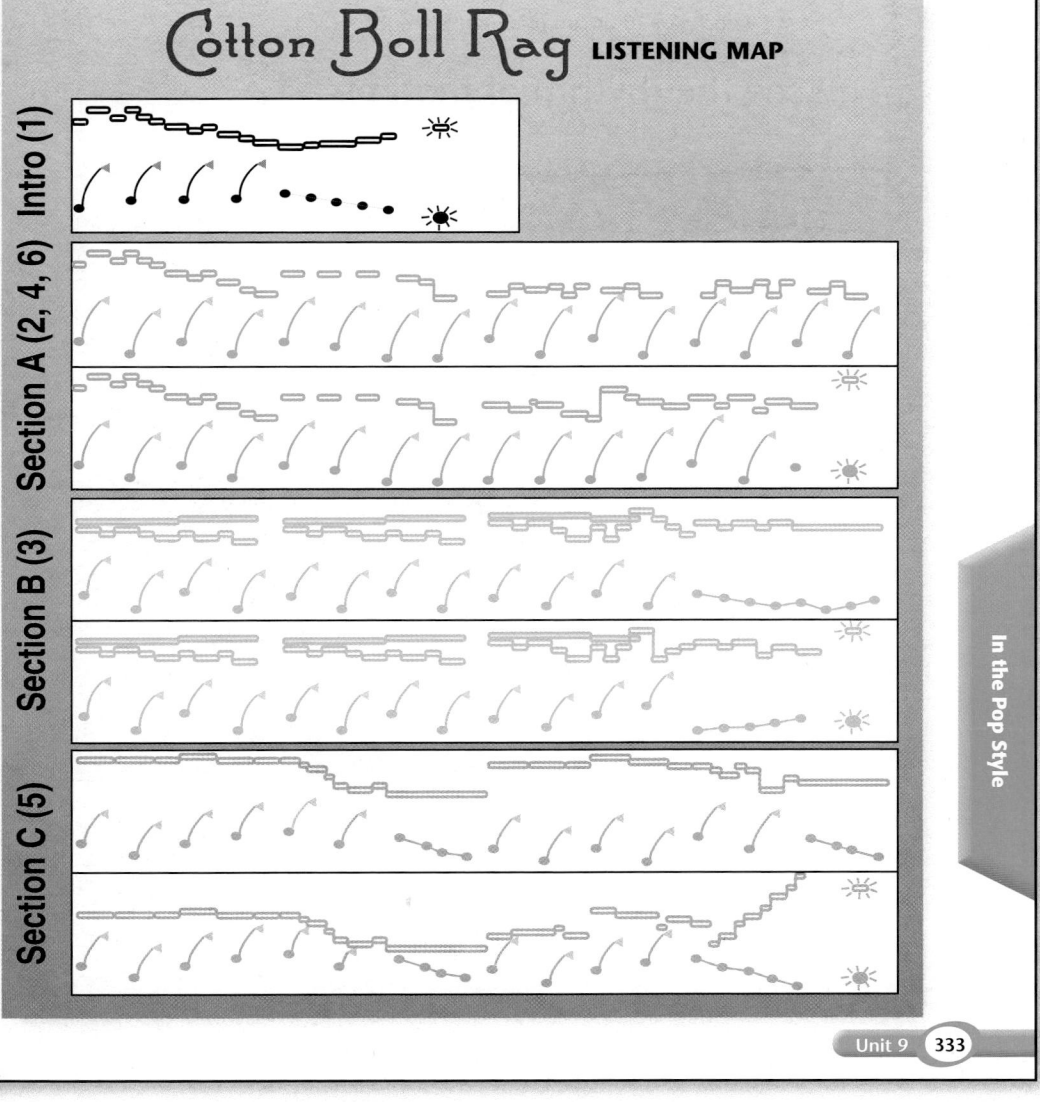

Cotton Boll Rag LISTENING MAP

Intro (1)
Section A (2, 4, 6)
Section B (3)
Section C (5)

In the Pop Style

Unit 9 **333**

1 INTRODUCE

Engage students in a discussion of various types of popular music. Inform students that popular music

- Is music favored by the majority of the people.
- Changes quite regularly.
- Is composed music but shorter than most classical pieces.
- Exists all over the world.

9a Ask students to read the information on p. 332 about a style of American popular music called ragtime. See Across the Curriculum, p. 332, for information on the player piano, which played a major role in popularizing this style.

8a Invite students to read the poem "Ragtime" on p. 334. Allow volunteers to perform individual dramatic readings for the class.

2 DEVELOP

Listening

Direct students' attention to the listening map on p. 333 for *Cotton Boll Rag*. ("Boll" refers to the seed pod of the cotton plant.) Point out and discuss the lower set of symbols, which depicts the left-hand steady beat, and the upper set, which depicts the right-hand syncopated melody.

Tell students that the order of the sections they will hear is (1) Introduction, (2) A, (3) B, (4) A, (5) C, (6) A.

Play the recording of *Cotton Boll Rag* **CD 15-18** as students follow the listening map.

ASK What is the form of the music? (rondo)

continued on page 334

SPOTLIGHT ON

▶ **The Composer** Charles Hunter (1876–1906) was born in Tennessee and taught himself to compose and play ragtime. Considered a pioneer among white ragtime composers, Hunter incorporated into his rags many of the characteristics of country marches and country band fiddle tunes. His most popular rag, "Tickled to Death," was published in 1899—the same year as Joplin's "Maple Leaf Rag." Hunter's early death was attributed to tuberculosis.

MOVEMENT

▶ **The Cakewalk Game** The cakewalk may refer to several kinds of dances and to a game as well. In the game, as in the dance, a cake was awarded to those who promenaded or danced with the most original steps. Over the years the movements to the game have become simpler, with people just walking in time to the music.

To prepare for the game, place numbered squares along a circle. A hat may be filled with small pieces of paper with corresponding numbers. Prizes may be cupcakes, cookies, stickers, or whatever is appropriate. To play the game, everyone walks counterclockwise around the circle. When the music suddenly stops, everyone freezes; someone pulls a number from the hat (or perhaps the number has been secretly chosen ahead of time) and whoever is on or is closest to that numbered square wins a prize.

Unit 9   In the Pop Style   333

Moving

Inform students that, at the turn of the century,

- People usually went to halls where they could dance and listen to rags.
- The dance most frequently performed to rags was the cakewalk, shown on p. 334.

Share with students the information on the cakewalk in Cultural Connection below. Then invite students to move to the music of *North Carolina Breakdown* **CD 15-19**, using the Dance Directions on p. 564 or the cakewalk game described in Movement on p. 333.

Listening

Have students read the information about Scott Joplin on p. 335 in their books.

 Invite students to listen to a rag by Joplin, *Scott Joplin's New Rag* **CD 15-21**. After repeated listenings, ask students to

- Choose a "steady-beat" partner.
- Isolate one of the syncopated motives in the rag (see below).
- Tap the motive with accurate rhythm while the partner keeps a steady beat.
- Switch roles with their partners.

Ragtime
by Toyomi Igus

I see the rhythm of ragtime.

In our fine top hats and gowns,
we celebrate our newfound freedom
at ballroom dances and festive jubilees
where we listen to Scott Joplin's "Maple Leaf Rag"
and dare to dream of an equal world.

I see the rhythm of ragtime—

the music of the cakewalk,
the happy, high–steppin' dance of former slaves,
mimicking the high–steppin' dances of their masters,
now danced by everyone.

I see the rhythm of ragtime—

in the fine, cultured places
and the optimistic faces
of free men and women.

Learn to do the cakewalk step and then **move** to this musical selection.

 CD 15–19
North Carolina Breakdown

by Leroy Arthur Smith
as performed by Sammy Shelor
The cakewalk became popular at the turn of the 20th century.

Dancing the cakewalk ▶

334

 Footnotes

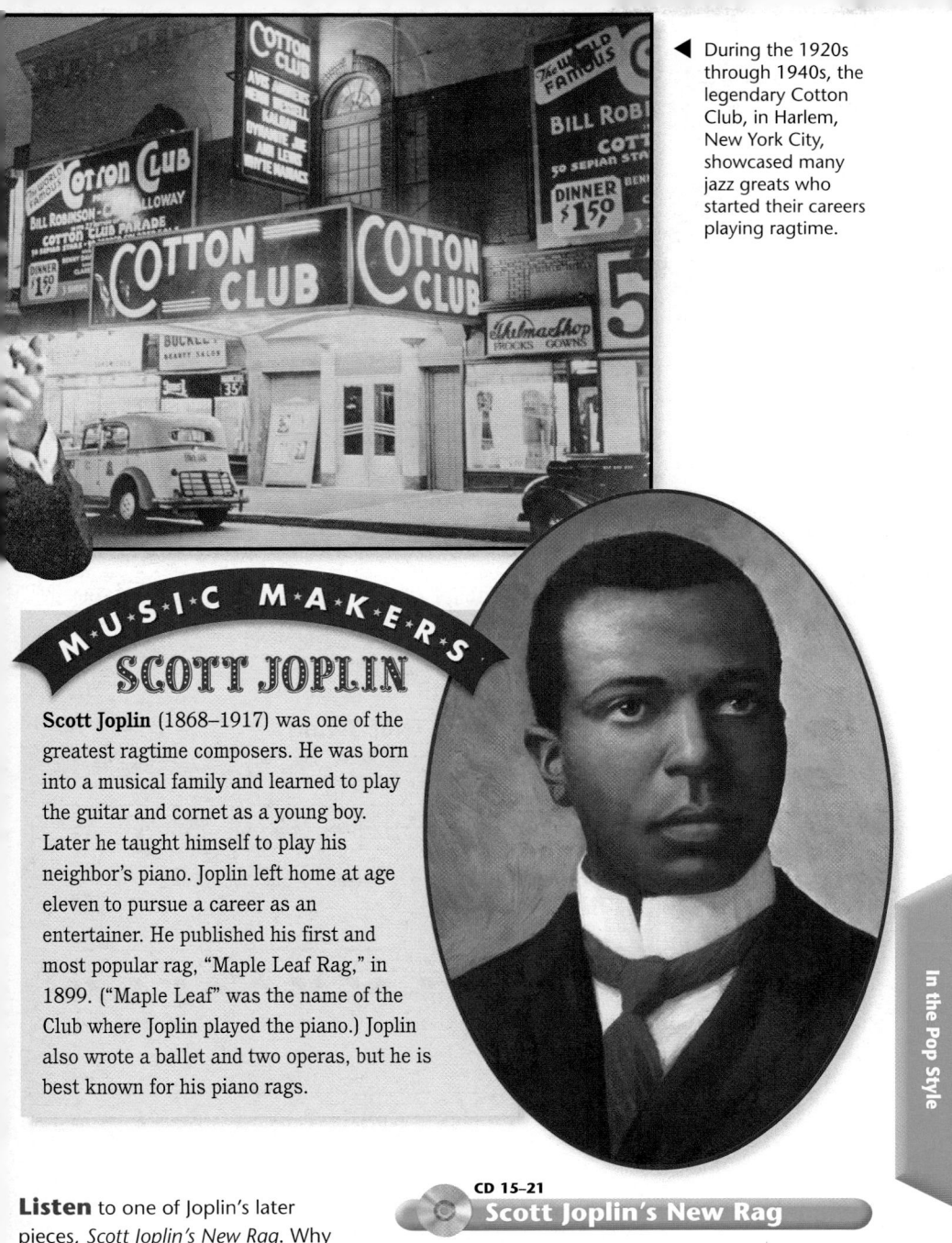

During the 1920s through 1940s, the legendary Cotton Club, in Harlem, New York City, showcased many jazz greats who started their careers playing ragtime.

M·U·S·I·C M·A·K·E·R·S

SCOTT JOPLIN

Scott Joplin (1868–1917) was one of the greatest ragtime composers. He was born into a musical family and learned to play the guitar and cornet as a young boy. Later he taught himself to play his neighbor's piano. Joplin left home at age eleven to pursue a career as an entertainer. He published his first and most popular rag, "Maple Leaf Rag," in 1899. ("Maple Leaf" was the name of the Club where Joplin played the piano.) Joplin also wrote a ballet and two operas, but he is best known for his piano rags.

Listen to one of Joplin's later pieces, *Scott Joplin's New Rag*. Why do you think most rags were written for the piano?

CD 15–21
Scott Joplin's New Rag

by Scott Joplin
This rag was written in 1912, the same year the *Titanic* made its fateful voyage.

In the Pop Style

Unit 9 **335**

Moving

Inform students that ragtime rhythms have inspired choreographers to invent new dance steps to rag music. One such newly created dance, entitled "Ragtime Dance," uses movements related to the Charleston. Students can learn the steps to this dance and move to *Scott Joplin's New Rag* **CD 15-21.** The Dance Directions can be found on p. 565.

3 CLOSE

Element: RHYTHM **ASSESSMENT**

6b **Music Journal Writing** Play the recordings of *Cotton Boll Rag* **CD 15-18** and *Scott Joplin's New Rag* **CD 15-21.** Ask students to move to or conduct the music as a way of determining the meter ($\frac{2}{4}$) and underscoring the offbeat quality of the melodic syncopation. Then have students write a description of each piece in their journals using standard terminology in explaining music performances. Their writing should include the following elements of ragtime music.

- Mostly in duple meter.
- Syncopated melody in the treble part.
- Steady beat in the bass part.
- Sounds like a jazzy version of a march.

SPOTLIGHT ON

▶ **Joplin's Rag** "Scott Joplin's New Rag" was written in 1912, near the end of Joplin's career. It is in ABC form. This composition was innovative in its use of the relative minor and scale passages in the B section. Patterns in the C section of the rag hint at the stride piano style to come, which was emulated by "Fats" Waller and James P. Johnson.

TECHNOLOGY/MEDIA LINK

Transparency Display the listening map transparency for *Cotton Boll Rag* as you play the recording. You may wish to point to each section of the piece on the first listening. On subsequent listenings, invite a student to point to the sections as you play the recording.

LESSON 2

LESSON AT A GLANCE

Element Focus   **MELODY** Repeated notes

Skill Focus   **SINGING** Perform a song from the swing era containing repeated notes

Connection Activity   **RELATED ARTS** Discover how swing era style can be expressed through the visual arts

MATERIALS

- "It Don't Mean a Thing (If It Ain't Got That Swing)"   **CD 15-23**

  Recording Routine: Intro (8 m.); vocal; interlude (32 m.); vocal; coda

- *It Don't Mean a Thing If It Ain't Got That Swing*   **CD 15-25**
- keyboard
- selected melody instruments

VOCABULARY

swing   big band   call and response

◆ ◆ ◆ ◆ National Standards ◆ ◆ ◆ ◆

1c Sing music from diverse genres
2c Perform instrumental music from diverse genres
4c Arrange, using electronic media
5b Sightread melodies in treble clef
6b Listen and analyze uses of rhythm, timbre, and form in music from diverse genres
7a Students evaluate the music they perform
8a Show how different arts portray the same idea in unique ways
8b Identify ways music relates to art and social studies
9a Describe characteristics of music styles from a variety of cultures

MORE MUSIC CHOICES

For more practice singing melodies from the swing era: "Sing, Sing, Sing!" p. 340

Element: MELODY   **Skill: SINGING**   **Connection: RELATED ARTS**

SWING with the BIG BANDS

Tune In

In 1931, big bands began sweeping the country. The style of music these big bands played became known as "swing." Many of these bands featured a singer or an instrumentalist as a soloist. These soloists were known as "sidemen."

Sing "It Don't Mean a Thing (If It Ain't Got That Swing)," which was popular during the swing era.

A typical big band of the 1930s featured saxophones, trumpets, trombones, piano, guitars and drums.

It Don't Mean A THING
(If It Ain't Got That Swing)

Words by Irving Mills   Music by Duke Ellington

It don't mean a thing, if it ain't got that swing,

Doo wah, doo wah, doo wah, doo wah, doo wah, doo wah, doo wah, doo wah.

It don't mean a thing, all you got to do is sing.

Doo wah, doo wah, doo wah, doo wah, doo wah, doo wah, doo wah, doo wah.

336

Footnotes

SPOTLIGHT ON

▶ **The Artist** The contemporary African American painter Michele Wood has gained recognition in Nigeria and Canada, as well as in the United States. Wood received the American Book Award for her first book, *Going Back Home: An Artist's Return to the South* (Children's Books, 1996), which is a beautiful and strong treatment of African American history.

BUILDING SKILLS THROUGH MUSIC

▶ **Language** Invite students to read the lyrics of "It Don't Mean a Thing (If It Ain't Got That Swing)" and suggest words that would be good antecedents for "It." Discuss reasons the choices are appropriate for the song and music. Assign a group of students to select one word from the suggestions as a substitute for "It" and write a new version of the song lyrics.

ACROSS THE CURRICULUM

8a ▶ **Art** Swing is the music of the Art Deco period—a period between World War I and World War II that is defined by its art and architecture. The period represents a graciousness of form. Artists were striving for elegant simplicity and used geometric shapes, exotic materials, and vibrant colors in their designs.

Buildings of architectural significance erected during this time include the Chrysler Building in New York City and the Collins Park Hotel in Miami Beach.

It makes no dif-f'rence if ___ it's sweet or hot. ___

Just give that rhy-thm ev - 'ry - thing you got,

Call

Oh, ___ it don't mean a thing, ___ if it ain't got that swing, ___

Response

Doo wah, ___ doo wah, doo wah, doo wah, doo wah, ___ doo wah, doo wah, doo wah.

Reprinted with permission of the publisher, Children's Book Press, San Francisco, CA.
Art copyright © 1998 by Michele Wood

In the Pop Style

Arts **Connection**

▲ Artist Michele Wood's illustration (from the book *i see the rhythm*) captures the rhythmic excitement of swing music in the 1930s.

Unit 9 **337**

1 INTRODUCE

Invite students to read the information on p. 336 and then direct their attention to the song "It Don't Mean a Thing (If It Ain't Got That Swing)" **CD 15-23.** Play the recording as students follow the music.

5b ASK Can you find any places in the song where the melody stays on the same pitch? (the "response" part—lines 2, 4, and 8)

What do you notice about the lyrics of those phrases? (They are scat syllables.)

For a more detailed discussion of the swing era, see Cultural Connection and Spotlight On, below, and Across the Curriculum, p. 338.

2 DEVELOP

Singing

1c Invite students to sing along on the "response" sections of the song as they listen to the recording **CD 15-23.** Then encourage students to sing the entire song with the recording.

9a Help students discover that

- The song is in call-and-response style.
- The beat is steady and the tempo stays the same.
- There is an abundance of syncopated rhythm.
- The rhythm has a bounce.
- The music is good for dancing.

Inform students that

- The song was popular during the big band era of the 1930s and 1940s.
- The strong beat and bounce of the rhythm is typical of music of the swing era.

continued on page 338

CULTURAL CONNECTION

▶ **Swing** Swing began gradually during the late 1920s and continued into the 1940s. Swing was usually played by big bands of ten musicians or more. The instruments of these bands were usually grouped into three categories: rhythm (piano, guitar, acoustic bass, and drums), brass (trumpets and trombones), and reeds (saxophones and clarinets). Most big bands had soloists, or "sidemen." Performers in big bands were required to read music because they played from elaborately written arrangements. Some of the well-known band leaders of the era included Benny Goodman, Count Basie, Duke Ellington, Jimmy Dorsey, Glenn Miller, Woody Herman, Stan Kenton, Harry James, and Lionel Hampton. Many believe swing was the most popular kind of jazz in the twentieth century and is still popular today.

SPOTLIGHT ON

▶ **Swing Dancing** Swing dance is a true United States folk dance. It started in the late 1920s in the ballrooms of Harlem in New York City. In the 1930s, it was called the lindy hop after the heroic American aviator, Charles Lindbergh, whose nickname was "Lucky Lindy."

Over the decades, the dance has also been called the jitterbug, the be-bop, and the boogie-woogie. Today, most people call it swing, with variations called East Coast swing, which is sometimes called lindy hop, as well as West Coast swing and shag.

Swing has experienced a big resurgence in recent years, with people taking dancing lessons and participating in big band dance events and competitions.

Analyzing

 Discuss with students the painting on p. 337—a stylized portrayal of the sights and sounds of 1930s swing. Share information about the artist in Spotlight On, p. 336.

Explain that visual elements of swing style could also be seen in the architecture of the period, as described in Across the Curriculum, p. 336.

Playing

 Encourage students to

- Learn to play the chords shown on p. 338 on the keyboard.
- Use the chords to accompany the recording or classroom singing of "It Don't Mean a Thing (If It Ain't Got That Swing)" **CD 15-23.**
- Improvise new rhythms in which to play the chords.

See Skills Reinforcement, p. 339 for additional keyboard accompaniment suggestions.

Listening

 Invite students to read the information about Duke Ellington on p. 339. Then play the recording of *It Don't Mean a Thing If It Ain't Got That Swing* **CD 15-25** performed by Ella Fitzgerald and the Ellington band. (See p. 341 for a Music Maker feature on Fitzgerald.)

ASK Was the song performed as a call and response or did Ella sing the complete melody by herself? (She sang the complete melody by herself.)

How many different instruments can you hear in the Ellington band? (in order of entrance—piano, drum, bass, tenor sax, baritone sax, trombone, trumpet, clarinet, and alto sax)

Play that Swing

Using a keyboard or another instrument of your choice, learn to **play** the chords shown below. These are the chords used in the response part of "It Don't Mean a Thing," on pages 336–337.

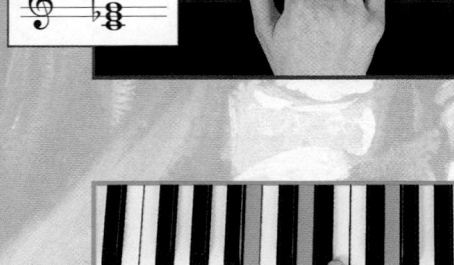

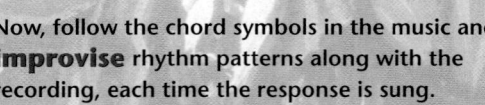

Now, follow the chord symbols in the music and **improvise** rhythm patterns along with the recording, each time the response is sung.

Hear that Swing

Listen to a recording of *It Don't Mean a Thing (If It Ain't Got That Swing)* by one of the great jazz singers of the twentieth century.

 CD 15–25
It Don't Mean a Thing If It Ain't Got That Swing

by Irving Mills and Duke Ellington
as performed by Ella Fitzgerald

This Ellington song also appeared in the Broadway musicals *Bubbling Brown Sugar* and *Sophisticated Ladies.*

338

Footnotes

ACROSS THE CURRICULUM

► Social Studies Many social changes accompanied the development of swing music. At the time, segregation was a reality for most people in the United States. Unfortunately, many Anglo Americans were leery of African American musical styles such as jazz and the blues. They were more receptive to these styles when they saw white performers such as Benny Goodman and Tommy Dorsey play them. A second change in lifestyle was the onset of the Great Depression in 1929. Swing music was decidedly upbeat, and people used the music and the dancing it inspired to escape their troubles. Finally, during World War II, large numbers of Americans left home to fight in other countries. The military sponsored countless U.S.O. tours of big bands, knowing that the homesick troops reveled in the nostalgic feel of the music.

CHARACTER EDUCATION

► Respect To encourage students to consider characteristics of a respectful person, challenge them to think of what such a person does or does not do that makes them respectful. Point out to students that listening to different styles of music and working with different people requires respect. Ask students how a respectful person acts and how do these actions demonstrate respect. Remind students that interacting with people who are different from them or listening to music that is different from their preferred music requires a respectful, accepting attitude.

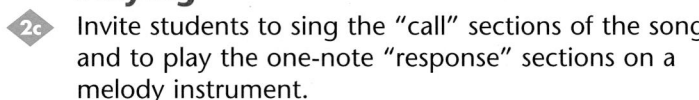

MUSIC MAKERS
DUKE ELLINGTON

Duke Ellington (1899–1974) helped to popularize scat singing in 1926 while performing "Heebie Jeebies." He dropped his music and couldn't remember the words. Rather than stop singing, Ellington sang the melody, using nonsense words. Jazz singers have been scatting ever since. In 1928, Ellington organized his band and performed at the Cotton Club, a famous dance club in Harlem, New York City. Ellington's band was the most popular of all swing bands.

In the Pop Style

Unit 9 **339**

Playing

2c Invite students to sing the "call" sections of the song and to play the one-note "response" sections on a melody instrument.

Moving

Refer students to the photo on p. 335.

8a **SAY** Big bands performed in places like the Cotton Club in Harlem, New York City. People sat at tables and listened to the music or joined their friends on the dance floor and danced.

Share the information in Cultural Connection on p. 337, and encourage students to move as they sing "It Don't Mean a Thing" once more.

3 CLOSE

Listening

6b Invite students to listen again to Ella Fitzgerald sing *It Don't Mean a Thing If It Ain't Got That Swing* **CD 15-25**.
9a

Help them list elements of swing they hear, including

- Constant tempo.
- Unified group sound of the orchestra.
- Rhythmic bounce of the music.
- Syncopated rhythms.
- Instrumentation.

Skill: SINGING   ASSESSMENT

7a **Performance/Peer Critique** Have students sing "It Don't Mean a Thing" in small groups, using a tempo and presentation appropriate for swing style. Encourage students in each group to comment on other groups' performances and offer suggestions for improvement.

SKILLS REINFORCEMENT

▶ **Keyboard** Use the following teaching suggestions to help all students perform a keyboard accompaniment for "It Don't
2c Mean a Thing (If It Ain't Got That Swing)."

Reinforcement Some students may have little experience playing keyboard. Allow these students to gain confidence by having them play a "two-beat" bass line using chord roots. Ask them to play two notes per measure, on the beat.

On Target Students who are proficient in playing keyboard can be asked to play the chords shown on p. 338.

Challenge You may wish to invite advanced keyboard players to play the Em, C_7, and B_7 chords in addition to those shown on p. 338 to accompany the song.

TECHNOLOGY/MEDIA LINK

4c **Video Library** Show the video *Jazz and Improvisation* to students to present a performance of "It Don't Mean a Thing If It Ain't Got That Swing" by jazz singer Diane Schuur.

Unit 9   *In the Pop Style*   **339**

LESSON AT A GLANCE

Element Focus **MELODY** Melodic ornamentation

Skill Objective **SINGING** Improvise using scat syllables and melodic ornamentation

Connection Activity **STYLE** Discuss scat singing and the sound of the big bands during the swing era

MATERIALS

- "Sing, Sing, Sing!" **CD 15-26**
  Recording Routine: Intro (12 m.); vocal; instrumental; coda
- *How High the Moon* **CD 15-28**
- *Pennsylvania 6-5000* **CD 16-1**
- **Dance Directions** for *Pennsylvania 6-5000* p. 566
- xylophones, bells, Autoharps, or keyboards
- **Resource Book** p. I-25

VOCABULARY

scat singing   dynamics   big band   instrumentation

◆ ◆ ◆ ◆ National Standards ◆ ◆ ◆ ◆

1d SIng music written in two parts
2c Perform instrumental music from diverse genres
6a Listen and describe events in music using appropriate terms
6b Listen and analyze uses of pitch, timbre, harmony, and form in music from diverse genres
7a Students evaluate the music they perform
8b Identify ways music relates to social studies
9a Describe characteristics of music styles from a variety of cultures
9b Classify high-quality musical works by genre

MORE MUSIC CHOICES

For more practice with scat singing:
"It Don't Mean a Thing (If It Ain't Got That Swing)," p. 336
"Now's the Time," p. 445

Scat Singing

During the 1930s, radio and phonograph records made it possible for swing to expand its boundaries from the dance hall to homes all across America.

Sing this popular swing song from that era. Can you **identify** a phrase in the song that duplicates the effect of scat singing?

CD 15-26

Sing, Sing, Sing!

Words and Music by Louis Prima

si (l) t, d r m s l

REFRAIN

Sing, sing, sing, sing, __ ev - 'ry-bod - y start to sing like __

dee dee dee, bah bah bah dah. Now __ you're sing - in'

with a ___ swing. _ Now _ you're sing-in' like ev-'ry - thing. ___

VERSE *Call*

When the mu-sic goes a - round, _ ev - 'ry-bod-y's gon-na go to ___ town.

Call   *Response*   *D.C. al Fine*

But here is one thing you should _ know; _ sing _ it high and sing it ___ low! Oh,

340

Footnotes

SKILLS REINFORCEMENT

▶ **Recorder** Invite students to learn to play the recorder part for "Sing, Sing, Sing!" found on p. I-25 in the Resource Book.

2c

BUILDING SKILLS THROUGH MUSIC

▶ **Social Studies** Share the information from the Cultural Connection, Spotlight On, and Teacher to Teacher footnotes. Have students develop a time line from 1877–1990. Ask them to list the information from the lesson, then add world events to their time line.

CULTURAL CONNECTION

8b ▶ **Technological Advances** The rapid development of technology affected the way people viewed the world around them. First, the phonograph allowed people to hear a variety of music in their own homes. In 1878, a year after its invention, Thomas Edison wrote that the phonograph could be used to teach elocution, to read to the blind, and to reproduce musical performances. The first records held a minimal amount of information. A full-length symphony might take up as many as 12 records. Beginning in 1920, with the advent of radio broadcasting, people were able to follow events as they happened. Radio broadcasts of classical and popular music promoted a new unity in musical taste. People stopped buying sheet music of popular songs and instead purchased records.

Sing and Swing

Scat singing can be used to express a variety of emotions and musical effects. In this example, **listen** to the wide range of dynamics and pitches performed by the soloist.

CD 15–28
How High the Moon

by Nancy Hamilton and Morgan Lewis as performed by Ella Fitzgerald

In describing her scat singing skills, Ella Fitzgerald said, "I just tried to do what I heard the horns in the band doing."

M·U·S·I·C M·A·K·E·R·S
Ella Fitzgerald

Ella Fitzgerald (1917–1996) is considered one of the finest jazz singers of the 20th century. She had a special gift for singing in the "swing style." Her ability to swing eighth notes and her perfect timing for singing syncopated rhythms made her the envy of other performers. One of the best scat singers of her time, Fitzgerald was able to make her voice sound like an instrument.

Create your own scat singing. Experiment with a song you already know. Use your voice as an instrument and scat the song on nonsense syllables instead of the words. "This Train," on page 27, would be a good song for scat singing.

In the Pop Style

1 INTRODUCE

Ask students to read the text on p. 340. Then invite them to listen to "Sing, Sing, Sing!" **CD 15-26.**

9a ASK Did you hear any scat syllables in this song? (yes, in the second phrase of the song)

Inform students that

9b
- Scat singing came about during the early part of the swing era (the 1920s).
- Performers frequently imitate jazz instruments when they scat sing.

2 DEVELOP

Analyzing

6b Have students

- Listen to "Sing, Sing, Sing!" again.
- Sing the scat syllables along with the recording.
- Listen for sections of the song that repeat.

ASK What is the form of this song? (ABA)

How do you know? (The refrain is performed at the beginning and end; the verse is performed in the middle.)

Help students identify F as *do.*

ASK What pitch does the refrain end on? (D, or low *la*)

What are the chords in the refrain? (Dm, A₇)

What pitch does the verse end on? (F, or *do,* on the word *low*)

What chords are in the verse? (F, C₇)

Help students determine that the refrain is in minor and the verse is in major—another way of highlighting the ABA form.

continued on page 342

SPOTLIGHT ON

▶ **The Performer** Scat singer Diane Schuur (born 1953) can be seen in the video *Jazz and Improvisation* performing "It Don't Mean a Thing." She has been acclaimed worldwide for her vocal versatility and her incredible 3½ octave range. Blind since birth because of a hospital accident, Schuur sang and learned to play the piano as a child. Schuur began her career when she was ten years old, singing at a local hotel. She originally sang country songs but switched to jazz early in her career. She performed at the White House in 1982 with Stan Getz, another famous jazz musician. Schuur has won several Grammy Awards for her jazz recordings, and she is well known for her talent in scat singing.

TEACHER TO TEACHER

9a ▶ **Big Band Instrumentation** Discuss the use of certain instruments and the way they were used to emphasize the musical style of this era. The traditional big band consisted of five reeds (clarinets and saxophones), four trumpets, and four trombones. Although big band leaders often featured different instruments, the saxophone became an important section in these groups. The saxophone was not widely accepted until the 1920s, although jazz musicians adopted the instrument as early as 1914. Glenn Miller's signature sound highlighted a clarinet lead doubled by the full saxophone section playing an octave lower. The saxophone is a reed instrument, although its body is made of brass. It was invented around 1840 by Antoine-Joseph (Adolphe) Sax, son of a Belgian woodwind manufacturer.

Singing

Invite students to sing the song. Help them discover that the refrain is in two-part harmony.

1d Encourage all students to sing the lower part as they sing the song again. Then have them sing the song in two parts.

Playing

2c Invite one group of students to play the Dm and A_7 chords during the refrain and another group to play the F and C_7 chords during the verse. Use xylophones, bells, Autoharps, or keyboards.

Listening

ASK Who are some famous musicians known only by their first names? (Cher, Elvis)

SAY Ella Fitzgerald is known to most music lovers by her first name.

Direct students' attention to the photograph of Ella Fitzgerald on p. 341 and have them read the accompanying Music Maker feature.

Invite students to

- Listen to Ella sing *How High the Moon* **CD 15-28.**

6a • Raise their hands when they hear her begin to scat sing.

ASK Did Ella only scat sing the melody or did she also improvise on, or ornament, the melody? (She did both.)

What did Ella do with the pitch as she sang? (She changed her scat singing by going into other octaves.)

Listening

6a Have students read the information on p. 342. Then play the big band recording of *Pennsylvania 6-5000* **CD 16-1**, performed by the Glenn Miller Orchestra. (See Spotlight On, below, for information on Glenn Miller.)

◄ Benny Goodman and his orchestra

▲ The Glenn Miller Orchestra

Trombonist and big band leader Tommy Dorsey ▶

And the Bands Played On

Not all of the big bands played swing or had a vocalist. Each band had a particular sound, depending on the instrumentation of the band.

Listen to *Pennsylvania 6-5000,* performed by the Glenn Miller Orchestra, as you follow the listening map on page 343. What instruments can you **identify**?

CD 16–1
Pennsylvania 6-5000

by Carl Sigman and Jerry Gray
as performed by the Glenn Miller Orchestra

The title of this selection is the phone number for Manhattan's Hotel Pennsylvania, located near Penn Station. This spot was a prime location in New York for big bands.

Footnotes

ACROSS THE CURRICULUM

8b ▶ **Social Studies** Swing music and dance were all the rage for young people in the 1930s and early 1940s. Ask students to write an article describing the popular music and dance "cultures" of today. Why is this music so popular? Encourage students to clip photos from popular music magazines and fan publications to help tell their "stories."

Portrait of America's Music by David P. Press (Marshall Cavendish, 1994) is a great teacher resource containing photos, cultural information, and historic settings surrounding the chronological development of jazz and other popular music styles in America.

SPOTLIGHT ON

▶ **The Performer** Glenn Miller (1904–1944) led one of the most popular big bands of the swing era. He organized his first orchestra in 1937. By 1939, through a series of radio broadcasts, the band had developed a nationwide following. In 1942, at the height of his fame, Miller disbanded his orchestra to join the military. While a captain in the U.S. Army Air Force, he assembled a dance band to entertain the troops. Miller is presumed to have died when his plane disappeared en route to Paris.

Miller's band had many hits with both sentimental ballads ("Moonlight Serenade") and swinging upbeat tunes ("In the Mood," "Little Brown Jug," "Tuxedo Junction"). "Pennsylvania 6-5000" was recorded in 1940.

Pennsylvania 6-5000 LISTENING MAP

Penn-syl-van-ia six five thou-sand.

Penn-syl-van-ia six five 0 - 0 - 0. ___

In the Pop Style

6b **ASK** What instruments are featured as a solo instrument? (trumpet and sax)

Share the information on big band instrumentation provided in Teacher to Teacher, p. 341. Then play *Pennsylvania 6-5000* again as students follow the listening map on p. 343.

For additional listening experiences with the saxophone, trombone, and trumpet, play **CD 21-50**, **CD 21-51**, and **CD 21-42** from the Sound Bank. Detailed descriptions and photos of the instruments are found on p. 517 and p. 519.

Moving

Encourage students to learn the basic swing dance pattern and perform it with *Pennsylvania 6-5000*. (See Movement below.)

3 CLOSE

Element: MELODY   **ASSESSMENT**

7a **Performance/Observation** Divide the class into several small groups. Invite each group to

- Choose a song students know well.
- Experiment with melodic ornamentation and scat singing.
- Rehearse its performance.
- Present its performance to the class.

Observe that members of each group understand melodic ornamentation and scat singing.

MOVEMENT

▶ **Popular Dance** The basic swing step is performed in a six-beat pattern. See Dance Directions on p. 566 in this book for the complete routine, to be performed with *Pennsylvania 6-5000*.

TECHNOLOGY/MEDIA LINK

Transparency Display the listening map transparency for *Pennsylvania 6-5000* as you play the recording. You may wish to point to the notated excerpts as they occur on the recording.

CD-ROM Divide students into small groups. Have them enter the chord progression for "Sing, Sing, Sing!" into *Band-in-a-Box*. Have students choose the Jazz Swing style for playback and then chant the song's rhythm using the syllable *du*. Discuss the "bouncy" feel of swing music. Have students change the playback to Rock style. Then ask them to describe how this changes the rhythmic feel of the song. (It no longer feels "bouncy.")

LESSON AT A GLANCE

Element Focus	**RHYTHM** Meter in 3
Skill Focus	**SINGING** Sing a song in triple meter that includes yodeling
Connection Activity	**SOCIAL STUDIES** Become aware of the role of cowboys in the expansion of the American West

MATERIALS

• "Cattle Call"   **CD 16-3**

   Recording Routine: Intro (12 m.); refrain; v. 1; refrain; bridge; interlude (12 m.); v. 2; refrain; coda

• *Cattle Call*   **CD 16-5**

• **Resource Book** pp. H-24, I-26

• mallet instruments, keyboard

VOCABULARY

grace notes   modulation   yodeling   falsetto

◆ ◆ ◆ ◆ National Standards ◆ ◆ ◆ ◆

1c Sing music from diverse genres
2a Play instruments accurately alone and in small ensembles
5c Identify standard notation symbols for pitch and rhythm
6b Listen and analyze uses of pitch and harmony in music from diverse genres
7b Students use specific criteria for evaluating their own performances
8b Identify ways music relates to social studies
9a Describe characteristics of music styles from a variety of cultures

MORE MUSIC CHOICES

For more practice with country music:
"Orange Blossom Special," p. 266
"Rocky Top," p. 348

ON THE LONE PRAIRIE

Cowboys expanded our western boundaries as they drove cattle in search of grazing land. They sang songs while out on the range. These songs were the inspiration for many later country pop ballads.

Feel the meter in 3 as you **sing** "Cattle Call."

CD 16-3

CATTLE CALL

Words and Music by Tex Owens

1. The cattle are prowl-in', the coy-otes are howl-in' way out where the do-gies bawl. Where spurs are a-jing-lin', the cow-boy is sing-in' ___ his lone-some cat-tle call.
2. For hours he would ride on the range far and wide when the night winds blow up a squall. His heart is a feath-er; In all kinds of weath-er ___ he sings his cat-tle call.

344

Footnotes

MEETING INDIVIDUAL NEEDS

▶ **Boys' Changing Voices** Some boys enter adolescence as early as the upper years of elementary school (grades 5–6). When a boy enters puberty his voice begins to change. Adolescent boys can avoid being limited to narrow vocal ranges by developing their head voice. Many boys need to find their head voice before they can learn to develop it. Yodeling is one method that will help boys discover their head voice.

BUILDING SKILLS THROUGH MUSIC

▶ **Language** Invite students to sing "Cattle Call" **CD 16-3** and list terms that describe the characteristics of the music and interpretation. Discuss which musical characteristics were the most important and have students list them in their music journals. Ask students to describe the interpretation they expect to hear on the recording by LeAnn Rimes and Eddie Arnold and list in their Music Journal.

ACROSS THE CURRICULUM

8b ▶ **Social Studies** The life of the cowboy, which has been glamorized in the media and arts, was often difficult and lonely. The most trying part of the job was the cattle drive, during which the cattle were herded from the ranches in Texas to livestock markets in Kansas, where they would be sold to the beef industry. On the journey, cattle had to swim through rivers and often stampeded. Cowboys often sang songs to the cattle, feeling that the music would calm them.

The "roundup" involved branding new calves and choosing older cattle for the market. After the work was done, cowboys would often demonstrate their skills in a "rodeo." The era of the cowboy, which lasted from the mid-1860s to the mid-1880s, ended with the loss of open range and the expansion of the railroads.

Tune In

Cowboys sang slow, gentle songs at night to calm the cattle and keep them from being frightened. The "cattle calls" quieted the cattle and kept them from running away.

REFRAIN

Ooh, _ ooh, _ do - gie,

Ooh, _ ooh, _ doo doot doo doo doo doo

doo _ doo _ do - gie.

1. *To next stanza* F 2. F *Fine*

Oh, oh - dl - oh dee dee dee. dee.

In the Pop Style

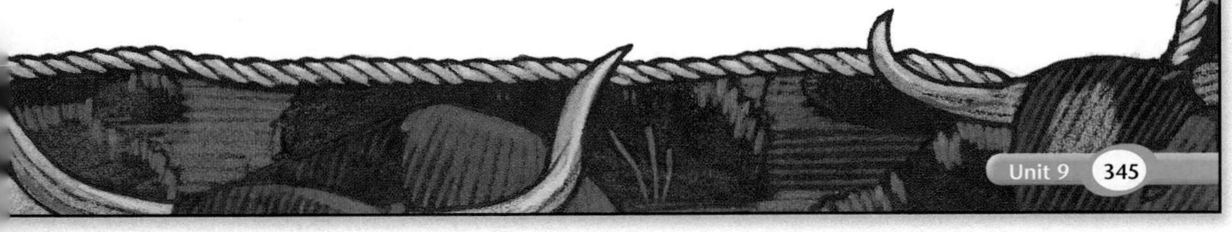

Unit 9 **345**

1 INTRODUCE

8b Engage students in a discussion of a cowboy's life. Inform students that

- Cowboys entertained themselves at night by singing.
- Cowboys' songs were about their life, the places they visited, and their friends.
- Cowboy songs are a type of country music called country-western.

Share information with students from Across the Curriculum on p. 344.

2 DEVELOP

Singing

Ask students to examine the song "Cattle Call." Help them discover that

5c
- The music is in meter in 3.
- There are grace notes in the refrain.

Inform students that cowboys often performed a waltz to cowboy songs in triple meter.

9a **ASK What instrument would you expect to hear in the accompaniment and why?** (guitar, because it was a favorite instrument of the cowboys)

6b Help students discover the yodeling effect in the refrain as they listen to the recording. Inform students that

- Yodeling is a shift between your regular voice and falsetto.
- Falsetto is a higher voice that is less powerful and has a lighter quality than the full voice.
- Yodeling is frequently used by country singers.

1c Invite students to practice yodeling. Then encourage them to sing "Cattle Call" **CD 16-3** with the recording.

continued on page 346

CULTURAL CONNECTION

▶ **Dance** Encourage students to learn about the various styles of American popular dancing. Invite country line dancers and other country musicians and dancers to your school. Add photos of these experiences to class bulletin boards and student portfolios as students continue to learn about the rich diversity of America's popular music and dance.

TEACHER TO TEACHER

▶ **Young Singers** Not all of today's popular singers use healthy vocal techniques to produce their unique sounds; therefore, young singers should be discouraged from imitating or modeling these singers. Instead, students should be encouraged to sing with a light voice that is free of vibrato, harshness, or pinching of the tone. When singing in groups, they should be encouraged to blend so that no single voice is heard above the others. Young singers should also learn to enunciate clearly, so that words are understandable, by using consonants that are clear and vowels that are uniform.

Lesson 4 Continued

Playing

2a Refer students to the instrumental accompaniment activity on p. 346 and have them

- Read standard notation to name the notes in each pattern.
- Find the notes on a keyboard or mallet instrument.
- Practice the movement involved in playing each pattern.
- Play the patterns alone and then accompany the singing or the recording of "Cattle Call" **CD 16-3.**

Listening

Inform students that

- Eddy Arnold, a famous country-western singer, made the song "Cattle Call" famous.
- LeAnn Rimes invited him to make a new recording of the song with her.

Invite students to listen to this recording of *Cattle Call* **CD 16-5.**

6b Help students discover that

- Each performer sings the verse alone.
- The singers sing the refrain together.
- The song changes key between the verse Rimes sings and the verse Arnold sings.

SAY The interlude between the verses is a *modulation*—a musical transition from one key to another. The modulation to a new key gives the music a "lift" and allows each singer to sing the verse in his or her most comfortable range.

Invite students to learn more about LeAnn Rimes by reading the Music Maker feature on p. 347. See Spotlight On, p. 347, for biographical information on Eddy Arnold.

He rides in the sun 'til his day's work is done, and he rounds up the cat-tle each fall. Ooh, __ ooh, __ do - gie. Sing-in' his cat-tle call.

To Verse 2

Playing Cowboy

Choose a mallet instrument or a keyboard and **play** the following part along with the refrain of "Cattle Call." How does this part stress the feel of meter in 3?

REFRAIN:
Lines 1 and 3 *(play 4 times)*

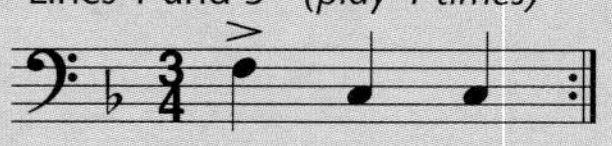

Line 2 *(play 4 times)*

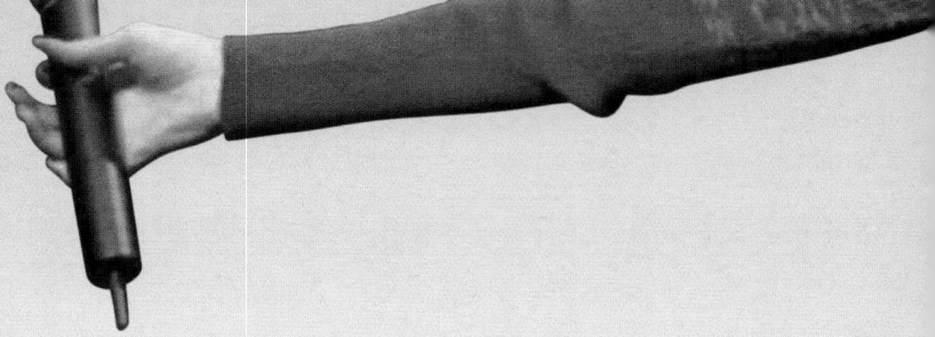

Line 4

Footnotes

 ▶ **Keyboard** See Resource Book, p. H-24, for a complete score of this ostinato accompaniment for "Cattle Call."

F position: C position:

Bb position: G7 position:

▶ **Recorder** Encourage students to learn the recorder part for "Cattle Call" on p. I-26 in the Resource Book.

TEACHER TO TEACHER

▶ **Resource Materials** For a comprehensive resource about American country music, see *A Century of Country: An Illustrated History of Country Music* by Robert K. Oermann (TV Books, 1999). This excellent teacher resource surveys the beginnings of hillbilly music in 1900 through its evolution into the many popular forms and fusion styles of today.

View a wonderful set of videos about the history and artists of American country music in *America's Music: Roots of Country* (Turner Home Entertainment, 1996).

A Shining Star

Just as some swing singers sing scat, some country and western singers **yodel**. **Listen** to this duet by country singers Eddy Arnold and LeAnn Rimes. What familiar vocal style can you **identify** in this version of *Cattle Call*?

> **Yodeling** is rapid shifts between a lower full voice and a high voice type of singing called *falsetto*.

CD 16–5
Cattle Call

by Tex Owens
as performed by Eddy Arnold and LeAnn Rimes
LeAnn Rimes was a fan of Eddy Arnold. In time, the two became great friends.

MUSIC MAKERS

LeAnn Rimes

LeAnn Rimes (born 1982) is a shining star of country music. Her albums have soared to multiplatinum status. The album *You Light Up My Life: Inspirational Songs* made her one of the first country artists to achieve number one status on three of the Billboard charts (country, pop, and contemporary Christian). Rimes has received two Grammy awards and was the first country artist to be named Best New Artist. Since Rimes recorded her first album at age eleven, she has indeed become a shining star.

Tune In

Eddy Arnold was the first country music performer to add an orchestra and strings to his music. He was also the first country singer to appear at Carnegie Hall in New York City.

In the Pop Style

---

3 CLOSE

Element: RHYTHM   ASSESSMENT

7b **Performance/Self-Assessment** Organize the class into two groups—singers and instrumentalists—and have students perform "Cattle Call" **CD 16-3** with the refrain accompaniment on p. 346. Invite students to evaluate their performances by posing the following questions:

- Did each group perform in an appropriate tempo?
- Did each group keep a steady tempo?
- Did each group's performance reflect the feel of meter in 3? How?
- Did each group sound "country"?

SPOTLIGHT ON

▶ **The Singer** Eddy Arnold (born 1918) is from the mountains of Tennessee, the son of a country fiddler and a guitarist. His mother taught him to play guitar. Although Arnold's voice lacked the nasal quality of most country singers, he recorded more number one country hits than any other country artist. Arnold is credited for taking country music from the country to the city. He was the first country singer to have his own television show. "Cattle Call" was one of his greatest hits of the 1950s. In 1966, Arnold was inducted into the Country Music Hall of Fame, the highest honor in country music.

TECHNOLOGY/MEDIA LINK

Video Library Show the video *String Instruments: Bowed* to students to present a country fiddle duet.

LESSON AT A GLANCE

Element Focus   **RHYTHM** Steady beat

Skill Objective   **MOVING** Perform steady-beat movements in a country line dance

Connection Activity   **RELATED ARTS** Explore country style line dancing

MATERIALS

- "Rocky Top"   **CD 16-6**

  Recording Routine: Intro (4 m.); vocal; interlude (16 m.); vocal
- *Tennessee River*   **CD 16-8**
- *I Love a Rainy Night*   **CD 16-9**
- **Dance Directions** for *I Love a Rainy Night* p. 567
- sandblocks, tambourine

VOCABULARY

country music

◆ ◆ ◆ National Standards ◆ ◆ ◆ ◆

1c Sing music from diverse genres

2b Perform easy instrumental pieces with technical accuracy

3b Improvise rhythmic variations on given melodies

5a Read quarter notes, eighth notes in duple meter

6b Listen and analyze uses of timbre in music from diverse genres

7b Students use specific criteria for evaluating their own performances

8b Identify ways music relates to other school subjects

9a Describe characteristics of music styles from a variety of cultures

MORE MUSIC CHOICES

For more practice singing country music:

"Home on the Range," p. 69

"Cattle Call," p. 344

Home Sweet Home

In the seventeenth and eighteenth centuries, British settlers came to the New World. Many settled in the mountains of Appalachia. They brought with them their folk songs. Many of these songs tell of heartaches. Accompanied by fiddles and guitars, they became the root of country music.

The lyrics for the song "Rocky Top" are typical of country music. The singer has moved to the city but misses the old homestead in Rocky Top, Tennessee. As you **sing** the song, notice that the lyrics are sad but the music is upbeat.

Ozark folk art: Wood carving by Mike Kotz ▶

CD 16-6

Rocky Top

Words and Music by Boudleaux Bryant and Felice Bryant

Wish that I was on ol' Rock-y Top, down in the Ten-nes-see hills;

Ain't no smog-gy smoke on Rock-y Top, Ain't no tel-e-phone bills.

Once I knew a girl on Rock-y Top, Half bear, oth-er half cat;

Wild as a mink, but sweet as so-da pop, I still dream a-bout that.

348

Footnotes

TEACHER TO TEACHER

▶ **Classroom Project** Encourage students to add their favorite country artists to bulletin board displays or portfolio projects about popular musical recording artists.

BUILDING SKILLS THROUGH MUSIC

▶ **Language** Review articulation styles (*legato, marcato,* and *staccato*) from p. 87. Ask students to chant phrases from "Rocky Top" in each style and describe the differences. Divide the class into groups to plan arrangements of "Rocky Top" that use one articulation style for the verse and a contrasting articulation style for the refrain. Invite students to perform their arrangements for the class. Discuss which arrangements were the most effective and why. Have students describe considerations the performer must make when selecting an articulation style for each section of the song.

CULTURAL CONNECTION

▶ **Country Music Roots** Country music was rooted in the folk traditions of the Southern and Western United States. The pioneer of today's country music was Jimmie Rodgers (1897–1933), country music's first recording artist. With the establishment of the Grand Ole Opry in 1925, Nashville, Tennessee, became the center of the country music scene. Roy Acuff popularized the Opry and the "old-timey" country sound of the 1940s. At the same time, Roy Rogers and Gene Autry brought cowboy music to a wide audience. The two styles fused into country-western music. Hank Williams' honky-tonk music told the stories of hard luck and lost love. The pop-influenced Nashville sound was developed in the 1950s.

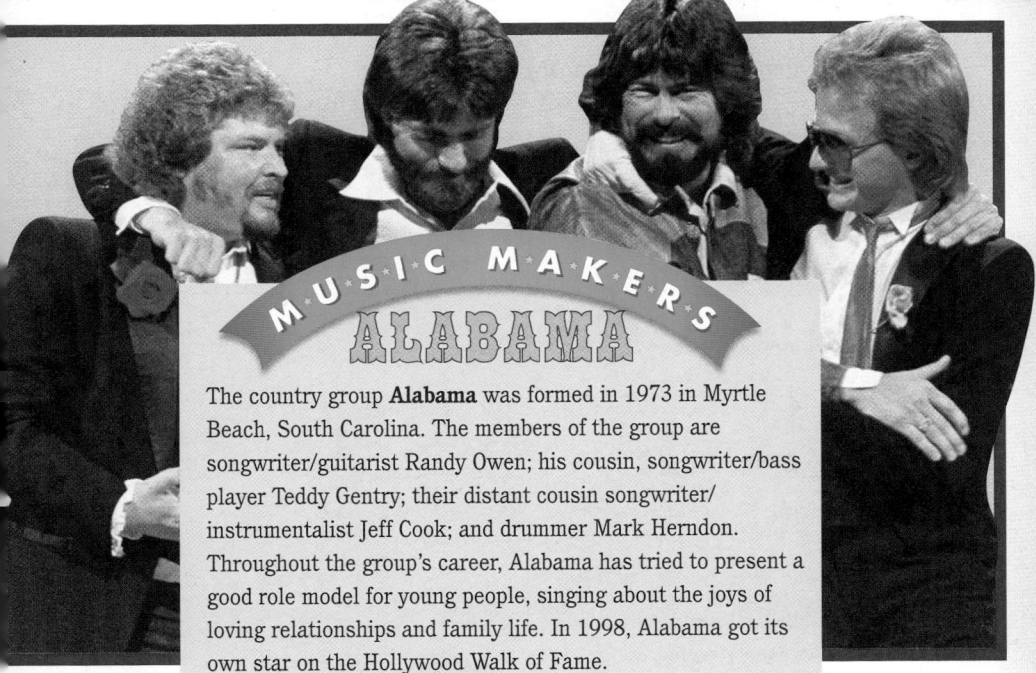

MUSIC MAKERS
ALABAMA

The country group **Alabama** was formed in 1973 in Myrtle Beach, South Carolina. The members of the group are songwriter/guitarist Randy Owen; his cousin, songwriter/bass player Teddy Gentry; their distant cousin songwriter/instrumentalist Jeff Cook; and drummer Mark Herndon. Throughout the group's career, Alabama has tried to present a good role model for young people, singing about the joys of loving relationships and family life. In 1998, Alabama got its own star on the Hollywood Walk of Fame.

My Country Home

From the cowboys to bluegrass to honky-tonk, country music has gone through many changes over a long period of time and is still being defined.

Listen to the popular country music group Alabama sing a song about their home.

CD 16–8
Tennessee River

by Randy Owen
as performed by Alabama

This song combines country-rock and honky-tonk styles.

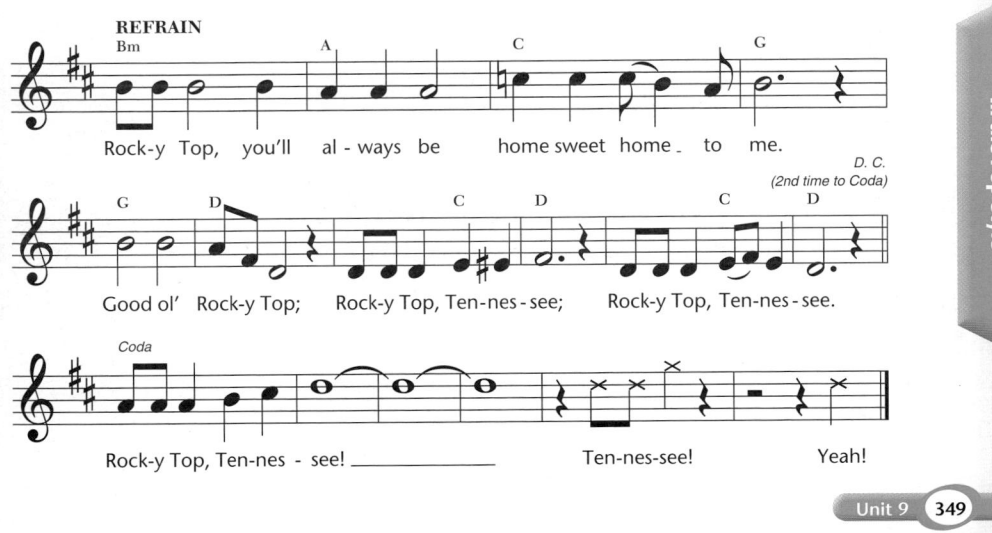

REFRAIN
Bm   A   C   G
Rock-y Top, you'll al-ways be home sweet home to me.

D. C.
(2nd time to Coda)
G   D   C   D   C   D
Good ol' Rock-y Top; Rock-y Top, Ten-nes-see; Rock-y Top, Ten-nes-see.

Coda
Rock-y Top, Ten-nes - see! _____ Ten-nes-see! Yeah!

In the Pop Style

Unit 9 349

---

1 INTRODUCE

ASK If you and your family move to another country, what are some of the things that you would want to take with you? (Accept a variety of answers.)

Explain that

- During the nineteenth century a move from one country to another was a really big event.
- People tried to take with them those things that represented their culture.
- People took their music, an important part of their culture, with them to their new home.

2 DEVELOP

Listening

Invite students to listen to the popular country song "Rocky Top" **CD 16-6.**

ASK Why does the singer miss Rocky Top? (He misses the clean air, not having to pay a phone bill, and his girlfriend.)

6b What instruments can you identify in the accompaniment? (fiddle, banjo, guitar, bass, harmonica, piano, tambourine, drums)

Point out to students that

- The fiddle is a violin played with a straight, penetrating tone.
- "Rocky Top" was adopted as an official song of Tennessee in 1982.

Singing

1c Invite students to sing "Rocky Top" with the recording. As they sing, have them tap a light, steady beat on beats 1 and 3.

continued on page 350

SKILLS REINFORCEMENT

2b ▶ **Recorder** Have students review the notes D, E, F♯, and G on their recorders. Remind them to gently whisper *daah* on the low notes. Students can play the pattern below on their recorders during the verse of "Rocky Top." They will need to play the phrase four times.

SPOTLIGHT ON

▶ **Country Music** Country music began as folk music but moved into the world of popular music after the invention of the radio and phonograph. Early radio broadcasts of country music, especially the broadcasts from the Grand Ole Opry, became popular with people living in rural and remote areas of the country. Country singers use a folk song style of singing and project an emotional sincerity in their voices. They sing with a clear tone. Their quality tends to be nasal and slightly tense or strained. Singers often let their voices "break" to add emotion to the song. The texts are usually sentimental and reflect nostalgia and loneliness.

Lesson 5 Continued

Performing

5a Invite students to

- Read the rhythms on p. 350.

2b • Play the rhythms on the instruments indicated.

3b • Perform the rhythms as an accompaniment to "Rocky Top" **CD 16-6.**

- Encourage students to improvise new rhythm accompaniments for the song.

Listening

1c Invite students to read about the popular country group Alabama, on p. 349. Then play the group's

9a recording of *Tennessee River* **CD 16-8.** Draw students' attention to the use of typical country music style elements, such as

- Sentimental, emotional lyrics.
- Nasal vocal quality.
- Vocal harmony above the melody.
- Pedal-steel guitar and fiddle.

Refer to Cultural Connection, p. 348, and Spotlight On, p. 349, for more information on country music history and style.

Moving

Inform students that

- Many people dance to country music.
- The steps of the dance depend on the song.
- A popular country dance is the "line dance" because it is performed in a line and the steps are easy.

8b Invite students to learn the line dance steps for *I Love a Rainy Night* **CD 16-9** and then move to the steady beat as they listen to the music. See Movement, below, for background information on country line dancing and dance directions.

"Rocky Top" Rhythms

Play these rhythm patterns to accompany "Rocky Top."

A Country Line Dance

Older generations "two-stepped" to songs like "Rocky Top." Line dances are popular today. **Perform** a line dance to *I Love a Rainy Night*.

CD 16-9
I Love a Rainy Night

by Eddie Rabbitt, Even Stevens, and David Malloy
as performed by Eddie Rabbitt

350

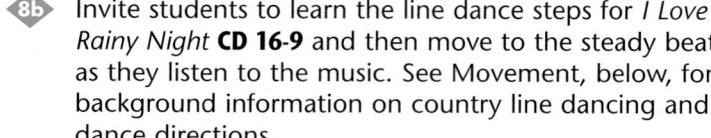

MOVEMENT

8b ▶ **Line Dance** Country line dancing is a relatively modern type of American dance style. In older generations as well as those of today, people did "two-steppin'" to popular country tunes. Line dances swept the United States in the 1980s and 1990s. The new millennium still finds the country line dance popular. For the line dance routine to accompany *I Love a Rainy Night,* see Dance Directions on p. 567 in this book.

SPOTLIGHT ON

▶ **The Musician** Singer-songwriter Eddie Rabbitt (1944–1998) was born in Brooklyn, NY, as Edward Thomas. During his career he achieved 26 No. 1 country singles and eight pop hits in the Top 40. Rabbitt discovered guitar at age 12. He moved to Nashville in the mid-1960s to try to sell his song, "Working My Way Up from the Bottom," which he sold within days. It became a hit for Roy Drusky. Eventually, Rabbitt wrote songs for Elvis Presley, Ronnie Milsap, and others. Rabbitt, whose baby died from liver disease, did much charity work for health groups. He worked with cerebral palsy and muscular dystrophy groups and became the honorary chairman of the American Council on Transplantation. Sadly, his untimely death came about as a result of lung cancer.

Country's Finest

The Grand Ole Opry in Nashville, Tennessee, is the home of country music. The Opry House provides a stage for performance, radio broadcasting, and recording studios. All of this helped popularize the country music style, and produced many recording stars. ▼

Hank Williams   Ernest Tubb   Patsy Cline

The Carter family, Jimmie Rodgers, Roy Acuff, Patsy Cline, and Hank Williams were some of the early country recording artists. Alan Jackson, Dolly Parton, Patty Loveless, Willie Nelson, George Strait, and Reba McEntire are just a few of the many performers who carry on the country music tradition today.

In the Pop Style

Unit 9   **351**

3 CLOSE

Listening

Ask students to read and view the material about the Grand Ole Opry on p. 351 and then share the related information in Cultural Connection below. Allow students to choose and then "reprise" one or more selections from this lesson or the previous one.

Skill: MOVING   **ASSESSMENT**

7b **Performance/Peer Critique** Organize the class into small groups. Have each group perform all or a portion of the line dance to accompany *I Love a Rainy Night* **CD 16-9.** After each performance, invite the dancers and the "audience" to evaluate the performance, using the following criteria.

- Did the movements follow the tempo and the steady beat of the music?
- Were the movements performed accurately and in unison?

CULTURAL CONNECTION

▶ **The Grand Ole Opry** Several country singers gathered in a hall on the fifth floor of the National Life and Accident Insurance building in Nashville, Tennessee, in 1925 to present a concert of country music. This was the humble beginning of the Grand Ole Opry. This regular Saturday evening performance became so popular with fans that it soon outgrew the space and had to find a new home. The Opry moved to a series of halls before finding a home in Ryman Auditorium. Country music performers called the Ryman home until 1974, when they moved into the new Grand Ole Opry House. Millions of fans from around the world travel each year to attend the live weekend performances. Performances of the Grand Ole Opry were first broadcast by radio in 1939.

SCHOOL TO HOME CONNECTION

▶ **Country Performers** Country music has produced many recording stars. Have students ask their parents, relatives, and friends to help collect pictures, information, and, if possible, sheet music or CDs of famous country stars. Have them bring the information in and make a bulletin board.

TECHNOLOGY/MEDIA LINK

Web Site Go to *www.sfsuccessnet.com* to learn more about country music and musicians.

Element: FORM | **Skill: PLAYING** | **Connection: STYLE**

LESSON AT A GLANCE

Element Focus **FORM** 12-bar blues

Skill Objective **PLAYING** Perform a 12-bar blues chord progression

Connection Activity **STYLE** Explore elements of blues style

MATERIALS

- "St. Louis Blues" **CD 16-11**
  Recording Routine: Intro (4 m.); v. 1; interlude (12 m.); v. 2; coda
- *St. Louis Blues* **CD 16-13**
- **Resource Book** pp. F-43, H-25
- resonator bells, keyboard

VOCABULARY

blues   chord progression   improvise

◆ ◆ ◆ ◆ **National Standards** ◆ ◆ ◆ ◆

2b Perform easy instrumental pieces with technical accuracy
3b Improvise melodic embellishments
4c Arrange, using electronic media
6c Understand and use basic principles of chords and harmonic progressions in music analysis
7b Use specific criteria for evaluating performances and offer constructive suggestions for improvement
9a Describe characteristics of music genres from a variety of cultures

MORE MUSIC CHOICES

For more practice with blues style:
"Good Mornin', Blues," p. 224

1 INTRODUCE

Have students read the text on p. 352 and then read the first verse lyrics of "St. Louis Blues."

Singing THE BLUES

The ancestors of many African Americans came to America against their will. Life in America was hard. Denied their freedom, many slaves found an emotional escape through singing. Their songs were often sad, and they would **improvise** on the spot. This tradition eventually led to a musical style called the blues.

> **Improvise** means to make up the music while performing.

"St. Louis Blues" is a 12-bar blues song with three phrases, each phrase being four measures long. The lyrics of the first and second phrases are the same. The third phrase is different.

Read the words of "St. Louis Blues" before you **sing** the song.

Create lyrics for a 12-bar blues. Make your phrases rhyme.

CD 16-11

St. Louis Blues

si, l, t, @ r ma m s
Words and Music by W. C. Handy

Swing

1. I hate to see __ the ev-'nin' sun go down. __
2. Feel-in' to-mor - row, __ like __ I feel to-day. __

Hate to see __ the ev-'nin' sun go down.
Feel to-mor - row, __ like __ I feel to-day. __

'Cause my ba - by, __ he done left this town. __
I'll pack my trunk, __ make my get - a - way. __

352

Footnotes

SPOTLIGHT ON

▶ **The Singer** If W. C. Handy was the father of the blues, then Bessie Smith (1894–1937) can be called the empress of the blues. Smith was the most important female blues singer of her time. She was born in Chattanooga, Tennessee, in 1894. She learned to sing and dance as a teenager. Her voice was so powerful that it could be heard over the sound of a band without a microphone. Her performances expressed the essence of the blues. Smith had enormous talent and influenced generations of singers.

BUILDING SKILLS THROUGH MUSIC

▶ **Language** Have students sing "St. Louis Blues" **CD 16-11** and move to show syllables or words that are accented. Ask students to look at the song notation and identify words that appear to be incorrect spellings and/or phrases that are not standard usage. Have students rewrite the words and/or phrases with correct style, grammar, and spelling.

SKILLS REINFORCEMENT

▶ **Recorder** Use the following suggestions to help all students play a recorder accompaniment for "St. Louis Blues."

2b
Reinforcement Some students may have limited experience playing the recorder. Ask these students to play C and D, following the chord progression of the song.

On Target Students who are confident playing the recorder may be asked to choose one of the chords from "St. Louis Blues" and then play the root note for four beats.

Challenge Interested students may be invited to improvise a four-beat pattern and perform their chords with the recording of "St. Louis Blues."

Blues Harmony

A blues harmony frequently has only three chords: I, IV, and V. Using a keyboard, **play** these chords in the key of F: F, B♭₇, C.

Now practice this chord progression:

F — B♭₇ — F — F

B♭ — B♭₇ — F — F

C₇ — B♭₇ — F — F

Perform this progression as you **sing** "St. Louis Blues."

Using your blues lyrics, **create** a melody for a 12-bar blues.

Listen to the great blues artist Bessie Smith sing *St. Louis Blues.*

CD 16–13
St. Louis Blues

by W. C. Handy
as performed by Bessie Smith

It's been said that Smith's performance of *St. Louis Blues* expresses the essence of the blues.

M·U·S·I·C M·A·K·E·R·S

Bessie Smith

Bessie Smith (1894–1937) sang many kinds of music, from vaudeville to blues. In 1923, she was the first major blues and jazz singer to make widely-distributed recordings. She is famous for her passionate and powerful voice that overcame the primitive recording quality of that era. The older blues style lost its popularity by the end of the 1920s and Smith's career declined, but she kept on working. Near the time of her death, she was starting to explore swing music, but Bessie Smith will always be known as the "Empress of the Blues."

CD-ROM Use *Band in a Box* to create your own song in blues style.

In the Pop Style

2 DEVELOP

Singing

 Help students discover that

- There are three phrases in the song, and each phrase is four measures long.
- There are a total of 12 measures, hence a 12-bar blues.

Invite students to sing "St. Louis Blues" **CD 16-11** with the recording. (Note that, as is appropriate in this style, the singer includes improvisation in her performance.)

Playing

 Help students identify the chords in the song (as shown on p. 353) and practice them on bells or keyboard. Then encourage students to accompany the song with the chords as they sing.

Listening

 Before students listen to Bessie Smith's performance of *St. Louis Blues* **CD 16-13**, have them read about her in Music Makers on p. 353. See Spotlight On, p. 352, for additional biographical information. Invite students to compare the two recordings of *St. Louis Blues* and determine which one they prefer.

3 CLOSE

Element: FORM   **ASSESSMENT**

Performance/Peer Critique Divide the class into small groups and invite each group to

- Create a blues-style text to fit the 12-bar blues chord progression.
- Chant the text while playing.

- Improvise a melody for the text, and play it for the class.

- Critique the performances by listening for the appropriate chord changes and blues style, and discuss how these elements contribute to the 12-bar blues form.

SKILLS REINFORCEMENT

▶ **Keyboard** A tritone accompaniment, with walking bass, for "St. Louis Blues" can be found in the Resource Book, p. H-25.

▶ **Mallets** Students will enjoy learning the Orff accompaniment for "St. Louis Blues" on Resource Book p. F-43. Encourage students to play the accompaniment as the class sings the song.

TECHNOLOGY/MEDIA LINK

CD-ROM Use *Band-in-a-Box* as a tool for learning improvisation. As students sing "St. Louis Blues," have them enter the jazz swing style accompaniment for this song. Have students

- Sing the song with the *Band-in-a-Box* accompaniment.
- Mark the keyboard's middle octave F, A♭, and E♭ with tape.
- Improvise at the end of measures 3 and 4, 7 and 8, and 11 and 12.

LESSON AT A GLANCE

Element Focus   **RHYTHM** Syncopated rhythmic motive

Skill Objective   **SINGING** Sing a blues song containing a syncopated rhythmic motive

Connection Activity   **GENRE** Recognize that not all blues are sad

MATERIALS

- "Basin Street Blues"   **CD 16-14**

  Recording Routine: Intro (8 m.); vocal; coda
- claves, tambourine, drum

VOCABULARY

blues   rhythmic motive   syncopation

◆ ◆ ◆ **National Standards** ◆ ◆ ◆

1c Sing music from diverse genres
2a Play instruments accurately in small ensembles
5c Identify standard notation symbols for rhythm
6c Understand and use basic principles of rhythm, chords, and harmonic progressions in music analysis
7a Students evaluate the music they perform
8b Identify ways music relates to social studies
9a Describe characteristics of music genres from a variety of cultures

MORE MUSIC CHOICES

For more practice with syncopated rhythmic motives:
"This Train," p. 27
"Mango Walk," p. 200

1 INTRODUCE

9a Invite students to list facts they already know about the blues genre. Have them read p. 354 and the lyrics of "Basin Street Blues." Discuss the many moods that blues songs can convey.

Not all blues songs are sad, a point proven by "Basin Street Blues." In what other ways is this song different from the "standard" blues song "St. Louis Blues"?

Listen for this syncopated rhythm as you **sing** this blues song.

CD 16-14

BASIN STREET BLUES

Words and Music by Spencer Williams

Swing
VERSE

Won't-cha come a-long with me,   to the Mis-sis-sip-pi?

We'll take the boat _ to the land of dreams, _ Steam down the riv-er, down to

New Or-leans; _ The band's there to meet us,   old friends to greet us,

We'll see the place the folks all meet, _ This is Ba-sin Street. _

354

Footnotes

ACROSS THE CURRICULUM

8b ▶ **Social Studies** View a wonderful video introduction to jazz history and artists in *The Story of Jazz* (BMG, 1994). The video includes rare performances, interviews, and narration about the cross-cultural influences that shaped this unique art form.

Ask students to use a map to trace the development of American jazz from its roots in West Africa to New Orleans and its migration north to cities along the Mississippi River.

BUILDING SKILLS THROUGH MUSIC

▶ **Social Studies** Invite students to sing "Basin Street Blues" **CD 16-14** and identify places named in the lyrics. On a map of the United States, locate the Mississippi River and New Orleans. Have students review information about blues from previous lessons (pp. 212, 224, 352) and identify additional cities (Chicago, Memphis, St. Louis) that are famous for the blues.

SPOTLIGHT ON

9a ▶ **New Orleans Jazz** New Orleans has a long history of instrumental music dating back to the 1700s. Brass bands commonly performed for funeral processions and parades. Small ensembles and orchestras played for society balls. Musicians became proficient in several styles of music and developed the ability to improvise. The jazz style was developed around the turn of the twentieth century. In a New Orleans jazz band, the cornet or the trumpet played the melody, the clarinet played the harmony, and the trombone punctuated the melody. Drums, string bass, and guitar combined to form the rhythm section, which kept the beat and filled in the chords.

"Basin Street Blues" is about a special street in New Orleans, Louisiana, where blues can be heard almost 24 hours a day.

REFRAIN

Ba-sin Street is the street where the e-lite always meet in New Or-leans, Land of dreams, you'll nev-er know how nice it seems or just how much it real-ly means. Glad to be, yes, sir-ee, where wel-come's free, Dear to me, Where I can lose My Ba-sin Street blues.

2 DEVELOP

Singing

1c Play the recording of "Basin Street Blues" **CD 16-14** and invite students to sing along.

6c **ASK** How do the blues elements in "Basin Street Blues" differ from those in "St. Louis Blues"? ("Basin Street Blues" is more than 12 measures long; it uses more chords than the I, IV, V₇; it doesn't have the same rhyme scheme; and it isn't sad.)

9a Share with students the information on New Orleans jazz in Spotlight On, p. 354.

Reading

Focus students' attention on the first measure of the refrain of "Basin Street Blues" and have them

5c • Clap the rhythm.

• Identify the measures in the refrain in which the same rhythmic motive is used (2–6, 9–13).

6c • Recognize the rhythm as a syncopated motive.

1c • Sing the song with the recording **CD 16-14** and clap the motive each time they sing it.

Playing

2a Distribute rhythm instruments, such as claves, tambourines, and drums, and have students play the motive along with the recording **CD 16-14**.

3 CLOSE

Element: RHYTHM **ASSESSMENT**

7a **Performance/Peer Critique** Divide the class into two groups. Have one group sing "Basin Street Blues" while the other group plays the rhythmic motive on the refrain. Then allow groups to switch roles. Invite students to critique each performance and offer suggestions for improvement.

CULTURAL CONNECTION

9a ▶ **The Blues Era** Washington Irving is credited with coining the term "blues music" in 1807. It referred to the songs created by African American slaves to describe the sadness and despair of their lives. Blues singers sang with altered pitches, or blue notes, and with improvisational vocal sounds. Blues were sung in prisons, in cotton fields, and in work camps. The field holler was a staple of the blues style. A soloist called out a sentence, and the other workers answered back as one voice. Later blues performers substituted guitar or banjo riffs for the choral response. Blues music was wildly popular in the 1920s, and it influenced the development of both jazz and swing music in later years.

TECHNOLOGY/MEDIA LINK

Video Library Show the video *Jazz and Improvisation* to students to present a blues performance of *Sweet Home Chicago*.

LESSON AT A GLANCE

Element Focus **TEXTURE/HARMONY** Blues chord progression

Skill Objective **PLAYING** Accompany a rock 'n' roll song using a standard blues chord progression

Connection Activity **RELATED ARTS** Perform the Twist, a dance that was popular during the early rock 'n' roll era

MATERIALS
- *Rock Around the Clock* — CD 16-16
- *Bye Bye Love* — CD 16-17
- *The Great Pretender* — CD 16-18
- *The Twist* — CD 16-19
- keyboard, guitar

VOCABULARY
blues chord progression   triplet

◆ ◆ ◆ National Standards ◆ ◆ ◆
2d Perform simple accompaniments by ear
6a Listen and describe events in music using appropriate terms
6b Listen and analyze uses of rhythm, harmony, form in music from diverse cultures
8a Show how different arts portray the same emotion in unique ways
8b Identify ways music relates to social studies
9a Describe characteristics of music genres from a variety of cultures

MORE MUSIC CHOICES
For more practice singing songs in the rock 'n' roll style:
"Hound Dog," p. 212
"Dancin' in the Street," p. 361

Rock 'n' Roll 'n' Sing

The differences between rhythm-and-blues and country music faded during the mid-1950s. Elvis Presley, Chuck Berry, Bill Haley, Buddy Holly, Fats Domino, and many others blended blues elements with country-western music to create a unique style called "rock 'n' roll."

With his group, called the "Downhomers," Bill Haley played local amusement parks that featured live entertainment. Even then he wanted to combine country and pop music. When he left this group he formed a new band, "Bill Haley and the Comets"— the first rock 'n' roll band in history.

Listen to Bill Haley's *Rock Around the Clock*, one of the first rock 'n' roll hits of the 1950s.

▲ Bill Haley and the Comets

CD 16–16
Rock Around the Clock

by M. Friedman and J. DeKnight
as performed by Bill Haley and the Comets
Since its release in 1955, *Rock Around the Clock* has sold over 16 million copies.

356

Footnotes

ACROSS THE CURRICULUM

▶ **Social Studies** Ask students to research everything they can find about rock 'n' roll artists of the 1950s to today. Challenge students to find pictures, old album covers, and recordings from parents, grandparents, and older friends. Students may wish to create a class bulletin board of "Rock Stars of the Past" or a time line of famous artists and the names of their greatest hits.

BUILDING SKILLS THROUGH MUSIC

▶ **Language** Have students select two of the performing groups featured on pp. 356-359 and complete a Venn Diagram (see Resource Book p. C-8), listing musical characteristics of each in a separate circle. Ask them to include common musical characteristics in the overlapping area. After completing the Venn Diagram, have students identify items that were frequently included and suggest reasons why.

CULTURAL CONNECTION

8b ▶ **The 1950s** The United States was the leading military power following World War II. The population boomed as families left the cities for new suburban housing. The television became a fixture in households during the 1950s, and Americans rejoiced that the economic challenges of the 1930s and 1940s were over. The 1950s were also marked by strife, however. American troops were sent to Korea to fight communism. African Americans protested against racial segregation in schools and businesses. Scientists and politicians scrambled to catch up to Russian advances in space technology. The world seemed black and white. The foundations for the dynamic social changes of the 1960s began in the 1950s.

Another group to popularize country and rock was Phil (born 1937) and Don (born 1939), better known as the Everly Brothers. Using two-part harmony, and elements of bluegrass country sounds and pop music, they became one of the most influential rock 'n' roll duos across the decades.

Listen to their first hit, *Bye Bye Love*.

CD 16–17
Bye Bye Love

by Felice and Boudleaux Bryant
as performed by the Everly Brothers
Bye Bye Love launched a three-year string of classic hit singles for this duo.

In the Pop Style

1 INTRODUCE

SAY There were many styles of rock 'n' roll music developing in the 1950s.

Select a student to read the information on p. 356. Then share with students information from Spotlight On, p. 359.

2 DEVELOP

Listening

Have students

- Listen to *Rock Around the Clock* **CD 16-16.**
- Clap the basic beat with the recording.

9a Point out to students that the chord progression of this early rock 'n' roll song (after the opening section) follows that of the standard 12-bar blues.

6b Write the progression (see Skills Reinforcement below) on the board. Play the recording of *Rock Around the Clock* again and point to the chords in time with the music.

Have students

9a
- Read about the Everly Brothers, on p. 357, and their particular style of rock 'n' roll.
- Listen to *Bye Bye Love* **CD 16-17.**
- Sing along with the recording.

continued on page 358

AUDIENCE ETIQUETTE

▶ **Get There Early!** Arriving early for a performance shows courtesy to the performers and other audience members. Help students list and describe the advantages of arriving early. For example, audience members who arrive early have time to

- Find their seats and get comfortable.
- Read the program (if available) to learn more about the music or performers.
- Look at and examine the surroundings—the architecture of the building, the design of the stage and scenery, the lighting. Identify how these features affect sound.
- Watch musicians on stage preparing for the performance or observe the set-up of instruments and equipment.

SKILLS REINFORCEMENT

▶ **Keyboard/Guitar** Encourage students to learn the following blues chord progression to accompany *Rock Around the Clock*.

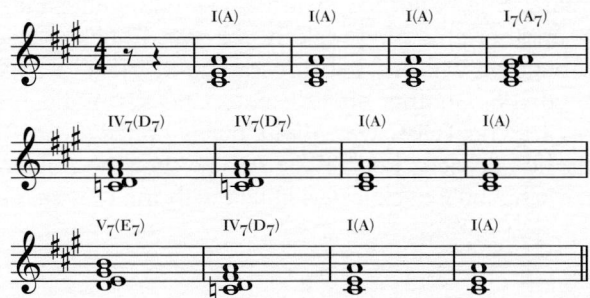

Lesson 8 Continued

Invite students to

- Read about the Platters, on p. 358, and their contribution to early rock 'n' roll.

6b • Softly tap the triplet rhythm notated on p. 358 as they listen to *The Great Pretender* **CD 16-18.**

8b Discuss the social background of the period 1955–1962 (see Cultural Connection, p. 356). Then have students read about Dick Clark and *American Bandstand,* on p. 359.

Moving

Invite students to

- Read about Chubby Checker on p. 359.
- Practice the movements for the Twist.

8a • Twist as they listen to Chubby Checker's recording **CD 16-19.**

6b Point out that *The Twist* follows the same blues chord progression (though in a different key) as *Rock Around the Clock.* See Skills Reinforcement below to have students transpose the progression to the new key.

THE PLATTERS

The Platters were one of the most popular singing groups of the 1950s. The group consisted of four male singers and one female singer. Tony Williams was the lead tenor. Other members of the group were David Lynch, Herb Reed, Paul Robi, and Zola Taylor. The group performed mostly slow rock 'n' roll tunes. The Platters toured the world as "international ambassadors of musical goodwill," and appeared in several movies, including *Rock Around the Clock* and *The Girl Can't Help It*. They are remembered for their crisp, impeccable harmonies and their string-laden accompaniments.

Triplets in the Background

Softer, slower rock 'n' roll songs divide the beat in three, resulting in triplets.

Listen to the Platters sing *The Great Pretender*. Tap the triplets as you listen.

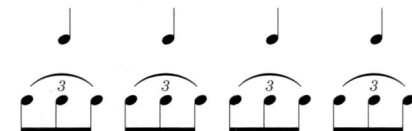
CD 16–18
The Great Pretender

by Buck Ram
as performed by the Platters
The Great Pretender was one of four number one singles from the Platters in the late 1950s.

358

Footnotes

American Bandstand

Dick Clark was neither a composer nor a performer, but was still very influential in the promotion of early rock 'n' roll. He was the host of *American Bandstand*, a TV show in Philadelphia that showcased local high school students dancing to popular hit records. Clark transformed the local show into a national phenomenon. He often interviewed recording artists on his show, which helped many of these young performers become stars. Clark was responsible for the popularity of Frankie Avalon, Bobby Rydell, Fabian, and Chubby Checker.

Move to a New Beat

Many new dance steps were introduced on *American Bandstand* — the Hucklebuck, the Pony, the Fly, and the Mashed Potato — but none became as popular as the Twist.

Learn to do the Twist, then **move** as you **listen** to Chubby Checker's performance.

Put one foot out and pretend you're crushing a bug with your big toe. At the same time, move your hands and body as though you're drying your back with a towel. Now, twist!

CD 16–19
The Twist

by Hank Ballard
as performed by Chubby Checker
The Twist dance craze went international and inspired a whole series of new songs, such as "Twist and Shout," "Twistin'," and "Twist Polka."

▲ Dick Clark from *American Bandstand*

▲ It's 1960 and Chubby Checker introduces a new dance craze — the Twist — at the Peppermint Lounge in Manhattan.

In the Pop Style

Unit 9 **359**

3 CLOSE

Element: TEXTURE/HARMONY — **ASSESSMENT**

2d **Performance/Observation** Play the recording of *Rock Around the Clock* **CD 16-16** and invite instrumentalists to accompany the song using the blues chord progression shown in Skills Reinforcement, p. 357. (The progression begins with the first verse.)

6a Observe students' abilities to hear the chord progression by asking them to hold up one finger for the I chord, four fingers for the IV chord, and five fingers for the V chord at the appropriate time in the music.

SPOTLIGHT ON

▶ **Rock 'n' Roll** Rock 'n' roll first appeared on the pop music charts in the mid-1950s. Early rock songs were often new arrangements of existing music. For example, Elvis Presley's first single, "That's All Right," was a blues song played at a fast tempo. Presley, Little Richard, Chuck Berry, and Buddy Holly were some of rock's first star performers. Their hits contained elements of rhythm and blues (R&B), country, and gospel music. Many artists became known for their onstage antics as well. Little Richard wore makeup and sequined vests. Chuck Berry "duck-walked" across the stage. Elvis shook his hips. Rock music spoke to teenagers, and their frenzied reaction created a youth market that is still courted by today's record companies.

SCHOOL TO HOME CONNECTION

▶ **Fifty Plus** Ask students to interview relatives or friends, over the age of 50, about their favorite rock 'n' roll artists from the 1950s, 1960s, 1970s, and beyond. Encourage students to ask their interviewees to play recordings of the music of the artists they mention. Have students write a report about "Rock 'n' Roll" memories to share with the class. Encourage students to develop a historical time line of rock 'n' roll hits and artists.

TECHNOLOGY/MEDIA LINK

Web Site Go to *www.sfsuccessnet.com* to learn more about the music and performing artists of the 1950s.

Unit 9 *In the Pop Style* **359**

LESSON AT A GLANCE

Element Focus **RHYTHM** Backbeat

Skill Focus **SINGING** Sing a soul song containing backbeat rhythms

Connection Activity **GENRE** Become familiar with the characteristics of classic soul music

MATERIALS
- "Dancin' in the Street" **CD 16-21**
  Recorded Routine: Intro (4 m.); vocal; coda
- *Dancin' in the Street* **CD 16-20**
- *Soulville* **CD 16-23**
- hand drums, tambourines

VOCABULARY

backbeat soul music

◆ ◆ ◆ ◆ National Standards ◆ ◆ ◆ ◆

1e In groups, sing moderately easy pieces with technical accuracy
2a Play instruments accurately in small ensembles
2c Perform instrumental music from diverse genres
5a Read quarter notes and eighth notes in duple meter
6a Listen and describe events in music using appropriate terms
6b Listen and analyze uses of rhythm in music from diverse genres
9a Describe characteristics of music genres from a variety of cultures

MORE MUSIC CHOICES

For more practice with strong backbeat:
"Get on Your Feet," p. 6

The Soul of the Music

Black gospel music crossed the boundaries of the church in the early 1960s to blend with rhythm and blues. The result was called *soul*. As in most styles of rock music, the backbeat is important in soul.

Martha Reeves and the Vandellas are the original soul artists who sang "Dancin' in the Street." **Sing** the song and clap to the backbeat rhythm.

Now **listen** to the original soul artists sing *Dancin' in the Street*.

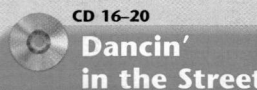

CD 16–20
Dancin' in the Street

by Marvin Gaye, Ivy Hunter, and William Stevenson
as performed by Martha Reeves and the Vandellas

The Vandellas were one of the favorite groups for dance music in the 1960s.

▼ Rosalind Ashford, Martha Reeves, and Annette Sterling

"A song has to become a part of you. It's something in you that you'll have for the rest of your life."
Martha Reeves

360

Footnotes

ACROSS THE CURRICULUM

▶ **Language Arts** For more about soul artists and music, see *The Ultimate Soul Music Trivia Book: 501 Questions and Answers About Motown* and *Rhythm & Blues, and More* by Bobby Bennett and Sarah A. Smith (Citadel, 1997).

BUILDING SKILLS THROUGH MUSIC

▶ **Language** Have students read the information on p. 360 and p. 363 to determine the meaning of the title "Queen of Soul." List suggested meanings on the board. Invite students to listen to *Soulville* **CD 16-23** and identify unique qualities of Aretha Franklin's performance. Discuss reasons why the title "Queen of Soul" is appropriate for her.

MOVEMENT

▶ **Popular Dances/Then** What popular dances did your parents or grandparents and other older relatives enjoy when they were younger? Ask older people to teach you a dance and bring in music to demonstrate that dance to members of your class. Include names of popular dances on the Rock 'n' Roll History Time Line your class creates for bulletin boards or student portfolios.

▶ **Popular Dances/Now** What are today's popular forms of dance that students like to do? Invite students to practice popular dances with older siblings and friends and teach these dances to their class.

Dancin' in the Street

l, ta d r ma m f

CD 16-21

*Words and Music by Marvin Gaye,
Ivy Hunter, and William Stevenson*

Call - in' out _ a - round _ the world, _ are you read - y for a brand new beat? _ Sum-mer's here _ and the time is right _ for danc - in' in the street. _ _ They're danc - in' in Chi - ca - go, _ _ down in New Or - leans, _ in New York _ Cit - - y; All _ we need _ is mu - sic, sweet _ mu - - sic, There'll be mu - sic ev - 'ry - where. _ There'll be

In the Pop Style

1 INTRODUCE

9a **ASK** **Which are the strong beats in rock 'n' roll?** (beats 2 and 4)

What are those strong beats called? (backbeats)

Select a student to read the information at the top of p. 360. Direct students' attention to the song on pp. 361–362 and help them understand how to follow the music.

2 DEVELOP

Listening

6b Invite students to clap the backbeat rhythm as they listen to and follow the music of "Dancin' in the Street" **CD 16-21.**

Singing

1e Have students sing the song with the recording while clapping the backbeat. Then play the "original artist" recording of the song **CD 16-20,** sung by Martha Reeves and the Vandellas.

continued on page 362

SKILLS REINFORCEMENT

▶ Guitar "Dancin' in the Street" has a "groove" on the chord G_7, which, with the exception of a few chord changes, remains constant throughout the song. This is a great opportunity to tune the guitar to an open "G" chord and let students try playing along with those parts of the song. Because they don't have to depress any strings with the left fingers, students can concentrate on experimenting with the right hand, finding a strumming rhythm that goes along with the rhythmic "feel" of the song. Share these resulting strumming rhythms with the class.

SPOTLIGHT ON

▶ The Performers Martha Reeves (b. 1941) grew up in Detroit. She said that she didn't want a singing career. Nevertheless, while in high school, she sang with Betty Kelly (b. 1944) and Rosalind Ashford (b. 1943) in a group called the Del-Phis. Reeves later got a job as a secretary at Motown Records. In addition to her secretarial tasks, she recorded songs for backup artists to learn. When one of the backup singers fell ill before a recording session for Marvin Gaye, Motown head Berry Gordy asked Reeves and her two friends to sing. He liked what he heard and in 1963, he signed them as featured artists known as "Martha and the Vandellas." The group produced many hit singles, including "Quicksand," "Jimmy Mack," and "Nowhere to Run," rivaling even the Supremes in popularity among female groups.

Reading

5a "Dancin' in the Street" is highly syncopated. The following pattern appears frequently throughout the song.

6a Challenge students to find the pattern (m. 7) and its variations (mm. 3, 32) in the song and to clap these rhythms when they hear them in the music.

Playing

2a Invite several students to play the rhythm of the melody on hand drum or tambourine while the rest of the class sings the song and claps the backbeats.

Encourage students to

9a
- Read about soul music and Aretha Franklin on p. 363 and discuss the characteristics of classic soul (short phrases; improvisation; loud, intense singing; and call-and-response form).
- Listen to Aretha Franklin's performance of *Soulville* **CD 16-23.**

ASK Which beats were the strongest? (the backbeats)

6b Would the rhythm pattern we clapped for *Dancin' in the Street* also fit *Soulville?* (yes)

Footnotes

SKILLS REINFORCEMENT

6b ▶ **Analyzing** Like early blues, early rock 'n' roll harmonies relied heavily on the three primary chords: I, IV, and V_7. Soul and later rock composers moved beyond the primary chords to include minor chords and altered chords. Some of the more musically advanced students might find it interesting to explore the various chords used to harmonize "Dancin' in the Street."

ACROSS THE CURRICULUM

▶ **Language Arts** Encourage students to read more about famous Motown soul artists and their music in *The Temptations (African-American Achievers)* by Ted Cox (Chelsea House, 1997) and *Diana Ross: Entertainer (Black Americans of Achievement)* by John Wyeth (Chelsea House, 1995).

The Queen of Soul

Soul music can express a performer's strong emotions. Some of the special musical techniques that singers use include repetition of short phrases; improvisation; loud, intense singing; and call-and-response form.

Listen to one of Aretha Franklin's soul classics. Which musical techniques listed above can you **identify** in this performance?

CD 16–23
Soulville

by T. Turner, M. Levy, R. Glover, and D. Washington
as performed by Aretha Franklin

Franklin recorded *Soulville* as part of a tribute to the great blues singer Dinah Washington.

M·U·S·I·C M·A·K·E·R·S

Aretha Franklin

Aretha Franklin (born 1942), known as the "Queen of Soul," is a member of the Rock and Roll Hall of Fame. She sang at the Inaugurations of Presidents Carter and Clinton, and also at the memorial service for Martin Luther King Jr. In 1999, VH1 named her one of the top 100 musicians of the twentieth century.

In the Pop Style

Unit 9 **363**

3 CLOSE

Skill: SINGING   **ASSESSMENT**

1e **Performance/Observation** As students sing "Dancin' in the Street," have

2c
- Half the class clap backbeats while singing.
- Half the class clap or play the melodic rhythm on a percussion instrument while singing.

Observe students' ability to sing while clapping and/or playing backbeats accurately.

CHARACTER EDUCATION

▶ **Emotional Expression** To help students understand the importance of expressing emotions appropriately, remind them that soul music used to communicate emotions. Discuss inappropriate and appropriate means of expressing emotions and the possible consequences of these actions. Identify strategies for practicing self-discipline when students are upset emotionally (for example, counting to ten, going for a walk, thinking about the consequences if they react inappropriately, and so on). Encourage students to notice situations in the coming days where they or someone else demonstrates self-discipline and appropriate emotional expression. Share and discuss these situations at the next class meeting.

TECHNOLOGY/MEDIA LINK

Web Site For more information on popular music of the 1960s, visit *www.sfsuccessnet.com*.

Lesson	Elements	Skills	
LESSON 1 **Watch the Stars** pp. 368-369 	**Element: Expression** **Concept:** Dynamics **Focus:** Musical expression **Secondary Element** Rhythm: meter **National Standards** 1a 6a 6b	**Skill: Listening** **Objective:** Identify expressive techniques in a listening selection **Secondary Skills** • **Listening** Listen to the recording and discuss the expressive lyrics • **Singing** Sing a song with meter changes	**SKILLS REINFORCEMENT** • **Listening** Identify the melodic variation in the listening selection
LESSON 2 **Where On Earth?** pp. 370-371 	**Element: Texture/Harmony** **Concept:** Harmony **Focus:** Two-part harmony **Secondary Element** Rhythm: $\frac{6}{8}$ meter **National Standards** 1c 1d 2a 6c 8b	**Skill: Playing** **Objective:** Accompany "Río, río" **Secondary Skills** • **Singing** Sing the song in Spanish • **Playing** Play an accompaniment for the song	**SKILLS REINFORCEMENT** • **Mallets** Play an accompaniment
LESSON 3 **Undersea Worlds** pp. 372-377  	**Element: Rhythm** **Concept:** Pattern **Focus:** Syncopated and nonsyncopated rhythms **Secondary Element** Harmony: chord progression **National Standards** 1a 1b 2a 3b 4c 5a 5c 6b 6c 8b	**Skill: Playing** **Objective:** Perform syncopated and nonsyncopated rhythms **Secondary Skills** • **Listening** Listen to a song and discuss interpretation; • **Singing** Sing a song in uneven rhythm while tapping the beat • **Reading** Read rhythm patterns of a song • **Playing** Improvise rhythm parts to accompany the song • **Listening** Listen to a selection and compare it to the song • **Creating** Create a short composition	**SKILLS REINFORCEMENT** • **Creating** Create a composition to describe underwater life

Connections

Music and Other Literature

Connection: Science

Activity: Discuss the relationship between heavenly bodies and specific geographical locations

ACROSS THE CURRICULUM **Language Arts** Create a class poem about wishes and dreams; reference book

SPOTLIGHT ON **An American Tail** Information about the movie

SCHOOL TO HOME CONNECTION **Take a Trip** Make a list of imaginary trip ideas

BUILDING SKILLS THROUGH MUSIC **Science** Research galaxies, solar systems, stars, and planets

Song "Somewhere Out There"

Listening Selection
Somewhere Out There

More Music Choices
"Get on Your Feet," p. 6
"The Voices of Pride," p. 86

ASSESSMENT

Music Journal Writing Compare the song and the listening selection and describe the expressive techniques

TECHNOLOGY/MEDIA LINK
Transparency Use listening map to display musical expression

Connection: Social Studies

Activity: Learn about the rivers of Chile

TEACHER TO TEACHER **Teaching Instrument** Patterns Use an aural model to learn instrument patterns

ACROSS THE CURRICULUM **Social Studies** Learn about the rivers in Chile

BUILDING SKILLS THROUGH MUSIC **Social Studies** Discuss the rivers in the United States

Songs
"Río, río"
"River, River"

More Music Choices
"Ev'ry Time I Feel the Spirit," p. 242
"Canción Mixteca," p. 326

ASSESSMENT

Performance/Observation Sing a song with harmony and an accompaniment

TECHNOLOGY/MEDIA LINK
Sequencing Software Record the two parts of the song to assess tone and pitch accuracy

---

Connection: Science

Activity: Compare a fantastic idea of life under the sea with the scientific reality

ACROSS THE CURRICULUM
Science Read a book about underwater scenes
Language Arts Read a book containing ocean and science activities
Language Arts Summary of a novel

MEETING INDIVIDUAL NEEDS **Vocabulary Building** Discuss vocabulary about sea life and the ocean

SPOTLIGHT ON
The Song-Writing Team Information about the songwriters
An Oceanographer Information about Jacques Cousteau
The Great Barrier Reef Geography and information about the reef

TEACHER TO TEACHER **Science Activities** Use activities from books to create an ocean bulletin board

SCHOOL TO HOME CONNECTION **A Family Trip** Take a trip to an aquarium or natural history museum

BUILDING SKILLS THROUGH MUSIC **Science** Discuss underwater plant and animal life

Song "Under the Sea"

Listening Selection *Carnival of the Animals,* "Aquarium"

More Music Choices
"Morning Comes Early," p. 13
"Day-O!" p. 18

ASSESSMENT

Performance/Observation Distinguish between steady beat and syncopation, and play syncopation

TECHNOLOGY/MEDIA LINK
Web Site More information on music for the movies

Lesson	Elements	Skills

LESSON 4 — Seasons of Life
pp. 378-381

Element: Form
Concept: Form
Focus: Verse/refrain

Secondary Element
Rhythm: pattern

National Standards
1a 6a 6b 6c 8b

Skill: Singing
Objective: Sing a song in verse/refrain form

Secondary Skills
- **Reading** Identify musical symbols in the song
- **Singing** Sing the song in two groups
- **Listening** Listen to the interview and describe music vocations
- **Analyzing** Listen to a poem and compare it to the song

SKILLS REINFORCEMENT
- **Creating** Create additional verses for a song

LESSON 5 — A Better World
pp. 382-385

Element: Texture/Harmony
Concept: Harmony
Focus: Chord Progressions

Secondary Element
Form: verse/refrain

National Standards
1a 1d 2a 6b 6c 7a 8b 9a

Skill: Playing
Objective: Play a three-chord song on keyboard, guitar, or resonator bells

Secondary Skills
- **Singing** Sing a song, identify phrases and their use
- **Analyzing** Analyze the chord progression of a song
- **Listening** Listen to and compare the message of the lyrics in two songs

SKILLS REINFORCEMENT
- **Singing** Exercises to learn harmony
- **Keyboard** Play accompaniment to the song
- **Guitar** Play a chord accompaniment

LESSON 6 — Same but Different
pp. 386-389

Element: Rhythm
Concept: Pattern
Focus: Syncopated and nonsyncopated rhythms

Secondary Element
Melody: phrase

National Standards
1a 3a 5a 6b 6c 7a 8a 8b

Skill: Singing
Objective: Sing a song using syncopated and nonsyncopated rhythms

Secondary Skills
- **Singing** Sing the song and pat the steady beat
- **Analyzing** Analyze different rhythms within the song
- **Comparing** Perform a song with and without syncopation; compare a poem to a song
- **Listening** Listen and identify examples of syncopated rhythm in related selection
- **Creating** Create a poem, song, or picture to express similarities and differences among people

SKILLS REINFORCEMENT
- **Vocal Development** Practice good vocal technique while singing

Connections

Music and Other Literature

Connection: Related Arts

Activity: Compare the form and message of a poem and a song

ACROSS THE CURRICULUM
Art Read and show artwork from the book which inspired the song
Language Arts Use the poem in a journal activity

SPOTLIGHT ON
Career in Music: Ethnomusicologist Explanation of the career
The "Folk Process" Quote from Pete Seeger on folk tradition

MOVEMENT
Creative Dramatization Move to interpret song lyrics

CULTURAL CONNECTION
Folk Instruments Evolution of folk music in instruments

BUILDING SKILLS THROUGH MUSIC
Language Select phrases and write their meaning

Song "Turn, Turn, Turn"

Listening Selection *Interview with Pete Seeger*

M·U·S·I·C M·A·K·E·R·S
Pete Seeger

Poem "Children Learn What They Live"

More Music Choices
"California," p. 52
"This Land Is Your Land," p. 118
"Loch Lomond," p. 140
"Blow the Wind Southerly," p. 178
"Ev'ry Time I Feel the Spirit," p. 242

ASSESSMENT

Performance/Observation
Sing another verse/refrain song and teach it to the class aurally

TECHNOLOGY/MEDIA LINK
CD-ROM Use software to explore harmony of the song

Connection: Social Studies

Activity: Discuss social themes in songs of the 1960s

ACROSS THE CURRICULUM
Language Arts Discuss and list social concerns
Language Arts Research folk musicians of the era

SPOTLIGHT ON
The Sixties History and culture of the decade

TEACHER TO TEACHER
Resonator Bell List List required bells for accompaniment

BUILDING SKILLS THROUGH MUSIC
Social Studies Describe characteristics that indicate the influence of another musician

---

Song "Blowin' in the Wind"

Listening Selections
Blowin' in the Wind
The Times They Are A-Changin'
Both Sides Now
Arts Connection *Friends*
M·U·S·I·C M·A·K·E·R·S
Bob Dylan
Joni Mitchell

More Music Choices
"Yakety Yak," p. 205
"Linstead Market," p. 241

ASSESSMENT

Performance/Peer Critique Select a song from the book, perform it with an accompaniment and evaluate the performance

TECHNOLOGY/MEDIA LINK
CD-ROM Use software to explore style, harmony, and accompaniment

---

Connection: Language Arts

Activity: Experience a poem that celebrates people's differences and similarities

ACROSS THE CURRICULUM
Social Studies Discuss ways to make a positive difference
Language Arts Read about children who make contributions to society

TEACHER TO TEACHER
Idioms Illustrate the meaning of the song lyrics

CHARACTER EDUCATION
Respect Discuss awareness of and respect for diversity within the school

MEETING INDIVIDUAL NEEDS
Including Everyone Discuss different ways to participate in the same activities

CULTURAL CONNECTION
Everyday People Display "Everyday People" photographs or illustrations in class

BUILDING SKILLS THROUGH MUSIC
Social Studies Describe how performers blend styles

Song "A World of Difference"

Listening Selection *Everyday People*
Poem "You and I"
M·U·S·I·C M·A·K·E·R·S
Sly and the Family Stone

More Music Choices
"Morning Comes Early," p. 13
"Funwa alafia" ("Welcome, My Friends"), p. 32

ASSESSMENT

Performance/Self-Assessment Sing a song with syncopated and nonsyncopated rhythms and evaluate the accuracy of the syncopated rhythm

TECHNOLOGY/MEDIA LINK
Electronic Keyboard Play root chords for song and improvise rhythm patterns

---

Lesson	Elements	Skills	
LESSON 7 **A Song of Hope** pp. 390-391 	**Element: Rhythm** **Concept:** Pattern **Focus:** Backbeat **Secondary Element** Harmony: chords **National Standards** 1c 2a 5a 6c 7b 8b	**Skill: Reading** **Objective:** Sing a song from notation that is based on two rhythmic motives **Secondary Skills** • **Listening** Listen to a selection and determine which instruments are playing the backbeat • **Singing** Sing a song and clap the backbeat • **Playing** Play a recorder accompaniment	**SKILLS REINFORCEMENT** • **Reading** Read notation to discover rhythmic motives • **Recorder** Play a countermelody to accompany the song
LESSON 8 **Sing of Freedom** pp. 392-395 	**Element: Timbre** **Concept:** Vocal **Focus:** Vocal timbre **Secondary Element** Harmony: chords **National Standards** 1c 2a 4b 6b 6c 8a 8b 9a	**Skill: Listening** **Objective:** Listen to and describe the vocal timbre of a folk singer **Secondary Skills** • **Singing** Sing two songs and find the similarities between both songs' lyrics and melodies • **Playing** Play a keyboard accompaniment • **Listening** Listen to two selections and compare range • **Performing** Perform both songs as one work	**SKILLS REINFORCEMENT** • **Listening** Use a Venn diagram to compare songs
LESSON 9 **A Song of Nature** pp. 396-399 	**Element: Melody** **Concept:** Pitch and direction **Focus:** Melodic contour **Secondary Element** Timbre: instrumental **National Standards** 1c 6b 6c 8a 9a 9c	**Skill: Listening** **Objective:** Listen to melodic contour in a Native American composition that celebrates the sunrise **Secondary Skills** • **Listening** Listen to the song and draw the contour of the melody in the air • **Singing** Sing a song using vocables and discuss related art on the page • **Listening** Listen and compare listening selections • **Listening** Compare listening selection to a poem • **Singing** Sing the song and analyze the melodic contour and repetition	

Connections

Music and Other Literature

Connection: Social Studies

Activity: Discover the connection between African American spirituals and the plight of enslaved people

TEACHER TO TEACHER **Inspiring Spontaneity** Model spontaneous movement

ACROSS THE CURRICULUM **Social Studies/Language Arts** Make lists of words to describe feelings, hopes and dreams relevant to the song

BUILDING SKILLS THROUGH MUSIC **Language** Discuss how changes in dynamics and tempo emphasize ideas in the lyrics of the song

Song "Come and Go with Me to That Land"

More Music Choices
"Dancin' in the Street," p. 361

ASSESSMENT

Performance/Peer Critique Sing a song with a backbeat to demonstrate accurate performance of rhythmic motives

TECHNOLOGY/MEDIA LINK
MIDI/Sequencing Software Experiment with tracks to create a different performance

---

Connection: Related Arts

Activity: Explore the use of textiles as an art form and means of expression

CULTURAL CONNECTION **The Song** Discuss the meaning and music techniques in spirituals

MEETING INDIVIDUAL NEEDS **Encouraging Participation** Help students perform movements with the song

ACROSS THE CURRICULUM
Social Studies Share background of spirituals and related reading
Art Learn about quilts and their secret codes

SPOTLIGHT ON
The Performers Information about the Boys Choir of Harlem
Voice Classification Four main classifications of voice

BUILDING SKILLS THROUGH MUSIC **Language** Write a paragraph about freedom

Song "Oh, Freedom"

Listening Selection *Oh, Freedom* and *Come and Go with Me*

M·U·S·I·C M·A·K·E·R·S Odetta

Arts Connection *Eighteenth- century cotton coverlet*

More Music Choices
"Oklahoma," p. 36
"Stand By Me," p. 46
Shenandoah, p. 265

ASSESSMENT

Music Journal Writing Compare and describe different types of vocal timbre

TECHNOLOGY/MEDIA LINK
CD-ROM Explore accompaniment styles

Connection: Culture

Activity: Discuss the importance and symbolic meaning of the flute in Native American culture

CULTURAL CONNECTION
Native American Flute Significance of the instrument
American Indian Dance Theater Information on the dance troupe

TEACHER TO TEACHER **Native American Music** Explanation of vocables in song

ACROSS THE CURRICULUM **Language Arts** Read and dramatize Zuni folktales

SPOTLIGHT ON
The Performer/Composer Information about R. Carlos Nakai
The Performer/Composer Information about Paul Winter

CHARACTER EDUCATION **Environmental Awareness** Discuss the impact individuals and groups have on the environment

BUILDING SKILLS THROUGH MUSIC **Art** Describe the elements of art in a photograph

Song "Zuni Sunrise Call"

Listening Selections
Daybreak Vision
Garden of the Earth
Listening Map Daybreak Vision
Poem "Garden of the Earth"
Arts Connection *American Indian Dance Theater*
M·U·S·I·C M·A·K·E·R·S Paul Winter

More Music Choices
"Jo'ashilá" ("Walking Together"), p. 108
Kokopelli Wandering Song, p. 110

ASSESSMENT

Music Journal Writing Write short descriptions comparing a song and a listening selection

TECHNOLOGY/MEDIA LINK
Transparency Use listening map to point to the sections in the music

Lesson	Elements	Skills

LESSON 10
Common Ground

pp. 400-401

Element:
Texture/Harmony
Concept: Texture
Focus: Melodic and rhythmic ostinato

Secondary Element
Form: verse/refrain

National Standards
1c 1d 2c 8b

Skill: Singing
Objective: Perform ostinato patterns to accompany a melody

Secondary Skills
- **Singing** Sing a song with an ostinato accompaniment
- **Playing** Play an ostinato on a melody instrument

SKILLS REINFORCEMENT
- **Recorder** Create and play ostinatos for a song
- **Mallets** Play an Orff arrangement

LESSON 11
One If By Land,
Two If By Sea
pp. 402-403

Element: Form
Concept: Form
Focus: Verse/refrain

Secondary Element
Melody: pitch and direction

National Standards
1a 2a 6b 8b

Skill: Singing
Objective: Sing a song in verse/refrain form

Secondary Skills
- **Listening** Listen to the song and identify the form
- **Listening** Listen to the selection and compare it to the song

SKILLS REINFORCEMENT
- **Keyboard** Perform a keyboard accompaniment

Connections

Music and Other Literature

Connection: Culture

Activity: Discuss that communities are made up of people who have common interests

ACROSS THE CURRICULUM **Social Studies** Read a book about a *kibbutz*

CULTURAL CONNECTION **Israeli Folk Music** Information on style and functions

BUILDING SKILLS THROUGH MUSIC **Math** Identify fractions for music notes

Songs
"Zum gali gali" (Hebrew)
"Zum gali gali" (English)

More Music Choices
"I Love the Mountains," p. 34
"O Music," p. 162

ASSESSMENT

Performance/Observation
Perform sections of a song to demonstrate texture

TECHNOLOGY/MEDIA LINK
Web Site More information about Israeli folk music

Connection: Science

Activity: Learn about the history of navigation

ACROSS THE CURRICULUM **Science** Discuss celestial navigation

SPOTLIGHT ON **The Performers** Information about the Kingston Trio

BUILDING SKILLS THROUGH MUSIC **Social Studies** Discuss the purpose of ships in the world today

Song "The Ship That Never Returned"

Listening Selection *M.T.A.*

More Music Choices
"Bound for South Australia," p. 22
"The Greenland Whale Fishery," p. 230

ASSESSMENT

Performance/Observation
Perform the song in groups with good tone quality

TECHNOLOGY/MEDIA LINK
MIDI/Sequencing Software Change the mood of the song by experimenting with tempo, dynamic, and orchestration changes

INTRODUCING THE UNIT

The unit presents songs that have made a difference in the lives of individuals and societies. The importance of friendship and love, the yearning for social progress and world harmony, and concern for the environment are expressed through the music.

Presented on p. 365 is a brief overview of the skills that are assessed in this unit. (See below and pp. 364–365 for unit highlights of related curricular experiences.)

For a more detailed unit overview, see Unit at a Glance, pp. 363a–363h.

UNIT PROJECT

Invite students to read the text at the top of p. 364 and discuss friendship from two standpoints:

- How to be a good friend
- How to choose a good friend

Help students visualize their world of friends. On a piece of paper, have them draw circles around their names. Then ask them to write the names of their closest friends on the line surrounding their names and draw circles around those names. Have them continue writing names and drawing circles for many different levels of friendship (for example, people you see once a year, people you see every day, and so on). Remind students that at the end of this exercise they are surrounded by a community of caring people, even if they only have one or two close friends.

Friends Forever

Friends like to share important moments with each other. Feelings about friendship can be expressed through music or poetry.

..."And the song from beginning to end, I found again in the heart of a friend."

Henry Wadsworth Longfellow

MUSIC MAKERS

Carole King

Carole King (born 1942) is one of the most successful singers and songwriters in our country's history. She is noted for her ability to express her genuine emotions through her songs. King co-wrote songs recorded by artists such as the Beatles, Aretha Franklin, the Monkees, and several "girl groups" of the 1960s. In 1971, after several unsuccessful albums, she released her own solo album, *Tapestry*. It sold over 13 million copies and secured King's place in music history as an important singer and songwriter.

▲ Willie Nelson and friends

Listen to *You've Got a Friend* as performed by Carole King.

 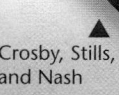

CD 17–1
You've Got a Friend

by Carole King
You've Got a Friend also became a top hit for singer James Taylor.

▲ Crosby, Stills, and Nash

(364)

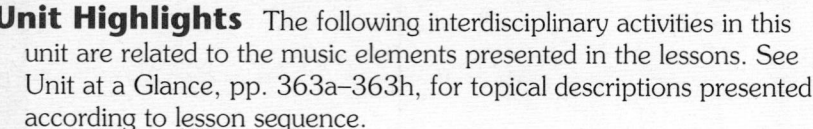

ACROSS THE CURRICULUM

Unit Highlights The following interdisciplinary activities in this unit are related to the music elements presented in the lessons. See Unit at a Glance, pp. 363a–363h, for topical descriptions presented according to lesson sequence.

▶ **ART**

- Share a book about artwork through the ages (p. 378)
- Read books about freedom quilts (p. 395)

▶ **LANGUAGE ARTS**

- Create a class poem (p. 368)
- Explore a book containing ocean/science activities (p. 374)
- Discover facts about author Jules Verne (p. 376)
- Record responses in a journal (p. 381)
- Discuss various problems in society (p. 382)

- Research folk music and musicians (p. 384)
- Read books about improving the world (p. 388)
- Share books about the Zuni people (p. 397)

▶ **SCIENCE**

- Read a book about undersea life (p. 372)
- Learn about the history of sea navigation (p. 402)

▶ **SOCIAL STUDIES**

- Explore facts about the geography of Chile (p. 370)
- List community and school activities that would make a positive difference (p. 386)
- Write words that describe the feelings expressed in an African American spiritual (p. 391)
- Explore facts about the text of African American spirituals (p. 393)
- Read a book about a *kibbutz* (p. 400)

◀ Neil Young

▲ Kris Kristofferson (left) performing at a Farm Aid Concert

Keepers of the Earth

Time spent with friends makes things around us special. Friends share in our joys and sorrows and stand by us when we need them the most. They are indeed the keepers of the earth.

▼ Willie Nelson (left) and Woody Harrelson

Unit 10 **365**

MUSIC SKILLS ASSESSED IN THIS UNIT

Reading Music: Rhythm

- Read and clap syncopated rhythms (p. 377)
- Read, analyze, and clap a syncopated phrase (p. 387)

Reading Music: Pitch

- Read notation to identify various musical symbols (p. 379)
- Read and sing pitches in a Native American song (p. 397)

Performing Music: Singing

- Sing a song in two-part harmony (p. 371)
- Perform a song in verse/refrain form (p. 381)
- Sing a folk song (p. 385)
- Sing a song with syncopation (p. 389)

Moving to Music

- Create a dramatization to interpret song lyrics (p. 379)
- Perform movements with an African American spiritual (p. 392)

Performing Music: Playing

- Perform an accompaniment on mallet instruments (p. 371)
- Accompany a folk song (p. 385)
- Perform a backbeat rhythm to accompany a song (p. 391)

Creating Music

- Compose a short piece describing life underwater (p. 375)
- Create additional verses for a classic folk song (p. 378)

Listening to Music

- Listen and compare two versions of a song (p. 369)
- Listen and compare various vocal timbres (p. 395)

CULTURAL CONNECTION

Unit Highlights The musical literature in this unit provides many opportunities for students to explore a variety of world cultures. See Unit at a Glance, pp. 363a–363h, for topical descriptions presented according to lesson sequence.

▶ AMERICAN REGIONAL

- Learn about folk instruments (p. 380)

▶ NATIVE AMERICAN

- Explore facts about the Native American flute (p. 396)
- Learn about the American Indian Dance Theater (p. 398)

▶ MIDDLE EASTERN

- Discover facts about Israeli folk music (p. 400)

OPENING ACTIVITIES

MATERIALS	
• "You've Got a Friend"	**CD 17-2**
Recording Routine:	
Intro (4 m.); vocal; coda	
• *You've Got a Friend*	**CD 17-1**
• Resource Book p. G-10	

Listening

Play *You've Got a Friend* **CD 17-1**.

ASK **What type of friend is the song about?** (A friend who is dependable, especially when things are not going well.)

Select a student to explain the routine of the song to the rest of the class.

Engage students in a brief discussion of the importance of friendship.

Focus students' attention on p. 364 and have them read about songwriter Carole King.

Singing

Invite students to follow the music on pp. 366–367 and sing "You've Got a Friend" with the recording **CD 17-2**.

Creating

Have students create a rhythm accompaniment for the song. Notate the rhythm(s) on the board or music staff paper. Select instruments for each rhythm. Students might consider one of the following suggestions:

• Eighth notes played on a tambourine, with the first and fifth notes accented.

• A dotted quarter note followed by an eighth note and a half note, played on a drum.

When You Need a Helping Hand

Some people express their feelings about friendship through music. **Sing** Carole King's song about friendship and think of someone you consider a friend.

You've Got a Friend

Words and Music by Carole King

When you're down ___ and trou - bled, And you need some love and care, ___
___ a - bove ___ you grows ___ dark ___ and full of clouds, ___

And noth - in' ___ noth - in' is go - in' right, ___
And that ol' ___ north wind be - gins ___ to blow, ___

Close your eyes ___ and think of me, and soon I ___ will be there ___ To
Keep your head ___ to - geth - er, and call my ___ name out loud; ___

bright - en up ___ e - ven your dark - est night. ___
Soon you'll hear ___ me ___ knock - in' at ___ your door. ___

REFRAIN
You just call ___ out my ___ name, ___ and you know ___ wher - ev - er I am, ___

I'll come run - nin' ___ to see you a - gain. ___ last time to Coda

Win - ter, spring, sum - mer or fall, ___ All you have to do is call, ___ and I'll be ___

366

Unit Highlights This unit includes a variety of strategies and methods, described below, to track students' progress and assess their understanding of lesson objectives.

▶ **INFORMAL ASSESSMENTS**

At the close of each Teacher's Edition lesson in this unit, one of the following types of assessments is used to evaluate the learning of the key element focus or skill objective.

• Music Journal Writing (pp. 369, 395, 399)

• Performance/Observation (pp. 371, 377, 381, 401)

• Performance/Peer Critique (pp. 385, 391)

• Performance/Self-Assessment (p. 389)

▶ **RUBRICS**

Visit *www.sfsuccessnet.com* for rubrics to assess students' achievement in music skills.

Students might wish to create a different rhythm for the verse, refrain, and bridge.

Moving

See Resource Book p. G-10 and invite students to add a sign interpretation of "You've Got a Friend" to a performance of the song.

INNOVATIVE TEACHER SUPPORT FOR THIS UNIT

- **MAKING MUSIC DVD, Grade 5** contains video segments that support lessons, including signing and movement.
- **MAKING MUSIC with Movement and Dance** provides more opportunities for large group activities in music or physical education classes.
- **MAKING MUSIC with Technology** provides lesson plans for many technology applications; includes MIDI files.
- *¡A cantar!* features recorded songs and lessons from around the Spanish-speaking world; includes strategies for bilingual classes and for English-speaking teachers working with Spanish-speaking students.
- **Bridges to Asia** features recorded songs and lessons from Asian and Pacific region cultures.
- *www.sfsuccessnet.com* provides an online lesson planner to conveniently create lesson plans at school or at home. Includes rubrics for assessment, lesson modifications to meet the needs of all students, performance musicals based on program content, and more.

Unit 10 **367**

TECHNOLOGY/MEDIA LINK

Unit Highlights The following components are used in this unit to reinforce and expand students' understanding of music elements and related themes. See Unit at a Glance, pp. 363a–363h, for a descriptive listing according to lesson sequence.

▶ **CD-ROM**

- Use *Band-in-a-Box* to help students understand style, harmony, and accompaniment (p. 381)
- Use *Band-in-a-Box* to help them play a chordal accompaniment (p. 385)
- Explore accompaniment styles using *Band-in-a-Box* (p. 395)

▶ **ELECTRONIC KEYBOARD**

- Play chord roots and improvise rhythm patterns (p. 389)

▶ **MIDI/SEQUENCING SOFTWARE**

- Record song parts and self-assess tone and pitch accuracy (p. 371)
- Use the MIDI file to emphasize different parts (p. 391)

- Play MIDI file to alter the tempo, dynamics, and orchestration of a song (p. 403)

▶ **TRANSPARENCY**

- Display a listening map to help students follow a selection (p. 369)
- Display a listening map to help students follow a recording (p. 399)

▶ **WEB SITE**

- Go to *www.sfsuccessnet.com* for more information about music for the movies (p. 377); Israeli folk music (p. 401)

Unit 10 *Keepers of the Earth* **367**

LESSON AT A GLANCE

Element Focus	**EXPRESSION** Musical expression
Skill Objective	**LISTENING** Identify expressive techniques in a listening selection
Connection Activity	**SCIENCE** Discuss the relationship between heavenly bodies and specific geographical locations

MATERIALS

- "Somewhere Out There"   **CD 17-4**
  Recording Routine: Intro (4 m.); vocal
- *Somewhere Out There*   **CD 17-6**
- world map

VOCABULARY

vocal timbre   dynamics   tempo   meter

◆ ◆ ◆ ◆ National Standards ◆ ◆ ◆ ◆

1a Sing accurately in small ensembles
6a Listen and describe events in music using appropriate terms
6b Listen and analyze uses of pitch, dynamics, and timbre in music from diverse genres

MORE MUSIC CHOICES

For more practice using expression:
"Get on Your Feet," p. 6
"The Voices of Pride," p. 86

1 INTRODUCE

Lead a discussion of what heavenly bodies can be seen from the locality where students live. Then invite students to tell the class about friends or relatives who live in other cities, states, and countries. Allow students to place colored pins on a world map to indicate where their friends or relatives live.

Establish the connection between the two topics by having one student read aloud the text on p. 368.

WATCH THE STARS

We miss our friends when they are far away, but we can stay in touch. We can share letters and phone calls. We can send them small gifts. Watching the sun and moon and stars reminds us that our friends are watching, too.

Listen to the song "Somewhere Out There."
Describe how the composers use words and melody expressively.

CD 17–4

Somewhere Out There
(from *An American Tail*)

Words and Music by James Horner, Barry Mann, and Cynthia Weil

Some-where out there be-neath the pale moon-light, some-one's think-in' of me and lov-ing me to-night. Some-where out there some-one's say-ing a prayer that we'll find one an-oth-er in that big some-where out there. And e-ven though I know how ver-y far a-part we are, it

368

Footnotes

ACROSS THE CURRICULUM

▶ **Language Arts** Ask students to think about someone special who is far away. Invite students to write down dreams and wishes they would share with this friend. Use their ideas to create a class poem.

For more teaching ideas see *Wishes, Lies, and Dreams: Teaching Children to Write Poetry* by Kenneth Koch (Harperperennial Library, 2000).

BUILDING SKILLS THROUGH MUSIC

▶ **Science** Share the information in the side column on p. 368. Have students describe the sky. Then ask them to research the difference between galaxies (systems of stars, dust, and gas held together by gravity), solar system, stars, and planets.

SKILLS REINFORCEMENT

6b ▶ **Listening** Inform students that "Somewhere Out There" has been recorded by many different performers. After students have listened to James Galway perform the song on flute, ask if he played it exactly as notated in their books. (no) Explain that musicians often add their own expressive changes to the performance. Invite students to follow the music and discover that the flutist made changes by

- Adding new pitches to the melody and omitting others.
- Playing parts of phrases at a different octave.
- Holding some pitches longer and others shorter.
- Using different music for the interlude.
- Making a greater *ritardando* (slowing the tempo) at the end.

Music of the Heart

Music can be comforting. In the movie *An American Tail*, two characters who are separated by a great distance sing this song as a duet. Through the song, they are united in their hearts. **Listen** to another version of *Somewhere Out There*.

 CD 17–6

Somewhere Out There

**by James Horner, Barry Mann, and Cynthia Weil
as performed by James Galway**

Somewhere Out There was nominated for a Golden Globe award and won two Grammy awards in 1986.

helps to think we might be wish-in' on the same bright star. And

when the night wind starts to sing a lone-some lul-la-by, it

helps to think we're sleep-ing un-der - neath the same big sky.

Some-where out there if love can see us through,

then we'll be to-geth - er some-where out there, out

where dreams come true. _____

Unit 10 **369**

2 DEVELOP

Listening

Have students listen to "Somewhere Out There" **CD 17-4**, focusing on the expressive lyrics of the song and the performance style of the singers.

 ASK Who sings the song? (a man and a woman)

What does the song describe? (feelings of separation and a desire to reunite with a friend)

What helps the friends feel closer to each other? (They share the same stars and sky.)

How does the music express the feelings described in the text? (use of soft dynamics, slow tempo, and flowing melody)

Help students discover that changes in vocal timbre result when male and female voices alternate in the recording.

Singing

 Invite students to sing "Somewhere Out There" **CD 17-4** with the recording.

 **ASK** What is the meter of the song? ($\frac{4}{4}$)

Is the meter always $\frac{4}{4}$? (no)

Help students locate the meter change on p. 369.

3 CLOSE

Skill: LISTENING   **ASSESSMENT**

Music Journal Writing Have students

 • Sing "Somewhere Out There" **CD 17-5** with the Stereo Performance Track.

• Listen to flutist James Galway's interpretation of *Somewhere Out There* **CD 17-6**.

 • Compare the two versions by writing descriptions of the expressive techniques used by Galway (see Skills Reinforcement, p. 368).

SPOTLIGHT ON

▶ **An American Tail** This 1986 movie tells the story of Fievel the mouse and his emigration to America. Fieval Mousekewitz and his family decide to leave Russia when their village becomes overrun with cats. Before the ship reaches New York City, Fievel is swept overboard during a storm and is separated from his family. At first he searches for them on his own, but he soon discovers that he needs the help of a friendly cat and bird to find his loved ones. "Somewhere Out There" expresses Fievel's sense of abandonment and his hope for a reunion with his family. *An American Tail* was produced by Steven Spielberg and directed by Don Bluth, a former Disney animator. "Somewhere Out There" was nominated for a Best Song Oscar.

SCHOOL TO HOME CONNECTION

▶ **Take a Trip** Invite students to think of an imaginary trip they would like to take with a friend or relative. Where would they go if they could go anywhere? What would they do there? Ask them to discuss their fantasy trip ideas with a friend or family member and to make a list of favorite destinations and activities.

TECHNOLOGY/MEDIA LINK

 Transparency To provide students with another example of how dynamics and tempo are used to create musical expression, display the listening map for *When Johnny Comes Marching Home* **CD 4-32** as you play the recording.

LESSON AT A GLANCE

Element Focus	**TEXTURE/HARMONY** Two-part harmony
Skill Objective	**PLAYING** Accompany "Río, río"
Connection Activity	**SOCIAL STUDIES** Learn about the rivers of Chile

MATERIALS

* "Río, río" **CD 17-7**
* "River, River" **CD 17-8**
  Recording Routine: Intro (8 m.); vocal; coda
* **Pronunciation Practice/Translation** p. 540
* **Resource Book** p. A-42, G-12
* alto and bass metallophones, soprano xylophone

VOCABULARY

melody   harmony

◆ ◆ ◆ ◆ **National Standards** ◆ ◆ ◆ ◆

1c Sing music from diverse cultures
1d Sing music written in two parts
2a Play instruments accurately in small ensembles, with good stick technique
6c Understand and use basic principles of intervals in music analysis
8b Identify ways music relates to social studies

MORE MUSIC CHOICES

For more practice singing songs in two parts:
"Ev'ry Time I Feel the Spirit," p. 242
"Canción Mixteca," p. 326

1 INTRODUCE

8b Ask students to read the English text of "Río, río" to discover what the singer is feeling and how the river plays a role. (The singer describes the river as wide, deep, and swift and if his or her tears would be added, the river would be even deeper.)

Have students identify Chile as the country of origin and locate it on a map. Lead students in a discussion about the rivers of Chile. For more information, see

Where on Earth?

The South American country of Chile is made up of many different landscapes. The Atacama Desert is located in the north, while the Andes Mountains serve as the eastern border with Argentina. Other features of the land include rivers, lakes, and glaciers.

The Chilean song "Río, río" shows how emotions can sometimes be expressed through images of nature—in this case, a swiftly-flowing river.

SOUTH AMERICA
Atacama Desert
Andes Mountains
Chile

CD 17-7

Río, río
(River, River)

English Words by Alice Firgau

Traditional Song from Chile

Qué gran-de que vie-ne_el rí-o, _____ qué
How wide __ and deep is the riv-er, _____ How

gran - de se va_a la mar. _____ Si lo_au-men-ta_el __ llan-to
swift-ly it flows to the sea. _____ Rí-o, rí-o, ____ rí-o,
If my tears should _ meet its
Riv-er, riv-er, ____ flow-ing

370

Footnotes

TEACHER TO TEACHER

▶ **Teaching Instrument Patterns** When teaching instrument patterns it is a great advantage if students can hear the pattern correctly while they are learning, not just before. Ask a capable student who learns quickly to play the pattern as an aural model while you assist in the learning process. This task can be shared among capable students.

BUILDING SKILLS THROUGH MUSIC

▶ **Social Studies** Have students name and discuss rivers located in the United States and the roles these rivers play in our society.

ACROSS THE CURRICULUM

▶ **Social Studies** Among the more interesting geographical features of Chile is its rivers. Due to the odd shape of the country, the rivers of Chile run from east to west and are not very long in length. Just like the climate, the rivers vary from region to region. Many rivers in the Northern Desert region do not flow to the sea. The one exception is the Loa, the only river in the Atacama Desert. In the Central Valley region of Chile, the rivers Aconcagua, Mapocho, Maipo, Maule, and Bío, Bío are fed by the Andes Mountains. Display a map of Chile and invite students to locate the country's many rivers.

Sing of South America

Follow the notation as you **listen** to "*Río, río.*"
Sing the melody part. Then learn to sing the harmony part. You'll be singing harmonies that are typical of Spanish music. What interval is used the most?

Play these parts on mallet instruments to accompany "*Río, río.*"

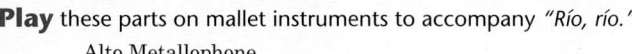

Alto Metallophone

Bass Metallophone

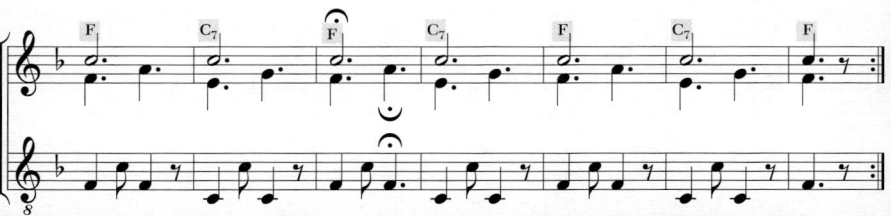

mí - o ____ co - mo gran - de ____ no ha de es - tar, ____ Si lo au -
rí - o, ___ De - vol - ved - me el __ a - mor mí - o. De - vol -
wa - ters, __ Oh, how deep it __ then would be. ____ If my
riv - er, __ Please re - turn my __ love to me. ____ Please re -

men - ta el __ llan - to mí - o ____ co - mo gran - de ____ no ha de es - tar.
ved - me el __ a - mor mí - o ____ que me can - so ____ de llo - rar.
tears should _ meet its wa - ters, _ Oh, how deep it __ then would be.
turn my __ love to me, Oh, _ from my sor - row _ set me free.

Keepers of the Earth

Unit 10 **371**

Across the Curriculum on p. 370.

2 DEVELOP

Singing

Play the recording of "*Río, río*" **CD 17-7** and ask students to follow the notation.

6c **ASK** Is "*Río, río*" sung in unison or two parts? (two parts)

1c Have students

- Practice singing the melody and harmony parts on a neutral syllable.
- Practice singing the Spanish words using Pronunciation Practice Tracks **CD 17-10, 17-11** and Resource Book p. A-42.

Playing

2a Have students practice the alto and bass metallophone accompaniment on p. 371 by isolating each part.

To help students learn to play the A section of the accompaniment, write the notes A F E G E F on the board. Sing this pattern while students playing the alto metallophone part play the pattern using an "air mallet" with the left hand. (Have them refer to a keyboard if necessary to establish direction.) Have students add the right hand "air mallet" on C.

Instrument patterns for the B section can be developed in a similar manner.

3 CLOSE

Element: TEXTURE/HARMONY **ASSESSMENT**

1d **Performance/Observation** Have the class prepare a performance of "*Río, río.*" Have students
2a divide into two groups to sing the melody and harmony parts. Invite students to perform the metallophone and xylophone parts to accompany the song.

Observe students' ability to accurately sing the song harmony and perform an accompaniment on mallet instruments.

SKILLS REINFORCEMENT

▶ **Mallets** Students may be invited to perform the following ostinato on soprano xylophone to accompany "*Río, río.*"

Soprano Xylophone

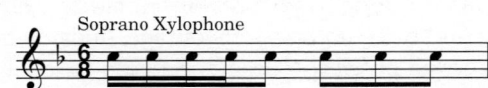

TECHNOLOGY/MEDIA LINK

Sequencing Software Have groups of four students record the two parts of "*Río, río*" on separate tracks of a digital recording program and then self-assess their tone and pitch accuracy.

Unit 10 *Keepers of the Earth* **371**

LESSON AT A GLANCE

Element Focus **RHYTHM** Syncopated and nonsyncopated rhythms

Skill Objective **PLAYING** Perform syncopated and non-syncopated rhythms

Connection Activity **SCIENCE** Compare a fantastic idea of life under the sea with the scientific reality

MATERIALS

- "Under the Sea"   **CD 17-12**
  Recording Routine: Intro (4 m.); vocal
- *Carnival of the Animals,* "Aquarium"   **CD 17-14**
- woodblocks, claves, cowbell, maracas
- selected melodic instruments

VOCABULARY

syncopation   ostinato

◆ ◆ ◆ ◆ National Standards ◆ ◆ ◆ ◆

1a Sing accurately with good breath control
1b Sing easy pieces with technical accuracy
2a Play instruments accurately alone and in small ensembles
3b Improvise rhythmic variations on given melodies
4a Compose short pieces, demonstrating unity and variety through music
5a Read eighth notes in alla breve time
5c Identify standard notation symbols for rhythm
6b Listen and analyze uses of rhythm, dynamics, and timbre in music from diverse genres
6c Listen and analyze uses of rhythm in music from diverse cultures
8b Identify ways music relates to science

MORE MUSIC CHOICES

For more practice with syncopation:
"Morning Comes Early," p. 13
"Day-O!" p. 18

Undersea Worlds

Scientists now know about animals and plants that live miles beneath the ocean. Some of them even thrive on volcanic heat. "Under the Sea" describes an imaginary world where the creatures yearn for a different home. **Listen** for calypso sounds and instruments as you **sing.**

CD 17-12

Under the Sea
(from Disney's *The Little Mermaid*)

Words by Howard Ashman

Music by Alan Menken

The sea - weed is al - ways green - er
Down here ___ all the fish is hap - py

in some-bod - y el - se's lake.   You dream _ a-bout
as off ___ through the waves they roll.   The fish _ on the

go - ing up there,   but that _ is a big mis - take.
land ain't hap - py,   they sad _ 'cause they in the bowl.

Just look _ at the world a - round you,   right here _ on the
But fish _ in the bowl is luck - y,   they in ___ for a

Footnotes

ACROSS THE CURRICULUM

8b ▶ **Science** Students will enjoy the following book regarding views of life under the sea.

3D Eyewitness: Ocean Life (no author) (Dorling Kindersley, 1999) is a collection of detailed underwater settings and scenes, which can be brought alive by placing a provided viewing mirror in the middle of each photographic display.

BUILDING SKILLS THROUGH MUSIC

▶ **Science** Ask the class to suggest names of plant and animal life that can be found under the sea and list them on the board or in their music journals. Then have students sing "Under the Sea" **CD 17-12** and identify which items from their list are mentioned in the song lyrics.

MEETING INDIVIDUAL NEEDS

▶ **Vocabulary Building** The song "Under the Sea" provides a great opportunity to build English vocabulary about sea life. You may want to bring in pictures of sea life and discuss them with students. Also, you may encourage students to draw what they understand about the ocean and then to label the living things that they draw.

Undersea Ostinatos

After you learn to sing "Under the Sea," choose percussion instruments and then **improvise** your own parts.

1 INTRODUCE

Invite a student to read aloud the text on p. 372. Ask students to give examples of when "the grass is always greener on the other side." (Possible answers may include examples such as: A little brother thinks that the ice cream cone his sister has is bigger and better than his, when in reality it isn't; a young child wants to play with a toy that a playmate has rather than his or her own, when in reality the wished for toy may not be suitable for the young child; and so on.)

2 DEVELOP

Listening

Tell students that they will listen to a song about life under the sea. Have students

- Listen to "Under the Sea" **CD 17-12.**
- Discuss how this song is an example of "the grass is always greener" idea.
- List the singer's reasons for staying at home under the sea.

8b Share with students information about the Great Barrier Reef. See Spotlight On, p. 375. Have interested students read the books recommended in Across the Curriculum, pp. 372 and 374, and Teacher to Teacher, p. 377, and give a presentation to the class. Then engage students in a discussion comparing the song's description of life under the sea with a scientific description.

Singing

1b Invite students to

- Sing "Under the Sea" with the recording **CD 17-12.**
- Tap the beat while they sing the first two measures of the song.

6c Help students discover that the rhythm is uneven in the first measure and even in the second measure.

continued on page 374

SPOTLIGHT ON

▶ **The Song-Writing Team** During their years of collaboration, Alan Menken and Howard Ashman won nearly every award presented by the film and theater communities. They first achieved fame for *Little Shop of Horrors* (1982), which became the most profitable off-Broadway musical ever. They then composed the film music for Disney's *The Little Mermaid* (1989). The musical score won two Academy Awards, two Golden Globe Awards, and two Grammy Awards. Two years later, Menken and Ashman wrote another film score for Disney's *Beauty and the Beast.* At the 1991 Academy Awards, three of the five nominees for the year's "Best Song" were from *Beauty and the Beast.* Menken and Ashman began work on the music for Disney's *Aladdin,* but sadly, Howard Ashman died in 1991.

CULTURAL CONNECTION

▶ **The Little Mermaid** *The Little Mermaid* was originally a fairy tale written by the Danish writer Hans Christian Andersen in 1836. It told the story of a young mermaid who chooses to become human to try to win an immortal soul. Andersen's little mermaid dies at the end of the story when she cannot convince her true love, the prince, to marry her. When Disney turned the story into an animated film, the moviemakers added several characters (including Sebastien, the singing crab) and a happy ending. The movie was released on November 14, 1989. It won Academy Awards for Best Song ("Under the Sea") and Best Score and became a popular franchise, inspiring several videos, books, and a sequel.

Lesson 3 Continued

Explain that the uneven rhythm is syncopated and the even rhythm is nonsyncopated.

5a **ASK Where else in the song can you find examples of syncopated and nonsyncopated measures alter-**
5c **nating?** (mm. 3–4; 5–6; 7–8, 9–10, 11–12; 13–14; 15–16)

Reading

Write the following rhythm pattern on the board:

5a Invite students to clap the rhythm.

ASK Is the rhythm syncopated or nonsyncopated? (nonsyncopated)

2a Encourage students to clap or play the rhythm pattern on a woodblock as an ostinato as they sing the first 16 measures of the song.

Help them discover that

- In the first part of the song syncopated rhythms alternate with nonsyncopated rhythms.
- The remainder of the song is mostly syncopated.

Out _ in the sun they slave _ a - way, ___ while _ we de -
Un - der the sea we off _ the hook. __ We _ got no

vo - tin' full _ time to float - in' un - der the sea.
trou-bles, life _ is the bub - bles un - der the

sea. Un - der the sea! Since _ life is

sweet here we _ got the beat here nat - u - ral - ly.

E - ven the stur-geon and _ the ray ___ they _ got the

urge 'n start _ to play. ___ We _ got the spir - it, you _ got to

(374)

Footnotes

ACROSS THE CURRICULUM

8b ▶ **Language Arts** Students will enjoy reading the following book containing interesting ocean/science activities.

The Down By the Sea Activity Book by Karen Aspinwall (The Cattail Company, 1993) includes countless science, ecology, and conservation activities about the ocean. Activities include games, crossword puzzles, math activities, poems, word puzzles, coloring pages, and more. Answers to the activity pages are included.

SPOTLIGHT ON

▶ **An Oceanographer** Jacques Cousteau (1910–1997), whose name became synonymous with undersea exploration, was born in Bordeaux, France. Cousteau and his colleagues began work on perfecting underwater breathing apparatus that would enable them to dive deeper and stay down longer. He fashioned a waterproof housing for a movie camera. Cousteau was the co-inventor of the Aqua-Lung, better known by the acronym "scuba" (self-contained underwater breathing appara-tus). Before this, only the diving bell and helmeted diving suits were available. The scuba gear set divers free to explore to depths of more than 100 feet. Cousteau was greatly interested in protecting the ocean environment and founded the Cousteau Society in 1974, which was dedicated to marine conservation.

Playing

Ask students to read the text on p. 373. Have students

 3b
- Improvise their own rhythm parts to accompany the song as the recording is played.

1a
- Sing "Under the Sea" **CD 17-12** with the improvised rhythmic accompaniment.

continued on page 376

▶ **The Great Barrier Reef** Found along the northeast Queensland coast of Australia, the Great Barrier Reef is the world's longest coral reef at 1,250 miles (2,000 km) in length. It is a complex ecosystem, unique in that it is the largest structure ever built by living non-human creatures. (An ecosystem is a balanced group of plants and animals in their environment that depend on each other for survival.) The reef is composed of limestone, the hard, rocklike material derived from water by the living coral polyps, plantlike sea animals that live in colonies on the reef. As the coral polyps die, their hard skeletons form the foundation of the reef. In 1979 the Great Barrier Reef was designated as a marine park.

Invite students to locate the Great Barrier Reef on a map or a globe.

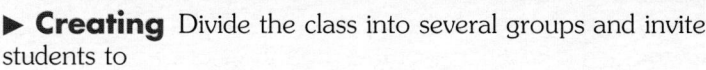

4a ▶ **Creating** Divide the class into several groups and invite students to

- Choose one or two melodic instruments and several percussion instruments to portray an underwater environment.
- Create a short composition describing life underwater. (There should be repetition of phrases and rhythms and contrasting material.)
- Prepare a score for their composition using notation or icons.
- Perform their compositions while the listeners decide the underwater habitat and explain their choice.

Listening

 6b Share with students that in *Carnival of the Animals,* composer Camille Saint-Saëns uses instrumental music to describe several different kinds of animals. *Aquarium* is a musical picture of life under the water.

Have students

- Listen to *Aquarium* **CD 17-14.**
- Identify the sounds that make them think of life under the sea.

Write the following terms on the board and invite students to decide which terms or phrases best describe *Aquarium* and which best describe "Under the Sea." (They may have to listen again to each selection.)

- Lively ("Under the Sea")
- Calm (*Aquarium*)
- Vocal ("Under the Sea")
- Orchestral (*Aquarium*)
- Syncopation ("Under the Sea")
- Even rhythm (*Aquarium*)
- Soft dynamics (*Aquarium*)
- Loud dynamics ("Under the Sea")
- String instruments (*Aquarium*)
- Brass instruments ("Under the Sea")
- Mallet instruments ("Under the Sea")
- Celesta and piano (*Aquarium*)

Creating

4a See Skills Reinforcement, p. 375, for a composing/performing activity based on the subject matter of "Under the Sea."

- fish she sings. The smelt __ and the sprat they know __

__ where it's at, an' oh, that blow-fish blow.

Un - der the sea. Un - der the sea.

When __ the sar - dine be - gin __ the be -

guine it's mu - sic to me. What __ do they

got, a lot __ of sand. We __ got a hot crus-ta - ce-an

Water Music

Listen to this musical description of aquatic life.

Compare the composer's use of rhythm with that of "Under the Sea."

CD 17–14
Aquarium

from Carnival of the Animals
by Camille Saint-Saëns

Other animals depicted in Saint-Saëns' [san(n)-sa(hn)] musical "carnival" include birds, elephants, lions, tortoises, kangaroos, and even practicing pianists.

376

Footnotes

ACROSS THE CURRICULUM

▶ **Language Arts** Jules Verne's novel *20,000 Leagues Under the Sea* (1870) is about the adventures of Captain Nemo and his crew aboard the submarine *Nautilus,* which Nemo built for revenge. The submarine is shaped like a fish with a large metal fin on top to ram and sink ships. One day, ships start sinking, particularly ones dealing with war. Nemo hated war and throughout the book he used his submarine to destroy all kinds of war-related ships. Woven into this story is Nemos' search for a man named Charles Denver. Nemo blames Denver for his daughter's death, has sought him for years, and has traveled over 20,000 leagues, or almost 60,000 miles, to find him.

Invite interested students to read the book and give oral book reports to the class.

SPOTLIGHT ON

▶ **The Author** Jules Gabriel Verne (1828–1905) was born in Nantes, France. His parents were of a seafaring tradition, a factor which influenced his writings. He ran off to be a cabin boy on a merchant ship, returned home and studied law. However, his passion was for the theater and writing, not law. His interest in geology, engineering, and astronomy is evident in his well-known novels *Five Weeks in a Balloon, Journey to the Center of the Earth, From Earth to the Moon,* and *20,000 Leagues Under the Sea.* He became a very rich man because of the popularity of these novels. His last novel was *The Invasion of the Sea.*

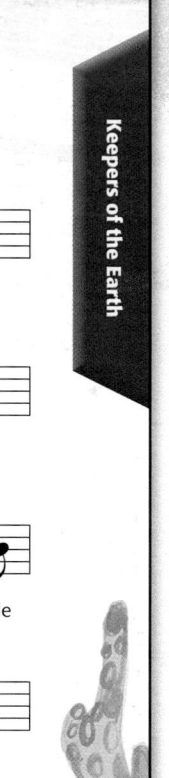

band. Each _ lit - tle clam here know _ how to jam here un - der the

sea. Each _ lit - tle slug here cut - tin' a

rug here un - der the sea. Each _ lit - tle

snail here know _ how to wail here that's _ why it's

hot - ter un - der the wa - ter. Ya _ we in

luck here down in the muck here un - der the sea. _____

"Under the Sea" won an Academy Award in 1989 for best song of the year. *The Little Mermaid* won a Golden Globe Award for best original score.

Unit 10 **377**

3 CLOSE

Element: RHYTHM | **ASSESSMENT**

2a
6c
Performance/Observation To provide an example for the assessment, instruct students to clap one measure of a steady $\frac{4}{4}$ beat pattern, followed by one measure of four beats rest. During the measure of rest, play four beats of syncopated rhythm on the woodblock. Practice the alternation between unison steady beat and solo syncopation several times.

4a Then have students take turns playing syncopated rhythm solos (on selected rhythm instruments) during the rests while the class claps the unison steady-beat measures.

Observe each student's ability to distinguish between steady beat and syncopation and to perform syncopation correctly.

TEACHER TO TEACHER

▶ **Science Activities** *Exploring the Oceans: Science Activities for Kids* by Anthony D. Fredericks *et al.* (Fulcrum, 1998) is a great source of activities, projects, and experiments to help students understand the importance of ocean ecosystems. Invite students to make a bulletin board of their completed experiments and activities. This is an excellent way to have students research and share their information.

SCHOOL TO HOME CONNECTION

▶ **A Family Trip** Students and their families may want to visit the nearest aquarium or natural history museum to gather information about ocean life. If such a trip is not feasible, parents and students may research ocean life at the local library or on the Internet.

TECHNOLOGY/MEDIA LINK

Web Site For more information on music for the movies, go to *www.sfsuccessnet.com.*

LESSON AT A GLANCE

Element Focus   **FORM** Verse/refrain

Skill Objective   **SINGING** Sing a song in verse/refrain form

Connection Activity   **RELATED ARTS** Compare the form and message of a poem and a song

MATERIALS

- "Turn, Turn, Turn"   **CD 17-15**

  Recording Routine: Intro (8 m.); vocal (four verses); coda
- *Interview with Pete Seeger*   **CD 17-17**
- "Children Learn What They Live" (poem)   **CD 17-18**

VOCABULARY

folk music   aural tradition   verse   refrain   *D. S. al Fine*

◆ ◆ ◆ ◆ National Standards ◆ ◆ ◆ ◆

1a   Sing accurately in small ensembles
6a   Listen and describe events in music using appropriate terms
6b   Listen and analyze uses of form in music
6c   Understand and use basic principles of chords and harmonic progressions in music analysis
8b   Identify ways music relates to language arts

MORE MUSIC CHOICES

For more practice with verse/refrain form:

"California," p. 52

"This Land Is Your Land," p. 118

"Loch Lomond," p. 140

SEASONS OF LIFE

Change is a part of life. Everyone at some point makes new friends, moves to a new school, or changes an address. "Turn, Turn, Turn" reminds us that every change has its purpose.

Look at any object around you. You'll see it has a shape, a form. A song has form, too. **Identify** the musical symbols that guide you through the song. Then follow the symbols as you **sing** "Turn, Turn, Turn."

CD 17-15

TURN, TURN, TURN
(To Everything There Is a Season)

Words Adapted from the Book of Ecclesiastes   *Adaptation and Music by Pete Seeger*

A REFRAIN *(tacet)*

To ev-'ry-thing _ (Turn, turn, turn) There is a sea-son (Turn, turn, turn) And a time for ev-'ry pur-pose un-der heav-en. _

B VERSE *(tacet)*

1. A time _ to be born, a time _ to die; A time to plant, _ a time _ to reap; A time to hurt, __ a time _ to heal; A time to laugh, a time to weep.

TRO–© Copyright 1962 (Renewed) MELODY TRAILS, INC., New York, NY Used by permission.

378

Footnotes

ACROSS THE CURRICULUM

8b ▶ **Art** Share with students *To Every Thing There Is a Season* by Leo and Diane Dillon (Scholastic, 1998). The verses from Ecclesiastes that comprise the lyrics to "Turn, Turn, Turn" are set within artwork from many cultures and historical periods, from Egyptian wall murals to aboriginal bark paintings. Invite students to create their own artwork. Then combine their artwork with the song's lyrics for display. (Note that the original wording of the phrase *A time to hurt* is *A time to kill*.)

BUILDING SKILLS THROUGH MUSIC

▶ **Language** After students discuss the lyrics of the song "Turn, Turn, Turn," have them select two of the least common phrases from the verses (for example, *a time to build-up; a time to break down; time to cast away stones*) and write the meaning of the phrases.

SKILLS REINFORCEMENT

▶ **Creating** The song "Turn Turn Turn" is deeply personal to all who know it. Try to inspire students to write additional verses based upon their views of what is most important in the world, using the general form of "opposites" to unify the phrases (for example, "a time to be born, a time to die"). Perform the song with the extra verses provided by students. Afterwards, ask them to critique the verses according to the "goodness of fit," and make sure to keep track of the criteria for making this judgment. These might include "thematic unity," or how well the new verses retain the spirit of the original verses, and "coordination," or how well the text rhythm conforms to the metric structure of the music.

1 INTRODUCE

Briefly review the lyrics of the first three songs of this unit. Help students discover that all three songs focus on the individual:

- "Somewhere Out There" (The speaker is lonely.)
- *"Don Alfonso"* (Someone is looking for his lost friend.)
- "Under the Sea" (One character tries to convince another to stay at home.)

Invite a student to read aloud the text on p. 378. Ask students to share their knowledge about rites of passage that occur to babies, children, teenagers, and adults. Encourage them to discuss rites of passage that are culture specific.

Choose a student to read aloud the first verse of "Turn, Turn, Turn."

ASK **What is this song about?** (the changes, at different times in life, that all people experience)

Who does this song talk about? (all people, humanity)

Help students discover that this song focuses on the human experience, not on one person's life. See Skills Reinforcement, p. 378, for a creating activity to enhance students' understanding.

2 DEVELOP

Reading

Ask students to look at the music to "Turn, Turn, Turn." Challenge them to locate the following musical symbols:

- *D.C.*
- *Fine*

continued on page 380

SPOTLIGHT ON

▶ **Careers in Music: Ethnomusicologist** Students might like to know that Pete Seeger has made a career of collecting folk songs from all over the world. People who collect and study traditional music and teach others about its history and performers are called ethnomusicologists. Ethnomusicologists also examine the role of music in a particular culture. They may travel to remote areas of the world in order to record people performing their traditional music. At times they transcribe, or write, this music on paper in some form.

MOVEMENT

▶ **Creative Dramatization** Students may enjoy using movement to interpret the lyrics of "Turn, Turn, Turn."

- Divide the class into four groups and assign each group one verse of the song.
- Encourage the groups to think of group movements for each key word set in their verse. For example, in verse 1 the key word sets are *born/die, plant/reap, hurt/heal, laugh/weep.*
- Have the entire class work together to create movements for the song's refrain.
- Allow each group to perform its verse as the rest of the class sings the song.
- Invite all students to sing and move to the refrain.

Lead students in explaining what each symbol means and how the symbols help guide singers through the song.

1a Singing

Invite the students to sing "Turn, Turn, Turn" **CD 17-15** with the recording.

6a ASK How many sections does the song have? (two—a verse and a refrain)

Which section does the song begin with? (the **6b** refrain)

How are the refrain and verse sections different from each other? (The words of the refrain are always repeated, but each verse has different words and a slightly different melody.)

Divide the class into two groups. Invite one group to sing the refrain and the other group to sing the verses with the recording.

Listening

Choose a student to read aloud the Music Makers feature on p. 380 about Pete Seeger.

ASK Who does Pete Seeger want to help with his music? (people who can't speak for themselves)

Invite students to listen to *Interview With Pete Seeger* **CD 17-17** and describe various music vocations.

MUSIC MAKERS
PETE SEEGER

Pete Seeger (born 1919) is one of the leaders of the folk-music revival in the 1940s and 1950s. He sang on college campuses, at folk concerts and festivals, radio, and television shows. Seeger is a folk musician who uses music to express his political views. His musical style and concern with ordinary working people, war, and social issues influenced many other folk singers. In 1948, he was one of the founders of the Weavers, a folk music group, and performed with them throughout the United States. Seeger loves and collects folk songs and performs many of them at concerts all over the world.

CD 17-17
Interview with Pete Seeger

Tune In

Pete Seeger helped create a group dedicated to cleaning up the Hudson River. The group's symbol is the *Clearwater*, a boat that monitors water quality on the Hudson.

380

Footnotes

CULTURAL CONNECTION

▶ **Folk Instruments** Pete Seeger and other folk singers often accompany themselves on the guitar or the banjo. These instruments are portable, lightweight, and easy to play. String instruments with frets date to ancient times, but the modern versions of guitars and banjos took shape a few hundred years ago. The modern acoustic guitar, with its six strings and metal tuning pegs, dates from the mid-1800s. An African prototype of the banjo was brought to the West by slaves, where it evolved into the banjo we know today. After the Civil War in the United States, the banjo became one of most popular instruments in America, and it became a staple of bluegrass, country, and folk music during the twentieth century.

SPOTLIGHT ON

▶ **The "Folk Process"** The version of "Turn, Turn, Turn" that appears in this lesson was prepared by Pete Seeger especially for classroom use. As part of this process, Mr. Seeger expressed the following thoughts:

"No two verses [of "Turn, Turn, Turn"] have the exact same melody. Many old folk songs have irregular rhythm and meter, and probably I was unconsciously carrying on an old tradition when I improvised this melody to some words originally put down about 2,256 years ago near Jerusalem, and translated about 400 years ago near London, England. This is my original tune; [but] Roger McGuinn, of the Byrds, sings it slightly differently. That's the 'folk process.'"

CHILDREN LEARN WHAT THEY LIVE

CD 17-18

by Dorothy Law Nolte

Keepers of the Earth

If children live with criticism, they learn to condemn.

If children live with hostility, they learn to fight.

If children live with fear, they learn to be apprehensive.

If children live with pity, they learn to feel sorry for themselves.

If children live with ridicule, they learn to feel shy.

If children live with jealousy, they learn to feel envy.

If children live with shame, they learn to feel guilty.

If children live with encouragement, they learn confidence.

If children live with tolerance, they learn patience.

If children live with praise, they learn appreciation.

If children live with acceptance, they learn to love.

If children live with approval, they learn to like themselves.

If children live with recognition, they learn it is good to have a goal.

If children live with sharing, they learn generosity.

If children live with honesty, they learn truthfulness.

If children live with fairness, they learn justice.

If children live with kindness and consideration, they learn respect.

If children live with security, they learn to have faith in themselves and in those about them.

If children live with friendliness, they learn the world is a nice place in which to live.

Unit 10 **381**

Analyzing

Choose several students to read aloud the poem "Children Learn What They Live" **CD 17-18** on p. 381.

Have students

8b
- Describe the form of the poem.
- Compare the use of repetition in the poem to that in "Turn, Turn, Turn."
- Describe how "Turn, Turn, Turn" uses the repeated text of its refrain to suggest that there is a purpose for the different things mentioned in the verses.
- Describe how the poem uses a parallel structure of the verses to convey the qualities that children learn from the input they receive.
- Discuss the message of the poem.

3 CLOSE

 **Element: FORM**   **ASSESSMENT**

1a
6b **Performance/Observation** Divide the class into small groups. Have each group find another song in their texts that uses verse/refrain form. (See More Music Choices in Lesson at a Glance, p. 378.)

Have each group

- Share its finding with the rest of the class.
- Perform its song for the class.
- Teach the song to the class using the aural teaching approach, and have the class sing the verse/refrain songs.

ACROSS THE CURRICULUM

▶ **Language Arts** The poem "Children Learn What They Live" describes the importance of the role models in a child's life. After listening to the poem, invite students to participate in this journal activity. Have students write

- The names of their role models, on the left side of the page.
- The traits that they have learned from each person, next to his or her name.
- Their name, at the bottom of the page.
- The traits that they want to teach others, next to their name.

TECHNOLOGY/MEDIA LINK

6c
CD-ROM Use the *Band-in-a-Box* software to help students understand style, harmony, and accompaniment.

- Prepare a *Band-in-a-Box* file containing the harmonic progression for "Turn, Turn, Turn."
- After students can sing the song, display the main screen of *Band-in-a-Box* and point out how the chords on the screen are in the same sequence as those in the student text.
- Choose a folk-rock accompaniment style in the program and then play it as the class sings.
- Display parts one at a time and help students discover that the notes shown are in the chords indicated in the music.

LESSON AT A GLANCE

Element Focus **TEXTURE/HARMONY** Chord progressions

Skill Objective **PLAYING** Play a three-chord song on keyboard, guitar, or resonator bells

Connection Activity **SOCIAL STUDIES** Discuss social themes in songs of the 1960s

MATERIALS

- "Blowin' in the Wind" **CD 17-19**
  Recording Routine: Intro (8 m.); vocal (three verses)
- *Blowin' in the Wind* **CD 17-21**
- *The Times They Are A-Changin'* **CD 17-22**
- *Both Sides Now* **CD 18-1**
- **Resource Book** p. H-26
- keyboards, guitars, resonator bells

VOCABULARY

harmony   chord progression

◆◆◆◆ National Standards ◆◆◆◆

1a Sing accurately in small ensembles
1d Sing music written in two parts
2a Play instruments accurately
6b Listen and analyze uses of harmony in music from diverse cultures
6c Understand and use basic principles of intervals and chords in music analysis
7a Students evaluate the music they perform
8b Identify ways music relates to language arts
9a Describe characteristics of music genres from a variety of cultures

MORE MUSIC CHOICES

For more practice using I, IV, V₇ chords:
"Yakety Yak," p. 205
"Linstead Market," p. 241

A BETTER WORLD

Some songs make us aware of the needs of others. The music of the 1960s reflects the people's yearning for social progress and world harmony.

"Blowin' in the Wind" asks many questions. Does the refrain have the answers? As you **sing** the song, focus on the meaning of the words.

Arts Connection

Friends by Diana Ong, 1940 ▶

CD 17-19

Blowin' in the Wind

t (d) r f s l

Words and Music by Bob Dylan

VERSE

1. How man-y roads must a man walk __ down be - fore they call him a man? ____ How man-y seas must a white dove __ sail be-
2. How man-y years must a moun-tain ex - ist be - fore it is washed to the sea? _____ How man-y years can some peo-ple ex - ist be-
3. How man-y times must a man look __ up be - fore he can see the __ sky? _____ How man-y ears must __ one man __ have be-

382

Footnotes

ACROSS THE CURRICULUM

8b ▶ **Language Arts** Bob Dylan's songs were often about things in the world that he questioned. Invite students to share the things in society that cause them concern. (Responses may include hunger, homelessness, disease, prejudice, treatment of the elderly, drugs, and violence.) Make a list of students' responses. From the list, have students create questions to be read aloud as a prelude to singing "Blowin' in the Wind."

BUILDING SKILLS THROUGH MUSIC

▶ **Social Studies** Have students review information about Woody Guthrie on p. 283. Discuss how a musician could influence someone in a later generation. Have students read about Bob Dylan on p. 384. Ask them to describe characteristics of his music that show the influence of Woody Guthrie. Invite students to listen to *Goin' Down the Road Feelin' Bad* **CD 13-10** and *Blowin' in the Wind* **CD 17-21** and identify similarities and differences in performance styles.

SKILLS REINFORCEMENT

1d ▶ **Singing** Students can sing the refrain to "Blowin' in the Wind" in two parts. The harmony is sung a third higher than the melody. To help students learn the harmony part, write the two parts on large staff paper or on the board. Then have students

- Sing the refrain melody alone and then again as you sing the harmony part.
- Echo-sing the refrain harmony as you model it.
- Sing the last phrase of verse 1 and continue singing the harmony as you sing the melody.

Divide the class into two groups and have one group sing melody while the other sings the harmony. Listen for the appropriate balance, making sure that the melody has aural prominence.

fore she sleeps in the sand? _____ How man-y times must the
fore they're al-lowed to be free? _____ How man-y times can a
fore he can hear peo-ple cry? _____ How man-y deaths will it

can-non balls fly be-fore they're for-ev-er _____ banned? __
man turn his head and pre-tend that he just does-n't see? _____
take till he knows that too man-y peo-ple have died? _____

REFRAIN

The an-swer, my friend, is blow-in' in the wind, The an-swer is blow-in' in the

1.,2. 3.

wind. _____ wind. _____ The an-swer is blow-in' _____ in the wind. _____

How Many Chords?

You can **play** these chords to add harmony to "Blowin' in the Wind."

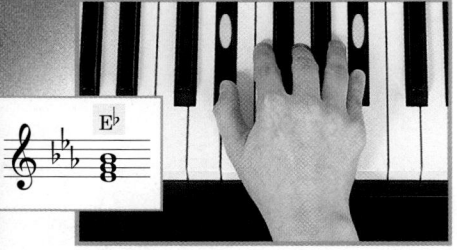

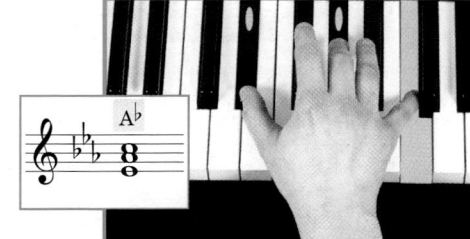

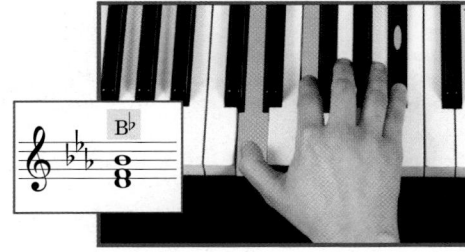

Unit 10 **383**

1 INTRODUCE

Invite students to describe their ideas of an ideal world. Explain that many of the songs written in the 1960s either protested the social conditions that the United States was facing or described the way life could be if the conditions were improved. Discuss with students what they may already know about the 1960s and then share the information in Spotlight On below.

2 DEVELOP

Singing

Invite students to

* Listen to the recording of "Blowin' in the Wind" **CD 17-19.**
* Identify the song's refrain.
* Listen to the song again, and join in singing the refrain.

SAY There are four phrases in the song. Three phrases make up the verse and the fourth phrase is the refrain.

ASK **In each verse, which two phrases are melodically the same?** (Phrases 1 and 3 are the same.)

How are the lyrics of the first three phrases similar? (The lyrics ask questions.)

What is the purpose of the fourth phrase? (It responds to the questions although there really is no answer.)

Divide the class into four groups. Ask each group to sing one phrase of "Blowin' in the Wind" with the recording.

ASK **What is the song about?** (the suffering caused by war and the need to stop all fighting)

continued on page 384

 ## SKILLS REINFORCEMENT

▶ **Keyboard** See Resource Book p. H-26 for a "strumming" accompaniment to perform with "Blowin' in the Wind."

 ## SPOTLIGHT ON

▶ **The Sixties** The 1960s were turbulent years in U.S. history. The Civil Rights movement stormed through the South, and racist traditions such as Jim Crow laws and segregation were questioned. As the Vietnam War escalated, young people organized peaceful demonstrations and sit-ins. The assassinations of John F. Kennedy, Martin Luther King, Jr., Malcolm X, and Robert Kennedy shocked the nation. Americans of all ages realized that the idyllic post World War II years were over. Many folk musicians of the 1960s were spokespeople for social reform. They wrote original folk songs and re-introduced traditional songs. Easy and pleasurable to sing, these songs could be performed anywhere by anyone. Singing folk songs reminded people of less tumultuous times, while expressing the hope for peace and equality.

Unit 10 *Keepers of the Earth* **383**

Lesson 5 Continued

Analyzing

6b Direct the students to find the chord symbols printed on top of the staves for the music to "Blowin' in the Wind" on pp. 382–383.

6c Distribute copies of the chord chart on Resource Book p. H-26 and help students follow the chord progression of "Blowin' in the Wind" **CD 17-19** as they listen to the recording. Have student volunteers write the chord symbols on the board in the order they are played.

ASK Which phrases have similar accompaniment chords? (phrases 1, 2, and 3)

Which phrase is different from the others? (phrase 4)

What do all phrases share? (They all use the same three chords.)

Playing

Organize the class into groups of three or more. Invite students to choose one of the following for each group: a keyboard, a guitar, a set of resonator bells. (Each bell set should include the appropriate bells for an E♭, A♭, and B♭₇ chord. See Teacher to Teacher, p. 385.) Then have the groups

- Practice playing the E♭, A♭, and B♭₇ chords on their instruments. (Refer keyboard players to the chord positions shown on p. 383.)

1a
- Sing "Blowin' in the Wind" and play the chords as accompaniment.

Listening

Choose a student to read aloud the Music Makers feature on p. 384 about Bob Dylan.

Then have students

- Listen to *Blowin' in the Wind* **CD 17-21** as performed by Bob Dylan.

9a
- Discuss the influences of folk music they hear in the song.

MUSIC MAKERS
Bob Dylan

Bob Dylan [DIH-lan] (born 1941) is a popular song writer and recording artist. He learned to play the guitar and harmonica when he was six years old and started his first band when he was in high school. Dylan started writing songs to protest governmental policies and social problems. His music is influenced by his love of country-western music, folk music, and the blues.

How Many Roads?

Listen to *Blowin' in the Wind* as performed by the original artist, Bob Dylan. How does Dylan convey his message?

CD 17–21
Blowin' in the Wind

written and performed by Bob Dylan
Blowin' in the Wind expresses the hopes and strong emotions of the 1960s generation. It also became an anthem of the Civil Rights movement.

Listen to *The Times They Are A-Changin'* by Bob Dylan. What is the message?

CD 17–22
The Times They Are A-Changin'

written and performed by Bob Dylan
Dylan wrote this song in 1963, the same year President John F. Kennedy was assassinated.

(384)

Footnotes

SKILLS REINFORCEMENT

2a

▶ **Guitar** "Blowin' in the Wind" is to many people the most significant folk rock song of its time. It is also in the basic repertoire of the folk guitarist. Students should find the I, IV, and V₇ chords relatively easy to play in D major, capo at first fret, because all three are in first position. The chords are:

D	G	D	D	D	G	D	A₇
D	G	D	D	D	G	A₇	A₇
D	G	D	D	D	G	D	D
G	A₇	D	D	G	A₇	D	D

After they have mastered the chord changes, encourage students to fingerpick the chords, the most commonly used technique for accompanying the song.

ACROSS THE CURRICULUM

▶ **Language Arts** Folk singers and songwriters of the 1950s and 1960s encouraged other musicians to perform their compositions. Bob Dylan's "Blowin' in the Wind," for example, was a hit for the group Peter, Paul, and Mary. Students might enjoy researching other folk musicians of this era. Invite students to use Web sites, books, and album covers to create a "Who's Who" file. Offer students the following list as a research starting point: Pete Seeger; Lester Flatt and Earl Scruggs; Bob Dylan; New Lost City Ramblers; Joni Mitchell; Chad Mitchell Trio; Leadbelly; Judy Collins; the Kingston Trio; Joan Baez; the Weavers; Arlo Guthrie; Crosby, Stills, Nash, and Young; and Peter, Paul, and Mary. Encourage students to share the research with the class.

M·U·S·I·C M·A·K·E·R·S

Joni Mitchell

Joni Mitchell (born 1943) is a visual artist turned folk singer. She is considered one of rock music's best songwriters. Mitchell's music career spans over three decades. Her work includes folk, pop, and jazz. Her music has both emotional and intellectual appeal.

Listen to *Both Sides Now.* How would you **describe** Joni Mitchell's music?

CD 18–1
Both Sides Now

by Joni Mitchell
as performed by Judy Collins

Many famous singers, such as Judy Collins, Willie Nelson, and Pete Seeger, have performed Mitchell's songs.

Unit 10 **385**

- Listen to *The Times They Are A-Changin'* **CD 17-22**.
- Discuss the message Dylan is sending his listeners.

6b
- Identify the instruments Dylan uses to harmonize the song.

Have students read the Music Makers feature on p. 385 about Joni Mitchell. Then invite them to

- Listen to *Both Sides Now* **CD 18-1**.

6b
- Identify the song's form (verse/refrain) and the instruments used.

- Say the words of the song's refrain.

ASK What three things does the singer look at "both sides" of? (clouds, love, life)

What message is Joni Mitchell telling her listeners? (Life and love, just like clouds, are difficult to understand.)

Invite students to describe Joni Mitchell's music and to compare it to the music of Bob Dylan.

3 CLOSE

Element: TEXTURE/HARMONY > **ASSESSMENT**

Performance/Peer Critique Organize the class into small groups. Guide the groups in finding folk songs in their books that include chord symbols. If you prefer, assign "Blowin' in the Wind" or "Turn, Turn, Turn," p. 378, to the groups. Have each group

2a
- Select instruments (keyboard, guitar) to accompany the song.

- Practice singing and accompanying the song.

1a
- Perform the song for the class.

7a
After each performance, have the class discuss how successfully the group provided harmony for the song.

TEACHER TO TEACHER

2a ▶ **Resonator Bell List** To assist students in playing a hand chime or resonator bell accompaniment to "Blowin' in the Wind," use the following list of bells needed to play each chord.

	I	IV	V₇
Top:	B♭	C	B♭
Middle:	G	A♭	A♭
Bottom:	E♭	E♭	D
Chord:	E♭	A♭	B♭₇

TECHNOLOGY/MEDIA LINK

CD-ROM As students learn to play chordal accompaniments to "Blowin' in the Wind," have them use the *Band-in-a-Box* software to help them gain a better understanding of style, harmony, and accompaniment.

- Prepare a *Band-in-a-Box* file containing the harmonic progression of "Blowin' in the Wind."

- When students are comfortable singing the song, display the main screen of *Band-in-a-Box* and demonstrate that the chords on the screen shown are in the same sequence as the chords in the student text.

- Choose a folk-rock accompaniment style for the program, and play it as the class sings the song.

LESSON AT A GLANCE

Element Focus **RHYTHM** Syncopated and nonsyncopated rhythms

Skill Objective **SINGING** Sing a song using syncopated and nonsyncopated rhythms

Connection Activity **LANGUAGE ARTS** Experience a poem that celebrates people's differences and similarities

MATERIALS

- "A World of Difference"   **CD 18-2**
  Recording Routine: Intro (4 m.); v. 1; refrain; v. 2; refrain; coda
- "You and I" (poem)
- *Everyday People*   **CD 18-4**

VOCABULARY

syncopation

◆ ◆ ◆ ◆ National Standards ◆ ◆ ◆ ◆

1a Sing accurately with good breath control
3a Improvise simple harmonic accompaniments
5a Read syncopated rhythms in duple meter
6b Listen and analyze use of rhythm in music from diverse genres
6c Understand and use basic principles of rhythm in music analysis
7a Students evaluate the music they perform
8a Show how different arts portray the same idea in unique ways
8b Identify ways music relates to social studies

MORE MUSIC CHOICES

For more practice with syncopation:
"Morning Comes Early," p. 13
"Funwa alafia" ("Welcome, My Friends"), p. 32

Same but Different

Every person has unique gifts, but we all share things that are the same. Our differences, though, are what often make us interesting.

Read the lyrics of "A World of Difference." What gifts do you have to offer?

CD 18–2

d r m f s l t d' r'

A World of Difference

Words by Joseph and Pamela Martin   *Music by Joseph M. Martin*

1. It takes the sun-shine and the rain _ to help a gar-den grow. _
2. Moun-tains need the val - leys, _____ the wa-ter needs the sand, _

The sun and moon _ to-geth-er work _ to make the o-cean flow. _
And we all need each oth - er _____ to lend a help-ing hand. _

Our strength is in our dif-'ren-ces, _ the gifts we have to share, _
So we must work to-geth - er; __ we can't do it a - lone. _

And to-geth-er we can build a bet-ter world _ for peo-ple ev - 'ry-where. _
Yes, __ we _ all __ need each oth - er __ to make this house a home. _

386

Footnotes

ACROSS THE CURRICULUM

8b ▶ **Social Studies** Ask students to think of ten things the class could do to make a positive difference in their school or community. (cleaning up a park or school playground, planting trees, visiting the elderly, or adopting a senior citizen pen pal) If time permits, arrange for the class to carry out one or more of the ideas.

BUILDING SKILLS THROUGH MUSIC

▶ **Social Studies** Distribute a chart entitled "Popular Music Genres" with columns labeled Soul, Rock, and Rhythm and Blues. Select students to suggest ways to distinguish each category. Have students listen to *Everyday People* **CD 18-4** and identify characteristics that match their list. Ask students to describe how the performers combined or blended the styles into one.

SKILLS REINFORCEMENT

1a ▶ **Vocal Development** "A World of Difference" is a good song to include in a class or chorus performance. It also provides opportunities for students to practice vocal techniques. While students are learning the song, help them to

- Avoid singing flat by having them lift one of their hands as they sing the ascending note patterns. (The upward physical motion reminds them to return to the "high side" of the opening pitch.)
- Determine where to breathe by using rests and punctuation marks as clues.
- Hold out the ends of phrases by "filling up the notes" with supported breath.
- Pronounce final consonants on words together.

REFRAIN

We're the col-ors of the rain - bow; we're the stars up in the sky.

No two of us are quite the same and here's the rea-son why:

We all have a pur-pose and a spe-cial place to serve,

For it takes a world of dif-f'ren-ces to make a dif-f'rence in our world.

It Takes Syncopation

The syncopated rhythm of "A World of Difference" adds interest to the song. **Perform** the first phrase without syncopation.

1.
It takes the sun-shine and the rain to help a gar-den grow.

Now **perform** the same phrase as written. **Describe** the difference.

2.
It takes the sun-shine and the rain to help a gar-den grow.

As you **sing** the entire song, notice how syncopation is used in other phrases.

1 INTRODUCE

Ask students to organize themselves into groups according to a color they are wearing. When the groups are established, have the group members make a list of the differences that exist within the group even though they share a common color. Some of the differences may include

- Shoe styles.
- Hair color and styles.
- Accessories.

Have the groups discuss their lists with the class. Then choose students to read aloud the text at the top of p. 386 and the lyrics to "A World of Difference." Engage students in a short discussion of the unique gifts each has to offer.

2 DEVELOP

Singing

Invite students to

- Listen to the recording of "A World of Difference" **CD 18-2** while patting the steady beat.
- Sing the song with the recording.
- Pat the steady beat while singing the first phrase.

Analyzing

Direct students' attention to the musical phrase at the bottom of p. 387. Have them

- Clap the rhythm of this phrase.
- Clap the rhythm of the first phrase of "A World of Difference" on p. 386.

ASK How is the phrase on p. 387 like the first phrase of the song? (It has the same pitches and words.)

How is it different? (Unlike the song's first phrase, the rhythm of the phrase on p. 387 is not syncopated.)

continued on page 388

TEACHER TO TEACHER

▶ **Idioms** To help students understand the lyrics of "A World of Difference," ask the class to illustrate the meaning of the song. Students may need some prompting in explanations in order to understand idioms such as "we're the color of the rainbows." Use the time in which students are illustrating to discuss the meanings of some of the song's idiomatic expressions.

CHARACTER EDUCATION

▶ **Respect** To help encourage students' awareness of and respect for people's differences, have them list the ways people in their school are similar to and different from each other. For example, physical or job-related (students, staff, teachers) differences might be noted. Similarities might include needs (love, acceptance) and goals (learning, personal development). Discuss the important role each individual plays in giving the school its identity and making it a successful, positive place to learn. Invite students to create a poster or banner encouraging awareness of and respect for diversity within the school.

Lesson 6 Continued

Have students

- Sing the phrase as it is written at the bottom of p. 387.
- Sing the first phrase of "A World of Difference" as it appears on p. 386.

6c **ASK** How does syncopation change the melody? (Syncopation adds a "punch" and energy to the rhythm.)

Comparing

5a Invite students to find rhythms in the song that are syncopated and rhythms that are not syncopated. Then encourage students to

- Sing "A World of Difference" without syncopation while listening to the Stereo Performance Track **CD 18-3.**
- Sing the song as written with the Stereo Performance Track.

Help students recognize that syncopation adds excitement, interest, and "bounce" to the song. It also helps to emphasize certain words and ideas that the songwriters want the listeners to remember.

Choose students to read aloud the poem "You and I" on p. 388.

8a **ASK** What message is the poem's author conveying? (Everything starts with one's self.)

SAY The lyrics of songs are often poems that are set to music.

Invite students to discuss the similarities between the poem "You and I" and the song "A World of Difference." Then encourage students to examine the photos on p. 388 and help them explain

- What the people are doing.
- How the people are alike and how they are different.

People in Harmony

In many ways, people are the same all over the world. There are some differences in culture, music, art, and language, but basically people have the same needs, hopes, and dreams. They are the keepers of the earth, and of themselves. Where does this all start? Read the poem and find out.

You and I

by Mary Ann Hoberman

Only one I in the whole wide world
And millions and millions of you,
But every you is an I to myself
And I am a you to you, too!

But if I am a you and you are an I
And the opposite also is true,
It makes us both the same somehow
Yet splits us each in two.

It's more and more mysterious,
The more I think it through:
Every you everywhere in the world is an I;
Every I in the world is a you!

388

Footnotes

ACROSS THE CURRICULUM

▶ **Language Arts** Encourage students to read *Kids with Courage: True Stories About Young People Making a Difference* by Barbara Lewis (Free Spirit Publications, 1992), a collection of stories about 18 kids and their brave, helpful, and kind contributions to the world.

You may want to introduce students to *52 Ways to Make a Difference* by Lynn Gordon (Chronicle, 1996). This is a collection of 52 colorful cards with ideas for actions that can improve the world.

MEETING INDIVIDUAL NEEDS

▶ **Including Everyone** Physical appearance is often the focus of students' attention when they think about how people are the same and different. Direct their attention to actions and the many ways people can participate in the same kinds of activities in school and life. Give concrete examples from classroom routines (for example, distributing books, instruments), daily life (brushing teeth; traveling to school), and making music (moving, playing instruments). With each example, ask how the same task can be accomplished in a different way. Use more complex examples and ask students to solve problems as to how the final task can be completed in a different way, either independently or with others.

What's the Difference?

Listen to and compare *Everyday People* and "A World of Difference."

CD 18–4
Everyday People

by Sylvester Stewart
as performed by Sly and the Family Stone
With its message promoting the brotherhood of all people, *Everyday People* became a number one hit in 1969.

Sly and the Family Stone

Sly and the Family Stone was a popular music group in the late 1960s and early 1970s. Sly Stone (Sylvester Stewart, born 1943) started the group. The band was one of the first to be made up of men and women of both African and European Americans, which was not common at that time. Their music is a fusion of soul, rock, rhythm and blues, and funk. In 1993, Stone was inducted into the Rock and Roll Hall of Fame.

Keepers of the Earth

Unit 10 **389**

8a Ask students to look at the photos again and

- Describe it in detail by picking out each color.
- Try to take in every image at one time.
- Discuss how the overall effect changes when they look at it through "different eyes."

Listening

Choose a student to read aloud the Music Makers feature on p. 389 about Sly and the Family Stone. Then have students

- Listen to *Everyday People* **CD 18-4.**
- Discuss the ideas expressed in the song.
- **6b** • Identify and pat examples of syncopated rhythm in the melody.

3 CLOSE

Creating

Organize the class into small groups. Have each group

- Make a list of the ideas expressed in *Everyday People,* "A World of Difference," and the poem "You and I."
- Identify the similarities and differences among the ideas expressed in the songs and poem.
- Create a poem, song, or picture that expresses the group's ideas about the similarities and differences among people.

Element: RHYTHM — **ASSESSMENT**

1a **Performance/Self-Assessment** Divide the class into two groups and have one group sing "A World of Difference" while the other group pats a steady beat.
7a Then allow groups to switch. For each performance, have students evaluate the accuracy of the syncopated rhythms.

CULTURAL CONNECTION

▶ **Everyday People** Students may not be aware of the fascinating, different people they meet every day. Help them celebrate their world by creating a bulletin board labeled "Everyday People Who Enrich Our World." Invite them to write about the "Everyday People" in their lives, including those seen at school, at club meetings, and at home. Then ask students to write descriptions of these "Everyday People." Have them bring pictures of family and friends and display them with pictures from music class.

You may want to host a party for parents, friends, and other classmates where your students can unveil the bulletin board and perform "A World of Difference," selected poetry, and other songs.

SCHOOL TO HOME CONNECTION

▶ **Everyday Heroes** Invite students to ask people of varying ages to share a story about a person (famous or not) whom they feel has made a difference in the world. Have students share the stories they collect with the class.

TECHNOLOGY/MEDIA LINK

Electronic Keyboard Have students play the chord roots for "A World of Difference" using a bass voice.

Students may improvise their own rhythm patterns to play the roots.

Invite advanced student pianists to play the song's melody.

LESSON AT A GLANCE

Element Focus   **RHYTHM** Backbeat

Skill Objective   **READING** Sing a song from notation that is based on two rhythmic motives

Connection Activity   **SOCIAL STUDIES** Discover the connection between African American spirituals and the plight of enslaved people

MATERIALS

• "Come and Go with Me to That Land"   **CD 18-5**

   Recording Routine: Intro (4 m.); v. 1; v. 2; v. 3; coda

• **Resource Book** p. I-27

• recorders

• selected rhythm instruments

VOCABULARY

backbeat   timbre   rhythmic motive

> ◆ ◆ ◆ **National Standards** ◆ ◆ ◆ ◆
>
> **1c** Sing music from diverse genres
> **2a** Play instruments accurately alone and in small ensembles
> **5a** Read quarter, eighth, and dotted notes in duple meter
> **6c** Understand and use basic principles of rhythm in music analysis
> **7b** Students use specific criteria for evaluating their own performances
> **8b** Identify ways music relates to social studies

MORE MUSIC CHOICES

For more practice with backbeat:
"Dancin' in the Street," p. 361

1 INTRODUCE

8b Tell students that African Americans who were enslaved often expressed their desire for freedom in songs called spirituals. See Across the Curriculum, p. 391, for a related activity.

A Song of Hope

People who are free choose the way they live, work, and play. When people experience discrimination, they lose some of their freedom.

African American spirituals often provided hope when freedom seemed only a dream. "Come and Go with Me to That Land" is a song of hope for freedom and the promise of a new land. **Listen** to the recording and **identify** the rhythm patterns in the color boxes each time they occur.

Sing this spiritual and respond to its energy by clapping and swaying to the music.

▲ Dr. Martin Luther King Jr. leading a civil rights march on Washington, D.C., 1963

CD 18–5 MIDI 24

Come and Go with Me to That Land

s, l, d r m s l

African American Spiritual

1. Come and go with me to that land, ____
2. There's ____ no suf - f'ring in that land, ____
3. Peace ____ and free - dom in that land, ____

Come and go with me to that land, ____
There's ____ no suf - f'ring in that land, ____
Peace ____ and free - dom in that land, ____

Come and go with me to that land ____ where I'm bound. ____
There's ____ no suf - f'ring in that land ____ where I'm bound. ____
Peace ____ and free - dom in that land ____ where I'm bound. ____

Footnotes

TEACHER TO TEACHER

▶ **Inspiring Spontaneity** African American spirituals and other folk idioms invite spontaneity in vocal and physical expression. Involving students in spontaneous clapping and swaying may be daunting, but it is also rewarding. As a teacher, you provide many behavioral cues that show students what you expect from them. Chances are that your students will mirror your reaction to music. They will more likely move spontaneously after they have seen you model the behavior in a variety of settings.

BUILDING SKILLS THROUGH MUSIC

▶ **Language** Have students sing "Come and Go with Me to That Land" and discuss how changes in dynamics or tempo could emphasize different ideas from the lyrics. Divide the class into two groups to plan a performance showing either changes in dynamics or tempo. Ask students to locate phrases that would be effective and describe changes that would make the performance expressive.

SKILLS REINFORCEMENT

5a ▶ **Reading** "Come and Go with Me to That Land" has two important rhythmic motives as shown in the color boxes above.

Help students recognize that the second pattern is syncopated. Divide the class into two groups. Invite students in group 1 to clap or play the first pattern on an instrument each time they sing it. Invite students in group 2 to clap or play the second pattern on a contrasting instrument each time they sing it. Encourage students to find other syncopated rhythms in the song, especially ♪ ♩.

▶ **Recorder** A countermelody for "Come and Go with Me to That Land" can be found on Resource Book p. I-27.

2a

Come and go with me to that land, ___
There's ___ no suf-f'ring in that land, ___
Peace ___ and free-dom in that land, ___

Come and go with me to that land, ___
There's ___ no suf-f'ring in that land, ___
Peace ___ and free-dom in that land, ___

Come and go with me to that land ___ where I'm bound. ___
There's ___ no suf-f'ring in that land ___ where I'm bound. ___
Peace ___ and free-dom in that land ___ where I'm bound. ___

Recorder Countermelody

Play this recorder part to accompany "Come and Go with Me to That Land."

Unit 10 **391**

2 DEVELOP

Listening

Play the recording of "Come and Go with Me to That Land" **CD 18-5** and have students tap the rhythm patterns in the color boxes as they occur in the music.

SAY In many African American spirituals, the second and fourth beats in each measure are stronger beats. They are called backbeats.

6c Have students listen to the song again and note which instruments play the backbeats. (drums, tambourine)

Singing

1c Invite students to

- Sing the first verse of "Come and Go with Me to That Land" with the recording.

- Clap the backbeats while singing the last two verses.

Playing

2a Introduce or review the recorder fingering for A, C, and D. Have students learn the part on p. 391 to accompany "Come and Go with Me to That Land."

3 CLOSE

Skill: READING   **ASSESSMENT**

1c
2a
7b **Performance/Peer Critique** Divide the class into two groups. Have one group sing "Come and Go with Me to That Land" while the other group plays a steady backbeat rhythm on available rhythm instruments. Allow groups to switch and evaluate each performance, using the following questions:

- Did the singers perform the rhythmic motives accurately?

- Did the players keep a steady beat and play only on beats 2 and 4?

ACROSS THE CURRICULUM

8b ▶ **Social Studies/Language Arts** Make three blank columns on the board or a large sheet of paper. Ask the class to think about what it would be like to be unjustly imprisoned or enslaved. Encourage students to suggest words to describe the feelings. (Answers may include *hopelessness, suffering, pain, anger, shame,* or *desperation.*) Write the answers in one of the columns. In the second column, list students' words or phrases to describe the dreams and hopes an enslaved person might have. (Answers may include *having a warm bed, living with family members, having enough food, being free to wander through the outdoors.*) In the third column, have students list the hopes and dreams expressed in "Come and Go with Me to That Land."

TECHNOLOGY/MEDIA LINK

MIDI/Sequencing Software Using the MIDI song file for "Come and Go with Me to That Land," have students solo, mute, and unmute various tracks to emphasize the different parts as the file plays.

LESSON AT A GLANCE

Element Focus **TIMBRE** Vocal timbre

Skill Objective **LISTENING** Listen to and describe the vocal timbre of a folk singer

Connection Activity **RELATED ARTS** Explore the use of textiles as an art form and means of expression

MATERIALS

- "Oh, Freedom" **CD 18-7**

  Recording Routine: Intro (4 m.); vocal (four verses); coda

- *Oh, Freedom* and *Come and Go with Me* **CD 18-9**
- **Resource Book** p. C-8
- keyboards, guitars

VOCABULARY

timbre modulate bridge alto range

◆ ◆ ◆ ◆ **National Standards** ◆ ◆ ◆ ◆

1c Sing music from diverse cultures

2a Play instruments accurately alone and in small ensembles

4b Arrange pieces for voices and instruments

6b Listen and analyze uses of harmony and timbre in music from diverse cultures

6c Understand and use basic principles of rhythm, tonality, and intervals in music analysis

8a Show how different arts portray the same idea in unique ways

8b Identify ways music relates to social studies

9a Identify characteristics of music genres from a variety of cultures

MORE MUSIC CHOICES

For more practice with vocal timbre:

"Oklahoma," p. 36

"Stand By Me," p. 46

Shenandoah, p. 265

SING OF FREEDOM

African Americans who were freed from enslavement frequently used spirituals to express the importance of freedom. As you **sing** "Oh, Freedom," notice the timbre of the singers who perform the vocal accompaniment.

CD 18–7

OH, FREEDOM

African American Spiritual

1., 4. Oh, _____ free-dom! Oh, _____ free-dom!
2. No more cry - in', No more cry - in',
3. There'll be sing - in', There'll be sing - in',

Oh, _____ free - dom o - ver me. _____
No more cry - in' o - ver me! _____
There'll be sing - in' o - ver me! _____

And be - fore I'd be a slave, I'll be bur-ied in my grave,

And go home to my Lord and be free. _____

392

Footnotes

CULTURAL CONNECTION

8b ▶ **The Song** Spirituals like "Oh, Freedom" express the desire for freedom from the bondage of slavery. This sentiment was strong. The quote by African American writer Ralph Ellison states, "For the art—the blues, the spiritual, the jazz, the dance—was what we had in place of freedom."

9a Musically, "Oh, Freedom" uses syncopation, repeated changing verses, repeated refrains, and I-IV-V$_7$ harmonic accompaniment.

BUILDING SKILLS THROUGH MUSIC

▶ **Language** Have students sing "Oh, Freedom" **CD 18-7**. Ask them to write a brief paragraph about freedom and the rights that we have as a "free" person.

MEETING INDIVIDUAL NEEDS

8a ▶ **Encouraging Participation** Use the following suggestions to help all students perform movements with "Oh, Freedom."

Reinforcement Some students may not be comfortable creating movements. Ask these students to move to the steady beat of the song.

On Target Students who are comfortable performing movement may be asked to create gestures that represent freedom using whole-body movements.

Challenge Encourage interested students to create a movement routine for "Oh, Freedom."

Keyboards Add Timbre

Add a new timbre by playing these three chords to accompany "Oh, Freedom."

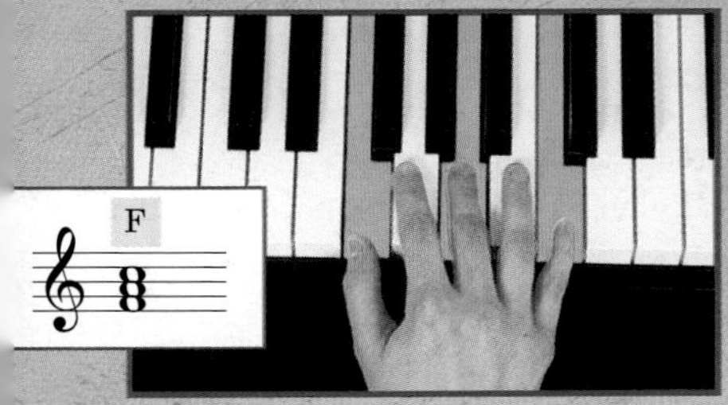

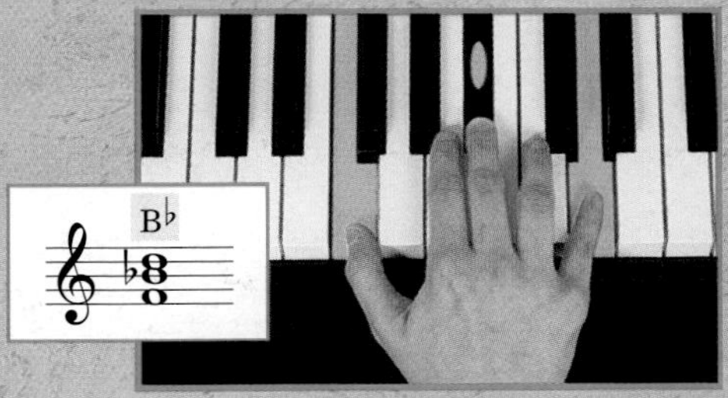

Unit 10 **393**

continued on page 394

1 INTRODUCE

Write the following on the board: "Spaghetti grows on trees." Ask students to close their eyes. Select three individuals and two small groups of students to read the sentence aloud. (Since students' eyes will be closed during the selection process, walk among them, tapping the shoulders of the readers.) After the readings, have the rest of the class identify the readers and the order in which they read the sentence. Explain that students were able to identify the readers because they recognized the sound, or timbre, of the voices.

2 DEVELOP

Listening

6b Have students listen to the recording of "Oh, Freedom" **CD 18-7,** paying attention to the vocal timbre of the singers. Help students discover that

- An adult female voice performs the melody for verse 1.
- Boys' voices (the Boys Choir of Harlem) sing the melody and adult voices sing harmony on verses 2 and 3.
- On verse 4 (which is a reprise of verse 1), the boys' voices sing the melody while the adult female improvises.

Share with students information about the Boys Choir of Harlem (See Spotlight On, below).

ACROSS THE CURRICULUM

8b ▶ **Social Studies** Share with students that African American spirituals such as "Oh, Freedom" and "Come and Go with Me to That Land" have their roots in the songs enslaved African Americans sang in early American times. Many biblical texts and references are found within spirituals. It is likely that the "land" to which singers refer in "Come and Go with Me to That Land" is the land of salvation beyond a life of good deeds. At the same time, that "land" probably refers to the northern "free" states to which slaves hoped to escape from their bondage.

After students take turns reading *Runaway to Freedom* by Barbara Smucker (HarperTrophy, 1979), invite them to write about their reactions to the story. Ask, "How did the people really escape? How did the story make you feel?"

SPOTLIGHT ON

▶ **The Performers** The Boys Choir of Harlem, featured on the recording of "Oh, Freedom," was founded in 1968 by Dr. Walter J. Turnbull. Approximately 250 young people between the ages of 8 and 18 are arranged into several different groups, including training and preparatory trebles and concert and girls choirs. The performing choir, the 35 to 40 boys who tour, are chosen from the concert choir on a rotating basis, using criteria such as desired vocal balance, academic performance, and attendance and progress at rehearsals. The repertoire ranges from classical music to contemporary songs, gospel music, and spirituals. The choir has traveled extensively throughout the United States and abroad, performed at the White House, and appeared at the United Nations and on major television networks.

Unit 10 *Keepers of the Earth* **393**

Select several students to read aloud the lyrics to "Oh, Freedom."

ASK What similarities do you find between the lyrics of "Oh, Freedom" and those of "Come and Go with Me to That Land" on pp. 390–391? (Both songs talk about the desire to be free in a beautiful place.)

To develop this discussion more fully, see Across the Curriculum on p. 393.

Singing

1c Have students sing "Oh, Freedom" **CD 18-7** with the recording.

6c **ASK** What similarities do you find between the melody of "Oh, Freedom" and that of "Come and Go with Me to That Land"? (They are both in F pentatonic, both use essentially the same notes, both include syncopation.)

Playing

2a Have students study the keyboard accompaniment diagram on p. 393. Then invite students to play the chords on keyboards in the order in which they occur in "Oh, Freedom."

If the number of keyboards is insufficient for the class, have students play the accompaniment chords on Autoharps or guitars (capo at third fret and play D, G, and A₇ chords).

Select students to play the keyboard accompaniment while the class sings "Oh, Freedom" **CD 18-7.**

Listening

Select students to read aloud the Music Maker feature about Odetta on p. 394. To help students understand Odetta's unique abilities, share with them the information in Spotlight On below.

Sing for Freedom

Performers and composers often combine several songs to create a longer work.

Listen to how Odetta combines *Oh, Freedom* and *Come and Go with Me (to That Land)* into one performance.

CD 18–9
Oh, Freedom and Come and Go with Me

African American Spirituals
as performed by Odetta

This example of Odetta's singing showcases the low alto range of her voice.

M·U·S·I·C M·A·K·E·R·S
Odetta

Odetta Holmes Felious Gordon (born 1930, in Birmingham, Alabama) is a much-loved singer of African American folk music. She is known by the single name, Odetta. Her parents recognized her musical talent and encouraged her to sing. As a child, she took singing lessons and taught herself to play the guitar. She became famous in the early 1950s as an exciting interpreter of African American folk music. She has made many recordings that show off her unusual vocal range, which runs from coloratura to low alto. In 1999, President Bill Clinton presented Odetta with the National Endowment for the Arts' Medal of Arts.

394

Footnotes

SKILLS REINFORCEMENT

6b ▶ **Listening** Once students have listened to Odetta sing *Oh, Freedom* and *Come and Go with Me to That Land* several times, have them use a Venn diagram (see Resource Book p. C-8) to

- Compare and contrast Odetta's interpretation of "Oh, Freedom" and "Come and Go with Me" to the versions in their book.

- Make a list of these differences and similarities.

SPOTLIGHT ON

▶ **Voice Classification** Students might be interested to know that there are four main classifications of voices: soprano, alto, tenor, and bass. Within each of these groups are the following subgroups: first and second soprano, mezzo-soprano and contralto, first and second tenor, baritone, and bass. A singer's range and timbre determine the classification of his or her voice. (Occasionally, individuals develop a range that is much broader than any one category. Odetta is one example.)

All of us were born with high voices that fit the soprano range. As we mature, our voices change. Some become lower and some become higher. The sound or timbre of our voices also changes as we get older. Although boys' voices make the most dramatic change in range, girls' voices change too.

Make Your Own Arrangement

Create your own choral arrangement. Use two songs that share a similar topic, and combine them into one larger work. Connect the two songs with an instrumental interlude.

6b Explain to students that they will hear Odetta singing an arrangement of "Oh, Freedom" and "Come and Go with Me to That Land," which features the singer's low alto range. Then invite them to listen to the recording of Odetta's performance **CD 18-9.**

ASK Which song was in a higher key—"Oh, Freedom" or "Come and Go with Me to That Land"? ("Come and Go with Me to That Land")

Share with students that in order to modulate (or move smoothly from one key to another) between songs, Odetta plays an instrumental interlude known as a "bridge."

3 CLOSE

Performing

Organize the class into several groups and encourage each group to

1c • Find two songs that are related thematically.

2a • Combine the two songs into a larger work.

4b • Provide keyboard, Autoharp, or guitar accompaniment for both songs. (MIDI accompaniments could be substituted for the guitar or keyboard accompaniments; see Technology/Media Link below)

• Use a different vocal timbre for each song.

8a Focus students' attention on the eighteenth-century coverlet shown on p. 395. Use the information and **8b** resources listed in Across the Curriculum below to explore the fascinating story of "freedom quilts."

Skill: LISTENING   **ASSESSMENT**

6b **Music Journal Writing** See Skills Reinforcement, p. 382, to assess the students' ability to compare and describe different types of vocal timbre.

Arts **Connection**

Appliquéd cotton coverlet from the mid-eighteenth century ▲

ACROSS THE CURRICULUM

8a ▶ **Art** Invite students to examine the coverlet shown above and then read about the secret codes incorporated into quilts that **8b** aided slaves in their journey to freedom.

• *Sweet Clara and the Freedom Quilt* by Deborah Hopkinson (Random House, 1995).

• *Hidden in Plain View: A Secret Story of Quilts and the Underground Railroad* by Jacqueline L. Tobin and Raymond G. Dobard (Doubleday, 2000).

TECHNOLOGY/MEDIA LINK

6c **CD-ROM** Allow students to explore accompaniment styles with *Band-in-a-Box.*

• Prepare a *Band-in-a-Box* file with the melody and chord progressions to "Oh, Freedom."

• Have students take turns selecting different accompaniment styles to apply to the file as the class sings a verse of the song. Then discuss the appropriateness of the selected style.

• Ask students to determine why they were able to sing the song, no matter what accompaniment style was played. (The song's melody and harmony never change; only the accompaniment pattern applied to the harmony changes.)

LESSON AT A GLANCE

Element Focus **MELODY** Melodic contour

Skill Objective **LISTENING** Listen to melodic contour in a Native American composition that celebrates the sunrise

Connection Activity **CULTURE** Discuss the importance and symbolic meaning of the flute in Native American culture

MATERIALS
- "Zuni Sunrise Call"   **CD 18-10**
  Recording Routine: Instrumental; vocal (twice); instrumental
- *Daybreak Vision*   **CD 18-11**
- *Garden of the Earth*   **CD 18-12**
- "Garden of the Earth" (poem)

VOCABULARY
melodic contour

◆ ◆ ◆ National Standards ◆ ◆ ◆ ◆
1c Sing music from diverse cultures
6b Listen and analyze uses of pitch, timbre, and form in music from diverse cultures
6c Understand and use basic principles of tonality in music analysis
8a Show how different arts portray the same idea in unique ways
9a Describe characteristics of music styles from a variety of cultures
9c Compare, in several cultures, functions music serves

MORE MUSIC CHOICES
For more experience with Native American music:
"Jo'ashilá" ("Walking Together"), p. 108
Kokopelli Wandering Song, p. 110

A Song Of Nature

Taking care of the earth is an important part of life. Native American art and music often reflect respect for the earth, animals, and people. As you **sing** "Zuni Sunrise Call," picture the earth at daybreak.

 CD 18–10

Zuni Sunrise Call

Zuni Native American Song

Noh ay loh ah noh ay loh ah

Wah ah day oh nah wee yahn nah lay

Ah _____ day oh nah wee yahn nah lay

Nah yah nah ah wee oh _____ mee tehn lah lay

Nah yah nah ah wee oh _____ mee tehn lah lay _____

Footnotes

CULTURAL CONNECTION

9c ▶ **Native American Flute** The flute is very popular among the Zuni, the Navajo, and other Native American groups. It is viewed as "the breath of life" and is played for many ceremonial gatherings. Native American flutes have three to six finger holes and are made out of clay, wood, bone, or cane. Some are decorated with leather, beads, and paints. (See Cultural Connection, p. 110, for more information on the Native American flute.)

BUILDING SKILLS THROUGH MUSIC

▶ **Art** Ask students to look at the photo on p. 397 of the Native American dancers. Have them describe the photograph in detail using technical terminology of the elements of art. Encourage students to list different colors including the shadings and tones.

TEACHER TO TEACHER

9a ▶ **Native American Music** Students may wonder what the text of "Zuni Sunrise Call" means. As with many Native American songs, the words have no literal meaning. The Native American tradition says that nonliteral syllables (vocables) recall a time when people and animals spoke to one another in an ancient language we have lost. Read the words to "Zuni Sunrise Call" aloud. Notice that there are no punctuation marks, but many syllables are repeated. Help students understand that Native American music is constructed according to rules and principles that are different from Western music; therefore, it will sound different. Students will take cues from you to determine how they will approach and react to this music.

◀ The American Indian Dance Theater is a large troupe of musicians and dancers that tours throughout the United States. Members perform dances that encourage a deeper understanding of Native American heritage.

Pictured are examples of Zuni traditional carvings from natural materials. The carvings of animals and people are very small. ▶

Utah

Colorado

New Mexico

Zuni Reservation

Arizona

Tune In

"One must rise early each day and greet the sun."
Zuni proverb

Unit 10 **397**

1 INTRODUCE

Invite students to share with the class descriptions of their favorite places to enjoy nature. Create a class description of daybreak in your area and in a nearby park.

Then choose a student to read the text on p. 396. Share with students the information about Native American lyrics in Teacher to Teacher, p. 396.

2 DEVELOP

Listening

Invite students to

- Listen to the recording of "Zuni Sunrise Call" **CD 18-10.**

6b
- Discover the highest and lowest pitches of the song. (A, above and below middle C)

- Draw the contour of the melody in the air with their hands.

Singing

1c Invite students to sing "Zuni Sunrise Call" with the recording, using a *loo* or *oo* syllable. Then have students sing the song with the recording, using the Native American vocables.

Invite students to study the pictures on p. 397 as selected students read the captions aloud.

8a ASK **How do the artwork and the dancers' costumes depict a relationship with nature?** (Both are made from natural materials and both represent things found in nature.)

continued on page 398

ACROSS THE CURRICULUM

▶ **Language Arts** Encourage students to read and dramatize the following books about the Zuni people:

- *Ahaiyute and the Cloud Eater* by Vladimir Hulpach (Harcourt Brace, 1996) is the story of a young Zuni boy who proves his ability to be a warrior by killing the huge snakelike monster, the bringer of the terrible drought.

- *The Boy Who Made Dragonfly: A Zuni Myth* by Tony Hillerman (University of New Mexico Press, 1986) is a Zuni myth about a boy and his sister who become leaders of their people through the help of a magical, mysterious dragonfly.

SPOTLIGHT ON

▶ **The Performer/Composer** R. Carlos Nakai has appeared on over 30 solo and compilation albums. He is one of today's most honored Native American musicians and is credited with reintroducing the cedar flute to modern audiences. Nakai, of Navajo-Ute descent, rarely quotes Native American melodies in his compositions. Instead, he chooses to create new works in the style of traditional music. In addition to making albums, Nakai has written a book on flute playing. He co-wrote the soundtrack for *How the West Was Lost,* a 1993 documentary produced for the Discovery Channel.

Listening

Remind students about the class description of dawn written earlier in the lesson.

SAY We will listen to another description of dawn. This one is a musical description by R. Carlos Nakai. (See Spotlight On, p. 397, for information on Nakai.)

Have students

- Close their eyes and imagine the dawn as they listen to *Daybreak Vision* **CD 18-11.**
- Share what they imagined as they listened to the piece.

Ask students to study the listening map for *Daybreak Vision* on p. 398 or have them look at the transparency as it is projected on the screen. (See Technology/Media Link, p. 399.)

6c Help students discover the melodic repetition in the piece, as represented by the icons.

SAY The shape created by a grouping of high and low pitches is called contour. The shape of the melody line is called melodic contour. In Native American songs this contour, plus the text, determines the form.

9a Help students understand that Native American music does not have an absolute pitch set with staff names that indicate a precise sound. It is all relative high and low.

Have students

- Follow the listening map while listening to *Daybreak Vision* **CD 18-11.**
- Identify the use of repetition in the piece.
- **6b** Listen to *Daybreak Vision* and draw the melodic contour on paper without referring to the listening map.
- Share their contour maps with a partner.

Celebrate Sunrise

Native Americans have a deep appreciation for nature. This composition for Native American flute also celebrates sunrise.
Listen to *Daybreak Vision* as you follow the melodic contour on the listening map.

CD 18–11
Daybreak Vision

written and performed by R. Carlos Nakai

Nakai blends traditional and contemporary elements in his compositions for Native American flute.

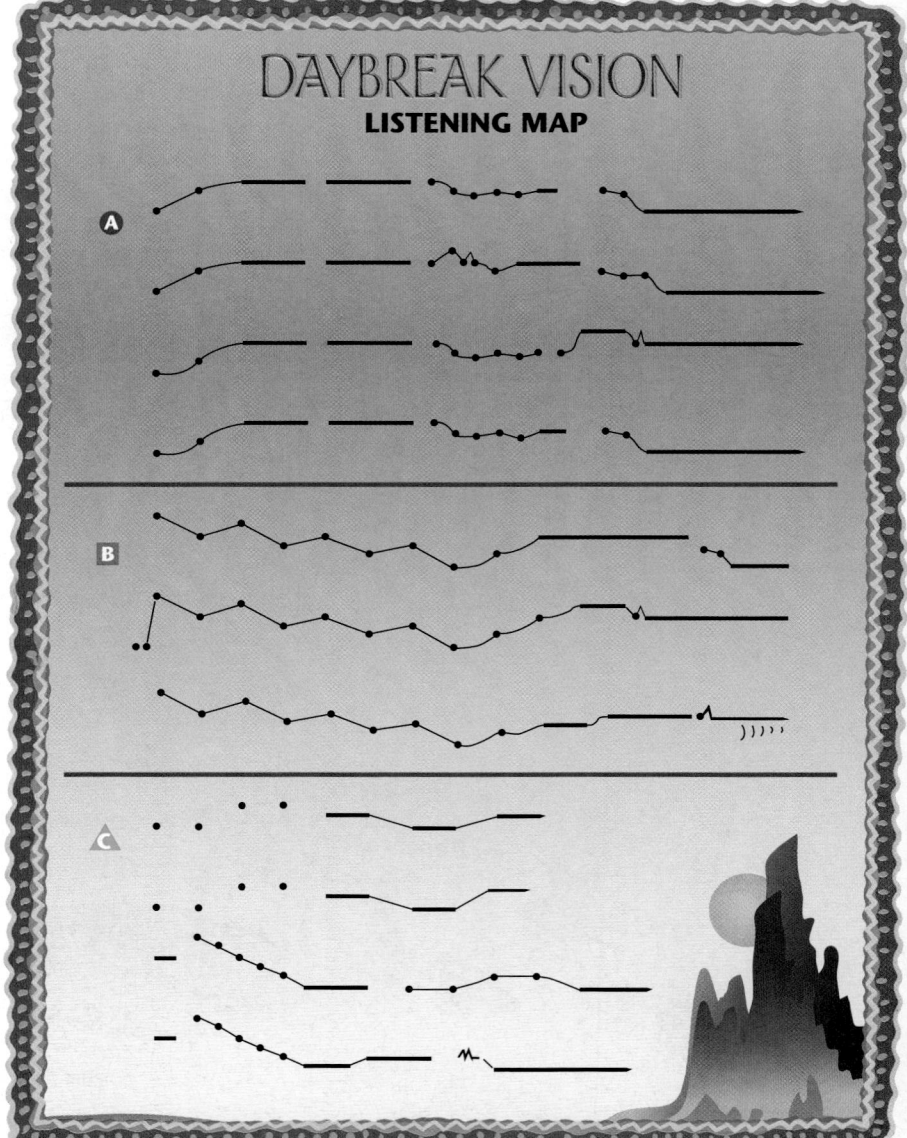

DAYBREAK VISION
LISTENING MAP

Footnotes

CHARACTER EDUCATION

▶ **Environmental Awareness** To help students understand the need to respect and protect nature, discuss the impact individuals and groups have on the environment. Remind students that if the quality of the earth is to be maintained for future generations, sacrifices may have to be made. Divide students into groups to consider ways they individually contribute to pollution. Then focus students' attention on sacrifices they might make by creating a list of ways they could reduce the amount of waste they generate. Encourage students to incorporate one means of reducing waste in their individual lives for the remainder of the school year.

CULTURAL CONNECTION

▶ **American Indian Dance Theater** Songs and dances play a very important role in ceremonies and rituals of Native Americans. Chester Mahooty, the soloist in the recording of "Zuni Sunrise Call," is with the American Indian Dance Theater. He belongs to a group of Native Americans who present dances and songs to an audience of non-Indian people. The members of this dance group belong to a number of Indian nations throughout the United States. "Zuni Sunrise Song" is a tribute to the rising sun, which, in Zuni belief, is the giver of each day's life on Earth.

Protecting the Earth

People who live in different countries share concern for the earth. **Listen** to *Garden of the Earth*, a song reflecting that sentiment.

 CD 18–12
Garden of the Earth

Traditional Folk Song from Russia as performed by the Dimitri Pokrovsky Singers with the Paul Winter Consort

Paul Winter traveled to Russia fifteen times to learn about the country's musical heritage before creating this arrangement of *Garden of the Earth.*

Garden of the Earth

by Paul Winter and Paul Halley

There's a garden 'round the Earth,
There's a home beneath the sun,
In the beauty of this garden,
We will hear a thousand songs.
Many voices, many tongues,
From the mountains to the sea,
Sing of beauty all around us
In this ancient harmony.
For the glory of the Earth,
For the glory of the sun,
We will sing of life together
And forever live as one.

M·U·S·I·C M·A·K·E·R·S
Paul Winter

Paul Winter (born 1931) is known for his fusion of world music from various cultures with jazz. He founded the Paul Winter Consort in 1967 and explored non-Western music through this group. Winter became interested in and involved with environmental issues and has worked to join music and nature together. He even attempted to communicate with whales and used those sounds in several of his works.

Listening

6b Play the recording of "Zuni Sunrise Call" **CD 18-10** again and ask students to

- Focus on the part played by the Native American flute.
- Compare the flute in this song with that in *Daybreak Vision.*

9c Share with students and discuss the information about the significance of the flute in Native American culture (See Cultural Connection, p. 396).

Select several students to read aloud the poem "Garden of the Earth" on p. 399. Then have students read the Music Makers feature about Paul Winter.

Share with students that the music for *Garden of the Earth* is a traditional Russian folk song. Then invite them to

- Listen to *Garden of the Earth* **CD 18-12.**

8a
- Discuss the similarities among the ideas expressed through "Zuni Sunrise Call," *Daybreak Vision, Garden of the Earth,* and the traditional Zuni carvings on p. 397.

3 CLOSE

Singing

Invite students to sing the English words of *Garden of the Earth* **CD 18-12** with the recording. Help them discover the melodic contour of the song and the melodic repetition in the song.

Skill: LISTENING   **ASSESSMENT**

6b **Music Journal Writing** Listen to "Zuni Sunrise Call" and *Daybreak Vision* with students. Ask them to write descriptions of each, comparing melodic contour, melodic repetition, and subject of lyrics.

SPOTLIGHT ON

▶ **The Performer/Composer** Paul Winter is known for using a variety of musical styles and for blending music and nature. He named his group the Paul Winter Consort and adopted certain non-Western instruments and performance styles. His compositions use elements of African, Asian, Russian, and Latin American music. His 1986 album *Canyon* was recorded in the Grand Canyon.

Winter's 1988 album *Earthbeat* was recorded in both Russia and America. To record *Garden of the Earth,* he first recorded a Russian choir performing the original tune. Next, he recorded an American choir performing his English adaptation. Finally, Winter and other musicians added accompaniment and improvisation. The different recordings were blended into a seamless whole.

TECHNOLOGY/MEDIA LINK

Transparency Display the listening map transparency for *Daybreak Vision* as you play the recording. Point to each section of the piece on the first listening to help students follow along. On subsequent listenings, invite a student to point to the sections as you play the recording.

LESSON AT A GLANCE

Element Focus   TEXTURE/HARMONY Melodic and rhythmic ostinato

Skill Objective   SINGING Perform ostinato patterns to accompany a melody

Connection   CULTURE Discuss that communities are made
Activity   up of people who have common interests

MATERIALS

- *"Zum gali gali"* (Hebrew)   **CD 18-13**
- *"Zum gali gali"* (English)   **CD 18-14**

  Recording Routine: Intro (4 m.); refrain; v. 1; refrain; interlude (4 m.); refrain; v. 2; refrain; interlude (2 m.); refrain

- **Pronunciation Practice/Translation** p. 540
- **Resource Book** pp. A-43, F-45
- bells, barred instruments, recorder or flute, finger cymbals, triangle

VOCABULARY

ostinato   *D.C. al Fine   Fine*

◆ ◆ ◆ ◆ **National Standards** ◆ ◆ ◆ ◆

1c Sing music from diverse cultures
1d Sing music written in two parts
2c Perform instrumental music from diverse cultures
8b Identify ways music relates to social studies

MORE MUSIC CHOICES

For more practice with ostinatos:
"I Love the Mountains," p. 34
"O Music," p. 162

1 INTRODUCE

Invite students to describe various groups to which they belong. Guide them to understand that such groups can be called communities.

Common Ground

What is a community? It's a group of people who share something in common. The people in these photographs work together in an Israeli *kibbutz.*

Learn to **sing** *"Zum gali gali."* Then sing the refrain and verse together to create a partner song. The repeated refrain creates a common ground that unites the song.

Footnotes

ACROSS THE CURRICULUM

8b ▶ **Social Studies** Share with students that in Israel there are communities of people who live together and work to make a better life for themselves and the country. Such a community is called a *kibbutz.* Encourage students to learn about these work communities in *Life on an Israeli Kibbutz (The Way People Live)* by Linda Jacobs Altman (Lucent Books, 1996).

BUILDING SKILLS THROUGH MUSIC

▶ **Math** Divide the class into two groups, one clapping the rhythm of the refrain of *"Zum gali gali"* and the other keeping the steady beat (1 beat=half note). Have them repeat the activity on the verse. Ask students to identify fractions for each note; quarter note or rest=1/2; eighth note=1/4 and so on. Have students compute the value for each beat, then for each measure.

CULTURAL CONNECTION

8b ▶ **Israeli Folk Music** Although Israel is viewed as a unified culture with a single folk tradition, the country is the birthplace of a variety of musical styles. *Ashkenazi* music traces its roots to Europe, the Americas, and other Western cultures. *Sephardi* music is related to the cultures of Greece, North Africa, Spain, and Portugal. *Mizrahi* music is rooted in the Jewish traditions of Syria, Lebanon, Iraq, and other Arab countries. Israeli music includes songs in Ladino (from medieval Spain), Arabic, Hebrew, and Yiddish (a German dialect interspersed with Hebrew words). Individual Israeli folk pieces are categorized according to function: *devotional music* refers to pieces used in public or private worship and *secular music* refers to pieces performed at festive events such as wedding feasts and parties.

CD 18–13
MIDI 25

Zum gali gali

English Words by David Eddleman

Folk Song from Israel

m l t, d r m

REFRAIN
Em

Zum ga - li, ga - li, ga - li, zum ga - li, ga - li,

Em   Fine

Zum ga - li, ga - li, ga - li, zum ga - li, ga - li.

VERSE
Em   D   Em

1. He - cha - lutz   le   'man   a - vo - dah;   A - vo - dah   le
2. He - cha - lutz   le   'man   ha - b'tu - lah;   Ha - b'tu - lah   le
1. We are build - ing, build - ing a land   Out of rock and
2. So that war and   hun - ger may cease,   We are work - ing,

D   Em   D   Em

'man he - cha - lutz.   A - vo - dah   le   'man he - cha - lutz.
'man he - cha - lutz;   Ha - sha - lom   le   'man ha' a - mim;
de - sert and sand;   Men and wo - men   la - bor in pride,
work - ing for peace.   Though the days   be   heav - y and long,

Em   D   Em   D.C. al Fine

He - cha - lutz   le   'man   a - vo - dah.
Ha' - a - mim   le   'man   ha - sha - lom.
We are work - ing   side   by _____ side.
We will make   our   na - tion _____ strong.

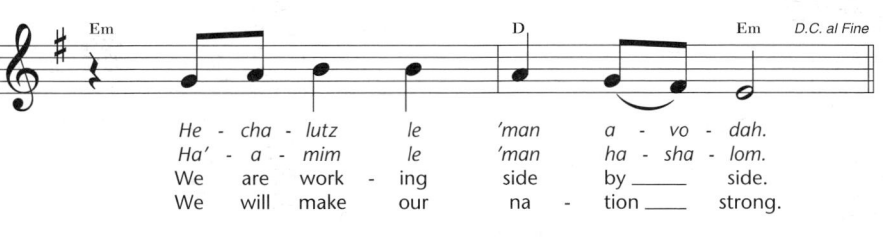

MIDI Use the MIDI song file of *"Zum gali gali"* to experiment with texture. You can duplicate tracks to add more layers or substitute instruments for other timbres.

2 DEVELOP

Singing

SAY People who have have common interests and who work together for a common goal create communities. *"Zum gali gali"* is an Israeli folk song about a community of pioneers working together to build a new country.

Invite students to listen to the recording of *"Zum gali gali"* **CD 18-13.** Locate the *D.C. al Fine* and *Fine* markings in the music and explain what they mean.

1c Invite students to sing the song in English with the recording. Then have students

- Echo-sing measures 1 and 2 of the refrain as an ostinato as you model it.
- Sing the ostinato while you sing the refrain.
- Practice the Hebrew lyrics using the Pronunciation Practice Track **CD 18-16** and Resource Book p. A-43.

1d Select a small group of volunteers to sing the ostinato while the rest of the class sings the song.

Playing

2c Select several students to play the ostinato on a melody instrument. Invite several other students to play the ostinato on finger cymbals or another rhythm instrument. Then have all students sing *"Zum gali gali"* and play one of the ostinatos on an instrument.

3 CLOSE

Element: TEXTURE/HARMONY **ASSESSMENT**

1c **Performance/Observation** Organize the class into four groups. Have students perform *"Zum gali gali"*
2c by layering the parts as follows. Group 1: Rhythmic ostinato; Group 2: Melodic ostinato; Group 3: Verse; Group 4: Refrain. Allow groups to switch parts. Observe students' ability to accurately and independently perform the melodic ostinato.

SKILLS REINFORCEMENT

 ▶ **Recorder** Students can play the two simple ostinatos below to accompany *"Zum gali gali."* Encourage students to create their own ostinatos to accompany the song, using only the notes E and B. (Remind students to move their fingers together when leaping between the two notes.)

▶ **Mallets** See Resource Book, p. F-45, for an Orff arrangement for *"Zum gali gali."*

TECHNOLOGY/MEDIA LINK

Web Site Go to *www.sfsuccessnet.com* to learn more about Israeli folk music.

LESSON AT A GLANCE

Element Focus **FORM** Verse/refrain

Skill Objective **SINGING** Sing a song in verse/refrain form

Connection Activity **SCIENCE** Learn about the history of navigation

MATERIALS

- "The Ship that Never Returned" **CD 18-17**
  Recording Routine: Intro (8 m.); v. 1; refrain; interlude (4 m.); v. 2; refrain; interlude (4 m.); v. 3; refrain; coda
- *M.T.A.* **CD 18-19**
- keyboard or Autoharp

VOCABULARY

verse refrain

◆ ◆ ◆ ◆ National Standards ◆ ◆ ◆ ◆

1a Sing accurately in small ensembles
2a Play instruments accurately in small ensembles
6b Listen and analyze uses of form in music from diverse cultures
8b Identify ways music relates to social studies

MORE MUSIC CHOICES

For more songs of the sea:
"Bound for South Australia," p. 22
"The Greenland Whale Fishery," p. 230

1 INTRODUCE

8b Invite students to read the text about ocean transportation at the top of p. 402. Ask students if any of them have ever traveled by sea or vacationed on a ship. Have volunteers share their experiences.

SAY Today ships rely on navigation systems to help them reach their destinations. In the past, sailors had to use other methods to guide their vessels.

Lead students in a discussion about the history of navigation. For more information, see Across the Curriculum below.

One If By Land, Two If By Sea

The earth's people travel in many ways. One popular form of travel is by ship on the ocean. Until the twentieth century, worldwide travel and commerce were possible only by ship. What impact did later forms of transportation have on the world's environment?

Sing "The Ship that Never Returned," a popular hit from the late nineteenth century. **Identify** the form of the song.

The Ship that Never Returned
Words and Music by Henry C. Work

Footnotes

ACROSS THE CURRICULUM

▶ **Science** Navigation has had an important role in the development of civilization. In earlier times sailors navigated by studying the sun and stars as well as wind direction. One early device used for navigation was the astrolabe. It was made up of a brass or bronze disk with a sight and was used to measure the angle between the horizon and a celestial body. British explorer James Cook was the first person to employ modern celestial navigation techniques.

BUILDING SKILLS THROUGH MUSIC

▶ **Social Studies** Share the information from Across the Curriculum with students. Lead them in a discussion of the purpose of ships in the world today. Ask students to include the bodies of water where ships sail.

SKILLS REINFORCEMENT

2a ▶ **Keyboard** Use the following suggestions to help all students perform a keyboard accompaniment for "The Ship that Never Returned."

Reinforcement Some students may have difficulty playing the B♭ E♭ B♭ F₇ chord progression. Write the progression on the board and have students practice playing each chord.

On Target Most students will be able to easily play the B♭ E♭ B♭ F₇ chord progression. Ask these students to play the progression while the rest of the class sings the song.

Challenge Invite interested students to improvise a counter-melody for the refrain of "The Ship that Never Returned" to perform on keyboard.

REFRAIN B♭

Did she ev - er re - turn? No, she

E♭ B♭

nev - er re - turned, and her fate is still un -

F₇ B♭ E♭

learned. And ___ one last man set sail, Com -

B♭ F₇ B♭

man - der, on a ship that nev - er re - turned.

A Variation in Words

Another way people travel is by railway, including subways and cross-country trains. **Listen** to this variation of "The Ship that Never Returned." This humorous version of the song tells of the effect of a subway fare increase on one unfortunate rider.

CD 18–19
M.T.A

by Jacqueline Steiner and Bess Lomax Hawes as performed by the Kingston Trio

This song is also known as "Charlie on the M.T.A."

◄ The Kingston Trio

MIDI Use the song file for "The Ship that Never Returned" to experiment with arranging the song in different styles.

2 DEVELOP

Listening

6b Have students look at the notation for "The Ship that Never Returned" and identify the verse/refrain or AB form.

ASK How are the refrain and verse sections different from each other? (The words of the refrain are repeated, while each verse has different words.)

Play "The Ship that Never Returned" **CD 18-17** and ask students to raise their right hand when they hear the refrain.

ASK How did the style of each verse differ? (Verse 1 is performed in a nineteenth century style; verse 2 is performed in a jazz style; verse 3 is performed in a contemporary country style.)

1c Invite students to sing "The Ship that Never Returned" with the recording **CD 18-17**.

Listening

Invite students to listen to *M.T.A.* **CD 18-19** performed by the Kingston Trio. Point out to students that this song is another version of "The Ship that Never Returned."

ASK What differences do you hear in this recording as compared to the one we listened to earlier? (The words are different; this version is in a "folk style" and sung by only male voices.)

For additional information about the Kingston Trio, see Spotlight On below.

3 CLOSE

ELEMENT: FORM **ASSESSMENT**

1a **Performance/Observation** Divide the class into two groups. Have one group sing the verses, the other
2a sing the refrain of "The Ship that Never Returned."

Observe students' ability to perform each section accurately and independently with good tone quality. Ask students to switch parts and sing the song again.

SPOTLIGHT ON

▶ **The Performers** During the folk music revival of the 1950s and 1960s, the Kingston Trio became one of the most popular groups in the world. The group was formed in Palo Alto, California by Dave Guard, Nick Reynolds, and Bob Shane. The group recorded their first album in the summer of 1958 and soon after the song "Tom Dooley" became a number one hit. Over the next four years, the Kingston Trio recorded ten albums. In 1961, Dave Guard left the group and in 1967 the Kingston Trio disbanded. Bob Shane later formed the New Kingston Trio.

TECHNOLOGY/MEDIA LINK

MIDI/Sequencing Software Play the MIDI song file for "The Ship that Never Returned." Ask students to suggest tempo, dynamic, and orchestration changes for the music. Play the file again, using various suggestions. After each hearing, ask students if the mood of the song changed.

Lesson	Elements	Skills

LESSON 1
A Greeting Song

pp. 410-413

Element: Rhythm

Concept: Pattern
Focus: Syncopated patterns

Secondary Element
Melody: pitch and direction

National Standards
1a　1c　2c　4c　5a　6c　7b
8b

Skill: Singing
Objective: Sing syncopated patterns

Secondary Skills
- **Listening** Listen to the song
- **Reading** Clap and speak syncopated patterns using rhythm syllables
- **Playing** Play syncopated rhythms on rhythm sticks
- **Performing** Perform the song with unpitched instruments and movement

SKILLS REINFORCEMENT
- **Performing** Practice syncopation with body percussion
- **Vocal Development** Perform warm-up exercises before singing
- **Playing** Play percussion ostinatos to accompany the song

LESSON 2
A Song of Freedom

pp. 414-417

Element: Form

Concept: Phrase
Focus: Phrase and section repetition

Secondary Element
Expression: dynamics

National Standards
1c　1d　1e　5e　6b　8b

Skill: Singing
Objective: Sing repeated phrases and sections with expressive variation

Secondary Skills
- **Listening** Listen for phrases and harmony in the recording
- **Reading** Compare rhythms and pitches in the song
- **Performing** Sing the song with dynamic changes

SKILLS REINFORCEMENT
- **Singing** Practice vocal techniques to develop expressive singing

LESSON 3
A Pledge of Loyalty

pp. 418-425

Element: Form
Concept: aba
Focus: aba form

Secondary Element
Expression: articulation

National Standards
1b　1d　4a　5c　6a　6b　7b
8b

Skill: Singing
Objective: Sing with expression a patriotic choral arrangement in aba form

Secondary Skills
- **Listening** Listen to identify significant text and key changes
- **Analyzing** Determine the form of the song
- **Describing** Discuss performing with emotion
- **Listening** Listen for singers' vocal timbre
- **Creating** Create a composition in ABA form
- **Performing** Perform the song with slide show
- **Listening** Listen to the selection and compare it to the song

SKILLS REINFORCEMENT
- **Vocal Development** Techniques for adding resonance; techniques for singing long phrases

Connections

Music and Other Literature

Connection: Culture

Activity: Explore Angolan culture and the music of southwestern Africa

CULTURAL CONNECTION **Bantu** Information about the language of Angola

SPOTLIGHT ON **Angola** Facts about the country and its instruments

TEACHER TO TEACHER
Song Form Discuss song form
Vocalises References for vocalises

BUILDING SKILLS THROUGH MUSIC **Social Studies** Substitute non-English greetings in the song text

Song "O, Desayo"

More Music Choices
"Funwa alafia" ("Welcome, My Friends"), p. 32
"Kokoleoko," p. 33
"Kum ba yah," p. 244
"Bantama kra kro," p. 308

ASSESSMENT

Performance/Peer Critique Sing in sections and evaluate rhythmic accuracy

TECHNOLOGY/MEDIA LINK
MIDI/Sequencing Software Arrange and record percussion parts

Connection: Social Studies

Activity: Discuss the history of apartheid in South Africa

ACROSS THE CURRICULUM
Social Studies Definition and background of apartheid
Social Studies Compare freedoms enjoyed currently with freedoms of earlier generations

SPOTLIGHT ON
South Africa Discuss the diversity of the nation
Freedom Songs Source for freedom songs

TEACHER TO TEACHER **Performance Tips** Ideas for how to sing the song with vitality and joy

MEETING INDIVIDUAL NEEDS **Inclusion** Color coding song sections

BUILDING SKILLS THROUGH MUSIC **Art** Discuss the elements that are similar between pieces of art

Song "Freedom is Coming"

More Music Choices
"This Train," p. 27
"Joshua Fought the Battle of Jericho," p. 101
"Go Down, Moses," p. 190
"Oh, Freedom," p. 392

ASSESSMENT

Performance/Self-Assessment Sing the song to demonstrate form and expression; compare to a recording

TECHNOLOGY/MEDIA LINK
MIDI/Sequencing Software Use the song file to help learn parts

---

Connection: Social Studies

Activity: Discuss the meaning and symbols of patriotism

ACROSS THE CURRICULUM
Social Studies Origin of "America"
Language Arts Write about freedom and pride in being an American
Science Discuss the planetary system

TEACHER TO TEACHER
Keyboard Accompaniment Use accompaniment to maintain pitch
Lyrics Help to understand word meaning

CULTURAL CONNECTION
Big Ben Description of England's famous clock and bell
White Cliffs of Dover Geography and facts of the cliffs

CHARACTER EDUCATION **Patriotism** Discuss patriotic behaviors

AUDIENCE ETIQUETTE **School Assemblies** Practice and reinforce audience behavior in school assemblies

BUILDING SKILLS THROUGH MUSIC **Reading** Discuss words and phrases in the song text that indicate loyalty

Song "I Vow to You, My Country"

Listening Selection The Planets, "Jupiter"

More Music Choices
"America, the Beautiful," p. 76
"This Land is Your Land," p. 118
"America," p. 486
"The Star-Spangled Banner," p. 488

ASSESSMENT

Performance/Peer Critique Sing a song to show form and expression

TECHNOLOGY/MEDIA LINK
Web Site More information about composer Gustav Holst
MIDI/Sequencing Software Use the file to experiment with expression, harmony, and transposition

Lesson	Elements	Skills	
LESSON 4 **A Conga from Cuba** pp. 426-429 	**Element: Form** **Concept:** Form **Focus:** AB form **Secondary Element** Rhythm: dotted rhythms **National Standards** 1c 1d 5a 5c 6b 7a	**Skill: Singing** **Objective:** Sing a song in AB form **Secondary Skills** • **Listening** Listen to the song and identify form • **Analyzing** Identify A and B sections from song notation • **Reading** Identify dotted rhythm and melodic patterns • **Playing** Play a steady beat and chordal accompaniment • **Moving** Perform a version of the conga	**SKILLS REINFORCEMENT** • **Vocal Development** Practice good posture and intonation • **Moving** Suggestions for performing the movement activity
LESSON 5 **In Search of Peace** pp. 430-433 	**Element: Form** **Concept:** Form **Focus:** AABA form **Secondary Element** Expression: articulation **National Standards** 1a 1c 1d 5a 5e 6a 6b 7b 8a 8b	**Skill: Singing** **Objective:** Sing a song in AABA form with expression **Secondary Skills** • **Listening** Identify the rhythmic motive and harmony in the song • **Reading** Practice rhythms and pitches with syllables; determine the form • **Moving** Move to show the ABA sections of the song	**SKILLS REINFORCEMENT** • **Vocal Development** Techniques for singing in tune • **Singing** Tips for pronouncing Hebrew vowels
LESSON 6 **A Carol from Spain** pp. 434-439 	**Element: Rhythm** **Concept:** Meter **Focus:** Mixed meter **Secondary Element** Expression: tempo **National Standards** 1a 1c 1d 2c 5a 5e 6b 6c 7b 8b 9a	**Skill: Singing** **Objective:** Perform a song notated in mixed meter **Secondary Skills** • **Listening** Identify rhythmic patterns in phrases • **Reading** Read and identify time signatures, tempo, and score markings • **Performing** Sing the song with recorder, drum, and finger cymbal accompaniment • **Listening** Compare two versions of the song	**SKILLS REINFORCEMENT** • **Analyzing** Clap a steady beat and say the changing rhythms of the vocal parts • **Keyboard** Play the melody of the song • **Singing** Techniques for maintaining proper vowel formation

Connections

Music and Other Literature

Connection: Social Studies
Activity: Learn about the design and construction of the conga drum

- **SPOTLIGHT ON** The Conga Background of the music genre
- **CULTURAL CONNECTION** The Conga Drum Information about the drum
- **MEETING INDIVIDUAL NEEDS** Inclusion Suggestions to help perform rhythm patterns
- **TEACHER TO TEACHER** Pronunciation Accuracy Invite a Spanish teacher to teach pronunciation of song text
- **MOVEMENT** Patterned Dance Perform a version of the conga with the song
- **BUILDING SKILLS THROUGH MUSIC** Dance Move to the steady beat of the music

Songs
"Uno, dos, y tres"
"One, Two, and Three"

More Music Choices
"Chiapanecas" ("The Girl from Chiapas"), p. 92
"Imbabura," p. 203
"Canción Mixteca" ("Mixteca Song"), p. 326

ASSESSMENT

Performance/Self-Assessment Perform the song and evaluate accuracy of rhythm, pronunciation, and balance

TECHNOLOGY/MEDIA LINK

MIDI/Sequencing Software Use the MIDI file to learn the voice parts

---

Connection: Culture
Activity: Discuss cultural influences in Jewish music and participate in a Jewish folk dance

- **ACROSS THE CURRICULUM** Social Studies Facts about Israel
- **CULTURAL CONNECTION** Jewish/Israeli Culture Facts about the people and their music
- **SPOTLIGHT ON** Pronunciation Tips for singing in Hebrew
- **TEACHER TO TEACHER** How to Sing a Descant Suggestions on how to introduce and produce good vowel sounds
- **MOVEMENT** Patterned Dance Steps and routine for movement to accompany the song
- **BUILDING SKILLS THROUGH MUSIC** Physical Education Perform a patterned dance

Song "Hine mah tov"

More Music Choices
"Dundai," p. 106
"Tzena, tzena," p. 298
"Joshua Fought the Battle of Jericho," p. 101
"Happy Days Are Here Again," p. 284
"Sing, Sing, Sing!" p. 340

ASSESSMENT

Performance/Peer Critique Select and perform another ABA song with movement; sing a song in small groups and evaluate the performance

TECHNOLOGY/MEDIA LINK

CD-ROM Arrange an accompaniment

MIDI/Sequencing Software Use the MIDI file to rehearse for performance of the song

---

Connection: Related Arts
Activity: Discuss elements of Renaissance style in a painting

- **SPOTLIGHT ON** Carols Facts about the origin of carols
  Spain in the Sixteenth Century Information about the era
- **CULTURAL CONNECTION** The Renaissance Facts about sixteenth-century culture
- **TEACHER TO TEACHER** Meter Changes Background on meter in Renaissance music
- **MEETING INDIVIDUAL NEEDS** Including Everyone Learn conceptual words
- **CHARACTER EDUCATION** Values Discuss values and behaviors that demonstrate them
- **ACROSS THE CURRICULUM** Art History Facts about the "School of Palma Vecchio"
- **BUILDING SKILLS THROUGH MUSIC** Art Compare a painting and an illustration

Song "Ríu ríu chíu"

Listening Selection Ríu ríu chíu
Arts Connection A Concert

More Music Choices
"Beyond Borders," p. 292
"A World of Difference," p. 386

ASSESSMENT

Performance/Peer Critique Sing the song with rhythmic stress to show meter

TECHNOLOGY/MEDIA LINK

Web Site More information on Renaissance music

MIDI/Sequencing Software Use the song file to help learn the song

Lesson	Elements	Skills	
LESSON 7 **A Wading Bird** pp. 440-443 	**Element: Melody** **Concept:** Pattern **Focus:** *Do-re-mi* and *do-mi-so* **Secondary Element** Form: phrases **National Standards** ◆1c ◆1d ◆1e ◆2c ◆5e ◆6a ◆6c ◆7a ◆8b ◆9a	**Skill: Singing** **Objective:** Sing *do-re-mi* and *do-mi-so* patterns **Secondary Skills** • **Listening** Listen to hear pronunciation of language • **Reading** Find and sing melodic patterns with pitch syllables, and discuss markings • **Performing** Perform the song with chord accompaniment	**SKILLS REINFORCEMENT** • **Creating** Improvise consequent phrases to given antecedent phrases • **Guitar** Suggestions on how to approximate a ukulele sound
LESSON 8 **Scat Cat!** pp. 444-451 	**Element: Rhythm** **Concept:** Beat **Focus:** Syncopated patterns **Secondary Element** Melody: motive **National Standards** ◆1a ◆1c ◆1d ◆1e ◆2c ◆3b ◆5a ◆5e ◆6b ◆7a ◆8b ◆9a	**Skill: Singing** **Objective:** Sing syncopation and tied rhythms in a scat-style song **Secondary Skills** • **Listening** Listen and identify syncopated beats and motives, listen for form • **Reading** Identify sections in the song • **Moving** Create gestures and facial expressions for the song • **Performing** Perform the song in a theatrical style • **Listening** Compare two recordings of the song • **Moving** Perform a "jazz strut" • **Performing** Suggestion for a performance theme	**SKILLS REINFORCEMENT** • **Singing** Techniques for energetic enunciation of scat syllables; add a third vocal part • **Keyboard** Play an accompaniment to song • **Singing/Vocal Dynamics** Exercises to enhance dynamic variation

Connections

Connection: Culture
Activity: Discuss aspects of Hawaiian culture

TEACHER TO TEACHER 'Ūlili E Examine the structural characteristics of the song

CULTURAL CONNECTION Hawaiian Culture Information about history and culture

SPOTLIGHT ON
Ukulele Information about the instrument
'Ūlili Bird Information about the Hawaiian seabird

ACROSS THE CURRICULUM Social Studies Facts about Hawaii

BUILDING SKILLS THROUGH MUSIC Language Write a descriptive sentence about the song and its subject

Connection: Style
Activity: Become acquainted with the jazz technique of scat singing

SPOTLIGHT ON
Scat Singing Information about the singing style
The Performers Louis Armstrong and Ella Fitzgerald
The Performer/Composer Information about Charlie Parker

MOVEMENT
Creative Movement Use body movements to accompany the song
Patterned Dance Perform the basic box step as a "jazz strut"

TEACHER TO TEACHER
Syncopation Mastering syncopation by feel
Vocal Techniques Learn scat singing techniques

CULTURAL CONNECTION The Swing Era Music of the 1930s–1940s

MEETING INDIVIDUAL NEEDS Pitch Accuracy Developing pitch sense

ACROSS THE CURRICULUM Social Studies Discuss the early twentieth century in the United States

BUILDING SKILLS THROUGH MUSIC Writing Create new lyrics for the song

Music and Other Literature

Song "'Ūlili E"

More Music Choices
"The Ship that Never Returned," p. 402

Song "Now's the Time"

Listening Selection Now's the Time
M·U·S·I·C M·A·K·E·R·S
Charlie Parker

More Music Choices
"Morning Comes Early," p. 13
"Éliza Kongo," p. 14
"Basin Street Blues," p. 354

ASSESSMENT

Performance/Observation Sing a song with pitch syllables to demonstrate melodic patterns

TECHNOLOGY/MEDIA LINK
MIDI/Sequencing Software Use file to teach the song
Web Site More information on the dance, instruments, and music of Hawaii

ASSESSMENT

Performance/Self-Assessment Perform the song and videotape the performance for evaluation

TECHNOLOGY/MEDIA LINK
CD-ROM Practice scat singing

INTRODUCING THE UNIT

The choral selections in this unit will challenge students vocally, musically, and artistically. As your students learn and perform this varied and exciting literature, their musical understanding and literacy will be enhanced. Each choral setting will touch your students in new and significant ways.

Presented on p. 405 is a brief overview of the skills that are assessed in this unit. (See below and pp. 406–407 for unit highlights of related curricular experiences.)

For a more detailed unit overview, see Unit at a Glance, pp. 403a–403f.

UNIT PROJECT

Point out to students that many of the songs in Unit 11 come from different countries and cultures. This musical potpourri offers many opportunities to capture the spirit of music and cultural influences through a number of classroom activities. Activities can be assigned to groups of students, resulting in a class project. Ask students to

- Read and write short reports about aspects of the cultural background for each song.
- Find pictures or create slides of images of the culture of each song.
- Find additional recorded songs representative of the culture of each song.
- Find recipes from the culture of each song that could be served at a party or social gathering.
- Find one example of apparel from the culture of each song.

When nearing the completion of Unit 11, have students plan a cultural fair where they can present their activities.

Sing Together in Harmony

Welcome to another year of choral music. This year, you will take a journey on a musical landscape composed of rhythm, melody, harmony, and form. With each new song, your awareness of how these musical elements relate to each other will help you understand the composer's technique for creating a song. At the end of this journey, you will no longer be just a visitor to the musical score. It will be a place where you will feel right at home.

Come, let's **sing** "Sail Away" and begin our musical tour.

CD 18–20
MIDI 27

Sail Away

Words and Music by Malcolm Dalglish (adapted)

Dark clouds hide the sun,

Rain comes down and the rivers run. Rivers run down to the sea,

and when you've got your liberty,

* Don't you want to sail away?

* "Don't you" is pronounced "donchiew"

404

ACROSS THE CURRICULUM

Unit Highlights The following interdisciplinary activities in this unit are related to the music elements presented in the lessons. See Unit at a Glance, pp. 403a–403f, for topical descriptions presented according to lesson sequence.

▶ **ART**
- Read about the School of Palma Vecchio (p. 438)

▶ **LANGUAGE ARTS**
- Write about national pride (p. 420)

▶ **SCIENCE**
- Discover facts about the solar system (p. 424)

▶ **SOCIAL STUDIES**
- Read about apartheid (p. 414)
- Write about the concept of freedom (p. 417)
- Explore the history of a patriotic melody (p. 418)
- Explore facts about Israel (p. 430)
- Learn about the geography of Hawaii (p. 443)
- Research the migration of African Americans in the early twentieth century (p. 450)

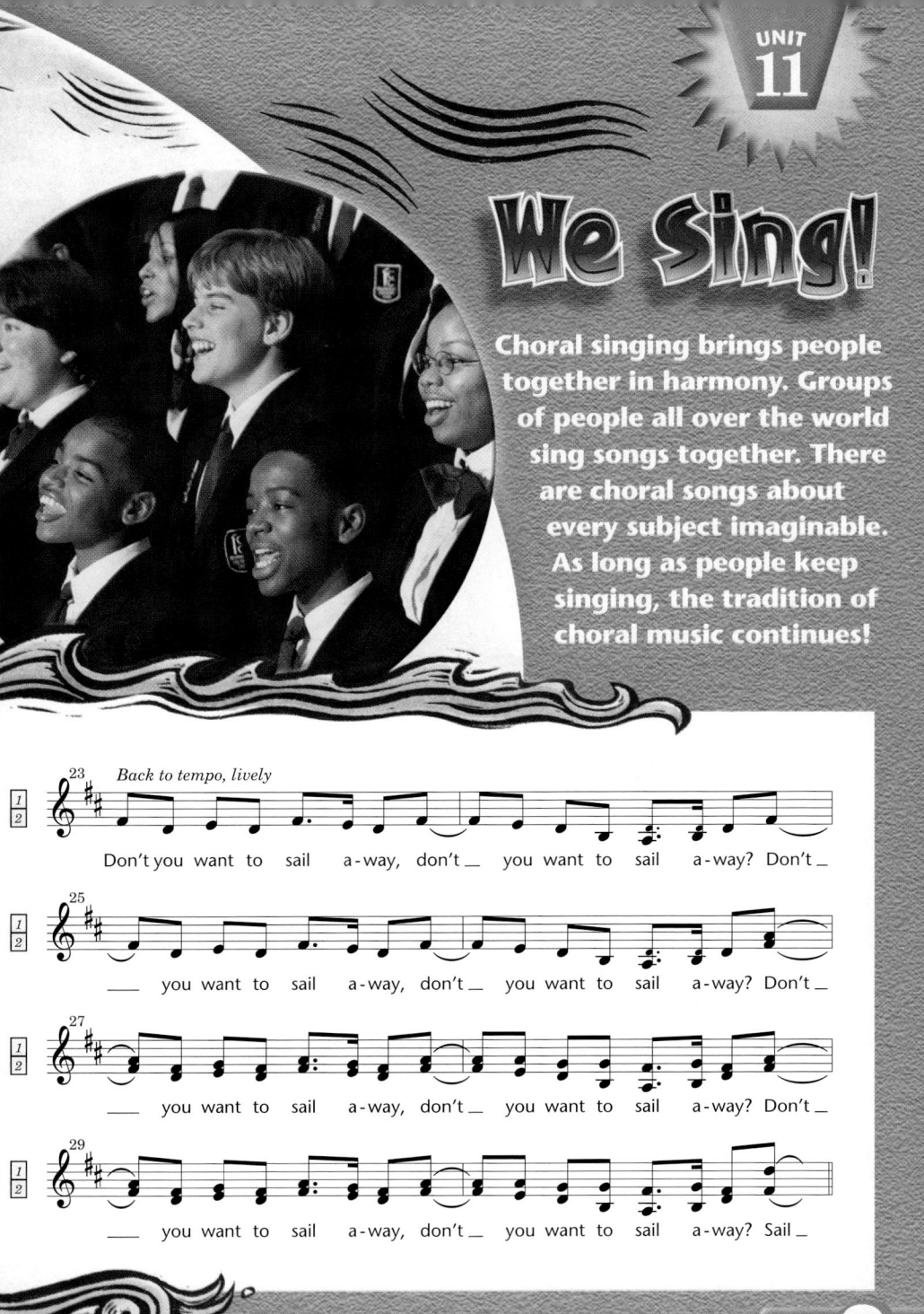

UNIT 11

We Sing!

Choral singing brings people together in harmony. Groups of people all over the world sing songs together. There are choral songs about every subject imaginable. As long as people keep singing, the tradition of choral music continues!

Unit 11 **405**

MUSIC SKILLS
ASSESSED IN THIS UNIT

Reading Music: Rhythm

- Read and clap rhythm patterns in a song (p. 411)
- Read and identify rhythm patterns in a song (p. 415)

Reading Music: Pitch

- Read and sing a song using pitch syllables (p. 443)
- Read and sing melodic phrases using pitch syllables (p. 416)

Performing Music: Singing

- Sing sections of a song with rhythmic and melodic accuracy (p. 413)
- Sing a freedom song (p. 417)
- Sing a patriotic song (p. 423)
- Sing a Spanish song about the conga (p. 429)
- Sing a Jewish folk song (p. 433)
- Perform a Spanish Christmas song (p. 438)
- Sing a Hawaiian song (p. 443)
- Perform a scat song in jazz style (p. 449)

Moving to Music

- Perform the conga (p. 428)
- Perform a Jewish folk dance (p. 432)

Performing Music: Playing

- Perform an accompaniment on nonpitched rhythm instruments (p. 412)
- Accompany a Spanish song (p. 437)

Creating Music

- Create ABA compositions (p. 422)
- Improvise consequent phrases (p. 441)

Listening to Music

- Listen to an orchestral selection (p. 422)
- Listen to a choral performance (p. 437)

CULTURAL CONNECTION

Unit Highlights The musical literature in this unit provides many opportunities for students to explore a variety of world cultures. See Unit at a Glance, pp. 403a–403f, for topical descriptions presented according to lesson sequence.

▶ **AFRICA**

- Learn facts about the Bantu language (p. 410)

▶ **AMERICAN REGIONAL**

- Explore facts about Hawaiian history and culture (p. 440)
- Read about the swing era of music (p. 447)

▶ **EUROPEAN**

- Discover facts about the clock Big Ben (p. 419)
- Learn about the white cliffs of Dover (p. 421)
- Read about the Cotswolds (p. 423)

- Explore information about Stonehenge (p. 425)
- Learn about the sixteenth century Renaissance (p. 435)

▶ **LATIN AMERICAN**

- Read about the conga drum (p. 426)

▶ **MIDDLE EASTERN**

- Explore facts about Jewish/Israeli culture (p. 431)

OPENING ACTIVITIES

MATERIALS	
• "Sail Away"	CD 11-20
Recording Routine:	
Intro (8 m.); vocal	

Discussing

Invite students to express their feelings about their desire to find adventure by sailing away to places unknown.

Unit Highlights This unit includes a variety of strategies and methods, described below, to track students' progress and assess their understanding of lesson objectives.

▶ **INFORMAL ASSESSMENTS**

At the close of each Teacher's Edition lesson in this unit, one of the following types of assessments is used to evaluate the learning of the key element focus or skill objective.

- Performance/Observation (p. 443)
- Performance/Peer Critique (pp. 413, 423, 433, 438)
- Performance/Self-Assessment (pp. 417, 429, 449)

Listening

Have students listen to the recording of "Sail Away" **CD 11-20** as they follow the score. They should be aware of the overall choral interpretation and the effect of tempo, phrasing, pronunciation of the words, harmony, and so on.

Unit 11 **407**

TECHNOLOGY/MEDIA LINK

Unit Highlights The following components are used in this unit to reinforce and expand students' understanding of music elements and related themes. See *Unit at a Glance*, pp. 403a–403f, for a descriptive listing according to lesson sequence.

▶ **CD-ROM**

- Arrange an accompaniment using *Band-in-a-Box* (p. 433)
- Practice scat singing using *Band-in-a-Box* (p. 451)

▶ **MIDI/SEQUENCING SOFTWARE**

- Arrange and record percussion parts (p. 413)
- Sing song parts with MIDI tracks (p. 417)
- Use a MIDI file to help students learn a song (pp. 425, 433, 439, 443)
- Isolate voice parts using a MIDI file (p. 429)

▶ **WEB SITE**

- Go to *www.sfsuccessnet.com* for more information about composer Gustav Holst (p. 425); Renaissance music (p. 439); dance, instruments, and music of Hawaii (p. 443)

Analyzing

Have students read through the lyrics of "Sail Away" and notice the use of nonsense syllables (vocables) in measures 50–55. Then as they look through the notation, have them point out the meter changes in the first four lines of music, which give a feel free to the music. The rest of the song is in duple meter, mainly $\frac{4}{4}$ meter.

Have students notice where the harmony part begins, the use of syncopation, the repeats, and other notational signs.

When the rhythm patterns and the melody and harmony parts have been learned, encourage students to perform this choral piece with the sense of freedom and abandon it suggests.

Encourage students to crisply enunciate the initial consonants of words such as *don't, you, want, to,* and *sail*.

LESSON AT A GLANCE

Element Focus **RHYTHM** Syncopated patterns

Skill Objective **SINGING** Sing syncopated patterns

Connection Activity **CULTURE** Explore Angolan culture and the music of southwestern Africa

MATERIALS

- "O, Desayo"   CD 18-22

   Recording Routine: Intro (8 m.); refrain; v. 1; refrain; v. 2; refrain; v. 3; refrain; coda

- rhythm sticks, tambourine, drum
- **Pronunciation Practice/Translation** p. 541
- **Resource Book** p. A-44

VOCABULARY

syncopation   descending intervals   refrain

verse   coda

◆ ◆ ◆ National Standards ◆ ◆ ◆ ◆

1a Sing accurately in small ensembles

1c Sing music from diverse cultures

2c Perform instrumental music from diverse cultures

4c Arrange, using electronic media

5a Read quarter, eighth, whole, and dotted notes in duple meter

6c Understand and use basic principles of pitch and rhythm in music analysis

7b Students use specific criteria for evaluating their own performances

8b Identify ways music relates to social studies

MORE MUSIC CHOICES

For more practice singing songs from Africa:

"*Funwa alafia*" ("Welcome, My Friends"), p. 32

"*Kokoleoko,*" p. 33

"*Kum ba yah,*" p. 244

"*Bantama kra kro,*" p. 308

A GREETING SONG

Nearly all cultures have songs to say hello and goodbye. "*O, Desayo*" is an Angolan "hello" song. In Angola, in southwestern Africa, Portuguese is the official language, but most Angolans speak Bantu. The word *menina* indicates "smallness" and in this song means "little girl."

Singing Tips

Look at the three syncopated rhythm patterns in the color boxes. Practice speaking each pattern before singing it. When you sing "*O, Desayo,*" separate *O* from *Desayo* with a tiny space of silence, and then accent the consonant *D*, of *Desayo,* to enhance the vocal expression of the syncopated rhythm.

Reading Music Tips

Before singing the song, practice the pitch patterns in measures 10–11. Practice speaking the rhythm patterns in the color boxes on a neutral syllable and then with the words of the song.

410

 Footnotes

CULTURAL CONNECTION

8b ▶ **Bantu** The language of Angola is Bantu. Sixty million people living in equatorial and southern Africa speak Bantu. The most widely spoken Bantu-derived language is Swahili, a language used by the various tribes to trade goods. In recent years, many Swahili songs have been brought to America. These songs have been included in concerts as part of the multicultural education of American students.

BUILDING SKILLS THROUGH MUSIC

▶ **Social Studies** Ask students to name non-English words that are used as greetings, for example *hola* (Spanish), *bon jour* (French), *guten Tag* (German), and so on. Have students perform "*O, Desayo*" and substitute any of the previously mentioned non-English greetings for the term *O, Desayo.*

SPOTLIGHT ON

8b ▶ **Angola** Angola is the third largest country in Sub-Saharan Africa. Although it is one of the poorest countries in the world, it has an abundance of natural resources, including iron ore and diamonds. Angolan dances and instruments, such as the marimba, were introduced to Latin America and the Caribbean as a result of the slave trade in the sixteenth and seventeenth centuries. Other popular instruments in this region of Africa include slit and skin drums, and several types of musical bow string instruments.

Knowing the Score

Music symbols and terms give you directions about how to sing the song. Find and discuss these symbols and terms: refrain, coda, and repeat signs. If you were drawing a map of how this song is to be performed, how would it look?

Sing a Greeting

Sing "O, Desayo," focusing on pitch and good breathing skills. Imagine that the pitch is an archery target and you are singing to the center of the bull's eye.

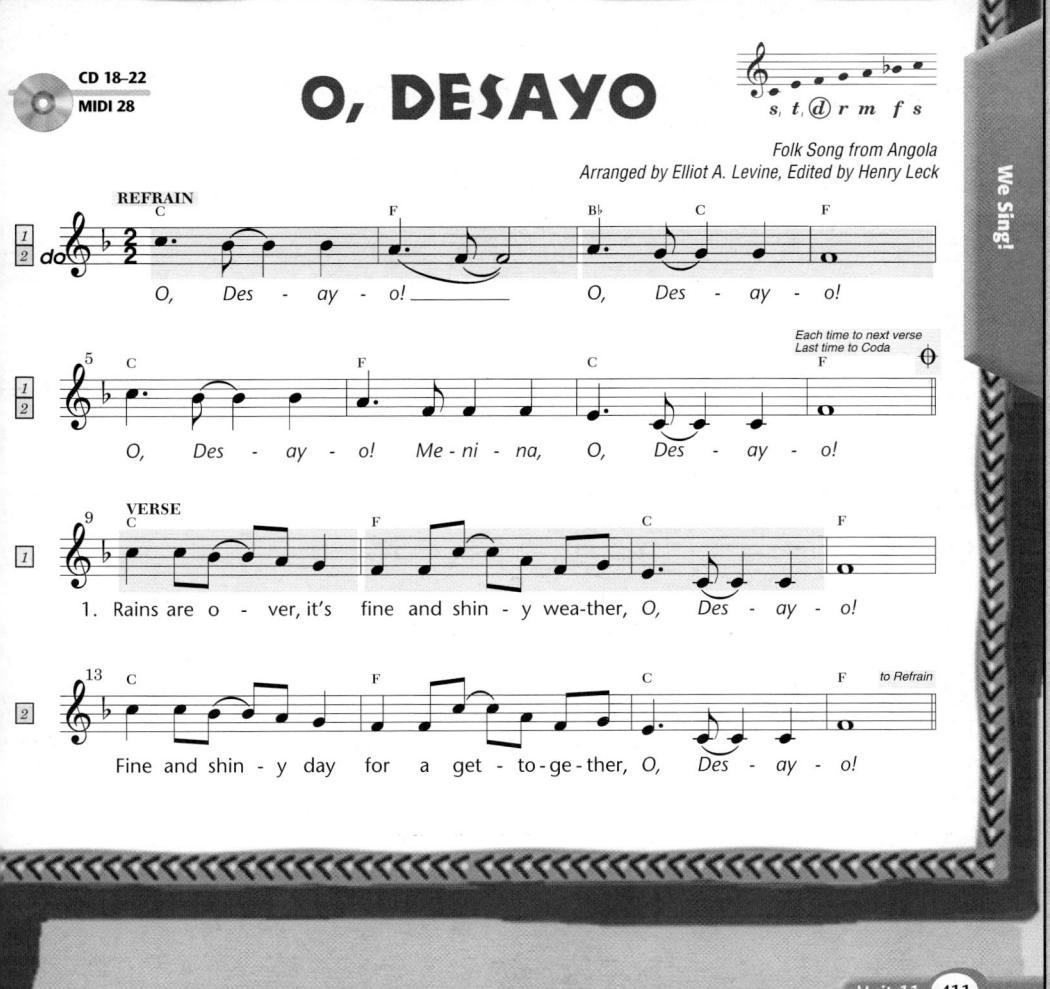

CD 18-22
MIDI 28

O, DESAYO

s₁ t₁ ⓓ r m f s

Folk Song from Angola
Arranged by Elliot A. Levine, Edited by Henry Leck

REFRAIN

O, Des - ay - o! _____ O, Des - ay - o!

Each time to next verse
Last time to Coda

O, Des - ay - o! Me - ni - na, O, Des - ay - o!

VERSE

1. Rains are o - ver, it's fine and shin - y wea - ther, O, Des - ay - o!

to Refrain

Fine and shin - y day for a get - to - ge - ther, O, Des - ay - o!

Unit 11 **411**

1 INTRODUCE

8b Discuss how students might greet each other before school in the halls and on the street. ("Hello," "Hi," "What's up?," "What's happening?," and so on.) Explain that "O, Desayo" is a greeting song from the African country of Angola. Share with students the information in Spotlight On and Cultural Connection, p. 410.

2 DEVELOP

Listening

Play the recording of "O, Desayo" **CD 18-22**.

ASK How many times is *menina* **("little girl") greeted each time the refrain is sung?** (four times in the Bantu language)

1c Share the literal translation of "O, Desayo" on p. 541. Teach students the Bantu words using the Pronunciation Practice Track **CD 18-24** and Resource Book p. A-44. When students are comfortable with the song, have them sing with the recording **CD 18-22**.

Reading

5a Have students

- Clap the rhythm patterns in mm. 1–8.
- Discuss where and how the syncopated rhythm patterns occur.
- Speak the text in rhythm for mm. 1–8.
- Clap and speak the rhythm patterns in mm. 9–16 using rhythm syllables.
6c
- Discuss where and how the syncopated rhythm patterns occur.
- Speak the text in rhythm for mm. 9–16.
- Read the text of the song in rhythm.

continued on page 412

TEACHER TO TEACHER

1a ▶ **Song Form** "O, Desayo" is a good example of a song with refrain, verse, and coda. The song's format offers an opportunity for students to perform "O, Desayo," emphasizing these musical characteristics. Have the girls sing bars 1–4 of the refrain and the boys bars 5–8. Repeat the refrain with the entire class. The verse can be sung by a soloist or by a few voices, followed by the same rendition of the refrain.

SKILLS REINFORCEMENT

6c ▶ **Performing** Use the following teaching suggestions to help students perform syncopated rhythms.

Reinforcement Some students may have difficulty performing syncopated rhythms. Have them clap a moderately-slow four-beat rhythm pattern while speaking "one AND, two AND."

On Target Most students will be able to perform syncopated rhythms. If they encounter problems, ask them to use the suggestion described above.

Challenge Invite interested students to create a body movement that emphasizes the syncopated accent.

Lesson 1 Continued

Singing

"O, Desayo" has a descending pattern of *so-fa-mi-re-do*. Create warm-ups by having students sing these intervals on the vowel *o*. Encourage students to listen carefully for in-tune singing.

Have students

- Sing the pitch syllables for mm. 7–8, 11–12, and 15–16. (The pitches and rhythms are the same for each pair of measures.)

- Sing the pitch syllables for mm. 1–2 and 5–6. (The pitches are the same but with a slight rhythmic variance.)

- Sing the pitch syllables for mm. 9–10 and 13–14. (The pitch and rhythms are the same.)

- Sing the entire song using pitch syllables and then the text.

Remind students of the singing tips presented on p. 410 in their books.

Playing

The syncopation of "O, Desayo" makes this song interesting and fun to sing.

Have half the class clap the rhythm of mm. 1–8 while the other half taps rhythm sticks to measures 9–16.

Repeat this exercise and assign several students to speak the Bantu and English text along with the clapping and stick tapping.

Performing

Have students

- Sing "O, Desayo" **CD 18-22** using rhythm sticks, tambourine, and drum.

- Include shoulder movements to match the rhythm of the melody.

Ninga drummers from Burundi, West Africa, in traditional dress ▶

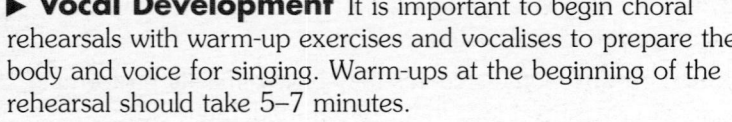

412

Footnotes

SKILLS REINFORCEMENT

 ▶ **Vocal Development** It is important to begin choral rehearsals with warm-up exercises and vocalises to prepare the body and voice for singing. Warm-ups at the beginning of the rehearsal should take 5–7 minutes.

Try the following sequence.

- Stretches (knees, neck, shoulder, arms, jaw).
- Breathing exercises (deep breathing, support, and control).
- Resonance and placement (hums, whirlies, glissandi, middle register vocalises using *m* and *n*).
- Range and agility (arpeggios and short scale passages).

TEACHER TO TEACHER

▶ **Vocalises** Use the following references for vocalises for young choirs.

- *Teaching Kids to Sing* by K. H. Phillips (Wadsworth, 1996)
- *Successful Warmups* by N. Telfer (Neil A. Kjos Music Co., 1995)
- *Group Vocal Technique* by J. Jordan and F. Haasemann (Hinshaw Music, 1992)

3 CLOSE

Element: RHYTHM — **ASSESSMENT**

1a **Performance/Peer Critique** Ask the boys to sing mm. 1–8 of *"O, Desayo"* and have the girls evaluate the rhythmic and melodic accuracy of their singing.

Ask the girls to sing mm. 9–16 and have the boys evaluate their musical accuracy.

1c Divide the class in half and have each half sing *"O, Desayo."* Have students listen for and discuss
7b rhythmic and melodic accuracy.

Ask students to evaluate

- Precision of the syncopated patterns.
- Clarity of enunciation.
- In-tune singing.

We Sing!

SKILLS REINFORCEMENT

2c ▶ **Playing** Invite students to play the following percussion parts as an ostinato to accompany *"O, Desayo."*

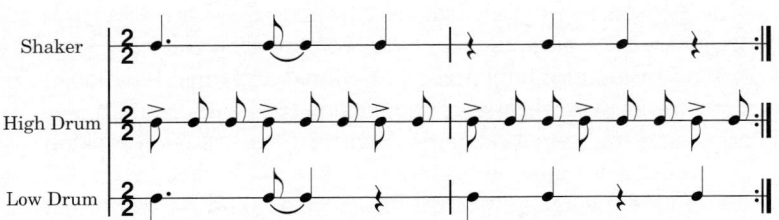

TECHNOLOGY/MEDIA LINK

4c **MIDI/Sequencing Software** After singing *"O, Desayo,"* have students

- Explore General MIDI percussion voices on the classroom keyboard.
- Arrange and record their own percussion parts for the song using the classroom computer, keyboard, and MIDI sequencing software.
- Sing the piece with various combinations of student percussion tracks.

LESSON AT A GLANCE

Element Focus   FORM Phrase and section repetition

Skill Objective   SINGING Sing repeated phrases and sections with expressive variation

Connection Activity   SOCIAL STUDIES Discuss the history of apartheid in South Africa

MATERIALS

- "Freedom Is Coming"   **CD 18-25**

  Recording Routine: Intro (2 m.); vocal; coda

VOCABULARY

repeat signs   pick-up

first and second endings

◆ ◆ ◆ ◆ National Standards ◆ ◆ ◆ ◆

1c Sing music from diverse cultures
1d Sing music written in three parts
1e In groups, sing moderately easy pieces with technical accuracy
5e In performance classes, sightread easy music accurately and expressively
6b Listen and analyze uses of pitch, rhythm, harmony, dynamics
8b Identify ways music relates to social studies

MORE MUSIC CHOICES

For more practice singing freedom songs:

"This Train," p. 27

"Joshua Fought the Battle of Jericho," p. 101

"Go Down, Moses," p. 190

"Oh, Freedom," p. 392

A Song of FREEDOM

Whenever groups of people have their liberties limited, they have developed songs that speak of their longing for freedom. "Freedom Is Coming" grew out of people's frustration with *apartheid,* a national policy of racial segregation once associated with South Africa.

Singing Tips

"Freedom Is Coming" can be sung while walking. Use good breathing skills and vowel shapes to help you sing with good intonation. When singing the word *freedom*, accent the first syllable.

Listen carefully to your fellow singers to maintain good blend within parts and good balance between voice parts.

Reading Music Tips

Read the shaded rhythm patterns in part 1 by clapping and speaking. Then sing them with words. **Read** and practice the shaded rhythm pattern in part 2.

Knowing the Score

Identify and discuss the purpose of repeat signs and the markings for ending 1 and ending 2. How many times is each section sung? Describe how the closing bar (or end bar) looks. How is it different from a repeat sign?

▲ *Peaceful Protest* by John Roome

Footnotes

ACROSS THE CURRICULUM

8b ▶ **Social Studies** The word *apartheid* means "separateness." In 1948, the Afrikaner-dominated party implemented the policy of apartheid. The result was a forced separation between whites and nonwhites, between Africans and other nonwhites, between one African ethnic group and all other African ethnic groups, and between rural and urban Africans. In 1994, apartheid was finally set aside, an event that inspired songs such as "Freedom Is Coming."

BUILDING SKILLS THROUGH MUSIC

▶ **Art** Ask students to look at the art examples on pp. 414–417 and describe the ideas represented. Have them identify concepts of line, color, texture, and shape that are common to the five examples. Lead students in a discussion on why each example portrays freedom.

SPOTLIGHT ON

▶ **South Africa** A one-word description of the Republic of South Africa would be "diverse." Located on the southern tip of Africa, it has nine provinces with 11 official languages. These include Afrikaans, English, Ndebele, Sepedi, Sesotho, Swazi, Tsonga, Tswana, and Zulu. It has three capitals (Pretoria, Cape Town, and Bloemfontein) and five national anthems. Religious groups are likewise diverse. They include Christian, Muslim, Hindus, and traditional religions. South Africa has been making good progress in many areas, such as health, literacy, and social justice. Life expectancy is up to 56.29 years, and 81.8% of the people over 15 can read and write. In addition, since 1994, there have been multiracial elections. In fact, a new flag was made to celebrate that event.

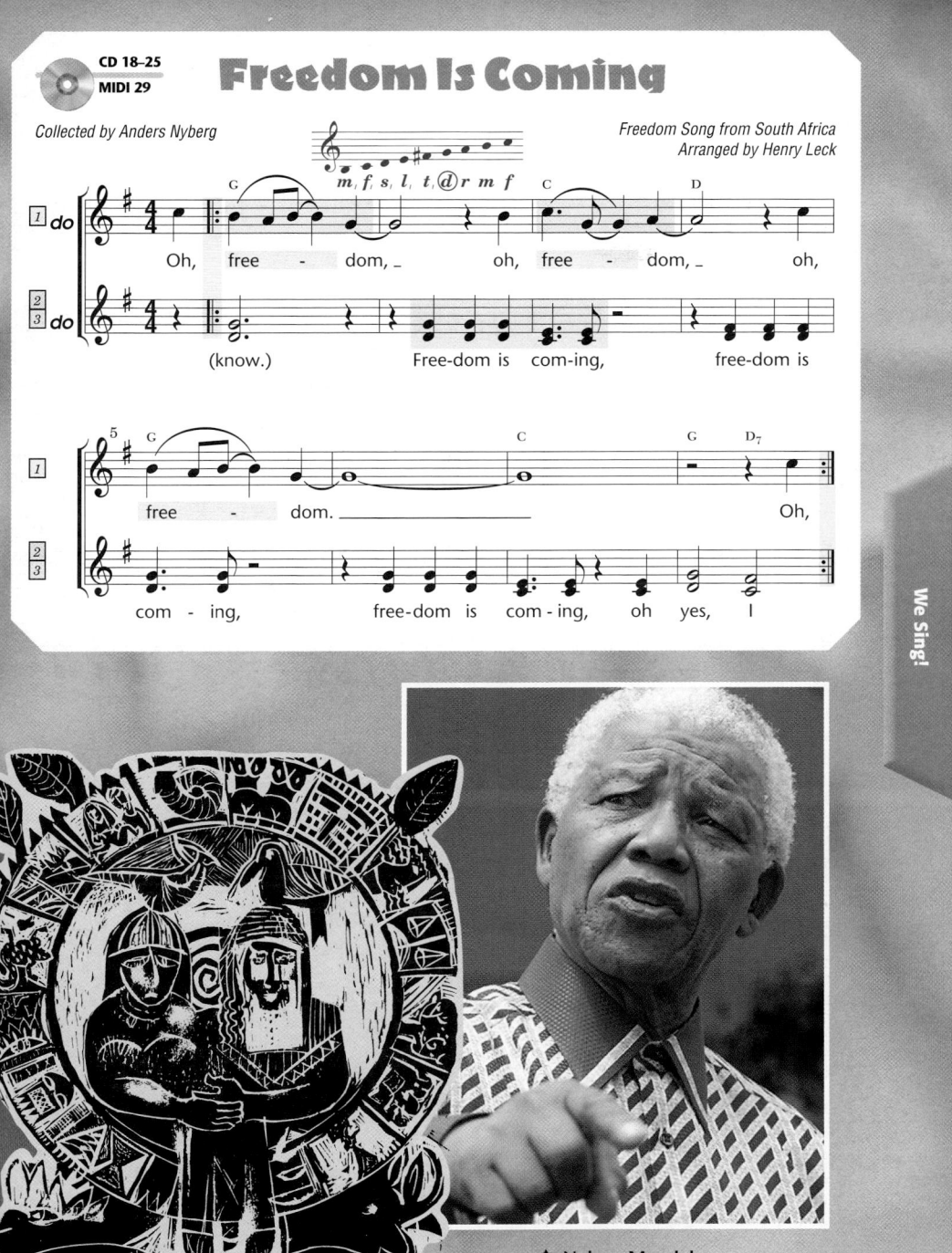

CD 18–25
MIDI 29

Freedom Is Coming

Collected by Anders Nyberg

Freedom Song from South Africa
Arranged by Henry Leck

Oh, free - dom, _ oh, free - dom, _ oh,

(know.) Free-dom is com-ing, free-dom is

free - dom. _____ Oh,

com - ing, free-dom is com - ing, oh yes, I

▲ A Fair Deal, woodcut
by Margaret Gradwell

▲ Nelson Mandela

We Sing!

Unit 11 415

1 INTRODUCE

Lead a discussion in the definition of freedom.

ASK What freedoms do we enjoy everyday in the United States?

SAY The founders of our country believed that all citizens are entitled to life, liberty, and the pursuit of happiness.

ASK What would it be like to have those liberties taken away? (We would feel trapped into living the life someone else told us we had to live.)

See Spotlight On and Across the Curriculum, p. 414 for information on apartheid and South Africa today.

2 DEVELOP

Listening

Play the recording of the first section of "Freedom Is Coming" **CD 18-25.**

ASK How many times is the phrase *Oh, freedom* sung? (six times)

Do the harmony parts move at the beginning of each phrase or at the end? (the end)

Reading

Tap the rhythm of the opening phrases *Oh, freedom, Oh, freedom.* Then play the complete recording of the song.

ASK Where do those two different rhythm patterns occur elsewhere in the music? (mm. 9–13, with slight variation; 17–21; 25–28)

Point out that in each example, there is a pick-up note (upbeat) in the preceding measure.

continued on page 416

SKILLS REINFORCEMENT

▶ **Singing** The phrase *Oh, freedom* should be sung by expressing surprise on *O*, then by pressing the upper teeth to the lower lips, creating a friction-like sound on the *F* of *freedom*. The first quarter note on *freedom* should be sung with a *crescendo* through the two eighth notes and quarter note (beats 2 and 3). The final *m* on the *dom* of *freedom* should be released on beat 3 (the quarter rest) by pitching the *m* in the rest beat. For rhythmic expression on the word *is*, create a tiny separation between *freedom* and *is*, emphasizing the initial vowel of *is*. Put vocal energy on the *c* of "coming" to achieve rhythmic sparkle. On *Oh yes, I know*, imagine that the notes for these words are pasted together so there is no stopping of sound. Sing the words smoothly (*legato*), creating vocal weight on each word.

TEACHER TO TEACHER

▶ **Performance Tips** "Freedom Is Coming" is a spirited song created by South Africans who believed that if and when Nelson Mandela would be freed from his island jail, they would be free. This song makes an excellent processional for a concert. Originally, the song was not written down, which means that the students do not have to take the notation literally. It would not have been uncommon for the singer to sing the refrain over and over, repetition being a form of musical expression. It is important that the students sing this song with vitality, feeling absolute joy for each word. The more expression they show on their faces, the more likely they will capture the essence and intent of "Freedom Is Coming."

Unit 11 *We Sing!* 415

Lesson 2 Continued

Have students

- Sing the pitch syllables for the *Oh, freedom, Oh, freedom* opening phrases.

1e

- Sing the pitch syllables for mm. 9–12, 17–20, and 25–28. (Notice that they are all the same.)

- Count how many repeat signs occur in the song and determine when to sing the second ending.

Singing

SAY The syncopation of the phrases gives this song its unique character.

1e Invite the class to sing the pitch syllables of the melody and then the words. When singing *freedom* be sure the upper teeth make contact with the lower lip for the consonant *F.* There should be a slight rush of air on the *F,* which will enhance a strong downbeat.

The second half of the second beat of *freedom* should be accented to bring out the syncopated rhythm.

1d All the harmony notes should be sung with a slight accentuation.

5e Performing

This song can be sung with many repeats. It could begin softly and become gradually louder and then gradually softer.

Have students perform the song *a cappella,* with added hand-clapping as the song gets increasingly louder.

The song could be used as a processional, bringing the choir into the auditorium to begin a concert. The processional could begin with one voice, and with each repetition, more voices could be added.

8b "Freedom Is Coming" might be part of a larger program of songs, especially during Black History Month.

Invite students to create costumes and incorporate classroom instruments when appropriate.

▲ *Life* **by William Zulu**

▲ *Freedom of religion, belief and opinion* **by Dina Cormick**

416

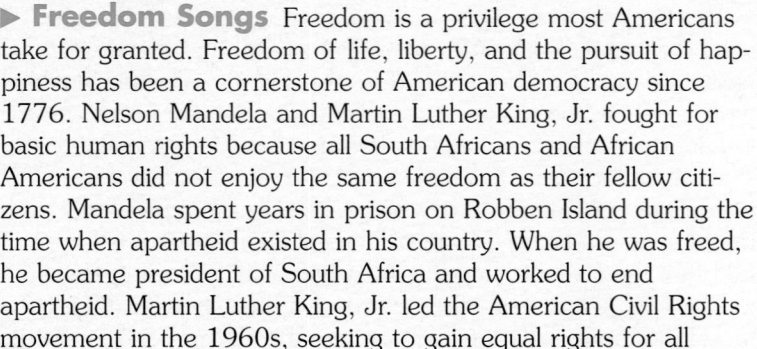

SPOTLIGHT ON

▶ **Freedom Songs** Freedom is a privilege most Americans take for granted. Freedom of life, liberty, and the pursuit of happiness has been a cornerstone of American democracy since 1776. Nelson Mandela and Martin Luther King, Jr. fought for basic human rights because all South Africans and African Americans did not enjoy the same freedom as their fellow citizens. Mandela spent years in prison on Robben Island during the time when apartheid existed in his country. When he was freed, he became president of South Africa and worked to end apartheid. Martin Luther King, Jr. led the American Civil Rights movement in the 1960s, seeking to gain equal rights for all African Americans.

MEETING INDIVIDUAL NEEDS

▶ **Inclusion** Some students may not be able to identify the repeat signs in the songs. You may want to color code these sections for students. Alternatively, you may want to write out the text of the song in exactly the order you want students to sing.

spir - it __ knows.

My

Oh,

knows, my spir - it knows, my spir - it

free - dom, __ oh, free - dom, __ oh,

know(s). Free-dom is com - ing, free-dom is

free - dom. __ Oh, __

com-ing, free-dom is com-ing, oh yes, I yes, I know.

We Sing!

▲ *Freedom and Security of the Person* by James Mphahlele

3 CLOSE

Element: FORM   **ASSESSMENT**

6b **Performance/Self-Assessment** Play the recording of "Freedom Is Coming" **CD 18-25.** Have students

- Follow the score, observing all repeat signs and endings.
- Discuss the vocal quality and style of the singers.
- Listen for the balance between the melody (part 1) and harmony (parts 2 and 3).
- Listen for dynamic contrast.

Then have students

1c
- Sing the song, following the repeat signs and endings.
- Compare their performance with the recorded performance.
- Discuss with students how the song has influenced their ideas and feelings about freedom.

ACROSS THE CURRICULUM

8b ▶ **Social Studies** Ask students to write about the freedoms they experience every day. Have them compare these freedoms to the freedom of past generations. Have students make a chart showing the development of freedom in this country. Then write down what they think America, their town or city, neighborhood, and school is doing in continuing the challenge to work toward freedom and brotherhood for all.

TECHNOLOGY/MEDIA LINK

1e **MIDI/Sequencing Software** Use the classroom computer, keyboard, and MIDI sequencing software to create a learning center for the song "Freedom Is Coming." Before class begins, record each of the song's voices onto a separate track using MIDI sequencing software. Remind students how to turn off and turn on individual tracks for MIDI playback. Divide the class into small groups and have them

- Listen to the entire MIDI tracks together while following their part in the book.
- Listen to their assigned parts alone.
- Sing their parts with the group's MIDI track.
- Sing their parts with all of the MIDI tracks together.

LESSON AT A GLANCE

Element Focus FORM aba form

Skill Objective SINGING Sing with expression a patriotic choral arrangement in aba form

Connection Activity SOCIAL STUDIES Discuss the meaning and symbols of patriotism

MATERIALS

- "I Vow to You, My Country" **CD 18-27**
  Recording Routine: Intro (5 m.); v. 1; interlude (3 m.); v. 2
- *The Planets,* "Jupiter" **CD 18-29**

VOCABULARY

upbeat   key change   phrase   enunciation
aba form

◆ ◆ ◆ ◆ National Standards ◆ ◆ ◆ ◆

1b Sing easy pieces with technical accuracy and expression

1d Sing music written in two parts

4a Compose short pieces demonstrating unity and variety through music

5c Identify standard notation symbols for pitch and rhythm

6a Listen and describe events in music using appropriate terms

6b Listen and analyze uses of form, timbre, pitch, rhythm in music from diverse genres

7b Students use specific criteria for evaluating their own performances

8b Identify ways music relates to social studies, science, and language arts

MORE MUSIC CHOICES

For more practice singing patriotic songs:

"America, the Beautiful," p. 76

"This Land Is Your Land," p. 118

"America," p. 486

"The Star-Spangled Banner," p. 488

A Pledge of Loyalty

This patriotic melody has become one of the most cherished in England. The lyrics speak of love for one's country. It was sung at Princess Diana's wedding and again at her funeral.

Singing Tips

Each verse of "I Vow to You, My Country" has three sections: **a** **b** **a**. Each section, in turn, is made up of two phrases. **Sing** the phrases *legato* on the syllable *noo* to achieve a flowing phrase line. Focus on good breathing skills to sing with accuracy and expression.

Reading Music Tips

Many measures in this song contain dotted rhythm patterns. Look in measure 7 and speak the rhythm pattern using rhythm syllables. **Identify** other dotted rhythms in the song.

Knowing the Score

The keyboard accompaniment for this song is included in your book. In which measures does the keyboard play alone?

CD 18–27
MIDI 30

I Vow to You, My Country

Words by Sir Cecil Spring-Rice

Melody by Gustav Holst
Arranged by R. Osborne

With emotion

Keyboard

418

Footnotes

ACROSS THE CURRICULUM

8b ▶ **Social Studies** One patriotic melody shared by the United States and Great Britain is "America." The hymn was first published in London in 1745 as "God Save the King"—the British national anthem. In 1832, Samuel Francis Smith came across the melody in a music book for German public schools, and was inspired to write the words that have become a permanent part of our national identity.

BUILDING SKILLS THROUGH MUSIC

▶ **Reading** Ask students to share what the lesson title "A Pledge of Loyalty" means to them. Then ask them to listen to "I Vow to You, My Country" **CD 18-27** while following the text. Have students identify words or phrases that correspond to those on the list of student suggestions.

TEACHER TO TEACHER

▶ **Keyboard Accompaniment** The introduction of "I Vow to You, My Country" is in the accompaniment, which presents the main theme of the song. It is important for the singers to listen to the theme to get their starting pitch and to feel the tempo that is set by the accompanist. The introduction also provides the singers with a sense of the style and rhythmic character of the main theme. When the singers begin to sing, the chords played by the accompanist support many of their pitches. When the voices divide into two-part singing in canonlike fashion, the keyboard part mirrors the voice parts, helping the choir to sustain correct intonation and rhythmic accuracy. Encourage students to examine the entire accompaniment to see how it supports the voice parts.

1. I___ vow to you, my coun-try, all

1. I___ vow to you, my coun-try, all

earth-ly things a - bove, En - tire and whole and per - fect, the

earth-ly things a - bove, En - tire and whole and per - fect, the

Westminster Abbey ▼

Houses of Parliament ▼

◀ **Big Ben**

1 INTRODUCE

Lead a discussion about the meaning of national pride and patriotism.

ASK When have you experienced patriotic feelings? (during a parade, during the singing of the National Anthem at a sports event, at the fireworks on July 4, when we see the flag blowing in the breeze, and so on.)

Have students list patriotic symbols. (the eagle, the American flag)

2 DEVELOP

Listening

Play the recording of "I Vow to You, My Country" **CD 18-27.**

Invite students to write down the words that could be considered "vow words" *(earthly things, service of my love, the love that asks no questions,* and so on). Have students raise their hands when they hear a key change (mm. 33–34).

6a ASK Why did the arranger write a key change at this point in the song? (It leads into the last verse of the song.)

Analyzing

6b Have students focus on verse 1 and find

- The a section (mm. 6–14).
- The b section (mm. 14–22).
- The a section (mm. 22–30).

5c ASK How many full measures are there in the introduction? (five measures)

How many measures are there in each phrase in this song? (four measures)

continued on page 420

SKILLS REINFORCEMENT

1b ▶ Vocal Development To create a warm, resonant sound, have students sing all the phrases on the vowel O. The lips should be fully rounded and the space inside the mouth big enough to accommodate the large end of an ice cream cone. Now sing the text with the feeling of the O mouth position to achieve the same vocal color. Words and syllables that have dotted quarter notes *(vow, entire, love)* should be sung with a slight *crescendo,* giving a forward, energetic flow to the music. When singing words set to a dotted eighth note followed by a sixteenth *(you, whole, lays, never),* separate the two notes with a wafer-thin silence. Imagine that the sixteenth note goes in the direction of the music and is attached to the note that follows it. Think of each phrase as being in the shape of a rainbow—*crescendo* to the top and then *decrescendo* to the bottom.

CULTURAL CONNECTION

▶ Big Ben One of England's most famous landmarks, the famous clock known as Big Ben, is located in the Palace of Westminster in London. (See the illustration above.) The four dials of the clock are 23 feet in diameter. The minute hand is 14 feet long, and the numbers are each two feet high. A light shining above the clock face signals when Parliament is in session.

Technically, the name Big Ben does not refer to either the clock or the clock tower. It refers only to the 13-ton bell inside the tower that strikes the hours. Named for the first commissioner of works, Sir Benjamin Hall, the bell was originally located in the Palace of Westminster. It was given to the Dean of St. Paul's by William III but returned to Westminster in 1858 after being refashioned in Whitechapel.

Lesson 3 Continued

SAY Each phrase begins with an upbeat.

ASK On what note does the upbeat appear in the first phrase of the A section? *(the note D)* In the B section? *(the note F)*

Ask students to identify the term and symbol referring to tempo found on p. 58. *(rit.)*

Then ask them to identify a symbol referring to articulation. *(slur)* Write the following three terms on the board: *legato, staccato,* and *marcato.* Ask students to identify the term referring to articulation, that describes how a slur should be performed. *(legato)*

Describing

SAY The instructions for singing this song are "With emotion."

ASK What are other words for "emotion"? *(feeling, excitement, empathy, compassion, passion, enthusiasm, and so on)*

Have one or more students read the text of the song aloud, emphasizing the verbs, adjectives, and nouns.

 (Hint: More vocal weight should be placed on the "emotion" words when speaking and singing them.)

ASK When singing this song, what vocal timbre (quality of voice) should be used? *(strong and confident)*

Listening

Have students

6b
- Listen again to the recording **CD 18-27** and analyze the vocal quality of the children's singing.
- Become familiar with the rhythm of the first full measure of the song.
- Clap the rhythm as a group and find that same rhythm in other places within the song.
- Clap that rhythm again, this time speaking the words for only that measure along with the clapping.
- Do the same for other measures in the song with that same rhythm.

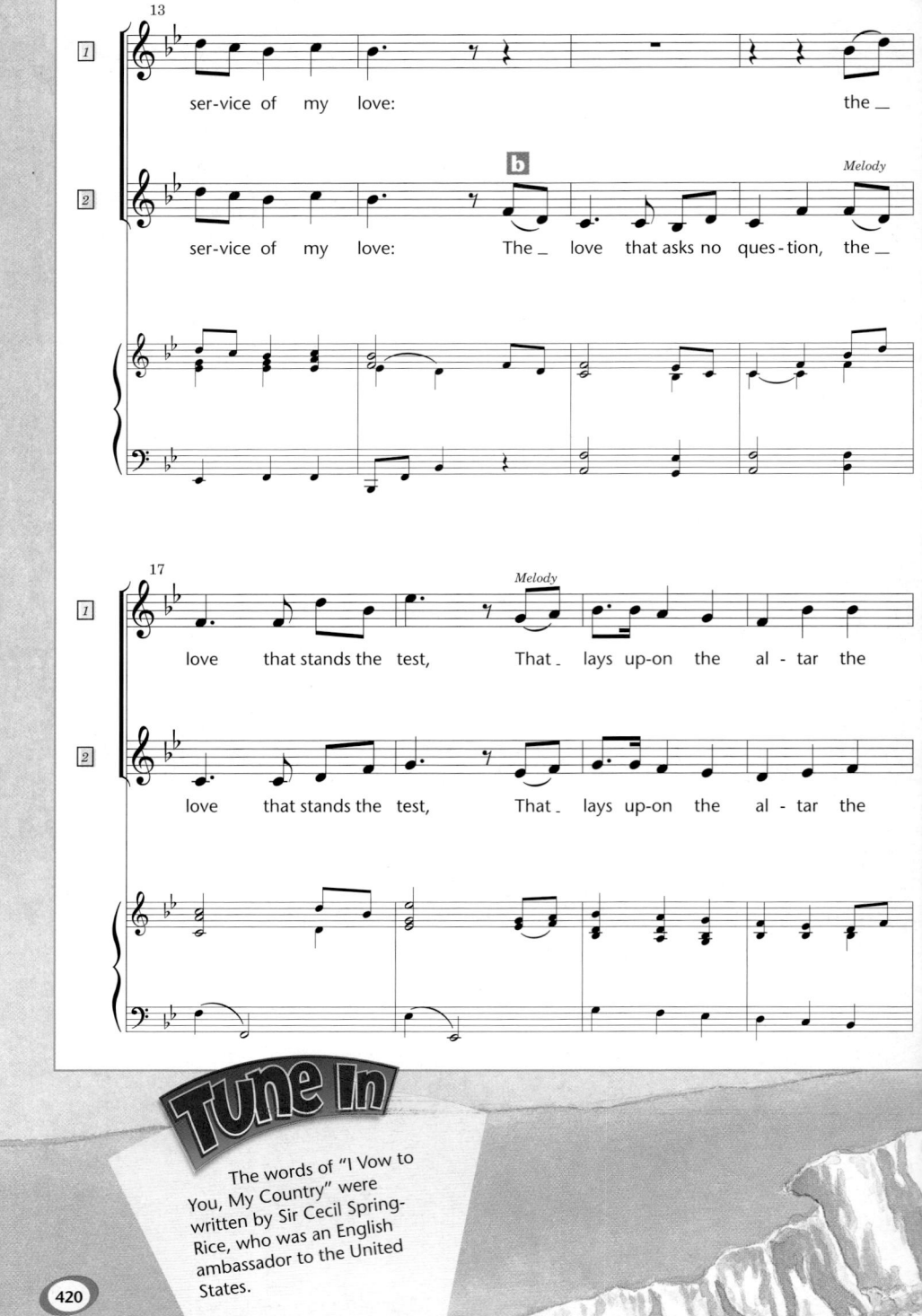

 Tune In

The words of "I Vow to You, My Country" were written by Sir Cecil Spring-Rice, who was an English ambassador to the United States.

420

Footnotes

CHARACTER EDUCATION

▶ **Patriotism** To help students understand patriotism, have them identify three people they view as patriotic and discuss the patriotic behaviors these individuals exhibit. Ask students to consult with three other people (parents, teachers, friends) about patriotism and compile a list of words describing patriotic behaviors. Compare and contrast students' lists, discussing those behaviors that show national pride.

ACROSS THE CURRICULUM

8b ▶ **Language Arts** Ask students to write a paragraph about their pride in being an American. Ask "What does freedom mean to you? What freedoms and rights do you have that people in other places of the world may not have? What is unique about America? What do you love about your town or city? What makes our homeland home?"

Pair selections from student writings with photographs, slides, or other visual technology to illustrate America and its diversity of people and customs.

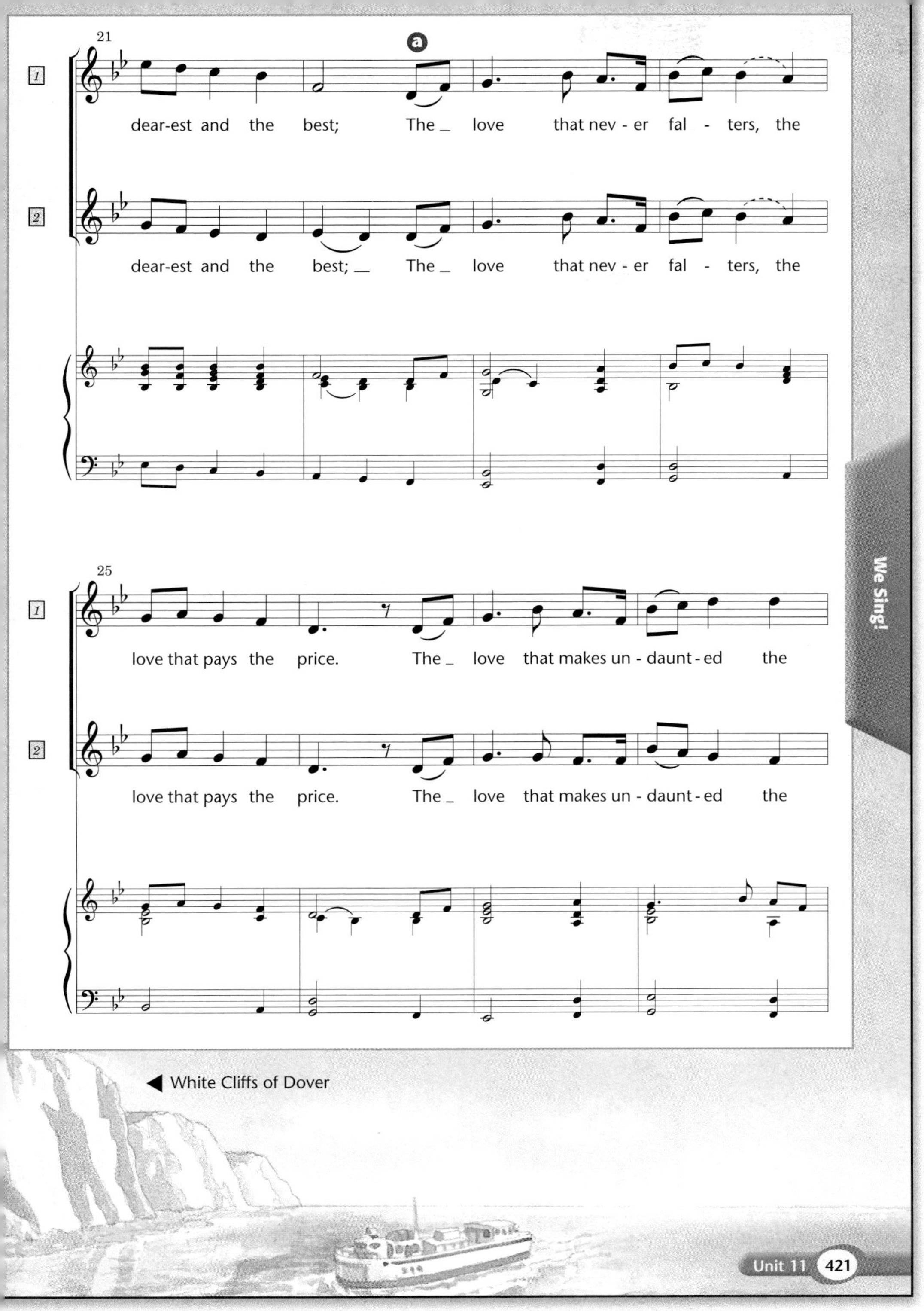

dear-est and the best; The __ love that nev - er fal - ters, the

dear-est and the best; __ The __ love that nev - er fal - ters, the

love that pays the price. The __ love that makes un - daunt - ed the

love that pays the price. The __ love that makes un - daunt - ed the

◀ White Cliffs of Dover

ASK **What do you notice about voices 1 and 2 from mm. 6–14?** (They are exactly the same, or in unison.)

What happens beginning with beat 3 of m. 14? (Voices 1 and 2 sing independently through the rest of the song, except in mm. 51–54.)

Singing

Have students sing voice part 1 along with the recording. When they are comfortable with that, have them sing voice part 2 along with the recording.

Divide the class in half and have one half sing voice part 1, and the other half sing voice part 2.

Have students switch voice parts and sing the entire song one more time.

Have students look at the last three notes of the song.

ASK **What interval are the two parts singing?** (They are singing the interval of a third.)

Have students practice all parts of the song that seem to be more difficult. Switch voice parts so that all students have ample opportunity to learn the tune and build their confidence.

continued on page 422

SKILLS REINFORCEMENT

▶ **Vocal Development** Singing long phrases requires a good supply of air in the lungs. To prepare for a deep, full breath, execute a long sigh, letting all the air out of the lungs. Now imagine you are about to dive into a swimming pool with the intention of swimming under water all the way to the other end of the pool. Slowly breathe in through your nose, imagining that your lungs are like a paper bag that needs to be completely filled. Close your eyes and swim under the imagined water for five seconds. Repeat the exercise adding a second at a time until you reach 10 to 12 seconds. Now take a deep breath and slowly release it for five seconds, then six seconds, and continue until you can do it for 10 to 12 seconds. Read one phrase of the song in one breath and then read two phrases in one breath. Now sing each phrase in a single breath.

CULTURAL CONNECTION

▶ **White Cliffs of Dover** A powerful image, England's white cliffs of Dover (illustrated above) have been immortalized in movie and song. Located in the southeast corner of Kent, the cliffs are only 20 miles from the European continent. A visitor to Dover could enjoy walking on the cliffs while watching one of the busiest waterways in the world.

The cliffs, however, are quite fragile. Made of soft white chalk, they are easily fissured by wind and water. Many tons of chalk have already collapsed. Scientists debate whether to protect the cliffs from nature.

Creating

8b Encourage students to find poems about pride and patriotism.

4a Have students create a composition in ABA form. Consider including one or more of the compositions on a concert program.

Performing

"I Vow to You, My Country" would be a wonderful selection for a patriotic program. Students could prepare slides of American scenery, national monuments, fireworks, flags, and so on. A slide show could be shown before the program or while the music is being sung. A map of the United States could be projected against the back wall of the stage. Small American flags could be held by the choir or placed around the stage.

Listening

6b Play the recording of *Jupiter* **CD 18-29** from Holst's suite *The Planets.* Point out to students that this piece is the origin of the melody used in "I Vow to You, My Country."

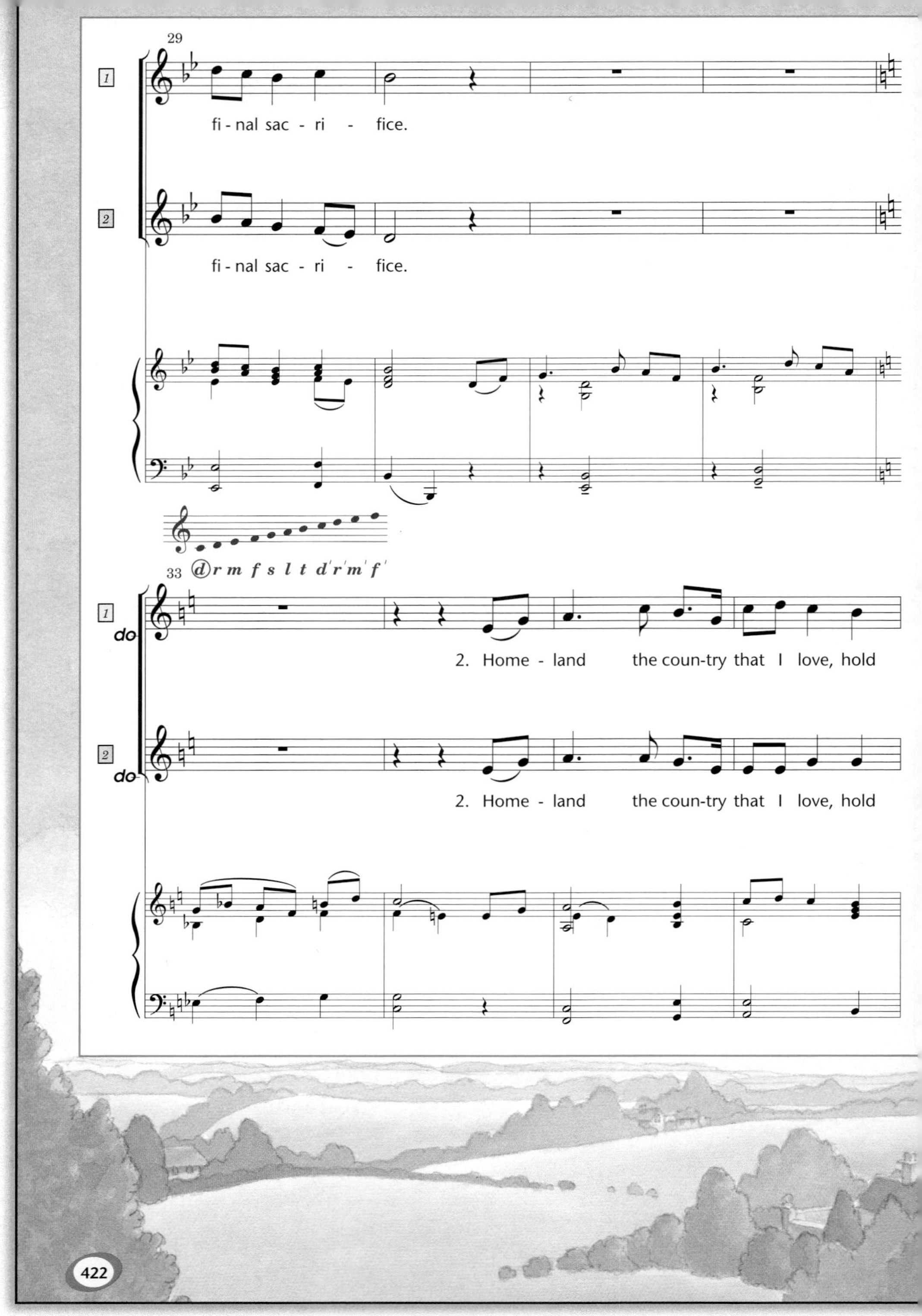

Footnotes

AUDIENCE ETIQUETTE

▶ **School Assemblies** School assemblies provide excellent opportunities for practicing and reinforcing audience behavior. Encourage students to

- Be attentive to their personal space, and respect the space of others.
- Use good eye contact and look attentively at the speakers or performers.
- Be active listeners. Concentrate and think about what they hear.
- Show appreciation by clapping at the appropriate time.

TEACHER TO TEACHER

▶ **Lyrics** Too often when choirs sing, they do not understand or think about what the words to a song mean. What ideas are being expressed and what feelings should the singers seek to draw from the audience? To help students become aware of the impact of song text,

- Invite the drama teacher to expressively read the song text to the students.
- Invite the English teacher to explain the power and purpose of the words in the song text that carry the meaning.
- Play recordings of songs that are expressively performed.

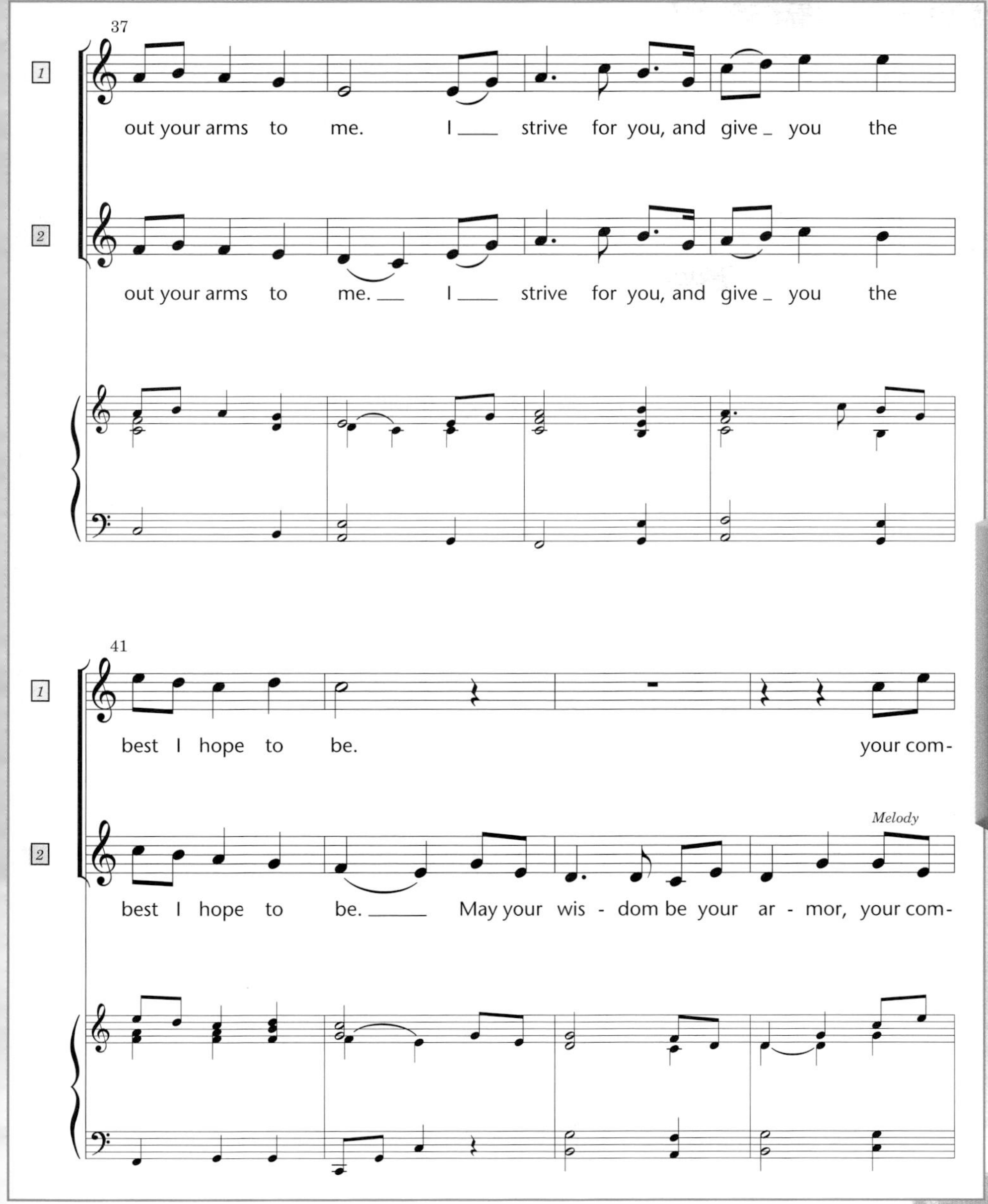

37

out your arms to me. I____ strive for you, and give_ you the

out your arms to me.___ I____ strive for you, and give_ you the

41

best I hope to be.   your com-

Melody

best I hope to be. _____ May your wis - dom be your ar - mor, your com-

▼ The Cotswolds

Unit 11 423

3 CLOSE

Skill: SINGING ASSESSMENT

7b **Performance/Peer Critique** Organize the class into three groups. Have each group sing "I Vow to You, My Country."

As each group performs, have the class signal to indicate ABA form then write evaluative comments about the

- Clarity of enunciation.
- Expressive singing of the words.
- Appropriate tone quality.
- Legato singing line.
- Rhythmic accuracy.

continued on page 423

CULTURAL CONNECTION

▶ **The Cotswolds** This garden spot of England (illustrated above) has been gently lived in for approximately 6000 years. The population changed gradually from Neolithic people to those of the Bronze and Iron Ages. Next came the Celts, the Romans, the Anglo-Saxons, the Normans, and then modern people. All valued nature and left the land basically unscathed. All left on view fascinating remnants of their lives.

After touring this region of southern England, one might enjoy spending some time at the Cotswolds' famous health spas. One might also want to purchase some locally made woolen sweaters, cloth, and superbly executed crafts.

MOVEMENT

▶ **Creative Movement** A sequential pattern, or "wave," is done by performing a single movement, person by person, down a line or around a circle. Simple movements—opening and closing, rising and sinking, moving forward and backward—can be very effective in this form. The movement appears to travel like an electrical current from person to person, adding a great deal of visual interest. Ask students to create a single movement representing a word in the text of a song. The movement should have a clear direction in space. Do the movement in a wave sequence, sweeping across or around the group. Next, add a contrasting movement representing another word from the song text. Do the first movement as a wave, and then add the second movement in the same way. Continue to add movements for a total of four to six.

Unit 11 *We Sing!* 423

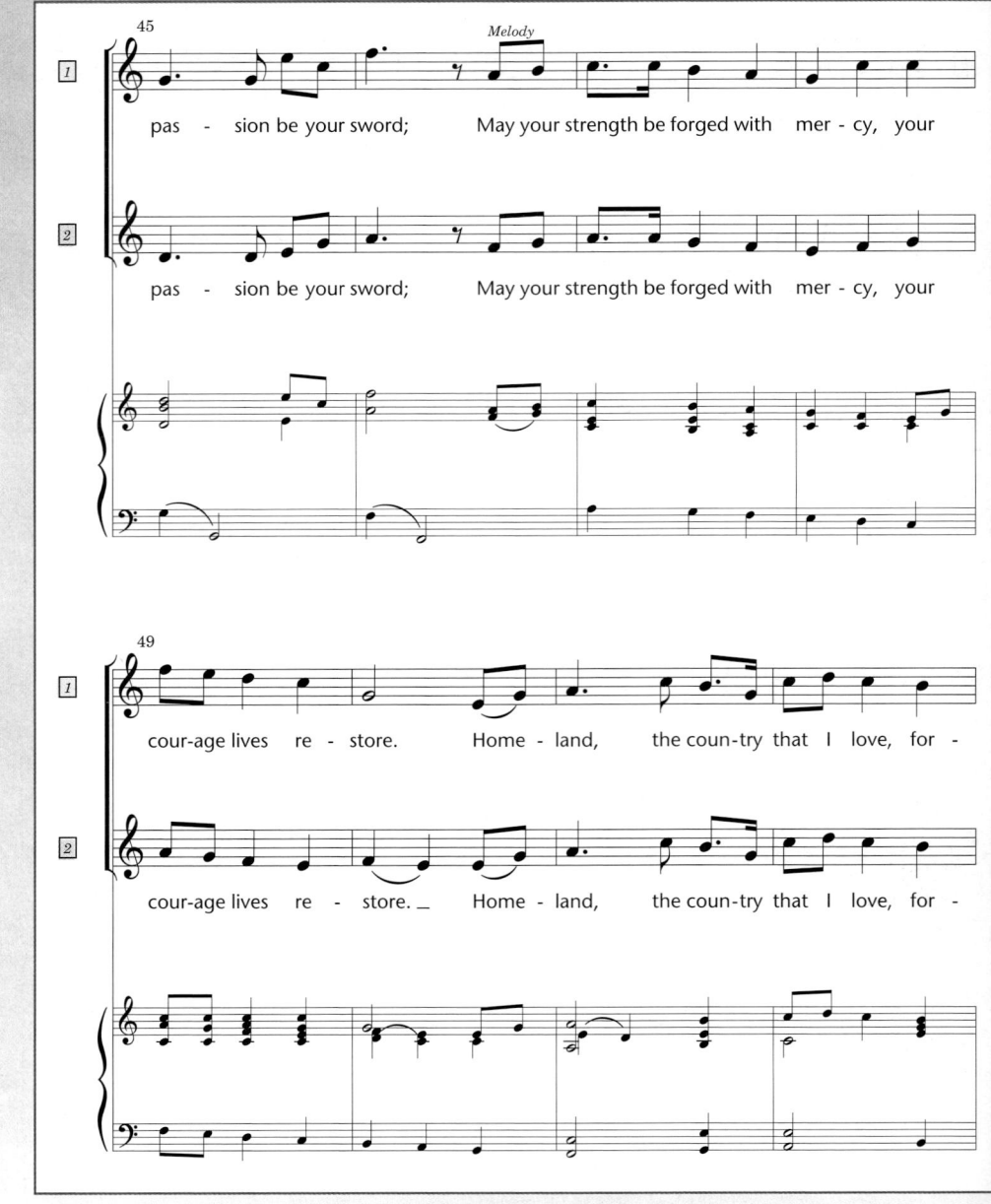

A Famous Melody

Listen to *Jupiter* by Gustav Holst. **Identify** where the melody of "I Vow to You, My Country" begins.

CD 18–29
Jupiter

from *The Planets*
by Gustav Holst

In *The Planets*, Holst composed a movement for each planet, except Earth and Pluto. (Pluto had not yet been discovered.) He composed *The Planets* between 1914 and 1916.

424

Footnotes

SPOTLIGHT ON

▶ **The Composer** Gustav Holst (1874–1934) was born at Cheltenham, near London. He composed as soon as he could hold a pen, and he played various instruments as fast as they came his way. His professional life began as a village organist and conductor of village choral societies. Later in life, he played the trombone in theater orchestras. He is best known for composing such pieces as *The Planets, The Hymn of Jesus, The Perfect Fool,* and *At the Boar's Head.*

ACROSS THE CURRICULUM

8b ▶ **Science** You never hear the song "Twinkle, Twinkle, Little Planet." That is because planets are celestial bodies that give off no light of their own. They merely reflect the light of their star (the sun). A group of planets revolving around the sun is called a "planetary system" or "solar system."

Our planetary system has nine planets. The inner ones—Mercury, Venus, Earth, and Mars—are made of rock. The outer ones—Jupiter, Saturn, Uranus, Neptune, and Pluto—are made mainly of gas. A tenth planet, Planet X is conjectured.

53

ev-er reign su-preme; And when time stands still, my home-land, may

ev-er reign su-preme; And when time stands still, my home-land, may

57

rit.

heav-en hold your dream. Home - land.

rit.

heav-en hold your _ dream. Home - land.

rit.

 Stonehenge

Unit 11 **425**

CULTURAL CONNECTION

▶ **Stonehenge** Nobody knows who built this circular mega-lithic structure (illustrated above) or why; yet there it stands on Salisbury Plain in Wiltshire, England, ready to taunt all comers with its mystery. The only thing that is known about this group of upright stones is that it was built in three phases sometime between 2800 B.C. and 1500 B.C.

Because Stonehenge's axis is pointed toward the sun at sunrise on both the summer and winter solstices, some think that the structure was used as an observatory to predict eclipses. Others think it was a site for religious ceremonies that were to take place on certain days of the year.

The builder is likewise shrouded in the mists of time. The monument was thought to have been built by the Druids (proven false), the devil, Merlin, or a group of giants. What do you think?

TECHNOLOGY/MEDIA LINK

Web Site To find out more information about composer Gustav Holst, visit *www.sfsuccessnet.com*.

MIDI/Sequencing Software Each choral arrangement in Unit 11 is accompanied by a MIDI song file. Use these MIDI files to play the tempo slower, isolate vocal parts, teach the harmony parts, highlight difficult measures to repeat and practice, and transpose the key, if desired. These files will assist students in learning the music and in rehearsing for performance.

LESSON AT A GLANCE

Element Focus	**FORM** AB form
Skill Objective	**SINGING** Sing a song in AB form
Connection Activity	**RELATED ARTS** Learn about the design and construction of the conga drum

MATERIALS

• "Uno, dos, y tres"   **CD 19-1**
• "One, Two, and Three"   **CD 19-2**
  Recording Routine: Intro (8 m.); vocal; interlude (8 m.); vocal; coda
• **Pronunciation Practice/Translation** p. 541
• **Resource Book** p. A-44
• keyboard, claves, maracas, conga drum

VOCABULARY

coda

> ◆ ◆ ◆ ◆ **National Standards** ◆ ◆ ◆ ◆
>
> **1c** Sing music from diverse cultures
> **1d** Sing music written in two parts
> **5a** Read dotted eighth and sixteenth notes in duple meter
> **5c** Identify standard symbols for pitch and rhythm
> **6b** Listen and analyze the uses of form
> **7a** Students evaluate the music they perform

MORE MUSIC CHOICES

For more practice singing songs in Spanish:
"Chiapanecas" (The Girl from Chiapas), p. 92
"Imbabura," p. 203
"Canción Mixteca" (Mixteca Song), p. 326

A Conga from Cuba

"Uno, dos, y tres" is a spirited conga from the Caribbean country of Cuba. The conga is a dance originally developed by enslaved Africans living in Cuba.

Move to the rhythm of the conga as you **sing** the song.

Singing Tips

Listen to the recorded Spanish Pronunciation Practice for this song. Words beginning with a q, such as quien, are pronounced with a k sound, as in kitchen. Words beginning with a c, such as con and Cuba, are also pronounced with a k sound.

Reading Music Tips

Compare the rhythm patterns in measures 4 and 12. Are they the same, or different? Practice tapping and speaking each pattern before singing it. **Compare** the pitch patterns in measures 4 and 12. Are they the same, or different?

Read the melody using pitch syllables and hand signs.

Knowing the Score

This song is arranged in **A** **B** form. In which measure does the B section begin? In which measure is D.C. al Coda located? What does this abbreviation mean?

▲ Cuban conga dancers and musicians

Tune In

In 1938, Cuban-born musician Desi Arnaz (1917-1986) performed a series of concerts in Miami, Florida. His performances made conga dance music popular in the United States.

◀ The Vinales Valley in western Cuba

Footnotes

SPOTLIGHT ON

▶ **The Conga** The conga is an Afro-Cuban dance music genre. It is an essential element of the Carnival celebration in Latin American countries. In the 1930s, it became popular as a ballroom dance in North America and Europe. The characteristic dance consists of three short steps and a forward leap.

BUILDING SKILLS THROUGH MUSIC

▶ **Dance** Invite students to perform the conga dance with the recording of "Uno, dos, y tres" **CD 19-1.** As students perform, make sure they are moving to the steady beat of the music.

CULTURAL CONNECTION

▶ **The Conga Drum** The conga drum consists of a long, barrel-shaped shell that can be up to 90 cm in depth and a single head approximately 25 to 30 cm in diameter. Early conga drums had a thick velum nailed to the shell. The shell is generally made of either wood or fiberglass. For a photo and sound sample of the conga drum, see Sound Bank p. 514 and **CD 21-26.**

Uno, dos, y tres
(One, Two, and Three)

English Words by Don Kalbach

CD 19–1
MIDI 31

Words and Music by Rafael Ortiz
Arranged by Carlos Abril

Al tam - bor ma - yor de a - lan - te _____
He's a won - der - ful drum maj - or, _____

_____ no hay quien lo pue - da i - gua - lar _____
There is none who can com - pare, _____

_____ con su rit - mo fas - ci - nán - te _____
With his fas - ci - nat - ing rhy - thm,

1 INTRODUCE

Lead students in a discussion about the conga. Explain that the conga is not only a dance, but also a type of drum. For more information on the design and construction of the conga drum, see Cultural Connection p. 426.

2 DEVELOP

Listening

6b Play the recording of *"Uno, dos, y tres"* **CD 19-1** and have students listen for the A and B sections. Ask them to raise their right hand when they hear repeated phrases.

Write the following two terms on the board: *adagio* and *allegro*. Ask students to identify the term referring to tempo that best describes *"Uno, dos, y tres."* (allegro)

Analyzing

Have the students look at the notation for *"Uno, dos, y tres"* and find the A and B sections.

ASK **Where does the A section begin?** (m. 1)

Where does the B section begin? (m. 17)

Where does the C section begin? (m. 37)

Then have students locate the *D.C. al Coda* and explain its meaning.

Reading

5a
5c **ASK** Ask students to identify dotted rhythm patterns that occur in *"Uno, dos, y tres."* Have students isolate and practice each of these patterns. Then ask them to tap the rhythm of the entire song.

Have students identify repeated melodic patterns that occur in the A and B sections. Ask them to sing mm. 1–8 using pitch syllables.

continued on page 428

MEETING INDIVIDUAL NEEDS

▶ **Inclusion** Some students may have difficulty performing the dotted rhythms tied to long notes. Pair students who can correctly say the rhythm syllables to these rhythm patterns with students who need extra reinforcement. You can also write the problematic rhythm patterns on the board and have students speak the appropriate rhythm syllables slowly. Have students increase their speaking speed until it matches the tempo of the song.

SKILLS REINFORCEMENT

▶ **Vocal Development** Correct posture is essential to good singing. Have students raise their arms over their heads as if they were reaching for the stars. Ask them to bring their arms down slowly to their sides while keeping their rib cage high. To help students perform with accurate intonation, demonstrating fundamental skills, ask them to

• Take a deep breath and then let the air out by hissing to a ten count, a fifteen count, and a twenty count.

• Repeat the exercise above, except release the air with staccato hisses.

• Sing selected phrases from *"Uno, dos, y tres"* at a slower than appropriate tempo to develop good breath support.

Lesson 1 Continued

Singing

1c Ask students to read the text on p. 426 about the pronunciation of Spanish words. Then play the Pronunciation Practice Tracks for *"Uno, dos, y tres"* **CD 19-4, CD 19-5** to help students learn the Spanish words. (For more information, see Teacher to Teacher p. 428)

1d Have students practice singing part 1 with the recording **CD 19-1.** Then have them sing part 2 with the recording. When they are comfortable singing each part, divide the class into two groups to sing the song.

Encourage students to

- Allow a brief space of silence between the dotted eighth note/sixteenth note rhythm.
- Listen for balance between parts 1 and 2.

Playing

Students may enjoy performing a steady beat accompaniment on nonpitched percussion instruments such as claves, maracas, and conga drums (if available). Advanced students may be invited to improvise their own rhythm ostinatos.

Students can also perform a chordal accompaniment on keyboard. *"Uno, dos, y tres"* can be accompanied by playing the B♭ and E♭ chords in closest position. (See p. 383 for chord photos)

Moving

Invite students to perform a simplified version of the conga with *"Uno, dos, y tres."* (See Movement footnote below.) For other movement teaching suggestions, see Skills Reinforcement p. 429.

[Musical notation with lyrics:]

de mi Cu - ba tro - pi - cal.
From the coun - try I hold dear.

de mi Cu - ba tro - pi - cal.
From the coun - try I hold dear.

B

Cuen - ten los pa - sos __ que a - quí lle - ga - mos. __
Count - ing the pac - es, __ All in our plac - es. __

Cuen - ten los pa - sos __ que a - quí lle - ga - mos. __
Count - ing the pac - es, __ All in our plac - es. __

U - no, dos, y tres, qué pa - so más ché - ve - re __ qué
One and two and three, what step can be bet-ter than, __ what

U - no, dos, y tres, qué pa - so más ché - ve - re __ qué
One and two and three, what step can be bet-ter than, __ what

428

Footnotes

TEACHER TO TEACHER

▶ **Pronunciation Accuracy** In addition to having students listen to the Pronunciation Practice Tracks **CD 19-4, CD 19-5,** invite a Spanish teacher to teach the words to students and then evaluate students' pronunciation accuracy. The Spanish teacher should also analyze the singing of the Spanish text to make sure all words are correctly sung.

It should also be noted that when the letter *c* appears before the vowels *e* and *i*, it is pronounced as *s* in Spanish America and the southwest of Spain, and as *th* in other parts of Spain.

MOVEMENT

▶ **Patterned Dance** Students may enjoy performing this simplified version of the conga with *"Uno, dos, y tres."*

Formation: Students stand in pairs, right shoulder against left shoulder, around the room (A section)

Students stand in a line of 4 to 8 pairs (B section)

A section

mm. 2–4: Partners walk to the right on the beat.
mm. 6–8: Partners walk to the left on the beat.
mm. 10–12: Repeat movement for mm. 2–4.
mm. 14–16: Walk to the beat, partner forming a line.

B section

mm. 17–20: Partners walk three beats, beginning on the right foot and kick left leg to the side. On repeat of mm. 19–20, students should form a longer line with 3 to 7 other pairs.

mm. 21–end: repeat movements for mm. 17–20.

Note: On the eight measure interlude, students should return to their original formation.

Children playing in the Miel River in eastern Cuba

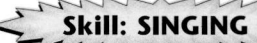

3 CLOSE

Skill: SINGING   Assessment

1d
7a **Performance/Self-Assessment** Invite students to give a performance of *"Uno, dos, y tres."* Videotape their performance so that students will be able to evaluate their

- Accurate performance of rhythm.
- Pronunciation of the Spanish words.
- Balance between part 1 and part 2.

SKILLS REINFORCEMENT

▶ **Moving** Use the following teaching suggestions to help all students perform a movement activity with *"Uno, dos, y tres."*

Reinforcement Some students may have difficulty performing the patterned dance. Ask these students to move to the beat, creating different movements for each section.

On Target Most students will be able to learn the patterned dance. Have these students practice the routine and perform it with the recording.

Challenge Invite interested students to create their own routine to perform with *"Uno, dos, y tres."*

TECHNOLOGY/MEDIA LINK

MIDI/Sequencing Software Using the MIDI file and sequencing software, record part 1 and part 2 on separate tracks. Remind students how to turn on and off individual tracks for MIDI playback. Have students

- Learn the appropriate voice part while listening to the MIDI track and following the song notation.
- Sing the appropriate voice part with the accompanying MIDI track.
- Sing the appropriate voice part while listening to both parts on the MIDI track.

LESSON AT A GLANCE

Element Focus **FORM** AABA form

Skill Objective **SINGING** Sing a song in AABA form with expression

Connection Activity **CULTURE** Discuss cultural influences in Jewish music and participate in a Jewish folk dance

MATERIALS

• "Hine mah tov" **CD 19-6**
  Recording Routine: Intro (4 m.); vocal
• **Pronunciation Practice/Translation** p. 541
• **Resource Book** p. A-46

VOCABULARY

AABA form   legato

◆ ◆ ◆ ◆ National Standards ◆ ◆ ◆ ◆

1a Sing accurately in small ensembles
1c Sing music from diverse cultures
1d Sing music written in two parts
5a Read dotted eighth and sixteenth notes in duple meter
5e In performance classes, sightread easy music accurately and expressively
6a Listen and describe events in music using appropriate terms
6b Listen and analyze uses of rhythm, harmony, and form in music from diverse cultures
7b Students use specific criteria for evaluating performances and offer constructive suggestions for improvement
8a Show how different arts portray the same idea in unique ways
8b Identify ways music relates to social studies

MORE MUSIC CHOICES

For more practice singing Israeli/Hebrew folk songs:
"Dundai," p. 106
"Tzena, tzena," p. 298
For more practice with ABA and AABA songs:
"Joshua Fought the Battle of Jericho," p. 101
"Happy Days Are Here Again," p. 284
"Sing, Sing, Sing!" p. 340

In Search of Peace

"Hine mah tov" is a traditional Jewish melody. This text is commonly known as a song of peace. The translation of the Hebrew text is: "Behold, how good and pleasant it is for brethren to dwell together in peace."

Singing Tips

Hebrew is an easy language to sing. **Listen** to the recorded Pronunciation Practice for this song. The *ch* sound in Hebrew is pronounced like the *ch* sound in Bach.

Reading Music Tips

Compare the rhythm patterns in measures 5 and 13. How are they different? Practice tapping and speaking each pattern before singing it.
Compare the pitch patterns in measures 5 and 13.

Knowing the Score

This song is arranged in Ⓐ Ⓐ Ⓑ Ⓐ form. In which measure does the Ⓐ section return? How is the Ⓐ section different the second time it appears?

430

Footnotes

ACROSS THE CURRICULUM

8b ▶ **Social Studies** Israel is an old-new country, small in size with a population of 5.9 million inhabitants. Because the people of Israel emigrated from many lands, it has absorbed many different cultures and social influences, including language, literature, the arts, science, media, and sports. Today, Israel participates in tours of dance troupes, art exhibits, orchestra concerts, book fairs, film festivals and sports competitions. *Areil* is the leading cultural magazine of the country.

BUILDING SKILLS THROUGH MUSIC

▶ **Physical Education** Invite students to perform the patterned dance described in the Movement footnote on p. 433. Monitor both groups of singers/dancers to ensure they are performing each movement accurately.

SKILLS REINFORCEMENT

1a ▶ **Vocal Development** Singing in tune requires hearing the phrase in one's mind. Have students practice singing *la₁ -ti₁- do- re- mi* and *mi- re- do- ti₁-la₁* in several different keys. Use hand signs to help see and feel the up and down relationship between each interval. Now, have students sing silently while using hand signs. When students get to the final note, have them sing it out loud and check with the piano to see if they are still in tune. Ask half the class to sing the initial *la* and hold it while the rest of the class sings the five-note scale up and down. The held *la* should help the singers sing the exercise in tune. Apply the above techniques to each phrase in *"Hine mah tov."*

Hine mah tov

d r m f fis ⓛ t d' r' m' f' s' l'

Hebrew Folk Song
Arranged by Henry Leck

CD 19–6
MIDI 32

We Sing!

Ⓐ mf
La la la la la la la la   la la la la la la

mp
La la la la la la la la   la la la la la la   Hi-

ne mah tov u-mah na-'im she-vet a-chim gam ya chad! _ Hi-

ne mah tov u-mah na-'im she-vet a-chim gam ya-chad! _ Hi-

Ⓐ
ne mah tov u-mah na-'im she-vet a-chim gam ya-chad! _ Hi-

Hi - ne she-vet a - chim gam ya-chad!

ne mah tov u - mah na-'im she-vet a-chim gam ya-chad!

Hi - ne she - vet a - chim gam ya-chad! Hi-

Unit 11 431

1 INTRODUCE

SAY The topic of peace has been written about in poems and songs. The idea of peace has inspired peace symbols and peace hand gestures.

Invite students to describe peace symbols and gestures they have seen. Discuss poems and songs that are primarily about peace. Then introduce *"Hine mah tov,"* with its message of peace, by asking students to read the opening text on p. 430.

Share information from Cultural Connection below with the class.

2 DEVELOP

Listening

Play the recording of *"Hine mah tov"* **CD 19-6.**

Have students

- Describe the tempo.
- 6a • Identify the main rhythmic motive by clapping it.
- 6b • Raise their hands when they hear harmony.
- Raise their hands when they hear a key change.

Reading

"Hine mah tov" has a great deal of repeated rhythm and melody patterns. The following steps will aid in learning the song more quickly.

- Have the girls speak the rhythm syllables of mm. 5–8.
- Have the boys speak the rhythm syllables of mm. 9–12.
- 5a • Simultaneously, have the boys speak the rhythm syllables of mm. 13–16, altos mm. 17–20, and sopranos mm. 21–24. (The rhythm for each part is the same.)

continued on page 432

▶ **Jewish/Israeli Culture** Jewish people and their music find their roots in the Middle East, especially in the land of Israel. For centuries, Jews have lived among Eastern and Western cultures: Iran, to Israel, the Western Mediterranean and North Africa, Europe, and the Americas. Jewish music defies a geographical location but has a unique property: intercultural synthesis. Because Jews have wandered the globe for over 2,000 years, they have assimilated foreign cultures into their art and daily lives. In short, Jewish music is cross-cultural—it has many faces.

Invite people of Jewish heritage (parents, grandparents, a rabbi or cantor, and so on) to talk to students about the culture, traditions, songs, food, and other features of Jewish and Israeli culture.

1a ▶ **Pronunciation** Singing *la la la la* can be done with a lazy tongue, where the tip of the tongue never makes firm contact with the hard surface of the mouth right behind the upper teeth. Lazy singing of this nature will result in singing *luh* instead of *lah* for *la*. Since this opening section is to be sung sprightly, the tip of the tongue must move quickly, giving very little time to the consonant "l" and moving rapidly to the vowel *ah*. The Hebrew words in this song contain many "m" and "n" consonants. In order for them to be heard, they must be pitched as in a hum-like effect. Two words end in *chad* and *chem: yachad* and *achem*. They require a "ch" sound similar to the "ch" in *Bach*.

Lesson 5 Continued

- Have students sing the pitch syllables for mm. 5–8 and mm. 13–16. (This will prepare them for most of the song.)
- Have students determine where sections A (m. 13), B (m. 37), and A (m. 50) are in the score.

Singing

Play the Pronunciation Practice Track **CD 19-8** for "Hine mah tov" to help students learn the Hebrew. (Refer also to Resource Book p. A-46.)

SAY When singing the *la la la* sections, place the tip of the tongue lightly on the hard surface behind the upper front teeth.

Some other pronunciation suggestions include:

- Enunciate every consonant.
- Do not connect the final consonants of words to words that begin with a vowel. For example *tov umah;* the *v* of *tov* is not connected to the *u* of *umah.*
- When singing the descant, the musical line should be sung *legato.*
- Make the sound that is formed in the throat when you say *Bach.*

Moving

Have students create movements to show the ABA sections of the song and then perform their movements with the recording **CD 19-6.**

Have students

- Research folk costumes that would be appropriate for an Israeli dance.
- Learn the Jewish folk dance presented in Movement, p. 433, and perform it with *"Hine mah tov."*
- Find other examples of Jewish folk songs that can be sung and danced to.

432

Footnotes

Refer also to Resource Book p. A-46.

 **SKILLS REINFORCEMENT**

1a ▶ Singing The vowels in Hebrew are pronounced like English vowels, produced by the tongue, teeth and lips in a similar way. "*Hine mah tov,*" for example, requires the vowels *e, eh, ah,* and *oh.* In saying and singing *e* the tip of the tongue is against the lower teeth. By rounding the lips slightly, a less bright, warmer *e* sound is produced. *Eh* requires the tip of the tongue to touch the lower teeth with the jaw dropped slightly. Place the tip of your finger on the bottom of your chin and say *e* then *eh.* You will observe a change in the jaw position. The *ah* vowel also requires the tip of the tongue to rest against the lower teeth, the tongue lies flat, and the jaw is in its lowest relaxed position.

 **TEACHER TO TEACHER**

1d ▶ How to Sing a Descant A descant is an additional treble part that decorates a melody. It is usually pitched higher than the melody and can be easily heard. Generally, it is a good idea to have only a few singers sing the descant, depending upon the size of the choir. In this song the range of the descant is narrow—only a 5th, from A to E. This descant is to be sung on the vowel *ah.* The singers should say *ah* to determine the shape of their mouth and the position of their tongue and lips. The tendency of singers is to change the mouth position, which will result in modifying the vowel to *uh.* The descant should float above the melody and never over balance it. If the singers know the song well and are secure, the descant singers can be placed throughout the choir, rather than in block formation, thereby helping to balance the melody and the descant.

432

Students may also enjoy performing movement from diverse cultures. Like the folk dance for *"Hine mah tov,"* the patterned dance for "Morning Comes Early" uses a circle formation. (See Dance Directions p. 554.)

Performing

1c
5e
"Hine mah tov" could be part of an entire program of folk songs and dances from many lands. Have students gather information about the various folk songs and introduce each one during the concert, explaining to the audience what they are about to hear.

3 CLOSE

Element: FORM   **ASSESSMENT**

6b
8a
Performance/Peer Critique Separate students into small groups. Have each group identify a song in their books that is in ABA form. (See More Music Choices in Lesson at a Glance.) Ask the groups to make a chart showing the A and B sections of the song; create movements for the song that reflect its form; practice singing and moving to a recording of the song; and perform the song and movements for the class.

7b
Select a small ensemble from the class (eight to twelve voices) to perform *"Hine mah tov"* for the class. Organize the remaining students into small groups. Assign each group the task of making written evaluations of the small-group performance.

Each group should comment about

- Clarity of diction.
- Accuracy of pitch and dotted rhythm patterns.
- Balance between melody and harmony.
- Degree of expressive singing.
- Facial expressions to match the meaning of the song text.

MOVEMENT

▶ **Patterned Dance** *Introduction:* Voice 1 singers (#1s) follow a leader and walk onstage to form a circle; Voice 2 singers (#2s) wait offstage.

A music: #1s join hands ("V" position) and circle counterclockwise. #2s, entering the stage on their vocal entrance, join the #1s in the circle. All continue circling counterclockwise.

B music: All face center and go in four steps, slowly raising arms high. Then go out four steps, slowly lowering arms. This is done three times during the B music.

A music: The #1 leader breaks from the circle, creating a curved line that opens up to a straight line facing the audience. Arms are slowly raised as the song ends.

TECHNOLOGY/MEDIA LINK

CD-ROM Encourage students to arrange a simple accompaniment for dancing to *"Hine mah tov"* using *Band-in-a-Box.* Have them

- Choose the key of G (one sharp) and a $\frac{2}{4}$ meter.
- Type the chord symbols.
- Choose various folk accompaniments.

If time allows, sequence a recorder part for performance.

MIDI/Sequencing Software Each choral arrangement in Unit 11 is accompanied by a MIDI song file. Use these MIDI files to play the tempo slower, isolate vocal parts, teach the harmony parts, highlight difficult measures to repeat and practice, and transpose the key, if desired. These files will assist students in learning the music and in rehearsing for performance.

LESSON AT A GLANCE

Element Focus **RHYTHM** Mixed meter

Skill Objective **SINGING** Perform a song notated in mixed meter

Connection Activity **RELATED ARTS** Discuss elements of Renaissance style in a painting

MATERIALS

- "Ríu ríu chíu" **CD 19-9**
  Recording Routine: Intro (4 m.); v. 1; refrain; v. 2; refrain; v. 3; refrain; v. 4; refrain; coda
- **Pronunciation Practice/Translation** p. 541
- Ríu, ríu, chíu **CD 19-12**
- **Resource Book** pp. A-46, H-27

VOCABULARY

Renaissance   mixed meters   *allegro moderato*
Fine   stanzas

◆ ◆ ◆ National Standards ◆ ◆ ◆

1a Sing accurately in small ensembles
1c Sing music from diverse cultures
2c Perform instrumental music from diverse cultures
5a Read quarter, half notes in mixed meter
5e In performance classes, sightread easy music accurately and expressively
6b Listen and analyze uses of pitch, rhythm, form, and timbre in music from diverse cultures
6c Understand and use basic principles of pitch and rhythm in music analysis
7b Students use specific criteria for evaluating performances, and offer constructive suggestions for improvement
8b Identify ways music relates to social studies and the visual arts
9a Describe characteristics of music from a variety of cultures

MORE MUSIC CHOICES

For more practice with mixed meter:
"Beyond Borders," p. 292
"A World of Difference," p. 386

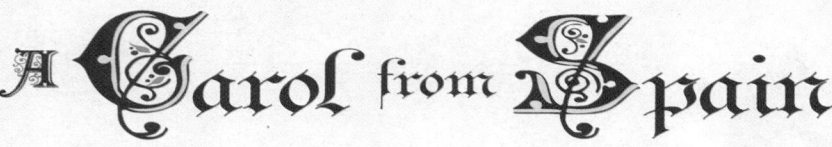

A Carol from Spain

"*Ríu ríu chíu*" is a Spanish Christmas carol from the Renaissance period, c. 1450–1600. It was sung in the courts of the nobility. It can be sung *a cappella*—without instruments—or with instruments *doubling* the parts.

Singing Tips

The tempo marking of *allegro moderato* indicates that this song should be sung moderately fast, as if you were singing it as part of a celebration. Use correct vowel shapes and good breathing skills, especially when singing the Spanish words in the refrain.

Reading Music Tips

This song has frequent meter changes that follow the rhythm of the words. The meter is felt as one, two, or three beats per measure.
Read the melody by using pitch syllables and hand signs.

Knowing the Score

At the end of the song you will see the Italian markings *D.C. al Fine*. What does that mean in English? In which measure does *Fine* appear by itself?

434

Footnotes

SPOTLIGHT ON

 ▶ **Carols** A carol was originally a dance during the twelfth and thirteenth centuries performed by people of the court and by popular society. It was common for the singers to dance to the refrain of a carol. Some scholars suggest that a carol is a circle dance. Other authorities suggest that there was no fixed choreography. Nevertheless, when the rhythmic characteristics of a carol have a dance-like feel, singers should represent that feeling in their singing.

BUILDING SKILLS THROUGH MUSIC

▶ **Art** Have students look at *A Concert* on p. 439 and the illustration on p. 434. Ask them to describe details of each example, such as the clothing worn by the people depicted. Have students compare and contrast the two examples.

SKILLS REINFORCEMENT

 ▶ **Analyzing** "*Ríu ríu chíu*" has four different time signatures in the score, making this a song in changing (mixed) meter. In most songs with changing meter, the underlying beat remains constant. In this song the quarter note remains constant. Ask half the class to clap the quarter notes steadily. Ask the other half of the class to say a neutral syllable to the rhythm of Voice 1, then ask the class to reverse roles. Use the same technique, but speak the words of the song and then sing them. Ask the singers to observe how important words—nouns, verbs, and adjectives—occur on strong beats or notes of greater rhythmic duration.

Río río chíu

CD 19-9
MIDI 33

Sixteenth Century Carol from Spain
Arranged by Henry Leck

s, si (l) t d r m

Allegro Moderato
REFRAIN

Rí-u rí-u chí-u la guar-da ri-be-ra,

Dios guar-do el lo-bo de nues-tra cor-

Dios guar-do el lo-bo, el lo-bo de nues-tra cor-

Hand Drum

Finger Cymbals

1 INTRODUCE

Invite students to discuss

• The sort of person a nobleman or noblewoman would be like.

• The type of clothes and parties the nobility would have at Christmas time.

8b Refer students to p. 439 to examine and discuss the artwork from the Renaissance period. The painting depicts three noblewomen in the leisurely activity of making music. (The instrument depicted is a lute.) Elements of Renaissance style seen in this painting are the subject matter, the natural, graceful position of the performers, and the realistic depiction of the drape and folds of the rich garments. Compare the clothing worn by the nobility with the informal wear depicted in the illustration on p. 434. To help students understand Renaissance culture, share with them the information from Cultural Connection below.

Then play the recording of *"Río río chíu"* **CD 19-9.**

ASK **Is this a song that could be danced to?** (yes) **Why?** (It has a strong beat and is very rhythmic.)

2 DEVELOP

Listening

Have students listen to *"Río río chíu"* again.

6b **ASK Do any phrases repeat exactly?** (Yes; mm. 6–11 in voice 2 repeat in mm. 12–17; mm. 7–11 in voice 1 repeat in mm. 13–17)

Do the English verses follow the same rhythmic patterns as in the refrain in Spanish? (no)

What instruments, if any, could accompany this song? (recorders, drums, and finger cymbals)

continued on page 436

CULTURAL CONNECTION

8b ▶ The Renaissance During the sixteenth century, many European cultures were experiencing a renaissance. *Renaissance* meant a rebirth—a return to the art, literature, music, sculpture, and architecture of ancient Greek and Roman times. It was expected that people of the court could sing madrigals, play instruments such as the recorder and mandolin, ride horses, fence, speak Greek and Latin, and be able to carry on a good conversation about a variety of subjects. The music of the day was influenced by what was occurring in society, politics, and religion. The clothing, plays, and poems reflected the daily life of Renaissance England and Europe. Today, much of the music that was written during the Renaissance era is still performed.

TEACHER TO TEACHER

9a ▶ Meter Changes Renaissance music is generally conducted in two. An exception to this is *"Río río chíu,"* an excellent example of a sixteenth-century song in which the feel of the rhythmic pulse is governed by word and syllable groupings. The composer of this song has a note for every syllable of each word. All the notes are not of the same rhythmic value. Sometimes the composer uses longer note values for certain syllables as a way of stressing their musical and textual meaning. In this song this emphasis can be seen on the syllables *chi, be-ra, lo, de,* and *de-ra.* Therefore, it is impossible to conduct this song in two. The meter changes were not originally written in the score; they have been added as an aid to interpretation and performance.

Lesson 6 Continued

Reading

Have students look at the score.

ASK How many different time signatures are there in the song? (4)

Help students notice that the word accents coincide with the changing meters. Share the information in Teacher to Teacher p. 435, and Skills Reinforcement, p. 434.

ASK Which voice has a D-sharp? (voice 2; m. 10)

How fast would *allegro moderato* be? (moderately fast but, not too fast, because of the meaning of the text)

Where does the double bar appear and what is its purpose? (It appears in m. 17; it marks the *Fine,* or what will eventually be the end of the song.)

Singing

Invite students to

- Speak the rhythm syllables of the first phrase (mm. 1–5).

- Sing the pitch syllables of mm. 1–5.

- Listen to the Pronunciation Practice Track **CD 19-11** and then sing mm. 1–5 in Spanish.

- Follow the procedures above for mm. 6–17 and voice 2.

- "Flip" the R for the words "*Ríu, guarda ribera, nuestra,* and *cordera.*

- Emphasize words and syllables that fall on half notes.

Have students learn voice 1 as a group. Then have them learn voice 2. Divide the class into two groups and assign one voice to each group.

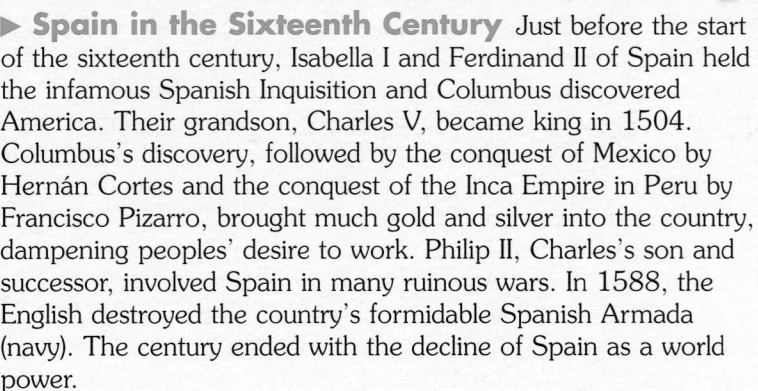

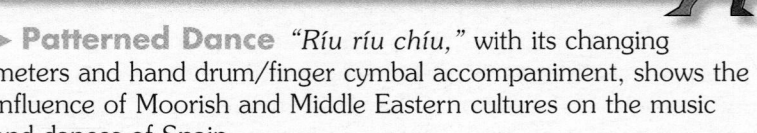

436

Footnotes

SPOTLIGHT ON

▶ **Spain in the Sixteenth Century** Just before the start of the sixteenth century, Isabella I and Ferdinand II of Spain held the infamous Spanish Inquisition and Columbus discovered America. Their grandson, Charles V, became king in 1504. Columbus's discovery, followed by the conquest of Mexico by Hernán Cortes and the conquest of the Inca Empire in Peru by Francisco Pizarro, brought much gold and silver into the country, dampening peoples' desire to work. Philip II, Charles's son and successor, involved Spain in many ruinous wars. In 1588, the English destroyed the country's formidable Spanish Armada (navy). The century ended with the decline of Spain as a world power.

MOVEMENT

▶ **Patterned Dance** "*Ríu ríu chíu,*" with its changing meters and hand drum/finger cymbal accompaniment, shows the influence of Moorish and Middle Eastern cultures on the music and dances of Spain.

A simple way to explore this influence in dance is through the use of a "serpentine," or snake-like floor pattern. A long line of dancers, hands linked, travels through the space making large curves. The image is of the head of the "snake" (line) leading the body and "tail" (end of the line). It is most effective when done with a walk in continuous arcs, scallops, and spirals, and is an excellent cooperative group task. This sinuous serpentine pattern is commonly found in the art and architecture of Northern Africa and the Middle East.

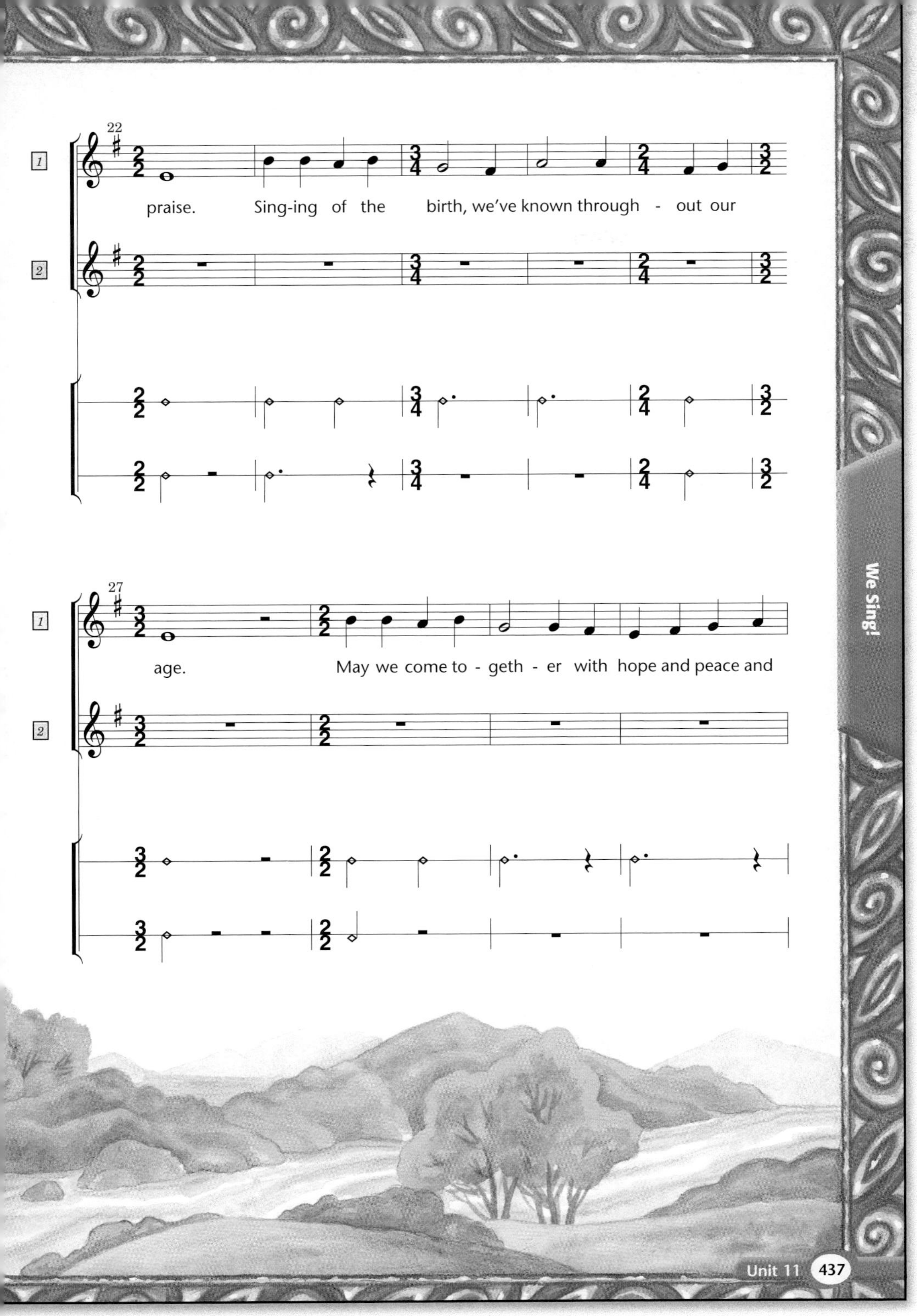

[Musical notation - measures 22-26]

praise.   Sing-ing of the   birth, we've known through - out our

[Musical notation - measures 27-31]

age.   May we come to - geth - er with hope and peace and

We Sing!

Performing

1c
5e
This song could be sung as part of a Christmas program. Students would dress in period costumes and make-up. Rather than sing on choral risers, the choir could sing in small groups or sitting at tables. Students could sing other songs and read poetry from the sixteenth century.

2c Have students sing "*Ríu ríu chíu*" with recorder, drum, and finger cymbal accompaniment. Give several students an opportunity to play instrument parts in mixed meter.

Some of the members of the choir could create a dance to accompany certain verses of the song. If performed on choral risers, voices 1 and 2 could be sung in a block formation or interspersed, depending how well the students know the song. A few voices or soloists could sing the various stanzas in English.

Listening

6b Invite students to listen to another version of "*Ríu, ríu, chíu*" **CD 19-12** performed by the choral group, The Sixteen.

ASK How is this version different from the version you just sang? (Accept various answers.)

continued on page 438

MEETING INDIVIDUAL NEEDS

▶ **Including Everyone** "*Ríu ríu chíu*" provides a great opportunity to build vocabulary. Many of the words in this song are conceptual and not concrete, including *forgiveness, hope, truth, love,* and *relation.* You may want to invite students to identify meanings for these words and create a visual dictionary for them. Alternatively, you may want to ask students to talk with a partner and then share with the whole class the meaning of each verse.

SKILLS REINFORCEMENT

▶ **Keyboard** To play a melody in mixed meters, students can play the melody of "*Ríu ríu chíu*" as shown in their books. Use
2c RH fingers 1, 2, 3, 4, and 5.

See Resource Book p. H-27 for a rhythm exercise to prepare students for this activity.

3 CLOSE

Skill: SINGING   ASSESSMENT

7b **Performance/Peer Critique** If enough students are available, divide the class into two choirs. Each choir should sing "*Ríu ríu chíu*" **CD 19-9** including the second stanza. The choirs may be accompanied by instruments, if enough performers are available.

Choirs 1 and 2 should evaluate each other for

- Rhythmic stress that reflects the mixed meter and agrees with the stress of the words in the song.
- Clarity of Spanish pronunciation and enunciation.
- Facial expressions that reflect the meaning of the song.
- Accurate performance of an *allegro moderato* tempo.
- A sprightly performance.

2. As we find this season clear with warmth within us,
Maybe we will see the meaning of forgiveness.

See in one another growing day by day,
Toward a closer, loving time we all would pray. *Refrain*

3. So with treasured gifts and hope for years to come,
May we seek the meaning of the newborn Son.

Living life together with hope and truth and love,
Sharing what we have through the love from up above. *Refrain*

4. Now with celebration we gather far and near,
Seeking new relation with those we hold most dear.

As we come together, we hope for bright days long,
So we join together and we sing this song. *Refrain*

Visit **Take It to the Net** at *www.sfsuccessnet.com* to learn more about Renaissance Music.

Footnotes

CHARACTER EDUCATION

▶ **Values** Invite students to discuss what *"Ríu, ríu, chíu"* is about. Ask students to find words that support their responses and delineate values (hope, love, peace, forgiveness, truth). Divide students into small groups and assign one word to each group. Have students compile a list of specific behaviors that demonstrate the value they have been assigned. For example, to show love, you could offer encouragement to someone who is having difficulty with schoolwork, talk with a classmate you don't know well who might be feeling lonely, or compliment someone for a job well done.

ACROSS THE CURRICULUM

8b ▶ **Art History** In the Arts Connection credit on p. 439, "School of Palma Vecchio" refers to the artists who studied with or painted in the style of Palma Vecchio (c. 1480–1528). Vecchio was born Jacopo Negreti in Serinalta, Italy. He studied under Bellini, originator of the Venetian High Renaissance style. Vecchio is known for his warm colors, transparent glazes, large forms, blond tonality, and fused soft-focus effects. Perhaps his most famous works are the type of religious paintings he specialized in, known as "holy conversations" and "Three Sisters." At his death, his students completed 62 of his unfinished paintings.

 **Connection**

▲ *A Concert* (16th century, School of Palma Vecchio). During the Renaissance (1450–1600) there was renewed interest in art, music, and the value of humankind. More scientific exploration occurred than ever before. Artists Leonardo da Vinci and Michelangelo, writer William Shakespeare, explorer Christopher Columbus, and scientist Galileo lived during this period. Many consider the Renaissance period the "Golden Age" of the arts.

A Renaissance Christmas

Listen to another version of *"Ríu ríu chíu."*

CD 19–12

Ríu ríu chíu

**Sixteenth Century Carol from Spain
as performed by The Sixteen**

The Sixteen is one of Great Britain's finest choirs. They have toured throughout Europe, America, and Asia.

SKILLS REINFORCEMENT

1a ▶ **Singing** Generally, vowels in singing should be similar to the way they are spoken. To help students perform with accurate intonation, demonstrating basic performance techniques, have them hold a mirror in front of their mouth to observe the way they form vowels with their lips, tongue, and teeth (articulators). Ask them to practice speaking *a, e, i, o,* and *oo,* while looking at the mirror. The tip of the tongue should be touching the lower teeth. The lips should be rounded for *o* and *oo.* Speak the five vowels on a pitch and observe the enunciation and articulators. Practice singing each vowel up and down the scale without changing the articulators. Imagine the shape of the vowels as capital letters inside the mouth, which allows for rounder, fuller vowel sounds. Sing only the vowels of the words in the song, maintaining proper vowel formation.

TECHNOLOGY/MEDIA LINK

9a **Web Site** For more information on Renaissance music, visit *www.sfsuccessnet.com.*

MIDI/Sequencing Software Each choral arrangement in Unit 11 is accompanied by a MIDI song file. Use these MIDI files to play the tempo slower, isolate vocal parts, teach the harmony parts, highlight difficult measures to repeat and practice, and transpose the key, if desired. These files will assist students in learning the music and in rehearsing for performance.

Element: MELODY | **Skill: SINGING** | **Connection: CULTURE**

LESSON AT A GLANCE

Element Focus **MELODY** *Do-re-mi* and *do-mi-so* patterns

Skill Objective **SINGING** Sing *do-re-mi* and *do-mi-so* patterns

Connection Activity **CULTURE** Discuss aspects of Hawaiian culture

MATERIALS
- "'Ūlili E"   **CD 19-13**
  Recording Routine: Intro (10 m.); vocal
- **Pronunciation Practice/Translation** p. 542
- **Resource Book** p. A-47
- keyboard, bells, or guitar
- *ukulele* (optional)

VOCABULARY
D.C. *(da capo)*   coda

first and second ending

antecedent (musical question)

consequent (musical answer)

◆ ◆ ◆ National Standards ◆ ◆ ◆
1c Sing music from diverse cultures
1d Sing music written in three parts
1e In groups, sing moderately easy pieces with expression and technical accuracy
2c Perform instrumental music from diverse cultures
5e In performance classes, sightread easy music accurately and expressively
6a Listen and describe events in music using appropriate terms
6c Understand and use basic principles of intervals in music analysis
7a Create standards for evaluating performance
8b Identify ways music relates to science and social studies
9a Describe characteristics of music from a variety of cultures

MORE MUSIC CHOICES
For more practice with antecedent-consequent phrase structure:

"The Ship that Never Returned," p. 402

A WADING BIRD

When Europeans first traveled to Hawaii, they found a people who sang beautiful songs about their beloved land and sea.

Singing Tips

Listen to the Pronunciation Practice to learn the lyrics. Pay special attention to the sounds of the vowels. Use good breathing skills to help maintain accurate intonation for the long, sustained tones and for repeated tones. (See page 442.)

Reading Music Tips

Each phrase begins with a *do-re-mi* or *do-mi-so* pattern. **Sing** these patterns using pitch syllables and hand signs at the beginning of each phrase before singing the song.

Knowing the Score

Notice the chord symbols that are written above certain measures. They are provided so that the song can be accompanied on the *ukulele*. What is the name of the first chord to be played by the *ukulele*?

► The *ukulele* has been a popular instrument in Hawaii since the late nineteenth century.

Footnotes

TEACHER TO TEACHER

► **'Ūlili E** This song provides a wonderful opportunity for students to study musical phrases, the purpose of first and second endings, *da capo,* ⊕ sign, and coda. Additionally, students can be shown how measures 1–16 represent the traditional Hawaiian song, while the remainder of the song is a harmonized trio followed by fragments of the opening theme and leading to the coda. Examining these structural characteristics of "'Ūlili E" will help students discover how a composition is put together.

BUILDING SKILLS THROUGH MUSIC

► **Language** Invite students to listen to "'Ūlili E" **CD 19-13** and discuss how the music reflects the movements of the bird. Ask students to write one sentence that describes the *'ūlili* and/or its movements.

CULTURAL CONNECTION

► **Hawaiian Culture** Before 1795, the Hawaiian Islands were ruled by many chiefs or "alii." King Kamehameha (born in 1758) united all of Hawaii. Today, Hawaii is a mixture of ethnic groups from all over the world. If you visit Hawaii, you will find the luau and hula are still part of the cultural tradition. The luau is an outdoor feast, which can include kalua pig roasted in banana leaves while buried in the sand, mahi mahi (a saltwater fish), sweet potatoes, and fresh fruits. The hula is an ancient native dance performed by women, and it is still studied and danced today. If you visit Hawaii wherever you go, you will be greeted with the traditional "aloha."

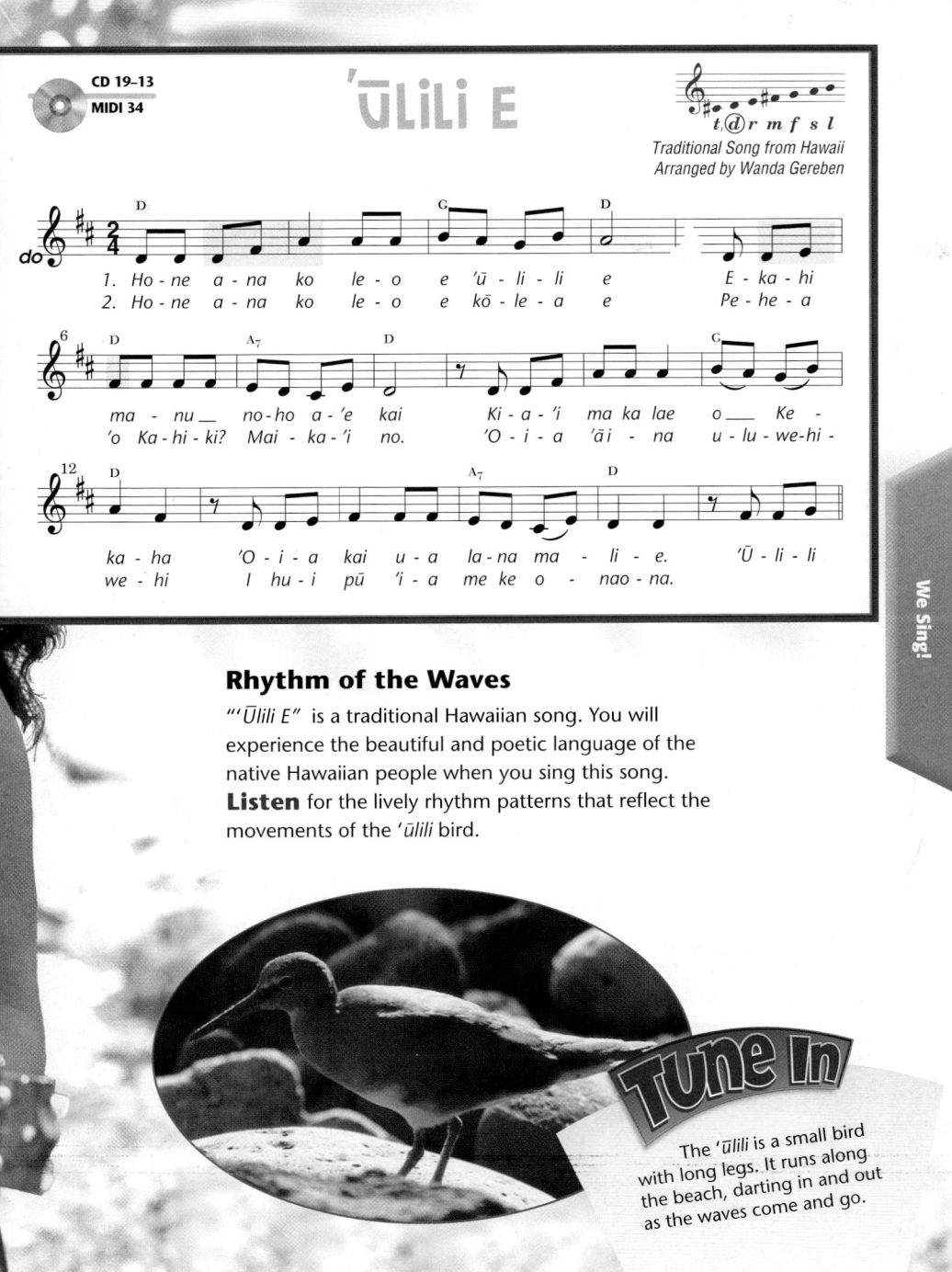

'ŪLILI E

CD 19–13
MIDI 34

Traditional Song from Hawaii
Arranged by Wanda Gereben

t @ r m f s l

1. Ho - ne a - na ko le - o e 'u - li - li e   E - ka - hi
2. Ho - ne a - na ko le - o e kō - le - a e   Pe - he - a

ma - nu__ no - ho a - 'e kai   Ki - a - 'i ma ka lae o__ Ke -
'o Ka - hi - ki? Mai - ka - 'i no.   'O - i - a 'āi - na u - lu - we - hi -

ka - ha   'O - i - a kai u - a la - na ma - li - e.   'Ū - li - li
we - hi   I hu - i pū 'i - a me ke o - nao - na.

Rhythm of the Waves

"'Ūlili E" is a traditional Hawaiian song. You will experience the beautiful and poetic language of the native Hawaiian people when you sing this song.

Listen for the lively rhythm patterns that reflect the movements of the 'ūlili bird.

The 'ūlili is a small bird with long legs. It runs along the beach, darting in and out as the waves come and go.

We Sing!

Unit 11 441

1 INTRODUCE

9a Bring a *ukulele* to class for students to examine.

SAY This is how the *ukulele* became part of Hawaii's musical culture: A boy on a ship from Portugal came to Hawaii in 1790, and was playing a small four-string instrument. The Hawaiian people loved the sound and the speed of the hands moving on the strings—like jumping fleas. The Hawaiians called this the *ukulele*, meaning "jumping flea." Since then it has become part of the Hawaiian culture.

Then share the information about this instrument from Spotlight On below, and the information about other aspects of Hawaiian culture from Cultural Connection on p. 440, and Across the Curriculum on p. 443.

2 DEVELOP

Listening

1e Play the Pronunciation Practice Track **CD 19-15** for "'Ūlili E" and ask students to

- Pay close attention to the sounds of the vowels and consonants.
- Practice them several times before singing the song.
- Listen for how the native singer stresses the syllables of each word.

Reading

6c Have students read the music for "'Ūlili E" and

- Identify the *do-mi-so* and the *do-re-mi-so* patterns in the song and sing them.
- Sing and hand sign all the pitch syllables.
- Identify the D.C. *(da capo)* direction in the score.
- Find the ⊕ sign to coda.
- Locate the first and second endings.
- Find the coda.

continued on page 442

SPOTLIGHT ON

9a ▶ **Ukulele** The *ukulele*, sometimes spelled *ukelele*, is usually associated with Hawaiian music. It is like a small guitar with four strings made out of nylon or gut. Like most string instruments, it can be tuned to different pitches, but it is usually tuned to G, C, E, and A. The Portuguese brought an instrument called the *bragha* (a small, four-string guitar-like instrument) to the Hawaiian Islands. This served as a forerunner of the *ukulele*. The *ukulele* appeared in the late nineteenth century and became popular in the United States during World War I and also in the 1940s and 1950s. It is not a difficult instrument to play and can be used to accompany many songs, especially folk songs.

SKILLS REINFORCEMENT

▶ **Creating** To extend the understanding of antecedent-consequent phrase structure, teachers can play a "call-and-response" game that allows students to improvise consequent phrases to teacher-provided antecedent phrases. Begin by writing out ten new antecedent phrases that are similar to those used in the song "'Ūlili E." Using a neutral syllable, sing these phrases to the students and ask them to "answer" them using the same neutral syllable. In classrooms in which solo singing is a less comfortable activity, the phrases may be played on the piano or other pitched instruments.

Lead a discussion exploring the musical purpose of the sign D.C. (*da capo,* meaning "at the head" or from the beginning), the first and second ending, and coda.

Have students review the phrase structure: antecedent (musical question)—phrase 1, mm. 1–4 and consequent (musical answer)—phrase 2, mm. 5–8.

6a **ASK How are the antecedent and consequent phrases similar and different?** (They are similar in that they are the same length. They are different in that the rhythms are not exactly the same, and the pitches of the consequent phrases are different.)

Are there other antecedent and consequent phrases? (yes; mm. 9–12 and mm. 13–16)

Singing

"*'Ūlili E*" has many words that have all vowels. Invite the students to sing carefully from one vowel to the next so that each vowel is clearly understood.

Play the recording **CD 19-13** and have students sing only the melody.

6a **ASK What do you see and hear when you sing mm. 1–4 and mm. 5–8?** (Mm. 1–4 is like a musical question—antecedent; and mm. 5–8 is like a musical answer—consequent.)

1e Have students include a two-bar *crescendo* and a two-bar *decrescendo* in each of the four-bar phrases.

1d When students are comfortable with the melody of "*'Ūlili E,*" teach the two harmony parts on p. 442.

▲ Big Island, Hawaii; view from inside a cave

442

Footnotes

SPOTLIGHT ON

8b ▶ **'Ūlili Bird** The *'ūlili* bird is a seabird found on the offshore islands of Hawaii. These locations offer safe nesting regions for these birds known as "wandering tattlers." They migrate annually over 2,000 miles from Alaska to Canada to Hawaii where they spend their winters foraging for insects and fish. They are usually solitary and can be seen hunting for food along rocky shorelines and tidal flats. The *'ūlili,* as well as several other seabird species, uses the protected offshore islands for roosting and nesting. Many seabirds build their nests under dense vegetation or in shallow, sandy burrows that cannot be seen by hikers or tourists. Their Hawaiian name, "*'ūlili,*" mimics their unique call.

SKILLS REINFORCEMENT

▶ **Guitar** The song "*'Ūlili E*" is intended for *ukulele,* but the sound of this instrument can be approximated in two ways. First, the chords can be played as written, using "Nashville tuning" on a standard guitar: replace the strings with the high-octave set of strings for a twelve-string guitar. This results in a quite authentic sound, as well as being very easy on the fingers. Second, the chords can be played with a capo placed on the fifth fret, and playing "A-D-E₇" in place of "D-G-A₇." This will require less reaching because the frets are closer together. The sound will be light and high.

'Ū - li - li   ho - lo   ho - lo   ka - ha - kai ____ e,

'O - i - a   kai   u - a   la - na   mā -

li - e.   'Ū - li - li   li - e.

li - e. ____

5e Performing

Have students play the chords indicated in the score above the staff to accompany the song. Chords can be played on keyboard, bells, guitar, or on ukulele by a proficient student.

For an introduction, play the chords of the first phrase to set the style of the song and the tonality for the choir.

Have a student introduce the song, explaining the meaning of "'Ūlili E" and why this song is a traditional Hawaiian song.

1c Have the class sing the song in parts with the accompaniment.

8b If this song were included in a multimedia concert focused on diversity, slides of Hawaii could accompany the performance.

3 CLOSE

Element: MELODY   ASSESSMENT

7a **Performance/Observation** Have students sing "'Ūlili E" **CD 19-13**, first with pitch syllables and then with the song text. Observe students' ability to sing the *do-re-mi* and *do-mi-so* patterns with accuracy.

▲ Waipio Valley, Hawaii, with waterfall

▲ Volcano steam on the Big Island

Unit 11 **443**

ACROSS THE CURRICULUM

8b ▶ **Social Studies** Have students locate Hawaii on a map. Hawaii became the fiftieth state of the United States on August 21, 1959. It was once an independent kingdom ruled by kings and a queen. The original Polynesian language of the Hawaiian people was made up of twelve letters: A, E, H, I, K, L, M, N, O, P, U, and W.

Hawaii is the only state made up completely of islands. The chain of Hawaiian islands covers a wide area of the Pacific Ocean. Hawaii has valleys, but the chief landform is steep mountains. The climate permits the growing of agricultural products such as sugar cane, pineapples, and coffee. Other products include fish, timber, beef cattle, and wheat. The manufacturing products include lumber for paper, petroleum, food processing (canning), and machinery.

TECHNOLOGY/MEDIA LINK

MIDI/Sequencing Software Each choral arrangement in Unit 11 is accompanied by a MIDI song file. Use these MIDI files to play the tempo slower, isolate vocal parts, teach the harmony parts, highlight difficult measures to repeat and practice, and transpose the key, if desired. These files will assist students in learning the music and in rehearsing for performance.

Web Site For more information on the dance, instruments, and music of Hawaii, visit *www.sfsuccessnet.com*.

Unit 11   *We Sing!*   **443**

Louis Armstrong

LESSON AT A GLANCE

Element Focus **RHYTHM** Syncopated patterns

Skill Objective **SINGING** Sing syncopation and tied rhythms in a scat-style song

Connection Activity **STYLE** Become acquainted with the jazz technique of scat singing

MATERIALS

- "Now's the Time" CD 19-16

  Recording Routine: Intro (4 m.); vocal; instrumental; vocal
- *Now's the Time* CD 19-18
- **Resource Book** p. H-28

VOCABULARY

scat singing   syncopation

melodic motive   rhythmic motive   call and response

◆ ◆ ◆ National Standards ◆ ◆ ◆

1a Sing accurately in small ensembles

1c Sing music from diverse genres

1d Sing music written in two and three parts

1e In groups, sing moderately easy pieces with expression

2c Perform instrumental music from diverse genres

3b Improvise rhythmic variations on given melodies

5a Read eighth notes, quarter notes in duple meter

5e In performance classes, sightread easy music accurately and expressively

6b Listen and analyze uses of rhythm, pitch, and form in music from diverse genres

7a Students use specific criteria for evaluating performances and offer constructive suggestions for improvement

8b Identify ways music relates to social studies

9a Describe characteristics of music genres from a variety of cultures

MORE MUSIC CHOICES

For more practice singing songs with tied syncopated rhythms:

"Morning Comes Early," p. 13

"*Éliza Kongo,*" p. 14

"Basin Street Blues," p. 354

Doo-doo n' doo-bee-doo! What an unusual way for the jazz "cats" to sing. These nonsense syllables, called scat, are meant to help the singer sound like a musical instrument. One of the most famous scat singers was Louis Armstrong. His *scat* singing made him world famous. Armstrong was also known for his trumpet playing and his distinctive, husky-sounding voice.

Singing Tips

When you **sing** "Now's the Time," emphasize the accented notes. The scat syllables should be slurred together and not cleanly separated when sung.

Reading Music Tips

Compare the lowest pitches in measures 7 and 8. Are they the same or different? Focus your attention on singing each pitch accurately. Using good vocal energy, enunciate the first consonant of each nonsense syllable with vigorous energy.

Knowing the Score

The third section of this song, which begins in measure 39, is written in call-and-response style. Which voice part is given the call, and which part the response?

◀ Louis Armstrong

444

Footnotes

SPOTLIGHT ON

9a ▶ **Scat Singing** In this technique of jazz singing, performers use nonsense syllables such as *bah doo'll yah do* in improvised melodies. In place of song lyrics, these nonsense syllables often imitate the sounds of instruments. Although the origin of scat singing is unknown, the first known recording was by Louis Armstrong in 1926 on "Heebie Jeebies." Other well-known scat singers include Ella Fitzgerald, Eddie Jefferson, and Sarah Vaughan.

BUILDING SKILLS THROUGH MUSIC

▶ **Writing** Have students listen to the scat singing in "Now's the Time" **CD 19-16.** Then ask them to think of words or phrases that could be substituted for some of the scat syllables. Have students work in groups to create new lyrics to "Now's the Time."

SKILLS REINFORCEMENT

1a ▶ **Singing** To achieve energy in enunciation of scat syllables, the lips and tongue must be active, full of life, and forceful in the delivery of all initial consonants. In scat singing, the clear and percussive enunciation of the consonants contributes to the rhythmic vitality of a scat song. The initial "b" in *bah* should be explosive. Pressing the lips together and accenting the "b" when singing *bah,* and letting the lips pop apart creates a good rhythmic effect. Use the tip of the tongue to say and sing *doo.* Create pressure with the tip of the tongue against the hard surface right behind the upper teeth; this is where "t" and "d" are produced in the mouth.

Sing "Now's the Time" in a *legato* style using the scat syllables.

Now's the Time

CD 19–16
MIDI 35

Music by Charlie Parker
Arranged by Norma Jean Luckey

We Sing!

1 INTRODUCE

9a Have students read aloud the information in their books about scat singing and Louis Armstrong. (See Spotlight On, pp. 444 and 446.)

5a Help the class create a phrase that incorporates syncopation. On the board

- Write four measures of even quarter notes in $\frac{4}{4}$. Ask the class to tap the even quarter notes as they count 1-2-3-4|1-2-3-4 steadily.
- Copy the four measures and change all the quarter notes to two eighth notes. Write 1 & 2 & 3 & 4 & under the beats. Have students tap and count aloud the even eighth notes.
- Tie together the second half of beat 2 and beat 3. Tap and count the subdivided beat aloud, emphasizing the "and" of beats 2 and 3. Strong beat 3 will be silent since it is held over. Have the class tap and count with you. Syncopation in the rhythm is the result.
- Have students copy the example and place it in their music portfolios.

3b
- Make up their own syncopated phrases, tying over other beats or writing rests on the strong beats in each measure.
- Demonstrate what they wrote.

continued on page 446

MOVEMENT

▶ **Creative Movement** Performing would not be as interesting if singers did not use animated facial expressions and body movements. Invite students to create a routine, using the following ideas, to accompany "Now's the Time."

- Move their heads from left to right and vice versa for the individual scat syllables.
- Move the shoulders in parallel motion with the head.
- Synchronize arm, hand, and head movements.
- Raise eyebrows to give an open-eye look.
- Shake head in rhythm to triplet and sixteenth-note patterns.
- Maintain a pleasant smile and "sell" the song.

TEACHER TO TEACHER

▶ **Syncopation** Music is probably easier to feel than it is to intellectualize or talk about. In preparing students for this song, have them practice the syncopated rhythms they created above. Divide the class in half, having one half tap 1-2-3-4 over and over, while the other half claps the second half (the "and") of each beat (1 & 2 & 3 & 4 &). Once this is mastered, have the class concentrate on & 1. This is the way the rhythm of the song begins, on a pick-up note. Have students transfer their understanding of syncopation to the song.

2 DEVELOP

Listening

Play the recording of "Now's the Time" **CD 19-16.**

9a **SAY** Scat singing uses syncopation and that is what you heard in the piece we just listened to.

ASK How is syncopation achieved in music? (Accents are shifted to the weak beats of the measure; notes are held over a strong beat; rests are often on the strong beat.)

6b On what part of the beat in the song does syncopation occur? (the second half; on one AND, or when two notes are tied together, as shown in mm. 7–8)

What syllables fall on the syncopated rhythm? (bah, dee, and bee)

6b Discuss the different ways a melodic and rhythmic motive is presented (use mm. 1–6).

- The melody is first presented with rests and the melodic pattern ends with a quarter note.
- The melody is then presented without rests and the quarter note is replaced with two eighth notes, which keeps the melody moving.

Discuss the new material in measure 12.

- The downbeat of the measure is an eighth rest.
- The melodic pattern is all stepwise.

Notice the new melodic and rhythmic motives, beginning in mm. 27–38.

- In the first three measures, the motive begins a step down from the prior measure.
- Syncopation is frequently used on the second and third beats of the measure.

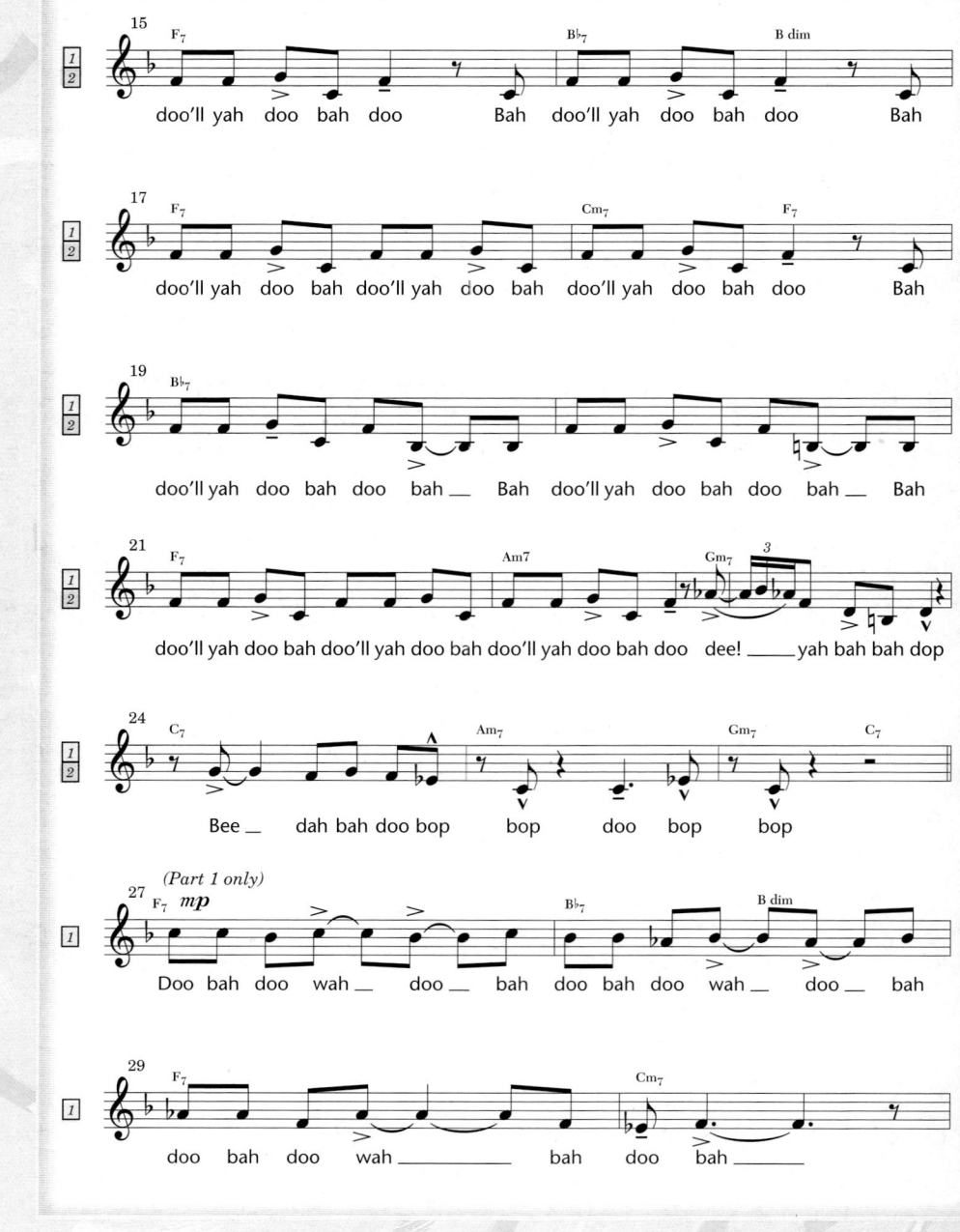

446

Footnotes

SPOTLIGHT ON

▶ **The Performer** Born in poverty in New Orleans, Louis Armstrong (1901–1971) was left in the care of his grandmother. Eventually he landed in the Colored Waif's Home where he learned to play the alto horn, the drums, and the cornet. In 1927 he switched to trumpet. From then on his life was filled with music. He studied with Joe Oliver in New Orleans and played with Oliver's band in Chicago. Later he went to New York and played with Fletcher Henderson's orchestra. In 1931 he started his own big band. Armstrong, nicknamed Satchmo, invented the virtuoso jazz solo. He recorded with jazz greats such as Ella Fitzgerald and Bessie Smith. Armstrong wrote two autobiographies and appeared on many television programs. Play for students Armstrongs' recording of *We Shall Overcome* **CD 21-14.**

TEACHER TO TEACHER

1a ▶ **Vocal Techniques** Help students become aware of the scat vocal techniques, such as scoops, portamentos, interval leaps up and down, consonant explosions, and how they are related to expressive movement. Encourage students to practice in front of a mirror in order to observe the relationship between their singing and expressive body movements.

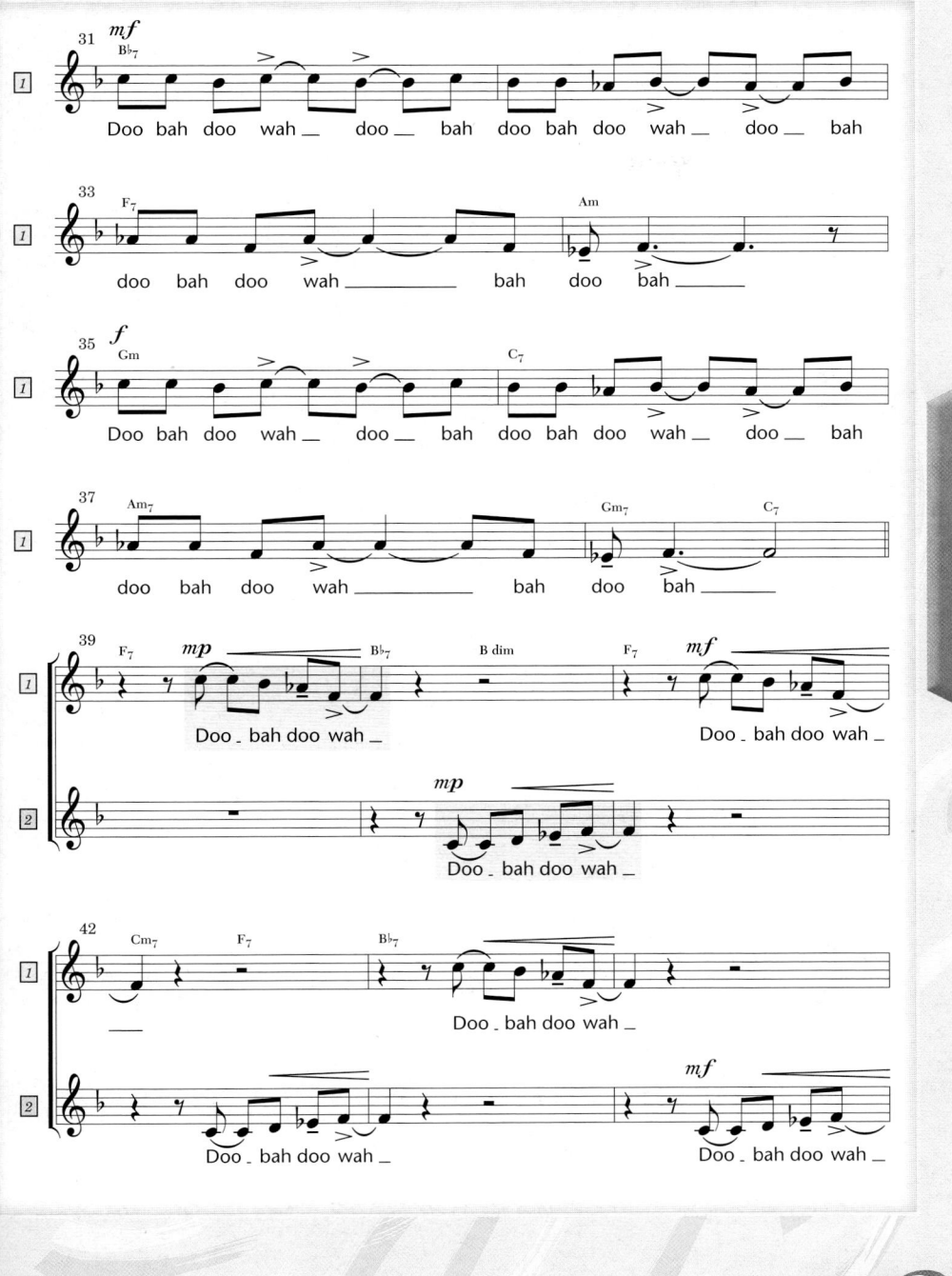

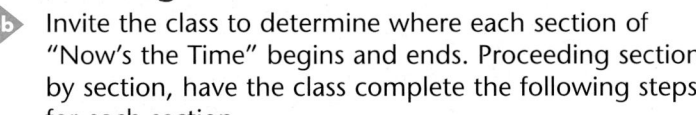

Point out the call and the response in mm. 39–50. Note that the rhythm pattern for the responses is similar to those in the call.

ASK How are the two patterns different? (The pattern in voice 1 is descending and the pattern in voice 2 is ascending.)

Discuss motive A in voice 1 and voice 2, and the pick-up to measure 75.

Reading

6b Invite the class to determine where each section of "Now's the Time" begins and ends. Proceeding section by section, have the class complete the following steps for each section.

- Identify the symbols referring to articulation. (accents)

5a
- Clap the rhythm of each phrase.
- Speak the rhythm of each phrase using rhythm syllables.
- Scat the rhythm of each phrase.
- Sing the pitch syllables of each phrase.
- Scat the melody of each phrase as written.

Singing

Play the recording of "Now's the Time" **CD 19-16** again. Invite students to listen for

- The vocal quality of the singers.
- The way the nonsense syllables are sung.
- Which notes and syllables get the accent.
- The rhythmic "swing feel" of the singing.

1c Have students apply each of the above singing techniques to each phrase and section of "Now's the Time" while singing along with the recording.

1d When students are able to sing each of the parts with the recording, divide the class into two groups and have one group sing voice 1 and one group sing voice 2.

See Skills Reinforcement below for an added third vocal part for measures 64–75.

continued on page 448

Unit 11 **447**

CULTURAL CONNECTION

▶ **The Swing Era (1930–1940)** During the Great Depression, America was ready for a new style of music, and found it in the new *swing* style. Swing is played by a large band, typically of 10–15 members divided into reeds, brass, piano, double bass, and drum set. The music is more orchestrated than improvised and is very often syncopated. It often featured a soloist who was backed up by the ensemble. Duke Ellington, Count Basie, Tommy Dorsey, Benny Goodman, and Fletcher Henderson were among the best. The swing era can be viewed not only as musical style but also as producing a culture. Most people knew the musicians the way kids know ball players. The jitterbug emerged, along with new clothing styles and a new slang. The era ended in the 1940s with the advent of Charlie Parker's bebop.

SKILLS REINFORCEMENT

1d ▶ **Singing** For more of a challenge, have students add a third vocal part to "Now's the Time" on mm. 64–75.

Unit 11 *We Sing!* **447**

Lesson 7 Continued

Moving

Scat singers rarely stand still while they are singing and their facial expressions are an extension of the music's expressive character. Have students find video-taped examples of scat singers to see how they use their facial expressions, hands, arms, and entire body.

Refer to the suggestions in Movement on p. 445 and invite students to create gestures and facial expressions for "Now's the Time."

7a If school policy permits, videotape the students' performance and then critique their gestures and facial expressions.

5e Performing

Scat singing does not necessarily lend itself to performing on choral risers. Encourage the class to create lighting and stage placement of the singers. Discuss with students what sort of dress would be appropriate for scat singing.

ASK How might voice 1 and voice 2 interact during the performance? (During the call-and-response mm. 39–50, singers can turn towards each other, as if in conversation.)

Listening

6b Before playing the recording of Charlie Parker's original performance of *Now's the Time* CD 19-18, have students read about him on p. 451. Share additional information about Parker from Spotlight On, p. 451.

Ask students to compare the two recordings of the song in this lesson and state which version they prefer and why.

Moving

See Movement below to have students perform a "jazz strut" with *Now's the Time*.

448

Footnotes

SPOTLIGHT ON

▶ **The Performer** One of the greatest jazz singers of all time, Ella Fitzgerald (1917–1996) was born into poverty. She was homeless when she entered a talent contest at the Apollo Theatre at age 16. She had planned to dance, but she froze. When coaxed to do something, she sang one of the few songs she knew and won the contest. Soon after that, she won a second contest at the Harlem Opera House. When band leader Chick Webb heard her, Fitzgerald's career began. She had an amazing quality to her voice that encouraged people to sing along with her. She was not intimidating, although her range was huge, her intonation perfect, and her feeling for harmony glorious. Her styles were as flexible as her voice; she sang swing, jazz, bebop, scat, and pop. Play for students Fitzgerald's recording of *How High the Moon* CD 15-28.

MOVEMENT

▶ **Patterned Dance** The basic box step can be done as a "jazz strut" along with Charlie Parker's *Now's the Time*. To do the box step, first visualize the four corners of a box. Step forward on the right foot—the first corner of the box Then cross the left foot over the right, stepping onto the left foot. Step back on the right foot, and then to the side with the left foot. These four steps have just created the box pattern. Repeat the box again by stepping forward on the right foot. Each step in the box step gets a count for a total of four counts. The pattern can also be reversed to the left side or done backwards. To give the step a jazz stylization, pick up the knees during the step and let the body lean into the direction of the steps. Students may enjoy giving the steps a jaunty, bouncing quality.

continued on page 450

3 CLOSE

5e **Performing**

A concert theme could be "Syncopation in Song" in which other syncopated songs could be programmed, including rap pieces created by the students. Rap pieces could be humorous and include such topics as "school rules," "teachers and the subjects they teach," and "musical qualities of choir members."

Skill: SINGING   **ASSESSMENT**

1c **Performance/Self-Assessment** Have students
7a give a performance of "Now's the Time." Videotape
their performance so that students will be able to
evaluate their

- Degree and accuracy of syncopated rhythms.
- Appropriateness of tempo.
- Swing feel of singing.
- Clarity of scat singing.
- Facial expressions and hand gestures.

We Sing!

SKILLS REINFORCEMENT

 ▶ **Keyboard** For a "comping" activity to accompany "Now's the Time," see Resource Book p. H-28.

2c Students will have an opportunity to play a walking bass and tritone harmony as other students create scat rhythms.

MEETING INDIVIDUAL NEEDS

1a ▶ **Pitch Accuracy** Singing out of tune can be the result of a variety of factors. If singers have not developed their "singing ears" while young, they will probably sing out of tune even as adults. If they have poor vocal technique, flatting or singing sharp may result. If they do not "listen ahead"—hear in their head where the phrase is going—they will sing out of tune. If the range of the song is too high or low, out-of-tune singing can result. Unfamiliarity with the vocal style can affect pitch accuracy, particularly in scat singing. Inaccurate singers tend to do better when placed between two accurate singers. Some singers do better when they hear a vocal exercise or line sung by a person who is of the same voice type. Voice lessons, peer and self-evaluation, plus positive reinforcement can produce accurate singing.

Lesson 8 Continued

Footnotes

 **SKILLS REINFORCEMENT**

1e ▶ **Singing/Vocal Dynamics** There are a variety of ways to achieve dynamic variations that result in artistic singing and will please the listener. Ask students to go through their score, highlight all the dynamic markings, and speak the syllables observing all dynamic changes. The phrase lengths in this song are varied, and should have their own dynamic shape based upon how the pitches are organized. All phrases should dynamically move to and away from a point. The amount of energy used to sing the initial consonants of each scat syllable can also influence dynamics. Find the syncopated rhythms and emphasize the consonants that occur on those rhythms. Analyze the song to determine which phrases are musically more important and then bring them out dynamically.

 ACROSS THE CURRICULUM

8b ▶ **Social Studies** During the early part of the twentieth century, the United States experienced a "Great Migration." Thousands of African Americans in the South traveled to Chicago, New York, and other northern cities in search of work and a better life.

Encourage students to research and share with the class information on the migration north of many African Americans in the early part of the twentieth century, and the impact this had on the development of jazz.

80 Bb7 / F7

doo'll yah doo bah doo bah __ Bah doo'll yah doo bah doo'll yah doo bah

82 Am7 / Gm *3*

doo'll yah doo bah doo dee! _____ yah bah bah dop

84 C7 / Am7 / Gm7 / C7 / F7 *ff*

Bee _ dah bah doo bop bop doo bop bop Yeah!

Listen to Charlie Parker's original recording of *Now's the Time*.

CD 19–18
Now's the Time

written and performed by Charlie Parker
Parker's recording of *Now's the Time* made this song famous.

MUSIC MAKERS
Charlie Parker

Charlie Parker (1920–1955) was a famous jazz performer on the alto saxophone. He and another musician, Dizzy Gillespie, contributed to the popularity of "bebop" in the 1940s and 1950s. Bebop, or "bop," was a change from the swing band sound that was popular earlier. Bop performers had more freedom in using off-beat accents (called syncopation), difficult harmonies, and solo improvisation. Bop was performed at such a fast tempo that it was almost impossible to dance to the music, so the audience had to sit and listen.

Unit 11 **451**

SPOTLIGHT ON

▶ **The Performer/Composer** Alto saxophone great Charlie Parker (1920–1955) was born in Kansas City, Missouri and lived life in the fast lane. His innovative music style, based on jazz, perhaps imitated his life. Called *bebop*, it was marked by explosions of unexpected phrasing, extended harmonic content, complex rhythms, as well as dazzling improvisations performed at breakneck tempos. Older jazz players despised his music, finding it intimidating, obnoxious, and unintelligible. Younger jazz players worshiped the new style that gave them an alternative to the big band music. Many of them tried to emulate not only Parker's musical style but also his style of living. Parker met an untimely end at age 35. After his death, he was elected to the Down Beat Hall of Fame.

TECHNOLOGY/MEDIA LINK

1c

CD-ROM To practice scat singing to a swing style accompaniment, have students

- Load a demo swing style melody into *Band-in-a-Box*.
- Mute the melody tracks.
- Record their singing (Windows only) as the accompaniment plays.

Lesson	**Elements**	**Skills**

LESSON 1

Fall Fun

pp. 456-457

Element: Melody
Concept: Pitch and direction
Focus: Melodic themes

Secondary Element
Rhythm: triplets

National Standards
1a 2a 4c 6a 6b 8a

Skill: Listening
Objective: Listen for melodic contrast in a symphonic (tone) poem

Secondary Skills
- **Singing** Sing the song accompanied by the recording
- **Playing** Play an accompaniment on recorder and xylophone

SKILLS REINFORCEMENT
- **Recorder** Play a countermelody to accompany a song
- **Mallets** Play an Orff arrangement to accompany the song

LESSON 2

Sing a Song of Thanks

pp. 458-459

Element: Texture/Harmony
Concept: Harmony
Focus: Two-part harmony

Secondary Element
Melody: pitch and direction

National Standards
1a 1d 5c 7a 8b

Skill: Singing
Objective: Sing a holiday song in two parts

Secondary Skills
- **Reading** Read accidentals in notation and describe how they affect pitch

SKILLS REINFORCEMENT
- **Notating** Practice changing pitches with accidentals

LESSON 3

An Autumn Song

pp. 460-461

Element: Melody
Concept: Pitch Patterns
Focus: Pentatonic Scale

Secondary Element
Expression: dynamics

National Standards
1c 6b 8b

Skill: Singing
Objective: Sing a pentatonic song in antiphonal style

Connections	Music and Other Literature	ASSESSMENT
Connection: Language Arts **Activity:** Compare a poem and a music selection **SPOTLIGHT ON** **The Show Family** Background information about *The Addams Family* **ACROSS THE CURRICULUM** **Language Arts** Read an eerie poem for Halloween **BUILDING SKILLS THROUGH MUSIC** **Language** Discuss how sounds can be used to enhance the song text	**Song** "The Addams Family" **Listening Selection** *Danse macabre* **Poem** "Dance of Death" (excerpt) **More Music Choices** *Carnival of the Animals*, "Aquarium," p. 376 *Havanaise for Violin and Orchestra*, p. 217	**ASSESSMENT** **Music Journal Writing** Listen to and compare two melodic themes **TECHNOLOGY/MEDIA LINK** **Sequencing Software** Create a percussion track to accompany the song
Connection: Social Studies **Activity:** Discuss the history and traditions of Thanksgiving celebrations **ACROSS THE CURRICULUM** **Language Arts/Drama** Create a Thanksgiving mini-drama with stories and poetry **SPOTLIGHT ON** **The Holiday** Facts about Thanksgiving **BUILDING SKILLS THROUGH MUSIC** **Language** Substitute words in song text	**Song** "Come, Ye Thankful People, Come" **More Music Choices:** "Canción Mixteca," p. 326 "Sing, Sing, Sing!" p. 340	**ASSESSMENT** **Performance/Peer Critique** Sing the song in two part harmony; use specific criteria to critique the performance **TECHNOLOGY/MEDIA LINK** **Sequencing Software** Create and record melodic sequences and percussion rhythms on individual tracks
Connection: Culture **Activity:** Explore Vietnamese Culture **SPOTLIGHT ON** **Antiphonal Singing** Information about the performance style **CULTURAL CONNECTION** **Vietnam** Facts about the culture and history of Vietnam **ACROSS THE CURRICULUM** **Language Arts/Social Studies** Read a book that describes the culture and geography of Vietnam **BUILDING SKILLS THROUGH MUSIC** **Social Studies** Research and discuss the crops of Vietnam	**Songs** *"Quâ câù gió bay"* "The Wind on the Bridge" **More Music Choices** "Arirang," p. 25 "Jasmine Flowers," p. 316	**ASSESSMENT** **Performance/Observation** Sing patterns in a pentatonic song accurately **TECHNOLOGY/MEDIA LINK** **Video Library** Watch a video to learn about different dance forms from various countries

Lesson	Elements	Skills	
LESSON 4 **A Harvest Song** pp. 462-463 	**Element: Melody** **Concept:** Pitch and direction **Focus:** Intervals **Secondary Element** Rhythm: meter changes **National Standards** 1c 2b 6b 6c	**Skill: Singing** **Objective:** Sing accurately the intervals of a Native American song **Secondary Skills** • **Reading** Identify intervals of a fourth in song notation	**SKILLS REINFORCEMENT** • **Singing** Sing intervals of a fourth, blending vocal tone between head and chest registers
LESSON 5 **A Chanukah Celebration** pp. 464-465 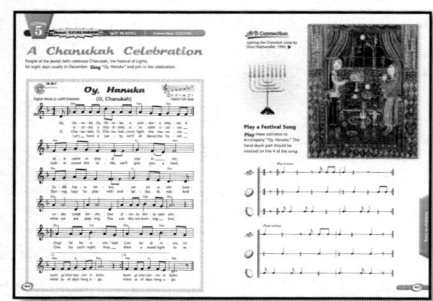	**Element: Texture/Harmony** **Concept:** Harmony **Focus:** I, IV, and V7 chords **Secondary Element** Rhythm: meter in 4 **National Standards** 1c 2a 6c 8b	**Skill: Playing** **Objective:** Play ostinatos to accompany a Chanukah song **Secondary Skills** • **Singing** Learn the Yiddish words to the song and sing with the recording	**SKILLS REINFORCEMENT** • **Keyboard** Play an accompaniment with the song
LESSON 6 **A Rockin' Holiday Song** pp. 466-467 	**Element: Form** **Concept:** Form **Focus:** AABA **Secondary Element** Rhythm: patterns **National Standards** 1a 2a 6b 8b 9a	**Skill: Singing** **Objective:** Sing a song in rock 'n' roll style **Secondary Skills** • **Analyzing** Listen and follow song notation to identify form • **Playing** Play a three-part percussion accompaniment	**SKILLS REINFORCEMENT** • **Singing** Sing in rock 'n' roll style maintaining proper vocal technique • **Playing** Play rock 'n' roll drum rhythms

Connections

Music and Other Literature

Connection: Culture
Activity: Learn about Native American harvest

> **SPOTLIGHT ON** **Corn** Historical information on the importance of corn

> **CULTURAL CONNECTION** **The Wabanaki** Discuss one of the earliest known Native American groups in North America

> **SCHOOL TO HOME CONNECTION** **Old Fashioned Popcorn** Recipe for making popcorn

> **BUILDING SKILLS THROUGH MUSIC** **Writing/Social Studies** Write new lyrics for the song

Song "Green Corn Song"

More Music Choices
"Haliwa-Saponi Canoe Song," p. 302
"Zuni Sunrise Call," p. 396

> **ASSESSMENT**
> **Performance/Observation**
> Sing intervals of a fourth accurately in a Native American song

> **TECHNOLOGY/MEDIA LINK**
> **Web Site** More information on Native American music

Connection: Culture
Activity: Discuss the traditions of Chanukah

> **SPOTLIGHT ON** **Yiddish** Facts about the language

> **CULTURAL CONNECTION** **Chanukah** Discuss holiday traditions

> **BUILDING SKILLS THROUGH MUSIC** **Art** Describe the elements of the painting

Songs
"Oy, Hanuka"
"O Chanukah"

Arts Connection *Lighting the Chanukah Lamp*

More Music Choices
"Yakety Yak," p. 205
"Good Mornin', Blues," p. 224

> **ASSESSMENT**
> **Performance/Observation**
> Sing the song with a keyboard accompaniment and rhythm ostinatos

> **TECHNOLOGY/MEDIA LINK**
> **Web Site** More information about Jewish music

Connection: Style
Activity: Explore rock 'n' roll style

> **MOVEMENT** **Popular Dance** Learn a basic swing step

> **ACROSS THE CURRICULUM** **Science** Discuss Christmas greenery: including evergreen trees, holly, and mistletoe

> **BUILDING SKILLS THROUGH MUSIC** **Dance** Perform a swing dance routine with a steady beat

Song "Rockin' Around the Christmas Tree"

More Music Choices
"Stand By Me," p. 46
"Hound Dog," p. 212

> **ASSESSMENT**
> **Performance/Observation**
> Sing a rock 'n' roll song in AABA form; sing solos during the B section

> **TECHNOLOGY/MEDIA LINK**
> **CD-ROM** Arrange an accompaniment for the song

Lesson	Elements	Skills

LESSON 7
A Musical Lullaby

pp. 468-469

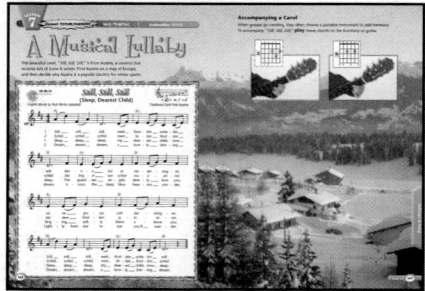

Element: Texture/Harmony
Concept: Harmony
Focus: Two-chord harmony

Secondary Element
Form: Phrases

National Standards
1c 2a 4c 6c 8a

Skill: Playing
Objective: Play a two-chord accompaniment to a carol

Secondary Skills
- **Analyzing** Analyze song notation and find same phrases; identify the chord progression
- **Singing** Sing a German carol from notation

SKILLS REINFORCEMENT
- **Guitar** Play a slow finger-picking pattern to accompany the song

---

LESSON 8
A Christmas Spiritual

pp. 470-471

Element: Form
Concept: Theme and variation
Focus: Call and response

Secondary Element
Rhythm: triplets

National Standards
1c 6a 6b 9a

Skill: Listening
Objective: Compare two versions of a call-and-response song

Secondary Skills
- **Singing** Sing a song in call-and-response form with a soloist performing the calls
- **Analyzing** Analyze and describe the form of the song

LESSON 9
Carols for Christmas

pp. 472-473

Element: Form
Concept: Melodic repetition
Focus: Repetition and contrast

Secondary Element
Rhythm: meter changes

National Standards
1c 2c 5c 8b

Skill: Analyzing
Objective: Analyze two Christmas songs containing repetition and contrast

Secondary Skills
- **Singing** Sing the song in Spanish; perform music from diverse cultures expressively

SKILLS REINFORCEMENT
- **Playing** Play a hand drum accompaniment

Connections

Music and Other Literature

Connection: Style
Activity: Recognize the harmonic style of traditional carols

ACROSS THE CURRICULUM **Language Arts** Explore poetry for choral reading and creative movement

SPOTLIGHT ON **Carols** Historical information about carols

BUILDING SKILLS THROUGH MUSIC **Language** Identify words from song text that suggest an instrumental accompaniment

Songs
"Still, Still, Still"
"Sleep, Dearest Child"

More Music Choices
"Day-O!" p. 18
"Simple Gifts," p. 184

ASSESSMENT

Performance/Observation
Play a two-chord guitar pattern while the class sings a carol

TECHNOLOGY/MEDIA LINK
CD-ROM Create a two-chord accompaniment for the song

Connection: Genre
Activity: Recognize call-and-response form in an African American spiritual

ACROSS THE CURRICULUM **Language Arts** Explore the Christmas story in an illustrated book of African American spirituals

CULTURAL CONNECTION **Call and Response** Background information on the genre

SPOTLIGHT ON **The Performers** Information about the Century Men

BUILDING SKILLS THROUGH MUSIC **Language** Write detailed descriptions of musical qualities

Song "Rise Up, Shepherd, and Follow"

Listening Selection *Rise Up, Shepherd, and Follow*

More Music Choices
"Day-O!," p. 18
"Go Down, Moses," p. 190
"Woke Up This Morning," p. 288

ASSESSMENT

Music Journal Writing
Listen to two performances of the same song; use a Venn diagram to compare the difference and similarities

TECHNOLOGY/MEDIA LINK
MIDI/Sequencing Software Use the MIDI song file to learn parts of the song

---

Connection: Culture
Activity: Learn about Christmas customs in Catalonia and Puerto Rico

CULTURAL CONNECTION **Christmas in Catalonia and Puerto Rico** Information about holiday customs

ACROSS THE CURRICULUM **Social Studies** Learn about Catalonia

BUILDING SKILLS THROUGH MUSIC **Reading** Compare ideas in two songs

Songs
"Las Navidades"
"The Christmas Season"
"El desembre congelat"
"Cold December"

More Music Choices
"Las estrellitas del cielo" ("Stars of the Heavens"), p. 175
"Don Alfonso," p. 177

ASSESSMENT

Performance/Observation
Sing the song and identify repetition and contrast

TECHNOLOGY/MEDIA LINK
Notation Software Notate a song that includes meter changes

Lesson	Elements	Skills

LESSON 10

Ring in the New!

pp. 474-475

Element: Texture/Harmony
Concept: Texture
Focus: Countermelody

Secondary Element
Timbre: electronic

National Standards
1d   4c   5e   6a   6b   7a   8b   9a

Skill: Singing
Objective: Sing a song with a countermelody

Secondary Skills
• **Analyzing** Identify sections of a song that are in unison or harmonized
• **Listening** Listen to a contemporary

LESSON 11

A Joyful Sound

pp. 476-477

Element: Melody
Concept: Pitch and direction
Focus: Interval of a fifth

Secondary Element
Rhythm: syncopation

National Standards
1c   2a   6c   7a   8b

Skill: Singing
Objective: Sing a holiday song featuring the interval of a fifth

Secondary Skills
• **Listening** Listen to discover the seven principles of Kwanzaa
• **Playing** Play phrases on a melody instrument

LESSON 12

Happy New Year!

pp. 478-479

Element: Melody
Concept: Tonality
Focus: Pentatonic scale

Secondary Element
Texture: melodic ostinato

National Standards
1c   2c   6a   6b   7a   8b   9a

Skill: Singing
Objective: Sing a pentatonic Japanese New Year song

Secondary Skills
• **Listening** Identify instrument timbres in a song recording

SKILLS REINFORCEMENT
• **Playing** Play an accompaniment on xylophone using the Japanese *Miyako* scale

Connections

Music and Other Literature

Connection: Culture

Activity: Learn about the tradition of the yule log

CULTURAL CONNECTION **Yule Log** Historical information about the tradition

ACROSS THE CURRICULUM **Language Arts** Read and dramatize a famous Christmas story; read about the history of a well-known Christmas carol

SPOTLIGHT ON **Mannheim Steamroller** Background information about the artist

BUILDING SKILLS THROUGH MUSIC **Social Studies** Compare two versions of the song using a Venn diagram

Song "Deck the Hall"

Listening Selection *Deck the Hall*

More Music Choices
"Roll On, Columbia," p. 116

ASSESSMENT

Performance/Peer Critique Sing a countermelody with a Christmas carol and evaluate the performance

TECHNOLOGY/MEDIA LINK
CD-ROM Explore various styles and create an accompaniment for the song

---

Connection: Culture

Activity: Explore the traditions of Kwanzaa and its seven principles

CULTURAL CONNECTION **Seven Principles of Kwanzaa** Description of each principle

ACROSS THE CURRICULUM **Social Studies/Art** Read about the traditions of Kwanzaa; make Kwanzaa gifts

SPOTLIGHT ON **Kwanzaa** Historical information about the celebration

BUILDING SKILLS THROUGH MUSIC **Art** Create a visual representation that shows the melody, pitch, or theme of the song

Song *"Heri za Kwanzaa"* ("Happy Kwanzaa")

More Music Choices
"The Voices of Pride," p. 86
"This World," p. 168

ASSESSMENT

Performance/Observation Accurately sing melodic phrases with an interval of a fifth

TECHNOLOGY/MEDIA LINK
Notation Software Create and notate a melody using Kwanzaa principles as text

---

Connection: Culture

Activity: Explore Japanese New Year celebrations

SPOTLIGHT ON **Temple Bells** Facts about temple bells

CULTURAL CONNECTION **Ōshogatsu (Japanese New Year)** Discuss information and traditions of the holiday

BUILDING SKILLS THROUGH MUSIC **Language** Identify English lyrics in the song that are not standard usage

Songs
"Hitotsu toya"
"Temple Bells"

More Music Choices
"Yüe liang wan wan" ("Cresent Moon"), p. 314
"Quâ câù gió bay" ("The Wind on the Bridge"), p. 460

ASSESSMENT

Performance/Self-Assessment Sing a pentatonic song while playing a pentatonic accompaniment on mallet instruments; write about the performance

TECHNOLOGY/MEDIA LINK
MIDI/Sequencing Software Use the MIDI song file to explore timbre

Lesson	Elements	Skills

LESSON 13
Three Kings Day

pp. 480-481

Element: Texture/Harmony
Concept: Harmony
Focus: Parallel and contrary motion in two-part harmony

Secondary Element
Melody: tonality

National Standards
1c 5e 6b 6c

Skill: Singing
Objective: Sing a song in two-part harmony that contains parallel and contrary motion

Secondary Skills
- **Listening** Identify the number of parts in vocal harmony; identify tonality (major or minor)
- **Analyzing** Analyze the parallel and contrary motion in melody and harmony
- **Playing** Accompany a song on guitar or Autoharp

SKILLS REINFORCEMENT
- **Guitar** Practice chord changes at a slower tempo to attain mastery

---

LESSON 14
A Song for Freedom

pp. 482-485

Element: Texture/Harmony
Concept: Harmony
Focus: Two-part harmony

Secondary Element
Expression: *legato* articulation

National Standards
1a 1d 3b 5e 6a 6c 7a 8a 8b

Skill: Singing
Objective: Sing a song about freedom in two-part harmony

Secondary Skills
- **Moving** Move to express the meaning of a phrase in the song
- **Listening** Identify and describe a specific phrase in a civil rights anthem

SKILLS REINFORCEMENT
- **Singing** Practice proper phrasing and breath control; introduce staggered breathing

---

LESSON 15
America Sings

pp. 486-489

Element: Melody
Concept: Pattern
Focus: Melodic phrases

Secondary Element
Texture/Harmony: countermelody

National Standards
1a 1d 2a 5a 5c 6b 6c 8b

Skill: Analyzing
Objective: Analyze and compare melodic phrases in two patriotic songs

Secondary Skills
- **Singing** Sing a song and analyze the phrases
- **Playing** Play a countermelody on hand chimes or resonator bells
- **Moving** Learn the sign interpretation of the song
- **Singing** Sing the song and analyze the sections
- **Listening** Identify and describe elements that contribute to the patriotic quality of a work for symphonic band

Connections

Music and Other Literature

Connection: Social Studies

Activity: Discuss the tradition of Three Kings' Day

CULTURAL CONNECTION *Tres Reyes Magos* Discuss the holiday traditions and background

TEACHER TO TEACHER **Singing Parallel Thirds** Tips on teaching vocal harmony in the classroom

BUILDING SKILLS THROUGH MUSIC **Language** Compare the musical elements of two songs

Songs
"Los reyes de Oriente"
"The Kings from the East"

More Music Choices
"De colores," p. 90
"Loch Lomond," p. 140

ASSESSMENT

Performance/Observation
Sing parallel and contrary harmony; move to show the parallel and contrary motion

TECHNOLOGY/MEDIA LINK

Web Site More information about Latin American instruments

Connection: Social Studies

Activity: Recognize songs as a means for expressing desire for freedom

MEETING INDIVIDUAL NEEDS **Inclusion** Create visual displays

CHARACTER EDUCATION **Freedom** Discuss the benefits and responsibilities of freedom

TEACHER TO TEACHER **A New Meter** Tips for teaching meter in 12

MOVEMENT **Creative Movement** Tips to help all students interpret phrases of the song

SPOTLIGHT ON **A Civil Rights Leader** Information about Dr. Martin Luther King, Jr.

ACROSS THE CURRICULUM **Language Arts** Read about tolerance and freedom

BUILDING SKILLS THROUGH MUSIC **Social Studies** Discuss how beliefs are expressed in two songs

Songs
"Lift Ev'ry Voice and Sing"
"For Children Safe and Strong"

Listening Selection *We Shall Overcome*

More Music Choices
"Go Down, Moses," p. 190
"Woke Up This Morning," p. 288

ASSESSMENT

Performance/Observation
Arrange a program for celebrating Martin Luther King; sing one song in two part harmony; sing another song with appropriate articulation

TECHNOLOGY/MEDIA LINK

MIDI/Sequencing Software Use MIDI song file to help singers learn harmony parts

---

Connection: Social Studies

Activity: Discuss the origins of the two principal patriotic songs of the United States

ACROSS THE CURRICULUM
Language Arts Read a book about our national anthem
Social Studies Discuss the war of 1812

CULTURAL CONNECTION "God Save the Queen" Background on the British national anthem

CHARACTER EDUCATION **Patriotism** Discuss ways to demonstrate patriotism

TEACHER TO TEACHER
Harmony Alternatives for boys with changing voices
Singing the National Anthem Pitch substitutions to avoid straining the voice

SPOTLIGHT ON **Francis Scott Key** Learn about the poet

BUILDING SKILLS THROUGH MUSIC **Language/Social Studies** Identify common themes in patriotic songs

Songs
"America"
"The Star-Spangled Banner"

Listening Selection *The Fourth of July*

More Music Choices
"The Voices of Pride," p. 86
"Battle Hymn of the Republic," p. 274

ASSESSMENT

Music Journal Writing
Compare the melodies of two patriotic songs; describe and explain the characteristics as "hymn-like" or "militaristic" in a journal

TECHNOLOGY/MEDIA LINK

Web Site More information on the history of patriotic songs

INTRODUCING THE UNIT

The selections in this unit are seasonal, holiday, patriotic, and special occasion songs. Many come from diverse ethnic sources or from American pop culture. Some songs tell of traditions and celebrations that are hundreds of years old. Others tell of newer celebrations.

Presented on p. 453 is a brief overview of the skills that are assessed in this unit. (See below and pp. 454–455 for unit highlights of related curricular experiences.)

For a more detailed unit overview, see Unit at a Glance, pp. 451a–451j.

UNIT PROJECT

Divide the class into small groups and assign a seasonal, holiday, or special occasion to each group (for example, winter, Christmas, harvest time, and so on). Ask each group to review the song(s) in Unit 12 that correspond to their season, holiday, or special occasion. Then encourage them to research information about their assigned holiday or season. Have each group organize a presentation, including a performance of song(s) from Unit 12, and any information gathered in their research.

Celebrate Winter

Winter festivals are popular in areas of the world where winter means snow and freezing temperatures. This picture envisions a beautiful snowy day. Imagine a sleigh ride down a long hill.

452

ACROSS THE CURRICULUM

Unit Highlights   The following interdisciplinary activities in this unit are related to the music elements presented in the lessons. See Unit at a Glance, pp. 451a–451j, for topical descriptions presented according to lesson sequence.

▶ **LANGUAGE ARTS**
- Read a Halloween poem (p. 456)
- Share a book about returning to a homeland (p. 461)
- Develop choral readings and creative movements to poetry (p. 468)
- Read about African American Christmas spirituals (p. 470)
- Read books about Christmas (p. 474)
- Share books about Dr. Martin Luther King, Jr (p. 485)
- Read a book about the history of the national anthem (p. 486)

▶ **SCIENCE**
- Read about the traditional American Christmas tree (p. 466)

▶ **SOCIAL STUDIES**
- Read about the geography of Catalonia (p. 472)
- Read a book about a Kwanzaa celebration (p. 476)
- Explore facts about American history (p. 489)

UNIT 12

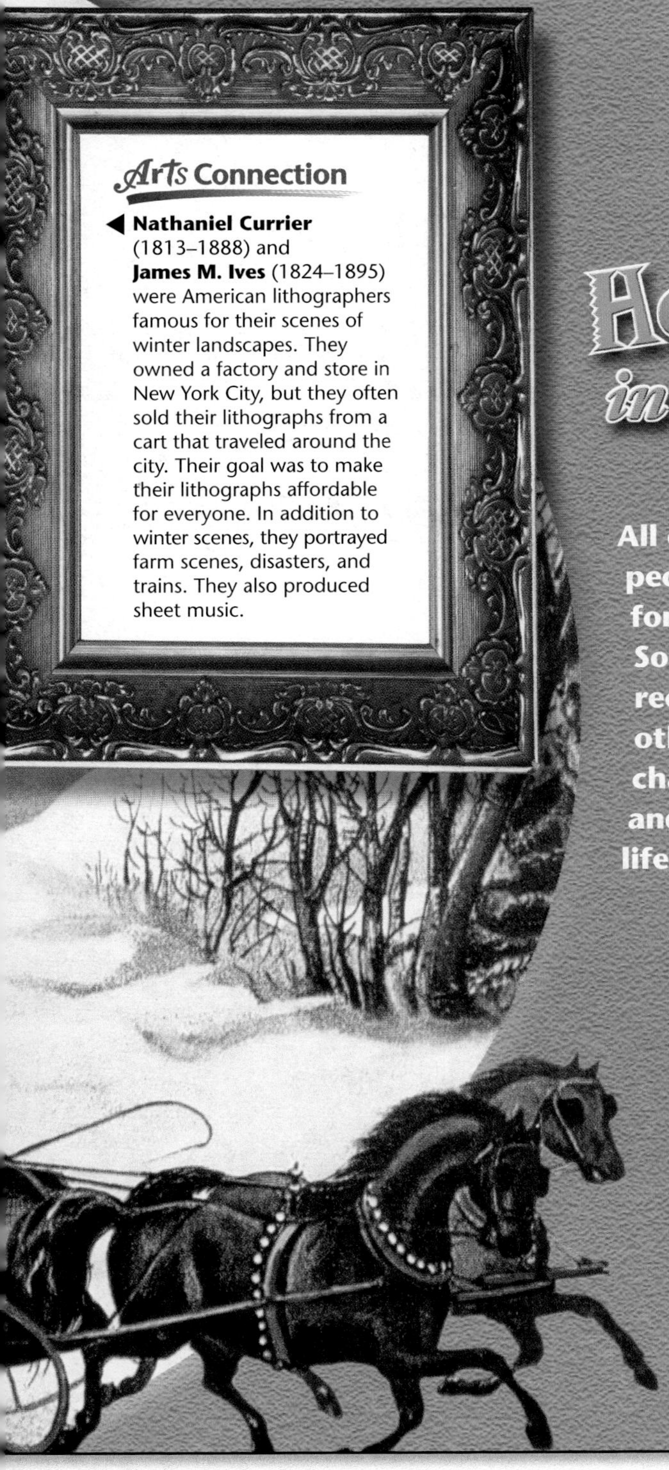

Holidays in Song

Arts Connection

◀ **Nathaniel Currier** (1813–1888) and **James M. Ives** (1824–1895) were American lithographers famous for their scenes of winter landscapes. They owned a factory and store in New York City, but they often sold their lithographs from a cart that traveled around the city. Their goal was to make their lithographs affordable for everyone. In addition to winter scenes, they portrayed farm scenes, disasters, and trains. They also produced sheet music.

All over the world, people come together for celebrations. Some celebrations recognize holidays, others observe the changing seasons, and still others honor life's milestones.

Unit 12 453

MUSIC SKILLS ASSESSED IN THIS UNIT

Reading Music: Rhythm

- Read and identify repeated rhythm patterns (p. 473)
- Read rhythm parts to perform with a song (p. 467)

Reading Music: Pitch

- Read and identify music notational signs (p. 459)
- Read and identify intervals in a song (p. 463)

Performing Music: Singing

- Perform a Thanksgiving song in two groups (p. 459)
- Sing a Vietnamese harvest song (p. 461)
- Sing a Christmas song (p. 467)
- Sing a Christmas song with a countermelody (p. 475)
- Sing a Kwanzaa song (p. 477)
- Perform a Japanese New Year song (p. 479)
- Sing songs celebrating Dr. Martin Luther King Jr.'s birthday (p. 485)

Moving to Music

- Perform a basic swing step (p. 466)
- Perform creative movement (p. 484)

Performing Music: Playing

- Perform a steady drum-beat accompaniment (p. 463)
- Perform a keyboard accompaniment (p. 465)
- Perform a chordal accompaniment (p. 469)

Creating Music

- Create pentatonic melodies (p. 479)

Listening to Music

- Listen and compare two melodic themes (p. 457)
- Listen and compare two versions of an African American Christmas song (p. 471)

CULTURAL CONNECTION

Unit Highlights The musical literature in this unit provides many opportunities for students to explore a variety of world cultures. See Unit at a Glance, pp. 451a–451j, for topical descriptions presented according to lesson sequence.

▶ **AFRICAN AMERICAN**

- Read about call and response in African-inspired music (p. 470)
- Discover the seven principles of Kwanzaa (p. 476)

▶ **ASIAN**

- Discover facts about Vietnam (p. 460)
- Learn about the Japanese New Year celebration (p. 478)

▶ **EUROPEAN**

- Read about Christmas in Catalonia (p. 472)
- Learn about the yule log tradition (p. 474)
- Learn about the melody of the British national anthem (p. 486)

▶ **LATIN AMERICAN**

- Read about Christmas in Puerto Rico (p. 472)
- Learn about the Puerto Rican celebration of *Tres Reyes Magos* (p. 480)

▶ **MIDDLE EASTERN**

- Explore facts about Chanukah (p. 465)

▶ **NATIVE AMERICAN**

- Learn about the Wakanaki (p. 462)

OPENING ACTIVITIES

MATERIALS

• "Winter Wonderland" **CD 19-19**
  Recording Routine:
  Intro (4 m.); vocal; interlude (8 m.); vocal; coda
• *A Musical Sleigh Ride* **CD 19-21**
• selected classroom instruments

Discussing

Have students define the term *celebration*. List on the board different types of celebrations. Explain that in most cultures throughout the world, people celebrate seasons. People who live in cold climates celebrate winter.

Focus students' attention on the Currier and Ives illustration on p. 452 and discuss events that might be included in winter celebrations.

Singing

Invite students to sing "Winter Wonderland" with the recording **CD 19-19.**

Encourage students to review the song and suggest sections of the song that might be sung by a soloist. (mm. 18-21 and mm. 22–25)

Moving

Have students suggest choreography for the song, relying on the text to help them plan the movements. Have the class sing the song with the choreography.

Listening

Have students read the information on p. 455. Invite students to listen to *A Musical Sleigh Ride* **CD 19-21** and determine how the composer used instruments to suggest a ride through the snow. (the constant jingle of the bells, the cracking of the whip)

Sing of Snow

Many people celebrate the beginning of the winter season. **Sing** "Winter Wonderland" and think of ways you might celebrate winter.

CD 19–19

Winter Wonderland

Words by Dick Smith

Music by Felix Bernard

Sleigh-bells ring, are you lis - t'nin'? In the lane snow is glis - t'nin', a beau - ti - ful sight, _ we're hap-py to - night, _ walk - in' in a win - ter won-der land! Gone a-way is the blue - bird; here to stay is a new bird. He sings a love song, _ as we go a - long, _ walk-in' in a win-ter won-der-land. In the mead-ow we can build a snow - man, then pre-tend that he is Par - son Brown.

454

Unit Highlights This unit includes a variety of strategies and methods, described below, to track students' progress and assess their understanding of lesson objectives.

▶ **INFORMAL ASSESSMENTS**

At the close of each Teacher's Edition lesson in this unit, one of the following types of assessments is used to evaluate the learning of the key element focus or skill objective.

• Music Journal Writing (pp. 457, 471, 489)
• Performance/Observation (pp. 461, 463, 465, 467, 469, 473, 477, 481, 485)
• Performance/Peer Critique (pp. 459, 475)
• Performance/Self-Assessment (p. 479)

▶ **RUBRICS**

Visit *www.sfsuccessnet.com* for rubrics to assess students' achievement in music skills.

He'll say, "Are you mar - ried?" We'll say, "No man, but

you can do the job when you're in town!" Lat - er on, we'll con-

spire, __ as we dream by the fire, __ to face un - a - fraid, __ the

plans that we made, __ walk - in' in a win - ter won - der - land.

Classical Sounds of Winter

Sleigh riding was very fashionable in the late 18th century. In some European countries snow was brought in from the mountains to the city for this purpose. Leopold Mozart, Wolfgang's father, wrote *A Musical Sleigh Ride* about this pastime.

Listen to the musical sounds of winter portrayed in this selection.

CD 19–21
A Musical Sleigh Ride

by Leopold Mozart
Mozart used brass instruments and jingle bells to add a festive sound to *A Musical Sleigh Ride*.

Unit 12 **455**

Creating

Divide the class into four groups and assign each group a different season of the year. Suggest that each group create a composition about its assigned season. Have the groups utilize classroom instruments to create their composition. Allow each group to perform its composition for the entire class.

INNOVATIVE TEACHER SUPPORT FOR THIS UNIT

- **MAKING MUSIC DVD, Grade 5** contains video segments that support lessons, including signing and movement.
- **MAKING MUSIC with Movement and Dance** provides more opportunities for large group activities in music or physical education classes.
- **MAKING MUSIC with Technology** provides lesson plans for many technology applications; includes MIDI files.
- *¡A cantar!* features recorded songs and lessons from around the Spanish-speaking world; includes strategies for bilingual classes and for English-speaking teachers working with Spanish-speaking students.
- **Bridges to Asia** features recorded songs and lessons from Asian and Pacific region cultures.
- *www.sfsuccessnet.com* provides an online lesson planner to conveniently create lesson plans at school or at home. Includes rubrics for assessment, lesson modifications to meet the needs of all students, performance musicals based on program content, and more.

TECHNOLOGY/MEDIA LINK

Unit Highlights The following components are used in this unit to reinforce and expand students' understanding of music elements and related themes. See Unit at a Glance, pp. 451a–451j, for a descriptive listing according to lesson sequence.

▶ **CD-ROM**

- Arrange an accompaniment using *Band-in-a-Box* (p. 467)
- Create an accompaniment using *Band-in-a-Box* (p. 469)
- Use *Band-in-a-Box* to explore various music styles (p. 475)

▶ **MIDI/SEQUENCING SOFTWARE**

- Sequence percussion parts (p. 457)
- Sequence voice parts (p. 459)
- Help students learn call-and-response form (p. 471)
- Reinforce the concept of timbre (p. 479)

- Use a MIDI song file to help students learn a harmony part (p. 485)

▶ **NOTATION SOFTWARE**

- Use notation software to learn about meter changes (p. 473)
- Create a melody using notation software (p. 477)

▶ **VIDEO LIBRARY/DVD**

- Share a video showcasing Cambodian dancing (p. 461)

▶ **WEB SITE**

- Go to *www.sfsuccessnet.com* for more information about Native American music (p. 463); Jewish music (p. 465); Latin American instruments (p. 481); history of patriotic songs (p. 489)

LESSON AT A GLANCE

Element Focus **MELODY** Melodic themes

Skill Objective **LISTENING** Listen for melodic contrast in a symphonic (tone) poem

Connection Activity **LANGUAGE ARTS** Compare a poem and a music selection

MATERIALS

- "The Addams Family" **CD 19-22**
  Recording Routine: Intro (5 m.); vocal; coda
- *Danse macabre* **CD 19-24**
- "Dance of Death" (poem) (excerpt)
- **Resource Book** p. H-29

VOCABULARY

symphonic poem

◆ ◆ ◆ National Standards ◆ ◆ ◆

1a Sing accurately in small ensembles
2a Play instruments accurately in small ensembles
4c Arrange, using electronic media
6a Listen and describe events in music using appropriate terms
6b Listen and analyze uses of pitch, rhythm, timbre in music from diverse genres
8a Show how different arts portray the same scene in unique ways

MORE MUSIC CHOICES

For other compositions by Camille Saint-Saëns:
Carnival of the Animals, "Aquarium," p. 376
Havanaise for Violin and Orchestra, p. 217

1 INTRODUCE

ASK What holiday is on October 31? (Halloween)

Ask students to read the paragraph on p. 456. Share information from Spotlight On below.

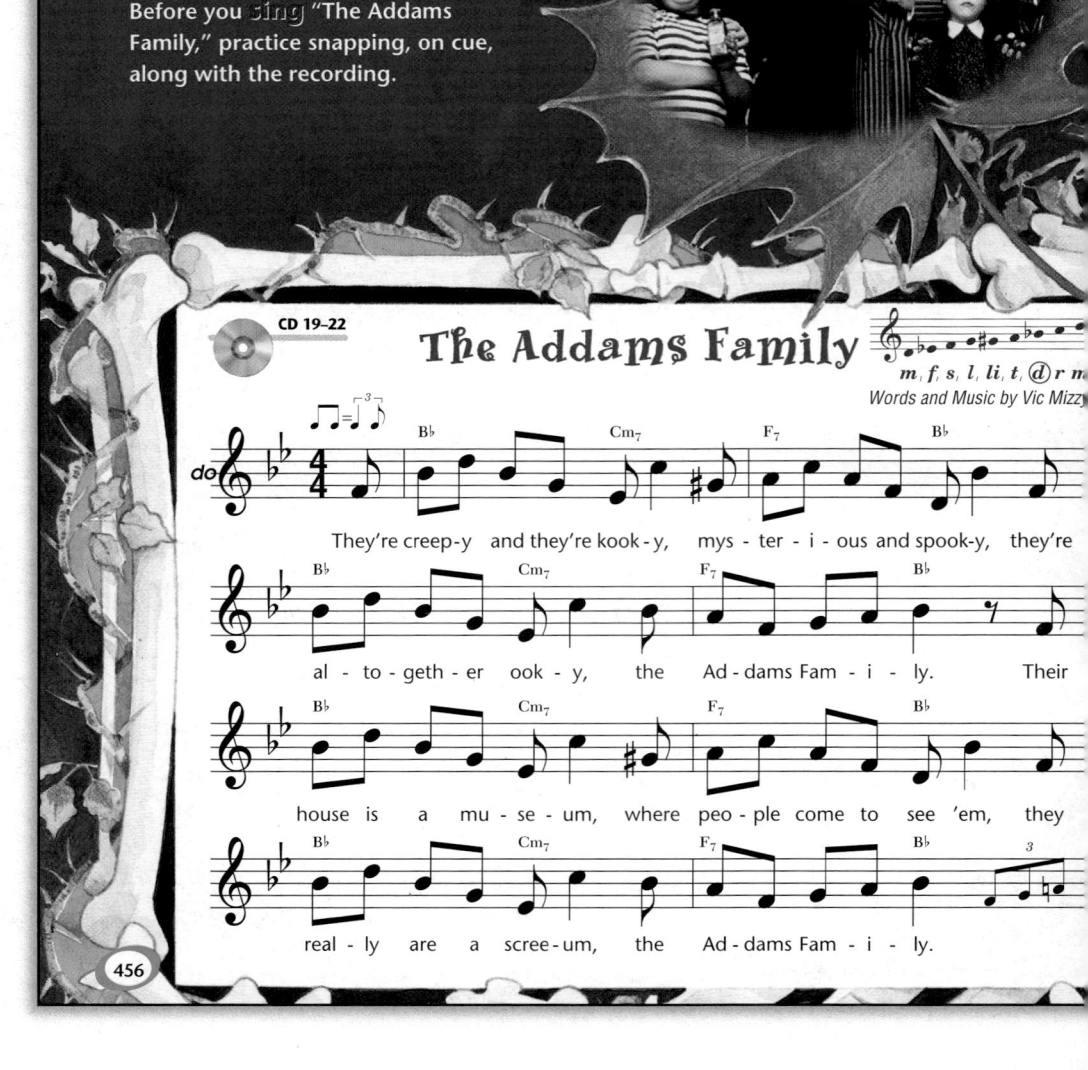

Fall Fun

It's a late October night. Unusual sounds can be heard in the distance. You may even detect a strange rhythmic snapping sound. Could it mean a Halloween visit from a certain "creepy" family?

Before you sing "The Addams Family," practice snapping, on cue, along with the recording.

CD 19–22

The Addams Family

Words and Music by Vic Mizzy

They're creep-y and they're kook-y, mys-ter-i-ous and spook-y, they're

al-to-geth-er ook-y, the Ad-dams Fam-i-ly. Their

house is a mu-se-um, where peo-ple come to see 'em, they

real-ly are a scree-um, the Ad-dams Fam-i-ly.

456

Footnotes

SPOTLIGHT ON

▶ **The Show Family** *The Addams Family* began as a cartoon series in *The New Yorker* magazine and was adapted into a TV series in the 1960s. "The Addams Family" was the theme song for this show. The show told the story of a wealthy family that celebrated all things macabre. It featured characters such as Lurch (the zombie butler), Thing (the disembodied hand), and Cousin It (an unintelligible being covered with hair).

BUILDING SKILLS THROUGH MUSIC

▶ **Language** Ask students to read the lyrics of "The Addams Family" and describe the kinds of sounds that could be used to enhance the lyrics. Then have them listen to the song recording **CD 19-22**. Have students describe ways the music enhances the text. Discuss which techniques were most effective.

ACROSS THE CURRICULUM

8a ▶ **Language Arts** Share *Dance of Death* by Henri Cazalis.

Zig-a-zig, zig-a-zig-a-zig,
Death sits on the tombstone and drums with his heel.
Zig-a-zig, zig-a-zig-a-zig,
Death tunes up his fiddle and plays a weird reel.

'Tis midnight and sadly the winter wind moans;
From shadowy lindens, with loud sighs and groans,
The skeleton dancers in white, whirling crowds
Come leaping and skipping and waving their shrouds.

Zig-a-zig, what a horrible sound
The rattle of bones as they dance 'round and 'round!
But hark! Bold young Chanticleer heralds the day
And Death and his dancers have vanished away!

A Spooky Dance

Listen for the "skeleton dancers" in this piece for orchestra. How many melodic themes do you hear?

CD 19–24
Danse macabre

by Camille Saint-Saëns
To give this symphonic poem a special "spooky" feeling, the composer instructs the solo violinist to adjust one of the instrument's strings to be out of tune.

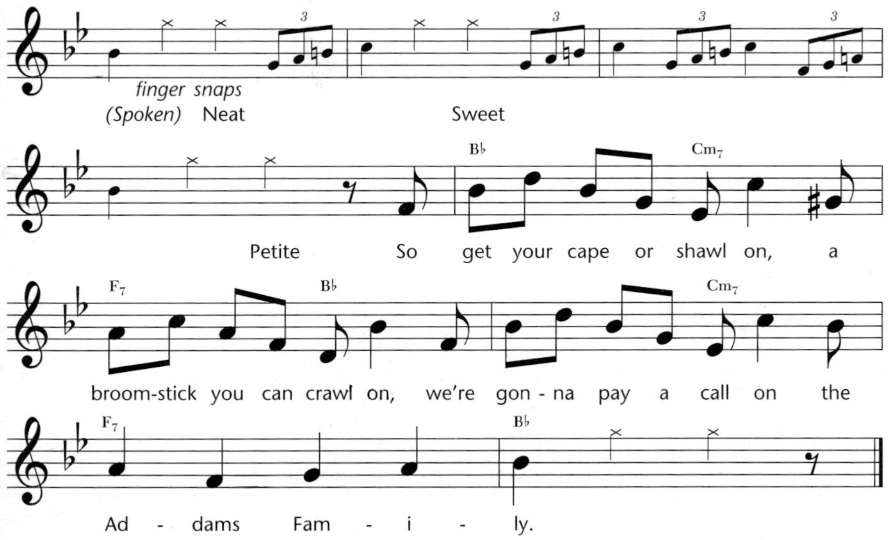

finger snaps
(Spoken) Neat Sweet Petite So get your cape or shawl on, a broom-stick you can crawl on, we're gon - na pay a call on the Ad - dams Fam - i - ly.

Holidays in Song

2 DEVELOP

Singing

1a Play the recording of "The Addams Family" **CD 19-22** and invite students to sing with the recording.

Playing

2a Encourage students to accompany the song on recorder and xylophone. (See Skills Reinforcement below.)

Listening

8a Read the excerpt from the poem "Dance of Death." (See Across the Curriculum, p. 456.)

SAY Symphonic poems are orchestral pieces based on a poetic idea or story.

Then play the recording of *Danse macabre* **CD 19-24.** Discuss the similarities between the listening selection and the poem.

6a Play the recording again.

ASK How many melodic themes did you hear? (two)

What instruments played the first melody? (first the flute and then the violins)

How did the second melody differ from the first? (The second melody was mournful.)

What instrument played the dance melody at the end? (xylophone)

3 CLOSE

Skill: LISTENING **ASSESSMENT**

6b **Music Journal Writing** Ask students to compare the two melodic themes of *Danse macabre* and add the written comparison to their music journals.

SKILLS REINFORCEMENT

 ▶ **Recorder** Using low C and D, students can play a simple countermelody to accompany "The Addams Family." During the four-measure rest, have students add the finger snaps indicated in their book.

2a

▶ **Mallets** Students will enjoy playing the interlude in "The Addams Family" on mallet instruments such as the xylophone. You will need to set up two xylophones in order to perform the B♭ and B natural.

TECHNOLOGY/MEDIA LINK

4c **Sequencing Software** Before class begins, sequence a bass track for "The Addams Family." Have students create and sequence a percussion track that can be used with the bass track for an accompaniment to their singing. Encourage them to listen to the recording to determine what each percussion instrument does, then sequence their percussion parts with one instrument on each track. Remind students to use track 10 for percussion.

LESSON AT A GLANCE

Element Focus   **TEXTURE/HARMONY** Two-part harmony

Skill Objective   **SINGING** Sing a holiday song in two parts

Connection Activity   **SOCIAL STUDIES** Discuss the history and traditions of Thanksgiving celebrations

MATERIALS

- "Come, Ye Thankful People, Come"   **CD 19-25**
  Recording Routine: Intro (6 m.); v. 1; interlude (2 m.); v. 2
- keyboard

VOCABULARY

interval   sequence

◆ ◆ ◆ ◆ **National Standards** ◆ ◆ ◆ ◆

1a Sing accurately in large ensembles
1d Sing music written in two parts
5c Define standard notation symbols for pitch
7a Students evaluate music they hear and perform
8b Identify ways music relates to social studies

MORE MUSIC CHOICES

For more practice singing songs in two-part harmony with accidentals:

"Canción Mixteca," p. 326
"Sing, Sing, Sing!" p. 340

1 INTRODUCE

8b Share with the class information about Thanksgiving from Spotlight On below. Then ask students to discuss Thanksgiving traditions celebrated by their families, and what part of the holiday they enjoy most. Select an activity from Across the Curriculum, below, to enhance the class performance.

Sing a Song of Thanks

Many cultures and countries celebrate a bountiful harvest. The United States Congress declared Thanksgiving a legal holiday in 1941 and set aside the fourth Thursday in November for its celebration.

458

Footnotes

ACROSS THE CURRICULUM

▶ **Language Arts/Drama** Create Thanksgiving mini-dramas and group choral readings from selections within *Thanksgiving: Stories and Poems* by Caroline Feller Bauer (HarperCollins, 1994). This book also includes wonderful ideas for crafts, songs, and holiday dishes.

BUILDING SKILLS THROUGH MUSIC

▶ **Language** Ask students to read the lyrics of "Come, Ye Thankful People, Come" and locate words or phrases that are not common usage today. Have students substitute standard usage words in the song lyrics for those that are not common usage.

SPOTLIGHT ON

8b ▶ **The Holiday** The Pilgrims arrived at Plymouth Rock on December 11, 1620, in the dead of winter. Forty-six of the original 102 settlers died that year. The following year, the remaining Pilgrims were able to celebrate a bountiful harvest, thanks to the help of the Wampanoag Indians, who taught them how to survive in their new home. The first Thanksgiving was a three-day feast, which included wild game, seafood, and fruit.

The thirteen colonies celebrated Thanksgiving in 1777 and 1789. However, it was not until 1863, after a 40-*year* campaign led by magazine editor Sarah Joseph Hale, that it became a common holiday in the United States. Thanksgiving was finally named an official national holiday in 1941.

Celebrate the Harvest

Sing the festive song "Come, Ye Thankful People, Come" in two-part harmony. Notice that part 2, the lower part, is highlighted.

 CD 19–25

Come, Ye Thankful People, Come

Words by Henry Alford

Music by George J. Elvey

1. Come, ye thank-ful peo-ple, come, Raise the song of
2. All the bless-ings of the field, All the stores the

har-vest home; All is safe-ly gath-ered in Ere the win-ter
gar-dens yield; All the fruits in full sup-ply, Rip-ened 'neath the

storms be-gin; God, our Mak-er, doth pro-vide For our wants to
sum-mer sky; All that spring with boun-teous hand Scat-ters o'er the

be sup-plied; Come to God's own tem-ple, come,
smil-ing land; All that lib-'ral au-tumn pours

Raise the song of har-vest home.
From her rich o'er-flow-ing stores.

Holidays in Song

Unit 12 **459**

2 DEVELOP

Singing

1a Invite students to sing "Come, Ye Thankful People, Come" **CD 19-25** with the recording.

ASK Where can you find a sequence in the song? (In the third phrase, the third and fourth measure is a sequence of the first and second measure.)

Select a group of students to sing the harmony part.

SAY Look for the sequence as you learn your parts. The interval pattern is the same.

1d Then play the harmony on keyboard to help students hear the part. When they are prepared, sing "Come, Ye Thankful People, Come" in two parts.

Reading

Encourage students to use standard terminology in explaining music notation.

5c **ASK What does a sharp do to a note?** (It raises it a half-step.)

What does a flat do to a note? (It lowers it a half-step.)

Draw students' attention to the natural sign in measures 7 and 8.

ASK Does the natural sign raise or lower the note? (It raises it, because it cancels the flat from the key signature.)

3 CLOSE

Element: TEXTURE/HARMONY — **ASSESSMENT**

7a **Performance/Peer Critique** Divide the class into two groups and have them perform "Come, Ye Thankful People, Come." Help students develop criteria for evaluating each other's performances, including balance of melody and harmony, pitch accuracy, and clear melodic sequences.

SKILLS REINFORCEMENT

5c ▶ **Notating** An accidental raises or lowers a pitch, usually by a half step. Rules govern what type of accidental is used. Help students understand that

- A sharp is used if the second note is higher than the first.
- A flat is used if the second note is lower than the first.
- A natural is used to cancel a flat or sharp.

Encourage students to identify the accidentals in "Come, Ye Thankful People, Come." Write the altered pitches on the board. (C♯, B♮, E♭, F♯) Invite students to add or remove the accidentals from the altered pitches in order to change the notes to their original pitches. Remind students there must be a half step between the altered note and the original note. (Answers: C♮, B♭, E♮, F♮)

TECHNOLOGY/MEDIA LINK

Sequencing Software Have students work in pairs to

- Sequence a Voice 1 track and a Voice 2 track, using excerpts from the vocal parts in their textbooks.
- Record additional percussion tracks (Channel 10) to accompany the song.
- Play their sequences for the class.

LESSON AT A GLANCE

Element Focus **MELODY** Pentatonic scale

Skill Objective **SINGING** Sing a pentatonic song in antiphonal style

Connection Activity **CULTURE** Explore Vietnamese culture

MATERIALS

- "Quâ câù gió bay" **CD 20-1**
- "The Wind on the Bridge" **CD 20-2**
  Recording Routine: Intro (8 m.); v. 1; v. 2; interlude (4 m.); v. 3
- **Pronunciation Practice/Translation** p. 543
- **Resource Book** p. A-49
- mallet instruments

VOCABULARY

pentatonic   accompaniment

◆ ◆ ◆ ◆ National Standards ◆ ◆ ◆ ◆

1c Sing music from diverse cultures
6b Listen and analyze uses of pitch in music from diverse cultures
8b Identify ways music relates to social studies

MORE MUSIC CHOICES

For more practice singing songs from Asian cultures:
"Arirang," p. 25
"Jasmine Flowers," p. 316

1 INTRODUCE

8b **ASK Why is harvest a time for celebration?** (Accept all reasonable answers.)

SAY In many cultures, it is customary to celebrate the harvest with parties and dancing. "Quâ câù gió bay" is a harvest song from Vietnam.

An Autumn Song

The song "Quâ câù gió bay" is the story of a boy who falls in love with a girl and gives her his coat, hat, and ring as tokens of his affection. When he returns home and is questioned by his parents regarding the missing articles, he tells them that the wind on the bridge took them away.

Sing this well-known song from Vietnam. It is often sung during spring and autumn harvest festivals.

CD 20–1

Quâ câù gió bay
(The Wind on the Bridge)

English Words by Bryan Louiselle   *Folk Song from Vietnam*

1. Yêu   nhau   còi___ áo   ý___ a   cho___ nhau.
1. My   love,   take my coat   as   a   sign   of my   love,

Về___ nhà   dối___ rằng   cha   dối___ mẹ___ a___ ý___ a.
Though, when I   go___ home, I   shall___ have to   tell___ this   tale:

Rằng   a   ý___ a___ qua___ cầu. Rằng   a   ý___ a___ qua___ cầu.
When   I   was___ stand-ing on the bridge, When   I   was___ stand-ing on the bridge,

460

Footnotes

SPOTLIGHT ON

▶ **Antiphonal Singing** Antiphonal singing used in "Quâ câù gió bay" is a performance style in which two choirs alternate singing. When singing is antiphonal, conductors sometimes position choirs with space between them or even move them to different places in the room. The Latin term, *antiphona*, was originally applied to this type of performance in Eastern cultures in the first century A.D. It referred to the specific practice of alternating between a men's choir and a women's choir.

BUILDING SKILLS THROUGH MUSIC

▶ **Social Studies** Share the information on p. 460. After students answer the question "Why is harvest a time for celebration?" have them research and discuss what crops are harvested in Vietnam and compare to their region of the United States.

CULTURAL CONNECTION

8b ▶ **Vietnam** Vietnam is an S-shaped, densely populated country that stretches along the Gulf of Tonkin, the South China Sea, and the Gulf of Thailand in Southeast Asia. It borders China, Laos, Thailand, and Cambodia. The country was considered a French colony from the late 1800s to the end of World War II. Ho Chi Minh seized control of North Vietnam in 1954 and created a communist regime that controlled the entire country by 1975.

Years of warfare have left the region economically poor, but the Vietnamese people have preserved a rich cultural heritage. Festivals highlighting music, the martial arts, folklore, and athletic competitions occur year-round in different regions of the country. *Trung thu*, a nationally-recognized September festival, honors the moon and features a procession of children carrying lanterns.

▲ During spring and autumn harvest festivals in Vietnam, participants dress in their finest, most traditional costumes to represent their villages.

Holidays in Song

Tình   tình   tình   gió_____   bay,   Tình   tình   tình   gió_____   bay.
A   strong wind blew the coat a - way,   A   strong wind blew the coat a - way.

2. *Yêu nhau cởi nón ý a cho nhau.*
   Về nhà dối rằng cha dối mẹ a ý a.
   Rằng a ý a qua cầu. Rằng a ý a qua cầu.
   Tình tình tình gió bay,
   Tình tình tình gió bay.

3. *Yêu nhau cởi nhẫn ý a cho nhau.*
   Về nhà dối rằng cha dối mẹ a ý a.
   Rằng a ý a qua cầu. Rằng a ý a qua cầu.
   Tình tình tình đánh roi,
   Tình tình tình đánh roi.

2. My love, take my hat as a sign of my love,
   Though, when I go home,
   I shall have to tell this tale:
   When I was standing on the bridge,
   When I was standing on the bridge,
   A strong wind blew the hat away,
   A strong wind blew the hat away.

3. My love, take this ring as a sign of my love,
   Though, when I go home,
   I shall have to tell this tale:
   When I was standing on the bridge,
   When I was standing on the bridge,
   A strong wind made me drop the ring,
   A strong wind made me drop the ring.

Unit 12 **461**

2 DEVELOP

Singing

1c Have students learn the Vietnamese words for *"Quâ câu gió bay"* using the Pronunciation Practice Track **CD 20-4** and Resource Book p. A-49. Then ask students to sing the Vietnamese lyrics with the recording **CD 20-1**.

Have students read the paragraphs and then look at the song notation while listening to the recording.

ASK What scale do you hear? How many pitches does it have? (pentatonic/five)

6b **Where do you hear echoes in this song?** (mm. 8 and 9 echo mm. 10 and 11; mm. 12 and 13 echo mm. 14 and 15)

Divide the class into two groups, one smaller than the other. Have the larger group sing the first two measures of the echo, and the smaller group sing the second two measures. Point out that the second group should be softer than the first.

ASK What do you call this style of singing? (antiphonal)

Using antiphonal style, have the groups sing both the Vietnamese **CD 20-1** and English **CD 20-2** versions of the song with the recordings. Switch students within the groups so that all have a chance to sing in the larger and smaller groups.

3 CLOSE

Element: MELODY   **ASSESSMENT**

Performance/Observation Have small groups of students sing *"Quâ câu gió bay."* Observe each group's ability to sing the pentatonic patterns accurately.

ACROSS THE CURRICULUM

▶ **Language Arts/Social Studies** Encourage students to read *Two Lands, One Heart: An American Boy's Journey to His Mother's Vietnam* by Jeremy Schmidt (Walker and Company, 1995). A young man, TJ, accompanies his mother to her homeland after a 25-year absence. The story is a narrative of a touching family reunion and details TJ's travel adventures. At the same time, the book paints a rich portrait of the culture, people, and land of Vietnam through its strikingly beautiful photography.

TECHNOLOGY/MEDIA LINK

Video Library Have students watch the video *Dancing* to help them understand different dance forms from Cambodia. As students watch the video, have them answer the following questions about the dance observed:

• What parts of the body are emphasized in the dance?

• Who do you think is performing, a professional or amateur?

• How are the dances taught?

LESSON AT A GLANCE

Element Focus **MELODY** Intervals

Skill Objective **SINGING** Sing accurately the intervals of a Native American song

Connection Activity **CULTURE** Learn about Native American harvest

MATERIALS
- "Green Corn Song" **CD 20-5**
  Recording Routine: Intro (7 m.); vocal

VOCABULARY
interval

◆ ◆ ◆ ◆ National Standards ◆ ◆ ◆ ◆

1c Sing music from diverse cultures
2b Perform easy instrumental pieces with technical accuracy
6b Listen and analyze uses of rhythm in music from diverse cultures
6c Understand and use basic principles of intervals in music analysis

MORE MUSIC CHOICES

For more practice singing Native American songs:
"Haliwa-Saponi Canoe Song," p. 302
"Zuni Sunrise Call," p. 396

1 INTRODUCE

Explain that long before the first Thanksgiving, Native Americans celebrated their harvest with singing and dancing.

Invite students to read the information on p. 462. Then share the information in Cultural Connection below.

A HARVEST SONG

Native American people on the East coast use song and dance to celebrate planting, growing, and harvesting food. The Native American "Green Corn Song" is sung by many tribes. Traditionally, the first part is sung by an elder woman, representing the corn-chooser; then other women join in. Today, the song can be sung by a combination of men and women.

Listen to "Green Corn Song," a harvest song that has been sung for hundreds of years.

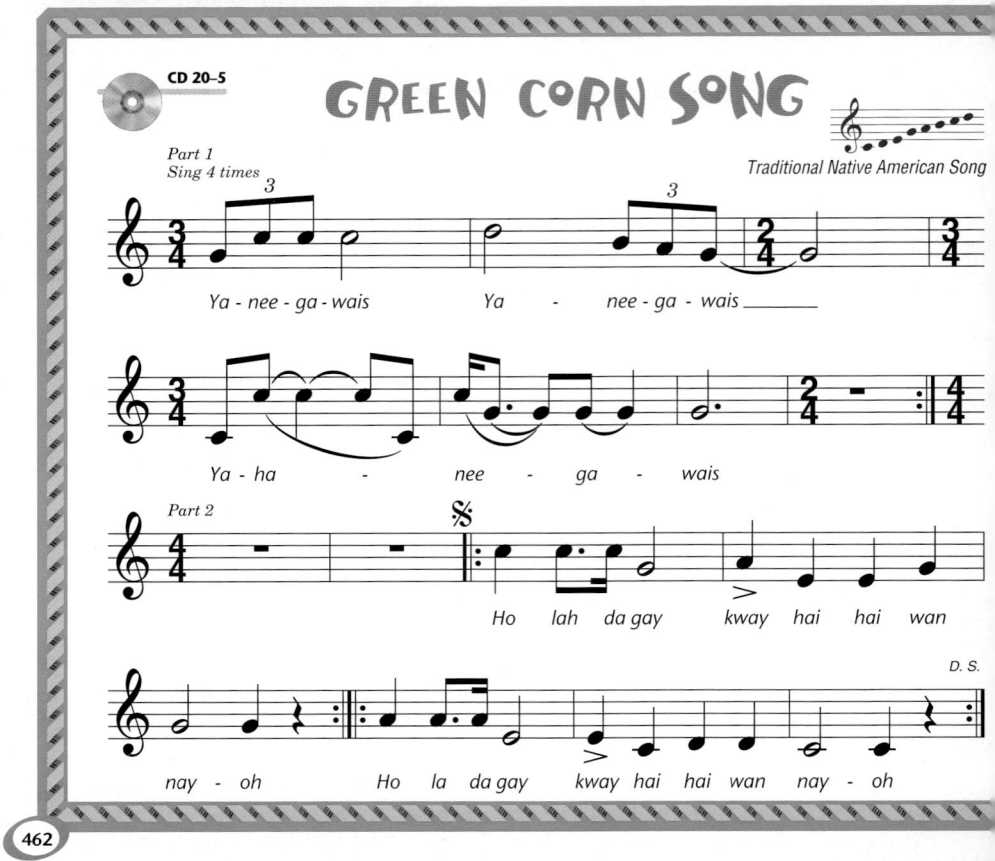

462

Footnotes

SPOTLIGHT ON

▶ **Corn** Corn, also called *maize,* is native to North and South America. Its edible grains grow in many colors, including yellow, red, blue, pink, and black. Historians estimate that it has been planted and harvested for 7,000 years. Corn has always been an important part of many Native American cultures.

Today, corn is one of the world's most popular crops, not only for its sweet grains, but also for its husks, fibers, and cobs.

BUILDING SKILLS THROUGH MUSIC

▶ **Writing/Social Studies** Invite students to sing "Green Corn Song" **CD 20-5.** Divide students into groups to create new lyrics using English words in place of the vocables. Possible subject ideas may include descriptions of the harvest, crops being harvested, and the coming of autumn.

CULTURAL CONNECTION

▶ **The Wabanaki** "Green Corn Song" is associated with the Wabanaki, descendants of the earliest known people to live in the region of New Brunswick, Canada. In the legends of these people, the first person was *Gloosk-ob,* meaning "good man." Gloosk-ob's grandmother taught him that the Great Power existed in the land and in all things. She also taught survival skills and the traits of sharing, respect, and cooperation. When Gloosk-ob grew, he traveled with his grandmother in a stone canoe. As he traveled, he created animals, fish, birds, and people. His creations traveled far and wide. Eventually, they landed in Wabanaki, the "Land of the Dawn."

2 DEVELOP

Reading

6c Direct students to look at the notation of "Green Corn Song."

ASK What interval begins the first line of the song? (fourth)

Have students find all of the fourths in the melody of the song.

ASK What interval begins the second line of the song? (octave)

Singing

Play the recording of "Green Corn Song" **CD 20-5** as students follow the notation.

1c Use the singing activity in Skills Reinforcement, below, to help students sing specific intervals in the song. Then invite students to sing again with the recording.

6b **ASK How do you know when part 2 begins?** (the drumbeat changes to half time)

Point out that the lyrics repeat many times.

SAY The text of "Green Corn Song" is composed of *vocables*—syllables that do not have a literal meaning but may, nonetheless, have specific meaning to the Native American performer and audience.

3 CLOSE

Element: MELODY **ASSESSMENT**

2b **Performance/Observation** Have small groups of students sing "Green Corn Song" with a steady drumbeat accompaniment. Assess students' ability to sing the intervals accurately.

A Native American dancer at the Schemitzun festival. This event features Native American dancers, drummers, and entertainers from more than 500 tribal nations across North America.

SKILLS REINFORCEMENT

▶ **Singing** Have students practice singing the intervals in "Green Corn Song." Ask them to

- Find and sing all the intervals of a fourth, both up and down.
- Find and sing the octaves.
- Practice singing the intervals again, focusing on keeping the pitches connected but energized.
- Remind students to keep the tone blended between chest and head registers.

SCHOOL TO HOME CONNECTION

▶ **Old-Fashioned Popcorn** Native Americans grew corn for popping more than 1,000 years before Europeans arrived in the fifteenth century. To make popcorn the "old-fashioned" way, select a large pan with a cover loose enough to allow steam to escape. Put in ⅓ cup oil in the pan for each cup of kernels. When the oil is hot, add enough popcorn to cover the bottom, cover the pan, and shake it over heat. Remove the pan when the popping slows down.

TECHNOLOGY/MEDIA LINK

Web Site Have students go to *www.sfsuccessnet.com* to learn more about Native American music.

LESSON AT A GLANCE

Element Focus **TEXTURE/HARMONY** I, IV, and V₇ chords

Skill Objective **PLAYING** Play ostinatos to accompany a Chanukah song

Connection Activity **CULTURE** Discuss the traditions of Chanukah

MATERIALS

- "Oy, Hanuka" — CD 20-7
- "O, Chanukah" — CD 20-8
  Recording Routine: Intro (4 m.); vocal; interlude (4 m.); vocal; coda
- **Pronunciation Practice/Translation:** p. 544
- **Resource Book** pp. A-50, H-30
- finger cymbals, tambourine, hand drum

VOCABULARY

ostinato

◆ ◆ ◆ **National Standards** ◆ ◆ ◆ ◆

1c Sing music from diverse genres
2a Play instruments accurately in small ensembles
6c Understand and use the basic principles of chords in music analysis
8b Identify ways music relates to social studies

MORE MUSIC CHOICES

For more practice singing songs with I, IV, and V₇ chords:
"Yakety Yak," p. 205
"Good Mornin', Blues," p. 224

1 INTRODUCE

8b Have students read the text on pp. 464 and 465 and look at the painting. Discuss some of the traditions associated with Chanukah (see Cultural Connection, p. 465).

Play the recording of "Oy, Hanuka" **CD 20-7** and invite students to follow the song notation.

A Chanukah Celebration

People of the Jewish faith celebrate Chanukah, the Festival of Lights, for eight days usually in December. **Sing** "Oy, Hanuka" and join in the celebration.

CD 20-7

Oy, Hanuka
(O, Chanukah)

English Words by Judith Eisenstein

Yiddish Folk Song

ⓛ t, d r m f l

Oy, Ha-nu-ka, Oy, Ha-nu-ka, a yom-tov a shey-ner, A lu-sti-ker, a frey-le-kher, ni-to nokh a-zoi-ner. __
O, Cha-nu-kah, O, Cha-nu-kah, come light the me-no-rah. __
Let's __ have a par-ty, we'll all dance the ho-rah. __

Al-le nakht in drey-dl shpi-ln __ mir,
Gath-er round the ta-ble, we'll give you a treat,

Zu-dik hey-se lat-kes, est on a shir. Gesh-
Shin-ing tops to play with and lat-kes to eat; And

vin-der, tsindt kin-der, Dee di-nin-ke likh-te-lekh ohn.
while we are play-ing, The can-dles are burn-ing __ low,

Zingt "Al Ha-ni-sim," loibt Gott far di ni-sim, Un
One for each night, they __ shed a sweet light to re-

1.
kumt gi-kher tan-tsn in kohn.
mind us of days long a-go,

2.
kumt gi-kher tan-tsn in kohn.
mind us of days long a-go.

464

Footnotes

SPOTLIGHT ON

▶ **Yiddish** Yiddish is known as a Germanic language, like English and German. It is written with Hebrew characters from right to left like two other Jewish languages, Hebrew and Aramaic. When Jews moved to German-speaking areas and eventually to Slavic regions, Yiddish evolved from the merging of German, French, Italian, Slavic, Hebrew, and Aramaic. Many Yiddish words have made their way into the English language, including *bagel* and *schmooze*.

BUILDING SKILLS THROUGH MUSIC

▶ **Art** Invite students to look at the Arts Connection, *Lighting the Chanukah Lamp* on p. 465. Ask students to describe the painting, citing such characteristics as color, form, and line.

SKILLS REINFORCEMENT

▶ **Keyboard** Have students play an accompaniment with "Oy, Hanuka." See Resource Book p. H-30.

2a

Lighting the Chanukah Lamp by
Dora Holzhandler, 1996 ▶

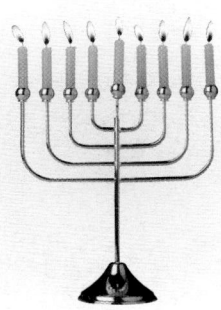

Play a Festival Song

Play these ostinatos to
accompany *"Oy, Hanuka."* The
hand drum part should be
omitted on line 4 of the song.

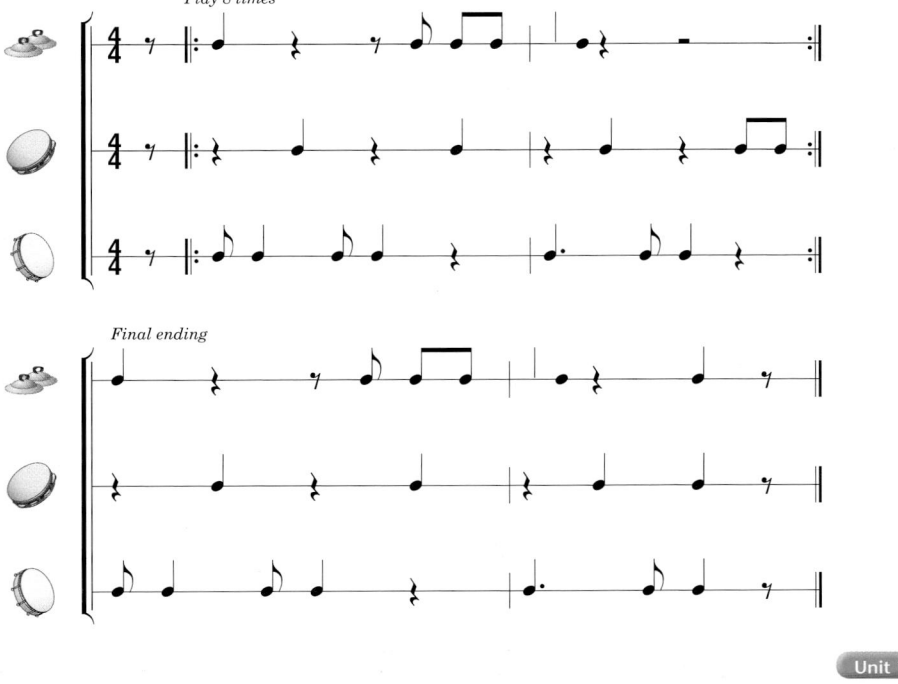

Play 8 times

Final ending

2 DEVELOP

Singing

1c Help students to learn the Yiddish words with
Pronunciation Practice Track **CD 20-10** and
Resource Book p. A-50. For more information on
Yiddish language, see Spotlight On p. 464.

Invite the class to sing *"Oy, Hanuka"* **CD 20-7** with the
recording.

Playing

Ask students to look at the song notation again.

6c **ASK What chords are used in** *"Oy, Hanuka"?* (Dm (I),
Gm (IV), and A₇ (V))

2a Have students review these chords by playing them on
the keyboard. Students may also be invited to perform
a keyboard accompaniment with *"Oy, Hanuka."* See
Skills Reinforcement on p. 464.

Point out the ostinatos on p. 465. Ask several students
to play the ostinatos with the indicated instruments
while the rest of the class sings the song.

3 CLOSE

Element: TEXTURE/HARMONY ▸ **ASSESSMENT**

1c **Performance/Observation** Divide the class into
small groups. Ask each group to accompany the class
2a with a keyboard accompaniment and/or the rhythm
ostinatos on p. 465.

Observe students' ability to accompany while the class
sings *"Oy, Hanuka."*

CULTURAL CONNECTION

8b ▶ **Chanukah** The Jewish holiday of Chanukah lasts for eight
days and nights. Families celebrate the holiday in their homes by
lighting an additional candle of the *menorah* each night until all
are lit. Jewish families recite special prayers, sing songs, play
Chanukah games, and exchange gifts each night. They may also
eat traditional foods such as apple fritters and cookies, crispy
potato latkes, and cheese-filled donuts.

TECHNOLOGY/MEDIA LINK

Web Site To learn more about Jewish music, visit
www.sfsuccessnet.com.

LESSON AT A GLANCE

Element Focus **FORM** AABA

Skill Objective **SINGING** Sing a song in rock 'n' roll style

Connection Activity **STYLE** Explore rock 'n' roll style

MATERIALS
- "Rockin' Around the Christmas Tree" **CD 20-11**

  Recording Routine: Intro (4 m.); vocal; interlude (8 m); coda
- sleigh bells/suspended cymbal, snare drum, bass drum

VOCABULARY
D. S. al Coda   *coda*

◆ ◆ ◆ ◆ **National Standards** ◆ ◆ ◆ ◆

1a Sing accurately in small ensembles
2a Play instruments accurately
6b Listen and analyze uses of form in music from diverse genres
8b Identify ways music relates to science
9a Describe characteristics of music genres from a variety of cultures

MORE MUSIC CHOICES
For more practice with rock 'n' roll songs:
"Stand By Me," p. 46
"Hound Dog," p. 212

1 INTRODUCE

8b Invite students to make a list of signs of Christmas, including season, weather, related holidays, and songs. Share the information in Across the Curriculum below.

A Rockin' Holiday Song

"Rockin' Around the Christmas Tree" was written in the 1950s, when rock 'n' roll was young.

Sing this upbeat song and **move** to the beat.

Create a rhythmic accompaniment that reflects the form of the song.

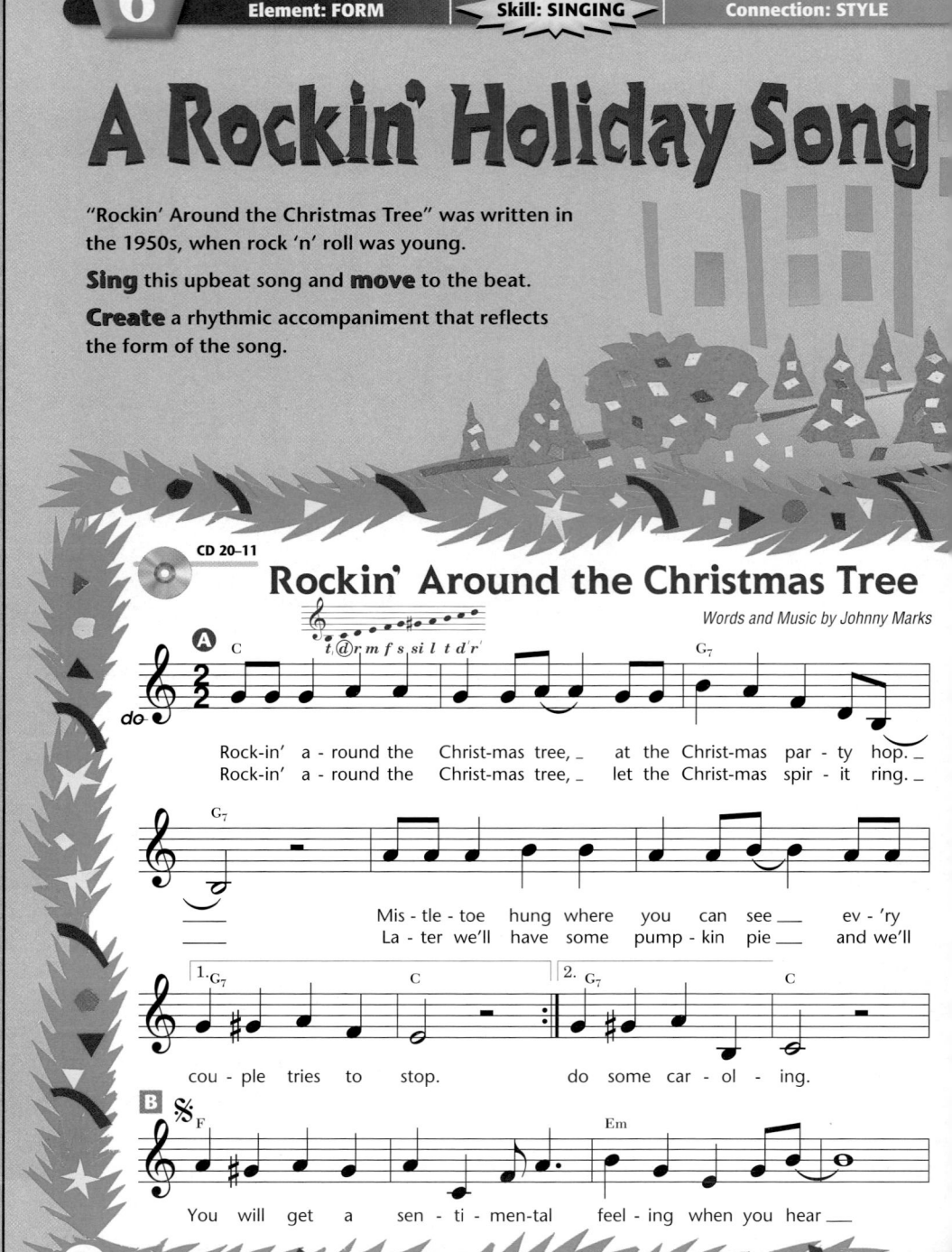

Footnotes

MOVEMENT

▶ **Popular Dance** The basic swing step for *Pennsylvania 6-5000* can be performed with "Rockin' Around the Christmas Tree." See Dance Directions on p. 566 for the complete routine.

BUILDING SKILLS THROUGH MUSIC

▶ **Dance** Invite students to perform a swing dance routine with "Rockin' Around the Christmas Tree" **CD 20-11.** Monitor students' movements to make sure they are performing with the steady beat of the song.

ACROSS THE CURRICULUM

8b ▶ **Science** "Rockin' Around the Christmas Tree" mentions three of the season's most famous symbols: Christmas trees, holly branches, and mistletoe. All three plants remain green throughout the year.

The traditional American Christmas tree is either a balsam or Douglas fir. They thrive in cold-temperate regions and have thick needlelike leaves that withstand freezing weather.

Holly grows as either a tree or a bush, from 40–50 feet tall. It has red or black berries.

Mistletoe is a small bush that grows on a branch of a host tree. It produces white berries in the winter that may be poisonous to people and animals.

Sheet Music (left side)

| Am | Am₇ | D₇ | G₇ |

voic - es sing - ing, "Let's be jol - ly, Deck the halls with boughs of hol - ly."

A C .... G₇

Rock-in' a - round the Christ-mas tree, have a hap - py hol - i - day. —

G₇ .... *Last time to Coda* ⊕ .... C *D. S. al Coda*

Ev-'ry-one danc-ing mer - ri - ly — in the new old - fash-ioned way.

⊕ *Coda* G₇ C

new old - fash - ioned way.

Holidays in Song

Unit 12 **467**

---

2 DEVELOP

Analyzing

6b Play the recording of "Rockin' Around the Christmas Tree" **CD 20-11** as students follow the notation. (Explain, if necessary, the directions *D.S. al Coda.*)

Help students map the basic form of the song (AABA): A: Lines 1–3; A: Lines 1–3; B: Lines 4–5; A: Lines 6–7.

Singing

1a Invite students to sing "Rockin' Around the Christmas Tree" **CD 20-11**, "swinging" the eighth notes.

Playing

2a Divide the class into three groups to play the following parts with "Rockin' Around the Christmas Tree."

Group 1: Sleigh bells (or suspended cymbal)

Group 2: Snare drum rim (or top of desk)

Group 3: Bass drum (or large hand drum)

See Skills Reinforcement below for additional playing suggestions.

Students may also be invited to create a rhythmic accompaniment in AABA form.

3 CLOSE

 Skill: SINGING   **ASSESSMENT**

1a **Performance/Observation** Organize the class into small groups. Have each group sing "Rockin' Around the Christmas Tree" with the recording. Encourage soloists to sing the B section of the song. Observe students' ability to accurately sing the song in AABA form.

SKILLS REINFORCEMENT

▶ **Singing** Singing in a pop style can sometimes cause singers to forget good vocal technique. Remind students to

- Use good posture.
- Take a good breath to "swing" the voice through the rhythm patterns.
- Make an effort to blend the chest and head registers.
- Sing with appropriate diction and vowel tones.

2a ▶ **Playing** Challenge students to play like a rock 'n' roll drum-
9a mer. Ask them to play the bell part with their left hand, the snare part with their right hand, and the bass drum part by tapping a foot on the floor. Suggest that they "swing" the eighth notes.

TECHNOLOGY/MEDIA LINK

CD-ROM Invite students to arrange an accompaniment for "Rockin' Around the Christmas Tree" using *Band-in-a-Box*. Have them

- Choose the key of C and a $\frac{2}{2}$ meter.
- Type the chord symbols.
- Choose a rock accompaniment.

LESSON AT A GLANCE

Element Focus **TEXTURE/HARMONY** Two-chord harmony

Skill Objective **PLAYING** Play a two-chord accompaniment to a carol

Connection Activity **STYLE** Recognize the harmonic style of traditional carols

MATERIALS

- "*Still, Still, Still*"   **CD 20-14**
- "*Sleep, Dearest Child*"   **CD 20-15**

  Recording Routine: Intro (4 m.); v. 1; interlude (4 m.); v. 2; coda

- **Pronunciation Practice/Translation** p. 544
- **Resource Book** p. A-51
- Autoharp, guitar

VOCABULARY

carol

◆ ◆ ◆ ◆ National Standards ◆ ◆ ◆ ◆

1c Sing music from diverse cultures
2a Play instruments accurately in small ensembles
4c Arrange, using electronic media
6c Understand and use basic principles of chords in music analysis
8a Show how different arts portray the same scene in unique ways

MORE MUSIC CHOICES

For more practice singing songs with two-chord harmony:
"Day-O!" p. 18
"Simple Gifts," p. 184

1 INTRODUCE

SAY "Still, Still, Still" is a traditional carol from Austria. Imagine the quiet of a snow-covered mountain as you listen.

A Musical Lullaby

This beautiful carol, "*Still, Still, Still*," is from Austria, a country that receives lots of snow in winter. Find Austria on a map of Europe, and then decide why Austria is a popular country for winter sports.

CD 20-14

Still, Still, Still
(Sleep, Dearest Child)

English Words by Ruth Martin (adapted)

Traditional Carol from Austria

do

1. Still, ___ still, ___ still, weils Kind - lein schla - fen
2. Schlaf, ___ schlaf, ___ schlaf, mein lie - bes Kind - lein
1. Sleep, ___ sleep, ___ sleep, my ___ dear - est ___ child, now ___
2. Dream, ___ dream, ___ dream, a ___ love - ly ___ shin - ing ___

will. Ma - ri - a ___ tut es nie - der - sing - en,
schlaf. Die Eng - el ___ tun schön mu - si - zie - ren
sleep. The guard - ian ___ an - gels dear - ly ___ love you,
dream. A - cross the ___ deep blue heav - ens ___ yon - der,

sei - ne ___ gro - sse Lieb dar - bring - en.
bei dem ___ Kind - lein ju - bi - lie - ren.
Sing - ing ___ soft - ly there a - bove you.
Light - ly from star to star you'll ___ wan - der.

Still, ___ still, ___ still, weils ___ Kind - lein ___ schla - fen ___ will.
Schlaf, ___ schlaf, ___ schlaf, mein ___ lie - bes ___ Kind - lein ___ schlaf.
Sleep, ___ sleep, ___ sleep, my ___ dear - est ___ child, now ___ sleep.
Dream, ___ dream, ___ dream, a ___ love - ly ___ shin - ing ___ dream.

468

Footnotes

ACROSS THE CURRICULUM

8a ▶ **Language Arts** Develop choral readings and creative movement to poetry selections from *Winter Poems* selected by Barbara Rogasky (Scholastic, 1999). Over 25 well-known poets have contributed to this fine collection of poetry about the sights, sounds, feelings, and textures of the season.

BUILDING SKILLS THROUGH MUSIC

▶ **Language** Ask students to look at the lyrics of "Sleep, Dearest Child" and identify specific words or phrases that should be considered in planning an accompaniment. Invite them to listen to **CD 20-15** and identify instruments heard in the accompaniment. Have students match specific words and phrases from the lyrics to the instrument.

SPOTLIGHT ON

▶ **Carols** The carol was created in England during the Middle Ages. It was a monophonic piece written in Latin, English, or a combination of the two. Carols were originally in verse-refrain form, but the term now refers to any kind of popular strophic song, usually with a Christmas-oriented text. The English were not alone in writing carols. The French *noël*, Italian *lauda*, and German *Weihnachtslied* are equivalents of the carol. The carol became associated with popular music instead of art music. Kings College, in Cambridge, started the tradition of pairing Christmas texts with Christmas carols in 1918. This became a staple of the Christmas season.

Accompanying a Carol

When groups go caroling, they often choose a portable instrument to add harmony. To accompany *"Still, Still, Still,"* **play** these chords on the Autoharp or guitar.

2 DEVELOP

Analyzing

Play the recording of *"Still, Still, Still"* **CD 20-14.** Share information about carols in Spotlight On, p. 468.

6c Have students look at the song notation for *"Still, Still, Still"* and find the phrases that are the same. (1 and 4, and 2 and 3) Then ask them to determine the chords in the song from the notation. (D and A₇, or I and V₇)

SAY Carols are traditionally written in a simple harmonic style, so that everyone can sing them.

Singing

1c Teach students the German lyrics to *"Still, Still, Still"* using the Pronunciation Practice Track **CD 20-17** and Resource Book A-51. Then have students sing the song with the recording **CD 20-14.**

Play the English version, "Sleep, Dearest Child" **CD 20-15,** and ask students to follow the notation. Remind them of the repeated phrases.

Playing

2a Assign students to play guitar or Autoharp. Point out the photographs of the guitar chord fingerings at the top of p. 469. (See also Skills Reinforcement below.) Then organize the class into small groups and have some members of the group sing the song and the others play the chord accompaniment.

3 CLOSE

Element: TEXTURE/HARMONY — ASSESSMENT

1c **Performance/Observation** Have students, individually or in small groups, play the chord accompaniment while the rest of the class sings the song. Assess students' ability to play the chords accurately.

SKILLS REINFORCEMENT

2a ▶ **Guitar** Students can play a slow fingerpicking pattern to accompany *"Still, Still, Still."* Finger the D and A₇ chords in the left hand as shown on p. 469. Play the notes of the finger-picked chords on even quarter notes in the right hand. The right hand fingers are: *p* = thumb, *i* = index finger, *m* = middle finger, and *a* = ring finger. The thumb *(p)* always picks the lower note (the root of the chord) with a downward motion. The other fingers pluck the strings with an upward motion.

On the D chord, finger-pick: *p* on open D string, *i* on 3rd string (G), *m* on 2nd string (B), and *a* on 1st string (E).

On the A₇ chord, finger-pick: *p* on open A string, *i* on open 3rd string (G), *m* on 2nd string (B), and *a* on open 1st string (E).

TECHNOLOGY/MEDIA LINK

4c **CD-ROM** Encourage students to create a two-chord accompaniment for *"Still, Still, Still"* in the appropriate style. Have students

- Start *Band-in-a-Box.* Under song settings, set the key to D.
- Type the chord symbols in each bar.
- Select a style from the Style (sty) menu.
- Under the Edit menu, select intro bars to generate an introduction for the song.
- Click play to hear the accompaniment and sing along.

LESSON AT A GLANCE

Element Focus   **FORM**   Call and response

Skill Objective   **LISTENING**   Compare two versions of a call-and-response song

Connection Activity   **GENRE**   Recognize call-and-response form in an African American spiritual

MATERIALS

- "Rise Up, Shepherd, and Follow"   **CD 20-19**
  Recording Routine: Intro (4 m.); v. 1; interlude (4 m.); v. 2; coda
- *Rise Up, Shepherd, and Follow*   **CD 20-18**
- **Resource Book** p. C-8

VOCABULARY

solo/chorus   call and response   spiritual
a cappella

> ◆ ◆ ◆ ◆ **National Standards** ◆ ◆ ◆ ◆
>
> **1c**   Sing music from diverse genres
> **6a**   Listen and analyze uses of form and timbre in music from diverse cultures
> **6b**   Understand and use principles of form in music analysis
> **9a**   Describe characteristics of music genres from a variety of cultures

MORE MUSIC CHOICES

For more practice with call and response:
"Day-O!," p. 18
"Go Down, Moses," p. 190
"Woke Up this Morning," p. 288

1 INTRODUCE

9a   **SAY** Christmas is a holiday celebrated around the world with special traditions, carols, and spirituals.

Ask students to read the paragraph at the top of p. 470. Share the information about call-and-response form in Cultural Connection below.

A CHRISTMAS *Spiritual*

Some African American spirituals are about Christmas. This spiritual, "Rise Up, Shepherd, and Follow," is in call-and-response form.

Sing the song, taking turns as the soloist for the "call" sections.

A Spirited Spiritual

Listen to this exciting performance of *Rise Up, Shepherd, and Follow.* What voice types do you hear in the choir?

> **CD 20–18**
> **Rise Up, Shepherd, and Follow**

African American Spiritual

This arrangement of *Rise Up, Shepherd, and Follow* is performed by The Century Men. Buryl Red is the conductor.

Can you hear a second African American spiritual in this recording? What is it?

Footnotes

ACROSS THE CURRICULUM

▶ **Language Arts** Share a book that re-tells the Christmas story through African American spirituals and accompanying full-page illustrations—*What a Morning: The Christmas Story in Black Spirituals,* edited by John Langstaff (Simon and Schuster, 1996). Simple musical arrangements for voice, guitar, and piano are included as well as helpful suggestions and notes for instrument players, teachers, parents, and administrators.

BUILDING SKILLS THROUGH MUSIC

▶ **Language** Ask students to write detailed descriptions of the musical qualities, including vocal timbre, style, and instrumentation, recorded in their Venn Diagram.

CULTURAL CONNECTION

9a   ▶ **Call and Response** The use of a lead singer alternating with a chorus is a trait of African-inspired music. Call and response became a popular form among African American field workers and was later used in gospel, jazz, and blues music. In its earliest form, the lead singer traditionally improvised a phrase, and the chorus responded using a short refrain. Call and response evolved into any alternation between two performers or two groups of performers. A blues singer, for example, might employ the technique by alternating between singing and playing the guitar. A gospel singer utilizes call and response when she encourages the audience to vocally respond to each phrase she sings. "Rise Up, Shepherd, and Follow" is traditionally performed with a solo singer and chorus. Encourage students to think of different ways to create the call-and-response effect.

Rise Up, Shepherd, and Follow

African American Spiritual

VERSE

1. There's a star in the East on Christ-mas morn,
2. If you take good heed of the an-gel's words,

Chorus

Rise up, shep-herd, and fol-low.

Solo

It will lead to the place where the babe is born,
You'll for-get your flocks, you'll for-get your herds,

Chorus

Rise up, shep-herd, and fol-low.

REFRAIN

Fol-low, fol-low, Rise up, shep-herd, and

fol-low. Fol-low the star of Beth-le-hem,

Rise up, shep-herd, and fol-low.

2 DEVELOP

Singing

Have students find the parts marked *Solo* and *Chorus* in the song notation on p. 471.

Play the recording of "Rise Up, Shepherd, and Follow" **CD 20-19**. Encourage students to sing the response (chorus) sections. Then invite students to sing the complete song with the recording.

Invite individual students to sing the call (solo) parts of the song while the rest of the class sings the response parts.

Analyzing

ASK What makes this call-and-response song unusual? (There are two different response melodies.)

Listening

Invite students to listen to the recording of *Rise Up, Shepherd, and Follow* **CD 20-18**.

ASK Who performed the music? (a men's chorus)

What instruments accompanied the voices? (None; they sang *a cappella*.)

What other familiar Christmas song did you hear? (*Go Tell It on the Mountain*)

3 CLOSE

Element: FORM   **ASSESSMENT**

Musical Journal Writing Play the recordings of "Rise Up, Shepherd, and Follow" **CD 20-19** and the listening selection *Rise Up, Shepherd, and Follow* **CD 20-18**.

Using the Venn diagram found on Resource Book p. C-8, have students compare and contrast the two selections. In addition to form, suggest that they consider vocal timbre, style or genre, rhythm, and melody.

SPOTLIGHT ON

▶ **The Performers** The Century Men, established in 1969, is a men's professional chorus directed by Buryl Red. The members of this group are themselves directors of music in Baptist churches from across the United States. Their public performances include extensive touring across the country, as well as nationwide telecasts. They have performed concerts in Brazil, China, Russia, Israel, Turkey, and across Europe.

TECHNOLOGY/MEDIA LINK

MIDI/Sequencing Software Use the MIDI song file for "Rise Up, Shepherd, and Follow" as a focus for call-and-response form. Ask students to

• Practice playing the solo parts.
• Practice playing the chorus parts.
• Practice playing the melody.
• Record rhythm accompaniments to the song in a new file.

LESSON AT A GLANCE

Element Focus   **FORM** Repetition and contrast

Skill Objective   **ANALYZING** Analyze two Christmas songs containing repetition and contrast

Connection Activity   **CULTURE** Learn about Christmas customs in Catalonia and Puerto Rico

MATERIALS

- "Las Navidades"   **CD 20-21**
- "The Christmas Season"   **CD 20-22**
  Recording Routine: Intro (8 m.); v. 1; interlude (4 m.); v. 2; coda
- **Pronunciation Practice/Translation** p. 544
- "El desembre congelat"   **CD 20-25**
- "Cold December"   **CD 20-26**
  Recording Routine: Intro (4 m.); v. 1; interlude (4 m.); v. 2; coda
- **Pronunciation Practice/Translation** p. 545
- **Resource Book** pp. A-52, A-53
- hand drum

◆ ◆ ◆ ◆ National Standards ◆ ◆ ◆ ◆

1c   Sing music from diverse cultures
2c   Perform instrumental music from diverse cultures
5c   Identify standard notation symbols for pitch and rhythm
8b   Identify ways music relates to social studies

MORE MUSIC CHOICES

For more songs from Spain:

"Las estrellitas del cielo" ("Stars of the Heavens"), p. 175

"Don Alfonso," p. 177

1 INTRODUCE

8b Lead students in a discussion about Christmas traditions in Puerto Rico and Catalonia. For more information, see Cultural Connection below.

Carols for Christmas

Christmas is celebrated with Spanish-language songs in many parts of the world. "Las Navidades" is from Puerto Rico, an island in the Caribbean that is a commonwealth of the United States.

Sing the rhythm of "Las Navidades" using rhythm syllables.

CD 20-21

Las Navidades
(The Christmas Season)

English Words by Shelley Belgard

Traditional from Puerto Rico

1. Por fin lle-ga-ron las Na-vi-da-des
2. Con tam-bo-ri-les güi-ro y ma-ra-cas,
1. The Christ-mas sea-son is here a-gain now,
2. We play the gui-ro and the ma-ra-cas,

las fies-tas rea-les de nues-tro lar.
mi se-re-na-ta a-le-gre va.
a cel-e-bra-tion with-in our home.
while we are sing-ing our joy-ful song.

Fies-ta de to-dos nues-tros an-he-los,
De-se-o a to-dos por des-pe-di-da
And we all long for this hap-py sea-son,
And so we wish you a Mer-ry Christ-mas,

nues-tros des-ve-los, y nues-tro a-fán.
a-ños de vi-da y fe-li-ci-dad.
with great ex-cite-ment and joy-ful hearts.
a joy-ful New Year, and hap-pi-ness.

472

Footnotes

CULTURAL CONNECTION

▶ **Christmas in Catalonia and Puerto Rico** In both Puerto Rico and Catalonia, children receive gifts on *El Día de Reyes*. (Three Kings Day). The presents are believed to be from the three Wise Men who brought gifts to the baby Jesus. Children leave water and grass for the kings' camels on the eve of *El Día de Reyes*. They awake the following morning to gifts left by the thankful kings. A popular Catalonian Christmas tradition is *caga tió*, a game in which a tree trunk stuffed with various treats is hit by children.

BUILDING SKILLS THROUGH MUSIC

▶ **Reading** Have students look at the English text for "Las Navidades" and the English text of "El desembre congelat." Ask them to identify ideas about Christmas or the celebration of Christmas found in each song and find similarities and differences.

ACROSS THE CURRICULUM

8b ▶ **Social Studies** The richest and most industrialized region of Spain is Catalonia. Its location on the Mediterranean Sea has made it an important area dating back to the Roman Empire. Catalonians achieved independence from Spain on December 18, 1979, when Barcelona, Tarragona, and Lérida were recognized as the autonomous community of Catalonia. The capital city, Barcelona, hosted the Summer Olympics in 1992. Catalonia has also produced many famous artists in the early twentieth century, including Salvador Dali, Pablo Picasso, and Antonio Gaudí.

You may wish to have students locate Catalonia and Barcelona on a map of Spain.

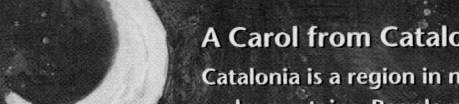

A Carol from Catalonia

Catalonia is a region in northeast Spain known for its beautiful beaches and mountains. People who live there speak both Spanish and Catalan.

Sing this Catalonian carol using pitch syllables.

How many examples of repetition can you **identify** in the melody?

CD 20–25

El desembre congelat
(Cold December)

English Words by Aura Kontra   Fifteenth-Century Melody from Catalonia

@ r m f s l t d'

do

1. El de - sem - bre   con - ge - lat,   Con - fós es re - ti - ra.
2. El pri - mer Pa - re caus - á,   La nit te - ne - bro - sa.
1. Cold De - cem - ber   days pro - claim   that the year is end - ing.
2. For   this night the   Child has come,   peace to man - kind bring - ing.

A - bril de flors   co - ro - nat,   Tot el món ad - mi - ra.
Que a tot el món   o - fus - cà   La vis - ta pen - o - sa.
And   a great re - splen - dent light   toward the Earth is   bend - ing.
An - gels greet Him   in a throng,   joy - ful prais - es   sing - ing.

Quan en un jar - di d'a - mor   Neix u - na di - vi - na flor. D'u - na
Mes en u - na   mit - ja - nit   bri - lla el sol que n'és eix - it. D'u - na
1., 2. God sent down His Son di - vine,   Gave to man a   gift sub - lime. And the

ro   ro   ro,   d'u - na   sa sa   **sa,**   d'u - na   ro,   d'u - na
bel bel bel,   d'u - na   la la   **la,**   d'u - na   bel,   d'u - na
shep - herds came   in the   dark of   night And the   kings brought their

sa, d'u - na ro - sa   bel - la,   Fe - cun - da i pon - cel - la.
la, d'u - na bel - la au -   ro - ra   que el cel en - a - mo - ra.
gifts where the Child lay   sleep - ing,   Sing - ing al - le - lu - ia.

Holidays in Song

2 DEVELOP

Analyzing

Ask students to look at the notation for *"Las Navidades."* Have them speak the rhythm of the first two measures using rhythm syllables.

5c **ASK How many exact repetitions of this pattern are there?** (five)

Where is it almost the same? (mm. 7–8)

Singing

1c Use Pronunciation Practice Track **CD 20-24** and Resource Book p. A-52. to help students learn the Spanish words of *"Las Navidades."* Then invite students to sing the song in Spanish.

Analyzing

Invite students to sing *"El desembre congelat"* **CD 20-25** with pitch syllables. Then ask them to look at the song notation.

5c **ASK How many times do you see repetition in the melody?** (four)

1c Use the Pronunciation Practice Track **CD 20-28** and Resource Book A-53. to assist students in learning the Catalan words.

Singing

Invite students to perform expressively, first from notation, then from memory, music from diverse cultures. Have them perform *"Las Navidades,"* then *"El desembre congelat."*

3 CLOSE

Element: ANALYZING   ASSESSMENT

5c **Performance/Observation** Ask students to look at the notation for *"Come, Ye Thankful People, Come"* on p. 459. Have students identify measures with repeated rhythm patterns. Then ask students to sing the song and raise their hand each time they hear a repeated rhythm pattern. Observe students' ability to recognize repetition and contrast.

SKILLS REINFORCEMENT

2c ▶ **Playing** Invite students to play the following pattern on hand drum to accompany the first two lines of *"El desembre congelat."*

Starting on line 3, play a quarter note on beat one of each measure.

TECHNOLOGY/MEDIA LINK

5c **Notation Software** Have students notate *"El desembre congelat."* This will give them an introduction to inserting meter changes. Demonstrate how to insert the changes; then have students

- Set up the program for the key of C and use standard symbols to notate $\frac{2}{4}$ meter.
- Create a lead sheet for the song using their favorite mode of note-entry.

LESSON 10

LESSON AT A GLANCE

Element Focus **TEXTURE/HARMONY** Countermelody

Skill Objective **SINGING** Sing a song with a countermelody

Connection Activity **CULTURE** Learn about the tradition of the yule log

MATERIALS

- "Deck the Hall" **CD 20-29**

  Recording Routine: Intro (8 m.); v. 1; interlude (2 m.); v. 2; interlude (2 m.); v. 3; coda
- *Deck the Hall* **CD 20-31**

VOCABULARY

countermelody

National Standards

1d Sing music written in two parts
4c Compose, using electronic media
5e In performance classes, sightread easy music accurately and expressively
6a Listen and describe events in music using appropriate terms
6b Listen and analyze uses of texture in music from diverse styles
7a Students evaluate the music they perform
8b Identify ways music relates to social studies and language arts
9a Describe characteristics of music from a variety of cultures

MORE MUSIC CHOICES

For more practice singing countermelodies:
"Roll On, Columbia," p. 116

1 INTRODUCE

9a Explain to students that the *fa la la*'s in "Deck the Hall" are typical of madrigals, which were popular songs that people sang in the evenings long before the existence of radios, televisions, or compact disks. Singers may have been gathered around the yule log. Share the Cultural Connection below.

LESSON 10 Element: TEXTURE/HARMONY | Skill: SINGING | Connection: CULTURE

Ring in the New!

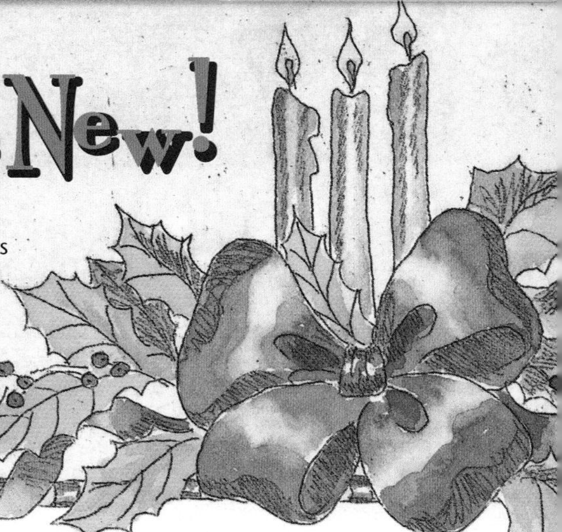

"Deck the Hall" was originally a New Year's carol. Now it is frequently performed at Christmas celebrations.

Sing "Deck the Hall" in unison. Then add the countermelody.

CD 20–29
MIDI 37

Deck the Hall

Traditional Carol from Wales

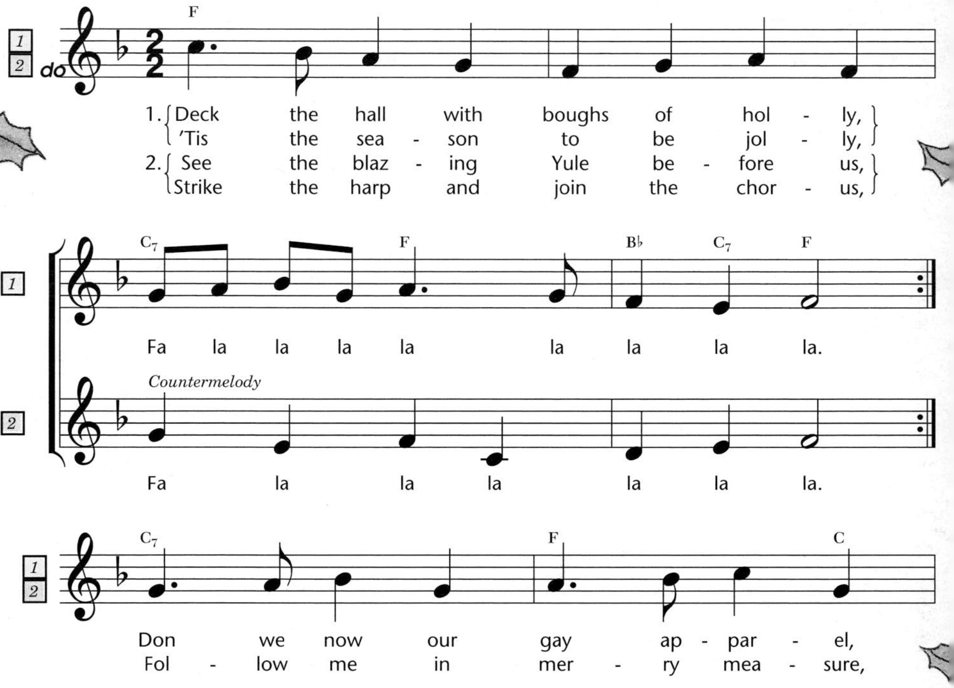

do
F
1. Deck the hall with boughs of hol - ly,
'Tis the sea - son to be jol - ly,
2. See the blaz - ing Yule be - fore us,
Strike the harp and join the chor - us,
C7 F B♭ C7 F
Fa la la la la la la la la.
Countermelody
Fa la la la la la la.
C7 F C
Don we now our gay ap - par - el,
Fol - low me in mer - ry mea - sure,

Footnotes

CULTURAL CONNECTION

8b ▶ **Yule Log** This tradition originated in Scandinavia. Scandinavians believed that the dead walked the earth at Yuletide, the night following the shortest day of the year. Each family chose a tree to burn in honor of the event. Family members and servants huddled around the fireplace, making sure the Yule fire lasted through the night. The modern practice of burning a single log on Christmas Eve hearkens back to the practice of bringing warmth and light into the cold dark winter night.

BUILDING SKILLS THROUGH MUSIC

▶ **Social Studies** Distribute copies of the Venn diagram from Resource Book p. C-8. Have students compare the two versions of "Deck the Hall" **CD 20-29, CD 20-31** using the Venn diagram.

ACROSS THE CURRICULUM

8b ▶ **Language Arts** Read aloud and dramatize portions of the famous Christmas story in *Christmas Carol: Charles Dickens' Tale* (Eyewitness Classics) by Charles Dickens (Dorling Kindersley, 1997). First published in 1843, this timeless story captures the true spirit of the season.

Travel back in time to the days of Charles Dickens, Scrooge, and Tiny Tim and discover the Victorian roots of many of our American Christmas symbols and traditions in *Victorian Christmas (Historic Community Series)* by Bobbie Kalman (Crabtree, 1996).

Learn about the history of a favorite Austrian Christmas carol in *Silent Night: The Song from Heaven* by Linda Granfield (Tundra Books, 1997).

1 F   Dm   C   G₇   C

Fa la la la la la la la la.

2

Fa la la la la la la la la.

1
2 F

Troll   the   an - cient   Yule - tide   car - ol,
While   I   tell   of   Yule - tide   trea - sure,

1 B♭   F   C₇   F

Fa la la la la   la la la la.

2

Fal la la la la la   la la la.

3.   Fast away the old year passes,   Sing we joyous all together,
     Fa la la . . .   Fa la la . . .
     Hail the new, ye lads and lasses,   Heedless of the wind and weather,
     Fa la la . . .   Fa la la . . .

Fa La La!

"Deck the Hall" uses an old Welsh melody called
"*Nos galan.*"

Listen to this modern version of *Deck the Hall*.

CD 20–31
Deck the Hall

**Traditional Carol from Wales
as performed by Mannheim Steamroller**

The driving beat in this "electric"
performance gives energy to the
repeating melody.

Tune In

In ancient times,
people burned a yule log
during the winter solstice.
They believed it brought
protection and good luck.

Holidays in Song

MIDI Use the song file for "Deck the
Hall" to practice the harmony part at a
slower tempo.

2 DEVELOP

Analyzing

6a Invite students to listen to "Deck the Hall" **CD 20-29** and
help them follow the routine of the notation.

     ASK Is "Deck the Hall" in unison or in harmony?
(harmony)

         In how many parts? (two)

         Which sections of the song are harmonized?
(only the *fa la la* parts)

     SAY The harmony part is written below the melody on
a two-staff system. It is called a countermelody.

Singing

5e Invite students to sing the melody of "Deck the Hall"
CD 20-29 with the recording, and then the countermelody.

1d Divide the class into two groups and have students sing
the song in two-part harmony.

Listening

6b **SAY** "Deck the Hall" has been a favorite carol for many
generations. The carol has been arranged for and performed by many different artists.

Share the information in Spotlight On below and then
invite students to listen to Mannheim Steamroller's version of the carol **CD 20-31**. Ask students to compare the
two versions of the song and describe which style they
prefer the best. Encourage students to use accurate
music terms in their descriptions.

3 CLOSE

Element: TEXTURE/HARMONY   **ASSESSMENT**

7a **Performance/Peer Critique** Divide the class into
two groups and have students sing "Deck the Hall"
with the countermelody. Allow groups to switch parts
and evaluate each other's performance.

SPOTLIGHT ON

▶ **Mannheim Steamroller** Mannheim Steamroller is the
creation of Chip Davis, a multitalented musician, composer, and
record producer. His idea is to blend classical and rock music elements to create a new sound. "Mannheim" (a city in Germany)
refers to the eighteenth-century orchestra noted for its intense
crescendos, and "Steamroller" is Davis's own term for the layering of sound, texture, volume, and timbres. In the years since its
creation, Mannheim Steamroller has sold over 28 million records
along with a successful series of Christmas albums.

TECHNOLOGY/MEDIA LINK

4c **CD-ROM** Have students use *Band-in-a-Box* to create an
accompaniment for "Deck the Hall" and explore various styles.
Under song settings, set the key to F major, the chorus to end
after 4, and total choruses to 2; and then set it to uncheck
"Overall Loop" and "Embellish Chords." Have students

- Type the chord symbols in each bar. To insert two chords in
the first half of a measure, type one chord symbol followed by
a comma and the next chord symbol.
- Select a style from the Style (sty) menu.
- Under the Edit menu, select intro bars to generate an introduction for the song.
- Click "play" to hear the accompaniment and sing along.

LESSON AT A GLANCE

Element Focus **MELODY** Interval of a fifth

Skill Objective **SINGING** Sing a holiday song featuring the interval of a fifth

Connection Activity **CULTURE** Explore the traditions of Kwanzaa and its seven principles

MATERIALS

- *"Heri za Kwanzaa"* ("Happy Kwanzaa") **CD 20-32**
  Recording Routine: Intro (4 m.); vocal; coda
- resonator bells, keyboard

VOCABULARY

harmony   interval

♦ ♦ ♦ ♦ National Standards ♦ ♦ ♦ ♦

1c Sing music from diverse cultures
2a Play instruments accurately in small ensembles
6c Understand and use basic principles of intervals in music analysis
7a Create standards for evaluating performances
8b Identify ways music relates to social studies

MORE MUSIC CHOICES

For more practice singing songs that are based on the interval of a fifth:
"The Voices of Pride," p. 86
"This World," p. 168

1 INTRODUCE

8b **SAY** Kwanzaa is a unique African American celebration with focus on African American culture, values, and traditions.

Invite students to discuss the celebration, and then share with them information about the holiday. See Cultural Connection below and Spotlight On, p. 477.

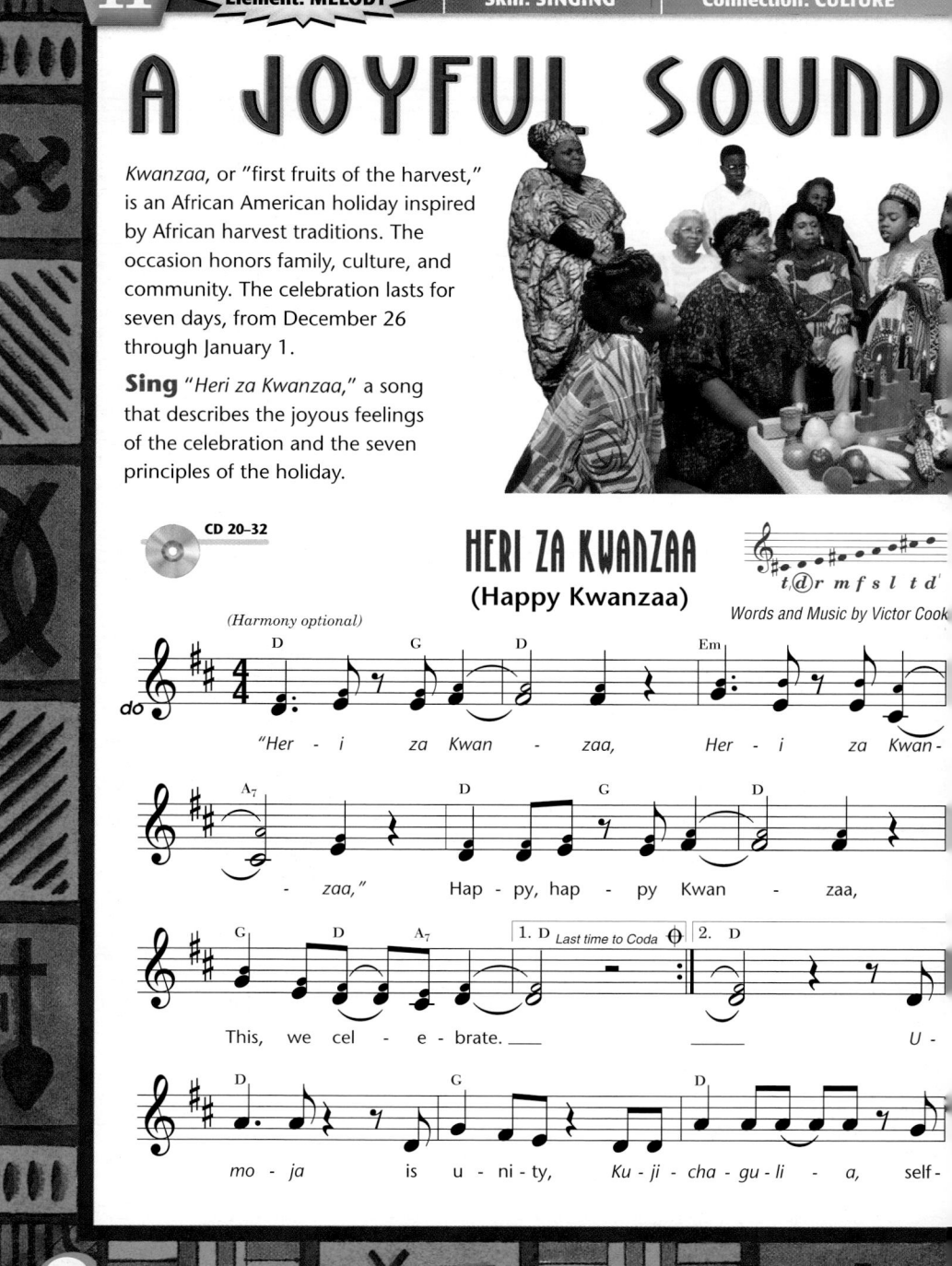

A JOYFUL SOUND

Kwanzaa, or "first fruits of the harvest," is an African American holiday inspired by African harvest traditions. The occasion honors family, culture, and community. The celebration lasts for seven days, from December 26 through January 1.

Sing *"Heri za Kwanzaa,"* a song that describes the joyous feelings of the celebration and the seven principles of the holiday.

CD 20–32

HERI ZA KWANZAA
(Happy Kwanzaa)

Words and Music by Victor Cook

(Harmony optional)

"Her - i za Kwan - zaa, Her - i za Kwan - zaa," Hap - py, hap - py Kwan - zaa, This, we cel - e - brate. ___ U - mo - ja is u - ni - ty, Ku - ji - cha - gu - li - a, self -

476

Footnotes

CULTURAL CONNECTION

8b ▶ **The Seven Principles of Kwanzaa** Kwanzaa celebrates seven social principles for relating to others and for being true to one's self-image. The principles are *Umoja* (unity); *Kujichagulia* (self-determination); *Ujima* (collective work and responsibility); *Ujamaa* (cooperative economics); *Nia* (purpose); *Kuumba* (creativity), and *Imani* (faith). Kwanzaa celebrants light a candle, or *mshumaa,* for each principle. The candles are held by a single candleholder, the *kinara.*

BUILDING SKILLS THROUGH MUSIC

▶ **Art** Ask students to create a visual representation using the three colors of Kwanzaa (black, red, and green) that depicts the song *"Heri za Kwanzaa."* Students' visuals may represent the melody, pitch, or theme of the song.

ACROSS THE CURRICULUM

8b ▶ **Social Studies/Art** Learn more about the traditions of Kwanzaa in *Celebrating Kwanzaa* by Diane Hoyt-Goldsmith (Holiday House, 1994). The book is centered around the true story of a Chicago family's holiday festivities. Kwanzaa's seven principles are explained in a day-by-day format with text and photographs showing what the family does to honor and commemorate the holiday.

Create great holiday gifts, cards, and decorations from ideas found in *Kwanzaa Crafts* by Judith Hoffman Corwin (Franklin Watts, 1995).

-de-ter-mi-na-tion, *U-ji-ma,* work re-spon-si-bil-i-ty,

This, we cel-e-brate. ___ *U-ja-ma,* co-op-'ra-

tive ec-o-nom-ics, *Ni-a* is your ___ pur-pose, *Ku-*

um-ba, cre-a-tiv-i-ty, *I-ma-ni* is ___ the faith. ___

Coda

This, we cel-e-brate, ___

This, we cel-e-brate. ___

Colors of *Kwanzaa*

The colors of *Kwanzaa* are black, red, and green. Black represents black people and their African heritage. Red represents their long struggle for freedom and equality. Green represents the hills of Africa and also the future.

Seven is a special number for *Kwanzaa*: 7 days, 7 symbols, 7 principles; and an extra *a* was added to *Kwanzaa* to give it 7 letters.

Holidays in Song

Unit 12 **477**

2 DEVELOP

Listening

Have students listen to *"Heri za Kwanzaa"* ("Happy Kwanzaa") **CD 20-32** to discover the seven principles of Kwanzaa and the translation of each principle.

SAY The seven principles of Kwanzaa are in Kiswahili, a language spoken in eastern and central Africa. It is the national language in Kenya, Tanzania, and Uganda.

Singing

1c Encourage students to sing *"Heri za Kwanzaa"* **CD 20-32** with the recording.

6c Help students discover that the melody for the first six principles of *Kwanzaa* uses only the notes D and A.

ASK What interval is D to A? (a fifth)

Playing

2a Invite students to play each of the Kwanzaa principles on a melody instrument as they sing the song with the recording.

3 CLOSE

Element: MELODY **ASSESSMENT**

1c **Performance/Observation** Invite individuals to sing one of the seven Kwanzaa principles in *"Heri za Kwanzaa"* as the rest of the class sings the English translation. Continue this for each of the principles.

7a Observe how well students sing on pitch, especially the interval of a fifth, and how accurately they sing the syncopated rhythms.

SPOTLIGHT ON

8b ▶ **Kwanzaa** Dr. Maulana Karenga initiated the first Kwanzaa holiday beginning on December 26, 1966. He founded it on the principle of Kawaida, which says that changes in society can occur when individuals learn about their cultural heritage. Dr. Karenga wanted African Americans to have a holiday that celebrates and honors the struggles of their ancestors. Over the years, Kwanzaa celebrations have invoked unique symbols, customs, and principles that encourage people to learn about the history of the African American experience. Among these is the *karumu,* a community-wide thanksgiving feast that is held on December 31.

TECHNOLOGY/MEDIA LINK

Notation Software Have students create a melody that incorporates the interval of a fifth, using the seven principles of Kwanzaa as text. Then ask them to notate their melodies using notation software.

Unit 12 *Holidays in Song* **477**

LESSON AT A GLANCE

Element Focus **MELODY** Pentatonic scale

Skill Objective **SINGING** Sing a pentatonic Japanese New Year song

Connection Activity **CULTURE** Explore Japanese New Year celebrations

MATERIALS

- "Hitotsu toya" **CD 21-1**
- "Temple Bells" **CD 21-2**

  Recording Routine: Intro (4 m.); v. 1; interlude (4 m.); v. 2; interlude (22 m.); instrumental; v. 3; coda
- **Pronunciation Practice/Translation** p. 547
- **Resource Book** p. A-55
- mallet instruments

VOCABULARY

pentatonic scale

◆ ◆ ◆ ◆ National Standards ◆ ◆ ◆ ◆

1c Sing music from diverse cultures

2c Perform instrumental music from diverse cultures

6a Listen and describe events in music using appropriate terms

6b Listen and analyze uses of timbre and pitch in music from diverse cultures

7a Students evaluate the music they perform

8b Identify ways music relates to social studies

9a Describe characteristics of music genres from a variety of cultures

MORE MUSIC CHOICES

For more practice singing pentatonic songs from Asia:

"Yüe liang wan wan" ("Crescent Moon"), p. 314

"Quả cầu gió bay" ("The Wind on the Bridge"), p. 460

1 INTRODUCE

8b Invite students to discuss their family New Year celebrations. Then have them read the information on p. 478 to discover how Japan celebrates this important holiday.

Happy New Year!

Many people around the world celebrate New Year's Day on January 1. New Year is Japan's most important holiday. *Shogatsu* is a three-day celebration. Most Japanese do not work during *O-Shogatsu*. House cleaning and food preparation are done earlier. Food is stored in special boxes. Many Japanese families wait up on New Year's Eve to hear the *Joya-no-Kan*, large temple bells that are rung 108 times at midnight to drive away evil thoughts.

Say It, Sing It

Sing "Hitotsu toya," an *O-Shogatsu* celebration song.

▲ Temple bell at the Chion-in Temple, Japan

CD 21–1
MIDI 38

Hitotsu toya
(Temple Bells)

English Words Anonymous

Folk Song from Japan

1. ひ と つ と や ＿＿＿＿ ひ と よ あ く れ ば
1. Hi - to - tsu to - ya, ＿＿＿＿ Hi - to - yo a - ku - re - ba
1. Tem - ple bells will chime, oh, ＿＿ chime for the bright new year that

に ぎ や か で に ぎ や か で
Ni - gi - ya - ka de, Ni - gi - ya - ka de,
comes to us to - night, Comes to us to - night.

お か ざ り た て た る ま つ か ざ
O - ka - za - ri ta - te ta - ru Ma - tsu - ka - za -
Now on ev - 'ry door there hangs a spray of love - ly

478

Footnotes

SPOTLIGHT ON

▶ **Temple Bells** In Japan temple bells are hung from the ceiling in an outdoor enclosure. They have no clapper inside. The sound comes from being hit from the side with a wooden log or pole suspended horizontally near the bell. One or more people pull the log backward and then push it forward and let go. The log strikes the bell and rings it. To ring the bell again, the log must be caught as it swings back and the movements above repeated.

BUILDING SKILLS THROUGH MUSIC

▶ **Language** Have students listen to the English version of "Hitotsu toya" **CD 21-2** while following the song notation. Ask students to identify places where the English lyrics do not follow standard usage. Select individual students to read phrases from the song lyrics as they would be spoken.

CULTURAL CONNECTION

8b ▶ **Ōshogatsu (Japanese New Year)** The Japanese New Year, the most important national holiday of the year, is celebrated for three days, January 1–3. Before the new year is welcomed, families and friends gather for *bonenkai* ("year-forgetting") parties to rid themselves of the past years' worries. They hang special bamboo, pine, or plum tree decorations in their doorways and on their cars. The practice began centuries ago when villagers hung a straw rope across their doors to keep out evil spirits. *Toshikoshi soba* (buckwheat noodles), symbols of long life, are traditionally served on New Year's Eve. Temples and shrines toll their bells 108 times at midnight that follows to drive away 108 evil thoughts. New Year's Day is believed to set the tone for the year to come, so it is a day free of stress and anger.

ri, _____ Ma - tsu - ka - za - ri.
pine, a _____ spray of love - ly pine.

2. ふたつとや
ふたばのまつは
いろよていろよて
さんがいまつは
かすがやまかすがやま

2. Futatsu toya,
Futaba no matsu wa
Iro yo te, Iro yo te.
Sangai-matsu wa
Kasuga-yama, Kasuga-yama.

2. Temple bells will chime, oh,
chime for the fragrance and the
green throughout the year.
  (2 times)
Of the fine and healthy pine on
Kasuga Yama, on Kasuga Yama.

3. みっつとや
みなさんこのひは
らくあそびらくあそび
ふるさきこまどで
はねをつくはねをつく

3. Mittsu toya,
Minasan kono hi wa
Raku-asobi, Raku-asobi,
Furusaki komado de
Hane o tsuku, Hane o tsuku.

3. Temple bells will chime, oh,
chime in the merriment, the
music, games, and dance.
  (2 times)
People swing the battledore.
This is the time to play.
This is the day to play.

Add an Accompaniment!

Play this melody on mallet instruments to accompany *"Hitotsu toya."*

Play 3 times

Get in Motion!

Move to show the ringing of the temple bells as you **sing** *"Hitotsu toya."*

Classical dance at the
O-Shogatsu festival ▶

Holidays in Song

Unit 12 479

2 DEVELOP

Listening

6a Invite students to listen to *"Hitotsu toya"* **CD 21-1** sung in Japanese and to raise their hands when they hear the temple bell. Direct students to the picture on p. 478. (See Spotlight On, p. 478.)

6b Mention the instruments on the recording: *koto*—popular Japanese string instrument; *shakuhachi*—a bamboo flute with four finger holes and a thumb hole; slit drum—a length of hollow bamboo with a slit on one side that is beaten with a stick.

Singing

1c Use the Pronunciation Practice Track **CD 21-4** and Resource Book p. A-55 to help students learn the Japanese lyrics. Encourage students to sing *"Hitotsu toya"* **CD 21-1** in Japanese with the recording.

Help students discover the importance of the F♯ in the song. (It ends on F♯.)

9a **SAY** The melody is based on an important Japanese pentatonic scale called the *Miyako* which uses the notes E, F♯, G, B, and C.

ASK How is this scale different from the *do* and *la* pentatonic scales? (It includes two half steps F♯–G; B–C.)

3 CLOSE

Skill: SINGING   **ASSESSMENT**

1c
2c **Performance/Self-Assessment** Encourage students to sing *"Hitotsu toya"* and play the instrumental pentatonic accompaniment, on p. 479, on mallet instruments. (See Skills Reinforcement below.)

7a

Have students evaluate their own performance and write about the experience in their music journals.

SKILLS REINFORCEMENT

2c ▶ **Playing** Use the following teaching suggestions to help all students play pentatonic patterns.

Reinforcement Some students may have difficulty playing the pentatonic melody shown on p. 479. Allow these students to gain confidence by practicing the *Miyako* scale (E, F♯, G, B, C). Arrange the scale on alto or soprano xylophone and have students play it ascending and descending.

On Target Most students will be able to perform the pentatonic melody on p. 479. Ask these students to perform the melody with *"Hitotsu toya."*

Challenge Invite interested students to create their own pentatonic melody to perform on keyboard or mallet instruments with *"Hitotsu toya."*

TECHNOLOGY/MEDIA LINK

6b **MIDI/Sequencing Software** Use the MIDI song file for *"Hitotsu toya"* to reinforce the concept of timbre. Ask students

- How are the General MIDI voices used in *"Hitotsu toya"*? (They imitate traditional Japanese instruments.)

- How do you think the traditional instruments imitated by the keyboard are played? (The *koto* and *shamisen*, string instruments, are plucked. The *shakuhachi*, a flute-like instrument, is blown.)

LESSON AT A GLANCE

Element Focus — **TEXTURE/HARMONY** Parallel and contrary motion in two-part harmony

Skill Objective — **SINGING** Sing a song in two-part harmony that contains parallel and contrary motion

Connection Activity — **SOCIAL STUDIES** Discuss the tradition of Three Kings' Day

MATERIALS

- "Los reyes de Oriente " — **CD 21-5**
- "The Kings from the East" — **CD 21-6**
  Recording Routine: Intro (8 m.); vocal; interlude (8 m.); vocal; coda
- **Pronunciation Practice/Translation** p. 547
- **Resource Book** p. A-56
- Autoharp, guitars

VOCABULARY

major   minor   harmony

◆ ◆ ◆ ◆ National Standards ◆ ◆ ◆ ◆

1c Sing music from diverse cultures

5e In performance classes, sightread easy music accurately and expressively

6b Listen and analyze uses of harmony in music from diverse cultures

6c Understand and use basic principles of tonality in music analysis

MORE MUSIC CHOICES

For more practice singing songs in two-part harmony:

"De colores," p. 90

"Loch Lomond," p. 140

1 INTRODUCE

Discuss the different ways holidays are celebrated. Encourage students to share traditions observed by their families. Then invite students to read the information about Three Kings' Day on p. 480.

Three Kings Day

Spanish-speaking children throughout the world celebrate *Día de los Reyes* (Three Kings Day). In Puerto Rico, Christmas celebrating begins on Christmas Eve and lasts until January 6. Children wake up on Three Kings Day to find toys and gifts. In some regions children leave empty shoes out so that visiting Wise Men can leave food or gifts.

Sing "*Los reyes de Oriente*." Is the song based on a major or a minor scale? Next, **sing** the harmony part. How does this part relate to the melody?

CD 21–5 MIDI 39

Los reyes de Oriente
(The Kings from the East)

English Words by Aura Kontra   *Aguinaldo from Puerto Rico*

De tie-rra le-ja-na ve-ni-mos a ver-te,
From a dis-tant land, we come in ad-o-ra-tion,

Nos sir-ve de guí-a la es-tre-lla de_O-rien-te.
Fol-low-ing a star, a star of fas-ci-na-tion,

¡Oh, bri-llan-te_es-tre-lla que a-nun-cias la_au-ro-ra,
Shin-ing star so bright, till dawn you rule the night, ____

No me fal-te nun-ca tu luz bien-he-cho-ra! ____
Nev-er cease to guide us with your kind-ly light. ____

480

Footnotes

SKILLS REINFORCEMENT

▶ **Guitar** The song "*Los reyes de Oriente*" is appropriate for guitar accompaniment. It has two easy chords (Dm and A₇) and can be played at an unhurried tempo with only one strum per measure. The chord changes form a very clear, repeated pattern in each of the four systems (three strums on one chord, followed by one strum on the other chord), which make the chord changes easier for the students to anticipate, and will lead to more efficient mastery of the song.

BUILDING SKILLS THROUGH MUSIC

▶ **Language** Invite students to listen to "*Las Navidades*" **CD 20-21** and "*Los reyes de Oriente*" **CD 21-5.** Then ask them to find similarities and differences, including timbre, rhythm, theme or idea, and so on.

CULTURAL CONNECTION

▶ *Tres Reyes Magos* The Puerto Rican celebration of Epiphany, a church festival commemorating the arrival of the Magi in Bethlehem, evolved into *Tres reyes magos*, or Three Kings' Day. According to Christian scripture, three Magi (wise men from the East)—Melchior, Balthasar, and Kaspar—traveled for many days to see the infant Jesus. In preparation for this day honoring the kings' travels, cities host elaborate parades on January 5, the night before Epiphany begins. The "three kings" appear at the end of the parade. Later that night, children put grass and water under their beds to feed the kings' camels. When they wake, they find presents left by the grateful kings.

Christmas Harmony

The *aguinaldo* [ah-ghee-NAHL-doh] is a folk song with lyrics that describe Christmas themes. Instruments such as the guitar, *cuatro*, *tiple*, *tres*, and *guiro* are used as an accompaniment that adds to the musical flavor of the culture.

▲ *Cuatro*

◀ *Guiro*

Participants in a Three Kings Day celebration, ▼ Puerto Rico

Holidays in Song

Unit 12 **481**

2 DEVELOP

Listening

Play the recording of *"Los reyes de Oriente"* **CD 21-5**.

ASK How many parts do you hear in the vocal line? What do you call that? (two/harmony)

6c **Is this song in major or minor?** (minor)

Analyzing

Have students read the text at the top of p. 480. Explain that the harmony moves in parallel and contrary motion. Parallel motion is movement in the same direction. Contrary motion is movement in the opposite direction. Draw lines on the board to illustrate.

6b Have students find where the parallel and contrary motion occurs between the melody and harmony. (parallel: lines 1-2; contrary: lines 3-4.)

Singing

1c Teach the Spanish lyrics using Pronunciation Practice Tracks **CD 21-8** (melody), **CD 21-9** (harmony) and Resource Book p. A-56. Have the class sing along in two parts with the recording **CD 21-5**. For tips on teaching the harmony, see Teacher to Teacher below.

Playing

6b Direct students' attention to the chord symbols in the music. Ask volunteers to play the chords on guitar or Autoharp as an accompaniment to the singing of *"Los reyes de Oriente."* (See Skills Reinforcement, p. 480.)

3 CLOSE

Element: TEXTURE/HARMONY — ASSESSMENT

Performance/Observation Have students draw the contours of the melody and harmony in contrasting colors in mm. 9–16. Divide the class into two groups to sing only the parts in contrary motion and then sing only those in parallel motion. Observe students' ability to perform contrary and parallel motion harmony.

TEACHER TO TEACHER

5e ▶ **Singing Parallel Thirds** Singing harmony parts written in parallel thirds poses a challenge for inexperienced singers. Harmony in contrary motion makes it easier for them to hold their parts. Have the class learn the last two phrases of the song in contrary motion before you introduce the parallel third harmony for the first and second phrases.

Also, bear in mind that talented singers who learn harmony parts quickly should not always be assigned to those parts. This might hinder the development of their upper range and cause overuse of the chest voice. To help all students sing harmony, begin by assigning easy harmony parts to the less experienced singers and the more challenging harmony parts to the independent singers.

TECHNOLOGY/MEDIA LINK

Web Site For more information about Latin American instruments such as *cuatro*, *tiple*, *tres* and *guiro*, visit *www.sfsuccessnet.com*.

LESSON AT A GLANCE

Element Focus	**TEXTURE/HARMONY** Two-part harmony
Skill Objective	**SINGING** Sing a song about freedom in two-part harmony
Connection Activity	**SOCIAL STUDIES** Recognize songs as a means for expressing desire for freedom

MATERIALS
- "Lift Ev'ry Voice and Sing"   **CD 21-10**

  Recording Routine: Intro (2 m.); v. 1; modulation; v. 2; coda
- "For Children Safe and Strong"   **CD 21-12**

  Recording Routine: Intro (4 m.); v. 1; v. 2; interlude (4m.); v. 3
- *We Shall Overcome*   **CD 21-14**
- keyboard or other melody instruments

VOCABULARY
legato   *staccato*   *dynamics*

◆ ◆ ◆ ◆ National Standards ◆ ◆ ◆ ◆
1a Sing accurately in small ensembles
1d Sing music written in two parts
3b Improvise rhythmic variations on given melodies
5e In performance classes, sightread easy music accurately and expressively
6a Listen and describe events in music using appropriate terms
6c Understand and use basic principles of meter in music analysis
7a Create standards for evaluating performances
8a Show how different arts portray the same event in unique ways
8b Identify ways music relates to social studies and language arts

MORE MUSIC CHOICES
For more practice singing songs about freedom:
"Go Down, Moses," p. 190
"Woke Up This Morning," p. 288

A Song For Freedom

The words to "Lift Ev'ry Voice and Sing" were written in 1900 by James Weldon Johnson to commemorate the birthday of Abraham Lincoln. The poet's brother, J. Rosamond Johnson, set the words to music. "Lift Ev'ry Voice and Sing" is regarded as the African American national anthem.

In what ways were Martin Luther King Jr. and Abraham Lincoln alike?

Sing "Lift Ev'ry Voice and Sing" in a slow, even tempo. How would you **describe** the appropriate expression?

CD 21-10 MIDI 40

Lift Ev'ry Voice and Sing

Words by James Weldon Johnson   *Music by J. Rosamond Johnson*

1. Lift ev-'ry voice and sing, till earth and heav-en ring,
2. Ston-y the road we trod, bit-ter the chas-t'ning rod

Ring with the har-mo-nies of lib-er-ty.
Felt in the days when hope un-born ___ had died.

Let our re-joic-ing rise high as the lis-t'ning ___ skies,
Yet with a stead-y beat have not our wea-ry ___ feet

Let it re-sound loud as the roll-ing sea.
Come to the place for which our fa-thers died.

482

Footnotes

MEETING INDIVIDUAL NEEDS

8a ▶ **Inclusion** Invite students to create visual displays of "Lift Ev'ry Voice and Sing." This will allow you to check for comprehension and understanding of the song material as well as provide you with great sources for the bulletin board or performance area. The words in this song focus on important concepts—liberty and hope—that could form the basis of a class discussion about the traditions of the United States.

BUILDING SKILLS THROUGH MUSIC

▶ **Social Studies** Have students read the lyrics to "Lift Ev'ry Voice and Sing" and "For Children Safe and Strong." Then discuss how the beliefs and ideals of Martin Luther King, Jr. and Abraham Lincoln are expressed in the two songs.

SKILLS REINFORCEMENT

1a ▶ **Singing** Encourage your students to sing each phrase of "Lift Ev'ry Voice and Sing" as musically as possible. Help them discover that a breath within the phrase distracts from the continuity of the music and the lyrics. To sing a long phrase, a singer must have good posture and good breath support. Breath control is dependent on the singer taking a deep breath, using the diaphragm, and controlling the release of air throughout the phrase. Not every singer has mastery of breath control. To give listeners the impression that the group sings each phrase on one breath, use the technique of staggered breathing. Some singers carry the phrase along, breathing only at the end of the phrase; while singers who have not yet mastered breath control take a quick breath under the other singers' sustained vocal line and continue to the end of the phrase.

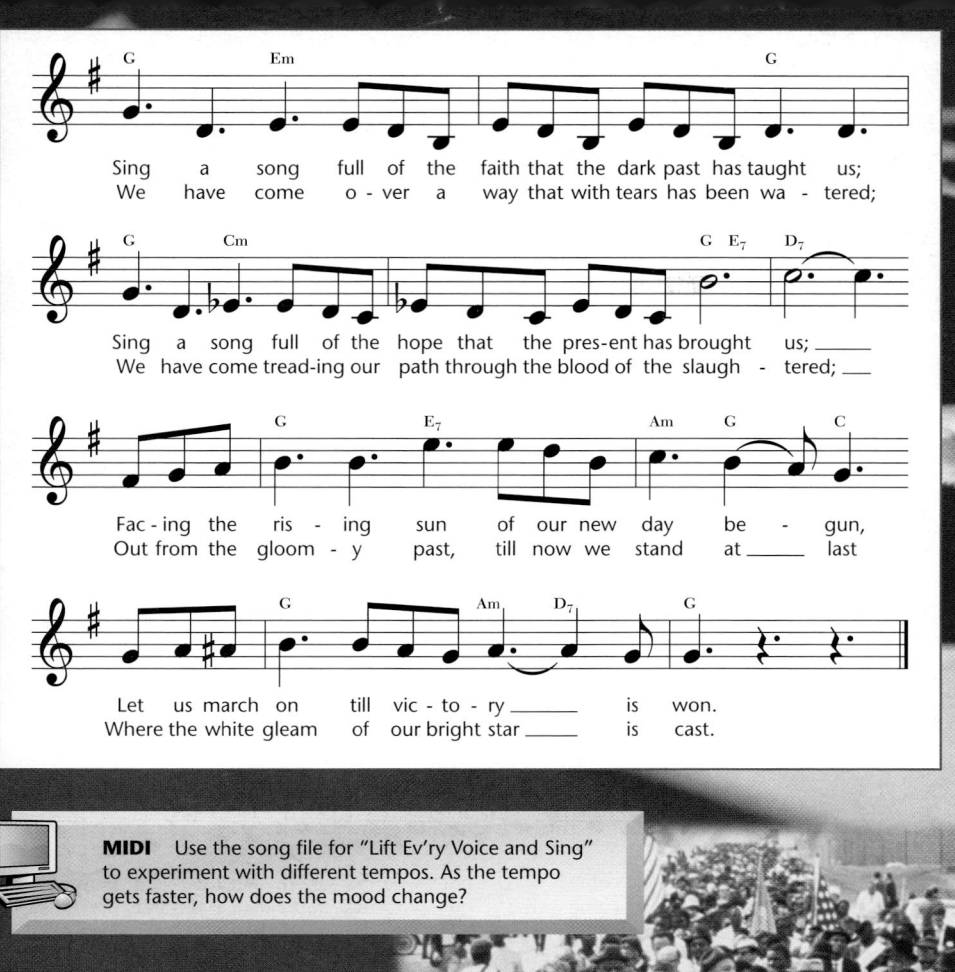

Sing a song full of the faith that the dark past has taught us;
We have come o - ver a way that with tears has been wa - tered;

Sing a song full of the hope that the pres-ent has brought us;
We have come tread-ing our path through the blood of the slaugh - tered; ___

Fac - ing the ris - ing sun of our new day be - gun,
Out from the gloom - y past, till now we stand at ___ last

Let us march on till vic - to - ry ___ is won.
Where the white gleam of our bright star ___ is cast.

MIDI Use the song file for "Lift Ev'ry Voice and Sing" to experiment with different tempos. As the tempo gets faster, how does the mood change?

Holidays in Song

Create a movement to accompany one of the eight different phrases of the song. Think about the meaning of the lyrics for your phrase.

Perform your movement while singing "Lift Ev'ry Voice and Sing." Stand motionless when you are not moving to your phrase.

Martin Luther King Jr. leading the March on Washington, D.C., March 25, 1965 ▶

Unit 12　483

1 INTRODUCE

8b Engage students in a short discussion of freedom. Have students describe the roles that both Abraham Lincoln and Martin Luther King, Jr. played in the fight for freedom. (Lincoln fought to free enslaved persons and King fought for equal rights. Both men were assassinated by men who opposed their views.)

Ask students to read the lyrics of "Lift Ev'ry Voice and Sing" and then list other songs that express a desire for freedom. ("Oh, Freedom," "Woke Up This Morning," "Free at Last," "Keep Your Eyes on the Prize," and so on)

2 DEVELOP

Singing

1a Invite students to sing "Lift Ev'ry Voice and Sing" **CD 21-10** with the recording.

Encourage students to experiment by singing the song at different dynamic levels and interpretive styles.

7a **ASK At what dynamic level should we sing this song?** (*forte*)

Remind students that *forte* means "loud, but not forced."

ASK Should the song be performed smoothly and connected or short and detached? (smoothly and connected)

What is the music term for smooth and connected? (*legato*)

6a **What happens between verses 1 and 2 on the recording?** (the music modulates, or changes key)

How many phrases are in the song? (eight)

continued on page 484

TEACHER TO TEACHER

6c ▶ **A New Meter** "Lift Ev'ry Voice and Sing" is written in $\frac{12}{8}$ meter, or compound quadruple time. The meter is compound because the beat is subdivided into three pulses. Quadruple time tells us that there are four beats per measure. The music is notated in $\frac{12}{8}$ meter to give it a majestic feel and a longer musical line, rather than in $\frac{6}{8}$, which would result in a choppier, less flowing rendition of the lyrics. The strong beats in $\frac{12}{8}$ coincide with the poetic meter of the lyrics. The three eighth notes on beat 4 provide a driving impetus to the music, which continues throughout the song.

Lesson 14 Continued

Moving

8a Divide the class into eight groups and assign each group one phrase of the song. Have each group

- Study the lyrics of its phrase.
- Choose a movement that best expresses the meaning of the phrase.
- Practice the movement as the group members sing the phrase, and then perform their movement in unison.

Instruct students to stand perfectly still while they sing the song and execute their movements only during their assigned phrases. They should freeze in position as statues at the end of their phrases and hold the position through the end of the song.

See Movement, below for additional teaching suggestions.

Singing

8b Invite students to read the information on p. 484.

Have students discuss the importance of freedom and why the fight for civil rights continues.

1a Invite students to sing "For Children Safe and Strong" **CD 21-12** with the recording.

Help students observe the rests in measures 2 and 10.

ASK What effect is created by the rests? (The rests make the melody sound *staccato*, and create syncopation.)

Should the rest of the song be sung staccato or legato? (*legato*)

1d Focus students' attention on the two-part harmony in the refrain and invite students to sing the harmony part with the recording **CD 21-12.**

5e Divide the class into two groups and invite students to sing the verses in unison and the refrain in harmony with the recording **CD 21-12.**

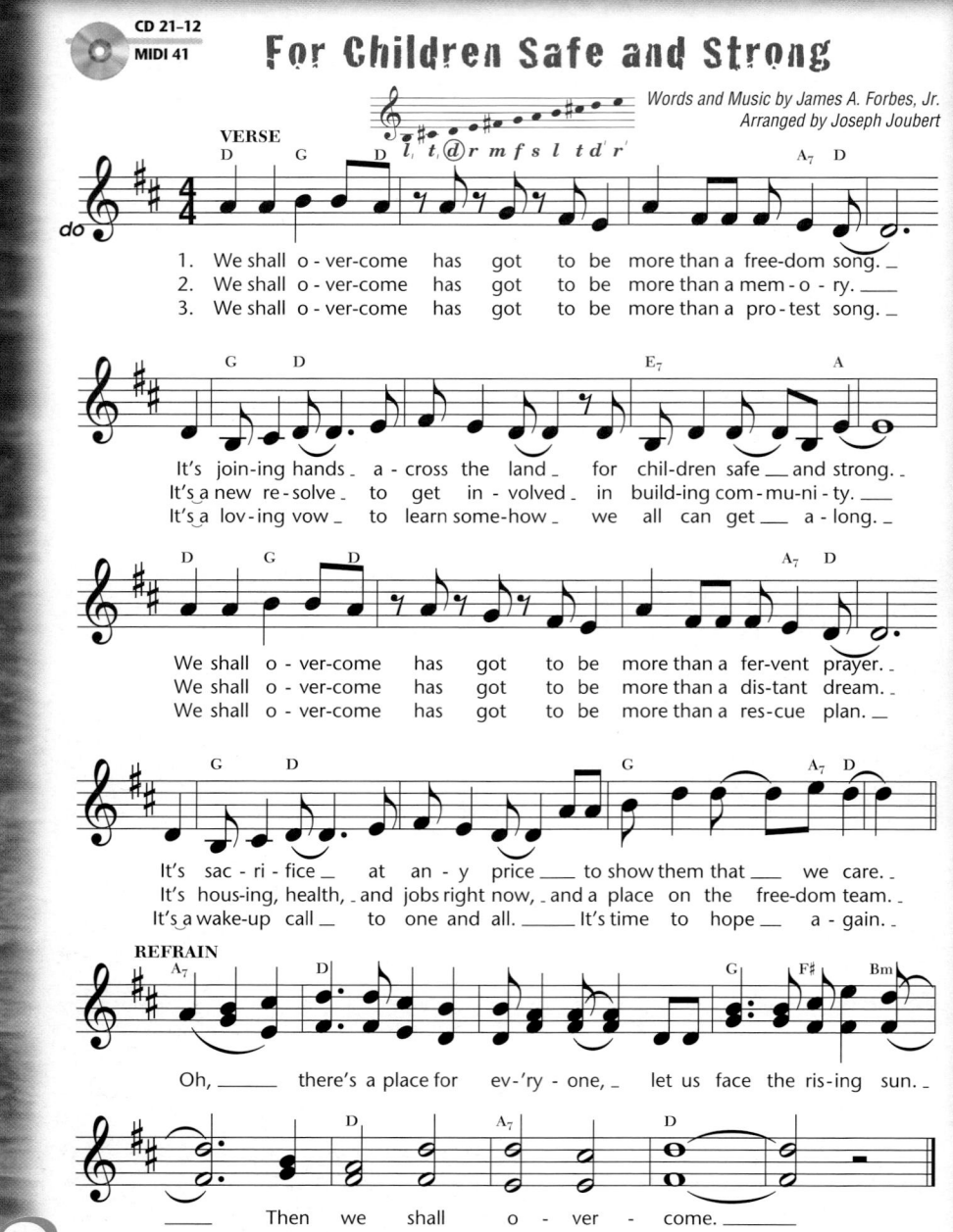

Let Freedom Ring!
The Civil Rights movement did not stop with the death of Dr. Martin Luther King. This song celebrates our freedom and reminds us that securing individual freedom and civil rights for all people is a continuous struggle.

CD 21–12
MIDI 41

For Children Safe and Strong

Words and Music by James A. Forbes, Jr.
Arranged by Joseph Joubert

VERSE

1. We shall o-ver-come has got to be more than a free-dom song. _
2. We shall o-ver-come has got to be more than a mem-o-ry. _
3. We shall o-ver-come has got to be more than a pro-test song. _

It's join-ing hands _ a-cross the land _ for chil-dren safe _ and strong. _
It's a new re-solve _ to get in-volved _ in build-ing com-mu-ni-ty. _
It's a lov-ing vow _ to learn some-how _ we all can get _ a-long. _

We shall o-ver-come has got to be more than a fer-vent prayer. _
We shall o-ver-come has got to be more than a dis-tant dream. _
We shall o-ver-come has got to be more than a res-cue plan. _

It's sac-ri-fice _ at an-y price _ to show them that _ we care. _
It's hous-ing, health, _ and jobs right now, _ and a place on the free-dom team. _
It's a wake-up call _ to one and all. _ It's time to hope _ a-gain. _

REFRAIN

Oh, _____ there's a place for ev-'ry-one, _ let us face the ris-ing sun.

_____ Then we shall o-ver-come. _____

484

MOVEMENT

3b ▶ **Creative Movement** Use the following teaching suggestions to help all students move to "Lift Ev'ry Voice and Sing."

Reinforcement Some students may not feel comfortable choosing a movement for an entire phrase from the song. Allow these students to identify one word from each phrase to choose a movement for. For example, "sing," "ring," or "rise."

On Target Most students will be able to interpret an entire phrase through movement. Monitor these students to make sure they are performing their movement on the assigned phrase.

Challenge Invite interested students to create a movement routine to perform with the entire song.

SPOTLIGHT ON

▶ **A Civil Rights Leader** Dr. Martin Luther King, Jr., (1929–1968) was the most prominent figure of the 1960s civil rights movement that swept the southern United States. He grew up in a segregated society that looked down on any interaction between people of different races. Dr. King followed in the footsteps of his father, by becoming a Baptist minister. In 1963, he gave his famous "I Have a Dream" speech to 250,000 civil rights activists in Washington, D.C. He won the Nobel Peace Prize in 1964 for advocating nonviolent means of protest. On April 4, 1968, Dr. King was assassinated while assisting a sanitation worker strike in Memphis, TN.

A Hymn for Civil Rights

"We Shall Overcome" became the anthem of the American Civil Rights movement during the early 1960s. It was also an anthem for workers in the 1940s and Chinese students in 1989.

CD 21–14
We Shall Overcome

African American Spiritual
as performed by Louis Armstrong
The words of *We Shall Overcome* have changed through the years but the spirit of the song remains the same.

Nobel Peace Prize Winners ▼

Rigoberta Menchú Tum

Mother Teresa

Yitzhak Rabin

Jane Addams

The Dalai Lama

Jimmy Carter

Holidays in Song

Unit 12 **485**

Listening

Explain that the text of "For Children Safe and Strong" refers to the song "We Shall Overcome," which became the anthem of the civil rights movement.

6a Have students play the first measure of "For Children Safe and Strong" on a keyboard or other melody instrument.

Invite students to listen to *We Shall Overcome* **CD 21-14** and raise their hands when they hear this motive.

ASK Is the motive exactly the same in both songs? (No, it was extended in *We Shall Overcome*.)

Invite students to listen to *We Shall Overcome* again and play or sing the motive each time they hear it.

3 CLOSE

Skill: SINGING **ASSESSMENT**

1d
7a
Performance/Observation Encourage students to prepare a program celebrating Dr. King's birthday that includes "Lift Ev'ry Voice and Sing," "For Children Safe and Strong," and several other songs from their books that deal with freedom and civil rights.

Have them

• Determine the order for performing the songs.

• Decide if any songs or parts of songs will be performed as solos or in small groups.

• Sing "For Children Safe and Strong" in two-part harmony.

• Research and write a narration to be read between each song.

If time and schedule permit, the students could perform their program for another class and invite their relatives and friends to attend.

ACROSS THE CURRICULUM

8b ▶ **Language Arts** Read aloud portions of Abraham Lincoln's Gettysburg Address and the Reverend Dr. Martin Luther King, Jr.'s "I Have a Dream" speech. Compare the ideas about freedom expressed in both. Martin Luther King, Jr. gave this speech at the foot of the Lincoln Memorial in Washington, D.C., during the civil rights March on Washington, August 28, 1963.

Read aloud selections from *Dear Dr. King: Letters from Today's Children to Dr. Martin Luther King, Jr.* by Jan Colbert and Ann M. Harms (eds.) (Jump at the Sun, 2000). This touching and poignant book is a collection of letters from Memphis school children, ages 6–12 years, telling the late Dr. King about their personal challenges in the quest for tolerance, freedom, acceptance, and understanding among all Americans.

TECHNOLOGY/MEDIA LINK

1d **MIDI/Sequencing Software** Use the MIDI song file for "Children Safe and Strong" to help inexperienced and dependent singers learn the harmony part. Using a computer or sequencer you can isolate just the refrain, and have individual or groups of students sing along with the

• Harmony part unaccompanied.

• Harmony part and the accompaniment.

• Harmony part and the melody.

• Harmony part, melody and the accompaniment

LESSON AT A GLANCE

Element Focus **MELODY** Melodic phrases

Skill Objective **ANALYZING** Analyze and compare melodic phrases in two patriotic songs

Connection Activity **SOCIAL STUDIES** Discuss the origins of the two principal patriotic songs of the United States

MATERIALS

- "America" **CD 21-15**
  Recording Routine: Intro (4 m.); v. 1; interlude (2 m.); v. 2; interlude (2 m.); v. 3; interlude (2 m.); v. 4
- "The Star-Spangled Banner" **CD 21-17**
  Recording Routine: Intro (4 m.); v. 1; v. 2; v. 3
- *The Fourth of July* **CD 21-19**
- **Resource Book** p. G-14
- hand chimes or resonator bells (with one mallet per bell)

VOCABULARY

countermelody   phrase   timbre
texture   fermata

◆ ◆ ◆ ◆ National Standards ◆ ◆ ◆ ◆

1a Sing music accurately in large ensembles
1d Sing music written in two parts
2a Play instruments accurately in small ensembles
5a Read quarter notes, eighth notes, and dotted notes in triple meter
5c Identify standard notation symbols for pitch and rhythm
6b Listen and analyze uses of pitch, rhythm, timbre, and form
6c Understand and use basic principles of rhythm, meter, and intervals in music analysis
8b Identify how music relates to social studies

MORE MUSIC CHOICES

For more practice singing about patriotism:
"The Voices of Pride," p. 86
"Battle Hymn of the Republic," p. 274

America sings

Tune In

The melody for "America" is the melody of "God Save the Queen," the national anthem of Great Britain.

"America" was written by Samuel F. Smith to celebrate Washington's birthday. It was performed for the first time on July 4, 1831, by a group of Boston children.

Play the part below on hand bells, chimes, or resonator bells to accompany verses one and two of "America."

CD 21-15

America

Words by Samuel Francis Smith   Traditional Melody

t d r m f s l

1. My coun-try! 'tis of thee, Sweet land of
2. My na-tive coun-try, thee, Land of the
3. Let mu-sic swell the breeze, And ring from
4. Our fa-thers' God, to Thee, Au-thor of

lib-er-ty, Of thee I sing; Land where my
no-ble free, Thy name I love; I love thy
all the trees Sweet Free-dom's song; Let mor-tal
lib-er-ty, To Thee we sing; Long may our

486

Footnotes

ACROSS THE CURRICULUM

8b ▶ **Language Arts** Ask students to research information about our national anthem in *The Star-Spangled Banner (Cornerstones of Freedom)* by Deborah Kent (Children's Press, 1995). Create a narrative about the anthem to be paired with "The Star-Spangled Banner" in patriotic musical performances.

BUILDING SKILLS THROUGH MUSIC

▶ **Language/Social Studies** Ask students to name other patriotic songs in addition to "America" and "The Star-Spangled Banner." (Answers may include "God Bless America," "America, the Beautiful," "Let Freedom Ring," and so on.) Have students identify common themes or ideas expressed in the songs; for example, praise of America's beauty or the bravery of fallen heroes.

CULTURAL CONNECTION

▶ **"God Save the Queen"** The melody of the British national anthem, "God Save the Queen," is the same as the music to "America." When singing the British anthem, it is traditional to change the gender words to reflect the current monarch. Here is the first verse of "God Save the Queen," first heard in 1744.

God save our gracious Queen,
Long live our noble Queen,
God save the Queen.
Send her victorious,
Happy and glorious,
Long to reign over us,
God save the Queen.

Samuel Francis Smith, seated at the desk of Edgar Silver, founder of Silver Burdett ▶

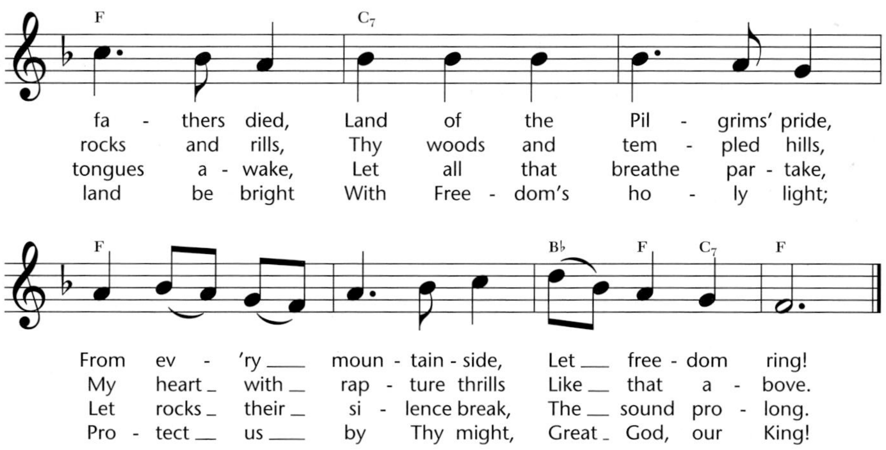

fa - thers died, Land of the Pil - grims' pride,
rocks and rills, Thy woods and tem - pled hills,
tongues a - wake, Let all that breathe par - take,
land be bright With Free - dom's ho - ly light;

From ev - 'ry ___ moun - tain - side, Let ___ free - dom ring!
My heart ___ with ___ rap - ture thrills Like ___ that a - bove.
Let rocks ___ their ___ si - lence break, The ___ sound pro - long.
Pro - tect ___ us ___ by Thy might, Great ___ God, our King!

Holidays in Song

1 INTRODUCE

8b Encourage students to create a list of patriotic holidays on the board. (Independence Day, Columbus Day, Veterans Day, Presidents Day, Memorial Day, Flag Day)

Invite students to read the information on p. 486.

2 DEVELOP

Singing

1a Invite students to sing "America" **CD 21-15** with the recording. Share with them information about the origins of the song in Cultural Connection on p. 486 and Spotlight On, p. 488.

Help students discover "America" has only one phrase of six measures and one phrase of eight measures.

5a Write the rhythm for the second measure of "America" on the board and have students find the rhythm in the song. (mm. 2, 4, 8, 10, and 12)

Have students quietly tap the rhythm each time it occurs as they sing the song with the recording.

Playing

Draw attention to the hand chime/resonator bell countermelody on p. 486.

6c **ASK How does the rhythm of the countermelody differ from the rhythm of the song?** (The countermelody uses only quarter notes.)

5c
2a Assign each of nine students one of the pitches in the countermelody and have them say the letter name of his/her assigned pitch when it occurs in rhythm while you count the beat. Then have students perform the countermelody on hand chimes or resonator bells.

6c Help students recognize that by adding the countermelody, they change both the texture and timbre of the music. (The countermelody should be performed with verses 1 and 2 only.)

continued on page 488

CHARACTER EDUCATION

▶ **Patriotism** Ask students to define patriotism. Discuss different ways people demonstrate patriotism in this country (wear red, white, and blue; fly a flag at their home; recite the Pledge of Allegiance). Have students rate their patriotism using a scale of 1 to 10 (1 being the lowest, 10 being the highest). Discuss students' responses, reminding them that overt behaviors like flying a flag are not the only way to determine patriotism. Challenge students to interview an older adult about how he or she was taught to demonstrate patriotism. Have students ask this individual about how he or she perceives the level of patriotism to be today compared to the time in which he or she grew up.

TEACHER TO TEACHER

1a ▶ **Harmony** The harmony part in "The Star-Spangled Banner," beginning on p. 488, provides a good alternative for singers who cannot sing the highest pitches of the melody. Another alternative would be to teach these singers to jump octaves (sing the melody at the top of the page an octave lower than written). Boys with changing voices will find this technique especially helpful. While jumping octaves does not always produce the most musical performance, it allows singers with limited ranges to participate in the singing of this important song and other songs with wide ranges.

Moving

Invite students to learn the sign interpretation for "America" found on Resource Book p. G-14.

Singing

Select a student to read the information at the top of p. 488 about "The Star-Spangled Banner." See Spotlight On below and discuss with students the origin of the song. Point out that "The Star-Spangled Banner" was adopted as the national anthem of the United States on March 3, 1931.

Invite students to sing the melody with **CD 21-17**.

6b **ASK What is the phrase form of this song?** (aabc: "a"—lines 1 ad 2; "a"—lines 3 and 4; "b"—lines 5 and 6; "c"—lines 7 and 8)

6c Help students discover that the first section of the song is in unison, its melody is lower, and it has more dotted rhythms. Help students learn that the second section is in harmony, its melody is higher, and it has fewer dotted rhythms.

Draw attention to the fermata on p. 489 and explain that it is held until the conductor releases it.

Invite students to sing the harmony part of the second section with the recording.

1d Select a group of students to sing the harmony part of our national anthem while the rest of the class sings the melody with the recording.

Our National Anthem

During the War of 1812, Francis Scott Key wrote the words to "The Star-Spangled Banner." In 1931 an act of Congress established "The Star-Spangled Banner" as the national anthem of the United States.

Practice both the melody and harmony parts for "The Star-Spangled Banner." Then sing in two-part harmony.

488

Footnotes

SPOTLIGHT ON

▶ **Francis Scott Key** The sight of the American flag still flying at dawn on September 14, 1814, over Fort McHenry after a long and heavy bombardment by the British fleet in Baltimore Harbor inspired Francis Scott Key (1780–1843) to scribble a poem on the back of an envelope. His patriotic words were published and later set to an old English song known as "Anacreon in Heaven" by John Stafford Smith (1750–1836).

Key had gone on September 13 to seek the release of a friend held captive on a British ship, but when the fierce naval attack erupted, he was stranded for about 25 hours aboard a sloop behind the British fleet. After a day and night of rockets bursting in air, he was ecstatic and relieved to see the huge American flag flying over the fort, indicating that the fort was still in American hands.

TEACHER TO TEACHER

▶ **Singing the National Anthem** "The Star-Spangled Banner" melody requires a range of an octave and a fifth. Many young singers are incapable of singing both extremes of this range; therefore, our national anthem is difficult for them to perform. Students for whom the A♭ below middle C is low may substitute the middle C for the A♭. This substitution will dissuade girls and boys with unchanged voices from developing a rasping chest sound that often occurs when children sing below their range.

Let's Celebrate

Music is often an important part of celebrations.

Listen to *The Fourth of July*. The music paints a lively picture of the holiday.

CD 21-19

 The Fourth of July

by Morton Gould
performed by Morton Gould and his Symphonic Band

Gould's "Yankee Doodle" celebration includes fireworks and a parade.

And the rock-ets' red glare, the bombs burst-ing in air,
Now it catch-es the gleam of the morn-ing's first beam,
Then __ con-quer we must, for our cause it is just,

Gave proof through the night that our flag was still there.
In full glo-ry re-flected now __ shines on the stream.
And this be our motto: "In ____ God is our trust!"

Oh, say, does that __ Star-Span-gled Ban-ner __ yet __ wave __
'Tis the Star-Span-gled __ Ban-ner, oh, long may __ it ___ wave __
And the Star-Span-gled __ Ban-ner in tri-umph _ shall _ wave __

O'er the land ____ of the free and the home of the brave?
O'er the land ____ of the free and the home of the brave!
O'er the land ____ of the free and the home of the brave!

Unit 12 **489**

Holidays in Song

Listening

Have students read on p. 489 in their books about Morton Gould's piece for symphonic band entitled *The Fourth of July* **CD 21-19.** Then play the recording.

6b **ASK** How does the music paint a picture of a Fourth of July celebration? (marching beat, patriotic tunes, brass and percussion instruments, lively rhythms)

Analyzing

6c Ask students to apply criteria in evaluating musical compositions. Have them compare the melody of the two patriotic songs in this lesson to discover that

- "America" is more like a hymn, while "The Star-Spangled Banner" is more militaristic.
- Both use $\frac{3}{4}$ meter and dotted rhythms.
- "America" has a small range; its melody is made up mostly of steps and repeated tones.
- "The Star-Spangled Banner" has a very wide range, with many large skips, and a rocketlike rising melodic figure in mm. 1–2 and mm. 9–10.
- "America" has two long phrases while "The Star-Spangled Banner" has eight phrases.

3 CLOSE

Element: MELODY  **ASSESSMENT**

Music Journal Writing Ask students to write in their music journals those characteristics that make "America" sound hymn-like and "The Star-Spangled Banner" more militaristic. ("America": narrow range, movement mostly by steps and repeated tones; "The Star-Spangled Banner": wide range, large melodic skips, a rocketlike rising melodic figure in mm. 1–2 and mm. 9–10)

ACROSS THE CURRICULUM

8b ▶ **Social Studies** Unresolved shipping and trade issues from the Revolutionary War created political tension in the United States in the first years of its existence. Americans feared that Britain would incite the Native Americans to attack settlers moving westward. Americans also suffered from a law that prevented free access to British ports. Almost 400 American ships were captured in two years, and some sailors were forced into service on British ships. The United States declared war on Britain on June 18, 1812. Some called the action America's "second war for independence." The War of 1812 involved Native American, American, and British troops in battles in Canada, in the U.S., and on the Great Lakes. Following the 1814 American victory at Fort McHenry, the British retreated to New Orleans and, in Europe, diplomats signed a peace treaty ending the war.

SCHOOL TO HOME CONNECTION

▶ **Pictures of America** Ask parents or other family members of students to loan the class pictures of various places, landscapes, landmarks, and people in America. Organize a slide show to accompany the singing of patriotic songs at concerts and performances.

TECHNOLOGY/MEDIA LINK

Web Site For more information on the history of patriotic songs go to *www.sfsuccessnet.com.*

SILVER·BURDETT

Making Music

Student Resources

CONTENTS

Unit 1
Music Reading Practice

👆 Reading Sequence 1, page 10

MATERIALS

- "Laredo" (Spanish), p. 10   **CD 1-9**
- "Laredo" (English), p. 10   **CD 1-10**
- Reading Sequence 1
  Rhythm part (drum)   **CD 1-14**
  Rhythm part with accompaniment   **CD 1-15**
  Accompaniment only   **CD 1-16**
- **Resource Book** p. E-2
- nonpitched percussion instruments

Rhythm: Reading Meter in 4

Review the definition of time signature. Direct students to Reading Sequence 1 and have them

- Identify the time signature of the exercise and the conducting pattern.
- Practice the exercise with the recording **CD 1-14**.
- Perform the exercise with "Laredo" **CD 1-9** while individual students take turns conducting the group.

👆 Reading Sequence 2, page 12

MATERIALS

- "Morning Comes Early," p. 13   **CD 1-17**
- Reading Sequence 2
  Rhythm part (drum)   **CD 1-19**
  Rhythm part with accompaniment   **CD 1-20**
  Accompaniment only   **CD 1-21**
- **Resource Book** pp. D-2, E-3
- nonpitched percussion instruments

Rhythm: Reading ♪ ♩ ♪

Ask students to identify the meter of Reading Sequence 2. Have students

- Describe the ♪ ♩ ♪ pattern as short-long-short.
- Identify the measures where the ♪ ♩ ♪ pattern is found. Reinforce this pattern by reading it with rhythm syllables.
- Practice the exercise with the recording **CD 1-19**.
- Perform the exercise on nonpitched percussion instruments to accompany the song **CD 1-17**.

👆 Reading Sequence 1, page 10   CD 1–14 / MIDI 42

Rhythm: Reading Meter in 4

Use rhythm syllables to **read** and **perform** this counter-rhythm for "Laredo."

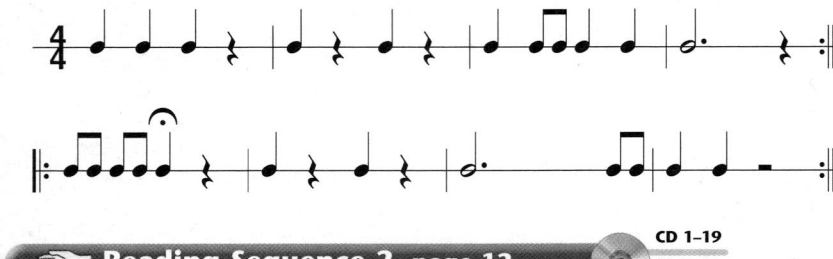

👆 Reading Sequence 2, page 12   CD 1–19 / MIDI 43

Rhythm: Reading ♪ ♩ ♪

Use rhythm syllables to **read** and **perform** this rhythm accompaniment for "Morning Comes Early."

Footnotes

▶ **The Reading Sequences and Its Formats** The music reading program within Units 1–6 of MAKING MUSIC Grade 5 develops fundamental musical concepts and skills through a sequenced body of activities and lessons. The Reading Sequences of the Music Reading Practice section provide opportunities to reinforce and extend students' music reading experiences.

The Reading Sequences appear as student pages within the Pupil's Edition. In addition, these exercises are available as blackline masters in the Resource Book. You may complete any Reading Sequence as a class project by creating an overhead transparency of the blackline master. You may also use the same Reading Sequence blackline master to prepare worksheets, on which students can make individual responses and for assessment. Let your own goals and the skill level of the students guide your choice of Reading Sequence formats.

 Reading Sequence 3, page 22
CD 2-3
MIDI 44

Melody: Reading Note Names (C-D-E-G-A)

Read and **sing** this countermelody for "Bound for South Australia." Use pitch syllables and hand signs.

Reading Sequence 4, page 26
CD 2-12
MIDI 45

Melody: Reading Pentatonic Patterns

For inner hearing practice, use pitch syllables and hand signs to **read** and **sing** this countermelody for "This Train."

491

Reading Sequence 3, page 22

MATERIALS
- "Bound for South Australia," p. 22 — **CD 2-1**
- Reading Sequence 3
  Melody part — **CD 2-3**
  Melody part with accompaniment — **CD 2-4**
  Accompaniment only — **CD 2-5**
- **Resource Book** p. E-4

Melody: Reading Note Names (C-D-E-G-A)

Have students sing the extended pentatonic scale using pitch syllables and hand signs. Direct students to Reading Sequence 3 and have them

- Find *do* on the staff and review the staff placement of the notes in the pentatonic scale.
- Point to each "middle" C in the exercise.
- Sing the exercise **CD 2-3** using pitch syllables and hand signs.

Invite students to sing this exercise as a countermelody to "Bound for South Australia" **CD 2-1**. Divide the class into two groups. Have one group sing the song while the other group sings the exercise as a countermelody. Invite students to switch parts and sing again.

Reading Sequence 4, page 26

MATERIALS
- "This Train," p. 27 — **CD 2-10**
- Reading Sequence 4
  Melody part — **CD 2-12**
  Melody part with accompaniment — **CD 2-13**
  Accompaniment only — **CD 2-14**
- **Resource Book** pp. D-4, E-5

Melody: Reading Pentatonic Patterns

Review the extended pentatonic scale. Invite students to refer to the hand signs along the side of the page. Have students

- Review $\frac{4}{4}$ meter and its conducting pattern.
- Clap and read the rhythms in Reading Sequence 4.
- Sing the exercise **CD 2-12** using pitch syllables and hand signs.
- Sing the exercise as a countermelody to "This Train" **CD 2-10**.

Notate the exercise on the board in D-*do,* then ask students to read it from staff notation.

▶ **Singing Flats and Sharps (Reading Sequences 3 and 4)** By now, students who are familiar with reading from pitch syllables (*do-re-mi*) can begin to sing melodies using note letter names, as well. This reinforces both interval recognition and staff reading, and prepares students for more advanced instrumental playing. When singing note names in keys with sharps or flats it may be helpful to use a system that gives a one-syllable name to notes like "B-flat," for instance. In keys with flats, the suffix -*ess* can be added to the note name for singing (pronounced *bess, dess, fess),* and so on. ("A" is sung as *oss.*) In sharp keys, the suffix (pronounced *ees*) can be added, so C-sharp is sung as *ceese.* Some other notes, for example, would be *fis, bis,* and *ais.*

▶ **Using the MIDI Files** MIDI files are provided for all Reading Sequence exercises. Each file contains individual tracks for specific melody or rhythm parts, as notated in the corresponding exercise on the student page, and a full accompaniment for the song on which the exercise is based. As an instructional tool, the files can be used to isolate individual parts, accompany any combination of parts, and transpose the pitches or change the tempo of the exercise and accompaniment.

Unit 2
Music Reading Practice

Reading Sequence 5, page 52

MATERIALS

- "California," p. 52   **CD 3-9**
- Reading Sequence 5
  Rhythm Part 1 (woodblock)   **CD 3-11**
  Rhythm Part 2 (tambourine)   **CD 3-12**
  Rhythm Parts 1 and 2   **CD 3-13**
  Rhythm Parts 1 and 2 with accompaniment   **CD 3-14**
  Accompaniment only   **CD 3-15**
- **Resource Book** p. E-6
- nonpitched percussion instruments

Rhythm: Reading ♩ ♫ and ♫ ♩

Review ²₄ meter and its conducting pattern. Direct students to Reading Sequence 5 and have them

- Read, clap, and count Part 1 using rhythm syllables.
- Analyze Part 1 and identify how it is similar to Part 2. (both parts use ♩, ♫, and ♩ ♫)
- Read, clap, and count Part 2 using rhythm syllables.

Use the recordings to practice each part of the exercise. Then, divide the class into three groups and have

- Group 1 perform Part 1 **CD 3-11**.
- Group 2 perform Part 2 **CD 3-12**.
- Group 3 sing the song **CD 3-9**.

Students can also perform the parts on nonpitched percussion instruments to accompany the song.

Reading Sequence 6, page 54

MATERIALS

- "Drill, Ye Tarriers," p. 54   **CD 3-16**
- Reading Sequence 6
  Rhythm part (claves)   **CD 3-18**
  Rhythm part with accompaniment   **CD 3-19**
  Accompaniment only   **CD 3-20**
- **Resource Book** p. E-7
- nonpitched percussion instruments

Rhythm: Reading ♩ ♫, ♫ ♩, and ♬♬

Ask students to identify the meter of Reading Sequence 6 and review the conducting pattern. Direct students to the exercise and have them

- Look at the notation and count how many times each sixteenth-note rhythm appears. (18 times)
- Clap and read the exercise using rhythm syllables.
- Practice the exercise with the recording **CD 3-18**.
- Perform the exercise on nonpitched percussion instruments to accompany the song **CD 3-16**.

Reading Sequence 5, page 52   **CD 3–11**   **MIDI 46**

Rhythm: Reading ♩ ♫ and ♫ ♩

Use rhythm syllables to **read** and **perform** this two-part rhythm accompaniment for "California."

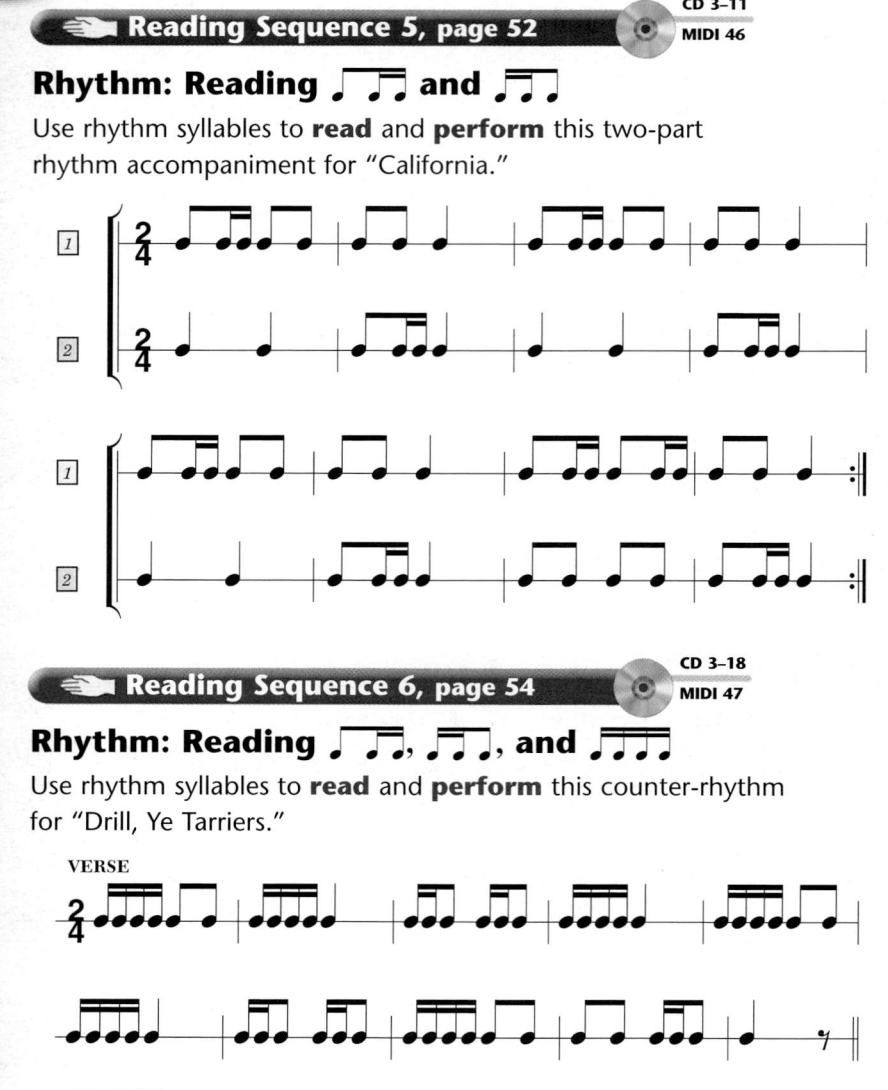

Reading Sequence 6, page 54   **CD 3–18**   **MIDI 47**

Rhythm: Reading ♩ ♫, ♫ ♩, and ♬♬

Use rhythm syllables to **read** and **perform** this counter-rhythm for "Drill, Ye Tarriers."

VERSE

REFRAIN

Footnotes

▶ **Creating (Reading Sequence 5)** Invite students to create harmony parts for "California" using the exercise as a rhythmic framework. Suggest that they create a countermelody by choosing *do, fa,* or *so* (D, G, or A) as the pitch for each beat, deciding which notes best match the melody. Students can then sing, notate, and play their new parts using recorders or melodic percussion instruments. This "limited" composition exercise serves as aural preparation for future harmonic work with I, IV, and V chords.

▶ **Rhythm Reading Practice (Reading Sequence 6)** For those students new to music reading in this grade, the rhythms in "Drill, Ye Tarriers" may be quickly introduced in one or two lessons. Reinforcing the activities over several lessons will allow students to practice rhythm reading while learning other musical skills.

Reading Sequence 7, page 60
CD 3–33
MIDI 48

Melody: Reading *fa*

Read and **sing** this two-part countermelody for *"A la puerta del cielo."* Use pitch syllables and hand signs.

Reading Sequence 8, page 62
CD 4–1
MIDI 49

Melody: Reading *do, re, mi, fa, so,* and *la*

Read and **sing** this countermelody for *"Da pacem, Domine."* Use pitch syllables and hand signs.

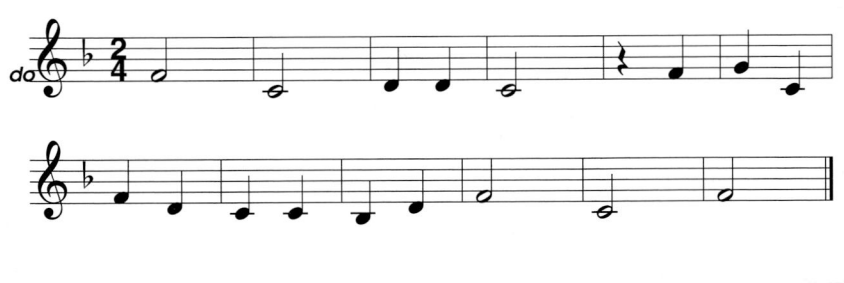

493

▶ **Aural Preparation (Reading Sequence 7)** *"A la puerta del cielo"* contains a new note, *ti,* which students will encounter consciously in later lessons. Singing the song provides aural preparation for that element. Teachers following the reading sequence may wish to have students read the reading sequence (which contains only known elements) instead of the full staff version of the song in the student book. Once the new note has been learned, students can revisit the song and read the actual notation from their books.

▶ **Reading Half Steps (Reading Sequences 7 and 8)** With the introduction of *fa,* students also encounter the interval of the half step for the first time. Reinforce the idea that, though a half step may look the same as a whole step on the staff, it is a smaller interval. The use of hand signs and pitch syllables, along with attention to in-tune singing, will help students accurately perform patterns containing the *mi-fa* melodic interval.

Reading Sequence 7, page 60

MATERIALS
- *"A la puerta del cielo,"* p. 60 — **CD 3-29**
- *"At the Gate of Heaven,"* p. 60 — **CD 3-30**
- Reading Sequence 7
  Melody Part 1 — **CD 3-33**
  Melody Part 2 — **CD 3-34**
  Melody Parts 1 and 2 — **CD 3-35**
  Melody Parts 1 and 2 with accompaniment — **CD 3-36**
  Accompaniment only — **CD 3-37**
- **Resource Book** pp. D-6, E-8

Melody: Reading *fa*

Direct students to Reading Sequence 7 and have them

- Read and clap the rhythm of Part 1 using rhythm syllables.
- Read and clap the rhythm of Part 2 using rhythm syllables.

Invite students to sing a *do*-pentachordal pattern *(so-fa-mi-re-do)* using pitch syllables. Have them hum *fa*. Ask them which two syllables *fa* falls between. *(mi* and *so)* Direct students again to the exercise and ask them to

- Identify *do* on the staff and review the notes of the F-*do* extended pentatonic scale (See Resource Book p. D-8).
- Analyze the notation and find *fa* each time it appears.

Use the recordings to practice each part of the exercise. Then, divide the class into two groups and have

- Group 1 perform Part 1 **CD 3-33.**
- Group 2 perform Part 2 **CD 3-34.**
- Group 3 perform the song **CD 3-29.**

Reading Sequence 8, page 62

MATERIALS
- *"Da pacem, Domine,"* p. 62 — **CD 3-38**
- *"Grant Us Peace,"* p. 62 — **CD 3-39**
- Reading Sequence 8
  Melody part — **CD 4-1**
  Melody part with accompaniment — **CD 4-2**
  Accompaniment only — **CD 4-3**
- **Resource Book** p. E-9

Melody: Reading *do, re, mi, fa, so,* and *la*

Invite students to look at Reading Sequence 8 and ask them to

- Identify *do* on the staff and the flat in the key signature (B♭). Sing the exercise using pitch syllables and hand signs. (For reference, direct students to the hand signs along the side of the page.)
- Sing the exercise as a countermelody to *"Da pacem, Domine"* **CD 3-38.**

Unit 3
Music Reading Practice

Reading Sequence 9, page 94

MATERIALS

- "Himmel und Erde," p. 94 — **CD 5-11**
- "Music Alone Shall Live," p. 94 — **CD 5-12**
- Reading Sequence 9
  Rhythm part (triangle) — **CD 5-15**
  Rhythm part with accompaniment — **CD 5-16**
  Accompaniment only — **CD 5-17**
- **Resource Book** pp. D-9, E-10
- nonpitched percussion instruments

Rhythm: Reading ♩. and ♪

Have students identify the time signature of Reading Sequence 9 and practice conducting meter in 3. Then have them

- Read and clap the exercise using rhythm syllables while individual students take turns conducting the group.
- Practice the exercise with the recording **CD 5-15**.

Invite students to harmonize the song by choosing either *mi* or *fa* as the pitch in each measure.

Reading Sequence 10, page 96

MATERIALS

- "Don't You Hear the Lambs?," p. 97 — **CD 5-19**
- Reading Sequence 10
  Rhythm part (triangle) — **CD 5-21**
  Rhythm part with accompaniment — **CD 5-22**
  Accompaniment only — **CD 5-23**
- **Resource Book** pp. D-11, E-11
- nonpitched percussion instruments

Rhythm: Reading Dotted-Rhythm Patterns

Ask students to identify the time signature of Reading Sequence 10. Invite students to look at the exercise and have them

- Analyze the notation and find the dotted eighth/quarter note pattern.
- Clap and read the exercise using rhythm syllables while individual students take turns patting the steady beat.
- Perform the exercise on nonpitched percussion instruments as an accompaniment to the song.
- Perform the exercise on nonpitched percussion instruments to accompany the song **CD 5-19**.

Reading Sequence 9, page 94
CD 5–15 / MIDI 50

Rhythm: Reading ♩. and ♪

Use rhythm syllables to **read** and **perform** this counter-rhythm for *"Himmel und Erde."*

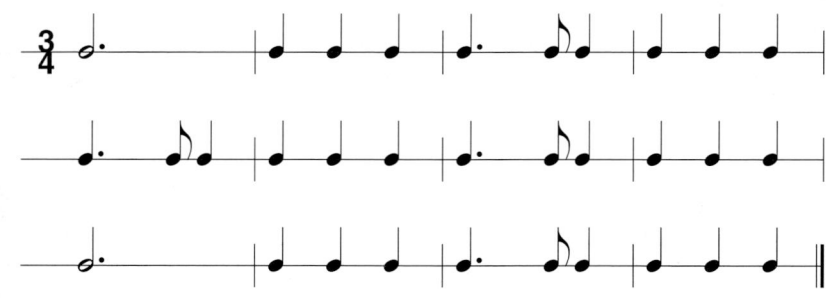

Reading Sequence 10, page 96
CD 5–21 / MIDI 51

Rhythm: Reading Dotted-Rhythm Patterns

Use rhythm syllables to **read** and **perform** this counter-rhythm for "Don't You Hear the Lambs?"

494

Footnotes

▶ **Aural Preparation (Reading Sequences 9 and 10)** *"Himmel und Erde"* contains a new note, *ti*, which students will encounter consciously in later lessons. "Don't You Hear the Lambs?" contains an altered tone, *ta*, or the lowered *ti*, which creates the mixolydian mode of this melody. Singing the songs provides aural preparation for those elements. Teachers following the reading sequence may wish to have students read the reading sequences (which contain only known elements) instead of the full staff versions of the songs in the student book. Once the new notes have been learned, students can revisit the songs and read the actual notation from their books.

▶ **Creating (Reading Sequences 9 and 10)** To create a two-part arrangement of "Don't You Hear the Lambs?," have students compose text for the exercise and sing it along with the melody. Students may also enjoy creating countermelodies for *"Himmel und Erde"* using only *mi* and *fa*.

Melody: Reading *low ti*

Read and **sing** this two-part countermelody for "All Through the Night." Use pitch syllables and hand signs.

Melody: Reading *low ti*

Read and **sing** this two-part countermelody for *"Dundai."* Use pitch syllables and hand signs.

▶ **Singing Tips** (**Reading Sequences 11 and 12**) The optional Part 2 of "All Through the Night" and *"Dundai"* is written to provide practice reading below the staff, along with developing a healthy tone in the lower part of students' vocal range. Care should be taken to sing with a rich and light sound without forcing the "chest voice."

▶ **Listening** (**Reading Sequence 12**) After they have read both parts of the exercise, have students listen to the accompaniment track for *"Dundai."* Ask them to identify which part can be clearly heard in the accompaniment and what instrument is playing it. (The tuba plays the melody of Part 2.) Have them look at the part and analyze how it is different from the part they hear on the recording. (The rhythm consists of quarter notes and rests instead of half notes.)

MATERIALS

- "All Through the Night," p. 105   **CD 5-28**
- Reading Sequence 11
  Melody Part 1   **CD 5-29**
  Melody Part 2   **CD 5-30**
  Melody Parts 1 and 2   **CD 5-31**
  Melody Parts 1 and 2 with accompaniment   **CD 5-32**
  Accompaniment only   **CD 5-33**
- **Resource Book** pp. D-12, E-12

Melody: Reading *low ti*

Review the placement of *low ti* using Resource Book p. D-12. Invite students to look at Reading Sequence 11 and have them

- Read and clap the rhythm of Part 1 using rhythm syllables.
- Read and clap the rhythm of Part 2 using rhythm syllables.
- Identify *do* on the staff and review the F-*do* scale.
- Sing each part using pitch syllables and hand signs, then with note letter names.
- Point to each *low ti* in the exercise.
- Perform the exercise with "All Through the Night" **CD 5-28.**

MATERIALS

- *"Dundai"* (Hebrew), p. 106   **CD 5-34**
- *"Dundai"* (English), p. 106   **CD 5-35**
- Reading Sequence 12
  Melody Part 1   **CD 5-38**
  Melody Part 2   **CD 5-39**
  Melody Parts 1 and 2   **CD 5-40**
  Melody Parts 1 and 2 with accompaniment   **CD 5-41**
  Accompaniment only   **CD 5-42**
- **Resource Book** pp. D-14, E-13

Melody: Reading *low ti*

Direct students to *"Dundai"* on p. 106 and ask them to sing m. 4 and m. 8 using pitch syllables and hand signs. Then, direct students to Reading Sequence 12 and have them

- Locate the measures in Part 1 that have the same pitch and rhythm pattern as m. 4 and m. 8 in the song.
- Identify *do* on the staff, then practice singing each part using pitch syllables and hand signs.
- Perform the exercise with *"Dundai"* **CD 5-34**.

Unit 4
Music Reading Practice

Reading Sequence 13, page 136

MATERIALS

- "Wabash Cannon Ball," p. 136   **CD 7-1**
- Reading Sequence 13
  Rhythm part (woodblock)   **CD 7-3**
  Rhythm part with accompaniment   **CD 7-4**
  Accompaniment only   **CD 7-5**
- **Resource Book** pp. D-16, E-14
- nonpitched percussion instruments

Rhythm: Reading ♩. ♪

Ask students to identify the meter of Reading Sequence 13 and review the conducting pattern. Direct students to the exercise and ask them to

- Identify each ♩. ♪ rhythm.
- Clap and read the exercise with rhythm syllables.
- Practice the exercise with the recording **CD 7-3**.
- Perform the exercise with "Wabash Cannon Ball" **CD 7-1** while individual students take turns conducting the group.

Invite students to perform the exercise on nonpitched percussion instruments as an accompaniment to the song.

Reading Sequence 14, page 138

MATERIALS

- "Scotland the Brave," p. 138   **CD 7-6**
- Reading Sequence 14
  Rhythm part (drum)   **CD 7-8**
  Rhythm part with accompaniment   **CD 7-9**
  Accompaniment only   **CD 7-10**
- **Resource Book** p. E-15
- nonpitched percussion instruments

Rhythm: Reading Dotted-Rhythm Patterns

Have students identify the meter of Reading Sequence 14. Invite students to look at the exercise and ask them to

- Locate the dotted eighth/sixteenth note pattern in the notation.
- Read the exercise with rhythm syllables.
- Perform the exercise with "Scotland the Brave" **CD 7-6**.

For additional practice, students may perform the exercise on nonpitched percussion instruments to accompany the song.

Reading Sequence 13, page 136   CD 7–3 MIDI 54

Rhythm: Reading ♩. ♪

Use rhythm syllables to **read** and **perform** this counter-rhythm for "Wabash Cannon Ball."

Reading Sequence 14, page 138   CD 7–8 MIDI 55

Rhythm: Reading Dotted-Rhythm Patterns

Use rhythm syllables to **read** and **perform** this counter-rhythm for "Scotland the Brave."

496

Footnotes

▶ ♩. ♪ and ♪ ♩. (**Reading Sequence 13**) "Wabash Cannon Ball" contains a new rhythmic element ♩. ♪. Ask students to analyze the new rhythm and describe it, comparing it to ♪ ♩.. While both are two uneven sounds on a beat, ♪ ♩. is arranged in a short-long pattern. Once they are given the rhythm syllable names, students should be able to read both figures easily.

▶ **Creating** (**Reading Sequence 14**) After they have read the exercise for "Scotland the Brave," have students speak the last eight measures of the exercise while listening to the recording of "Loch Lomond" **CD 7-13**. Invite students to suggest changes that might improve the exercise as a countermelody for "Loch Lomond." Then have them notate the exercise on the board or on staff paper.

Reading Sequence 15, page 146 CD 7–22 MIDI 56

Melody: Reading a Diatonic Major Scale

Read and **sing** this countermelody for *"Las velitas."* Use pitch syllables and hand signs.

Reading Sequence 16, page 148 CD 7–27 MIDI 57

Melody: Reading a Melodic Sequence

Read and **sing** this countermelody for "Autumn Canon." Use pitch syllables and hand signs.

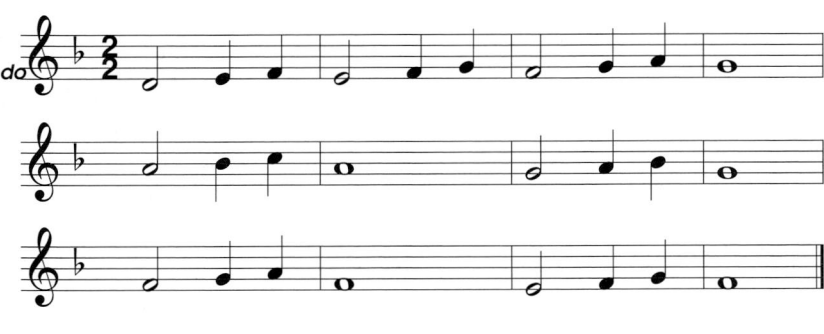

497

▶ **Half Steps (Reading Sequences 15 and 16)** Invite students to find the half steps in Reading Sequences 15 and 16. Remind them that half steps are always found between *mi* and *fa*, and *ti* and *do*. Then ask them to identify scale fragments in each exercise. Remind students that scale passages move stepwise, using both whole and half steps. Both of these songs are based on scale passages. *"Las velitas"* is based on the *do*, or major scale; "Autumn Canon" is based on the *la*, or minor scale.

Reading Sequence 15, page 146

MATERIALS

- *"Las velitas,"* p. 147 **CD 7-18**
- "Candles Burning Bright," p. 147 **CD 7-19**
- Reading Sequence 15
  Melody part **CD 7-22**
  Melody part with accompaniment **CD 7-23**
  Accompaniment only **CD 7-24**
- **Resource Book** pp. D-20, E-16
- keyboards

Melody: Reading a Diatonic Major Scale

Review the C-*do* scale using Resource Book p. D-21. Ask students to identify where half steps in the scale occur. Invite students to look at Reading Sequence 15 and have them

- Read the rhythms in the exercise using rhythm syllables.
- Identify *do* on the staff and then sing the C-*do* scale.
- Sing the exercise using pitch syllables and hand signs.
- Perform the exercise with *"Las velitas"* **CD 7-18**.

Invite students to perform the exercise on keyboards as an accompaniment to the song.

Reading Sequence 16, page 148

MATERIALS

- "Autumn Canon," p. 148 **CD 7-25**
- Reading Sequence 16
  Melody part **CD 7-27**
  Melody part with accompaniment **CD 7-28**
  Accompaniment only **CD 7-29**
- **Resource Book** p. E-17
- recorders or other melody instruments

Melody: Reading a Melodic Sequence

Direct students to Reading Sequence 16 and have them

- Clap and read the rhythm of the exercise.
- Sing m. 1 using pitch syllables and hand signs.
- Identify other measures in which both the melodic contour and rhythm match those of m. 1.
- Sing the entire exercise with pitch syllables and hand signs, then with note letter names.
- Sing the exercise as a countermelody to "Autumn Canon" **CD 7-25**.

For additional practice, students can play the exercise on recorders or other melody instruments as an accompaniment to the song.

Unit 5
Music Reading Practice

Reading Sequence 17, page 174

MATERIALS

- "Las estrellitas de cielo," p. 175   **CD 8-29**
- "Stars of the Heavens," p. 175   **CD 8-30**
- Reading Sequence 17
  Rhythm Part 1 (drum)   **CD 8-33**
  Rhythm Part 2 (triangle)   **CD 8-34**
  Rhythm Parts 1 and 2   **CD 8-35**
  Rhythm Parts 1 and 2 with accompaniment   **CD 8-36**
  Accompaniment only   **CD 8-37**
- **Resource Book** pp. D-23, E-18
- nonpitched percussion instruments

Rhythm: Reading in Compound Meter

Ask students to identify the meter of Reading Sequence 17 and the conducting pattern (§; meter in 2). Direct students to the exercise and have them

- Read and clap Part 1 using rhythm syllables.
- Read and clap Part 2 using rhythm syllables.

Use the recordings to practice each part of the exercise. Divide the class into three groups and have

- Group 1 perform Part 1 **CD 8-33**.
- Group 2 perform Part 2 **CD 8-34**.
- Group 3 sing the song **CD 8-29**.

For additional practice, students can play the exercise on nonpitched percussion instruments as an accompaniment to the song **CD 8-29**.

Reading Sequence 18, page 178

MATERIALS

- "Blow the Wind Southerly," p. 178   **CD 9-8**
- Reading Sequence 18
  Rhythm part (tambourine)   **CD 9-10**
  Rhythm part with accompaniment   **CD 9-11**
  Accompaniment only   **CD 9-12**
- **Resource Book** p. E-19
- nonpitched percussion instruments

Rhythm: Reading in § Meter

Invite students to look at Reading Sequence 18 and have them identify whether it is in simple or compound meter. Ask students how many beats per measure in § meter. (Two beats, each with three pulses, for a total of six eighth notes per measure) Then have them

- Read the exercise with rhythm syllables.
- Practice the exercise with the recording **CD 9-10**.
- Perform the exercise with "Blow the Wind Southerly" **CD 9-8** while individual students take turns patting the steady beat.

Reading Sequence 17, page 174
CD 8–33   MIDI 58

Rhythm: Reading in Compound Meter

Use rhythm syllables to **read** and **perform** this two-part rhythm accompaniment for "Las estrellitas del cielo."

Reading Sequence 18, page 178
CD 9–10   MIDI 59

Rhythm: Reading in § Meter

Use rhythm syllables to **read** and **perform** this rhythm accompaniment for "Blow the Wind Southerly."

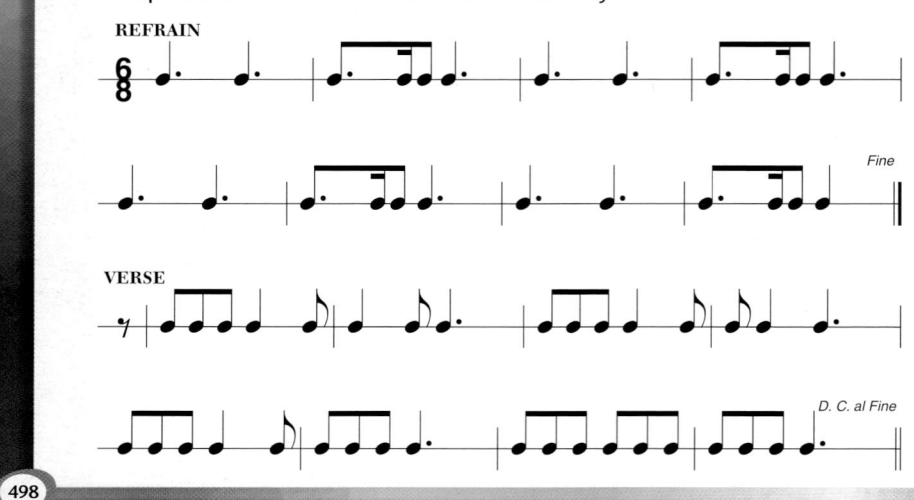

Footnotes

▶ **§ Meter (Reading Sequence 17)** After students can feel and describe the difference between simple and compound meter, they can learn to read rhythmic figures that occur in §. Teachers following a reading sequence may wish to use the Reading Sequences to introduce rhythm syllables for common § patterns. Later, students can revisit the songs in these lessons for additional reading practice.

Reading Sequence 19, page 188

CD 9–23
MIDI 60

Melody: Reading the Natural Minor Scale

Read and **sing** this countermelody for "Johnny Has Gone for a Soldier." Use pitch syllables and hand signs.

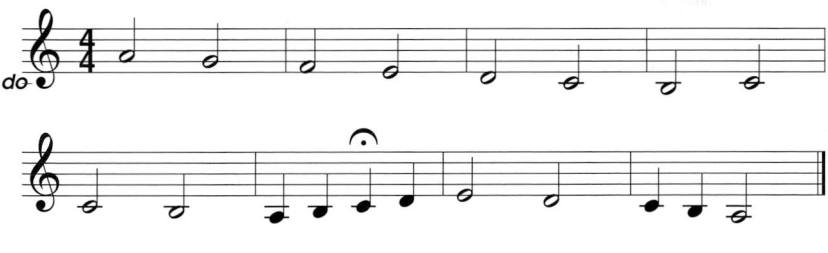

Reading Sequence 20, page 190

CD 9–28
MIDI 61

Melody: Reading the Harmonic Minor Scale

Read and **sing** this two-part countermelody for "Go Down, Moses." Use pitch syllables and hand signs.

499

▶ **Singing Half Steps** (**Reading Sequence 20**) For most students, hearing and singing half steps in tune requires extra reinforcement and practice. Echo-singing patterns containing half steps (including those with altered tones) sung or played by the teacher will help to ensure that students can perform those intervals accurately. Sing on neutral syllables and have students echo. Then sing pitch names, then note names in various keys.

Reading Sequence 19, page 188

MATERIALS

- "Johnny Has Gone for a Soldier," p. 188   **CD 9-21**
- Reading Sequence 19
  Melody part   **CD 9-23**
  Melody part with accompaniment   **CD 9-24**
  Accompaniment only   **CD 9-25**
- **Resource Book** pp. D-25, E-20
- keyboards

Melody: Reading the Natural Minor Scale

Ask students to identify the meter of Reading Sequence 19 and review the conducting pattern. Direct students to the exercise and have them

- Read the rhythms in the exercise using rhythm syllables.
- Find *la* on the staff. (Review the staff placement of the notes in the natural minor scale.)
- Sing the exercise **CD 9-23** using pitch syllables and hand signs.
- Perform the exercise as a countermelody with "Johnny Has Gone for a Soldier" **CD 9-21.**

Invite students to play this exercise on keyboards to accompany the song.

Reading Sequence 20, page 190

MATERIALS

- "Go Down, Moses," p. 190   **CD 9-26**
- Reading Sequence 20
  Melody Part 1   **CD 9-28**
  Melody Part 2   **CD 9-29**
  Melody Parts 1 and 2   **CD 9-30**
  Melody Parts 1 and 2 with accompaniment   **CD 9-31**
  Accompaniment only   **CD 9-32**
- **Resource Book** pp. D-27, E-21

Melody: Reading the Harmonic Minor Scale

Review the notes of the harmonic minor scale using Resource Book p. D-27. Remind students that in this scale, the pitch syllable *si* is used instead of *so*. Invite students to look at Reading Sequence 20 and have them

- Read and clap Part 1 using rhythm syllables.
- Read and clap Part 2 using rhythm syllables.
- Find *la* on the staff and review the staff placement of the notes in the natural minor scale.
- Use the recordings to practice each part of the exercise.
- Perform the exercise with "Go Down, Moses" **CD 9-26.**

Unit 6
Music Reading Practice

🖐 Reading Sequence 21, page 216

MATERIALS

- "Oh, Watch the Stars," p. 216   **CD 10-29**
- Reading Sequence 21
  Rhythm part (drum)   **CD 10-31**
  Rhythm part with accompaniment   **CD 10-32**
  Accompaniment only   **CD 10-33**
- **Resource Book** pp. D-29, E-22
- nonpitched percussion instruments

Rhythm: Reading Triplets

Review $\frac{4}{4}$ meter and its conducting pattern. Invite students to look at Reading Sequence 21 and have them

- Read and clap the exercise using rhythm syllables.
- Point to each triplet in the exercise.
- Practice the exercise with the recording **CD 10-31**.
- Perform the exercise with "Oh, Watch the Stars" **CD 10-29** while individual students take turns conducting the group.

For additional practice, students can play the exercise on nonpitched percussion instruments as an accompaniment to the song.

🖐 Reading Sequence 22, page 222

MATERIALS

- "Old Abram Brown," p. 222   **CD 10-38**
- Reading Sequence 22
  Rhythm Part 1 (woodblock)   **CD 11-1**
  Rhythm Part 2 (drum)   **CD 11-2**
  Rhythm Part 3 (claves)   **CD 11-3**
  Rhythm Parts 1, 2, and 3   **CD 11-4**
  Rhythm Parts 1, 2, and 3 with accompaniment   **CD 11-5**
  Accompaniment only   **CD 11-6**
- **Resource Book** pp. D-31, E-23
- nonpitched percussion instruments

Rhythm: Reading Augmentation and Diminuation

Ask students to identify the meter of Reading Sequence 22 and the conducting pattern. Direct them to the exercise and have them

- Read and clap Part 1 using rhythm syllables.
- Read and clap Part 2 using rhythm syllables.
- Read and clap Part 3 using rhythm syllables.
- Compare the rhythm of the 3 parts to discover augmentation and diminuation.

Use the recordings to practice each part of the exercise. Divide the class into four groups and have

- Group 1 perform Part 1 **CD 11-1**.
- Group 2 perform Part 2 **CD 11-2**.
- Group 3 perform Part 3 **CD 11-3**.
- Group 4 conduct the performance.

🖐 Reading Sequence 21, page 216   CD 10-31   MIDI 62

Rhythm: Reading Triplets

Use rhythm syllables to **read** and **perform** this counter-rhythm for "Oh, Watch the Stars."

🖐 Reading Sequence 22, page 222   CD 11–1   MIDI 63

Rhythm: Reading Augmentation and Diminution

Use rhythm syllables to **read** and **perform** this three-part rhythm accompaniment for "Old Abram Brown."

Footnotes

▶ **Inner Hearing Practice (Reading Sequence 21)** To reinforce inner hearing and part work skills, as well as rhythmic reading, have students count silently while tapping a steady beat, saying only *triplets* out loud. Isolate other rhythmic figures in the same manner, or assign each student one rhythm to clap or play on a instrument each time it occurs.

▶ **Practice with Augmentation and Diminution (Reading Sequence 22)** Students can practice augmenting and diminishing the rhythm of other known songs. For example, have them augment or diminish the exercises for "Laredo" (p. 10) and "Morning Comes Early" (p. 12).

Melody: Reading in Mixolydian Mode

Read and **sing** this countermelody for "The Greenland Whale Fishery." Use pitch syllables and hand signs.

Reading Sequence 24, page 232

CD 11–23
MIDI 65

Melody: Reading in Dorian Mode

Read and **sing** this countermelody for "Connemara Lullaby." Use pitch syllables and hand signs.

501

Reading Sequence 23, page 230

MATERIALS

• "The Greenland Whale Fishery," p. 230   **CD 11-16**
• Reading Sequence 23
   Melody part   **CD 11-18**
   Melody part with accompaniment   **CD 11-19**
   Accompaniment only   **CD 11-20**
• **Resource Book** pp. D-32, E-24
• recorders or other melody instruments

Melody: Reading in Mixolydian Mode

Ask students to

• Identify the meter of Reading Sequence 23
• Clap and read the rhythm of the exercise using rhythm syllables.
• Find *so* on the staff. (Review the staff placement of the notes in the mixolydian scale.)
• Sing the exercise **CD 11-18** using pitch syllables and hand signs.
• Perform the exercise with "The Greenland Whale Fishery" **CD 11-16**.

Invite students to play this exercise on recorders or other melody instruments as a countermelody to the song.

Reading Sequence 24, page 232

MATERIALS

• "Connemara Lullaby," p. 232   **CD 11-21**
• Reading Sequence 24
   Melody part   **CD 11-23**
   Melody part with accompaniment   **CD 11-24**
   Accompaniment only   **CD 11-25**
• **Resource Book** pp. D-33, E-25
• keyboards

Melody: Reading in Dorian Mode

Review $\frac{6}{8}$ meter and its conducting pattern. Invite students to

• Clap and count the rhythm of the exercise with the recording **CD 11-23**.
• Find *re* on the staff and review the staff placement of the notes in the dorian scale.
• Sing the exercise **CD 11-23** with pitch syllables and hand signs, then with note letter names.
• Perform the exercise as a countermelody with "Connemara Lullaby" **CD 11-21**.

For additional practice, students can play the exercise on keyboards to accompany the song.

▶ **Mixolydian and Dorian Modes (Reading Sequences 23 and 24)** Both of the reading exercises above can be used to reinforce students' hearing and understanding of modes. Point out that while the notes from *so* to *so^l* form the mixolydian scale, it is also easy to transform a *do* scale from major to mixolydian by using the altered tone *ta* instead of *ti*. Lowering the seventh scale degree of the *do*, or major scale, creates the pattern of whole and half steps that occur naturally in the *so* scale.

The same rule applies to the dorian mode. While it occurs naturally from *re* to *re^l*, the dorian scale can easily be formed by transforming the *la*, or natural minor scale. Using the altered tone *fi* instead of *fa* raises the sixth scale degree of the minor scale, creating the pattern of whole and half steps that occur naturally in the *re* scale.

Have students read the exercises both ways: "The Greenland Whale Fishery" in G=*so* and in G=*do* (F will be the altered tone, *ta*); "Connemara Lullaby" in D=*re* and in D=*la* (B will be the altered tone, *fi*).

Playing the Recorder

MATERIALS
- *The Honiesuckle*   CD 21-20
- **Resource Book** pp. I-1 through I-29
- recorders

VOCABULARY
countermelody   consort

ACTIVITIES

Getting Ready

Review with students how to hold the recorder with their left hand on top. Refer to Recorder Playing Position below.

Have students use the diagrams on p. 502 to review the fingerings for G, A, and B.

If some students are new to the recorder, pair them with more advanced players. In groups, students can play four-beat patterns using G, A, and B that can be echoed by the entire group. Encourage students to take turns being the group leader. Remind students to

- Cover holes securely.
- Whisper *daah* on each note.
- Blow gently.

To reinforce the reading and playing of G, A, and B, have students compose and notate their own three-note melodies. Have students share their compositions with classmates. If possible, record the performance and have students write in their music journals about their compositions.

Playing the Recorder

This section of your book will help you develop your skill at playing the soprano recorder.

Getting Ready

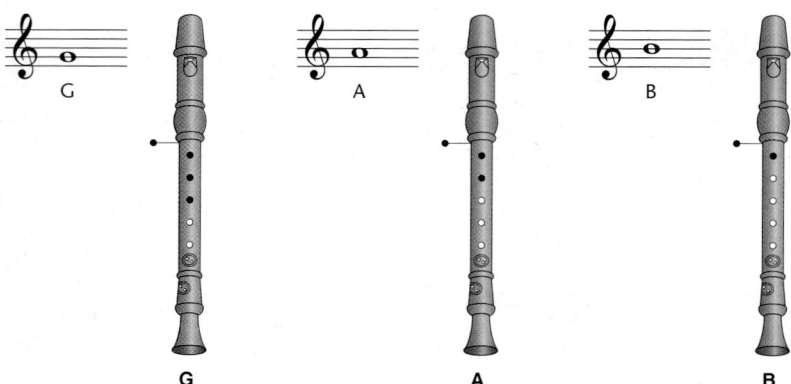

Look at the diagram for the note G. Using your left hand, cover the holes that are darkened. Press hard enough so that the holes make a light mark on each finger and thumb. Cover the tip of the mouthpiece with your lips. Blow gently as you whisper *daah*. **Play** a steady beat on the note G. After you can play G, try practicing A and B. The diagrams will help with finger placement.

Soprano, alto, tenor, and bass recorders are played together to form a consort. Sometimes the higher sound of the sopranino recorder is added.

Soprano ▶

◀ Alto

Tenor ▶

502

Footnotes

▶ **Recorder Playing Position** Here are some general guidelines for proper recorder technique.

- Hold the recorder at about a 45 degree angle with the holes facing out and the single thumb hole closer to the body.
- Place the left thumb on the hole in the back and curve the left fingers over the first, second, and third holes.
- Place the right thumb on the back of the recorder between the fourth and fifth holes.
- When covering holes, use the cushions (pads) of the fingers. Fingers should be slightly curved.
- Each hole is covered by a specific finger.
- Rest the mouthpiece lightly on the lower lip.
- Press the upper lip against the mouthpiece with a slight amount of pressure.

Beginning with a "B-A-G" Song

Now that you can play B, A, and G, **play** a countermelody to accompany the song "Wabash Cannon Ball," page 136. It can be played during the verse or the refrain. Choose which section you want to **sing** and which section you want to **play**.

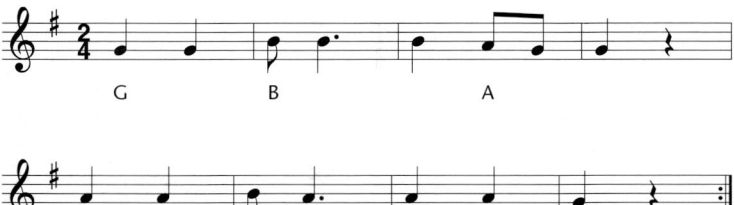

Building Right Hand Strength

Here are two new notes. Cover the holes securely with your fingers flat, not arched, and whisper *daah*. When playing notes in the low register of the recorder, remember to use very little air.

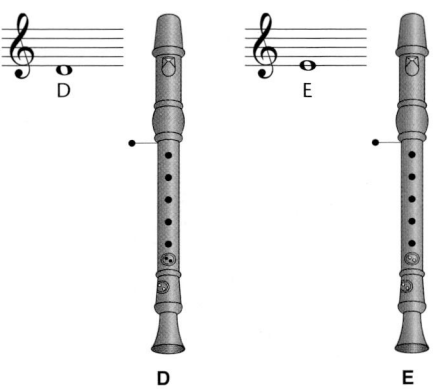

Below is a recorder countermelody that you can **play** during the verses of "California," page 52. Find a way to tap the beat as you **sing** the refrain. Does the recorder countermelody use mostly steps, leaps, or repeats?

Beginning with a "B-A-G" Song

Have students look at the countermelody for "Wabash Cannon Ball" on p. 503. They should notice that it uses only G, A, and B. Then have students

- Sing the letter names of the notes in rhythm.
- Sing the letter names of the notes while fingering their recorders.
- Play the recorder countermelody.

Have students play the recorder with the recording of "Wabash Cannon Ball," **CD 7-1**. Since the recorder part can be played during the verse or the refrain, divide the class so that some students are singing while others are playing.

For additional practice playing G-A and B-A-G, students may play ostinatos and countermelodies found in the Teacher's Edition and Resource Book for the following songs.

- "Morning Comes Early," p. 13
- "Kokoleoko," p. 33
- "Down by the Riverside," p. 256
- *"La Jesusita,"* p. 322
- "Bound for South Australia," p. 22

For additional resources, refer to the Recorder Index on p. 634.

Building Right Hand Strength

In order to build right hand strength, introduce students to D and E. Explain to them that they need very little air when playing notes in the low register. When first playing notes that use the right hand, students may forget to completely cover the left hand holes. Remind them to check that all their fingers are firmly covering the necessary holes.

Have students look at the countermelody on p. 503 for "California." Have them identify the steps, leaps, and repeats, and read the countermelody for "California."

They should play during the verse of the song and sing and feel the steady beat during the refrain.

▶ **Care of Plastic Recorders** After playing, dry the interior with a swab such as a large feather or small cloth attached to a cleaning rod. If the mouthpiece becomes clogged, blow into the recorder while covering the top hole or window of the mouthpiece. Plastic recorders can be washed in the top shelf of most dishwashers or by hand with warm soapy water. Be sure to rinse and dry the recorder after washing.

▶ **Care of Wood Recorders** Warm up the instrument before playing. Each time you play, take the recorder apart and dry the inside with a swab. Do not expose the wood recorder to extreme temperature changes or water. Use cork grease sparingly for easier assembly of the instrument and to prevent the cork from drying. Wood recorders will require a "break in" period.

▶ **Inclusion** A soprano recorder is available for students with finger disabilities. Sections are put together and the holes are rotated and plugged according to the needs of the player.

continued on page 504

Adding High C and High D

Have students look at the fingering illustration on p. 504 to learn to play high C and high D. Remind students to move their thumb only slightly away from the hole when playing D.

When students can play high C and high D, have them play the countermelody for "Drill, Ye Tarriers" on p. 504. They should sing the verse and accompany the refrain with their recorders.

Invite students to listen to a recorder consort play *The Honiesuckle* **CD 21-20.** Share with students that the music was written by Anthony Holborne in the Renaissance Period (16th century).

Adding High C and High D

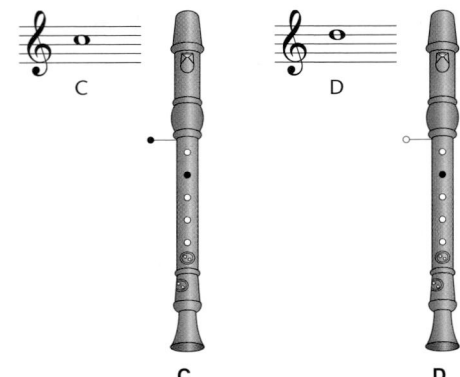

Practice playing high C and high D. (Remember to move your thumb slightly away from the hole when playing D.) When you can **play** these notes, accompany the refrain of the song "Drill, Ye Tarriers," page 54, on your recorder. How is the recorder part different from the main melody? How is it the same?

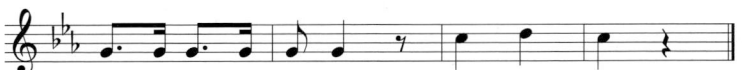

Listen to this Renaissance piece played by a recorder consort.

CD 21–20
The Honiesuckle

by Anthony Holborne
as performed by the Flanders Recorder Quartet

The English composer Anthony Holborne lived during the sixteenth century and was described as having been a "Gentleman usher" to Queen Elizabeth I.

A child in sixteenth century costume playing a Renaissance descant recorder

504

Footnotes

▶ **Recorder Identification** If possible, each student should have his or her own recorder. To help identify the instruments, use an electric engraving tool to carve the initials or name of each student on the recorder below the thumb hole. As an alternative, have students place a unique sticker on the front of their recorders below the window.

▶ **Listening** Provide students with opportunities to listen to music that includes a recorder or similar aerophone. Some examples to choose from are

• *"Ríu ríu chíu,"* **CD 19-9**, recorder

• *"Eliza Kongo,"* **CD 1-23**, penny whistle

▶ **Playing** Besides the ostinatos and countermelodies listed in the Recorder Index on p. 576, some students may be able to play entire song melodies from the student book. Here are a few suggestions to get them started.

• *"Éliza Kongo,"* p. 14

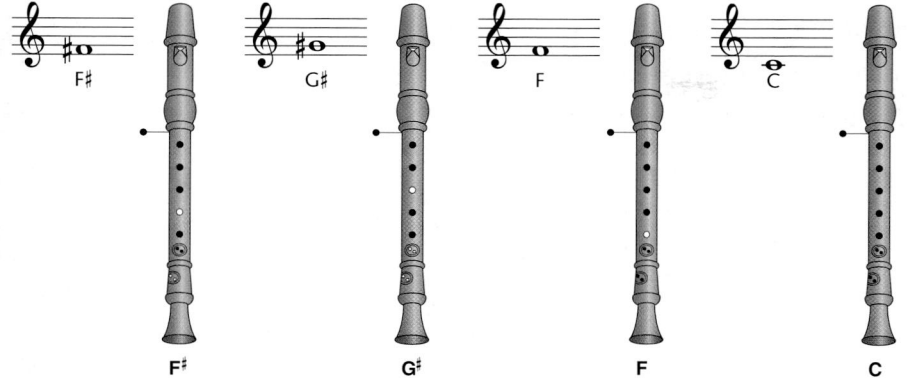

F♯   G♯   F   C

Learning Notes in Pairs

Try learning these new notes paired with notes you already know: F♯ with G; G♯ with A; F and C. This half-step rule will help you remember how to finger F♯ and G♯.

1. Think of the fingering for the note that is a half step higher than the note with the sharp.
2. Skip a hole on your recorder and then cover the next two holes.

New Recorder Challenges

When you can play F♯ and G♯, play this countermelody with "Laredo," page 10.

G♯   F♯

Use the diagrams above to learn to play F and low C. **Play** this countermelody during the refrain of *"A la puerta del cielo,"* page 60.

F   C   D

Practice each countermelody slowly as you become familiar with these new notes.

Learning Notes in Pairs

Relating new fingerings to those learned previously will aid students in remembering new notes. Relate F♯ to G; G♯ to A; and F to C. Have students learn the half-step rule for notes with accidentals. They should read the directions for the half-step rule in their books and then experiment with the fingerings for F♯ and G♯ before using the fingering chart.

New Recorder Challenges

When they can play F♯ and G♯, have students look at the recorder part for "Laredo" on p. 505. See Resource Book p. I-2 for another countermelody to play with "Laredo."

Have students relate the fingerings of F and low C.

ASK How many fingers do you need to move when leaping from F down to C? (One)

Are there any other leaps that require you to move only one finger? (A to high C)

Students can play the countermelody on p. 505 while others sing *"A la puerta del cielo."* Remind students to whisper *daah* gently when playing notes in the low register.

- "Morning Has Broken," p. 29
- "Don't You Hear the Lambs?" p. 97

▶ **Music Notation Software** Have students compose a recorder melody using the notes of the G pentatonic scale. Each student should compose an eight-measure composition with four beats in each measure. To begin, have the class notate on the board some four-beat rhythm patterns that they can read. Then have each student select one note from the pentatonic scale for each of their eight measures. They will need to use some notes more than once. Using notation software, notate each measure copying a rhythm pattern from the board and placing it in the correct position for the note selected for that particular measure. Continue until all eight measures are completed. Have students play their compositions using the computer and their recorders.

Mallet Instruments

MATERIALS
- "Tumba," p. 161
- "The Greenland Whale Fishery," p. 230
- "Garden of the Earth" (poem), p. 399
- **Resource Book** pp. F-1 through F-46
- soprano and alto glockenspiels; soprano, alto, and bass xylophones; soprano, alto, and bass metallophones; a variety of mallets

VOCABULARY
bordun

ACTIVITIES

Moving and Playing

Upper grade students may have varying levels of ability and experience. Prepare them for coordinated playing of Orff mallet instruments with movement, body percussion, and small percussion practice. Have students pat a steady beat with both hands on their legs, then have them pat with alternating hands. When students show proficiency, have them pat with a crossover movement left, right, then left-over-right. These movement activities help prepare students to play simple, alternating, and crossover borduns on xylophones, metallophones, and glockenspiels. It is also beneficial to pat tricky rhythm patterns before playing them on instruments.

Listening

Choosing Mallets Have students read about mallets on p. 506 of the student text. Then demonstrate the various timbres that can be produced when different mallets are used on the instruments. For example, play a metallophone with a soft yarn-headed mallet. Then play with a hard rubber-headed mallet. Have students compare the timbres.

Improvising

Mallet instruments can be used creatively and to reinforce music reading skills. Instruments can be set up in the following scales.

- C *do* pentatonic: C-D-E-G-A
- F *do* pentatonic: F-G-A-C-D
- G *do* pentatonic: G-A-B-D-E
- e *la* pentatonic: e-g-a-b-d
- d *la* pentatonic: d-f-g-a-c
- D dorian mode: D-e-f-g-a-b-c-D
- G mixolydian mode: G-a-b-c-d-e-f-G

Have students improvise with specific rhythms on unspecified pitches. The rhythms used can be derived from words in poetry, song lyrics, or other sources.

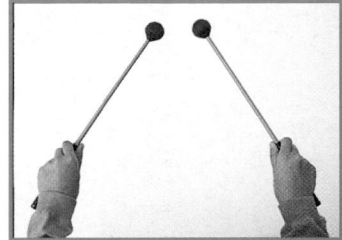

Mallet Instruments

Playing Mallets

When using mallets to play barred instruments, follow these simple suggestions.

Holding the Mallets

Fold your fingers and thumbs around the mallet handle—the thumb should lie alongside the handle, but the pointer finger should not sit on top of the mallet. The backs of your hands should face the ceiling. Grip the handles on the hand grips, but not at the very end. (Smaller hands may need to grip further up toward the mallet head.) Elbows should hang easily at your sides. Avoid elbows that stick out to the side or hug the body.

Striking the Bars

Strike each bar at its center, not at either end. Let your mallet strike quickly and then bounce away. If you let the mallet stay on the bar, the sound is stopped.

Matching Mallets to Instruments

It is important to choose the appropriate mallet for each instrument to make the best sound.

For special effects, use hard wood mallets or mallet handles. Avoid anything that would damage the surface of the bars.

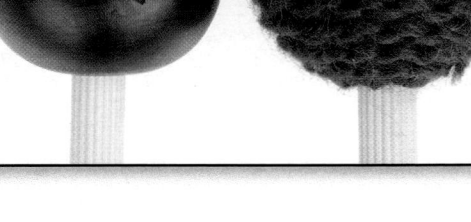

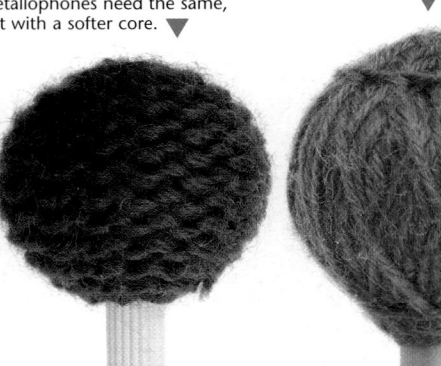

Glockenspiels need small wood, hard rubber, or composition heads.

Alto/soprano xylophones need medium-sized felt or yarn heads with a hard core. Alto/soprano metallophones need the same, but with a softer core.

Bass instruments need larg felt or yarn heads. Choose softer mallets for metallophones, and harder mallet for xylophones.

Footnotes

▶ **Care of Mallet Instruments** Show students how to set up the instruments in specific scales. Have them lift the bars up carefully with two hands, one hand at each end of the bar. Caution them to make sure the nails that hold the bars in place do not get bent. Explain to students that the bars are being removed so that they can make "good" sounding music together. Have students practice walking to the instruments by "moon-walking" slowly around them. They should not step over the instruments because their toes can easily get hooked on them and cause injury to the student and damage to the instrument.

▶ **Position and Technique** Students should kneel, stand, or sit in front of an instrument. Have them hold the mallets by wrapping their fingers in a relaxed way over and around the grip of the mallet, arms slightly away from their sides. Have students strike the bars at the center and "pull" the sound from the instrument with a light, upward, and buoyant stroke. If students push downward into the bars, the vibration of the bars will be muted, making a dull sound.

Position

You may sit or stand while playing mallet instruments. This depends on the distance of the top of the instrument from the floor. Your body should stay straight with your arms placed easily in front of you to strike the bars.

Sit on the floor. ▶

◀ Sit in a chair to play bass instruments.

Stand ▶

◀ Sit in a chair.

507

The instruments can also be used to play sound effects to enhance meaning in poetry. Have students read the poem "Garden of the Earth" on p. 399. Invite them to explore non-tonal setups on glockenspiels, metallophones, and xylophones. Encourage students to use various mallet types and techniques, such as *glissandos*, as they accompany the poem.

Playing Borduns

A simple bordun is the first and fifth pitches of a scale played together or alternated. In *do* pentatonic on C, the bordun would be C and G. In d *la* pentatonic, the bordun would be d and a. Students should always use two hands when playing.

Have students play the alto metallophone or bass xylophone/metallophone simple borduns on p. 161 as the class sings "Tumba." Invite them to experiment with playing with various types of mallets.

Playing Harmony

Have students play a harmonic accompaniment with the song "The Greenland Whale Fishery" on p. 230, following the chords shown above the music. When the chord is G, students play the pitches G and D. When the chord is F, they play the pitches F and C.

Composing

Students can compose songs using a pentatonic scale of their own choosing. To get started, have them choose a poem that can be read rhythmically in a specific meter, for example, "You and I" on p. 388. Have students use the word rhythm of the poem and invent a pentatonic melody. Allow time for the students to experiment on instruments that have been set up in a pentatonic scale. Coach them to use repetition and patterns in their melodies.

▶ **Orff Instrumentarium** See Resource Book p. F-46 for a key to instrument abbreviations on a score. Set up the instruments in the classroom as an ensemble, grouping the families together in the following manner. Place a bass xylophone for you to play in the center, facing the group. On the left, set up the soprano and alto glockenspiels in two rows. Similarly, to the right, set up the soprano and alto metallophones, with a bass metallophone in a third row. Set up the xylophones in similar formation to the metallophones. Then set up other percussion and drums to the right and behind the xylophones.

Playing the Guitar

MATERIALS

Guitars	
Sound Bank	CD 21-21
I Love a Rainy Night	CD 16-19
Bye Bye Love	CD 16-17
Blowin' in the Wind	CD 17-21

This section introduces three types of guitars and their parts, some applications, and proper playing position.

Why Play the Guitar?

Ask students if they know anyone, a family member or friend, who plays the guitar. Briefly discuss when the instrument is played by this person.

ASK When have you seen a guitar played other than in this class? (Accept all answers.)

Types of Guitars

Ask students to remove guitars from their cases. Point out the major parts of the instrument as captioned in the student text. Ask students to locate these parts on their guitars. Ask how their guitars compare to the types shown on p. 508.

Write out a list of acoustic guitar parts on the board or distribute to help students remember the parts of the guitar and their purpose.

- Soundhole: Allows the string vibrations amplified in the resonator to project outward.
- Bridge: Allows vibrations to enter the resonator.
- Tuning pegs: Tighten and loosen the strings to change pitch.
- Nut: Keeps strings spaced properly on the finger-board above the frets, and takes some of the string tension off the tuning pegs.

Add the following list for electric guitar.

- Pick-ups: Pick up, or amplify, the string vibrations, since there is no resonance on a solid body guitar.
- Tone/volume controls: Change the sensitivity of the pickups.
- Tremelo arm: Allows string tension to be controlled by the right hand.

Discuss with students some of the many uses of the guitar in music. Suggestions include accompaniment for voices, a rhythm instrument, or a melodic or "lead" instrument. Also briefly discuss in which music styles the guitar is used. Suggestions include classical, folk, blues, rock, and alternative.

Use the listening selections listed in the Materials section to explore the sound of the different instruments.

Tuning the Guitar

Explain string numbers to students. Try to avoid referring to strings as "low" and "high." Since the higher pitched string is nearer the floor, this can be confusing to the inexperienced player. Refer to strings instead by size or thickness until the students learn the numbers.

Why Play the Guitar?

The guitar is perhaps the most loved instrument in the United States, especially among young people. Most popular and folk music includes the guitar. You can very quickly learn how to begin making music with the guitar by following the suggestions included in these pages.

Types of Guitars

There are three types of guitars—nylon-string classical, steel-string acoustic, and electric. Look at these photographs and learn the names of their parts.

▲ Nylon-String Classical Guitar

▲ Steel-String Acoustic Guitar

▲ Electric Guitar

Tuning the Guitar

- Guitar strings are numbered 1, 2, 3, 4, 5, 6, with the sixth string being the lowest in pitch. (It is also the thickest string.)
- You can tune the guitar using the keys of the piano. The illustration to the right shows what keys to use for tuning each guitar string.

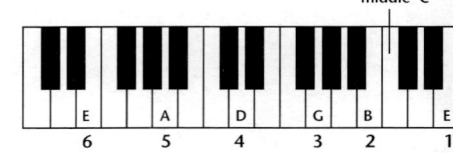

Footnotes

▶ **Selecting Guitars for Classroom Use** If you are able to provide guitars for your students, the best choice is a nylon-stringed classical guitar. The design of these guitars promotes proper playing habits and technique. They are economical, and nylon strings are easier on the fingertips until callouses are developed.

If students supply some of their own instruments, you will most likely be using an assortment of guitar types in your class. Take advantage of this situation by asking students to help you classify them according to the three guitar types. Steel-stringed acoustic guitar players will likely experience the most difficulty because of the string material and tension, but will have a slimmer neck, which makes playing chords a little easier. Electric guitars should not present a problem, since they can be set at the same volume as the other guitars being played and need a relatively light touch.

- You can also tune your guitar by using an electronic tuner, which allows you to "see" when each string is in tune.
- You can also tune the guitar by using a method called "relative tuning." Follow these steps:

1. Tune the sixth, or lowest-pitched, string to E on the piano or pitch pipe.
2. Press the sixth string on fret 5 and pluck it with your right thumb, producing the note A, which you use to tune the next, or fifth, string.
3. Reach your right hand over to the tuners, and turn the fifth-string tuner until the two sounds match. Now the fifth string is in tune.
4. Press the fifth string on fret 5, and use the pitch to tune the fourth string, repeating the tuning process as before.
5. Press the fourth string on fret 5, and use the pitch to tune the third string.
6. Press the third string on fret 4, and use the pitch to tune the second string.
7. Press the second string on fret 5, and use the pitch to tune the first string. Now you are in tune!

The Best Playing Positions

There are three ways to hold your guitar comfortably and correctly. Notice the different ways that are pictured here:

- Always raise the guitar neck slightly, because this allows the left hand to play chords without extra tension and effort.
- Always keep the front of the guitar completely vertical, because this also helps the left hand to play chords easily.
- Place the thumb of your left hand behind the neck. Keep your fingers arched as you reach around the neck to press the strings. Press the strings down onto the fingerboard by trying to pinch your thumb and fingers together. Keep your palm away from the neck.

509

Guitar

Have students strum the strings with the right thumb. Then have the class play and count each string one at a time, using the text on the bottom of p. 508.

ASK Do all the guitars sound the same? (They won't if the guitars aren't tuned.)

Explain the general rules for using tuning pegs: Tightening the string *raises* the pitch. The player turns the tuning peg away from himself or herself. Loosening the string *lowers* the pitch. The player turns the tuning peg toward him or her.

Then have students practice tuning with a keyboard. This is a pitch-matching skill for your students that will take some time. Make sure the process is *aural*. In other words, ask students whether strings need to be higher or lower to match the target pitch, and therefore if the strings should be tightened or loosened.

Consider using an electronic tuner for those students who are visual learners.

Demonstrate relative tuning following the steps on p. 509. This is the method that students will most likely use the most as they continue learning, so practice the steps carefully. Since this process introduces left-hand technique, draw the students' attention to the specific area that the fingers press in each fret (for example, in the space above an indicated fret, rather than directly on it).

The Best Playing Positions

It is best for the students to use a proper playing position from the very beginning. Have the class read the instructions on p. 509. Then, referring to the photographs on p. 509, ask students to experiment until they find the position that is most comfortable for them.

Point out the optimal position of the neck, which properly aligns the left-hand for chording.

The inside of the right elbow should straddle the widest part of the guitar body, and the right hand should be placed directly over the sound hole.

▶ **Reading Guitar Chord Diagrams** Observe the detailed chord diagrams on p. 510. Help students identify the various features of these diagrams. The best way to help students orient the diagram to what they see on their own guitars is to have them hold the guitar vertically at an arm's distance, then turn it so that they are looking squarely at its front.

continued on page 510

Playing the Guitar

Playing Basics

Have students wrap the thumb of the left hand around the neck of the guitar as they practice the right thumb strum described on p. 509. Then teach a strum which uses the thumb and index finger. Explain that the thumb will play the bass note on string 6, and the rest of the strings are scraped with the nail of the index finger, using a smooth downward motion. Try these patterns with your students.

Thumb-Strum-Thumb-Strum ($\frac{2}{4}$, $\frac{4}{4}$, and $\frac{6}{8}$ meter)

Thumb-Strum-Strum ($\frac{3}{4}$ meter)

As before, practice playing as a group first. Then ask each student to play the strum individually. It is important that each student hears himself or herself individually. This builds confidence and a discriminating ear, which is essential to rapid improvement. Students should aim for increased accuracy and speed with practice.

For more advanced strumming patterns, try the calypso, rhythm and blues, and compound brush strums. Diagrams are provided below and on the next page.

Ask students to select one song from the textbook that could be played with one of these strums.

Playing Guitar Chords

To begin developing left-hand technique, have the students observe and then repeat the numbering of the left-hand fingers, as illustrated on p. 510.

Remind students to press the strings down only before actually playing the strings to reduce finger fatigue. When not playing, the fingertips can be simply rested on the appropriate strings.

Guitar Chords Used in This Book

Ask students to look at the chords fingered on p. 510. Have them locate the fingers on the neck, keeping the fingers of the left hand relaxed and "round," with space between the guitar neck and the hand. The palm should not touch the neck of the guitar. For each chord, give students a moment to find the position, then have them strum the chord as a group and then individually.

Strum Diagrams

Teach these strum patterns to the students as part of their chord mastery. Draw the diagrams on the board, or duplicate and distribute.

Calypso Strum

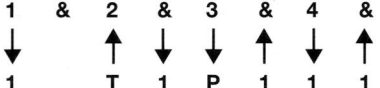

1 = first finger
T = thumb
P = palm, slapping down on strings

Playing Basics

Here is some basic information on how to **play** the guitar:

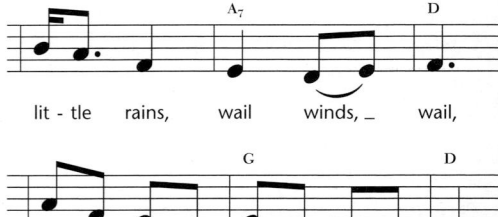

- The left-hand fingers press the strings on the frets to produce chords, which are used to accompany songs.
- The right-hand thumb brushes the strings to make the sounds.
- Notice how the left-hand fingers are numbered; you will use these numbers when you begin reading the guitar chords.

Playing Guitar Chords

- All chords have note names—these are indicated in many song scores in this book, as shown on the right. The position of the chord names tells you what chords you will use, and when you will be changing chords in the song.

lit - tle   rains,   wail   winds, _   wail,

Guitar Chords Used in This Book

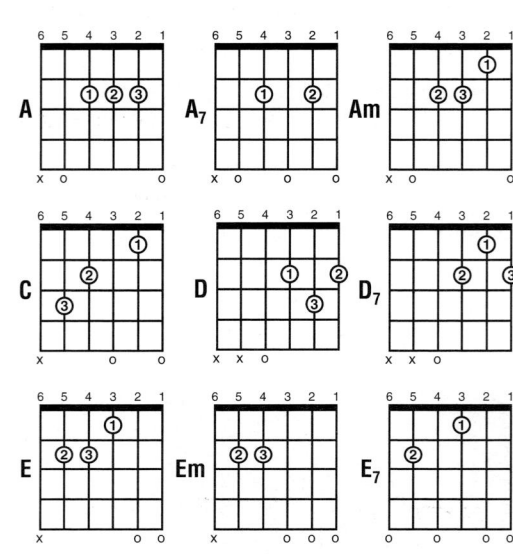

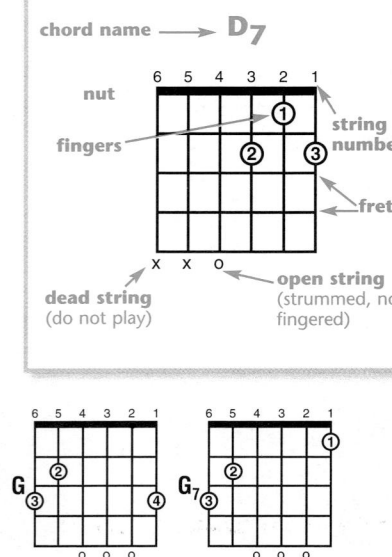

Footnotes

▶ **Developing a Repertoire** Below is a list of songs in the student text that can be played well on the guitar.

Songs in the Key of C

Imbabura, p. 203
Yakety Yak, p. 205
De colores, p. 90
Morning Comes Early, p. 13

Orange Blossom Special, p. 266
Scotland the Brave, p. 138
Bound for South Australia, p. 22

Songs in the Key of D

Don't You Hear the Lambs?, p. 97
Colorado Trail, p. 276
Camptown Races, p. 270
Linstead Market, p. 241

If I Had a Hammer, p. 287
Shenandoah, p. 264
Still, still, still, p. 468
Adelita, p. 50

Some Hints on Practicing

- Practice right and left hand separately if it helps you, but always try to "put everything together" (both hands playing while singing the song) each time you practice. This will help you develop the "feeling" of playing, which you will never forget!

- If possible, watch yourself play in the mirror, so that you can "see" that you are actually playing and doing a great job!

- It is better to play songs slowly at an even pace and gradually build up the tempo, than to play quickly through the easy parts and slow down at the difficult parts. Playing evenly helps your mind and hands stay together!

How You Can Tell You're Improving

You are improving if you answer "yes" to more and more of these questions:

- Can you make chord changes without looking?
- Can you play at an even tempo?
- Can you sing along while you play?
- Do your fingertips hurt less when you play?
- Can you play for longer periods of time?
- Can you play some songs from memory?

Guitar

511

Some Hints on Practicing

By far the most challenging aspect of beginning left-hand technique is *changing chords*, which can be made much easier for students by offering them fingering "shortcuts," or common fingerings used when moving from chord to chord. For instance, when forming the D chord, the first and second fingers keep their basic position, moving up one string then to A7. Aim for increased accuracy and speed with more practice.

Review the suggestions for practicing at the end of each lesson. Consider providing a full-length mirror in the classroom to demonstrate how to practice with it.

How You Can Tell You're Improving

Review the questions in this section at the end of each lesson. Also review posture and technique each week. Individual weekly assessments are useful in determining which students may need extra help.

Strum Diagrams

Compound Brush Strum

First, play this rhythm on the middle strings of the guitar with short, quick downstrokes of the index finger.

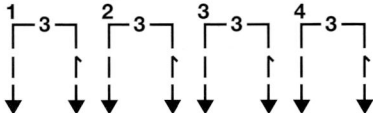

Now, add an upstroke with the index finger in between each downstroke.

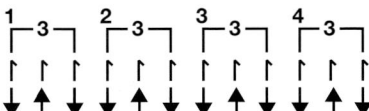

Rhythm-and-Blues Strum

Use the thumb to brush down on the strings with the rhythm. Add a fuller strum on "F" by scraping all the nails of the fingers across the strings in a downward motion.

Finally, play on the bass notes on "T."

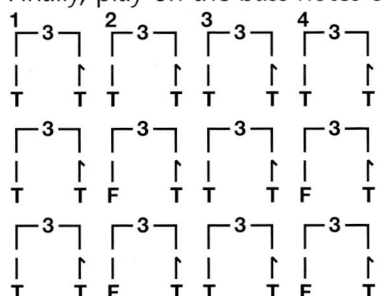

Playing the Keyboard

MATERIALS
- Textbook
- Keyboards

This section is designed to assist you in class piano instruction, in addition to or in place of private instruction.

Sitting Position

Have each student (or as many as you have keyboards) sit facing the keyboard, as far forward on the bench as is necessary for the student's feet to reach the floor. The edge of the bench should touch just below the top of the leg. If a student's feet do not comfortably reach the floor when he or she is properly seated, provide a large telephone book or other support for under the feet. It is important that the upper body be high enough for the forearms to be on the same level as the keyboard, with wrists parallel to the keyboard.

Hand Position

Ask students to stand with arms down at their side. Have them look down and observe the shape of the hand in a relaxed position. Then, ask students to sit at the keyboard and put their hands above the keys, holding their hands loosely in that same position. You can ask them to lightly swing their elbows to check flexibility. Point out that the curved fingers need to rest far enough in on the keys so that the thumb touches a white key.

If necessary, have students switch places so that all have a chance to find their playing position.

Finger Numbers

Ask students to hold up their hands and count off 1, 2, 3, 4 and 5, while wiggling that finger. You may wish to have students count off each hand separately first, and then together.

Fingering for Melodies

Ask students to look at the diagrams at the top of p. 513. Then, after checking students for proper playing position, ask them to locate the illustrated keys on their keyboards. Using first the right and then the left hand, ask students to play the patterns first individually, then as a group. Have students switch places if necessary so that all have a turn.

Sitting Position

For maximum support from your arms, shoulders and back, sit slightly forward on the bench with your feet resting on the floor at all times. Your knees should be just under the front edge of the keyboard. Sitting too close will push the elbows back which in turn will cause the shoulders to go up and tension to develop. You should feel a center of gravity, which will allow you to lean from side to side if necessary.

Hand Position

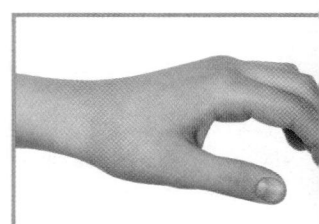

The most supportive hand position is the shape of your hand as it hangs naturally at your side. When you bring your hand up to the keyboard, the fingers should be slightly curved at the middle joint and the wrist should be parallel to the keyboard. You should feel a certain amount of "flexibility" in your elbows as they hang near your side. Don't be a hugger – one who keeps the elbows too close to the sides at all times. The elbow should follow through with the natural movement of your wrist.

Finger Numbers

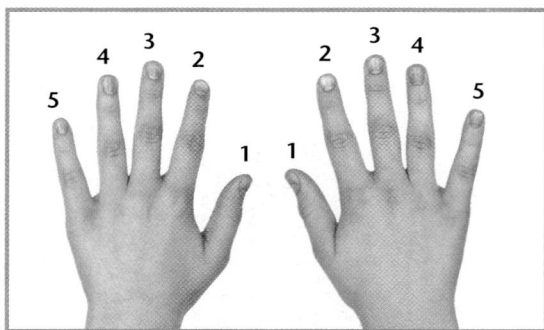

Fingering for Steps and Skips

How a melody moves determines the fingering on the keyboard. Look at the diagrams at the top of page 513. By translating the keyboard examples to one- and two-line staves, it is easy to see how right/left movement on the keyboard relates to up/down movement on the staff.

Footnotes

▶ **Chording** Many songs can be accompanied with just three or four chords. Beginning keyboard players who can play basic chords in the keys most often favored by beginning guitar players can often play in a group. Consider teaching the class root position chords for C, G, D, and Am. You can have them experiment with I-IV-V-I chord progressions (G-C-D-G), and expand to include the minor 2nd (G-C-Am-D-G) chord progression.

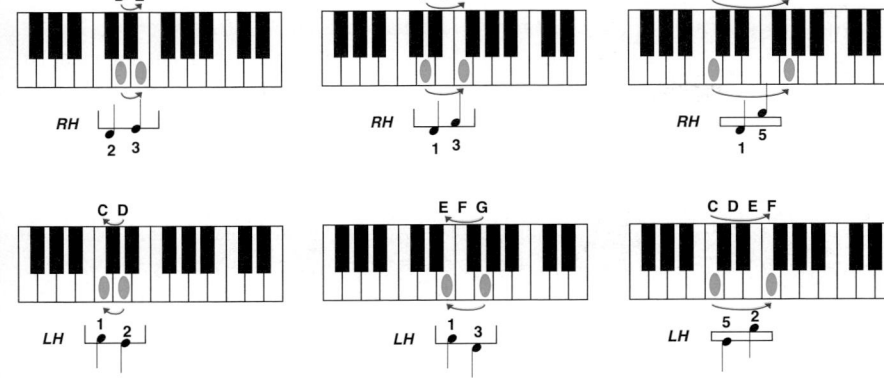

Three-Line Reading

Play the following examples. Determine a logical fingering before you begin each one.

RH   Begin on D:

LH   Begin on D:

Playing from Treble and Bass Clefs

When singing music, you have learned to follow the upward/downward direction of a melody and to determine if it moves by step, by leap, or if it stays on a repeated tone. When playing music, you must read music in the same way as well as determine where to play the notes on the keyboard. Each note in printed music indicates one place, and only one place, where it can be played.

Three-Line Reading

Ask students to look at the three-line examples on p. 513. Point out the last measure in the right-hand line. Note that the last pitch and the first pitch of the pattern are the same.

ASK What is the distance between the highest and lowest note? (a fifth)

Have students place the thumb and fifth finger of the right hand on these keys.

Note for the class the accidental in the pattern. Check each student for proper playing position, then ask them to play each pattern as a group.

Repeat the question and positioning for the left hand pattern and have students play again as a group.

ASK In what meter is the first example? ($\frac{2}{4}$) The second? ($\frac{6}{8}$)

Is this duple or triple meter? (duple)

Playing from Treble and Bass Clefs

Ask students to look at the examples at the bottom of p. 513, and find the lowest and highest notes in each example. Point out that those pitches will use the outer fingers of the hand. Check each student for proper playing position, then ask them to play each line separately, then together. Again, have students switch places if necessary so that all have a turn.

ASK What do you notice about the melody patterns? (They are the same for each hand.)

As a review, consider duplicating the pattern at the bottom of the page and asking the students to mark the fingering numbers above each pitch. Remind them to pay attention to which clef and hand they are working with in making their determination.

▶ **Integrating the Curriculum** Students may be interested in maintaining a bulletin board filled with images of famous keyboard players past and present. Performers may be grouped according to time period, style, or specific instrument. The bulletin board may be updated as the year progresses. Encourage students to bring in photographs or articles of performers to include in the class bulletin board.

Sound Bank

MATERIALS
- Sound Bank   **CD 21**, tracks 21–55

VOCABULARY

percussion	vibration	pitch	resonance
timbre	tension	bow	reed
valve			

USING THE SOUND BANK

Sound Bank is a glossary of the principal instruments discussed in this book. Text, pictures, and recordings are designed to be used together to help students integrate the definitions, illustrations, and sounds.

Ready Reference When an instrument is studied in the book, reinforce the learning by having students

- Look at the illustration.
- Listen to the sound.
- Read the definition.

Evaluation Test students' comprehension by playing the recorded examples in random order and having students respond orally or on paper.

Instrument Families The instruments shown in the student text are listed alphabetically but are divided into families—strings (orange), percussion (blue), woodwinds (purple), brass (green), and keyboard (red). The color codes will help students immediately identify the family to which an instrument belongs.

ACTIVITIES

Vibrations and Sound

SAY All sound sources make vibrations. Vibrations are back-and-forth movements that come to our ears through the air. Our ears "hear" the vibrations as sound.

To demonstrate vibration, hit a cymbal or pluck the free end of a ruler that is braced on a desk.

Use the following instruments for additional demonstrations of vibration and sound. Allow students to touch the instruments lightly, in order to feel as well as see the vibrations.

- drumhead
- Autoharp strings
- guitar strings
- piano strings

Guide students in experimenting with other classroom percussion instruments to feel vibrations. Point out that

- On some instruments, the vibrations may be obvious.
- On others, such as the maracas, the vibrations may be very delicate and difficult to feel. (On the sand blocks, they cannot be felt at all.)

See p. 516 for another experiment with vibrations.

Sound Bank

◄ *Arpa* [AHR-pah] A folk harp that has 34–36 nylon strings and spans almost five octaves. It is a diatonic instrument and must be retuned to play in a different key. The arpa is used especially for the *jarocho* music of Veracruz, Mexico. CD 21–21 p. 131

◄ *Axatse* [ahks-AHT-see] An African rattle made from a gourd that is cut, emptied of its seeds, dried in the sun, and covered with loose-fitting net. Small beads or shells woven into the net create loud sounds as they hit the hollow gourd. CD 21–22 p. 66

◄ *Bodhran* [boh-RAHN] A drum from Ireland made of animal skin nailed to a single-headed frame; hand-held, using a criss-cross system of cord, wire, or sticks over the open end. CD 21–23 p. 157

◄ **Bongo Drums** A pair of small Afro-Cuban single-headed drums made from hollowed tree trunks that are joined together horizontally. The larger drum is placed to the player's right. The drums are played with bare hands. CD 21–24 p. 305

◄ **Clarinet** A cylinder-shaped wind instrument, usually made of wood. There are holes and metal keys on the side of the clarinet and a reed in the mouthpiece. Low notes on the clarinet are soft and mellow. The middle notes are open and bright, and the highest notes are thin and resonant. CD 21–25 p. 186

◄ **Conga Drum** An Afro-Cuban elongated drum. The muleskin head is struck with the hands. Pressing the head with the hand, elbow, or wrist raises the pitch. CD 21–26 p. 156

Instrument Key: strings   percussion   woodwind   brass   keyboard

Footnotes

▶ **Playing Percussion Instruments** Almost anything that makes noise can be used as a percussion instrument. Percussion instruments can be struck, shaken, or scraped.

- Struck: most percussion instruments; struck with hands, mallets, sticks
- Shaken: maracas (seeds or pebbles strike the inside)
- Scraped: sand blocks, *guiro*

The percussion section of a concert band or a symphony orchestra is usually placed toward the rear, since it can be heard easily. In addition to adding specific effects and colors to the ensemble, percussion instruments help provide a rhythmic foundation.

Percussion instruments can also be grouped according to those that make a definite pitch (timpani, mallet percussion) and those that produce a sound of indefinite pitch (drums, maracas, triangle).

◀ **Doumbek** [DOHM-bek] Arab and Turkish music feature the doumbek. It is a goblet shaped drum with a combination of a deep bass tone ("doum") and fiery, crisp treble tone ("bek"). Formally, the doumbek has a goatskin or fishskin head stretched and glued to the top. Now they are being made of cast aluminum with a synthetic head. The focus is on both high and low tones. CD 21–27 p. 297

◀ **Dulcimer: Plucked** A soundbox with strings across it. The strings are usually plucked with a quill. The sound of a dulcimer is quiet and sweet. CD 21–28 p. 258

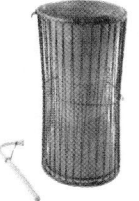

◀ **Dundun** [DOON-doon] West African double-headed drums some having an hourglass shape. The ends are covered with goatskin drumheads that are fastened together with leather cords stretched down the length of the drum. These drums are known as talking or singing drums because they can match the pitch and rhythm of spoken language. CD 21–29 p. 66

◀ **Erhu** [EHR-hoo] A Chinese string instrument with a long, round, hardwood neck that has two tuning pegs at the upper end. The lower end is inserted into a resonator. The instrument has two steel strings and is played with a horsehair bow that is supported by a bamboo neck. CD 21–30 p. 310

◀ **Flute** A small metal instrument shaped like a pipe, with holes and keys in its side. The player holds the flute sideways and blows across the open mouthpiece. The sound of the flute is pure and sweet. Its low notes are the same ones that fifth graders sing, but it can also go much higher. CD 21–31 p. 113

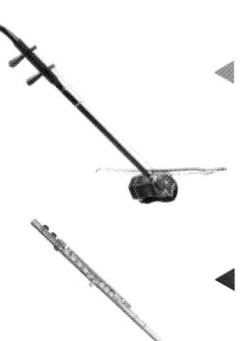

◀ **Guitar: Acoustic** A wooden string instrument with six strings. The player strums or plucks the strings with a pick or the fingers to play a melody or chords. When played softly, the guitar is gentle and sweet. It sounds lush and powerful when it is played louder. CD 21–32 p. 384

(515)

▶ **Playing String Instruments** String instruments make sounds when the strings vibrate. The strings are stretched over sound boxes of various shapes. Most string instruments are held between the chin and shoulder or rested on the floor. Some, such as the guitar and harp, are plucked or strummed with the fingers or a pick. The orchestral strings (violin, viola, cello, and string bass) may also be plucked or even strummed, but they are usually bowed.

String players press the strings with their left hand to make different pitches. The right hand draws the bow across the strings or plucks the strings, creating sound. String players (including guitarists) must do two very different things—one with each hand—to make music.

During the eighteenth century, the string family became the foundation of the orchestra. A symphony orchestra today might have 20 to 30 violins (divided between "first" and "second"), 8 to 12 violas, 8 to 12 cellos, and 6 to 10 string basses.

Timbre

SAY Every instrument—and every voice—has its own timbre. Usually, we can tell who is speaking or what is being played just by the sound—we don't even have to look. Let's listen to the timbres of our voices.

Divide the class into two parts. Face the "listeners" away from the "speakers." Have the

- Speakers take turns saying the same sentence or phrase at about the same dynamic level.
- Listeners try to identify the speaker from the timbre.
- Groups switch roles.

Turn this activity into a game by keeping score.

Repeat this activity, using instruments featured in the Sound Bank. Use the recordings to review, if necessary.

Resonance

SAY Resonance can make sounds louder and fuller. Let's try this experiment to hear resonance.

Have students

- Say something—"hello," or their names—into the air.
- Say the same thing into a resonating chamber—an empty cardboard box or an empty wastebasket.

ASK What happened to the sound? (It got louder and fuller.)

Making a Pitch

ASK Some of the percussion instruments pictured in your book have a definite pitch. Can you tell which they are? (hand bells, *mbira*, piano, steel drums, timpani, xylophone)

SAY Other percussion instruments have an indefinite pitch, although some can make high or low sounds. The conga, for instance, is larger than the *doumbek* and makes a lower sound.

SAY The pitch of an instrument results from the number of vibrations: the more vibrations, the higher the pitch. The pitch can be made higher or lower in three ways: size, tension, and thickness. If the sound sources are equal in two of the ways, the third will determine the pitch.

continued on page 516

Size

SAY A large drum makes a lower sound than a small drum. A large dog barks at a lower pitch than a small dog. You might also be able to see how size determines pitch in your own family: A man's voice will sound lower than your own voice or a woman's voice.

Tension

SAY Tension means tightness; the tighter you make the string or the drumhead, for instance, the higher the pitch.

ASK On some instruments, like the triangle, the player can't change the tension. How can the player get different pitches? (by using larger or smaller triangles)

Guide students in experimenting with tension using rubber bands.

ASK What happens to the sound of a rubber band when you pull it to make it longer—increase the tension? (The pitch gets higher.)

Is the sound loud? (no) **Is it attractive?** (no) **How can it be made louder and more attractive?** (Add resonance.)

Have students work in pairs to demonstrate tension, pitch, and resonance. One student stretches a rubber band across the open end of a glass, cup, or box. Another student plucks the rubber band.

SAY When resonance is added, it is easier to hear the sound of the rubber band.

ASK How can you raise the pitch? (Stretch the rubber band more.)

What happens to the sound when the rubber band is stretched? (It gets higher.) **When it is relaxed?** (It gets lower.)

Thickness

Experiment by playing individual strings of an Autoharp or a guitar.

ASK What happens when you pluck a string that is thicker? (It makes a lower sound.) **Thinner?** (It makes a higher sound.)

Guitarrón [gee-tahr-ROHN] A large, round-backed, non-fretted bass guitar of Chile and Mexico. It is strung with six harp strings, and was invented around the beginning of the twentieth century. The guitarrón is either strummed or plucked, and has a rich, deep sound. CD 21–33 p. 51

Hand Bells Each bell has a handle to hold for ringing. It is swung to produce a sound and has a clapper inside. They are used in sets for pitch, rhythm and tone-color. These sets can range from six to sixty that cover a range of a short melodic scale to five chromatic octaves. The music is performed by a team of four to 15 ringers, each ringer holding one hand bell in each hand. CD 21–34 p. 158

Harp The symphonic harp is a large instrument with strings stretched vertically in an open, triangular frame. The player plucks the strings and operates foot pedals to play chromatic tones. Rippling chords are characteristic sounds of the instrument. CD 21–36 p. 198

Harpsichord A small keyboard instrument shaped something like a piano. Because the strings are plucked, not hammered like piano strings, the sound of the harpsichord has a light, transparent quality. CD 21–35 p. 197

Jarana [hah-RAH-nah] An eight-string guitar used to strum rhythmic accompaniments in various *son* (sohn), or "folk music," ensembles in Mexico. It is used especially in the central Gulf Coast area in playing *jarocho* (pertaining to Veracruz) music. CD 21–37 p. 131

Koto [koh-toh] A 13 to 17-string zither with movable frets. It is known as the national instrument of Japan. The player sits on the floor, either cross-legged or in a kneeling-sitting position. Sound is produced when the player plucks the silk strings, using the fingers and thumb of the right hand, with a bamboo, bone, or ivory pick. The sound of the koto is a little like that of a harp. CD 21–38 p. 196

(516) **Instrument Key:** strings | percussion | woodwind | brass | keyboard

Footnotes

▶ **Playing Woodwind Instruments** All wind instruments make sound when the air inside them vibrates. The tubes and bells of wind instruments contain the vibrating air and give the sound resonance. Woodwind players make sounds by blowing across a hole (flute), by vibrating a reed (clarinet, saxophone), or by vibrating two reeds against each other (oboe, bassoon). The player changes the size of the instrument, making it longer or shorter by opening or closing holes along the instrument's length.

Flutes, oboes, and bassoons can be traced back to the 1400s. Composers since the 1700s have incorporated them in the orchestra because each woodwind is easily capable of playing melodies and because each brings a unique timbre to the orchestra. Clarinets are relatively new and were not added to the orchestra until the late eighteenth century (the time of Mozart and Haydn). Although the recorder is a woodwind instrument, it was replaced by the more popular and more powerful flute in the 1700s. The saxophone is used mostly in stage bands, jazz ensembles, and concert bands.

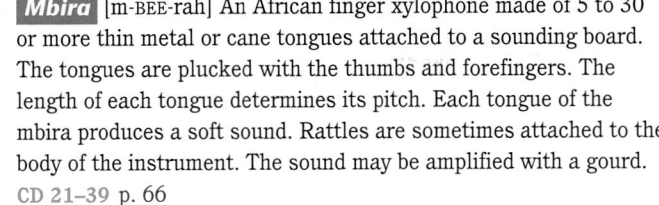

Mbira [m-BEE-rah] An African finger xylophone made of 5 to 30 or more thin metal or cane tongues attached to a sounding board. The tongues are plucked with the thumbs and forefingers. The length of each tongue determines its pitch. Each tongue of the mbira produces a soft sound. Rattles are sometimes attached to the body of the instrument. The sound may be amplified with a gourd. CD 21–39 p. 66

Piano A large keyboard instrument with 88 keys and many strings on the inside. When the player presses the keys, hammers inside the piano strike the strings to make the sounds. The piano can play music in a quiet mood as well as in a loud "military style." CD 21–40 p. 237

Requinto [reh-KEEN-toh] A small guitar that is used to play fast, highly improvisational melodies. The strings are plucked with a long, thin plastic pick. Like the jarana, the requinto is used in playing *jarocho* songs in the Veracruz area. CD 21–41 p. 131

Saxophone A woodwind instrument invented by Adolphe Sax in the nineteenth century by placing a clarinet-type reed mouthpiece on a piece of brass tubing. The saxophone has a warm, brassy-but-mellow sound that makes it ideal in jazz ensembles. CD 21–42 p. 342

Shakuhachi [shah-koo-hah-chee] A Japanese end-blown bamboo flute with a thumbhole and four finger holes. The early eighth-century instrument had five front finger holes, one thumbhole, and was made from stone, jade, or ivory. CD 21–43 p. 112

(517)

Sound Bank

▶ **Playing Brass Instruments** Brass players make the air inside the instrument vibrate by buzzing their lips against the mouthpiece. The lips must be tight and the air forced through them.

Brass players change pitches by tightening their lips even more or by pressing one valve or a combination of valves (except the trombone, although valve trombones can sometimes be found). Each time a valve is pressed, another length of tubing is added, changing the instrument's size by making it longer.

Although brass instruments existed from the 1400s, they are the last instrumental family to become full-fledged members of the orchestra. Prior to the early 1800s, brass instruments were used only for special effects or on special occasions. As the orchestra became larger, however, more brass instruments were included. Now, it is common to see two to four of each member of the family. Due to its mellow sound and ease of blending, the French horn, derived from the hunting horn, won acceptance before the others.

Playing Keyboard Instruments

The piano, organ, and synthesizer are keyboard instruments. All keyboard instruments are played the same way, but the sound is made in different ways.

SAY When the piano keys are pushed down, padded hammers strike the strings inside the instrument, in much the same way that the bars are struck on the glockenspiel and marimba.

Demonstrate, if possible, by exposing the inside mechanism of a piano, allowing students to see the hammers strike the strings.

SAY When electronic keyboard or electronic organ keys are pushed down, circuits in the machine are turned on in a way that makes sound. Both instruments are really synthesizers, since these circuits can be made to produce many different sounds, even some not available in nature.

Playing Longer and Shorter Sounds

ASK Which percussion instruments make sounds that last for a short time? (*axatse, bodhran,* bongo drums, conga, *doumbek, dundun, mbira,* snare drum, *taiko,* xylophone)

How can you make the sound of a drum longer? (by hitting it repeatedly, as in a roll on the snare drum)

Experimenting with Sound

Some instruments can be played in more than one way. For instance, an Autoharp can be played by

• Strumming in the usual way, using a pick or, for comfort, a door stop.
• Striking the strings with a mallet.
• Scraping with a guitar pick or other object.
• Plucking individual strings.

ASK Can you use an instrument to make a sound like corn popping, or trees rustling, or a sound of your choice? (Allow students to experiment with different ways to play the instruments as well as different volumes.)

When students have discovered how to create sounds in new ways or to imitate another sound, encourage them to create sound effects to accompany a poem in the book.

For another sound experiment, have students try to make a bottle "play." They should use a bottle with a small neck and blow across the top toward the other side, trying to aim the air so that it is split in half.

ASK Are there any instruments in the Sound Bank that make sound the same way? (Yes; the modern flute is played that way. The *shakuhachi* uses the same principle, but is end-blown. The mouthpiece divides the air.)

continued on page 518

Sound Bank (517)

INSTRUMENTS FEATURED IN THE RECORDINGS

Many of the listening selections, songs, and illustrations in this book may be used to supplement the lessons on timbre. See the specific references below for selected instruments in the Sound Bank.

- ARPA: *La bamba* **CD 6-25**
  Illustration: p. 131

- AXATSE: *"Ye jaliya da"* **CD 4-7**
  Illustration: p. 66

- BODHRAN: *O'Sullivans March* **CD 8-6**
  Illustration: p. 157

- BONGO DRUMS: *"El carite"* **CD 14-6**

- CLARINET: "Oh, Watch the Stars" **CD 10-29**
  Illustration: p. 89

- CONGA DRUMS: "Day-O!" **CD 1-28**
  Illustration: p. 156

- DOUMBEK: *"Ah ya Zane"* **CD 13-16**
  Illustration: p. 297

- DULCIMER (mountain): *Amazing Grace* **CD 12-14**
  Illustration: p. 259

- DUNDUN: *"Funwa alafia"* **CD 2-19**
  Illustration: p. 33

- ERHU: *"Yüe liang wan wan"* **CD 14-23**
  Illustration: p. 310

- FLUTE: *Somewhere Out There* **CD 17-6**
  Illustration: p. 113

- GUITAR: *Bye Bye Love* **CD 16-17**
  Illustration: p. 357

- GUITARRÓN: *"Adelita"* **CD 3-4**
  Illustration: p. 51

- HARP: "Morning Has Broken" **CD 2-16**
  Illustration: p. 186

- HARPSICHORD: *Two-Part Invention in A Major* **CD 11-27**
  Illustration: p. 236

- JARANA: *La bamba* **CD 6-25**
  Illustration: p. 131

- KOTO: *"Hitotsu toya"* **CD 21-1**
  Illustration: p. 196

- MBIRA: *"Ye jaliya da"* **CD 4-7**
  Illustration: p. 66

- PIANO: "You've Got a Friend" **CD 17-2**
  Illustration: p. 197

- REQUINTO: *La bamba* **CD 6-25**
  Illustration: p. 131

- SAXOPHONE: *Yakety Yak* **CD 10-16**
  Illustration: p. 451

- SHAKUHACHI: *Shika no tone* **CD 21-1**
  Illustration: p. 112

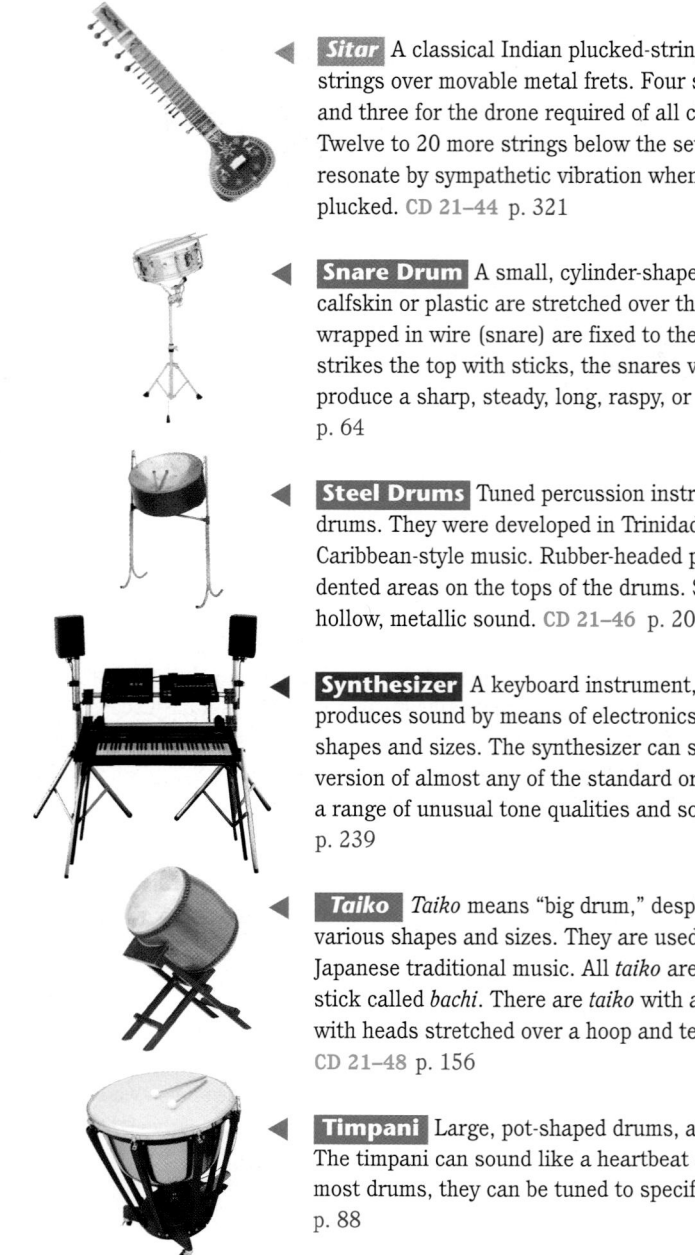

Sitar A classical Indian plucked-string instrument with seven strings over movable metal frets. Four strings are for the melody and three for the drone required of all classical Indian music. Twelve to 20 more strings below the seven, are not plucked but resonate by sympathetic vibration when the melody strings are plucked. CD 21–44 p. 321

Snare Drum A small, cylinder-shaped drum. Two heads made of calfskin or plastic are stretched over the metal shell and strings wrapped in wire (snare) are fixed to the bottom. When the player strikes the top with sticks, the snares vibrate in response. It can produce a sharp, steady, long, raspy, or rolling sound. CD 21–45 p. 64

Steel Drums Tuned percussion instruments made from oil drums. They were developed in Trinidad and are used for Caribbean-style music. Rubber-headed pan sticks are used to strike dented areas on the tops of the drums. Steel drums produce a hollow, metallic sound. CD 21–46 p. 200

Synthesizer A keyboard instrument, with keys like a piano that produces sound by means of electronics. Synthesizers come in all shapes and sizes. The synthesizer can sound like an electronic version of almost any of the standard orchestral instruments. It has a range of unusual tone qualities and sound effects. CD 21–47 p. 239

Taiko *Taiko* means "big drum," despite the fact that there are various shapes and sizes. They are used in various styles of Japanese traditional music. All *taiko* are struck with some sort of stick called *bachi*. There are *taiko* with a nailed head, and others with heads stretched over a hoop and tensioned with ropes. CD 21–48 p. 156

Timpani Large, pot-shaped drums, also called "kettledrums." The timpani can sound like a heartbeat or a roll of thunder. Unlike most drums, they can be tuned to specific pitches. CD 21–49 p. 88

(518) **Instrument Key:** strings | percussion | woodwind | brass | keyboard

Footnotes

► **Active Listening** At the same time that they are listening to the recorded Sound Bank or supplementary examples, students should also look at the illustration of the instrument either in the Sound Bank or on the cited page. This will help them to remember the sound of the instrument when they see it, and vice versa. Reinforcing this association will help students' future listening.

Begin with two examples. Test students' ability to differentiate the instruments. Use dissimilar sounds at first, then gradually make them more similar.

When several instruments are learned in this way, divide the class into teams and have students challenge each other. Keep score of correct answers.

 **Trombone** A large brass instrument with one of the loudest voices in the orchestra. The trombone is a long, narrow, curved tube with a bell at one end and a cup-shaped mouthpiece at the other. It has a movable metal tube, called a slide, that lengthens or shortens the tubing. The trombone can project a huge, brilliant sound, but its soft voice is mellow. CD 21–50 p. 342

 **Trumpet** The smallest brass instrument. It has a bell at one end and a cup-shaped mouthpiece at the other. There are three valves, or buttons, on top. In its loudest voice, the trumpet has an important-sounding, brilliant tone. It can also sound soft, warm, and sweet. CD 21–51 p. 342

 **Tuba** The largest brass instrument, with a very large bell that usually points upward. The tuba is so heavy that it may be set on a metal stand while the player sits behind it to blow into the cup-shaped mouthpiece. The tuba's low notes, the lowest of any brass instrument, are deep and dark sounding. The higher ones are hearty and warm. CD 21–52 p. 180

 *Vihuela* [vee-WEH-lah] The vihuela is linked with the guitar and viol. The strings are plucked with six or seven pairs of unison strings. It is a large instrument with very little inward curve. Multiple roses set into the soundboard add to the unique appearance. The size suggests low pitch. It was extremely popular in Spain during the 15th and 16th centuries. CD 21–53 p. 322

 **Violin** A small wooden string instrument that is held under the chin. The player uses a bow or plucks it with the fingers. The violin has many different voices, from a beautiful "singing" quality to a bright, playful sound. CD 21–54 p. 159

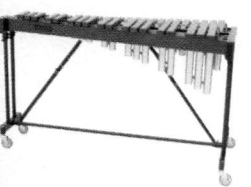 **Xylophone** A pitched percussion instrument that has a keyboard of wooden bars and is played with mallets. The xylophone has a bright, brittle sound that makes it effective in lively or humorous passages. CD 21–55 p. 65

- SITAR: *Sindhi-Bhairavi* **CD 15-1**
  Illustration: p. 320
- SNARE DRUM: *Rock Around the Clock* **CD 16-16**
  Illustration: p. 65
- STEEL DRUMS: "Linstead Market" **CD 11-32**
  Illustration: p. 240
- SYNTHESIZER: *Come Out and Play* **CD 11-30**
  Illustration: p. 238
- TAIKO DRUM: *Yaudachi* **CD 8-4**
  Illustration: p. 156
- TIMPANI: *Theme and Variations for Percussion* **CD 4-5**
  Illustration: p. 65
- TROMBONE: *"Da pacem, Domine"* **CD 4-4**
  Illustration: p. 342
- TRUMPET: *"Da pacem, Domine"* **CD 4-4**
  Illustration: p. 343
- TUBA: "When Johnny Comes Marching Home" **CD 9-13**
  Illustration: p. 355
- VIHUELA: "Laredo" **CD 1-9**
  Illustration: p. 323
- VIOLIN: *Sonata in A Major*, Movement 4 *(Allegretto poco mosso)* **CD 8-11**
  Illustration: p. 159
- XYLOPHONE: *Danse macabre* **CD 19-24**
  Illustration: p. 65

CONTENTS

SILVER·BURDETT

Making Music

Teacher Resources

Pronunciation Practice

Phonetic Respellings for Pronunciation of Non-English Songs

These simplified phonetic guides will assist you and your students in pronouncing non-English words. All pronunciation phonetics are matched to those of the native singer on the Pronunciation Practice Track and have been verified by the CP Language Institute. The Pronunciation Practice Guide provides a phonetic respelling in syllabic form, based on sounds in the English language that most nearly approximate the non-English sounds. When words do not have an English equivalent, we have provided the nearest approximation or instructions for making the sound. The Key to Pronunciation below refers to the system used in the Pronunciation Practice Guides.

Where possible, vowel sounds have been written with beautiful vocal tones in mind. For example, it is difficult to sing a sustained long *i* sound. Instead students are taught to sustain an *ah* sound, adding a small touch of *ee* to the release of the vowel.

Key to Pronunciation

ah	as in f<u>a</u>ther		(m)	French nasal <u>m</u>; not articulated as a distinct letter but as an open nasal sound
ah‿ee	as in l<u>i</u>ght (diphthong; a long *ah* sound with a hint of *ee* at close)		n	as in <u>n</u>ote
aw	as in <u>awe</u>		(n)	French nasal <u>n</u>; not articulated as a distinct letter, but as an open nasal sound
eh‿ee	as in d<u>ay</u> (diphthong; a long *eh* sound with a hint of *ee* at close)		(ng)	as in sa<u>ng</u> (sometimes sounded as a prolonged nasal tone)
b	as in <u>b</u>utton		oh	as in t<u>o</u>ne
ch	as in <u>ch</u>urch		oo	as in sp<u>oo</u>n
d	as in <u>d</u>ad		ow	as in p<u>ow</u>der
dj	as in ju<u>dg</u>e		p	as in <u>p</u>at
ee	as in s<u>ee</u>d		r	as in <u>r</u>an
eh	as in l<u>e</u>t		(r)	as in tu<u>r</u>n (combined with another vowel sound in German)
ew	used for French <u>u</u> (pronounce a bright *ee* and round the lips as if to whistle)		rr	rolled <u>r</u>
f	as in <u>f</u>ace		rrrr	extended trilled <u>r</u>
g	as in <u>g</u>oat		s	as in <u>s</u>ong
h	as in <u>h</u>at		t	as in <u>t</u>ell
hkh	guttural, aspirant <u>h</u> of German, Hebrew <u>ch</u>, and Spanish j		th	as in <u>th</u>at
			thh	as in fea<u>th</u>er
ih	as in f<u>i</u>t		uh	as in <u>u</u>p
I	as in l<u>i</u>ght (a harsh *i* sound; where possible an *ah‿ee* has been suggested for singing the I sound)		v	as in <u>v</u>an
k	as in <u>k</u>ite		w	as in <u>w</u>ay
l	as in <u>l</u>et		wh	as in <u>wh</u>at
ll	prolonged <u>l</u> sound		y	as in <u>y</u>es (not a vowel sound)
m	as in <u>m</u>an		z	as in <u>z</u>one
			zh	as in a<u>z</u>ure

English Translations by CP Language Institute

The English translations for these songs were provided by CP Language Institute. For over two decades, the Institute has been one of the leading language consultants for clients in the New York City area and in other locations. The Institute specializes in translation, interpretation, typesetting, graphic design, language instruction, and voice overs. Its highly qualified staff of native translators guided and monitored the pronunciation and recording of each Pronunciation Track for Silver Burdett MAKING MUSIC.

Laredo, **p. 10** CD 1–12, 13
Folk Song from Mexico

Pronunciation Practice

Verse 1

Phrase 1. *Ya me voy pa-ra_el La-re-do, mi bien,*
yah meh voh_ee pah-rah_ehl lah-reh-doh, mee byehn,

2. *Te ven-go_a de-cir a-diós.*
teh vehn-goh_ah deh-seerr ah-dyohs.

3. *Ya me voy pa-ra_el La-re-do, mi bien,*
yah meh voh_ee pah-rah_ehl lah-reh-doh, mee byehn,

4. *Te ven-go_a de-cir a-diós.*
teh vehn-goh_ah deh-seer ah-dyohs.

5. *De a-llá te man-do de-cir, mi bien,*
deh ah-yah teh mahn-doh deh-seer, mee byehn,

6. *Co-mo se man-cuer-nan dos.*
koh-moh seh mahn-kwehr-nahn dohs.

7. *De a-llá te man-do de-cir, mi bien,*
deh ah-yah teh mahn-doh deh-seer, mee byehn,

8. *Co-mo se man-cuer-nan dos.*
koh-moh seh mahn-kwehr-nahn dohs.

Verse 2

Phrase 1. *To-ma e-sa lla-vi-ta de_o-ro, mi bien,*
toh-mah eh-sah yah-vee-tah deh_oh-roh, mee byehn,

2. *Abre mi pe-cho y ve-rás:*
ah_breh mee peh-choh ee veh-rahs:

3. *To-ma e-sa lla-vi-ta de_o-ro, mi bien,*
toh-mah eh-sah yah-vee-tah deh_oh-roh, mee byehn,

4. *Abre mi pe-cho y ve-rás:*
ah_breh mee peh-choh ee veh-rahs:

5. *Lo mu-cho que yo te quie-ro, mi bien,*
loh moo-choh keh yoh teh kyeh-roh, mee byehn,

6. *Y_el mal pa-go que me das.*
ee_ehl mahl pah-goh keh meh dahs.

7. *Lo mu-cho que yo te quie-ro, mi bien,*
loh moo-choh keh yoh teh kyeh-roh, mee byehn,

8. *Y_el mal pa-go que me das.*
ee_ehl mahl pah-goh keh meh dahs.

Translation

Verse 1 I am going to Laredo, my love,
I have come to tell you goodbye.
From there I will tell you, my love,
How the two of us are tied together.

Verse 2 Take this little key of gold, my love,
Open my heart with it and see
How much I love you, and
The bad repayment you give me.

Éliza Kongo, p. 14 CD 1–26

Traditional Song from Dominica

Pronunciation Practice

Phrase 1. *Nou ka mou-té*
noo kah moo-tah

2. *an-ro-a c'est la-peé*
ahn-roh-ah seh lah-peh

3. *É-li-za Kon-go*
eh-lee-zah kohn-goh

4. *Nou ka mou-té*
noo kah moo-tah

5. *an-ro-a c'est lap-eé*
ahn-roh-ah seh lah-peh

6. *É-li-za Kon-go*
eh-lee-zah kohn-goh

7. *Ay jou-joup,*
ah_ee joo-joop,

8. *jou-joup, jou-joup nou ka-man-dé*
joo-joop, joo-joop noo kah-mahn-deh

9. *É-li-za Kon-go*
eh-lee-zah kohn-goh

10. *Ay pawé-ou,*
ah_ee pahweh-oo,

11. *pawé-ou, pawé-ou mwen ka-vi-ni*
pahweh-oo, pahweh-oo mween kah-vee-nee

12. *É-li-za Kon-go.*
eh-lee-zah kohn-goh.

Translation

We can climb,
And find (it is) peace up there,
Eliza Congo
We can climb,
And find (it is) peace up there,
Eliza Congo;
Oh! Get ready,
Get ready, get ready,
We can ask.
Oh! Get ready, get ready, get ready, I am coming;
Oh! Get ready,
Eliza Congo.

Arirang, p. 25 CD 2–9

Folk Song from Korea

Pronunciation Practice

Phrase 1. *A-ri-rang, A-ri-rang,*
ah-ree-rahng, ah-ree-rahng,

2. *a-ra-ri-yo,*
ahr-rah-ree-yoh,

3. *A-ri-rang ko-ge-ro-nuh-muh-kan-da.*
ah-ree-rahng koh-geh-roo-noh-moh-kahn-dah.

4. *Chung-chun ha-nul-en*
chuhng-chuhn hah-nehl-ehn

5. *pyul-do man-ko,*
pyeeah-doh mahn-koh,

6. *I-neh ka-sem-en*
ee-neh kah-seeoom-ehn

7. *su-sim-do man-ta.*
soo-sheem-doh mahn-tah.

Translation

Arirang, Arirang, Arirang,
Going over the hill,
Leaving me behind.
[You are] going, dear.
[You are] going, dear.
You won't reach ten miles
Before you become lonesome [for me].

Funwa alafia (Welcome, My Friends), p. 32 CD 2–22

Folk Song from West Africa

Pronunciation Practice

Phrase 1. *Fun-wa a-la-fia,*
foon-wah ah-lah-fee_ah,

2. *Ah-shay, Ah-shay.*
ah-sheh, ah-sheh.

3. *Fun-wa a-la-fia,*
foon-wah ah-lah-fee_ah,

4. *Ah-shay, Ah-shay.*
ah-sheh, ah-sheh.

Translation

Welcome, my friends;
I greet you in peace.
Welcome, my friends;
I greet you in peace.

Adelita, p. 50 CD 3–7, 8
Folk Song from Mexico

Pronunciation Practice
Verse (Unison)
Phrase 1. *A-de-li-ta se lla-ma la jo-ven,*
    ah-deh-lee-tah seh ya-mah lah hoh-vehn,

    2. *A quien yo quie-ro_y no pue-do ol-vi-dar.*
    ah kyehn yoh kyeh-roh_ee noh pweh-doh ohl-vee-dahr.

    3. *Y_en el cam-po yo ten-go_u-na ro-sa,*
    ee_yehn ehl kahm-poh yoh tehn-goh_oo-nah roh-sah,

    4. *Y con el tiem-po la voy a cor-tar,*
    ee kohn ehl tyehm-poh lah voh_ee ah kohr-tahr,

(Harmony)
Phrase 1. *Si_A-de-li-ta qui-sie-ra ser mi_es-po-sa*
    see_ah-deh-lee-tah kee-syeh-rah sehr mee_ehs-poh-sah

    2. *Si_A-de-li-ta fue-ra mi mu-jer.*
    see_ah-deh-lee-tah fweh-rah mee moo-hehr.

    3. *Le com-pra-rí a_un ves-ti-do de se-da,*
    leh kohm-prah-ree ah_oon vehs-tee-doh deh seh-dah,

    4. *Pa-ra lle-var-la_a bai-lar al cuar-tel.*
    pah-rah yeh-vahr-lah bah_ee-lahr ahl kwahr-tehl.

Translation
Adelita is the name of the young woman
Whom I want and cannot forget.
And in the meadow I have a rose,
And with time I am going to cut it.
If Adelita would like to be my wife,
If Adelita would be my woman,
I will buy her a dress of silk
So I can take her to dance at the barracks.

La ciudad de Juaja (The City of Juaja), p. 58 CD 3–27
Folk Song from New Mexico

Pronunciation Practice

Verse 1
Phrase 1. *Des-de la ciu-dad de Jua-ja,*
    dehs-deh lah see_oo-dahd deh hwah-hah,

    2. *me man-dan so-li-ci-tar,*
    meh mahn-dahn soh-lee-see-tahrr,

    3. *que me va-ya que me va-ya,*
    keh meh vah-yah keh meh vah-yah,

    4. *de_un te-so-ro a dis-fru-tar.*
    deh_oon teh-soh-roh ah dees-froo-tahr.

Refrain
Phrase 1. *¿Qué di-ces, a-mi-go? va-mos*
    keh dee-sehs, ah-mee-goh? vah-mohs

    2. *a ver si di-cen ver-dad,*
    ah vehr see dee-sehn vehr-thahth,

    3. *Si_es ver-dad de lo que di-cen*
    see_ehs vehr-thahth deh loh keh dee-sehn

    4. *nos que-da-mos por a-llá.*
    nohs keh-dah-mohs pohr ah-yah.

Verse 2
Phrase 1. *Los ce-rros son de tor-ti-llas,*
    lohs seh-rrohs sohn deh tohr-tee-yahs,

    2. *las que-bra-das de bu-ñue-los,*
    lahs keh-brah-dahs deh boo-nweh-lohs,

    3. *y las pie-dras, fru-tas cu-bier-tas,*
    ee lahs pee_eh-drahs, froo-tahs koo-byehr-tahs,

    4. *pi-nos son los ca-ra-me-los.*
    pee-nohs sohn lohs kah-rah-meh-lohs.

Translation
Verse 1 From the city of Juaja;
    They are calling me to go,
    To go there is some
    Treasure to enjoy.

Refrain What do you say, my friend?
    Let's go to see if they tell the truth,
    If what they say is true,
    We may stay there.

Verse 2 The hills are made of tortillas,
    The canyons are made of rolls,
    And stones, fruit with overlay,
    And the pine trees are the candies.

A la puerta del cielo (At the Gate of Heaven), p. 60 CD 3–32

Folk Song from Spain

Pronunciation Practice

Verse 1

Phrase 1. *A la puer-ta del cie-lo*
ah lah pwehrr-tah dehl see_eh-loh

2. *ven-den za-pa-tos,*
vehn-dehn sah-pah-tohs,

3. *Pa-ra an-ge-li-tos*
pah-rrah ahn-heh-lee-tohs

4. *que an-dan des-cal-zos,*
keh ahn-dahn dehz-kahl-zohs,

Refrain

Phrase 1. *Duér-me-te, ni-ño,*
dwehrr-meh-teh, nee-nyoh,

2. *duér-me-te, ni-ño,*
dwehrr-meh-teh, nee-nyoh,

3. *Duér-me-te, ni-ño, a-rrú, a-rrú.*
dwehrr-meh-teh, nee-nyoh, ah-rroo, ah-rroo.

Verse 2

Phrase 1. *A los ni-ños que duer-men*
ah lohs nee-nyohs keh dwehrr-mehn

2. *Di_os los ben-di-ce*
dee_ohs lohs behn-dee-seh

3. *A las ma-dres que ve-lan*
ah lahs mah-drrehs keh veh-lahn

4. *Di_os les a-sis-te.*
dee_ohs lehs ah-sees-teh.

Translation

Verse 1 At the door of heaven they sell shoes
For angels that walk bare foot.

Refrain Sleep child, sleep child,
Sleep child, arrú, arrú*

Verse 2 Children who sleep
Are blessed by God;
Mothers who keep watch
Are assisted by God.

Refrain

Arru, arru—lulling sounds made to help a baby sleep

Da pacem, Domine (Grant Us Peace), p. 62 CD 3–41

Prayer in Latin; Music by Melchior Franck

Pronunciation Practice

Phrase 1. *Da pa-cem, Do-mi-ne,*
dah pah-chehm, doh-mee-neh,

2. *Da pa-cem, Do-mi-ne,*
dah pah-chehm, doh-mee-neh,

3. *in di-e-bus nos-tris.*
een dee-eh-boos nohs-trees.

Translation

Give peace, Lord,
Give peace, Lord,
In our days.

Ye jaliya da, p. 67 CD 4–9

Folk Song from West Africa

Pronunciation Practice

Phrase 1. *Ye ja-li-ya da*
yeh djah-lee-yah dah

2. *Al-lah le-ga ja-li-ya da.*
ahl-lah leh-kah djah-lee-yah dah.

3. *Ye ja-li-ya da*
yeh djah-lee-yah dah

4. *Al-lah le-ga ja-li-ya da.*
ahl-lah leh-kah djah-lee-yah dah.

Translation

The brotherhood of storytellers
God created the brotherhood of storytellers.
The brotherhood of storytellers
God created the brotherhood of storytellers.

De colores, p. 90 CD 5–4, 5

Folk Song from Mexico

Pronunciation Practice

Phrase 1. *De co-lo-res,*
deh koh-loh-rehs,

2. *de co-lo-res se vis-ten los cam-pos*
deh koh-loh-rehs seh vees-tehn lohs kahm-pohs

3. *en la pri-ma-ve-ra,*
ehn lah pree-mah-veh-rah,

4. *De co-lo-res,*
deh koh-loh-rehs,

5. *De co-lo-res son los pa-ja-ri-tos*
deh koh-loh-rehs sohn lohs pah-hah-ree-tohs

6. *que vie-nen de a-fue-ra,*
keh vee-eh-nehn deh_ah-foo_eh-rah,

7. *De co-lo-res,*
deh koh-loh-rehs,

8. *De co-lo-res es el ar-co i-ris*
deh koh-loh-rehs ehs ehl ahr-koh ee-rees

9. *que ve-mos lu-cir,*
keh veh-mohs loo-seer,

10. *y por e-so los gran-des*
ee pohr eh-soh lohs grahn-dehs

11. *a-mo-res de mu-chos co-lo-res*
ah-moh-rehs deh moo-chohs koh-loh-rehs

12. *(1st and 2nd endings) me gus-tan a mí.*
meh goos-tahn ah mee.

Translation

Of colors, of colors the fields dress in the spring.
Of colors, of colors are the little birds that live outside.
Of colors, of colors the rainbow that we see illuminates,
And that is why the great loves of young men are pleasant to me.

Chiapanecas (The Girl from Chiapas), p. 92 CD 5–10

Folk Song from Mexico

Pronunciation Practice

Phrase 1. *Un cla-vel co-rté,*
oon clah-vehl kohr-teh,

2. *por la sie-rra fui*
pohr lah syeh-rah fwee

3. *ca-mi-ni-to de mi ran-cho.*
kah-mee-nee-toh deh mee rahn-choh.

4. *Co-mo_el vien-to fue*
koh-moh_ehl vee_ehn-toh fweh

5. *mi ca-ba-llo fiel*
mee kah-bah-yoh fee-yehl

6. *á lle-var-me_has-ta su la-do,*
ah yeh-vahr-meh_ah-stah soo lah-doh,

7. *Lin-da flor de_a-bril*
leen-dah flohr deh_ah-breel

8. *to-ma_es-te cla-vel*
toh-mah_ehs-teh klah-vehl

9. *que te brin-do con pa-sión.*
keh teh breen-doh kohn pah-see_ohn.

10. *No me di-gas no,*
noh meh dee-gahs noh,

11. *que_en tu bo-ca_es-tá*
keh_ehn too boh-kah_eh-stah

12. *el se-cre-to de mi_a-mor.*
ehl seh-kreh-toh deh mee ah-mohr.

13. *Cuan-do la no-che lle-gó*
kwahn-doh lah noh-cheh yeh-goh

14. *y con su man-to de_a-zul*
ee kohn soo mahn-toh deh_ah-sool

15. *el blan-co ran-cho cu-brió*
ehl blahn-koh rahn-choh koo-bree_oh

16. *y_a-le-gre_el bai-le_em-pe-zó.*
ee_ah-leh-greh_ehl bah_ee-leh_ehm-peh-soh.

17. *Bai-la, mi Chia-pa-ne-ca,*
bah_ee-lah, mee chee_ah-pah-neh-kah,

18. *bai-la, bai-la con gar-bo,*
bah_ee-lah, bah_ee-lah kohn gahr-boh,

19. *Bai-la sua-ve ra-yo de luz.*
bah_ee-lah swah-veh rah-yoh deh loos.

20. *Bai-la, mi Chia-pa-ne-ca,*
bah_ee-lah, mee chee_ah-pah-neh-kah,

21. *bai-la, bai-la con gar-bo,*
bah_ee-lah, bah_ee-lah kohn gahr-boh,

22. *que_en el bai-le la rei-na_e-res tú,*
kehn ehl bah_ee-leh lah reh-nah_eh-rehs too,

23. *Chia-pa-ne-ca gen-til.*
chee_ah-pah-neh-kah gehn-teel.

Translation

I cut a carnation on the mountain path of my ranch.
My loyal horse rode like the wind to take me to your side.
Beautiful flower of April, take this carnation that I offer you
passionately.
Don't tell me no, because a kiss tells the secret of my love
for you.
When the night arrived and with its blue cloak covered the
white ranch,
the dance began happily.

Dance, my Chiapaneca, dance, dance with grace,
Dance, smooth ray of light.

Dance, my Chiapaneca, dance, dance with grace,
Because you are the queen of the dance, gentle Chiapaneca.

Pronunciation Practice
and Translations

Himmel und Erde (Music Alone Shall Live), p. 94 CD 5–14
Round from Germany

Pronunciation Practice

Phrase 1. *Him-mel und Er-de*
hihm-mehl oondt eer-duh

2. *müss-en ver-gehn;*
moos-ehn fehr-gehn;

3. *a-ber die Mu-si-ca,*
ah-buhr dee moo-see-kah,

4. *a-ber die Mu-si-ca,*
ah-buhr dee moo-see-kah,

5. *a-ber die Mu-si-ca*
ah-buhr dee moo-see-kah

6. *blei-bet be-stehn.*
bll-beht beh-shtehn.

Translation
Sky and earth
Sky and earth must pass by;
But the music,
But the music
That final continues.

Dundai, p. 106 CD 5–37
Folk Song from Israel

Pronunciation Practice

Verse
Phrase 1. *E-rets Yis-ra-el,*
eh-reets ees-rah-ehl,

2. *b'li To-rah.*
beh-lee toh-rah.

3. *Hi k'-guf*
hee kay-goof

4. *b'li n'sha-ma.*
beh-lee nuhshah-mah.

5. *Yal-de Yis-ra-el,*
yahl-deh ees-rah-ehl,

6. *lim-du To-rah.*
leem-doo toh-rah.

7. *Hiz-ku*
shees-koo

8. *im-tsu nish-mat ha-u-ma.*
eems-tsoo nee-shmaht hah-oo-mah.

Refrain 1. *Dun-dai*, dun-dai,*
doon-dah-ee, doon-dah-ee,

2. *dun-dai dai,*
doon-dah-ee dah-ee,

3. *Dun-dai, dun-dai, dun-dai dai.*
doon-dah-ee, doon-dah-ee, doon-dah-ee dah-ee.

Translation
*Dundai – A word with no meaning

Israel without the Torah is like a body without a soul.
Children of Israel, learn the Torah and strengthen the soul
of the nation.

Note: "Dundai" is typically sung at Shavuot. This festive
springtime holiday is celebrated to commemorate the
giving of the Ten Commandments at Mount Sinai.

Jo'ashila, p. 108 CD 5–45
Traditional Song of the Navajo

Pronunciation Practice

Phrase 1. *Jo-'a-shi-lá,*
joh-ah-shee-lah,

2. *Jo-'a-shi-lá,*
joh-ah-shee-lah,

3. *Jo-'a-shi-lá,*
joh-ah-shee-lah,

4. *hei yei' yun ga.*
heh yeh yoon gah.

5. *T'oo ga' ni-zhon-ni-go*
toh gah nee-zohn-nee-goh

6. *bah ho-zhó lá hei ya' hei',*
bah hoh-tzoh lah heh yah heh,

7. *nee ya.*
neh yah.

Translation
Walking together, Walking together,
Walking togther,
Happy about beauty;
Walking together, walking together.

Pronunciation Practice and Translations   **527**

La bamba, p. 128 CD 6–23
Folk Song from Mexico

Pronunciation Practice

Verse 1

Phrase 1. *Pa-ra bai-lar la bam-ba.*
   pah-rrah bah_ee-lahrr lah bahm-bah.

   2. *Pa-ra bai-lar la bam-ba-*
   pah-rrah bah_ee-lahr lah bahm-bah-

   3. *se ne-ce-si-ta un-a po-ca de gra-cia.*
   seh neh-seh-see-tah_oon-ah poh-kah deh grrah-see_ah.

   4. *Un-a po-ca de gra-cia pa-ra mi pa-ra ti*
   oon-ah poh-kah deh grrah-see_ah pah-rrah mee pah-rrah tee

   5. *y'a a-rri-ba a-rri-ba;*
   yah ah-rree-bah ah-rree-bah;

   6. *y'a-rri-ba y'a-rri-ba por ti se-ré*
   yah-rree-bah yah-rree-bah; pohrr tee seh-rreh

   7. *por ti se-ré por ti se-ré*
   pohrr tee seh-rreh pohrr tee seh-rreh

   8. *yo no soy mar-i-ne-ro.*
   yoh noh soh_ee mahrr-ee-neh-rroh.

   9. *Yo no soy mar-i-ne-ro, soy cap-i-tan;*
   yoh noh soh_ee mahrr-ee-neh-rroh, soh_ee kahp-ee-tahn,

   10. *soy cap-i-tan, soy cap-i-tan.*
   soh_ee kahp-ee-tahn, soh_ee kahp-ee-tahn.

Translation

In order to dance the bamba,
In order to dance the bamba,
You need a bit of grace and another thing,
Oh, up and up
And up and up I will go.
I am not a sailor, I am not a sailor,
[But] for you I will be,
For you I will be, for you I will be.

Refrain

Dance the bamba, dance the bamba,
dance the bamba…

Las velitas (Candle Burning Bright), p. 147 CD 7–21
Folk Song from Mexico

Pronunciation Practice

Phrase 1. *Her-mo-sas ve-li-tas,*
   hehr-moh-sahs veh-lee-tahs,

   2. *en la_ob-scu-ri-dad.*
   ehn lah_ahb-skoo-ree-dahd.

   3. *Ha-blan de la_es-tre-lla*
   hah-blahn deh lah_ehs-treh-djah

   4. *de la Na-vi-dad.*
   deh lah nah-vee-dahd.

   5. *Ved nues-tras ve-li-tas,*
   vehd nwehs-trahs veh-lee-tahs,

   6. *ved que_a-lum-bran bien.*
   vehd keh_ah-loom-brahn bee_ehn.

   7. *Ha-blan de la_es-tre-lla*
   hah-blahn deh lah_ehs-treh-djah

   8. *que bri-lló_en Be-lén.*
   keh bree-djoh_ehn beh-lehn.

Translation

These beautiful candles in the darkness speak of
The Christmas star.
Have a look at our candles,
See how they illuminate.
They speak of the star that shone in Bethlehem.

Pollerita, p. 151 CD 7–33
Folk Song from Bolivia

Pronunciation Practice

Phrase 1. *Po-lle-ri-ta, po-lle-ri-ta de mi cho-li-ta,*
poh-yeh-ree-tah, poh-yeh-ree-tah deh mee choh-lee-tah,

2. *Po-lle-ri-ta, po-lle-ri-ta co-lor ro-si-ta.*
poh-yeh-ree-tah, poh-yeh-ree-tah koh-lohr roh-see-tah.

3. *Que bien se bai-la,*
keh byehn seh bah_ee-lah,

4. *que bien se can-ta,*
keh byehn seh kahn-tah,

5. *con mi cha-ran-gui-to.*
kohn mee chah-rahn-ghee-toh.

6. *Sa-ra ma-la-gu ta tu*
sah-rah mah-lah-goo tah too

7. *ma-na tri-go pe-la-cu*
mah-nah tree-goh peh-lah-koo

8. *Ma-na chu-ño pun-ti-co.*
mah-nah choo-noh poon-tee-koh.

9. *Que bien se bai-la*
keh byehn seh bah_ee-lah

10. *que bien se can-ta*
keh byehn seh kahn-tah

11. (1st ending) *con mi cha-ran-qui-to.*
kohn mee chah-rahn-ghee-toh.

12. *Que bien se bai-la*
keh byehn seh bah_ee-lah

13. *que bien se can-ta*
keh byehn seh kahn-tah

14. (2nd ending) *con mi cha-ran-qui-to.*
kohn mee chah-rahn-ghee-toh.

Translation

Little skirt, little skirt of my cholita,*
Little skirt, little pinkish skirt;
How well you dance, how well you sing
With my charanguito,* with my charanguito.

Cholita—Bolivian woman
Charanguito—five-string instrument

Ego sum pauper (Nothing Do I Own), p. 158 CD 8–10
Traditional

Pronunciation Practice

Phrase 1. *E-go sum pau-per,*
eh-goh soom pah-pehrr,

2. *Ni-hil ha-be-o*
nee-heel hah-bay-oh

3. *Cor-me-um da-bo.*
kor-meh-oom dah-boh.

Translation

I'm a poor man.
I have nothing.
I give my heart.

Las estrellitas del cielo (Stars of the Heavens), p. 175 CD 8–32
Folk Song from Spain

Pronunciation Practice

Phrase 1. *Las es-tre-lli-tas del cie-lo*
lahs ehs-treh-yee-tahs dehl syeh-loh

2. *Bri-llan con su luz de pla-ta.*
bree-yahn kohn soo loos deh plah-tah.

3. *San-tia-go las fué sem-bran-do*
sahn-tee-ah-go lahs fweh sehm-brahn-doh

4. *Con sus es-pue-las de pla-ta.*
kohn soos ehs-pweh-lahs deh plah-tah.

Translation

Stars in the sky
Shine with their silvery light.
Santiago sowed them
With his silver spoon.

Don Alfonso, p. 177 CD 9–5, 6
Folk Song from Spain

Pronunciation Practice

Verse 1
Phrase 1. *De-los ár-bo-les fru-ta-les*
deh-lohs ahr-boh-lehs froo-tah-lehs

2. *Me gus-ta el me-lo-co-tón,*
meh goos-tah ehl meh-loh-koh-tawn,

3. *Y de los rey-es de Es-pa-ña,*
ee deh lohs reh-yehs deh ehs-pah-nyah,

4. *Don Al-fon-so de Bor-bón.*
dohn ahl-fahn-soh deh bohr-bawn.

Verse 2
Phrase 1. *"¿Dón-de vas, Al-fon-so Do-ce?*
dohn-deh vahs, ahl-fahn-soh doh-she?

2. *¿Dón-de vas, tris-te de ti?"*
dohn-deh vahs, trees-teh deh tee?

3. *"Voy en bus-ca de Mer-ce-des*
voh ee ehn boos-kah deh mehr-seh-dehs

4. *Que ha-ce tiem-po no la vi."*
keh ah-seh tyehm-poh noh lah vee.

Verse 3
Phrase 1. *Ya Mer-ce-des e-stá muer-ta,*
yah mehr-seh-dehs eh-stah mwehr-tah,

2. *Muer-ta es-tá que yo la vi,*
mwehr-tah ehs-tah keh yoh lah vee,

3. *Cua-tro du-ques la lle-va-ban*
kwah-troh doo-kehs lah yeh-vah-bahn

4. *Por las ca-lles de Ma-drid.*
pohr lahs kah-yehs deh mah-dreed.

Translation

Verse 1 Of the fruit trees,
I like the peach,
and of the kings of Spain,
Mr. (Don) Alfonso de Barón.

Verse 2 Where are you going, Alfonso, where?
Where are you going [looking so sad]?
I am going in search of Mercedes
Whom I have not seen for a while.

Meng Jian Nu, p. 194 CD 10–4
Folk Song from China

Pronunciation Practice

Phrase 1. *Zheng yu mei hua,*
djuhng yeh meh eh hwah,

2. *shi xing chung,*
shee seeng chwuhng,

3. *Jia jia hu hu*
jee ah jee ah hoo hoo

4. *tian hon deng,*
tee ehn hohn duhwng,

5. *Ran jia zhang fu*
rehn jee-ah djuhng foo

6. *tuan yuan ju,*
tuh ehn yuh ehn joo,

7. *Meng Jian Nu de zhang fu*
mehng zhuhng noo duh djuhng foo

8. *zou chan cheng.*
zow chahn chuhwng.

Translation

January is new year with plum blossoms blooming.
Every family lights the red lantern.
Other women are drinking wine with their husbands;
I dreamt that my husband was traveling far away.

Imbabura, p. 203 CD 10–15
Folk Song from Ecuador

Pronunciation Practice

Verse 1, 4
Phrase 1. *Im-ba-bu-ra de mi vi-da,*
eem-bah-boo-rah deh mee vee-dah,

2. *tú se-rás la pre-fe-ri-da,*
too seh-rahs lah preh-feh-ree-dah,

3. *por-que_a to-das das al-ber-gue*
pohr-keh_ah toh-dahs dahs ahl-behr-geh

4. *co-mo si fue-ran tus hi-jos.*
koh-moh see fweh-rahn toos ee-hohs.

Verse 2
Phrase 1. *To-dos los e-cua-to-ria-nos*
toh-dohs lohs eh-kwah-toh-ree_yah-nohs

2. *te de-di-ca-mos can-cio-nes,*
teh deh-dee-kah-mohs kahn-see_oh-nehs,

3. *pa-ra tus her-mo-sos la-gos,*
pah-rah toos ehr-moh-sohs lah-gohs,

4. *que nos brin-dan sus ha-la-gos.*
keh nohs breen-dahn soos ah-lah-gohs.

Verse 3
Phrase 1. *De mi co-ra-zón la due-ña*
deh mee koh-rah-sohn lah dweh-nyah

2. *has de ser, Im-ba-bu-re-ña,*
ahs deh sehr, eem-bah-boo-reh-nyah,

3. *por-que yo_ad-mi-ro tus pren-das,*
pohr-keh djoh_ah-dmee-roh toos prehn-dahs,

4. *tus mu-jé-res y tus flo-res.*
toos moo-heh-rehs ee toos floh-rrehs.

Translation

Imbabura of my life, you will be my favorite,
Because you give refuge to all as if they are your children.
We Ecuadorians dedicate songs to you
For your beautiful lakes, that offer us delights.
Imbabureña, you will be the owner of my heart,
Because I admire your jewels, your women, and your flowers.

Viva Jujuy, p. 228 CD 11–14
Folk Song from Argentina

Pronunciation Practice

Phrase 1. *Vi-va Ju-juy, viva la puna,*
vee-vah hoo-hoo-ee, vee-vah lah poo-nah,

2. *Viva mi a-ma-da.*
vee-vah mee ah-mah-dah.

3. *Vi-van los ce-rros*
vee-vahn lohs seh-rrohs

4. *pin-ta-rra-jea-dos*
peen-tah-rah-he_ah-dohs

5. *De mi que-bra-da.*
deh mee keh-brah-dah.

6. *De mi que-bra-da*
deh mee keh-brah-dah

7. *Hu-ma-hua-que-ña.*
hoo-mah-hwah-keh-nyah.

8. *No te se-pa-res*
noh teh seh-pah-rehs

9. *De mis a-mo-res*
deh mees ah-moh-rehs

10. *Tu_e-res mi due-ña.*
too_eh-rehs mee dweh-nyah.

Translation
Long live Jujuy, long live the puna,*
Long live my beloved one.
Long live the double hills
Of my canyon.
Of my Humahuaca canyon.
Don't get far from my love,
You are my owner.

Puna—highland

¡Qué bonita bandera! (What a Beautiful Banner!), p. 294 CD 13–23, 24

Folk Song from Puerto Rico

Pronunciation Practice

Verse 1

Phrase 1. *A-zul, blan-ca y co-lo-ra-da,*
ah-sool, blahn-kah ee koh-loh-rah-dah,

2. *y en el me-dio tie-ne un es-tre-lla.*
yen ehl meh-dyoh tyeh-neh_oon ehs-treh-jah.

3. *Bo-ni-ta, se-ñor-es,*
boh-nee-tah, seh-nyohr-ehs,

4. *es la ban-de-ra Puer-to-ri-que-ña.*
ehs lah bahn-deh-rah pwehr-toh-ree-keh-nyah.

Refrain

Phrase 1. *¡Qué bo-ni-ta ban-de-ra!*
keh boh-nee-tah bahn-deh-rah!

2. *¡Qué bo-ni-ta ban-de-ra!*
keh boh-nee-tah bahn-deh-rah!

3. *¡Qué bo-ni-ta ban-de-ra*
keh boh-nee-tah bahn-deh-rah

4. *es la ban-de-ra Puer-to-ri-que-ña!*
ehs lah bahn-deh-rah pwehr-toh-ree-keh-nyah!

5. *¡Qué bo-ni-ta ban-de-ra!*
keh boh-nee-tah bahn-deh-rah!

6. *¡Qué bo-ni-ta ban-de-ra!*
keh boh-nee-tah bahn-deh-rah!

7. *¡Qué bo-ni-ta ban-de-ra*
keh boh-nee-tah bahn-deh-rah

8. *es la ban-de-ra Puer-to-ri-que-ña!*
ehs lah bahn-deh-rah pwehr-toh-ree-keh-nyah!

Translation

Verse
Blue, white and red,
And in the middle there's a star.
Pretty, gentlemen,
Is the Puerto Rican flag.

Refrain
What a pretty flag! (Repeat once.)
What a pretty flag is the Puerto Rican flag!

Ah ya Zane (Zane from Abedeen), p. 297 CD 13–29

Arabic Folk Song

Pronunciation Practice

Phrase 1. *Ah ya Zane,*
ah yah zeen,

2. *Ah ya Zane,*
ah yah zeen,

3. *Ah ya Zane el A-be-deen*
ah yah zeen ehl ah-bee-deen

4. *Ya ward,*
yah wahrd,

5. *Ya ward-im-fet-tah,*
yah wahrd-ihm-feht-tah,

6. *bay-nil-ba-sa-teen.*
bee-neel-beh-seh-teen.

Translation

Ah thou rose, ah thou rarest flower 'midst the garden seen.
Ah, sleep, ah sleep, ah sleep had fled my eyes,
As when, as when my loved one had forsaken me.
And thou and thou, who stand to judge and blame,
The cup, the cup of sorrow no more can I drain.
One day one day in a garden fair I saw,
A gazelle, whose eyes of dark black did my soul enthrall.

Tzena, tzena, p. 298 CD 13–34, 35
Music by Issachar Miron; Hebrew Words by Yehlel Haggiz
Arabic Words by Salman Natour

Pronunciation Practice

Verse 1   **Hebrew:**
Phrase 1. *Tze-na, tze-na, tze-na, tze-na,*
tzehn-nah, tzehn-nah, tzehn-nah, tzehn-nah,

2. *ha-ba-not ur-e-na*
hah-bah-naht oor-ee-nah

3. *cha-ve-rim ba-im la-ir.*
hkhah-vah-reem bah-eem lah-eerr.

4. *Al-na, al-na, al-na, al-na,*
ahl-nah, ahl-nah, ahl-nah, ahl-nah,

5. *al-na teet-cha-be-na*
ahl-nah teet-hkhah-beh-nah

6. *u-miz-mor yach-dav na-shir.*
oo-meez-mohr yahkh-dahv nah-sheerr.

Verse 2
Phrase 1. *Tze-na, tze-na, ha-ba-not ur-e-na*
tzehn-nah, tzehn-nah, hah-bah-naht oor-ee-nah

2. *cha-ve-rim ba-im la-ir.*
hkhah-vah-reem bah-eem lah-eerr.

3. *Al-na, al-na, al-na, teet-cha-be-na*
ahl-nah, ahl-nah, ahl-nah, teet-hkhah-beh-nah

4. *u-miz-mor yach-dav na-shir.*
oo-meez-mohr yahkh-dahv nah-sheerr.

Verse 3
Phrase 1. *Tze-na, tze-na, tze-na, tze-na, tze-na,*
tzehn-nah, tzehn-nah, tzehn-nah, tzehn-nah,
tzehn-nah,

2. *Tze-na, tze-na, tze-na, tze-na, tze-na,*
tzehn-nah, tzehn-nah, tzehn-nah, tzehn-nah,
tzehn-nah,

3. *Tze-na, tze-na, tze-na, tze-na, tze-na,*
tzehn-nah, tzehn-nah, tzehn-nah, tzehn-nah,
tzehn-nah,

4. *Tze-na, tze-na, tze-na, tze-na, tze-na,*
tzehn-nah, tzehn-nah, tzehn-nah, tzehn-nah,
tzehn-nah,

5. *Tze-na!*
tzehn-nah!

Verse 1   **Arabic:**
Phrase 1. *Zei-na, zei-na, zei-na, zei-na,*
zee-nah, zee-nah, zee-nah, zee-nah,

2. *Ma-had yuw-kaf bei-ni w'be-na*
mah-hahd yoo-awf beh-nyoo beh-nah

3. *b'lel let t'wa-ad na.*
blee lee twah-ahdt nah.

4. *Yal-la ma'a-na ma'a-na yal-la*
yuh-lah mah-nah mah-nah yuh-lah

5. *Nyd-buk deb-ka nur-kus ho-ra*
need-book dahp-kih noor-oos hoh-rrah

6. *ma-as ad na.*
mah-uhs ahdt nah.

Verse 2
Phrase 1. *Zei-na, zei-na,*
zee-nah, zee-nah,

2. *Yal-la ghan-nu ma'a-na*
yuh-lah kuhn-noo mah-nah

3. *ah-lan bi-kom ya-as-ha-ab*
ah-hlahn bih-kohm yuh-ahs-hah-ahb

4. *Zei-na, zei-na,*
zee-nah, zee-nah,

5. *Yal-la rud-du ma'a-na*
yuh-lah roodt-doo mah-nah

6. *yal-la ya kul lell ah bab*
yuh-lah yuh kool lehl_ah(H) bahb

Verse 3
Phrase 1. *Zei-na, zei-na,*
zee-nah, zee-nah,

2. *Nur-kus ho-ra*
noorr-oos hoh-rrah

3. *nyd-buk deb-ka yal-la*
need-book dahp-kih yuh-lah

4. *hu-bi ad u'-ma ba-ad-na*
hoo-beh ahd oo-ma bah-hahd-nah

5. *Zei-na, zei-na ghan-nu ma'a-na*
zee-nah, zee-nah kahn-noo mah-nah

6. *ghan-nu ma'a-na, ghan-nu*
kahn-noo mah-nah, kahn-noo

7. *Zei-na, zei-na, zei-na!*
zee-nah, zee-nah, zee-nah!

Translation

Traditional Verse
Daughters, go forth and see the pioneers in the colony.
Do not shirk toil and labor.

Hebrew Words of Yehlel Haggiz
Go out,
Young girls, and see friends coming to the city.
Don't hide, and a song together we will sing.

El carite (The Kingfish), p. 305 CD 14–9

Folk Song from Venezuela

Pronunciation Practice

Verse

Phrase
1. *A-yer sa-lió*
   ah-yehrr sah-lee_oh

2. *la lan-cha Nue-va_Es-par-ta.*
   lah lahn-chah noo_eh-vah_ehs-pahrr-tah.

3. *Sa-lió con-fia-da*
   sah-lee_oh kohn-fee-ah-dah

4. *a re-co-rrer los ma-res.*
   ah rreh-koh-rrehr lohs mah-rrehs.

5. *En-con-tró_un pez*
   ehn kohn-troh_oon pehz

6. *de fuer-zas muy li-je-ro.*
   deh foo_ehr-sahs moo-ee lee-hehr-rroh.

7. *Que_a-ga-rra los an-zue-los*
   keh_ah-gah-rrah lohs ahn-soo_eh-lohs

8. *y re-vien-ta los gua-ra-les.*
   ee reh-vee_ehn-tah lohs gwah-rrah-lehs.

Refrain
1. *Co-mo la cos-ta_es bo-ni-ta,*
   koh-moh lah kohs-tah_ehs boh-nee-tah,

2. *Yo me ven-go di-vir-tien-do;*
   joh meh vehn-goh dee-veerr-tee_ehn-doh;

3. *Pe-ro me vie-ne si-guien-do*
   peh-rroh meh vee_eh-neh see-gee-ehn-doh

4. *de fue-ra_u-na pi-ra-gui-ta.*
   deh foo_eh-rrah_oo-nah pee-rrah-gwee-tah.

Translation

The Nueva Esparta boat went out yesterday.

It when out confident to travel over the seas.

It found a fish of quick strength that grabs the fish hooks and smashes the crates

Because the coast is pretty I have been having fun

But there has been a canoe following me from outside.

Se va el caimán (The Alligator), p. 306 CD 14–13

Dance Song from Colombia

Pronunciation Practice

Verse 1

Phrase
1. *Voy a_em-pe-zar mi re-la-to*
   voh_ee ah_ehm-peh-zahr mee reh-lah-toh

2. *con a-le-gría_y con a-fán,*
   kohn ah-leh-gree_ah_ee kohn ah-fahn,

3. *Voy a_em-pe-zar mi re-la-to*
   voh_ee ah_ehm-peh-zahr mee reh-lah-toh

4. *con a-le-gría_y con a-fán,*
   kohn ah-leh-gree_ah_ee kohn ah-fahn,

5. *Por el rí-o Mag-da-le-na*
   pohr ehl ree-oh mahg-dah-leh-nah

6. *se_vol-vió_un hom-bre cai-mán,*
   seh_vohl-vee_oh_nohm-breh kah_ee-mahn,

7. *Por el rí-o Mag-da-le-na*
   pohr ehl ree-oh mahg-dah-leh-nah

8. *se_vol-vió_un hombre cai-mán.*
   seh_vohl-vee_oh_ nohm-breh kah_ee-mahn.

Se va el caimán (The Alligator), p. 306 CD 14–13 (continued)

Pronunciation Practice

Refrain
Phrase 1. *Se va͜el cai-mán, Se va͜el cai-mán,*
seh vah͜ehl kah͜ee-mahn, seh vah͜ehl kah͜ee-mahn,

2. *Se va pa-ra Ba-rran-qui-lla,*
seh vah pah-rah bah-rrahn-kee-djah,

3. *Se va͜el cai-mán, Se va͜el cai-mán,*
seh vah͜ehl kah͜ee-mahn, seh vah͜ehl kah͜ee-mahn,

4. *Se va pa-ra Ba-rran-qui-lla.*
seh vah pah-rah bah-rrahn-kee-djah.

5. *Se va͜el cai-mán, Se va͜el cai-mán,*
seh vah͜ehl kah͜ee-mahn, seh vah͜ehl kah͜ee-mahn,

6. *Se va pa-ra Ba-rran-qui-lla,*
seh vah pah-rah bah-rrahn-kee-djah,

7. *Se va͜el cai-mán, Se va͜el cai-mán,*
seh vah͜ehl kah͜ee-mahn, seh vah͜ehl kah͜ee-mahn,

8. *Se va pa-ra Ba-rran-qui-lla.*
seh vah pah-rah bah-rrahn-kee-djah.

Verse 2
Phrase 1. *Lo que co-me͜es-te cai-mán*
loh keh koh-meh͜ehs-teh kah͜ee-mahn

2. *yo le ten-go͜ad-mi-ra-ción,*
yoh leh tehn-goh͜ahd-mih-rah-see͜yohn,

3. *Lo que co-me͜es-te cai-mán*
loh keh koh-meh͜ehs-teh kah͜ee-mahn

4. *yo le ten-go͜ad-mi-ra-ción,*
yoh leh tehn-goh͜ahd-mih-rah-see͜yohn,

5. *Co-me que-so͜y co-me pan*
koh-meh keh-soh͜ee koh-meh pahn

6. *con re-fre-scos͜de li-món,*
kohn reh-freh-skohs͜deh lee-mohn,

7. *Co-me que-so͜y co-me pan*
koh-meh keh-soh͜ee koh-meh pahn

8. *con re-fre-scos͜de li-món.*
kohn reh-freh-skohs͜deh lee-mohn.

Verse 3
Phrase 1. *Al o-tro la-do del rí-o*
ahl oh-troh lah-doh dehl ree-oh

2. *pes-car-on u-na mo-ja-rra,*
pehs-kah-rohn oo-nah moh-hah-rrah,

3. *Al o-tro la-do del río*
ahl oh-troh lah-doh dehl ree-oh

4. *pes-car-on u-na mo-ja-rra.*
pehs-kah-rohn oo-nah moh-hah-rrah.

5. *Y del bu-che le sa-car-on*
ee dehl boo-cheh leh sah-kah-rohn

6. *él͜que to-ca la gui-ta-rra,*
eh͜keh toh-kah lah gee-tah-rrah,

7. *Y del buche le sa-car-on*
ee dehl boo-cheh leh sah-kah-rohn

8. *él͜que to-ca la gui-ta-rra.*
ehl͜keh toh-kah lah gee-tah-rrah.

Refrain

Translation

I'll start telling my story with gladness and enthusiasm.
On the Magdalena river a man turned into a cayman.
What this cayman eats is surprising:
He eats cheese and bread with cold lemon drinks.
There the cayman goes, there the cayman goes.
He is leaving for Barranquilla.
There the cayman goes, there the cayman goes.
He is leaving for Barranquilla.
On the other side of the river
They fished a *moharra*,
And from its belly they
Removed the guitarist.

Bantama kra kro, p. 308 CD 14–17, 18

Song from the Akan People of Ghana

Pronunciation Practice

Melody

Phrase 1. *Ban-ta-ma kra kro,*
bahn-tah-mah krah kraw,

2. *meh yeh den na m'an-ya*
meh yeh dehn yah mahn-yah

3. *bi ma-dzi*
bee mehd-zee

4. *Kra kro deh deh iyi*
krah kraw deh deh yih

5. *meh yeh den na m'an-ya*
meh yeh dehn yah mahn-yah

6. *bi ma-dzi*
bee mehd-zee

7. *Kra kro kra kro,*
krah kraw krah kraw,

8. *meh yeh den na m'an-ya*
meh yeh dehn yah mahn-yah

9. *bi ma-dzi*
bee mehd-zee

10. *me nyi si-ka*
meh nyee see-kah

11. *meh yeh den na m'an-ya*
meh yeh dehn yah mahn-yah

12. *bi ma-dzi.*
bee mehd-zee.

Translation

Bantam cookie.
How can I afford one to eat?
Cookie sweet, sweet.
How can I get some to eat?
Cookie, cookie. How can I get some to eat?
I don't have money, so how can I get some to eat?

Yüe liang wan wan (Crescent Moon), p. 314 CD 14–26

Folk Song from China

Pronunciation Practice

Phrase 1. *Pao ma liu liu di shan shang*
pah‿oh mah lee-oh dee shahn shahng

2. *Yi duo liu liu di yün yo*
ee dwaw lee-oh lee-oh dee yeen yaw

3. *Duan duan liu liu dee zhao zai*
doh-ahn doh-ahn lee-oh dee dzah-oh dzah‿ee

4. *Kang ding liu liu cheng yo*
kahng deeng lee-oh lee-oh dee chung yoh

5. *Yüe liang wan wan*
yew-eh lee-ahng wahn wahn

6. *kang ding liu liu di cheng yo*
kahng deeng lee-oh lee-oh dee chuhng yoh

Translation

Above the Paoma Mountain floats a cloud,
The crescent moon is shining on Kangding City,
Oh, the crescent moon,
Oh, Kangding City.

Lahk gei mohlee, p. 317 CD 14–31

Folk Song from Taiwan; Adapted by Rebecca Schwann

Pronunciation Practice

Phrase 1. *Lahk gei moh lee*
   lahk geh-ee moh lee

2. *jeen jee-ahn shwee,*
   jeen jee-ahn shwee,

3. *Long goon sheen jway lee go*
   lawng goon sheen jwah-ee lee goh

4. *jeen go jwee.*
   jeen goh jwee.

5. *Hoh hway lahn dee*
   hoh hweh lahn dee

6. *sheen shiong dwee,*
   sheen shee⌣ahng dwee,

7. *Sheen bean nah moh new-ah lee-goh*
   sheen been nah moh noo-ah lee-goh

8. *shiong keh kwee.*
   shee⌣ahng keh kwee.

Translation

June jasmine is really beautiful,
Watching you makes me very happy,
It's hard for a nice flower to find her match,
Without you beside me makes me very sad.

Choi hát bội (The Theater Game), p. 318 CD 14–35

Traditional Song from Vietnam; Collected by Phong Nguyen

Pronunciation Practice

Phrase 1. *Rủ nhau ra đám*
   roo now rah dahm

2. *kìa mú u*
   kee-ah moo oo

3. *kìa mú u kìa nọ mú u.*
   kee-ah moo oo kee-ah noo moo oo.

4. *Cha kêu mẹ hú*
   chah keh⌣oo meh ah⌣oo

5. *mầy còn ngủ tao còn ngủ*
   mah⌣ee kawn noo tou kawn noo

6. *trống lịnh đánh hát bội đó*
   trahng lee(n) duh(n) haht boh⌣ee duh

7. *thừc rồi còn ngồi đây*
   too⌣kuh raw⌣ee kawn (n)gaw⌣ee deh⌣ee

8. *sao chẳng đi coi họ hát chơi.*
   shah-ow chahng dee kaw⌣ee haw haht chaw⌣ee.

Translation

Get up. Let's go to the grove of *mu u* trees.
Father and mother wake us up. Don't sleep too long!
Don't you hear the drum?
It signals that the *hát bôi* theater game is about to begin.
Get up! Let's go there to see the play. It's fun.

Ragupati Ragava Raja Ram, p. 321 CD 15–4

Traditional Hindu Song

Pronunciation Practice

Refrain

Phrase 1. *Ra-gu-pa-ti ra-ga-va*
rah-goo-pah-tee rah-gah-vah

2. *ra-ja Ram*
rah-jah rahm

3. *Pa-ti-ta pa-va-na*
pah-tee-tah pah-vah-nah

4. *Si-ta Ram.*
see-tah rahm.

Verse 1

Phrase 1. *Si-ta Ram jai*
see-tah rahm jah‿ee

2. *Si-ta Ram,*
see-tah rahm,

3. *Pa-ti-ta pa-va-na*
pah-tee-tah pah-vah-nah

4. *Si-ta Ram.*
see-tah rahm.

Verse 2

Phrase 1. *Ish-ware Al-lah*
ee‿eesh-wehr ah-lah

2. *te-re nam,*
teh-reh nahm,

3. *Sub-ko sun-mut-ti*
sah-buh-koh suhn-muh-tee

4. *de bha-ga-wan.*
deh bah-gah-vahn.

Translation

Oh Lord, Oh King Ram, you are supreme.
Oh God (Sita & Ram), purify the sinner.
We pray, Sita Ram, we pray, Sita Ram;
Your name is the same; it can be called God or Allah.
Oh God (Sita & Ram), shall purify [the] sinner.
Oh God Ram, give good wisdom to every one.

La Jesusita, p. 322 CD 15–8

Folk Song from Mexico

Pronunciation Practice

Verse

Phrase 1. *Va-mos al bai-le‿y ve-rás que bo-ni-to*
vah-mohs ahl bah‿ee-leh‿ee veh-rahs keh boh-nee-toh

2. *Don-de se‿a-lum-bran con vein-te lin-ter-nas,*
dohn-deh seh‿ah-loom-brahn kohn vehn-teh leen-tehr-nahs,

3. *Don-de se bai-lan las dan-zas mo-der-nas,*
dohn-deh seh bah‿ee-lahn lahs dahn-sahs moh-dehr-nahs,

4. *Don-de se bai-la de mu-cho va-ci-lón.*
dohn-deh seh bah‿ee-lah deh moo-choh vah-see-lohn.

Refrain

Phrase 1. *Y quié-re-me, Je-su-si-ta,*
ee kyeh-reh-meh, heh-soo-see-tah,

2. *Y quié-re-me, por fa-vor;*
ee kyeh-reh-meh, pohr fah-vohr;

3. *Y mi-ra que soy tu‿a-man-te*
ee mee-rah keh soh‿ee too-ah-mahn-teh

4. *Y se-gu-ro ser-vi-dor.*
ee seh-goo-roh sehr-vee-dohr.

Translation

Verse Let's go and dance, and you will see how nice it is.
Where twenty lanterns give off light,
Where they dance the modern dances;
Where they dance, swinging and swaying, having a good time.

Refrain And love me, Jesusita, and please love me.
Look that I am your loved one and your faithful servant.

Canción Mixteca (Mixteca Song), **p. 326 CD 15–14,15**

Words and Music by José Lopez Alavés

Pronunciation Practice

Melody & Harmony

Phrase 1. *!Que le-jos es-toy*
keh leh-hos ehs-toh_ee

2. *del sue-lo don-de_he na-ci-do!*
dehl sweh-loh dohn-deh nah-see-thoh!

3. *In-men-sa nos-tal-gia_in-va-de*
een-mehn-sah noh-stahl-hyah_een-vah-theh

4. *mi pen-sa-mien-to!*
mee pehn-sah-myehn-toh!

5. *Y_al ver-me tan so-lo_y tris-te*
yahl vehr-meh tahn soh-loh_ee tree-steh

6. *cual ho-ja_al vien-to,*
kwahl oh-hahl vyehn-toh,

7. *qui-sie-ra llo-rar,*
kee-syeh-rah djoh-rahr

8. *qui-sie-ra mo-rir de sen-ti-mien-to.*
kee-syeh-rah moh-reer deh sehn-tee-myehn-toh.

9. *!Oh tie-rra del sol!*
oh tyeh-rrah dehl sohl!

10. *Sus-pi-ro por ver-te*
Soo-spee-roh pohrr vehr-teh

11. *a-ho-ra que le-jos*
ah-oh-rah keh leh-hohs

12. *yo vi-vo sin luz sin a-mor.*
yoh vee-voh seen loos seen ah-mohr.

13. *Y_al ver-me tan so-lo_y tris-te*
yahl vehr-meh tahn soh-loh_ee tree-steh

14. *cual ho-ja_al vien-to,*
kwahl oh-hahl vyehn-toh,

15. *qui-sie-ra llo-rar,*
kee-syeh-rah djoh-rahr

16. *qui-sie-ra mo-rir de sen-ti-mien-to.*
kee-syeh-rah moh-reer deh sehn-tee-myehn-toh.

Translation

How far I am from the ground where I was born,
Immense nostalgia invades my thought,
And upon seeing myself so lonely and sad like a leaf in the wind,
I would like to cry, I would like to die of feeling.
Oh, land of the sun,
I breathe to see you now, how far away I live without light, without love,
And upon seeing myself so lonely and sad like a leaf in the wind,
I would like to cry, I would like to die of feeling.

Río, río (River, River), p. 371 CD 17–10, 11

Traditional Song from Chile

Pronunciation Practice

Melody & Harmony

Phrase 1. *Qué gran-de que vie-ne␣el rí-o,*
keh grahn-deh keh vyehn-ehl ree-oh,

2. *qué gran-de se va␣a la mar.*
keh grahn-deh seh vah lah mahr.

3. *Si lo␣au-men-ta␣el llan-to mí-o,*
see loh␣ah␣oo-mehn-tah-ehl yahn-toh mee-oh,

4. *co-mo gran-de no␣ha de␣es-tar.*
koh-moh grahn-deh noh␣ah dehs-tahr.

5. *Si lo␣au-men-ta␣el llan-to mí-o,*
see loh␣ah␣oo-mehn-tah-ehl yahn-toh mee-oh,

6. *co-mo gran-de no␣ha de␣es-tar.*
koh-moh grahn-deh noh␣ah dehs-tahr.

7. *Rí-o, rí-o, rí-o, rí-o,*
ree-yoh, ree-yoh, ree-yoh, ree-yoh,

8. *de-vol-ved-me␣el a-mor mí-o.*
deh-vohl-vehd mehl ah-mohr mee-oh.

9. *De-vol-ved-me␣el a-mor mí-o*
deh-vohl-vehd mehl ah-mohr mee-oh

10. *que me can-so de llo-rar.*
keh meh kahn-soh deh yoh-rahr.

Translation

How big comes the river,
How big it goes to the sea.

If my tears add to it,
How big it then would be.
If my tears add to it,
How big it then would be.

River, river, river, river,
Return my love to me.
Return my love to me
Because I am getting tired of crying.

Zum gali gali, p. 401 CD 18–16

Folk Song from Israel

Pronunciation Practice

Refrain

Phrase 1. *Zum ga-li, ga-li, ga-li,*
zoom gah-lee, gah-lee, gah-lee,

2. *zum ga-li, ga-li,*
zoom gah-lee, gah-lee,

3. *Zum ga-li, ga-li, ga-li, zum ga-li, ga-li.*
zoom gah-lee, gah-lee, gah-lee, zoom gah-lee,
gah-lee.

Verse 1

Phrase 1. *He-cha-lutz le 'man a-vo-dah;*
heh-khah-loots luh-mahn ah-voh-dah;

2. *A-vo-dah le 'man he-cha-lutz.*
ah-voh-dah luh-mahn heh-khah-loots.

3. *A-vo-dah le 'man he-cha-lutz.*
ah-voh-dah luh-mahn heh-khah-loots.

4. *He-cha-lutz le 'man a-vo-dah.*
heh-khah-loots luh-mahn ah-voh-dah.

Verse 2

Phrase 1. *He-cha-lutz le 'man ha b'tu-lah;*
heh-khah-loots luh-mahn hahb-too-lah;

2. *Ha-b'tu-lah le 'man he-cha-lutz;*
hahb-too-lah luh-mahn heh-khah-loots;

3. *Ha-sha-lom le 'man ha'a-mim;*
hah-shah-lohm luh-mahn hah-ah-meem;

4. *Ha'-a-mim le 'man ha-sha-lom.*
hah-ah-meem luh-mahn hah-shah-lohm.

Translation

Refrain   Zum gali, gali, gali, zum, gali, gali...*

Verse 1   The pioneer is meant for work; work is meant
for the pioneer.

zum gali, gali — These words have no meaning.

O, Desayo, p. 411 CD 18–24

Folk Song from Angola

Pronunciation Practice

Phrase 1. *O, Des-ay-o!*
oh, deh-sI-yoh!

2. *O, Des-ay-o!*
oh, deh-sI-yoh!

3. *O, Des-ay-o! Me-ni-na,**
oh, deh-sI-yoh! meh-nee-nah,

4. *O, Des-ay-o!*
oh, deh-sI-yoh!

Translation

"O Desayo" offers a greeting to one another.

The word *menina** is a diminuitive, meaning "little girl."

Uno, dos, y tres (One, Two, and Three), p. 427 CD 19–4, 5

Words and Music by Rafael Ortiz

Pronunciation Practice

Phrase 1. *Al tam-bor ma-yor de͜a-lan-te*
ahl tahm-bohr mah͜yohr deh-ah- lahn-teh

2. *no͜hay qui-en lo pue-da͜i-gua-lar*
noh͜ah ee kee-ehn loh pweh-dah͜ee-gwah-lahr

3. *con su rit-mo fas-ci-nán-te*
kohn soo reet-moh fah-see-nahn-teh

4. *de mi Cu-ba tro-pi-cal.*
deh mee koo-bah troh-pee-kahl.

5. *Cuen-ten los pa-sos*
kwehn-tehn lohs pah-sohs

6. *que͜a-quí lle-ga-mos.*
keh͜ah-kee djeh-gah-mohs.

7. *U-no, dos, y tres*
oo-noh, dohs, ee trehs

8. *que pa-so más ché-ve-re,*
keh pah-soh mahs cheh-veh-reh,

9. *qué pa-so más ché-ve-re,*
keh pah-soh mahs cheh-veh-reh,

10. *el de mi con-ga es,*
ehl deh mee kohn-gah ehs,

11. *el de mi con-ga es, el de mi con-ga es.*
ehl deh mee kohn-gah ehs, ehl deh mee kohn-gah ehs.

Translation

One, two, and three!
There is no one who can equal the drum major,
With his fascinating rhythm from my tropical Cuba.
Count the steps as we arrive.
One, two, three! what better step!
What better step than that of my conga, of my conga, of
my conga!

Hine mah tov, p. 431 CD 19–8

Hebrew Folk Song

Pronunciation Practice

Phrase 1. *Hi-ne mah tov*
hee-neh mah tohv

2. *u-mah na-'im*
oo-mah nah-eem

3. *she-vet a-chim*
sheh-veht ah-hkheem

4. *gam ya-chad!*
gahm yah-hkhahd!

5. *Hi-ne mah tov u-mah na-'im*
hee-neh mah tohv ooh-mah nah-eem

6. *she-vet a-chim gam ya-chad!*
sheh-veht ah-hkheem gahm yah-hkhahd!

Translation

How good and pleasant it is for "brothers" to dwell together
in unity!

Ríu, ríu, chíu, p. 435 CD 19–11

Sixteenth Century Carol from Spain

Pronunciation Practice

Phrase 1. *Rí-u, rí-u chí-u*
rree-oo rree-oo chee-oo

2. *la guar-da ri-be-ra,*
lah gwahr-dah ree-beh-rrah,

3. *Dios guar-do el lo-bo*
dee͜ohs gwahr-doh ehl loh-boh

4. *de nues-tra cor-de ra.*
deh noo͜ehs-trrah kor-deh rrah.

Translation

Ríu, ríu, chíu protected it,
God protected our lamb from the fox.

'Ūlili E, p. 441 CD 19–15

Traditional Song from Hawaii

Pronunciation Practice

Verse 1

Phrase 1. *Ho-ne a-na ko le-o*
hoh-neh ah-nah koh leh-oh

2. *e 'ū-li-li e*
eh oo-lee-lee eh

3. *E-ka-hi ma-nu*
eh-kah-hee mah-noo

4. *no-ho a-'e kai*
noh-hoh ah-eh kah‿ee

5. *Ki-ā-'i ma ka lae*
kee-ah-ee mah kah lah-eh

6. *o Ke-ka-ha*
oh keh-kah-hah

7. *'O-i-a kai u-a*
oh-ee-ah kah‿ee oo-ah

8. *la-na ma-li-e.*
lah-nah mah-lee-eh.

9. *'Ū-li-li e,*
oo-lee-lee eh,

Vocal Part 2 and Melody
(Vocal Part 2)

Phrase 1. *'A-ha-ha-na 'ū-li-li 'e-he-he-ne*
ah-hah-hah-nah ee-lee-lee
eh-heh-heh-neh

2. *'ū-li-li 'a-ha-ha-na*
oo-lee-lee ah-hah-hah-nah

(Melody)

3. *'Ū-li-li ho-'i*
oo-lee-lee hoh-ee

4. *'E-he-he-ne 'ū-li-li 'a-ha-ha-na*
eh-heh-heh-neh oo-lee-lee
ah-hah-hah-nah

5. *'ū-li-li 'e-he-he-ne*
oo-lee-lee eh-heh-heh-neh

6. *'Ū-li-li 'Ū-li-li*
oo-lee-lee oo-lee-lee

7. *ho-lo ho-lo ka-ha-kai e,*
hoh-loh hoh-loh
kah-hah-kah‿ee eh,

8. *'O-i-a kai u-a*
oh-ee-ah kah‿ee oo-ah

9. *la-na mā-li-e*
lah-nah mah-lee-eh

10. *'Ū-li-li e,*
oo-lee-lee eh,

Vocal Part 3 and Melody
(Vocal Part 3)

Phrase 1. *'A-ha-ha-na 'ū-li-li 'e-he-he-ne*
ah-hah-hah-nah ee-lee-lee
eh-heh-heh-neh

2. *'ū-li-li 'a-ha-ha-na*
oo-lee-lee ah-hah-hah-nah

(Melody)

3. *'Ū-li-li ho-'i*
oo-lee-lee hoh-ee

(Vocal Part 3)

4. *'E-he-he-ne 'ū-li-li 'a-ha-ha-na*
eh-heh-heh-neh oo-lee-lee
ah-hah-hah-nah

5. *'ū-li-li 'e-he-he-ne*
oo-lee-lee eh-heh-heh-neh

6. *'Ū-li-li 'Ū-li-li*
oo-lee-lee oo-lee-lee

7. *ho-lo ho-lo ka-ha-kai e,*
hoh-loh hoh-loh
kah-hah-kah‿ee eh,

8. *'O-i-a kai u-a*
oh-ee-ah kah‿ee oo-ah

9. *la-na mā-li-e*
lah-nah mah-lee-eh

10. *'ū-li-li e,*
oo-lee-lee eh,

Verse 2

Phrase 1. *Ho-ne a-na kō le-o*
hoh-neh ah-nah koh leh-oh

2. *e kō-le-a e*
eh koh-leh-ah eh

3. *Pe-he-a 'o Ka-hi-ki?*
peh-heh-ah oh kah-hee-kee?

4. *Mai-ka 'i no.*
mah‿ee-kah ee noh.

5. *'O-i-a 'āi-na*
oh-ee-ah ah‿yee-nah

6. *u-lu-we-hi-we-hi*
oo-loo-veh-hee-veh-hee

7. *I hu-i pū- 'i-a*
ee hoo-ee poh ee-ah

8. *me ke o nao-na.*
meh keh oh nah‿oo-nah.

*'Ūlili E, p. 441 CD 19–15 (continued)

Translation

So sweet is your call, oh sandpiper!
Numerous residents by the sea shore,
A guardian along the peninsula at Kekaha*
With the sea's calm serenity.
Oh sandpiper, calling tra-la-la, tra-la-la,
Oh yes Sandpiper, calling rea-la-la, tra-la-la
Sandpiper running along the shore
With the sea's calm serenity,
So sweet is your call, of plover
"How was the journey?" "very fine!"

It is a lane green and lush
"Filled with a fragrance sweet to me."

*'Ūlili is a sandpiper bird that lives along the shore and run up and down along the sand.
*Kekaha is a district of the island of Hawaii near Hilo.
*Kolea is the golden plover, a migrating bird who summers in Alaska and winters in Hawaii.

Quâ câu gió bay (The Wind on the Bridge), p. 460 CD 20–4

Folk Song from Vietnam

Pronunciation Practice

Verse 1
Phrase 1. *Yêu nhau cở-i áo ý-a cho nhau.*
     ee_ew nyah_oo koh-ee ow ee_ah tchoh nyah_oo.
    2. *Về nhà dối rằng cha dối mẹ a ý_a.*
     veh nyah zoh_ee zuhng tchah zoh_ee meh_eh ah ee_ah.
    3. *Rằng a ý_a qua câù. Rằng a ý_a qua câù.*
     zuhng ah ee_ah kwah kuh_oh. zuhng ah ee_ah kwah kuh_oh.

Refrain
Phrase 1. *Tình tình tình gió bay,*
     teen teen teen soh_hoh beh_ee,
    2. *Tình tình tình gió bay.*
     teen teen teen soh_hoh beh_ee.

Verse 2
Phrase 1. *Yêu nhau cở-i nón y_a cho nhau.*
     ee_ew nyah_oo koh-ee naw(tn)
     ee_ah tchoh nyah_oo.
    2. *Về nhà dối rằng cha dối mẹ a ý_a.*
     veh nyah zoh_ee zuhng tchah zoh_ee meh_eh ah ee_ah.
    3. *Rằng a ý_a qua câù. Rằng a ý_a qua câù.*
     zuhng ah ee ah kwah kuh_oh. zuhng ah ee ah kwah kuh_oh.

Refrain
Phrase 1. *Tình tình tình gió bay,*
     teen teen teen soh_hoh beh_ee,
    2. *Tình tình tình gió bay.*
     teen teen teen soh_hoh beh_ee.

Verse 3
Phrase 1. *Yêu nhau cở-i nhan y_a cho nhau.*
     ee-ew nyah_oo kuhr-ee nyuhr(n)
     ee_ah tchoh nyah_oo.
    2. *Vế nhà dối rằng cha dối mẹ a ý_a.*
     veh nyah zoh-ee zuhng tchah zoh_ee meh_eh ah ee_ah.
    3. *Rằng a ý_a qua câù. Rằng a ý_a qua câù.*
     zuhng ah ee_ah kwah kuh_oh. zuhng ah ee_ah kwah kuh_oh.

Final Refrain
Phrase 1. *Tình tình tình dánh ro-i,*
     teen teen teen dah-(n) zuh-ee,
    Tình tình tình dánh ro-i.
     teen teen teen dah-(n) zuh-ee.

Translation

Verse 1 Loving you, I give you my coat (shirt).
    Coming back home I tell my father and mother,
    "On the bridge, the wind has taken it away."
    Tinh tinh tinh gio bay . . . (The sound of the wind)
Verse 2 Loving you, I give you my hat…
Verse 3 Loving you, I give you my ring.
    Coming back home I tell my father and mother,
    "On the bridge, because of the wind, it has dropped into the river."

Oy, Hanuka (O, Chanukah), p. 464 CD 20–10

Yiddish Folk Song

Pronunciation Practice

Verse 1

Phrase 1. *Oy Ha-nu-ka, Oy Ha-nu-ka, a yom-tov a shey-ner,*
oh_ee khah-nih-keh, oh_ee khah-nih-keh,
ah yuhn-tehv ah sheh_ee-nehrr,

2. *A lu-sti-ker, a frey-le-kher, ni-to nokh a-zoi-ner.*
ah loo-stih-kehr, ah free-leh-kher, nih-toh nohkh
ah-zoh_ee-nehrr.

3. *Al-le nakht in drey-dl shpi-ln mir,*
ah-leh nahkt ihn dreh_ee-duhl shpih-(ln) meerr,

4. *Zu-dik hey-se lat-kes, est on a shir.*
zoo-dihk heh_ee-seh laht-kehs, ehst ohn ah sheerr.

5. *Gesh-vin-der, tsindt kin-der,*
gehsh-vihn-dehr, tsihndt kihn-dehrr,

6. *Dee di-nin-ke likh-te-lekh ohn.*
dee dee-nihn-keh lihkh-teh-lekh ohn.

7. *Zingt "Al Ha-ni-sim," loibt Gott far di ni-sim,*
zih(ng)t ahl hah-nih-suhm, loh_eebt guht fahr dee
nih-suhm,

8. *Un kumt gi-kher tan-tsn in kohn.*
uhn-kuhmt gih-khehr tahn-tsn ihn kohn.

Second Ending

1. *Un kumt gi-kher tan-tsn in kohn.*
uhn-kuhmt gih-khehr tahn-tsn ihn kohn.

Translation

Tonight is Hanukah, the joy of the holiday is unending.
Father will light a candle and will raise his voice in song.
Also the children raise their voices in song loudly,
And Mother bakes holiday pancakes for all.

Chorus Rise up, o flame,
Rise up, o flame, and grow!
Please tell, o candle, about a day of bravery,
About a night of lights in the sanctuary.

Tonight is Hanukah, we will gather here in the room,
We will rejoice and play very tastefully and neatly,
And like the shining Hanukah candles,
About a day of bravery, we will tell in song.

Still, Still, Still (Sleep, Dearest Child), p. 468 CD 20–17

Traditional Carol from Austria

Pronunciation Practice

Verse 1

Phrase 1. *Still, still, still,*
shteel, shteel, shteel,

2. *weils Kind-lein schlaf-en will.*
vI_ehls keend-lah_een shlahf-ehn veel.

3. *Ma-ri-a tut es*
mah-ree-ah toot ehs

4. *nie-der-sing-en,*
nee-dehr-tzeeng-ehn,

5. *sei-ne gro-sse*
tzI_ee-neh kgroh-seh

6. *Lieb dar-bring-en.*
leepb dahr-breeng-ehn.

7. *Still, still, still,*
shteel, shteel, shteel,

8. *weils Kind-lein schla-fen will.*
vI_ehls keend-lah_een shlahf-ehn veel.

Verse 2

Phrase 1. *Schlaf, schlaf, schlaf,*
shlahf, shlahf, shlahf,

2. *mein lie-bes Kind-lein schlaf.*
mI_een lee-behs keend-lah_een shlahf.

3. *Die Eng-el tun schön*
dee ehng-ehl toon shuh(r)n

4. *mu-si-zie-ren*
moo-zee-tzee-rehn

5. *bei dem Kind-lein*
bI_ee dehm keend-ll_een

6. *ju-bi-lie-ren.*
yoo-bee-lee-rehn.

7. *Schlaf, schlaf, schlaf,*
shlahf, shlahf, shlahf,

8. *mein lie-bes Kind-lein schlaf.*
mI_een lee-behs keend-lah_een shlahf.

Still, Still, Still (Sleep, Dearest Child), p. 468 CD 20–17 (continued)

Translation

Silent, silent, silent, because [her] little child wants to sleep.
Maria does it downsing [lull], her big love present
Silent, silent, silent, because [her] little child wants to sleep.

Sleep, sleep, sleep, my dearest little child, sleep.
The angels make beautiful music by the little child that
"brims over" with joy.
Sleep, sleep, sleep, my dearest little child, sleep.

Las Navidades (The Christmas Season), p. 472 CD 20–24

Traditional from Puerto Rico

Pronunciation Practice

Verse 1
Phrase 1. *Por fin lle-ga-ron*
    pohr feen djeh-gah-rrohn

2. *las Na-vi-da-des*
    lahs nah-vee-thah-thehs

3. *las fies-tas rea-les*
    lahs fee‿eh-stahs rreh‿ah-lehs

4. *de nues-tro lar.*
    theh noo‿eh-stroh lahrr.

5. *Fies-ta de to-dos*
    fee‿eh-stah theh toh-thohs

6. *Nues-tros an-he-los,*
    noo‿eh-strohs ahn-eh-lohs,

7. *nues-tros des ve-los, y*
    nues-tro‿a fán.
    noo‿eh-strohs thehs veh-lohs,
    ee noo‿eh-stroh‿ah-fahn.

Verse 2
Phrase 1. *Con tam-bo-ri-les,*
    kohn tahm-bohr-ee-lehs,

2. *güi-ro‿y ma-ra-cas,*
    gwee-rroh‿ee mah-rah-kahs,

3. *mi se-re-na-ta*
    mee seh-reh-nah-tah

4. *a-le-gre va.*
    ah-leh-greh bah.

5. *De-se-o‿a to-dos*
    theh-seh‿oh ah toh-thohs

6. *por des-pe-di-da*
    pohrr theh-speh-thee-thah

7. *a-ños de vi-da‿y fe-li-ci-dad.*
    ah-nyohs theh vee-thah‿ee feh-lee-see-thahth.

Translation

Verse 1 Christmas time
    Has finally arrived,
    The regal parties
    Of our home.
    Party of all of
    Our longing,
    Our sleeplessness,
    And our eagerness.

Verse 2 With little drums,
    Guiro and maracas,
    My serenade
    Happily goes.
    I wish to all
    As a farewell
    Years of life
    And happiness.

El desembre congelat (Cold December), p. 473 CD 20–28

Fifteenth-Century Melody from Catalonia

Pronunciation Practice

Verse 1

Phrase 1. *El de-sem-bre con-ge-lat,*
ahl deh-zehm-breh kohn-djeh-laht,

2. *Con-fós es re-ti-ra.*
kohm-fooz ehs reh-dee-rah.

3. *A-bril de flors co-ro-nat,*
ah-breel deh flohs koh-roo-naht,

4. *Tot el món ad-mi-ra.*
toht ehl mohn aht-mee-rah.

5. *Quan en un jar-dí d'a-mor*
kwahn ehn oon djahr-dee dah-mohr

6. *Neix u-na di-vi-na flor.*
nehsh oo-nuh dee-vee-nah floh.

7. *D'u-na ro ro ro, d'u-na sa sa sa,*
doo-nah rroh rroh rroh, doo-nah sah sah sah,

8. *d'u-na ro, d'u-na sa, d'u-na ro-sa bel-la,*
doo-nah rroh, doo-nah sah, doo-nah rroh-zah beh-yah,

9. *Fe-cun-da_i pon-cel-la.*
fah-koon-deh_ee poon-seh-yah.

Verse 2

Phrase 1. *El pri-mer pa-re caus-à,*
ahl pree-meh pah-reh kow-zah,

2. *La nit te-ne-bro-sa.*
lah neet teh-neh-broh-zah.

3. *Que_a tot el món o-fus-cà*
kuh toht ehl mohn oh-foos-kah

4. *La vis-ta pen-o-sa.*
lah vees-tah peh-noh-zah.

5. *Mes en u-na mit-ja-nit,*
mehz ehn oo-nah meed-jah-neet,

6. *bri-lla_el sol que n'és eix-it.*
bree-yuhl sohl kuh nehz uh-sheet.

7. *D'u-na bel bel bel, d'u-na la la la,*
doo-nah behl behl behl, doo-nah yah yah yah,

8. *d'u-na bel, d'u-na la, d'u-na bel-la_au-ro-ra*
doo-nah behl, doo-nah yah, doo-nah behl -yah_ow-roh-rah

9. *que_el cel en-a-mo-ra.*
kuhl sehl eh-nuh-moh-rah.

Translation

Frozen December
Frozen December
Confused it retires.
April crowned with flowers,
The whole world admires.
When in a garden of love
A divine flower is born.
From a beaut', beaut', beaut'
From a ful, ful, ful
From a beaut', from a ful
From a beautiful rose
Fertile and budding.

The first father caused
the gloomy night
that blinded the entire world
the sad sight;
but in one midnight,
the risen sun shined
from a beaut' beaut' beaut',
from a ful ful ful,
from a beaut', from a ful,
from a beautiful dawn
that makes the skies fall in love.

Hitotsu toya (Temple Bells), p. 478 CD 21–4
Folk Song from Japan

Pronunciation Practice

Verse 1
Phrase 1. *Hi-to-tsu to-ya,*
hee-toh-tsoo toh-yah,

2. *Hi-to-yo a-ku-re-ba*
hee-toh-yah uh-koo-ruh-bah

3. *Ni-gi-ya-ka de,*
nee-geh-yah-kah deh,

4. *Ni-gi-ya-ka de,*
nee-geh-yah-kah deh,

5. *O-ka-za-ri ta-te ta-ru*
oh-kah-zah-ree tah-tuh tah-roo

6. *Ma-tsu-ka-za-ri,*
mah-tsoo-kah-zah-ree,

7. *Ma-tsu-ka-za-ri.*
mah-tsoo-kah-zah-ree.

Verse 2
Phrase 1. *Fu-ta-tsu to-ya,*
foo-tah-tsoo toh-yah,

2. *Fu-ta-ba no ma-tsu wa*
foo-tah-bah noh mah-tsoo wah

3. *I-ro yo te,*
ee-roh yoh-oo teh,

4. *I-ro yo te.*
ee-roh yoh-oo teh.

5. *Sa-n-ga-i ma-tsu wa*
sah-(n) gah-ee mah-tsoo wah

6. *Ka-su-ga ya-ma,*
kah-soo-gah yah-mah,

7. *Ka-su-ga ya-ma.*
kah-soo-gah yah-mah.

Verse 3
Phrase 1. *Mit-tsu to-ya,*
meet-tsoo toh-yah,

2. *Mi-na-san ko-na hi wa*
mee-nah-sah-(n) koh-nah hee wah

3. *Ra-ku-a-so-bi,*
rah-koo-ah-soh-bee,

4. *Ra-ku-a-so-bi,*
rah-koo-ah-soh-bee,

5. *Fu-ru-sa-ki ko-ma-do de*
foo-roo-sah-kee koh-mah-doh deh

6. *Ha-ne o tsu-ku,*
hah-neh oh tsoo-koo,

7. *Ha-ne o tsu-ku.*
hah-neh oh tsoo-koo.

Translation

It is the first day of the first month of the year.
People decorate their houses with pine branches and
happily celebrate a new year.
The best pine is the pine of Futaba (two leaves).
If you prefer the pine of Sangai, you go to Mt. Kasuga
Not only you and me but everyone enjoys games
on New Year's Day.
How about playing hanetsuki outside?

Los reyes de Oriente, p. 480 CD 21–8, 9
Aguinaldo from Puerto Rico

Pronunciation Practice

Phrase 1. *De tie-rra le-ja-na*
deh tyeh-rrah leh-hah-nah

2. *ve-ni-mos a ver-te,*
veh-nee-mohs ah vehrr-teh,

3. *Nos sir-ve de guí-a*
nohs seer-veh deh ghee-ah

4. *la_es-tre-lla de_O-rien-te.*
lah_ehs-treh-jah deh_oh-ryehn-teh.

5. *¡Oh, bri-llan-te_es-tre-lla*
oh, bree-jan-teh_ehs-treh-jah

6. *que_a-nun-cias la_au-ro-ra,*
keh_ah-noon-syahs lou-roh-rah,

7. *No me fal-te nun-ca*
noh meh fahl-teh noon-kah

8. *tu luz bien-he-cho-ra!*
too loos byehn-eh-choh-rah!

Translation

From a foreign land we come to see,
The star serves as our guide from the Orient.
Oh, shine brightly, you that announces the dawn,
Do not falter your beneficial light.

Movement Glossary

A

action words Words (verbs) that readily evoke movement. Examples include *freeze, flutter, melt, pop, crumple, swivel, creep, ripple, dart,* and *explode.*

allemande left In square or contra dances, corners grasp left forearms, wrists, hands, or elbows and walk around clockwise back to place. They bend left elbows and pull away a bit.

allemande right The same movement using right forearms, etc.

arch Two people raise one or two joined hands for others to duck under.

B

ballroom A partner hold in which the man's right arm is around the woman with his right hand firmly in the middle of her back. (See **hand holds**.)

basket (or basket hold) Dancers join hands with second person on one side, as well as a person beside them. Baskets can be formed in front of the body or in back. Longer arms may be on top, or arms may weave with left arm under and right over, or vice versa. (See **hand holds**.)

bend A basic stationary movement, bend brings two body parts closer together. The opposite of stretch, bend is done in the joints of the body.

body percussion Sounds produced by the contact of two or more body parts.

    clap body percussion in which hands strike.

    pat body percussion in which both hands tap the thighs simultaneously or alternately.

    snap body percussion in which the sound is produced by friction between the thumb and third finger.

    stamp body percussion in which the foot strikes the floor.

bow In classroom dances, an acknowledgment of the partner with a dip of the head or a quick bend at the waist. Although in traditional dances the man may bow more dramatically while the woman acknowledges with a bend of knees or curtsy, the simple bow described here is appropriate for both genders.

buzz step (or buzz turn) A movement with a down-up motion in an uneven rhythm (slow-quick). When turning clockwise, dancers step on right foot with slightly bent knee and then push with ball of left foot as though on a scooter. Use opposite footwork for counterclockwise. Movement is smooth with feet close to the floor and no leaps. Partners keep the outsides of their right feet close.

C

CW, CCW Movement directions clockwise and counterclockwise. (See individual listings.)

cast off Dancers at head of longways set turn away from each other and lead their lines around the outside to the foot of the set.

CAST OFF

circle formation A dance in a ring with hands joined or not. Examples of circles include single, double, concentric, closed, and open. (See individual listings.)

classroom choreography A dance pattern arranged for successful teaching in school settings. It may be based on traditional movements but made more appropriate for schoolchildren. (See **traditional dances**.)

clockwise A movement direction that progresses as do the hands of the clock, or around the circle to the left. Referred to in most dance notes as CW.

close A movement when the free foot comes up next to the supporting foot and takes weight. Also referred to as "together," as in step-together.

closed circle A circular formation that has no beginning or end. Hands may be joined or not.

collapse A basic stationary movement, collapse is the complete release of the body or body part into gravity.

concentric-circle formation Closed circles within circles, sometimes each moving to a different pattern or in opposite directions. Hands may be joined or not.

CONCENTRIC-CIRCLE FORMATION

contra dance A traditional dance form, originally from the U.S. New England region. It is called "contra" because it is usually performed in longways sets with partners opposite (from the French *contre*).

contrast The diversity or variety between adjacent movements or patterns.

corner In contra dance or square dance, the person next to you who is not your partner.

counterclockwise A movement direction that progresses opposite to the hands of the clock, or around the circle to the right. Referred to in most dance notes as CCW.

crawl A basic locomotor movement, crawl is a weight transfer on a low level in space, using hands and knees or hands and feet.

creative dance Within the context of music education, a form of dance that develops skills related to the elements and concepts of movement while exploring possibilities for kinesthetic self-expression.

D

direction The spatial orientation of the line of motion. Directions include forward, backward, sideways, up, and down.

do-si-do Dancers face and pass right or left shoulders, then go around each other back-to-back and return backwards, with no turns, to place. Originally, and sometimes still, called in square dancing do-sa-do (named for the French *dos-á-dos* or *back-to-back*).

double circle A couples formation in which partners stand side by side facing the same direction, or front-to-front with one person's back to the center and the other facing into the center.

DOUBLE CIRCLE

DOUBLE CIRCLE

E

effort actions The twentieth century movement theorist Rudolf van Laban's terms referring to basic qualities of movement. The eight effort actions are slash, press, thrust (punch), glide, wring, flick, float, and tap (dab). (See individual listings.)

elbow swing (or elbow turn) Two dancers link right or left elbows and move in a circle.

ELBOW SWING

energy One of the basic elements of dance, energy provides the "texture" or "color" of movement. Although variously described through the terms *force, dynamics, weight,* and *movement qualities,* energy refers to the way muscular power is used to produce qualities of motion.

entrance/exit The range of possibilities for entering and leaving the performing space.

F

flick A light, quick movement that is scattered or curved; one of the Laban effort actions. An example is the quick movement of butterfly wings.

float A light, slow, drifting movement; one of the Laban effort actions. An example is the movement of astronauts in outer space.

focus The direction of attention in movement. Focus most commonly refers to the gaze of the eyes.

formation Arrangement of dancers in the space. Examples include scattered, line, circle, Sicilian circle, concentric circle, double circle, longways set, and square set.

G

gallop A basic locomotor movement with a forward step and a closing step in an uneven rhythm (slow-quick or quick-slow). Either of the steps can be leaps. The leading foot does not alternate. It is also possible to gallop backward.

general space (also shared-space) The larger space in which movement can occur.

gesture A movement of a single part of the body usually on the periphery. Examples include a nod of the head, a tap of the foot, and a wave. Gestures can have predetermined meanings, many of these translate worldwide.

glide A smooth, sustained, linear movement; one of the Laban effort actions. An example is the movement of skating or sledding.

grand right and left (also right and left grand or grand chain) A movement sequence in which partners progress around the circle in opposite directions by joining right hands and pulling past each other's right shoulder, then giving left hands to next person and passing left shoulders. They continue to alternate rights and lefts until they meet their partner, or the seventh or eighth person, as designated in the dance pattern.

grapevine pattern or step An intertwining 4-step movement pattern that can have several combinations and move clockwise or counterclockwise: step to side/cross in front/step to side/cross in back, or cross in front/step to side/cross in back/step to side, or other weaving patterns. In country-western "line" dances, grapevine means a 3-step pattern: side/back/side/touch.

group shape (group design) The sculptural grouping of more than one body in space, also known as "tableau," "portrait," or "stage picture."

H

hand holds Different ways to connect hands for dancing. Examples include ballroom, basket, pinkie, skater's, T, V, and W. (See individual listings.)

HAND HOLDS

Ballroom   Basket   Pinkie   Skater's

T   V   W

hand jive A nonlocomotor movement activity in which hand motions are performed to the musical beats.

head couple (or top couple) In a longways set, the couple closest to the band and caller or CD player and teacher.

hop A basic locomotor movement in even beat that has a takeoff and landing from one foot to the same foot.

I

improvise Movement that is created spontaneously, ranging from free-form to highly structured form. Improvisation always has an element of chance.

in place Movements performed without traveling.

J

jig A musical meter in $\frac{6}{8}$ as well as a set dance or solo exhibition dance, traditionally from the British Isles, in $\frac{6}{8}$ meter.

jump A basic locomotor movement in even beat that has a take-off and landing from one or both feet to both feet.

L

leader/follower In this versatile relationship, the follower imitates or copies the movement of a leader. The imitation can be sequential or simultaneous. Simultaneous leader/follower exercises can be done as mirrors where the leaders and followers are face-to-face, or as shadows where the followers are behind the leader. (See individual listings.)

leap A basic locomotor movement in even beat that has a take-off from one foot with a landing on the other, usually higher than that of a walk or run.

levels High, medium, and low areas of space.

line A formation in which dancers are side by side, facing the same direction. Hands are joined, using a variety of hand-holds. Lines can be short and straight or long and curved (sometimes called **open circles**).

locomotor movement (or traveling movement) Movement that carries the body from place to place using a transfer of weight. Examples include run, walk, skip, hop, jump, gallop, turn, crawl, and leap. (See individual listings.)

longways/contra set A dance formation that consists of partners facing in two parallel lines. The part closest to the caller and the music is the top or head, farthest away is the bottom or foot. Dancers travel up toward the top, or down toward the bottom.

LONGWAYS / CONTRA SET

M

march To walk with a rhythmic stride to the steady beat.

mirroring To follow in unison the movements of a partner or leader as if looking in a mirror.

mixer A group dance or singing game in which participants change partners each time the pattern repeats.

MIRRORING

movement echo Echoing repeats or copies a movement after the movement is done by a leader.

movement exploration To experiment with movements using variations on time, space, and energy.

movement phrase Similar to a grammatical phrase, a movement phrase is a natural grouping of movements with a sense of completion.

movement qualities Styles of movement created by the way force is used to begin and continue the actions.

> **percussive** characterized by sharp, forceful, explosive attack.
>
> **suspended** movement characterized by a momentary hanging of the body or a body part in space, followed by a collapse to gravity.
>
> **sustained** movement begun and continued with smooth, even force.
>
> **vibratory** movement in which the body or body part(s) shivers and shakes as a result of rapid contractions and releases of muscles.

movement rondo Like the musical form, a movement rondo alternates contrasting movements or patterns with a recurring movement or pattern. For example, ABACAD.

N

nonlocomotor movement (or **stationary movement**) Movements that do not involve traveling from place to place. Some examples are bend, drop, swing, and twist.

O

open circle A nonclosed circular formation that has a leader at one or both ends.

OPEN CIRCLE

P

pathway The line or trajectory created by movement in the air or on the floor. Spatial (air) pathways or floor pathways may be straight or curved.

pattern The smallest unit of form. Pattern usually involves several movements and makes use of repetition.

patterned dances Dances with a prescribed sequence of steps and/or movements.

peel off The movement enacted when individuals in a single file or column reach a designated spot and turn back down the line alternately to the right or left.

personal space (or **self-space)** The sphere or "bubble" of space that immediately surrounds the body in stillness or motion.

pinkie hold A hand hold, usually in the W position, in which little fingers are joined. Generally it is right under and left over ("right under the leftovers"). (See **hand holds**.)

pivot A turn clockwise or counterclockwise on the ball of one or both feet.

play-party A music game, originating in nineteenth-century U.S. in response to religious prohibitions against dancing. Traditionally, the accompaniment was only singing and foot stomping, as the fiddle was "the devil's instrument."

press A strong, slow, sustained linear movement where the force is focused in direction; one of the Laban effort actions. An example is the movement of rowing a boat.

progression Mostly in contra dances and those of the British Isles, the movement of each couple is to the next position in the set.

promenade A figure in which partners join hands and walk together around the circle.

promenade position (or **skater's position**) A partner position in which individuals stand side by side, facing the same direction, with right hands joined over left hands in front of the body. There are also other promenade positions; this is best for school-age students.

pull A basic stationary movement that moves toward the center of the body. Beginning with a stretch, pull moves into a bend with the use of force.

push A basic stationary movement that moves away from the center of the body. Beginning with a bend, push extends into a stretch with the use of force.

R

reel A musical meter in $\frac{4}{4}$ as well as a set dance from the British Isles and the U.S. in $\frac{4}{4}$ meter. A reel is also a way to join arms in traditional longways dances, sometimes called "strip the willow."

right-hand star A figure in which four or more dancers join right hands and circle clockwise. A left-hand star goes counter-clockwise. Also called a wheel, a mill, or right-hands-across, hands may be joined by piling them in the middle, grasping the one opposite, or holding the wrist ahead.

RIGHT-HAND STAR

ring Another way to refer to circle formations, especially in historic dances.

run A basic locomotor movement in even rhythm that transfers weight from one foot to the other with a moment when both feet are off the ground.

S

sashay (or chassé, side gallop, slide, slip) A sideways locomotor movement in uneven rhythm (slow-quick, slow-quick) in a side-close, side-close pattern.

scattered formation A random arrangement of dancers within the assigned space.

set An arrangement of dancers in square, longways, or groups-of-three formations. Also refers to the setting step, or balance step, in English country dances.

shadow To imitate the movements of a person from behind him or her.

shape The sculptural line or design of one or more bodies in space. (See **group shape**.)

Sicilian circle A dance formation in which couples face other couples around the circle, with one pair facing and progressing counterclockwise, the other facing and progressing clockwise.

SHADOW

SICILIAN CIRCLE

single circle A ring formation with dancers usually facing the center of the circle; hands may be joined or not.

skater's hold A partner hold in which right hands join over left hands in front of or behind the body. (See **hand holds**.)

skater's position (or promenade position) A partner position where individuals stand side by side, facing same direction, with right hands joined over left hands in front of or behind the body.

skip A basic locomotor movement that combines a step and a hop with alternating feet in an uneven rhythm (slow-quick, slow-quick).

slash A sharp, strong, curved movement; one of the Laban effort actions. An example is the movement of whirling helicopter blades.

slide See **sashay**.

space A basic dance element, referring to the area through which one moves.

square dance A traditional U.S. form performed by four couples in a four-sided or box formation.

square set An arrangement of four couples in an imaginary box formation, each couple standing on a different side of the box, all facing center. In U.S. and British Isles squares, couple 1 has its back to the music, then count counterclockwise for couples 2, 3, and 4. Couples 1 and 3 are head couples, 2 and 4 are side couples.

stage directions:

    down stage portion of the performance area closest to the audience.

    stage left portion of stage area to left of performer.

    stage right portion of the performance area to right of performer.

    up stage portion of the performance area most distant from the audience.

stamp As used in patterned dances, placing the foot firmly on the floor and lifting it slightly so as not to take weight (see also **stomp**); the next movement is done on the same foot. As body percussion, a stamp takes weight.

stationary movement (or nonlocomotor movement) Movement done in place. Stationary movement does not travel. Examples include bend, stretch, twist, swing, sway, push/pull, and collapse. (See individual entries.)

step-close A step pattern in which the dancer steps on one foot and brings the other foot beside the first foot (step-together), taking the weight also on the second foot.

step-hop A basic step pattern that includes a step and a hop in an even rhythm.

step-in-place Walking without traveling through space.

step-together See **step-close**.

step-touch A step pattern where the dancer steps on one foot and brings the other foot beside the first foot, touching it to the floor but not putting weight on it.

stomp As used in patterned dances, placing the foot firmly on the floor and taking weight on it. (See also **stamp**.) The next movement will be on the other foot.

stretch A basic stationary movement in which there is full extension of a body part or the whole body.

sway A stationary movement that moves side to side, or front and back. Sway is a gentle, rocking movement of one body part or the whole body shifting weight in place.

swing A basic stationary movement that occurs when the body or a body part moves in an arc or circle. Swinging includes several phases: the release of the body/body part into gravity, and the lift and suspension of the body/body part on the other side of the arc.

swing As used in patterned dances, turning with various hand or arm holds such as a two-hand swing or elbow swing. Also, swing is a nonlocomotor movement in which one knee lifts as its foot lightly swings across the other leg. (Also, swing is, of course, the popular couple dance that used to be called the jitterbug.)

T

T hold The shoulder hold in which dancers, usually in a circle formation, place their hands on their neighbors' nearest shoulders. Arms are somewhat extended to form a "T". (See **hand holds**.)

tap A quick, light, staccato movement that moves to one point; one of the Laban effort actions. An example is the movement of knocking on the door.

thrust A fast, strong, linear movement that moves to one point; one of the Laban effort actions. An example is the movement of a karate blow.

top-of-the-set The end of the set closest to the band and caller or the music source.

traditional dances Dances that have roots in a culture, or have been passed down through generations mostly unchanged, or have some claim to historical accuracy.

turn A locomotor movement that indicates the body revolving around its vertical axis while traveling through space.

Turning can be done while walking, skipping, hopping, galloping, or leaping.

twist A nonlocomotor movement in which the body or body part rotates on its axis.

two-step A movement pattern in which the dancer steps forward on the first foot, closes with the second foot, steps forward again on the first foot, and holds for a beat. It may also be done in other directions.

U

unison movement Two or more dancers performing the same movement at the same time.

V

V hold A partner or group position in which individuals stand side by side with hands joined and held down, making "Vs" between them. (See **hand holds**.)

W

W hold A partner or group position in which individuals stand side by side with hands joined at shoulder level and elbows down, making "Ws" between them. (See **hand holds**.)

walk A basic locomotor movement in even rhythm in which weight is transferred from one foot to the other, keeping continual contact with the floor. There is a wide range of possibilities for varying the walk. Examples include character walks, inventive walks, walks of varying tempos and directions, and walks expressing various emotions.

weaving (or winding) A movement pattern in which some dancers go around other dancers who are standing still, often with arms raised in arches or windows.

weight The concept of weight includes several different meanings. In the context of transferring weight, it refers to the downward force of the vertical axis of the body as it moves in space. Laban's use of the term refers to weight as the intensity of force used in the muscles as in light or heavy. Weight can also refer to the quality of the body giving in to gravity or allowing gravity to work on it.

wring A strong, sustained, twisting movement; one of the Laban effort actions. An example is the movement of squeezing water from a towel.

wring the dishrag Partners face, joining two hands and swinging them overhead in the same direction to complete a circle while turning the bodies back-to-back and ending up face-to-face.

Dance Directions

Morning Comes Early, p. 13 CD 1–17, 22

Choreography by Sanna Longden, based on traditional figures

Routine: Intro (4 m.); v. 1; interlude (4 m.); v. 2; coda (4 m.)

Formation: Girls stand in a closed circle facing into the center, hands joined down by their sides in "V" position. Boys form a circle around the girls, hands on their own waists with fingers back.

Verse—Girls' Pattern

Measures 1–4
- Move clockwise. They step forward with the right foot in front of the left foot, and step on the left foot to the left side, then repeat the same pattern two more times. Then they stomp right-left-right. This is called a *rida* step.

Measures 5–8
- Repeat measures 1–4, but cross with the left foot, step to the side with the right foot, then stomp left-right-left.

Verse—Boys' Pattern

Measures 1–4
- Move counterclockwise. They step to the side with the right foot, close with the left, repeat the same pattern two more times, then stomp right-left-right.

Measures 5–8
- Repeat measures 1–4 moving clockwise with opposite footwork.

Interlude—Girls' Pattern

Measures 1–4
- Facing center, four touch-steps: Touch R heel forward, step on R foot; touch L heel forward, step on L foot; repeat. Keep hands joined, or place fists on own waists.

Interlude—Boys' Pattern

Measures 1–4
- Facing center, stand proud, fists on waists: Step R, L, R, lift L knee and slap it (with L or R hand); step L, R, L, lift R knee and slap it. Variations encouraged.

Refrain—Girls' Pattern

Measures 1–8
- Still in a closed circle, move counterclockwise for four measures, then clockwise for four measures, using same side-close pattern as boys above.

Measures 9–16
- Repeat pattern for measures 1–8.

Refrain—Boys' Pattern

Measures 1–8
- Facing counterclockwise, each boy puts his left hand on the left shoulder of the boy in front of him, with right hands on their waists. Starting on their right foot, boys walk 14 steps, then turn to face the other direction while stomping right-left-right.

Measures 9–16
- Each boy puts his right hand on the right shoulder of the boy in front of him, with left hands on their waists. Starting on the left foot, boys walk 14 steps; then turn and face center while stomping left-right-left.

Coda
- Repeat movements of Interlude. On last beat, raise arm and shout "hey!"

Drill, Ye Tarriers, p. 54 CD 3–16, 21

Choreography by Sanna Longden

Routine: Intro (4 m.); three verses with turnarounds; coda

Dancing is a natural part of Irish culture. Legend has it that when two Irishmen meet at a crossroads, they do a little jig. Irishmen who worked on the railroads would sing and dance during breaks. There weren't many women at the work camps, so the men danced with one another. Here is a dance that can be performed by men only, women only, or both together.

Formation: Students stand in a circle, facing center, not holding hands. Have them number off into 1's and 2's. 1's and 2's are partners.

Verse

Ev'ry morning at seven o'clock
- 1's take four steps into circle.

There's twenty tarriers a-working at the rock,
- 1's take four steps backward to place, as 2's take four steps into the circle.

And the boss comes along and he says, "Keep still . . .
- 2's take four steps backward to place, as 1's take four steps into the circle.

And come down heavy on the cast iron drill.
- 1's take four steps backward to place, as 2's take four steps in place.

Refrain

So drill, ye tarriers, drill.
- Partners face and walk toward each other as follows: Forward, 2, 3, stamp, (pat partner's hands once).

And drill, ye tarriers, drill!
- Partners move apart backward 2, 3, stamp-stamp (clap-clap own hands).

Oh, it's <u>work</u> all day for the <u>sugar</u> in your tay, down beyond the <u>railway</u>, and <u>drill</u>, ye tarriers, <u>drill</u>!

- Partners face, prepare to pass right shoulders and progress in opposite directions. 1's move clockwise on the outside; 2's move counterclockwise on the inside. Students "high-five" or pat right hands with each person they pass (six in all). Students pat hands with partner on "work," then another person on each strongly accented word.

Dance Directions

Ms. Maggie's Jig, p. 139 CD 7–11, 12

Traditional Scottish dance, notated by Sanna Longden

Routine: section A (8 m.); section B (8 m.); section A (8 m.); section B (8 m.); section C (8 m.); section D (8 m.); section C (8 m.); section D (8 m.); section E (8 m.); section F (8 m.); section E (8 m.); section F (8 m.)

Scottish country dances are social and friendly. They are similar to other longways dances of the British Isles, but have more elegance because of the influence from seventeeth- and eighteenth-century French court dances. *Ms. Maggie's Jig* is based on the traditional Scottish *Cumberland Jig.*

Formation: Assign partners and have students stand in longways sets (see Movement Glossary, p. 548) of six couples. Begin the dance with groups of four people joining hands, that is, couples 1 and 2, 3 and 4, and so on. This is called setting up "four hands from the top." The top of the set is traditionally closest to the music-the band and caller, or other source of music (compact disc player).

Basic Step	• Practice this traveling step before beginning the dance. The step, called a "skip change of step," is like an elegant polka step. Have students take a small hop on the left foot while stretching the right leg a bit up in front with a pointed toe (skip); step onto the right foot; close the left foot to the right foot; and step forward onto the right foot. Repeat with a skip on the right foot while stretching the left in front. It is also all right to walk through the figures.
Measures 1–4	• Have each group of 4 make a right-hand-star (see Movement Glossary, p. 548) by joining hands with the person across from them. (Scottish dancers say, "Right hands across to make a wheel.") Everyone walks eight steps clockwise or takes 4 skip changes of step.
Measures 5–8	• Students make a left-hand-star, and walk eight steps counterclockwise or dance 4 skip changes of step.
Measures 9–12	• Couples 1, 3, and 5 walk down the middle of the set in eight steps or dance 4 skip changes of step, holding closest hands. Couples 2, 4, and 6 stand in place.
Measures 13–16	• Couples 1, 3, and 5 return to their places in eight steps or 4 skip changes of step.
Measures 17–22	• Top couple casts off (see Movement Glossary, p. 548) and leads the others down each side of the set.
Measures 23–28	• Couples meet at the bottom of the set and follow the top couple back to place. On the last step, the top couple turns to face down the center of the set and joins closest hands. All others face their own partners and join both hands to form an arch.
Measures 29–32	• Top couple walks or does the traveling step down the set under the arches to become the bottom couple. On the last step, the others drop hands and step backward into a wider set.
	The dance begins again with a new top couple, formerly couple 2. All others are also in a new position, ready to make a star with a new couple. This is called a "progression."

Tumba, p. 161 CD 8–12, 14

Choreography by Sanna Longden, based on traditional dance figures

Routine: Intro (4 m.); vocal (3-part round); coda

Formation: Three concentric circles.

There is no traditional dance to "Tumba." It is an excellent song to encourage creative movements. Here is a progression to help teacher and students create a dance canon:

1) Students learn to sing the song as a round or canon.

2) Each group may walk around the room as a unit, connected by joined hands, elbows, shoulders, and so on, continuing to sing the canon.

3) Now everyone moves around the room by themselves, still singing their own parts.

4) Teacher asks singers to try movements to go with the melodies—mention hands, feet, direction, levels, and feelings to provide structure; if possible, model some ideas.

5) Teacher keeps an eye out for three good ideas to incorporate into the canon dance. Try for contrasting directions and levels for each of the melodies. Suggested pattern:

    A. Walk CCW while pressing palms down alternately and bending from waist.

    B. Join hands and move sideways CCW with eight slides or side-close steps.

    C. Turn individually to R while clapping hands high overhead (two counts per clap).

    (from "Toemba" taught by Femke van Doorn, shared by Karleen Manwaring)

End dance canons in the same manner as song canons. When it feels right the first group should repeat the last movement until all three groups are doing the same movement—end on a *crescendo!*

Dance Directions

Don Alfonso, p. 177 CD 9–2, 7

Sevillana-style choreography by Sanna Longden

Routine: Intro (8 m.); v. 1; interlude (4 m.); v. 2; interlude (4m.); v. 3; coda (4 m.)

"Don Alfonso" is a folk song in the flamenco song style and dance style called *sevillana* [she-vee-AH-nah], named for the Spanish city of Seville where it originated in medieval times. The *sevillana* is sung and danced accompanied by guitar and castanets. The words and music often express pain and other sad emotions with strong movements and stern facial expressions. Dancers may stamp, clap, and snap their fingers. The audience shows appreciation and encouragement by shouting *"Olé!"*

Formation: Assign boy-girl or red-blue partners. Have students stand in a double circle, facing their partners. Boys' or reds' backs are to the center. Girls or blues are facing the center.

Basic steps	• Girls move the right foot in, left foot out, right foot out, then repeat, starting on left foot. They snap their fingers on each step in. Boys stomp with right foot in place, clap twice above head, stomp with the left foot in place, and clap twice above head.
Introduction	• All pose like statues with heads high, backs straight, hands on waists. They may also have one hand on waist and the other across body holding first hand, or hands up in air in clap or snap position. On guitar strum, perform many fast heel hits (step-hit heel, step-hit heel), a movement known as *maquina escribir* or "typewriter" because of the way it sounds. (This movement is not effective in sneakers.)
Verse 1	• Perform basic step 16 times. Girls may swish their skirts with one hand.
Interlude	• Turn in place to the right with four basic steps, then to the left with four basic steps. On the last two measures pose as in the introduction, and prepare for verse 2.
Verse 2	• Girls dance around boys, performing eight basic steps counterclockwise, then do eight basic steps clockwise. Boys perform their basic step, either in place or turning in the opposite direction from girls.
Interlude	• Repeat as above.
Verse 3	• Couples stand side-by-side, facing another couple, ready to progress counterclockwise or clockwise. With basic steps, couples weave past one another around the circle, first passing on the right as a couple, then on the left, and so on around the ring. All perform 14 basic steps. On the last two measures, all face center to re-form the circle.
Coda	• Facing the center, all do the *maquina escribir* into the center 12 times, and backward 12 times. After final chord, everyone stomps and shouts *"Olé!"*

Ali Pasha, p. 218 CD 10–35, 36

Based on a dance by Bora Özkök, notated by Sanna Longden

Routine: Intro (16 m.); Part I (8 m.); Part II (8 m.); Part III (8 m.);
(Part I, II, and III repeat 3 times—total 4 times)

All over the world throughout history, people who are oppressed, or feel put down, try to deal with their misery by making up satirical songs about their oppressors. This folk song makes fun of a very cruel military general of the Ottoman Turkish Empire named Ali Pasha, who lived in the late eighteenth and early nineteenth centuries. The dance has movements that are typical of folk dancing in Turkey.

Formation: Students stand in one or more lines or open circles with hands joined at shoulder height in a "W" position. Sometimes people hook little fingers in a pinkie hold (see Movement Glossary, p. 548). The leader is at the right end holding a scarf in their free hand to signal changes in the step.

Style: Dancers should be close, almost arm to arm. Movements are up-and-down with steps directly under the body. Keep knees flexible so torso and arms can bounce with the beat. When foot touches in front, the style is to lean back a bit; all touches are on a flat foot. When figures change, the leader may call *"geç, geç"* (pronounced "getch, getch," which means "change, change") and wave the kerchief.

The music is meter in 5, which can be counted 1-2-3-4-5, or 1-2-3-1-2.

Part I

Introduction	• Stand and pulse to the meter. Toward the end of the introduction, face slightly counterclockwise and get right foot ready.
Measure 1	• Step with right foot, left foot, right foot (counts 1, 2, 3), then touch left foot in front (on flat foot while leaning back a bit, counts 4, 5).
Measure 2	• Step backward, left foot, right foot, left foot (counts 1, 2, 3), then touch right foot (counts 4, 5), while turning a bit to face center.
Measure 3	• Walk into the center, right foot, left foot, right foot (counts 1, 2, 3), then touch left foot (counts 4, 5).
Measure 4	• Walk backward out of the center, left foot, right foot, left foot (counts 1, 2, 3), then touch right foot (counts 4, 5) while turning to face in the original direction.
Measures 5–8	• Repeat Part I, measures 1–4.

Part II

Measure 1	• Perform grapevine step (see Movement Glossary, p. 548). Face center and step right foot to right side, left foot in back, right foot to right side, left foot crosses in front of right.
Measure 2	• Continue in the same direction, right foot to right side, left foot back, right foot to right side, touch left foot next to right.
Measures 3–4	• Repeat Part II, measures 1–2, starting with left foot to left side.
Measures 5–8	• Repeat Part II, measures 1–4.

Part III

Measure 1	• Face center and step in place, right foot in, left foot out, right foot out, touch left heel in front and lean back a bit.
Measure 2	• Continue facing center and step in place, left foot out, right foot out, left foot in, then stamp right foot.
Measures 3–8	Repeat Part III, measures 1–2, three times.

Erie Canal, p. 262 CD 12–18, 20

Arranged and notated by Sanna Longden, based on traditional dance figures

Routine: Intro (4 m.); vocal; interlude (4 m.); vocal; coda

When bargemen and their families got together to relax, they enjoyed singing work songs. Often a fiddler or a banjo player would start playing, and everyone would get up and dance. Here is a dance they might have done.

Formation: Assign partners and have students make a Sicilian circle (see Movement Glossary, p. 548). Each set of partners faces another set around the circle. One set faces and progresses clockwise, the other counterclockwise. Partners are side-by-side; the person directly across from each partner is the "opposite."

Verse	***I've got a mule, her name is Sal, . . . on the Erie Canal.*** • Partners do-si-do (see Movement Glossary, p. 531) past right shoulders (eight counts), then past left shoulders (eight counts). ***She's a good old worker and . . . on the Erie Canal.*** • Do-si-do with opposite past right shoulders (eight counts), then past left shoulders (eight counts). ***We've hauled some barges in our day, . . . coal, and hay,*** • Hook right elbows with partner and walk around until they get back to place (eight counts); repeat with left elbows. ***And we know ev'ry inch of the way, . . . to Buffalo.*** • Repeat elbow turns with opposite.
Refrain	• All join inside hands with partners. Partners facing clockwise raise hands in a bridge and move apart as they walk forward and over the other pair. Those facing counterclockwise walk forward as they duck under. Take four steps to go over and/or under. Everyone now faces a new pair and they switch positions-those who ducked under the first time make a bridge, and those who made a bridge duck under. Continue to move forward, alternating the bridge and the ducking under, taking four steps for each meeting. Each pair should meet and pass eight others.
Interlude	• Make sure couples are facing another couple and going in the correct direction. As they meet a new pair, they acknowledge them with a nod and smile. Then partners face each other to begin again from the verse.

Orange Blossom Special, p. 269 CD 12–27, 28

Arranged by Sanna Longden, based on traditional dance figures

Routine: Harmonica (freely); intro (4 m.); v.1–3; v. 1–3; coda

The Orange Blossom Special is a well-known Appalachian dance tune. Musicians often start the tune by making train sounds, then play slowly, like a train pulling out of the station, and increase the tempo as the train gathers speed. Some play very fast to show their virtuosity. Here are some dance figures to use with this music. They are based on Grand March figures, and simulate a railroad tunnel. The figures will fit the music differently, depending on the size of the group and the dance space. Figures may be repeated as necessary to fill out the time while the music plays.

Introduction

- During the long introduction, students can try this modified clogging step. Encourage them to think "shuf-fle STEP," counting "1 and 2," then "shuf-fle STEP" again on 3 and 4. On "1," brush the ball of one foot sharply forward brush it backward; on "and," step firmly on that same foot with a slightly bent knee; on "2," repeat with the other foot. Continue the shuffle step, alternating feet until the vocal begins.

Verses

From single line to pairs

- Everyone falls into line behind a leader who guides the single line around the room, then up the center of the dance space toward the music. The first person in line peels off to the right (or left), second person peels off the other way, third goes the first way, fourth the second, and so on. As everyone peels off, alternating directions with the person ahead, they turn back and march down the side of the line, away from the music, to the end of the room. There they face toward the center line to meet those coming from the other side, and together they proceed up the center in a column of pairs, linking arms to stay in close formation.

Arches and Tunnels

- To begin the tunnel, leaders turn to face others as they join inside hands to make an arch over the others' heads and walk back the other way. Each couple in turn ducks under the forming arch, then stands to make their own arch and follow the leaders back the other way.

Continuing Arches and Tunnels

- When the leaders reach the end, they drop their arch and turn to duck under the tunnel and burrow their way up to the other end. Each pair follows in turn.

Variation on Arches and Tunnels: Dip and Dive

- Leaders make an arch over the first couple, then duck under the arch made by the next couple coming toward them. Everyone keeps moving as they alternate over and under. To end the action, the lead couple goes under the last arch and keeps walking in the same direction to start a new figure.

Coda

Promenade to Single Circle

- Leaders guide everyone into a straight column of couples going toward the music. When they reach the top, each couple separates, one student goes right, and one goes left. They go out and down to the bottom of the set. When they meet again, instead of going side by side up the set again, they step one behind the other, alternating boy-girl-boy-girl, or one-two-one-two.

Tzena, tzena p. 298 CD 13–30, 36

Traditional Israeli dance, contributed by Sanna Longden

Routine: Intro (4 m.); Hebrew verse; interlude (8 m.); Arabic verse; interlude (8 m.); English verse

People dance the *hora* as they sing *"Tzena, tzena."* The dance came to Israel in the early twentieth century when the land was called Palestine (Israel became a nation in 1948). Settlers brought the dance from Romania, where *horas* are popular circle dances. In fact, the word *hora* means "circle dance." The Israeli hora was originally done in closed circles with hands joined and held down at the sides in a "V" position or with hands on neighbors' shoulders in a "T" position. In Israel, the traditional *hora* moves clockwise, although today *horas* can move in any direction. The steps are high and joyous, with leaps and kicks.

Note: The *hora* has a six-beat pattern, while the music for *"Tzena, tzena"* has four beats per measure.

Formation: Students in a single circle, holding hands down by sides or on neighbors' shoulders as described above.

Dance Pattern • Move to the left as follows: step (or leap) with the left foot, step with the right foot, step with the left foot, lift (or kick) with the right foot, step with the right foot, lift (or kick) with the left foot. Repeat as needed.

Ala Da'lona, p. 301 CD 14–1, 2

Traditional Middle Eastern dance

Routine: Intro (improvisation, then 4m.); instrumental; interlude; vocal; coda

The *debke* (also called *debky, dubka,* or *debka*) is one of the most common dances of the Lebanese, Jordanian, Syrian, and Palestinian people. The word *debke* means "line dance," and traditional *debkes* are often done in short lines. Hands are generally joined down at the side, with dancers moving counterclockwise, shoulder to shoulder in a tight formation. Although the step pattern is almost the same as the Israeli *hora, debke* steps are more up-and-down, as well as sharp and powerful, with stamps and knee movements. Like the *hora*, the *debke* is a six-beat pattern danced to music with four beats per measure.

People also do the same dance pattern in other Eastern European and Western Asian countries. In Bulgaria, it is called *horo;* in Hungary, *kor;* in Serbia and Croatia, *kolo;* in Macedonia, *oro;* in Greece, *choros.*

Formation: Students stand in short lines, with hands joined down at sides, as described above.

Basic Arabic *Debke*

Dance Pattern • Move counterclockwise as follows: step with the right foot, step with the left foot, step with the right foot, stamp with the left foot, step with the left foot, and stamp with the right foot. Repeat pattern as needed.

North Carolina Breakdown, p. 334 CD 15–19, 20

Cakewalk game from Southern United States, notated by Sanna Longden

Routine: Intro (16 m.); section A (16 m.); section B (16 m.); section C (16 m.); repeat sections A, B, C; section D (16 m.); sections A, B, C, D; coda (8 m.)

The term "cakewalk" refers to several kinds of dances. In the late nineteenth and early twentieth centuries, African American vaudeville dancers performed a solo exhibition dance called the "cakewalk." The term also refers to a music game that originally awarded cakes to those who promenaded with the most complex or unusual steps. That music game has become simpler over the decades, now people just walk around to music, hoping to be in the right place to win a cake when the music suddenly stops.

Formation: First mark big numbered squares on the floor or other ways to indicate numbered stops along the circle, and fill a container with numbered pieces of paper for someone to choose. Colors, animals, or other items may be used instead of numbers. You may wish to have cupcakes, cookies, stickers, pencils, or other appropriate prizes. Then have students stand in a single circle, facing either clockwise or counterclockwise. Have one volunteer be in charge of stopping the music (the "conductor") and another in charge of drawing numbers from a container (the "judge").

Cakewalk Game

- When the music begins, students walk to the beat around the circle. The "conductor" pauses the music and everyone freezes. The "judge" reaches into the container for a number. Whoever is on or closest to that number wins a prize. The "conductor" plays the music again and the game continues.

Scott Joplin's New Rag, p. 335 CD 15–21, 22

Notated by Sanna Longden, based on the "Twelfth Street Rag"

Routine: Intro (4 m.); Section A—Part I (32 m.); section B—Part II (32 m.); section A (16 m.); section C—Part III (32 m.); interlude (20 m.); section A (16 m.); coda

Section A—Part I	• Perform the following patterns for eight beats each: Move counterclockwise. Start on left foot and walk forward four steps, then stop and touch left foot forward, left foot to the side, then step left, right, left. (*ta, ta, ta, ta, ta, ta, ti-ti, ta*) Repeat the pattern starting with the right foot. Continue this pattern throughout Section A.
Section B—Part II	• Perform the following patterns for eight beats each: Face counterclockwise and move sideways toward the center stepping on the beat. Start with left foot and alternate feet, side, back, side, back, side, back, side, and scuff. Repeat the pattern starting on the right foot move away from center. Repeat this pattern throughout Section B.
Section C—Part III	• Perform the following patterns for four beats each: Face counterclockwise and step with left foot, point or kick right foot forward, step on right foot, touch left foot in back, and repeat the pattern through Section C. This pattern mimics the basic Charleston step. A jazzy Charleston feel is encouraged here.
Interlude	• Perform the following patterns for eight beats each: Raise hands shoulder high with palms out, and wave hands and arms left and right. Then perform toe and heel swivels to the right, then wave left and right, then toe and heel swivels to the left, and then wave left and right.
Coda	• Wave left and right for four beats. On last beat, reach both arms up with hands open and fingers straight up.

Pennsylvania 6-5000, p. 342 CD 16–1, 2

Swing dance, notated by Sanna Longden

Routine: There is a six-count pattern called the East Coast swing and an eight-count pattern called the West Coast swing. Sometimes the more active "aerial" moves are called the "Lindy Hop."

Swing dancing is a type of folk dance that developed in the United States in the late 1920s in the ballrooms of Harlem, New York. In the 1930s, it was called the "Lindy Hop" after the American aviator Charles Lindbergh, whose nickname was "Lucky Lindy."

Formation: Assign partners and have students scatter throughout the dance space. Traditionally, men and women dance together as partners, with the man as "leader" and woman as "follower." For the classroom, however, students can be paired in whatever way works best. You may wish to have everyone practice as both "leaders" and "followers." When students are confident, they may also create their own moves.

Swing Dance Patterns

Swing Dance Patterns • This is the basic six-count pattern for the East Coast swing. The dance steps are performed in a three-beat pattern while the music is in a four-beat pattern: *ta ta ti-ti ta | ta ti-ti ta ta | ti-ti ta ta ti-ti |* It might be helpful for the students to think "slow, slow, quick-quick" as they dance. This pattern repeats, always beginning on the same foot, leader on the left foot and follower on the right foot.

Individual Practice • Imagine a small square. For leader: Stand with feet in bottom right corner.

1. Step with left foot in top left corner.

2. Step right foot in lower right corner.

3. Step left foot directly behind right foot and step right foot in lower right corner.

For follower: Stand with feet in bottom left corner and reverse feet.

I Love a Rainy Night, p. 350 CD 16–9, 10

Choreography by Sanna Longden

Routine: Intro (4 m); v. 1; v. 2; refrain; v. 3; v. 4; refrain; interlude (2 m.); refrain; interlude (6 m.); refrain (4 times)

Country line dancing is a modern American dance style but many of the songs that accompany line dances are a lot older. People also do the "two-step" to the same type of music. Line dancing became very popular in the United States in the 1980s and 1990s, and is still popular today.

Formation: Students stand in lines or scattered facing the same direction. When students are comfortable with the basic pattern, add the "cool moves".

Note: as in all "four-wall dances," each time students end a pattern, they should be facing the next wall to the right.

The Vine

Measures 1–2
- Step sideways with right foot (count 1), cross in back with left foot (count 2), step with right foot (count 3), touch left foot and clap (count 4), step sideways to the left (count 5), cross in back with left foot (count 6), step with left foot (count 7), touch right foot and clap (count 8). For a "cool move," lift left foot behind right knee and slap sole of the foot with right hand (count 4). Do the same on count 8 with opposite hands and feet.

The Two-Step

Measures 3–4
- Step forward on right foot (count 1), close left foot to right foot (count 2), step forward on right foot (count 3), touch left foot and clap (count 4), step backward on left foot (count 5), close right foot to left foot (count 6), step backward on left foot (count 7), touch right foot and clap (count 8). For a "cool move," lift left knee and slap it with left hand. Then do the same on count 8 with the right knee and hand. Try slapping their knee with the opposite hand for an even "cooler move."

Turns

Measures 5–6
- Make a full circle to the right, stepping with the right foot (count 1), left foot (count 2), right foot (count 3), stamp left foot and clap (count 4). Then make a 360-degree turn to the left, stepping with the left foot (count 5), right foot (count 6), left foot (count 7), stamp right foot and clap (count 8).

Step-Stamps

Measures 7–8
- Stand in place and step with right foot (count 1), stamp left foot without putting weight on it (count 2), step with left foot (count 3), stamp right foot with no weight (count 4), step with right foot (count 5), stamp left foot (count 6), step with left foot (count 7), stamp right foot (count 8). Snap fingers on each stamp. On beats 5–8 make a quarter turn to the right to face a different wall.

Repeat patterns throughout the song.

Dance Directions

Adolescent Voice

Introduction

The care and training of the adolescent voice is of primary importance. If proper vocal habits can be achieved in the adolescent years, a lifetime of healthy singing will result. These pages present practical information about the changing voice and how the young voice can be developed during maturation.

Male Voice Classification and Part Assignments

Certain developmental stages of adolescent male voices can be identified during puberty, but several criteria must be taken into account. **Range** (not including *falsetto*) is the single most potent indicator of voice development. Other important criteria are **tessitura** (most comfortable singing area of the range), **voice quality** (amount of natural breathiness and constriction; resonance characteristics), **register development** (modal, *falsetto*, whistle registers; also lift point: where the *falsetto* register begins*), and **average speaking voice pitch.**

Voice classification involves applying these criteria in assigning voice parts to different developmental stages. This range/*tessitura* chart identifies the developmental stages for males. (The bracketed notes indicate *tessituras*; the term *baritone* does not connote adult sound.)

Stages of the Changing Voice

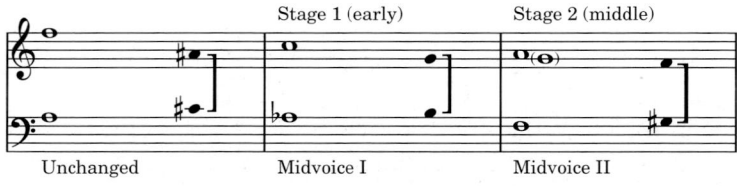

| Unchanged | Stage 1 (early) Midvoice I | Stage 2 (middle) Midvoice II |

| Stage 3 (climax) Midvoice IIA | Stage 4 (new developmental) New Baritone | Stage 5 (cont.) Settling Baritone (Developing) |

In using the range chart, several points should be kept in mind.

- Lower limits of ranges move down generally by plateaus of thirds.

- There tends to be more stability and less individual variation in the lower range limits throughout the different stages.

- In the upper pitch limits, there are great variations (even in individuals) throughout Midvoice I, II, and IIA; but stabilization takes place in the New Baritone stage.

- The stages represent transitions that may last a few weeks, a few months, or—in some cases—a year or longer.

The sequence of changes may also be thought of in the following way.

Early	Middle	Climax	New Development
Midvoice I	Midvoice II	Midvoice IIA	New Baritone Settling (Developing) Baritone

Group voice-testing procedures have been developed to help the teacher identify the various stages of change. (See Group Testing Procedures, p. 570.)

In the sixth, seventh, and eighth grades, one finds many voices in the Midvoice II, Midvoice IIA, and the New Developing Baritone stages. There may be exceptions to this, but there are no true basses or tenors at this point. (Some voices may begin to approximate these classifications, but most voices must still mature a great deal.) In a choral setting, consider the stages in terms of high, middle, and low.

High	Middle	Low
Unchanged Midvoice I	Midvoice II Midvoice IIA	New Baritone Settling (Developing) Baritone

Have the boys sing "America," p. 486, in the key of C or B. The low voices (those singing in the lower octave) can be grouped together. Now transpose the song to the key of F or G. The high voices will be easy to separate because they will sing very easily in this range:

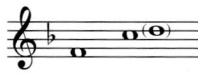

---

*The *falsetto* register emerges during Midvoice II. The lift point or beginning of the *falsetto* is sometimes difficult to detect, especially in trained voices or those just beginning the stage. For rapidly changing voices, the *falsetto* may be difficult to produce, particularly in the range C^4–G^4.

Their voices will be lighter and less mature.

The remaining voices will sound very strong in the key of B♭ or A singing in the following range:

These are Midvoice II's and IIA's. The keys that work best for these stages are C, B, and B♭. Low voices will double the pitches one octave below.

Group lighter voices together (Unchanged and Midvoice I) and place them in a section where they can sing an upper part easily. The following diagram shows one way to seat students in a mixed choir arrangement.

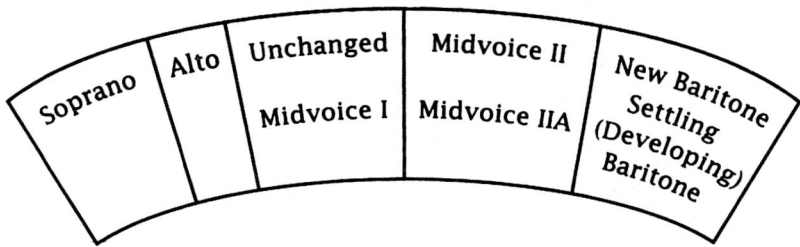

If the changing voices are grouped properly, students can be assigned to parts that fit their singing ranges and *tessituras*. Not all parts of each song will necessarily fit these stages but certain sections or parts will. Sometimes notes must be changed or omitted for certain voices, but if the teacher understands the range capabilities of each student, songs that match the criteria mentioned earlier can be selected.

Unison and two- and three-part songs often do not offer part-assignment flexibility; however, the principles of finding "singable" areas within all songs still apply. Unison songs are especially troublesome. Try to find tunes with a composite range of a sixth or minor seventh.

Baritones can double these pitches one octave lower. Although Midvoice II's may have some trouble in this key, they will be able to sing most of the notes.

Composite Vocal Ranges

For boys' choruses, apply the same principles of the group audition process from which four-part divisions can easily be derived.

Tenor 1 = Unchanged, Midvoice I's

Tenor 2 = Midvoice I's, Midvoice II's, and some Midvoice IIA's

Baritone 1 = Midvoice IIA's, New Baritones

Baritone 2 = Settling (Developing) Baritones (Basses)

In the first few meetings of the class, however, the teacher may wish to divide the group into three parts—high, medium, and low.

High—Unchanged, Midvoice I's

Medium—Midvoice II's, some IIA's (if the upper register is still stronger than the lower register)

Low—New Baritones, Settling (Developing) Baritones

Female Voice Classification and Part Assignments

Girls' voices do not undergo the dramatic changes that boys' voices do during puberty; however, care must be taken to help them develop good vocal habits during this period. The female vocal folds do lengthen and grow, and the thyroid cartilage shows more vertical growth than it does in males. While the Adam's apple is not as prominent in girls as it is in boys, this does not mean that maturation is not occurring. In the seventh and eighth grades, girls' voices begin to show distinct personal qualities, and the chest, middle, and head registers become more obvious. There is less variability in the range of girls' voices. Therefore, there is more flexibility in assigning choral parts. Guard against assigning them exclusively to one part, such as alto. It is essential that their entire vocal range be developed and exercised. Girls' voices do not approximate or equal the adult alto or soprano classification during junior high years.

The chart shows the typical female range during seventh and eighth grades as well as register lift points.

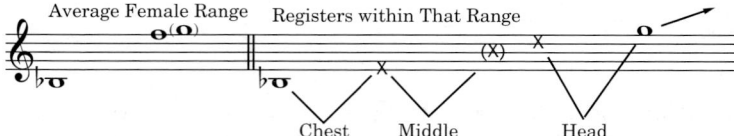

Average Female Range   Registers within That Range

Chest   Middle   Head

It is important that the chest register not be carried too high; that is, to the breaking point, typically.

This often occurs when girls sing too heavily in the alto range.

Have girls alternate singing soprano and alto parts so that they exercise their voices through the normal pitch range. Exclusive assignment to alto may harm the growth of the range and cause voice—pushing, forcing, and neglecting the upper part of the range. (See Group Testing Procedures below.)

After the girls have been assigned to two groups, they can sing either the high or the low treble part.

Group Testing Procedures

Individual and group voice testing are crucial processes that need to take place in every choral class. The following practical approach will permit the teacher to classify students (both girls and boys) by voice part.

1. Divide the class into two groups—boys and girls.

2. Have both groups sing "America," p. 486, in the key of C (B♭ will also work if there are boys who are physically more mature in the class). The primary range of a sixth fits the vocal ranges reasonably well for all parts (with changed voices singing an octave below the rest).

3. Have the boys sing alone in the key of C or B♭. Listen for voices singing in the octave below middle C. These are your New and Settling Baritones. (Some Midvoice IIAs will sing some notes in the lower octave, and some will not match pitch. Assign them to the upper tenor or baritone line.) Check for boys singing in *falsetto* register; some Midvoice IIs and Midvoice IIAs and even baritones do this.

4. Have the baritones sing as a group. Listen for notes sounding below the correct pitch. If you have chosen voices that have not yet reached the baritone stage, you

will hear their sound above the pitch level being sung by the others.

F⁴   G⁴

5. Have the other boys sing "America" in F or G. Note those who sing in the upper octave with ease and light vocal quality. These are Midvoice Is and Unchanged Voices. They should be assigned to alto in an SATB mixed chorus situation or possibly tenor if the range is high and does not go below G³ or A³. Watch for boys singing in *falsetto*; some may be Midvoice IIs or baritones. Expect to hear some voices doubling the pitch an octave below. (Midvoice IIs will do this.)

G³   A³

6. Have the remaining voices sing "America" in B♭. They should sing their notes with ease. Assign them to the tenor part.

B♭3

7. Have the girls sing "America" in C or B♭. Note those who have the strongest voices and sing the notes with ease. Then have them sing "America" again in F or G, noting those girls who have the strongest, most mature voices and are not forcing the sound. Voices identified in both segments may be divided evenly between the soprano and alto parts. Listen for balance, uniformity, and clarity of sound between the groups. Voices identified in the low key but not in the upper key should be assigned to alto and vice versa for those identified in the upper key but not in the lower key. Assign the rest evenly to the alto part and soprano parts.

C⁴

8. Have the girls sing in several keys (low to high). There should not be much difference in balance or quality of sound between the two groups, although the soprano may be lighter in quality.

9. Finally, have all sing "America" in B♭, B, or C.

This procedure will enable you to establish a positive rapport with the students immediately. Voices can be assigned parts, and a lesson in "voice maturation" can be given in a practical, applied setting. Students are interested in understanding the growth process in their singing voices and will listen attentively if they are involved throughout the audition process. Most will achieve some degree of success and will look forward to the next class with enthusiasm.

Principles for Voice Development

- Establish proper body alignment and breathing for singing.

- Help students achieve the proper coordination between subglottic air pressure, extrinsic and intrinsic muscular control of the vocal folds, and articulation within the resonance areas. This will happen if students do not allow excessive tension to develop in the jaw and throat areas.

- Begin exercises in the area of the students' range that is most comfortable, regardless of the variety of stages of vocal development in the class.

- Give enough vocal practice in the proper modal registers (normal voice ranges) as the voices develop.

- Teach the students to understand the process of voice maturation and to consider the changing voice a healthy, natural phenomenon.

- Teach the students to listen for resonant tones and good pitch, and to feel relaxation in the breathing process.

- Help students (particularly Midvoice II's, IIA's, New Baritones, and Settling Baritones) develop the transition area between modal (chest) register and *falsetto* (C^4–G^4 in particular).

- Develop exercises to improve pitch agility. (See Vocalises, p. 572.)

- Have students work for precise vowel and consonant articulation.

- Help students watch for visible and audible signs of vocal stress. Avoid practicing for too long a period of time.

- Be aware of the need for motivation and other psychological aspects of singing.

- Always give positive reinforcement to student efforts. Be supportive and honest throughout all aspects of singing.

Teaching Good Body alignment

Proper body alignment ensures increased efficiency of the vocal and breathing mechanism. Below are two basic techniques for teaching good posture.

- Rest the body weight easily on the balls of the feet. Stand with the feet a little apart, one foot slightly in front of the other.

- Raise the arms above the head, then lower them slowly (still extended) on either side of the body, with chest up and shoulders back. As the students raise their arms, have them rise to tiptoes, then return to normal as the arms descend. Rest on heels with weight evenly distributed and be sure the students are relaxed. This will ensure proper body balance and good body position for singing.

Teaching Correct Breathing

Have the students

- Place hand on abdomen and expel air, utilizing hissing sound. Feel relaxation response, or release, upon inhalation.

- Slowly inhale by audibly sucking air in through slightly puckered lips. Count to four or indicate the length of the inhalation by conducting beats. At the end of inhalation, expel the air by making a hissing sound, *ssss*. Inhalation and expiration should be considered a continuous action.

- Repeat and check for relaxation in the upper body and throat.

- Suck air for a count of two. Exhale and connect with a voiced (sung) sound, *sah*—at a comfortable pitch for all voices.

- Inhale and then expel the air on a whispered *hah*. This eliminates the lip area as the focal point and permits feeling the upward flow of air in the back of the throat. Next, inhale on a whispered *ah* and exhale, connecting immediately with *hah* on a comfortable tone.

- Gradually eliminate the whispered *ah* inhalation. Along with the elimination of inspiratory air noise, there should develop a well-coordinated intercostal, diaphragmatic-abdominal action that serves to direct the air pressure at the proper rate and intensity through the glottis. The resulting tone should be rich and unforced.

Vocalises for the Changing Voice

These exercises begin in the composite range for changing male voices. They will work well with girls' developing voices, but should be transposed higher (girls only) to account for the female pitch range. While it is good for an SATB choir to begin with these pitches, at some point brief vocalises should be done with girls separate from the boys. For adolescent girls it is very important to devise vocalises, such as arpeggios, to exercise register transitions and to develop vocal efficiency throughout the singing range. Over time, this can easily be done in the mixed chorus situation.

Repeat each exercise several times in a moderate tempo at the given pitch. Then continue, raising the starting pitch by half steps until the upper limit of the vocal range is reached. For flexibility, increase the tempo of each exercise.

Exercise 1   To energize sound:

(hiss) ssssssss   Sah _____

Exercise 2   To develop energy:

Whisper on "*h*" for four counts

Kah,   kah,   kah,   kah,   kah,   kah,   kah,   kah

Exercise 3   To build resonance and projection:

Lug - ge - dy   lug - ge - dy   lug - ge - dy   lug - ge - dy   lah

Exercise 4   For flexible jaw, vital sound projection, and proper energy level:

Bah,   bah,   bah,   bah,   bah,   bah,   bah,   bah,   bah

Exercise 5   To develop glottic pressure and breath support:

Whisper on "*h*" for four counts

H _____   ah _____

and sing *hah, hoh, hee* on sustained tones.

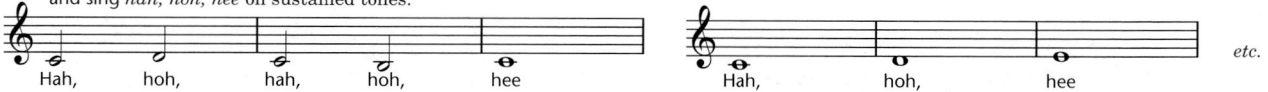

Hah,   hoh,   hah,   hoh,   hee   Hah,   hoh,   hee   *etc.*

Exercise 6   For lightness, good vocal cord approximation for expanding the range, and rhythmic-pitch agility:

Coo coo coo coo coo coo   coo   Coo coo coo coo coo coo   coo

Exercise 7   For precise articulation, pitch agility, and energy:

Tah - kah,   tah - kah,   etc. _____

Tip   of   the tongue.   etc. _____

Bub - ble,   bub - ble,   etc. _____

Exercise 8   For sustained notes with gradual *crescendos, decrescendos,* and dynamic control:

Nah _____   Nah _____

Exercise 9   For lip articulation, lightness, and building consistency throughout range without strain:

Tip   of   the tongue,   etc. _____

Exercise 10   For resonance and pitch agility:

Noo - mee,   noo - mee,   noo - mee,   etc. _____

Exercise 11   For consistent tone throughout the range, dynamic flexibility, and developing richness and depth of tone:

Yoh   Hoh _____

Exercise 12   For rhythmic flexibility:

Nah _____   Nah _____

Song Analyses for Changing Male Voices

All of the songs presented in this text have been analyzed for meeting the unique needs of changing male voices. It is important to note that some accommodation has to be made for the various voice change stages so that adolescent singers will experience success in classroom singing activities. Due to the developmental process, primarily of the larynx and vocal tract, the capabilities of individual voices can vary quite widely, thus the reason for suggesting specific options for these voices with every song.

The following observations for each voice change stage can assist in modifying ranges, changing octaves or part assignments, and so on, to ensure the successful performance of each song:

Midvoice I

These voices are in the first stage of change, and thus are losing higher pitches in the range, notably C^5–F^5. Avoid singing pitches in this part of the range. Often singers can produce the notes, but must strain to do so. This causes many vocal problems, especially later in the maturation process. Stay in the comfortable *tessitura* as much as possible. In some cases, when the top part is very high, the Midvoice I can double the pitches one octave below. See the charts for suggestions.

Midvoice II

The second stage of change presents many challenges. These voices should be singing primarily in the G^3–F^4 range, although some can handle higher *tessituras* in the early part of this stage. Some voices may have an easy transition to *falsetto* (lift point typically G^4–B^4). Other voices may have trouble even producing the *falsetto* register. Check the charts for performance suggestions. Some transposition may be possible, or doubling higher parts an octave below. Sometimes some sections or individual notes may have to be eliminated. There are a variety of performance options, however, and voices in this stage should be encouraged to creatively explore possibilities.

Midvoice IIA

This is the climax of voice change. The stage does not last long (perhaps a few months in most cases). Voices are extremely vulnerable during this time and care must be taken to ensure good breath support and efficiency. A good range for these voices is E^3–C^4 (D^4), although some individuals might be able to produce notes outside this parameter. Explore performance options. Some alto parts might fit the range, and many lower parts of three-voice arrangements work very well. In many of the songs of this text, chorus versus verse writing can be taken into account. Midvoice IIAs may sing both or either section and still receive much satisfaction. The song charts offer a variety of performance options.

New Baritone

The New Baritone range offers a number of possibilities for performance. Top parts and in some cases alto can be sung an octave lower. Melodic writing often suits this voice. One must avoid singing A^3–D^4 (E^4) as a *tessitura*. Some three-part songs (part III) in this text contain this high range. It is better to assign Midvoice IIs and IIAs to this part and allow the New Baritone to sing the top or in some cases the middle part an octave below. This avoids strain, poor intonation, and inaccurate pitch acuity. If the performance options are followed, most of the songs in this text can be sung quite easily.

Settling Baritones (Emerging Adult Voice)

Basically these voices are gaining flexibility and range during this stage. Some may have tendencies toward tenor or baritone, but still do not have adult capabilities. Individuals may be able to sing lower or higher parts with ease, while some will have difficulties producing *falsetto* in the C^4–G^4 range. In this regard, the same is true for New Baritones; thus, some of the same suggestions for New Baritone, particularly about avoiding high *tessituras*, apply to this voice change stage. The significant differences between the two stages are that Settling Baritones often have much lower ranges and are more flexible in upper pitch areas.

Composite Vocal Ranges

Song Title	Midvoice I	Midvoice II	Midvoice IIA	New Baritone	Settling Baritone
A la Puerta del cielo, p. 60		+•refrain	same as II	•	•
Addams Family, The, p. 456		•	•	•	•
Adelita, p. 50	alto	•lines 2, 3; alto as written or •top pt	same as II	•either pt	•either pt
Ah ya Zane, p. 297		•except last 2 beats, m3+last 2m, line 3	•	•	•
All Through the Night, p. 105		•line 3	same as II	•	•
Ama-Lama, p. 142		•p1 omit low Cs, p2 line 2 •high Cs	•p1 omit low Cs, p2 •last 2m	•	•
Amazing Grace, p. 250	omit high D	•except low Ds remain at original pitch	•	•	•
America, p. 486	transpose to B or B♭, basses sing one octave lower				
America, the Beautiful, p. 76	•line 2, last 3m	•line 2, last 3m •lines 3, 4	same as II	•last 3m ••	same as N.B.
Arirang, p. 25		•m1–2, line 3	same as II	•	•
Ash Grove, The, p. 114	omit 1st 3m, p2	• descant	•descant	•melody	•melody
Autumn Canon, p. 148	omit high Ds	•lines 1, 2	•lines 1, 2	+	•
Away to America, p. 57		•line 4	•omit low Cs	+	•
Bantama kra kro, p. 308	either pt	lower pt	lower pt	•lower pt	same as N.B.
Basin Street Blues, p. 354	+refrain	+refrain •lines 3, 4	same as II	•	•
Battle Cry of Freedom, p. 272	omit lines 1, 2, p 2	+refrain •lines 1–3	same as II	•	•
Battle Hymn of the Republic, p. 274	melody	+refrain •descant	same as II	•	•
Beyond Borders, p. 292	alto	•lines 2–5, p1 •alto, p2	same as II	•alto	•alto
Blow the Wind Southerly, p. 178	+refrain	+•verse	+•verse	•	•
Blowin' in the Wind, p. 382	+refrain	•	•	•	•
Bound for South Australia, p. 22		+•1st response +2nd response •refrain/except 2nd ending	same as II	•	•
California, p. 52			•	•	•
Camptown Races, p. 270	melody or alto	omit solo alto	omit solo alto	•	•
Canción Mixteca, p. 326	alto	alto, omit unison section	same as II	•alto	•alto
Cattle Call, p. 344	+lines 3–4	+refrain; alto or •top part	same as II	•alto	•alto
Chiapanecas, p. 92	omit high Ds	•m23 (beat 2)–31, p2 lines 4–7	•omit low C♯s	•	•
Cho'i hát bội, p. 318		•omit low Ds	•	•	•
Choo Choo Ch'Boogie, p. 44		•some low notes	•	•	•
Colorado Trail, p. 276		+last 2m each line	•	•	•
Come and Go with Me to That Land, p. 390		•line 1, p2	same as II	•	•
Come, Ye Thankful People, Come, p. 458	alto	alto	alto	•either pt	•either pt
Connemara Lullaby, p. 232	omit high Ds & Es	•omit low Ds & Es	•	•	•
Da pacem, Domine, p. 62		•	•	•	•
Dancin' in the Street, p. 361		•	•	•	•
Day-O!, p. 18		•smaller notes	same as II	•	•
De colores, p. 90	either pt	alto	•top pt	•alto	•alto
Deck the Hall, p. 474	pt2	+line 1 +pt1	same as II	•pt2	•pt2
Don Alfonso, p. 177	either pt	alto	alto	•either pt	same as N.B.
Don't You Hear the Lambs?, p. 97			•verse	•	•
Down by the Riverside, p. 256			•	•	•
Drill, Ye Tarriers, p. 54	omit high Ds, Es	last m p2 +line 2	same as II	•	•
Dundai, p. 106	omit high Ds	•except last m, p1 & 3	•	•	•
Ego sum pauper, p. 158	omit high Ds	•except last note, line 1	same as II	•	•
El carite, p. 305		+•lines 2, 3, 4, 5	•	•	•
El desembre congelat, p. 473		+refrain •line 3	same as II	•	•
Éliza Kongo, p. 14	pt2	pt2	pt2	•pt2	•pt2
Erie Canal, p. 262	lower pt, refrain	+chorus •upper notes	same as II	•melody	•melody

Key:

• = melody or part to be sung one octave lower
•• = melody or part to be sung two octaves lower
+ = sing only this section
m = measure number
p = page
pt = part

Song Title	Midvoice I	Midvoice II	Midvoice IIA	New Baritone	Settling Baritone
Ev'ry Time I Feel the Spirit, p. 242	alto	alto or •top part	same as II	•alto	•alto
Fifty Nifty United States, p. 250		•p1 •p2, lines 1–3 •p4 lines 3–4 p5 lines 2, 3	same as II	•	•
For Children Safe and Strong, p. 484		verse •last 2m, line 4; refrain; alto	same as II except •lines 1, 3	•alto	•alto
Freedom Is Coming, p. 415	any pt	alto	alto	•	•
Funwa alafia, p. 32	omit high Ds	•except last measure	•	•	•
Get on Your Feet, p. 6	pt2 on coda	•omit low Ds	•coda: alto	•coda: alto	•coda: alto
Go Down, Moses, p. 190		•m1–2, lines 1, 2 •lines 3, 4 except last 2m	same as II	•	•
God Bless America, p. 4		•verse except m7–8, 15–16; •m11 (beat 4)–19	•verse, •m11 (beat 4)–22	•	•
Goin' Down the Road Feelin' Bad, p. 282		•line 1	same as II	•	•
Good Mornin', Blues, p. 224				•	•
Green Corn Song, p. 462		•lines 1–3	•lines 1–3	•	•
Greenland Whale Fishery, The, p. 230	omit high Ds	•omit low Ds	•	•	•
Haliwa-Saponi Canoe Song, p. 302		omit m2, lines 3, 4	same as II	•	•
Happy Days Are Here Again, p. 284	omit high Ds	•some notes too low	•	•	•
Heri za Kwanzaa, p. 476	lower pt	lower pt	lower pt	•lower pt	•lower pt
Himmel und Erde, p. 94		•except m3–4, m11–12	same as II	•	•
Hine mah tov, p. 430		+alto, p2 lines 1–2; •top part, except lines 3–4	same as II	•	•
Hitotsu toya, p. 478		•lines 1, 2	same as II	•	•
Home on the Range, p. 68		•omit low Ds, Cs	+omit low Cs	•	•
Hosanna, Me Build a House, p. 132	omit high Ds	•omit low Ds and Cs	•	•	•
Hound Dog, p. 212		•	•	•	•
I Believe I Can Fly, p. 170		•except or omit low Cs & Ds	•except or omit low Cs	•	•
I Love the Mountains, p. 34		•lines 2, 3	•lines 2, 3	•	•
I Vow to You, My Country, p. 418		+pt2B •pt1, beg. m38	same as II	•pt 2	•pt 2
If I Had a Hammer, p. 287		•except line 4, 5; •high D	same as II	•	+
Imbabura, p. 203	omit high D	•high As & Cs, lines 2–3, 6; •m18–25	•except or omit low Cs	•	•
It Don't Mean a Thing, p. 336		•omit low Es	•	•	•
Jasmine Flowers, p. 316	omit high Ds	•	•	•	•
Jo'ashilá, p. 108		•for high B♭s	same as II	•	•
Johnny Has Gone for a Soldier, p. 188		•lines 1, 3	•lines 1, 3	•	•
Joshua Fought the Battle of Jericho, p. 101	omit high Es	•	•	•	•
Kokoleoko, p. 33		•	•	•	•
Kum ba yah, p. 244	pt2 or 3 no solo	• pt1 or pt 3	• pt1 or pt3	•pt3	•pt3
La bamba, p. 128		•except lines 3, 6, on p2	same as II	•	•
La ciudad de Juaja, p. 58		•	•	•	•
La Jesusita, p. 322	omit high Ds	•omit low Ds	•	•	•
Lahk gei mohlee, p. 317	omit high Ds, Es	•	•	•	•
Land of a Thousand Dances, p. 330	alto	omit verse or sing • if comfortable, alto and unison on refrain	•verse, refrain same as II	•, alto on refrain	•, alto on refrain
Laredo, p. 10	alto	•top part except Cs, Fs	•top part except Cs & Fs	•	•
Las estrellitas del cielo, p. 175		•last line as written	•	•	•
Las Navidades, p. 472		•high Bs & C♯ option: •last line	same as II	•	•
Las velitas, p. 147		•except last 2m	•	•	•
Let Freedom Ring, p. 77	omit high Ds, Es	•	•	•	•
Lift Ev'ry Voice and Sing, p. 482	omit high Ds, Es	•except p2, •last 2 notes line 2 •lines 3, 4	same as II	•	•
Linstead Market, p. 241	alto: refrain	•verse alto: refrain	same as II	•alto	•alto

Key:

• = melody or part to be sung one octave lower   + = sing only this section   p = page

•• = melody or part to be sung two octaves lower   m = measure number   pt = part

Song Title	Midvoice I	Midvoice II	Midvoice IIA	New Baritone	Settling Baritone
Live in the City, p. 71	omit high Ds	•omit low Ds, Cs	•	•	•
Loch Lomond, p. 140	alto	+•chorus: alto	•verse •refrain: top part	•	•
Los reyes de Oriente, p. 480	alto	alto	alto	•alto	•alto
Love Is on Our Side, p. 324		•omit low Ds, Cs	•	•	•
Mango Walk, p. 200	+lines 2, 4	••+lines 1, 3	same as II	•	•
Meng Jian Nu, p. 194	omit high Ds	•omit low Ds	•	•	•
Morning Comes Early, p. 13	omit high Ds, Es	•lines 2, 3	•lines 2, 3	•	•
Morning Has Broken, p. 29	+lines 2, 3, 4	+lines 2, 4	same as II	•	•
Now's the Time, p. 444		•m27, 28, 31, 38 pt2, top part; +m57–58, pt2 to end	same as II		
O, Desayo, p. 411	pt2	+p2; •top part, line 1 •pt2, line 2 •pt2, lines 1–3, p3	same as II	•	•
O Music, p. 162	+lines 1, 3	•lines 1, 2	•lines 1, 2	•	•
Oh, Freedom, p. 392		•lines 2, 3	same as II		
Oh, Watch the Stars, p. 216		•line 2	•	•	•
Oklahoma, p. 36	+sing harmony pts p38	same as I	same as I	•harmony parts	same as N.B.
Old Abram Brown, p. 222	•high Ds	•line 2: m2 •line 3	•line 2, m2 •line 3, 4	•	•
One Small Step, p. 126	•line 7, p1 omit high Ds, Es	•lines 6–7, p1 •p2	same as II	•	•
Orange Blossom Special, p. 266		•line 3, p1 •line 2, p2	•	•	•
Over There, p. 279		•lines 3, 4, 7, 8	•	•	•
Oy, Hanuka, p. 464		•omit low Ds option: lines 2–3, 6 at pitch	•	•	•
Pat Works on the Railway, p. 182		pt2 on refrain	same as II	•	•
Play a Simple Melody, p. 72		+omit low Bs, Cs, Ds	•omit low Bs, Cs	•	•
Pollerita, p. 151		•lines 1–3, p1 •lines 2, 4, p2	same as II	•	•
Promised Land, The, p. 258		omit high As & Ds	•	•	•
Quâ câù gió bay, p. 460		•line 2	•sing low As as written	•	•
¡Qué bonita bandera!, p. 294	alto	+refrain, alto	same as II	+•refrain, alto	same as N.B.
Ragupati Ragava Raja Ram, p. 321		•last line 4	same as II	•	•
Río, río, p. 371	alto	alto option: •line 3	same as II	•alto	•alto
Rise Up, Shepherd, and Follow, p. 471		•verse except last 2 beats, line 3, 4, refrain •line 1, m2, 3	same as II	•	•
Ríu ríu chíu, p. 434		•top part +	•top part	•	•
Rockin' Around the Christmas Tree, p. 466		•except last 2 notes p1, 2	same as II	•	•
Rocky Top, p. 348		•except last 2m of each line	•	•	•
Roll On, Columbia, p. 116	pt1, p2	•descant	•descant	•verse, pt2	same as N.B.
Sail Away, p. 404		alto	alto	•	•
San Antonio Rose, p. 134	•p1 last 2m, p2 first 3m	•high As & C♯s, p1 line 5, p2 line1	same as II except p2 •line 4	•omit low As	•
Scotland the Brave, p. 138	omit line 1, p2	•high Es	+•refrain	•	•
Se va el caimán, p. 306		•		•	•
Shady Grove, p. 260	omit high Ds	•m4–5, 12–13	•	•	•
Shenandoah, p. 264		•lines 2, 3	•lines 2, 3	•	•
Ship that Never Returned, The, p. 402		+•refrain, except line 1, line 2, m1–2, line 4, m4	same as II	•	•
Simple Gifts, p. 184		•possible for some in spots	•omit low Es	•	•
Sing, Sing, Sing!, p. 340	alto	•verse refrain: alto	same as II	•	•
Somewhere Out There, p. 368	omit high Ds	+line 5 •line1, p2 •line 6	same as II	•	•
St. Louis Blues, p. 352		•m1	•m1	•	•

Key:

•	= melody or part to be sung one octave lower	+	= sing only this section	p	= page
••	= melody or part to be sung two octaves lower	m	= measure number	pt	= part

Song Title	Midvoice I	Midvoice II	Midvoice IIA	New Baritone	Settling Baritone
Stand By Me, p. 46	omit 1st line of refrain	•	•	•	•
Star-Spangled Banner, The, p. 488	alto	•top part beg. last beat, p1	same as II	•	•
Still, Still, Still, p. 468		•1st 2 notes	•1st 2 notes •line 3	•	•
Teach Me to Swing, p. 84	omit high Ds	•	•	•	•
There's a Place, p. 210	alto, p1 omit lines 1, 2, p3	alto p2, •lines 2, 3, p2	same as II	•alto, p1 • •lines 1, 2, p2	same as N.B.
This Land Is Your Land, p. 118	melody	•top part last 5m as written	same as II	•melody	•melody
This Train, p. 27	omit high E♭	•lines 2, 3 last 4 notes, line 3 as written	same as II	•	•
This World, p. 168		•lines 3–5, p1 •lines 1, 2, 4, p2	same as II	•	•
Tumba, p. 161	take lower octave D, line 3	•line 3	•	•	•
Turn, Turn, Turn, p. 378	omit high Ds	•refrain	•refrain	•	•
Twelve Gates to the City, p. 280		•m3–4, •verse except m20–22, 32–34	•refrain except m8–10, verse same as II	•	•
Tzena, tzena, p. 298		•pt II, III	•pt II, III	•	•
ʻŪlili E, p. 441	pts2 or 3	+pts2 or 3	same as II	•	•
Under the Sea, p. 372	omit high Ds	•line 1, 4, p1 •p2–6	same as II	•	•
Uno, dos, y tres, p. 426	alto	alto	alto	•melody or alto	same as N.B.
Viva Jujuy, p. 228		•m3, 5, 13	same as II	•	•
Voices of Pride, The, p. 86	omit high Ds, Es	•p2, lines 1, 2, 4	same as II	•	•
Wabash Cannon Ball, p. 136	omit high Ds	•omit low Ds	•	•	•
When Johnny Comes Marching Home, p. 180			•lines 2, 3	•	•
Winter Wonderland, p. 454	omit high Ds, E♭s	•	•	•	•
Woke Up This Morning, p. 288		•except line 3	•	•	•
World of Difference, A, p. 386		•line 3, p1, •last m, p1 •lines 1–2, p2 •m1, line 3, p2	same as II	•	•
Yakety Yak, p. 205	•	•	•	••	••
Ye jaliya da, p. 67		omit high Es	omit high Cs	•	•
You've Got a Friend, p. 366		•1st phrase as written; also last 3 phrases, p2	same as II	•	•
Yüe liang wan wan, p. 314		•lines 1, 2	•lines 1, 2	•	•
Zum gali gali, p. 401		•verse	•verse	•	•
Zuni Sunrise Call, p. 396				•	•

Key:

- • = melody or part to be sung one octave lower
- •• = melody or part to be sung two octaves lower
- \+ = sing only this section
- m = measure number
- p = page
- pt = part

Teacher Notes

RESEARCH
Validates the Program

Making Music Research Base

Silver Burdett MAKING MUSIC incorporates the rich tradition and history of a company that has served the music education profession for almost 120 years. Because this experience has been merged with applications of the most recent research on learning in music, teachers may safely rely on the curriculum, instructional models, and methods that comprise the program. The strong, empirical base of the program is strengthened by the considerable number of authors who are themselves researchers in music teaching and learning and have published works in their specific fields. Many of the authors have specialized in and researched areas such as curriculum design, perception, acquisition of music skills, and repertoire for music learning. Authors for Orff Process, Listening Maps, Signing, Child Voice, Adolescent Voice, and other specific areas, a Multicultural Advisory Panel, and a Teacher Advisory Panel also helped to shape MAKING MUSIC.

Research documents the ways in which children perceive and respond to music, how individuals approach the task of learning, and how they gain insights through involvement with music materials. MAKING MUSIC takes into account that every child is inherently musical and has the potential for musical growth. It also reflects the research in how that growth occurs. For example, MAKING MUSIC recognizes that children go through several stages in their ability to sing accurately and expressively. Therefore the program provides effective strategies and materials for nurturing vocal growth at every stage of development.

Research in music learning shows that students often understand a concept before they can accurately perform the related skill. For example, the concept of beat is often attained at a fairly young age, but the ability to maintain a steady beat at a variety of speeds or tempos does not occur until around the age of nine. MAKING MUSIC was created to distinguish between skills development and conceptual understandings. Skills strands are introduced, developed slowly, and practiced over time. Analogous concepts are introduced and interwoven as appropriate so that meaning is not separated from practice.

According to Howard Gardner, children come to school already knowing a great deal about music. Children are usually able to apply to music the concepts of loud/soft, high/low, fast/slow, and long/short. They respond readily to style and can often name different styles. They know the names and sounds of many instruments and are eager to manipulate sounds to create interesting effects and patterns. Students are open to a wide range of music. They have a strong sense of the syntax of music from their own cultures. Most importantly, they do not question whether they are musical but naturally employ the human language of music.

> ### MAKING MUSIC
> takes into account that every student is inherently musical and has the potential for musical growth.

When children begin formal schooling, the challenge for the music educator is to ensure that children grow musically from their intuitive knowledge to discipline-specific knowledge. The National Standards for Arts Education provide guidelines for this process. These standards, issued by MENC: National Association for Music Education, identify the music elements and skills that should be covered at each grade level, and these same elements and skills form the foundation of MAKING MUSIC.

Activities for skills development, written by many excellent teachers who understand the development of music skills, are woven through the series. Complementing the skills strand is an in-depth focus on concept development. MAKING MUSIC has dedicated an entire section of each grade to the development of music elements and skills, using an appropriate and pedagogically sound sequence. Elements are introduced through discovery, expanded, assessed, reviewed, and applied, using new materials that demand increasingly sophisticated listening and perception.

Skills Acquisition

- Many research studies related to music skills acquisition have agreed that students learn more about music when they use keyboards. This has proven to be true for both elementary and middle school students. Therefore, a keyboard skills strand has been incorporated into grades K-8 of MAKING MUSIC.
- In another skills area, the Listening Map Transparencies included in this program are visuals designed to represent musical sounds. By using simplified scores students are provided a greater awareness of specific elements of music. Listening map transparencies in MAKING MUSIC are of this type, and while they illustrate the sound, they are careful not to apply any subjective meanings to the listening selections.
- Common sense tells us that reading notation, or in the case of songs, reading notation with lyrics simultaneously, can be a difficult skill to acquire. MAKING MUSIC always prints songs (with lyrics and notation) against a white background. Also, color-coded identification of vocal parts is placed before the music staff begins instead of surprinting the actual vocal part.

Assessment Practices

- Recent research also suggests that assessment practices reflect and document the range of behaviors specific to the discipline being studied. Studies on the value of written assessment as a self-teaching tool have encouraged the addition of writing projects to lessons. Ideas for reflective thinking and self-assessment through maintenance are particularly appropriate to music instruction. Ideas for use of video, audio, and written entries that may comprise portfolios are given throughout the series.

Contemporary/Popular Music

- One aspect of student motivation and involvement in music learning is subjective task value, which includes attraction as a source of enjoyment for its own sake. Music preference and attitude studies show that students prefer music styles that are popular and regarded as their own. The shift to preference for popular music may begin as early as age five or six. MAKING MUSIC offers students contemporary and popular music that speaks to students' interests outside the classroom, while it also offers more traditional, multicultural, and "classical" selections than any other program. Interviews with popular musicians of proven ability and appeal further relate students' daily music with music learning and help them recognize the commitment necessary to become a "pro."

Culturally Diverse Music

- MAKING MUSIC also recognizes that music literature representing a diversity of cultures and countries is an important contributor to multicultural education, now mandated in many schools.

> **The inclusion of music literature from a student's own culture increases his or her sense of self-esteem.**

With the advancement of cultural pluralism, there is increased necessity for students to understand and appreciate music of cultures different from their own. Also, the inclusion of music literature from a student's own culture increases his or her sense of self-esteem. Research shows that students learn more and have a greater appreciation for diversity in music when they are actively involved. MAKING MUSIC actively involves students in music literature from many different cultures and countries.

Teaching Style Concepts

- Studies have confirmed the effectiveness of teaching style concepts by comparing pieces and excerpts of the style being studied as well as pieces of a contrasting style. This practice is incorporated into all levels of MAKING MUSIC.

Music Literacy

- MAKING MUSIC is a program that sustains students' interest as it brings them to music literacy and proficiency. Research on these different factors has been integrated into MAKING MUSIC by authors who were selected for their strong credentials in the various fields of music learning. This outstanding group of music professionals has created a program with which teachers can accomplish the goal of all music instruction—enthusiastic, musically literate students capable of a lifetime of active involvement in music.

QUALITY RECORDINGS in the Classroom

Today's Children and the Contemporary Sound

Since first becoming aware of its power, people throughout the ages have listened to music through "mental earphones." These earphones have always delivered music to us with sound that originates from the technological, environmental, and social conditions of the era. Whether a log drum in the jungles of Africa or a harpsichord in an eighteenth-century French drawing room, the sound of an instrument is fashioned by the available material from which it was made, the shape to which that material was transformed, the way in which the performer plays, and the site of the performance. The social context in which the music takes place also influences our way of listening. In church, at a high tea, in a salon, at a sporting event—each of these situations influences how we hear and respond to music.

Though we may not like to think of music as a product of technology, it nevertheless is colored by technology in critical and profound ways. The electronic organ, for example, has changed the sound of African American music so much that its special "electric" tone color has become a natural part of our perception of the gospel sound.

Electronics has had a deep and lasting impact on the ways we listen to music. Whether we listen through sound speakers or a headset, in an arena or in a Broadway theater, music is often heard through electronic reproduction. Even symphony concerts and opera performances, once the haven for unamplified performances, are sometimes assisted

 True To The Music
—*A Commentary by Buryl Red*

Few musicians are as well known in nearly every niche of the music industry as Buryl Red. He has an international reputation as a composer, arranger, conductor, and producer. Not surprisingly, he is also a staunch advocate of music education, serving most recently as Executive Producer of recordings for Silver Burdett MAKING MUSIC. The following article contains his beliefs regarding the role and purpose of recordings in music education, both past and present.

through subtle electronic enhancement. This "electronicization" of contemporary music has produced a generation of children steeped in the electronically amplified sound. Such children have difficulty as they first encounter the traditional venues of the concert hall and opera house when amplification is not being employed. The sound, to these children, sounds somehow distant and without presence. The common complaint is, "It isn't loud enough!" Some of these children grow up to become recording engineers who have never heard the sound of a real acoustic violin or flute or piano. Having never been to a concert, they are unacquainted with the pure sound of those instruments unembellished by electronic wizardry. Even some adult concertgoers are beginning to complain that the Mahler symphony they hear in the concert hall is not as compelling sonically as what they hear on their CD players at home.

These, then, are our children—reared in a new tradition and accustomed to a

sound that their elders did not experience as they grew up. So in presenting recordings to today's children, especially in a classroom series, it is of greatest importance that those recordings have the intensity and energy that young contemporary ears want to experience and have come to expect. In MAKING MUSIC, the full weight of modern recording technology has been brought to bear on the wonderful songs that are the backbone and strength of this program. Instrumental tracks have been created that favorably compare to the sound of recordings children hear at home and on the street.

Recording for Authenticity in All Cultures and Styles

In MAKING MUSIC, concern and sensitivity have gone into the recordings to ensure that they provide authenticity in the program's multicultural songs and listening selections. Care has been taken to create recorded performances that reflect the style and conditions of each culture. Recording an ethnic selection involves making subtle choices. In recording a blues song, for example, I must ask myself a number of questions: Is the song a blues from the old folk tradition? Is it a modern blues composed for a Broadway show? Is it a hybrid of the two, or perhaps something in-between? Once that has been decided, an arrangement must be written to create that exact sound and flavor, and the performance and recording must represent the subtleties of the particular tradition. The days are now past when that traditional blues song can be recorded with flute, harp, and vibraphone and sung by young children who do not represent and cannot produce the sound of the singers who would sing that blues song. We might record it, but our children wouldn't "buy" it.

I believe, too, that as we recognize and respect the styles of various non-Western cultures and ethnic groups, we must be equally zealous in maintaining the stylistic integrity of the varied musical expressions of Western cultures. Presenting a song from a Broadway musical would mean that we have recorded the tune as it sounds on Broadway rather than as it would sound were it recorded in some concocted manner that suits "children's music." We have made a very special effort to represent the traditions of all types of music in their proper context.

The Myth of Children's Music

The recordings of contemporary popular music in MAKING MUSIC sound like contemporary popular music rather than watered-down imitations. In the not-so-distant past, such imitations served to make this style of music more suitable as "children's music" or, worse, "textbook music." We have too long subscribed to the idea that music for children must be "dumbed down" to ensure that they grasp it easily. That idea may be one of the most damaging of myths about children and their ability to hear and perceive music aesthetically. Children are eager to demonstrate that they can handle almost any music that excites them; textbook recordings have, in the past, often failed to do this.

I don't believe there is such a thing as "children's music." There is only music that reaches out and touches people, both young and old. A friend once pointed out to me that children's music is any music that children enjoy singing or hearing. Children need not be talked down to musically. They are capable of listening to and enjoying pieces that may strike adults as technically complex, because they listen with open ears and no preconceived notions. These pieces need to be recorded for them with full attention to their expressive content, authenticity, and validity. Even if the purpose of the arrangement is to place emphasis on a particular musical concept, we do not want to say that the performance of the music itself doesn't really matter, or that it doesn't need to be artistically or emotionally convincing. Even with those pieces that have been composed with a pedagogical point in mind, we want to communicate to our young audience the emotional impact of the music. After all, isn't that what it's all about?

> ...children's music
> is any music
> that children enjoy
> singing or hearing.

Most children already have some skill in perceiving stylistic differences in music by the time they arrive at school. They know the difference between a pop song and a rap, for example. It is equally important to present music that is not so familiar to them, such as concert (or "serious") music, folk music from diverse cultures, and music from distant historical periods. To do that properly, these styles must be presented with equal intensity, as well as emotional and artistic integrity. If this is not done, children will gain the impression that music recorded offhandedly or with obvious lack of care has no feeling and is not worthy of attention. That would

do a great deal of harm. For this reason, all genres of music must be presented within their broadest definitions. For example, African American music is so rich in its varied styles that even a spiritual can be presented in many different ways, all of which are valid from historical viewpoints. That spiritual might have been performed as a church or field song, or an Underground Railroad song in the nineteenth century. Today it might be performed as a gospel song.

Recording Performances

Recordings in MAKING MUSIC contain performances that capture this integrity and intensity. We asked our instrumentalists and singers to perform with the same attention to artistic detail that they would bring to any concert, recording date, or theatrical performance. The music dominated and the musicians played more than dots on paper. They paid attention to the stylistic and dynamic nuances of any professional performance. There were *rubatos* and *ritardandos*, shades of loud and soft, and the artists lent their own deeply felt interpretations. In short, the performers came to the studio to make *real* music. Best of all, thanks to the superb quality of the arrangements and original compositions, we were freed from the "jingle" sound that has for too many years dominated the educational music recording field.

Communication is what good musical performance is, and we tried never to forget it. Often this effort to communicate the style and feeling of the music determined the choice of vocalists. In the majority of cases we featured children's choruses on the song selections, but at times we realized that children's voices could not always communicate the energy and the intensity of the music—in a gospel song, for instance. In such situations it was clear that adult voices could more adequately acquaint children with the goal we were aiming for—to demonstrate what the music is really supposed to sound like. Appropriately, both children and adults have often been used together, a very felicitous combination.

In using adult voices, only the very best from their stylistic fields were chosen to perform for these recordings. A song from India called for singers who were associated with a Hindu temple, who knew the song from personal experience, and who knew how it was supposed to be sung. An African song brought in singers from the African continent— singers such as South African stars Thuli Dumakude and Blondie Chaplin, who brought true authenticity and feeling to the music.

Folk songs from South America were beautifully recreated by the group Andes Mata, who arrived at the studio with panpipes and *charongas*. When we wanted a more contemporary South American sound, we found the best in Gustavo Moretto, whose studies in this country have led to his recognition as a serious concert composer in the United States but who is considered a pop and jazz performer in South America.

For an African American gospel song, we chose performers who could represent that style impeccably— Carol Woods, for example, one of our finest African American singing stars of Broadway and film.

Other world-class musicians whom we involved in these recordings were Yomo Toro, the great guitarist well known in the Latino community; Joseph Joubert, who has been musical director for Judy Collins and accompanist for Wynton Marsalis, Kathleen Battle, and Ben Vereen; and Linda Twine, who has conducted such hit musicals as *Jelly's Last Jam*, *Big River*, and *The Wiz*.

Notation—A Matter of Interpretation

In many ways we are just beginning to be comfortable with other ways of producing sound. This is an issue, especially in vocal music, for those of us who have been schooled in the purest Western choral tradition, which includes jazz and pop styles as well as the Western "classical" tradition. The multicultural movement has shown us that there are other equally valid ways of producing vocal sound, although some of these styles may make us uncomfortable because of our lack of experience with them. Our first impulse is to try to notate the songs and melodies of these non-Western cultures. Notation was conceived and developed specifically to record on paper the music of Western Europe. Unfortunately, most non-Western music cannot be contained, rhythmically or tonally, within the Western notational system.

It's a dilemma. But I feel we have been too much a slave to notation in past music series. After all, even within the context of Western music of all eras and styles—especially in jazz and popular music—music is rarely performed exactly as it is printed on the page. Music is dependent on an interpretation by a performer, unless the composer has written for a computer and has been in control of every nuance. This is why we have chosen the very best performers to make these recordings. We know that their interpretations will be valid ones, even though there might be elements that another musician might have done a little differently. I think we have addressed very well that dilemma between notation and interpretation and provided an example for every student of the ways in which notation becomes a "blueprint" for performance without being a dictator.

Pick-A-Track™ vs. Stereo Performance Track

The Pick-A-Track technique, introduced over two decades ago by Silver Burdett, was handy for teaching songs using the recorded voices and then "dialing them out" so that children in the classroom could sing the song with the instrumental track only. Teachers loved this recording feature. The problem with Pick-A-Track is that it is unnatural. Music is not naturally heard the way it is presented in Pick-A-Track. When you attend a live performance, the sound from the singers and the instrumentalists is heard from roughly the same source. No one hears the singers' sound coming from one sole spot and the instrumentalists from another.

A better way of dealing with the "voices versus instrumentalists" question is provided by the stereo vocal and the stereo performance tracks. In the stereo vocal, the sound is recorded and mixed just as it is in commercial recordings, providing a rich, full stereo sound that has depth, balance, and clarity. Songs in MAKING MUSIC are recorded as full stereo vocals with techniques used in the best commercial recordings.

A Philosophy of Recording

We have approached the recording process of MAKING MUSIC with a definite philosophy in mind: to create recordings that are true to the music—recordings that will stimulate a child's interest and create an exciting response in a way that the old textbook recording philosophy, with its super-simple accompaniments, basic harmonic structure, unmusical interpretations, and babyish singers, did not. We know now that children need to be able to hear "classroom" music in the same aurally exciting way they hear their favorite recording artists.

Classroom Management

As we know, unresolved classroom discipline and management issues can often be at the heart of teacher stress and dissatisfaction. How can we begin to improve our own music classroom discipline and management strategies in order to increase student learning and also increase our own happiness and satisfaction in our classrooms?

Creating Positive Environments for Musical Learning

The rewards of teaching music to young students are obvious, but may deserve focus here as we balance a discussion of the ever-present discipline and management concerns in many of our music classrooms. We music teachers enjoy frequent reminders of the success of our hard work in the classroom. Among these joys are the treasured moments when we actually see and hear evidence of our students' musical development—the satisfying sounds of their active music making; their faces reflecting their hard work and accompanying sense of personal and group accomplishment; the pride of increasing music skills and knowledge; and, of course, our group performance goals well met and received. However, we also know that these and other rewarding moments don't come easily. They are often accompanied by recurring challenges involving music classroom discipline and management.

As music teachers, we are aware of the need for constructive suggestions and direct action toward improving our music classroom environments. Evidence of successful hard work in this area often includes the following teacher-centered events:

• careful pre-thought and classroom organizational planning

• the establishment and practice of positive and effective discipline and management techniques

• consistent expectations and appropriate reinforcement of students' efforts

• reflection with other teachers resulting in classroom experimentation, growth, and development of discipline and management skills throughout one's career.

Simply put, many music teachers seek some guidance about their discipline and management practices including the enhancement of communication skills and relationships with students. Furthermore, they need to talk and listen to one another, especially those closest to the problems at hand.

The following sections of this article will offer a variety of practical suggestions and strategies for planning/organizing, implementing, evaluating, and reflecting upon discipline and management techniques in the classroom.

Organizing for a Successful Year (Pre-planning)

Try some of the following ideas for increased organization and communication at your school site.

• **Plan ahead for less performance stress.**
Meet with your appropriate school-site administrator before the school year begins. Outline your needs for rehearsal space, dates, and times, as well as tentative dates and times for actual performances and assemblies. Once you have these agreed dates, be sure they actually appear on the school's master calendar. Create a brief flyer with this information to share with classroom teachers, administrators, and parents. Make it known that all is scheduled.

• **Toot your own horn.**
Share a one-page description that highlights selected activities and learning which will take place in your classroom. Be sure to list performance dates. Share this information at faculty meetings. The more opportunities you have in which you can share your teaching with others, the better. Invite peers and administrators to your classroom to witness what the students can do in music class.

• **Open the door to communication about music's solid role within the entire school curriculum.**
Invite administrators, school board members, parents, and classroom teachers to join in your performance efforts. Administrators might be willing to greet parents. Other teachers might be willing to narrate or join your efforts by displaying at actual performances student artwork, poetry, and other projects related to your performance themes and song texts.

Classroom Management *continued*

Music Classroom Tips: Selected Strategies for Positive Environments

One overriding goal within a well-managed, positive learning environment is the development of individual student self-discipline and self-control. The following suggestions are also meant to increase your positive interactions with the students, and students with each other.

- **Avoid chaos upon entry to the music classroom.**

  Many teachers experience problems with misbehavior right at the start of the music lesson. What may be needed is a non-verbal focus activity. Try posting a chart with interesting, different ways for students to enter your classroom each day. For example, "Walk in very slow motion, no talking… and be seated by the end of the metallophone music." Greet your class outside the door, point to the sign, and start the entry. Be sure to reward students who follow the suggestion. You might ask students to think of interesting ways to enter. For example, "Tip-toe to the table, get your music books, open to page 53, and wave." Write these suggestions on cards and start a collection of ideas!

- **Every good meal has a tempting menu!**

  Create a very brief outline "menu" of your lesson. Write key words (make them interesting) on the board and go over the plan with the students. Let them know where the lesson is going. For example, "New partner dance from a surprise desert country" or "New note on the recorder=?" Menus provide a way to keep the class moving forward time-wise and, at the same time, involve students in looking forward to what will happen next.

- **Use your classroom space to increase student focus.**

  Consider using different areas of your classroom for different general music activities. These areas can be very close together. For example, students may learn that musical listening is near the AV equipment, recorder practice and reading/notation drill is near a chart area, movement is in an open space, related children's literature and dramatization is in a reading/visuals corner, and Orff instruments is in another corner. If you do not have your own music room, consider how this idea can be adapted to other classroom spaces, usually within more confined spaces. Simply changing direction and focus may be a way of increasing interest in your lesson activities.

Specific Activity Tips

- **Singing**

  Behavior problems often occur when students do not know what to do next, particularly when beginning new song material using printed music. Try asking students to work with a partner to survey a new song by saying to them, "Point to the first ending and show your partner where we are" or "Point to the words of the song text as we listen to the CD recording" or "Point to the words as we say them together in rhythm," and so on. You might also say, "I may stop the recording. If I do, please silently show your partner where we are in the music. Then we will go on." Also, ask students to take turns with a partner and read song texts aloud, or sing phrases back and forth for extra practice. Reward pairs who can do this well.

- **Movement**

  Many teachers desire to teach movement on a frequent basis but may dread the possible chaos. You may wish to try the following.

  Bus Stop Designate a known area in the front of your room (for example, in front of the piano or table) as the "bus stop." During movement activities where students must find a partner, there are two simple rules— no one can say no if asked, and if you cannot find a partner, simply go to the "bus stop" and wait. The first person you meet there is your partner, as the person can't say no.

  Specific Commands Students can misuse a lot of valuable class time to form one or more dance circles. Try saying to them, "We need a standing-up single circle in the middle of our space by the time I finish counting to 10. Please go there without talking. Let's see if you can do it. Let me know when you are ready." Then count to "10" slowly. Look away and let the students tell you the circle is ready. Lavish them with praise. If unsuccessful, have the class do it again. They will want to please you.

- **Listening**

  Try structuring your music listening episode into three parts by using simple non-verbal cues and known responses (depending on the type of listening you are doing). For example, if students are listening to a recorded instrument featured within pictures in the student books, tell them, "We will have a signal for three things. When you see one finger up, listen quietly. Two fingers up means you are to point to the picture of the

Aim for increasingly positive feedback!

instrument you hear. Three fingers up means you are to write the name of the instrument and some words describing its sound." Observe how closely students pay attention to your non-verbal signals!

- **Instrument Buddies**
  Most of us must have our students share Orff and other classroom percussion instruments. Pair up students (including those with special needs) with another before instruments are assigned. One student plays while the other watches and sings. When it is time to change instrument players, take a moment of class time for the first buddy to "teach" their part to the next. Buddies can also help the new players by conducting the actual playing motion, steady beat, and so on. Students can then repeat the same routine by going to different instruments, always with the former "player" teaching the new player.

Remember you are not alone!

When things go wrong, consider. . .

- **Are you as positive as you think you are?**
  Research points to the fact that effective teachers make positive comments approximately three out of four times to their students. Video tape yourself on a typical day and tally your comments to your students (negative, positive, neutral). You may be surprised!

- **Aim for increasingly positive feedback.**
  Provide positive comments for student behavior that are actually appropriate for the task at hand. These positive re-enforcements do not need to be artificial or forced in nature and can include a nod of the head, a "thumbs-up," and a smile. Verbal comments can include "That recorder descant is really coming along," or "Way to go! I didn't have to ask you to put away the instruments." Aim to increase your positive comments in class, and your students will in turn desire to behave in order to hear your praise. Remember to reserve praise for true growth and effort.

Try the following.

- **Younger children**
  Choose an indestructible item such as a beanbag, stuffed animal, plastic cup, and so on. Keep this colorful item in the same place, visible to all students to the front and side of the classroom. Teach your students that the object will be handed to anyone who is talking, off-task,

and so on. If given the item, they must hold it silently until they stop what they are doing and are willing to join the group again. They simply must put the object back in its regular place. Then, when and if a student misbehaves, simply hand the student the object (saying nothing) and let them determine when to physically put it back. Follow up with a discussion with that student (after class) about what behavior they changed.

- **Older children**
  Sometimes a student must be isolated from the group. Make this isolation time productive by putting that student to work. Provide a piece of paper with two columns. One is "What went wrong today," the other is "What I will do next time instead." After class, discuss the student's responses, tear up the "wrong" side, and have the student keep (or send to the parent with return signature and/or phone call home) the "What I will do next time instead" side.

Invite discussion and reflection about discipline and management.

Remember, you are not alone. Many teachers report that some of their best solutions to discipline and management problems come from other teachers—music teachers, classroom teachers, and specialists. Try the following suggestions.

- Don't depend on others to start a dialogue on this subject! Invite a peer to listen to your situation and give you feedback and suggestions. Let them know how it went when you implemented suggestions. Keep track of things that work well. Offer the same help to them and others in person, over the phone, via e-mail, and so on. We often can help others more than we can help ourselves, and, in doing so, end up solving some of our own challenges along the way.

- Ask your school-site administrator and music/arts coordinators for professional time to observe others teach and exchange discipline strategies.

- Request that decision-makers create opportunities at professional growth days and meetings for teachers to talk to other teachers about discipline and management ideas. Encourage teachers to share their strengths in this area.

- Reach out to student teachers and new teachers who many times are in great need of your experience with discipline and management. Offer to mentor others.

MEETING INDIVIDUAL NEEDS

INCLUSION

Legislative mandates have resulted in hundreds of thousands of children with disabilities receiving a free, appropriate education—a free, appropriate music education—that had previously been denied to them. Children with disabilities are now singing, playing instruments, listening to music, dancing, and making friends in inclusive music classrooms.

Since the passage of *The Individuals with Disabilities Education Act* (formerly *The Education for All Handicapped Children Act of 1975*), concerned parents, guardians, teachers, administrators, and other professionals have continuously worked to provide in inclusive settings the highest quality education for children with and without disabilities. These efforts are documented by a wealth of printed literature, clinics, and in-service programs that focus on educational opportunities that will result in children with disabilities living maximally independent, happy, and productive lives in their homes, schools, and communities.

> **A challenge of inclusive classrooms is to maintain the highest expectations for each student.**

Music can enrich the quality of life of all children, and children with disabilities can participate, or partially participate, in the same meaningful music activities as their peers. The inclusive music classroom may be the only opportunity for children with disabilities to learn music skills and apply knowledge that will enhance the quality of their musical lives. In some cases, children with disabilities may be gifted or musically talented. Because of the high emphasis on verbal and motor skills in school, these children are not easily identified.

A challenge of inclusive classrooms is to maintain the highest expectations for each student and to carefully observe, assess, and nurture a wide range of music responses, from the simple to the more complex. Children may be different in many ways, but what remains constant are the long-term values that we hold for their well-being, happiness, and musical development.

Collaboration, Communication, and Support

The long-term effectiveness of any music program for a child with disabilities requires communication and collaboration with others who are knowledgeable about the individual. Time spent at the beginning of the school year, and ongoing contact, can build an important support group for the student as well as the music teacher. The particular type of disability category is relatively unimportant compared to knowing pertinent information about the student's safety. Information that will specifically affect instructional decisions includes the nature of any physical disabilities or health impairments, medications, or medical procedures.

Children with disabilities are important resources because they can communicate ways in which the teacher can structure activities for inclusion. In conversations with others, no matter how brief, teachers should inform parents (and others, including the child) about the child's successes in the music classroom—no matter how small they may seem at the time.

Teachers should communicate music and social goals to classroom aides and define the ways in which they can help the child progress socially and musically. Likewise, it is important that tolerance and social problem solving are taught to classrooms of students throughout the year. Students without disabilities should be taught when and how to help their disabled peers, although each student with a disability should be given every opportunity to participate successfully and as independently as possible.

Planning and Implementing Lessons

Children with and without disabilities are exposed to essentially the same music curriculum for each grade level, and expectations should be high for each child. A flexible curriculum that provides multiple ways of expressing competency and achievement will not lower standards. Specific adaptations for any child should be minimal and in keeping with the intent of the lesson and the lesson's activities. In some cases, adaptations that are necessary to meet the individual needs of a child may be appropriate for all students and can be incorporated easily into the lesson.

Well-established teaching principles apply to teaching all children in every situation, and yet the success of each child's learning is dependent upon individualizing those principles. Some examples of these principles are:

- knowing what is important to teach and when

- knowing what will motivate a child
- knowing when and what kind of questions or tasks to ask of a child
- knowing when and how to give a child feedback
- knowing how to teach skills, knowledge, and confidence.

Individualizing instruction remains at the core of excellence in teaching and learning. Planning individually focused accommodations facilitates instruction that is aligned with the music curriculum and relevant to individual needs.

Strategies

Here are several principles and specific strategies to consider in planning and implementing lessons.

- Encourage children to perform music, even simple choral accompaniments or improvisation, at home when they are alone or for family and friends.

- Provide opportunities to make choices and decisions about music and music making that are similar to those that are given to non-disabled peers.

- Provide frequent opportunities for social interactions with peers in small groups and with a kind partner.

- Communicate and greet the child in the same manner as you would other children of the same age from the same class. Monitor your proximity and interactions with the child and make adjustments when needed.

- Use small groups and partners early in the school year. Place no more than one child with a disability in any group, along with kind, sensitive children who are good musical models.

- Analyze sequences and implement relevant steps that move from simple tasks to more complex ones. Even the simplest task should be experienced in an age-appropriate context.

- Provide an adequate range of examples to exemplify a concept.

- Provide adequate practice across activities that are interesting and engaging. When children perform a rhythm or sing a phrase correctly, have them repeat that experience as a class, in small groups, individually, and in a variety of related activities.

- Although some children may have specific behavioral programs that require individual procedures, develop a set of classroom rules, routines, and management techniques that are consistently applied with all children.

- Teach children what to do when they lose their place or make a mistake. Good musicians develop skills for recovering from errors.

- Give individual specific praise and corrective feedback as a matter of routine.

- If a child cannot participate fully, develop minimal adaptations to allow him or her to participate as completely and independently as possible.

- Some children may have difficulty with tasks involving printed materials (such as tracing musical phrases or locating music symbols). Single word cues at the beginning of lines may help organize the search. Have children work in pairs on some occasions, tracing and locating symbols and words together.

- Have children with physical disabilities play a variety of instruments and instrumental parts for accompaniments and in ensembles. First, observe physical movements as children perform simple and more complex patterns on different "silent instruments." Then provide choices of instruments that you know the children will be able to play, and give them choices of rhythms they have performed successfully during "silent practice."

- In many cases, assessment can be the same as for non-disabled students. In other cases, children simply may need more time or a change in the assessment context or modality. Alternative forms of assessment might include providing a cassette tape recorder, an enlarged version of printed material, an extended time, a separate room, a scribe, a reader, a computer, or a sign-language interpreter. In all cases, assessment should be consistent with the individual goals that are set for the child and should include both effort and individual achievement.

- If peer tutors are used, help them understand the importance of showing sensitivity about how and when to help their peers with disabilities.

- In some cases, teacher aides may provide support for students with more severe disabilities. Instruct aides as to how and when to help. The aide should allow the child to participate as independently as possible. Children who come with aides from special education classrooms should arrive for class and leave class at the same time as their non-disabled peers.

> Individualizing instruction remains at the core of excellence in teaching and learning.

Teaching for Thinking

Graphic organizers are overt strategies that can help make students' thinking visible and concrete by organizing information visually. They employ various levels of thinking skills and effectively advance vocabulary and concept development.

The main objective of teaching for thinking is to help children understand how they know what they know. Critical thinking can be taught, practiced, learned, and assessed. There is much to think about in music, and teaching for thinking should be an integral part of the music program.

Teaching for thinking can happen simply and in a few minutes through modeling the thinking process. Think aloud about the content of a lesson or problem and how you would solve it. For example, "I'm not sure which of these instruments I want to use for the accompaniment. Let me think about their sounds as I try them out to see how each would fit the style of the song." Structure brief, but frequent opportunities for students to practice thinking and to talk about their decisions with partners or in small groups.

Before students can think creatively and critically, however, they must have a solid knowledge base of meaningful concepts and ideas and a basic understanding of their connections and relationships. As you work with the strategies listed below, carefully choose activity material, concepts, and ideas that students have thoroughly learned. Remember that thinking critically can involve active music making as well as verbal activities.

GRAPHIC ORGANIZERS

Graphic organizers are overt strategies that can help make students' thinking visible and concrete by organizing information visually. They employ various levels of thinking skills and effectively advance vocabulary and concept development. They can be used by individuals, pairs, and small groups or with the whole class as an instructional tool, extension activity, or evaluation.

It is important to model the process for using the graphic organizers before asking the children to use them on their own. Adapt materials to meet your specific purpose. It is not necessary to fill in all the spaces each time. If necessary, add lines or boxes to accommodate the needed information.

The graphic organizers found in the Resource Book can be made into transparencies for use on the overhead projector or reproduced. They may include any of the following: Story Map, Semantic Map, Comparison Chart, Venn Diagram, KWHL Chart, and Semantic Feature Analysis Chart.

STORY MAP

Story maps are simple vertical flow charts that identify the main story elements. They are usually a post-reading or post-listening activity, but can also be used as a formula for creating a story. They can also be used with ballads, such as "Don Gato," and program music, such as Peter and the Wolf.

Key Elements of Story Maps

WHEN (time)

WHERE (place)

WHO (characters)

WHAT (the dilemma that the main characters try to solve)

HOW (the series of steps taken to solve the problem)

ENDING (the resolution of the story's problem and new understandings created by it)

Teaching Sequence

1. Using a transparency of the story map, explain to the students that using a story map will help them see how the parts of a story or ballad fit together and help them remember the story line. Discuss the map headings to make sure the students understand them.

2. Listen to a ballad, stopping at the end of each verse to discuss the story map headings and fill in any information. Ask students, "Were the WHO, WHAT, WHERE, and WHEN introduced? Was the problem introduced? Could you infer any information?" Sometimes the information isn't available in the lyrics.

3. It is important to have the students predict and summarize each time. Have students give reasons for their predictions. Ask questions sequentially and logically so that the students can identify the most important information in the story.

4. Now listen to the selection all the way through and discuss their responses.

5. After they have worked through several story maps with your help, have students work in pairs or small groups to map another ballad or to create one of their own. Always discuss the completed map with them, leading them to think about how all the parts of the story are related.

SEMANTIC MAP

A semantic map graphically illustrates the relationships among a group of words or concepts. Surrounding the central concept are categories related to it.

Teaching Sequence

1. Select a central word or concept related to the lesson and write it in the center circle; for example, classroom instruments.

2. Ask the children to think of words related to the central word and write them down on a sheet of paper.

3. Select children to share orally some of the words they have written. List these on the chalkboard. Assist the children in categorizing the words and naming the categories. To reinforce or assess concepts previously taught, provide the category headings and ask the children to list related words under the appropriate headings.

4. Discuss the map and, most importantly, help children understand how they arrived at their choices. Help them think about their thinking (meta-cognition).

COMPARISON CHART

A comparison chart simply lists how two things are alike and how they are different by writing similarities in the left-hand column and differences in the right-hand column.

VENN DIAGRAM

With two overlapping circles, Venn diagrams illustrate the relationships among categories of items as students examine unique characteristics and common characteristics.

Teaching Sequence

1. Select two categories that share common characteristics familiar to your children, such as two songs.

2. Label each circle with its category or composition title.

3. Ask the children to suggest items or words that belong in at least one of the categories. If the word belongs in only one category, place it in the outer area of that circle. If it is common to more than one category, write it in the overlapping area of the circles.

KWHL CHART

A KWHL chart is used for gathering and organizing information. It is helpful as a pre- and post-reading or pre- and post-listening activity for the recorded interviews.

Teaching Sequence

1. **K** stands for **what I already know**. In the first box list what is already known about the subject being studied or the person to be interviewed.

2. **W** stands for **what I want to know**. Help the students generate questions about the subject matter or develop interview questions for the individual to be interviewed and list them in the second box.

3. **H** stands for **how am I going to learn this**. Help students brainstorm and list ways to learn; for example, read books or magazines, watch videos, interview someone, and listen to recorded interviews. In the third box, write the method(s) they are going to use.

4. **L** stands for **what I learned**. In the last column list the information gathered from reading, listening, and so on. Review the questions listed in the second box to see if they were answered sufficiently.

SEMANTIC FEATURE ANALYSIS CHART

Semantic maps show how items or words are alike. Semantic feature analysis shows how they are alike and different by using a grid design to graphically display the common features. In this way, items can be compared and contrasted by specific features or characteristics.

Teaching Sequence

1. Begin with a list of known words that share several common features. Write these in the left-hand column; for example, musical instruments.

2. Ask students to suggest features common to several of the words. Write the features in a row across the top of the grid; for example, metal, wood, strings.

3. Complete the grid by putting plus (+) or yes, or minus (–) or no, beside each word beneath each feature to indicate if a word does or does not incorporate a listed feature. Students may find a feature that may not apply precisely to one or more words in the category. Use this discovery as a spark for lively discussion.

4. Encourage students to discuss the unique meaning of each word. Point out that no two words share exactly the same pattern of features.

Character Education in Our Music Classroom

"What does it mean to teach children lifelong skills to develop positive character traits? Are we now responsible to teach this, too?

Toward Lifelong Skill Development

Among the many terms currently used around the nation to describe lifelong skill goals toward positive character development are the following: trustworthiness, truthfulness, listening to others, achieving your personal best, responsibility, effort, perseverance, friendship, controlling anger, fairness, cooperation, conflict management and resolution, and citizenship.

Most of us are in agreement that our students need repeated opportunities in continuing to develop these and other positive character traits. We recognize that our students may naturally exercise these lifelong skills as members of their families, as participants in their class and school communities, and as future adult members and citizens of their surrounding community, state, and nation. But what responsibility do we have as teachers to make sure these concepts and skills are taught? Why does this responsibility have to be added to our list of things to accomplish in the music classroom?

As music teachers, we may naturally feel overwhelmed in tackling such skill development because of the multiple requirements and accountability systems we already must meet and document. Furthermore, we may be frustrated by what we believe to be powerfully negative influences of the media, popular culture, and trends in youth social behavior on any efforts toward the development of a child's good character— character that was once primarily developed and shaped at home and within many forms of religious education and community life.

At the same time, we also know that we already provide many opportunities toward character skill development through activities in our daily music classroom. We may simply need to highlight ways to communicate what is innate in our music classroom learning environments in order to point out the natural connections to the character development of our students.

> **When you build character, you must address. . . the head, the heart, and the hand.**

Toward this goal, it may be helpful to understand what it means to educate character in others. It has been said that teaching good character involves teaching toward knowing the good, loving the good, and doing the good. These are powerfully motivating concepts which move many educators, administrators, parents, community and religious leaders, and other child advocates toward educative action designed to benefit the common good of not only the child, but of our entire society.

Of course, there are many approaches to action in meeting these goals. One truth may be that there is more involved than just saying and reminding children of good character words and traits. When you build character, you must address the cognitive, the emotional, and the behavioral—the head, the heart, and the hand. Music learning activity, as we know, involves all three realms. In so doing, it provides daily opportunities for

our students to develop good character traits and skills.

The remainder of this article will offer you specific connections between selected character or lifelong skills concepts and concrete examples found in music classroom activities. What is important here are not the specific terms themselves, but rather the overall concepts and connections. We hope these connections may serve to help you in your communications with others about how music education is vitally linked to and an active reinforcement of character education for children.

Connections Involving Self

Responsibility We require students to arrive on time, put away their supplies, follow directions, be well-behaved, and and prepared musically. Successful musical rehearsal and performance requires and rewards personal responsibility toward a group effort.

Curiosity Students are exercising this trait when they are asked to find the new note and its fingering on the recorder, figure out what beats are missing in a particular measure, guess the cultural origin of a recorded listening segment, and so on. When we ask older students to explore and find out information about instruments, composers, styles of music, or have them ask new probing questions about what they play, sing, or hear, students are exercising their curiosity in an active, productive manner.

Effort and Perseverance The act of practicing music alone or in a group requires continual effort and the exercise of perseverance. Students cannot give up on practicing and must "try again and again" if they are to improve the musical sound. Music teachers motivate by modeling these traits for their students, as music making itself is a natural composite of both perseverance and effort.

Courage When we praise and reward students for their ability to overcome being self-conscious and nervous in performance, we are helping them develop this trait of courage. The need for courage never ends. In reviewing how far a student or group has come, we are pointing out that courage is what this effort demanded in order to succeed. Also, many music teachers teach about famous composers and performing artists who overcame impossible odds to develop their skills and performance talents. Determination and resolve are companion traits with courage.

Connections Involving Others

Listening to Others The ability to listen is at the heart of all musicianship. Cooperative group projects and partner work in music class involve shared decision-making and compromise. Students must listen to the teacher for direction and criticism, as well as to one another in order to complete a specific group project or task. Also, we listen to others making music to learn how to make music for others and with others.

Friendship One of the best motivators for student participation in music and music performance groups is reported simply as, "We get to make friends." Research indicates that many at-risk students value school because of their participation in music. Friendships in the music classroom often naturally evolve from working together toward a rewarding common goal. A community of friends is established because our stu-

dents enjoy working with others who enjoy the same things they do.

Caring Students help other students to learn music, critique and support others' efforts, and take care of one another within the larger group. Students are actively caring for one another when they offer to help, lend a hand to and include students with special needs, and understand when others need their assistance.

> *The ability to listen is at the heart of all musicianship.*

Cooperation All music making requires active cooperation with the leader and other performers. Students are exercising this skill continually in the music classroom by making sound together, moving, trading instruments, picking partners, setting up and cleaning up, and countless other activities.

We ask our students to share and work together in the music classroom. We model and expect students to be fair to others as we give everyone a turn. We ask students to work out their different points of view in making decisions for a group project. We say to younger children, "Show me that you and your partner know how to share and put away the instruments." Many music teachers ask older students to work out a class problem and lead others to do the same.

Truthfulness We encourage our students to critique one another with the goal of helping others improve their music making. We ask students to tell us the truth about what they think of a

performance. "Which part needs to be louder?" "What needs to be done for this to sound better?" "Where's the hard part and what do we need to do to be able to play or sing it?"

Flexibility and Sense of Humor We can teach our students to be flexible by modeling this trait ourselves, especially in our ability to laugh at our mistakes and the world around us. We model flexibility by accepting human error, being accommodating, and adapting to the needs of individuals and the group. Many teachers and students learn to exercise this important skill when working with students with special needs. We learn to adapt and not be inflexible in demanding that all students do musical tasks in the same way. We are open to students who often think of alternative ways to make music as they compose and experiment with musical sounds.

Controlling Anger Students are asked to exercise individual control over their physical and emotional reactions to others and less-than-perfect events in the music classroom. We ask and reward students for controlling themselves and being patient with others during music making.

Building Community and Citizenship A well-managed music classroom is a model for future adult citizenship in the larger community. In this classroom, individuals have a role to add to the composite community effort by learning their part through hard work and self-discipline, directly participating in constructive and creative action with others, electing and supporting leaders, respecting the rights of the majority, and caring about the overall goal and effort of the many. Simply put, students work toward projects and performance in community, every member offering an important and valued addition to the whole.

Assessment Strategies

Evaluation Criteria and Procedures Built Into MAKING MUSIC

At every grade level of MAKING MUSIC, evaluation criteria (referred to as assessments throughout the program) are provided within lessons and at the ends of units. Assessments incorporated into each lesson affect perceptions of students, teachers, administrators, and all who care about what is accomplished by studying music, and they serve to provide essential information about what students achieve from taking a music course based on MAKING MUSIC.

Because individual teachers seldom have the time or resources to develop truly comprehensive assessments, and because effective assessments must include a rich diversity of methods and strategies that encourage all students to be successful, the authors and editors of MAKING MUSIC have incorporated the following types of assessment into the program.

• Observations
Teachers observe individuals, small groups, or the entire class during an activity to assess some aspect of student learning. Students may also observe one another for peer assessment. Possibilities for observations include checklists of elements or skills, anecdotal comments, and student performances.

• Performances
Teachers assess progress on or attainment of skills and behaviors through individual or group performances, including composition, movement activities, sound pieces, projects, demonstrations, cooperative learning, and, of course, all performing skills.

• Self-Assessments
Students are asked to think about themselves as musicians. These self-assessments may include

descriptions of things they have learned to do well, are continuing to work on, are planning to do, or would like to learn. Self-assessments may be reflections, checklists, journal writing, interest inventories, attitudinal surveys, or descriptions of students' feelings and values.

• Interviews
Teachers formally or informally talk with students individually or in groups in order to better understand students' thinking processes and attitudes. Interviews may be conferences or discussions that demonstrate processing, problem solving, critical thinking, and so on.

• Music Journals/Journal Writing
Opportunities are provided for students to write as they formulate, organize, internalize, and evaluate concepts. Writing provides a good record of the student's thinking, an indicator of what the student is learning and how the student feels. Writing may be a separate activity or may be part of a larger project. Journals may include students' written evaluations of music, specific assignments, or actual compositions. Musical compositions may be in the form of notated compositions, compositional sketches, or graphic notations.

• Audio Journals and Video Journals
Opportunities are provided for students to make recordings of their performances, interviews, and so on. A student's audio or video journal may be a record of his or her "critical incidents" in music making or listening.

Portfolios

A music portfolio will include examples of a student's musical work. Examples may include representative work, "best" work, mandatory assignments, and so on. Examples often reflect the variety of contexts in which the learning occurs. Portfolios in music might include audio recordings, video recordings, photos, graphic notation leading to actual notation, examples of tests or "What Do You Hear?" exercises, graphic organizers, and so on. Teachers may have students develop individual portfolios or may create group portfolios for the whole class.

> Assessments demonstrate what is accomplished by studying music and show what students learn from a course using MAKING MUSIC.

What Do You Hear?

Cognitive assessments provide an objective way to measure students' understanding of music concepts. "What Do You Hear?" exercises are provided at every grade level. They include blackline masters for student answer sheets and recorded excerpts that the student must listen to and analyze.

Reaction Letters or Reaction Memos

Students might be asked to write letters to "Old Dan Tucker" or to the Boys Choir of Harlem or to Mozart. In setting up the activity, the Teacher's Edition provides the "stem" to get the student started, such as "I wish I could be part of your group because...." Also, students might write reaction letters or memos to each other regarding their work in class.

Peer Critiques

Students might provide, either by discussion or in writing, critiques of interviews, in-process work, final work, or performances.

Written Assessments

Written assessments include quizzes and tests, activity sheets, and graphic organizers. Opportunities for assessment using written language are found at the ends of units and within each lesson of MAKING MUSIC, where they help to focus the entire lesson and help teachers and students to conceptualize the learning that is taking place.

Attitude Inventory

Students respond to a checklist or provide written responses to music. Attitude inventories may be used as pretests and posttests to learning. In this way, teachers learn the attitudes students had before studying a particular selection and compare it to how students' attitudes might have changed.

CONTENTS

to the National Standards for Music Education

"Because music is a basic expression of human culture, every student should have access to a balanced, comprehensive, and sequential program of study in music." This goal, as expressed by the authors of the National Standards for Arts Education, is the driving force behind MAKING MUSIC and the correlation chart below. The chart, and the corresponding on-page National Standards references in this Teacher's Edition (shown with the icon **1a**), will provide valuable assistance in tracking your students' progress and making this goal a reality.

Organization

The National Standards have been developed and organized according to two specific grade-level clusters: Grades K–4 and Grades 5–8. Within each cluster, students may work towards a degree of competency in the skills described in any of the Standards. Full competency, however, is not expected until students have exited the last grade of each cluster. The process of meeting each Standard, then, is a cumulative one in which some Standards may not be fully applicable until the last grade of the cluster.

The page references in the chart below reflect this understanding. The musical activities presented in the earlier grades of MAKING MUSIC engage students in developmentally appropriate learning experiences, which are designed to prepare students to achieve specific Standards by the end of Grades 4 and 8.

Content Standard	Achievement Standard	Teacher's Edition Page
1 Singing, alone and with others, a varied repertoire of music	**1a** Students sing accurately and with good breath control throughout their singing ranges, alone and in small and large ensembles	29, 30, 35, 61, 88, 99, 130, 137, 144, 153, 163, 181, 183, 189, 191, 192, 204, 222, 223, 230, 231, 261, 263, 267, 285, 369, 375, 380, 381, 383, 384, 385, 386, 387, 388, 389, 403, 411, 412, 413, 430, 431, 432, 436, 439, 444, 446, 449, 457, 459, 467, 482, 483, 484, 487
	1b Students sing with expression and technical accuracy a repertoire of vocal literature with a level of difficulty of 2, on a scale of 1 to 6, including some songs performed from memory	7, 27, 55, 69, 77, 119, 149, 172, 279, 283, 419, 420
	1c Students sing music representing diverse genres and cultures, with expression appropriate for the work being performed	11, 13, 15, 19, 21, 23, 25, 27, 33, 47, 51, 52, 57, 59, 60, 61, 63, 66, 67, 73, 75, 87, 89, 91, 92, 93, 102, 103, 105, 107, 109, 130, 131, 133, 134, 135, 140, 141, 147, 152, 161, 175, 176, 177, 179, 185, 189, 191, 193, 195, 198, 201, 203, 205, 213, 215, 217, 225, 229, 231, 233, 235, 241, 243, 245, 257, 259, 265, 273, 277, 281, 287, 288, 296, 297, 299, 300, 301, 303, 304, 305, 306, 307, 309, 315, 316, 317, 319, 321, 323, 327, 337, 345, 349, 350, 355, 371, 373, 391, 394, 395, 397, 401, 411, 412, 413, 417, 428, 433, 437, 443, 447, 449, 451, 461, 463, 465, 469, 471, 473, 477, 479, 481
	1d Students sing music written in two and three parts	37, 47, 48, 51, 70, 78, 79, 115, 116, 117, 121, 140, 149, 159, 161, 163, 182, 243, 245, 271, 274, 296, 297, 309, 342, 382, 401, 416, 421, 428, 429, 432, 442, 447, 459, 475, 484, 485, 488

Content Standard	Achievement Standard	Teacher's Edition Page
	1e Students who participate in a choral ensemble sing with expression and technical accuracy a varied repertoire of vocal literature with a level of difficulty of 3, on a scale of 1 to 6, including some songs performed from memory	30, 31, 361, 362, 415, 416, 417, 441, 442, 480
2 Performing on instruments, alone and with others, a varied repertoire of music	**2a** Students perform on at least one instrument[1] accurately and independently, alone and in small and large ensembles, with good posture, good playing position, and good breath, bow, or stick control	6, 10, 11, 12, 14, 17, 22, 23, 29, 30, 34, 35, 52, 64, 66, 90, 98, 99, 104, 106, 13, 114, 117, 120, 137, 144, 145, 158, 160, 161, 178, 179, 185, 188, 195, 203, 215, 216, 229, 233, 234, 243, 244, 245, 257, 270, 300, 346, 355, 362, 371, 374, 377, 383, 384, 385, 390, 391, 394, 395, 402, 403, 457, 464, 465, 467, 469, 477, 487
	2b Students perform with expression and technical accuracy on at least one string, wind, percussion, or classroom instrument a repertoire of instrumental literature with a level of difficulty of 2, on a scale of 1 to 6	36, 39, 48, 55, 74, 133, 135, 157, 173, 182, 183, 199, 261, 349, 350, 352, 463
	2c Students perform music representing diverse genres and cultures, with expression appropriate for the work being performed	20, 21, 33, 50, 59, 60, 108, 135, 138, 174, 177, 190, 201, 205, 224, 226, 241, 281, 295, 296, 297, 305, 306, 307, 316, 317, 323, 324, 325, 338, 339, 340, 342, 361, 363, 401, 412, 413, 437, 442, 449, 479
	2d Students play by ear simple melodies on a melodic instrument and simple accompaniments on a harmonic instrument	68, 100, 102, 103, 111, 117, 119, 120 128, 131, 266, 268, 277, 282, 283, 300, 324, 359
	2e Students who participate in an instrumental ensemble or class perform with expression and technical accuracy a varied repertoire of instrumental literature with a level of difficulty of 3, on a scale of 1 to 6, including some solos performed from memory	148, 287, 305
3 Improvising melodies, variations, and accompaniments	**3a** Students improvise simple harmonic accompaniment	102, 120, 205, 224, 227, 241, 316, 389
	3b Students improvise melodic embellishments and simple rhythmic and melodic variations on given pentatonic melodies and melodies in major keys	21, 23, 24, 25, 53, 112, 113, 179, 182, 278, 307, 350, 353, 375, 445, 484
	3c Students improvise short melodies, unaccompanied and over given rhythmic accompaniments, each in a consistent style, meter, and tonality	226, 265, 321
4 Composing and arranging music within specified guidelines	**4a** Students compose short pieces within specified guidelines,[2] demonstrating how the elements of music are used to achieve unity and variety, tension and release, and balance	8, 9, 17, 19, 73, 74, 92, 153, 185, 375, 376, 377
	4b Students arrange simple pieces for voices or instruments other than those for which the pieces were written	70, 395

Content Standard	Achievement Standard	Teacher's Edition Page
	4c Students use a variety of traditional and nontraditional sound sources and electronic media when composing and arranging	11, 21, 31, 35, 57, 59, 61, 64, 66, 67, 75, 90, 93, 95, 103, 105, 113, 137, 145, 163, 177, 183, 187, 189, 201, 215, 217, 221, 223, 235, 239, 243, 245, 277, 339, 353, 413, 457, 469, 475
5 Reading and notating music	**5a** Students read whole, half, quarter, eighth, sixteenth, and dotted notes and rests in $\frac{2}{4}$, $\frac{3}{4}$, $\frac{4}{4}$, $\frac{6}{8}$, $\frac{3}{8}$, and alla breve meter signatures	13, 19, 53, 55, 60, 61, 63, 73, 91, 95, 97, 98, 99, 105, 107, 133, 134, 139, 140, 141, 144, 147, 151, 153, 157, 175, 181, 182, 183, 217, 223, 257, 273, 287, 288, 299, 300, 303, 304, 306, 309, 350, 362, 374, 387, 388, 390, 411, 412, 427, 431, 436, 445, 447, 487
	5b Students read at sight simple melodies in both the treble and bass clefs	25, 26, 27, 63, 133, 151, 171, 188, 189, 327, 337
	5c Students identify and define standard notation symbols for pitch, rhythm, dynamics, tempo, articulation, and expression	7, 8, 13, 15, 17, 19, 23, 63, 87, 88, 92, 117, 120, 147, 149, 172, 189, 193, 231, 235, 288, 316, 324, 345, 355, 374, 419, 427, 459, 473, 487
	5d Students use standard notation to record their musical ideas and the musical ideas of others	15, 55, 66, 95, 96, 99, 100, 105, 106, 138, 148, 149, 163, 271, 279
	5e Students who participate in a choral or instrumental ensemble or class sightread, accurately and expressively, music with a level of difficulty of 2, on a scale of 1 to 6	416, 433, 437, 443, 448, 449, 475, 481, 484
6 Listening to, analyzing, and describing music	**6a** Students describe specific music events[3] in a given aural example, using appropriate terminology	35, 38, 55, 59, 63, 66, 67, 88, 89, 99, 100, 108, 111, 113, 115, 129, 153, 154, 171, 193, 226, 227, 229, 261, 265, 267, 274, 288, 313, 342, 359, 362, 369, 380, 419, 431, 442, 457, 471, 475, 479, 483, 485
	6b Students analyze the uses of elements of music in aural examples representing diverse genres and cultures	8, 9, 15, 16, 19, 20, 21, 29, 33, 37, 46, 47, 57, 59, 66, 67, 74, 78, 79, 95, 97, 101, 102, 112, 113, 119, 120, 131, 137, 145, 152, 153, 155, 159, 161, 173, 182, 186, 187, 191, 197, 198, 199, 201, 203, 221, 225, 227, 238, 239, 265, 268, 269, 271, 274, 277, 281, 285, 291, 311, 312, 317, 319, 321, 334, 335, 338, 339, 341, 343, 345, 346, 349, 357, 358, 361, 362, 368, 369, 376, 381, 383, 384, 385, 389, 393, 394, 395, 397, 398, 399, 403, 4125, 417, 419, 420, 422, 427, 431, 433, 435, 437, 446, 447, 448, 457, 461, 463, 467, 471, 475, 479, 481, 488, 489
	6c Students demonstrate knowledge of the basic principles of meter, rhythm, tonality, intervals, chords, and harmonic progressions in their analyses of music	11, 13, 51, 53, 61, 69, 70, 77, 86, 91, 92, 93, 95, 96, 97, 98, 99, 107, 109, 137, 139, 140, 141, 146, 147, 149, 174, 175, 176, 179, 191, 192, 193, 201, 202, 203, 205, 213, 214, 215, 216, 217, 219, 220, 221, 222, 223, 227, 229, 230, 231, 233, 240, 241, 243, 245, 257, 258, 259, 263, 299, 316, 324, 327, 353, 355, 371, 373, 377, 381, 384, 387, 388, 391, 384, 387, 388, 391, 394, 398, 411, 434, 441, 463, 465, 469, 477, 481, 483, 487, 488, 489
7 Evaluating music and music performances	**7a** Students develop criteria for evaluating the quality and effectiveness of music performances and compositions and apply the criteria in their personal listening and performing	33, 57, 131, 157, 159, 163, 183, 221, 285, 297, 307, 317, 339, 343, 385, 389, 429, 443, 448, 449, 459, 475, 477, 479, 483, 485

Content Standard	Achievement Standard	Teacher's Edition Page
	7b Students evaluate the quality and effectiveness of their own and others' performances, compositions, arrangements, and improvisations by applying specific criteria appropriate for the style of the music and offer constructive suggestions for improvement	31, 39, 49, 71, 112, 115, 117, 121, 145, 161, 173, 243, 289, 309, 325, 347, 351, 353, 391, 413, 423, 433, 438
8 Understanding relationships between music, the other arts, and disciplines outside the arts	**8a** Students compare in two or more arts how the characteristic materials of each art[4] can be used to transform similar events, scenes, emotions, or ideas into works of art	16, 20, 28, 94, 95, 103, 120, 136, 138, 140, 142, 143, 144, 158, 162, 163, 175, 186, 219, 220, 221
	8b Students describe ways in which the principles and subject matter of other disciplines taught in the school are interrelated with those of music[5]	11, 12, 13, 15, 17, 18, 19, 21, 22, 25, 26, 27, 28, 29, 32, 33, 34, 35, 36, 37, 46, 47, 52, 54, 56, 57, 58, 60, 62, 63, 64, 66, 67, 69, 70, 72, 76, 77, 78, 86, 97, 98, 99, 101, 102, 103, 104, 109, 10, 111, 113, 114, 115, 116, 117, 118, 119, 136, 139, 146, 148, 149, 150, 154, 170, 178, 180, 182, 184, 185, 188, 189, 191, 192, 194, 195, 196, 198, 202, 214, 216, 217, 218, 220, 222, 223, 226, 232, 233, 236, 237, 238, 239, 240, 241, 242, 244, 256, 257, 258, 260, 262, 264, 265, 266, 267, 268, 270, 271, 273, 274, 276, 278, 279, 282, 283, 284, 285, 286, 289, 295, 297, 298, 299, 300, 302, 303, 308, 309, 310, 311, 312, 314, 318, 319, 320, 332, 340, 342, 344, 345, 350, 354, 356, 358, 370, 372, 373, 374, 378, 381, 382, 383, 386, 390, 391, 392, 393, 395, 400, 402, 410, 411, 414, 416, 417, 418, 420, 422, 424, 430, 435, 438, 442, 443, 450, 458, 460, 464, 465, 466, 472, 474, 476, 477, 478, 483, 484, 485, 486, 487, 489
9 Understanding music in relation to history and culture	**9a** Students describe distinguishing characteristics of representative music genres and styles from a variety of cultures[6]	16, 129, 141, 200, 204, 213, 214, 215, 219, 225, 229, 242, 257, 267, 288, 295, 319, 321, 323, 324, 333, 339, 341, 345, 350, 353, 354, 355, 357, 361, 362, 384, 392, 396, 398, 433, 435, 439, 441, 444, 445, 446, 467, 470, 474, 479
	9b Students classify by genre and style (and, if applicable, by historical period, composer, and title) a varied body of exemplary (that is, high quality and characteristic) musical works and explain the characteristics that cause each work to be considered exemplary	72, 78, 214, 225, 278, 279, 341, 357
	9c Students compare, in several cultures of the world, functions music serves, roles of musicians,[7] and conditions under which music is typically performed	87, 309, 321, 396, 399

	K	1	2	
Expression				
Dynamics	Loud/soft Getting louder/getting softer Soft dynamics	Loud/soft Getting louder/getting softer	Loud/soft Dynamics and dynamic markings including *p*, *f*, *crescendo/decrescendo* Getting louder/getting softer Sudden changes	
Tempo	Fast/slow Getting faster/getting slower Changes in tempo	Fast/slow Getting faster/getting slower Changes in tempo	Getting faster/getting slower Tempo markings: *fermata* ⌢ Changes in tempo	
Articulation	Smooth and connected Short and detached *Legato/staccato*	Smooth and connected Short and detached *Legato/staccato*	Smooth and connected Short and detached *Legato/staccato* Accents	
Mood	Variety of moods	Variety of moods	Variety of moods	
Rhythm				
Beat	Steady beat Steady beat/no beat Beat/rhythm Beat/silent beat (rest)	Steady beat Steady beat/no beat Beat/rhythm Sound/silence Beat/silent beat (rest)	Steady beat Steady beat/no beat Beat/rhythm Beat/offbeat	
Duration	Long and short sounds Longer/shorter One sound per beat = ♩ Two sounds per beat = ♫	Longer/shorter One sound per beat = ♩ Two sounds per beat = ♫ No sound on a beat = 𝄽	Longer/shorter Tie One sound per beat = ♩ Two sounds per beat = ♫ No sound on a beat = 𝄽 Four sounds on a beat = ♬♬ ♩	
Meter	Strong beat/weak beat	Strong beat/weak beat Meter in 2 Meter in 3	Strong beat/weak beat Meter in 2 $\frac{2}{4}$ meter Meter in 3 $\frac{3}{4}$ meter	

3	4	5	6
Dynamics and dynamic markings including *p*, *f*, *crescendo/ decrescendo*, sudden changes (*subito*, *p*, *f*), *mezzo* (*mp*, *mf*), *pp*, *ff* Dynamic contrasts Dynamics as an expressive choice	Dynamics and dynamic markings including *crescendo/decrescendo*, *subito*, *p*, *f*, *mezzo* (*mp*, *mf*), *pp*, *ff* Changes in dynamics Appropriateness of dynamic choices Dynamics as an expressive choice	Dynamics and dynamic markings including *crescendo/decrescendo*, *subito*, *p*, *f*, *mezzo* (*mp*, *mf*), *pp*, *ff* Changes in dynamics Appropriateness of dynamic choices Dynamics as an expressive choice	Dynamics and dynamic markings including *crescendo/decrescendo*, *subito*, *p*, *f*, *mezzo* (*mp*, *mf*), *pp*, *ff* Balancing dynamics Changes in dynamics Appropriateness of dynamic choices Dynamics as an expressive choice
Tempos and tempo markings including *accelerando*, *ritardando*, *allegro*, *moderato*, *adagio* Changes in tempo Tempo as an expressive choice	Tempos and tempo markings including *accelerando*, *presto*, *andante*, *subito* Changes in tempo Sudden changes in tempo Appropriateness of tempo choices Tempo as an expressive choice	Tempos and tempo markings including *allegretto*, *lento* Changes in tempo Appropriateness of tempo choices Tempo as an expressive choice	Tempos and tempo markings including *rubato*, *fermata* ⌢ Changes in tempo Appropriateness of tempo choices Tempo as an expressive choice
Articulations and articulation markings including *legato/ staccato*, accents, *pizzicato/arco* Articulation as an expressive choice	Articulations and articulation markings including *legato/ staccato*, accents, *pizzicato/arco*, various slurs, *marcato* Phrasing Articulation as an expressive choice	Articulations and articulation markings including *legato/ staccato*, accents, *pizzicato/arco*, various slurs, *marcato* Articulation as an expressive choice	Articulations and articulation markings including *legato/ staccato*, accents, *pizzicato/arco*, various slurs, *marcato* Vocal/instrumental methods Articulation as an expressive choice
Variety of moods	Variety of moods	Variety of moods	Variety of moods
Beat/rhythm Beat/offbeat Upbeat	Beat/offbeat Upbeat	Beat/offbeat Upbeat Backbeat	Backbeat Anacrusis
Tie	Tie	Tie Augmentation Diminution	Tie Augmentation Diminution Relative duration
$\frac{2}{4}$, $\frac{3}{4}$, $\frac{4}{4}$ meters	$\frac{2}{4}$, $\frac{3}{4}$, $\frac{4}{4}$, $\frac{6}{8}$ meters Changes in meter	$\frac{2}{4}$, $\frac{3}{4}$, $\frac{4}{4}$, $\frac{6}{8}$ meters Meter in 5 Meter in 7 Mixed meter	$\frac{2}{4}$, $\frac{3}{4}$, $\frac{4}{4}$, $\frac{6}{8}$, $\frac{3}{8}$, $\frac{2}{2}$ meters Mixed meter Compound meters Changing meters

	K	1	2	
Pattern	Sound/silence Same/different Combinations including: ♩, ♫, ‰ Repeated patterns	Sound/silence Same/different Ostinato Combinations including: ♩, ♫, ‰ Repeated patterns	Ostinato Combinations including: ♩, ♫, ‰, ♩, ♬	
Form				
Phrase Form	Same/different phrases Echo (imitation) Call and response Introduction	Same/different phrases Question/answer phrase Long and short phrases Echo (imitation) Call and response Repetition/contrast Phrase forms including: ab, aba Introduction and coda Cumulative song	Same/different phrases Question/answer phrase Long and short phrases Repetition/contrast Phrase forms including: ab, aba, aaba, aabb Solo/chorus Call and response Introduction and coda Cumulative song	

Section Form	Same/different sections	Same/different sections
		Introduction and coda
		Verse/refrain (AB)
		Section forms including: AB
		   (binary), ABA
			Same/different sections
			Introduction and coda
			Verse/refrain (AB)
			D.C. al fine (ABA)
			Section forms including: AB, ABA,
			   AABA, ABACA (rondo)	

Composite Form				
Melody				
Pitch & Direction	High/low Higher/lower Upward/downward Low to high High to low	High/low Higher/lower Upward/downward Low to high High to low Steps, skips, and repeated pitches	Melodic direction Higher/lower Upward/downward Steps, leaps, and repeated pitches	

3	4	5	6
Ostinato Even and uneven rhythm patterns (dotted rhythms) Syncopation/no syncopation Combinations including [whole note], [sixteenth notes], [dotted half], [eighth notes, eighth]	Even and uneven rhythm patterns (dotted rhythms) Syncopation/no syncopation Combinations including [dotted quarter, eighth], [sixteenth notes], [eighth notes], [eighth, dotted quarter] Swing eighths	Even and uneven rhythm patterns (dotted rhythms) Syncopation/no syncopation Motive Combinations in simple meter: [triplet], [dotted eighth sixteenth] Combinations in compound meter: [eighth], [quarter], [dotted quarter], [quarter], [eighth], [beamed sixteenths] Combinations of 2 and 3 in mixed meter: [triplet] and [eighth sixteenth]	Syncopation Motive Combinations in duple meter: [triplet], [dotted eighth sixteenth] Combinations in compound meter: [eighth], [quarter], [dotted quarter], [quarter], [eighth], [dotted quarter], [beamed sixteenths] Combinations of 2 and 3 in mixed meter: [triplet] and [eighth sixteenth] Layered patterns Rock 'n' roll shuffle Even rock rhythms
Question/answer phrase Long and short phrases Repetition/contrast Phrase forms including ab, aba, aaba, aabb Solo/chorus Call and response Introduction, interlude, and coda Cumulative song	Question/answer phrase Long and short phrases Repetition/contrast Motive Phrase forms including ab, aba, aaba, aabb Solo/chorus Call and response Introduction, interlude, and coda Cumulative song Ballad	Question/answer phrase Long and short phrases Repetition/contrast Motive Phrase forms including ab, aba, aaba, aabb, abac Solo/chorus Call and response Introduction, interlude, and coda Ballad 12-bar blues	Motive Phrase forms including ab, aba, aaba, abbb, aabb, abac Solo/chorus Call and response Introduction, interlude, and coda Ballad 12-bar blues Canons and rounds Fugue
Same/different sections Introduction and coda Interlude Verse/refrain (AB) *D.C. al fine* (ABA) First and second endings *D.S. al fine* Section forms including AB, ABA, AABA, ABACA (rondo)	Introduction and coda Interlude Verse/refrain (AB) *D.C. al fine* (ABA) First and second endings *D.S. al fine* Section forms including AB, ABA, AABA, ABACA (rondo) Theme/variations	Section forms including AB, ABA, AABA, ABACA Theme/variations March Overture Finale Movement	Section forms including AB, ABA, AABA, ABACA, ABCA, AABAA Theme/variations Overture Finale Movement Through-composed Fugue Minuet and Trio Bridge
	Opera, operetta, musical theater, piano prelude, symphony	Opera, operetta, musical theater, piano prelude, symphony, sonata-allegro, concerto	Opera, operetta, musical theater, piano prelude, symphony, sonata-allegro, concerto
Melodic sequence Melodic direction Steps, skips, and repeated pitches Intervals: unison, octave Pitch letter names	Melodic imitation Melodic sequence Melodic contour Steps, skips, and repeated pitches Intervals: unison, octave, third Pitch letter names Range and register Definite and indefinite pitch	Melodic imitation Melodic sequence Melodic contour Intervals: unison, second, third, fourth, fifth, sixth, seventh, octave Pitch letter names Range and register Definite and indefinite pitch Ornamentation Whole and half steps	Intervals: unison, second, third, fourth, fifth, sixth, seventh, octave Pitch letter names Range and register Definite and indefinite pitch Ornamentation Whole and half steps Accidentals Blues notes Manipulation of pitches as compositional devices: sequence, repetition, contrast; melodic ideas and development; theme, motive, melodic ostinato

Melody (continued)	K	1	2	
Tonality		Tonal center *do*-pentatonic	Tonal center *do*-pentatonic *la*-pentatonic	
Pattern	Same/different	Same/different Combinations including *so-mi, la, so-mi-la, do, so-mi-la-do*	Same/different Motive Pentatonic pitch patterns, including *so-mi, so-mi-la, do, so-mi-la-do, mi-re-do, re, la-so-mi-re-do*	
Timbre **Environmental**	Nature sounds Found sounds Machine sounds	Nature sounds Found sounds Machine sounds	Nature sounds Found sounds Machine sounds	
Vocal	Various tone qualities produced by individuals and groups Individual: sing, speak, shout, whisper	Various tone qualities produced by individuals and groups Individual: sing, speak, shout, whisper; adult, child	Various tone qualities produced by individuals and groups Individual: male, female, child Group: duet, trio, quartet, chorus	

3	4	5	6
Tonal center *do*-pentatonic *la*-pentatonic *so*-pentatonic Major/minor	Tonal center Key signature *do*-pentatonic *la*-pentatonic *so*-pentatonic Major/minor Whole and half steps Scales: pentatonic, major, minor Changes of key (modulation)	Tonal center Key signature *do*-pentatonic *la*-pentatonic *so*-pentatonic Major/minor Whole and half steps Scales: pentatonic, major, natural minor, harmonic minor Modes: aeolian, dorian, mixolydian Changes of key (modulation) Cadence	Major/minor Whole and half steps Scales: pentatonic, chromatic, major, natural minor, harmonic minor, whole-tone, blues Modes: aeolian, dorian, mixolydian Atonality (chance music) Changes of key (modulation)
Motive Melodic ostinato Pentatonic pitch patterns, including *mi-re-do, so-mi-re-do, la-so-mi-re-do, so₁-la₁-do-re-mi-so-la-do'*	Motive Melodic ostinato Melodic sequence Diatonic pitch patterns including *la-so-mi-re-do, la₁, so₁, do', so-do', fa', so₁-la₁-do-re-mi-fa-so-la-do', ti*	Motive Melodic ostinato Melodic sequence Diatonic pitch patterns including *la-so-mi-re-do, la₁, so₁, do', so-do', fa', so₁-la₁-do-re-mi-fa-so-la-do', ti* *la* diatonic (natural minor) *si* in melodic minor *ti* in dorian mode *te* in mixolydian mode	Motive Melodic ostinato Melodic sequence Melodic repetition Motive manipulation Diatonic pitch patterns including *so₁-la₁-do-re-mi-fa-so-la-ti-do'* *la* diatonic (natural minor) *si* in melodic minor *ti* in dorian mode *te* in mixolydian mode Pitches in compositional devices: sequence, retrograde, imitation, inversion, repetition, transposition, modulation
Nature sounds Found sounds Machine sounds	Nature sounds Found sounds Machine sounds	Nature sounds Found sounds Machine sounds	Nature sounds Found sounds Machine sounds Elemental acoustics Sound quality determined by the sound source Sound quality affected by the material, shape, and size of the source Sound quality affected by the way the sound is produced
Various tone qualities produced by individuals and groups Individual: male, female, child Group: duet, trio, quartet, chorus	Various tone qualities produced by individuals and groups Individual: soprano, alto, tenor, bass Group: large and small ensembles Vocal blending *A capella* singing Variety of vocal styles including: opera, operetta, musical theater, and popular singers	Various tone qualities produced by individuals and groups Individual: soprano, alto, tenor, bass Group: large and small ensembles Vocal blending *A capella* singing Variety of vocal styles including: opera, operetta, musical theater, and popular singers Vocal production	Various tone qualities produced by individuals and groups Individual: soprano, alto, tenor, bass Group: large and small ensembles Vocal blending *A capella* singing Variety of vocal styles including: opera, operetta, musical theater, and popular singers Vocal production Vocal production and style of diverse cultures

Timbre (continued)	K	1	2	
Instrumental	Body percussion Classroom percussion Various tone qualities produced by individual instruments and groups of instruments Individual instruments including flute, trumpet, snare drum, piano, guitar Group: large and small ensembles	Body percussion Classroom percussion Various tone qualities produced by individual instruments and groups of instruments Tuned percussion Individual instruments including trombone, violin, timpani, trumpet, clarinet, flute Group: large and small ensembles	Various tone qualities produced by individual instruments and groups of instruments Individual instruments including timpani, clarinet, African percussion, trumpet Group: large and small ensembles Families: strings, percussion, winds Instrumentation from diverse cultures	
Electronic			Synthesized sounds	

Texture & Harmony

	K	1	2	
Texture	One sound/more than one sound Accompaniment/no accompaniment Layers of sound Thick/thin	One sound/more than one sound Accompaniment/no accompaniment Layers of sound Thick/thin Ostinato Bordun	Accompaniment/no accompaniment Layers of sound Thick/thin Ostinato Bordun	
Harmony				

3	4	5	6
Various tone qualities produced by individual instruments and groups of instruments Individual instruments Group: large and small ensembles Families: strings, percussion, winds, keyboards Instrumentation from diverse cultures including: Cambodian pinpeat orchestra, Irish instruments, Japanese instruments	Various tone qualities produced by individual instruments and groups of instruments Individual instruments Group: large and small ensembles including orchestra, concert band, *jarocho, gamelan,* symphony orchestra Families: strings, percussion, winds, keyboards Instruments from diverse cultures including: Irish instruments, Indian instruments, Chinese instruments	Various tone qualities produced by individual instruments and groups of instruments Individual instruments Group: large and small ensembles including orchestra, symphony orchestra, *jarocho, gamelan,* bands (marching, symphonic, dance, military, rock) Families: strings (chordophones), percussion (idiophones and membranophones), winds (aerophones)	Various tone qualities produced by individual instruments and groups of instruments Individual instruments Group: large and small ensembles including orchestra, symphony orchestra, concert band, *jarocho, gamelan,* bands (marching, symphonic, dance, military, rock), jug band Families: strings (chordophones), percussion (idiophones and membranophones), winds (aerophones) Folk instruments Instrument making: student-made instruments Instruments from diverse cultures including: West African percussion, Middle Eastern percussion, Caribbean percussion, drums from around the world
Synthesized sounds	Synthesized sounds Electric guitar	Synthesized sounds Electric guitar	Synthesized sounds Electric guitar Sampling
Layers of sound Thick/thin Ostinato Partner songs Echo songs Countermelodies and descants	Layers of sound Thick/thin Ostinato Partner songs Echo songs Countermelodies and descants Rounds and canons Monophonic, homophonic, polyphonic textures	Ostinato Partner songs Countermelodies and descants Rounds and canons Monophonic, homophonic, polyphonic textures	Ostinato Partner songs Countermelodies and descants Rounds and canons Change in texture density Combining independent melodies Monophonic, homophonic, polyphonic textures
Harmony/no harmony Unison/chordal harmony Major/minor Chord changes including: 　I–V$_7$ 2-part singing	Harmony/no harmony Unison/chordal harmony Major/minor Chord changes including: 　I–V$_7$ 　I–IV 　I–IV–V$_7$ Chord roots 2-part singing Harmony in thirds and sixths Harmonic styles including: parallel and contrary motion	Major/minor Chord changes including: 　I–V$_7$ 　I–IV 　I–IV–I–V$_7$ 　I–IV– V$_7$ Construction of triads and other chords Chord intervals: root, third, fifth, seventh Chord progressions Cadence 2-part singing Harmony in thirds and sixths 3-part singing Harmonic styles including: organum, parallel motion, contrary motion, countermelodies	Major/minor triads and inversions Chord changes including: 　I–V$_7$ 　I–IV 　I–IV–I–V$_7$ 　I–IV–V$_7$ Construction of triads and other chords Chord intervals: root, third, fifth, seventh Chord progressions Cadence 2-part harmony Harmony in thirds and sixths 3-part harmony SATB Harmonic styles including: organum, parallel motion, contrary motion, countermelodies

Skills Scope and Sequence

	K	**1**	**2**	
Singing **Vocal Development**	Vocal range C4–A4; *tessitura* D4–A4 Engage in vocal exploration using speaking, singing, calling, and whispering Engage in vocal exploration using high, middle, and low registers Explore producing head voice sounds and sustaining tones Engage in vocal exploration using descending and ascending *glissandi* on vowel *oo* Expand vocal range upward Sing a variety of simple songs in various keys and meters, alone and with a group Practice good vocal health	Vocal range D4–D5; *tessitura* D4–B4 Engage in vocal exploration using speaking, singing, calling, and whispering and descending and ascending *glissandi* Engage in vocal exploration using high, middle, and low registers Develop head voice sounds in the upper register and sustain tones Expand vocal range upward Develop good singing posture Sing a variety of simple songs in various keys and meters, alone and with a group Practice good vocal health	Vocal range C4–D5; *tessitura* D4–B4 Engage in vocal exploration, blending chest and head voice throughout the vocal range to produce uniform tonal quality in each register Practice producing head voice sounds in the upper register and sustaining tones Expand vocal range upward Practice good singing posture Sing a variety of simple songs in various keys and meters, alone and with a group, responding to cues from a conductor Practice good vocal health	
Intonation	Develop aural perception of different tones, patterns, and/or sounds Develop inner hearing of rhythms, tones, patterns, and melodies Develop pitch matching skills	Develop aural perception and inner hearing of different tones, patterns, rhythms, melodies, and/or sounds Develop pitch matching skills for *so-mi, so-la-so-mi,* and *do* Develop aural perception of melodic steps and skips	Develop aural perception and inner hearing skills Develop resonance singing on a neutral syllable (*oo*) Practice pitch matching for *mi-so-la* and expand to include *do-re-mi* Develop aural perception of home tone or tonal center Develop correct intonation singing *do*-pentatonic songs	
Expression	Sing songs using dynamics of *mp*	Sing songs using dynamics of *mp*	Expand dynamics range *mp–mf*, maintaining appropriate vocal quality Develop articulation skills of singing with connected and separated notes (legato and staccato) Develop singing in complete phrases with energy and direction Practice singing ritardando following a conductor	
Part Singing	Sing melodic echoes and dialogue songs	Sing melodic patterns in echo and call-and-response forms	Sing melodic patterns in echo and call-and-response forms Perform speech pieces in canon Sing simple drones and melodic ostinatos	
Diction	Develop good diction through modeling	Develop good diction through modeling Sing on a neutral syllable (*oo*) to develop resonant singing	Improve good diction through modeling Sing on a neutral syllable (*oo*) to develop resonant singing	
Song Repertoire	Sing songs representing genres and styles from diverse cultures Memorize a repertoire of songs	Sing songs representing genres and styles from diverse cultures Memorize a repertoire of songs	Sing songs representing genres and styles from diverse cultures Memorize a repertoire of songs	

3	4	5	6
Vocal range B3–E5; *tessitura* D4–D5 Engage in vocal exploration, blending chest and head voice throughout the vocal range to produce uniform tonal quality in each register Expand vocal range upward Develop correct breathing techniques Practice good singing posture Sing a variety of songs in various keys and meters, alone and with a group, responding to cues from a conductor Practice good vocal health	Vocal range A3–G5; *tessitura* C4–D5 Expand core vocal range Practice blending chest and head voice throughout the vocal range to produce uniform tonal quality in each register Develop deep breathing skills and breath control Practice good sitting and standing postures for singing Build confidence in solo singing Sing with sensitivity to blend in a group or choral ensemble, responding to cues from a conductor Practice good vocal health	Vocal range A3–G5; *tessitura* C4–D5 Sing vocalises using basic arpeggios to expand core vocal range Perform warm-up exercises and sing vocalises to prepare for singing Practice blending chest and head voice throughout the vocal range to produce uniform tonal quality in each register Improve deep breathing skills and breath control Build confidence in solo singing Refine good sitting and standing postures for singing Sing with sensitivity to blend in a group or choral ensemble, responding to cues from a conductor Practice good vocal health	Average vocal range G3–G5; *tessitura* D4–D5 Understand and adapt vocal range to accommodate changing voices Perform warm-up exercises and sing *mi-re-do* and *do-re-mi-fa-so* vocalises in varied keys Practice blending chest and head voice throughout the vocal range Refine deep breathing skills, breath control, and staggered breathing techniques for long notes or phrases Refine good sitting and standing postures for singing Build confidence in solo singing Sing with sensitivity to blend in a choral ensemble, responding to cues from a conductor Practice good vocal health
Develop aural perception and inner hearing skills Develop resonance singing on a neutral syllable (*oo*) Develop pitch matching skills Develop correct intonation singing *do-*, *la-*, and *so-* pentatonic songs Develop octave singing	Develop aural perception and inner hearing skills Develop correct intonation, singing extended pentatonic patterns and scales Develop singing half steps in tune using *do*-pentatonic scale Identify and sing *do*-pentatonic intervals	Develop aural perception and inner hearing skills Perform vocalises to improve resonance and placement Sing with correct intonation Identify and sing intervals in *do*-pentatonic and major scales	Develop aural perception and inner hearing skills Perform vocalises to improve resonance and placement Sing with correct intonation Recognize change of mode Sing dorian and mixolydian modes and harmonic minor scales Identify natural and harmonic minor scales
Expand dynamics range *p–mp–mf–f*, maintaining appropriate vocal quality Practice singing complete phrases on neutral syllables	Expand dynamics range, maintaining appropriate vocal quality Develop *legato* singing	Develop techniques for incorporating *crescendo* and *diminuendo* into singing expressively while maintaining the appropriate tempo Practice *legato* singing Develop *staccato* singing using proper breath support Sing songs using appropriate phrasing	Expand dynamics range, incorporating *crescendo* and *diminuendo* into singing expressively while maintaining the appropriate tempo Practice *legato* and *staccato* singing Sing with *rubato* while maintaining the appropriate dynamic level Sing using appropriate phrasing Sing major scales, arpeggios, and chords
Sing echo songs, melodic ostinatos, partner songs, rounds, countermelodies, descants, and easy 2-part canons Add harmony to songs by singing chord roots	Sing melodic ostinatos, partner songs, rounds, canons, descants, countermelodies, and 2-part songs Add harmony to songs by singing chord roots Add harmonic endings to songs in preparation for singing parallel harmonies Experience 3-part singing	Sing melodic ostinatos, partner songs, rounds, canons, countermelodies, descants, and 2- and 3-part songs Add harmony to songs by singing chord roots and 2- and 3-part chordal accompaniments using the following chords: I, IV, V_7, I Sing in parallel thirds	Sing melodic ostinatos, partner songs, rounds, canons, countermelodies, descants, and 2- and 3-part songs Add harmony to songs by singing chord roots and 2- and 3-part chordal accompaniments in major and minor modes using the following chords: I, IV, V_7, I; i, V_7 Sing in parallel thirds and sixths
Develop correct production of uniform vowel sounds and well-articulated consonants Sing on a neutral syllable (*oo*) to develop resonant singing	Sing vocalises of pure vowels: *a(ah)*, *e(eh)*, *i(ee)*, *o(oh)*, and *u(oo)* to develop resonant singing Practice correct production of uniform vowel sounds Develop correct articulation of consonant *r* Develop correct articulation of voiced and unvoiced consonants	Refine correct production of uniform vowel sounds Practice correct articulation of consonant *r* and voiced and unvoiced consonants Develop correct articulation of diphthongs Learn and apply basic rules for correct English diction	Refine correct production of uniform vowel sounds Refine correct articulation of consonant *r* and voiced and unvoiced consonants Practice correct articulation of diphthongs Develop techniques for singing sustained words correctly
Sing songs representing genres and styles from diverse cultures Memorize a repertoire of songs	Sing songs representing genres and styles from diverse cultures Memorize a repertoire of songs	Sing music from diverse genres and cultures, with appropriate expression and tone quality Memorize a repertoire of songs	Sing music from diverse genres and cultures, with appropriate expression and tone quality Memorize a repertoire of songs

	K	1	2	
Playing **Percussion** **(Mallets, unpitched, drumming)**	Explore timbre possibilities using body percussion and nonpitched instruments Learn correct playing techniques for pitched and nonpitched percussion Use instruments as "sound effects" for stories, poems, and dramatizations Play a steady beat using bilateral motions Play rhythm patterns on nonpitched percussion instruments, individually and in unison with others Play melodic patterns on mallet instruments Play and invent simple rhythm patterns Use patterns as introductions, interludes, and codas for songs and speech pieces	Expand instrumental sound resources, playing each with appropriate technique Explore techniques for playing mallet instruments and nonpitched percussion Use body percussion in different levels Play a steady beat using bilateral and alternating motions Imitate and invent rhythmic and melodic patterns, individually and in unison with others Play melodic patterns (ostinatos, melodic fragments) Play elemental harmonies (simple bordun) Repeat simple rhythmic and melodic patterns to accompany songs Play instruments in combination with each other (ensemble) Incorporate expressive elements into playing Develop awareness of timbre categories: woods, metals, shakers, scrapers, and so on	Play a steady beat and strong beat using bilateral and alternating lateral motions Play rhythmic patterns and ostinatos from notation Imitate and invent rhythmic and melodic patterns both in isolation and to accompany songs, speech pieces, and movement Develop basic mallet techniques Play melodic patterns to accompany songs (ostinatos, melodic fragments) Play simple melodies by rote on mallet instruments Play elemental harmonies (simple bordun, moving bordun, crossover bordun) Play instruments in groups (ensemble)	
String Instruments **(Autoharp, Guitar)**			Play one-chord and two-chord strums on the Autoharp	

3	4	5	6
Develop "crossover" mallet technique for playing borduns and ostinatos Play accompaniments for songs and speech pieces using body percussion, nonpitched percussion, and/or mallet instruments. Play combined patterns in ensemble to accompany songs, speech pieces, and movement, including borduns, melodic ostinatos, rhythmic ostinatos, and melodic/rhythmic fragments Develop a knowledge base for selecting accompaniment instruments appropriate to the style and culture of a song Develop original accompaniments as a group	Refine mallet techniques Include syncopation in rhythmic and melodic patterns Use body percussion and/or non-pitched percussion instruments to perform rhythm rounds, and create question/answer rhythmic phrases Use mallet instruments, keyboard, and/or recorder to create question/answer rhythmic phrases Play accompaniments on mallet instruments involving two chords—I–V, I–VI, I–VII Develop familiarity with chromatic structure of the keyboard Play melodies on mallet instruments by rote and by reading Develop simple instrumental pieces	Include offbeat rhythms in rhythmic and melodic patterns Play accompaniments on mallet instruments involving the I–IV–V_7 harmonic progression Develop more extended instrumental pieces. Include opportunities for rhythmic and/or melodic solos (composed or improvised) Provide opportunities for individuals to play small pieces alone, demonstrating good technique and style Develop ability to play culture-specific instruments and styles; e.g., various African drumming genres	Incorporate harmonization into the development of accompaniments using mallet instruments Play accompaniments on mallet instruments involving the I–IV–V_7 harmonic progression Expand familiarity and capability with culture-specific styles and instruments Provide opportunities for individuals to play small pieces alone, demonstrating good technique and style Develop ability to play culture-specific instruments and styles; e.g., various African drumming genres Play basic rock rhythm patterns with popular songs
Play two-chord Autoharp accompaniments for songs using simple strums	Play Autoharp accompaniments, both major and minor, using three chords and simple strums Identify types of guitars (nylon-string classical, steel-string acoustic, electric) Identify parts of the guitar Tune the guitar from a piano Develop proper guitar playing posture Use finger numbers for the left-hand Learn how to form chords Learn fundamental right-hand techniques (basic strumming patterns, picking) Learn fundamental left-hand techniques (chords A, D, E_7, G, C, D_7) Learn half chords Learn techniques for smooth transitions between chords Learn open tuning Begin use of the capo Create simple accompaniments to songs including short introductions, refrains, and ostinatos Play songs in the keys of C, D, and G	Play Autoharp accompaniments, both major and minor, using three or more chords Review types of guitars (nylon-string classical, steel-string acoustic, electric) Review parts of the guitar Tune the guitar using relative tuning Reinforce proper guitar playing posture (three different approaches) Learn to read chord diagrams Review and reinforce techniques for smooth transitions between chords Continue using the capo Play common chord progressions Learn alternative playing techniques Continue to learn and use open tuning Learn classic songs from guitar repertoire Continue left-hand techniques (review chords and learn A_7, E_7, G_7, Em, Am, Dm) Create accompaniments to songs including introductions, verses, refrains, and ostinatos Play songs in the keys C, D, G, F, Em, and Dm Discuss guidelines for improving practice time Discuss guidelines of self-assessment of skill progress	Use Autoharp accompaniments in conjunction with other string band instruments such as guitar Review parts of the guitar Tune the guitar from a piano Tune the guitar using relative tuning Reinforce proper guitar playing posture (three different approaches) Review and learn to read chord diagrams Review and reinforce techniques for smooth transitions between chords Continue using the capo Learn right-hand techniques (strumming patterns, picking) Continue to learn and use open tuning Learn alternating bass string technique Play music from the classical, pop, and folk genres Begin playing the electric guitar Learn to use mallet chords Continue left-hand techniques (review chords and learn Bm, B_7, $B\flat$, Gm) Create accompaniments to songs including introductions, verses, refrains, and ostinatos Play songs in the keys C, D, G, F, and several minor keys

	K	1	2	
Keyboard and MIDI	Identify black and white keys Maintain a steady beat Locate high and low sounds Play with supported index fingers Identify and play basic pulse Use timbre to identify range Play a two-handed accompaniment Discover and play pitches that move up and pitches that repeat Play strong beats Play an ostinato Play repeated phrases	Play with supported fingers Discover and play rhythm patterns Identify and play high and low sounds Accompany reinforcing a steady beat Play an ostinato Play call-and-response melodies Play a melodic phrase with ascending and descending skips Play a two-handed accompaniment Play a refrain	Play a two-handed accompaniment using supported index fingers Identify and play specific pitches Play duet accompaniments Read prestaff notation Discover and play *mi-re-do* patterns Determine melodic direction and play steps, skips, and repeats Determine appropriate finger numbers Play phrases using *do-re-mi-so* Play an ostinato Play melodies Accompany in various styles Read note values	
Recorder				

3	4	5	6
Read prestaff notation Read finger numbers and note values Play rhythm patterns to show high and low sounds on specific pitches Read a five-line staff Show timbre by playing a duet accompaniment Play sixteenth notes Play accompaniments using harmonic intervals Play extended range with melodies divided between hands Identify and accompany songs in different meters Play broken chord accompaniments Play melodies with an octave range Play I and V₇ chords	Review prestaff notation Review five-line reading and fingering Identify and play same and different phrases Play triads Expand five-finger position to achieve "closest position" Play ensembles Play walking bass lines Play broken chord accompaniments Improvise using pentatonic scales Play fingering shifts Play melodies with a large stretch Play ♩. ♪ rhythm patterns Play using thumb crossing Improvise on a given pentascale and rhythmic pattern Play I, IV, and V₇ chords	Review five-line reading and fingering Play syncopated rhythm patterns Play two-handed broken chords Play a strumming accompaniment Play a descant Play a tritone accompaniment for blues Play a two-handed accompaniment with crush notes Play a three-part round "Comp" a blues accompaniment Improvise on a blues pentascale and scat syllables Play an accompaniment using triplets Play an introduction and an interlude	Review five-line reading and fingering Play a rhythmic ostinato Play a harmonic ostinato Play a broken-chord accompaniment Play a tritone blues accompaniment Determine and play different dynamic levels Play a strumming accompaniment Determine and play multiple fingering positions Play a countermelody using finger crossing Play closest position chords Play a trio Play I, IV, and V₇ chords Play a piano piece
Read notes B, A, G, E, D Play with holes properly covered Use proper hand position with left hand on top Play with the pads of slightly curved fingers Move fingers together Play one-, two-, and three-note tonal patterns, ostinatos, and countermelodies Show phrases by breathing Blend sound with other recorder players Blend sound with singers and/or other instruments	Read new notes C¹, D¹, and F♯ Play with holes properly covered Use proper hand position with left hand on top Play with the pads of slightly curved fingers Move fingers together Build right-hand strength Play two-, three-, four-, and five-note tonal patterns, ostinatos, melodies, and countermelodies Play syncopated rhythm patterns Play melodic phrases using steps, skips, and repeats Accompany 2-chord songs in keys G, D Create ostinatos Create introductions and interludes Improvise using notes E, G, A, B Show phrases by breathing Blend sound with other recorder players Blend sound with singers and/or other instruments Blend harmony with melody	Read new notes G♯, C, F, and B♭ Improve playing and breathing techniques and hand dexterity Develop right-hand strength Play melodic phrases using steps, skips, and repeats Play ostinatos, abbreviated melodies, melodies, and countermelodies Play syncopated rhythm patterns Play contrasting sections Play a phrase of a round as an ostinato Play partner songs Create introductions, interludes, and codas Improvise in major and la-pentatonic (G and e) Create ostinatos Create melodies based upon a rhythm Practice proper articulation Blend sound with other performers Practice proper breathing and phrasing Blend harmony with melody Learn to read ahead Listen to recorder music played in different styles	Read the new note E¹ Introduce alto recorder Read C, D, E, F, and G for alto recorder Improve playing and breathing techniques and hand dexterity Play ostinatos, abbreviated melodies, melodies, and countermelodies Blend sound with other performers Blend harmony with melody Play enharmonic tones Play a phrase of a round as an ostinato Play ensemble recorder music Play vocal scores for recorder consort Play partner songs Create ostinatos Improvise in phrases as contrasting sections to melodies Improvise 12-bar blues in A using pentatonic scale tones A, C, D, E, and G Improvise recorder parts following chord progressions Create melodies based upon a rhythm Practice proper articulation Refine playing in the low register Add breath marks at phrase endings and practice proper breathing and phrasing Learn to read ahead Listen to recorder music played in different styles

	K	**1**	**2**
Creating **Improvising**	Improvise patterns, using sound and movement Improvise rhythmic ostinato accompaniments Improvise introductions to songs, stories, poems, and dramatizations, using patterns of sound and movement Explore a range of sound possibilities with voices, body percussion, instruments, and environmental and electronic sound sources Improvise sound pieces to describe moods or images Improvise sound pieces and/or sound effects to accompany stories, poems, and songs	Improvise simple rhythms, using sound and movement, in call-and-response form Improvise a contrasting or B section in an AB or ABA form, using sound and/or movement Improvise rhythmic, melodic, and movement patterns and use as accompaniments to songs and speech pieces Improvise, using sound and movement, backgrounds or settings for poems, stories, songs, and speech pieces Use tempo and dynamic changes and contrasts in improvisations Improvise simple sound pieces for voices, body percussion, instruments, and environmental and electronic sounds	Improvise the b phrase in an aaba form Improvise body percussion patterns to accompany songs or speech pieces Invent strumming patterns for one-chord Autoharp accompaniments Improvise melodic phrases using the pentatonic scale Improvise sound pieces and music to accompany movement, poetry, and storytelling, using a variety of media, including technology sources	
Composing	Create movements and dramatizations for songs and poems Create new words and movements for familiar songs Compose soundscapes for voices, body percussion, instruments, and environmental sounds	Compose, using sound and movement, backgrounds or settings for poems, stories, songs, and speech pieces Create introductions for songs and speech pieces, using sound and movement Invent systems for notating musical ideas Compose original verses to familiar songs Use tempo and dynamic changes and contrasts in compositions Compose simple sound pieces for voices, body percussion, instruments, and environmental and electronic sounds	Create settings, sound effects, or accompaniments for songs, poems, dances, and speech and creative movement pieces, using a variety of sound sources and movement ideas Compose simple AB and ABA pieces, using sound and movement Compose introductions and codas for songs and speech pieces, using sound and movement Compose B and C sections to create an ABACA piece Compose and notate rhythmic and melodic ostinato accompaniments to pentatonic melodies, using classroom percussion or technology sources	
Reading/Notating **Rhythm**	Beat icons Long/short icons	Interpret icons representing beat/strong beat, long/short, and tempo and dynamic changes Durations including: ♩, 𝄽, ♫ Follow and create listening charts	Iconic notation Durations including: ♩, 𝄽, ♫, ♬, ♩ Meters including: $\frac{2}{4}$, $\frac{3}{4}$ Tie	

3	4	5	6
Improvise contrasting B and C sections in a rondo (ABACA) form, using sound and movement Improvise rhythmic, melodic, and movement ostinatos in accompaniments for songs or speech pieces Improvise simple pieces that show thick and thin texture contrasts; use movement to show texture Improvise simple melodies based on the pentatonic scale Use variation in dynamics, tempo, and articulation in improvisations Experiment with various electronic and environmental sound sources and alternative ways to play instruments	Use melodic sequences in improvisations Improvise music to accompany movement or dance Improvise introductions, codas, and interludes Improvise melodies in major and minor Improvise simple sound and movement variations on a theme Improvise pieces in rondo (ABACA) form, using a variety of sound sources, including technology and movement Invent playing techniques (strumming, mallet) for I-V and I-IV accompaniments	Improvise extended phrases in question/answer form, using movement, rhythms, and melody Improvise melodies over accompaniments, using the I, IV, and V chords Improvise melodies, using various scales Experiment with strumming or other playing techniques to create rhythmic variety in chordal accompaniments	Use melodic sequences in improvisations Improvise answer phrases when given question phrases Improvise music to accompany movement and movement to accompany music Improvise chordal accompaniments for familiar songs Use given and original motives and themes as the basis for improvising with sound and movement Use acoustic and electronic instruments to improvise melodies over given chord patterns including rock and blues
Compose accompaniments and dramatizations for songs and readings, using a variety of sound sources and movements Compose rhythmic, melodic, and movement ostinatos in accompaniments for songs or speech pieces Compose simple melodies based on the pentatonic scale Create AB, ABA, and ABACA pieces, using speech, instruments, voices, and movement Compose and notate two short rhythm pieces that can be performed together as partners Compose simple pieces that show thick and thin texture contrasts; use movement to show texture Use variation in dynamics, tempo, and articulation in compositions Compose simple percussion and wind instrument pieces to explore sound sources and timbres	Compose music to accompany movement or dance Compose accompaniments of or backgrounds and dramatizations for songs, poems, and stories, using music and movement Create, notate, and perform a pentatonic melody Create and perform speech, rhythm, and movement canons Compose introductions, codas, and interludes Use melodic sequences in compositions Create, notate, and perform rhythmic, speech, or movement variations on a theme Compose pieces in rondo (ABACA) form, using a variety of movement and sound sources, including technology options	Compose and arrange accompaniments for songs, poems, stories, and dramas, using music and movement Compose, notate, and perform compositions in AB, ABA, and ABACA forms Compose a music or movement theme and variations on the theme Compose, notate, and perform melodies in major and minor mode, using various media, including technology Invent a scale, using classroom instruments and technology options, and compose a melody using that scale	Compose, notate, and perform original songs, instrumental works, speech pieces, and dramatizations Compose music to accompany dance or dramatic presentations Use given and original motives and themes as the basis for composing with sound and movement Compose chordal accompaniments for familiar songs Create new verses for a song Invent new arrangements of simple pieces, using voices, acoustic instruments, or electronic instruments other than those for which the music was originally written Compose and notate short arrangements, using computer software Experiment with found sounds and new sound sources to create music Compose accompaniments in different musical styles using auto-accompaniment on MIDI keyboards
Durations including: Meters including: $\frac{2}{4}$, $\frac{3}{4}$, $\frac{4}{4}$	Upbeat Durations including: Meters including: $\frac{2}{4}$, $\frac{3}{4}$, $\frac{4}{4}$	Upbeat Durations including: Meters including: $\frac{2}{4}$, $\frac{3}{4}$, $\frac{4}{4}$, $\frac{6}{8}$	Steady beat/back beat Durations including: tied notes Meters including: $\frac{2}{4}$, $\frac{3}{4}$, $\frac{4}{4}$, $\frac{2}{2}$, $\frac{6}{8}$ Compound, changing, and asymmetrical meters Syncopation

	K	1	2
Melody	Upward/downward melodic motion icons Preparation for *so-mi* patterns	Interpret icons representing melodic motion Patterns including: *so-mi, so-mi-la, so-mi-la-do* *do*-pentatonic in C, F, G for playing on mallet instruments	Patterns including: *so-mi, so-mi-la, so-mi-la-do, mi-re-do, so-mi-re-do, la-so-mi-re-do* *do*-pentatonic in C, F, and G *la*-pentatonic in e

Listening/Analyzing/Describing

Respond to characteristics of phrase form: same and different Respond to characteristics of rhythm: steady beats, strong beats, silent beats, long/short sounds, repeated rhythm patterns Respond to characteristics of melodies: high/low pitches; upward/downward melodic direction; repeated melodic patterns Identify accompaniment/no accompaniment Identify environmental sounds: animals, machines, and weather Identify instrumental sounds of classroom percussion instruments, keyboards, flute, and trumpet Identify differences between vocal sounds: speaking, singing, shouting, whispering, humming Respond to expressive qualities in music: fast/slow and loud/soft Listen to music of diverse cultures and styles Demonstrate appropriate audience behavior while observing classroom performances Discuss appropriate audience behaviors	Respond to characteristics of phrase form: same/different, call and response, and solo/chorus Respond to characteristics of sectional form: verse and refrain Respond to characteristics of rhythm: steady beats, strong beats, silent beats, absence of beats, long and short sounds, rhythm patterns Respond to characteristics of melody: high/low pitches, upward/downward direction, melodic patterns Identify and describe various accompaniments Identify various found sounds Identify sounds of nonpitched and pitched percussion instruments; trombone, violin, flute, clarinet, and trumpet Identify vocal timbres: male, female, child Identify qualities of speech, singing, shouting, whispering Respond to expressive qualities in music: fast, slow, and changing tempos; loud, soft, and changing dynamics Describe mood and style in a variety of music Identify music of diverse cultures and styles Listen to music that suggests a story or subject Demonstrate appropriate audience behavior while observing classroom performances Discuss appropriate audience behaviors	Identify characteristics of phrase form: same and different, call and response, aab, and aaba Identify characteristics of sectional form: verse and refrain, AB, ABA, and ABACA Identify rhythmic elements: steady beat, long and short sounds, repeated rhythm patterns, $\frac{2}{4}$, $\frac{3}{4}$ meters Identify high/low pitches, steps/skips, melodic direction, and melodic patterns Contrast styles of two pieces Identify melodic and rhythmic ostinatos Identify vocal timbres of individuals and groups: male, female, child Identify various instrumental timbres, including nonpitched and pitched percussion, strings, woodwinds, brass, and electronic instruments Respond to expressive qualities in music: fast, slow, and changing tempos; loud, soft, and changing dynamics Perceive and respond to articulation changes (*legato* and *staccato*) Identify and respond to section changes Describe mood and style in a variety of music Identify music of diverse cultures and styles Listen to music that suggests a story or subject Demonstrate appropriate audience behavior while observing classroom performances Discuss appropriate audience behaviors

3	4	5	6
Patterns including: *mi-re-do*, *so-mi-re-do*, *la-so-mi-re-do*, *la*$_{\vert}$, *so*$_{\vert}$, *do*$^{\vert}$, *so*$_{\vert}$-*la*$_{\vert}$-*do-re-mi-so-la-do*$^{\vert}$ *do*-pentatonic scale *la*-pentatonic scale *so*-pentatonic scale Letter names for pitches	*do*-pentachordal Patterns including: *la-so-mi-re-do*, *la*$_{\vert}$, *so*$_{\vert}$, *so-do*$^{\vert}$, *fa*, *ti*, *so*$_{\vert}$-*la*$_{\vert}$-*do-re-mi-fa-so-la-ti-do*$^{\vert}$ *do*-pentatonic scale *la*-pentatonic scale *so*-pentatonic scale Letter names for pitches	Major/minor diatonic Dorian Mixolydian *do*-pentachordal Patterns including: *la-so-mi-re-do*, *fa*, *so*$_{\vert}$-*la*$_{\vert}$-*do-re-mi-fa-so-la-ti-do*$^{\vert}$ *do*-pentatonic scale *la*-pentatonic scale *so*-pentatonic scale Letter names for pitches	Half/whole steps Accidentals; intervals Ornamentation Major/minor scales Pitch sets (12-tone, whole-tone) Motive Repetition and contrast *do*-pentatonic scale *la*-pentatonic scale *so*-pentatonic scale Letter names for pitches
Identify AB, ABA, AABB, and ABACA forms Identify rhythmic elements: steady beat, $\frac{2}{4}$ and $\frac{3}{4}$ meters, patterns Identify same/different, longer/shorter, higher/lower, upward/downward, louder/softer, faster/slower Identify patterns and themes Identify chord changes in two-chord songs Distinguish between major and minor tonality Analyze and describe how tempo, dynamics, and timbre affect the mood of a piece Identify various vocal timbres of individual performers and groups Identify instrument families in the orchestra: strings, woodwinds, brass, percussion Respond to expressive qualities in music: fast, slow, and changing tempos; loud, soft, and changing dynamics Identify music of diverse cultures and styles Listen to program and nonprogram music Listen to standard orchestral and chamber music Demonstrate appropriate audience behavior while observing classroom performances Discuss appropriate audience behaviors	Identify form in instrumental pieces Identify rhythmic elements in $\frac{2}{4}$, $\frac{3}{4}$, and $\frac{4}{4}$ meters Identify same/different, longer/shorter, higher/lower, upward/downward, louder/softer Distinguish between major and minor tonality Analyze and describe how tempo, dynamics, and timbre affect the mood of a piece Identify vocal timbres of groups Identify individual instruments Identify families of instruments from diverse cultures: strings, woodwinds, brass, percussion Analyze and describe differences between orchestra and band sound Respond to expressive qualities in music: fast, slow, and changing tempos; loud, soft, and changing dynamics Compare and describe the elements of style in two contrasting pieces Analyze music of diverse cultures and styles Analyze standard orchestral and chamber music Listen to choral works Demonstrate appropriate audience behavior while observing classroom performances Discuss appropriate audience behaviors	Identify and analyze sectional, theme and variations, and ABACA/rondo form Identify rhythmic elements of meter in $\frac{2}{4}$, $\frac{3}{4}$, $\frac{4}{4}$, and $\frac{6}{8}$ Identify chords Distinguish between major, minor, and other modes Analyze and compare rhythmic elements in terms of steady beat, meter, rhythm patterns, and relative duration Analyze and compare melodic structure in terms of movement, contour, sequence, phrase, cadence, and mode Analyze and compare pieces in terms of texture and chordal and linear harmony Identify timbres of individual singing voices and vocal ensembles Identify timbres of individual instruments and ensembles Respond to expressive qualities in music: fast, slow, and changing tempos; loud, soft, and changing dynamics Respond to show form in music Respond to show interpretation of lyrics in music Analyze and compare elements of style in several contrasting pieces Analyze music of diverse cultures and styles Identify complete sections from longer musical forms Compare program and absolute music Listen to chamber groups Demonstrate appropriate audience behavior while observing classroom performances Discuss appropriate audience behaviors	Identify repetition and contrast Identify sectional forms: AB, ABA, ABACA/rondo, and theme and variations Identify chords Distinguish between major, minor, and other modes Identify intervals: thirds and sixths Identify cadence Identify and describe how the words of a song affect the form and expressive qualities Identify *rubato* Recognize appropriateness of tempo choices Identify tempo category for selection: *largo*, *adagio*, *andante*, *moderato*, *allegro*, *vivace*, *presto*, *prestissimo* Discern individual and group timbres Discern vocal timbres from a variety of cultures Identify similarities and differences among string instruments from different cultures Move to show form, melodic contour, tempo changes, and changes in dynamics Respond to expressive qualities in music: fast, slow, and changing tempos; loud, soft, and changing dynamics Identify and describe style differences determined by rhythm, melody, and timbre Analyze music of diverse cultures and styles Recognize composite forms: opera, cantata, mass, and others Identify dance styles Recognize and describe a variety of vocal styles Identify various styles of drumming Demonstrate appropriate audience behavior while observing classroom performances Discuss appropriate audience behavior while listening to peers and guest musicians perform for the class

	K	**1**	**2**
Moving			
Nonlocomotor	Acquire a repertoire of nonlocomotor movements: pat, clap, stamp, bend, stretch, twist, shake Perform nonlocomotor motions in finger plays and action songs	Practice basic repertoire of nonlocomotor movements in finger plays and action songs Develop these alternating patterns: pat-clap, pat-tap, pat-stamp	Practice nonlocomotor movements Practice alternating patterns Develop repertoire of bilateral movements: snap and hand jive motions
Locomotor	Develop a repertoire of locomotor movements: walk, run, hop, jump, twirl Coordinate locomotor movements during singing games and circle dances	Practice basic locomotor movements: walk, run, hop, jump, twirl Practice coordinating locomotor movements during singing games and circle dances Develop these locomotor movements: skip, slide, leap, gallop	Practice basic locomotor movements during singing games and circle dances Develop facility with basic patterned locomotor movements: line and folk dances
Time	Perform creative movements while exploring concepts of time: rhythm (pulse, beat, speed-time or tempo); accent (light or strong); and duration (length)	Perform creative movements while exploring concepts of time: rhythm, accent, tempo, and duration	Perform creative movements while exploring concepts of time: rhythm, accent, tempo, and duration
Space	Perform creative movements while exploring concepts of space: level (low, middle, high); direction (forward, backward, sideways, up, down); size (large or small); place-pathways (on the floor, in the air); focus	Perform creative movements while exploring concepts of space: level, direction, size, place-pathways, focus	Perform creative movements while exploring concepts of space: level, direction; size, place-pathways, focus
Energy	Perform creative movements while exploring concepts of energy: attack (smooth, sharp); weight (heavy, light); strength/tension (tight, loose); flow (sudden or sustained, bound or free) Experiment with qualities of movement including effort actions such as flick, tap, thrust, slash, float, glide	Perform creative movements while exploring concepts of energy: attack, weight, strength/tension, and flow Experiment with qualities of movement including effort actions such as flick, tap, thrust, slash, float, glide	Perform creative movements while exploring concepts of energy: attack, weight, strength/tension, and flow Experiment with qualities of movement including effort actions such as thrust, slash, float, glide, wring, press

Refine nonlocomotor movements Practice alternating patterns Develop these alternating patterns: clap-snap, stamp-snap, pat-clap-snap Practice bilateral movements	Refine nonlocomotor movements Refine alternating patterns Develop these alternating patterns: alternating snap, stamp-pat-clap, stamp-pat-clap Refine bilateral movements	Refine nonlocomotor movements Refine alternating patterns Develop these alternating patterns: alternating pat-snap, clap-snap, stamp-snap, pat-clap-snap, stamp-pat-clap-snap Refine bilateral movements	Refine nonlocomotor movements Refine alternating patterns Refine bilateral movements
Practice basic locomotor movements Practice patterned locomotor movements in singing games; circle, line, and folk dances Develop this pattern of locomotor movement: square dance	Refine basic locomotor movements Practice patterned locomotor movements Develop these patterns of locomotor movements: social and popular (or contemporary) dances	Refine basic locomotor movements Refine patterned locomotor movements Develop these patterns of locomotor movements: social and popular (or contemporary) dances	Refine locomotor movements Refine patterned locomotor movements Develop these patterns of locomotor movements: social and popular (or contemporary) dances
Perform creative movements while exploring concepts of time: rhythm, accent, tempo, and duration	Perform creative movements while exploring concepts of time: rhythm, accent, tempo, and duration	Perform creative movements while exploring concepts of time: rhythm, accent, tempo, and duration	Perform creative movements while exploring concepts of time: rhythm, accent, tempo, and duration
Perform creative movements while exploring concepts of space: level, direction; size, place-pathways, focus	Perform creative movements while exploring concepts of space: level, direction; size, place-pathways, focus	Perform creative movements while exploring concepts of space: level, direction; size, place-pathways, focus	Perform creative movements while exploring concepts of space: level, direction; size, place-pathways, focus
Perform creative movements while exploring concepts of energy: attack, weight, strength/tension, and flow Experiment with qualities of movement including effort actions such as thrust, slash, float, glide, wring, press	Perform creative movements while exploring concepts of energy: attack, weight, strength/tension, and flow Experiment with qualities of movement including effort actions such as thrust, slash, float, glide, wring, press	Perform creative movements while exploring concepts of energy: attack, weight, strength/tension, and flow Experiment with qualities of movement including effort actions such as thrust, slash, float, glide, wring, press	Perform creative movements while exploring concepts of energy: attack, weight, strength/tension, and flow Experiment with qualities of movement including effort actions such as thrust, slash, float, glide, wring, press

Skills Scope and Sequence

Pitch Syllable Systems

Several systems of both pitch and rhythm syllables are available for use in the music classroom. The purpose of using syllables is to ensure that students develop the ability to associate musical notation with a corresponding sound. When choosing a system, consider the developmental level of the students and the ease with which they can achieve success. Also, take into account consistency between grade levels and performance-based music programs.

Solfeggio or *so-fa*

There are two types of solfége systems. Both systems use the following syllables and their chromatic alterations.

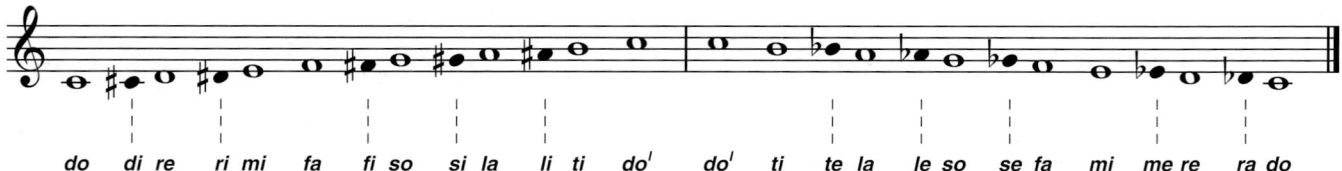

do di re ri mi fa fi so si la li ti do¹ do¹ ti te la le so se fa mi me re ra do

Moveable *do*

The syllable *do* is the tonic pitch in any major key. Minor keys are based on *la*. The advantage to this system is that it establishes patterns that can easily be adapted to any key (for example, a minor third always exists between *so* and *mi*, and there is always a half-step between *mi* and *fa*). This method tends to favor early success particularly for younger students, since the introduction of letter names and key signatures can be postponed until a more age-appropriate time.

Moveable Major Scale

do re mi fa so la ti do¹

Relative Harmonic Minor Scale

la₁ ti₁ do re mi fa si la

Fixed *do*

The pitch C is always *do*, regardless of key. Proponents of this system argue that it more accurately represents true music reading, since the lines and spaces of the staff are always associated with the same sound. Knowledge of key signatures is required for success with this system.

Fixed Major Scale

do re mi fa so la ti do¹

Fixed Harmonic Minor Scale

do re me fa so le ti do¹

Moveable Numbers

Similar to moveable *do*, this system uses numbers (usually 1–7) with 1 functioning as the tonic. Students can often achieve success early on because of their familiarity with numbers, although the numbers themselves can be less musical to sing than *so-fa* syllables. This system does not allow for half step alteration, and rhythmic accuracy can be a factor when using 7.

Moveable Major Scale – Numbers

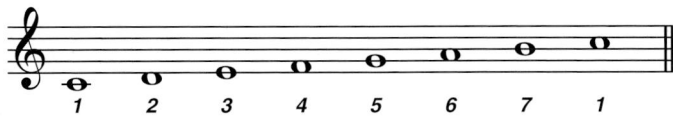

Moveable Harmonic Minor Scale – Numbers

Fixed Numbers

Similar to fixed *do*, the numbers correspond to a specific pitch class. C is usually 0 and this advanced system is often reserved for twelve-tone music.

Fixed Major Scale – Numbers

Neutral Syllable

This system uses a neutral syllable such as *la, lu, du,* etc. It is most beneficial for students who are already proficient readers and possess a strong aural sense of intervallic relationships. These students appreciate the lack of need to transfer pitches to any type of syllable.

Pitch and Rhythm Syllable Systems

Rhythm Syllable Systems

	Traditional	Kodály-based	Gordon
	This numbers-based method reinforces meter by starting each measure with *1*. Each beat is numbered and subdivisions of the beat are represented by the use of syllables *&* and *e*. A variation of this system uses *ta, te, la,* and *lee*. The most widely used system in instrumental music programs, this method is less singable because it incorporates multi-syllable numbers.	Although Zoltán Kodály used these syllables, they were developed by Emil Chevé in nineteenth century France. Rather than using numbers, each beat is represented by *ta*. Subdivision of the beat is based on *ti* and each rhythmic pattern is assigned a distinct syllable. This method lends itself to singing and/or playing patterns without having to distort melodies by using numbers.	Gordon's syllables are designed to promote audiation, or the ability to hear a musical sound when looking at notation. Like the Kodály-based syllables, the use of *du, da,* and *de* are easily singable.
Simple Meter			
♩	1	ta	du
♫	1-& OR 1-te	ti-ti	du-da
♬♬	1-e-&-a OR 1-ta-te-ta	ti-ri-ti-ri OR ti-ka-ti-ka	du-ta-de-ta
♩♫	1-&-a OR 1-te-ta	ti-ti-ri OR ti-ti-ka	du-de-ta
♬♩	1-e-& OR 1-ta-te	ti-ri-ti OR ti-ka-ti	du-da-de
♬♩	1-e-a OR 1-ta-ta	ti-ri-ti OR ti-ka-ti	du-ta-ta
♩.♪	1-a OR 1-ta	teem-ri OR teem-ka	du-ta
♪♩.	1-e OR 1-ta	ti-reem OR tik-um	du-ta
♩	1-2	ta-am OR to-o	du-
♩.♪	1-2 & OR 1-2 te	tam ti	du de
♪ ♩.	1 &-2 OR 1 te-2	ti tam	du da
♪♩ ♪	1 &-2 & OR 1 te-2 te	syn-co-pa OR ti ta ti	du-du de
♩.	1-2-3	ta-a-am OR to-o-om	du-u-u
o	1-2-3-4	ta-a-a-am OR toe	du-u-u-u

Compound Meter

♩.	1	ta	du
♫	1-&-a OR 1-la-lee	ti-ti-ti	du-da-di
♬♬	1-e-&-a-&-a OR 1-ta-la-ta-lee-ta	ti-ri-ti-ri-ti-ri OR ti-ka-ti-ka-ti-ka	du-ta-da-ta-di-ta
♬♪	1-e-&-& OR 1-ta-la-lee	ti-ri-ti-ti OR ti-ka-ti-ti	du-ta-da-di
♪♬	1-&-a-& OR 1-la-ta-lee	ti-ti-ri-ti OR ti-ti-ka-ti	du-da-ta-di
♪.♬	1-e-& OR 1 -ta-lee	teem-ri-ti OR teem-ka-ti	du-ta-di

Breath Impulse

A variation of the traditional method, the breath impulse system uses numbers to represent each beat in a measure. When performing longer durations or sustained notes, the numbers are extended *(Wu-un, Two-oo,* and so on) with pulses of air that correspond to the underlying rhythmic pulse. The pulses vary to achieve the correct subdivision *(Wu-uh-uh-un* for sixteenth notes; *Wu-uh-un* for compound meter). Supporters of this method maintain that it emphasizes rhythmic subdivision, promotes good breath control, and contributes to success in vibrato development. This method is more widely used by instrumental teachers, since it does not lend itself to singing melodies expressively.

Glossary

A

a cappella A term used to indicate unaccompanied choral singing.

AB form A musical plan that has two different parts, or sections.

ABA form A musical plan that has three sections. The first and last sections are the same. The middle section is different.

accent Indicates that a note should be sung or played with more emphasis than the other notes. (>)

accidental A sign used to show an altered pitch. The most common signs (which raise or lower a pitch by a half step) are sharps (♯), flats (♭), and naturals (♮).

accompaniment Music that supports the sound of the featured performer(s).

alto Female voice, the range of which lies below that of a soprano.

aria A song for solo voice in an opera, an oratorio, or a cantata; often designed to show off the singer's vocal ability.

articulation A form of musical expression, using *legato, staccato,* or *marcato*.

augmentation The lengthening of note values of a melody. The opposite effect—the shortening of note values—is called diminution.

B

backbeat An emphasis on the offbeats: 1 **2** 3 **4**.

ballad A song that tells a story.

baritone Male voice, the range of which lies between that of the tenor and the bass.

bass The lowest range of the male voice.

beat A repeating pulse that can be felt in most music.

blues A twentieth-century jazz style characterized by a 12-bar blues harmonic structure, flatted third and seventh notes, and slow, syncopated rhythms.

brass A group of wind instruments, including trumpets, French horns, trombones, and tubas, used in bands and orchestras.

C

cadence A group of chords or notes at the end of a phrase or piece that gives a feeling of pausing or finishing.

call and response A follow-the-leader process in which a melody is introduced by one voice or instrument (call) and then immediately answered by other voices or instruments (response).

calypso A style of folk music from the Caribbean that tells a story about an event or experience.

canon A musical composition in which the parts imitate each other. One part begins, or leads, and the other part follows.

chamber music Music written for small groups, often having only one voice or instrument for each part, as in a string quartet.

changing meter A grouping of beats that changes throughout a composition; for example, the music may begin in $\frac{3}{4}$ and then change to $\frac{6}{8}$ or any other meter.

chord Three or more different tones played or sung together.

chord progression The order of chords in a segment of a piece of music.

chorus A large group of singers.

chromatic scale A consecutive succession of 12 half tones.

coda A "tail" or short section, added at the end of a piece of music.

composer A person who creates music by putting sounds together in his or her own way.

compound meter A meter in which the beat is subdivided into groups of three.

concerto A composition written for solo instrument(s) with orchestra.

contour The "shape" of a melody, determined by the way it moves upward and downward in steps and leaps, and repeated tones.

contrast Two or more things that are different. In music, slow is a *contrast* to fast; section A is a *contrast* to section B.

countermelody A melody that is played or sung at the same time as the main melody.

crescendo Gradually getting louder.

D

decrescendo Gradually getting softer.

descant Another melody that decorates the main tune, usually placed above the main melody.

diatonic scale An arrangement of seven different notes. It is called "major" when the *tonic*, or home note, is *do*.

duet A composition written for two performers.

duple meter The way beats in music are organized into groups of two.

duration The length of sounds, from very short to very long.

dynamics The degrees of loudness and softness of sound.

E

embellish To decorate the melody and take freedom with the rhythm.

ensemble A group of players or singers.

F

fermata A sign ⌢ indicating that a note is held longer than its written note value, stopping or "holding" the beat.

form The overall structure, or plan, of a piece of music.

forte (*f*) Loud.

fortissimo (*ff*) Very loud.

G

gamelan Ensembles consisting of gongs, gong-chimes, metallophones, xylophones, and drums, found in Indonesia, Malaysia, and in scattered places around the Western world.

glissando A continuous movement from one pitch to another.

H

half step The distance between one key and the next, black or white.

harmonic minor scale An arrangement of eight tones with a pattern of steps as follows: whole, half, whole, whole, half, whole + half, half.

harmony Two or more different pitches sounding at the same time.

I

improvise To make up the music while performing.

interlude Music inserted between verses of a song; also, music played between the scenes of a play or opera.

interval The distance from one tone to another.

introduction Music played before the main part of a composition begins.

irregular meter A grouping of beats that moves in an irregular number of beats, such as $\frac{5}{4}$.

J

jazz A style that grew out of the music of African Americans, then took many different substyles, such as ragtime, blues, cool jazz, swing bebop, rock. It features solo improvisations over a set of harmonic progression.

K

key The scale on which a piece of music is based, named for its tonic, or "home-base" tone.

key signature The musical symbol, comprising sharps or flats placed on the staff, that defines the key of a piece of music.

L

legato Music performed in a smooth and connected style.

M

major scale An arrangement of eight tones according to the following pattern of steps or intervals: whole, whole, half, whole, whole, whole, half.

marcato Music performed with stressed or accented notes.

measure A grouping of beats set off by bar lines.

melodic rhythm The rhythm of the words.

melody A line of single tones that moves upward, downward, or repeats.

meter The way beats of music are grouped, often in sets of two or three.

meter signature The symbol, such as $\frac{2}{4}$ or $\frac{6}{8}$, that tells how many beats are in a measure (top number) and the kind of note that gets one beat (bottom number).

mezzo forte (*mf*) Medium loud.

mezzo piano (*mp*) Medium soft.

mood The feeling that a piece of music gives. The *mood* of a lullaby is quiet and gentle.

motive A phrase that repeats in different ways.

movement Each of the smaller, self-contained sections (usually three or four) that together make up a symphony, sonata, concerto, string quartet, or suite.

Glossary

N

natural minor scale An arrangement of eight tones with a pattern of steps as follows: whole, half, whole, whole, half, whole, whole.

O

opera A theatrical production combining drama, vocal and orchestral music, costumes, scenery, and sometimes dance.

oratorio A musical drama for voices and orchestra, often based on a religious narrative; usually performed without scenery or action.

ornamentation In music, the decoration or embellishment of a melody, usually by the addition of notes, to make the work more beautiful or to demonstrate the abilities of the performer.

ostinato A repeated rhythm or melody pattern played throughout a piece or a section of a piece.

overture An instrumental introduction to an opera, oratorio, or other stage work; the term is sometimes given to an independent orchestral composition.

P

partner songs Two or more different songs that can be sung at the same time to create harmony.

pentatonic Music based on a five-tone scale. A common pentatonic scale corresponds to tones 1, 2, 3, 5, and 6 of the major scale.

percussion Pitched or nonpitched instruments that are played by striking, scraping, or shaking.

phrase A melodic idea that is a complete musical thought.

pianissimo (*pp*) Very soft.

piano (*p*) Soft.

pitch The location of a tone with respect to highness or lowness.

pizzicato On a string instrument, the plucking of the strings.

polyphonic texture Music created when two or more separate melodies are sung or played together.

prelude An instrumental introduction to a musical drama, usually shorter than an overture; also, a short, independent composition.

program music Music that is inspired by an extramusical idea—a person, place, story, scene, and so on.

Q

quartet A composition for four voices or instruments, each having a separate part; a group of four singers or instrumentalists, each playing or singing a different part

R

ragtime An early form of jazz popular from around 1890 to World War I.

range In a melody, the span from the lowest tone to the highest tone.

rap A form of music based on recitation of rhythmic poetry over an incessant beat. An occasional melodic phrase may occur.

refrain The part of a song that repeats, using the same melody and words.

register The pitch (highness or lowness of a tone) location of a group of tones. If the group of tones are all high sounds, they are in a high *register*. If the group of tones are all low sounds, they are in a low *register*.

repeated tones Two or more tones in a row that have the same sound.

rest Symbol for silence in music.

rhythm The way movement is organized in a piece of music, using beat, no beat, long and short sounds, meter, accents, no accents, tempo, syncopation, and so on.

rhythm pattern A combination of sounds and silences in the same or differing lengths.

rondo A musical form in which the first section always returns. The most common rondo form is ABACA.

root The tone on which a chord is built.

round A composition in which the parts enter in succession, singing the same melody.

S

scale An arrangement of pitches from lower to higher according to a specific pattern of intervals or steps.

scat singing A jazz vocal style in which syllables are used instead of words.

score The musical notation of a composition, with each of the instrumental and vocal parts shown in vertical alignment.

sequence A pattern of pitches that is repeated at a higher or lower pitch level.

shanty A sailor's work song.

simple meter A meter in which the beat is subdivided into groups of two.

slur Indicates that a syllable is sung on more than one pitch.

solo Music for a single singer or player, often with an accompaniment.

soprano The highest range of the female voice.

spiritual An African American religious folk song that originated during the period of enslavement.

staccato Music performed in a separated, detached style.

steady beat Regular pulses.

step To move from one tone to another without skipping tones in between.

strings A term used to refer to string instruments that are played by bowing, plucking, or strumming.

strong beat The first beat in a measure.

style In music, style refers to the unique way in which the elements of melody, rhythm, timbre, texture, harmony, and form are handled to create a special "sound."

swing A jazz style developed in the 1930s and played by big bands.

symphony In Western art music, an ensemble consisting of multiple strings plus an assortment of woodwinds, brass, and percussion instruments.

syncopation An arrangement of rhythm in which important sounds begin on weak beats or weak parts of beats, giving a catchy, "off-balance" movement to the music.

T

tempo The speed of the beat in music.

tenor The highest-pitched adult male voice.

texture The layering of sounds to create a thick or thin quality in music.

theme An important melody that occurs several times in a piece of music.

theme and variations A musical form in which each section is a modification of the initial theme.

tie A musical symbol that connects two notes of the same pitch.

timbre The special sound or tone color, that makes one instrument or voice sound different from another.

time signature Musical symbol that indicates how many beats are in a measure (top number) and which note gets the beat (bottom number).

transpose To play a composition or musical passage in another key.

trio A composition for three voices or instruments, each having a separate part; a group of three singers or instrumentalists, each playing or singing a different part.

triple meter The way beats in music are organized into groups of three.

triplet A symbol used to show three even sounds on a beat in simple meter.

U

unison The simultaneous playing or singing of the same notes by two or more performers either at the same pitch or in octaves.

upbeats Beats that are sometimes called weak beats because they lead to the next note, a strong beat.

V

variation Music that changes a theme in some important ways.

verse Refers to a section of a song that is sung before the refrain.

vocables Sung or spoken syllables that do not have a specific meaning.

W

whole step On a keyboard, the distance between any two keys with a single key between.

woodwinds A term used to refer to wind instruments, now or originally made of wood.

Y

yodeling A style of singing using a rapid shift between a lower full voice and a high voice style of singing called *falsetto*.

Glossary

CONTENTS

SILVER·BURDETT

Making Music

Indexes

Themes Index

The content of MAKING MUSIC can be used to support teaching thematically in an integrated curriculum. This list shows many of the topical ideas that you might use from this program. We encourage you to consider this list as a starting point only, a framework that can be enlarged upon easily. In this way, you can help deepen the meaning that your students derive from the music literature, and enrich their work in other disciplines.

THEME	PAGE
Movement	7, 16, 28, 48, 51, 57, 87, 136, 143, 151, 172, 186, 220, 303, 309, 360, 379, 392, 403, 423, 433, 436, 445, 448
Our Country	68, 70, 76, 78, 114, 118, 122, 180, 183, 259, 266, 270, 440
Poems and Ballads	42, 95, 98, 110, 114, 121, 149, 152, 163, 166, 207, 303, 305, 306, 334, 381, 388, 399, 456
Related Arts	9, 12, 16, 42, 48, 54, 63, 95, 96, 98, 102, 110, 112, 114, 121, 136, 139, 143, 145, 149, 151, 152, 160, 163, 166, 172, 178, 185, 186, 202, 207, 219, 221, 231, 260, 262, 265, 269, 273, 277, 296, 300, 301, 303, 305, 306, 312, 315, 319, 334, 335, 337, 342, 350, 359, 368, 370, 371, 378, 379, 381, 382, 388, 395, 397, 399, 403, 414, 415, 416, 417, 419, 421, 422, 423, 424, 425, 433, 436, 439, 442, 443, 445, 448, 456, 463, 472
Science	29, 34, 90, 114, 116, 148, 170, 178, 196, 197, 198, 199, 216, 230, 236, 238, 239, 314, 316, 368, 372, 376, 396, 399, 402, 424, 452, 454, 458, 462, 466
Self-Esteem	151, 152, 156, 184, 185, 203, 252, 253, 381, 382, 383, 386, 387

THEME	PAGE
Social Studies	14, 15, 22, 24, 25, 32, 33, 50, 51, 60, 62, 66, 67, 90, 91, 94, 106, 107, 112, 128, 129, 138, 139, 147, 151, 152, 158, 160, 178, 228, 240, 241, 294, 295, 296, 298, 299, 300, 304, 305, 306, 308, 310, 311, 314, 315, 318, 319, 320, 322, 323, 324, 370, 371, 392, 394, 395, 400, 401, 434, 435, 436, 437, 438, 472
Theater and Film	9, 28, 36, 38, 168, 277, 278, 313, 319, 369, 372, 456

Pitch and Rhythm Index

The Pitch and Rhythm Index provides a listing of songs for teaching specific pitches and rhythms. Specific measure numbers are indicated in parentheses when the rhythms or pitches apply to only a portion of a song. The letter *a* indicates that the anacrusis to the measure is included.

The Pitch Index is organized by the teaching sequence used in MAKING MUSIC. Pitch categories are listed in the order in which they are presented in the series.

The Rhythm Index is also organized by the teaching sequence used in MAKING MUSIC. The songs or portions of songs that are listed contain only rhythms that have been taught up to that point in the sequence.

An asterisk (*) next to a song title indicates that the song is used to present the pitch or rhythm in this grade level.

Pitch Index

la

mi so la
Camptown Races (m. 1–12, 5–8, 11–12, 17–18), p. 270
Pollerita (m. 5–6, 9–10), p. 151
Viva Jujuy (m. 17–20), p. 228

do

do mi so
If I Had a Hammer (m. 1–2, 5–6), p. 287

re

do re mi
Day-O! (Banana Boat Loader's Song) (m. 3–4, 7–8, 11–12, 15–16, 19–20, 23–24), p. 18
Sail Away (m. 9–14), p. 404

do re mi so
Imbabura (m. 1–8), p. 202

do re mi so la
California (m. 1–8), p. 52
Camptown Races (m. 1–16), p. 270
Rocky Top (m. 1–16), p. 348
Sail Away (m. 15–20), p. 404
Sing, Sing, Sing! (m. 17–24), p. 340
Stand By Me (m. 1–16), p. 46

do re mi so la do[|]
Imbabura (m. 9–16), p. 202

re mi so la
Yüe liang wan wan (m. 1–6), p. 314

la_|

la_| do re mi
Dancin' in the Street (m. 1–13), p. 361
Drill, Ye Tarriers (m. 1–4), p. 54
Land of a Thousand Dances (m. 1–8), p. 330
Pollerita (m. 7–8, 11–12), p. 151
Sail Away (m. 27–29), p. 404

la_| do re mi so la
Goin' Down the Road Feelin' Bad (m. 1–11), p. 282
Pollerita (m. 1–12, 21–28), p. 151
Yüe liang wan wan (final: la1), p. 314
Yüe liang wan wan (m. 7–13), p. 314
Zuni Sunrise Call (final: do), p. 396

so_|

so_| la_| do re mi
I Believe I Can Fly (m. 1–9), p. 170
Sail Away (m. 23–30, voice 2 - melody), p. 404
Under the Sea (m. 17–32), p. 372

so_| la_| do re mi so
Arirang (final: do), p. 25
Meng Jian Nu (final: so), p. 194

so_| la_| do re mi so la
Come and Go with Me to That Land (final: do), p. 390
El carite (m. 1–8), p. 305
Love Is on Our Side (final: la), p. 324
Oh, Freedom (final: do), p. 392

so_| do re mi so
Ama-Lama (m. 1–4), p. 142

so_| do mi
Over There (m. 1–7, 16–23), p. 279

so_| do mi so
La Jesusita (m. 1–2, 9–10), p. 322

do[|]

do re mi so la do[|]
Bound for South Australia (final: do), p. 22
California (final: do), p. 52
California (m. 9–16), p. 52
Camptown Races (m. 17–24), p. 270
Funwa alafia (final: do), p. 32
Jo'ashila, p. 108
Oh, Watch the Stars (final: do), p. 216
Shady Grove (final: re), p. 260

do so la do[|]
This World (m. 1–15), p. 168

mi so do[|]
Day-O! (Banana Boat Loader's Song) (m. 9–10, 13–14, 33–34, 37–38), p. 18

la_| do re mi so la do[|]
Colorado Trail (final: do), p. 276

so_| la_| do re mi so la do[|]
Sail Away (m. 31–38, voice 1 - melody), p. 404

do re mi so la do[|] re[|]
Bound for South Australia (final: do), p. 22

re mi so la do[|] re[|] mi[|]
Jasmine Flowers (final: so), p. 316
Lahk gei mohlee (final: so), p. 317

do mi so do[|] mi[|]
Happy Days Are Here Again (m. 1–7), p. 284

so_| la_| do re mi so la[|] do[|]
Ev'ry Time I Feel the Spirit (final: do), p. 242
This Train (final: do), p. 26

fa

do re mi fa
Da pacem, Domine (m. 1–4, 9–12), p. 62
Freedom Is Coming (m. voice 1 - melody) (final: do), p. 415
Kokoleoko (m. 1–2), p. 33

do re mi fa so
Beyond Borders (m. 1–8), p. 292
Da pacem, Domine (final: do), p. 62
Get on Your Feet (Melody only, m. 1–8), p. 6
Morning Comes Early (m. 1–4, 13–16, 21–24), p. 13
O, Desayo (m. 1–6), p. 411
Tzena, tzena (m. 1–16), p. 298

do re mi fa so la
Battle Cry of Freedom (m. 9–12), p. 272
Blowin' in the Wind (final: do), p. 382
God Bless America (m. 30–39), p. 4
Kum ba yah (final: do), p. 244
O Music (m. 5–12), p. 162
One Small Step (m. 1–11), p. 126
Turn, Turn, Turn (To Everything There Is a Season) (m. 1–15), p. 378

Pitch and Rhythm Index

632

Rhythm Index

Recorder Index

Classified Index

O

P

Classified Index

T

TECHNOLOGY/MEDIA
CD-ROM

Teacher Notes

Acknowledgments and Credits

Design and Electronic Production: Kirchoff/Wohlberg, Inc.
Listening Maps and Music Reading Practice: MediaLynx Design Group

Photograph Credits

Parent/ Archive Photos 452 The Granger Collection, New York 456 Orion/ Paramount/ Kobal Collection 461 Dr. Barbara Cohen 462 Toni Parker Johnson/ Mashantucket Pequot Tribal Nation 463 Mashantucket Pequot Tribal Nation 464 CMCD/PhotoDisc 465 (TR) Bridgeman Art Library International Ltd. 465 (TL) CMCD/PhotoDisc 468 © Paul Almasy/Corbis 470 © Frere Marc, Taize/ Gene Plaisted, OSC/The Crosiers 471 © Frere Marc, Taize/Gene Plaisted, OSC/ The Crosiers 476 Lawrence Migdale/Stone 478 Kenneth Hamm/Photo Japan 478 © Images Colour Library-ImageState Ltd 479 Michael S. Yamashita/Corbis 481 AP/Wide World 482 Corbis 482 PhotoDisc 483 Bettmann/Corbis 484 © Jim Zuckerman/Corbis 485 Fernando Morales/© AFP 485 Bettman/ Corbis 485 Hulton - Duetsch Collection/Corbis 485 Reuters/Ian Waldie/Archive Photos 485 Ron Sachs/CNP/Archive Photos 485 © Bill Wittman 486 Jeff Greenberg/ PhotoEdit

Design and Electronic Production: Kirchoff/Wohlberg, Inc. Listening Maps and Music Reading Practice: Medialynx.

(A) TAB1 ©Mary Kate Denny/PhotoEdit (B) TAB 2 ©Dannielle Hayes/ ©Fotopic/Omni-Photo.Com (C) TAB 3 ©David Young-Wolff/PhotoEdit (D) TAB 4 ©John Garrett/Getty Images

Illustration Credits

6 Tony Caldwell 6 Steve Barbaria 8 Steve Barbaria 14 Patrick O'Brien 17 Patrick O'Brien 18 Elizabeth Rosen 20 Elizabeth Rosen 22 Arvis Stewart 26 Vilma Ortiz-Dillon 26 Nancy Freeman 28 Vilma Ortiz-Dillon 32 Donna Perrone 32 Beatrice Lebreton 35 Michael Di Giorgio 42 Michael Dinges 44 Michael Dinges 50 Fabricio Vanden Broeck 56 Marni Backer 58 Fabricio Vanden Broeck 60 Gail Piazza 65 Tony Nuccio 68 Tom Leonard 86 David Galchutt 88 David Galchutt 98 Bob Karalus 100 Enrique O. Sanchez 103 Enrique O. Sanchez 103 Vilma Ortiz-Dillon 107 Neecy Twinem 108 Todd Leonardo 123 Vilma Ortiz-Dillon 134 Donna Perrone 136 Don Madden 178 Arvis Stewart 184 Tom Leonard 194 Oki Han 200 Jennifer Bolten 202 Michael Di Giorgio 207 Jennifer Bolten 213 Tuko Fujisaki 216 Eileen Hine 222 Tuko Fujisaki 226 Michael Di Giorgio 228 Michael Di Giorgio 230 Craig Spearing 233 Michael Di Giorgio 248 Annette Cable 248 Antonio Cangemi 249 Debbie Maze 266 Chris Duke 267 Chris Duke 268 Tony Nuccio 268 Bob Berry 269 Chris Duke 270 Joe Boddy 290 Sarah Larson 294 Antonio Cangemi 296 Antonio Cangemi 298 Bradley Clark 300 Bradley Clark 302 Gerardo Suzan 304 Michael Di Giorgio 304 Gerardo Suzan 306 Michael Di Giorgio 306 Gerardo Suzan 314 Jean & Mou-Sien Tseng 328 Roger Leyonmark 344 Craig Spearing 346 Craig Spearing 354 Steve Barbaria 359 Dan Brawner 370 Michael Di Giorgio 372 Pat Paris 374 Pat Paris 376 Pat Paris 392 Linda Wingerter 396 Jennifer Bolten 397 Michael Di Giorgio 399 Jennifer Bolten 400 Antonio Cangemi 402 Andrew Wheatcroft 406 Jennifer Hewitson 408 Jennifer Hewitson 418 Bob Karalus 420 Bob Karalus 422 Bob Karalus 424 Bob Karalus 430 Ron Himler 431 Ron Himler 432 Ron Himler 434 Debbie Maze 436 Debbie Maze 456 David Galchutt 458 Arvis Stewart 460 Chi Chung 466 Claude Martinot 472 Marni Backer 474 Esther Baran 476 Beatrice Lebreton 480 Vilma Ortiz-Dillon 481 Vilma Ortiz-Dillon

Acknowledgments

Credits and appreciation are due publishers and copyright owners for use of the following:

4: "God Bless America," Words and Music by Irving Berlin. Copyright 1938, 1939 by Irving Berlin. Copyright © 1965, 1966 (Renewed) by Irving Berlin. Copyright Assigned to the Trustees of the God Bless America Fund. This arrangement Copyright © 2003 by the Trustees of the God Bless America Fund. International Copyright Secured. All Rights Reserved. Used by Permission. 6: "Get on Your Feet" Words and Music by John DeFaria, Clay Ostwald and Jorge Casas. Copyright © 1988 Foreign Imported Productions & Publishing, Inc. (BMI) International Rights Secured. All Rights Reserved. Reprinted by permission. 10: "Laredo" English Words (©) 1988

Silver Burdett Ginn. 14: "Éliza Kongo" from *Brown Girl in the Ring* by Alan Lomax. Copyright © 1997 by Alan Lomax. Reprinted by permission of Pantheon Books, a division of Random House, Inc. 18: "Day-O," from *Folk Songs of Jamaica*. Complied by Tom Murray. © 1951 Oxford University Press. Used by Permission. All Rights Reserved. 25: "Arirang" English Words (©) 1995 Silver Burdett Ginn. 28: "Morning Has Broken". Reprinted by permission of Harold Ober Associates Incorporated. Copyright (©) 1957 by Eleanor Farjeon. 32: "Funwa alafia" (Welcome, My Friends) English Words © 2002 Pearson Education, Inc. 36: "Oklahoma" from *Oklahoma!* Music by Richard Rodgers, Words by Oscar Hammerstein II. Copyright 1943 by Williamson Music. Copyright Renewed. This arrangement Copyright © 2001 by Williamson Music. International Copyright Secured. All Rights Reserved. Used by Permission. 42: "Be Bop" by Toyomi Igus from *I SEE RHYTHM* p. 19. Text copyright © 1988 by Toyomi Igus. Reprinted with permission of the publisher, Children's Book Press, San Francisco, CA. 44: "Choo Choo Ch'Boogie," Words and Music by Vaughn Horton, Denver Darling and Milton Gabler. Copyright 1945 (Renewed) RYTVOC, Inc. This arrangement © 2001 RYTVOC, INC. All Rights Reserved. Reprinted by permission of Hal Leonard Corporation. 46: "Stand By Me" featured in the Motion Picture *Stand By Me*. Words and Music by Ben. E. King, Jerry Leiber and Mike Stoller. © 1961 (Renewed) Jerry Leiber Music, Mike Stoller Music and Mike & Jerry Music LLC. This arrangement © 2001 Jerry Leiber Music, Mike Stoller Music and Mike & Jerry Music LLC. All Rights Reserved. Used by Permission. 50: "Adelita" English Words © 1988 Silver Burdett Ginn. 57: "Away to America" Words and Music by Linda Williams. Copyright © 1983 by Hal Leonard Corporation. This arrangement copyright © 2001 by Hal Leonard Corporation. International Copyright Secured. All Rights Reserved. Used by Permission. 58: "La Ciudad de Juaja" (The City Of Juaja), English Words by Ruth De Cesare, John Donald Robb Archives of Southwestern Music, College of Fine Arts, University of New Mexico. Used by Permission of John Donald Robb Trust. 60: "A la puerta del cielo" (At the Gate of Heaven) English Words © 2002 Pearson Education, Inc. 67: "Ye jaliya da" a folk song from West Africa. Used by Permission, DWADD. 71: "Live in the City" Music by Buryl Red, Words by Bryan Louiselle. © 2000 Generic Music and Frog Prince Music. Used by permission. 72: "Play a Simple Melody" from the Stage Production *Watch Your Step*. Words and Music by Irving Berlin. Copyright © 1914 by Irving Berlin. Copyright Renewed. This arrangement © 2001 by the Estate of Irving Berlin. International Copyright Secured. All Rights Reserved. Used by Permission. 77: "Let Freedom Ring" Words and Music by Buryl Red. © 2000 Generic Music. Used by Permission. 84: "Teach Me To Swing" Words and Music by Kirby Shaw. Copyright © 1997 Kirby Shaw Music. International Copyright Secured. Reprinted by permission. 86: "The Voices of Pride" Words and Music by Ned Ginsburg. © 1991 by Ned Ginsburg. Reprinted by permission. 90: "De colores" English Words © 1988 Silver Burdett Ginn. 92: "Chiapanecas" English Words © 2005 Pearson Education, Inc. 95: "Music" from *What is That Sound!* by Mary O'Neill. Copyright © 1966 by Mary O'Neill. © renewed 1994 by Abigail Hagler and Erin Baroni. Reprinted by permission of Marian Reiner. 97: "Don't You Hear the Lambs?" from *Folk Songs North America Sings* by Richard Johnston. 1984 by Caveat Music Publishing Ltd., copyright assigned 1988 to G Ricordi & Co. (Canada) Ltd. Used with permission. 106: "Dundai" English Words © 2002 Pearson Education, Inc. 108: "Jo'ashila" (Walking Together) Traditional Navajo song from *Roots and Branches*. Courtesy World Music Press. 114: "The Ash Grove" Arrangement © 2002 Pearson Education, Inc. 116: "Roll On, Columbia" Words by Woody Guthrie. Music based on GOODNIGHT, IRENE by Huddie Ledbetter and John A. Lomax. TRO- © Copyright 1936 (Renewed) 1957 (Renewed) and 1963 (Renewed) Ludlow Music, Inc., New York, NY. Used by Permission. 126: "One Small Step" Words and Music by Jay Althouse and Sally K. Albrecht. 1997 © Alfred Publishing Co. Inc. Used by Permission of the publisher. 128: "La bamba" adapted and arranged by Richie Valens. © 1958 (Renewed) Picture Our Music. All Rights for USA administered by EMI Longitude Music Co. All Rights for the World excluding USA administered by Warner-Tamerlane Publishing Corp. All Rights Reserved. Used by Permission. WARNER BROS. PUBLICATIONS U.S. INC.,

Teacher Notes

LISTENING INDEX

Listening Selections by Composer

Listening Selections by Title

SONG AND SPEECH

PIECE INDEX